P9-AOH-692

GUSTAV MAHLER

JENS MALTE FISCHER

GUSTAV MAHLER

TRANSLATED BY STEWART SPENCER

YALE UNIVERSITY PRESS
NEW HAVEN AND LONDON

First published in English by Yale University Press in 2011

English translation copyright © 2011 Stewart Spencer

Originally published under the title *Gustav Mahler: Der fremde Vertraute* by Jens Malte Fischer © 2003 Paul Zsolnay Verlag, Vienna

All rights reserved. This book may not be reproduced in whole or in part, in any form (beyond that copying permitted by Sections 107 and 108 of the U.S. Copyright Law and except by reviewers for the public press) without written permission from the publishers.

For information about this and other Yale University Press publications, please contact:
U.S. Office: sales.press@yale.edu   www.yalebooks.com
Europe Office: sales@yaleup.co.uk   www.yalebooks.co.uk
Library of Congress Cataloging-in-Publication Data

Fischer, Jens Malte.
  Gustav Mahler / Jens Malte Fischer.
    p. cm.
  ISBN 978-0-300-13444-5 (cl : alk. paper)
  1. Mahler, Gustav, 1860-1911. 2. Composers—Austria—Biography. I. Title.
  ML410.M23F45 2011
  780.92—dc22
  [B]
                                                                    2011011115
Set in Minion Pro by IDSUK (DataConnection) Ltd
Printed in Great Britain by the MPG Books Group, Bodmin, Cornwall

A catalogue record for this book is available from the British Library.

The Publishers acknowledge the generous assistance of The Hampsong Foundation in the publishing of this book

10 9 8 7 6 5 4 3 2 1

For Thomas Hampson,
friend, and great interpreter of Mahler's music

For the chief goal of biography appears to be this: to present the subject in his temporal circumstances, to show how these both hinder and help him, how he uses them to construct his view of man and the world, and how he, providing he is an artist, poet, or author, mirrors them again for others.

JOHANN WOLFGANG VON GOETHE,
From the Preface to *From My Life: Poetry and Truth* (1811–13)

Contents

List of Illustrations ix

1   What Did Mahler Look Like? An Attempt at a Description   1

2   Small Steps: Kalischt and Iglau (1860–75)   12

3   Studies in Vienna (1875–80)   42

4   The Summer Conductor: Bad Hall (1880)   90

5   Emotional Ups and Downs in Laibach (1881–2)   99

6   For the Last Time in the Provinces: Olmütz (1882–3)   108

7   Presentiment and a New Departure: Kassel (1883–5)   114

8   The Avid Reader: Mahler and Literature   125

9   Becoming Mahler: Prague (1885–6)   140

10   The First Symphony   148

11   Life's Vicissitudes: Leipzig (1886–8)   157

12   Notes on Mahler's Songs   168

13   Lowland Dreams: Budapest (1888–91)   178

14   The Conductor   191

15   The Second Symphony   202

16   Self-Realization: Hamburg (1891–7)   208

17   Jewishness and Identity   251

18 The Third Symphony   274

19 The God of the Southern Climes: Vienna (1897–1901)   282

20 Mahler's Illnesses: A Pathographical Sketch   321

21 The Fourth Symphony   333

22 Vienna in 1900: Alma as a Young Woman (1901–3)   340

23 The Fifth Symphony   385

24 'Nothing is lost to you': Faith and Philosophy   392

25 The Sixth Symphony   409

26 Opera Reform – Early Years of Marriage – Mahler's
    Compositional Method (1903–5)   416

27 The Seventh Symphony   458

28 The Administrator – Contemporaries – Signs of Crisis (1905–7) 464

29 The Eighth Symphony   519

30 *Annus Terribilis* (1907)   527

31 *Das Lied von der Erde*   562

32 Starting Afresh: New York (1908–11)   568

33 The Ninth Symphony   611

34 Crisis and Culmination (1910)   620

35 The Fragmentary Tenth Symphony   662

36 'My heart is weary' – The Farewell   666

37 Mahler and Posterity   691

    List of Abbreviations   707

    Notes   709

    Select Bibliography   734

    Index   740

    Acknowledgements   765

Illustrations

(*between pages 246 and 247*)

1 Mahler walking at Fischleinboden, near Toblach, 1909. (Österreichische Nationalbibliothek, Vienna)

2 Bernhard Mahler. (Médiathèque Musicale Mahler, Paris)

3 Marie Mahler. (Médiathèque Musicale Mahler, Paris)

4 A postcard showing Mahler's birthplace in Kalischt, Moravia. (Österreichische Nationalbibliothek, Vienna; 460.707-B)

5 Mahler, 1865 or 1866. (Österreichische Nationalbibliothek, Vienna)

6 The Main Square in Iglau, Moravia, mid- to late nineteenth century (Muzeum Visočyni, Jihlava, Czech Republic)

7 Siegfried Lipiner. (Internationale Gustav-Mahler-Gesellschaft, Vienna)

8 Mahler in 1881. (Österreichische Nationalbibliothek, Vienna)

9 The 'Zum Höllengebirge' guest house at Steinbach on the Attersee. (Österreichische Nationalbibliothek, Vienna)

10 Gustav Mahler and his sister Justine, 1899. (Österreichische Nationalbibliothek, Vienna)

11 Anna von Mildenburg as Brünnhilde in Wagner's *Die Walküre*. (Österreichische Nationalbibliothek, Vienna)

12 Selma Kurz, May 1900. (Baron Nathaniel Rothschild, Vienna)

13 Mahler's house at Maiernigg. (Photo by Eric Shane)

14 Alma Schindler, *c.* 1898. (Österreichische Nationalbibliothek, Vienna)

15 Mahler on his way to or from the opera house, Vienna, *c.* 1904. (Österreichische Nationalbibliothek, Vienna)

16 Mahler triumphs over his predecessor Wilhelm Jahn: a cartoon by Theo Zasche, 1897. (Österreichische Nationalbibliothek, Vienna)

17 The Vienna Court Opera House, *c.* 1900. (Österreichische Nationalbibliothek, Vienna; 233.127-C)

(*between pages 502 and 503*)

18 Mahler, Vienna, 1907, photographed by Moriz Nähr. (Médiathèque Musicale Mahler, Paris)

19 'Reichmann is going too!' Cartoon of Mahler from the *Wiener Zeitung*, *c.* 1902.

20 Alfred Roller's design for the prison courtyard in Beethoven's *Fidelio*, mixed technique (1904). (Österreichische Theatermuseum, Vienna)

21 Natalie Bauer-Lechner. (Arthur Spiegler, Vienna)

22 Detail from Gustav Klimt's Beethoven frieze, Secession Building, Vienna. (Österreichische Galerie Belvedere, Vienna)

23 Mahler, Max Reinhardt, Carl Moll and Hans Pfitzner in the garden at Carl Moll's villa, 1905. (Österreichische Nationalbibliothek, Vienna)

24 Alma Mahler with her two daughters, Maria and Anna, 1906 (Österreichische Nationalbibliothek, Vienna)

25 Mahler with his daughter Anna at Toblach, 1909. (Österreichische Nationalbibliothek, Vienna)

26 Mahler, New York, 1909, photographed by A. Dupont. (Kaplan Foundation, New York)

27 Cartoon from the time of the first performance of the Sixth Symphony in Vienna, *Die Muskete*, 19 January 1907. (Internationale Gustav-Mahler-Gesellschaft, Vienna)

28 Mahler conducting a rehearsal for his Eighth Symphony in the Munich Exhibition Hall, 1910. (Internationale Gustav-Mahler-Gesellschaft, Vienna)

29 Mahler, possibly October 1910 on his final voyage from Europe to New York or on the return journey, April 1911. (Internationale Gustav-Mahler-Gesellschaft, Vienna)

30 Auguste Rodin's bust of Mahler (1909). (Brooklyn Museum of Modern Art)

31 Mahler's grave, Grinzing,Vienna. (Österreichische Nationalbibliothek, Vienna)

1

What Did Mahler Look Like?
An Attempt at a Description

I T IS ONE of the many curious aspects of Alma Mahler's reminiscences of her husband that she never attempts to describe his physical appearance. In her own memoirs she deals with Mahler in a remarkably cursory manner, and yet even in the volume nominally devoted to her recollections of her husband we are not told what he looked like. True, she lacked the art of physical description, although she was certainly capable of highlighting certain features, notably in her thumbnail sketch of Alexander Zemlinsky: 'He was a hideous gnome. Short, chinless, toothless, always with the coffee-house smell on him, unwashed'[1] – a sketch of this kind would at least have offered the reader a clue, but Mahler himself is not given a face by her. Readers may make of this what they like. We are obliged, therefore, to rely on other eyewitnesses:

> Small in stature, pale and thin: the lofty forehead of his long face framed in blue-black hair, and behind glasses, remarkable eyes; lines of sadness and of humour furrowed a countenance across which an astonishing range of expression passed as he spoke to the various people round him. Here was the incarnation of Kreisler, the arresting, alarming, demoniac conductor envisaged by the youthful reader of E. T. A. Hoffmann's fantastic tales.[2]

Bruno Walter's first impression of Mahler was entirely typical: this is how many people saw him when they met him for the first time. Time and again the name of Kreisler is invoked by contemporaries attempting to give literary expression to their impressions – and not just their physical impressions. At a somewhat later date, Ferruccio Busoni was similarly – and even more implausibly – compared to Kreisler, even though the two composers bore absolutely no resemblance to one another. None the less, Mahler and Busoni shared a love of Hoffmann, and it is unfortunate that these two great will-o'-the-wisp-like figures did not become better acquainted until the very end of Mahler's life, when Busoni was on the ship that brought the fatally ill Mahler back to Europe. Observers who, like the music critic Ferdinand Pfohl, regarded Mahler with scepticism and hostility or at least with profound bewilderment described him as a 'Lucifer' figure. Pfohl thought that Mahler looked like someone who had despaired in God and who in consequence had been cast down from the light into the darkness – in particular, Pfohl was thinking of the Lucifer figure of Abadona in Klopstock's religious epic *The Messiah*. His description also includes a reference to Mahler's Jewishness:

> What did this Lucifer look like? During his time in Hamburg, his head, tapering to a pyramid-like point, and his oval face still revealed the rounded lines of youth. His gaze from his dark, flashing, Semitic eyes was penetratingly keen, his lids slightly reddened, as is often the case with people who have to do too much reading and who work too much at night. In his appearance, he was small, dainty, elegant; there was a hint of gracefulness about him.[3]

Numerous other impressions could be cited, all of them surprisingly similar: Mahler was not the sort of person who left different impressions on different people. Time and again we encounter the same characteristics: the small, slim body, the unusually animated features and the nervous, uncoordinated movements, including the 'twitching foot' that clearly struck every observer and to which we shall shortly return. And just as commentators repeatedly referred to the 'magic' of Mahler's conducting, so they frequently fell back on the term 'demonic' when seeking to describe his personality and outward appearance. Not even Bruno Walter, who knew Mahler as few others did, could avoid the term. At the same time Walter added a further Hoffmannesque character to that of Kapellmeister Kreisler: the archivist Lindhorst in *The Golden Pot*, whom the student Anselmus thinks he can see flying away into the dusk in the form of a vulture.[4]

If we want to move away from the predictable unanimity of these superficial descriptions and probe a little deeper, we need to turn to two texts that bring us much closer to Mahler's physical appearance. The first consists of the reminiscences of Natalie Bauer-Lechner, who was Mahler's closest confidante over a period of many years. (Like Alma Mahler and the composer's sister, Justine, she will generally be referred to by her first name only in the course of the following narrative.) The other is the preface to the iconographic study of the composer that was published by Alfred Roller eleven years after Mahler's death under the title *The Portraits of Gustav Mahler*.[5] This last-named volume is rightly regarded as the finest description of Mahler by a colleague and friend who, as stage and costume designer, worked closely with Mahler on his operatic reforms in Vienna. Although Roller got to know Mahler at a relatively late date, he had the advantage not just of knowing him personally over a period of several years but of being able to bring to bear on him the trained eye of a painter and draughtsman, allowing him to register bodies and faces considerably more precisely than normal people, who tend to be much less observant. Roller's descriptions are a stroke of good fortune for those of us who want to know something about Mahler. And if we look at surviving portraits of the composer, which we can do most manageably and comprehensively through Gilbert Kaplan's *Mahler Album*,[6] we shall come much closer to an understanding of what Mahler actually looked like.

Mahler was unprepossessing, ugly and weak and a twitching bundle of nerves – thus Roller quotes received opinion. All in all, this suggests the picture of a degenerate older Jew from a family marked out by illness and prematurely decimated, very much the sort of person against whom well-meaning friends warned the young Alma Schindler.[7] Roller and Natalie offer a different picture, and even if we need to take account of the fact that both of them were writing from the standpoint of affection and friendship, the picture that emerges from Roller – a highly respected colleague, rather than a friend – seems entirely objective and certainly at odds with the usual clichés. True, Mahler was not tall, but this needs to be seen in the context of average heights at the turn of the century, rather than judged by today's standards; Roller, who was himself very tall, reckoned that Mahler was just 5 feet 3 inches in height. At no point in his life did Mahler tend to corpulence, but was well-proportioned and slim, in other words, never gaunt. The first time that Roller saw Mahler swimming – he himself uses the word 'naked', which may be taken literally or it may refer to a swimming costume – he was surprised and, indeed, impressed by the masculine proportions of Mahler's body. His admiration finds expression in a hymnic description of Mahler's physique, which is innocent of all homoerotic feelings but reflects the expert's appreciation of naked, well-proportioned bodies – as a teacher at Vienna's School of Applied Arts, Roller was used, after all, to drawing nudes. But his surprise stemmed above all from the fact that like most of Mahler's circle he had assumed that beneath the voluminous clothes typical of the turn of the century was a spindly little man with no muscles. Roller attests that the forty-year-old Mahler had a 'flawlessly beautiful, powerfully slim man's body',[8] toughened from his youth by a regular regimen of walking, hiking, swimming and cycling. Mahler had remarkably broad shoulders, narrow hips and straight, muscular legs. His chest, too, was muscular and powerfully bulging, his stomach showed no trace of fat, the musculature being clearly visible. Roller was particularly impressed by Mahler's well-formed, sun-burnt back, which reminded him of a 'trained racehorse'.[9]

Roller's enthusiastic account gains in credibility when we recall Mahler's physical activities, which were a source of astonishment chiefly to those who cultivated the picture of an enfeebled 'neurasthenic', as observers generally referred to their degenerate and decadent contemporaries. (A satirical couplet, popular at the time, runs: 'Haste nie und raste nie,/Dann haste nie Neurasthenie', literally, 'Never make haste and never rest, and you'll never suffer from neurasthenia'.) When he was not on holiday during the summer, Mahler would keep in shape by walking long distances every day: whether in Budapest, Hamburg or Vienna, he went virtually everywhere on foot, while outside built-up areas he would stride along at such a brisk pace that few of his companions could keep up with him. In Hamburg he also went cycling, a pursuit he maintained with great enthusiasm over a period of several years, even taking his bicycle on holiday with him. Together with the Austrian writer Arthur Schnitzler, Mahler was one of the pioneers of this form of locomotion. When his sister Justine fell ill after nursing their fatally ill parents, Mahler would carry her, fully clothed (including coat and furs), up and down several flights of stairs to his apartment in Budapest, even though she was taller and heavier than he. As a swimmer, too, he was feared: no one could compete with him when he leapt into the water, swam beneath the surface and then reappeared some distance from the shore, splashing around and snorting with laughter – a sign that his lungs were exceptionally capacious. When rowing, he would drive his fellow oarsmen to despair as he ignored all their attempts to establish an efficient stroke. His own stroke was far too short and quick, making it enormously tiring, and yet he could maintain this energy-wasting technique over longer periods than those who adopted a more sensible and ergonomic approach. Many of his colleagues report that during rehearsals at the opera house he would run tirelessly between the orchestra pit and the stage, often hauling himself up from the pit to the footlights with the help of a small flight of steps, before leaping back down again. Once he was onstage and needed to show the performers their moves, he could push around even the heaviest Wagner singers as though they were balls of cotton wool. Against this background we can understand Roller's horror when, at a *Lohengrin* rehearsal in Vienna in 1904, he saw Mahler furtively clutch his heart after one such exertion.

Mahler moved at an allegro furioso. He literally ran up mountains, staying the course till the end, whereas Roller, four years his junior, was unable to keep up with him. Roller attributed to Mahler's gait an impetuousness bordering on triumphalism. If, in spite of his nature, Mahler had to walk more slowly out of consideration for Alma or other companions who could not walk as quickly, he would place one foot elegantly in front of the other and keep to a narrow path – Pfohl's reference to 'gracefulness' comes to mind here.

But if he could set his own pace, then he would 'press ahead', to borrow a favourite phrase from his scores. Pfohl also saw a thrusting movement, Mahler's chin protruding like a battering ram and his head thrown back, a posture also ascribed to Beethoven. But the most striking aspect of his gait, which was occasionally also observed when he stood still, was the uncontrolled movement of his right leg. Uncontrolled, but not unnoticed. In his letters to Alma, Mahler himself sometimes referred to this as his 'Totatscheln', an onomatopoeic expression of unknown origin used only between the two of them. Anyone unfamiliar with Mahler might gain the impression that this was a conscious use of body language, Mahler stamping his foot on the ground much as someone might bang his fist on the table in order to make a point. But this tic, which Roller called Mahler's 'twitching leg' and which other friends such as Bruno Walter described more discreetly as an irregular way of walking, had nothing to do with such conscious body language. When he was walking, Mahler would take between one and three short steps that would fall out of the regular rhythm, whereas when he was standing still, he would mark time on the spot with his right foot, sometimes quite lightly, but at other times more markedly. He never did so when he was concentrating, notably when conducting, but if his concentration lapsed, the tic might suddenly reappear. That it had nothing to do with anger and indignation is clear from the fact that it was often most pronounced whenever Mahler laughed uncontrollably. He would then clean his glasses, which had become misted over with tears of laughter, and his right leg would take on a life of its own – according to Natalie, it was like a wild boar pounding the earth. Whenever he was out walking and stopped to note down some musical idea or other in his sketchbook, his leg would perform a syncopated rhythm before he started walking again.

Roller thought that the origins of this tic – and it is hard to avoid the term – lay in the involuntary movements of Mahler's extremities during his childhood. (We would nowadays speak of a 'hyperactive child'.) But Roller is the only writer to report on this childhood phenomenon, which he saw as an early stage of St Vitus's dance, or Sydenham's chorea. 'Chorea minor', which appears in childhood, is triggered by an infection and may be accompanied by symptoms of rheumatism. The idea of such an aetiology is not entirely absurd as it is fairly certain that Mahler's heart-valve defect – discovered later – can be traced back to rheumatic fever. 'Chorea major', also known as Huntington's disease, can safely be dismissed in Mahler's case as its symptoms are accompanied by irritability, insecurity and lack of inhibitions. Be that as it may, it is understandable that to the superficial observer this tic was Mahler's most noticeable physical trait and that it did much to reinforce the cliché of the composer as neurasthenic.

Roller reports an additional feature that he thought might be connected with Mahler's 'twitching foot': he had sometimes observed the composer standing on one leg in the middle of a room, one hand on his hip, his head resting on his other hand and the foot of one leg placed in the hollow of the knee of his other leg, creating the impression of a flamingo. This impression is reinforced by a number of photographs of Mahler standing either in the photographer's studio or outside in the open air and revealing his preference for a position in which his left leg was placed nonchalantly against his right leg, either over it or beneath it, a position that is relatively normal when sitting but not so common when standing as it can seem nonchalant or even precious. Mahler can hardly have intended to create this impression. As it is almost always the left leg that grips the right one, holding it firmly and preventing it from twitching, we may not go far wrong in interpreting this position, too, like his standing on one leg, as an attempt – conscious or otherwise – to domesticate his tic. We see this posture in a studio photograph dating from Mahler's time in Budapest. We also see it in a photograph of both Mahler and Justine in Vienna, although here it is the right leg that grips the left one. It is also apparent in a photograph taken during Mahler's walking holiday to the Fischleinboden near Sexten during the summer of 1907. And, sadly and distressingly, we see the same stance in the very last photograph of Mahler that was presumably taken on board the ship bringing him back to Europe, already terminally ill. In spite of his failing strength, he is once again fully dressed, his face marked by illness, but still adopting the familiar position, leaning apparently nonchalantly against the deck rail, resting on a walking stick in his right hand and for the last time assuming the elegant pose that he remained fond of all his life, the 'gracefulness' still apparent as a memory of earlier times, while his face shows the listlessness of a man marked out by death.

One sign of tenseness was Mahler's tendency to bite his fingernails, a tendency which in his bachelor days he evidently took to such extreme lengths that he would often bite his nails right down to the flesh so that he drew blood. This was an unattractive habit from which Alma managed with some difficulty to wean him, albeit never entirely successfully.

Arguably the most expressive representation of Mahler's head was Auguste Rodin's. It shows an extreme example of brachycephalism, an anatomical feature generally not apparent in photographs, whether full-face or profile, as the shape of the skull is concealed by the luxuriant growth of black hair. Alma was inordinately fond of Mahler's hair, which started to recede only towards the end of his life, growing thinner at the temples and on his crown, while never really turning grey. It was Alma, too, who insisted that the hair on either side of his temples should appear as full as possible in order to make the very narrow skull seem more rounded. But it is clear from the few snapshots that show him with short hair that he had virtually no exterior occipital protuberance, a peculiarity even more evident in the famous caricatures of Mahler produced in New York by Enrico Caruso, not only the greatest tenor of his day but also an accomplished draughtsman. The obverse of this 'absence' was the massive brow and powerful lower jaw, with its striking chin. In this way even the shape of Mahler's skull reflected his aspirations both forward and upward: there are very few photographs that show Mahler looking down in thought. On his temples were two protruding veins that Natalie described as his 'zigzag lightning veins', which stood out even more prominently whenever he was angry: 'There can be little more terrifying than Mahler's head when he's in a rage. Everything about him burns, twitches and emits sparks, while every single one of his raven-black hairs seems to stand on end separately.'[10] His nose was powerfully developed, narrow and noticeably curved – the usual term is 'hooked' – and uncommonly characteristic, without appearing disproportionate. (In this respect, Mahler's death mask gives a distorted picture.) His eyebrows were fine and mobile, lending emphasis to his expressive facial features, a point so often described by observers.

Particularly striking in photographs of the older Mahler are the deep lines on his face, above all those running down from the sides of his nose to his mouth and that are most pronounced in the final photograph of all, where they convey a sense of the greatest bitterness. But even more exceptional are the lines that run almost vertically down the middle of his cheeks from the cheekbone to the lower jaw, more pronounced on the right than on the left. It was above all these lines which, together with the clear downward curve of his mouth, gave Mahler's face its oft-cited similarity to the tragic masks of classical antiquity. The mouth itself was relatively thin-lipped, without, however, giving the impression of being pinched, as it does with his sister Justine, who was definitely disadvantaged from this point of view. Often described as eerie, the mobility of Mahler's facial expressions is reflected in the fact that in some photographs his mouth seems to have been cut into his face with a knife, appearing narrow and implacable (Pfohl summed this up in a graphic image: 'he eats and devours his lips'[11]), whereas in other photographs his lips appear full, making their owner seem gentle and forbearing – most movingly in the photograph taken in Amsterdam in October 1909.

Apart from his twitching leg and tendency to bite his nails, Mahler had a third habit, albeit not so striking as the other two: he would chew on his cheeks, sucking them in between his teeth, sometimes so violently that the flesh inside his cheeks began to bleed. He often did so when deep in thought. The habit can be clearly seen in the snapshot that shows him in Vienna on his journey between the opera house and his apartment, when he thought that he was unobserved, although – for whatever reason – he also chewed his cheeks in official photographs.

We have already had occasion to refer to photographs of the early Mahler in which the viewer is struck above all by the changing appearance of his beard. The luxuriant beard that Mahler still wore at the age of twenty, undoubtedly in an attempt to appear older than he was, was reduced to a Van Dyke beard in Kassel, becoming a thin moustache in Prague. Mahler continued to have a moustache during his early months in Budapest but then dispensed with facial hair entirely. During the summer he was sometimes too lazy to shave every day and would then have a hint of a moustache that can be seen in the photographs taken in Maiernigg on the Wörthersee during the summer of 1905. Alfred Roller reports that one summer he suddenly discovered Mahler with a full beard the colour of iron but with two grey strands running down from the corners of his mouth, but following protests from those around him, Mahler quickly abandoned this experiment. Although there is no photographic evidence to support Roller's claim, it is none the less entirely plausible.

Mahler was short-sighted, something especially clear from the photographs taken during his youth, when he sat for the camera without wearing spectacles. He started to wear glasses when he was eighteen, if not earlier, a rimless pair that now looks positively fashionable. But we soon find him using a pince-nez, too, an arrangement that went on for some time: in private he continued to prefer a pince-nez, but this was impracticable on the conductor's podium, where for a long time his gestures remained extremely violent, so that here he had to use spectacles. He continued to wear these rimless glasses until the end of his life, further accentuating the shape of his expressive skull. It is impossible to know if their reduced weight made his migraine attacks more bearable or whether he preferred them for aesthetic reasons, but his lack of vanity makes the first alternative more likely.

Mahler set little store by decent clothing. During his years as a Kapellmeister he had too little money to afford to buy good-quality clothes, nor did he have the time or inclination to go shopping. Instead, his absent-mindedness and disregard for the 'trumpery' of the world encouraged him to neglect his appearance, a negligence that extended to his household at least as long as his sister was not living with him. He maintained this attitude even after he could afford to buy better-quality clothes. Initially it was his sister who tried to persuade Mahler to mend his ways, a role subsequently taken over by Alma, who herself dressed with exceptional taste and lavished considerable expense on her wardrobe. Mahler allowed himself to be guided by her at least to the extent that he was now prepared to spend more money on clothes but was not willing to waste time buying them. What Alma did not do for him was not done at all.

Later he had his shirts and nightshirts tailor-made, a practice that was then more common and less expensive than it is now. Contrary to contemporary practice, Mahler wore thigh-length nightshirts, claiming that the longer type was irksome and that he could sleep better when he was a little bit cold.

It emerges from a number of surviving photographs that the clothes he wore when hiking comprised a grey rustic suit with waistcoat and a white shirt with a bow tie – there is no question of the carelessness of today's tourist clothing. If the weather was warm, he would remove his jacket and hang it over his left shoulder, using a piece of string. Mahler was a sun-worshipper who always returned sun-burnt from his summer holidays. To prevent himself from catching sunstroke he would wear a lightweight white cap with a narrow eye-shield, as may be seen on the wonderful photograph of Mahler and his daughter Anna Justine taken in Toblach during the summer of 1909. For shorter walks in summer, he wore ordinary shoes, but for the mountains he preferred more robust mountaineering boots. He was almost always photographed wearing a waistcoat, the only exceptions being the photographs taken in Maiernigg in 1905, in which he is seen wearing an open-necked pleated shirt. New coats were carelessly buttoned only at the top, while new hats were forcibly adapted to fit the shape of his skull and soon ceased to look new. For weeks on end he could wander around with the lining of his coat torn, the state of disrepair being a matter of total indifference to him.

The extent of his indifference emerges particularly clearly from the famous series of photographs taken at the Vienna Court Opera in 1907. Even in these official photographs, in which Mahler's bow tie has evidently been tied with a little more care than usual, it is still possible to see a kind of notebook poking out of the top of his breast pocket in at least one of the photographs, while various scraps of paper can be observed peering out of the side pocket of his waistcoat. But this carelessness should not be confused with uncleanliness. Mahler was painstaking about physical cleanliness. With the exception of his badly bitten fingernails and tousled, uncombed hair, no one ever saw him unkempt or dirty. His body had to be clean (he washed himself from head to foot, including his hair, every day), as did his clothing and underwear. The only item of clothing that was genuinely important to him was his footwear. For a passionate walker like Mahler, shoes were the tools of his trade and as such could decide whether or not he was enjoying his walk. The only other item of professional clothing that was subject to his strict control was the tail coat that he wore to conduct. His regard for the composers and the works in his repertory seems to have persuaded him to show his respect in this way.

According to Ferdinand Pfohl, Mahler's laughter could sound remarkably like snarling. Apparently it was never warm-hearted and cheerful but always scornful and harsh. But this seems to reflect the sense of bitterness felt by the forgotten fan. Pfohl is equally negative about Mahler's voice, which is said to have been cutting, cold and grating. His evidence is called into question not least by his claim that Mahler always spoke with a pronounced Austrian accent and even revelled in the more trivial colloquialisms of Vienna's suburban dialect.[12] But this account is contradicted by other reports, which insist that Mahler spoke a pure German free from all dialectal impurities. Only the most sensitive ear could detect Mahler's Bohemian origins from his pronunciation of the trilled [r], which he articulated as a dorso-uvular trill, rolling it slightly more noticeably than speakers from other regions. Of course, Mahler's long period of residence in Vienna makes it entirely plausible that he was able to speak a Viennese dialect whenever he wanted to, and it is possible that he culti-vated this folk idiom in Hamburg, where Pfohl got to know him. Mahler's voice was evidently extremely euphonious, baritonal in colour and capable of carrying some distance, especially when he raised it and shouted across at the stage from his position on the conductor's podium. On those occasions when he became more animated than usual in private conversation his voice would assume a tenor-like quality, and when he was beside himself with anger, it immediately rose to a higher octave and could become cutting. Those who knew him well could tell whether his anger was feigned, in which case his voice retained its baritonal colouring, or genuine, when his voice rose markedly in pitch. It is a shame that we have no recordings of Mahler's voice to complement the Welte-Mignon recordings of his piano playing. The technology certainly existed at this time, as there are surviving recordings of the voices of Arthur Schnitzler, Hugo von Hofmannsthal and even Kaiser Franz Joseph, all of whom were recorded in Vienna during the period when Mahler was director of the Court Opera. It was a missed opportunity.

Mahler remained Mahler, and his appearance changed only imperceptibly between the thirtieth and fiftieth years of his life. Only in the photographs taken in New York in 1909 do we detect a very slight difference, for here he seems more mellow, an observation confirmed by those of his friends who saw him again at this time. A slight but noticeable increase in weight is reflected in the outlines of his face. But this was only a temporary change, for the following photographs again show Mahler looking tense and, finally, careworn and exhausted by suffering, as he was at the time of his final fatal illness.

The legend that Mahler is not seen laughing on any of the photographs of him cannot be sustained, even though the surviving photographs show him smiling at best. Of course, all the surviving images of Mahler are marked by a gnawing seriousness that is unsettling but which is not the same as melancholy or depression. Two snapshots taken in Maiernigg in the summer of 1905 are typical. One of them, which is not posed, shows Mahler playing with his daughter Maria, holding her head and looking almost cheerful, while the other, posed for the photographer, shows him again with his daughter, but this time he has relapsed into the state of brooding earnestness that the life-loving Alma found so hard to bear. All the more remarkable, and almost touching, are the pictures that show a tender, relaxed Mahler, which is how his surviving daughter Anna remembered him: sensitive, humorous, full of understanding. But few people saw this side of him. The picture that he presented to the outside world was inevitably very different.

Small Steps: Kalischt and Iglau
(1860–75)

Surroundings and General Ambiance

At the end of the eighteenth century the border between the margravate of
Moravia, with its capital in Brünn (modern Brno), and the kingdom of
Bohemia, with its capital in Prague, ran only a few kilometres north of Iglau
(Jihlava), a situation that was still unchanged by the middle of the nineteenth
century. A century earlier, both countries had been members of the Holy
Roman Empire of the German Nation, whose Habsburg emperor resided in
Vienna. To the south, Moravia was bounded by the archdukedom of Austria, to
the east by the kingdom of Hungary. Some twenty-five miles to the north-west
of Iglau and, as such, part of Bohemia, lay the village of Kalischt (now Kaliště),
where Gustav Mahler was born on 7 July 1860. By then, the Holy Roman
Empire no longer existed, Franz II having ceased to be its emperor in 1806,
when, as Franz I, he became the emperor of Austria. By 1815 Austria had
assumed the presidency of the German Confederation and by 1848 its emperor
was Franz Joseph. The 1848 revolution sent shock waves across the whole
Empire, rocking it to its very foundations, while in Hungary the Imperial Diet
was dissolved. The following year Hungary declared its independence from
Austria but was soon brought back into line. Following the Austro-Prussian
War of 1866, the new nationalist and separatist aspirations of the Slavs and
Magyars were accommodated within the 'Ausgleich' of 1867 (Mahler was then
seven years old), which established the Dual Monarchy of Austro-Hungary, a
remarkably long-lived construct that survived until the First World War. Under
its terms, Austria and Hungary were constituted as independent states enjoying
equal rights, a status which in Hungary's case led to jealousy among the
Bohemians and Moravians. The emperor of Austria ruled over the Cisleithan
lands, in other words, those lands that lay on the western side of the Leitha river
and that included Bohemia and Moravia, while the apostolic king of Hungary

reigned over the Transleithan lands beyond the Leitha. As stipulated by the constitution of the double monarchy, Franz Joseph remained emperor of both Austria and Hungary: two monarchies, one emperor and one king. A linguistic atlas of the time shows that German was the first language of the majority of the population in north-west and south-west Bohemia, while Czech was the predominant language elsewhere. In the case of Moravia, the north-eastern part of the region, beginning in the area around Olmütz (modern Olomouc), was German-speaking, virtually the whole of the rest of the country preferring Czech. There was, however, a small linguistic enclave where German was spoken close to the border between Bohemia and Moravia approximately halfway along its length: this was the area around Iglau.

Some twenty-five miles separate the village of Kalischt from Iglau, a town which, although not large, was none the less important. Mahler's family moved to Iglau in October 1860, and so it is reasonable to regard Mahler himself as one of its sons. Kalischt was a village on the windswept high plateau, although the immediate countryside was attractive enough. The house in which Mahler was born was a squat, single-storey building not unlike the equally modest house in which Verdi was born in Roncole near Busseto. Much later, when Mahler was in his mid-thirties and was out walking with his close confidante, Natalie Bauer-Lechner, they passed a group of similarly miserable-looking peasant cottages, reminding Mahler of his own origins: 'Look, I was born in just such a wretched little house; the windows didn't even have glass in them. There was a pool of water in front of the house. Nearby was the tiny village of Kalischt and a few scattered huts.'[1] It emerges from this that the house occupied by Mahler's parents did not even lie in the village itself, assuming that we can speak of a village at all, but was some distance away. The register of births maintained by the Israelitic community at Unter-Kralowitz (Dolní Kralovice) records that on 7 July 1860 a son, Gustav, was born to the tradesman Bernard Mahler (in early documents his first name is often spelt thus, rather than the more usual Bernhard) and to his wife Marie, the daughter of Abraham Hermann and Theresia née Hermann from Ledetsch (were the two related?), at house no. 9 in Kalischt (villages like this one did not have street names). The entry is dated 23 July, the child having been circumcised on the 14th.[2]

The family moved from Kalischt to Iglau on 22 October. It was more than a mere accident that on the previous day the Emperor Franz Joseph had issued a decree 'To my peoples', granting them additional rights and in the process allowing Austrian Jews greater freedom of movement. Of course, Bernhard Mahler's family did not suddenly decide on this date to move house the very next day. As early as February 1860 an imperial decree had made it possible for Jews – including those in Iglau – to acquire property, and the immediate establishment of the most important Jewish institutions, including a synagogue destroyed in March 1939, reflects the town's attractiveness for Jews, who until then had been more or less scattered along the border between Bohemia and Moravia. With some seventeen thousand inhabitants, Iglau was then the second-largest town in Moravia after Brünn. Compared to the six hundred inhabitants of Kalischt, it was a large town, although the yardstick by which we measure such a town has, of course, changed considerably since Mahler's day. Until 1848 Jews were not allowed to settle in Iglau, but the change in the law encouraged more and more to move there: by 1869 there were already 614, and by the outbreak of the First World War that figure had risen to 1,450, a total that represents some 6.4 per cent of the population.

Described in the register of births as a tradesman, Bernhard Mahler traded in alcoholic beverages both in Kalischt and Iglau. He was also a Jew. Mahler's own Jewish background was to be a lifelong problem for him, and even after his death it has continued to exercise supporters and opponents of his music. It will play a not unimportant role in the course of the following pages.

Throughout the nineteenth century and even later, the Jews of Bohemia and Moravia differed from those who lived further to the east in that they did not live in the usual ghettos cut off from the rest of the population. Even in Prague, where the ghetto could look back on a particularly long tradition, this shtetl was no impervious enclave but a particular quarter that was relatively open. The classic picture of shtetl Jews that enjoyed such dubious popularity only after such a picture had largely been destroyed does not apply to the Jews in nineteenth-century Bohemia and Moravia.[3] Outside Prague, Bohemia's Jews lived in small communities in Czech-speaking Central Bohemia and spoke Czech and German in addition to their own Western Yiddish dialect. If the surrounding area was predominantly German-speaking, as it was in the region around Iglau, then this Yiddish dialect would become increasingly assimilated with the language of the region, even if its speakers did not abandon it entirely. In Moravia there were more small, Jewish-dominated towns that were independently administered. Kalischt was simply a small village in which Jews and non-Jews lived together in a largely harmonious way. The area around Kalischt, like that around Iglau – in spite of the barely perceptible border between Bohemia and Moravia, the two virtually formed a single region – was predominantly German-speaking, with the result that Mahler grew up in a Jewish family that spoke German. As we have already noted, he himself spoke standard Austrian, his own particular idiolect notable for its general excellence, elaborate sentence structures and lively imagery. It was not, however, the language of the Austrian aristocracy.

The Jews of the period sought their livelihood for the most part by working in the textile, brewing and sugar industries, including manufacturing. Typical of their number was Bernhard Mahler and the latter's father, Simon, who ran a distillery, selling his produce both on and off the premises. The Jews in Bohemia and Moravia had not only emerged from their ghettos at a relatively early date but had also tried to shake off the remnants of that existence by increasingly assimilating themselves with their non-Jewish surroundings, the stability of their situation helped in no small part by the fact that they had not been uprooted or persecuted since the Middle Ages. Bohemian Jews tended to gravitate towards Prague and for the most part spoke Czech, while Moravian Jews opted for Vienna and generally spoke German. From this point of view, Mahler was more of a Moravian, although he always regarded himself as a German-speaking Austrian. There were proportionately more Jews in Moravia than in Bohemia and there were a number of relatively large Jewish centres there, whereas in Bohemia the Jewish centre of Prague dominated all others. The figures for the period around 1850, ten years before Mahler was born, are as follows: in Bohemia there were 3 million Czechs, 1.1 million Germans and 66,000 Jews, whereas in Moravia there were 1.3 million Czechs, 600,000 Germans and 38,000 Jews. Here the term 'Jewish minority' seems particularly appropriate, some 100,000 Jews making up 2 per cent of a population of 6.1 million. Prague and Vienna both drew Jews into their sway, which helps to explain why upper-class Jewish families were to be found mainly in Vienna and to a lesser extent in Prague, while the Bohemian and Moravian provinces were the home of middle-class and working-class Jews, including the Jewish lumpenproletariat of pedlars and day labourers.

The relaxation of religious ties that can be observed among Central European Jews in general and that went hand in hand with the process of acculturation with the surrounding non-Jewish world may also be found, of course, among the Jews of Bohemia and Moravia, where it can be seen a whole generation earlier than in Germany. Among the reasons for this is the fact that the Rabbis were badly trained and often incapable of maintaining their congregations' interest in the Jewish religion by means of compelling arguments and by setting an example for others. Internal migration to the larger towns and cities with their more powerful liberal influences often undermined and finally destroyed the attitudes that had seemed unshakable in smaller towns and villages. In the years around the middle of the nineteenth century the liberal Jews who could have steered this trend in the direction of greater reform played virtually no role in Bohemia and Moravia. Joseph II's 1781 Edict of Toleration not only bore within it politically expedient considerations alongside its Enlightenment ideas about the equality of men and, hence, of religious denominations, it also resulted in a growing tendency towards Germanicization that was in increasingly stark contrast to the first stirrings of Czech nationalism. This led to an increase in anti-Jewish attitudes on the part of that portion of the population that felt itself to be Czech, attitudes that gradually developed into open anti-Semitism.

All these tendencies were aspects of what might be termed the general weather pattern and were not necessarily equally apparent in every place and at every time. Certainly, they were clearly not such burning issues in Kalischt and Iglau that they left their mark on the day-to-day lives of Mahler and his family. We know relatively little about Mahler's forebears, although the family can be traced back to the small town of Chmelná in Bohemia, close to the modern town of Dolní Kralovice. Mahler's great-great-grandfather on his father's side was originally called Abraham Jacob, in other words, Abraham the son of Jacob. When all the Jews living in the Habsburg Empire were required to assume 'regular' surnames following Joseph II's decree of 1787, Abraham Jacob took the name of Abraham Mahler, perhaps because he ground spices, the German verb for 'to grind' being *mahlen*. He also sang in his local synagogue and oversaw the kosher slaughter of animals. Abraham Mahler (1720–1800) thus appears to have been the only previous member of the family to evince any interest in music. He lived with a freeborn peasant by the name of Matous Gilig, and the same was true of his son Bernard. (As with Mahler's own father, the form 'Bernard' was initially more prevalent than 'Bernhard'.) Bernard Mahler was described as a grocer, a profession pursued by several members of the family. He was Mahler's great-grandfather. The composer's grandfather, Simon, was born in Chmelná in the district of Benesov in 1793 and died in Lipnitz (Lipnice) in 1855. Mahler's grandmother was called Marie (or Maria) Bondy and was born in 1801. She died at a ripe old age in 1883, also in Lipnitz. Her father, Abraham Bondy, was a butcher in Lipnitz. Simon and Marie Mahler were married without the permission of the state authorities, with the result that their marriage was not legally recognized. Their ten children were not legitimized until 1850.

Gustav's father, Bernhard, was born – illegitimately – at Lipnitz near Deutsch-Brod (Nemecký Brod) on 2 August 1827. That same year Bernhard's family moved to house no. 52 in Kalischt, where there was an existing distillery that his father-in-law, Abraham Bondy, leased and that Simon Mahler bought in 1828. Here Bernhard learnt everything that there was to know about the business of distilling and selling alcohol, and even as a young man he was already delivering his father's produce to the surrounding area. Sometimes he had to spend the night in Iglau, in which case he had to report his arrival and departure to the police. (Three such stays are recorded in 1856 and 1858.) It was no doubt during one of these business trips that he met his wife Marie, née Hermann, who was born in Ledetsch on 2 March 1837. Both socially and financially, her family was more successful than the Mahlers. Indeed, her father, Abraham, was evidently a well-to-do businessman and soap manufacturer. Manufacturing soap was certainly more respectable than distilling alcohol. The term 'soap boiler', which is occasionally used to describe Abraham, sounds condescending and even comical to modern readers, but it covered a wide range of possibilities, from simple manual worker to successful industrialist: Abraham belonged to the second group. Brandy distillers and soap boilers – of such stuff are geniuses made. The parents of Mahler's mother, Abraham and Theresia Hermann from Ledetsch, create a more prosperous impression than his father's family on their two surviving photographs.

Bernhard and Marie married in 1857, Marie bringing to the marriage a size-able dowry of 3,500 florins, which allowed the family to buy a somewhat larger and better house in Kalischt, no. 9 in the town. This was the house in which Mahler himself was born. His date of birth is given in several contemporary documents as 1 and 14 July 1860, but the records of the local Jewish commu-nity help to shed light on this discrepancy: 14 July was the day of Mahler's circumcision, a ceremony performed by David Kraus of Ledetsch, with two local godparents in attendance, Ignatz Weiner and Anton Kern. The child was born on the 7th. It remains unclear why Mahler's school reports invariably state that he was born on the 1st, although the simplest explanation is that the numeral 7 – written at the time without a cross-bar, as in modern English – was misread as a 1, an error that was then perpetuated.

As we have already noted, Mahler's grandfather and father were both active as distillers, an occupation frequently found among Jews at this time. It was not a disreputable calling. In an earlier age, it had been a privilege accorded to feudal lords, and even Christians pursued it, not that this prevented them from criticizing Jews for doing so, just as they upbraided them for lending money, often going so far as to accuse Jews of seeking to ruin them by forcing them to consume alcohol. Documents have survived in which attempts are made to defend distilling against such accusations. Bernhard Mahler's father does not in fact appear to have been very successful as a distiller. According to information given by Mahler to Natalie Bauer-Lechner, it was his grandmother, rather than his grandfather, who contributed to the upkeep of the family by going from house to house selling mercery goods. Possibly deterred by his father's lack of success in the business, Bernhard Mahler himself turned to distilling only at a relatively late date, having begun his professional life as a carrier, working his way up with what his son described as exceptional resolve. Initially things were not easy for the family. When Mahler was born, the 'wretched little house', as he called it, did not even have glazed windows, and even in the refurbished state in which it appears in later photographs, it still leaves a pitiful impression. This does not mean, however, that the family that Bernhard and Marie Mahler started here lived in grinding poverty. Rather, we must assume that they rapidly rose from modest beginnings and were soon enjoying a certain affluence.

According to Alma, Bernhard Mahler already owned a distillery in Kalischt and transferred it to Iglau immediately after Gustav's birth. His firm's headed paper indicates that he owned a 'Rum, Punch, Rosolio, Liqueur and Essence

Manufactory', a fine-sounding name for what was initially a small-scale enterprise. ('Rosolio' or 'rosoglio' is the Italian word for liqueur, no doubt indicating
a different type of taste from the one conjured up by the French term.) Such
businesses were known as liqueur manufactories rather than schnapps distill-
eries, not least because the term implied greater respectability. It was also
customary at this time to sell the distillery's produce both over the counter and
at a bar attached to the premises. But Mahler was entirely right to protest when
the writer Richard Specht referred to his father simply as a 'publican' in one of
his publications, finding the term 'businessman' more fitting.[4] When Bernhard
Mahler moved to Iglau, he had to reapply for permission to manufacture and
distribute his produce. The document in question has survived. He was
allowed to manufacture and sell spirits but not to sell them over the counter on
account of existing competition. But this permission, too, was granted in 1861,
and from then on Bernhard Mahler was able to sell spirits over the counter
on the ground floor of the house in which he lived. Other shops were gradually added, Bernhard Mahler's alcohol production and bar eventually being
extended to embrace a whole chain of such establishments.

Bernhard Mahler's choleric temperament repeatedly got him into trouble.
On one occasion he sold bread, which he was not allowed to do, and on
another he traded in alcohol in places where he was not authorized. He also
adopted a very liberal attitude to closing times in his various retail outlets. And
he succeeded only with difficulty in avoiding a hefty fine when he insulted a
local official. It is not hard to imagine volcanic eruptions within the family
circle. Bernhard Mahler's plans were inventive if not always successful. He
tried running a lottery under the over-optimistic name of 'God's Blessing',
although the lottery itself signally failed to enjoy the Almighty's blessing, and
it was not until a second such scheme was floated, this time called 'Luck', that
good fortune smiled on Bernhard Mahler. In spite of all the setbacks and problems that he encountered, he was ultimately successful in his chosen line of
business. If we may briefly turn the clock forward: in 1872, when Mahler was
twelve, Bernhard Mahler was able to buy the adjoining property at 264
Pirnitzergasse from Anna Proksch for 10,000 florins, by no means a small sum
of money – almost three times Marie's dowry, it was the equivalent of over
£40,000 at today's prices. The building had a large courtyard with a barn, and
Bernhard Mahler soon built on to the first storey, an extension made necessary
by the increasing size of his family. The ground floor was reserved for his business operations, while the family lived on the first floor, facing the street. The
servants occupied the first-floor rooms at the back, overlooking the courtyard,
and the floor above was let to another family.

The following year Bernhard Mahler evidently felt that the time had
come to place his existence in Iglau on a bureaucratically sound footing as

he was still a citizen of Kalischt, living in Iglau virtually as a guest of the town. No one could automatically acquire civil rights in a town simply because they lived there, and not even the ownership of a house was enough. But every citizen of the Empire could apply for such rights after he had lived in a community for ten years, a state of affairs that was extended to cover Jews, too, after 1860. Three years after he was officially entitled to do so, Bernhard Mahler duly applied for these rights, arguing that not only was he a house-holder but that he was also running a successful business. The itinerant schnapps dealer had reached the peak of his middle-class career, his application being accepted without question. On payment of a large fee he and his family became citizens of Iglau, and later that same year he took up an impor-tant post in the town's Jewish community, although the exact nature of his function is unclear.

For at least a section of the Jewish population, acculturation and the ascent of the social ladder went hand in hand with a veritable thirst for education, a desire for cultural improvement evident from the autobiographical accounts of many Bohemian and Moravian Jews. In particular, those who had attended grammar schools retained a lifetime commitment to the ideal of education and learning. They read more enthusiastically and more intensively than the Czech population and owned a treasured collection of books which in middle-class families was carefully kept in a glass-fronted cupboard in the living room. Central to these small private libraries were generally the German classics, Lessing, Goethe, Schiller and, above all, Heinrich Heine, a writer whom they regarded as one of their own, preferring to ignore his somewhat awkward rela-tions with Judaism. Although it was only in Iglau that Bernhard Mahler was really able to feel a member of the middle classes, he too clearly shared this desire to improve his mind. Mahler himself rarely had a good word to say about his father, and yet he reports that even as a carrier Bernhard used to have books about his person and that he came to be known as a 'coach-box scholar'. It was only logical, therefore, that his sons would attend a grammar school if at all possible.

Bernhard Mahler did nothing to encourage his son's later rejection of Judaism. From 1873 Bernhard played a role in the town's Jewish community and from 1878 he was a member of its committee on education, a position that he could scarcely have assumed unless he had been active for some time in municipal affairs. He was on terms of such close friendship with the local cantor that the latter stood godfather to Mahler's favourite sister, Justine. As always, it was the mother on whom devolved the task of providing her children with a religious education, and she cannot have been negligent in this regard as Mahler received his best mark – 'very good' – for religion in his first school report, which qualified the subject parenthetically as 'Mosaic'.

Our first evidence of Mahler's musical sensibilities is bound up with the town's synagogue. He told Natalie Bauer-Lechner, for many years his closest friend, that when he was about three he was taken to the synagogue but interrupted the singing of the congregation with shouts and screams: 'Be quiet, be quiet, it's horrible!' He then apparently insisted that they should sing the old Bohemian song, 'At'se pinkl házi' ('The bundle swings to and fro'), even singing it to them first in order to give them the tune.[5] So Mahler grew up in a family that embraced the religion of its forefathers. His estrangement from Judaism evidently took place only after he moved to Vienna to study.

Mahler also spoke to Natalie about his father's character and his parents' marriage. His mother did not love his father and barely knew him before they were married. She had had her eye on another man, but contemporary practice demanded that young women be dragged into marriage by their parents and by the tenacity of their suitor. It would not be cynical to claim that, judging by numerous eyewitness accounts, some of the resultant matches were less happy than others. In the case of Mahler's parents, the marriage certainly seems to have been an unhappy one. Mahler himself claims that his parents were as ill-matched as fire and water, his father being the very epitome of brute obstinacy, while his mother was gentleness itself. There were good reasons for this. Alma also reports that his mother limped from birth, although this is supported by no other testimony. Mahler's father, conversely, is said by Alma to have been a creature of instinct and a sensualist, brooking no inhibitions in this area.[6] In his virtuoso, iconoclastic and, in part, revealing film about Mahler, Ken Russell shows us the father as a debauched lecher lurching from bouts of alcoholism to sexual violations of his female servants, the sensitive little Mahler fleeing his father's beatings by seeking refuge in nature. A fundamental point that needs to be made at the outset is that Alma's reminiscences of her first husband, together with the corresponding passages in her memoirs, need to be treated with the utmost caution. The number of manifest distortions and falsifications of the truth is legion, whether the result of calculation or failing memory or the passage of time. Alma based her picture of Mahler on the principle that her own recollections were paramount and that she was writing from the perspective of a survivor who saw herself as a victim. As a point of principle, we shall do better to regard Natalie's reminiscences as far more substantial and credible as she wrote down Mahler's remarks immediately after their walks or other encounters. Her later revisions, undertaken at a time when, to her infinite sadness, she and Mahler went their separate ways, seem not to have led to any distortions. To that extent, the portrait of Mahler's father that is painted by Alma may be questioned.

There is no doubt, conversely, that there was a far closer bond between Mahler and his mother than with his father, but this, too, is entirely normal. It was also entirely normal, unfortunately, that the health of many young women was undermined by a succession of births as rapid as those that we nowadays associate with so-called primitive peoples. It is not entirely certain how many children Marie Mahler bore – this, too, is not unusual, given the state of documentation at this time, especially in lower middle-class families living in rural areas. Gustav was her second son after a brother, Isidor, who was born in 1858 and who was only a few weeks old when he died, apparently from an accident. Six children are believed to have died in infancy, although this, too, was by no means exceptional, diphtheria and other infectious diseases having a devastating effect on infant mortality. Apart from Gustav, six children survived. Ernst, who was born in 1862 and to whom Mahler was particularly close, died of a heart ailment in 1875. Mahler's mother, too, is said to have had a congenital heart defect, so that Mahler's own problems with his heart, which were directly related to his final fatal illness, may have been hereditary. His sister Leopoldine died in Vienna of a brain tumour in 1889 at the age of twenty-six. According to Alma, she too had been married off to a husband she did not love. Another brother, Alois, emigrated to America, evidently the black sheep of the family. For a long time he had to be supported there, but by the time of his death in Chicago in 1931 he was thoroughly respectable, if entirely unknown.[7] Mahler's favourite sister, Justine Ernestine, shared a house with Mahler until he married Alma Schindler. The very next day she married the violinist Arnold Rosé, who was the leader of the Vienna Philharmonic and, hence, of the Vienna Court Opera Orchestra, as well as being the leader of the Rosé Quartet. Justine died in Vienna in August 1938. Although she lived to witness Austria's annexation by Germany, she was spared its appalling aftermath. Conversely, Justine's daughter Alma, named after her mother's sister-in-law, was not spared the horrors of the Second World War. In 1932 she had founded a ladies' orchestra, the Wiener Walzermädel (literally, the Waltzing Girls of Vienna), that toured the whole of Europe. When Arnold Rosé, by then a widower, emigrated to London in 1939, Alma followed him but returned to the continent for professional reasons, visiting first the Netherlands and then France. She was arrested in Dijon and deported to Auschwitz in July 1943. There she founded a women's orchestra, her uncompromising stance providing an inspiration for the other women in the orchestra. Mahler's niece died in Auschwitz in April 1944, probably from food poisoning.[8] His favourite brother, Otto, was in Mahler's view an extremely talented musician. Otto took his own life in Vienna in February 1895. Emma Marie Eleonor, Mahler's youngest sister, who for a time lived with Mahler and Justine, died in Weimar in May 1933.

The town of Iglau, to which the Mahlers moved in 1860 from the more than modest farmstead in Kalischt – it was really no more than a cottage – was quite different from the backwater where Mahler was born. Their first home in the town was at Pirnitzergasse C no. 265/4, where they rented first-floor rooms from the house's owner, Anastasia Kampfova. Although Iglau was known then – and now – as Jihlava in Czech, this name was of little significance as the population spoke mostly German, Czech being the language used by the servants. Iglau was a beautiful, even neat and tidy town clustered around St Jakob's Church which, situated on a hill, was visible from far around. From there, the streets fell away steeply to the idyllic Heulos valley. The town was surrounded by a double circumvallation and from a military standpoint was regarded as secure. The contemporary historian Christian d'Elvert has particular praise for the town square, also known as the Stadtring, which certainly creates an imposing impression on old maps of the town as well as on photographs. Even today, it remains largely unaltered. On maps it seems positively disproportionate, as its size – more than 400,000 square feet – bears no relation to that of the town but seems to occupy a sixth of its overall area. This jewel in the municipality's crown was lined by beautiful two- and three-storey private houses, while the square itself contained two fountains and a large statue of the Virgin Mary. There were three suburbs outside the town walls: the Spital-Vorstadt, the Frauen-Vorstadt and the Pirnitzer Vorstadt. The last-named lay to the south of Iglau and was directly connected to the main square by the Pirnitzergasse. As is clear from a town plan dated 1862, the property on the western side of the street nearest the square is a long complex of buildings numbered 266, with numbers 265 and 264 immediately to the south of it. Inasmuch as the respectability of these houses was defined by their proximity to the town centre, we may well be entitled to claim that in moving to Iglau the Mahler family had finally made it.

Within the context of the Austro-Hungarian provinces, having made it did not mean living in the lap of luxury. Theodor Fischer, the son of one of the Mahlers' neighbours, whose father later became municipal director of music and gave harmony lessons to the young Gustav, has left a description of the Mahlers' first apartment in Iglau. The family lived on the first floor, which consisted of a large kitchen, a vestibule and two other rooms. The larger of these two rooms was furnished as a salon, with the usual rep trimmings, a glass display cabinet for ornaments and porcelain and, later, the framed letter according Bernhard Mahler his patent of citizenship in Iglau, an important and valuable document for a Jew who had previously enjoyed far fewer civic rights but who now had the freedom to settle wherever he wanted. The room also contained a bookcase in which the 'coach-box scholar' kept works by both classical and contemporary writers, and a grand piano made by the firm of Vopaterny on which Mahler practised his first five-finger exercises. If Theodor Fischer's memory served him and allowing for misunderstandings, the second room was the communal bedroom for parents and children, in other words, Gustav, Ernst, Leopoldine,

Alois and Justine, making a total of seven, for it was not until 1872 that the family moved next door to 264 Pirnitzergasse, a house which – as is clear from the map of the town – was no wider at the front but which extended further back and presumably provided the family with more space.

The former apartment had been rented, but Bernhard Mahler was able to buy the adjacent property, suggesting that he was extremely successful as a businessman and that Mahler's pride in his father's status was fully justified. Later renamed the Znaimergasse and now known as Malinovského, the Pirnitzergasse was not a very long street and fell away fairly steeply towards the town wall. The first block, between the town square and a narrow street crossing the Pirnitzergasse at right angles, comprised only five properties, the second block between the side street and the town wall only six more, at which point the world of Iglau came to an end. A surviving photograph shows clearly that the two houses in which the Mahlers successively lived were relatively narrow, being only three windows wide and having only two storeys, whereas the corner house was more imposing and had a Renaissance gable. A photograph of the entrance hall has also survived: it shows a dark stairwell with a vaulted ceiling and well-worn stone steps. In the Fischers' house next door there were abandoned workshops and dark attics calculated to create an eerie impression, and here the children's maid would tell her charges appropriate fairytales and horror stories, including perhaps the story of the sad song on which Theodor Fischer claims that Mahler's first real work was based.

A Child in Iglau

The first surviving photograph of Bernhard Mahler shows him in the typical attitude of the conquering hero standing beside a table and wearing a coat, with a top hat in his hand. The photograph is so blurred that all that we can really make out is a man in his mid-thirties – it could be about the time of Gustav's birth. Measured by the size of the table against which he is supporting himself, he appears to be relatively small in stature, a feature inherited by his son. He is also sporting a walrus moustache. But, apart from that, it is impossible to make out any other details. A second, later photograph shows a much older man with grey streaks in his beard and tired, almost lifeless eyes. His wife, seen standing by the same table in the same photographer's studio, is wearing a voluminous black satin dress and looks larger and more compact than her husband. There is as yet no sign here of the heart disease from which she suffered, nor of the exhaustion caused by bringing so many children into the world. If we are to speak of family resemblances, then Mahler clearly looks much more like his mother than his father, not just physically but in terms of the close emotional ties between them.

The earliest surviving photograph of Mahler himself shows him at the age of about six, dressed in a dark, tight-fitting suit, with a white round collar (Ill. 5). In his right hand, he is holding a lighter-coloured flat hat. On a chair is something that looks like a large sheet of paper or a newspaper but which is in fact a sheet of music that the child is holding firmly in his left hand. Mahler later explained to Natalie Bauer-Lechner his fear of being swallowed up by the intimidating photographic apparatus and of finding himself fixed to a sheet of cardboard behind the camera. Only when his father was similarly photographed without anything untoward happening was it possible to calm the boy. But the unfathomable sadness that all the adults present must have tried to dispel cannot be explained simply in terms of the child's fear of being photographed and remains deeply disturbing. It is the boy's dark, deep-set eyes in combination with the corners of the mouth that are turned down as far as possible that characterize his face and that were to remain essentially the same until the end of his life. Mahler's short-sightedness and the glasses that he wore to alleviate this condition meant that his eyes were not so expressive in later life, but the downward-turning corners of his mouth continued to dominate his features even when he smiled, which he rarely did in photographs. The result is always a smile against a background of sadness or at least of melancholy reserve. It is an aspect of his expression that Mahler clearly inherited from his mother, even if it was not as pronounced in her case.

What kind of a child was Mahler? Alma's tragically heroic picture of a terrified child beaten every day by his father and barked at for being untidy so that he sought refuge in daydreams reflects only one side of his character and behaviour. As with all the facts and explanations that Alma offers for the period before she knew Mahler, it is impossible to decide if they are a truthful reflection of what he said (which is not necessarily the same as the truth) or whether, deliberately or otherwise, she falsified the truth. There is no doubt that Mahler was a particularly sensitive child, although this in itself is hardly surprising. After all, where is the genius of whom it is said that as a child he was rough, unfeeling and lacking in imagination? Whenever his mother was ill in bed, as she often was with a migraine, he would kneel behind her and pray intently, before asking her if she felt any better. In order not to undermine his self-confidence, she would claim that she was already feeling a little better, even when this was not the case. He would then crawl back behind the bed and continue praying in order to complete her recovery.

The fact that a sheet of music was pressed into the six-year-old Mahler's little hand in the photographer's studio clearly indicates the importance that his family attached to his musical interests. Was Mahler a child prodigy? When judged by the standards of the time, the answer must be no. Mozart was five when he began to write music and six when he first appeared before the elector of Bavaria as a keyboard virtuoso. By the age of eight he had learnt notation and written four violin sonatas. The young Beethoven received his first keyboard lessons from his father at the age of four or five, but the latter's limited abilities as a teacher prevented the child from attaining his true potential as a prodigy. In spite of this, Beethoven was still only eight when he was thrust into the limelight at a public concert in Cologne, even though this did not lead to a continuous career. Brahms was ten when he first appeared in public as a pianist, but his piano teacher, Otto Cossel, wisely prevented him from embarking on a career as a child pianist, and it was not until he was seventeen that he wrote his first real compositions. Wagner was even more of a late developer and was sixteen when he first tried his hand at composition, these early works proving far inferior to Brahms's in terms of their expressive power and technical sophistication. Mahler occupies the middle ground between child prodigy and late developer.

When judged by the scant evidence that has survived from the period that Mahler spent as a young student in Vienna, we are relatively well informed about his burgeoning feelings for music. He himself clearly attached so much weight to these experiences and to related episodes and anecdotes that he recounted them to Natalie Bauer-Lechner. (Some of them do not appear in the most recent edition of her recollections but only in the autograph copy.[9]) He himself will not have taken entirely seriously the claim that he gave his first proof of his musical gifts as a new-born infant on the journey from Kalischt to Ledetsch, where he was to be shown off to his grandparents. The two villages were a day's journey apart, and Mahler screamed so insistently that his mother and father took it in turns to sing to him and rock him, even having to walk alongside the carriage, singing the same song, in an attempt to calm him down. More significant is the fact that at an age when he could barely walk he could already repeat each song he heard and that when he was about three he began to play the accordion: a substitute for the piano, this was then the most popular instrument in this particular part of the world. Mahler's accordion was presumably a smaller version more appropriate to his age. On it he would pick out the notes of the music he had just heard, acquiring a certain proficiency on the instrument within a short space of time. But the child's greatest love was band music, which was part of the sound world that left its mark on Mahler's childhood and adolescence and that it requires little imagination to hear in the marches of his symphonies. Iglau was home to a military garrison, and it appears that its band marched along the Pirnitzergasse before playing in the town square. One morning when Mahler was not yet four years old, he ran after the band, dressed only in his shirt, with his accordion slung round his neck. The neighbours' wives caught him in their arms, determined to enjoy a good joke at the child's expense. They set him down on a fruit stall and asked him to repeat what the band had just played. Only then, they said, would they take him home, Mahler having in the meantime lost his sense of direction. He did as they bade him, whereupon he was carried back home to his worried parents with a great deal of commotion. On another occasion, when he was already attending school, he stopped to watch a passing band, remaining fascinated by the sight and sound of them for so long that he dirtied himself and the smell drove the bystanders away.

It was only logical that the accordion should be followed by the piano. Mahler's acquaintance with this last-named instrument cannot have been as spontaneous as it was in the lives of most other musicians, where the small child might discover the piano in his parents' music-loving household and coax from it his first enchanted sounds. The Mahler family however – untypically for a lower middle-class household of the period and untypically even for a businessman like Bernhard Mahler – did not own a piano. It required another journey to Ledetsch by the now somewhat older Mahler and his parents to visit his grandparents, whose piano had been banished to the attic – another sign of the marginal role played by music in Mahler's family. The keyboard of this 'musical monster', as Mahler called it, was still so high that he had to raise his hands above his head to reach it. Even so, he managed to pick out a tune on it, causing considerable amazement among the adults downstairs. This was undoubtedly a special day in Mahler's life, for his family was finally forced to acknowledge the child's exceptional talent. His grandfather asked if the instrument gave him pleasure, and a day later it arrived in Iglau on an ox-drawn cart. Mahler must then have been four or five years old. It seems to have been Czech members of a dance band that played in one of his father's bars who gave him his first lessons on the piano, but a proper teacher was soon engaged in the person of Jan Broz, who was followed by Franz Sturm.

By his own account, Mahler made such rapid progress that by the age of six he was in a position to make his first public appearance, when the instrument's pedals had to be extended by means of wooden blocks so that he could reach them with his feet. There are no surviving records of this concert, and it was not until October 1870, when Mahler was ten, that any notice was taken of one of his public appearances. In 1866 his audience presumably consisted of members of his own family. He himself had no memory of the event but relied on the accounts of other family members, who recalled that at this and similar appearances he did not bow to the audience in the way usually associated with child prodigies but made straight for the piano and began to play. At the end of the performance he would then disappear again without waiting for the applause. He was little more than six when he became a piano teacher in his own right. Even at that early date there were already signs of the implacably high demands that he made of his musicians as he held his hand close to his pupil's cheek, ready to cuff him whenever he played a wrong note. As an alternative, or possibly in addition, the pupil was required to write out the line 'I must play C sharp and not C' one hundred times, a method that soon frightened off the young Mahler's first pupil. He was somewhat more successful with his second pupil, even if he was once reduced to running home, howling, to tell his mother: 'I don't want to teach the piano any longer to this stupid boy, who plays so badly, no, no, no.' The five kreuzers an hour that he received for his lessons were his first income as a musician. Never again, however, was he to be active as a teacher, either on the piano or as a conductor or composer – at least if we disregard his detailed work with orchestras and singers. He simply did not have the time for teaching in addition to composition.

Mahler dated his first compositions to his sixth year. Although it was subsequently unnumbered and has not survived, his op. 1 was a curious but entirely typical combination of a polka and an introductory funeral march. At the age of six, Mahler accepted paid commissions as a composer, something he was never to do in later life, his mother having promised him two kreuzers on condition that he did not make any ink blots on the expensive music manuscript paper. Such blots were common at this time as neither the ink nor the pens met present-day standards of quality and reliability. (Nietzsche spent his whole life wrestling with his writing materials.) In fact, Mahler did use one of the very latest safety pens, but he still managed to produce an ink blot in spite of praying to God to help him to avoid such a disaster. He later recalled with a laugh that his faith in God had received a considerable knock as a result of this incident.

His op. 2 was another commissioned piece, a song that he wrote for his father, again in the hope of receiving a fee. Somewhat surprisingly, he chose a poem by Lessing, a writer whose works he may have found in his parents' bookcase. Certainly the author of the two plays *The Jews* and *Nathan the Wise*, and a friend of Moses Mendelssohn, was one of the most popular classical writers among German and Austrian Jews. Mahler quoted the poem from memory in conversation with Natalie, who transcribed it as follows:

> Die Türken haben schöne Töchter,
> die hüten strenge Keuschheitswächter,
> ein Türke darf viel Mädchen freien.
> Ich möchte wohl ein Türke sein.
> Der Liebe ganz ergeben,
> der Liebe nur zu leben.
> Doch: Türken trinken keinen Wein,
> nein, nein, ich will kein Türke sein!

[The Turks have beautiful daughters who are guarded by strict harem guards, a Turk may woo lots of girls. I'd like to be a Turk. Devoted entirely to love and living for love alone. But: Turks don't drink wine, no, no, I don't want to be a Turk!]

This is how the meticulous Natalie transcribed it.[10] In fact, Lessing's original departs from this transcription at several points:

> Die Türken haben schöne Töchter
> Und diese scharfe Keuschheitswächter;
> Wer will, kann mehr als eine frei'n:
> Ich möchte schon ein Türke sein.
> Wie wollt' ich mich der Lieb ergeben!
> Wie wollt' ich liebend ruhig leben
> Und . . . doch sie trinken keinen Wein;
> Nein, nein, ich mag kein Türke sein.

[The Turks have beautiful daughters and these in turn have strict harem guards; he who wants to can woo more than one: I'd like to be a Turk. How I'd devote myself to love! How I'd like to lead a quiet life of love and . . . but they don't drink wine; no, no, I don't want to be a Turk.]

These lapses of memory are relatively unimportant, of course, although it is worth noting that Lessing's 'Wie wollt' ich liebend ruhig leben' ('How I'd like to lead a quiet life of love') becomes 'der Liebe nur zu leben' ('to live for love alone'), one of the central passages from the love duet in Act Two of Wagner's *Tristan und Isolde*, a borrowing that neither Mahler nor Natalie nor later readers appear to have noticed. Mahler merely adds that the notion of living for love alone, which is not in Lessing's original, struck him as terribly poetical, prompting Natalie to comment pointedly that this was a remarkable choice of text for someone who had such an ascetic approach to wine and women. Mahler remained a teetotaller all his life, but as far as women were concerned, he was by no means as abstinent as Natalie believed – not that he chose to contradict her on this point.

Some of Mahler's later attempts at composition date from his years at the Vienna Conservatory: a sonata for violin and piano, a nocturne for cello, several solo piano pieces and finally an opera to a text by his closest school friend, Josef Steiner, *Herzog Ernst von Schwaben* (Duke Ernst of Swabia). What would we not give to have an opera by Mahler, however childish or fragmentary! But unfortunately the incomplete *Herzog Ernst* has not survived, even though it played a crucial role in Mahler's acceptance to study at the Vienna Conservatory in the autumn of 1875. All in all, the information that is available to us conveys a picture of a highly gifted child expressing himself with increasing independence as a performer and composer. He was not, however, a precocious child prodigy like Mozart, astounding connoisseurs and artists of the time. It is difficult to judge if there was a basic difference in Mozart's and Mahler's gifts or whether it was simply their differing family backgrounds and social circumstances that led their talents to develop at different rates. Perhaps the most decisive difference was that Mozart was supported by his father Leopold, with all the latter's ambitions and connections, whereas Bernhard Mahler had no musical interests and was taken completely unawares by his son's talent, a talent repeated in Mahler's brother Otto, while the other people around Mahler were equally inadequately prepared to deal with such gifts. A cautious comparison between the subsequent development of both composers shows Mozart developing at a markedly slower rate than Mahler, who was twenty when he completed his first version of *Das klagende Lied*, on which he had already been working for two years. At a similar age Mozart wrote *La finta giardiniera*. Of course, such comparisons between two compositions that are so remote in time are problematical, and yet it remains a fact that *Das klagende Lied* reveals a composer in no way inferior to the Mozart of *La finta giardiniera* either creatively or in terms of its orchestration.

Mahler was six when he started school, attending the Imperial and Royal Primary School in the Brünnergasse. He will have started more or less regular music lessons at the same time, initially with Franz Sturm. Later teachers, both at school and elsewhere, included the conductor at the Iglau Municipal Theatre, Franz Victorin, the aforementioned Jan Broz (also known as Johannes Brosch), Wenzel Pressburg, the double-bass player Jakob Sladky and, above all, Heinrich A. Fischer. As stated, the Fischers were the Mahlers' neighbours in the Pirnitzergasse. Heinrich Fischer was also the music director of the local male-voice choir and the father of Mahler's childhood friend, Theodor, who many years later published his reminiscences of the composer.[11] It was Heinrich Fischer who gave Mahler his first lessons in harmony. The composer later told Natalie that his parents borrowed music scores for him from the town's lending library, this, too, being a middle-class tradition not least because then, as now, scores were prohibitively expensive to buy. Each week a portfolio of symphonies, salon pieces, sonatas and operatic arrangements would arrive before having to be returned to the library a week later. (This practice also recalls the custom of the 'reading circle' that has now almost entirely died out.) These scores filled the child with unparalleled delight, and he would quickly play through them, finding everything equally wonderful. Later, Mahler expressed surprise at his indifference to the fact that some pieces were musically better than others, but he no doubt worked it all out so well that his lively imagination made up for any deficiencies.[12]

Mahler's field of vision grew considerably more extended between his sixth and his tenth year of life. Iglau, a town of nearly 20,000 inhabitants, had enormous cultural potential. The town's theatre seated 1,020 and, like many theatres of the time, staged spoken drama, operas and operettas but not ballet. Ten years before Mahler's birth it had been built into the former Capuchin Church, an act of secularization rich in symbolic significance. Edited by the local prompter, a Herr Borzutzky, the almanach for the Iglau Municipal Theatre for the 1870/71 season lists mainly spoken plays, but the operatic repertory included Bellini's *Norma*, Meyerbeer's *Robert le diable*, Mozart's *Don Giovanni* and Hérold's *Zampa*. Two years after the theatre was opened, the Iglau Male-Voice Choir was founded, the years leading up to Mahler's birth revealing considerable new momentum in the municipal culture of the community. The choir's motto was 'Fest und treu, froh und frei' ('Steadfast and true, happy and free'). The significance of this and similar associations for the musical life of towns relatively remote from Vienna and Prague cannot be overemphasized. Even Meistergesang had a tradition in Iglau, a singing school having been established in the town as early as 1571. But the Iglau Music Association in which professional and amateur musicians played orchestral music was disbanded in 1862. Nor should we forget performances in St Jakob's Church. According to Theodor Fischer, its activities included performances of Mozart's *Requiem*, Beethoven's *Christus am Oelberge* and Rossini's *Stabat Mater*, all of them works requiring more than merely amateur enthusiasm to perform them.

But the world of music in which Mahler grew up included not only the foregoing official institutions, it covered a much wider range of activities. As we have already seen, the young Mahler was particularly fascinated by military music. The garrison was stationed close to the town's main church, and there was always an infantry regiment in Iglau, involving the inevitable colourful uniforms in the town square, reveille and tattoo, the shouts and exercise signals and, on special occasions, music played in the town square, the size of which helped to create a particularly magnificent impression. A regimental band normally consisted of eight soldiers. At the front was the conductor with his large stick to beat time, a stick that he would flourish with a great show of virtuosity. Behind him were a trumpet and cornet, then generally a baritone horn and a tuba and, finally, cymbals and two sets of drums. The musicologist Guido Adler, who was a friend and fiercely loyal supporter of Mahler, also grew up in Iglau, although he was five years older than the composer. In his book on Mahler he describes the importance of military music for Mahler's later career, while the composer's childhood friend Theodor Fischer additionally drew attention to the significance of the dance bands that performed at fairs in Iglau and the surrounding area. Even though children were not allowed to dance, they could listen until it was time for them to go to bed. The typical Iglau dance band consisted of a string quartet comprising a four-string 'Klarfiedel', a three-string 'Grobfiedel', a viola and a 'Platschperment', the latter a small double bass that the player rested diagonally on his upper legs and played with a bow. There was even a traditional local dance, the two-part *hatscho*, the first section of which was in a relatively solemn 3/4 metre, while the second was a galop in 2/4 time, inevitably reminding us of the polka with an introductory funeral march that Mahler wrote as a child. Theodor Fischer was even reminded of such a *hatscho* when hearing the third movement of Mahler's First Symphony.

The klezmer music performed by groups of Jewish musicians that is regularly associated with Mahler's childhood is not mentioned at all in eyewitness accounts of this period. The term derives from a Yiddish version of two Hebrew words, *klej* = 'tools', and *semer* = 'song', and means 'music instruments'. This kind of music is now universally popular, the annihilation and disappearance of the Eastern European Jews having belatedly contributed to its popularity. Although there is a widespread belief that virtually all Jewish music from the region east of the Elbe was klezmer music, it needs to be stressed that such music was chiefly found among Eastern European Jews, in other words, among the Jews who lived in parts of present-day Poland, Byelorussia, Lithuania, Romania, Moldavia and the Ukraine. The Jews of Bohemia and Moravia should be regarded not as Eastern European but as Central European Jews. The region around Iglau where Mahler grew up was no 'klezmer area'. This does not mean that there were no Jewish musicians who played at public events and other celebrations, or even individual musicians of Jewish descent who played in bands and brought their very specific clarinet sonorities to the sound world of such a band. There were undoubtedly such musicians in the Iglau area, and the sporadic traces of the world of Jewish music that we find in Mahler's works and to which we shall return in due course are presumably bound up with such trace elements. However, neither in Mahler's case nor in that of Guido Adler, who was subjected to the very same influences, can there be any question of the influence of specifically Jewish music. Rather, it is symptomatic of the world into which he was born and, more especially, of the world of music at this time that Moravian and Bohemian dance music, the folksongs of the region (which were later to inspire Janáček) and the instrumental mastery of popular Jewish musicians combined to produce a stimulating and exciting blend.[13]

A second photograph of the young Mahler survives from the time when he first appeared as a pianist before a wider public. The features that were later to appear clear-cut and striking are still immature and lacking in definition, while the eyes, which even here seem to suggest short-sightedness, are dreamily unfocused and appear to imply introspection rather than peer inquisitively out into the world. Here is the description of Mahler left by Theodor Fischer, who probably knew him better at this time than anyone apart from his own family:

> At school, Mahler was easily distracted and absent-minded – one of his secondary-school teachers called him 'quicksilver personified'. He was often immersed in his own thoughts, pensive and lost to the world, drawing down on him the censure of his teachers. Even though he was often able to impose his will on his brothers and sisters and playmates, acting in the process like a little tyrant, he was in fact characterized by a superior sense of justice, which could neither commit nor condone unfairness, while at the same time demonstrating forbearance, philanthropy and sympathy with people suffering from poverty and distress.[14]

Although Natalie knew Mahler as well as his sisters, even she had difficulty imagining this curious combination of mercurial volatility and dreamy introspection in the young composer. She once asked him if he had not been a terribly unruly child, but Mahler insisted that he had spent his whole time daydreaming. This introspection recalls Rückert's poetic description of himself as being 'lost to the world' and clearly goes well beyond anything that might be regarded as 'normal' in a child, giving rise to concern and ultimately anger on the part of Mahler's parents, especially his father. As a boy, Mahler was often so self-absorbed that he had to be physically shaken to bring him back to reality. It was a genuine torment to him to be constantly reminded of this and to be threatened with dire reprisals for not taking such an active interest in the world as other children of his age. 'You can't imagine how I was tormented by this,' he told Natalie:

> And, of course, I felt very guilty at my introspection. Only much later did it occur to me how parents and grown-ups sin against a child that clearly needs this sense of introversion more than anything for its own intellectual development. As a comic example of my sitting there and dreaming, I was later told that one day when I was a small boy I disappeared, and after they had been looking for me for hours, I was found in the empty pigsty. God knows how I had got there, but since I was unable to open the door, I just sat there calmly, without crying out, until in their despair they finally came looking for me. On hearing their calls, 'Gustav! Gustav!', I replied from the pigsty, thoroughly contented, 'Here I am!'[15]

As a child, Mahler was a voracious reader, taking his passion to the same extreme lengths as his interest in music and retaining that addiction until the end of his life. With the exception of Wagner, Schumann and Berlioz, there can have been no other composer born in the nineteenth century who was as well-read as Mahler. As a child he could forget all other concerns if the right books were to hand. In order not to be disturbed, he once climbed out on to the roof of his parents' house through the skylight and spent hours up there. As before, search parties were sent out to look for him, and he was finally spotted from the house opposite. His father went up to the attic, trembling with fear and anger but not daring to call to the child in case he fell from the roof in his fright. An hour later, Mahler left his idyllic refuge of his own accord and was greeted by his father with a sound thrashing.[16]

Mahler's own recollections and those of his childhood companions have left us with a comprehensive picture of the conditions under which he spent these early years. Conversely, we know very little about the period between his starting school and his move to Vienna in 1875. Only with the recent publication by the Iglau Municipal Archives of surviving documents relating to Mahler's time in the town do we know the dates and raw facts about his time at school.[17]

Mahler first attended school in the autumn of 1866, when he enrolled at the Imperial and Royal Primary School in the Brünnergasse. After three years – the usual period of time spent at such a school – he transferred to the town's Imperial and Royal Grammar School, or German Grammar School, in the street known as Im Jesuitengarten, where he made an initially promising start. At the end of his first year he was twenty-second out of forty-nine pupils – once again, this was the normal way of indicating a pupil's position – and he was thus in the middle of his class. Since he had been thirty-first out of fifty-one halfway through his first year, his position had evidently improved. He received his best mark in religion ('Mosaic') from Dr Unger: 'excellent'. Remarkably for a dreamy bookworm, his standard of achievement in physical education was felt to be 'praiseworthy', and the same was true of his marks in German. In Latin he was 'satisfactory', but in geography and history (taught as a single subject), maths and science, he was only 'adequate'. The 'outward form of his written essays' was described as 'somewhat careless'. During his second year at the school, his achievements in the gym and on the sports field dropped to 'adequate', whereas in the new subject of singing he was said to be 'excellent'. The musical career of the gifted child first impinged on the world at large on 13 October 1870, the date on which Mahler gave his first public recital for an audience that went beyond his family circle, when one of the local newspapers reported that a nine-year-old keyboard virtuoso – Mahler was in fact ten at the time – had appeared at the Municipal Theatre and that he was the son of a local Jewish businessman: 'The success scored by the future piano virtuoso with his listeners was considerable and did him credit, leaving us wishing only that a decent instrument had been placed at his disposal to complement his attractive playing.'[18] We do not know Mahler's programme on this occasion, nor even whether the recital took place in the afternoon or evening.

A remarkable episode occurred in the autumn of 1871, when Mahler was eleven. His father enrolled him at the Neustadt Grammar School in Prague, where he lodged with the leather dealer Moritz Grünfeld. It is unclear how Bernhard Mahler came to know this family, still less why the child was sent away to school. Modern readers may baulk at the idea of packing off an eleven-year-old boy to a relatively distant city only a short time after he had started secondary school, but in Mahler's day this was not unusual. It looks as if he had difficulties at school in Iglau and that for this and other reasons the dreamy child and his strict father were often at loggerheads. The Prague episode ended unhappily, for after six months at the city's Grammar School, Mahler was sixty-fourth in a class of sixty-four. It also appears that the Grünfelds were uncaring and unloving hosts, although once again we do not know whether Alma exaggerated her husband's account of the matter. None the less, her report that Mahler was left to go hungry and unshod is certainly impressive, however unlikely it must seem that a child staying with a businessman's family in Prague was allowed to run around barefoot not only in the street but also at school. We also learn from Alma that Mahler witnessed an incident in the Grünfeld household whose archetypal character not even Freud could have depicted with greater explicitness: unobserved in a dimly lit room, Mahler apparently saw one of Moritz Grünfeld's sons engaging in brutal sex with a servant girl. Thinking that the woman was being violently attacked, Mahler tried to intervene, only to be brusquely rebuffed by the couple. Whatever the truth of the matter – perhaps Freud would have discussed this episode if he had had more time to speak to Mahler and to analyse him at greater length in 1910, for the incident would surely have appealed to him – Mahler's family noticed that his stay in Prague was doing him no good, and so he returned to Iglau in March 1872, when he was just in time to start the second semester of the 1871/2 school year.

In order to complete our account of Mahler's schooling, we need to antici-pate the events of our next chapter, for his education moved along two parallel lines from the autumn of 1875: from mid-September he studied at the Vienna Conservatory while simultaneously continuing his classes at the Iglau Grammar School. The words 'Private student' have been added in a flowing hand in the columns in his school report that should have contained his marks for 'Manners' and 'Diligence'. Two of the thirty-two pupils in his class were external pupils. It is impossible to say how Mahler contrived to pursue these two courses in parallel. His school report makes no mention of any missed classes, so that we can only assume that he presented himself at the Iglau

Grammar School at the end of each semester and did what he could to meet the school's end-of-term requirements by taking a special oral and written examination that replaced the continuous observation of the other pupils. This twofold burden soon took its toll and by July 1876, when Mahler had completed his first full year as an external student, his marks were still only middling: 'excellent' for religion, 'praiseworthy' for history, geography and maths, 'satisfactory' for science and German, and 'adequate' for Latin and Greek. All in all, this was not a bad result for a youth who had just turned sixteen and who, thrown back on his own devices, was studying music in the relatively faraway city of Vienna.

But by the end of the first six months of the following academic year, it is clear from surviving records that in the examinations that he sat in February 1877 Mahler's results were no longer quite so respectable. Rabbi Unger was still satisfied with his charge in matters of the Jewish religion, but Herr Pappenberger was disappointed in Mahler's knowledge of Latin: 'Grammar barely adequate, written assignment unsatisfactory.' (The topic was 'How the Greeks honoured their poets'.) His Greek was scarcely any better, his written examination being 'barely adequate' – he got bogged down in his Greek text after only a few lines – although his oral examination was better. In German, too, his written examination was 'barely adequate'. In this case, Mahler expatiated on the influence of the Orient on German literature, hardly an easy subject for a sixteen-year-old, and the essay duly peters out in a helpless list of a few relevant names lacking in any overall context. Mahler's spoken German, by contrast, was 'satisfactory'. He began his written maths examination with some cheery logarithms, but these quickly gave way to attempts to form meaningful sequences of numbers, most of them struck out, the whole exercise condemned by his teacher as 'inadequate'.

All this boded ill for the external school-leaving examination that Mahler sat before the same board on 14 July 1877. In German, he was asked to write on the question 'What motives persuaded Wallenstein's various supporters to desert him in Schiller?', a classical subject in a classical German-language grammar school. It is remarkable that a boy who was later to be so well-read should have had such difficulties in this subject, but this was no doubt due to the lack of imagination on the part of his German teachers at this time. Be that as it may, his approach to the topic was surprising, to say the least. Every teacher, whether at school or university, is familiar with the student who by a process of more or less tortuous reasoning ends up answering a different – and more congenial – question from the one set. None the less, Mahler's response is certainly one of a kind. Boldly and resolutely he retitles the essay 'On the motives that persuaded Wallenstein to desert', eliminating both the general's supporters and Schiller at one fell swoop. His teacher, Dr Langhals, clearly noticed this, leading him to write the words 'Topic arbitrarily altered' on the first page of the answer. It made little difference that at the end of his essay Mahler fell back on his knowledge of classical antiquity, spoke of crossing the Rubicon and concluded, pithily, 'Alea iacta est'. Whether the answer was dictated by dreamy introspection or arrogance, it was still marked 'inadequate'.

Just two months later, Mahler's teachers at the Iglau Grammar School turned a blind eye on his failings and following a further examination on 12 September 1877 judged him ready to proceed to the next stage of his educational career or at least to study music in Vienna – presumably none of them thought him capable of studying a branch of philology. Music was not one of the subjects that was taught at grammar school, and even 'singing' had disappeared from the timetable after only one term. Mahler's schooling had thus come to an end after a fashion. When we consider that an immature youth had been required to grapple with the influence of the Orient on German literature, we shall have no difficulty in seeing that Mahler's relations with the Iglau Grammar School were very similar to those between Thomas Mann's fictional anti-hero, Felix Krull, and the penal institution that he was obliged to attend:

> The only circumstances in which I can live presuppose the untrammelled life of the spirit and the imagination, and so it is that my memory of my many years in prison strikes me as being less irksome than my memory of the bonds of servitude and fear induced in my sensitive child's soul by the apparently more respectable discipline of the chalk-white, box-shaped house down there in the little town.

The final marks that Thomas Mann received on leaving the Katharineum in Lübeck were in fact even worse than those of Mahler, his elder by fifteen years. Almost all were 'satisfactory', including his marks in written and spoken German. Both men received their best marks in religion, although in Mann's case this was still only 'very satisfactory'. No great writer can have embarked on life with such middling qualifications.

What was Mahler like outside school? What impression did he leave on other people, including his friends, his fellow pupils and adults? We know from Theodor Fischer's reminiscences that he was strong-willed to the point of unruliness but that he was also compassionate by nature. His musical gifts were striking and, indeed, far above the average, although he was by no means treated as a child prodigy. As for his child's powers of imagination, he later told Natalie that he thought up entire novels to accompany the music that impressed him and that he then recounted these novels to his parents and friends in a mysteriously darkened room in the style of a theatrical performance, sometimes being so taken by his own account that he was moved to tears.

In the case of Beethoven's Piano Trio op. 121a, for example, which uses a theme from Wenzel Müller's 'Ich bin der Schneider Kakadu' ('I am Kakadu the tailor'), he devised a narrative recounting the tailor's whole life and death. Another anecdote illustrates the self-discipline of the older composer, a quality without which Mahler would have been unable to make any progress on his vast compositional output in the face of the administrative and conducting commitments that wore him down. He was waiting outside the school building for the reports to be handed out. His nervousness finally became so unbearable that he resolved to confront the demon of impatience once and for all. Later he would recall that even this disagreeable moment had passed and that this would help him to possess his soul in patience in future.

Mahler made frequent appearances as a pianist during this period. At a concert that he gave in 1872 at the Iglau Grammar School he performed Liszt's paraphrase of the Wedding March and Dance of the Elves from Mendelssohn's incidental music to *A Midsummer Night's Dream*, a piece within the grasp only of players with an exceptional technique. And in April 1873 the wedding of the Habsburg Archduchess Gisela and Prince Leopold of Bavaria preoccupied Iglau's cultural world to an unusual degree, prompting the town to push the boat out: there were services in the leading churches and also in the synagogue (a sign that Iglau's Jews were keen to demonstrate that they too were loyal subjects of the emperor, a keenness entirely typical of Central European Jewry at this time), a tattoo, soup kitchens and, of course, a concert at the Municipal Theatre. Mahler's contribution to the concert was the Fantasy on motifs from Bellini's *Norma* by Sigismond Thalberg, another famous mid-nineteenth-century piano virtuoso who, like his rival Liszt, was noted for his paraphrases and who had died only relatively recently. That the twelve-year-old Mahler scored a success with so demanding a piece in the presence of the town's dignitaries is an indication of his considerable talent as a pianist. He was able to repeat the programme a few weeks later at a concert at the Hotel Czap. Even if we have no hard evidence for such a claim, we may none the less assume that his parents and, for a time, Mahler himself envisaged a career as a pianist, a career that could be pursued with a very real sense of purpose, unlike that of a conductor. (No one would have considered for him a career as a composer.) It should also be borne in mind that for two years the piano was Mahler's main subject at the Vienna Conservatory. (Conducting was not a subject that was taught at this time.)

In mid-April 1875 the family was convulsed by an event that affected all their lives: Gustav's younger brother died of an illness variously described as pericarditis and hydrocardia. This was a similar diagnosis to that accorded to Mahler's illness in 1911, namely, endocarditis. In both cases, the lack of a cure in the form of antibiotics meant that the illness was fatal, especially where the heart was already diseased. We do not know how healthy Ernst Mahler was as a child or whether his mother's heart condition was inherited by some of her children. But the number of heart conditions in the Mahler family is certainly striking. Ernst was bedridden for a long time, and Mahler seems to have kept his brother company, reading stories and talking to him. A famous passage in a long letter that the nineteen-year-old Mahler wrote to his friend Josef Steiner reveals the close connection between his memories of his brother and his work on his early opera, *Herzog Ernst von Schwaben*, the hero of which shared his brother's first name. Mahler must have come across this character from Swabian history either through the anonymous late medieval *Volksbuch* or through the tragedy by the widely read Romantic poet Ludwig Uhland. Ernst was around five when he became duke of Swabia. Placed under the guardian-ship of his mother, Gisela, whose second husband became the Emperor Konrad II, the young Ernst rebelled against his stepfather. Twice he was defeated by Konrad, and twice he broke his promise to submit to him. On the third occa-sion he sided with his best friend, an outlawed vassal, and was killed in battle at the age of only twenty. The motif of unconditional love between friends must have had a powerful appeal for the young Mahler, while that of the prematurely deceased youth provided a link with his own similarly named brother:

> Then the pallid shapes that people my life pass by me like shadows of long-lost happiness, and in my ears again resounds the chant of yearning. – And once again we roam familiar pastures together, and yonder stands the hurdy-gurdy man, holding out his hat in his skinny hand. And in the tuneless melody I recognized Ernst of Swabia's salutation, and he himself steps forth, opening his arms to me, and when I look closer, it is my poor brother; veils come floating down, the images, the notes, grow dim.[19]

Several aspects of this passage are notable. First, there is the identification of Duke Ernst with Mahler's brother, both of whom died young, and both of whom had a talent for friendship. Here the planned opera and the death of Mahler's brother several years earlier merge to form a single image. And, second, there is the remarkable way in which Mahler 'stages' the whole episode. It is no accident, for example, that he uses the phrase 'veils come floating down', a highly theatrical stage direction. And Mahler is evidently thinking in terms of music theatre: the hurdy-gurdy man, taking time off from his appearance in the final song of Schubert's *Winterreise*, is evidently playing a melody from Mahler's opera. We do not, however, know what point Mahler had reached before he broke off work on the score.

With the best will in the world, it is impossible for us to form a coherent or detailed picture of Mahler between the ages of ten and fifteen, a period of decisive importance in terms of his own development, as it is in that of any individual, and yet we do have some powerful sketches that may contribute towards such a picture. Mahler was a sensitive child gifted with a lively imagination, a clear propensity for music and considerable talent as a pianist. At the grammar school that he attended in Iglau he clearly failed to live up to his father's expectations and struck observers as being dreamy and lacking in concentration, things his unhappy stay in Prague did nothing to alter. The family's large brood of children evidently suffered from precarious health, although we do not know whether Mahler himself was regarded as a sickly child. It would be wrong to imagine him hiding away behind the piano, wide-eyed and puny, like some prototypical Hanno Buddenbrook. Even as a child he seems to have been physically tough, with the almost superhuman energy that characterized him as an adult and which right up to the onset of his final fatal illness enabled him to a large extent to compensate for his genetically weak constitution. At all events, his childhood friend Theodor Fischer confirms that he always won the games they played together, be it 'cops and robbers' or whipping a top. Bernhard Mahler must have realized that he could not look to his son to succeed him in his distillery. And yet, in spite of his son's successes as a pianist, Bernhard lacked the knowledge and imagination to see any alternative career for him. For this, an independent authority was needed.

In 1875, during his summer holidays, Mahler visited some family friends who lived near Caslau, a small town some eight miles north of Iglau and, as such, halfway between Iglau and Prague. He went there with Josef Steiner, his closest friend after Theodor Fischer, and must have spent a few days on the Ronow estates. Together with another neighbouring farm by the name of Morawan, this was one of the places that Mahler could still recall in great detail many years later. Although we do not know exactly where and with whom Mahler stayed, a surviving letter indicates that he must have been in Ronow for a few days and that there seems to have been a Herr Steiner here, perhaps Josef's uncle. The latter drew the attention of Gustav Schwarz, the local steward, to the phenomenal pianist from Iglau. So isolated were such estates that talented performers who could entertain their audiences were always extremely welcome. Together with other inhabitants of the estate, the lady of the manor – she was presumably a widow – was able to enjoy Mahler's piano playing, and it was Schwarz who set the course for Mahler's subsequent career, thus becoming arguably the most decisive figure in what was one of the most momentous years of his life. Gustav Schwarz evidently understood something about music – certainly more than Bernhard Mahler – and once he had heard the youth perform, it was clear to him that here was a musician whose talent deserved encouragement. But far from leaving it at that, Schwarz now took the initiative. We know all this from Mahler's first surviving letter, which he wrote

to Gustav Schwarz on 28 August 1875.[20] Mahler must have made it clear to
Schwarz that it would not be enough for him to return to Iglau and say to his
parents: 'There's a gentleman at Ronow who thinks I should study music!'
Let us not forget that Mahler had only just turned fifteen and was still at
school: then, as now, the examinations that he sat there would be of decisive
importance for the rest of his life.

   Not even Gustav Schwarz could have been as irresponsible as to advise
Mahler to abandon his schooling and become a pianist, but he none the less
seems to have taken an unusual interest in the boy. Not only did he write to
Bernhard Mahler, he also responded to the youth's urgent entreaties and travelled to Iglau to convince Bernhard of the need to act. Mahler had asked
Schwarz to do so, comparing his father with one of the characters in Gottfried
August Bürger's ballad *The Wild Huntsman* who is pulled in different directions by two knights. Schwarz was needed to urge Bernhard Mahler in the
right direction. (Mahler speaks of 'our project', suggesting something of a
conspiracy between him and Schwarz.) In fact, Mahler twists the meaning of
Bürger's ballad as the good knight warns the count against everything he
thinks of doing at the instigation of the wicked knight, but his warnings fall on
deaf ears. In the case of Mahler's father, by contrast, the point was not to warn
him but to encourage him to allow his son to study music in Vienna as there
was no conservatory in Iglau where music could be studied to an advanced
level. We can hardly blame Bernhard Mahler for harbouring the sort of doubts
that his son faithfully reports in his letter to Schwarz, namely, that Mahler
would neglect his school work in Vienna and might fall into bad company, for
a fifteen-year-old was still a child at that time, just as he is now. It says much
for Schwarz's powers of persuasion that Bernhard Mahler gave his permission
for his son to go to Vienna. (As usual at this time, Mahler's mother had little
more than an advisory role to play in such decisions.) He did, however, place
a provisional barrier in the way of such a move: Schwarz was no expert in the
field of music, and so Bernhard Mahler demanded that such expertise should
first be sought.

   Things now moved quickly, not to say precipitately. Schwarz arrived in Iglau
on 4 September, and the new academic year at the Vienna Conservatory was
due to begin in mid-September. Speed was of the essence. It must have been
only a few days after the 4th that Schwarz once again intervened to help set the
young Mahler on the right path. He drove with him to Baden just outside
Vienna in order to call on Julius Epstein, a pianist of some renown, who since
1867 had taught at the Conservatory run by the Gesellschaft der Musikfreunde
in Vienna and who had also edited Schubert's piano sonatas. It is clear from a
contemporary caricature that he also had a reputation as a talent scout. In
1911, immediately after Mahler's death, Epstein, by then almost eighty, was

asked by a Viennese newspaper to recall his young piano pupil, and Epstein responded with a remarkably precise account. But he recalled being visited only once at the Conservatory by Bernhard Mahler and his son, whereas Schwarz, equally precisely, remembered taking Mahler to see Epstein in Baden. Their two accounts differ in another respect, too. Schwarz reports that Epstein was not especially taken by Mahler's piano playing and pricked up his ears only when Mahler played him some of his own compositions, whereas Epstein remembered exactly the opposite: the piece of his own composition that Mahler played did not impress him, but he was in no doubt that he was in the presence of a born musician. 'He won't be taking over your distillery,' he allegedly told Bernhard Mahler. Whatever the truth of the matter, Julius Epstein and Gustav Schwarz managed to persuade Bernhard Mahler to allow his son to study music and to do so, moreover, at one of the leading conservatories in Europe, that of the Gesellschaft der Musikfreunde in Vienna. It appears that lodgings were soon found for Mahler because Bernhard owned several apartments in the Viennese suburb of Fünfhaus (today the 15th district). From the autumn of 1875 until the autumn of 1877 the young Mahler seems to have lived there.

Studies in Vienna
(1875–80)

Vienna in the 1870s

The Vienna of 1875 that greeted the fifteen-year-old provincial youth who, bashful and proud only of his talents as a musician, had fallen out of the family nest in Iglau at an unusually early date, was completely unlike the Vienna of 1897, when, confident of his coming victory, Mahler arrived in the city from Hamburg to take up one of the leading posts in the musical life of Europe and, hence, of the world. Just as Mahler's own situation in 1875 could hardly have been more different from that in 1897, when the thirty-seven-year old was unrivalled as a conductor and administrator, only his gifts as a composer having as yet failed to achieve the acclaim for which he strove, so the city itself changed irreversibly during this period. True, the changes that took place were not as radical as those that had been observed between 1850 and 1875, but important coordinates had shifted perceptibly. As a result, hand-me-down opinions on 'Vienna around 1900' will not bring us any closer to an adequate understanding of Mahler's twofold 'conquest' of the city. We may begin, therefore, by attempting to sketch a portrait of the city in which the young Mahler arrived on the threshold of his adolescence.

Shortly after the end of the Second World War, Hermann Broch wrote an essay, 'Hofmannsthal and his Age', which in spite of a number of unevennesses remains one of the most readable analyses of late nineteenth-century Viennese culture, not least because Broch himself knew certain of its aspects at first hand. In it, he examined the city's culture from an architectural standpoint and found it one of the most pitiful in the whole history of the world.[1] The false splendours of the Neo-Baroque, Neo-Renaissance and Neo-Gothic buildings that typified this age of eclecticism had borne within them the essentially incompatible characterstics of constraint and pomp, stifling oppression and security, and a poverty that was concealed behind a wall of wealth. Certainly, the stylistic endeavours of these decades reveal the most remarkable mixture of rationalism, individualism, historicism, Romanticism, eclecticism and scepticism, a mixture that was not to be seen again until the end of the twentieth century, a period nebulously described as 'post-modern'. In the light of post-modernism, historicism is now viewed with greater tolerance than was shown by a purist like Hermann Broch, who was writing in the wake of Adolf Loos and Karl Kraus. In spite of this, his diagnosis remains remarkable. The more uninhibited was society's espousal of technological progress not only in Vienna and Austria, but elsewhere too, all the greater appears to have been the need to conceal and transcend it by means of theatrical gestures, spoken drama and opera being the leading media of the age. Vienna regarded itself as the centre of the arts in the German-speaking world, but, as Broch convincingly demonstrates, it was above all a city of ornament. In its extravagant traditionalism, it confused art with decoration and as a result became a museum, decline in a world of poverty leading in Broch's view to a persistent vegetative state, whereas decline in a world of great wealth leads inexorably to the museum. Ornament was not a Viennese invention but determined the stylistic attitude of the entire age, whether it was known nationally and regionally as the Gründerzeit or the Second Empire. For its Austrian variant Broch used the mocking term 'Backhendl' Age, an expression which, even if he did not coin it, he none the less helped to popularize. (The word means 'fried chicken', the dish in question being regarded as the height of culinary affluence in Biedermeier Austria.)

Between 1860 and 1890, ornament characterized the domestic interiors of the upper middle classes throughout central Europe, cheaper imitations trickling down into the middle classes and soon typifying their interiors, too. The over-ornateness of the fabrics used and the finish of the armchairs and of curtains that barely let through the daylight, the imitation Renaissance light fittings and pediments above the doorways, the uncomfortable chairs whose proud description as 'old German' only with difficulty concealed the fact that it was impossible to sit on them for any length of time without damaging one's posture, the important part played by reproductions of large-scale paintings, few individuals apart from eminent painters and financiers being able to afford the originals, and the unscrupulous sway of advisers who, initially known as decorators, later came to be called interior designers – all this was influenced by the burgher's attempt to leave his mark on every corner of his home and to occupy every niche, suggesting to his visitor that the latter had no right to be there at all. By the turn of the century, opposition had arisen to this over-ornate style of interior decoration in the form of the Vienna Secession, the Vienna Werkstätte, art nouveau, 'Modern Style', Jugendstil and, later, the Bauhaus. The most mordant critic of this decorative and ornamental art was the Viennese architect Adolf Loos, who in 1898 inveighed against all this tawdriness:

The artisan was now expected to make Greek, Romanesque, Gothic, Moorish, Italian, German, Baroque and Neoclassical cupboards and chairs for his clients depending on their intellectual beliefs. Even worse: one room was to be furnished in one style, the next room in another. . . . The decorator – that worthy individual who in an earlier age had busied himself with the stitching needle and stuffed mattresses now washed his hair, donned a velvet jacket and a dangling necktie and became an artist. He removed the word 'Upholsterer' from his firm's hoarding and described himself instead as an 'interior decorator'. It sounded impressive. With that there began the reign of the interior designer, a reign of terror that continues to haunt us to this day.

The doyen of interior designers in Vienna at this time was Hans Makart. He had been born in Salzburg in 1840 and studied with the Munich history painter Karl von Piloty, arriving in Vienna in 1869 and in the fifteen years that were left to him – he died at the age of forty-four, probably as the result of syphilis – becoming the leading representative of both the age and the city. By 1875, the year in which Mahler first arrived in Vienna, Makart had achieved the first high point in his career in the capital, painting the portraits of the most prominent women from high society and commanding fees that eventually approached those demanded by Franz von Lenbach, whose financial demands were the yardstick by which every self-respecting portraitist of the period was judged. But as an entrepreneur and entertainer Makart outdid Lenbach and all the others. As the Viennese art critic Ludwig Hevesi observed around 1900, Makart's skills as an artist were inferior to those of his contemporaries, including Böcklin, Menzel, Lenbach and Klinger, but in disseminating the insane notion of 'tawdry beauty' he was second to none. Makart took over from his mentor Karl von Piloty the tendency to cover entire walls with history paintings that anticipate the monumental formats of the twentieth-century cinema, but he surpassed him in his titillating depiction of female flesh and in this respect he influenced those members of the Vienna Secession who had otherwise turned their backs on him. Hevesi's 'dream of the optic nerve' was an epidermal dream, Makart being the Rubens that Viennese society of the 1870s and 1880s truly deserved.

In 1879, while the young Mahler was working on *Das klagende Lied*, Makart was organizing the celebrations to mark the silver wedding of the Austrian emperor and his wife. With twenty-nine floats and thousands of participants, the procession was a three-dimensional re-enactment of Makart's monumental painting, *The Entry of Charles V into Antwerp* of 1878, a sophisticated mixture of art and life, the scantily clad women and girls whom Charles received in Antwerp in 1520 being lent the features of well-known beauties from Vienna's salons. Most provocatively of all, Makart turned himself into the tacit focus of the pageant, wearing dark blue velvet and riding a richly caparisoned horse, thereby suggesting an analogy between himself and Charles V. The homage intended for the imperial couple was thus redirected at the prince of art, whom the crowds greeted with cries of 'Long live Makart!' By taking to its furthest extreme a skilfully organized exoticism and historicism Makart became, as it were, the interior designer of a whole ornamentally obsessed world. His studio style also came to influence interior design in general. Every afternoon his studio near the Ringstraße was open to visitors, while the evenings were given over to the famous studio parties in which the old salon culture was taken to megalomaniac extremes. Guests included not only Makart's fellow artists, Piloty and Lenbach from Munich, but also Wagner, who during a visit to Vienna in 1875 made a point of calling on Makart. Others who looked in included the actress Sarah Bernhardt and the architect Gottfried Semper, another friend of Wagner's, while the limelighters of Viennese society and (would-be) leading figures from the worlds of art, science and politics jostled for attention. Makart's studio reminded critical contemporaries of an Oriental bazaar, and it became the setting for constant rearrangements of armour, chairs, busts, animal skeletons, musical instruments, polar-bear skins and the by now emblematic Makart bunches of dried reeds, autumnal leaves, palm fronds and wheat sheaves. His studio was a masked ball frozen in time, while the orgy of ornament that it embodied was reminiscent of a still life, and for good reason: Makart's masked balls were the high point of the Viennese season. No parties in the city could be more elegant, more timely or more sophisticated, not least because Makart was by now a wealthy man and a strikingly generous host.

A phenomenon like Makart was probably possible only in the Vienna of this period. 'Happy the man who forgets what can't be changed' – this line from Johann Strauß's *Die Fledermaus* reflected the hedonistic frenzy of an entire city, at least to the extent that property conditions allowed the population to pursue such a lifestyle at all. By the end of the 1850s, the death of the elderly field marshal Josef Radetzky and the announcement that the city was to be redeveloped and expanded brought to an end the age of 'good old Vienna' that had survived from the Josephinian era – or at least it did so for more sensitive observers. To the superficial onlooker the Habsburg Empire seemed an island of stability. Contemporaries who preferred to turn a blind eye to the true situation continued to identify with Franz Joseph, who was born at Schönbrunn in 1830 and who came to power in December 1848 at the age of only eighteen. By the time of his death at Schönbrunn in November 1916 at the age of eighty-six, he had ruled for sixty-eight years, a period that undoubtedly attests to a remarkable degree of stability, and yet it would be wrong to infer from the longevity of the monarch and of his constitution and system that all was well with the wider picture. By the mid-1870s there were already signs that the foundations were no longer as secure as they seemed to be at first sight. The country's humiliating defeat by the Prussian army at Königgrätz in 1866 was still a recent memory, while the old rivalry between Austria and Prussia had now been replaced by inner tensions within the dual monarchy's multiracial state. Robert A. Kann, one of the leading historians of the Habsburg Empire, has summed up the years between the Congress of Vienna in 1814–15 and the Austro-German dual alliance of October 1879 in terms of stasis, decline and stabilization, for all that this last-named stage was merely temporary, the term itself ignoring the fact that, as we shall see, the crisis did not simply end in 1879. The period began with the Habsburg Empire regaining its former position as an important European power, a position it owed more to its place in the field of political tension between East and West than to its purely military might. It was none the less a position of some strength, only Russia and Great Britain being more powerful at this time. But by 1879 Austria had fallen to fifth position in the rankings, having been overtaken by Germany and France. The alliance of 1879 saw Austria effectively taking refuge beneath the umbrella of a country that had triumphed over the dual monarchy in 1866 and over France in 1871, the Franco-Prussian War famously leading to the establishment of the German Reich. In terms of the country's internal politics, these years also witnessed a transition from the final throes of enlightened absolutism to a constitutional government that was a direct result of the – failed – revolution of 1848 and of political and economic liberalism. But the liberalism of this period soon went into decline, with far-reaching consequences not least for the role of the Austrian Jews whose assimilation and acculturation had owed much to the triumph of liberalism. The emergence of political anti-Semitism in the years around 1879 was no accident, but was bound up with the end of the age and with the waning of liberal influence.

The year 1879 brought with it the political defeat of the liberals in the Austrian half of the dual monarchy, and from now on the tone was set by more radical forces in the form of the Christian Socialists and Social Democrats, by the Pan-Germans among the Austro-Germans who sought union with Wilhelminian Germany and by the Young Czechs in Bohemia and Moravia who were the most striking manifestation of the new nationalism that was an important factor in the dual monarchy's dissolution. Not only was there a particular brand of Czech nationalism, there were similar forces at work in Slovakia, Romania, Italy, Croatia, Slovenia and Serbia. All these separatist and nationalist movements benefited from the consequences of the Ausgleich of 1867, which was itself a direct consequence of the defeat of 1866. This agreement established the basic rules of the dual monarchy that were to be effortfully upheld until 1918. Under the terms of this arrangement, two independent states – Austria and Hungary – were constituted along the lines of a single entity under a single ruler who functioned in Austria as emperor and in Hungary as king. The two states' common concerns included foreign policy, defence and the budget, at least to the extent that this affected their common interests. In the main, therefore, their shared concerns were foreign policy and defence. There is no doubt that the Ausgleich helped to underpin the hegemony of the Magyars and Austro-Germans, a linguistic, cultural and organizational supremacy that took little account of the Czech population whose role had none the less been important from both a cultural and a historical point of view. In this way the seeds were sown for the centrifugal forces that were soon to emerge within the dual monarchy. The dual alliance of 1879 merely expressed the fact that German-Hungarian hegemony was now properly acknowledged and consolidated in the monarchy's relations with the outside world, a guarantee against the increasingly vociferous demands of Pan-Slavism to which the nationalists among the Slav population naturally lent a willing ear. And yet in spite of this, the decline of the monarchy was by no means inevitable. Commenting on the situation in the years around 1879, Robert Kann writes that 'in Austro-Hungary there was still the possibility of peaceful constitutional and social change, assuming only that appropriate national and, above all, social reforms were implemented. These opportunities were for the most part missed.'[2]

Vienna's role as the Austrian capital and as home of the emperor was constitutionally established by 1848, but this does not mean that the city found its role an easy one to play. In the eyes of many leading thinkers, Vienna had proved far too progressive during the 1848 revolution, a hotbed of subversive aspirations and a haven for refractory students and Jewish agitators – a good deal of Vienna's later anti-Semitism can be traced back to the myth of the powerful Jewish involvement in the subversive activities of 1848, a myth that lived on in countless malicious caricatures. The aristocracy had no wish to see their city as the home of people who could not be trusted, and Schönbrunn was in any case outside the city's confines. According to Friedrich Hebbel, Prince Friedrich Schwarzenberg is said to have remarked that it was a shame that when Prince Alfred von Windisch-Graetz retook Vienna from the insurgents, he did not burn down the whole of this 'den of iniquity', but the emperor was resolved 'to turn Vienna, that great machine room of the bureaucratic mechanism, into the true centre of the monarchy, towering above all other capitals in terms of its outward appearance too', to quote an official release. Such a transformation required far-reaching changes to the physical form of the city. A plan of 1844 shows a crowded city enclosed within fortifications that were surrounded in turn by an almost circular glacis of open, untilled land that was suitable for country walks but which also served a military purpose as it was impossible for any attacker, including the Turkish armies of an earlier age, to approach the city walls undetected. Beyond the glacis, however, settlements had sprung up like a belt around the city, and it was only a question of time before these suburbs merged with the city centre. This development was resisted by the army, in whose eyes the Turks had now been replaced as a threat by the revolutionary inhabitants of the suburbs. But in 1857 the emperor refused to be dissuaded any longer and appointed a commission to enlarge the city. In giving the go-ahead to build on the glacis, the commission effectively created the Ringstraße and its whole culture: even now, the Ring continues to be lined with the key buildings that embody the Austria of Franz Joseph and that still allow us to see very clearly where the city's defences once stood and where the glacis began.

Vienna's Ringstraße remains the clearest symbol of the early years of the dual monarchy. In 1875, when the young Mahler arrived in the city, it was still far from complete. A competition to design the street had been held in 1858, and during the next seven years this road was duly built. Some 6.5 kilometres in length and 57 metres wide, it was officially opened on 1 May 1865. Between 1869 and 1888 – a relatively short space of time, when we recall the size of the task and the building techniques of the period – the State Opera, Natural History Museum, Museum of Art History, Votive Church and New University, the Stock Exchange, the Parliament and the Town Hall were built to plans by many of the leading architects of their day, including August Siccard von Siccardsburg, Eduard van der Nüll, Gottfried Semper, Karl von Hasenauer, Heinrich von Ferstel and Theophil Edvard von Hansen. Inspired by the prevailing spirit of eclecticism, each building reproduced a different style, all of them together representing the stylistic history of humankind or at least attempting to do so: the Town Hall was imitation Gothic, the Burgtheater faux early Baroque and the University was in the style of the Renaissance, while the Parliament building set out to present an image that was simultane-ously Greek, noble and classical. The present-day observer will have no diffi-culty in understanding what appalled the generation of Adolf Loos and the Secessionists about this theme park *avant la lettre*. But we must not forget the many residential houses on the Ringstraße, private homes that did more than merely meet the needs of the upper classes and the aristocracy – the majority of these houses were to be found in the Schwarzenbergplatz, close to the street where Mahler lived when he later became director of the Court Opera. Many of the other buildings were blocks of flats for the middle classes provided by the liberally minded town council.[3]

The monumental buildings along the Ringstraße were the liberal bour-geoisie's way of celebrating its own achievements, dating, as they did, from the heyday of liberal influence on Austrian politics. The historian Heinrich

Friedjung, who was himself a child of the age of liberalism, saw in the Ringstraße a reminder of generations of ordinary Viennese men and women who, effortfully and at the cost of great self-sacrifice, had once helped to shape the face of the city in spite of adverse conditions. Now power was placed in the hands of the middle classes, at least in part, and this transfer found expression in the redevelopment of Vienna, the social and aesthetic values of liberalism being literally carved in stone. By the time that the Ringstraße was completed, it was already a monument to an era that was drawing to an end. Barely finished, it was already old-fashioned in the eyes of its critics, or else it was felt to bear witness to a false view of the world and of life in general. Some observers complained that the Ringstraße was too untraditional, having sacrificed the venerability of tradition to the needs of a sybaritic lifestyle. Others, including modernists such as the leading architect Otto Wagner, who was later to leave his mark on the city, felt that it was little short of mendacious to conceal modern civilization behind the fake stylistic walls of the past. But the tragedy of the Ringstraße and its culture lay above all in the fact that the liberalism that had brought it into being was already in decline both politically and economically, while continuing to celebrate its own achievements on an architectural level and seeming as if it would continue in power for ever. It had no answer to the question of nationality or to the social problems of the day.

Not least as a result of various electoral reforms, the right to vote was now extended to members of the population who were traditionally hostile to the interests of the liberal bourgeoisie and upper classes. The elections held in the wake of the reforms of 1873 brought serious losses to the liberals for the first time in their history, and by 1879 the liberals had lost their majority in the lower house and became the party of opposition in a country governed by Eduard von Taaffe. The party's subsequent defeat in the elections of 1897 sealed the fate of liberalism as a political force that had been worn away by the reactionary Christian Socialists on the one hand and by the workers' movement on the other. There is a profound symbolism to the fact that the year that witnessed the end of liberalism also saw Mahler's return to Vienna as director of the Court Opera. After all, it was liberalism that had made possible his own acculturation as the son of provincial Jewish parents. And it is no coincidence that at the same time that he was taking up his office in Vienna as the first high point of his career, an anti-Semitic campaign was to be launched against him that was to dog him until his departure for America in 1907. Not only did the liberals lose the 1897 elections, but the year was also notable for the election of the anti-Semitic Karl Lueger to the important post of mayor of Vienna, a post he continued to fill until his death in 1910.

Let us return to the mid-1870s. In 1873, some two years before Mahler began his studies in Vienna, two events had taken place that marked the culmination

and crisis of liberalism and of contemporary attitudes to life. The first was the
Vienna World Fair, the second the collapse of the stock market, with all its
long-term consequences. It is no exaggeration to claim that 1873 and, in consequence, the years between 1875 and 1880, which appear to us now in the wan
light that still penetrates the dust stirred up at the time and that were so decisive in determining the young Mahler's future development, were the fulcrum
on which the age's sense of security was supported and that once that support
had been removed, the age was incapable of recovering its sense of equilibrium.
This sudden reversal in the country's fortunes can be reduced to just two dates:
the World Fair opened on 1 May 1873, and the stock exchange crashed just a
week later, nadir following apogee with extraordinary, positively portentous
speed. The Vienna World Fair was the fifth in the series of twelve that had
begun in London in 1851 and that ended in Paris in 1900. Originally intended
as a mere display of a country's achievements, these exhibitions increasingly
became a way of measuring its self-assurance, pontifical masses for the secular
religion of the nineteenth century, namely, progress, a measure based on the
liberal beliefs of the middle classes. In 1870, when Franz Joseph gave his
blessing to the ambitious plans for a World Fair in Vienna, one of his ulterior
motives had naturally been to increase the prestige of the monarchy, a move
desperately needed in the wake of the military defeats of 1859 and 1866. Not
least, it was an opportunity to show off the Ringstraße to the rest of the world.
The Prater was chosen as the site for the exhibition, which was symbolized by
a gigantic rotunda that was 108 metres in diameter and 84 metres in height and
which the Viennese, in a typical mixture of dismissal and affection, referred to
as the 'Gugelhupf'. The increasing tendency to speculate in buildings and land
that had started with the Ringstraße, and that had by now become a typical
phenomenon of the time both in Austria and elsewhere, was encouraged by the
World Fair. It was hoped that as soon as the exhibition opened, everything that
had been built on credit would pay for itself overnight. Virtually all the city's
large luxury hotels date from this period. They include the Imperial on the
Ringstraße, which was converted from a former ducal palace. As the guiding
principles of liberalism, culture and education were central to the exhibition's
programme. In the event, the exhibition itself was still unfinished at the time of
its official opening, while the crowds of visitors expected during its first few
weeks remained obstinately absent, a state of affairs for which the poor weather
and the astronomically high cost of hotel rooms were conjointly to blame. The
result was that many a castle in the air came crashing to the ground. A week
later 110 insolvencies were reported on the stock exchange, a further 120 the
following day, 'Black Friday', 9 May 1873. By the time that the exhibition closed
in November, it had managed to turn round its fortunes, but its reputation
continued to be dogged by the events of six months earlier. As if Vienna had not

suffered enough misfortune, cholera broke out in the city in July 1873, resulting in almost three thousand deaths, a figure that had been thought impossible in such a civilized age and in so progressive and modern a city. The impact of the epidemic on visitors from abroad does not need to be spelt out.

The events of 9 May 1873 were described by a journalist of the time as 'the big crash', probably the first – but certainly not the last – time that such a term had been used in financial circles. It was soon taken over into other languages. The economic boom of the years around 1870 seemed deceptively secure: there were excellent harvests in the dual monarchy, but poor ones elsewhere in Europe; the rail network had doubled in size within a matter of only a few years (it was during this period that the first trains arrived in Iglau); and the engineering, iron and construction industries all enjoyed a period of rapid growth. The building boom in Vienna required banking services and finance companies, resulting in a broad stratum of capitalists and gentlemen of leisure, who in turn invested their new-found wealth in extremely lucrative ways and who could afford to buy the more luxurious houses on the Ringstraße or in almost equally magnificent squares and streets: these were the Rothschilds, the Königswarters, the Epsteins, the Todescos, the Gomperzes and the Springers. The fact that some of them were Jewish merely fuelled the anti-Semitism that stemmed from the stock market crash. The lower house of Parliament contained many men who had won money and influence during these years. Rumour had it that the lower house was a public limited company whose board was run by the ministry. 'Railways are not built with moral sentiments' was another popular saying of the time, reflecting the fact that the views on morality of an older generation who had been conditioned by the revolution of 1848 had been rendered obsolete by the frenzy of the Gründerjahre. The World Fair with its catastrophic opening was by no means the only cause of the stock market crash. Rather, hopes that it would prove a success had only delayed the consequences of a lengthy period of excessive speculation.

A single set of figures is enough to indicate the extent to which the market had become overheated and how it was already cooling down: during the boom years between 1868 and 1873, seventy new banks were founded in Vienna, whereas only eight of these banks were still in business in 1883. Of course, this great crash was far from being a local phenomenon, as the seismic tremors in Vienna affected the whole of Europe or, rather, the psychological impact of the explosion in Vienna caused buildings run up for speculative gain to come crashing down all over the Continent. The greatest upheavals were caused in the neighbouring Reich that had only recently been created in a spirit of high-minded optimism. The boom of the Gründerjahre gave way to a general feeling of depression, the low point of which was not reached until the end of the 1870s but whose repercussions were felt throughout the 1870s and 1880s. At the time there were no economic models to explain such events, causing all that happened to seem all the more mysterious and threatening. Economic historians tell us that from today's perspective the raw facts and data are not enough to explain the tremendous consequences of these events, but this is not what mattered. What mattered was the dull sense of a deep depression, and this feeling of depression led in turn to the real thing: the irrational ways in which stock markets react today can give us an idea of such mechanisms without any need for a great depression. Economic historians argue that it was only in 1896 that a new upturn in the country's fortunes began. In Vienna and in the Austrian provinces, in Kassel and in Prague – in short, wherever Mahler spent these decisive years of his life and where his musical abilities and wishes were shaped alongside his whole outlook on life and on the world – the 1870s and 1880s were marked by a profound sense of insecurity, by a lack of trust in the optimism that had hitherto sustained the belief in progress, by a constant eye on possible social unrest and by an ideological dynamism and aggression that found expression in increasingly radical political extremism, including the political anti-Semitism that raised its ugly head at the end of the 1870s, one of its principal arguments being the Jews' alleged complicity in the economic crisis of 1873. And, without wishing to draw premature parallels, it is hard to deny that Mahler's music is marked by the juxtaposition of extreme triumphalism and a profoundly shaken sense of self-assurance, especially the early symphonies whose seeds were sown at this time.

It is no accident that Johann Strauß's *Die Fledermaus* opened at the Theater an der Wien on 5 April 1874 and that its internationally celebrated lines, 'Happy the man who forgets what can't be changed', were first heard less than a year after the great crash. And yet the basic idea behind the work is not Viennese at all. In 1872 Henri Meilhac and Ludovic Halévy, two librettists best known for their exceptionally successful collaboration with Jacques Offenbach, had written a comedy, *Le Réveillon* (the title refers to a midnight supper party traditionally held on New Year's Eve), for Paris's Théâtre du Palais-Royal. In turn, *Le Réveillon* was based on an 1851 farce, *Das Gefängnis* (The Prison), by the popular Berlin playwright Roderich Benedix. Karl Haffner and Richard Genée adapted the text for a Viennese audience, and by the end of 1873 – the year of the stock market crash – they were able to entrust it to Johann Strauß, who allegedly set it to music in the space of forty-two days. Quite apart from its international acclaim – in spite of the absence of reliable statistics, *Die Fledermaus* is regularly said to be the most successful work ever written for the musical theatre – it is hard to imagine a more striking or more obvious expression of the brilliance and tawdriness of the Gründerjahre in Vienna. Strauß's operetta is a mixture of irresistible champagne-driven verve, a rampant male sexuality apparently untouched by the fear of sexually transmitted diseases, and female attempts to emulate their menfolk. The principal male character is like something out of a fairytale: Eisenstein, a young gentleman of leisure, convincingly embodies the age's oft-cited ability to lead a carefree existence on the strength of a private income. As such, his life is safe from economic crises and the very opposite of that led by those who had lost their entire fortunes and been hoisted by the petard of their own speculations. Eisenstein, too, is hoisted by his own petard, but only by way of a joke: he manifestly does not have to worry about his fortune, which allows him to pursue the most lavish of lifestyles.

It is enough to consider the sets for the opening act in the Viennese première: they show the home of a relatively young man who clearly does not need to work – he is described in the cast list as a 'man of independent means' – but who none the less has a vast fortune at his disposal and who can afford to maintain a splendid villa 'in a spa resort near a big city', to quote the libretto. Presumably, then, the action takes places in Baden bei Wien, as the city can only be Vienna. No one does an honest day's work in *Die Fledermaus*, even the prison governor evidently having nothing to do, while his plenipotentiary in the prison, the jailer Frosch, is permanently tipsy. And alcohol, with its amnesiac effects, certainly reigns supreme in a world addicted to pleasure. At Prince Orlofsky's party, held in another luxury villa in this 'slum district', the guests all hail champagne as 'the crowned head of the entire land'. And yet it is also made clear at this party, if only covertly, that however attractive all this may be, it is still transient: pleasure is no more permanent than the boom of the Gründerjahre. In the almost unbearable melancholy of the 'Brüderlein und Schwesterlein' chorus, it is brought home to us that enjoyment is as short-lived as the euphoria of the early 1870s: 'Laßt das traute Du uns schenken, für die Ewigkeit, immer so wie heut', wenn wir morgen noch dran denken!', literally, 'Let's confer on each other the familiar "you" for all eternity, just like today, as we still think about it tomorrow' – eternity lasts only this one night. And with their unsettling sentimentality the opening words of this chorus inevitably reminded Viennese listeners of another song, this one sung by Youth to Fortunatus Wurzel in Ferdinand Raimund's *Das Mädchen aus der Feenwelt, oder Der Bauer als Millionär* (The Girl from the Fairy World, or The Peasant as Millionaire), before Wurzel adds his voice, turning it into a duet: 'Brüderlein fein, Brüderlein fein, mußt mir ja nicht böse sein! Scheint die Sonne noch so schön, einmal muß sie untergeh'n' ('Dear little brother, you shouldn't be cross with me! Though the sun still seems so fair, it still has to set.'). 'Through such a potent lack of seriousness,' wrote Hermann Broch:

Viennese frivolity acquired that special note that distinguished it from that of every other city, a note lacking in all aggression but bringing together the

whole audience in a spirit of delightful thoughtlessness and quintessential
Gemütlichkeit. Of course, such sentiments also contained a grain of wisdom,
Gemütlichkeit and wisdom traditionally going together: the end may be
nigh, but that end is willingly accepted. And yet it was the wisdom of the
world of operetta, and in the shadow of the approaching end it acquired a
ghostly presence, becoming Vienna's high-spirited apocalypse.[4]

Young Mahler and his Friends

The Vienna Conservatory was already a well-respected institution in the
city's musical life even before Mahler began his studies there in September
1875. It was neither a municipal nor a state-run institution but a private
college managed by the Gesellschaft der Musikfreunde, the city's most important musical institution based on private initiative, its magnificent building
containing what remains one of the finest concert halls in the world –
indeed, the Viennese themselves claim that the Musikvereinssaal has no equal.
Situated near the Karlsplatz and within a stone's throw of the Ringstraße, the
Musikverein had been designed by Theophil von Hansen, one of the leading
architects of the Ringstraße, and, three years in the building, had been officially opened in 1870, the Conservatory being housed in one of its wings.
Although it received financial support from the privy purse, it was essentially
a private organization, and like all conservatories of every period, it employed
a whole range of teachers, some of them better than others. It had been
founded as long ago as 1821, when its first director had been Antonio Salieri,
no less, but it was not until 1909 that it acquired the status of a state-run institution, thereby becoming the forerunner of today's University of Music and the
Performing Arts. The Vienna Conservatory was not quite as highly regarded
as its counterpart in Leipzig, which at this date was arguably the world's finest
music college, but it still had a whole series of famous teachers on its books. Its
director was the violinist and conductor Joseph Hellmesberger Senior, whose
pupils included Leopold Auer and Arthur Nikisch and who was famous for his
wit. Although he accused his professor of harmony, Robert Fuchs, of plagiarism, Fuchs was evidently a good teacher whose pupils numbered not only
Mahler himself but also Franz Schreker, Alexander Zemlinsky (an early rival
of Mahler's for the hand of Alma Schindler), Jean Sibelius and Franz Schmidt.
Julius Epstein – the man who officially discovered and fostered Mahler's
talent – was the best known of the Conservatory's piano teachers but, however
good he may have been, it was his misfortune that there was an even better
piano teacher working in Vienna at this time, albeit only privately, Theodor
Leschetitzky, whose pupils included Paderewski and Schnabel. The institute's
principal composition teacher was Franz Krenn, who also taught Mahler but

whom history has judged unfavourably, his views and methods being criticized for being too backward-looking. It seems as if the more liberal Fuchs
introduced greater compositional contraband into his harmony classes than
was officially permitted. Anton Bruckner, finally, gave organ lessons at the
Conservatory in addition to his classes at the University.

Leaving aside Mahler's three-month stint as conductor in Bad Hall during
the summer of 1880, his first continuous stay in Vienna lasted six years, from
September 1875 to the summer of 1881, at which point he took up a post in
Laibach (Ljubljana). This six-year period, between the ages of fifteen and
twenty-one, is a decisive phase in the life of any artist and, indeed, of any individual. Unfortunately, these are also the worst-documented years in Mahler's
life, so that we have no choice but to attempt to reconstruct them on the basis
of other, disparate sources. There were in fact two phases to Mahler's education in Vienna, each of them associated with a different circle of friends. The
first such circle, and the more intimate of the two, was made up of Mahler's
fellow pupils from the Conservatory and provided him with a specifically
musical stimulus, whereas the second was more important in terms of his
general outlook on the world and resulted from his contacts with the circles
associated with Siegfried Lipiner and Engelbert Pernerstorfer.

Mahler's circle of friends at the Conservatory initially consisted of no
more than four or five individuals, some of them more interesting than
others, but all in all a good indication of Mahler's ability to attract important
people of his own age. The individuals in question were Anton Krisper, Rudolf
Krzyzanowski and, to a lesser extent, his brother Heinrich, Hans Rott and
Hugo Wolf. It is also possible that Mahler briefly made the acquaintance of
the mezzo-soprano Rosa Papier at this time. She later became a well-known
member of the Vienna Court Opera and, following her early retirement on
health grounds, a distinguished singing teacher whose pupils numbered Anna
von Mildenburg. She also exerted considerable influence on Vienna's musical
scene, helping in no small way to bring about Mahler's appointment as director
of the Court Opera. The wife of the pianist Hans Paumgartner, she was the
mother of Bernhard Paumgartner, later to become well known as a Mozart
scholar and as president of the Salzburg Festival. For a time, this group of
friends was very small, an unsurprising state of affairs as Mahler was looking
for something like a substitute family in the city. Epstein took considerable
interest in the boy and could play the part of a fatherly friend, but he inevitably
had little time for the lad from Iglau, quite apart from his understandable
reluctance to show undue preference for any one particular student. Of greater
importance were friends of Mahler's own age: Wolf was born in the same year
as Mahler, Hans Rott was two years older, Anton Krisper three years older, and
Rudolf Krzyzanowski a year older. In comparison to today's state-run colleges

of music, the Vienna Conservatory was a tiny institution, so that students of different ages very soon met on its various courses.

Anton Krisper came from Laibach, where he had been born into a well-to-do family of businessmen. He matriculated at the Conservatory in 1876 but remained there for only two years before moving to Leipzig and enrolling at the city's University, where he read musicology. He is said to have written an opera during his youth, but no such work has come down to us. He was more successful academically, his dissertation on 'Art Music in Terms of its Origins, Development and Consequences' being praised by one of the leading figures of the as yet young discipline of musicology, Hugo Riemann. The multitalented Krisper later studied mining and worked as an engineer. He died in a sanatorium near Graz in 1914, evidently as the result of some venereal disease, and was buried in Laibach. His friendship with Mahler is documented in a series of important letters written between 1878 and 1880, but thereafter the two friends lost contact. It seems that Krisper also played the cello, with Wolf as his accompanist.

Mahler was closer to the brothers Rudolf and Heinrich Krzyzanowski than he was to Krisper. The younger of the two brothers, Rudolf, died, like Mahler, in 1911, only a few weeks after his friend. He was evidently highly gifted as a musician, equally talented not only as a violinist and pianist but also as an organist and as a composer. The close links between Rudolf Krzyzanowski and Mahler were reciprocal, and the two men's paths frequently crossed in later life. Mahler did much to help his older friend, especially when the latter's career as a conductor got off to a shaky start. The Krzyzanowski family came from Eger. Rudolf's elder brother, Heinrich, was born in 1855 and was enrolled not at the Conservatory but at the University, from where he graduated in German Studies in 1877, his teacher being the eminent Germanist Richard Heinzel. After teaching in a series of grammar schools, he married and moved to Germany, working as a freelance writer in Starnberg, Munich and Berlin. His short story *Im Bruch* was published in 1885. He later moved back to Vienna, where he worked as a private tutor, for a time supported by Mahler, and lectured on literary topics. By the 1920s he was living in the Tyrol. During Mahler's early years in Vienna, the Krzyzanowski brothers appear to have been his closest friends.

The two composers among Mahler's early friends are far more fascinating figures than Krisper and the Krzyzanowskis – fascinating but also problematical. When Hans Rott's Symphony in E major of 1878/80 received its first performance in Cincinnati in 1989, more than a century after it had been written, the event was little short of a sensation. Experts and – following further performances and some gramophone recordings – the public at large recognized that this hour-long symphony, the final movement of which alone lasts almost twenty-five minutes, is a key work in the evolution of the 'New Symphony', representing, as it does, an attempt to make a fresh start in the field of the symphony that was then being tilled by Bruckner and Brahms. The most famous exponent of this new style was none other than Mahler himself, and it is to him in fact that we owe the term 'New Symphony'. Even at a first hearing it was obvious to many listeners that there were astonishing similarities between the musical language of Rott's one and only symphony and that of Mahler's First, which was not composed until 1885–8, in other words, at least five years later than Rott's work. It also gave pause for thought that Rott and Mahler studied at the Vienna Conservatory at exactly the same time. A remark that Mahler made about Rott to Natalie Bauer-Lechner now received greater attention. Mahler had taken the score of Rott's symphony with him on holiday during the summer of 1900 in order to see whether it was worth performing at one of the Vienna Philharmonic's concerts:

> What music has lost in him is immeasurable. His First Symphony, written when he was a young man of twenty, already soars to such heights of genius that it makes him – without exaggeration – the founder of the New Symphony as I understand it. It is true that he has not yet fully realized his aims here. It is like someone taking a run for the longest possible throw and not quite hitting the mark. But I know what he is driving at. His innermost nature is so much akin to mine that he and I are like two fruits from the same tree, produced by the same soil, nourished by the same air. We would have had an infinite amount in common. Perhaps we two might have gone some way together towards exhausting the possibilities of this new age that was then dawning in music.[5]

Mahler also mentions a number of anecdotes about Rott's activities as organist at the Piarist Monastery in Vienna, where he played for a pittance in return for free accommodation. Mahler remembered seeing a string of sausages hanging on a nail in his room, like a kind of a wreath. He would eat them one by one in order to appease his hunger. He ostensibly lost his post when the monks accused him of stealing their books.

Rott was born in Vienna in 1858, the son of an actor. He enrolled at the Conservatory in 1874, a year before Mahler, and studied the organ with Bruckner, harmony with Hermann Grädener rather than Fuchs and composition with Krenn. Like so many others, Rott was introduced to Wagner by Bruckner and in this way became a member of the Vienna Academic Wagner Society about which I shall shortly have more to say. He also attended the first Bayreuth Festival in 1876. Bruckner held Rott in high regard and was deeply shaken by his early death in 1884. It is reported that he spontaneously took up the cudgels for Rott when the latter was defeated by Mahler in the Conservatory's competition for composers. It seems probable that Rott submitted the opening movement of his symphony, while Mahler's entry was a movement from a lost piano quintet. Mahler, who had not previously been smiled on by good fortune, was awarded the first prize, while Rott was laughed out of court by the jury that awarded the prize. The normally shy Bruckner is said to have leapt to his feet and exclaimed: 'Don't laugh, gentlemen, you'll hear great things about that man!' Because of Rott's premature death, Bruckner's prophecy did not come true, but Rott's surviving symphony shows that the older composer was right. In another conversation with Natalie, Mahler confused this competition with a later one when he unsuccessfully submitted *Das klagende Lied* for the 1881 Beethoven Prize. The jury on this later occasion included Brahms, whom Mahler later came to respect but who was regarded at this time as a traditionalist with no time for the 'New Symphony' and a positive loathing of all that smacked of Wagner and Bruckner. Mahler was guilty of exaggeration when he later blamed this jury for plunging him into the wearying career of an opera conductor as a means of earning his living, instead of writing an opera called *Rübezahl* and making his breakthrough as a composer.

Legend has it that Brahms was also responsible for blighting Rott's career but in a far more serious way than was the case with Mahler. Rott entered his name for the 1880 Beethoven Prize, submitting not only his complete First Symphony but also a Pastoral Prelude that remained unperformed until 2000. In the run-up to such awards, composers were expected to call on the members of the jury to pay them their respects. And so Rott dutifully went to see Brahms, but if we may believe his account of their meeting, he received a brusque rebuff. Brahms is said to have commented 'You cannot possibly have written this yourself' – a remark that may even have been intended as a compliment. Profoundly depressed, the unsuccessful Rott tried in vain to obtain work as an organist, but the only post that he was offered was as a choral conductor in Strasbourg, and he did not want to leave Vienna. In late October 1880 he reluctantly boarded a train to Strasbourg. Symptoms of pathological nervousness and extreme eccentricity that had evidently been apparent for some time now came to a disastrous head, and when a fellow passenger tried to light a cigar, Rott is said to have threatened him with a gun, claiming that smoking was strictly forbidden on the train as a certain Johannes Brahms – the name meant nothing to the smoker – had filled it with dynamite. Rott was removed from the train and taken back to Vienna, where he spent the last four years of his short life in a series of psychiatric institutions. He was only twenty-five when he died in June 1884, apparently from tuberculosis, although it is possible – if impossible to prove – that venereal disease and the resultant mental imbalance were to blame.[6]

It seems unlikely that Rott and Mahler were close. Heinrich Krzyzanowski, who was a close friend of both men, maintains that it was Rott in particular who preferred to keep his distance as he was jealous of Rudolf Krzyzanowski, Rott's own best friend who was also a very close friend to Mahler. Heinrich offers a particularly striking account of the very different impression left by Rott and Mahler as they walked along the street together, the former blond, immensely tall and tending to corpulence, while the short, swarthy, fidgety Mahler lolloped along beside him, his long coat trailing on the ground.[7] It remains unclear why Mahler did not perform Rott's symphony after he had taken the trouble to examine the score in the summer of 1900. We cannot say whether he harboured doubts as to its immaturity or whether he was taken aback by the similarities with his own early works and wanted to avoid any discussion about an unduly obvious debt. Be that as it may, the relationship between Rott and Mahler remains a remarkable phenomenon, but the rumour that has begun to circulate since its rediscovery that Mahler's early works are clearly modelled on Rott's one and only symphony is without foundation. True, there are surprising points of agreement in terms of both composers' tone of voice, but such similarities may also be observed between Brahms and Friedrich Gernsheim, between the young Wagner and Meyerbeer, and between the young Schoenberg and Wagner. In the case of Rott and Mahler, they may perhaps go even further than this and provide eloquent proof of the fact that both composers were able to achieve similar results because they shared common goals and had both been influenced by Bruckner and Wagner. None the less, it is impossible to ignore Hans Rott in any account of Mahler's development as a composer, while Rott's music undoubtedly merits our attention for its independent qualities.

At least as remarkable is the relationship between Mahler and Hugo Wolf. Here, too, it is difficult to speak of a close friendship between the two adolescents, even though both were in very close contact and even shared an apartment. Both men were born in 1860, Mahler being some four months younger than Wolf. Wolf hailed from Windischgrätz (now Slovenjgradec), a very small town in what was then southern Styria with a large Slovene population. Both men were fifteen when they arrived in Vienna from the Austrian provinces, where their musical talents had attracted attention at a very early date. They appear to have got to know one another in Robert Fuchs's harmony class at the Conservatory, although their initial contacts were desultory, and it was not until later that their acquaintance deepened, a development that had presumably taken place by the summer of 1877, when they probably began to share rooms. Both men regularly attended performances at the Court Opera as standees, and both became fanatical Wagnerites. Wolf first saw *Tannhäuser* at the Vienna Court Opera in November 1875 and in the middle of December he even managed to obtain an audience with Wagner, who was then staying at the Hotel Imperial, a meeting on which he reported with great enthusiasm in a long letter to his parents, even if Wagner politely but firmly declined his invitation to look at his compositions. Wolf became a lifelong Wagnerian, taking over his hero's anti-Semitism in addition to his aesthetic ideals. Mahler, too, became an inveterate Wagnerian but did not share his idol's anti-Semitism, although he could certainly have done so in the form of Jewish self-hatred. As we shall later have cause to note, it is a remarkable fact that he never once mentions Wagner's anti-Semitism, even though he was not unaware of the anti-Jewish sentiments that were rampant at this time and of which he was a principal victim. The cult of Wagner played an important role in Vienna's cultural life, leaving a mark on Mahler that went far beyond mere questions of musical taste.

Wagner had been a frequent visitor to Vienna, not least at the time of the 1848 revolution, when the city had been a hotbed of unrest. Strangely enough, it was Johann Strauß who introduced Wagner's music to Viennese audiences when he conducted excerpts from *Tannhäuser* and *Lohengrin* at a concert in 1853. From then on, Wagner's works were a staple of the repertory, provoking the same violent responses for and against them as those found throughout the rest of the world of music. The first performance of *Lohengrin* at the Kärntnerthor-Theater in 1858 helped to consolidate Wagner's reputation in the city in spite of the embittered resistance of the critic Eduard Hanslick, who had begun his career as a Wagnerian only to become his most powerful and intransigent adversary. There were also plans to give the first performance of *Tristan und Isolde* at the Vienna Court Opera in 1861, but in the event they came to nothing, and it was not until four years later that the work was finally unveiled in Munich. Conversely, the concerts that the composer organized in Vienna to replace the aborted première proved immensely successful but could not prevent Wagner, who had temporarily found refuge at Penzing in the city's suburbs, from having to flee Vienna in March 1864 in order to escape from his creditors. From Vienna he travelled to Stuttgart, where he was finally tracked down by an emissary of King Ludwig of Bavaria, who invited him to Munich, an unsuspected high point in his career that was not, however, to last. Quite apart from events such as these, Wagner was from then on a regular talking point in aesthetic and even political discussions in Vienna. By 1875, when Mahler and Wolf arrived in the city, a critical point had been reached in these discussions, leading in part to Wagner's breakthrough in the capital, for between March and May the composer had conducted three concerts of his own works in the city, followed in the autumn of that year by a return visit to superintend productions of *Tannhäuser* and *Lohengrin* at the Court Opera. (It was on this occasion that Wolf called on Wagner.) It was the Court Opera's new director, Franz Jauner, who had made it possible for Wagner to be crowned the new king of opera in Vienna after all the botched opportunities of the past. True, Jauner was no Wagnerian, but he knew the merits and drawing power of Wagner's operas and was firmly resolved to help them achieve their break-through at the Court Opera, an aim in which he and his successor Wilhelm Jahn were successful. By 1883/4 all the composer's works from *Rienzi* onwards were in the Court Opera repertory, while the house's principal conductor, Hans Richter, was closely associated with Bayreuth. Singers from the Court Opera also appeared on Bayreuth's Green Hill.

It was against this background that Wolf and Mahler grew up, Mahler's later cultivation of a sparer production style and his reassessment of Wagner's music during his period as director being inconceivable without this phase from 1875 to 1883. But Wagner's works were also explosive in terms of musical politics. Brahms had moved to Vienna in 1862 and taken over the running of the city's Singakademie, finally settling there in 1868 and becoming artistic director of the Gesellschaft der Musikfreunde from 1875 to 1878. (As we have already seen, it was in this capacity that he sat on various committees and competition juries.) A late developer, he had yet to complete his First Symphony, but thanks to his great choral works, his First Piano Concerto, Alto Rhapsody, lieder, chamber works and piano music he was the most famous composer then living in Vienna, a European figure who, although a native of Hamburg, was already being claimed by the Austrians. Brahms was also regarded as a 'conservative' composer (this is not the place to argue the merits of such an assessment) and hence as one of the figureheads of the party that opposed the 'musicians of the future', as members of the New German School were often called. This antagonism had come to the fore at the latest by 1860, when a Berlin newspaper published a declaration by a handful of signatories informing the world that they could 'only deplore and condemn as contrary to the most fundamental essence of music the products of the leaders and disci-ples of the so-called New German School'. Among the protest's signatories were Brahms himself and his friend Joseph Joachim, the most famous German violinist of his day. Only a short time earlier a whole series of musicians and music critics under Liszt's organizational and intellectual aegis had coined the term 'New German School' with reference to themselves, going on to form an association which from 1861 was known as the Allgemeiner Deutscher Musikverein. They viewed themselves as the party of progress and felt that they could overcome the hegemony of Viennese Classicism only by abandoning traditional sonata form and symphonic form in the conservative sense of those terms and by espousing new forms of expression, namely, the Wagnerian music drama and programme music. (The symphonic poem played an important role here, and it is no accident that Berlioz and his *Symphonie fantastique* were much touted by Liszt.)

Wagner was a great deal more controversial than Berlioz, so that after 1860 an individual's attitude to Wagner helped to clarify his or her position: progressives were expected to revere Wagner, Liszt and Berlioz, while reactionaries were convinced of the unsurpassable greatness of Mendelssohn and Schumann, and they composed in the style of Brahms. (This is a highly abbreviated and simplified account of a complex situation.) As a naïve child of his age, Bruckner was involuntarily caught in the crossfire, his idolatrous admiration for Wagner and use of multiple trombones instantly aligning him with the New German School, without leaving any scope for a more subtle analysis of his music. In Vienna, Eduard Hanslick and Ludwig Speidel, the city's two most powerful critics, lent their weight to the 'Brahmins', as Brahms's supporters were called, their interventions invariably proving intelligent, witty and effective.

Until the mid-1870s, it seemed unlikely that Wagner would ever gain a foothold in the Austrian capital, a state of affairs apparently confirmed by the unfortunate events of the last twenty or thirty years. But the situation then changed, the Wagnerians having a great advantage over their adversaries: at least to the extent that they were musically inclined, all who regarded themselves as progressive, whether socially, politically or morally, and all who felt that they were still young or at least behaved as if they were must necessarily side with the New Germans and, hence, with Wagner. As a venomous music critic, Wolf lost no opportunity to unleash torrents of abuse on Brahms, summing up the positions of the two armies on the occasion of an all-Liszt concert: 'On the one hand, youth, intelligence, idealism, judgement, enthusiasm, conviction; on the other, obtuseness, frivolity, lack of principles, ignorance and arrogance.' It was as simple as that. Many other young music enthusiasts adopted an equally black-and-white view of the situation, and this is certainly true of Mahler, who can scarcely have heard a note of Wagner's music in Iglau. He soon became one of Wagner's most fanatical followers, and we may well be right in assuming that it was in this way that he became friendly with Wolf or, more accurately, became Wolf's ally in matters Wagnerian. In her memoirs, Alma has given a colourfully embroidered account of the lives led by Mahler, Wolf and Rudolf Krzyzanowski in the room that they rented together. All three, she writes, were sensitive to noise. When one of them was composing and needed to use the piano, the others had to wander the streets and on one occasion even sleep outside on a bench in the Ringstraße. They are also said to have played through *Götterdämmerung* from the vocal score – this was no doubt around the time of the first performances of the work in Vienna in February 1879 – and to have made such a noise singing and playing the second-act Vengeance Trio for Brünnhilde, Gunther and Hagen that they were given immediate notice to quit.

There was also an institutional side to the Wagnerian enthusiasms of Vienna's young musicians: it was known as the Viennese Academic Wagner Society and was founded in 1872 by Guido Adler, later to make a name for himself as a musicologist and as one of Mahler's most unquestioning supporters, and by the sixteen-year-old Felix Mottl, later a distinguished Wagner conductor. They were reacting to the fact that in keeping with its name, the Conservatory did not include Wagner's music in its syllabus. Indeed, it could hardly have done so, given the influential Brahms's aversion to Wagner. (Conversely, Wagner felt only an irrational loathing of Brahms. On the one occasion when Nietzsche brought a Brahms score with him to Wagner's home in Bayreuth, he was greeted with open contempt.) But the Wagnerian enthusiasm of Vienna's young musicians also had a distinctly political aspect to it. Criticism of Wagner came above all from the liberal camp, not least on account of his anti-Semitism, while that same anti-Semitism made him all the more popular with certain of his supporters, among whom we must unfortunately number Wolf. These same supporters also held Pan-German ideas which, in terms of party politics, inevitably implied allegiance to the German nationalist party. It was not necessary, of course, for all who harboured German nationalist beliefs in Austria to become Wagnerians, but Austria's Wagnerians necessarily thought in terms of German nationalism, Mahler himself later being one of the few exceptions. German nationalist views had evolved in the wake of the German Confederation and the Frankfurt National Assembly of 1848/9 and implied a Pan-German empire under Austrian rule. Following Prussia's victory in the war of 1866 and the establishment of a German Reich without Austria, German nationalist attitudes became radicalized in Austria. After 1871 the majority of those who held such beliefs no longer demanded that Austria be incorporated into the German Reich as this would have been tantamount to acknowledging Prussian hegemony and the end of Austria as an independent nation. Rather, they believed in the overwhelming superiority of all things German in matters of language, culture and national sentiment within the multiracial dual monarchy, with the result that they looked down with contempt on other sections of the population who spoke different languages and who were felt to be racially different. In turn, their contempt was bound up with political attempts to express this sense of superiority on a political and constitutional level. For the German nationalists there could never be any question of reconciliation with the Magyars or even with the Czechs.

By the end of the 1870s Georg von Schönerer had worked his way up to the position of leader of the German national movement, and by 1882 he had formulated a programme in Linz with Adler and Pernerstorfer, both of whom went on to become prominent Social Democrats and whom we shall meet again as members of Siegfried Lipiner's circle of friends, which also included

Mahler. But when Schönerer began to promote anti-Semitism as an essential doctrine of the German national movement, he lost increasing numbers of supporters, a development that turned the German Nationalists, some of whom called themselves 'Pan-Germans', into a right-wing party. It is clear that although Mahler, unlike Otto Weininger, never became a Jewish anti-Semite, he sympathized with German national ideas, at least for a time. Wagner was the musical and political hero of all young Austrians with German national views. In their eyes, his music and his music dramas were a superior, ultra-modern art form, in addition to which they were German in the sense that Wagner himself had defined that term, most notably in his essay 'What is German?'. Elsewhere, in his series of articles 'Religion and Art', Wagner advocated vegetarianism, which Wolf and Mahler both espoused for a time. But Mahler may ultimately have found the German nationalism and anti-Semitism of the Viennese Academic Wagner Society too much to stomach, for it is clear from surviving documents that by 1879 he had already resigned his membership as part of a concerted action that also included Anton Krisper, Rudolf Krzyzanowski and Hans Rott, but not Wolf, who remained true to his beliefs until the end of his life.

It is no disrespect to Rott to argue that Wolf was the most important composer whom Mahler encountered prior to Richard Strauss. As with Strauss, relations between the two men remained problematical, but in Wolf's case they additionally ended on a shrilly discordant note. Does this suggest that Mahler was incapable of accepting compositional greatness in anyone other than himself? In the case of Wolf, there is something to be said for this claim, whereas with Strauss we know that he ungrudgingly recognized the importance of a work like *Salome*, no doubt in part because he himself no longer had any ambitions in the field of opera. Although Wolf was still describing Mahler as his 'friend' in a letter that he wrote to his parents in 1879, the first cracks in his relations with him may already have appeared in the autumn of that year when the two of them discussed their plans for an opera on the subject of Rübezahl, a legendary giant from the Riesengebirge on the boundary between Silesia and Bohemia. It seems that they failed to reach an agreement on the subject. According to Mahler's version of events, as recounted by Natalie, Wolf had told him about his plans for an opera, to which Mahler had responded by insisting that the subject could be treated only as a comedy. True, Wolf's only completed opera, *Der Corregidor*, is a 'comic' opera, although the humour has never managed to achieve its desired effect with every section of its audience. But with the best will in the world, Wolf was incapable of imagining Rübezahl as a subject for a comedy, a conviction shared by the present writer, too. Fired by the conversation, Mahler, however, spent the next week committing a libretto to paper. When the two friends next met – and it is significant that in discussing these events with Natalie, Mahler referred not to 'my friend' but to 'your friend' – Mahler asked Wolf how he was getting on with *Rübezahl*. Wolf reported that he had found some interesting material in the library, whereupon Mahler triumphantly drew his finished libretto from his pocket, causing Wolf to fly into a rage and declare that *Rübezahl* was now dead to him as an opera.[8] From the summer of 1880 onwards, there is no real trace of any further contact between the two composers. Mahler had in any case left Vienna, whereas Wolf remained in the city. No letters appear to have passed between them. Alma claims that the two men later met by chance in Bayreuth and walked past each other with no more than a cool word of greeting, but we have no means of knowing whether this account is correct. That their relations left a deeper mark on both parties than this pitiful end to their contacts might otherwise suggest emerges from a number of other pieces of evidence.

Wolf's nervous breakdown as the result of a syphilitic infection appears to have been triggered by a meeting with Mahler in September 1897, nearly twenty years later. (This statement of fact implies no apportionment of blame.) Mahler was already running the Vienna State Opera as Wilhelm Jahn's representative and had expressed an interest in *Der Corregidor*. Almost certainly he saw the difficulties involved in staging what remains a problematic piece, but he also recognized the merits of Wolf's hugely ambitious opera and felt an obligation to his former friend. But when Wolf called on him in the hope that a production could quickly be mounted, Mahler was obliged to put him off, arguing that the house's schedule, for which he was not responsible, prevented the piece from being staged in the foreseeable future. (The work had received its first performance in Mannheim in June 1896, only months after its completion.) Wolf had pinned all his hopes on Mahler and found it impossible to accept his reasons for not staging the work. In addition, it seems that the two men argued over Anton Rubinstein's opera *The Demon*, which Mahler may well have held in higher regard than *Der Corregidor*. As Dietrich Fischer-Dieskau has pointed out in his life of the composer, Wolf was already in an agitated state of mind caused by his incipient paralysis when he turned up in Mahler's office at the Court Opera on 18 September 1897.[9] Mahler was evidently forced to draw his attention to the work's shortcomings, and the two men parted on a note of acrimony. Alma claimed that as soon as he was outside, Wolf started to shout that he was Mahler and director of the Vienna Opera, whereupon he was restrained on the Ringstraße, but her account appears to be exaggerated. More reliable witnesses state that Wolf hurried to Mahler's rooms in the Auenbruggergasse claiming that he was director of the Vienna Opera and demanding admittance from the cook, who slammed the door in his face. He then invited his closest friends to his rooms to play through his latest opera, *Manuel Venegas*, for them. As he was doing so, he started to cry uncontrollably in a scene that Thomas Mann took over in describing Adrian Leverkühn's breakdown in *Doktor Faustus*. Wolf then delivered himself of a prepared speech directed at the staff of the Court Opera, taking tremendous delight in showing Mahler the door. According to an alternative account, Wolf went to see the tenor Hermann Winkelmann and likewise declared that he was the Court Opera's new director. Winkelmann retorted that this title belonged to Mahler, whereupon Wolf mysteriously whispered that he had 'already got rid of Mahler'. The day after these events, Wolf was taken by friends to a private psychiatric hospital under the pretext that as the Court Opera's new director he had to be introduced to the lord chamberlain. 'So you're playing games with me,' Wolf presciently told his doctors when they admitted him to the clinic.

Mahler, too, was not unaffected by these events. In his reminiscences of the composer, the writer on music Ernst Decsey – significantly enough, Wolf's first major biographer – recalls visiting Mahler's country retreat at Maiernigg on the Wörthersee. As a keen champion of Wolf, Decsey naturally brought the conversation round to his idol, who at this date, around 1900, was still alive, immured in a psychiatric institution in Vienna. Decsey was understandably taken aback when in no uncertain terms Mahler questioned whether Wolf's songs, including 'Weylas Gesang', had any artistic merit. He claimed not to be able to find in them any of the basic rules of composition, namely, the statement of a theme and its working out. A song, he insisted, should be characterized by singing and by music, not by the word-setting, which is of course paramount in Wolf. Mahler grew increasingly agitated, striking his open palm with his fist and refusing to calm down. Decsey left under the clear and no doubt correct impression that 'Wolf was a sore point with him'.

Conservatory and University

We are now more familiar with the world in which the fifteen-year-old distiller's son from Iglau found himself in 1875. It would be foolish to assume that from his first day in the city, Mahler conquered cultural Vienna and felt at home in every corner of this vast city. Rather, we should imagine a young boy from a town of nearly twenty thousand inhabitants finding himself in a city with a population that had just passed the one million mark – until then, the largest city he had known was Prague, an experience he had found profoundly disturbing. The term 'culture shock' is entirely appropriate here. We do not know all the details of Mahler's life during this period – with a few exceptions, his surviving letters do not predate 1879 – but certain conclusions are none the less possible. According to the matriculation register of the 'Conservatory for Music and the Performing Arts of the Gesellschaft der Musikfreunde in Vienna' (to give it its official title), Mahler's main subject was the piano, which he studied, of course, with his paternal patron Julius Epstein. The same register gives no indication of Mahler's subsidiary subjects, but we know that he studied harmony with Robert Fuchs and counterpoint and composition with Franz Krenn. (We should not forget that at the same time Mahler was attempting to complete his course as an external pupil at the Iglau Grammar School.) But the University's records also show that when he completed his studies at the end of the 1877/8 academic year Mahler's main subject was no longer the piano but composition, which he had been studying with Krenn. It is unclear why he changed courses in September 1877, but it cannot have been because of his inadequacies as a pianist for in the competition held in 1876 he won first prize for his performance of a Schubert sonata. A few days later, on 1 July 1876, he also won the first prize in composition for the opening move-ment of a quintet. There is no indication that he fell out with Epstein, and so his decision to change courses was presumably a reflection of his increasingly apparent interest in composition.

And with whom did Mahler study conducting? The answer is simple: with no one, for at this date conducting was not taught at any conservatory or college of music. When Peter Heyworth once asked Otto Klemperer how a conductor learnt to conduct, Klemperer replied: 'What one can teach and what one can learn is so minimal that I could explain it to you in a minute.' And Shaw's famous comment, in *Man and Superman*, that 'He who can, does. He who cannot, teaches', could also be applied to conducting. The most gifted of Mahler's 'disciples', Bruno Walter, who was a whole generation younger than his mentor, studied conducting at the Stern Conservatory in Berlin, but this was in 1890, by which date such courses were gradually being set up. They eventually included all the canonical aspects of the discipline that remain part of such courses even now: continuo, score-reading, the ability to play from a full score, the theory of musical form, composition and instrumentation. Otherwise, young conductors learnt their trade almost in passing by means of chorus and orchestral rehearsals with conservatory orchestras, accompanying singers and, most important of all, attending concerts given by the leading conductors of their day – Walter's great model was Hans von Bülow. Mahler managed to achieve all this without attending a class in conducting, just as Walter would have done. Conductors acquired the tools of their trade not only by watching the great conductors of their age, which in Mahler's case meant Bülow, Nikisch, Strauss and, to a lesser extent, the somewhat stolid Hans Richter, but also, and above all, by gaining practical experience in the provinces. The young Mahler could hone his skills on the screeching violins and croaking bassoons in Bad Hall and Laibach, where technical shortcomings in his stick technique were not so immediately apparent and could quickly be remedied. By the time that he arrived in Kassel at the age of twenty-three, he was already fully proficient as a conductor, documentary evidence from this period leaving us in no doubt on the matter: here was a conductor who measured everything by the standards of the works that he was interpreting, driving not only his comrades-in-arms but also any refractory adversaries in the orchestra to the very limits of their often modest abilities, persuading them to go along with him, however reluctantly, and sweeping his audience along with him. There is no doubt, too, that from first to last he felt a sense of profound inadequacy in the face of the great works by other composers, a feeling that frequently left him terminally depressed.

Financially speaking, Mahler was better off than many of his fellow pupils. (Given their youth, the word 'pupil' seems more fitting here than 'student'.) In financing his studies, he even demonstrated considerable astuteness, just as at a later date the otherworldly Mahler could show great cunning in monetary matters. It emerges from a request that he made for financial help during his second year at the Conservatory and that refers back to an alleged application from the previous academic year that he had told the authorities that his family was starving and had asked for half his school fees to be remitted, leaving them with a bill of only sixty florins, which could be paid in instalments: 'My father is not in a position to support me, still less to pay my school fees.' To put it mildly, this was less than the truth. Four years earlier, Bernhard Mahler had bought one of the better houses in Iglau and was clearly in a position to finance his son's studies, but presumably he had no wish to do so as he was still not convinced that his investment in a career in music would ever pay for itself. On this occasion, the application was successful, no doubt in part because Epstein added a note, guaranteeing that the fees that had not been remitted would be paid in full. Like many of the other pupils at the Conservatory, Mahler also earned some extra money by giving piano lessons – not only the subject at which he himself was best but also the one most sought after by the sons and daughters of the upper middle classes. According to Mahler's childhood friend Theodor Fischer, who was currently studying law at the University of Vienna, Mahler was also well regarded as an accompanist and worked with young singers and violinists in need of a pianist. That he additionally performed in the Bösendorfersaal suggests that he also accompanied established artists. On one occasion, at least, the dreaminess that we recall from his days in Iglau must have reasserted itself as we find a Polish violinist having to stamp his foot to remind his accompanist of his duties.

But there was also an incident that may well be related to Wolf's enforced departure from the Conservatory at some date during the 1876/7 academic year. According to the latest writings on Wolf, the Conservatory's director, Joseph Hellmesberger, received a letter that contained an unequivocal threat

on his life and that was signed 'Hugo Wolf'. Wolf was apparently not responsible for the letter, but when he went to see Hellmesberger and tried to defend
himself, the director is said to have screamed at him: 'I want nothing more to
do with you. You are no longer attached to the Conservatory.' It is more than
possible that Wolf, who was even smaller than Mahler and barely 5 feet 1 inch
in height but as vicious as a terrier, refused to be intimidated but expressed his
anger in no uncertain terms, an anger that is fully understandable if the
signature was indeed forged. (On the other hand, such was Wolf's character
that it is entirely possible that he *was* the author of the letter.) This seems to be
the only plausible explanation for a remarkable letter that Mahler wrote to
Hellmesberger. Undated, it contains nothing that would allow us to place it in
any wider context, but perhaps it was the result of a spontaneous gesture of
solidarity over which Mahler had then had second thoughts:

> I very much regret my overhasty decision and make so bold as to ask you to
> ignore my ill-considered action and allow me to return to the Conservatory.
> I shall endeavour to deserve this favour by my unremitting hard work and by
> satisfying not only you yourself, Herr Director, but the other teachers, too.[10]

The two prizes that Mahler won during his first year at the Conservatory were
a considerable boost to his self-esteem, and on 12 September 1876, when he
was still only sixteen, he organized a benefit concert at the Hotel Czap in his
native Iglau, the beneficiary being the local grammar school where he was still
a pupil – the gesture was no doubt much appreciated. Mahler did not appear
on his own but brought with him two violinists from the Vienna Court Opera
Orchestra, Eugen Grünberg and August Siebert, and his friend and fellow
student, Rudolf Krzyzanowski, who played the viola. The programme was a
demanding one and shows that Mahler could now rely on his technique as a
pianist, for Schubert's *Wanderer Fantasy* is a technically challenging piece, as
are the Chopin Ballades, one of which he also played on this occasion. But the
concert additionally featured two of his own works, a lost violin sonata and a
piano quartet – or possibly only a single movement from such a piece, in which
case it may have been his first surviving composition, a movement headed 'Not
too fast. Resolutely' and dating from 1876/7.

Although Mahler's first year at the Conservatory may have been successful,
his second year clearly turned out to be more problematical. For the first time
in his life, Mahler appears to have undergone a kind of crisis, albeit one whose
nature and causes remain a mystery. This was presumably the year in which he
abandoned his studies, only to resume them very soon afterwards, while his
admissions register also reveals certain irregularities in his studies. On the one
hand, he was allowed to continue his classes at the Iglau Grammar School,

while on the other he had difficulties with his course in counterpoint. While winning another first prize for the piano, he performed poorly in counterpoint, arriving late for the examination that he was required to resit, failing to complete the exercise and being unable to submit any course work, a failure that he attempted to cover up by submitting what his examiners dismissed as the 'first part of a fictitious piece', with the result that they refused to allow him to compete for the composition prize. It was around this time, too, that Mahler failed his school-leaving examination in Iglau, passing it only at the second attempt. In a priceless letter that he wrote to Julius Epstein and that relates specifically to these events and to Mahler's embarrassing setback in Iglau, we see the first instance of his stylistic grasp of Romantic irony in the sense understood by Schlegel and Jean Paul – the latter an author for whom Mahler retained a lifelong affection. To the multifarious demands that were being placed on the seventeen-year-old youth and that included the attractions of the big city, Wagnerism and the evenings that he spent at the Opera, the piano lessons that he was giving and his duties as an accompanist and, finally, his workload at the Conservatory and the classes that he was concurrently following at the grammar school in Iglau, Mahler reacted not with despair but with irony:

> Your 'Well-Tempered Highness' will excuse me if I modulate from the gentle adagio of my feelings through the dissonance of my anger to a wild finale, which is to be played moltissimo rubato. [Mahler is alluding here to his Piano Quartet of 1876, the first movement of which includes the performance marking 'moltissimo rubato and impassioned' towards the end.] The fact is that my entry in the leavers' concert here in Iglau was a few bars too late or, rather, I arrived a few days too late so that I have not been able to take the examination and have had to put it off for two months. None the less I hope to complete the homework that you set me for the vacation and to do so, moreover, to your complete satisfaction.[11]

For a seventeen-year old, this is a remarkably polished letter demonstrating a real satirical wit, so that it is easy to understand why, according to a number of his friends, Mahler for a time considered a career as a writer rather than as a musician. But, just as we saw with his letter complaining about his father's alleged poverty, young Mahler was not over-punctilious about the truth: he had not arrived too late for his examination in Iglau but had simply failed it, a point he clearly preferred not to disclose to his revered teacher. Although we should not attach too much importance to this, we shall have repeated occasions to note that whereas Mahler applied only the strictest moral standards to himself and others and that he generally came up to those standards, he was

willing for tactical reasons to play fast and loose with the truth and to manipulate facts and figures, the better to achieve his desired goals.

Before examining the rest of Mahler's period of study in Vienna, about which
we know so little, and before taking a closer look at the circle around Siegfried
Lipiner, we must take another step back and consider Mahler against the background not only of Wagner and Brahms but also of Brahms and Bruckner, for
it was these three composers – together with Johann Strauß, of course – who
dominated the musical world of Vienna in the 1870s and who impregnated the
air that Mahler and his friends breathed. We have already given a brief account
of the battle lines between the Wagnerians and the 'Brahmins'. On the one hand
was progress, the 'new' and an aesthetic outlook bound up with expression,
on the other, reaction, the 'old' and a formal aesthetic culled from Eduard
Hanslick's opusculum *On the Beautiful in Music*. (The fact that Hanslick was
Wagner's most bitter critic helped even the most slow-witted observer to see the
situation clearly.) And whereas the progressives promoted the symphonic poem
and music drama, the party of reaction sought to perpetuate the Beethovenian
form of the symphony, chamber music and lieder of a kind that had been traditional since the late eighteenth and early nineteenth centuries. The allegedly
academic and dry-as-dust Brahms had many friends, especially among the
older generation, but he also had many enemies, most of whom belonged
to a younger generation. It was left to Schoenberg in his 1933 lecture 'Brahms
the Progressive' to point out that the Wagner-Brahms alternative was not
in fact a genuine one and that it was more sensible to speak of 'Brahms *and*
Wagner':

> It is the purpose of this essay to prove that Brahms, the classicist, the
> academician, was a great innovator in the realm of musical language, that, in
> fact, he was a great progressive. . . . Gustav Mahler and Richard Strauss had
> been the first to clarify these concepts. They had both been educated in the
> traditional as well as in the progressive, in the Brahmsian as well as in the
> Wagnerian philosophy of art. Their example helped us to realize that there
> was as much organizational order, if not pedantry in Wagner as there was
> daring courage, if not even bizarre fantasy in Brahms.

And Schoenberg goes on to demonstrate by means of a series of detailed examples that Brahms's music contains a vast amount of intricate motivic writing,
but also a marked economy in his handling of complex material coupled with
clear logic and imagination. Without eschewing beauty and emotion, Brahms
had shown the creative forces that could be unleashed by his detailed treatment of the musical material, by wrestling with ideas and with that material
and by the technique of 'developing variation' that may strike the listener as a

conceptual process. Brahms 'the progressive' ushered in a period of progress in the direction of an absolute musical language that Schoenberg himself claimed finally to have put into practice.[12]

On the other hand there was Bruckner. Or perhaps it would be more accurate to describe Bruckner as occupying a place apart, for the opposing camp was home to Wagner and the 'New Germans'. Brahms had no time for Bruckner and even less understanding, notoriously dismissing his works as 'symphonic boa constrictors'. To the extent that Vienna's critics were almost all on the side of Brahms rather than that of Wagner and the New Germans (although this dualism was less marked among the general public), Bruckner, who had dedicated his Third Symphony to Wagner, was misinterpreted as a Wagnerian and showered with scorn and contempt. Mahler himself was present when the Third Symphony was given its first performance in Vienna on 16 December 1877 and saw Bruckner suffer one of the worst setbacks of his career. He was not only the composer of the work but was also obliged to conduct it, when the planned conductor, Johann Herbeck, for some years the director of the Court Opera and the principal conductor of the Gesellschaft der Musikfreunde's concerts, had died unexpectedly in the October of that year. The first performance of the Third Symphony turned out to be a disaster, the audience laughing and shouting protests, before leaving the hall in droves during the work's final movement, a 'Farewell Symphony' of a kind hardly envisaged by Haydn. 'Let me out,' a tearful Bruckner is reported to have exclaimed, 'people don't want to know about me.' In his review of the performance, Hanslick made no attempt to spare the composer's feelings: the symphony, he wrote, sounded as if Beethoven's Ninth had been crossed with Wagner's *Die Walküre* and then been trampled underfoot. Some two years later an arrangement of the symphony for two pianos was published. It was the work of Mahler and Rudolf Krzyzanowski, who had received the commission at some date during 1878. It was a great honour for a barely eighteen-year-old youth, and the first time that his name had appeared on a piece of music. Mahler and Krzyzanowski were among the youngest and at the same time the closest admirers of Bruckner, a point that Mahler himself repeatedly emphasized. In a letter probably written in 1902, he dated his contacts with Bruckner to the years between 1875 and 1881, in other words, the exact period when he was studying in Vienna. He insisted that in spite of claims to the contrary he had never been a 'pupil' of Bruckner but was 'one of his most enthusiastic admirers and publicists'.[13] In comments that were not intended for public consumption, conversely, we find a more critical attitude to Bruckner on Mahler's part. In around 1900 he told Natalie fairly bluntly: 'If it were up to me, I should scarcely perform any Bruckner at the Philharmonic concerts, which are so limited in scope and intended only for the best: one really cannot expect an audience to listen to these scraps of music and appalling absurdities, for all that they are often interrupted by divine ideas and themes.'[14] And when Mahler heard the Ninth Symphony in Salzburg in August 1906, he wrote to Alma: 'The work is the last word in absurdity. Salzburg was a-tremble with enthusiasm. It was a kind of musical midday snack in Bavarian style.'[15]

If Mahler adopted an increasingly critical view of Bruckner that we could sum up as 'wonderful themes inartistically developed', then his attitude to Brahms and his music changed from austere reserve to great respect, while falling short of genuine enthusiasm. As a Wagnerian and an advocate of Bruckner's music, Mahler was the born enemy of Brahms or at least he should have been. But this was not the case. In later years, when Brahms was already an old man, the two composers grew closer as human beings, Mahler frequently visiting the older man at his summer retreat at Bad Ischl. Although he assured Natalie that these visits were of limited appeal as they failed to provide him with any intellectual or professional stimulus, he justified them by claiming that the elderly composer was anxious to avoid all intellectual exertion that did not flow directly into his work. But Mahler's respect for Brahms's music increased as he grew older. From an early date he concentrated on the symphony to the virtual exclusion of all other genres, tending to the 'Brahmin' camp in his rejection of the symphonic poem and music drama, for all that he felt a spiritual affinity with the former, at least in his first two symphonies, whereas his commitment to the latter went no further than performing such works in the opera house. It would never have occurred to him to write a violin concerto, and when he heard a performance of the Brahms concerto in Berlin with the composer's friend Joseph Joachim as the soloist, he almost literally exploded with anger: 'How can anyone write anything as ante-diluvian as a violin concerto?' he asked Natalie. 'It's Zarathustra's tightrope walker flogging himself to death and ready to be buried.'[16] And yet, as Schoenberg indicated, Mahler was able to be both a Wagnerian and a Brahmsian at one and the same time, no doubt because, like Schoenberg, he recognized the progressive features in Brahms's music, a point that emerges with particular clarity from a comparison between Bruckner and Brahms that took place – presumably in the early 1890s – within the context of a discussion with his brother Otto. Otto argued simplistically that with Bruckner the content was greater, whereas with Brahms the form was more perfect. Mahler countered this by insisting that:

In order to judge a work you have to look at it as a whole. And in this respect, Brahms is indisputably the greater of the two, with his extraordinarily compact compositions which aren't at all obvious, but reveal greater depth and richness of content the more you enter into them. And think of his immense productivity, which is also part of the total picture of an artist! With Bruckner, certainly, you are carried away by the magnificence and wealth of his inventiveness, but at the same time you are repeatedly disturbed by its fragmentary character, which breaks the spell. *I* can permit myself to say this, because you know how deeply I revere Bruckner in spite of it, and I shall always do whatever is in my power to have his works played and heard.[17]

But, as principal conductor of the Vienna Philharmonic, he exercised this power only hesitantly and without any real sense of inner conviction.

Mahler's intellectual curiosity, which he retained throughout his life, extended far beyond the world of music. His father's example as a 'coachman-scholar', the classical authors in the family's bookcase and his knowledge of history, literature and philosophy, which he picked up at school alongside all the cramming, sometimes putting down unintentional roots, all exercised his young mind. The Conservatory could offer no counterpart to this or provide him with any intellectual stimulus as it was too much of a training ground for future musicians, with too narrow a syllabus. Mahler had scarcely passed his school-leaving examination, albeit at the second attempt, when his intellectual energy drove him to the city's University, where he enrolled in September 1877 at the age of seventeen.[18] During his first term there it was mainly German language and literature that he studied – interestingly, he read Middle High German language and literature with Richard Heinzel, later adding courses in philosophy, history and the history of music. It appears, too, that he studied harmony with Bruckner, although this was later deleted from his University records. As an institution, the University of Vienna enjoyed a considerable reputation, although the lecturers in the courses that Mahler attended were not necessarily adept at firing the young hothead's interests. At all events, Mahler was already following completely different courses by his second term: classical sculpture, the history of Dutch painting and the 'philosophy of the history of philosophy', which he studied with Franz Brentano, who was the nephew of the poet Clemens Brentano and arguably Vienna's leading teacher in the field of the humanities. And yet here, too, Mahler's appetite was evidently not whetted, for he failed to register for any course at all for what would have been his third term at the University. Instead, he took a year off, resuming his course only in the autumn of 1879, when he read archaeology, European history of the Napoleonic Age and the 'history of music since the death of Beethoven'. In this last-named subject, his teacher was none other than Eduard Hanslick, who had founded the tradition of musicology in Vienna, occupying a chair that was still called 'Aesthetics and the History of Music' and that was later to be filled by Mahler's friend and champion Guido Adler.

The very choice of subjects that Mahler studied indicates the wide range of his interests, while also attesting to the fact that the University and the subjects on offer there ultimately failed to satisfy him. His intellectual energy needed to find other outlets and open other valves. His closest friends at the

Conservatory were shortly joined by two further groups of acquaintances, the first of which was Vienna's Literary Club, an organization concerned with everything not directly bound up with music and, as such, likely to be of interest to a young reader like Mahler. Friends such as Rudolf Krzyzanowski, Rott and Wolf had been interested only in music, whereas the Literary Club consisted of three young people closely associated with Mahler's Moravian homeland: his cousin Gustav Frank, who was attending the Academy of Fine Arts in Vienna and whom Theodor Fischer described as an 'engraver'; Theodor Fischer, who was the son of Iglau's director of music and later the well-heeled president of the district court and who has left us such a colourful account of Mahler's childhood; and, finally, Emil Freund, who on leaving the Iglau Grammar School was similarly studying law at the University of Vienna and who was to remain Mahler's confidant and lawyer until his death. Unfortunately we have absolutely no idea what literary topics the Iglau Four discussed. In his reminiscences, Fischer reports only that 'at our meetings there were debates on literary questions and the issues of the day; they generally ended in our walking the streets for half the night, when in a spirit of romantic effusiveness we would abandon ourselves to the spell cast on us by the wonderful moonlit buildings of old Vienna.'[19]

If the Literary Club was a loose continuation of the literary enthusiasms of grammar-school pupils fired by Romantic interests, the second circle in which Mahler found himself – probably from the autumn of 1879 – was of incomparably greater importance, affecting the whole of the rest of his life. Certainly, it was more important than the University and, intellectually speaking, more important than his friends at the Conservatory. This was the Pernerstorfer circle, a group that in Mahler's case could also be called the Lipiner circle. Mahler was a member of it, on and off, until 1883, when he finally left Vienna to take up his post in Olmütz. These three years and the circle itself were the most crucial of all in terms of Mahler's literary and philosophical formation and his whole outlook on life, so that a lengthy excursus is more than justified, not least because Lipiner was of tremendous importance in Mahler's life, first in the years leading up to the breach following his marriage to Alma Schindler, and again in the final years of Mahler's life. (The fact that Alma Schindler was born in the autumn of 1879, at the very time that Mahler was becoming involved in the Lipiner circle, also serves to underline the generation gap between Mahler and his wife.)

The Lipiner Circle

The history of the Lipiner circle predates Mahler's entry into it,[20] beginning, as it does, in March 1867, when a group of grammar-school pupils from the Schottengymnasium in Vienna formed an association that called itself the

Telyn Society, its fine-sounding name inspired by the word for an ostensibly Celtic form of harp played by the old bards of Britain – the Ossianic fabrications of James Macpherson had not yet entirely lost their impact. The members of the Telyn Society were interested not only in literary history but also in politics, their name implying that they were picking up a tradition that was Germanic in its wider sense. In doing so, they were emphatically not appealing to the Nibelung myth, which Wagner was then in the process of reviving. (The first performance of his *Ring* had yet to take place.) Wilhelm Jordan's epic version was only just starting to appear in print and had found only a small audience in Austria. If the pupils at the Schottengymnasium knew about the *Nibelungenlied*, it was because one of their teachers, Hugo Mareta, was an enthusiastic champion of the poem. However powerful Wagner's impact may have been on Vienna's young academics and intellectuals some ten years later, there must have been some other point for them to latch on to in the 1870s. Celtic culture was thus a kind of preparation for the *Nibelungenlied*. But the idea of German nationalism was none the less a driving force behind the formation of this club. Austria had just been defeated by Prussia, making a Pan-German solution no more than a distant prospect, so that the increasingly apparent attempts to revive Celtic national feeling in Britain in the years around the middle of the century evidently encouraged a similar movement in Austria. The founder members of the Telyn Society were all destined to play important roles in Austrian society and history, but they were also important for Mahler. They included Victor Adler, the son of a wealthy Jewish businessman, Salomon Adler, who had come to Vienna from Prague and who later became one of Austria's leading Social Democrats; Max von Gruber, the son of one of the pioneers of otology and later a famous hygienist who conducted important research in the field of typhoid infections; and Heinrich Friedjung, who went on to become a historian and a central figure in the Austrian German National Party, only to find himself excluded from it on account of his Jewish descent and additionally discredited as a historian for not checking the reliability of historical sources that turned out to be inauthentic. Last but not least was Engelbert Pernerstorfer. Unlike his fellow pupils, he came from a poor background and was the son of a tailor. Together with Adler, he went on to found the Austrian Social Democratic Party. First, however, he became a German Nationalist, an affiliation that followed naturally from his membership of the Telyn Society. It needs to be emphasized, however, that these young German nationalists had not yet signed up to an anti-Semitic agenda, not least because such a move would have been problematic in view of Adler's and Friedjung's Jewish origins. The Telyn Society came to reflect a very special blend of Germanocentric and German national thinking, Socialist fantasies, sympathy with the Paris Commune and solidarity with the fate of the emerging proletariat. This mixture of nationalism and socialism, both of which were still in their infancy, inevitably led most members of the Telyn Society to embrace German national ideas, only Pernerstorfer and Adler going on to espouse the cause of social democracy. If social democracy in Austria was always more nationalistic than in Germany, it was because of these origins.

By the time that the members of the Telyn Society had left school and gone on to university, their adolescent infatuation with Celtic and Germanic Romanticism had waned, and the Welsh telyn soon lost its significance. All its members were considerably older than Mahler, Adler having been born in 1852, Pernerstorfer in 1850. But they all remained in close contact and in 1872 founded a 'Reading Society of Viennese German Students', with the emphasis on 'German'. With the exception of the usual student societies, this was the most important student organization in Vienna in the 1870s, and certainly the most intellectually influential. One of the few University professors to exert any authority over this small group of student intellectuals was Lorenz von Stein, whose brilliant writings straddled the disparate disciplines of economics, politics and sociology, and included *Socialism and Communism in Present-Day France* and a handbook on sociology. Adler and Pernerstorfer played leading roles in the Reading Society, which soon evolved into far more than a mere continuation of the Telyn Society under another name. By 1874 Adler was its librarian and Pernerstorfer its secretary. Its members discussed not only the theories of Darwin but also the philosophy of Schopenhauer, debating the differences between them on the basis of a sensationalist tract of the time, Carl von Rokitansky's *The Solidarity of All Animal Life*. Adler's diaries contain lengthy notes teeming with concepts such as 'fellow suffering', 'world suffering' and 'weltschmerz' – it comes as no surprise to learn that only a few years later many of these young people felt drawn to Wagner and to his religion of compassion as expressed in some of his late essays such as 'Religion and Art' of 1880 and in *Parsifal*. It is also clear why Mahler, too, should have been attracted to this group. Thanks not least to the additional influence of Dostoevsky, Mahler subscribed all his life to a personal religion of compassion. Socialism, German nationalism and the interest in compassion and solidarity that predisposed a number of these students to pin their colours to the Social Democratic mast led them far away from the liberal spirit that still dominated the age but whose roots were already cankered. In this way the Reading Society came within the purview of the authorities and at the end of 1878 was disbanded as politically suspect. From this point of view it was entirely logical that its members, including, at a later date, Mahler too, should have stumbled across the writings of Nietzsche and done so, moreover, at an exceptionally early date.

We need to remember that Nietzsche's first full-length publication, *The Birth of Tragedy*, had first appeared in 1872 and that it had met with little interest except in specialist circles and among Wagnerians. It says much for the perceptiveness of Vienna's student population that one of their number, Josef Ehrlich, had already made contact with Nietzsche by April 1876 and expressed his enthusiasm for the philosopher's *Untimely Meditations*, the fourth and final one of which – 'Richard Wagner in Bayreuth' – was about to appear. The main members of the Reading Society had been very much waiting for Nietzsche, even though he was neither a German nationalist nor a writer noted for a particular interest in the religion of compassion, but his radical philosophy was now struggling to emerge from the cocoon of his *Untimely Meditations*. Vienna's students must have made a second attempt to get in touch with Nietzsche the following year, for in June 1877 we find Erwin Rohde writing to the philosopher and mentioning a student whom he had met in Vienna and who had introduced himself as a member of what Rohde called the 'Nietzsche Society of Vienna'. The student, Rohde claimed, had sent Nietzsche a copy of a book titled *Prometheus Unbound*, the very title of which was a flattering tribute to the Basel Professor of Classical Philology, for the title page of *The Birth of Tragedy* had included a vignette depicting the unbound Prometheus. Nietzsche received the book only after some delay, for it had been sent to his mother's home in Naumburg and only from there was it forwarded to the philosopher, who was currently on holiday at Rosenlauibad. But his reaction on finally reading it was entirely positive, and in his reply we find him telling Rohde that the poem had provided him with 'a day of true celebration' and that its author must be a veritable 'genius'. The name of this genius was Siegfried Lipiner.

Who was this Siegfried Lipiner, who was to become Mahler's leading authority on all intellectual matters? The son of Jewish parents, he had been born in Jaroslav in Galicia in 1856 and had moved to Vienna in 1871, completing his schooling at the city's Leopoldstadt Grammar School in 1875 – the Leopoldstadt was then the quarter with the largest Jewish population in Vienna. He officially matriculated at the University in the autumn of 1875, although he had already attended a number of lectures there, his main interests being philosophy, literature and religion. (Meanwhile, Mahler, his junior by four years, was beginning his studies at the Conservatory.) He wrote *Prometheus Unbound* when he was only eighteen, and the volume was published, with a dedication to Heinrich Laube, in 1876. During the summer of that year Lipiner moved to Leipzig to hear Gustav Theodor Fechner lecture – another writer who exerted a powerful influence on Mahler, a point to which we shall return in due course. On his return to Vienna, Lipiner interrupted his studies, and it was not until some time later that he completed a doctorate with the promising title of 'Homunculus: A Study of Faust and Goethe's Philosophy', the text of which appears not to have survived.

Contact with Nietzsche did not develop along the lines that Lipiner must secretly have hoped. But at all events it seems likely that it was Lipiner who drew Mahler's attention to the early writings of a philosopher whose name cannot have been known in his home town of Iglau. Indeed, it is even questionable whether it was familiar in circles attached to the University of Vienna. As Mahler himself was later obliged to admit, Lipiner had an annoying way of insinuating himself into other people's lives. Just as he later reproached Mahler for seeing Alma Mahler, whose immaturity he considered unworthy of his friend, so he demonstrated considerable arrogance in attempting to advise Nietzsche on where to live and spend his holidays. This was something that Nietzsche loathed, and not even his closest friends were allowed to interfere in this area of his life. But Lipiner was merely a distant admirer who was much younger than the philosopher, and so he was kept at a distance. It seems not to have troubled Nietzsche that Lipiner was Jewish – he had a markedly ambivalent attitude to Jews but was certainly not anti-Semitic like Wagner, feeling only a loathing of anti-Semites such as his later brother-in-law Bernhard Förster. For reasons that remain unclear, Lipiner forfeited Nietzsche's sympathies even though the latter continued at least for a time to acknowledge the younger man's significance. But within a year it was all over, and by August 1878 we find Nietzsche writing to his mother and sister: 'A letter from Lipiner, long, significantly speaking *for* him, but of unbelievable impertinence towards me. I have broken free from my "admirer" and his circle – and I can breathe freely again. His future development is very close to my heart, I am not confusing him with his Jewish characteristics, about which he can do nothing.'[21] But Nietzsche was unable to maintain this tolerant attitude towards Lipiner, and when the latter sent him his *Renatus* six months later, his reaction was brief and to the point: it was a ghastly aberration. Thus the personal contacts between Lipiner and Nietzsche came to an end, although Lipiner's lifelong enthusiasm for the philosopher remained unaffected by all this.

Much the same happened to Lipiner when he visited Bayreuth. He was introduced to Wahnfried by Malwida von Meysenbug, the principal intermediary between Nietzsche and Wagner. As with Nietzsche, Lipiner tested the water by sending one of his writings, in this case his lecture 'On the Elements of a Renewal of Religious Ideas in the Present Day', which he had delivered at the Reading Society in January 1878 and which he had then had printed at his own expense. The lecture bore clear parallels with some of the ideas that Wagner himself was to express more fully in 'Religion and Art' in 1880, although Lipiner had of course read Schopenhauer and the earlier writings of Wagner and had combined them with Nietzsche's ideas, so that it is no surprise to find that Wagner and his wife were much taken by the lecture. In September 1878 Lipiner finally had an opportunity to meet the Wagners at Wahnfried. The conversation naturally revolved around his lecture and the ideas on religion that were then preoccupying Wagner, as well as touching on the writings of the anti-Semitic academic Paul de Lagarde. It seems that differences in their views were already apparent at this stage and that the Wagners were evidently dismayed by certain 'Israelite' elements in Lipiner's view of religion, a point on which they differed from Nietzsche. Three days later – 23 September 1878 – Lipiner was invited back to Wahnfried, and on this occasion another contentious subject came up: socialism. As we have seen, socialist ideas were rife among Vienna's students, but Wagner had long since suppressed his past as a revolutionary, and so he had little time for Lipiner's socialist sympathies. The power of such a movement could lie only in destruction, Wagner insisted, adding that constructive ideas were always childish. His tone was even more intemperate when Lipiner returned two days later and tried to draw attention to inconsistencies in Schopenhauer's thinking. Wagner became 'very heated' in his discussion with the young disciple from Vienna, although he afterwards regretted his outburst and tried to make it up with Lipiner, but the latter had already left town. This was Lipiner's only visit to Bayreuth. He later sent a number of his books and articles to Wahnfried, but Wagner was no longer interested. Anyone who revealed Jewish aspects in his view of religion or who supported socialism and criticized Schopenhauer had emphatically forfeited his respect and was clearly of no further use to him as a disciple or propagandist. Wagner's outright hostility towards Jews inevitably played a decisive role in this.

Lipiner twice had an opportunity to draw closer to the two men whom he regarded as the most illustrious minds of their day, but in spite of starting out from a strong position, both attempts ended in disaster. It is difficult to know whether it was because of these setbacks that his initial triumphs, both inspired and inspirational, ended in the gloom of obscurity. In 1881 he found a niche for himself as librarian to the German Senate, later becoming the library's director, but he published very little. In 1891 he converted to Protestantism. His monumental magnum opus, written under the influence of his newly discovered Christianity, was to be a trilogy on the life of Christ, but although he is believed to have completed several drafts of it, he later destroyed them all. Only a prologue, *Adam*, has survived and was published posthumously. His knowledge of Polish helped him to translate two works by the Polish national poet Adam Mickiewicz, one of which, 'Todtenfeier', impressed Mahler enormously and left its mark on his Second Symphony. Lipiner also wrote a libretto for an opera on the subject of Merlin for the Viennese composer Karl Goldmark, who was immensely successful in his own day. But after that Lipiner fell silent. Only after his reconciliation with Mahler, about which we shall have more to say in due course, did he write a touching poem to mark the composer's fiftieth birthday. It was called 'The Musician Speaks'. He died on 30 December 1911 after a lengthy struggle against cancer of the larynx, only months after the death of the man with whom he had been such a close friend during the promising years of his adolescence.

The phenomenon of a writer who causes a stir with an early work but then fails to live up to expectations – although the expectations may also be false – is certainly not unknown in the history of literature. There are also writers who enjoy a tremendous reputation as intellectual heroes or scintillating conversation-alists or respected authorities within a small and exclusive circle, a reputation that is not reflected by their published works. The Schwabing magus of the turn of the century, Alfred Schuler, was one such writer and was additionally comparable to Lipiner in that he too tended towards spiritualism and the occult. Lipiner's published writings seem unimpressive today but appear, rather, to be high-flown and even half-baked, and yet readers familiar with late nineteenth-century litera-ture will have little difficulty in identifying typical features of this style and in understanding why Nietzsche was so impressed. At a time when Nietzsche's impact was virtually non-existent, Lipiner took up and developed one of the ideas in *The Birth of Tragedy*, in which Nietzsche had proposed his own interpretation of Aeschylus's *Prometheus Bound* and expressed the hope that Prometheus's subsequent release would come from the unleashing of the Dionysian element in Wagner's works. Lipiner is by far the earliest and at the same time the most monumental instance of the impact of the early Nietzsche on circles other than those of classical philologists and Wagnerians. Nor is there any doubt that he was the earliest writer to respond poetically to Nietzsche's thinking and to give epic expression to those ideas, a development particularly welcome to a thinker who could make nothing of the dramas of his day. As for the content of his epic, we can do worse than quote from an enthusiastic review by Johannes Volkelt, professor of aesthetics at the University of Vienna and an influential figure in the Pernerstorfer circle:

> The evolution of humanity, its titanic struggle for self-emancipation, its fall from what it thought were the heights of absolute intellectual freedom into the depths of lawlessness and inhumanity, the mind's ability to rouse itself from this state of degradation and its victorious flight to the ultimate goal of true freedom and reconciliation – it is this that the poet places before our mind's eye with his broad brushstrokes.

Lipiner's *Prometheus* symbolizes humankind's rebellious self-awareness, while the figure of Christ represents our attempts to overcome every urge towards individuation. When Nietzsche looked at this more closely, he cannot have been pleased by what he saw, and to the extent that Lipiner's next work, his epic poem *Renatus*, which appeared in 1878 with a dedication to Malwida von

Meysenbug, reflected identical ideas, it is not surprising that Nietzsche was now convinced that his hopes in Lipiner had been misplaced. Indeed, had he looked more closely at *Prometheus Unbound* in the first place and not allowed himself to be blinded by the belief that he had found his first disciple, both men would have been spared their later sense of disillusionment.[22]

Be that as it may, Mahler was profoundly influenced by Lipiner, which is why the foregoing excursus was so necessary. Nor was Mahler alone in attesting to Lipiner's remarkable impact. Writing in the aftermath of Mahler, Bruno Walter offers us a much more succinct description:

> Siegfried Lipiner, a rather short man with Zeus-like curly blond hair, a full beard of the same colour, and radiant blue eyes, was a poet endowed with vision, force, and eloquence. Carried away by a topic of conversation, by a memory, or by a picture, he was likely to be 'seized with the spirit.' On such occasions, a wealth of thoughts and wisdom, improvised, but perfect in form, would flow from his lips.[23]

Another leading member of the Reading Society, Richard Kralik, has also left a lively portrait of Lipiner in his recollections, a portrait that reflects his charisma while at the same time revealing that not everyone felt it in the same way. Kralik later made a name for himself as a dramatist, poet and cultural historian. In 1905 he founded the Grail Alliance, an organization which, Teutonic and anti-Jewish, was intended to revitalize Catholicism and which drew heavily for its ideas on Wagner's regeneration essays. Recalling the late 1870s, Kralik had the following to say about Lipiner:

> His first work, *Prometheus Unbound*, very quickly made his name better known and even famous. It was held out as a foil to Goethe's *Faust*. We – his friends – did not entirely understand it, but we were uncommonly impressed by it, not least because its author was able to declaim it and comment on it in such fiery, self-confident terms. It was not easy for anyone in our circle to escape from the spell of this superior idealism. Even sceptics such as the poetess Betty Paoli called him a prodigy, albeit not without a hint of irony. But a minority among us considered his poetry to be fabricated, inauthentic, unoriginal, a 'schoolbook gone mad', as one keen and critical mind expressed it. In short, it was vapid, hollow and meaningless.[24]

It is unclear whether Kralik himself belonged to this minority, although his anti-Semitic outlook may well have influenced his views. At all events, it is remarkable that the negative epithets applied here to Lipiner were later taken over word for word and applied to Mahler by contemporary critics. Deriving from one of Wagner's favourite arguments in his essay 'Jews in Music', they stemmed from the belief that Jews were incapable of any kind of creative endeavour. Unsurprisingly, Kralik refers to Mahler only a few pages later and mentions his membership of the Lipiner circle, dismissing his music in identical terms. (Conversely, Kralik's son Heinrich later became one of Mahler's great apostles in Vienna.) Quite apart from the failure of Lipiner's career as a poet, at least as far as its public manifestation was concerned, it is important to note that as the germ cell of the Reading Society and like the Telyn Society before it, the Pernerstorfer circle held ideas clearly bound up with cultural reform. The materialism and laissez-faire liberalism that had dominated Austrian culture since the middle of the century were now to be offset by root-and-branch reforms, starting with the country's culture.

In Nietzsche the Pernerstorfer circle had chosen the most eloquent advocate of this critique of liberal ideas. This group of Viennese students, which Mahler joined in 1879, enthusiastically accompanying their strident German national songs on the piano, was the first in Europe to take a real interest in Nietzsche, going beyond the individual responses to the philosopher's early writings on the part of a handful of solitary freethinkers and in that way forming one of the very first 'Nietzsche Societies'. German national thinking found a strange bedfellow in the desire for social justice in a future reformed society. Indeed, there was an element of 'national socialism' about this outlook, long before this nexus of ideas evolved to such devastating effect. It is no surprise to find a large number of young Jews sharing these aspirations, for the sort of willpower advocated by Nietzsche could also imply abandoning their unwanted Jewishness and embracing a loftier idea of humanity which, no longer bedevilled by 'race' and religion, would come into being in the wake of their assimilation and acculturation. From this point of view, one can understand why Wagner's idea of regeneration, as championed in his essays of the years around 1880, found so many admirers and advocates among Jewish intellectuals and artists, the anti-Semitic implications of his writings being wilfully ignored or at least trivialized as the waste products of a process of fermentation. When Wagner's essay 'Religion and Art' appeared in the *Bayreuther Blätter* in 1880, it had a tremendous impact in Vienna, too, especially among members of the group associated with Pernerstorfer and Lipiner. The vegetarianism that Wagner preached in this essay suddenly became de rigueur, and for a time Mahler, too, became a committed vegetarian. As with Wagner himself, however, the enthusiasm proved short-lived: an acquaintance of his reports seeing him tucking into a joint of meat with horseradish sauce at a restaurant in Budapest. The parameters of this group could no doubt be circumscribed by reference to Nietzscheanism, Wagnerism, vegetarianism and socialism, and it was this witches' brew of ideas that left its mark on the young Mahler and constituted his true schooling at this time. It was

presumably Lipiner who introduced him to the Pernerstorfer circle, and he had
certainly been introduced to Victor Adler by 1878 at the latest. The Viennese
polymath Friedrich Eckstein, who was one of the most colourful and distinctive characters in fin-de-siècle Vienna, saw these events unfold and noted the
impression that Mahler left on outsiders at this time. Here he describes the
vegetarian restaurant where members of the circle met:

> One of them was shortish, betraying an unusual irritability in his curiously
> uneven gait. His narrow face, framed by a brown beard, was intellectually
> alive and animated; he spoke wittily in a strong Austrian accent. He always
> carried a bundle of books or scores under his arm and conversation with him
> was sporadic. His name was Gustav Mahler. He had studied law [Eckstein is
> wrong on this point] and completed a course at the Vienna Conservatory. He
> came to our notice because he was the first to make a piano transcription of
> a Bruckner symphony.[25]

A Time of New Departures

This, then, was the intellectual environment in which Mahler spent his formative years between adolescence and manhood. Numerous detailed observa-
tions will later indicate the extent to which his whole outlook was shaped by
his years in Vienna between 1875 and 1881, when his musical, philosophical,
political and literary ideas were formed. (We shall later have more to say about
Mahler's reading habits.) There is, however, surprisingly little evidence about
the state of Mahler's health, or perhaps it is not so surprising after all as he was
not yet the compulsive correspondent that he was later to become. Letters to
his parents appear to have gone missing, and in Vienna he threw himself head
over heels into the physical and intellectual demands of his threefold course of
study at the Conservatory, the University and the 'private university' of the
Pernerstorfer and Lipiner circle. We are relatively ill-informed about the whole
of this decisive period, but especially about the years between 1878 and 1881.
Virtually the only letters that have survived from this time are those that
Mahler wrote during his summer vacations and sent to his friends who were
still in Vienna. He continued to compose, of course, and wrote an overture,
The Argonauts, which he submitted for the Beethoven Prize in July 1878, but
his entry was unsuccessful, and no prize was awarded that year. Conversely, a
Scherzo from a Piano Quintet which, like the overture, is no longer extant,
earned him a first prize from the Conservatory at this time. And with that he
completed his studies at this last-named institution on 2 July 1878.

In the autumn of 1879 he began work on his opera *Rübezahl*, leading to his
falling-out with Wolf. Of this particular project, only a kind of libretto has

survived, but the impression that it leaves is one of immaturity, which is hardly surprising. We do not know how much progress Mahler may have made on the score or whether he started work on it at all. Nor do we know how far he got with his plans for an opera on Duke Ernst of Swabia. But with that we leave the realms of speculation and find ourselves dealing with Mahler's first complete surviving compositions. The text of his cantata, *Das klagende Lied*, had been completed by the spring of 1878, but it was not until November 1880 that he put the finishing touches to the score of what is a very substantial work. I shall have more to say about this in the next chapter. In the summer of 1879, while he was back at home in Iglau, Mahler had fallen in love with Josephine Poisl, the daughter of the manager of the local telegraph office – we may assume that he already knew her before this date. Josephine Poisl was the second woman with whom we know Mahler fell in love – the first was a certain Pauline, whom he got to know on the estates at Morawan and Ronow in the two summers of 1875 and 1876 – and it was she who inspired his first three songs, 'Im Lenz' (In Spring), 'Winterlied' (Winter Song) and 'Maitanz im Grünen' (May Dance in the Country), which he completed in quick succession in February and March 1880. During the summer of 1879 Mahler gave piano lessons to Josephine and her sister, Anna, but there was never any prospect of a long-term relationship: as a twenty-year-old impecunious music student, he stood no chance of being accepted as a suitable suitor by Josephine's parents. Three letters to her have survived. The first dates from March 1880 and still addresses her with the formal 'Sie'. In it, Mahler recalls the previous summer when the two of them sat in a little house in the Föhrenwald and he told her the stories of two of the heroic legends from Germany's distant past, the Lay of Horn-Skinned Siegfried and the tale of Wayland the Smith. In his final letter, he reacts to the news that her father had evidently declared the relationship over. In it, he strikes what is already a typical note of outrage that we shall find again and again in similar situations:

Despair dictates these lines. . . . I have never humbled myself before another person! See! I am kneeling before you! – Oh, by all that is dear to you – if you have ever felt even the least spark of love for me – I beg you – give me a sign to say that I should not despair . . . I am scarcely in control of myself any longer – my blood runs cold in my veins – and I am wandering round like a corpse! . . . Yes, yes! You still love me! – You must still love me – otherwise I must despair of the light and of heaven – nay, of everything that is beautiful and dear! – O my sweet child, whom I love so ardently! Hear me – across all the lands and mountains that lie between us I call out to you in my hour of greatest need! Give, O give me a sign![26]

Few letters have survived from this period, but most of those that have are detailed and powerfully expressed. This is especially true of the letters that Mahler wrote to his fellow student at the Conservatory, Anton Krisper, and to Josef Steiner, who had been two classes above him at the Iglau Grammar School and who wrote the words for his planned opera *Duke Ernst of Swabia*. Steiner had remained in Iglau, and when Mahler spent a few weeks in Puszta-Batta near Budapest between early June and mid-August 1879, earning some money by giving piano lessons to the children of his host, Moritz Baumgarten, it was Krisper and Steiner to whom he opened his heart, telling them of his loneliness in Hungary and pining equally for Iglau and Vienna. Like his correspondence with Josephine Poisl, these letters allow us a deeper insight into the nineteen-year-old Mahler's frame of mind than most of his later letters, which tend to be more to do with his career and other daily concerns. Not until the unhappy summer of 1907, when Mahler was in Maiernigg, and the catastrophic marital crisis that overtook him in Toblach during the summer of 1910 does it again become possible for posterity to gaze more deeply into his troubled psyche.

The letter that Mahler wrote to Josef Steiner between 17 and 19 June 1879 – one of the longest that he ever sent – is a remarkable confession.[27] It reveals a young man filled with an extreme and emphatic love of life but also plagued by depression and a death wish. Of course, we also need to pay due heed to the literary stylization that is clearly influenced by his reading of Jean Paul and of eccentric Romantics such as E. T. A. Hoffmann, even down to his choice of particular words, making it hard to decide where to locate the dividing line between literature and real life. The blurred distinction between them is typical of Mahler, as is the emotional life which, lived to extremes, characterizes his music. Although he later learnt to moderate its expression in his day-to-day activities, it vented itself all the more explosively at critical junctures in his life. His letter to Steiner is a three-movement symphony in epistolary form and could be headed 'The Sufferings of Young Mahler'. The opening movement is an Allegro furioso ed estatico, the second an Andante lugubre and the third an Allegretto grazioso. The three movements represent the three sections of the letter, which was written on three consecutive days, each section reflecting the mood of the day. The first is dominated by a sense of wild agitation: 'The greatest intensity of the most joyful vitality and the most consuming yearning for death dominate my heart in turn.' Mahler then strikes a note of despair at life and art in general, showing him to be well prepared for the mood of the circle around Pernerstorfer and Lipiner that he was to enter only a few weeks later:

When the abominable tyranny of our modern hypocrisy and mendacity has driven me to the point of dishonouring myself and when the inextricable web of conditions in art and life has filled my heart with disgust for all that is sacred to me – art, love, religion – what way out is there except by self-annihilation? Wildly I wrench at the bonds that chain me to the loathsome, insipid swamp of this life, and with all the strength of despair I cling to sorrow, my only consolation.

The young Mahler seems to be suicidal, much like Goethe's Werther or even Faust as the latter raises the phial of poison to his lips at the beginning of the tragedy that bears his name. And yet Mahler never really considered committing suicide, for even in the darkest periods of his life, there was always a ray of light that promised salvation. And the same is true in the present case:

Then all at once the sun shines upon me – and gone is the ice that encased my heart, again I see the blue sky and the flowers swaying in the wind, and my mocking laughter dissolves in tears of love. Then I needs must love this world with all its deceit and frivolity and its eternal laughter. Oh, would that some god might tear the veil from my eyes, that my clear gaze might penetrate to the marrow of the earth! Oh, that I might behold this earth in its nakedness, lying before its Creator without adornment or embellishment.

Implicit in these lines, and barely concealed at all behind a pseudo-literary veil, is the erotically ecstatic, pantheistic idolization of nature that was to characterize Mahler's view of nature for a long time to come and that left its mark above all on his first four symphonies.

The second section of the letter is less strident, less eccentric, less effusive. As Mahler himself points out, it is as if 'assuaging tears' have welled up in his eyes after the previous day's outburst. The role that he now adopts is that of Eichendorff's good-for-nothing:

But in the evening when I go out on to the heath and climb a lime tree that stands there all on its own and gaze out into the world from the topmost branches of this friend of mine, the Danube winds her old familiar way before my eyes, her waves flickering in the glow of the setting sun; from the village behind me the chime of the eventide bells is wafted to me on a kindly breeze, and the branches sway in the wind, rocking me to sleep like the Erlkönig's daughters, and the leaves and blossoms of my favourite tree tenderly caress my cheeks. – Stillness everywhere! The most sacred stillness! Only from afar comes the melancholy croaking of the toad that sits mournfully among the reeds.

Particularly striking are the echoes of Schubert's two songs, 'Der Lindenbaum' from *Winterreise* and 'Erlkönig'. At the same time, however, there are also pre-echoes of the *Lieder eines fahrenden Gesellen*, in which we likewise find the motif of a lime tree ('Auf der Straße steht ein Lindenbaum'). And when Mahler then adds some delightful reminiscences of the farms at Morawan and Ronow, where he fell in love with Pauline, then 'two eyes that once made a thief of me' peer over the horizon, and we see 'my sweetheart's two blue eyes' from the *Lieder eines fahrenden Gesellen*. Although the third and shortest section of the letter still speaks of loneliness, it confirms that Mahler's mood is now 'serenely cheerful', a change scarcely credible after the earlier outbursts but none the less symptomatic of a young man in extremis. A few weeks later, while still giving piano lessons to the Baumgarten children, Mahler wrote to Albert Spiegler in a very similar vein. But what is most striking here is his longing to hear a Christian service, especially the sound of peasants praying before the altar and the strains of an organ playing. The fact that it is emphatically not the sounds of a synagogue that Mahler was longing to hear indicates that even at the age of nineteen he had already begun to distance himself from the Judaism of his forebears.[28] And in March 1880, when he was shaken to his very core by his unrequited love of Josephine Poisl and seized by a tremendous feeling of loneliness even in the hurly-burly of Vienna ('I am so alone! I do not know whether I shall be able to bear it for much longer. I feel as if I am about to collapse at any minute! I have just been fighting a great battle – and have still not got to the end of it'[29]), he sent Anton Krisper a copy of a poem that is a remarkable mixture of things that he had read and others he had experienced for himself, the former category including reminiscences of Wilhelm Müller and Schubert (once again, there are clear references to Schubert's *Winterreise*), Eichendorff and Jean Paul, as well as the literary style that was typical of Mahler during this period and later. As before, one can understand why Mahler hesitated for a time between the careers of poet and musician. As such, his poem may usefully bring to an end our survey of his adolescence:

Vergessene Liebe
Wie öd' mein Herz! Wie leer das All'!
 Wie groß mein Sehnen!
O! wie die Fernen Tal zu Tal
 sich endlos dehnen!
Mein süßes Lieb! Zum letzten Mal!?
Ach, muß ja ewig diese Qual
 in meinem Herzen brennen!

Wie strahlt' es einst so treu und klar
 in ihren Blicken!
Das Wandern ließ ich ganz und gar

trotz Winters Tücken!
Und als der Schnee vergangen war,
Da tat mein Lieb ihr blondes Haar
        wohl mit der Myrthe schmücken!

Mein Wanderstab! Noch einmal heut'
        komm aus der Ecken!
    Schliefst du auch lang! Nun sei bereit!
        Ich will dich wecken!
    Ich trug es lang' – mein Liebesleid
    – Und ist die Erde doch so weit –
    So komm, mein treuer Stecken!

Wie lieblich lächelt Berg und Tal
        in Blütenwogen!
    Kam ja mit seinem süßen Schall
        der Lenz gezogen!
    Und Blumen blüh'n ja überall
    – Und Kreuzlein steh'n ja überall –
        – die haben nicht gelogen![30]

[*Forgotten Love* / How desolate my heart! How empty the world! How great
my longing! O, how the distances stretch out endlessly from valley to valley!
My sweet love! For the last time!? Ah, this torment must burn in my heart for
ever! How her eyes once shone so true and clear! I gave up my wanderings
completely, in spite of winter's wiles! And when the snow had gone, my love
decked her blonde hair with myrtle! My staff! Come out from your corner
again today! You have slept long! Prepare yourself! I shall waken you! How
long I endured love's anguish, and yet the earth is broad enough – so come,
my faithful staff! How lovely mountains and valleys smile in their flowery
billows! Spring came with its dulcet strains! And flowers are blossoming
everywhere – and everywhere there are little crosses – they have told no lies!]

The Summer Conductor: Bad Hall (1880)

BAD HALL IS a health resort in Upper Austria, about twenty miles to the south of Linz, between Kremsmünster and Steyr and, as such, in the northern half of the Traun. As with Hallein, the name is derived from the Celtic word for 'salt' and reflects the fact that this tiny town has one of the highest concentrations of iodine bromine in any salt-water springs in Central Europe. As early as 1873 a local physician, Hermann Schuber, proudly published a pamphlet on the town's merits. Schuber was a man of many parts: not only a doctor of medicine and a surgeon but also an expert on midwifery and ophthalmology. Indeed, so exceptional was his versatility that the town required no other physicians as it was suitably prepared for all life's vicissitudes. Schuber was rewarded for his services by being appointed the spa doctor, and as if this were not enough, he was also senior consultant to the Imperial and Royal Hospital for Military Pupils. In addition to all these details, the title page of his pamphlet includes an attractive picture of the tree-lined town square, although it is a distinctly modest affair when compared to the one at Iglau. The first mention of Hall as a spa dates back to the end of the fourteenth century, but it was not until around 1820 that its medicinal role was revived. Within thirty years the town was a flourishing community, and by the turn of the century – by which time Mahler had almost forgotten about his stay in the town – Bad Hall had really come into its own, a development reflected in its many attractive Jugendstil buildings.

Bad Hall was far from being Bad Ischl, but by the end of the 1870s it had a summer theatre – a concept hard for today's readers to grasp. True, there are still spa orchestras, and plays are performed in multi-functional venues, generally by visiting companies. But the concept of a small theatre with its own ensemble that was summoned into existence during the summer months, when the town was used both as a spa and as a holiday resort, is now no more than a distant memory. Tiny ensembles were formed, made up of singers and actors who were cheap to engage because they were either young and unknown or old and otherwise unemployable. A scratch band was assembled that could also play at spa concerts and that was fifteen- or twenty-strong. In this way, the theatre was able to mount comedies, musical farces, vaudevilles and even operettas that required minimal casts – operas were out of the question, of course. The repertory during Mahler's months in Bad Hall comprised shorter pieces in the tradition of the Viennese folk theatre (Gleich, Meisl and Bäuerle rather than the more demanding works by Nestroy or Raimund, which required stage machinery of often Baroque complexity). Above all, however, it featured the operettas of Jacques Offenbach, which were enormously popular in Vienna, too, and probably also pieces by Lecocq and Planquette. Viennese operetta was only just emerging as a recognizable genre at this time, the works of its founder, Franz von Suppé, having recently received their successful first performances. We should not underestimate the value of these theatres for visitors from towns that had no theatres of their own, for this was their one and only opportunity to be introduced to this kind of art form. This was also true of children, who had not yet been taken to the theatre in larger towns and cities but who had their first experience of the theatre during their summer holidays at performances that may have been regarded as harmless but which were often quite the opposite.

Mahler was nineteen when he took up his first professional appointment. By today's standards, he was still extremely young, less so by the standards of his own day. As we have seen, he had spent several stimulating and productive years in Vienna before travelling to Bad Hall for the months of mid-May to mid-August 1880. Photographs of the period attest to the change that had taken place in him. The twelve-year-old boy seen standing next to his cousin Gustav Frank in a photograph taken in Iglau that shows him in regulation dress – in other words, like a grown-up, with a trilby in his right hand – is still the bashful melancholic familiar to us from his first surviving photograph. The eighteen-year old has abandoned the dutiful parting slightly to the left of centre and now combs his thick dark hair backwards and for the first time is seen wearing rimless spectacles to correct a short-sightedness that was already evident in earlier photographs. From then on he was obliged to wear a whole series of different spectacles, concealing a profound sadness in his eyes that was never to disappear, so that in the few surviving photographs that show him without glasses, this quality emerges all the more clearly and to all the more disturbing effect. The next surviving photograph was taken in 1881 and shows Mahler at the age of twenty-one at his home in Iglau, a year after his engagement in Bad Hall and no doubt shortly before he took up his interim appointment in Laibach. Again he is seen without glasses. But what a change has taken place in him during these three years! His hair, which remained full and dark until his death, is longer and more luxuriant. He has what at the time was called an 'artist's head'. Above all, he has a beard, which he was to retain until he moved to Kassel, where his facial hair was progressively reduced to a Van Dyke beard and thence to a simple moustache, before disappearing for good, the only exception being the months that he spent in Maiernigg during the summer of 1905. Although still short-sighted, he now radiates a feeling of great self-confidence. His years of apprenticeship were now over, and his intellectual and musical development had reached its first high plateau. Photographed from an angle, he gazes past us, a young artist staring into a promising future – and the word artist does not need to be placed in quotation marks (Ill. 8).

Mahler owed his engagement in Bad Hall to his Viennese agent Gustav Lewy, with whom he had signed a five-year contract only days before he took up his post. Then, as now, agents were a tiresome but unavoidable aspect of cultural life, as they were uniquely well placed to know what positions were available for conductors, singers and actors at the countless theatres in the German-speaking world. Administrators in search of such artists did not advertise in the press but appealed to agents, who leafed through their files and made recommendations as well as organizing auditions. The artist's fees could be considerable and involved a certain percentage of the sum that the agent was able to negotiate, the size varying according to the circumstances. Mahler was evidently tired of eking out a living by giving piano lessons and presumably had no wish to continue to be a burden on his parents' finances at a time when his younger siblings were costing more and more money. It cannot have been a love of operetta that took him to Bad Hall, as he was wholly indifferent to the genre. Rather, it was his first opportunity to conduct an orchestra, however small. It appears that he had already given up the idea of earning his living as a pianist, so that only conducting remained, not least in the light of his enthusiasm for opera. (Composition already fascinated him, of course, but this was highly unlikely to provide him with a source of any real income.) And he was seething with impatience, a restlessness that also finds expression in his constant changes of address at this period. Although some of his addresses can no longer be identified, it seems that when he started studying in Vienna, he lived in the Margarethenstraße near the Naschmarkt, within walking distance of the Conservatory, but from there he moved to the Salesianergasse near the Schwarzenbergplatz, a quarter that evidently appealed to him as he later took rooms at the Auenbruggergasse, just round the corner from here, during his tenure as director of the Vienna Court Opera. In the autumn of 1879 he moved round the corner to the Rennweg, a major thoroughfare that leads out of the town from the Schwarzenbergplatz, past the Belvedere Gardens, but by the end of November he was once again outside the city, living in one of Vienna's suburbs. When he left, Hugo Wolf moved into the room. By February 1880 Mahler was living at 39 Windmühlgasse in the sixth district of Mariahilf, a street that leads off the Mariahilferstraße. Within only a matter of weeks, he had moved again, this time to 12 Wipplingerstraße in an entirely different part of the city, a street that runs past the Judenplatz. There were also practical reasons for this restlessness: moving was easy, as pianos could be hired without difficulty, and Mahler's belongings could be packed away in a few cases, consisting, as they did, in a small amount of cash, books, scores and not many clothes – a young enthusiast like Mahler needed nothing more, a modesty that he retained throughout his life. He was also sensitive to noise. True, he occasionally reduced his fellow tenants and neighbours to a frenzy of despair by practising loudly on the piano, but he was easily disturbed by others. And so we find him writing to his friend Anton Krisper from the Windmühlgasse: 'In the next room lives an old maid who stays at her spinet the whole day long. Of course, she does not know that on account of this I am going to have to take up my walking stick again, like Ahasuerus. Heaven knows whether I shall ever settle down anywhere. There is always some heedless fellow to drive me from one room to another.'[1] (It is worth adding that this is the first occurrence of the Ahasuerus motif in Mahler's letters, here without any reference to the fate of the Jews as a nation.)

Mahler's emotional life was subject to extremely powerful mood swings that go far beyond anything that might be thought of as normal in late pubescence. His acute sensitivity is clear from the few surviving letters that he wrote to four of his friends in the period around 1880: Josef Steiner, Emil Freund, Albert Spiegler and Anton Krisper. We have already quoted passages from the longest of these letters, which Mahler wrote to Steiner in June 1879 while giving private piano lessons to Moritz Baumgarten's children in Hungary. The family estates outside Nagytétény near Budapest provided him with little stimulus, forcing him back into his own inner world and a mood of world-weariness brightened only by the intensity of his experience of nature. The final section of his three-part letter to Steiner reveals the remarkable way in which his fervent love of nature was combined with a musical experience, our first evidence of the intimate bond between these two different worlds in Mahler's emotional life:

> It is six o'clock in the morning! I have been out on the heath, sitting with Fárkas the shepherd, listening to the sound of his shawm. Ah, how mournful it sounded, and yet how full of rapturous delight – that folk-tune he played! The flowers growing at his feet trembled in the dreamy glow of his dark eyes, and his brown hair fluttered around his sun-tanned cheeks. Ah, Steiner! You are still asleep in your bed, and I have already seen the dew on the grasses.[2]

Linguistically speaking, this scene recalls a number of central motifs in *Das klagende Lied*, the words of which were already essentially complete by this date: these include the flower, the heath and the solitary song on the shawm. Erotically speaking, however, Mahler's longings are not yet fixed but cling to nature, as if seeking to suck it dry: 'Oh, that I might behold this earth in its nakedness, lying there without adornment or embellishment before its Creator,' he writes towards the beginning of the same letter.[3] But his longings are just as much directed at the friends of his youth. When Emil Freund wrote to him in Puszta Batta during that frustrating summer of 1879, Mahler replied: 'Your letter found me in a state of the most terrible longing – I simply can't stand it any longer.'[4] He fervently hoped to see his friend back at home before long. When he met Josephine Poisl in the autumn of 1879, his longing acquired a more concrete sense of direction, and so we now find him writing to Anton Krisper:

> I have just arrived in Vienna and am visiting the places where together we so often shared our joys and sorrows. I am the *unhappiest of fortune's favourites* ever to have writhed among roses. A new name is now inscribed in my heart alongside yours – true, only whisperingly and blushingly, but no less powerfully for that.[5]

Two months later he wrote to Krisper again:

> Dear friend, I have been quite dreadfully entangled in the delightful fetters of the darling of the gods. [. . .] For the most part I have really spent the time wallowing in sweet sufferings in the most varied ways, arising in the mornings with 'Ah' and going to sleep with 'Oh'; dreaming, I have lived, and waking, I have dreamt. [. . .] In a week I shall be in Iglau and shall awake from my rosy dreams into a still rosier daylight.[6]

He is referring, in other words, to when he will see Josephine Poisl again in Iglau. Needless to add, these ecstatic confessions and stifled longings are to a large extent a reflection of Mahler's reading, Goethe's *Werther* first and foremost:

> It is so strange how, when I came here first and looked out upon that lovely valley from the hills, I felt charmed with everything around me – the little wood opposite – how delightful to sit in its shade! How fine the view from that summit! – that delightful chain of hills, and the exquisite valleys at their feet! – could I but lose myself amongst them!

And again:

> Ah, how often then did the flight of the crane, soaring above my head, inspire me with the desire to be transported to the shores of the immeasurable ocean, there to drink the pleasures of life from the foaming goblet of the Infinite,

and to realize, if but for a moment with the confined powers of my soul, the bliss of that Creator who accomplishes all things in Himself, and through Himself![7]

Other literary borrowings may be traced to Mahler's reading of Lenau and Jean Paul. World-weariness, the anguish of love and the cult of nature combine to create an erotic blend of emotions. Like Büchner's Lenz, Mahler liked to walk in the mountains. In later life these hearty hikes were confined to his summer holidays and remained his principal physical exercise apart from swimming in mountain lakes, an activity he pursued with great tenacity and skill, at least until such time as his doctor's diagnosis destroyed his pleasure in this pursuit as well. Time and again the young Mahler undertook extended hikes. During the summer of 1880, for example, he planned to accompany Anton Krisper and the Krzyzanowski brothers on a walking holiday that would have taken them to the Bohemian Forest and the Fichtel Mountains, culminating in visits to 'Baireuth' and the Oberammergau Passion Play – a thought-provoking combination. In the event, these plans had to be abandoned when Mahler was offered his summer appointment in Bad Hall, and although he later attended the Bayreuth Festival, he never visited Oberammergau.[8]

In the mid-1890s, Mahler was asked by the music journalist Max Marschalk – one of the first to respond favourably to his work as a composer – to provide him with some biographical information about himself: 'The first work in which I really came into my own as "Mahler", he replied, 'was a fairytale for choir, soloists and orchestra: "Das klagende Lied". I am describing this work as my op. 1.'[9] Even though Mahler gave none of his works opus numbers, it is clear that what he meant by this is that in his own eyes *Das klagende Lied* was the first of his works that he felt to be worthy of the name. No more than a draft libretto of his *Rübezahl* has come down to us (we cannot say how much more of it was written, although we do know that Mahler continued to work on it even after completing *Das klagende Lied*), while his surviving chamber works from his days at school and at the Conservatory include only a single movement from a Piano Quartet in A minor ('Nicht zu schnell. Entschlossen'). We know only the title of a planned opera on the Argonauts and a possible overture to it. And his first three songs for Josephine Poisl, finally, are little more than student exercises, for all that they already anticipate the tone of the *Lieder eines fahrenden Gesellen*. But *Das klagende Lied* is entirely different from these. In the complete form in which it is once again performed today (in other words, including the 'Waldmärchen' movement that Mahler himself cut in 1893), it lasts a good hour in performance and is scored for an impressive array of resources, including chorus, off-stage band and five vocal soloists.

For a first work, *Das klagende Lied* is undoubtedly a tremendous achievement, conceived along the grandest lines and representing an enormous effort on the part of a twenty-year-old composer, its resultant grandeur utterly breathtaking. If Mahler had written nothing after *Das klagende Lied* and become just a world-famous conductor, we should have to lament the loss of a great talent. He completed the text as early as 1878, setting 'Waldmärchen' the following year and during the early months of 1880, putting the finishing touches to 'Der Spielmann' in March 1880 and completing the third and final section, 'Hochzeitsstück', in the October and November of that year. In his letter to Max Marschalk he referred to the whole piece as a 'fairytale', and there is no doubt that it is permeated by the 'old scent from the age of fairytales', to quote from Albert Giraud's words to Schoenberg's *Pierrot Lunaire*.

The reader will recall that as an old man, Theodor Fischer remembered his nursemaid Nanni telling him and Mahler the tale of the 'mournful song' when they were children. We do not know which version of the tale she used, still less what her philological approach to the material may have been or even whether she knew it from a published collection of fairy stories or if she herself had heard it as a child and now passed it on in the tradition of oral poetry – this latter alternative seems more likely as it is not even certain that Nanni could read. The best-known written version was recorded by Wilhelm Grimm in January 1812, and his source was Dortchen Wild. A native of Kassel, she was one of the wise women who provided the Brothers Grimm with their repository of fairytales. In this particular case, the tale was recounted by the stove in the summerhouse at Nentershausen one cold winter's day. In their notes to the 1856 edition of their famous fairytales, the brothers draw attention to earlier versions of the narrative that told of two or even three princes who are made to compete with each other to decide which of them will succeed his old and ailing father: the one who captures a bear or a wild boar with a little gold lock shall become king. It is, of course, the most foolish of the sons who wins. No one, moreover, is murdered in this version. But in another version, the elder brother murders his more fortunate younger sibling in order to achieve success. Yet another version tells of a brother and a sister, and the wild boar is a flower that the sister finds, whereupon she is killed by her brother. A young shepherd finds a bone from her buried body and carves a flute from it. But it starts to sing and reveals the crime. In a Scottish folksong transmitted by Walter Scott, a harper makes a harp from the sternum of a murdered woman, and the harp starts to play of its own accord. In this version the murderess and her victim are sisters. According to another song, the harp's strings are made from the victim's hair. The Grimms' version turns the rival princes or princesses of other versions into two brothers from a poor family to whom the king promises his daughter if they can capture or kill a wild boar that is laying waste to his kingdom. The younger brother encounters a black mannikin who gives him a spear that allows him to kill the beast. His elder brother envies him his success and murders him on a bridge over a stream. He buries the body beneath the bridge, takes the wild boar as his trophy and marries the king's daughter. Years later a shepherd finds a bone beneath the bridge and carves from it a mouthpiece for his horn. The bone then starts to sing by itself, so that the tale is called 'The Singing Bone':

> Ach, du liebes Hirtelein,
> du bläst auf meinem Knöchelein,
> mein Bruder hat mich erschlagen,
> unter der Brücke begraben,
> um das wilde Schwein,
> für des Königs Töchterlein.[10]

[Ah, you dear little shepherd, you are playing on my little bone. My brother slew me and buried me beneath the bridge for the sake of the wild boar, in order to win the king's little daughter.]

The shepherd hurries off to see the king and produces the singing bone, and the king understands what has happened. He has the rest of the body dug up beneath the bridge, has the wicked brother drowned and arranges for the remains of the good brother to be buried in the cemetery 'in a beautiful grave'. This, then, may be the version of the tale that Nanni told the young Theodor Fischer and his friends in Iglau, although she may alternatively have transmitted a more elaborate account familiar from Ludwig Bechstein's *New Book of German Fairy Stories* from the middle of the nineteenth century. Here it is a queen who decides whether a brother or his sister shall succeed to the throne by sending them out in search of a rare flower. The sister finds the flower. The brother kills her. One of her bones becomes a flute that reveals the crime to the queen. The murderer collapses on his throne beneath the weight of the revelation. Bechstein's version has the merit of already bearing the same title as Mahler's cantata, *Das klagende Lied*. But this title is also shared by a six-part ballad by Martin Greif, a successful playwright and poet who divided his time between Munich and Vienna and who was at the height of his fame in the 1870s, writing poems that reflect the influence of Lenau and Mörike combined with older balladesque traditions. Greif dresses up the succinct fairytale versions of Grimm and Bechstein with all manner of theatrical effects, considerably expanding them and larding them with numerous passages of undeniably effective direct speech and a use of contrast by no means lacking in dramaturgical skill. Although it cannot be proved, it is relatively certain that

Mahler attended a 'performance' of Greif's ballad, probably a semi-staged rehearsed reading in which he may even have been actively involved at the Vienna Conservatory in May 1876. When combined with his memory of the children's fairytale that he had heard in Iglau, this performance will have laid the foundations for his own attempt to dramatize the subject. A fourth influence is also likely in the form of Robert Schumann's choral ballads. Nowadays virtually forgotten, they were still a part of the repertory in the 1870s and 1880s, especially with choral societies with any claims to distinction. Schumann's Geibel-inspired ballad *Vom Pagen und der Königstochter* (Of the Page and the Princess), op. 140, includes two comparable basic motifs: the murder out of envy and the revelatory power of music.[11]

Ever since he had been able to read, Mahler had felt at home in the world of the fairytale and of German Romanticism, even though it was only at a later date that he began to explore the world of *Des Knaben Wunderhorn*. Drawing on a poetic vein that he had started to tap as a youth and that he quickly mastered to an astonishing degree, he drew up his own independent version of the story based on all these sources, the first draft of which he enclosed with a letter to Anton Krisper probably written in February or March 1878. (The accompanying letter has not survived, making it impossible to date the draft any more accurately.) With only a few retouchings, this 'Ballad of the Flaxen- and Auburn-Haired Horsemen' provided Mahler with the basis for the first section of *Das klagende Lied*, 'Waldmärchen'. Mahler subsequently cut this movement. The words were first reproduced by Hans Holländer but with a number of transcriptional errors.

This ballad formed the first part of what was originally the three-part version of *Das klagende Lied*. In the second part, headed 'Der Spielmann', the eponymous minstrel finds one of the bones of the buried skeleton and carves a flute from it. On this occasion, the bone does not start to sing of its own accord but needs to be woken into life by being played, at which point it goes its own way and reveals the heinous deed. The third part of the work is headed 'Hochzeitsstück' (Wedding Piece) and begins with a description of the queen's wedding with the auburn-haired knight. The Minstrel appears and is welcomed as a musician, but his flute then starts to sing its denunciatory song. Mahler reveals a certain dramatic skill in building to a climax. The murderer himself 'takes up the flute in impious scorn' and plays on it. (Mahler was clearly inspired by Heinrich Heine's *Belsatzar* here: 'And the monarch straight seized on a sacred cup / With impious hand, and fill'd it up.') But the flute adds a new strophe to its existing accusation: 'Ah brother, dear brother mine! This must I now deplore! / It was you who struck me dead! / You're playing on my dead bone! / This must I lament for ever!' The wedding ends as the walls collapse and the guests scatter.

Emotional Ups and Downs
in Laibach
(1881–2)

A GLANCE AT a map of the area covered by Mahler in the course of his pere-
grinations between school, conservatory and vacation shows how surprisingly close all these places were. Mahler's birthplace of Kalischt lies eight miles
to the south of Ledetsch and twenty miles to the north-west of Iglau. The village
from which his father came, Lipnitz, lay four miles to the east of Kalischt, while
his mother came from Ledetsch. Prague, where the young Mahler was particularly unhappy, lies some eighty miles to the north-west, Vienna a little further
to the south-east. Iglau lies almost halfway between the two largest cities in
the monarchy and was then on one of the major railway lines, making it a suitable place at which to start and end journeys. The farmsteads at Ronow and
Morawan where the fifteen-year-old Mahler spent one of his first relatively
extended vacations with his friend and classmate Josef Steiner lie seven and ten
miles to the south-east of Caslau (Cáslav), some forty miles to the north-west
of Iglau. Puszta Batta near Budapest, where Mahler gave private piano lessons
to Moritz Baumgarten's children during the summers of 1879 and 1882, was the
furthest he had ever been from home. For him, a summer without returning
home to see his parents and siblings was inconceivable. He was deeply attached
to the melancholic, elegiac countryside around Iglau, and when he was in
Hungary he tried to rediscover that mood, albeit in a 'flatter' form. Seelau
(Zeliv), where he visited Emil Freund on a number of occasions, also lay within
this area, some seven miles to the south-west of Kalischt. Seelau was not on
the rail network but could be reached in three hours by wagon. Wlaschim
(Vlašim), where he spent the summer of 1881 with his cousin Gustav Frank,
was no more than forty miles to the north-west of Iglau, and from Wlaschim,
Mahler could travel to Seelau before returning to Iglau, the attractiveness of
which was briefly increased during the summer of 1879, when he fell in love
with Josephine Poisl. Mahler also spent the summer of 1882 in Iglau and Seelau,
by which date he was already twenty-two. These close regional ties began to

loosen only in 1883, when Mahler went to Kassel. Thereafter his visits to Iglau and the surrounding area grew briefer and more infrequent. By 1889, when Mahler's parents both died within a short period of each other and he arranged for his brothers and sisters to live in Vienna, such visits had virtually ceased altogether, and from then on he had surprisingly little contact with a region that he had loved so much. He now felt drawn to the Alps, which he visited first with his brothers and sisters, then with his sisters and finally with his wife and children. Here he settled beside mountain lakes in order to be able to write music in the seclusion of his 'composing houses'. The mountains for walking, the lakes for swimming in and an isolated hut in which to work – this remained his ideal until the end of his life. His reasons for breaking free from his close links with his native Iglau are undoubtedly to be found in part in the loosening of his family's ties with the region but also in his recognition that his family background had become oppressively restrictive and that – as he once admitted to Natalie – he now felt that he had outgrown it.

Mahler left Bad Hall on 19 August 1880 and returned to Vienna. His agent, Gustav Lewy, had nothing lined up for the coming season. It is clear from his few surviving letters from this period that Mahler – already suffering from melancholia, not to say depression – was plunged into the depths of despair. (The twelve months between the autumn of 1880 and the autumn of 1881 are again exceptionally poorly documented.) Virtually all these letters are addressed to Mahler's small circle of adolescent friends, although his contacts with Lipiner, with whom he had previously been so close, were noticeably distant at this period. Perhaps the most eloquent of these letters is the one that he wrote to Emil Freund in Seelau in response to a particularly upsetting piece of news from Freund: on his first visit to Freund's house in Seelau during the summer of 1878, he had met a young woman who was related to his host and who fell in love with Mahler – we do not even know her name. According to Freund's later account of the matter, Mahler did not return her feelings but appears, rather, to have been annoyed by the strength of her emotions. Instead, he advised her to beware of unduly passionate feelings, a warning that must have made Mahler seem both precocious and cold. But subsequent develop-ments seem to have proved him right, for in October 1880 Freund wrote to tell him that the young woman had killed herself out of unrequited love. Although Mahler himself appears not to have been responsible, the news arrived at a time when he was already feeling profoundly upset as Rott had just been committed to an asylum and the first signs of Anton Krisper's syphilitically induced mental illness had made themselves felt to devastating effect.

In spite of the fact that he had just completed *Das klagende Lied*, all three events, together with his evidently unrequited love for Josephine Poisl and his inability to decide between the careers of piano virtuoso, conductor and composer, plunged Mahler into a state of deep depression. His reply to Emil Freund is dated 1 November 1880 and reveals his state of mind in no uncertain terms:

I have been dealt so many emotional blows in recent weeks that I find it almost impossible to speak to anyone who knew me in happier times. I can counter your news with some that is unfortunately just as upsetting: my friend Hans Rott has gone mad! – And I'm bound to fear a similar fate for Krisper. – Your lines reached me at the same time as this last piece of news – at a time when I myself was in need of comfort [no doubt Mahler is referring to his feelings for Josephine Poisl]. Misery is everywhere. It wears the strangest guises to mock us poor human beings. If you know a single happy person on this earth, tell me his name quickly, before I lose the little courage to face life that I still have. – Anyone who has watched a truly noble and profound individual struggle with the most vapid vulgarity [here Mahler is clearly referring to Rott] can scarcely suppress a shudder when he thinks of his own poor skin; today is All Saints' Day – if you'd been here at this time last year, you would know in what mood I welcome this day. Tomorrow will be the first All Souls' Day of my life! Now I too have a grave on which to lay a wreath. For the last month I have been a total vegetarian. The moral impact of this way of life, with its voluntary castigation of the body and resultant lack of material needs, is immense. That I am completely taken by this idea you can infer from the fact that I expect of it no less than the regeneration of the human race.[1]

There is a clear link here between Mahler's mood of world-weariness and his interest in Wagner's notion of regeneration. (Wagner's essay on 'Religion and Art', in which these ideas, including vegetarianism, play a central role, had just appeared in the October issue of the *Bayreuther Blätter*.) Mahler had felt something similar in the spring of 1880, when he wrote to Anton Krisper to complain that the world had affected him for the first time on a 'material' level, a remark that relates in part to his feelings of unrequited love but that was valid in other ways too.

Nor should we forget what the awakening of Eros matutinus meant for a young man of Mahler's generation. A good twenty years his junior, Stefan Zweig left a vivid and – in the circumstances – extremely outspoken account of this in his reminiscences. In Hugo Wolf, Hans Rott and Anton Krisper, Mahler now had no fewer than three deterrent examples of the dangers of venereal disease among his own immediate circle of friends. Fear of such diseases was so great that uninhibited contact with the opposite sex was impossible outside marriage. Sex with a prostitute was accompanied by the constant fear of infection. As Zweig points out, there was a notice on the door of every sixth or seventh house in Vienna that read 'Specialist for Skin and Venereal Diseases'. Those infected had to undergo painful courses of treatment with little prospect of recovery. For weeks on end their entire body was rubbed with mercury, with the inevitable side effect that their hair and teeth fell out, and yet not even this could guarantee a complete cure: the insidious disease could break out again at any time and lead to a 'softening of the brain', as was the case with Rott and Krisper and probably also with Wolf. It was by no means unusual for young men diagnosed with syphilis to take their own lives. Zweig reports that he could not recall a single comrade of his youth who at one time or another did not come to him 'with pale and troubled mien, one because he was ill or feared illness, another because he was being blackmailed because of an abortion, a third because he lacked the money to be cured without the knowledge of his family, the fourth because he did not know how to pay hush money to a waitress who claimed to have had a child by him, the fifth because his wallet had been stolen in a brothel and he did not dare go to the police'.[2] Arthur Schnitzler says much the same in his early autobiography, while the 'problem' is even more clearly spelt out in his diaries. (He, too, had a friend – Richard Tausenau – whose health was being undermined by syphilis.)

It is easy to imagine what all this must have meant for a young man like Mahler, even if he did not share Schnitzler's erotomania. Unlike Schnitzler, who repeatedly indulged his priapic desires in countless fleeting affairs with wait-resses, seamstresses, ladies of more or less ill repute and married women and who was evidently extremely fortunate in never becoming infected, Mahler equally evidently pursued a very different course. Even if Alma was later to give the impression that it was she who roused him to manhood – or perhaps this was the impression that Mahler himself wanted her to give – this was not in fact the case. Conversely, there is no doubt that as a young man he was exception-ally reserved in the matter of sex. The reasons for this must be sought not only in his fear of infection but also in his feelings of world-weariness, in a scepti-cism unusual in one so young and in a seriousness of purpose that extended beyond mere morality and embraced his whole philosophy in life. Wagner's *Parsifal* preached not only respect for animals but also sexual abstinence, sex being regarded as sinful. And like Parsifal, Mahler will have felt obliged to keep his distance from many a seductive Flowermaiden, to say nothing of women like Kundry, a corrupter of morals whom Parsifal rejected just as surely as Mahler would have done – only in the case of Anna von Mildenburg did Mahler fail to emulate Parsifal.

Mahler arrived in Laibach (Ljubljana) in September 1881 for the second engagement that he owed to his agent, Gustav Lewy. Now the main city of the

Republic of Slovenia, Laibach was then the centre of the Duchy of Krain (Kranjska), one of the crown territories of the Imperial and Royal Monarchy some sixty miles to the south of Klagenfurt. It was much larger than the spa resort of Bad Hall, and its theatre – the Landschaftliches Theater or 'Provincial Theatre' – was correspondingly larger in turn, the multi-functional preserve of the German-speaking population that dominated a town in which Slovene nationalism was none the less on the increase. By the date of Mahler's arrival, the town had some twenty-six thousand inhabitants, 60 per cent of whom were Slovene, the remainder German. Some fifteen years later the coalition government of Alfred August von Windischgrätz and Ignaz von Plener was to founder on the Slovene question. We do not know to what extent Mahler learnt about these problems during the six months that he spent in Laibach between taking up his appointment on 3 September 1881 and leaving the town at the beginning of April 1882. His post was as principal conductor, certainly a significant advance on his position in Bad Hall. His lodgings, too, had the advantage of a certain homeliness as he boarded with Anton Krisper's parents. It is unclear whether Krisper himself spent the winter in Laibach, although this seems unlikely.

Mahler's first appearance in the pit was on 24 September, when the regional assembly was opened and a play by Eduard von Bauernfeld was performed, prefaced by Beethoven's *Egmont* Overture under Mahler's direction. According to the laconic report in the local paper, it was a 'precise' performance. A week later he conducted his very first opera, Verdi's *Il trovatore*, which in keeping with standard practice in the German-speaking world at this time was performed in German as *Der Troubadour*. This was also the first performance under the theatre's new director, Alexander Mondheim-Schreiner. The local paper reported that it passed off 'without any untoward disruption' – one wonders what other performances were like if this point had to be specially made. 'The orchestra under Herr Mahler's direction held its ground.' This remark, too, will have failed to satisfy the young conductor, whose burning ambition and growing awareness of his own merits and abilities were in stark contrast to the modest potential of these tiny theatres where he had to muddle through as best he could. His lifelong loathing of routine performances cobbled together with the help of inadequate artists, which he resisted with an iron will and a fanatical belief in art at the great theatres where he worked from 1883 onwards, was fuelled by his experiences in Bad Hall, Laibach and Olmütz, all three of them appointments that he took over at the eleventh hour when the previous incumbent had found it impossible to stick at his post. The young student from the Vienna Conservatory who had never learnt how to conduct was thrown in at the deep end with inadequate orchestral musicians, largely untalented singers and amateur choristers, all of them lacking in enthusiasm. They were generally much older than their conductor and unwilling to be told what to do by a greenhorn.

Needless to add, there was no 'general music director' in Laibach. As principal conductor, Mahler was responsible for all the opera performances. Usually, a colleague shouldered the burden of the operettas that were in the repertory, although even here Mahler occasionally had to help out. There is no doubt that Mahler learnt the repertory here, but it is noteworthy that he had to conduct works that he spent the rest of his life avoiding: Rossini's *Il barbiere di Siviglia*, Gounod's *Faust* (always performed in German as *Margarethe*), Flotow's *Alessandro Stradella* and the operas of Donizetti. Among the operettas that he conducted were works by Lecocq, Suppé and Johann Strauß. Mahler was relieved that Wagner's works could not be performed in so small a theatre, nor could French grand opera, in other words, Halévy, late Rossini and Meyerbeer, whose staging and casting demands ruled them out of court – and again Mahler was happy at this. Mahler also made two further public appearances as a pianist. Otherwise, we know little about the months he spent in Laibach as no letters have survived from this period. At the same time, however, the words 'we know very little about this period' will soon no longer be necessary: with the beginning of 1883 the number of surviving documents grows from a mere trickle and no longer incorporates the gaps that have been so evident until now. Such were Mahler's artistic ideals and the enormous demands that he placed on himself that this repertory could never satisfy him. He retained a lifelong aversion to everything in the world of opera that was lacking in substance. Operetta naturally fell victim to this verdict. (Whether the verdict is justified is another question.) The operas of Flotow, Rossini and Gounod were little more than dross in his eyes, and in this respect he was very much Wagner's man, although even Wagner held Rossini in higher regard than Mahler did. Against Verdi he harboured all the reservations that were common at this time, and at no point in his life was he able to accept that the Italian was an important composer who could stand comparison with Mozart and Wagner. A year later in Olmütz he was happy to be allowed to conduct only Verdi and Meyerbeer, rather than Wagner and Mozart, as he felt that he would not have to besmirch and sully the great composers through inadequate performances with singers, players and chorus who were simply not up to the mark. His attitude to Meyerbeer was clearly the one adopted by Wagner in his essay 'Jews in Music', first published in 1850 and reissued in pamphlet form in 1869. For a Jewish conductor, this is a depressing observation, and it was not until much later that we find Mahler moderating his judgement.[3] His attitude to Verdi, too, changed in later life, when we find him admitting to Natalie that in his final operas Verdi achieved a much greater degree of concentration. Of the works that he conducted in Laibach, only Mozart and Weber can really have been to his liking, although it was presumably a matter of much regret to him that he had to perform their works with the resources of a provincial theatre, so that he drew the logical conclusion in Olmütz and declined to conduct them at all. With Weber's music he was then to develop a much closer and more remarkable relationship in Leipzig.

Again, we know next to nothing about another frustrating experience that can have done little to lighten his mood at this time: on 16 December 1881, Vienna's annual Beethoven Prize was awarded by a jury that included Brahms, Karl Goldmark and the Wagner disciple and principal conductor at the Vienna Court Opera, Hans Richter. Mahler had submitted *Das klagende Lied*, but it left no impression on the members of the jury. The winner was Mahler's harmony teacher, Robert Fuchs, with a Piano Concerto in B flat minor. In his letter to Emil Freund, Mahler announced that his main concern was to arrange for this tremendously ambitious and monumental work to be performed. He can have been in no doubt about the difficulty of achieving this aim, given the vast resources involved, including offstage orchestra, soloists and several choirs. Victory in this prestigious competition would undoubtedly have helped him as the prize-winning work was assured of a performance, quite apart from the prize money of five hundred florins. (In Bad Hall, Mahler had earned thirty florins a month.) In all, seventeen works were submitted by twelve different composers. It is no longer possible to say why the prize was awarded to Fuchs, who was then thirty-four and needed neither the money nor the prestige. From today's perspective, his compositions are notable for their impressive command of the tools of the composer's trade but there is little about them that is personal or original, still less do they display any obvious trace of genius. A whole world separates his works from *Das klagende Lied*, but a jury that set store by Fuchs was bound to view Mahler's work as a ragbag of eccentricities. Of the eminent members of the jury, only Goldmark seems to have suspected that Mahler's submission was the work of a talented composer. (Not until much later was Mahler to draw closer to Brahms.) Although Goldmark yielded nothing to Fuchs in his championship of traditionalism, he seems to have sensed Mahler's originality. Or at least posterity may hope that he had Mahler in mind when he asked for a rider to be added to the report: 'Herr Goldmark considers it desirable that, in assessing the works that have been submitted, the awarding committee should agree on certain principles with regard to the priority to be given either to the dexterity and skill shown in the construction of the works, or to talent, even if it shows less technical proficiency.' This pronouncement was answered unanimously by the jury's award of the first prize to Robert Fuchs, not even Goldmark having the courage to express his misgivings in a minority report. That he raised the point at all none the less redounds to his credit.

The subsequent fate of *Das klagende Lied* – the first work of which Mahler could legitimately be proud, for all that it was to remain a problem piece – is briefly told. All his attempts to have it performed came to nothing. Following his failed attempt to win the Beethoven Prize, he quickly realized that his chances of gaining a hearing were slim. In the summer of 1883 he sent the score to Liszt in Weimar, asking whether he would consider performing it at a meeting of the Allgemeiner Deutscher Musikverein. The score was returned to him with a note to the effect that Liszt did not like the 'poem'. Mahler could understand why the work should have found little favour with Vienna's 'Brahmins', but he must have been profoundly depressed to discover that the head of the New German School, whose son-in-law, Wagner, had just died, had no time for the work's audacities. For a while he returned the score to his bottom drawer, but in 1891, during his time as conductor in Hamburg, he made a third attempt to promote the piece and offered it to the publishing house of Schott in Mainz, but in vain. As a result of these multiple setbacks, Mahler set about revising the work. It was not that he doubted in himself or in the score, for he remained convinced that what he had written thirteen years earlier still had merit. And so we find him writing in 1893 to his sister Justine to express his astonishment at taking out the work again: 'The nuts which I have given to crack here are perhaps the toughest that my soil has yet brought forth.'[4] In spite of this, Mahler undertook an initial series of revisions to the score in an attempt to make it more accessible, principally reducing its length and cutting the whole of the opening movement, 'Waldmärchen'. He also simplified the instrumentation, removing some of the vocal soloists and simply omitting the offstage orchestra, in spite of its dramatic importance and undoubted effectiveness. This was a painful amputation, and it certainly reduces the work's impact. Mahler clearly saw that he had gone too far here, for in 1898 he revised the work again and restored the offstage orchestra in the final movement. That same year he told Natalie that he had unfortunately not had time to prepare the score for the printer, but in spite of this he had realized that the offstage orchestra must be reintroduced at this point, 'whether they play it for me or not'.[5] In general, Mahler toned down the more audacious passages when revising the work at this time, notably at the point at which the Minstrel carves his flute from the bone and the offstage orchestra and onstage bells allow past, present and future to merge together in the manner of a phantasmagoria – one of the boldest passages that Mahler ever composed.

The first performance finally took place at a special concert by the Vienna Singakademie and the Court Opera Orchestra in the city's Musikvereinssaal on 17 February 1901. It was conducted by the composer himself, who was otherwise extremely hesitant to mount performances of his own works in Vienna, and the soloists included the best that the Court Opera could offer:

the sopranos Elise Elizza and Anna von Mildenburg, the contralto Edyth Walker and the tenor Fritz Schrödter. The audience was impressed, not least by the lavish forces for which the work is scored. (As if anticipating the later publicity surrounding the 'Symphony of a Thousand', reviewers drew attention to the fact that there were some five hundred performers onstage.) The press, conversely, was dismissive, Max Kalbeck – an intimate of Brahms – summing up the views of his 'superiors', as Mahler used to call his critics, as follows: '*Das klagende Lied* seems to us more a skilfully laid out assortment of more or less crude or subtle acoustic effects than an artistically moulded and inspired musical organism.'[6] Natalie reports that even the choir included anti-Semitic elements and that Mahler had to contend with a certain amount of opposition, as he did throughout his whole time in Vienna. Mahler himself never heard the original three-movement version and conducted the two-movement alternative only twice.[7]

For the Last Time in the Provinces: Olmütz (1882–3)

THE THIRD AND final stage on Mahler's painful journey through the world of late nineteenth-century provincial music-making began in Olmütz in January 1883. It had been clear from the outset that he was able and willing to remain in Laibach for only a single season, for he had accepted the appointment knowing that it was a temporary one. In spite of this, he chalked up a number of successes in the town, both as a conductor and as the soloist at a concert by the local Philharmonic Society. In March 1882 he was able to conduct a benefit performance at the opera, a common practice at a time when conductors' salaries desperately needing boosting. But by early April his Laibach intermezzo was over. Before returning to Vienna, he made a brief detour to Trieste in order to see a city that he did not yet know. He spent the summer in what was already his traditional way, first with his family in Iglau, then with Emil Freund in Seelau and, for the last time, as piano tutor to the Baumgarten family at Nagytétény near Budapest. On 19 September he made his one and only appearance as a conductor in Iglau, conducting Suppé's overture to *Boccaccio* in a performance at the town's theatre described by the local press as 'rousing', as if he had been conducting a work by one of the great composers of the German repertory. On his return to Vienna, he resumed his inconstant lifestyle, working on *Rübezahl* and changing his address with a frequency that took his former restlessness to new heights, so that even his otherwise tolerant and commonsensical mother was moved to remonstrate shortly before Christmas, which he spent with his parents in Iglau:

Why these endless changes of apartment? I don't believe that there can be a single person apart from you who changes his apartment every 2 weeks. Will you end up changing your apartment every time you change your under-clothes? And in the end won't you find yourself without any underclothes or clothes? For as I know you, you will forget something in each place – and will continue to move until you have nothing left.[1]

Mahler's brief tenure in Olmütz also marked the last time he stepped in at the last minute to replace a colleague, the principal conductor, Emil Kaiser, having thrown in the towel in mid-season, whereupon Mahler's agent, Gustav Lewy, had once again played his joker. (The Olmütz Theatre, a building designed by the eminent architect Josef Kornhäusel, was run by Emanuel Raul, to whom it was a matter of indifference who replaced Kaiser.) Mahler arrived in Olmütz on 10 January 1883, and two days later his appointment was reported in the local press. In moving to the town, Mahler was in fact returning to his roots, Olmütz lying some forty miles north-east of Brünn and about twice as far to the east of Iglau. He lost no time in moving into the first available lodgings and dropping a quick postcard to his new friend in Vienna, Friedrich Löhr ('I'm in the worst possible mood'). By the 16th he had already conducted his first opera in the town, Meyerbeer's *Les Huguenots*, the epitome of French grand opera, which at least indicates that Olmütz was a step up from Laibach, where Meyerbeer's works were not performed at all. We would know even less about Mahler's time in Olmütz than we do about his period in Laibach if it had not been for the fact that the company included in its ranks a young and ambitious Hungarian baritone, Jacques (or Jakob) Manheit, with whom Mahler later worked in Budapest as well. Ludwig Karpath, who for a time was a follower of Mahler, interviewed Manheit on the subject of the time that Mahler spent in Olmütz, producing in the process one of the liveliest accounts of the young conductor's life. Manheit recalled Mahler's arrival in Olmütz and the company's first encounter with its new conductor:

The following day, at nine o'clock in the morning, the new conductor, whose name was Gustav Mahler, held a rehearsal for the chorus. When we went to a full ensemble rehearsal an hour later, the chorus singers came to us in absolute despair, claiming that they were completely hoarse and refusing to work with the new conductor any more. Full of curiosity, we soloists entered the rehearsal room, where Mahler was already sitting at the piano and warming his hands with his coat-tails. His head was covered in long, unkempt hair, he had the beginnings of a black beard, and he wore a large horn-rimmed pince-nez on his very prominent nose. He started the rehearsal without bothering to introduce himself to anyone. All his colleagues, men and women alike, regarded the new conductor with unconcealed hostility, which they expressed loudly and without reserve. Mahler, however, did not react to any of the interruptions, but demanded strict compliance with his orders. No one dared to contradict the young man. Two days later we saw him on the podium for the first time. We were performing *Les Huguenots*. After the first act the bass who was singing Marcel stormed breathlessly into the dressing room shouting, 'I can't sing with this man. He holds his baton now in his right hand, now in his left, and keeps on passing his free hand over his face, so that I can't see any of his cues.' When Mahler heard this serious complaint he replied quite equably, 'Yes, my dear friend, conducting makes me very hot and I perspire too much, so my pince-nez keeps slipping off and I have to catch it with my free hand. But I'll put it right straight away.' So he went to the wardrobe master for a broad piece of ribbon, fastened his pince-nez to it, and hooked it round his ears. But now he looked so comic that when the singers looked down on him from the stage, they were convulsed with laughter. Somehow we got to the end of the performance.[2]

Manheit not only describes this curious beginning to Mahler's stint in Olmütz, he also explains how he succeeded in making contact with the aloof and stand-offish Mahler outside the theatre, too, offering a graphic account of Mahler's ability to excite the contempt of his colleagues at the local inn. He would order water instead of beer or wine and boiled spinach and apples instead of the usual helpings of meat, a practising vegetarian in the spirit of Wagner, although, as Manheit later noted, by the time that he was living in Budapest Mahler had already abandoned his vegetarian principles. No less impressive is Manheit's account of a meeting with Mahler on 13 February 1883. Shortly before this, Mahler had told him that his father was in poor health. On the 13th, Manheit found the conductor sobbing loudly in the street, his hand-kerchief held to his eyes. Manheit was about to offer him his condolences on the death of his father, but Mahler interrupted him: his father was still alive, but something far worse had happened – Wagner had died. For the next few days no one could speak to him. Manheit's memoirs provide us with a complete picture of the young Mahler: uncompromisingly devoted to his art but with little interest in the more superficial aspects of his profession, heedless of his effect on others, exuding a powerful authority and even charisma in spite of his youth and lack of height and, as a Wagnerian of the most enthusiastic kind, holding radical views and leading a commensurate lifestyle. Manheit leaves us in no doubt that all who had eyes and ears could tell that they were dealing with an altogether exceptional individual in Olmütz. At the end of his brief stay in the town, Mahler was again offered the opportu-nity to conduct a benefit performance, the proceeds of which would be his to pocket. In spite of advice to the contrary, he insisted on conducting Méhul's hugely challenging opera *Joseph*, a work designed to test the resources of a small company to their limits. Manheit's account of Mahler getting his way, leaping over the double-bass players on to the stage during the rehearsals, a diminutive figure fired by nervous energy, not only conducting the score but simultaneously moving the singers around the stage and taking charge of the production, allows us a glimpse of the man who was later to revolutionize the operatic stage in Vienna, where he single-handedly invented the modern approach to opera production. It was a working method that Mahler retained throughout the whole of his life.

The extent to which Mahler was tormented by the conditions under which he had to work and which he regarded as unworthy of his art and his abilities emerges from a letter to Friedrich Löhr, who for many years was one of his closest friends. The two men met at the University in Vienna, where Löhr was studying philology and archaeology. Their contacts deepened during the summer of 1882, resulting in a lasting friendship, albeit one that never recaptured the intensity of its early months. In the letter that he wrote from Olmütz in mid-February 1883, Mahler made no secret of his feelings but struck a note of complete self-confidence: 'Take a thoroughbred horse and yoke it to a cart with oxen – all it can do is pull and sweat along with the rest of them. I hardly dare to appear before you – I feel so besmirched', and we may well believe that Mahler was being sincere here, rather than merely fishing for compliments. He then expresses his delight at having to conduct 'virtually only' Meyerbeer and Verdi, rather than Wagner and Mozart, but finally gives vent to his despair at having to suffer at the hands of his fellow artists and their 'unspeakable lack of sensitivity', for all that he is grateful to them for occasionally making an effort to please their conductor rather than serving the cause of their art:

> for the idea that an artist can become consumed by a work of art is quite beyond them. At times, when I'm all on fire with enthusiasm and am trying to sweep them along with me to greater heights – I see these people's faces, see how surprised they are, how knowingly they smile at each other – and then my ardour cools and all I want is to run away and never return. Only the feeling that I am suffering for my masters' sake and that some day I may perhaps kindle a spark in these poor wretches' souls fortifies me, and in some of my better hours I vow to endure all this with love – even in the face of their scorn.[3]

His ability to inspire even inadequate opera companies, orchestras and choruses to raise themselves to a higher than normal level will have made it clear to him from an early date that he would one day be able to make a living as a conductor and in the process serve his great masters, though he was, throughout his life, haunted by the nightmarish vision of the starving composer with no other resources to fall back on. (The example of Hugo Wolf was undoubtedly a particular deterrent in this regard.) The drudgery of life in an opera house about which he later complained so frequently and that kept him from composing was undoubtedly the result of clear, cold calculation during this earlier period. He knew, moreover, that the schedules of the opera houses of the period would allow him a certain amount of free time to indulge his love of composition. All this helps explain why, at the end of his brief period in Olmütz, Mahler made a concerted effort to find a better and, above all, a long-term position in a larger house. Nor was it long before fortune smiled on him, a development engineered by his admittedly self-interested agent Gustav Lewy, a man whom Mahler later preferred to airbrush out of his life.

And it was the hated town of Olmütz that played a decisive part in this development, the audience at the aforementioned performance of Méhul's *Joseph* including, as it did, one Karl Überhorst, who later became stage manager at the Dresden Court Theatre. As chance would have it, Überhorst was acquainted with Baron Adolph von und zu Gilsa, the intendant of the Theatre Royal in Kassel – as we know from the figure of Botho von Hülsen at the Berlin Court Opera, such posts were the appanage of retired members of the nobility. In May 1883 Lewy heard that Kassel was looking for a second conductor who would also take charge of the chorus: the official title was 'music and chorus director'. Scarcely had Lewy's letter of recommendation been received in Kassel when a letter from Überhorst arrived on the intendant's desk, evidently written at Mahler's request and warmly recommending the 'quite outstanding young conductor', whom he had had the good fortune to observe at work in Olmütz where 'through energy and circumspection' he had been able to 'weld his rather weak forces into an harmonious whole'.[4] Gilsa was so impressed by this praise from the pen of a qualified commentator that during the last week of May he invited Mahler to conduct a number of performances in Kassel on a trial basis. Mahler was in Vienna, where he had taken a few choral rehearsals at the Carltheater during an Italian season of operas, but was once again leading a relatively aimless existence in the city – the last time he was to do so. He seized the chance with his typical purposefulness and resolve. In his reply to the letter from Kassel asking him to reflect on the matter, he did not hesitate to manipulate dates, another feature typical of an artist so often described as unworldly. When he wrote to Kassel in May 1883, he was twenty-two and therefore in his twenty-third year, but he brazenly announced that he was in his twenty-fifth year – by contemporary criteria, and even by today's standards, he was still relatively young for the Kassel appointment. It is a little surprising that he was not worried that his papers would expose his mendacity if he were appointed, but he was evidently not concerned about this and, indeed, his act of deception went unnoticed. By the end of May he was in Kassel, the trial performances passed off creditably and he was offered a three-year contract running from 1 October 1883 to the end of September 1886, although, in the event, circumstances dictated that he remained in Kassel for only two seasons. His annual salary was 2,100 marks, a princely sum for the period. It was also his first regular income.

In July he and Heinrich Krzyzanowski undertook a walking tour from Eger to the Fichtel Mountains, whither he was drawn in particular by the prospect of visiting Wunsiedel, the birthplace of one of his favourite writers, Jean Paul. He also spent a few days in Iglau, where he found his elderly parents in poor health – 'poor and gloomy', he told Löhr: it was impossible, he went on, to show them any love or affection. Prior to this, however, he had been deeply shaken by an experience of a wholly different order, for he had been in Bayreuth, where he had attended a performance of *Parsifal* that had affected every fibre of his being. Wagner's self-styled 'farewell to the world' had received its world première only twelve months earlier in sets by Max and Gotthold Brückner based in part on designs by Paul von Joukowsky, with the Munich Court Opera Orchestra under the direction of its principal conductor, Hermann Levi. (The painfully strained relationship between the Wagners and Levi, who was the son of a rabbi from Gießen, is a particularly embarrassing chapter in the story of German culture.) Overseen by Cosima, the production was the work of Wagner himself, a stage director *avant la lettre*. Six months after Wagner's death, the production was revived by Emil Scaria, who shared the role of Gurnemanz in these performances. As in 1883, the conducting duties were divided between Levi and the less experienced Franz Fischer. (Mahler does not say which conductor he heard.) And in the principal roles Mahler was able to hear some of the finest Wagnerian voices of the age. Above all, however, the Wagners' exclusivity clause meant that he could hear *Parsifal* only in Bayreuth in a performance so intense that he was rendered speechless by it. In a letter to Löhr, he describes a feeling of rapt enchantment in barely articulate terms: 'When I emerged from the Festival Theatre, incapable of uttering a word, I knew I had come to understand all that is greatest and most painful in the world and that I would have to bear it within me, inviolate, for the whole of the rest of my life.'[5] A few days later he gave his final concert in Iglau, performing Beethoven's 'Kreutzer' Sonata and other works with the violinist Mila Ott von Ottenfeld – never again was he to appear in public in the town. He arrived in Kassel on 21 August, giving himself ample time to prepare for his first performance on 19 September. A new era was beginning: Mahler was just twenty-three.

Presentiment and a New
Departure: Kassel
(1883–5)

FOR THE FIRST time Mahler was now able to work continuously in a theatre over a period of years rather than just for months or even weeks; for the first time, too, he was employed by a theatre in which his talents and ambition could be given free rein, and for the first time he at last had a passionate affair with a woman. This love affair fired his imagination as a composer, and he wrote his *Lieder eines fahrenden Gesellen,* the earliest of his works to have remained in the repertory. When Mahler arrived in Kassel, he had just turned twenty-three. His period of employment ended a day before his twenty-fifth birthday.[1]

Mahler's first address in Kassel – furnished, as usual – was a second-floor apartment at 17 Mittlere Carlstraße, where his landlord was a master tailor by the name of Adolf Frank. During his second season he lived at 22 Frankfurter Straße in a property owned by a piano teacher, Caroline Liese. And from November 1884 he stayed with a Frau Lauckhardt at 13 Wolfsschlucht, an address that must have had a particular resonance for a lover of Weber's *Der Freischütz,* quite apart from the fact that Weber's works and especially his descendants were soon to enter Mahler's life in not entirely positive ways. At the time of Mahler's arrival, Kassel numbered some 62,000 inhabitants. It had long been the residence of the landgraves and, later, the electors of Hesse, becoming the capital of the new province of Hesse-Nassau following the province's secession to Prussia in 1866. (Even today, the city's most important buildings date from these two periods in its history, an era that came to an end in 1918.) Kassel was also a centre of industry with particular emphasis on the production of railway engines, carriages and textiles. The art gallery in the Museum Fridericianum enjoyed a European reputation, as did the regional library, which was likewise housed in the Fridericianum at this date in its history. It was here, after all, that Jacob and Wilhelm Grimm had worked as librarians in the early years of the century, Mahler himself following in their footsteps with *Das klagende Lied*. The Carlsaue along the Fulda was a recreational area of great natural beauty.

The theatre and music had always played an important role in Kassel, the local orchestra in particular being able to look back on a five-hundred-year tradition. Heinrich Schütz had been trained as a boy chorister in the town and had also been active as an organist and assistant conductor – Mahler's position – before leaving for Dresden in 1615. Beethoven would have become Court Kapellmeister there in 1809, if the Viennese aristocrats had not persuaded him to stay with a better offer. The Kassel Court Theatre had seating for over a thousand, was well equipped in terms of its stage machinery and enjoyed a particular upturn in its fortunes between 1822 and 1857, when Louis Spohr – not only one of the leading conductors of his day but also active as a composer working in the German Romantic tradition – left his mark on the town's musical life as Kapellmeister, an appointment that he owed to none other than Weber. In Mahler's day the principal conductor at the Kassel Theatre was Wilhelm Treiber, who was soon to become his bitter enemy. Following Kassel's promotion to the status of a Prussian provincial capital, the theatre had been renamed the Königliche Schauspiele, a title it shared with the theatres in Wiesbaden and Hanover. As such, it staged both opera and spoken drama. Its intendant was nominally subordinate to Botho von Hülsen, the general administrator in Berlin, but in practice he had a largely free hand. For the past eight years he had been the aforementioned Baron Adolph von und zu Gilsa, a retired army major and the first real intendant that Mahler encountered in the course of his work in the theatre. Although his appointment ended prematurely and was beset by numerous disagreements, Mahler retained fond memories of his superior, who was not particularly popular with his company but feared and respected rather than hated. Not unexpectedly, he ran his company with military precision, but it is significant that his bohemian assistant conductor learnt to respect an attitude which, however much it may have rubbed him up the wrong way, was none the less based on a motto to which he could relate: 'Subordination of individual interests to the interests of the whole.' When Mahler was later obliged to run an equally tight ship in Vienna, he will have recalled his superior in Kassel. The strictness that Gilsa evinced emerges from a surviving punishment book that records how Mahler was reprimanded for causing a number of ladies in the chorus to burst into peals of laughter. What would now be regarded as an important part of a good working relationship was grounds for rebuke in Mahler's day. It seems that in Kassel the sort of loose morals that have always been regarded as a part of theatre life flourished only under the most adverse conditions. For example, male conductors and répétiteurs were forbidden to hold solo rehearsals with female members of the company – there had to be at least three people present in the room. Mahler's courtship of the women in his life (all singers apart from Marion von Weber and Alma Schindler) was subjected to tiresome restrictions, at least in Kassel.

By today's standards, the Kassel Theatre's repertory was almost unimaginably wide-ranging: during the two seasons that Mahler spent in the town, there were fifty-eight different operas, including local premières, new productions and revivals, and a similar number of plays, most of which were 'classics' by Shakespeare, Goethe and Schiller, although Kleist, Hebbel, Lessing and Raimund were also represented, while the operatic repertory consisted in the main of German works by Gluck, Weber, Marschner, Nicolai, Lortzing, Wagner and, of course, Mozart, whose Italian operas were given in German in keeping with contemporary practice. The French repertory was represented by grand opera, especially Meyerbeer, a genre by no means dead in spite of Wagner's polemics against it. And there were also a handful of Italian works by Rossini and other bel canto composers as well as some Verdi. As music director and chorus master, Mahler was subordinate to both Treiber and the senior stage manager, a situation that soon led to problems. Mahler's surviving conditions of service would be enough to instil a sense of sheer terror in anyone holding such a position today, for the assistant conductor's duties defy belief: not only did he have to conduct everything left after the principal conductor had taken his pick, he also had to engage any additional performers needed at the performances that he himself conducted; adapt large-scale works to the resources of the local company, which meant arranging the existing parts for forty-seven permanent orchestral musicians and a chorus of thirty-eight; rehearse and conduct the overtures and entr'acte music in plays, a task that Mahler particularly hated; rehearse the chorus for at least an hour a day; take music calls; and write and conduct music for particular occasions – one such task was incidental music for *Der Trompeter von Säkkingen*, a stage adaptation of Joseph Victor von Scheffel's tremendously popular epic 'in seven scenes'. The result was a combination of duties which in a house of comparable size would now be divided up among at least four different people: the first Kapellmeister (Mahler's colleague, Wilhelm Treiber, would now be general music director or at least principal conductor), the assistant conductor, the chorus master and the head of the music staff. It is clear from surviving records that during his two seasons in Kassel Mahler conducted 160 opera performances and superintended the incidental music at one hundred performances of plays, making a total of 260 performances, a figure that is scarcely conceivable, especially when we recall that the seasons were then shorter than today.

Mahler also had to conduct an enormously wide-ranging repertory, but it was here that he prepared the ground for his later ability to work at far larger houses, from the Vienna Court Opera to the Metropolitan Opera in New York, and to do so, moreover, with sovereign authority. The highlights of the repertory were inevitably the preserve of the first Kapellmeister, but Mahler was still able to take charge of Meyerbeer's *Robert le diable* – the opera with which he made his Kassel debut on 19 September 1883 – and Verdi's *Un ballo in maschera*. Although neither of these composers was a favourite of Mahler's, they still ranked higher in his eyes than Rossini's *Il barbiere di Siviglia*, Donizetti's *La Fille du régiment* and Lortzing's *Der Waffenschmied*, works that he was simply unable to take seriously, so rigorous were his artistic standards. All this meant something of a step backwards when compared with Olmütz, where he had effectively been principal conductor but where the repertory had been far more limited in scope. His burning sense of ambition and his – undoubtedly justified – conviction that he was a better conductor than his superior, Wilhelm Treiber, led sooner than expected to conflicts that ultimately contributed to his premature departure from his post in Kassel, a development in which complications of a more private nature also played a part.

Kassel's music lovers soon realized or at least suspected that their new conductor was a man of no ordinary talent. The reviews of his early performances – for a time his name was misspelt as 'Maler' – were very good and in some cases positively euphoric. Curiously enough, he was described, among other things, as 'extremely experienced', which, given his previous experience, was something of an exaggeration, but the assessment does at least show the extent to which ardour, enthusiasm and tremendous talent can make up for a lack of experience. Equally curious and from a future standpoint more significant are the critical comments that were made at this time and that were to accompany the whole of Mahler's career as a conductor, later acquiring anti-Semitic associations: he was accused of a nervous style of conducting and rebuked for his extreme tempi and for unusual and surprising crescendos and sforzatos. Indeed, he was even censured by his intendant for stamping his feet during performances. Mahler's lifelong ability to spur on his players and singers with élan, enthusiasm and unassailable authority until they achieved standards of which they had scarcely thought themselves capable – with the drawback that he was resisted and even hated by those musicians who preferred a life of philistine lethargy – had been apparent from the very beginning but it was in Kassel that it first found such clear expression. We must never lose sight of the fact that even if Mahler had never written a note of music he would still have been ranked alongside Bülow and Nikisch as one of the most brilliant conductors of his age.

Problems with Wilhelm Treiber were not slow to emerge. On the very day that Mahler faced the orchestra for the first time in Kassel, we already find him writing to his closest friend at this time, Friedrich Löhr, complaining that his superior was 'the cheerfullest four-square time-beater ever to have come my way', by which he meant a conductor who, lacking in inspiration and imagination, was content to keep the orchestra more or less together by means of economical, unvarying gestures.[2] Mahler must have reached this snap judgement very quickly as he can have had few opportunities to observe Treiber at work, the season having only just started. The fact that he was already tending to overestimate his own merits and sometimes even overstepping the mark and expressing hurtful and hateful sentiments is clear from another letter written during these early weeks in Kassel, this time to his agent in Vienna. It is with a certain insolence, not to say outright mendaciousness, that he begins by claiming that administration, audience and critics already rate him more highly than Treiber, before going on to adopt an even more arrogant tone: 'Admittedly, Herr Treiber's contract cannot be overturned out of hand, so he naturally has more to conduct than I do. But it is not entirely impossible that something unpleasant might befall the above-mentioned gentleman. I prefer not to express myself more clearly.'[3] This is a new aspect of Mahler's personality, but it is clear from this example that whenever it was a question of pursuing artistic and even personal goals, Mahler could show a surprising sense of purpose and that he had no hesitation in elbowing rivals out of the way with positively brutal force. This particular passage reveals something amounting to an annihilation fantasy and certainly a lively imagination in relation to his advancement in Kassel, an imagination unsupported by any authenticated fact. There are no surviving reviews praising Mahler at the expense of Treiber or demanding that Treiber be replaced by his assistant. Still less did Gilsa or Hülsen think for a moment of dismissing the tried and tested and popular Treiber and appointing in his place a twenty-three-year-old nobody who had been in his post for only four weeks.

That Mahler spent these weeks and months in Kassel in a state of agitation, not to say mild hysteria, is clear not only from his letters to Löhr, with their complaints about his life among pygmies, by which he meant not just his excessive workload but also and above all the lack of any intellectual and personal exchange with like-minded individuals, but also from the intense passion that he felt for Johanna Richter and that drove him to unprecedented extremes of effusiveness. Above all, however, it emerges from a remarkable incident with Hans von Bülow that took place at this time. Bülow arrived in Kassel with his Meiningen Orchestra at the end of January 1884, preceded by an exceptional reputation on at least three different fronts. Not only was he one of the most accomplished and technically brilliant pianists of his day and, as such, the dedicatee of Tchaikovsky's Piano Concerto no. 1 in B flat minor, a work notorious for its horrendous technical difficulties that Bülow had unveiled in Boston in October 1875, but he was also the most impressive conductor of his day, having initially championed the works of Wagner by conducting the world premières of *Tristan und Isolde* and *Die Meistersinger von Nürnberg* in Munich in the 1860s, only to become an early advocate of Brahms when Wagner showed his gratitude by appropriating Bülow's wife, Cosima, née Liszt-d'Agoult. Thirdly, he was widely regarded as one of the most malicious and acerbic men of his age, a point evidenced by his surviving writings and letters. Bülow gave two concerts in Kassel with the Meiningen Orchestra, whose later conductors were to include Richard Strauss and Max Reger. The first was an all-Beethoven concert, while the second comprised works by Beethoven, Brahms and the locally revered Louis Spohr. In the wake of the first concert Mahler wrote a letter to Bülow that was to have dramatic repercussions. He had attempted to see Bülow at his hotel but had been turned away, and so he immediately wrote an exuberant letter, beginning with the admission:

> I am a musician who is wandering without a guiding light in the dreary night of present-day musical life, and who is prey to all the dangers of doubt and confusion. At the concert yesterday, when I beheld the fulfilment of my utmost intimations and hopes of beauty, it became clear to me that I had found my spiritual home and my master, and that my wanderings would come to an end now or never. And now I am here to beg you to take me along in any capacity you like – let me become your *pupil*, even if I had to pay my tuition fees with my blood.[4]

The letter ends with a brief note on Mahler's career to date and with the sigh: 'At least send me a reply!'

We do not know exactly what Bülow made of this letter, although we can infer what he thought about it from his reaction to it, a reaction that made it clear that Mahler had poured out his enthusiasm and effusiveness to the wrong person. A cynic and a sceptic like Bülow, who in spite of his successes as an artist had been bruised and disillusioned by life, was incapable of seeing this remarkable fantasist's letter in the right light and unable to understand the predicament and the ardour that lay behind it. He could react only by shaking his head in disbelief and by embarking on two courses of action that must have had a profoundly dispiriting effect on Mahler. First, Bülow handed the letter to Wilhelm Treiber and, second, he replied to Mahler a few days later, on his return to Meiningen, a letter whose coldness was no doubt intentionally wounding: 'Dear Sir, it is possible that your wish might come true in eighteen months' time, assuming that I receive sufficient evidence of your abilities both as a pianist and as an orchestral and choral conductor in order to be able to recommend you. I am, however, unable to offer you an opportunity to provide this evidence.'[5] Although we have no direct testimony to his reactions, Mahler must have been deeply upset by all this. Be that as it may, it was not until several years later, in Hamburg, that there was any kind of artistic rapprochement between the two men, Bülow finally having learnt to appreciate the sort of person he was dealing with. Conversely, it is all too easy to imagine what Mahler's fan letter must have meant in the hands of his arch-enemy, Wilhelm Treiber, who could never have served as Mahler's 'guiding light', and who with some justification must have seen himself as the butt of his assistant's comments on the 'dreary night of present-day musical life'. He duly forwarded the letter to his intendant, no doubt in the hope of making life more difficult for his young rival. But Gilsa merely filed it away without comment, an action that helps to explain Mahler's continuing respect for the dry old civil servant.

Another episode that was to have far-reaching consequences for Mahler's life and work was his affair with the singer Johanna Richter. Initially there seem to have been two options of an erotic nature that presented themselves to the assistant conductor, whose appointment coincided with that of two young sopranos, Virginia Naumann-Gungl and Johanna Richter herself. There is some evidence that Mahler's feelings were first fired by Naumann-Gungl, but she was already married and the mother of two children and, indeed, considerably older than Mahler. In short, she was less attainable. With Johanna Richter, by contrast, the situation was very different. Although we know little about her and have no idea what she looked like, making it impossible to say whether there is any truth to the claim that she was a noted beauty, it seems likely that she was indeed physically attractive as Mahler's susceptibility to female beauty is clear from pictures of the young Alma Mahler and of all the other women with whom he was in any way associated. Anna von Mildenburg is the only woman in his life who cannot be said to have been conventionally beautiful: in her case the critical factor was, rather, the power of a woman who can only be described as demonic. Johanna seems to have been more or less the same age as Mahler and was a coloratura soprano who excelled in parts such as Mozart's Konstanze and the Queen of the Night but whose repertory also included Leonora in *Il trovatore* and even Wagner's Venus. She was a popular favourite with Kassel audiences and also with local critics. It appears that there were initial misgivings about her vocal technique, but these were quickly silenced, and we may assume that Mahler worked closely with her: it was no doubt at this period in his career that he developed his partial understanding of vocal technique and of voices in general, an understanding that can be observed on repeated occasions in the course of his later career. Johanna Richter's subsequent career was far from insignificant. She left Kassel a year after Mahler and sang first in Rotterdam and then in Cologne, where she remained a member of the local ensemble for a period of many years, subsequently appearing in smaller houses and ending her professional career in around 1905, while remaining active as a teacher. She died in Danzig in 1944.

It is clear from his letters to Löhr that Mahler fell in love with Johanna Richter as soon as he arrived in Kassel, leading to a period of the most turbulent emotional upheaval. It was the first genuinely intense experience of love that he had known and at the same time a liaison that brought him more pain than pleasure, a point that emerges not from any direct evidence, for the only surviving letter from Johanna Richter to Mahler is decidedly non-committal, but from Mahler's letters to Löhr, among others, in which he reports on the highs and, more frequently, the lows of his liaison. It transpires from these letters that Mahler was exposed to a veritable whirlwind of emotions in which fear prevailed over hope. His own surviving account of the relationship gives the impression of a via dolorosa, a time of a 'continuous and altogether intolerable struggle'.[6] On his return to Kassel following the summer break of 1884, he told Löhr that he was once again 'in thrall to the terrible old spell'.[7] Johanna Richter seems to have expended all the wiles of feminine coquettishness on Mahler, leaving the completely inexperienced assistant conductor utterly helpless, an observation that implies no moral judgement, as the ability to reconcile the career of a singer with an affair involved a difficult balancing act, given the unsettled life led by such singers and the risk of an unwanted pregnancy that might put an end to that career. The course of Mahler's relationship with Johanna Richter may be illustrated by a passage from a letter that he wrote to Löhr on 1 January 1885. He had spent New Year's Eve with the soprano:

I spent yesterday evening alone with her, both of us silently awaiting the arrival of the new year. Her thoughts did not linger over the present, and when the clock struck midnight and tears gushed from her eyes, I felt terrible that I, I was not allowed to dry them. She went into the adjacent room and stood for a moment in silence at the window, and when she returned, silently weeping, a sense of inexpressible anguish had arisen between us like an everlasting partition wall, and there was nothing I could do but press her hand and leave. As I came outside, the bells were ringing and the solemn chorale could be heard from the tower.

As so often with the young Mahler, his effusive style has a literary ring to it, in this case an obvious allusion to a passage from Tannhäuser's Rome Narration: 'The new day dawned; the bells were ringing – celestial songs came floating down.' Appropriately enough, Mahler concludes his description with a clear reminiscence of Heine: 'Ah, dear Fritz – it was all just as if the great director of the universe had intended it all to be artistically apt. I spent the whole night crying in my dreams.'[8] But such effusions did nothing to move the relationship forward, and Mahler was left to traverse his vale of tears alone: 'I am torn apart, my heart is bleeding, all is lost' – these are the phrases that keep on recurring.

Mahler addressed several poems to Johanna Richter, the final line of the first of them already containing a reference to a 'solitary wayfarer'[9] and illustrating the link with the *Lieder eines fahrenden Gesellen*. Mahler composed this set of four songs, probably in December 1884, and dedicated them, at least tacitly, to Johanna Richter. There were originally six poems, all of them written by Mahler himself, but he set only four of them. The two that were not set to music include the following, a poem that offers arguably the most striking illustration of the composer's inner vacillation between the cynicism of Jean Paul's Schoppe in *Titan* and the openness of the twin brothers Walt and Vult in his *Flegeljahre*, while also including allusions to some of Wilhelm Müller's poems that Schubert set to music in *Winterreise*:

> Die Nacht bricht mild aus stummen ewigen Fernen
> Mit ihren tausend goldenen Augen nieder,
> Und müde Menschen schließen ihre Lider
> Im Schlaf, auf's neu vergessnes Glück zu lernen.
>
> Siehst du den stummen fahrenden Gesellen?
> Gar einsam und verloren ist sein Pfad,
> Wohl Weg und Weiser der verloren hat
> Und ach, kein Stern will seinen Pfad erhellen.
>
> Der Weg ist lang und Gottes Engel weit
> Und falsche Stimmen tönen lockend, leise –
> Ach, wann soll enden meine Reise,
> Wann ruht der Wanderer von des Weges Leid?
>
> Es starrt die Sphynx und droht mit Rätselqualen
> Und ihre grauen Augen schweigen – schweigen.
> Kein rettend Wort, kein Lichtstrahl will sich zeigen –
> Und lös' ich's nicht – muß es mein Leben zahlen.[10]

[With her thousand golden eyes, night falls gently from mute, eternal distances, and weary men and women close their lids in sleep to learn lost happiness anew. Do you see the silent wayfarer? All lonely and forsaken is his path, his way and signpost he has doubtless lost and, ah!, no star will light his path. The way is long, God's angels far away, and siren voices call enticingly and softly – ah, when will my journey end, when will the traveller rest from his journey's anguished sufferings? The sphinx stares blankly and threatens riddling torments, her grey eyes silent – silent. No saving word, no ray of light appears – if I fail to solve them, it will cost me my life.]

This painful relationship lasted until Mahler left Kassel and seems never to have transgressed the bounds of formal, polite behaviour, for all that Mahler would have liked it to have done so. In the only surviving letter that Johanna wrote to Mahler after he had already left for Prague, she addresses him as her 'dear good friend' and uses the respect for pronoun 'Sie'. Mahler spent his final hours in Kassel with Johanna in June 1885, but neither party was capable of finding a way out of the hopeless crisis of their unrequited love.

There is little more to be said about Kassel. Mahler's first summer break from the town, in 1884, was spent partly in Iglau and partly with Friedrich Löhr in Perchtoldsdorf. He returned to Kassel in late August, breaking his journey in Dresden, where he attended two performances at the Court Opera and was introduced to the company's principal conductor, Ernst von Schuch, who went on to champion the operas of Richard Strauss. Mahler admired Schuch's technical virtuosity on the podium but did not know where to begin to make sense of his interpretations. In January 1885 the Kassel newspapers reported a sensational event in the world of the theatre: the young assistant conductor had a new contract in his pocket, having successfully applied for a vacant position at the Leipzig Stadttheater, albeit not until his Kassel contract had expired, which in the normal course of things would not have been until the end of the 1886/7 season. As it turned out, things did not run their normal course, for Mahler was progressively worn down by the torments associated with his relations with Johanna Richter and by his confrontations with Treiber. In the spring of 1885 he asked for his contract to be prematurely terminated, a request that was eventually granted. His dismissal had to be approved by the central office in Berlin, and Gilsa, evidently perceptive and sympathetic to Mahler's situation, wrote a series of tactical letters to the capital expressing criticism of his assistant conductor. An interim solution had to be found for the months during which Mahler was otherwise unoccupied between Kassel and Leipzig, and in this he was helped by Angelo Neumann, Wagner's erstwhile comrade-in-arms, who was now director of the German Theatre in Prague. Having heard good things about the musical firebrand in Kassel, he signed a contract with Mahler in early April, an engagement formally announced in the newspapers two months later. But there was another major event in Mahler's life before he left the town.

For some time he had – with his intendant's permission – taken on the additional post of chorus master in the nearby town of Münden, where a series of successful concerts, coupled with his work as chorus master at the theatre, had led to an invitation to conduct a performance of Beethoven's Ninth Symphony at the opening concert of a Grand Music Festival to be held in Kassel on and around 1 July 1885. Gilsa had already agreed that the theatre orchestra would take part, a decision that inevitably left the town's principal conductor, Wilhelm Treiber, feeling snubbed. Treiber mobilized all his resources against Mahler, including a regular campaign against him in the local papers. Particularly remarkable is the fact that for the first time in his life, but by no means the last, Mahler found himself the butt of anti-Semitic barbs – we shall return to them in the context of our later examination of the whole complex of Jewishness and anti-Semitism. The entire episode caused quite a stir. Gilsa did not want to lose Treiber, especially at a time when Mahler was already on the point of leaving Kassel, and so he saw himself obliged to side with Treiber and, in spite of his sympathy for Mahler, to stop the orchestra from appearing. A scratch band was hastily assembled, and the Grand Music Festival began not with Beethoven but with Mendelssohn's oratorio *Saint Paul*, a performance that proved a triumph for all concerned, Mahler being praised in particular for his 'all-encompassing energy'. The soloists were all of the first order, including, as they did, Rosa Papier-Paumgartner, Mahler's friend from his days in Vienna.

Mahler returned to Münden to work with his choir on 5 July, his last day in Kassel, and wrote afterwards to Löhr: 'So far as I am concerned everything has turned out extremely well up to now. Honours & love have been simply showered upon me.'[11] The next day he returned to Iglau to spend some time with his family and to recover from recent upheavals, although he was unable to stay long in the town as his engagement in Prague was due to begin on 1 August. It had been a time of great agitation for Mahler, a time when he had suffered a great deal but also learnt a lot. He had also completed his *Lieder eines fahrenden Gesellen*, his first work after the great exertions of *Das klagende Lied* and the major disappointments that had followed.

The Avid Reader: Mahler
and Literature

THE SON OF the 'coachman scholar' Bernhard Mahler enjoyed books as others enjoy food: 'I am "devouring" an increasing number of books! They are, after all, the only friends that I keep by me! And what friends! Heavens, if I had no books! I forget everything round about me whenever a voice from "one of us" reaches me! They become ever more familiar and more of a consolation to me, my real brothers and fathers and lovers.'[1] Thus Mahler ends one of his letters to Friedrich Löhr, probably written in Hamburg during the winter of 1894/5. In using the phrase 'one of us' – in German, 'unsere Leut' – Mahler was parodying an expression regularly used by German and Austrian Jews to describe other Jews. From our earliest account of the young boy withdrawing to the ridge of his parents' roof, where he sat, totally engrossed in his reading, to the fatally ill Mahler capable of holding in his enfeebled hands only odd sections torn from Eduard von Hartmann's *The Problem of Life*, we have the picture of a man fired by a passionate love of books and reading. It was a passion greater than that normally found in nineteenth- and early twentieth-century composers and even in conductors of the period. There are few who can be compared with him in this respect: among composers, there were Schumann, Berlioz, Wagner and, above all, Busoni, a contemporary and a colleague with whom he was friendly, while among conductors, there was only Hans von Bülow. Unlike his colleagues, however, Mahler did not express himself in literary terms, except in his letters, unless it was a question of preparing a text to set to music, as was the case with his *Lieder eines fahrenden Gesellen*, or when he wrote poems to express his extreme emotional tension, poems generally addressed to the women he loved. All who knew him attested to his passion for reading. Especially at times of storm and stress in his life, Mahler's letters are filled with requests to his friends to send him books, either as gifts or as a loan, for they were expensive and even beyond the reach of a student. Later he surrounded himself with books wherever he lived and worked: an edition of Goethe's works, or at least the conversations with Eckermann, and a few volumes by Jean Paul were always to hand in his various composing houses or accompanied him on his vacations from Vienna. Books helped him to pass the time on long railway journeys, they were recommended to friends, and friends in turn recommended titles to him, recommendations by which he set great store. His reading was wide-ranging, extending, as it did, from the classics of world literature to rather more recondite works. Apart from occasional glances as far back as the ancient Greeks and, in particular, to Euripides, Shakespeare was the earliest playwright to engage his attention, which was focused in the main on German classical and Romantic writers, notably Goethe but also Hölderlin and E. T. A. Hoffmann. Among the great humorists whose works he enjoyed were Cervantes, Sterne, Jean Paul and Dickens, while Dostoevsky and the Dutch novelist Multatuli were likewise a source of abiding interest. As for more recent literature, Mahler's reading list was relatively brief, being largely dictated by friendship (Siegfried Lipiner and Gerhart Hauptmann), acquaintanceship (Frank Wedekind) or chance encounters (the Russian novelist Dimitri Merezhkovsky, who wrote a successful novel about Leonardo da Vinci and whose essay championing Dostoevsky at the expense of Tolstoi must have appealed to Mahler). His reading was not limited to belles lettres, however, but also included texts of a more philosophical nature, from Kant, whose works formed part of his reference library, to Frederick August Lange's *History of Materialism* and Alfred Edmund Brehm's *Life of Animals*, which he is said to have owned in its entirety. His friend Arnold Berliner, who successfully popularized modern science, provided him with information about developments in this field. Unfortunately, Mahler's library has not survived: when Alma had to flee from Vienna in 1938, his books were left behind to be plundered, destroyed and sold. Although a catalogue of them was never drawn up, we are none the less well informed about its contents.

Mahler's relationship to literature is best examined from the standpoint of his attitude to the texts that he set to music, in particular his *Wunderhorn* songs and those based on poems by Friedrich Rückert.[2]

The world of *Rübezahl* and of the 'Waldmärchen' that we find in Mahler's early plans for an opera and in *Das klagende Lied* was soon transformed into that of *Des Knaben Wunderhorn*, which left its mark on an entire complex of works in the form of several songs and the first four symphonies. The uncertain date of the *Lieder eines fahrenden Gesellen* initially led writers to assume that Mahler wrote the words to these songs before he read *Des Knaben Wunderhorn*, but it was only a matter of time before it was discovered that the first of the four *Gesellen* songs reveals verbal parallels with two of the *Wunderhorn* poems, Arnim's and Brentano's collection containing two strophes which, although they do not belong together, are printed one after the other:

> Wann mein Schatz Hochzeit macht,
> Hab ich einen traurigen Tag:
> Geh ich in mein Kämmerlein,
> Wein um meinen Schatz.
>
> Blümlein blau, verdorre nicht,
> Du stehst auf grüner Heide;
> Des Abends, wenn ich schlafen geh,
> So denk ich an das Lieben.[3]

[The day on which my sweetheart marries will be a sad day for me: I shall go into my little room and weep for my sweetheart. Little blue flower, do not fade, you are growing on a green heath; in the evening, when I go to bed, I shall think of love.]

Mahler turned these lines into the following:

> Wenn mein Schatz Hochzeit macht,
> fröhliche Hochzeit macht,
> hab' ich meinen traurigen Tag!
> Geh' ich in mein Kämmerlein, dunkles Kämmerlein!
> Weine! Wein! Um meinen Schatz,
> um meinen lieben Schatz!
> Blümlein blau! Blümlein blau!
> Verdorre nicht! Verdorre nicht!
> Vöglein süß! Vöglein süß!
> Du singst auf grüner Heide!
> Ach! Wie ist die Welt so schön!
> Ziküth! Ziküth!
> Singet nicht! Blühet nicht!
> Lenz ist ja vorbei!
> Alles Singen ist nun aus!
> Des Abends, wenn ich schlafen geh,
> denk ich an mein Leid'! An mein Leide!

[The day on which my sweetheart marries, is happily married, will be a sad day for me! I shall go into my little room, my dark little room! Weep! Weep! For my sweetheart, for my dear sweetheart! Little blue flower! Little blue

flower! Do not fade! Do not fade! Sweet little bird! Sweet little bird! You are
singing on the green heath! Ah! How beautiful the world is! Cheep-cheep!
Cheep-cheep! Do not sing! Do not bloom! For spring is over! All singing is
over and done with! In the evening, when I go to bed, I shall think of my
anguish! My anguish!]

Mahler's approach to his present source was to be typical of all his later
settings, hence its exemplary nature. His ability to assimilate a particular tone
or, rather, his ability to give his own tone of voice to what was initially another
tone was combined with an essentially unscholarly permissiveness with regard
to the texts he set, a freedom ranging from minimal changes, as was the case
with the Rückert settings, to free reworkings, most notably in the case of his
elaboration of Klopstock's 'Resurrection Song' in his Second Symphony. But all
the changes that Mahler made, whether to the Klopstock song or to the later
Wunderhorn poems, serve a simple aim, namely, to add to the intensity of the
poem's emotional content. The 'sad day' becomes a matter of personal import
for the man who has been forsaken, his little room becomes 'dark' when the
phrase is repeated, and the 'love' of the original becomes 'anguish' in Mahler's
revisions. The repeated phrases have a largely compositional function, giving
the text a greater emphasis, and much the same is true of the numerous exclamation marks with which Mahler liberally sprinkles these poems. Here, too,
however, he remains true to his principle of using contrast for dynamic ends:
the musical expression is not redoubled in an attempt to add greater emphasis
to the words, as it is so often in the case of Strauss's lieder. The exclamation
marks are not written into the music. Rather, the singer is instructed to remain
'quiet and sad till the end', not to underline the exclamation marks by means of
vocal emphasis. Such punctuation marks should be felt, but then suppressed:
the sob should be swallowed before it can be expressed.

   It is in the central section of the poem ('Blümlein blau') that Mahler departs
furthest from his source, for here he needed to enhance the impact of the quiet
and plaintive outer sections by means of a kind of scherzo. But the 'Gently
animated' performance marking of the central section represents no more
than a glimmer of life that is all too quickly extinguished. The agony of the
poet's emotional life finds expression in the individual song as it does in the
cycle as a whole where grim self-mortification ('Ich hab ein glühend Messer')
appears alongside a sense of lethargy that longs for death ('Die zwei blauen
Augen von meinem Schatz').

   The aspect of *Des Knaben Wunderhorn* that appealed to Mahler so disarm-
ingly and so directly was what might be termed its emotional polyphony.
Natalie Bauer-Lechner reports that while he was attending a fair near the
Wörthersee during the summer of 1900, Mahler was so taken by the combined

sounds of the shooting galleries and Punch and Judy show, the military band music and the singing of a male-voice choir, that he exclaimed:

> You hear? That's polyphony, and that's where I get it from! [. . .] Just in this way – *from quite different directions* – must the themes appear; and they must be just as different from each other in rhythm and melodic character (everything else is merely many-voiced writing, homophony in disguise). The only difference is that the artist orders and unites them all into one concordant and harmonious whole.[4]

To Mahler, the world also seemed to resonate with music in the *Wunderhorn* texts, with their polyphonic interplay of the sublime and the audacious, the bold and the understated, an amalgam of dance, lovelorn lament and dirge. In particular, Mahler was drawn to the figure of the deserter condemned to death, a figure who acquired a special resonance during the Revolutionary Wars of 1792–9 and above all during the Napoleonic Wars, repeatedly raising his voice in a moving lament in those of the *Wunderhorn* songs in which the singer steps into the character's role. Mahler's sympathy for humiliated, wounded souls, nurtured by his reading of Dostoevsky, inspired his greatest songs, including 'Revelge' and 'Der Tamboursg'sell', both of them late products of his enthusiasm for Arnim and Brentano's collection of poems. The deserter is a figure who was to preoccupy him from the time of his early song, 'Zu Straßburg auf der Schanz'. The fear of the soldier who, driven by homesickness and love to neglect his duties, has been condemned to death and who now awaits the firing squad, is grounded in the dull and unconsoling sounds of a march in which battlefield and place of execution eerily overlap. Mahler gave musical expression to the anguish of those who are bereft of speech, features that were later to be stressed by Berg in the principal male character of his opera *Wozzeck* which, Mahlerian in spirit, represents an intensification of Büchner's original. Adorno has convincingly demonstrated the way in which on the level of the work's musical design this characteristic reflects a plebeian element that rebels against the bourgeois musical tradition: 'Desperately it [Mahler's music] draws to itself what culture has spurned, as wretched, injured, and mutilated as culture hands it over. The art-work, chained to culture, seeks to burst the chain and show compassion for the derelict residue; in Mahler each measure is an opening of arms.'[5]

When Mahler wrote his *Kindertotenlieder* and his five other Rückert songs between 1901 and 1904, his elder daughter was still healthy and happy. We do not know whether he later discovered that Rückert's own children, Ernst and Luise, died from the same illness or at least from one similar to that from which Maria died in 1907. That a father who was also a poet might pen a poem to mark such an event is entirely to be expected, but for him to write several such poems a day over a period of six months until he had finally completed almost five hundred is almost certainly unique in world literature. Unlike the earthy *Wunderhorn* texts, Rückert's poems seem at first sight to have all the faded charm of pressed flowers, but it was this that attracted Mahler at a time when his symphonies – the Fifth and the Sixth – were characterized by immense contrasts and vast resources. By 1900 Rückert's poetry had been largely forgotten by readers and composers, their author seen as a sterile and unduly didactic orientalist by the champions of Naturalism and Symbolism, Jugendstil and Décadence. Mahler's interest in him reflects the composer's total independence in his poetical tastes and in the texts he chose to set to music.

Like the *Kindertotenlieder*, the five other Rückert settings that are nowadays normally taken together as the Rückert Lieder are notable for their reduced orchestration, their chamber-like transparency looking forward to the composer's later period, the wild march rhythms and droll humour of the *Wunderhorn* songs giving way to a greater sophistication and sensitivity. Webern made a note of his conversations with Mahler during their first encounter in February 1905, including the following remarkable comment on Rückert: 'After *Des Knaben Wunderhorn* I could not compose anything but Rückert – this is lyric poetry from the source, all else is lyric poetry of a derivative sort.'[6] This is a surprising remark when we recall that at this period Rückert was generally suspected of writing derivative verse, quite apart from the fact that there is no evidence that Mahler took any interest in the poetry that was being written around 1900 by Hofmannsthal, George and others, and that nowhere does he mention the names of Baudelaire, Rimbaud and Verlaine. In short, his literary judgements were based on a very small body of evidence. Rather, his affinity with Rückert attests to an understanding of language in general and of poetry in particular similar to that found in the case of Karl Kraus and Rudolf Borchardt. Kraus saw in poetry the most direct linguistic expression of a spiritual message, be it felt or thought, seen or reflected. There was no sense of coquettishness in Kraus's own description of himself as derivative in his poem 'Bekenntnis': 'I am merely one of those epigones dwelling in the ancient house of language.'[7] For him, the ancient word could seem new-born if it came close enough to the source of language, the 'well-spring' around which his own poetry constantly revolved. For his part, Borchardt brought out an anthology titled *Everlasting Storehouse of German Poetry*, the afterword of which singles out Rückert for particular mention: on the one hand, there were long sections of Rückert's verse that consisted of pure improvisation that failed to scale the literary heights, while on the other he was said to represent a faithful reflection of the German tradition, a tradition imbued with heartfelt beauty, caprice and playfulness, maturity and kindness, generally illustrating a wondrous world of inner life such as no other nation had created.[8] Anyone reading Borchardt's characterization will find it impossible to resist the temptation to turn back a few pages and check that it is not *Des Knaben Wunderhorn* that he is referring to here, but Rückert. But in the process he helps to make Mahler's fascination with Rückert more intelligible. The German writer Hans Wollschläger, who was as familiar with Rückert's writings as he was with Mahler's music, had the following to say about the *Kindertotenlieder*:

> Mahler was familiar from his own nature with panic-stricken terror and sensed it in Rückert's nature, too, allowing it to speak by removing its glibness. His music surrounds the text with the surreal timelessness of the death for which the death of a child is merely a metaphor; its linearity moves beyond the period that produced it, and in the final song the sounds of lamentation of all cultures seem to combine together.[9]

Herta Blaukopf has called Mahler a 'relatively conservative reader', a view with which one can only concur.[10] He registered the existence of the literature of his own day only if he was in personal contact with the writer, as he was with Gerhart Hauptmann, and yet even here sympathy for the author was generally followed only by a cursory reading of a sample selection. That he took an interest in the writings of Frank Wedekind is not generally known. He saw a production of *Spring Awakening* at Max Reinhardt's Kammerspiele in Berlin in 1907 and was introduced to the author who, as he explicitly stressed, struck him as not entirely unsympathetic. One might have thought that he would have been put off by the powerful emphasis on adolescent sexuality that caused Wedekind such problems with the censor, but this was not in fact the case. Mahler was filled with enthusiasm, writing to Alma: 'You know, I was bowled over! Immensely powerful, talented and full of poetry!' But he then went on to qualify his remark: 'What a shame! To think what that man might have made of his career! Just think of the company he keeps: whatever came over him?'[11] It is not clear if Mahler knew about Wedekind's subsequent development and whether he was familiar with *Pandora's Box*, still less whether he attended the famous world-première production of the piece by Karl Kraus at Vienna's Trianon Theatre on 29 May 1905 – conceivably Mahler had already left Vienna by this date in order to attend the Tonkünstlerfest in Graz. A seating plan of the second performance on 15 June has survived, showing the names of the members of the audience. Among them were Alban Berg, whose impressions of the evening later found expression in his second opera, *Lulu*, and even a certain 'Maler'. But by this date Mahler was in Maiernigg for the start of his summer holiday. Although he found both Arthur Schnitzler and Hugo von

Hofmannsthal sympathetic as individuals, his contacts with them were not sufficiently deep to inspire him to immerse himself in their works. When Strauss told Mahler that he was working on a setting of Hofmannsthal's *Elektra*, Mahler commented mockingly to Alma about the questionable delights of being 'modern'.[12] He viewed with suspicion the works of Maeterlinck and Oscar Wilde and, indeed, every author whose writings smacked of décadence and the fin de siècle, which he equated with perversion and sexual pathology. He even forbade Alma to read Wilde's *Picture of Dorian Gray*.[13] He loathed every form of obscenity and smut, evincing a degree of reserve which, entirely untypical of his age, was offended by the wholesale eroticization and sexualization of culture in the years around 1900; and if he held Strauss's *Salome* in such high regard, it was only by being untrue to his fundamental nature, for Wilde's play had nothing to say to him, his position being comparatively close to that of the Viennese court censor's office, which was distinctly hostile to the piece's underlying tendencies. On the other hand, he shared the view, held by his colleagues in the Secession, that art should be unconstrained by censorship, so that in recognizing the artistic merits of *Salome* and *Spring Awakening*, he was clearly willing to lower his own moral standards.

Mahler's lack of sympathy for turn-of-the-century Viennese literature, with what Hermann Bahr termed its 'defeat of naturalism', and his complete ignorance of French and English Symbolism, becomes more understandable when we consider his far more positive assessment of the now largely forgotten figure of Peter Rosegger, an assessment that many a Mahlerian now finds intensely puzzling. Even on his fiftieth birthday, which the composer spent alone at Toblach in 1910, he could still take pleasure in the fact that 'the heavens have been raining down volumes of Rosegger' in the form of a gift from his mother-in-law that pre-empted his own idea of giving Anna Moll a similar set of volumes. The critic Ernst Decsey recalled that in the summer of 1909 Mahler had hailed Rosegger as the leading poet of the age: 'He's the greatest. With all the others it's more or less just a case of birth pangs . . . cum grano salis, of course, cum grano salis'.[14] In conversation Mahler could sometimes get carried away but there is no escaping the fact that he thought highly of an ideologically blinkered poet from Styria famous for upholding traditional rural values at the expense of urban society. Mahler seems not to have been disturbed by the aura of earthiness and the poet's evident anti-Jewishness (for Rosegger, Jewish shopkeepers and speculators threatened the very existence of the peasants who dwelt in the forests). Perhaps the stylistically sophisticated simplicity and rustic values of a writer whose autobiographical tales are still capable of impressing us with their descriptions of the world of nature struck a chord with Mahler, recalling the experiences of his own lost childhood and adolescence.

Mahler's literary tastes seem to have been influenced in the main by the books contained in his parents' library in Iglau, thereafter by the anthology of texts used by his local grammar school. As Herta Blaukopf assumes, this volume must have been the one edited by Joseph Mozart and was made up for the most part of the German classics. Indeed, it was these that formed the unshakeable basis of Mahler's later literary judgements, not that this prevented him from devouring the works of other writers during his Sturm und Drang period: Jean Paul was certainly no schoolboy classic. Later he lacked the time and receptivity to discover other new writers. Shakespeare was an unassailable authority for Mahler. When he saw a production of *Romeo and Juliet* in Mannheim in 1904, he wrote to tell Alma that for all its bungled mediocrity the performance had opened his eyes once again 'to the greatest of all writers and perhaps of all human beings'.[15] On another occasion he played off Shakespeare against Ibsen, a playwright he held in relatively low esteem as a member of the modernist school: 'Shakespeare is *positive* and *productive*, while Ibsen is nothing but analysis, negation, infecundity.'[16]

If Lessing played no further discernible role in Mahler's intellectual world following his boyhood setting of 'Türken haben schöne Töchter', the same cannot be said of Goethe, whose works occupied the position of a central sun in the composer's literary firmament. If we may allow for several suns in this galaxy, then Jean Paul and Dostoevsky would have to be conceded a place alongside Goethe. *Faust* was naturally central to Mahler's enthusiasm, but he was almost equally enthusiastic about the conversations with Eckermann and *Wilhelm Meisters Lehrjahre* and *Wanderjahre*. He knew whole sections of *Faust* by heart – when Ernst Decsey visited him at Toblach in 1909, Mahler prevailed on the critic to read to him from *Faust*, declaiming many of the lines from memory to the delight of the critic, who recalled that in the half-lit room the composer looked uncannily like Goethe, a somewhat puzzling suggestion, for at first sight there was no physical similarity between Mahler and Goethe, but Decsey was not the sort of writer to indulge in mystification.[17] It was during this same visit that Decsey discovered a complete set of Alfred Edmund Brehm's multi-volume *Life of Animals* on one of the shelves in Mahler's house in Toblach. Mahler also preferred to re-read books that he had already enjoyed rather than risk disappointment with others that were unfamiliar, and so we find him revisiting Goethe's *Dichtung und Wahrheit*, *Die Leiden des jungen Werthers* and the life of Goethe by Albert Bielschowsky, published in two volumes between 1896 and 1904. He also had a multi-volume edition of Goethe's correspondence on his shelves but told Alfred Roller that he was keeping it for his old age. What drew Mahler to Goethe was more than just the poet. Rather, he saw Goethe as a profound thinker and philosopher whose wide-ranging interest in the natural sciences Mahler found particularly fascinating. And, flying in the face of the then traditional picture of Goethe as a classical figure, he was no less fascinated by the constant sense of striving in Goethe's life: 'He was never finished,' he told Decsey; 'he remained an apprentice right up to the end – that's an open secret.'[18] This sense of never achieving closure but of constantly developing towards a higher state is one that Mahler recognized in himself, too, and it was this that drew him to Goethe. Bruno Walter gives numerous examples of Goethe's towering importance for Mahler, mentioning in particular the conversations with Goethe recorded by the writer Johann Daniel Falk, especially the one that took place on the occasion of the burial of the poet Christoph Martin Wieland, with whom Goethe had been friendly, and that revolved around the subject of immortality. Far too little attention has been paid to this reference until now. Together with Mahler's extremely important letter to Alma about the end of Part Two of *Faust*, it will form the nucleus of a later chapter about Mahler's whole outlook on the world.

We have already seen how Jean Paul was second to none in influencing not only the young Mahler's effusive epistolary style but also his whole way of relating emotionally to the world. By 1880, when Mahler first discovered him, Jean Paul was far from being the fashionable writer that he had been eighty years earlier. By 1830 his reputation was already in decline. Ludwig Börne's hymn-like tribute to him was intended to encourage a reassessment, but it merely sealed the older view, the emergence of naturalism leading to the eclipse of a writer whose emotional outpourings and fantastical tales sometimes seem to anticipate Surrealism. The grotesquerie that the Weimar Classicists saw in his writings, encouraging Goethe to define the author of the novel *Hesperus* as a 'tragelaph' – a fabulous beast compounded of a goat and a stag – left its mark on the whole of the second half of the nineteenth century, Nietzsche's well-known dismissal of the writer as 'a fatality in a dressing gown' being only the most familiar and handy expression of a view that veered between bewilderment and disparagement. Given the fact that Mahler's tastes were relatively traditional, it is perhaps surprising to find him swimming against the tide long before Jean Paul was rediscovered by Stefan George and his circle. When Mahler made the pilgrimage to Bayreuth in 1883, it was not just for the sake of Wagner but for Jean Paul, too, for it was here in Bayreuth that Jean Paul had spent the final years of his life, here, too, that he was buried. Mahler also visited the writer's birthplace at Wunsiedel some twenty-five miles to the north-east. As late as 1894, when Bruno Walter first met Mahler in Hamburg, it was clear that *Siebenkäs* was one of the conductor's favourite novels.

If Mahler was drawn to Goethe by the latter's open-endedness and by the sense that he was not interested in achieving closure, then these same qualities must also have fascinated him about Jean Paul, who never intended his readers to regard his longer narrative works and his manifold shorter prose writings as finished but as works in progress. His self-irony, his whimsical and even grotesque humour, the emotional depth of his lyrical outbursts, his intense descriptions of nature, his political insights and satirical acuteness, his inward inspiration, his hymn-like accounts of friendship and his inexhaustible linguistic imagination must have struck the young Mahler as the work of a kindred spirit. Among the characters who must have seemed to the highly strung young conductor to be accurate reflections of his own emotional existence are Firmian Stanislas Siebenkäs – the lawyer who helps the poor in the novel of the same name and who once changed names with his friend Leibgeber, while Leibgeber himself then finds his way into the author's main work, *Titan*, as the humorist and mocking wit, Schoppe – and the dazzling fallen angel, Roquairol, in *Titan*, who as the main character in his own tragedy shoots himself in full view of the audience. (It will be recalled that for a time Mahler's First Symphony was called *Titan*.) All the questions about God and His adversaries, about the meaning of life and death, about the durability of love and friendship and about the unfathomable depths of human feelings, whether good or bad – these were all questions that Jean Paul asked with such eloquence and invariably answered with his inimitable mixture of humour, sadness and tearful consolation, a mixture that was largely responsible for his success with his readers. They also exercised Mahler.

There was something else about Jean Paul that was bound to appeal to Mahler in a way that not even Shakespeare or Goethe could, inasmuch as the young composer was keen to break down the symphony's old generic boundaries, much as Jean Paul had done with the novel, and to bring together elements of the classical symphony and the symphonic poem. When he told Natalie that the symphony, as he imagined it and as he planned to redefine it, should be as inexhaustible as the world and as life itself, encompassing everything,[19] then this mission statement of his reflects the programme underpinning Jean Paul's novels: common to them all is the infinite subjectivity that finds expression here and the creation of a sense of epic totality from top to bottom, from the emotionally charged to the humorous. Like the novelist, the writer of symphonies combines within his breast a multiplicity of different souls, including the humorist, the satirist, the parodist (think of his performance markings 'with humour' and 'in a spirit of parody'), the contemplative philosopher, the reflective observer of the world, the sensitive lover (as in the Adagietto of the Fifth Symphony), the nature worshipper ('Like a sound of nature', we read in the opening movement of the First Symphony), the enthusiast (the 'Veni, creator spiritus' of the Eighth Symphony), the elegist with a gift for fathoming the world's profundities and seeing through its veil of illusion (the Adagio of the Ninth Symphony): all of this can be rediscovered in the world of Jean Paul, taking us far beyond the relatively superficial borrowing of the word 'Titan' as the title of the First Symphony. If, in his essay 'The Storyteller', Walter Benjamin claims that to write a novel means 'to carry the incommensurable to extremes in the representation of human life', then he also, albeit unwittingly, provides the best possible definition of the Mahlerian symphony – it is no accident that Benjamin was also familiar with the writings of Jean Paul.

Following his return to Vienna after his second season in New York in the summer of 1909, Mahler found himself surrounded by a group of young admirers, including Schoenberg and Zemlinsky, and asked them their opinion of Dostoevsky, only to discover that they knew the writer merely by name. Mahler is then said to have turned to Schoenberg and exclaimed: 'But Schoenberg, what's all this? Let the young people who are studying with you read Dostoevsky – that's more important than counterpoint.' Webern apparently then got to his feet and like some hesitant schoolboy said, 'But we've got Strindberg.' It was hardly a comment calculated to endear his disciples to their revered master.[20] If Ibsen was at least worthy of criticism in Mahler's eyes, Strindberg simply failed to register with him at all: he presumably never read a line of Strindberg or saw any of his plays in the theatre.

Dostoevsky was the third of the fixed stars in Mahler's literary firmament, although it remains unclear how the composer came across him. True, the Russian novelist's name cannot have been unknown to the Sturm und Drang circles that Mahler frequented during his formative years in Vienna, for he was very much a contemporary writer, controversial and much discussed: *The Brothers Karamazov* did not appear in the original Russian until 1879/80, and it was not until 1884, when Mahler was in his mid-twenties, that the first German translation was published. None the less, there is no evidence that Mahler read Dostoevsky at this time, although it is possible that one of his friends, Nina Hoffmann-Matscheko, who published a monograph on the novelist in 1899, drew the writer to his attention. Drawing on his first-hand knowledge of the matter, Richard Specht adjudged that:

> Mahler's encounter with his books was an experience of determinative force for him. Even though Mahler spoke about Dostoevsky as often as he could and sought to coerce all whom he valued into reading the great Russian's writings, far too little weight has been placed on his relations with a writer who exerted the same sort of revelatory, even fateful influence on him as Beethoven did on Wagner and as Kleist did on Hebbel. Anyone who has genuinely responded to Dostoevsky will have a different attitude to Mahler's music – at least to his first four symphonies – than was formerly the case.[21]

Mahler's grief at the world's suffering, his search for consolation and spiritu-
ality, and his constant quest for an answer to the question as to how one could
be happy as long as a single creature suffered on earth – all of this drew its
intensity from his reading of Dostoevsky, which appears to date from his decisive years in Hamburg. If Goethe was his preferred reading towards the end of
his life, when he adopted a philosophical approach to the Sage of Weimar's
writings, and if Jean Paul preoccupied him during the intellectual turmoil of
his adolescence, then Dostoevsky left his mark on Mahler chiefly during his
thirties, when he encouraged all who were close to him to share his enthusiasm
for the Russian novelist. Bruno Walter was made aware of this state of affairs
when Mahler's sister, Emma, suddenly asked him: 'Who's right, Alyosha or
Ivan?' To her surprise, Walter, who did not yet know the novel, failed the test.
The American pianist Olga Samaroff, who married the conductor Leopold
Stokowski, once sat next to Mahler at a dinner held by the Steinways in New
York. Her attempts to engage him in conversation proved unsuccessful and
seemed even to make him more uncivil than ever until she remembered that
prior to the meal she had seen him take down a copy of *The Brothers
Karamazov* from his hosts' bookcase. Very fond of the novel herself, she none
the less wanted to provoke Mahler and, feigning innocence, asked him
whether he did not think that the book was much overrated. That saved the
evening, at least for Mahler and Olga Samaroff, as he spent the next few hours
convincing her of the novel's merits.

   The great conversation between Ivan and Alyosha to which Emma Mahler
was referring and that occurs in Book Five, immediately before the legend
about the Grand Inquisitor, revolves around some of Dostoevsky's central
concerns during the final years of his life. The earlier implacable analyses of a
life without God and without transcendence are now offset by Alyosha's belief
in the Resurrection, and there is no doubt that Mahler must have been struck
by the idea of the immortality of the human soul in the writings of an author
branded at the time as a misanthropic pessimist. It is an idea that may also be
seen as the basis of his own view of the world and as the source of his belief in
entelechy, the vital principle that guides the development of an organism and
that also causes the emotional force of a creative artist to be rekindled in his
work – it was very much this that later struck him about Goethe's writings. In
short, Mahler was bound to recognize himself in a part of Ivan's character, the
inner divisions of which were laid bare in this conversation with his brother
when he says that he must reluctantly acknowledge the existence of God but is
not prepared to acknowledge the world that this God created. And then comes
the central passage on the world's suffering, a passage from which Mahler drew
his answer to his own oft-cited question, 'How can one be happy as long as a
single creature suffers on earth?':

I am convinced that our sufferings will be healed and smoothed away, that the whole offensive comedy of human conflict will disappear like a pathetic mirage, like the infamous fabrication of the Euclidean human mind, as weak and undersized as an atom, and that ultimately, during the universal finale, at the moment of eternal harmony, there will occur and become manifest something so precious that it will be sufficient for all hearts, for the soothing of all indignation, the redemption of all men's evil-doings, all the blood that has been shed by them, will be sufficient not only to make it possible to forgive but even to justify all the things that have happened to men – and even if all that, all of it, makes itself manifest and becomes reality, I will not accept it and do not want to accept it.[22]

But Mahler believed that Alyosha was right: he not only knew and hoped that this was the case, he also acknowledged it in order to be able to endure the world's suffering and to give it artistic expression.

Mahler was attracted not only to the more philosophical writers, he could also work up considerable enthusiasm for E. T. A. Hoffmann, and there is no doubt that he discussed Hoffmann with Ferruccio Busoni, who was an expert on the subject. Certainly, we know that Mahler read the 'ghostly' Hoffmann at an early age, later emphasizing the fact that Hoffmann had achieved greatness as a music journalist and critic. Individual poems by Hölderlin, including 'The Rhine', excited Mahler's admiration, while he also evinced great affection for Clemens Brentano's fairytale *Gockel, Hinkel and Gackeleia*, which his daughter Anna later recalled him reading to her on frequent occasions. Anyone who likes Jean Paul, with his exceptionally profound approach to the theory of humour, is also bound to enjoy the other great humorists of world literature, and this was certainly true of Mahler, whose own caustic sense of humour was whetted by his reading of Sterne's *Tristram Shandy*, Dickens's *The Pickwick Papers* and Cervantes's *Don Quixote*. Whenever he read the episode of the windmills to his family and friends during his summer holidays, his laughter would often prevent him from completing the passage, so much did he enjoy the comic situation, while also deriving new strength from Don Quixote's idealism – for who can doubt that his own life was also a struggle with the sails of manifold windmills, both as director of several opera houses and, even more so, as a composer?

It is no accident that it is one of Jean Paul's aphorisms that brings to an end this portrait of Mahler as a reader:

How different and how wonderful is the friendship that can be forged with printed people – books – rather than with real ones! How loyally attached to us they remain when all else falls away, and how infinitely they can console us! How they are always the same, criticizing our weaknesses without committing weaknesses of their own! – And why should I not bring friends with me from the previous world, even though they have lost their bodies, but which contain all that is genuine, their soul? These friends alone have no sense of time, no self-interest, they are intimately related to us, part of our soul, two souls within one body.[23]

Becoming Mahler: Prague
(1885–6)

THE MONTHS THAT passed between the premature end of Mahler's Kassel engagement in the summer of 1885 and the start of his new appointment in Leipzig in the autumn of 1886 seemed initially as if they would be no more than an embarrassing but necessary interlude in his life, and yet in the event they turned out to be an exceptionally important year in his career. 'I am on the point of, as they say, making a name for myself,' he told his friend Friedrich Löhr in early July 1885, following a brief trip from Iglau to Prague to sort out the necessary arrangements.[1] His Prague contract must have been concluded by the end of May, although it was not announced by the local press until 5 June – presumably Mahler did not want the newspapers mentioning his name once again only weeks after the announcement of his Leipzig appointment, but on this occasion in the context of another city.

Theatrically speaking, the situation in Prague was confused at this time. Mahler had already spent a miserable few months in the city when he was eleven and had boarded with the Grünfelds, a family that was to produce two eminent instrumentalists, the pianist Alfred Grünfeld and his cellist brother, Heinrich. Heinrich, who was five years older than Mahler, later published his memoirs, from which it emerges that even in 1923 he still had little idea who his lodger had been: 'At home I repeatedly found the opportunity to make music with like-minded individuals, including a pale, slim youth who was boarding with my parents and who struck me in particular because of his shock of pitch-black hair. Otherwise none of us thought that there was anything remarkable about him. He was studying music in Prague and was modesty personified. His name was Gustav Mahler.'[2] This is the only reference to Mahler in the whole of Grünfeld's book. But it is by no means untypical of the public perception of Mahler in the 1920s. When Mahler returned to Prague in 1885 – presumably for the first time since 1872 – he was twenty-five years old and a completely different person, for he was now a young conductor with excellent prospects, arriving in the second-largest city in the Austro-Hungarian Empire (it now numbered 280,000 inhabitants), albeit one increasingly shaken by nationalist divisions between its Czech and German populations: by their own estimation, three-fifths were Czech and two-fifths were German-Austrian, although the linguistic disparity between the two groups was even greater, for some 80 per cent spoke Czech, whereas only 20 per cent spoke German even though this was the official language.

Mahler's new post was at the Royal German Regional Theatre – the Landestheater – whose new director, Angelo Neumann, was also joining the company at this time. Neumann was one of the most colourful theatrical figures in the second half of the nineteenth century. A native of Vienna, he began his career as a baritone, even appearing at the Vienna Court Opera, but he soon became an impresario. While still working as a singer in Vienna, he had taken part in Wagner's own productions of *Tannhäuser* and *Lohengrin* and become an enthusiastic Wagnerian, while also, no doubt, recognizing the box-office appeal of the composer's operas. With the exception of Wagner himself, no one did as much as Neumann at this time to promote Wagner's works. In Leipzig, where he ran the local opera company from 1876 to 1882, Neumann performed all of Wagner's operas, including the *Ring*, which he staged between April and September 1878. In 1882 he took the whole of his Leipzig company to London for four cycles of the work. Later that year he left Leipzig and formed his own touring company, the 'Richard Wagner Theatre', which was a kind of peripatetic Bayreuth Festival featuring some of the Festival's leading artists. (The theatre at Bayreuth itself remained dark from 1876 to 1882.) Wagner was forced to admit that Neumann, a Jew, had done a lot to further his cause and that, like most Jews at this period, he did not take his anti-Semitism amiss. Neumann later published his memoirs, including in them a number of the letters that passed between him and Wagner. He took over as director of the Prague Landestheater at the start of the 1885/6 season and, like Mahler, was therefore new to the company. Unlike Mahler, he was to remain there for many years and end his career in the city. The company was housed in the building now known as the Tyl Theatre. It had opened as long ago as 1783, when it had been called the Count Nostitz National Theatre. It was here, for example, that *Don Giovanni* had received its legendary first perform-ances in 1787, an event whose centenary was to be commemorated soon after Neumann and Mahler took up their new appointments.

Throughout the nineteenth century the theatre was at the centre of musical life in Prague, while at the same time encapsulating all the problems bound up with the coexistence of Germans and Czechs in this part of the Empire. Over the course of many decades plays and opera performances in Czech were increasingly marginalized, although in the case of the opera, there was of course still only a limited repertory. In the eyes of the city's German speakers, the Czech-speaking population belonged to the lower orders, their language dismissed as 'kuchelböhmisch', in other words, a Bohemian dialect spoken by kitchen maids. Performances in Czech were given in the afternoons, while the evenings were reserved for German plays and Italian operas. This increasing tendency of the two factions to drift apart culminated in 1862 in the founding of a Provisional Theatre at a time of incipient Czech nationalism. (It was here that Smetana worked from 1866 to 1874 and here, too, that *The Bartered Bride* was first performed in 1866.) In 1881 the Národní Divadlo or National Theatre opened its doors with a performance of Smetana's *Libuše*. Although the house burnt down later that same year, it was rebuilt within two years thanks to an impressive fund-raising campaign on the part of the city's Czech population. Since then it has been a shrine to Czech opera. A year after Mahler's departure from Prague, a second major house (the German Theatre was a small house on a Rococo scale) was opened. Now known as the Smetana Theatre, the New German Theatre performed German works under Neumann's direction and was intended as a counterweight to the Czech National Theatre. Mahler probably spoke no more than a few words of broken Czech but was still sufficiently open-minded to pay the occasional visit to the Czech Opera and see works by Smetana, Dvořák and Fibich. Whereas we now tend to rate Dvořák more highly than the 'more primitive' Smetana, Mahler felt greater enthusiasm for the latter, whose works he could not have heard in Vienna but which he later went on to champion. Neumann remained director of the German Theatre until his death in December 1910, only a few months before Mahler's own death.

Mahler was therefore working for a company with a long-established tradition, excellent singers and a decent orchestra. Above all, he soon found himself in a situation with which he could not have reckoned but which, completely unexpectedly, allowed him at least provisionally to realize his ambitions and to conduct the great works of the mainstream repertory, above all the operas of Gluck, Mozart and Wagner. He owed this in the main to Anton Seidl, who had worked with Neumann for many years and who was widely regarded as the leading Wagnerian conductor after Hans Richter and Hermann Levi. (In 1897 he was even allowed to conduct *Parsifal* in Bayreuth.) Seidl had assisted Neumann on all his Wagnerian projects, but within weeks of the latter's taking up his appointment in Prague, Seidl had broken the terms of his contract and gone to New York to assume control of the Wagner repertory at the Metropolitan Opera. Mahler having made his Prague debut with a gala performance of Cherubini's *Les Deux Journées* held to mark the emperor's birthday and having impressed Neumann with his fiery conducting, the way was now open for him to conduct all Wagner's major works in Prague. (His close contemporary, Karl Muck, who was to conduct *Parsifal* at every Bayreuth Festival from 1901 to 1930, did not join the company until the following season.) Mahler had in fact made contact with Neumann while he was still in Kassel and had been engaged on the strength of a meeting. He moved to Prague on 13 July 1885, taking rooms initially at 24 Rittergasse and later at 18 Langegasse, where he shared a flat with the Swedish bass Johannes Elmblad. Neumann had evidently bought a pig in a poke when signing up Mahler, but it soon turned out that his trust was not misplaced, and, having proved himself in *Les Deux Journées* (as always performed at this time in the German-speaking world as *Der Wasserträger*), Mahler proved no less adept in *Das Rheingold* and *Die Walküre*, which received their local premières on 19 and 20 December 1885. Thanks to his excellent connections, Neumann was able to use the sets that had been designed by Joseph Hoffmann for the Bayreuth performances in 1876 and that had been executed in the Coburg studios of Max and Gotthold Brückner. He also had access to the costumes, weapons and props designed for Bayreuth by Carl Emil Doepler.

In this way Prague's German Theatre became a sort of winter Bayreuth and in this guise it enjoyed considerable success, not least as a result of the fact that Mahler was able to conduct not only *Das Rheingold* and *Die Walküre* but also *Tannhäuser* and *Die Meistersinger von Nürnberg*, and because the company was able to draw on the talents of a more than respectable Wagnerian ensemble. The Wagnerian tenor Adolf Wallnöfer was already embarked on a distinguished career that was later to take him to the Met. (He was also a composer in his own right and a well-known recitalist for whom Brahms, among others, wrote songs.) The soprano Laura Hilgermann was still singing smaller roles in Prague, but Mahler later engaged her at the Budapest Opera and later still at the Vienna Court Opera, where she enjoyed a major career. And Johannes Elmblad, a good-natured giant of a man who shared rooms with Mahler in the city, sang Fafner, Hunding and Hagen in the Prague *Ring*, later becoming one of the most sought-after Wagnerian basses of his day. And finally there was Betty Frank. As a coloratura soprano, she was suited to only a handful of Wagnerian parts but she was an outstanding interpreter of coloratura and lyric roles in operas from Mozart to Meyerbeer. Above all, she was the love of Mahler's life in Prague, prompting him to write to Fritz Löhr in early December 1885: 'I keep stumbling from one idiocy into another. In this short pause I have landed myself in something it will take a long time to get out of',[3] suggesting that after the whirlwind of his affair with Johanna Richter in Kassel, he was now expecting something similar with Betty Frank. But these negative expectations failed to materialize.

Betty Frank hailed from Breslau. She herself claimed that she had been born in 1864, making it likely that the true date was somewhat earlier and that she was the same age as Mahler. She had studied in Paris with the famous Mathilde Marchesi, who had been friendly with Rossini, and had in this way borne witness to the tail end of the bel canto tradition of the late eighteenth century. Unlike Mahler, Betty Frank was already a star when she came to Prague, but her career ran along rather less auspicious lines than Mahler's. She became involved in a lengthy running battle with Neumann but remained in Prague and found herself increasingly sidelined. Other singers were given preference and she was compared with visiting stars such as Sigrid Arnoldson. She later tried to move to the Vienna Court Opera, but her attempts were unsuccessful, and in 1891 she finally took her leave of the German Theatre in Prague. She was still in her early thirties, but her career was effectively over. She married and had a child, and it is possible that her voice suffered as a consequence. After the First World War her name appears only as a singing teacher at one of Berlin's conservatories. With that, we lose all trace of her and do not even know when she died.[4] The only surviving portrait of her shows a small woman tending to portliness but with a mischievous expression in her eyes.

When Löhr visited Prague in January 1886, he discovered that Mahler was so overwhelmed with his work that he had little time to be sociable or to enjoy himself. As for Betty Frank, one has the impression that the relationship soon cooled and that by the time Mahler left Prague, it was all over. At all events, the two seem not to have seen each other again. Back in 1885, the liaison was manifestly the only distraction that he allowed himself. The numerous new operas that he had to conduct took up the rest of his time, and the bohemian lifestyle that he had adopted in Kassel gave way to a much more rigorous regime. Not only Wagner demanded his undivided attention, so too did *Don Giovanni*, *Fidelio*, *Norma*, *Le nozze di Figaro*, *Die Entführung aus dem Serail*, Marschner's *Hans Heiling* and Goldmark's *Die Königin von Saba* – all of them notoriously difficult works to conduct and nearly all of them first perform-ances for Mahler. It is no wonder, then, that none of the letters that Mahler wrote during his months in Prague even so much as mentions the beauties of the city, let alone its distinguished history – the court of Rudolf II, Rabbi Löw, the Golem and the secrets of the ancient Jewish cemetery. None of these played any part in Mahler's life. Rather, he missed his friends and had no opportu-nity to commune with like-minded individuals, who almost certainly did not include Betty Frank and Johannes Elmblad.

Mahler took care to ensure that he now looked to be fully mature and an artist to be reckoned with. When he arrived in Kassel, he still had a bushy black beard. There are young people who, no matter what they intend, look even younger with a beard, and in 1883 Mahler was one such person. In Kassel, it is clear from photographs taken in 1884 that he shaved off his beard and never wore one again, preferring a kind of handlebar moustache instead. In Prague, this handlebar moustache was reduced yet further to the usual close-cropped moustache, a development trailed by Mahler in one of his letters to Löhr. During his summer holidays in later life he occasionally reverted to this particular display of facial hair. As a conductor, Mahler was a sensation in Prague, and Neumann was initially proud of his skills as a talent scout, not least because he had already discovered Arthur Nikisch, with whom Mahler was to have a problematical relationship the following season in Leipzig. As Neumann later recalled, both he and Seidl felt that the young Mahler 'moved about too much when he was conducting, and in this way reminded us strongly of Bülow', whose nervous, fidgety manner was equally notorious and by no means uncontroversial. This is an interesting observation, as it remained a basic reproach throughout the whole of Mahler's career as a conductor and was later invested with an anti-Semitic subtext – a kind of *mauscheln* of the podium.

Another recurrent theme dates from this period, for it was in Prague that we first find the origins of the expression 'tradition is slovenliness' ('Tradition ist Schlamperei'), a phrase attributed to Mahler and usually believed to refer to the Vienna Court Opera Orchestra or, rather, the Vienna Philharmonic but which was in fact coined in Prague. Its full form reads: 'What you call tradition is mere convenience and slovenliness for you.' Mahler first conducted *Don Giovanni* on 6 September 1885 in the house where it had received its first performance in 1787. It was a piece, he believed, that the people of Prague had never really understood. That same day he wrote to his family in Iglau:

> It is a foregone conclusion that the papers, and especially the *Tageblatt*, will pounce on me, for I can tell you in advance that they will all cry 'Woe, woe, "Tradition" has gone to the devil.' By 'tradition' they mean the time-honoured (i.e., slovenly) way of staging a work. I have not let it bother me in the least, and shall quietly go my *own* way this evening.[5]

For the most part, this remained Mahler's maxim in life. He was resolved quietly to go his own way, and in Prague this attitude paid dividends. Most of the major reviews that have come down to us give at least a vague indication that here was an extremely gifted conductor, a point that emerges with particular clarity from the reports of the benefit concert that Mahler gave on 21 February 1886, when he conducted Beethoven's Ninth Symphony. The first part of the concert – a piece of programming that is almost inconceivable by today's standards – had featured the Dawn Duet from the Prelude to *Götterdämmerung* conducted by one of Mahler's colleagues and followed by excerpts from Act One of *Parsifal* under Mahler himself. The review that appeared in *Bohemia* deserves to be quoted at length as it is the first to give any clear indication not only of Mahler's particular style of conducting but also of his tremendous memory, which allowed him to conduct both the Wagner excerpts and the Beethoven symphony without a score, a feat almost unprecedented at this period. Also worth noting are the ways in which Mahler shaped the music with his hands and his ability to invest it with an unheard-of vitality thanks to the living, breathing tempo modifications generally referred to as 'rubato':

> Herr Mahler conducted both the long extract from *Parsifal* and the symphony from memory, a magnificent testimony to his detailed knowledge of the two works. He shaped every nuance in the air with his hands, recalling the tradition of the peculiar manner of conducting the religious choral music of the Middle Ages, which included shaping the melody by movements and gestures of the hand. It was universally recognized that Herr Mahler's conducting showed every part of the work to its best advantage. He subtly and artistically brought out the colouring of the first movement by stressing certain notes by means of crescendi and diminuendi and by a careful use of light and shade. By his choice of a moderate tempo for the passages in $3/4$ time he introduced a brilliant contrast into the second movement and made a clear-cut distinction between the adagio and the yearning of the D major episode.[6]

There is no doubt that in Prague, Mahler was already developing into the greatest conductor of his age and was finally becoming aware of this fact by being tested by the greatest works of the operatic repertory and by the reactions of critics and audiences alike. Friedrich Löhr, who probably knew Mahler better than anyone else at this time, attended this concert and wrote to an unknown correspondent afterwards, not only acknowledging Mahler's gifts as a conductor but also revealing an even deeper understanding of Mahler as a person: 'Now I must say that Mahler's conducting gave me enormous pleasure. You will not believe how great and mature and enthralling his conducting is; there is no longer any trace of fidgetiness, and he combines overwhelming energy with youthful fire.'[7] Even though Mahler had had a terrible row with Angelo Neumann immediately before the concert (the argument evidently concerned his choice of tempi in the ballet in Gounod's *Faust*, which had caused the dancers to stumble), he got his way and received an apology from Neumann, an apology that represented a triumph for the inexperienced young conductor over an ambitious impresario who was known throughout Europe. It is no wonder that Mahler suddenly lost the desire to go to Leipzig and to leave Prague after only a single season. It had also become clear to him that in view of his abilities and ambitions it was inevitable that in Leipzig he would come into conflict with Nikisch, who was his elder by five years and who was generally regarded as Leipzig's star conductor. And so he tried to persuade the director of the Leipzig Opera, Max Staegemann, to release him from his contract. But Staegemann had of course realized that with Mahler he would be gaining a talented new conductor. He had no intention of releasing Mahler from his contractual obligations. In April, Mahler also had an opportunity to perform some of his own music in Prague, when, at a further benefit concert, Betty Frank sang three of his early songs – 'Frühlingsmorgen', 'Hans und Grete' and 'Ging heut morgen über's Feld', the last of them from the *Lieder eines fahrenden Gesellen*. In early July he conducted performances of works by two of his household gods, Gluck's *Iphigénie en Aulide* in Wagner's adaptation, and, for the first time in his life, Beethoven's *Fidelio*, a work that he was later to stage in Vienna with Alfred Roller as his designer. The season came to an end for Mahler on 15 July. It had initially been a stopgap or interim solution for him, but in the end it proved a decisive turning point in his career as a conductor and opera director. After a short break in Iglau he set off for Leipzig on 25 July. The 1886/7 season was due to begin in early August. With so little time to rehearse, there was a sense of urgency bordering on panic.

The First Symphony

ALTHOUGH WE KNOW exactly when the First Symphony was finished, it is unclear when Mahler first thought of writing it and when he began to plan it in connection with his four *Lieder eines fahrenden Gesellen*, two of which are quoted in it. But it could have been in 1884 or 1885. The bulk of his work on the score, however, dates from the early months of 1888. By now Mahler was working at the Leipzig Opera. He wrote to his best friend, Friedrich Löhr, at the end of March 1888:

> Well! My work is finished! Now I should like to have you by my piano and play it to you! Probably you are the only person who will find me unchanged in it; the others will doubtless wonder at a number of things! It has turned out so overwhelming it came gushing out of me like a mountain torrent! This summer you shall hear it! All of a sudden all the sluice-gates in me opened! Perhaps one of these days I shall tell you how it all happened![1]

Unfortunately Mahler never made good this promise, at least in writing. His First Symphony is a tempestuous, urgent, rebellious work, the composer's first contribution to the medium and without doubt the boldest symphonic visiting card in the whole history of western music. According to Natalie Bauer-Lechner, the explosive outpouring that produced the piece lasted a mere six weeks and was closely bound up with Mahler's love for Marion von Weber, a point that Mahler merely hinted at when discussing the work's origins with Natalie but to which he admitted with astonishing candour when speaking to the Berlin critic Max Marschalk. In his analysis of the work, which was published in 1896 and, as such, the first in a whole series of analyses of the composer's symphonies, Marschalk mentioned a 'love affair' which, he claimed, provided the work with a kind of 'content'. Mahler gave his blessing to Marschalk's introduction, thanking him for it profusely, while stressing the fact that the content did not originate in his affair: in his own emotional life the relationship had preceded his work on the symphony but was certainly not its all-decisive starting point.

Mahler's relationship to his First Symphony was a complicated one. Not only was its period of creative incubation unusually long, he was also uncertain what to call the piece. Or perhaps we could say that it took an unusually long time for him to decide what the work actually was. This is the piece that first allowed him to engage with his concept of programme music and with the whole idea of programmes for symphonic music, a point that can merely be summarized here. At its first performance in Budapest in November 1889, the work was still described as a 'Symphonic Poem in Two Parts'. Although the two parts did not as yet have independent titles, the five movements were given the following headings: 1. Introduction and Allegro comodo; 2. Andante (later described as 'Blumine', this movement was removed – definitively – at the time of the work's Berlin première in 1896); 3. Scherzo; 4. A la pompes funèbres; and 5. Molto appassionato. For the Hamburg performance in October 1893, Mahler subjected the work to a thorough revision and discarded the term 'Symphonic Poem', a decision that no doubt reflected his awareness of the problems associated with it: after all, it implied a debt to the model established by Liszt, who had sought to establish the genre as an alternative to the traditional symphony, an orchestral work with a programme and a basic poetic idea to it, Liszt's *Tasso* of 1849 being seen as the natural successor of Berlioz's *Symphonie fantastique* of 1830.

Above all, Mahler's younger colleague and rival, Richard Strauss, had been launched on his remarkably successful career as a composer of symphonic poems with *Don Juan*, which had received its first performance in 1890, only a year after the Budapest première of Mahler's First Symphony. But Mahler was now keen to distance himself from Strauss's piece, with which his own composition had little in common. Still virtually unknown as a composer, he needed to see a stretch of clear blue water between the two works. But he still seems to have been reluctant to use the word 'symphony', and it was not until the Berlin performance of 1896 that this term first appears and not until the first printed edition of 1899 that the work was described as its composer's 'First Symphony'. Much could be written on the reasons for Mahler's reluctance to use the term 'symphony'. Quite clearly he was anxious not to impose unduly restricting shackles on himself and to burden himself with the weight of the Beethovenian symphonic tradition that had culminated in the Ninth Symphony. He knew how long Brahms had hesitated before writing his first symphony and he may also have been familiar with Brahms's famous comment, made with reference to Beethoven: 'I'll never write a symphony. You've no idea what people like me feel like when they can hear a giant like him constantly striding along behind them.' Although the actual wording of this remark may not have been known to Mahler, its essence was felt by all the young musicians of the 1870s and 1880s. This also explains the scope of the term 'new symphony' that Mahler later applied to himself and Hans Rott. For the present, however, he believed that by using the terms 'symphonic poem' and 'tone poem' he was giving himself substantially greater freedom. At the same time, Mahler himself claimed that in his first great tone painting (*Das klagende Lied* was something entirely different) he had also attempted to learn the lessons of the Wagnerian music drama. Meanwhile, he was becoming increasingly aware of the differences between his own works and Strauss's subsequent symphonic output. Perhaps, too, he was assailed by self-doubts as to whether his art of instrumentation was equal to a work of this length. Even as late as December 1909, when he conducted his early symphony for the last time in New York, he made further revisions to the score both before and after the performance, still dissatisfied with the result. *Don Juan* was called a 'tone poem for large orchestra'. In Hamburg in 1893, Mahler showed a certain boldness in using the same word ('Tondichtung') for his own piece, but added the phrase 'in symphonic form', an addition sanctioned by the fact that whereas Strauss's work was in a single movement, his own was in five.

In Hamburg, Mahler also added the heading 'Titan', a title that continues to this day to puzzle writers on the subject. The first part (the first three movements, including 'Blumine') was additionally headed ' "From the Days of Youth": Flower-, Fruit- and Thorn-Pieces', inevitably inviting comparisons with Jean Paul and his novel *Titan*, as every half-educated person at this time knew that Jean Paul had written a novel with this title and that the same writer's *Siebenkäs* – one of Mahler's favourite books – had the typically whimsical subtitle of 'Flower-, Fruit- and Thorn-Pieces or Married Life, Death and Wedding of the Advocate of the Poor, Firmian Stanislas Siebenkäs'. Even the strange title 'Blumine', although it does not come directly from Jean Paul, is undoubtedly related to his 'Flower Pieces'. In 1900, when he was preparing the work for its Viennese première, Mahler discussed the work at some length with Natalie Bauer-Lechner and in doing so denied any connection with Jean Paul. All that he had had in mind, he insisted, was a powerfully heroic individual, including his life and sufferings and his struggle in the face of a fate to which he eventually succumbed: 'The true, higher redemption comes only in the Second Symphony.'[2] Mahler had no reason to deny Jean Paul's influence, and so we would do well to believe Natalie's account, at least from the perspective of 1900 – whether he thought of the novel in 1888 or was still thinking of it in 1893 must remain an open question.

The Hamburg performance is noteworthy from a further point of view, for not only did the work now have a poetic title but this was the first and last time that the programme booklet included an 'explanation' of the work's 'content', Mahler evidently feeling that he could not trust the work to create an impression unaided. In summary, the programme was as follows. The opening movement was headed 'Spring without End' and described nature waking up from a long winter sleep. The second movement was still the Andante, but now – for the first time – it was called 'Blumine'. The third movement was a Scherzo headed 'In Full Sail'. Part Two was titled 'Commedia humana' after Dante and began with a 'Funeral March in the manner of Callot'. (Mahler had been introduced to the work of the French humorist and illustrator Jacques Callot by E. T. A. Hoffmann, who refers to him many times in his writings.) It bore the title 'Aground!' In the longest of the explanations that he appended to this programme, Mahler referred to a parodistic woodcut, 'The Hunter's Funeral Procession', that was familiar to every child in Austria. In it, the animals of the forest can be seen accompanying a huntsman's coffin. At the head of the procession is a group of Bohemian musicians. (In 1850 Moritz von Schwind made a famous engraving of this image in which the musicians themselves are animals.) The fifth and final movement is headed 'Dall'inferno' – another allusion to Dante – while the tempo marking is 'Allegro furioso'. This programme was never again used in this form. Occasionally we find references to 'the so-called Titan', but eventually these too disappear as Mahler distanced himself from anything that might resemble a programme. It was not, however, a question of rejecting particular ideas that might help to explain what was effectively inexplicable, for in his conversations with Natalie Bauer-Lechner in Vienna in 1900 there are still many such ideas, and interpretations of this and other works cannot avoid them altogether. But Mahler had been forced to realize that the sort of ideas he could entrust to his intimates were not suitable for any wider dissemination. Regardless of Jean Paul, the hero of the First Symphony is not one to whom we can give a name as we can to Strauss's *Till Eulenspiegel* or *Don Quixote*.

In two important letters to the Berlin critic Max Marschalk, with whom he was friendly, Mahler expressed his views on the problem of programmes and of programme music. Both letters were written in the wake of the Berlin performance of 1896. Marschalk was familiar with the Hamburg introduction and wanted to know why the work was now described simply as a 'Symphony in D major for large orchestra', why it was no longer divided into two parts, with corresponding headings, and why it no longer had a main title 'Titan'. Mahler replied with a candour that he was to demonstrate at no subsequent period in his life, as he grew increasingly mistrustful of critics. The Hamburg programme, he explained, had been written at the urging of his friends in order to make the piece more comprehensible, but unfortunately he had soon come to realize that such a programme contributed little to its understanding and much to its obfuscation. In symphonic music, he went on, there were of course programmes: even Beethoven's symphonies had such 'inner programmes', but these could be explained only by the audience's increasing familiarity with the works in question and had nothing to do with anything that might appear in any programme booklet. In a second letter that he sent to Marschalk only a few days later, Mahler adopted an even more emphatic tone: 'I know that, so far as I myself am concerned, as long as I can express an experience in words I should never try to put it into music. The need to express myself musically – in symphonic terms – begins only on the plane of *obscure* feelings, at the gate that opens into the "other world", the world in which things no longer fall apart in time and space.'[3] What this means is that Mahler was unable to write music to suit an existing programme, on which point he differed from Strauss. But nor could he provide a programme for an existing piece of music, as he had unfortunately tried to do in Hamburg. Moreover, any work of music must necessarily be based on something that the composer himself has experienced, but by 1896 Mahler had reached the point where he was no longer willing to entrust his acknowledgement of such experiences to the printed page. It was different when explanations showed understanding of the work in question. For new and unusual works such as Mahler's own, such explanations could be useful signposts or celestial maps, especially during the weeks and months immediately after their first perform-ances. One such explanation, in Mahler's view, was Marschalk's analysis of his First Symphony, which Mahler had liked precisely because it was straightfor-ward and had dispensed with poetic and biographical interpretative models.

Mahler took a close interest in the evolving problem of programme music, a problem which in the years around 1900 was a favourite topic with critics, who were equally exercised by the question of the extent to which it was still possible to write operas after Wagner. It was a problem that troubled Mahler greatly, not least because he was forced partly to blame himself for the situa-tion. Time and again he felt the need to sum up his own position. But his approach was never consistent, a point that emerges with some clarity from the programme that he drew up for his Second Symphony and that he distributed among his friends. Mahler often expressed his views on the subject, both in writing and in person. Suffice it to draw attention to an important letter that Bruno Walter wrote in December 1901 to the musicologist and critic Ludwig Schiedermair, who earlier that year could boast of having published the very first book on Mahler. The letter was undoubtedly written at Mahler's instiga-tion. Schiedermair had asked the composer to explain the ideas underpinning his Fourth Symphony, prompting Walter to begin his letter with the bald state-ment that 'Mahler emphatically rejects all programmes'. He then went on to offer an accurate summary of the composer's views:

If we were to wish to put it into words, all that is most profound and most inexpressible in our lives would seem at best like a bad translation but it finds its altogether perfect interpreter in music, whereas, as I have already mentioned, music is never in a position to describe with the same clarity whatever can be accurately described in words, with the result that in programme music it plays a doubly pitiful role, in the first place because it forsakes its own higher realm, which is that of the original life of the emotions (that has no other language) and now becomes incomprehensible in an alien world (that of the individual events) or because at best it stammers semi-incomprehensibly.[4]

In his impotent rage at not being able to escape from the subject, Mahler exclaimed 'Let all programmes perish' following a performance of his Second Symphony in Munich in October 1900, an imprecation that he repeated in a letter to the critic Max Kalbeck.[5] This is all that can be said on the subject.

Mahler himself cited the opening bars of the symphony's first movement as an example of the fact that not everything that gushed out of him like a mountain torrent was instantly fixed for all time. The performance marking at this point in the score is: 'Slow. Dragging. Like a sound of nature.' But it was only while Mahler was rehearsing this passage in Budapest that he was struck by this extraordinary opening for the strings. A normal A played by all the strings entering together sounded far too substantial to express that shimmering and flickering in the air that he was wanting to create here. It was at this point that he thought of the possibility of using harmonics, which are produced when the player touches the string very lightly at certain points along its length, causing it to vibrate in a way that produces a strangely ethereal tone very different from that of its usual frequency. No symphony before Mahler had begun in this altogether remarkable manner. None the less, if we ignore the harmonics, the principle of creating a layer of sound against which the dragging fourths of the winds stand out before the signal-like calls of the clarinets break free from it, is by no means without precedent. After all, the opening movement of Beethoven's Ninth Symphony proceeds along very similar lines, while Mahler was also familiar with a natural description of flickering, shimmering light in Wagner's *Siegfried*. But from these very first bars his handling of this effect is quintessentially Mahlerian. The musical material that Mahler sets forth here, juxtaposing it with apparently paratactical abandon, grows increasingly dense, as if in a jigsaw puzzle gradually assembled from the outer edges to the centre, before being distilled in a clear quotation from the second of the *Lieder eines fahrenden Gesellen*, 'Ging heut morgen über's Feld'. This opening seems to illustrate an important remark that Mahler made to Natalie Bauer-Lechner in 1899: 'Composing is like playing with bricks, continually making new

buildings from the same old stones. But the stones have lain there since one's
youth, which is the only time for gathering and hoarding them. They are all
ready and shaped for use from that time.'[6] Structurally speaking, this opening
movement resembles nothing so much as a set of bricks or stones.

The movement as a whole is structured around a large-scale theme that
Mathias Hansen terms a 'Groß-Thema' and that is formed during the movement's opening section. It is made up of three components, the first of which is
'Ging heut morgen über's Feld'.[7] A weighty march instils in the hero a Dionysian
mood which, as Mahler himself explained, is as yet untroubled and unclouded.[8]
The impulsive forward momentum continues to increase, culminating in what
Adorno and others have termed a 'breakthrough', the moment when the energy
that has been held back breaks loose and there is a sense of a force being
unleashed, a sense that provides a feeling of fulfilment as the physical paragon
of freedom.[9] This is not the place to discuss the complex nature of this concept,
but even the relatively inexperienced Mahlerian can quickly discover the relevant passages and observe the way in which in the later symphonies, too, these
breakthroughs always occur at an exposed point in the score. Such breakthroughs often emerge from march rhythms and their climaxes, recalling the
moment when in the wars of the eighteenth and early nineteenth centuries,
attacking troops would break free from their march rhythm and start to run
towards the enemy, screaming and shouting, drunk on the prospect of victory.
This is the moment of breakthrough in Mahler's symphonies. Adopting a
musicologically more precise definition, Mathias Hansen describes the breakthrough as the moment when the movement's formal structure explodes.[10]

When compared with the opening movement, the two middle movements
are distinctly conventional in character, as if Mahler had been vaguely afraid
that he had gone too far and curbed his own aspirations, confining himself to
a more domesticated environment, especially in the Scherzo whose pounding
dance rhythm recalls the specifically Austrian tradition of Schubert, Bruckner
and their intermediaries. It was only much later that Mahler realized that the
opening bars of the Scherzo are almost identical to those of a Brucknerian
Scherzo, with the result that he altered them slightly for the Vienna performance of 1900 in order to avoid the suspicion of plagiarism. The youth whose
development and desires are expressed in the First Symphony rushes out into
the world at the end of the final movement with a laugh of ebullient high
spirits. Such explanations may legitimately be quoted here, but only when we
bear in mind that they were offered to Natalie Bauer-Lechner within the
context of the Viennese performance. In short, they have nothing of an official
programme about them but are merely private descriptions of experiences
that preceded or accompanied the act of composition. Above all, we must
remember that they date from a period when Mahler had long since

withdrawn all his programmes, including those to the First Symphony. Yet in a way this very circumstance invests them with all the greater significance. In the second movement, this youth blusters through the world with all the greater vigour and earthiness and a correspondingly increased ability to cope with life.[11] The third movement takes as its starting point the popular song known in France as 'Frère Jacques' and in Germany as 'Bruder Martin'. It was this movement that encountered the greatest hostility on the part of Mahler's contemporaries. Even in Vienna in 1900 there were objections to the opening movement (it was customary at this period to react to individual movements, especially in the case of new works).

For its part, the Scherzo was well received, whereas the third movement was greeted with mocking laughter. Over a century ago audiences certainly found it difficult to digest a movement that begins with the rhythm of a funeral march on the muffled timpani and, over it, a *strascinando* double-bass solo playing the theme of 'Frère Jacques'. In this movement, Mahler explained, the hero has already lost his appetite for life because he has found a hair in his soup. Mahler imagined a funeral procession passing in front of the hero at this point in the symphony, its unchanging *pianissimo* avoiding any sense of artifice as the band is supposed to be a poor one, its strains mixing with the screeching and exuberant high spirits of another band of Bohemian musicians that passes by, outside the cemetery walls. The hero certainly sees the bitter irony and implacable polyphony of life in this brutal juxtaposition as the individual sections are assembled using the sort of straight cuts familiar from the cinema. The hero's anguished lament is heard above it all. The dreamily quiet middle section draws on the fourth of the *Lieder eines fahrenden Gesellen*, 'Die zwei blauen Augen von meinem Schatz'. In particular, it is the consoling second section that is used here, 'Auf der Straße steht ein Lindenbaum'. The glumly comic canon then demands its due again, after which it is overlaid by the other elements. The movement ends with a bewildered after-song – Adorno's *Abgesang*.

After only the briefest pause to catch its breath, the work then continues with its fourth and final movement, which begins with what Mahler termed a 'terrible outburst' that indicates the way in which the hero has become caught up in a bitter struggle with the pain and sorrow of the world. 'Time and again,' he explained, 'the hero and, with him, the triumphant motif are struck on the head by fate.' It is only in death that the hero achieves true victory. The victorious youthful theme from the opening movement returns, and the movement ends with a 'glorious victory chorale'. As with the Scherzo, we cannot help but notice that for the last time in Mahler's output this final movement is relatively conventional, a conventionality that has nothing to do with the composer's notorious 'banality'. Formally, too, he relies more heavily on elements of first-movement sonata form, such elements – exposition, development section, recapitulation and often a coda, too – normally being found in the opening movement of a solo sonata, quartet or symphony. In the opening movement of his First Symphony, Mahler had struck out boldly in a new direction, and it seems almost by way of compensation that he sought to ensure that the final movement was more firmly embedded within the existing tradition. But a more detailed analysis would be bound to conclude that however much the formative forces may assert their ability to forge a bond between the disparate elements, they never really succeed in achieving that goal.

Audiences were left largely at a loss by the new work. As a representative of the older generation, the critic Eduard Hanslick shook his grizzled locks in considerable perplexity when he heard the symphony in Vienna in 1900 – only three years earlier he had vigorously championed Mahler's cause as the new director of the Vienna Court Opera: 'As a genuine admirer of Director Mahler, to whom the Opera and the Philharmonic concerts are so profoundly indebted, I do not wish to judge his strange grand symphony with undue haste. But on the other hand, I owe it to my readers to be honest and so I sadly confess that this new symphony belongs to a type of music that in my own view is not music at all.'[12] The first performance in Budapest in 1889 had produced very similar reactions, and the respected conductor was advised to stick to what he did best, interpreting the works of the great composers rather than writing music of his own. In Hamburg, Ferdinand Pfohl, who at this date was still friendly with Mahler, disagreed with the widely held view and saw in the First Symphony an outstanding, inspired work, while regretting that it lacked any sense of overall structure that would have implied a specific goal and a sense of proportion.[13] For a long time, critics – rather than audiences – continued to fret over the First Symphony and to chew over the problem of programme music, taking exception to the cuckoo calls, to the 'Frère Jacques' canon and to the final move- ment, whose mixture of disruptive and conservative elements left them floun- dering. Even by the date of the work's final performance during its composer's lifetime, which Mahler himself conducted in New York in December 1909, the situation remained unresolved, the critic of the *New York Tribune*, for example, complaining that Mahler was a composer of programme music, albeit one unwilling to admit to that fact. He was also 'a naive though unoriginal melodist'.[14] By this date in his career, Mahler no longer had any patience with this and similar criticisms. But he was aware that the performance had elicited little response in its audience, and two days later he wrote to Bruno Walter:

> I myself was pretty pleased with that youthful effort! All these works give me a peculiar sensation when I conduct them. A burning pain crystallizes: what a world this is that rejects such sounds and patterns as something antago- nistic! Something like the funeral march and the storm that then breaks out seem to me like a burning denunciation of the Creator.[15]

Life's Vicissitudes: Leipzig (1886–8)

A ND SO WE come to Leipzig. It was Mahler's first visit to a city whose geographical location and urban landscape could not remotely compare with those of Prague, but as a centre of music it was infinitely more important. Even so, its importance had little to do with Johann Sebastian Bach, whose activities as Thomaskantor and *director musices* from 1723 to his death in 1750 were too remote to have had any deep or lasting influence on the city's musical life, at least beyond the world of religious music. And even by the 1880s the Bach revival still had a long way to go, in spite of the efforts of Felix Mendelssohn, who had directed the famous Gewandhaus Orchestra from 1835 until his death in 1847. It is perhaps worth adding at this point that as a student Mahler had had little contact with Bach's music, and many more years were to pass before he discovered it for himself. The Gewandhaus was arguably the city's greatest musical asset at this time, and both then and now it was certainly more important than the opera. Its principal conductor at the time of Mahler's arrival in Leipzig was Carl Reinecke, who remained the Gewandhaus's music director until 1895, evincing a particular predilection for the music of Brahms, who appeared regularly in the hall both as a pianist and as a conductor. It was here in 1879, for example, that Joseph Joachim gave the first public performance of Brahms's Violin Concerto under the composer's own direction. But the most outstanding figure in the musical life of the city was Mendelssohn, to whom Leipzig additionally owed its conservatory, an institution that moved into its splendid new premises in the Grassistraße in 1887. So crucial was the role played by Mendelssohn and, later, Ferdinand Hiller and Joseph Joachim that in 1869 Richard Wagner, who was born in Leipzig in 1813, used the second edition of his diatribe *Jews in Music* to fulminate against what he called 'the capital of the world of Jewish music'. By the end of the century the Leipzig Conservatory was the country's leading music college, enjoying a reputation far higher than those of Munich and Berlin.

Schumann had once taught there, as had Ignaz Moscheles, Max Reger and Joseph Joachim, while their pupils included musicians of the eminence of Niels W. Gade, Edvard Grieg, Arthur Sullivan, the magnificent if pugnacious Ethel Smyth and, finally, Frederick Delius: as an institution, the Leipzig Conservatory enjoyed a reputation that extended far beyond the country's confines.

Finally, there was the Leipzig Opera, which had found a home for itself in the city's Schauspielhaus in 1766. Its successor, the Neues Stadttheater on the Augustusplatz, opened in 1867 and was designed by the famous Berlin architect Karl Ferdinand Langhans. The orchestra was provided by the Gewandhaus, an arrangement similar to that found in Vienna, where the Vienna Philharmonic also performs in the opera house. Albert Lortzing had worked here, Schumann had conducted the first performances of his opera *Genoveva*, and Angelo Neumann had built up the Wagner repertory before leaving for Prague. Among Neumann's assistants in Leipzig were Anton Seidl, a conductor who, long associated with Wagner's works, followed Neumann to Prague. And then there was Arthur Nikisch, of whom Mahler was not a little afraid but whose challenge to his authority he was none the less determined to see off. Of the many anecdotes about Nikisch, the most famous is no doubt the one about a female member of Berlin's social elite at a time when Nikisch was principal conductor of the Berlin Philharmonic. The woman apparently sat down in one of the front rows in the Philharmonic Hall and, turning to her neighbour, said: 'Please wake me when he starts to become fascinating.' Nikisch certainly had charisma, although this is not clear from his few surviving recordings, which reveal a very matter-of-fact approach to the score. (What would one not give to have a recording of Mahler conducting? His Welte-Mignon piano rolls unfortunately tell us far too little about his work on the podium.) A native of Hungary, Nikisch was five years older than Mahler and had studied in Vienna, before joining the rank-and-file violins of the Court Opera orchestra. He was still only eighteen. If the experience of hearing Wagner conduct Beethoven's Ninth Symphony at the ceremony accompanying the laying of the foundation stone of the Bayreuth Festival Theatre in 1872 etched itself indelibly on his memory, he was no less enthusiastic about Verdi as a conductor when he heard him conduct *Aida* in Vienna in 1875. Nikisch was also gifted as a composer, but such was his fear of being branded a writer of 'Kapellmeister music' that he soon abandoned this alternative string to his bow. He joined the Leipzig Opera as chorus master in 1878, while Neumann was still running the company, and was soon its undisputed principal conductor. On the podium, he was notable for the extreme economy of his gestures, a point that applied to Mahler only in the very last years of his life. His colleague Erich Kleiber later used to wonder how Nikisch was able to unleash such powerful crescendos merely by slowly raising his left hand. Like Mahler, Nikisch left his players considerable latitude in terms of rubato. His secret seems to have been to suggest a whole world of expression by means of the most understated of gestures. Mahler was fully aware of what he might expect in Leipzig. (It is unclear if the two men had met in Vienna.)

Once again we have a chance to observe the skill and sophistication but also the ruthlessness with which Mahler sought to turn the situation to his own advantage. Even while he was still in Prague, he attempted to take soundings and prepare the ground. He was convinced that Nikisch was a 'jealous and capable rival'. But perhaps he himself had cause to be jealous as the younger and less well known of the two?[1] As the young star of Leipzig's musical scene, Nikisch was undoubtedly 'capable', but why should he be jealous of a largely unknown conductor from Prague? Mahler then attempted to persuade the company's director, Max Staegemann, to let him make his debut with *Tannhäuser*, a piece with which he was sure he could make his mark, but his démarche backfired and instead he was offered *Lohengrin*, a work in which the conductor has fewer opportunities to shine, even though it is a much more difficult piece to conduct. When Mahler finally arrived in Leipzig and was able to observe Nikisch at work, he was honest enough to admit that his colleague was an excellent conductor, albeit with an important qualification: 'His conducting often gives me considerable pleasure and so I can watch a performance under him as confidently as if I were conducting it myself – even though the greatest heights and the greatest depths are a closed book to him.'[2] Ultimately, Mahler may have been right, of course, but his verdict seems hasty and far too definitive when we recall what little opportunity he had had to observe his colleague at work. Consumed by his own enthusiasm, he also complained that Nikisch was cold and reserved towards him – but this was only to be expected.

True to form, Mahler lost little time in seeking to take control of the situation, while at the same time overestimating his own abilities – this, too, was symptomatic of a conductor who was convinced of his own youthful genius, even if not everyone shared that view of him. He had been in Leipzig for only three months, and he was already looking for trouble. And so we find him writing to Staegemann and demanding to be allowed to conduct two of the four *Ring* operas alongside Nikisch, brazenly claiming that there had been a tacit agreement between them,[3] an agreement presumably so tacit that Staegemann could not even remember it. But Mahler had certainly not been sold short, for he was allowed to conduct all the major works from Meyerbeer's *Le Prophète* and *Les Huguenots* to Halévy's *La Juive*, a work about which he was hugely enthusiastic. Wagner's *Der fliegende Holländer* and *Tannhäuser* also fell to his fiefdom. But the *Ring* has always been the preserve of a company's principal conductor, and a division of labour is as unusual now as it was in the 1880s. In an attempt to exert more pressure, Mahler even threatened to resign. Matters quickly came to a head. Nikisch received an offer to run the Budapest Opera, although in the event Mahler himself went to Budapest before Nikisch, who did not take up the post there until 1893. Meanwhile, Mahler himself seems to have had three different irons in the fire in the form of offers of work from the Hamburg Opera, the Karlsruhe Opera, where he would have succeeded the self-avowed Wagnerian Felix Mottl, and Prague, where Neumann was trying to lure him back. Later he also received a call from New York, where he was invited to take over Anton Seidl's old position. For some of these offers we have only Mahler's own testimony, but we may well believe him, not least because his reputation as an immensely gifted opera conductor was already beginning to spread with tremendous speed. In the event, the crisis passed. Nikisch did not go to Budapest, and for the present Mahler remained in Leipzig, even contriving to work out a tolerable modus vivendi with Nikisch. During the early months of 1887 Nikisch even had cause to be grateful to Mahler when a pulmonary infection reduced him to weeks of inactivity and Mahler had to take over all his commitments, appearing almost every evening in the pit of the Leipzig Opera.

Never before had Mahler had to work so hard, and it is unlikely that he ever learnt as much professionally as he did in these few short weeks between February and May 1887. He could now show what he was worth in the works that had previously been Nikisch's preserve. He felt that to all intents and purposes he was Nikisch's equal, and in this he was undoubtedly justified. Above all, he was allowed to conduct the whole of the *Ring*, a privilege which only a short time earlier he had fought to achieve for entirely selfish ends. The orchestra liked Nikisch and however much the players may have admired Mahler's abilities, they kept their distance, a distance that was to remain a feature of Mahler's career throughout the rest of his life. He was not the sort of conductor who could quickly gain the affection of his players. There was always more respect and even fear than love. A comment by one of his orchestral players later did the rounds: 'It's as if we'd been plain daft before Herr Mahler came along, as if it had needed him to come from Prague to show us what *piano* means, as if we could never get on without new flashy tricks all the time – if Nikisch doesn't get better soon, the whole orchestra's going to be off sick.'[4] The Leipzig Council records also contain a complaint from the orchestra's committee, asking for the council's 'protection and support' in the face of 'the unworthy way' in which it was allegedly being treated by its new conductor, who was said to be placing 'impossible demands' on them, while those who failed to meet his unreasonably high standards were accused of 'malice and stubbornness'.[5] Mahler could count himself fortunate that his boss,

Max Staegemann, stood by him and protected him. With the thoughtlessness that was typical of him, Mahler even claimed in a letter to Löhr that the battle over control of Leipzig's operatic life would soon be resolved in his favour thanks to his own 'physical superiority. I don't think that Nikisch will stand the pace, and sooner or later he will take himself off.'[6] This was the Darwinian spirit of the age speaking, and Mahler made no secret of his feelings when discussing a colleague he did not like and who was standing in his way – this characteristic, too, is part of our picture of a man who, for all his genius, was often far from philanthropic in his dealings with others. In the event, Mahler's predictions proved unfounded, and Nikisch saw off his rival, leaving Mahler to quit the battlefield in defeat. Nikisch later took over the Gewandhaus Orchestra and, later still, the Berlin Philharmonic, increasingly turning away from opera and concentrating instead on concerts. For his part, Mahler ran three companies, in Budapest, Hamburg and Vienna, and it was only at the end of his life that he became a proper concert conductor in New York. Previously he had conducted concerts only when it was a question of promoting his own works, while his brief stint as principal conductor of the Vienna Philharmonic brought him more annoyance than pleasure. That the 'physically inferior' Nikisch outlived Mahler by more than a decade is another story. Be that as it may, Nikisch and Mahler were the two leading conductors of the years between 1890 and 1911, however remote their fields of activity, so it is a pity that the pressure on them to appear as rivals was so great.

Mahler led a lonely life in Leipzig, where his watchword was 'work, and more work'. It was in any case not in his nature to forge friendships quickly, and, unlike so many other members of opera-house ensembles, he was never the life and soul of the company canteen. The complaints levelled at him by the players were presumably shared by their colleagues among the singers. But if there were singers who he felt were making a serious artistic effort, then he could be cordial and even friendly – this was certainly true of the bass Karl Perron, who sang Ochs in the first performances of *Der Rosenkavalier* in Dresden in 1911, and the young Paul Knüpfer, who went on to become principal bass at the Berlin Court Opera. But if Mahler felt that the singers were pretentious or idle, vain or only superficially interested in their art, he found it almost physically impossible to conceal his revulsion. At no point in his life did he find it easy to admit his indebtedness to others, and in gaining an audience for his own music he had to learn the hard way that it is unwise always to speak one's mind. Once, at a party in Leipzig, a man who played a not unimportant part in the city's musical life and who at this date was certainly more influential than Mahler ventured a mild criticism of one of Wagner's opinions, prompting Mahler to reply, tight-lipped: 'When Wagner has spoken, one holds one's tongue.' Sometimes he managed to cloak his negative views in sarcasm or, at best, irony.

At another party, an ambitious young composer performed a new piece called *Im stillen Tal* (In the Quiet Vale) in the most romantic salonesque style of the period. Mahler suffered unspeakably, but even the other guests realized that the piece had little merit. When the young composer ended his rendition and was greeted by an embarrassed silence, Mahler leapt to his feet and enthusiastically shook the younger man's hand: 'That was the real thing! I recognize the valley, I think I know where it is. It's in Styria! Thank you so much.'

The first person in Leipzig to welcome the recalcitrant Mahler with open arms and accept him into his own family circle was his boss, Max Staegemann, whose two attractive daughters provided an agreeable diversion for Mahler, whose feelings were always easily inflamed, although in the present instance nothing came of it all. In the case of his contact with another local family, by contrast, there were to be far-reaching consequences of both a personal and an artistic nature. The family in question was that of Carl von Weber, a captain in a Leipzig regiment. Mahler had hitherto felt no great affection for members of the military, but Carl von Weber was no ordinary captain, for he was the grandson of Carl Maria von Weber, whose unpublished papers he owned. In 1821 Carl Maria von Weber had worked intensively on an opera, *Die drei Pintos*, that was intended to be his contribution to the comic operas of his age. Although he continued to work on the project between then and his death in 1826, the opera was far from complete. There were musical drafts for seven out of a total of seventeen numbers, although even these were hard to decipher and sketched out in only the most rudimentary form. Of the surviving 1,700 or so bars, only eighteen had been orchestrated. Weber's widow, Caroline, was not very hopeful when she passed on the surviving material to Giacomo Meyerbeer – an early friend of her husband's – and asked him to take it with him to Paris in 1826 and, if possible, complete it. Whatever his reasons, Meyerbeer returned it to Caroline twenty-five years later, without any indication that he had worked on the sketches or even that he had looked through them. Weber's son, Max Maria, made a second attempt to have the opera completed and asked the composer and conductor Vincenz Lachner to undertake the task, only for Lachner, too, to decline the invitation. Mahler, whose great admiration for Weber's music was due in part to the fact that Wagner, too, had set such great store by it, was introduced to Weber and his wife at Max Staegemann's house, and it was not long before he was a regular visitor to the Webers' home as well, the frequency of his visits encouraged not only by Carl Maria's unpublished papers but also by the lady of the house, Marion von Weber, who was four years older than Mahler and the mother of three children aged between six and nine.

Marion von Weber was undoubtedly the first great love of Mahler's life, his violent passion for Johanna Richter and his more temperate infatuation with

Betty Frank being no more than the usual adolescent affairs on the part of a hot-blooded young man. But the present liaison was different, or perhaps it would be more accurate to say that it appears to have been different, for we know even less about the present relationship than we do about its two prede- cessors. Little documentary evidence has survived that would allow us to say much that is certain about the precise course and character of the affair, and yet what evidence there is is irrefutable. Whether or not we may believe every- thing that we read in the reminiscences of the distinguished English composer and suffragette Ethel Smyth, who was a frequent visitor to the Webers' home at this time, will probably never be ultimately established, but her comments on the impression that Mahler made on her appear to be an accurate reflection of her keen-eyed powers of perception and ability to turn an apposite phrase. After all, what she writes is merely a more pointed expression of the impres- sions left on many other of Mahler's contemporaries. She was, she explains, 'too young and raw then to appreciate this grim personality, intercourse with whom was like handling a bomb cased in razor-edges'.[7]

In one of the first letters that he wrote to Friedrich Löhr from Leipzig, Mahler mentions having met 'a beautiful person – the sort that tempts one to do foolish things'. According to Löhr himself, Mahler was referring here to Marion von Weber, and although this is by no means certain, it is not improb- able. Löhr, after all, must have known the true facts of the matter as he was probably the only person at this time with whom Mahler discussed his heartache. Conversely, a second letter from early January 1888 undoubtedly refers to his ménage à trois with Carl and Marion von Weber. The few lines that he writes to Löhr are 'all I can manage now in this trilogy of the passions and whirlwind of life! Everything in me and around me is in a state of *becoming*! Nothing *is*! Let me have just a little longer to see it through! Then you shall know all!'[8] Unfortunately no subsequent letter makes good this promise, and so we remain in the dark. Should we believe Ethel Smyth when she writes that Carl von Weber was robbed of his reason by Mahler's affair with his wife, so much so that he suddenly pulled out his revolver in a train and started taking potshots at the headrests between the seats before being dragged away to an asylum? According to a more credible version of events, the couple planned to elope, but Mahler could hardly have kept his lover in the style to which she was accustomed, quite apart from the problem of her three children. The couple did not elope, therefore, and with Mahler's departure from Leipzig, his passion seems to have waned. None the less, there is no doubt that Mahler's love of Marion von Weber was an important factor in the genesis of his First Symphony, on which he began work in January 1888. The affair seems, more- over, to have been an open secret, Leipzig's artists being prone to gossip, and it is said that Carl von Weber tolerated his wife's affair only out of fear of a scandal that could have cost him his military career. Certainly, it seems remarkable that he did not forbid Mahler to set foot in his house, which he could have done without causing a scandal. Not only the First Symphony, but the swift, even hasty genesis of *Die drei Pintos* was inspired by Marion von Weber. Other composers may have turned down the challenge, but Mahler succeeded in completing the sketches during a few brief weeks in the summer of 1887, a summer additionally interrupted by visits to see his family in Iglau, to Friedrich Löhr in Vienna and Perchtoldsdorf and a walking tour from Bad Reichenhall to Innsbruck, where Mahler met Rudolf and Heinrich Krzyzanowski, with whom he continued his journey on foot to Lake Starnberg.

A private performance of the as yet unfinished score of *Die drei Pintos* took place at Max Staegemann's home on 28 August, and only a few weeks later Staegemann was able to inform Carl von Weber that the score was complete. The opera received its first official performance to loud acclaim at the Leipzig Theatre on 20 January 1888, Mahler himself conducting. Shortly beforehand, Mahler had had an encounter with a younger colleague that was to prove momentous. The twenty-three-year-old Richard Strauss was then the third conductor at the Munich Court Opera. The Gewandhaus Orchestra was performing his early symphony in F minor, and Strauss came to Leipzig for the occasion. Mahler and Strauss were presumably introduced by Max Steinitzer, who was then one of Mahler's few friends in Leipzig and who went on to become a committed Straussian, writing one of the earliest biographies of the Munich-born composer. The encounter must have taken place at around the time of the concert, possibly on 13 October 1887, and it led to contacts between the two composers which, although marked by tensions, lasted until Mahler's death. Their dealings could never be described as a true friendship, for both men were too different in terms of their character and compositional aims, but in their very different ways they felt a mutual respect for each other's work.

Mahler's completion and adaptation of *Die drei Pintos* is an undoubted masterpiece, as readers can judge for themselves following a recording of the work in 1976. In the final years of the nineteenth century the opera enjoyed a tremendous vogue and was staged by many leading companies, although its star then set with equal rapidity. As Natalie Bauer-Lechner noted, Mahler proudly informed his family and friends that large sections of the score were his own work. It had taken him a long time, he explained, to decipher the sketches, which were written in a kind of shorthand, but once he had found the key, everything had proceeded more or less automatically. He had initially been worried that he had, as it were, been commissioned by Weber himself to complete the score, but the more he worked on it, the more confident he became, adopting a freer approach and adding material of his own so that in the end two-thirds of the finished opera could reasonably be said to be by

Mahler, albeit Weberian in spirit. Mahler was hugely amused by the fact that the passages that were most Mahlerian were regarded by the critics as particularly typical of Weber. The work was later described as an opera 'by Mahler out of Weber', a description that is by no means wholly inaccurate. And to the extent that Mahler never wrote another opera – Mahlerians continue to argue over whether this is a good or a bad thing – we must regard *Die drei Pintos* as the composer's particular legacy. When listening to it on a recording, we are bound to wonder why the work is not performed more often. After all, there is hardly such a glut of German comic operas as to justify this neglect.

Mahler spent no more than six weeks completing *Die drei Pintos* and immediately threw himself into a further round of feverish activity, conducting a performance of *Tannhäuser* in the presence of Cosima Wagner on 13 November 1887 that marked the start of her interest in his work. It was an interest that lasted until well after Mahler had moved to Vienna as director of the city's Court Opera. The effect of the performance on her emerges from a letter that she wrote some months later to Hermann Levi. Or perhaps it would be more accurate to refer to the impression left on Cosima by Mahler himself, for there is no doubt that he will have been introduced to her: after all, Cosima's visits to German opera houses resembled nothing so much as state occasions. Levi had evidently drawn her attention to a fellow Jewish conductor as he knew that Bayreuth and, in particular, Cosima Wagner was always on the lookout for talented young musicians. 'I know Kapellmeister Mahler', Cosima replied. 'I heard a *Tannhäuser* of his; the performance was worse than I would have thought possible in the light of all that we now know; but he himself left a not insignificant impression.'[9] Given the circumstances and in the wake of Wagner's pamphlet on *Jews in Music*, this was no mean praise from the composer's widow.

The triumphant opening of *Die drei Pintos* in Leipzig was followed by productions of Weber's 'new' opera in many other houses, the work proving a veritable sensation, while the royalties that Mahler secured for himself provided him for the first time in his life with more money than he required for his immediate needs and for the support of his family in Iglau. A few days after the first night, he met Tchaikovsky, who was attending a performance of *Don Giovanni* in Leipzig – the two men were to get to know each other rather better in Hamburg. In mid-February 1888 he went back to work on his First Symphony, which he completed in a frenzy of inspiration in a matter of only six weeks. In this he was additionally helped by the theatre's ten-day closure following the death of Kaiser Wilhelm I on 9 March 1888. Later, in conversation with Natalie Bauer-Lechner, Mahler adopted a far more discreet tone, speaking of the way in which Marion von Weber's 'musical, radiant and aspiring nature gave my life new meaning'.[10] Natalie, who was herself unhappily and hopelessly in love with Mahler, will have drawn her own conclusions from his unusually effusive expression. 'All of a sudden all the sluice-gates in me opened!' Mahler wrote to Friedrich Löhr in the context of his First Symphony.[11] At no other point in his life did the creative process prove so abrupt and volcanically eruptive.

But it suddenly seemed as if his stay in Leipzig would be brought to a premature end. Perhaps the hopelessness of his feelings for Marion von Weber left him disenchanted with the city and with his work there. Moreover, Nikisch's illness had meant that he had now conducted all the works that interested him, while *Die drei Pintos* had proved a sensation far beyond the city, his reputation as the man who completed Weber's opera for a long time outweighing that of the conductor and composer. But he had failed to achieve one of his principal goals, which was to supplant Nikisch and persuade his rival to move on. One has the impression that Mahler himself may even have provoked the Goldberg Affair that ultimately led to his departure from Leipzig, for only in this way could he find an excuse for behaving as he did towards Max Staegemann, who had welcomed him into his family circle with such warmth and cordiality. Albert Goldberg was the senior stage manager at the Leipzig Opera and according to the company regulations was Mahler's superior. It seems that the two men had a very public row in the course of which Goldberg screamed at his subordinate: 'You won't be conducting here again!'[12] Thus, at least, we gather from Mahler's letter to Staegemann. Mahler sought to interpret this as a dismissal, which it was not, because only Staegemann could dismiss his assistant conductor. But Staegemann had evidently realized that he could no longer keep his young firebrand of a conductor and may also have seen the problems raised by Mahler's association with the Webers. Whatever the answer, Staegemann agreed to Mahler's request, and at the end of May the local newspapers reported on the conductor's dismissal. A few days earlier Mahler had asked to be relieved of all his remaining duties throughout the rest of the season, and this wish, too, was granted. By 17 May 1888 his stimulating and fruitful stint in Leipzig was over.

Within days Mahler had left for Munich, where he met Heinrich Krzyzanowski. The two men then visited Lake Starnberg, as they had done the previous year. Mahler spent the month of June in Iglau and, having broken the symphonic ice, worked on 'Todtenfeier', which was to become the opening movement of his Second Symphony. But he had no new post to look forward to, and as always this made him extremely nervous. He knew what he was worth and what he could do. Nor was he in any doubt about his own genius. Long after he had taken up his post at the Vienna Court Opera, he continued to suffer from a sense of existential anxiety due in part, but not entirely, to the fact that initially he also had to look after his brothers and sisters and, later, his own family. And yet he must have known that in the light of the reputation that he had already acquired, it would be easy for him to find a new post. But his fears outweighed all other considerations. An interim solution presented itself in the form of a part-time contract with his former place of employment in Prague, where he was initially to rehearse and conduct five performances of *Die drei Pintos*, which opened on 18 August. Other work was also envisaged, but here, too, Mahler fell out with his employer, his old patron Angelo Neumann, so that these plans, too, came to nothing. In addition to all these worries, Mahler was also preoccupied with the first performance of his First Symphony. He had realized that it was not the sort of work that would be welcomed with open arms by every court orchestra in the land. With typical skill he exploited his contacts with his 'dear colleague' in Munich, Richard Strauss, and asked whether Hermann Levi, the Court Kapellmeister whose attention had already been drawn to him, might be persuaded to perform the piece. A reply from Strauss has not survived, but we know from a much later account that he and Levi played through the symphony's Funeral March on the piano and that both men were much taken by its originality. Even so, their interest did not lead to a performance of the work in Munich, and it was not until over a year later, on 20 November 1889, that the First Symphony – with 'Blumine' as its second movement – was heard in Budapest, where Mahler had been working since October 1888, following an unexpected offer that he hesitated before accepting.

Notes on Mahler's Songs

MAHLER WAS A composer who did not just write lieder on the side, as Strauss or Wagner did. Nor did he compose only lieder, as his student friend Hugo Wolf did. His emotionally powerful songs stand somewhat apart from those of his contemporaries and of his immediate predecessors such as Brahms, Wolf, Pfitzner and Reger, for all that they reflect his attempts to gain a firmer foothold with his audiences than he was able to achieve with his symphonies. In this he was only partially successful, his songs enjoying a hierarchy of popularity extending from the much-loved *Lieder eines fahrenden Gesellen* at the one extreme to the Rückert Lieder at the other. Mahler's songs stand apart from those of his contemporaries not only by dint of their compositional style but also in their choice of words. The predominance of the *Wunderhorn* poems on the one hand and the poetry of Rückert on the other (no other song composer seems as restricted in his choice of words as Mahler) appeared strange even in Mahler's own day. Even Brahms, who could hardly be described as a keen advocate of the latest trends in literature, set the words of contemporary poets such as Hermann Allmers, Karl Lemcke and Detlev von Liliencron. Strauss, for his part, was at the very forefront of the avant-garde in *his* choice of poets: John Henry Mackay, Otto Julius Bierbaum, Richard Dehmel, Oskar Panizza, Carl Busse, Christian Morgenstern – no composer of Strauss's generation could possibly have done more to promote contemporary poetry. Hans Pfitzner set verse by Dehmel and Ludwig Jacobowski, while only Hugo Wolf reveals a comparably conservative tendency in anthologies such as his *Spanisches* and *Italienisches Liederbuch* and Michelangelo Lieder. Mörike was for Wolf what Rückert was for Mahler, and yet even Mörike was more modern as a poet than Rückert.

A further aspect of Mahler's songs is their dovetailing of the old and the new. None of these songs reveals any of the audacities in their formal design or metrical subtleties or even the harmonic experiments found in his later works. As we have already seen, Mahler was in general no revolutionary keen to explore and extend the language of music. Rather, he used a largely traditional language to express unusual ideas that had previously been thought of as inexpressible. His famous claim that writing symphonies was synonymous with creating a world using all the resources of an existing technique makes sense only if the reader consciously underlines the word 'existing'. The world of Mahler's songs is more limited, 'smaller' and easier to grasp than that of his symphonies, so that the technique involved in writing them is also more restricted. In his symphonies – or at least from the Fifth onwards – he explores the outer limits of his musical world, whereas in his songs he remains well within those confines. But within this context of a certain simplicity in terms of both the material and the musical language, Mahler achieves a degree of expression that comes close to that of his symphonies, especially in his later songs. In Wagner's *Die Meistersinger von Nürnberg*, Hans Sachs broods on Walther's Trial Song: 'It sounded so old, and yet it was new, like birdsong in sweet May.' This same feeling is engendered in the listener by Mahler's songs. Much of what we hear sounds superficially familiar, but the sheer force of the expression then creates an impression that is both strange and deeply disturbing.

And there is something else: the songs and symphonies are related in ways that are sometimes covert and sometimes overt, but with no other composer in the whole history of music are these links as close. It would never have occurred to Brahms, for example, to use material from his many songs in one of his symphonies. For him, the boundaries between the two genres were too strict, just as they were for Beethoven. But for Mahler the situation was altogether different, a point that emerges with particular clarity from those of the later songs that come closest to the symphonies in terms of their sonorities and expressive power. And of no songs is this more true than it is of 'Revelge' and the last of the *Kindertotenlieder*, 'In diesem Wetter, in diesem Braus'. But even in the first four symphonies, which for good reason have been dubbed the *Wunderhorn* symphonies, we can see how even far more innocuous songs may acquire a symphonic weight that had initially seemed improbable. Writers on the later symphonies have repeatedly observed that the *Kindertotenlieder* represent a kind of hidden germ cell. If the fourth of them, 'Oft denk ich, sie sind nur ausgegangen', plays such a key role in the final movement of the Ninth Symphony, a vast power must have been concentrated within its formal confines. *Das Lied von der Erde*, finally, is the culmination of this increasing dovetailing of song and symphony, a process realized in a large-scale song that is subtitled a symphony.[1]

If we ignore Mahler's earliest songs from the period around 1880, his lieder can be divided into three major groups. First, there are the four *Lieder eines fahrenden Gesellen* of 1884–5. Second, there are the songs from *Des Knaben Wunderhorn*, which can be subdivided in turn into three smaller groups: first, the nine early songs that were published in 1892 together with some of the even earlier *Lieder und Gesänge* but which are not part of the corpus of songs generally heard in the concert hall under the title 'Wunderhorn Lieder'; they include 'Ich ging mit Lust durch einen grünen Wald', 'Zu Straßburg auf der Schanz' and 'Scheiden und Meiden'. The second part of this subgroup comprises the more famous *Wunderhorn* songs such as 'Der Schildwache Nachtlied', 'Das irdische Leben', 'Des Antonius von Padua Fischpredigt' and 'Wo die schönen Trompeten blasen'. And the third subgroup is made up of just two songs, the late *Wunderhorn* settings of 'Revelge' and 'Der Tamboursg'sell', both of which date from 1899–1901 and represent the high point of Mahler's enthusiasm for *Des Knaben Wunderhorn*. The third group, finally, comprises the ten Rückert settings, a group that can again be divided into two separate subgroups, namely, the five songs generally known as the Rückert Lieder and the five *Kindertotenlieder*.

The *Lieder eines fahrenden Gesellen* are unlikely to have been written before 1885. At the start of that year, Mahler wrote to his friend Friedrich Löhr from Kassel:

> I've written a cycle of songs, six of them so far, all of them dedicated to her [Johanna Richter]. She doesn't know them. What can they tell her but what she already knows? I'll enclose the final song herewith, although the inadequate words cannot render even a small part of it. – The idea of the songs as a whole is that of a wayfaring man who has been stricken by fate and who now sets forth into the world, travelling wherever his road may lead him.[2]

These lines do not necessarily prove that Mahler had completed these songs by this date, for the opening phrase may simply mean that he had written the words. Certainly, his reference to the 'inadequate words' of the final song would suggest that he was thinking only of the poems here, a suggestion underscored by the mention of six songs: as we know, Mahler set only four of them. Even so, he must have worked on the music in parallel with the poems and completed all four settings in the course of 1885. The words of the first song have given rise to much head-scratching. By his own account, Mahler did not get to know Arnim and Brentano's anthology of *Des Knaben Wunderhorn* until 1887, by which date he was already in Leipzig, and yet, as we have noted, this song already includes verbal borrowings from two dance songs from the collection, borrowings that cannot be the result of mere chance. Perhaps, then, this first song was written somewhat later than the rest. Mahler's achievement becomes all the more striking when we compare his settings with Rudolf Baumbach's successful collection of poems that appeared under the same title in 1878. We do not know whether Mahler knew this anthology, but he may have come across its title, even if he then forgot where he found it. At all events, he evidently had no qualms about taking it over. Baumbach introduces his wayfarer with the lines:

> Bin ein fahrender Gesell,
> Kenne keine Sorgen.
> Labt mich heut der Felsenquell,
> Tut es Rheinwein morgen.
> Bin ein Ritter lobesan,
> Reit auf Schusters Rappen,
> Führ' den lockren Zeisighahn
> Und den Spruch im Wappen:
> Lustig Blut und leichter Sinn,
> Hin ist hin, hin ist hin.
> Amen.[3]

[I'm a wayfaring fellow and have no cares. If the mountain spring refreshes me today, then Rhineland wine will do so tomorrow. I'm a worthy knight and ride on Shanks's pony, I'm a bit of a lad, and the motto on my coat of arms is: Merry blood and carefree mind, what's done is done. Amen].

Baumbach peers through industrially manufactured bull's-eye windows and sees a synthetic world full of wandering scholars and itinerant journeymen in which the different centuries merge according to the whim of the poet, the worlds of medieval minstrelsy and the mail coach entering into a kind of forced marriage. (The song 'Hoch auf dem gelben Wagen' that is still popular today comes from Baumbach's collection.) For his part, Mahler goes back to Wilhelm Müller and Schubert and transforms the verse of *Des Knaben Wunderhorn* into confessional poetry based on personal experience. Its linguistic autonomy may be poorly developed, but there is no denying the immediacy of the experiences in which it is grounded.

In Schubert's cycle, the miller's apprentice announces his delight in travelling the countryside. In Mahler's case this delight is transferred to the wayfarer. There is no doubt that this debt to Schubert's song cycle has played a role in the abiding popularity of Mahler's *Lieder eines fahrenden Gesellen*. Of all his songs, these are the ones that comply most obviously with the formal demands of the traditional German lieder repertory. With their regular form, the first two songs adopt a 'leisurely' tone, whereas the third song – 'Ich hab ein glühend Messer' – is already typically Mahlerian, the wayfarer expressing his jealousy and his unhappiness in outbursts remarkable for their wildly jagged lines. Here, too, the model is readily identifiable, of course: in both 'Der Jäger' and 'Eifersucht und Stolz' in *Die schöne Müllerin*, Schubert had already depicted these same moods in the form of two concentrated miniatures, but now the miniature has become a profoundly expressive theatrical monologue. (It may be added in passing that Mahler never developed a deeper understanding of Schubert's music.) The final song, 'Die zwei blauen Augen', is in marked contrast. It is as if the wayfarer has fallen into a catatonic state, the song's narrow range bordering on the monotonous and approaching Sprechgesang. And yet Mahler asks the singer to perform the song 'with a mysteriously melancholic expression', a demand that is almost impossible to meet, so clearly circumscribed is the range of expression. Any attempt to meet the composer's demand risks sliding into caricature. Even in his earliest fully fledged songs, the young Mahler already poses more riddles than the sheer verve of their performance can solve.

As we have already noted, the *Lieder und Gesänge* from *Des Knaben Wunderhorn* do not form a coherent group, still less do they constitute a cycle. They accompanied their composer over a period of some dozen years and ceased to interest him only once he was working on his middle-period symphonies. In March 1905, at the height of this phase, he wrote retrospectively to the critic Ludwig Karpath, offering a detailed account of the world of the *Wunderhorn* songs. Here he stresses that he was the only composer who for a long time took his song texts from this book. Mahler was right to insist on this point. There are other settings of *Wunderhorn* poems, even by Strauss and Eugen d'Albert. But they remain exceptions. The only composer who set a larger group of *Wunderhorn* texts was the now almost entirely forgotten Theodor Streicher, whom Mahler knew, even if he held him in low esteem. The pseudo-archaic tone that was otherwise so popular in the second half of the nineteenth century is one that composers clearly preferred to adopt at third hand: Strauss, for example, set poems by Felix Dahn, and a number of composers set verse by Rudolf Baumbach. But Mahler goes on:

> Another difference is that I have devoted myself heart and soul to that poetry (which is essentially different from any other kind of 'literary poetry', and might almost be called something more like Nature and Life – in other words, the sources of all poetry – than art) in full awareness of its character and tone.[4]

Mahler's view of *Des Knaben Wunderhorn* as 'natural poetry' may strike modern readers as strange. After all, we now have a clearer idea than Mahler of the Romantic and highly artificial view of 'Nature' and tradition held by Arnim and Brentano, but a composer fond of reading Brentano's fairytale *Gockel, Hinkel and*

Gackeleia to his daughter clearly believed unconditionally in the Romantic notion of the folk and of Nature. Our earlier chapter on Mahler's literary leanings has already addressed the question of his response to the *Wunderhorn* poems, a response notable for its mixture of shock and immediacy.

The full range of Mahler's *Wunderhorn* world becomes clear to listeners only when they can hear all his settings one after the other. Mathias Hansen had convincingly argued that these songs should be subdivided into three smaller groups. The first contains all the songs dominated by dance rhythms drawn from the world of folk music. Examples include 'Trost im Unglück', 'Rheinlegendchen' and 'Es sungen drei Engel', a song better known as the fifth movement of the Third Symphony. (This is not the place to discuss the complex relationship between the piano and orchestral versions of the *Wunderhorn* songs.) A second subgroup comprises songs that are satirical, critical or admonitory in tone. 'Des Antonius von Padua Fischpredigt' is undoubtedly the best known of this subgroup, once again familiar from its orchestral manifestation in the third movement of the Second Symphony. The third and smallest subgroup is none the less the most important and deals with soldiers, deserters and drummer boys, with the plebeian world of those downtrodden individuals who until then had had no voice of their own. In short, it is the world of Büchner's Woyzeck and Berg's Wozzeck. Among this subgroup are some of Mahler's greatest songs: 'Der Schildwache Nachtlied', 'Lied des Verfolgten im Turm', 'Wo die schönen Trompeten blasen', 'Revelge' and 'Der Tamboursg'sell'. In the case of the last of these, Mahler provided Natalie Bauer-Lechner with an insight into his own creative process. The song, he explained, occurred to him on the spur of the moment, as he was leaving the dining room in Maiernigg in August 1901. He sketched it out in the entrance hall, entering it in the sketchbook that he always carried around with him in his jacket pocket, then running to a favourite spot of his next to a spring. It soon became clear to him that this was not an idea for a symphony, which is what he had been looking for, but for a song. He remembered 'Der Tamboursg'sell' in *Des Knaben Wunderhorn* – a clear indication of how well he knew the collection, a copy of which he kept in his 'composing house'. When he arrived there and compared the musical idea with the words, he discovered that they were a perfect match.

Countless similar examples of this ability to husband his artistic resources may be observed in Mahler's work. It was a quality of which he was always as proud as any anxious husbandman watching over his land.[5] A glance at 'Revelge' – one of the most astonishing of his songs – may serve as an example of the whole complex of *Wunderhorn* settings. Goethe emphasized the charm of these poems in a famous review, a charm that subjugated even those who were relatively well educated, their view of the songs being comparable to that of old age's view of youth:

Here Art is in conflict with Nature, and this developing process, this reciprocal influence and this sense of striving seems to seek out a goal, a goal that
it has already in fact achieved. Wherever it manifests itself, the true poetic
genius is complete unto itself; although it may encounter imperfection on a
linguistic, technical or other level, it possesses that higher inner form that is
ultimately at the disposal of all, and even in the dark and dismal element it
often creates a more glorious impression than it may later do when that
element is clear and transparent. The lively poetic contemplation of a limited
state raises the individual to a universe that may itself be limited but which is
none the less untrammelled, so that we believe that we can see the whole
world within this tiny space.

In his brief characterization of the individual poems, Goethe writes of
'Revelge' that it is 'invaluable for him whose imagination can follow it'.[6] What
is so great about Mahler's setting is its ability to see the whole world within its
confines. (Arnim and Brentano spell the word 'Rewelge', while Goethe prefers
the form 'Revelje'. It derives from the French verb 'réveiller', meaning 'to wake
up', so that the correct spelling is 'Réveille', a military waking signal.) Listening
breathlessly to the song, most audiences will fail to notice that it is cast in a
hybrid form comprising both dialogue and narrative. It begins with the
desperate cry of a fatally wounded regimental drummer, who sings the first
two verses, in the course of which he asks a comrade to carry him to his quarters. But in the third verse the comrade refuses to help him: his company has
been defeated, and he faces certain death. In the fourth and fifth verses the
drummer complains about the lack of solidarity and decides that in the face of
death he will play his drum again. According to writers on Mahler, the last
three verses describe the dying man's febrile visions. But text and music tell a
different story, for what they in fact depict is the formation of a procession of
the living and the dead in the spirit of a dance of death. With his constant
drumming, the drummer wakes his dead comrades, and this company of
corpses succeeds where their living comrades fail, the terrible sight of them
causing the enemy to flee. Led by the drummer, the victorious regiment of
corpses passes in front of his lover's house, so that when she wakes up in the
morning, she sees the assembled company, with her drummer boy at its head.

Mahler turns this ghostly sequence into a powerful funeral march in the style
of Callot and Büchner. More than once he described the opening movement of
his Third Symphony as a kind of rhythmic study for this song, encouraging the
suggestion that the first and final movements of his Sixth Symphony may be the
logical consequence of 'Revelge'. Grounded in the implacable beat of the drum,
the musical argument moves with fatal logic towards the military dance of
death. From the line 'Ich muß wohl meine Trommel rühren' ('I think I have to

beat my drum'), the funeral march acquires a demonic dimension that seems almost disproportionate in the context of a song lasting only eight minutes. This company of skeletons marches along, as though whipped into a frenzy by the Furies, while maintaining the strict rhythm of the drumbeat. Meanwhile, the orchestra cries out in a paroxysm of apocalyptic distress. Each verse ends with a positively mindless refrain, 'Trallali, trallaley, trallalera'. In the final strophe, the skeletal soldiers take up their positions in front of the house of the drummer's sweetheart. Here Mahler encapsulates the whole of the song with its funereal rhythms. The trumpets and strings are now muted, the cymbals attached to the bass drum, everything clattering and scurrying past in a hushed *pianissimo* as the dead ride along, quickly but almost soundlessly. Nowhere does Mahler come closer to his favourite author, Jean Paul, than he does here:

All the graves gaped wide, and the iron gates of the charnel house were opened and closed by invisible hands. Along the walls flitted shadows cast by no living creature, while other shadows walked upright in the open air. Only the children still slept in their open coffins. In the heavens a grey and sultry mist hung in large folds, drawn closer and tighter like a net by a giant shadow, while the heat continued to grow. Above me I heard the distant crash of the avalanches, beneath me the first step of a mighty earthquake.[7]

Mahler himself regarded 'Revelge' as the greatest of his works 'of this kind'.[8]

The Rückert settings date from the final phase of Mahler's interest in the lied – only in the light of 'Revelge' does one hesitate to describe them as the high point of that interest. Rückert's importance for Mahler has already been mentioned. Once Mahler had left behind him the world of *Des Knaben Wunderhorn*, his only possible alternative – however surprising this may seem – appeared to him to be the more intimate and far more artful poetry of Friedrich Rückert. The atmosphere of *Des Knaben Wunderhorn* having left its mark on the composer's conception of his first four symphonies and having merged inextricably with it, it seems as if the discipline and self-denial of Rückert's poetry was a necessary counterweight that allowed him to achieve the conceptual audacities of the middle-period symphonies. Certainly, the ten Rückert settings coincide exactly with the period when Mahler was working on these symphonies.

Mahler himself spoke only rarely about his five Rückert Lieder, but when he did, it was to stress their intimate character. Natalie Bauer-Lechner felt that 'Blicke mir nicht in die Lieder' was so characteristic of Mahler's world of emotion that he could have written the words himself. He himself thought that it was the least significant and most innocuous of the set but that precisely for this reason it could expect to generate a response. In his view, 'Ich atmet' einen linden Duft' reflected the sense of understated happiness that people feel in the presence of a loved one on whom they

can count without the need for a single word to pass between them. 'Ich bin der
Welt abhanden gekommen' was 'brim-full of emotion but does not overflow'. It was,
he said, his 'very self'.[9] Alma also claimed that in writing this song Mahler had
thought of the tombs of cardinals in Italian churches, where the bodies of the men
in question lie on flat stones with their hands clasped and their eyes closed. 'Liebst
du um Schönheit', he added on another occasion, was a particularly private expression of his feelings for his wife.[10] Mahler clearly took pleasure in returning to a
greater intimacy and purity of expression as a counterbalance to the expressivity
of the middle symphonies and the later *Wunderhorn* songs and, indeed, he may
even have felt a need to recapture the simplicity of the earlier songs and of the
Fourth Symphony. This greater simplicity is also reflected in the compositional
style, with its filigree, porcelain-like orchestration: this is chamber music rather
than symphonic music, with atmospheric values and a reduced emotional and
dynamic range instead of the large-scale drama of works that pack a heavier
emotional punch. Mahler's subjectivism, which is markedly extrovert in the middle
symphonies, is here turned inwards, withdrawing into its shell. Voice and accompaniment become interwoven motivically and thematically. In 'Revelge', the vocal
line struggles for supremacy with the march rhythm, groaning, screeching and
whispering. In 'Ich atmet' einen linden Duft', by contrast, vocal line and orchestra
are impeccably well-behaved, each permanently granting the other precedence,
becoming entwined with a delicacy that none the less leaves a bitter aftertaste.

Only the fourth song, 'Um Mitternacht', causes us any difficulties. Most
writers on Mahler give this song a wide berth, only Mathias Hansen taking the
bull by the horns and describing it as an 'extraordinarily problematical piece'.[11]
Mahler certainly abandons the interiority of the other four songs and reveals a
lack of concern that is positively bewildering. The opening, it is true, conforms
in character to what has gone before it, while standing apart in terms of its
unusual instrumentation, which dispenses entirely with the strings. But at the
words 'Um Mitternacht hab' ich die Macht in deine Hand gegeben! Herr über
Tod und Leben' ('At midnight I handed over all power to You, Lord of life and
death'), Mahler generates a state of extreme frenzy that resembles nothing so
much as one of Adorno's 'breakthroughs', using the full force of the brass and
glissandos on the harp and piano. (Curiously enough, the piano is fully integrated into the orchestra here, an effect that was to be a favourite of Erich
Wolfgang Korngold and that he presumably learnt from Mahler.) The song
ends powerfully, as if underscoring a celebratory triumph, so that the work as
a whole sounds more like Elgar than Mahler. Indeed, we could even speak of a
'soul of hope and glory' that was being illuminated here. The puzzle that this
song represents has yet to be solved.

The *Kindertotenlieder* raise fewer questions and, indeed, are among Mahler's
most perfect and straightforward compositions. Ignoring Alma's foolish reproach

that Mahler anticipated the death of their elder daughter in these songs, we shall find few voices raised in dissent, few divergent opinions. For all their grief, these songs breathe a spirit of gentle serenity that is abandoned only at the start of the fifth and final song. Otherwise, the mood is one of extreme restraint and discreet contemplation. The listener barely discovers what has happened. No sense of catastrophe casts its jagged-toothed flames over the battlefield of fate. Instead, the father observes the night's sad events as if through a sheet of frosted glass. The strophic form of the songs is distinctly old-fashioned and creates a sense of traditional values, but Rückert himself had already led the way in breaking down the formal structures by means of a virtuoso variation technique, while additionally linking lines and verses together. In Mahler's hands, the sense of freedom is complete. The narrator has learnt to control his feelings to the utmost, rather than weeping convulsively. The asceticism of the emotional expression increases the sense of inner tension until it is almost unbearable. Unhappy the performer who externalizes these emotions. But asceticism and self-control do not acquire a mask-like rigidity in the *Kindertotenlieder*, as they might easily do. Rather, they assume an immensely enhanced melodic and thematic flexibility. The final song briefly lets itself go, only to retreat once again into a state of suppressed emotion. The 'restlessly anguished expression' of the beginning increases, only for it to fade away again. By bar 101, the performance marking is 'slow, like a lullaby'. This ending has a great model – not that this diminishes its own greatness for even a moment. The final song in Schubert's *Die schöne Müllerin* is 'Des Baches Wiegenlied' (The Brook's Lullaby) and begins with the words 'Gute Ruh, gute Ruh! Tu die Augen zu!' ('Rest, rest! Close your eyes!'). The brook has welcomed into its watery embrace the miller's unhappy apprentice and sings him a final lullaby. With Rückert and Mahler, it is the father who sings to his dead children, hoping that they may find eternal rest. The melody is infinitely consoling, a lullaby of overwhelming tenderness.

Lowland Dreams: Budapest
(1888–91)

UNTIL NOW, MAHLER had never managed to remain for as long as two and a half years with a single company and in a single town or city. Either he himself failed to stay the course, or others failed to stay it with him – generally the first alternative occurred with such speed that the second had no time to take effect. Budapest marked a new departure in his life as a conductor and director. It was also his most turbulent and eventful period to date, qualities that it acquired not least because in retrospect it may seem like a dress rehearsal for Mahler's years at the helm of the Vienna Court Opera. Although he spent only two years in Budapest, compared with ten in Vienna, we find the same line of development in both cases, the events that unfolded in Budapest constituting a much condensed version of those that took place in Vienna some ten years later: he began enthusiastically enough, with hugely impressive plans and a string of startling successes, while evincing boundless energy in dealing with the resistance that he encountered. Slowly, but surely, however, he grew increasingly tired and disenchanted, no longer prepared to assert himself in the face of resistance and gradually losing interest in the task in hand. In both cases he then made secret contact with outside organizations in an attempt to prepare the next stage in his career. At the same time it is difficult to avoid the impression that he sought to precipitate his premature departure, a departure that ultimately became the be all and end all of his existence.[1]

It is curious to note how quickly Mahler could lose all pleasure in the tasks that bound him to the world of the theatre and the music industry. As a composer, he showed an almost incredible degree of energy and determination over a period of twenty-two years, writing nine symphonies of vast dimensions, not to mention *Das Lied von der Erde* and the initial sketches of a tenth symphony, all of these works composed as a virtual sideline during his summer vacations, while the rest of the year was given over to his work as an administrator and conductor; and yet this energy could soon start to wane in the opera house if he felt that the effort and commitment that he brought to the task in hand had failed to produce the desired result as quickly as he had wanted. This same trajectory is observable in all his engagements, whether it was the nine months he spent in Laibach or his ten years in Vienna. Indeed, one could even argue that it also influenced his final engagement in New York, for all that he entered upon that engagement under very different auspices.

Buda and Pest had been merged in 1872, and yet it is clear from the headings to his letters that when Mahler arrived in the city in 1888, he still viewed it as Pest. One half of the city was called 'Ofen' in German, 'Buda' in Hungarian, and lay on the right bank of the Danube, on the slopes of the limestone hills that overlook the city. It was the older part of Budapest and was notable architecturally for its castle, coronation church and citadel. To the left of the river lay Pest, the less hilly part of the city, its monumental buildings dating for the most part from the nineteenth century and including the vast Houses of Parliament, St Stephen's Church and the opera house, which had opened in 1884 and which bore a striking and by no means fortuitous similarity to the Vienna Court Opera of 1869. The building still exists and now houses the Hungarian State Opera.

When Mahler arrived in the city, its population numbered some four hundred thousand. It was a genuine city, not far short of a metropolis. Nor was it an accident that architecturally speaking Pest sought to rival Vienna. Budapest's view of Vienna was in many ways distorted by the country's vicissitudinous history and by local – and objectively justified – perceptions of the city as inferior in status to Vienna. The Hungarian half of the monarchy was divided into estates, and the Hungarian estates promoted an increasingly nationalist, Magyar standpoint that reflected nineteenth-century trends in general and that was combined with powerful anti-Viennese and anti-imperial sentiments – the Kaiser in Vienna was also the king of Hungary. As in Bohemia, Hungarian nationalism had a notable linguistic component, a component that is additionally reflected in the way in which politics played a part in the day-to-day running of the Budapest Opera. While the singers performed in every conceivable language, German was frowned on and, if not officially banned, was at least felt to be intolerable. If Mahler intended to perform Wagner's works and to introduce them to Hungarian audiences, then he would have to perform them in a language other than German. His first victory in Budapest was his decision to grasp this nettle and perform Wagner's stage works in Hungarian.

Relations between Vienna and Budapest had certainly not improved in the wake of the revolutions of 1848–9. Under Lajos Kossuth, the Hungarians had risen up against Austria but in 1849 had been forced beneath the Austrian yoke, or that, at least, was how they saw the situation. The settlement of 1867 ensured that the Hungarian half of the dual monarchy enjoyed the maximum degree of independence that was possible under such an arrangement, but in the eyes of many this was still far from adequate, not least because many of the promises made in 1867 were not kept. Mahler's failure in Budapest was due in part to the fact that on taking up office he became caught in the crossfire between the two camps: as a twenty-eight-year-old German-speaking Bohemian Jew (Budapest, too, was a hotbed of fetid anti-Semitism), he was far from being the ideal candidate in the view of those members of the educated middle classes who harboured Magyar aspirations and for whom only a Hungarian director would have been acceptable. True, Mahler grandly announced that he would be learning Hungarian, but he never made good this promise, a failure that lost him much of the support that he would otherwise have enjoyed if he had made a serious attempt to engage with the Hungarian language, rather than merely repeating a few words of welcome that he had learnt to mimic like a parrot.

In spite of his national and linguistic handicap, Mahler was initially made to feel welcome in the city, at least by those who were not strident nationalists. The non-nationalist press, too, was supportive. He owed the warmth of his reception not only to the reputation that had preceded him from Kassel, Prague and Leipzig but also to the desperate state of the Budapest Opera. Magnificent though the new opera house may have been, its artistic and organizational state left much to be desired. The intendant, Count István Keglevic, was typical of the opera-house administrators of the nineteenth century, a former soldier and a member of the aristocracy, whose administration was so incompetent – to put it mildly – that by the beginning of 1888 he had been relieved of his post. Responsibility for running the opera passed to the Secretary of State, Ferenc von Beniczky, who was to become one of Mahler's most devoted friends. The day-to-day running of the house lay in the hands of Sándor Erkel, an ineffectual director who presumably owed his appointment to the fact that he was the son of Ferenc Erkel, now in his late seventies and something of a national institution. Of his eight operas, two – *Hunyadi László* (1844) and, especially, *Bánk bán* (1861) – have come to be regarded as typical national operas. He had also written the Hungarian national anthem. Exceptionally sprightly for his age, Ferenc Erkel continued to play an important role in the musical life of his country, whereas his son, who occupied the joint posts of general administrator and principal conductor at the Royal Hungarian Opera, was rather less favoured by fortune. During the early 1870s, the company's music director had been Hans Richter, who, even without conducting the works of his idol Wagner, had cast a long shadow from which Sándor Erkel was unable to escape. The singers were all Hungarian, but with few exceptions they failed to do justice to the great works in the repertory – and Budapest audiences, being widely travelled, knew what vocal standards were like in Vienna, for example. In principle, there was enough money to engage foreign stars, who were happy to exercise their larynxes in Budapest and to pocket the resultant fees. But the result of this reliance on foreign singers meant that the international repertory was sung in at least two languages, sometimes even more. When Verdi was performed, the visiting stars would sing in Italian, while the comprimarii and the chorus sang in Hungarian. All concerned had grown used to this state of affairs, but artistically sensitive souls were inevitably disturbed by it. Sándor Erkel was clearly competent as a conductor but too weak and submissive to be able to change a system notable for its endemic inefficiency and wilfulness, with the result that the company's standards sank perceptibly.

Beniczky was the most honest of men and by no means inexperienced as a politician but he had next to no idea how to run a theatre, still less an opera house. In seeking to replace Richter, who had moved on to Vienna, he thought along Wagnerian lines and approached Felix Mottl, who was the leading Wagner conductor of his day after Richter and Hermann Levi and who had been principal conductor in Karlsruhe for a number of years. Mottl had also conducted at Bayreuth. But he quickly turned down Beniczky's approach. Meanwhile, a young and ambitious conductor was whiling away the summer of 1888 in his home town of Iglau, with the odd foray to Munich and Prague, where he worked on the local première of *Die drei Pintos*. He had been released from his contract in Leipzig in May 1888, but had no new appointment in prospect, and it was not long before he started to worry about his future, afraid, as usual, that he would have no work in the coming season. A letter that he wrote from Iglau to Max Steinitzer, who was close to him at this time, strikes a dramatic note, although we need to remember that the uncertain fate of his First Symphony and the cooling of his feelings for Marion von Weber will have contributed to this mood of despair: 'Steinitzer, I'm in a bad way! . . . For now I can say only that I've no prospects of obtaining another engagement, and I freely admit that this worries me a lot. I now need some *intense* activity if I'm not to go under! Write soon! Please! And don't give up on your extremely muddled friend, Gustav Mahler.'[2] Mahler was not the man to adopt such a tone lightly but intended this as a serious diagnosis of his current mental confusion and chaotic lifestyle. The insane enthusiasm with which he threw himself into a whole series of new appointments during these years was due to the fact that he regarded them as lifelines that he hoped would help him to escape from his state of emotional confusion and his muddled private life, only for him to plunge even deeper into the swirling whirlpool of existence. None the less, his years in Budapest were at least free from any serious erotic involvements.

The triumvirate that laid the tactical ground for Mahler's appointment in Budapest consisted of an old friend and two complete strangers. The old friend

was Guido Adler, at this date in his career a music historian – he later went on
to become a musicologist at the University of Vienna, where he did much to
promote Mahler's posthumous reputation. Like Mahler, he grew up in Iglau
but was five years older. In 1888 he was already teaching the history of music
at Prague University. The two other members of the group were David Popper
and Ödön von Mihalovich. Popper was an eminent cellist from Prague who
had been teaching at the Budapest Academy of Music since 1886, while
Mihalovich – the only Hungarian member of the group – had been the
director of the Academy of Music since 1887. He felt powerfully drawn to
German music and, more especially, to the New German School associated
with the names of Wagner and Liszt. A pupil of Hans von Bülow, he avoided
the blinkered views of the Hungarian nationalists.[3] Surviving letters suggest
that it was almost certainly Adler who championed Mahler's appointment,
appealing to Popper, whom he knew from Prague and who was one of the
leading cellists of his day as well as being active as a composer. Adler asked
Popper to make it clear to Mihalovich that Mahler was well suited to a post
that had already attracted considerable interest. Within weeks of Mottl's decision not to accept the offer, the terms of Mahler's appointment were already
being discussed. The contract was probably ready for signature by the middle
of September, and by the 30th of the month Mahler was already striding into
the offices of the Royal Hungarian Opera with all his typical élan.

An eyewitness account of his arrival is provided by Ludwig Karpath, a native
of Budapest who went on to become a writer on music in Vienna and whose
memoirs, *Begegnung mit dem Genius* (1934), are a source of prime importance,
especially for Mahler's years in Vienna – self-important, garrulous and gossipy
by turns, these reminiscences none the less need to be treated with considerable caution. In his colourful account of 30 September 1888, Karpath recalls
wandering around outside the opera house in his native city, hoping to catch a
glimpse of famous artists:

> Then I saw a clean-shaven little man who, without taking notice of anyone,
> came through the office with rapid step and dashed up the stairs to the
> Director's office. 'That's the new Director!' observed the lanky porter.
>
> 'What? There's a new Director, and nobody knew about it? Surely
> the opera has a long-standing Director, Alexander [Sándor] Erkel, isn't he in
> office any more?'
>
> 'More than that I don't know,' replied the porter. 'I was just told that
> I should let this gentleman into the building – he came here this morning
> too – because he's the new Director.'
>
> 'What is his name?' I enquired further.
>
> 'Gustav Mahler,' replied the porter.

It was the first time in my life I had heard the name, and I was rather unwilling to credit the appointment as Director of the Royal Opera House of this man who looked so young. [. . .] The appointment had been prepared with the greatest of care, and so secretively that literally no one had any idea of it. Let it not be forgotten that Mahler was at that time still a Jew – he was baptized only later, in Hamburg – and this fact alone was such as to cause a sensation. Just as great a commotion was raised over the salary, by the standards of the time exorbitantly high, of ten thousand florins per annum for a period of ten years.[4]

Mahler brought to his new post a mixture of extreme enthusiasm and brilliant tactical skill. He began by summoning to the opera house representatives of the leading local papers and played the nationalist card. Knowing that as a German-speaking Austrian Jew, he would be viewed with distrust by members of the growing nationalist and separatist movements in Hungary and would not be protected by the aura of a famous name, he presented himself as a champion of the Magyar cause. Although it was no secret in the dual monarchy that opera performances in Hungary were often given in two languages, Mahler feigned ignorance and pretended to be disagreeably surprised by the news. This was an unfortunate state of affairs, he noted, and one that needed addressing without delay, both on artistic grounds (only in this way could the composer's intentions be realized) and on nationalist grounds: 'I shall consider it my first and foremost duty to exert all my energy in making the opera a truly Hungarian national institution.'[5] He also announced that he would not be appearing as a conductor – and also, we may add, as a stage director – until December, when he would be staging *Das Rheingold* and *Die Walküre* in Hungarian with a cast made up entirely of local singers. (In the event, the performances did not take place until late January 1889.)

A few days after meeting the press, Mahler addressed the company itself, delivering a speech that has survived in the form of a draft. In the course of his address, which was delivered on 10 October, Mahler adopted a far more general tone than he had done when talking to local journalists. After all, the members of the Royal Hungarian Opera had no doubt had their fill of platitudes about 'performing our tasks with the utmost rigour and demonstrating complete absorption in and devotion to the work as a whole'.[6] But they were soon to discover for themselves that their young director was entirely serious, a seriousness that was to fill them with a mixture of astonishment and dismay following his decision to force them out of the rut into which their lives had sunk. Mahler's principal fight was with the orchestra, less so with the singers, who felt that their honour as artists had been impugned. In spite of these attempts to reform the situation, Mahler found much of the press against him.

Not without reason, a number of local journalists made fun of the conductor from Bohemia who did not speak a word of Hungarian but who wanted to turn the Royal Hungarian Opera into a Magyar institution. But Mahler had the backing of a number of influential figures on the city's cultural scene, most notably Ferenc von Beniczky and Ödön von Mihalovich. Beniczky had introduced Mahler to the company with a welcoming speech remarkable for its warmth, while the hopes and trust that were placed in the new director were clear from his salary and ten-year contract. That Mahler came nowhere near fulfilling the terms of this contract is another story.

One of the terms of this contract stipulated that the house must employ a new stage manager and a new stage director, both of whom must be Hungarian. Beniczky was particularly keen on this clause as he, too, was ambitious and wanted to raise the profile of the Budapest Opera. It seems from newspaper reports of the period that both of these new employees had the additional task of improving the standard of sung Hungarian. Apparently, then, the company included non-Hungarian singers who learnt to sing Hungarian more or less phonetically. The first opera to be staged under Mahler's direction was Bizet's *Les Pêcheurs de perles*, a work of which he was particularly fond, just as he was of Bizet's music in general. The performances were not conducted by Mahler, nor was he responsible for the stage production. For reasons that remain unclear, the production turned out to be a fiasco. Perhaps the composer's sense of drama, as yet not fully developed in this work, struck local audiences as too anaemic, accustomed as they were to brighter colours. The next production, Donizetti's *La Fille du régiment*, proved more successful, while Konradin Kreutzer's Biedermeier idyll *Das Nachtlager von Granada* was even better. The fact that Mahler failed with Bizet's opera but succeeded with Kreutzer's was bound to cause him to reflect on the taste of audiences at the Budapest Opera, and the result of his reflections could hardly have pleased him. But, however much he may have brooded on this new situation, the difficulties and the hostility that he had to face left his fighting spirit initially intact.

In December 1888 he wrote to his old employer and benefactor in Leipzig, Max Staegemann, mentioning 'the most ridiculous difficulties in all directions' and adding, significantly: 'But I shall not give up!'[7] He would not give up until he had scored his first success, which could mean only the local premières of *A Rajna Kincse* and *A Walkür* – *Das Rheingold* and *Die Walküre* – on 26 and 27 January 1889, in a Hungarian translation specially prepared for the occasion by Antal Rado and Gergely Cziky. As was usual at this period, neither the stage director nor the conductor was mentioned on the playbill, but the director of the Royal Hungarian Opera naturally assumed both of these tasks, in the former case assisted by the new stage manager, Ede Ujházy, who no doubt also acted as an interpreter for Mahler and the rest of the company.

Towering above the ensemble was a single star singer, the soprano Arabella Szilágyi, who sang Brünnhilde in 1889 and who went on to become one of the house's best-loved singers. The first two parts of the *Ring* proved a resounding triumph and at least for a time they helped to consolidate Mahler's position. Beniczky, who had been largely responsible for Mahler's appointment, was immensely relieved, for if Mahler had been a failure, his own fate would no doubt have been sealed as well. In an open letter, he thanked his new director:

> With the production of *Das Rheingold* and *Die Walküre* you, Sir, have brilliantly achieved two points of your artistic programme, for on the one hand you have shown what one is capable of achieving through sheer hard work, while on the other hand you have also proved that with our national resources, so often and so unjustifiably disparaged, even the most difficult artistic tasks may be carried out; you have shown that it is possible to produce the greatest artistic creations of the present day, without the addition of people from outside, and in the Hungarian language. This circumstance will certainly fill every patriot with real joy and contentment.[8]

Local journalists, whether German- or Hungarian-speaking, fell over each other in their praise of the house's achievement in performing the first two parts of the *Ring* on consecutive evenings, and of performing them, moreover, in Hungarian with an ensemble that had not previously sung these works. The liberal newspapers praised the achievement as such, concentrating on the artistic success of the performances, while the nationalist papers stressed the fact that both works had been sung in Hungarian with an entirely home-grown company. All observers agreed that Mahler's conducting had swept all before it, a demonstration of the highest musical competence and overwhelming power, even if there had been a number of disagreements with the orchestra during the rehearsal period. Comments on the staging are comparatively rare, but it seems that both productions borrowed heavily from the ones that Wagner himself had staged in Bayreuth in 1876 – Mahler was currently on good terms with the composer's widow, Cosima. Mahler's victory was total, and yet it was to prove astonishingly short-lived, a circumstance that emerges not least from the fact that he was not even able to complete the *Ring*: the local premières of *Siegfried* and *Götterdämmerung* took place without him. He made the mistake of announcing that the *Ring* would be completed during the 1889/90 season but then – for reasons that are not entirely clear – he abandoned those plans, a change of programming that played straight into his enemies' hands. Although those enemies had fallen temporarily silent, they had not given up their fight. Wagner had died only a few years earlier, and his works – especially the *Ring* – were regarded as quintessentially Germanic, so that, even if sung in Hungarian, they could hardly be passed off as Hungarian national operas. But where were these national operas? Apart from the afore-mentioned works by Ferenc Erkel, there was no real operatic tradition in Hungary. Not even the cosmopolitan Liszt had made any real contribution to the genre, while the fact that Hungary's leading twentieth-century composer, Béla Bartók, wrote only a single opera that occupies a place apart in his output is an indication of the problematical nature of the situation. And here was Mahler, a Bohemian Jew obsessed with Wagner, an obsession that was far from being shared by all. Wilhelm Kienzl, the composer of the *Der Evangelimann*, visited Budapest in the spring of 1889 and was introduced to Mahler, who apparently told him that he felt an 'unutterable longing for German singing'.[9] But it was a longing that he was unable to express to outsiders, of course.

Kienzl also met Ferenc Erkel, whose son, Sándor, was unhappy with his post as assistant conductor and making life difficult for Mahler. Ferenc Erkel was not only disgruntled at the fact that his son had failed to achieve the position that he felt was his due at the Budapest Opera, he also told Kienzl that although he did not know Mahler as an artist, he regarded him as a 'Germaniser, who does not represent a benefit to Hungarian musical life'.[10] The Erkels exerted a powerful influence on the cultural life of the capital, for although Sándor's contribution may have been insignificant, his father was unanimously regarded as a national institution. It is easy to imagine, therefore, that Mahler's chauvinistic enemies would have fallen silent only briefly, quite apart from the issue of anti-Semitism, which was a problem in Hungary no less than it was elsewhere. Although the local journalists may have lacked the courage to express their views on this point, Ferenc Komlóssy had no such inhibitions when addressing the Hungarian House of Parliament during a debate on the opera house's budget in May 1889, in the course of which he proudly informed his colleagues that it was his 'duty' to make his 'anti-Semitic views' known.[11]

It looks as if the new productions of *Das Rheingold* and *Die Walküre* more or less exhausted Mahler's enthusiasm, although we would probably be doing him an injustice if we insisted on this point. After all, he conducted a number of other outstanding performances in the course of the following seasons. Foremost among these was *Don Giovanni*, with which he opened the new season in mid-September 1890. Later that same season, *Lohengrin* can also be numbered among his major successes. Lilli Lehmann, the greatest dramatic soprano of the turn of the century, gave several performances in Budapest during the winter of 1890/91, including Donna Anna in *Don Giovanni*. Even today, her recording of 'Or sai chi l'onore' still has the power to astonish us, revealing, as it does, the full dramatic force of which this great singing actress was capable. As such, she was no doubt the model for Mahler's protégée, Anna von Mildenburg. In her colourful reminiscences, translated into English as *My Path Through Life*, Lehmann describes her time in Budapest, including an account of the young Mahler's fiery, unbridled temperament and his curious errors of judgement in his choice of tempos for *Don Giovanni*:

> We often walked, rested, and leaped with him over hedges and ditches in the beautiful environs of Budapest, and had a jolly time. I was a friend to Mahler, and retained affection for him always. I honoured him for his great talent, his tremendous capacity for work, and his rectitude towards his art, and I stood by him in all the vicissitudes of his life, because of his great qualities, that were often mistaken and misunderstood. I comprehended even his nervous conditions, that sometimes unjustly afflicted those who could not keep pace with his talent and his indomitable ambition and industry, because I, also, formerly believed that only a strong will was needed to perfect what one is able to perfect himself, that is, to strive beyond his strength. I have known for a long time now that that is not so. We were good friends, even if we were of opposite opinions.[12]

Lilli Lehmann's initial impression of Mahler dates from December 1890, only three months before he left the Budapest Opera. The performance of *Don Giovanni* on 16 December in which she appeared as Donna Anna – for a star like Lehmann, Mahler was willing to make an exception, so that she sang the part in Italian, while the rest of the cast performed in Hungarian – was also attended by Brahms, who was in Budapest to play his Second Piano Concerto on the 17th. Brahms's friends in Budapest finally managed to talk him into attending the performance of *Don Giovanni* – he had initially turned down their invitation, arguing that he preferred to read the score and had never seen or heard a decent performance of the work. He would even prefer a cold beer, he insisted. But in the end he allowed his friends to drag him along to their box, where he demonstratively settled down on a sofa at the back in the hope of enjoying a rest. But it was not long before he was making increasingly inarticulate noises indicative of his enthusiasm, and at the end of the first act he was heard to shout out: 'Most excellent, admirable, what a deuce of a fellow!' He then ran on to the stage and embraced Mahler with typically grumpy cordiality. It was thanks, in part, to this impression that Brahms later supported Mahler's candidature when the latter was being considered for the post of director of the Vienna Court Opera.

By December 1890, when Lilli Lehmann and Brahms expressed their enthusiasm for his conducting, Mahler was already resolved to leave Budapest. Secret negotiations with the director of the Hamburg Opera, Bernhard Pollini, had begun the previous October, but still too late for him to take up his new post at

the start of the 1890/91 season, so that it was not until the end of March 1891
that he joined the Hamburg company. In fact, his increasing lack of commitment
to the Royal Hungarian Opera was due to factors not entirely related to
Budapest, its opera house and Hungary in general. Rather, family commitments
and health problems played a part in his decision. His father had died in Iglau
on 18 February 1889. Mahler's relations with his father had never been particularly close, and it may well be that his death after a long illness left Mahler
comparatively unaffected. But the same could not be said of his mother, who
died on 11 October 1889, even if we have no direct evidence to support this
claim. Whatever the truth of the matter, Mahler had no time to grieve. His father
died during his first season in Budapest, his mother shortly after the start of his
second, leaving him little opportunity to return to Iglau to make the necessary
arrangements. Moreover, his sister Leopoldine had died in Vienna only two
weeks before his mother, apparently from a brain tumour. Just twenty-six years
old, she was married to a Ludwig Quittner, and the couple had two children.
Mahler was now the head of the family and had to care for his brother Alois, who
was twenty-two and idling away his life in Brünn; for his sister Justine, who, only
twenty, had shouldered the burden of looking after their ailing and then dying
parents and who had suffered a physical and mental breakdown in consequence;
for his brother Otto, an artistically gifted sixteen-year-old who was studying
music at the Vienna Conservatory but whose erratic behaviour was already
causing concern; and for his fourteen-year-old sister Emma, who, like Otto, was
taken in by the Löhrs. Following her parents' death, Justine moved to Budapest
to be with her brother, who had finally abandoned his usual hotel rooms and was
then living in rented accommodation at 3 Theresienring.

A second source of worry arose at this time, for it was in Budapest that Mahler's
lifelong medical problems began, starting with a recurrent problem with haemorrhoids usually dismissed as tiresome and painful but not life-threatening. This
is certainly true today, when the condition is generally no cause for concern. Even
in Mahler's day the condition was operable, albeit at considerable discomfort to
the patient. The first such operation on Mahler took place in Munich in mid-July
1889, but two months later he was still in pain and had to take morphine, a drug
which, for want of any alternative, was then prescribed with negligent liberality.
This was by no means the end of Mahler's rectal discomfort, for in February 1901
he suffered such massive internal bleeding that he almost died. These bouts of
illness all take their place within an aetiology of inflammatory diseases. In short,
the bacterial endocarditis that killed him in 1911 was by no means an unfortunate but isolated incident at the end of his life but the culmination of a long
history of illness to which we shall be returning from time to time.

Given all these emotional worries and other demands on his time, it comes
as no surprise to learn that Mahler had no private life at this period. And he had

little time for composition either. True, his First Symphony received its first performance in Budapest on 20 November 1889 under the innocuous title of 'A Symphonic Poem in Two Parts'. Shortly before this he had performed three of his *Wunderhorn* songs at a concert with the coloratura soprano Bianca Bianchi. He wrote a number of other songs during the summer of 1890, which he spent with his brothers and sisters and the Löhrs at Hinterbrühl near Vienna. But he made little progress on his Second Symphony, the opening movement of which – 'Todtenfeier' – he had completed in Prague. Compositionally speaking, the time that he spent in Budapest was the most unproductive of his entire life, and even if there is no evidence to confirm this, we may be certain that this was one of the reasons why he became so disenchanted with the city. Running the opera company consumed him, leaving him no time for what he had long since realized was his true calling.

Mahler's final months in Budapest are quickly summarized. Press reactions to the first performance of his First Symphony were negative at worst and neutral at best. In November 1889 there was an argument in the press over changes that he had made to Meyerbeer's *Les Huguenots*. Exceptionally, we have to concede that Mahler was wrong and that the journalist, although far less significant a figure, was right. The matter is of sufficient interest to merit a more detailed discussion, but we must content ourselves with noting that Mahler, echoing Wagner's dismissal of a work whose merits he failed to recognize, peremptorily cut the whole of the final act, justifying his decision by pointing out that it was likewise usual at this time to cut the whole of the final scene of *Don Giovanni*, following the hero's descent into Hell. Few directors would risk cutting this sextet today, and yet this scene is by no means as important as the fifth act of *Les Huguenots*. At the beginning of 1890 a Hungarian-language newspaper demanded that Mahler make good the promises that he had made with regard to the championship of Hungarian operas, including his announcement that he would learn Hungarian. For all its polemical tone, the piece in question raised a number of legitimate points. By the autumn of 1890 it had become clear that Ferenc von Beniczky, one of Mahler's most important allies, would shortly be leaving his post. His prospective successor was Count Géza Zichy, a member of one of Hungary's foremost families and an important figure in the musical life of the country. Although Zichy had lost an arm in a hunting accident, he went on to train as a concert pianist, just as Paul Wittgenstein was later to do. He had also written a number of operas, none of which was performed under Mahler's directorship. Unlike the cosmopolitan Beniczky, Zichy made no secret of his Hungarian nationalism. His appointment was announced on 30 January 1891. Central to the speech that he delivered on taking up his new office was a passage that was repeated in all the newspapers and that must have made it clear to Mahler that his days in Budapest were numbered: 'You know my past, which may have been poor in achievements but which in *its direction and its aspirations* has always been consistently Hungarian. Here, too, I can only say that I mean to create a Hungarian art on a European level, for the present still with the help of foreigners, but later by dint of our own efforts alone.'[13]

As a foreigner, Mahler must have felt under personal attack, but he could take a relaxed view of the situation, because a week before Zichy had taken up his new post, he had signed a contract as principal conductor at the Hamburg Opera, an appointment as yet known to very few people in Budapest. It was a regressive step in terms of his position within the Hamburg hierarchy, but it represented a considerable advance in terms of the artistic potential of a house which, although only a municipal theatre, was extremely well financed, with a number of outstanding singers on its books. Once again Mahler had played his cards exceedingly well. After all, he had signed a ten-year contract, of which he had served only a quarter. He saw his chance within days of Zichy's appointment, when the rights of the director were severely curtailed and many of his powers transferred to the company's intendant, amounting to a provocative snub of Mahler, who used the opportunity to turn the tables on the count. Knowing that Zichy wanted to get rid of him and that he had no wish to endure him for another seven and a half years, he generously offered to leave early on condition that he received compensation amounting to two and a half times his annual salary, a total of twenty-five thousand florins. Zichy agreed, and on 14 March Mahler announced his resignation, while omitting to inform the good people of Budapest that he had already signed a contract with Hamburg. Be that as it may, many members of the audience realized too late what they were losing, even though there was nothing that they could have done to prevent it: on 16 March 1891 Sándor Erkel conducted a performance of *Lohengrin*, undoubtedly Mahler's most important new production in Budapest. Mahler's supporters were left to regret the departure of a director who, as a number of German newspapers pointed out, had been 'forced out of his position by the new Commissioner, Count Zichy, because he is a German'. The first act was repeatedly interrupted by calls for Mahler until 'detectives restored order in the gallery'. But wherever Mahler may have spent the evening, his heart was already in Hamburg.

14

The Conductor

Er reicht den Violinen eine Blume
Und ladet sie mit Schelmenblick zum Tanz.
Verzweifelt bettelt er das Blech um Glanz,
Und streut den Flöten kindlich manche Krume.

Tief beugt das Knie er vor dem Heiligtume
Des Pianissimos, der Klangmonstranz.
Doch zausen Stürme seinen Schwalbenschwanz,
Wenn er das Tutti aufpeitscht, sich zum Ruhme.

Mit Fäusten hält er fest den Schlußakkord.
Dann staunt er, hilflos eingepflanzt am Ort,
Dem ausgekommenen Klang nach wie ein Clown.

Zuletzt, daß er den Beifall, dankend, rüge,
Zeigt er belästigte Erlöserzüge,
Und zwingt uns, ihm noch Größres zuzutraun.[1]

[He hands a bouquet to the violins and with a mischievous look invites them to dance. Desperately he begs the brass to produce more sheen and like a child offers many a crumb to the flutes. He bends his knee before the shrine of the *pianissimo*, that monstrance of sonority. But storms tear his tail coat to shreds when he whips up a tutti to his own greater glory. With his fists he sustains the final chord. Then, helplessly rooted to the spot, he stands there like a clown, listening to the note as it dies away. Finally, as if to reprehend the applause, by way of thanks he reveals the offended features of a redeemer and forces us to expect yet greater things of him.]

As a lyrical poet, Franz Werfel has been almost completely forgotten. If German scholars still mention him at all, it is in the context of German Expressionism, but a poem like the one that he wrote in 1938 under the title 'The Conductor' continues to lie undetected in complete editions of his writings. And yet this sonnet is a masterpiece of gentle irony aimed at the typical maestro. There are hardly any poems about conductors in German literature, the only two that come to mind being Werfel's and one by Stefan Zweig that is directly connected with Mahler. It would be easy to assume that Werfel's poem, too, was inspired by Mahler, but its subject is in fact Bruno Walter, a not entirely uncritical friend of Alma's from the days of her marriage to Mahler and also a friend of Werfel. Walter played the organ at Werfel's funeral in Beverley Hills, by now an old man who had survived the much younger Werfel. Alma's third husband, Werfel was a musically gifted amateur tenor who knew Verdi's operas by heart and who joined forces with Fritz Busch in Dresden in the 1920s and helped to pioneer the Verdi revival in Germany, not least through his new German translations of a number of Verdi's operas. In the present poem he casts a keen but loving eye at the typical maestro who genuflects before the 'monstrance of sonority', a wonderful metaphor for the floating *pianissimo* of a full orchestra producing the gentlest of sounds. He also writes of 'the offended features of a redeemer' who forces his audience to expect even greater achievements. In both cases Werfel's language is equally witty and apt as a description of the facial expressions that all conductors, famous or otherwise, tend to reveal to their audiences at the end of a concerto, symphony or opera.

But Werfel's picture of a conductor is that of a demonstrative, narcissistic, amiable and polite representative of the profession and, as such, far closer to Bruno Walter than to Mahler, who did not leave the same impression either on his audiences or on his various orchestras. The picture of Mahler that emerges from the eyewitness accounts of his contemporaries is similar to the one that Elias Canetti sketches in a handful of pages in his main theoretical work, *Crowds and Power*, a passage that is undoubtedly the most penetrating ever to have been written about a conductor from the standpoint of the 'power' that he exerts. True, music was never central to Canetti's life, but he was briefly connected to the Mahler family by dint of his intense emotional entanglement with the conductor's daughter Anna. (His demeaning account of Alma will be quoted later.) For Canetti, there was no more graphic expression of power than the activity of the conductor. We may assume that like Werfel he often heard Bruno Walter conducting in Vienna, in addition to which he was friendly with Hermann Scherchen. According to Canetti, a person who knows nothing about power can deduce all its component parts by observing a conductor at work, at least if that person is willing to abandon the view that the principal function of conducting is to produce music. The first point to note is that the conductor is the only person in the whole room who stands, and who stands, moreover, on a raised podium. The score is a statute book for the performance. The orchestral players have only their individual parts, the audience normally only a programme booklet. The conductor alone knows the full impact of what he is doing. Mahler would punish latecomers by staring at them and he allowed weak singers to feel the full force of his disappointment by making stabbing movements at them with his baton. Throughout the performance, the conductor is seen by the crowd in the hall or auditorium as a leader. He stands at the front and leads the way, but instead of his feet, it is his hands that lead them:

> His eyes hold the whole orchestra. Every player feels that the conductor sees him personally, and, still more, hears him. The voices of the instruments are opinions and convictions on which he keeps a close watch. He is omniscient, for, while the players have only their own parts in front of them, he has the whole score in his head, or on his desk. At any given moment he knows precisely what each player should be doing. His attention is everywhere at once, and it is to this that he owes a large part of his authority. He is inside the mind of every player. He knows not only what each *should* be doing, but also what he *is* doing. He is the living embodiment of law, both positive and negative. His hands decree and prohibit. His ears search out profanation.
>
> Thus for the orchestra the conductor literally embodies the work they are playing, the simultaneity of the sounds as well as their sequence; and since, during the performance, nothing is supposed to exist except this work, for so long is the conductor the ruler of the world.[2]

Although Canetti never saw Mahler conduct, his description, intentionally or otherwise, brings us a little closer to the phenomenon that was Mahler, certainly closer than Werfel's poem. Another description comes from the internationally famous contralto Ernestine Schumann-Heink who, it is claimed, pursued Mahler with her obvious amorous intentions, intentions which, exceptionally, he ignored. In her memoirs she offers a relatively critical account of the conductor, while none the less helping to explain the tyrannical side of his conducting that many observers noted. Her memoir makes it clear how the diminutive conductor exploited the powers invested in him and carried that abuse of power to the point where many orchestras and many players came to hate him:

> But Mahler – poor Mahler! He was thin and nervous and sensitive, trembling to all music. It was always that he wanted and sought endlessly for perfection. He forgot that there is no perfection in this world. In his own mind and ideals, yes, but he forgot that when the orchestra was before him it was only eighty or

a hundred men who were not geniuses like himself, but simply good workers. They often irritated him so terribly that he couldn't bear it; then he became a musical tyrant. And this people couldn't understand or forgive. They didn't see why he was so merciless, and so it was that he was misjudged wherever he went. It was a tragedy for him, this attitude, for deep in his heart he had charity, and he was the most lovable and kindest creature you could imagine – except when conducting. When the baton was in his hand, he was a despot![3]

It is clear from this why Mahler always had difficulty with orchestras and choirs and why his engagements as a concert conductor in Hamburg and later with the Vienna Philharmonic ended prematurely on a note of embittered stridency.

Mahler clearly had no idea how to deal with what we would now call a collective in the theatre. In the case of many singers, but by no means all of them, he was able to communicate his ideas so well that they later recalled him with affection and gratitude. He forged a musical bond while preparing their parts with them and could influence them either individually or in small groups, making his intentions clear and inspiring them with his enthusiasm for the masterpieces of the repertory, assuming that they themselves were susceptible to such enthusiasm. But his approach to the orchestral collective quickly degenerated from the dictatorial to the aggressive, a development that may have been due to his own awareness of his lack of leadership skills. In his calmer moments he saw the problem very clearly. On one occasion in Hamburg, Natalie Bauer-Lechner asked him why the local musicians were so hostile towards him, when he was merely urging them on in the service of the music. Instead of being hostile, she argued, they really should have been grateful to him:

> There you're quite wrong! Do you really think these people are interested in learning and making progress? For them, art is only the cow which they milk so as to live their everyday lives undisturbed, as comfortably and pleasantly as possible. And yet, there are some amongst them who are more willing and better than the rest; one ought to have more patience with them than I am able to manage. For if one of them doesn't immediately give me what is on the page, I could kill him on the spot; I come down on him, and upset him so much that he really hates me. In this way I often demand more of them than they are capable of actually giving; no wonder they don't forgive me for it![4]

Canetti's psychological profile of the power-hungry conductor is of course incomplete if we fail to take account of the music, whether in the concert hall or the opera house. One cannot say that Mahler felt uncomfortable with his position of power on the podium, for he was undoubtedly conscious of his influence, a point that emerges with some force from his ambitious rise; but his

deep despair and the way in which he exercised control – a way that was counterproductive and certainly not suited to cementing and extending his position
of authority – show beyond doubt that for him the music was more important
than the power that was derived from it.

In order to appreciate what was so unsettling and controversial about
Mahler's conducting, we need to recall that until the end of the nineteenth
century, conductors remained relatively static and calm on the podium. In an
age when important symphonic works were increasingly being interpreted as
a substitute religion, conductors were gradually turning into the high priests of
this art. Their office acquired a hieratic aspect, and the larger the orchestras
that they conducted in ever bigger halls, the more cloud-girt their position on
the dais became. It was even said of Berlioz – that eccentric genius among
composers in the middle of the nineteenth century – that the concerts at which
he performed his own works were remarkable for their majestically measured
gestures, even if his mane of luxuriant hair created the impression of eccentricity. Mahler's immediate predecessors at the Vienna Court Opera, Wilhelm
Jahn and Hans Richter, were also said to be undemonstrative on the podium,
especially when they remained seated, as they normally did at opera performances. Only in the concert hall did they stand. Mahler followed their precedent
in both these respects. A calm deportment on the podium also has something
to do with physical size, of course. Even today, relatively small conductors tend
to gesticulate wildly, as is clear from film clips that allow us to compare two
of the leading Mahler conductors of the twentieth century, the extremely tall
Otto Klemperer and the comparatively small Leonard Bernstein. Quite apart
from his other affinities with Mahler, Bernstein arguably comes closest to his
revered idol in terms of his extreme mobility, even if Mahler avoided the
sort of air-borne leaps that Bernstein famously favoured. One of the few
composers before Mahler who was similarly said to engage in effusive gestures
was Beethoven, but, unlike Mahler, he was not a professional conductor. The
composer Louis Spohr, who played the violin under Beethoven's own direction, reports on the conductor's strange and unusual movements:

> When he wanted a *sforzando* he would vehemently throw out both his arms,
> which previously he had held crossed across his breast. For a *piano* he would
> crouch down, going down deeper as he wanted the sound to be softer . . . Then,
> at the beginning of a *crescendo* he would rise gradually and when the *forte* was
> reached he would leap up into the air. Occasionally he would shout with the
> music in order to make the *forte* stronger, without being conscious of doing so.[5]

Other accounts of Beethoven as a conductor likewise describe an exceptionally
animated figure who paid no heed to the usual way of conducting. The baton

was introduced only in the course of the nineteenth century, slowly displacing the older method of beating a stick on the ground or of using a slightly less heavy piece of wood that was struck against the conductor's desk in order to beat time. Spohr was one of the first conductors to dispense with this stick and to paint delicate lines in the air using a piece of rolled-up paper and, later, a baton similar to the ones in use today. Wagner, too, is said to have been extremely animated as a conductor, causing a stir and at the same time eliciting dissent. As with Mahler, this may have been due to his lively temperament and relatively small size. Hans von Bülow and Arthur Nikisch were regarded as the most modern conductors of their day. Mahler was in close contact with both men. But in both cases, their carefully choreographed movements on the podium were comparatively calm, while remaining highly effective. Another professional conductor of this period was Richard Strauss, who, although friendly with Mahler, was in many ways his opposite. He too made his mark by the extreme calmness of his demeanour. Tall and thin, Strauss was initially a somewhat fidgety conductor, but he quickly adopted a far more economical approach that struck contemporaries as particularly incongruous in the context of the floods of sound that he unleashed in works such as his own *Salome* and *Elektra*. He would stand perfectly still on the podium, his left arm and hand dangling motionlessly at his side and giving the impression that he would prefer to place his hand in his trouser or waistcoat pocket. He used his right hand only from the wrist, true to his own maxims, which he later formulated as ten golden rules. According to the second of them, 'You should not perspire when conducting: only the audience should get warm.' (The sixth rule reads: 'If you think that the brass is now blowing hard enough, tone it down another shade or two.')

Throughout much of his career, Mahler was the exact opposite of this, taking his place in the Beethovenian and Wagnerian tradition, while going far beyond it, suggesting that it is a peculiarity of composers who are also conductors that their approach to conducting is extremely animated, Strauss being the exception that confirms the rule. At the height of his career, Mahler was described by friends and enemies alike as a dervish on the podium. One small but by no means unimportant detail is worth noting: Mahler was the only famous conductor of his age to appear completely beardless, a point that further underlined his 'modernity'. All other conductors, including Bülow and Nikisch, wore beards of various kinds, and even the no less 'modern' Strauss had a luxuriant moustache that he was later to trim back to less ostentatious proportions. Quite apart from the fashionable trends of the years around 1900, a conductor's beard was regarded as a sign of authority and dignity. Anyone who dispensed with a beard had to find other means of maintaining what Max Weber describes as the individual's charismatic hold over orchestras and audiences alike.

In March 1901 a caricature by Hans Schließmann appeared in the humorous journal *Fliegende Blätter*. It was headed 'An ultramodern conductor' and subtitled 'Kapellmeister Kappelmann conducts his Symphonie diabolica'.[6] Although Mahler is not mentioned by name, every contemporary observer would have recognized him in a caricature that is particularly informative for the masterly way in which Schließmann uses it for a series of movement studies depicting the conductor in no fewer than seventeen different poses. Even though Schließmann clearly set out to caricature the conductor, he does so in a way which, exceptionally, is innocent of any anti-Semitic associations. The name 'Kappelmann' suggests a portmanteau neologism made up of the German words 'Kapellmeister' and 'Zappelmann' = 'a fidget'. As such, the caricature says much about the phenotype of Mahler as a conductor, revealing, as it does, a wide range of movements and positions, extending from a crouching position in which the legs are held apart to another in which the legs are placed close together, with the result that the conductor, balancing on the tips of his toes, is able to achieve a height of which he was otherwise incapable. Sometimes the left arm is left nonchalantly hanging at the conductor's side, while on other occasions both arms are raised ecstatically aloft, apparently attempting to draw down the music from the heavens. The baton whips through the air or is held calmly, while the left hand coaxes the necessary *espressivo* from the orchestra.

Even more expressive, of course, are the silhouettes of Mahler that Otto Böhler produced, presumably at the same time as Schließmann's caricature.[7] Böhler, who was famous for his silhouettes, depicted Mahler on the podium at the Vienna Court Opera and shows him conducting sitting down, although this did not, of course, prevent him from occasionally leaping to his feet whenever he became excited. There is no sense of a caricature in Böhler's work but a far greater degree of observation and a more subtle form of delineation. Once again, several images appear together on the same page, the technique that Böhler uses allowing the essential aspects of the conductor's movements to find even clearer expression. In two of the silhouettes, Mahler is depicted turning to the observer, and Böhler brings out to admirable effect the threatening character of Mahler's flashing, reflecting spectacles, a feature described by many other eyewitnesses. (We should recall at this point that anti-reflective spectacles did not exist at this period.) Again the observer is struck by the uncommonly animated nature of the conductor's body and flapping arms. Above all, however, we can appreciate the decisive function of the left arm and hand which, in contradistinction to Strauss, were used to calm the players down, to excite them, to dampen and fire them, to underscore a particular passage or to tease out even more subtle emotions from the body of players that was the orchestra.

Mahler was evidently the most unusual conductor of his age. Even those who barely understood what he was trying to achieve with his orchestras – and these people must have been in a majority – were both baffled and fascinated by his wild movements on the podium. It cannot be denied, of course, that anti-Semites seized hold of this circumstance and claimed that such movements were typical of Jewish conductors. Jews, it was said, gesticulated wildly when speaking and gesticulated equally wildly when conducting, whether they did so sitting or standing. In welcoming Mahler to Vienna the local *Reichspost* used the term *mauscheln* to describe the conductor in its edition of 14 April 1897, transferring to his body language the characteristics of those speech patterns that Jews were said to use in their futile attempts to speak correct German. A caricature like the one by Fritz Gareis emphasizes this aspect and depicts a 'Jew in the Thornbush', performing a veritable St Vitus's dance on the podium.[8] The fact that especially when he was conducting his own music, of course, Mahler was regarded as an 'ultramodern' conductor in the sense of nervous, decadent, overwrought and sickly is an indication of the link between anti-Semitism and anti-modernism that repeatedly affected perceptions of Mahler.

As many eyewitnesses noted, Mahler himself attempted in the course of his career to find a simpler style of conducting, later admitting that as a young conductor he had adopted far too artificial and studied an approach to the great works that were close to his heart, pouring into them far too much of his own personality. Only as a mature conductor did he achieve complete truth, simplicity and straightforwardness.[9] Anna von Mildenburg recalls how intensively he worked with his singers and with individual sections of the orchestra. But it was the critic Ernst Decsey – the author of biographies of Wolf and Bruckner – who wrote one of the liveliest accounts of Mahler conducting, stressing the tyranni-cally creative element of his conducting when he noted that he re-instrumented a work by following the inspiration of the moment and bringing out particular groups of instruments, while reducing the dynamic level of other groups, not out of a sense of preciousness or arbitrariness but because he was intuitively conscious of an alternative balance. Decsey places a positive gloss on the argu-ments raised by reactionary critics and insists that as a modern, nervous and sensitive individual Mahler was anxious not to miss any nuances. Whereas conductors of the older generation such as Hans Richter used broad brushstrokes to paint a broad line composed of almost unbroken swathes, Mahler produced a series of dots, a kind of pointillism of the conductor's podium, which Decsey saw as something entirely positive. His impression of Mahler is atmospherically dense and graphic, making it clear what attentive and unbiased observers could see when they looked down into the pit of the Vienna Court Opera:

> His body was racked with movement and in the semi-darkness he looked like
> some kind of fairy-tale goblin engaged in a flurry of hocus-pocus. In the harsh
> spotlight that lit up the rostrum his face was fascinatingly ugly and had a

ghastly pallor, ringed as it was by his waving hair. Every little shift in the orchestra was reflected in his sensitive features: one moment he would be dampening something down, which would knot the skin round his eyes into grim folds accompanied by a lifting of his nose; the next moment he would be smiling in confluence with the sweet strains of the orchestra, radiating his approval and enjoyment, so that it was a case of both devils and angels crossing his visage in turn. Lightning flashed from his spectacle lenses with each sharp movement of his head, and from behind the lenses his eyes shone forth, watchful, assertive and demanding attention – every inch of his frame was simultaneously both an instrument of command and a means of expression.[10]

Decsey observed something else, too, and it is a point that helps to explain the enthusiasm that many great singers felt for the allegedly insufferable conductor: Mahler was all eyes and missed nothing in the pit or on the stage, having memorized the works in his repertory so well that he could sing along with the performers and indeed did so at important passages. At the end of Act Two of *Tristan und Isolde*, for example, Tristan has to sing the words 'O König, das kann ich dir nicht sagen' ('O king, that I cannot tell you'). Here Mahler would not only prompt the words, duplicating the efforts of the prompter, but the hypnotic, mesmerizing quality of his cue would also give the singer an idea of how to interpret these words, an understanding evidently communicated as if by telepathy. Mahler's magnetism on the podium clearly conveyed itself to his singers, or at least to those whom he liked and who liked him in turn and who were willing to work with him on the score and on their own interpretations. Leo Slezak, Anna von Mildenburg, Selma Kurz and Marie Gutheil-Schoder were all immensely fond of him, convinced as they were that they had never worked with so great a conductor and would never do so again.

Mahler's fellow conductor and disciple Bruno Walter was in an even better position than Decsey to assess his mentor's gifts. Walter, whose talents as a composer do not concern us here, confirms Decsey's evaluation, while adding other aspects based on his detailed knowledge of conducting. He, too, stresses the improvisatory nature of Mahler's style of conducting, an aspect that was grounded, of course, in the most meticulous preparation – this also is a point that he shared with Bernstein. The more deeply Mahler explored the works that he conducted, the more spontaneous his interpretation appeared and the more he seemed to be conducting a piece for the first time. Even his thirtieth performance of a work seemed freshly minted and free from all routine. But his apparent spontaneity was based on the most ruthless respect for the note values, tempo, dynamics and other performance markings – it is no accident that as a composer anxious to ensure that his own works were correctly performed, he liberally scattered his scores with such markings to a degree hitherto unknown because he was tormented by the not entirely unjustified fear that his fellow conductors would otherwise fail to realize his intentions. This fear reached the point where he finally came to feel that he alone could conduct his own works, with the result that he increasingly took time off from his work in Vienna to conduct his music elsewhere, absences that irked the Viennese and ultimately contributed to his resignation from office.

Perhaps the most astonishing aspect, however, is that in spite of his tremendous mobility on the podium, Mahler's beat was never unclear – countless generations of orchestral players can confirm that precision is compromised by over-hectic movements on the part of a conductor. Bruno Walter recalls that singers and orchestral musicians were often guilty of minor imprecisions, albeit far fewer than with other conductors, but that there were never any of the usual problems of coordination between stage and pit, Mahler's exemplarily clear beat guaranteeing that they stayed together. Not even during the most extreme emotional outbursts did that beat forfeit its clarity and precision. But Walter also noted that in the course of time Mahler's conducting grew increasingly calm and mellow: 'In his last period in Vienna, the picture was one of almost uncanny calm, with no loss in intensity of effect. I remember a performance of Strauss's *Symphonia domestica* in which the contrast between the wild storms in the orchestra and the immobility of the conductor who unleashed them made an almost ghostly impression.'[11] The true essence of Mahler's conducting and of his influence as a conductor has of course been irretrievably lost. We have no recordings of him conducting, as we do of Nikisch, Strauss and Pfitzner, for example (although the technology existed to make such recordings). The only thing we have – and its value is all the greater in consequence – are the famous piano rolls made on a Welte-Mignon piano which contain excerpts from his own works. But the nature of that recording means that interpretative subtleties are difficult to hear, while the unusual speeds – almost all the pieces are played considerably faster than we are used to in modern interpretations – are all too apparent. But even if we had recordings of Mahler conducting, the technology was still in its infancy at that time, and many of the nuances would be lost. The most knowledgeable of his contemporaries knew, of course, that not even a description in words could really bring them to life. For all his linguistic sensitivity, the composer Josef Bohuslav Foerster, who was one of Mahler's confidants, could only touch on the impression the conductor must have made when he describes the

> incomparably balanced scale introducing the *Leonore* Overture no. 3 via the unusually long, breathtaking rest before the strings leap jubilantly up: a word about the mystic impression left when in the final movement of the Ninth Symphony, those thrilling bars rang out, introduced by a low B flat on the

contrabassoon and seeming to come from a mysterious distance, so that when they heard it listeners felt that invisible hosts of rapt enthusiasts were approaching with an exultant 'Hosanna' on their lips, just as they did on the very first Palm Sunday.[12]

Even Bruno Walter, who was otherwise noted for his precise way with words, ultimately fails to convey the immediacy of the impression left by Mahler when he concludes his account of Mahler as a conductor by noting that:

I want, however, to stress once more the fact that the decisive quality of his conducting and the source of its power was the warmth of his heart. That gave his interpretation the impressiveness of a personal message. That rendered unnoticeable the meticulous study lying behind the result he achieved: its virtuosity and accomplishment; that made his music-making what it was – a spontaneous greeting from soul to soul. Here, on the borderland between art and humanity, the nobility and potency of his mind were revealed. The secret of his lasting fame as conductor and director is his ideal combination of high artistic gifts with the ardent sensibility of a great heart.[13]

We must be content with this and try to understand what it was about Mahler that led so many people to report their impressions of this hot-headed conductor in words of such emotive impact and almost intoxicated enthusiasm so long after his death. It is an impression that perhaps emerges most powerfully when we listen to Mahler's music. The implacable expressive power that is conveyed by his own works, at least when they are adequately performed, must also have been apparent in his interpretations of the works of other composers. We must surely be allowed to draw this conclusion.

15

The Second Symphony

IN MAHLER'S MIND, there was an extraordinarily close link between his First and Second Symphonies, at least as far as the opening movement of the later work was concerned. In 1896 he left Max Marschalk in no doubt that the hero who is borne to his grave in this movement is the same person as the one who dies at the end of the First Symphony, where he is still attended by victory fanfares. Now he is retrospectively laid to rest, and in the course of the next four movements questions about the meaning of life and suffering are posed, albeit not always with the same urgency, for there are digressions and moments of rest on the journey that Mahler described as intermezzos. These questions are answered in the fifth and final movement.[1] The genesis of the Second Symphony is longer and more complicated than one might assume even for a work as ambitious and as long as this – it lasts some eighty minutes in performance. The First Symphony had already been completed when Mahler, staying in Prague where he was rehearsing *Die drei Pintos*, put the finishing touches to the opening movement in September 1888. For the present, however, that was all. His move to Budapest and all the wearisome duties bound up with it, together with the inordinate dimensions of a work that Mahler planned from the outset would be his magnum opus, left him little opportunity to make any further progress on the score. But his decision to call the opening movement 'Todtenfeier' did not stem from any vague prospect of completing a work that was in any case planned to be a complete symphony. The title was fixed soon after he completed the movement in September 1888 and is a clear reference to a key work of Polish literature, Adam Mickiewicz's *Dziady*, a remarkable mixture of epic and drama completed in 1832 and occupying a curious halfway house between messianic mysticism and a profoundly nationalistic critique of Russian hegemony in Poland, the narrative peppered with allusions to contemporary political events. Mahler's Second Symphony has no programme that is directly attributable to Mickiewicz's epic poem, but the poet's views on the power that the souls of the dead exert over the living must have chimed with the composer's view of the world, both then and later. There is no mystery surrounding Mahler's discovery of Mickiewicz: the first German translation of the work had been undertaken by Siegfried Lipiner and was published in Leipzig in 1887, a year before Mahler began work on his symphony. He also began sketching the second movement in 1888, whereas the third, fourth and fifth movements were not written until the summers of 1893 and 1894, when Mahler was staying at Steinbach on the Attersee. He completed the work in June 1894.

The first three movements were heard for the first time at a concert given by the Berlin Philharmonic on 4 March 1895. Although the rest of the programme was conducted by Strauss, Mahler himself took charge of his own composition, the performance proving sufficiently successful for him to be invited back to Berlin to conduct the entire work with the same orchestra on 13 December 1895. Mahler's involvement in an incomplete performance, without the decisive final movement, can be attributed only to his scepticism as to whether he would ever have a chance to perform the entire piece. Natalie Bauer-Lechner was unable to attend the performance, but Justine wrote to her to report on the powerful impression that the complete work left on its listeners – it was the first time that one of Mahler's works had had such a decisive and unequivocal impact on an audience, and it was no doubt this concert that convinced Mahler that he could captivate people's hearts with his music, a certainty that he never lost, in spite of all the setbacks that he suffered. This also explains his dictum, 'My time will come.' Even the opening movement was greeted with tremendous acclaim, but this was surpassed by the impact of the final movement, an impact achieved by means of the huge resources involved: older men were not ashamed to be seen crying, while younger men and women fell into each other's arms. The fluttering notes of the 'bird of death', as Mahler called it (on another occasion he spoke of a nightingale), that are played on the flute before the *pianissimo* entry of the chorus were heard in total silence, even though Mahler had feared that the audience would lack the requisite concentration. It turned out to have been fortunate that not many seats had been sold in advance, with the result that most of the tickets had been given away to students from the Conservatory and to local musicians – knowledgeable members of the public whose reaction was gratifyingly different from the usual response of subscribers to new and unfamiliar works.

Mahler himself offered a detailed account of the inner programme of his Second Symphony and did so, moreover, on more than one occasion. Although he had told the world that 'all programmes should perish', the fact that he considered it necessary and meaningful to draw up yet another such programme in 1901 attests to his inability to make up his mind on this point. On this occasion, however, he was resolved not to allow any of these texts to enter the public domain. Curiously enough, the 1901 explanations were intended for the king of

Saxony on the occasion of the first performance of the symphony in Dresden, a performance conducted not by Mahler but by the Court Opera's general music director, Ernst von Schuch. Mahler also sent a copy to his sister, who in turn passed it on to Alma. The 1901 programme agrees in the main with the others that Mahler drew up for the critic Max Marschalk, for Natalie Bauer-Lechner and, finally, for the first performance of the work in Berlin.[2] In essence, they all run as follows:

The opening movement is an Allegro maestoso that accompanies listeners and mourners to the coffin of a man they once loved. His life and his sufferings and aspirations pass before their mind's eye, encouraging them to collect their thoughts on the questions of life and death and of the afterlife, but above all on the question as to the meaning of what we call life. The second movement is marked 'Andante moderato' and, like the third and fourth, is intended as an intermezzo. Its idyllic ländler-like tone is in such stark contrast with the obsequies of the opening movement that even Mahler himself came to have doubts about its appropriateness. It encapsulates the memory of a single sunlit moment in the hero's life, when this life still seemed to him to be open-ended, unclouded and full of promise. The memory of this moment almost leads the survivors to forget what really happened and to lose sight of the hero's death. The third movement is headed 'With a calmly flowing motion' and is the work's Scherzo, revealing the hero in a sombre mood, beset by life's tribulations and losing his grip. In his own account of this movement, Mahler was unable to decide whether his diagnosis applies to the deceased or to those who are standing beside the grave. The threads of life become eerily confused. Disgust seizes hold of the individual, and suddenly everything seems meaningless and confusing. Mahler found an impressive image to explain the expressive quality that he had in mind when writing this movement: when we return to the bustling world from an exceptional situation such as the one that exists at the graveside of a person we love, the milling mass of life may strike us as terrifyingly alien. It is as if we are looking into a brightly lit ballroom at night and can see only the fleeting, turning shapes but are unable to hear the music. The movements in the room seem meaningless and ghostly, leading us to start up with a scream of disgust. The fourth movement, 'Urlicht', is headed 'Very solemn, but simple' and is a setting of a song of the same name from *Des Knaben Wunderhorn*. In it we hear a single emotionally affecting voice, the voice of naïve hope on the part of a soul that acknowledges its descent from God and reveals its desire to return there.

The final movement has several tempo markings, starting with 'In the tempo of the Scherzo. Flaring up wildly'. It restores the mood of the end of the opening movement. A voice calls out, proclaiming the Last Judgement. The Apocalypse is at hand. In conversation with Natalie Bauer-Lechner – and this is important – Mahler stressed that the first three movements have a narrative function, even if that function is retrospective, whereas 'Urlicht' is so short as to be little more than a brief meditation. The final movement, conversely, represents an inner event. Drumrolls are followed by the Last Trump, the graves fly open and humanity draws near, rich men and poor, kings and popes are all indistinguishable, recalling the Baroque *theatrum mundi*, Calderón and Hofmannsthal's *Großes Welttheater*. There is the sound of screaming, the very earth quakes, then a sudden a ghostly silence. A solitary bird calls out once again in the flute and piccolo and then, quietly and simply, *pianissimo* and *misterioso*, the unaccompanied chorus intones the phrase 'aufersteh'n, ja aufersteh'n, wirst du, mein Staub, nach kurzer Ruh!' ('You will rise again, yes, you will rise again, my dust, after brief repose'). God appears in all His glory, and the Last Judgement is replaced by omnipresent love. Mahler himself later admitted that he had no idea how he had achieved the culminating climax of the work. The words of this chorale are based on a hymn by Klopstock that Mahler heard at the memorial service for Hans von Bülow in St Michael's Church in Hamburg – writers have repeatedly, if erroneously, referred to it as an ode, Josef Bohuslav Foerster even claiming that it comes from Klopstock's verse epic *Messias*. Mahler used only the first two verses, adding the remaining two-thirds himself, so that the result may be regarded as a genuine poem by Mahler inspired by Klopstock's original and differing markedly from the attitude of humility and orthodox Christianity typical of Klopstock's hymn. Instead, it comes closer to the sort of individualized, pantheistic position characteristic of Mahler's own faith. It is worth noting in passing that more than a century before Mahler, Georg Christoph Lichtenberg, the great German aphorist, copied out Klopstock's text in his *Sudelbücher*. Even though he added no commentary of his own, it seems clear that Lichtenberg was motivated by the same enthusiasm and emotion as Mahler.[3]

It is evident that such a programme goes far beyond anything found in music before this period – and it remains a programme even if it was intended for only a limited readership and even if it is difficult to compare it with the normal type of programme associated with normal programme music. Even the instrumental resources on which the symphony calls go beyond anything demanded by Wagner and Strauss, more especially the off-stage orchestra in the final movement, which consists of four additional trumpets and trombones and an extra set of percussion. Mahler also demands three steel rods, two female soloists (soprano and contralto) for the fourth and fifth movements and a choir of mixed voices – at the first performance in Berlin this choir contained no fewer than two hundred singers. All in all, this looks forward to the yet more lavish resources of the Eighth Symphony. But the work's ambitions go even further. For the first time, Mahler tried to realize an ideal that he was to formulate on more than one occasion, namely, the idea of creating a world using all the means at his disposal. And these resources not only include orchestral and vocal forces that go to the very limits of what is feasible, but to tame and ultimately yoke together the most extreme forms of musical and textual expression, forms which had hitherto tended to create their effects independently of one another. He adopted an identical attitude towards the traditional repertory and in doing so went far beyond Beethoven, who had crossed the symphony with the cantata in the final movement of his Ninth Symphony. Mahler does the same in the final movement of his Second Symphony, which is a vast independent symphonic movement up to the entry of the chorus, and then a brief cantata. But he also adds a simple *Wunderhorn* song as an independent movement for the contralto soloist ('Urlicht') and paraphrases a further *Wunderhorn* song, 'Des Antonius von Padua Fischpredigt', in the third movement. Here Mahler felt that the poem's ironical attitude to life and to the activities of fish (and human beings), which listen attentively to the saint's sermon only to return, unrepentant, to their former lives, was the best way of criticizing a world that goes round and round in a circle of stupidity and self-interest. As Mahler effectively admitted when he gave the opening movement the title 'Todtenfeier' and separated it off from the rest of the work, this movement is a symphonic poem like Strauss's *Death and Transfiguration*, only without the transfiguration that comes in the final movement. It goes without saying that this hubristic desire to compel the world to listen to the work of a composer still in his mid-thirties was bound to involve inhomogeneity and heterogeneity. It is impossible, after all, to reconcile elements of sonata form with a simple folksong or to combine a ländler with a chorale and the caustic irony of St Anthony's sermon to the fishes with the 'Resurrection' chorus.

The most heterogeneous element of all is the second movement, a point that Mahler himself conceded, without, however, contemplating any changes here. In a letter to the conductor Julius Buths, who was planning to perform the work in Düsseldorf, Mahler effectively apologized for the fact that the second movement seemed out of place after the first, rather than as a necessary contrast. That was his mistake, he went on, a weakness in the work's structure: the planned intermezzo had turned out to be too disruptive.[4] The same letter contains another interesting remark. According to all existing versions of the full score, the fifth movement follows on from the fourth without a break, a point that is nowadays respected in all performances of the symphony. Buths had said that he wanted to have the concert's main interval at this point in what was already a long evening. Mahler agreed. It would surely be worth while putting this suggestion into practice, at least once.

The hybrid aspects of the work are relatively easy to identify. The Second Symphony has in no small way helped to fuel long-held prejudices against Mahler's music, which is said to be overblown and hollow and as such to be a reflection of the years of rapid industrial and economic expansion of the new German Reich. In his compelling examination of the work, Rudolf Stephan argues, conversely, that:

> The extreme subjectivity that is raised to a yet higher degree in this work, acquiring a cosmic, soteriological dimension, now strikes us as strange and is difficult to grasp any longer. But it was this dimension alone that suggested and perhaps even demanded the use of all the available expressive resources without regard for questions of taste or genre. The work's striking syncretism is not a sign of eclecticism or even a lack of discrimination but documents the composer's insight into the need for objective necessity. Anyone who wants to create a world needs many different means.[5]

Adorno adopted a more critical attitude to the piece, noting on the one hand that the Second Symphony is the work that allows most listeners to get to know Mahler and to love him, a point on which many would agree, but at the same time arguing that, unlike almost all Mahler's other works, it loses some of its impact. For all his enthusiasm for Mahler's music, Adorno even uses the term 'prolixity' in discussing the opening movement and observes 'a certain primitiveness' in the final movement. And yet even here he cannot avoid imputing to the *pianissimo* entry of the chorus at 'aufersteh'n, ja aufersteh'n' a suggestive power that remains undimmed, a point that listeners can still put to the test today.[6]

A far more moving and immediate response was that of the young Alban Berg, who attended Mahler's last concert in Vienna in November 1907, by which date Mahler had already left the Court Opera. The work on the programme was the Second Symphony. After the concert, Berg wrote to Helene Nahowski, whom he was later to marry:

> It happened in the finale of the Mahler symphony, when I gradually felt a sense of otherworldliness, as if in all the world there were nothing left but this music – and me enjoying it! But when it came to its shattering and uplifting conclusion, I suddenly felt a slight pang, and a voice within me said: What of Helene? It was only then that I realized that I had been unfaithful to you, so I now implore your forgiveness. Tell me, darling, that you understand and forgive me!?[7]

Berg was not wrong: Helene understood very well what he meant.

Self-Realization: Hamburg
(1891–7)

Different Forms of Loneliness

On an inclement January day in 1894 a still relatively young Czech composer set off for 14 Fröbelstraße, a street in Hamburg with a view of the as yet undeveloped marshland on the outskirts of the city. Josef Bohuslav Foerster was a few months older than Mahler and had already written two symphonies and a *Stabat Mater* but without achieving his breakthrough as a composer. If he had moved from Prague to Hamburg, it was because his wife, the dramatic soprano Berta Lauterer, whose career was moving faster than his own, had taken up an engagement at the Hamburg Opera. By the date of his death in 1951, conversely, the then ninety-one-year-old composer was one of the most distinguished of Czech composers, with a work-list that includes several important symphonies and operas such as *Eva*, works which, like those of his friend Josef Suk, have been rediscovered in recent years. Berta Foerster-Lauterer soon came to the attention of the company's principal conductor, Gustav Mahler, when she took over the role of Eva in *Die Meistersinger* at short notice and arrived at the rehearsals uncommonly well prepared. Mahler asked her with whom she had studied the part. 'With my husband,' she replied, whereupon Mahler turned to the orchestra with the words: 'Gentlemen, this is how a musician studies.' Addressing the soprano, he expressed the wish to get to know her husband. Foerster was understandably nervous when he set out to visit Mahler, for he too had heard of the conductor's reputation for rigour and inflexibility, a reputation acquired during his three years as the Hamburg Opera's senior conductor. Mahler was living alone in his third-floor apartment in the Fröbelstraße – it was not until later in the year that his sister Justine joined him there. Foerster rang the bell hesitantly. Like most bachelors, Mahler did not occupy the whole floor, but only two rooms. A friendly fellow lodger directed the visitor to a door at the end of the corridor. Foerster knocked but received no reply. Curiously enough, the first room that he entered was the bedroom, an arrangement presumably due to Mahler's need for extreme quiet while he was composing – evidently he preferred to have his bedroom, rather than his workroom, adjoining the corridor. The only objects in this first room were a simple bed and a slightly dusty laurel wreath with a ribbon bearing the inscription: 'To the Pygmalion of the Hamburg Opera – Hans von Bülow.' The great conductor, who lived in Hamburg, had presented Mahler with this wreath in recognition of his work in breathing new life into the city's opera house. Foerster finally found the tenant in the second room.

Mahler soon set his visitor at ease, and when Foerster returned home, it was in the knowledge not only that he had found a new friend but that he had met the most important person he had hitherto encountered in his life. This initial encounter forms the starting point for several chapters in Foerster's autobiography. Although Foerster later regretted not taking notes on his conversations with Mahler in the way that Natalie Bauer-Lechner did, these chapters are among the most vivid accounts of Mahler and are an important source especially for his years in Hamburg. This was the first time in his life that he was continuously and sympathetically observed by a friendly eye. A second important source for the Hamburg period is the memoir of the music critic Ferdinand Pfohl, although its value is diminished by the fact that for various reasons Pfohl broke off all contact with Mahler following the conductor's departure from Hamburg and adopted a highly critical tone motivated by wounded pride. (Such an attitude can, of course, have the advantage of allowing the observer a clearer view of his subject.)

The second room that Foerster saw on the day that he first met Mahler was the conductor's living room. It was almost completely filled with a piano, a library and a desk. There was also a pianino next to the wall. Foerster's terminology needs explaining. At the end of the nineteenth century, a piano – Foerster uses the word *Klavier* – was the successor of the fortepiano, a horizontal, rectangular instrument that was strung in a horizontal plane (hence Foerster's ability to see that the instrument was covered in scores and sheet music), while the pianino was what we would nowadays describe as an upright piano with vertical strings. If Mahler preferred the pianino, it was no doubt because of its fuller sound. Open on the music rest was the score of a Bach cantata, a composer whom he was studying with a degree of interest that not even musicians evinced at this time. On the walls were no family photographs or the usual objects of devotion but only three reproductions: Albrecht Dürer's *Melancolia*, 'the photograph of a drawing' depicting Saint Anthony preaching to the fishes – presumably a reproduction of Paolo Veronese's painting (Mahler had recently set the *Wunderhorn* song 'Des Antonius von Padua Fischpredigt') – and *The Concerto*, a painting formerly ascribed to Giorgione but now believed to be the work of Titian. It depicts a monk playing a keyboard instrument, a rapt, otherworldly expression on his face, and looking over his shoulder at a second figure holding a viol-like instrument, while a third figure wearing an elaborate hat stands to their right. Mahler told Foerster: 'I could go on composing this picture for ever.'[1] Others, too, noted the profound similarity between the monk and Mahler. In his own reminiscences of the composer, Bruno Walter reports that even before he met him for the first time he had repeatedly drawn a parallel between Mahler, about whom he had heard a great deal, and the monk in Titian's famous portrait, which by the end of the nineteenth century hung in countless middle-class houses in the form of a reproduction. When the two men finally met, Walter was even more struck by the similarity, which was typological rather than purely physiognomic:

> The picture gave the point of departure for our talk. Whether we then touched on Giorgione's strange prevision I do not remember, but I do recall our often speaking about it later. I also know that Mahler's likeness to the pious player enhanced my sense of the mystery prefigured in the fifteenth-century portrait.[2]

During his early years in Hamburg, Mahler lived on his own, his lifestyle giving many observers the impression of a monastic and even anchoritic existence. Certainly, there is no evidence of any goings-on with female members of the Hamburg ensemble of a kind familiar from the earlier and later periods. Not until Anna von Mildenburg entered Mahler's life in the autumn of 1895 does this situation appear to have changed. Even this affair was for a long time veiled in obscurity, because their relationship had already been broken off by the time that the soprano joined the Vienna Court Opera, while Mahler did all in his power to prevent details from reaching the public. Anna von Mildenburg likewise maintained a discreet silence, a silence surprising in view of her impulsive and passionate nature both onstage and in her private life with Mahler. In her reminiscences, which she published in 1921, she mentions Mahler, but not her affair with him, even if its existence may be inferred from a close reading of her remarks.

For a complete exposé we need to turn to the one hundred or so letters that Mahler wrote to her and that were published by Franz Willnauer in 2006. Together with the reminiscences of Foerster and Pfohl, these letters are the third source of our information about Mahler's time in Hamburg, and in terms of their intimacy, they are, of course, unparalleled. A letter preserved in Vienna indicates that in the 1920s Alma Mahler tried to regain these letters. Fortunately, Anna von Mildenburg, long since married to Hermann Bahr, refused to agree, not least because there is no doubt that Alma would have burnt them in her attempt to prove to the world that she was the one and only love in Mahler's life – anyone knowing only her own view of the matter would be bound to conclude that Mahler was a virgin when he married her. Conversely, Anna von Mildenburg's letters to Mahler have not survived. Presumably Mahler himself destroyed them before or shortly after his marriage.

Mahler had already been working in Hamburg for three years when Foerster got to know him. He had entered into negotiations with the director of the Hamburg Stadttheater, Bernhard Pollini, as early as October 1890, while he was still in Budapest, a démarche prompted either by his realization that his position in the Hungarian capital was untenable or by his own unwillingness to test that tenability. By January 1891 he had signed a contract as principal conductor. On paper this looks like a demotion – after all, he had been opera director in Budapest. But his post was the equivalent of what we would nowadays call 'general music director' and meant that he would hold the highest musical post in the company, while shedding the irksome duties that came with his administrative responsibilities in Budapest. Above all, Mahler could once again rehearse his favourite core repertory in German and rely on the resources of a well-funded company that was held in great affection by Hamburg's middle-class music lovers.

Hamburg could lay claim to having the first public opera house after Venice. It had opened on the Gänsemarkt as early as 1678, and by the years around 1700 was already an important centre of Baroque opera associated with three composers above all: Reinhard Keiser and his opera *Croesus*; the young George Frideric Handel, who played in the orchestra and wrote his opera *Almira* for Hamburg; and, above all, Georg Philipp Telemann, who composed some twenty operas for the company. In 1825 a new opera house was opened in the Dammtorstraße, where it still stands to this day. Designed by no less an architect than Karl Friedrich Schinkel, it witnessed only the second production in Germany of Wagner's *Rienzi* in 1844, a production conducted by the composer himself. Bernhard Pollini, who became its director in 1874, was born Baruch Pohl and was fully assimilated into the German community, but in spite of his change of name, he was unable to avoid the anti-Semitism of his age. With his keen eye for young and talented artists such as Mahler and Anna von Mildenburg, he raised the company to new artistic heights and placed it on a sound financial footing. None the less, relations between Pollini and Mahler were soon soured. According to Anna von Mildenburg's Mahlerian view of the situation, Pollini was an intriguer who ruthlessly exploited his discoveries, while none the less paying them handsomely. She reports that many young singers had to perform every other day to the greater glory of the house and its intendant. If they failed to survive this ordeal, they were quickly and unsentimentally dropped. Pollini's only interest was in a singer's voice, with the result that all of Mahler's attempts to work with his singers on questions of musical and dramatic interpretation were dismissed as completely pointless and disruptive to the smooth running of his company.

Mahler, too, was tremendously overworked, albeit not in such a way that he risked losing his voice. He soon saw through Pollini's tactics and, realizing how thoughtless his actions were, sought to counter them. But in order to achieve his ends, he had to keep Pollini in a good mood and avoid open confrontation. For his part, Pollini was no doubt vaguely aware of Mahler's genius, prompting him to seek his senior conductor's advice and to familiarize him with his plans and decisions. The result was a relationship in which hatred simmered beneath the deceptively calm surface of cooperation between colleagues. Gossip-mongers were not slow to go running to Pollini and inform him that his principal conductor had described the Stadttheater as a penitentiary. Pollini reacted by making Mahler conduct *Cavalleria rusticana* ten times, while more congenial tasks were allotted to a more complaisant colleague. In the longer term, however, Pollini was unable to sustain his punitive measures for it soon became clear to critics and audiences alike that the company had no other conductor who was anywhere near as good as Mahler. There is a symbolic rightness to the fact that Mahler's departure for Vienna in 1897 coincided with Pollini's death. But Hamburg later had other outstanding conductors such as Nikisch and Klemperer, who helped to maintain the house's musical standards in the wake of Mahler's departure – Mahler had wanted to compete with Nikisch in Leipzig, while Klemperer became one of the most enthusiastic of Mahlerian conductors alongside Bruno Walter and Willem Mengelberg.

The speed with which the people of Hamburg recognized Mahler's exceptional standing emerges from a review that appeared in the *Hamburgischer Correspondent* on 1 April 1891. Its author was Josef Sittard, a member of the conservative camp, who attended Mahler's first two performances in the city. Mahler's reputation was based on the successes that he had previously achieved conducting Wagner and in works like *Fidelio* and *Don Giovanni*, with the result that whenever he took up a new appointment he set the greatest store by introducing himself to his new audience with one of these works – throughout his whole life he was conscious of his impact as a conductor. In Hamburg he persuaded Pollini to let him make his debut with *Tannhäuser* on 29 March 1891, following this up with *Siegfried* two days later. Sittard's review appeared on 1 April – at this period it was still usual for reviews to appear the day after the performance. In it he wrote that the new conductor had surpassed all the expectations placed in him – after all, Mahler had previously run the Budapest Opera – and electrified his audiences with his performances:

> Herr Mahler is a conductor who has in his command not only the notes in the score, but, what is more, the spirit of the artistic work; and he also

possesses the gift of transmitting this spirit to the entire cast and carrying them along with him. There is no entry that is not cued by him, no dynamic shading that remains unobserved; Herr Mahler holds the reins in his hand with an energy which binds the individual firmly to him, draws him, we might say, with magical force into his own world of thought. The spiritual and artistic influence that such a conductor exerts on an orchestra was particularly easy to recognize yesterday [at the performance of *Siegfried*]; at times we thought we had before us a completely new instrumental ensemble. How clearly, rhythmically defined, carefully nuanced and phrased everything seemed; how the great climactic moments in the last two acts were enhanced! If Herr Mahler displays the same qualities in classical opera as in Wagner's music dramas, then our Opera may count itself fortunate to have such a brilliant conductor at its head.[3]

This review is extremely enlightening, which is why it has been quoted at length. When judged by the standards of the day, it is couched in unusually informative and precise terms, containing, as it does, a summary of all the positive qualities that were to typify Mahler throughout the rest of his life, at least whenever he conducted works by other composers. First, there was his ability to grasp the essence of the work that he was conducting and to communicate that view to the other members of the cast and orchestra, inspiring them to give of their best; second, there was the extreme precision of his cues to the singers and players; third, the vast dynamic range of his performances; fourth, his extreme care in his treatment of nuance and phrasing; fifth, his ability to bring out the work's rhythms with altogether exemplary clarity; sixth, the climaxes were overpoweringly dramatic and well placed; and, finally, he had an almost magical effect on his performers, especially his orchestral players, who played as if transformed by the spiritual energy of his conducting.

There were two other people who were enthusiastic about Mahler's conducting and whose opinion is even more significant than Sittard's. Tchaikovsky honoured Hamburg with a visit in January 1892, when he came to the city to conduct the local première of his opera *Eugene Onegin*. But the orchestra and the singers realized at the rehearsals that as an opera conductor the Russian composer had certain shortcomings. Wisely admitting to his own limitations, he handed over the conducting duties at short notice to Mahler, writing to his nephew shortly before the opening night: 'The conductor here is not merely passable, but actually has genius, and he ardently desires to conduct the first performance.'[4] The success of the first night fully justified Tchaikovsky. The other musician to be impressed by Mahler was not a composer (except of a handful of minor works) but a pianist and a conductor and, as such, arguably the most important figure in the generation before Mahler: Hans von Bülow. It is a source of great regret that no lasting friendship developed between the two men, but Bülow died in February 1894, during Mahler's years in Hamburg. At the same time Bülow's Brahmsian lack of sympathy for Mahler's music would have militated against such a friendship. (Much the same would have been true of Brahms himself.)

Mahler told Foerster about an incident as typical as it was embarrassing for both the parties concerned. Encouraged by Bülow's enthusiasm for his conducting at the Hamburg Opera – it was to this enthusiasm that Mahler owed the laurel wreath that hung above his bachelor's bed in Hamburg – he paid a visit to his famous colleague at the end of 1891 in order to show him the full score of his 'Todtenfeier', later to become the first movement of his Second Symphony. Bülow asked Mahler to play him excerpts from it, as this would give him a better idea of the work than merely reading the score. Mahler began, and after a while turned to observe his listener and was appalled to see him holding his hands to his ears. Bülow, it has to be said, was known for his eccentricities. And so Mahler continued to play, only to make the same observation again a few moments later. Was Bülow perhaps suffering from one of the migraines to which he was notoriously prone? Mahler stopped playing but was immediately urged to continue. When he had finished, Bülow, who was known for his implacable put-downs (one recalls the time when Nietzsche showed him one of his own compositions and Bülow described it as 'the rape of Euterpe'), gestured dismissively, adding: 'Well, if that's music, then I know nothing about music.'[5] In an earlier version of his reminiscences, Foerster offers a slightly different wording, 'then I no longer understand anything about music', suggesting a milder reaction to the score: if Bülow failed to understand the work, it was because he belonged to an older generation. But as a conductor, Bülow held his colleague in the highest regard. He himself had held the post of conductor in Meiningen in the early 1880s, becoming principal conductor of the Philharmonic Concerts in Hamburg in 1886. (The concerts were the brainchild of the great Berlin impresario, Hermann Wolff.) Bülow moved to the banks of the Elbe in 1887.

In short, there were many opportunities for Bülow to hear the young and brilliant Mahler conducting at the Hamburg Opera and also at the occasional concert in the city. True, Bülow's initial contacts with Mahler had been unfortunate – at Strauss's recommendation he had obtained a copy of the score to *Die drei Pintos*, only to dismiss the whole work as an 'infamous, outmoded concoction'.[6] But of his subsequent enthusiasm for Mahler as a conductor there is no doubt. As we have already had occasion to observe, Bülow's eccentricities were legendary – one recalls the time when he performed Beethoven's then rarely heard Ninth Symphony twice in succession in Meiningen, informing the audience that they would be wasting their time fleeing the building as all the doors had been locked. None the less, Mahler was evidently embarrassed by

Bülow's reaction to *Die drei Pintos* and felt that on this occasion his colleague had gone too far. And yet he was able to appreciate the praise that Bülow reserved for his work as a conductor. In late November 1891, for example, we find Mahler writing to Friedrich Löhr:

> Bülow lives here, and I go to all his concerts; it is droll how he takes every opportunity of sensationally 'distinguishing' me *coram publico* in his abstruse fashion. At every fine passage he casts me coquettish glances (I sit in the front row). – He hands the scores of unknown works down to me from the dais so that I can read them during the performance. – The moment he catches sight of me he ostentatiously makes a deep bow! Sometimes he addresses me from the dais, and so on.

Mahler then gives an edited version of the 'Todtenfeier' incident, adding an interesting variant on Foerster's account of the episode: 'When I played my "Todtenfeier" to him, he became quite hysterical with horror, declaring that compared with my piece *Tristan* was a Haydn symphony, and went on like a madman.'[7]

There is no doubt that Bülow was the most important musician before Strauss to recognize Mahler's genius, even if that recognition was very one-sided. But Bülow was already suffering from chronic ill-health. Like Strauss, he travelled to Egypt in the hope that the southern climate would lead to an improvement, but he died in a hotel room in Cairo on 12 February 1894 as the result of a stroke. His memorial service was held in Hamburg's St Michael's Church on 29 March and was attended by Mahler, among others. The service included music by Bach as well as a chorale sung to words by Klopstock, who had spent his most important years in Hamburg and died in nearby Ottensen in 1803, *Aufstehen wirst du mein Staub nach kurzer Ruh* ('You will arise, my dust, after brief repose'). Later that same afternoon, Foerster called on Mahler unannounced and found him bent over a score. He knew that until then Mahler had not been sure about the shape that the final movement of his Second Symphony should take. But when he entered Mahler's apartment, the latter exclaimed: 'Foerster, I've got it!' 'I know,' Foerster replied: 'Arise, yea, arise!' Mahler had found the initial spark for his final movement, and Foerster had guessed what it was. Hans von Bülow was the cause.

Mahler's letters from his early years in Hamburg, when he was still living on his own, reveal a sombre view of the world characterized by feelings of loneliness and by worries about his family and about money – these last two worries were closely connected. For much of his life he was tormented by very real fears about his livelihood, fears that were finally allayed only when he felt adequately provided for by his Viennese pension and by the handsome fees that he received in New York. He hated the coercive constraint of having to earn his living as an opera conductor, even if the opportunity to conduct the great masterpieces of the repertory remained a source of pleasure to him. His fear of not having a job continued to torment him even when it was clear that his growing fame as a conductor reduced the risk of unemployment. His fear was too deep-seated to be amenable to rational argument. Nor can it be fully explained on the basis of childhood experiences, for as far as we can tell, his parents' finances were never critical, however short of money they may initially have been. Mahler arrived in Hamburg from Budapest with a golden handshake of 25,000 florins, while his annual salary in Hamburg was 12,000 reichsmarks, before deductions were made for taxes and pension contributions, Mahler having negotiated the relevant details with great financial tenacity. In short, his finances were by no means precarious, although it has to be remembered that he not only had to look after himself, he also had to care for four of his brothers and sisters. (Ernst had died in 1875, his married sister Leopoldine in 1889. Mahler's links with the latter appear to have been relatively tenuous. Certainly, there is no evidence that her death provoked any reaction in him.) Of the four survivors, Alois was a good-for-nothing; his favourite sister, Justine, was unmarried and lived in Vienna, the only family member on whom Mahler could rely when he tried to keep the family together; Emma was both prematurely old and childlike; and, finally, there was the problem child, Otto.

Mahler's letters to Justine from this period are filled with worries of the most basic and yet depressing kind. On one occasion, Emma wanted a doll, and so Justine bought one for her. Otto spent two weeks on holiday with Mahler but no sooner had he returned than he was keen to set off again, and, as before, it was Justine who paid for him to do so. It is easy to understand that Mahler, having to foot each bill, complained about his siblings' egoism and lack of consideration. It is clear from all these letters that as the eldest of the other family members capable of dealing with the situation (Alois's inconstant lifestyle ruled him out of court), Justine was effectively the head of the family in Vienna whenever Mahler himself was absent. Friedrich Löhr and his wife, Uda, assumed the role of guardians in all matters that went beyond everyday practicalities. The younger members of the family lived for a time with the Löhrs, at least until such time as Justine and Emma moved to Hamburg in 1894. Otto's fate was sealed with his suicide in February 1895. The only other member of the family to show a talent for music, Otto had never been capable of sticking to his studies. When Mahler went to Hamburg, he hoped that his brother, then eighteen, would spend twelve months as a volunteer in the army and learn a sense of discipline and order, but it turned out that he was unfit for military service, and so he returned to his life as a wastrel.

Together with Justine, it was above all Friedrich Löhr and Mahler's old friend and legal adviser Emil Freund who shared the burden of responsibility involved in caring for the composer's family. In a letter that Mahler wrote to Löhr from Hamburg in November 1891, we find him expatiating on this theme:

> I wish from the bottom of my heart that the time were near when at long last Otto would have his examination and his year of military service behind him, so that this infinitely complicated process of providing money would become simpler for me; – it is beginning to wear me down and I long for the day when I am no longer obliged to earn so much money. Besides, it is very doubtful how much longer I shall be in a position to do so.[8]

Mahler's final remark was another example of sheer defeatism, for a conductor who had not only received a laurel wreath from Hans von Bülow but whom Brahms and Tchaikovsky had praised to the skies and who had held a leading position in Budapest and now in Hamburg had little cause to be afraid for his future. But his defeatism stemmed from his negative mood during his early period in Hamburg: 'Only there is now too much winter in me – if only spring would come again,' he writes, significantly, in his letter to Löhr.[9] This mood emerges even more forcefully from a letter to Emil Freund, suggesting that Mahler was suffering from what we would now call a midlife crisis. Now in his early thirties, he had – according to the life expectancy of the time – reached the halfway mark. (That he had in fact already passed the halfway point is another matter.) It was a crisis that was bound up with several factors, including his current burden of responsibility for his brothers and sisters; his despair at the state of the musical world ('Believe me, German artistic life the way it is at present holds no more attractions for me,' he wrote to Löhr in 1894. 'In the last analysis it is always the same hypocritical, corrupt, dishonest behaviour wherever one turns'[10]); his despair at his continuing lack of success as a composer – by holding his hands to his ears during Mahler's performance of 'Todtenfeier', Bülow had made it clear that not just ignorant critics but even his musical heroes failed to understand him; and, above all, his sense of loneliness in a remote and inhospitable part of the country, a loneliness inspired not least by his memory of his unhappy affairs in Kassel and Leipzig. And so we find him writing to Freund:

> I have been through so much in the last few weeks – without any evident material cause – the past has caught up with me – all I have lost – the loneliness of the present – all sorts of things – you know these moods of mine from earlier years – when I would be overcome by sadness even while among my

friends – when I was still all youth, vigour and stamina – so you can well imagine how I spend these long, *lonely* afternoons and evenings here. – *No one* with whom I have anything in common – whether a share in the past or shared hopes for the future. – [...] Oh, anything, anything, but this eternal, eternal loneliness! It was there when I was up in Norway, roaming about for weeks on end without speaking a word to a living soul – and that after already having had my fill of keeping silence – and now back in this atmosphere in which I cannot get so much as a single breath of fresh air.[11]

If we did not know that Mahler was never visited by thoughts of self-harm, we should have to describe this mood as suicidal. It is certainly indicative of his current state of depression.

It is altogether remarkable that Mahler's manifold triumphs as a conductor at the Hamburg Opera could do nothing to lighten his mood, but it is clear from this that however seriously he took his role there and however impassioned his performances, he did not see this as his true task in life but at best – namely, in the case of the great masterpieces that he saw it as his duty to serve – as a source of pleasure and at worst as a burden imposed on him by his need to provide for his family and, later, for his wife and children. In both cases, it helped him to spend his summer vacations composing. Even at this stage it was already clear to him that he would never be able to survive on his income as a composer. And on this point he was to be proved right. His successes in Hamburg were considerable, as is clear not only from the reactions of Brahms, Tchaikovsky and Bülow but also from the reviews by all the leading local critics.

In Hamburg, Mahler made his mark above all as a Wagner conductor. In contrast to Budapest, he had at his disposal an excellent team of Wagner singers among whom the most prominent was the heldentenor Max Alvary. In his short life, Alvary excited attention not so much through the solidity of his technique as through his youthful and virile timbre and a physique that was ideal for the young Siegfried. He had also studied architecture, allowing him to bring to his operatic interpretations an unusual and striking physicality. An idiosyncratic and intelligent artist, he was born Maximilian Achenbach, the son of a famous painter in Düsseldorf, and was the first tenor to sing Wagner's tenor roles without a beard, a revolutionary development clear from a comparison of photographs of Alvary and the great Albert Niemann, Wagner's Paris Tannhäuser and Bayreuth Siegmund. Alvary had been the Met's first Siegfried in 1887 and four years later sang Tristan and Tannhäuser in Bayreuth. He joined the Hamburg company six months after Mahler and from then on was regarded as the ideal and most modern interpreter of Wagner's heavier tenor roles. Two years later, however, his career suffered a serious setback when he was involved in an accident onstage in Mannheim, an accident from which he never recovered. He died in 1898.

His work with Mahler culminated in a series of guest appearances in London in the summer of 1892. It was Mahler's only visit to the city. He had been engaged to conduct the German opera season and conducted eighteen performances between the end of May and the end of July at both Covent Garden and Drury Lane. The great French composer Paul Dukas attended a performance of his *Fidelio*, his enthusiasm continuing to resonate even many years later:

> One of the most wonderful musical memories of my life is of a perform-
> ance of *Fidelio* in London, in the course of which he [Mahler] conducted
> the *Leonore* Overture no. 3, interpreting Beethoven's genius so marvellously
> that I had the feeling of being present at the original creation of this
> sublime work.[12]

The high point of this brief German season was a series of two complete cycles of the *Ring*, only the second time that the work had been staged in the capital; the first had been ten years earlier, when Angelo Neumann – Mahler's former director in Prague – had given four complete cycles under the direction of Anton Seidl, who was later to become the leading Wagner conductor at the Metropolitan Opera. The 1892 performances were a kind of co-production between Covent Garden and the Hamburg Opera or, to be more accurate, between the Royal Opera's director, Augustus Harris, and Bernhard Pollini of the Hamburg Opera. The orchestra was the Covent Garden band reinforced by a number of players from Hamburg, and the cast was headed by Alvary – curiously enough, the cycles were both prefaced by single performances of *Siegfried* designed to showcase Alvary's talents. The role of Wotan was divided between Karl Grengg and Theodor Reichmann, that of Brünnhilde between Katarina Klafsky, Pegalie Greeff-Andriessen and Rosa Sucher, who only recently had left Hamburg for Berlin. Until then Mahler had been unable to speak a word of English but took private lessons with a new friend of his, the physicist Arnold Berliner. However ambitious his intentions, the results were modest, to judge by a touching and comic little letter that he wrote to Berliner from London in June 1892:

> Dear Berliner!
>   I shall only to give you the adresse of my residence, because I hope to hear
> by you upon your life and other circumstances in Hambourg.
>   I myself am too tired and excited and not able to write a letter.
>   Only, that I found the circumstances of orchestra here bader than thought
> and the cast better than hoped.
>   [. . .]
>   I make greater progress in English as you can observe in this letter.[13]

We do not know what Berliner thought about his pupil's progress in English, but to the extent that Mahler evidently had to begin from a state of total ignorance, he may not have been entirely dissatisfied. The English critic Herman Klein, who got to know Mahler during this visit in 1892, later reported that 'for a man who knew so little English, I never came across any one so bent on speaking that language and no other. [. . .] He would rather spend five minutes in an effort to find the English word he wanted than resort to his native tongue or allow any one else to supply the equivalent.'[14] Eyewitness accounts of Mahler's time in New York likewise indicate that his English was poor and heavily accented. Clearly he had no gift for languages. But he could be satisfied with his success as a conductor in London. The *Ring* was well received, and there was universal acclaim for the conducting of a musician completely unknown in the capital – Hans Richter had originally been intended to conduct the season. He was the star or, as he wrote home in English, striking an ironical note: 'Me top again!'[15]

After the performance of *Fidelio* on 2 July, the audience even started to chant Mahler's name, although some of the critics were shocked that the conductor had had the temerity to perform the *Leonore* Overture no. 3 before the second act. (Even in Hamburg, Mahler had already performed this piece before the final scene, a practice he continued in his epoch-making production with Roller in Vienna.) The most distinctive critic on the London musical scene at this period was a certain Corno Di Bassetto – the pen-name of Bernard Shaw, who attended the performance of *Siegfried* on 8 June. His detailed review is a mine of important information about the standard of the performance, above all that of the singers. Curiously, he was of the mistaken belief that Mahler had brought the Hamburg Opera orchestra with him, leading him to conclude that the Covent Garden band could have turned in a better performance. And his only comment on the 'energetic conductor, Herr Mahler' was that 'he knows the score thoroughly, and sets the *tempi* with excellent judgment', suggesting that he was rather underwhelmed by the conducting.[16] A more enthusiastic response was that of the opera fanatic Herman Klein, who retrospectively recalled the 'magnetic power and technical mastery' of Mahler's conducting.[17] It is remarkable that, as we saw with Josef Sittard in Hamburg, critics were already using the term 'magnetism' to describe Mahler's conducting. The use of such a term is not entirely unexpected, of course, in describing the effect of a conductor both then and now, but the number of times with which it was applied to Mahler is none the less striking.

The various eyewitness accounts of Mahler's years in Hamburg, including the supremely important reminiscences and jottings of Natalie Bauer-Lechner, allow us to form a far more detailed picture of Mahler's personality than we have been able to do until now. At all events, it is clear that impartial observers generally had the impression that they were in the presence of an extremely important person, albeit one who, initially at least, did not excite great sympathy. As we have already had occasion to note, the critic Ferdinand Pfohl was far from impartial when recording his own recollections, but he was presumably merely exaggerating a point that other observers could sense less clearly and less intensely. Pfohl had got to know Mahler in Leipzig, but it was only in Hamburg that there was any closer contact between the two men. When Mahler left Leipzig and took his leave of Pfohl, the latter 'had the feeling' that he had met 'the most unsympathetic person of all time, and yet in spite of this he filled me with the sort of interest that one feels for a snake or a piece of fruit, when one does not know if it is poisonous and if one may die from eating it'.[18] When Pfohl and Mahler met each other again in Hamburg, Pfohl's opinion soon changed, not least because he was flattered when Mahler drew him into his confidence. At no point in his life, conversely, did Mahler ever really become friendly with a critic. Pfohl continued to find Mahler a strange individual, as slow to praise others as he was to criticize them. The most sharply worded of his reproaches was the Austrian word 'Trottel' ('simpleton' or 'idiot') and its superlative, 'Trottel aller Trottel', a term that Mahler once applied to the elderly Eduard Hanslick when the latter wrote an uncomprehending review of a work by Richard Strauss. Another, less articulate reaction was a bleating, almost snarling 'ah-ah-ah', with particular stress on the final syllable, implying amazement, interest and even incredulity.

Many eyewitness accounts attest to Mahler's otherworldliness – 'ich bin der Welt abhanden gekommen' ('I am lost to the world') is without doubt one of the most personal lines he ever set to music, even if it applies to only one aspect of his personality. If passers-by addressed him in the street, he would involuntarily knit his brows as he was generally deep in thought and walked at a considerable speed, walking being his preferred form of locomotion. Anecdotes on the subject abound from his time in Vienna, while famous photographs, taken of him in 1904 on his way to and from the Court Opera, give us some idea of his blindness in this regard. One wonders whether he was even aware of the tramcar that can be seen in one of these pictures. His love of animals could assume the most delightful aspects. Pfohl recalls how on one occasion Mahler took him with him on one of his walks, a secretive expression on his face, in order to show him something special. The object in question turned out to be a cow, grazing in a meadow not far from the opera house, a sight that left Pfohl distinctly unimpressed. When a stray dog attached itself to Mahler, he took it with him to his favourite restaurant at the Hotel Belvedere and was inconsolable when the dog was driven away by the hotel staff. He was also uncertain how to respond to a Hamburg prostitute when she accosted him and Pfohl in the street and wondered whether he should rescue her from her fate, but in the end he settled for a donation of three marks.

There are also countless examples of Mahler's absentmindedness. One day he was dining at his favourite restaurant with other guests. A large bowl of stewed fruit was passed round as the dessert, and when it came to his turn, Mahler filled his bowl, then licked the ladle before replacing it in the fruit, not because he had been badly brought up but simply out of thoughtlessness. A few years later two other eyewitnesses, including the composer Karl Goldmark, reported a very similar story to Pfohl: 'Just imagine what happened to Mahler when he was invited to a formal dinner with us!' Pfohl already knew the answer: 'He licked the ladle!'[19] Bruno Walter reports something similar. At a stage rehearsal in Hamburg the stage manager needed some time to make certain arrangements and the orchestra had to wait. Mahler waited by his stand, then lapsed into thought and failed to hear the shouts from the stage, telling him that he could continue. In the ensuing silence Mahler suddenly came to his senses again and, striking his baton on the music stand, called out: 'Waiter, the bill!' 'A deep confusion of this kind is the compensation for, and perhaps the condition of, concentration as absolute as his. For so-called distractions as cards or any other game, he had no use.'[20]

Walter also noted that Mahler's lifestyle was chronically disorganized and characterized by a grasshopper volatility. The iron discipline that allowed him to compose his monumental symphonies in the summer months was something that he evolved only in the course of time, probably starting in 1893, when he spent his first vacation on the Attersee. But for Mahler such volatility was by no means synonymous with a lack of concentration or carelessness. Walter, who knew him better than most other people, used to say that he was always ready for the next move once the raging floodtide of his thoughts and emotions had come to rest again, but the moment of rest was short-lived, and it required only some new idea to open the floodgates again. Not untypical of this characteristic was his attitude to eating. Throughout his life Mahler tried various diets, no doubt on account of his weak stomach, which repeatedly caused him problems, but also because of his recurrent bouts of haemorrhoids and his tendency to suffer from migraines, which he generally ascribed to an incorrect diet. These migraines were sometimes so severe that he had to lie in a darkened room – one such incident occurred in Paris in 1900, shortly before a concert with the Vienna Philharmonic, with the result that the concert began half an hour late. But it is impossible to discern any consistency to his eating habits. Here, too, we find the same volatility. We have already noted that for a time he was a vegetarian, a regime he adopted under the influence of Wagner, but, as with Wagner, it was a passing phase. During his time in Budapest, his favourite dishes appear to have included salted and smoked meat, whereas according to Pfohl, it was pot roast with dumplings and dried fruit that he preferred, a dish that one would hardly describe as part of a calorie-controlled diet. His alcohol intake, conversely, was extremely moderate, and there is no mention of his ever being drunk or even tipsy. In Budapest and Hamburg he seems to have enjoyed the odd glass of Pilsen beer (it may be recalled that the town of Pilsen was not far from Iglau), whereas he later preferred fine wines. When concentrating on his work during his vacations, he would drink only spring water.

Mahler smoked, but only in moderation. In Hamburg he tended to prefer cigarettes, but after a good meal he also smoked cigars given to him by his friends. If he had spent the morning composing to his satisfaction, he would take out a cigar and with a smile of contentment place it on the table that had been set for lunch. The famous photographs taken in 1905 and depicting him with Max Reinhardt, the architect Josef Hoffmann, Alfred Roller and Hans Pfitzner in the garden of his father-in-law Carl Moll are among the few that show him smoking, and here he is certainly in good company, for both Reinhardt and – surprisingly – Pfitzner are seen smoking cigars, Moll a cigarillo. Such pleasures were entirely typical of groups of men of their standing. Following the discovery of his heart insufficiency, Mahler was told not to smoke, a ban that he found so intolerable that he took up smoking again soon afterwards. Letters that he wrote from New York to his parents-in-law during the final months of his life contain requests for cigarettes and cigar holders and also for 'Nachmann's smoker's wool', which was placed in the holders as a filter. But it would be wrong to think of Mahler as an addict, except in the case of his addiction to his work as a composer. And even here, in the context of creative work, the word is best avoided.

A Difficult Man

One can well imagine that Mahler was not an easy person to work with – in theatrical and musical circles, such a person is generally described as a 'good colleague', usually implying certain deficiencies as an artist. Even before the young Anna von Mildenburg began preparing for her Hamburg debut as Brünnhilde in *Die Walküre* in 1895, she had already heard alarming things about the company's principal conductor. During a session with one of the répétiteurs, a small man with a sun-blackened face rushed in and, without introducing himself or welcoming anyone, simply hissed 'Carry on', then pushed the répétiteur away and sat down at the piano himself. The singer was so nervous and tense and so perplexed by Mahler's lack of any reaction that she burst into tears. Far from comforting her, he began to shout at her, then, seeing her tear-stained, terrified face, he burst into laughter, assuring her that so far she had done very well. But then he started to shout at her again: 'You'll have

to go on crying until you just sink into the general theatrical mire of mediocrity. Nobody cries then!'[21] He then resumed his former friendly concern –
a reaction that was soon to develop into a passionate affair. Mahler was not
the sort of man whose life was ruled by harmony, balance and the need for
appeasement. Rather, his life was tumultuous, tempestuous and remarkable
for its excesses and immoderation, to paraphrase the critical Pfohl, who was
referring in the process to both the man and his music. For orchestral musicians, he was a thorn in the flesh – it is easy to appreciate why the Vienna
Philharmonic soon tired of him, an attitude all the more understandable
when we recall the mentality of orchestral players then and now. The average
German and Austrian orchestral musician was badly off: at the Hamburg
Stadttheater, for example, musicians in the 1890s received little more than
subsistence wages. While Mahler was earning some 850 reichsmarks a month,
the second bassoonist was being paid eighty, a sum insufficient to feed him
and his family if his wife were not also working as a greengrocer, for example.
By way of comparison, this would be the equivalent of a present-day conductor
receiving 5,000 euros a month, while the second bassoonist received 500,
whereas in reality the latter earns between five and seven times that amount.
Mahler was justifiably indignant about this state of affairs and, like Meyerbeer
before him, he repeatedly tried to raise his players' level of income, at least to
the extent that it was in his power to do so.

In theory Mahler was able to see that lack of enthusiasm and slovenliness
were the inevitable result of such conditions, but once he was hard at work and
encountered a lack of commitment or even thick-skinned obstructiveness, he
could quickly lose his composure. Most orchestral musicians and many singers
trembled in his presence and felt terrorized – not until he was working in New
York did this situation improve, when he grew more mellow and realized that
he was wasting his energy on such fruitless battles. Both Pfohl and Anna von
Mildenburg report that he had a way of spreading an atmosphere of icy terror
during his rehearsals and performances. During a rehearsal in Hamburg, Pfohl
recalls that he tormented a flautist whose performance was not to his liking,
making him repeat the phrase until he was so tired that he left the rehearsal in
tears. At the end of the rehearsal the orchestral attendant told Mahler that the
player was waiting outside with a large group of friends, fully intent on beating
the living daylights out of him. Mahler sent for the police and left the building
with an armed guard. On another occasion, this time during rehearsals for the
first performance of the revised version of his First Symphony in Hamburg
in September 1893, Mahler found himself at loggerheads with the timpanist,
who was unable to bring the necessary weight to the transitional passage that
leads into the final movement. Incandescent with fury, Mahler leapt down
among the players, seized the timpanist's sticks and belaboured the drum with

terrifying force, achieving precisely the effect that the passage required. At its climax, the sticks flew out of his hands, describing a wide arc over the orchestra and prompting the remaining players and Mahler's friends in the rehearsal room to break into a round of applause.

During the actual performances, Mahler was unable to express his emotions in this way, but he had other means in his armoury. If a musician played a passage incorrectly or a singer sang a wrong note or came in at the wrong time, Mahler stabbed at the miscreant with his baton, as though with a rapier, turning his head and fixing the person in question with a furious look, a position he maintained for several seconds, while continuing to conduct with his free left hand. If he did not agree musically with what a singer was doing, he would begin to gesticulate wildly on the podium, shrugging his shoulders, looking questioningly at the person concerned, shaking his head and finally, if all else failed, sinking back with a resigned expression and a tired beat, making it clear to the singer that the chosen tempo was a musical and moral disaster and that he was abandoning the fight only to ensure that the performance continued. But the evildoer could be certain that at the end of the act or performance he or she would receive a furiously worded note in his or her dressing room.

In Vienna, Mahler was notorious for the fact that whenever latecomers tried to slip into their seats at the front of the house unnoticed, he would lower his raised baton and transfix the persons concerned with a piercing, stigmatizing stare, confident that they would never again arrive late. He soon ensured that latecomers were not admitted to the stalls until the act was over, a revolution at the Vienna Court Opera, where anything was permissible, as long as the ushers were adequately bribed. Many of the arrangements that we now find codified in present-day programme booklets go back to Mahler (as does the total darkening of the auditorium following Wagner's example). Few contemporaries realized that these measures were not an attempt on the part of an undersized individual to assert his authority by repressive means but that his obsessions and fanaticism sprang from his constant endeavour to ensure the musical integrity of the performance, a point that even Pfohl was forced to concede. Bruno Walter, who understood Mahler on the deepest level, expressed this same idea in rather more flattering terms:

His abrupt impulsiveness perhaps explains the excitement nearly everybody felt who came near him; especially, of course, singers and members of the orchestra. He diffused an atmosphere of high tension. This was communicated to those with whom he worked, and induced devout admiration in the best of them. It produced performances illuminated by the fiery glow within him which raised the Hamburg Opera to the top rank in Germany. Of course, there were weaker spirits, men of second-rate gifts, who were injured by his absolutism; good will or ill, however, none could resist his sway.[22]

Anyone who knew Mahler only from contexts such as these would be astonished to read Walter's claim that Mahler's most striking characteristic was his warm-heartedness, but there is no doubt that he was fired by a deep sense of compassion and fellow suffering, which finds expression not only in his love of animals – although, curiously enough, he never kept a pet – but also in his great empathy for the sufferings of the world and its inhabitants. Coupled with this, however, was a certain blindness towards the realities of that world and an assertiveness which, as we have seen, could occasionally be ruthless whenever his own interests were at stake. As such, this last-named quality amounted to a kind of naïve and immoral egoism. Many of his closer friends and associates attest to his sense of humour, but it was humour in the spirit of his favourite writer, Jean Paul, who writes in § 32 of his 'Vorschule der Ästhetik' (literally, 'Preliminary School of Aesthetics'):

> As the inverted sublime, humour does not destroy what is individual but, rather, it destroys what is finite through its contrast with the idea. For such humour, there is no individual folly, there are no fools, but only folly in general and a foolish world. Unlike the common joker with his sideswipes, it does not single out any individual folly but belittles what is great in order to place the petty beside it, on which point it differs from parody; or it raises the petty in order to place what is great beside it, in which regard it differs from irony. In this way it destroys both, because in the face of infinity everything is both the same and nothing.[23]

According to this definition, humour is the inverted sublime. No matter how much Mahler was a metaphysician searching for the infinite, for the metaphysical and for the meaning of a life that tormented him, he still enjoyed keen wit and brilliant ideas, having both of these at his command and being capable of laughing until he cried. What he loathed were obscene jokes and the sort of Jewish jokes that many Jews used to tell in a display of auto-aggression. If such jokes were told in his presence, he could be brusquely and icily dismissive. The cliché of the man of sorrows bearing the grief of the world upon his shoulders, which was peddled above all by Alma, is misleading. Even in extreme old age, Mahler's only surviving daughter, Anna, who was a sculptor by profession, could still recall her father's gentle smile, even if that smile always appeared against the background of a profound seriousness. But we need to recall that Anna knew her father only as an old man. She was six when he died and remembered him only as a tired old man who was none the less very affectionate towards her and who understood her much better than her mother.

Mahler enjoyed wrong-footing other people to humorous effect, but often failed to consider the feelings of the individual involved. However much she may have loved him, Anna von Mildenburg was forced to admit that:

> He hurt many unintentionally with his humour. Like most people when they talk in jest, he did not always weigh his words. For in the next moment he had quite forgotten about the individual who aroused his mirth and had forsaken the particular for the universal, for the deepest, most painful and self-denying introspection and the living truth.
>
> It was not a common humour, avoiding cheap suggestiveness and preventing him from sharing ordinary conviviality. . . . And they would look affronted and disgruntled, forever scenting a personal attack in his words. He noticed it and had to laugh at their darkened, suspicious, rejecting expressions. That really offended them.[24]

Unfortunately, too few of Mahler's surviving remarks attest to his sense of humour, for such remarks are dominated either by the other aspect of his personality or by purely routine concerns. As a result, two of the few examples from his correspondence must serve as evidence for the rest. Even so, both instances are sufficiently striking to demonstrate his gift for verbal humour. Mahler was one of the first people in Hamburg to take up what was then the new form of transport of cycling. In May 1895 we find him writing to a friend, Wilhelm Zinne, and describing his earliest experiences of a velocipede:

> I'm admired by all and sundry on my bike! I really do seem to be a born cyclist and shall certainly be appointed Geheimrad once more.
>
> I'm at the stage when all horses get out of my way – it's only with *bell-ringing* that I have trouble: if this becomes necessary I dismount (very smartly) – I can't yet bring myself to run down a taximeter, although they deserve it, stationing themselves in the middle of the road with no consideration for the fact that every road is too narrow for such an energetic cyclist.
>
> Well, then – all hail, once more!
>
> Yours sincerely
>
> Gustav Mahler
>
> Bicy-Clerk and Road Hogger.[25]

Many years later he sent a telegram to his wife, a woman singularly deficient in even a vestige of a sense of humour. In style, it recalls the sort of letters that Mozart sent to his cousin:

in very best of health today to the hotel did make my way then took a bath so
nice and hot and drunk of coffee one whole pot poetic is today my cable as
only munich makes one able for here the arts are more than fable one feels
transposed to arcady and thats a thing that pleases me gustav.[26]

Mahler remained in Hamburg for six whole years, a period that on closer
inspection turns out to have witnessed some of the most decisive changes in
his life. His lifestyle in particular underwent a profound transformation when
his sisters Justine and Emma joined him in Hamburg in the autumn of 1894.
Justine continued to run his household for him until he married Alma in 1902,
the same year as that in which Justine herself married Arnold Rosé. It was in
1893 that Mahler began what was to turn into a lifelong habit of spending the
summer months working in one of his 'composing huts' with a regular daily
routine – in 1893 the place that he chose was Steinbach on the Attersee. He
also had a passionate affair with Anna von Mildenburg – the first affair in his
life of any seriousness. And, finally, he converted to Catholicism shortly before
the end of his appointment in Hamburg.

Until Anna von Mildenburg's appearance on the scene, Justine Mahler –
eight years younger than her brother – was the most important woman in
Mahler's life. When their parents both died in 1889, Justine was the only
person whom Mahler trusted implicitly on all practical matters. And he was
entirely right to do so. Only once did he show any irritation when he discovered that she had for some time been conducting a clandestine affair with the
leader of his orchestra, Arnold Rosé, an affair that she legitimized immediately
after her brother was married. Emma, Justine's precocious and yet childlike
sister, to whom Mahler had never been particularly close, had married Rosé's
brother, Eduard, a cellist, in 1898. Two surviving photographs show Gustav
and Justine together. The first dates from 1889 and was taken in Budapest,
while the second was taken in Vienna ten years later. Neither of these two
photographs nor the later ones that depict the married Frau Rosé show her off
to the best advantage. Like her brother, she inherited the family's narrow lips
and also the myopic-seeming eyes. Unlike Mahler, however, these features did
not form part of an uncommonly characteristic and sharply contoured whole.
It is difficult to describe her as attractive. As Mahler himself put it, she was a
simple, defenceless soul, but, unlike her three brothers and sisters, she had
inherited the family's finer qualities. As such, she was very like her brother,
albeit not always equal to the challenges to which she was exposed. When she
effectively became the head of the family in 1889, she was only twenty-one but
the constant care that she had for some considerable time been lavishing
on her ailing parents had impaired her health, in spite of which she survived
her brother by twenty-seven years. Natalie Bauer-Lechner shared Justine's

veneration for Mahler and in a previously unpublished passage in her reminiscences left a clear diagnosis of the family situation, which she knew intimately from the inside:

Justi, who was in charge of Mahler's brothers and sisters and also of his household, immediately filled me with interest and every feeling of sympathy. She was not equal to the task that was allotted to her so prematurely, for she herself needed guidance and education, advantages that neither she nor the others – there had been thirteen children in all – had ever enjoyed, such was the utter neglect and impoverishment that they all suffered at home. Her sickly state of health, which was the result of the three years that she spent self-sacrificially nursing her parents, both of whom were seriously ill, together with her youth and her temperament, which, like Gustav's, was quick-tempered, passionate and far from pedagogically inclined, meant that she was really not suited to mentoring either Otto or Emma. And then there was the worst of them all, Alois, who was serving as a common soldier in Brünn, doing his three years' military service and constantly bombarding Gustav and her with worries and demands of the most outrageous kind. To deal with these three would have required the most all-powerful paternal authority – and even this might not have been sufficient to deal with an almost pathological intractability and unmanageability and even unbridled licentiousness on the part of Mahler's little tribe, who seemed to be possessed by a wicked demon.[27]

Justine's relationship with her later sister-in-law, Alma, can be described only as difficult, a state of affairs attributable to a combination of understandable jealousy on the part of a woman who for a long time had loved no one with greater intensity than the brother she idolized and the not entirely unfounded conviction that for various reasons Mahler and Alma were far from ideally matched as a couple. The young Alma's radiant and voluptuous beauty may also have caused further resentment on the part of the rather less prepossessing Justine. At all events, there seems little reason to doubt the truth of a remark that Alma imputes to Justine: during the second interval at the first night of the legendary Mahler-Roller production of *Tristan und Isolde* at the Vienna Court Opera in February 1903, Mahler lay down in his dressing room, exhausted and ashen-faced, wishing that some one else would conduct the third act for him. Justine is said to have gazed down at her brother as he lay there, almost unconscious, and to have whispered to Alma, who was standing beside her: 'One thing delights me – I had his youth, you have him now he's old.'[28]

Changes to the way in which Mahler spent his vacations were also far-reaching. Until then, he had tended to divide up his summer months. As long as his parents were still alive and the family was living together in Iglau, he would spend at least part of the summer there. He also went hiking with friends, notably through the Fichtelgebirge, an area of northern Bavaria not far from Iglau and very similar to it in terms of its rural character. In 1890 – his first summer following the death of his parents the previous year – he travelled to Italy in May, then spent some time with the Löhrs at Hinterbrühl near Vienna. In August 1891 he set off on his own on a tour of Scandinavia, visiting Copenhagen, Gothenburg and Oslo, the previous months having been spent rushing between Vienna, Marienbad and Bayreuth, where he is believed to have seen both *Parsifal* and *Tannhäuser*. But Mahler seems to have become increasingly conscious of the fact that this way of spending his holidays was ill suited to his nature, quite apart from the mind-numbing loneliness that he felt in Scandinavia, where days would pass without his speaking to a living soul. It may seem surprising that a loner like Mahler did not seek out loneliness. Rather, he preferred to spend his holidays in a quiet place, surrounded by his family, with frequent visits from friends, provided that he had sufficient time and space to work on his scores undisturbed. Once he had finished the allotted period of time working alone at his desk, he would positively seek out contact with other people. And this was how he arranged his summer vacation in 1892, travelling to Berchtesgaden from London in the company of Justine and Natalie Bauer-Lechner. His visit to Scandinavia seems to have shown him that the coast was not for him. Instead, he preferred a combination of Alpine scenery and mountain lakes, where he could hike and swim – mountaineering, by contrast, gave him no pleasure at all.

In the spring of 1893 Justine set out to find an alternative resort, Berchtesgaden having failed the test on account of its poor weather and other inconveniences. She stumbled upon the Attersee, some thirty miles to the east of Salzburg, just beyond the Mondsee and the Wolfgangsee. At this date, the Attersee was less fashionable and less crowded than the Wolfgangsee and the Wörthersee in Carinthia, but no less beautiful, relatively quiet and eminently affordable. On the eastern shore of the lake Justine found a guest house 'Zum Höllengebirge'. (It is now the Gasthof Föttinger and is in Seefeld near Steinbach.) Here she rented five rooms at a reasonable price – five rooms were needed not only for Mahler but also for Justine, Natalie, who was not in fact there the whole time, Emma and Otto. They had their own kitchen and could eat in their own dining room. The rooms were furnished in a simple, almost primitive, way, and missing items of furniture were made by a local carpenter and covered with a throw by the inventive sisters. The pièce de résistance was a leather sofa that was moved around and placed wherever it was needed.[29] On the opposite shore lay Nußdorf, where two of Mahler's friends from his students days in Vienna were staying with their families: Victor Adler and Engelbert Pernerstorfer.

Mahler arrived in Steinbach around 20 June 1893 after brief visits to Vienna and Berlin and made himself at home. But his principal reason for making this change to his holiday arrangements is that it had become painfully clear to him during his time in Hamburg that he had had only sporadic opportunities to devote himself to composition in any orderly way. Since taking up his appointment in the city, he had done little more than write a number of *Wunderhorn* songs and revise his First Symphony and the *Lieder eines fahrenden Gesellen*. He must have realized to his horror that his true aim in life, composition, was being reduced to short-breathed phases that would never allow him to create the 'new symphony' that he had been wanting to write since his days with Hans Rott. His new type of vacation proved him right: within a matter of only a few weeks he wrote no fewer than four *Wunderhorn* songs and, above all, the Andante and Scherzo of his Second Symphony, a task in which he was helped by the loan of a baby grand piano placed at his disposal by a local piano manufacturer. Even so, the guest house was insufficiently quiet for Mahler as it was situated on the main road, and even at this early date, the region was not entirely free from tourists. As a result, a local architect, Josef Lösch from Schörfling, was asked in the autumn of 1893 to build a simple brick house overlooking the water on the extensive meadow between the guest house and the lake – on this side of the lake such an open space was very much the exception. From the following summer, this would ensure that Mahler could work completely undisturbed.

According to the original estimate, this modest building, which was described in the plans as a 'music pavilion', cost 395 florins and 94 kreuzers. Mahler was able to move into it as soon as he arrived in Steinbach in June 1894. The building also housed the aforementioned baby grand, together with a table, a few chairs and a simple stove that could provide heating if the weather was cold. The first of Mahler's 'composing huts', it still exists, more or less unchanged. For decades it was used for other purposes, including – apparently – a laundry and a slaughterhouse and, according to the guest house's records, 'for sanitary purposes', but all these traces have now been removed, and in 1984 it was restored to its original form. And yet Mahler's refuge now lies in the middle of a campsite on which Austrian and German tourists, above all, perpetuate their particular kind of caravan culture, their taste in music reminding the observer that Mahler's is not the only type of music to give pleasure to its listeners. It was here in 1894 that Mahler realized his idea for the final movement of his 'Resurrection' Symphony and placed the coping stone on the work. Here, too, he wrote much of his Third Symphony in 1895, the work representing a response to the surrounding Attersee and Höllengebirge – in this context one recalls Mahler's comment to Bruno Walter, when the latter visited him in Steinbach during the summer of 1896, at a time when he was working on the vast opening movement of the symphony, the last of the work's movements to be composed:

> I arrived by steamer on a glorious July day; Mahler was there on the jetty to meet me, and despite my protests, insisted on carrying my bag until he was relieved by a porter. As on our way to his house I looked up to the Höllengebirge, whose sheer cliffs made a grim background to the charming landscape, he said: 'You don't need to look – I have composed all this already!' He went on to speak of the first movement, entitled, in the preliminary draft, 'What the Rocks and Mountains Tell Me'.[30]

But 1896 was the last summer that the Mahlers and their entourage spent in Steinbach. New tenants took over the inn, and it proved impossible for Mahler to reach an agreement with them. When he climbed the Alpine meadow for the last time and gazed back on his little hut, Natalie remembered him bursting into tears. The 'Schnützelputz-Häusel', as Mahler called the property after a line in one of the more whimsical poems from Des Knaben Wunderhorn, now belonged to his past. Unlike the house in the poem, his own hut was not filled with dancing mice and barking snails, but the time that he had spent there had proved to be exceptionally productive, demonstrating once and for all that he could work like this in the future, if possible using the whole of his summer vacation – in Hamburg, this amounted to the three months from the beginning of June to the end of August – and for whole periods cutting himself off from the family and friends whose company he otherwise welcomed. Generally he would get up at around six, then go for a swim in the lake, before making his way to his 'composing house', where breakfast was already laid out for him. As soon as he had finished eating, he would set to work. At around midday, he would be called to lunch, after which he would have a brief rest, then spend the afternoon walking in the mountains. The evening meal was taken relatively early, followed by a 'convivial get-together', involving reading, conversation and piano playing, after which the participants would retire for the night at a comparatively early hour.

Anna von Mildenburg

Anna von Mildenburg left only a single recording: the recitative to Rezia's aria, 'Ocean, Thou Mighty Monster', from Weber's Oberon. It remains a mystery why she did not leave more recordings at a time when the studios were full of singers less famous than the leading dramatic soprano at the Vienna State Opera and one, moreover, who had also appeared at Bayreuth. For all the recording's acoustic inadequacies, the dramatic thrust and vocal sovereignty of her 1904 recording are plain for all to hear. None the less, she appears not to have possessed a true *hochdramatisch* voice of the kind we generally associate with Wagner's heroines. Rather she seems to have had what German writers would now describe as a *jugendlich-dramatisch* voice of a particularly penetrating kind. At the time of the recording, the singer was thirty-two and at the height of her powers, revealing a fresh-toned, radiant voice that may, however, have been ill-suited to the heavy Wagner roles in her repertory. The relatively early decline in her vocal powers only ten years later may be connected with the unduly heavy roles that she sang, and there is no doubt that she essayed some of these roles too soon. It must be admitted that Mahler did little to protect her from this, for all that he frequently warned her not to sing on consecutive evenings, as the ruthless Pollini repeatedly demanded. The 1904 recording not only reveals her vocal authority, it also hints at a quality at least as important as her purely vocal gifts: the overwhelming drama that she brings even to as brief an extract as this. Like Lilli Lehmann, Anna von Mildenburg was one of those singers who in an age dominated by marmoreal vocalism, already looked forward to the sort of singing actor that we demand today, a stage performer for whom singing is merely one expressive means among many, the overriding concern being dramatic truth.

In October 1896, only a year after he had got to know the soprano, Mahler wrote to Cosima Wagner, recommending her as Kundry and Brünnhilde. Anna von Mildenburg was duly invited to sing Kundry at the 1897 Bayreuth Festival. She returned to sing the same part in 1911, 1912 and 1914, and in 1909 she was also heard as Ortrud in *Lohengrin*. Although she never sang Isolde or Brünnhilde in Bayreuth, she made her mark in these roles at the Vienna Opera, where she became the leading dramatic soprano of the Mahler era. Although Mahler's eyes may have been blinded by love in 1896, his comments to Cosima were almost certainly an accurate reflection of the young singer's vocal qualities:

> As for her voice, it has such strength and staying power, that she overcomes all difficulties with ease; her youth, therefore, does not present any obstacle but rather sets off her own individuality to rare advantage. With her, you would believe Wotan when he says: 'Nicht kos' ich dir mehr den kindischen Mund' ['Nevermore shall I fawn on your childlike mouth']. For roles such as Sieglinde she lacks the so-called 'femininity'. (Please do not misunderstand me – but when one speaks of 'femininity' one usually stresses the passive and surrendering nature of woman – it is this, and only this, that I mean.) On the other hand, when the heroic, the demonic – when action is required, she is in her element.[31]

In the light of Mahler's comments about the 'heroic' and 'demonic' element in Anna von Mildenburg's stage manner, it is hardly surprising that Strauss and

Hofmannsthal regarded her as the ideal Clytemnestra in *Elektra*, a point that emerges with some force from the few surviving photographs of her in this role. A singer who studied at the Munich Academy of Music in the mid-1930s told the present writer that her dramatic training with Anna Bahr-Mildenburg – she took the name on marrying the Viennese writer, Hermann Bahr, in 1909 – left an indelible impression. On one occasion the then elderly Bahr-Mildenburg showed her class how to sing and act the part of Clytemnestra, and even though her voice was then in ruins, the result had been one of the greatest theatrical experiences in the student's life.

Anna von Mildenburg was born Anna Mildenburg von Bellschau in Vienna in 1872 and was not quite twenty-three when she joined the Hamburg Opera in the autumn of 1895. She came from a military background and thanks to her father's postings had already travelled extensively by this date. The family was living in Görz when her voice was discovered by the well-known writer of comedies, Julius Rosen. As she recalls in her memoirs, Anna had already had a few voice lessons but had no thought of becoming a singer. Only when she moved to Vienna did she seek advice on the subject. Thanks to her father's connections, she even managed to see the director of the Vienna Court Opera, Wilhelm Jahn, whom Mahler was later to replace. Jahn put her in touch with one of the company's leading dramatic mezzo-sopranos, Rosa Papier, although only in her early thirties, had recently been forced to abandon her career as the result of a vocal crisis and quickly became one of the most sought-after voice teachers in the city, her pupils including a whole series of prominent singers. We have already quoted Anna von Mildenburg's colourful account of her first encounter with Mahler in early September 1895, when the latter had just returned from his summer vacation in Steinbach, hence the singer's reference to the conductor's sun-blackened features. The occasion of their meeting was Mahler's interference in a coaching session for the role of Brünnhilde, a role that would tax the resources of any young soprano. The first surviving letter from Mahler to Anna von Mildenburg was even included by Alma Mahler in her 1924 edition of Mahler's letters, but it is entirely innocuous in tone, being one of the numerous notes that Mahler dashed off to singers generally during a performance, criticizing their contribution to the proceedings. The few subsequent letters that Alma reproduced were edited in such a way either by Alma or by the singer so that all matters of personal import were removed. Only the informal pronoun 'du' was retained, a form of address that Mahler never used towards any of his other singers. Even so, the attentive reader will be aware of a significant undertone to Mahler's comment regarding the singer's first Aida in Hamburg: 'None but myself (who draws every breath with you) noticed that you were labouring hard in your singing this evening.'[32] By 29 November the fate of the lovers was sealed, for the letter that Mahler wrote to the singer that morning to congratulate her on her twenty-third birthday marks the beginning of an impassioned correspondence that makes it clear that the intensity of his feelings for her was matched only by his feelings for the woman who was later to become his wife.

This letter already strikes the note of unbridled ecstasy that was to characterize this correspondence between the end of 1895 and Mahler's departure from Hamburg less than two years later. The laconic exchanges that followed the end of their affair were in crass contrast to it. The letter of 29 November was almost certainly written after their first night together:

My dearest Anna,

My greetings to you this morning! How happy I feel at being able to tell you what today means for me. It is my birthday in the truest sense of the term! – You see, my love? I've let slip my birthday. You hinted a few days ago that the number 23 is a significant one in your life. – Did you have any inkling what your 23rd birthday would mean for you? In only a few hours' time I shall gaze into those dear eyes of yours. I can barely wait. Will the day come when I may always do so? Come soon! – I shan't break off at today's rehearsal. I'm very much afraid that I'm now going to be a very 'unconscientious' conductor. – Since gaining such blissful knowledge, I have lost my conscience. Tell me today, when we're unobserved, whether you love me. My beloved, you'll often have to tell me that you do before I'm absolutely certain. You are the 'enemy' before whom I've capitulated so quickly – and to whose tender mercies I've abandoned myself! Will you show me favour or disfavour? How happy I'd be if it were to be your favour! Yes? Yes? Tell me! My love! Until later! Your Gustav![33]

Curiously enough, Alma claims in her memoirs that Mahler never had an 'intimate relationship' with Anna von Mildenburg. Although Alma was unaware of the content of these letters, it must have been clear to her what had taken place in Hamburg, even if Mahler himself had denied it for tactical reasons. He was clearly not one of those men who boast to their fiancées about their premarital escapades. That she knew about his relationship is suggested by her attempts to belittle the singer, whom she refers to only as M. After all, Anna von Mildenburg was engaged at the Vienna Court Opera from 1898 and was one of Mahler's closest colleagues there. For a time she even lived close to the Mahlers. She was no beauty. In the first place, she was extremely tall, although this was a positive attribute in the heroic roles that she assumed onstage. She was also large-boned and powerfully built, without, however, seeming overweight. Mahler later told Natalie Bauer-Lechner that when she joined the company in Hamburg she had to work hard to seem less ungainly both on and off the stage: she moved awkwardly and trod on all her dresses if they were not tied up. Mahler trained her to walk properly and urged her to go out without an umbrella and muff in order to learn how to use her hands. Once she had acquired a certain poise, he rehearsed her detailed moves onstage and in that way turned her into the greatest singing actress of her age, a performer repeatedly compared to Eleonora Duse.[34] With its angular features, her large face had something masculine about it. As is clear from surviving photographs, her eyes were large and eloquent, dominating and domineering, blazing and impassioned. This does not mean that she was not feminine – the aforementioned passage from Mahler's letter to Cosima Wagner refers, rather, to the fact that she was not passive by nature and that she lacked the melting, self-sacrificial quality needed to play a part like Wagner's Sieglinde. Mahler's close correlation between the personality of the performer and the interpretation of the role that he or she was playing is bound to strike the modern reader as strange.

Anna von Mildenburg was clearly no shrinking violet but a wild, domineering woman, an aspect of her personality that her lover initially had no reason to bemoan. Mahler's letters to her leave us in no doubt about the intensity of their passion, an intensity missing from the letters that he exchanged with Alma during the early stages of their courtship. Not until the crisis that affected their marriage in 1910 does their correspondence strike a similar note of passion. Nor is there any doubt about the physical intensity of the feelings between the young soprano and a man who, already several years older, can scarcely have had much experience in such matters. But it was not only sexual desire that bound Mahler and Mildenburg together. His letters also suggest that this was probably the first and – at the risk of soundly callously dismissive of Alma – the last time in his life that he loved a woman and was loved in return by someone who on the strength of her own artistic gifts understood him as an artist and as a musician. Only Natalie Bauer-Lechner understood him better, but, much to her dismay, Mahler's feelings for her amounted to no more than respect, and when Alma arrived on the scene, Mahler coolly discarded her – one of the great mistakes in his life. Anna's letters to Mahler have not survived, and so it is only from his letters to her and from her later reminiscences that we can deduce that she understood him. For all their brevity, these reminiscences breathe a greater degree of understanding than the whole of Alma's garrulous memoir. If he had not presupposed so much interest on Anna's part, he would not have written to her in such detail whenever they were apart, most notably in December 1895, when he was in Berlin to prepare for the first performance of his Second Symphony and wrote to her almost every day.

Even deeper insights into Mahler's creative process were vouchsafed to Anna during the summer of 1896, when he was working on his Third Symphony at

Steinbach on the Attersee. His most important letters on the subject were
written to Anna and include explanations of the programmatical titles to the
individual movements, titles he later discarded. On each occasion he asked his
correspondent to understand that he had to concentrate on his work and that
he did not have much time for her, in spite of which he wrote to her almost
daily. The decisive factor was that he was dealing with an exceptionally gifted
performing artist capable of great emotional intensity and could assume an
understanding which, if not intellectual, was certainly intuitive. But intellectually, too, Anna von Mildenburg revealed what for a singer was an above-average
degree of intelligence, an intelligence that emerges from her later autobiographical writings – even if we concede that her husband, the writer Hermann Bahr,
may have helped to edit them – and above all from her important book on
the interpretation of Wagner's music dramas. Taking *Tristan und Isolde* as its
starting point, this substantial study very much breathes the spirit of Mahler's
operatic reforms.[35]

The fact that Anna was still young when she met Mahler caused him a great
deal of problems, just as Alma was later to do, but it also gave him a chance to
act as her mentor and avuncular guide, a role that he likewise assumed with
Alma. Neither woman will have found this easy. On 10 December 1895,
shortly before the first orchestral rehearsal for the first performance of his
Second Symphony in Berlin three days later, Mahler wrote to Anna:

> If I speak of the battles that lie ahead, I do so on the basis of my experience
> of life, an experience that allows me to foresee many of the things of which
> you yourself still have no inkling. Look, Anna, this must surely prove to you
> that I am utterly serious about my love for you. – If I were younger and more
> thoughtless, I'd regard the beautiful present as sufficient and not weigh down
> my mind with anything else. – Only bear in mind that what we are wanting
> to do together is no summer excursion or passing pleasure but a whole great
> life which (especially from my own side) is bound up with sacred duties – the
> obligations towards ourselves are so great and serious that even if there were
> no other considerations, these alone would demand that we examine
> ourselves in all seriousness. You must also consider my mission, which I am
> bound to regard as sacred above all else! But more on this at another time,
> this is something you first have to learn to understand.[36]

How must a twenty-three-year-old soprano have reacted to this tone of voice,
which is more appropriate to an itinerant preacher or a school inspector than
to an enamoured conductor? Could she really work out how serious he was in
speaking of 'sacred duties' and his 'mission'? Mahler was to strike a similar
note in the letters he wrote to the young Alma shortly before and after they

married. He was clearly unable to resist the temptation to adopt this tone, yet
his reason for doing so was not to bend a woman to his will by intimidating
her but simply because he was deadly serious. At least on an intuitive level,
Anna von Mildenburg seems to have understood exactly what Mahler thought
and what he wanted.

The fact that there were no more letters from Mahler to Anna von
Mildenburg is due, of course, to their close daily contact in Hamburg. Most of
the letters that passed between them date from the periods when Mahler was
away on tour or on holiday during the summer. Their affair had to be kept a
secret – whether or not they succeeded is another matter. Mahler's two sisters,
who were by now living with him in Hamburg, were not allowed to find out
what was going on. Yet it seems certain that Justine had her suspicions,
although, if Mahler is to be believed, she felt a great deal of sympathy for the
singer, which must have made their contacts somewhat easier. But Mahler was
also keen to ensure that the liaison was kept from his colleagues at the theatre.
After all, he had a certain experience of untidy relationships of this kind, and it
would have embarrassed him if there had been any gossip on this point. There
is, however, no evidence of this. When Anna travelled to Berlin for the first
performance of the Second Symphony in the company of Mahler's sisters, he
urged her not to betray them. He could meet her only at her own apartment,
where she lived alone, and whenever he sent her unsealed notes to her dressing
room, they were necessarily couched in a rather more formal language.

Unsurprisingly, the relationship between two such passionate people was
beset by scenes of great turbulence. Alma claims that it was these endless
scenes in Hamburg that finally turned Mahler against 'M.'. She had allegedly
begun by tormenting him and then, when he had turned his back on her,
stopped at nothing to win him back. That Anna von Mildenburg was capable
of such scenes is certainly credible, the elemental force of one particular
incident seemingly utterly believable: when Mahler and Alma were already
married and staying on the Wörthersee, it is said that the soprano, who was
living nearby, often turned up at their rented accommodation with a large
mangy dog, a creature that Mahler the animal-lover could not abide. Once,
during a severe storm, she drew him out on to the terrace, while the pregnant
Alma remained indoors: 'The great Wagnerian soprano let her hair fall about
her face and played Valkyrie and Ortrud in the same breath. She called to
me to come and when I made a sign of refusal she turned in scorn to Mahler:
"She's a coward." '[37] Mahler's surviving letters to Anna von Mildenburg
contain little to support this accusation. Conversely, a letter that he wrote on
7 February 1896 within months of the start of their affair speaks of a deep-
seated crisis and profound sense of injury on his part – not until Mahler wrote
to Alma at the height of their crisis over Walter Gropius was he to pen an

equally wounded and impassioned letter. A few key sentences are worth quoting:

> Anna! What I've been through in these last few days – and what I shall go through in the future – I simply can't begin to say! Anna! I've never felt such pure and sacred love for another human being – you don't love me! My God! I shall never get over this! . . . I must keep away from you – there's nothing more I can be to you! My very life is at stake! Believe me! Anna, if you'd asked me to sacrifice my life to you – I could have done so. But – oh, God! – how could you pretend to love me? How did you manage to do so? Have I deserved this from you? Do you know what you've stolen from me in doing so? I have lost my faith! May God help me – how can I go on living? – Didn't you see how deep and serious was my love for you? A love that I maintained so pure and inviolate throughout the time when I did not yet know you! . . . I am in a hell from which there is no release! . . . Anna, have no regard for me! Be the person that you feel most comfortable as! – You can't do anything for me! Whatever you do, it is like a red-hot knife plunged into my heart! Oh, God! Anna, my beloved! May God protect you! May God be with you! Forget that I ever existed! Don't write to me any more! Fare well! Fare well! My darling![38]

If we needed further proof of the importance and profound significance of this passion for Mahler, it would be this letter, even if we have no idea what caused him to be so distraught. In the event the breach between them was by no means final. A short poem that Mahler wrote on 19 May indicates that all was well again – as was later to be the case with Alma, Mahler often wrote poems in moments of great agitation, not least whenever he was attempting to sort out his own feelings and build bridges:

> Ein Reuevoller liegt zu deinen Füssen;
> das Wort, das seinem tollen Mund entsprang
> in seines frohen Mutes Überdrang –
> O, lass es nicht den armen Sünder büssen!
>
> Mein Lieb, nicht wahr, du wirst verzeih'n?!
> Das schnelle Wort, das dich gekränkt, vergessen?
> Könnt'st du nur meine Reu' und Scham ermessen,
> Lieb, diesmal sagtest sicher du nicht: 'Nein'!
>
> Vom 'Schelm von Bergen' kennst du ja die Mär'!?
> Die Königin verlor an ihn die Ehr'; –

der König macht gleich eine Tugend aus der Not:
Schlug lieber schnell zum Ritter ihn – statt todt![39]

[He lies, repentant, at your feet; the word that passed his foolish lips in happiness's unrestraint – oh, let the sinner not atone for it! My love, you'll surely find forgiveness and forget the rash offending word?! Could you but gauge my self-reproach and shame, my love, you'd surely not say 'No'! You know the story of 'the mountain rogue'!? To him the queen her honour lost; the king, however, turned the ill to good by dubbing him a knight – and not by killing him!]

The love between Mahler and Anna von Mildenburg was at its most intense in 1896. He shared everything with her – thoughts on his works and their genesis, and reflections on his subsequent career. No doubt he meant well, but he saw no harm in pointing out the vast gulf that separated a singer from a composer: 'You yourself know what art means in our lives – but you know only how to *reproduce* art! Just think what *producing* art must be like!'[40] This was typical of Mahler – he always had difficulty showing consideration for sensitive souls around him. Essentially, he was right, but there was surely no need for him to blurt out the truth so implacably and so imperiously. Even by the summer of 1896 it was already becoming clear that his days in Hamburg were numbered and that things could not go on as they were between him and Pollini. Although he said nothing to Anna about his concrete prospects, he had long been thinking about Vienna and of the 'god of the southern climes', as he would henceforth refer to his ultimate goal as an opera director and conductor. When she auditioned as Kundry in Bayreuth in early December 1896, he was with her in his thoughts. And even as late as 1897, the letters that he wrote to her from Moscow, where he was conducting a Russian Music Society concert, still reveal all the old warmth and affection.

It is unclear from the surviving sources what led to a cooling of these feelings. Had the scenes between them really become intolerable, as Alma insinuates? Had he suddenly noticed that Anna was not sufficiently attractive for his demands, not sufficiently 'feminine'? Was her exceptional height unsuited to a man of his relatively short stature? Certainly, the woman whom he went on to marry was the very opposite of Anna: Alma was of medium height, voluptuous and markedly feminine, albeit not as passive and submissive as he felt that Sieglinde should be. Above all, she was a dazzling beauty – in a letter to his parents, Bruno Walter even described her as the most beautiful young woman in turn-of-the-century Vienna, and Walter undoubtedly had a greater understanding of women than his great model. None of Alma's comments on this relationship deserves to be taken seriously, not least when she gives the distinct impression that Mahler left Hamburg to escape from the soprano's attentions.

There were undoubtedly other, more compelling reasons for his departure. The first evidence that his relationship with the singer was under strain comes in his letters of May 1897, by which date he had already taken up his new post in Vienna. 'Your question as to whether I intend to see you again is really rather silly'[41] – such a cold attempt to appease his love, who had remained behind in Hamburg, must give the reader pause for thought.

There is little doubt that by May 1897 their love was no longer what it had been, and the course that it was to take must already have been clear during the final months of Mahler's appointment in Hamburg. In his letters to the singer, he offers her advice concerning her future career, even suggesting Vienna as a possible showcase for her *hochdramatisch* gifts. But he also mentions other opera houses, suggesting that while Anna von Mildenburg was understandably waiting for the call to Europe's leading operatic centre, Mahler, conversely, was stalling, unable to bring himself to make Vienna seem a wholly unattractive proposition. He clearly had mixed feelings on the matter. In terms of his own emotional well-being, it would have been better if she did not join him in Vienna, as he knew her temperament and the possessive nature of the demands that she placed upon him – and he no longer loved her. But for the institution that he was now running, the engagement of the most gifted dramatic soprano of her day could only have been a good thing. Indeed, his plans to reform the city's operatic scene could only benefit from her involvement. The situation became critical in the summer of 1897, when Pollini declared his willingness to release her from her contract in Hamburg, leaving the Vienna Court Opera free to engage her. At that date Mahler was not yet the new director, nor even the acting director. Moreover, he was recovering from a severe attack of angina and an operation to remove an abscess from his neck and had had to cancel his planned appearances at the Court Opera. Instead, he had travelled with Justine and Natalie to the Tyrol to recover, and it seems that only now did the news of the Court Opera's plans to engage the singer reach him.

Alarm bells ringing, Natalie wrote to Rosa Papier to report that the news had been a bombshell and had left Mahler devastated, and yet it must be said that if this was indeed the impression that he gave, he must have dissembled as he knew very well what was being planned. The singer's hold over Mahler was boundless, Natalie went on, and there was nothing that he could do to resist it. From the moment that she first set foot in Hamburg, the soprano had tried repeatedly to ensnare Mahler, which was precisely why he had left the company. But Natalie was seriously overstating her case, for the main reason for Mahler's departure was the tremendous opportunity to work in Vienna, although it cannot be denied that the difficult situation with regard to Anna von Mildenburg will have confirmed him in his desire to move. Natalie urged the influential Rosa Papier to do everything in her power to prevent the soprano from moving to Vienna. Her letters are demonstrably dictated by jealousy – the same jealousy which, coupled with her possessiveness and her unrequited love for Mahler, finally precipitated the break between them. But the fact that they were not simply the brain-spun creation of an overwrought mind is clear from a letter that Mahler wrote to Rosa Papier at this same time, in which he presciently noted that Natalie had undoubtedly gone too far. He had to admit, he went on, that the Vienna Court Opera could not forgo the services of such an outstanding singer merely because of the personal problems between them. They should simply wait to see which way the wind was blowing. In any case, Anna von Mildenburg's contract was not due to take effect until the autumn of 1898 and so they still had a year in which to deal with any obstacles that might lie in the way of their future collaboration, a statement that clearly demonstrates that Mahler had until then wanted to prevent the singer's engagement.[42]

Mahler must have written the decisive letter to his former lover in July 1897, explaining what was to happen. If she had been in any doubt as to the nature of Mahler's true feelings for her, this letter will have opened her eyes, for its logic is unconvincing. In Hamburg, Mahler had been the company's principal conductor and yet he had had an affair with the ensemble's dramatic soprano, an affair that they had evidently managed to keep a secret. If there had been the occasional gossip, this had manifestly not disturbed him. Why should things be different in Vienna? In his letter to the singer, he suggests with some-what hollow pathos that if she were to accept the offer that she was about to receive from Vienna, it was necessary for them

to restrict our personal dealings as far as possible in order to prevent life from once again becoming a torment to us both. Even now the entire company is alarmed by the various titbits of gossip that have been reaching Vienna from Hamburg, and news of your engagement would have the effect of a bomb-shell. If we were to give them the least cause to mistrust us and so on, *my own position* would become *impossible* within a very short space of time and I would have to set off on my travels again, just as I did in Hamburg. You too would suffer as a result, assuming that your entire raison d'être were not like-wise called into question. I ask you now, my dearest Anna: do you feel that you have the strength to accept an engagement in Vienna with me and – at least during the first year – to renounce all personal contacts and refuse all favours on my part? I hope that you are convinced that this will be *no less difficult for me* than it is for you, and that only the most bitter necessity obliges me to ask this question of you. . . . I am almost inclined to think that we shall be subjecting ourselves to an *intolerable* ordeal: and in the event of your feeling the same, I would ask you simply to *decline* the offer and to accept one from *Berlin*, which you will be receiving very soon.[43]

Mahler's letter is extremely revealing, and if Anna von Mildenburg was as clever as her former lover repeatedly claimed, then she must have realized by now that it was all over between them. Mahler was not being honest with himself in this letter. There is absolutely no evidence, for example, that 'life was a torment' to them both in Hamburg or that they were the subject of widespread gossip, while it is altogether unlikely that their affair was already the talk of the town in Vienna. At the same time, Mahler's claim that he would have had to resign his position at the Court Opera if his liaison with the soprano became known is wildly exaggerated. Both of them were unmarried and both were adults, so their affair would not have mattered. Indeed, if a prohibition on such affairs had been the general rule in the cultural capitals of Europe, the arts would simply have ceased to function – after all, even the old Kaiser had had an affair with the actress Katharina Schratt. And what was Anna von Mildenburg to make of Mahler's demand not to speak to him privately for an entire year? Did he really think that this was a convincing request? And why should the situation change after a year if they were then to resume their affair? Gossip and the threat of dismissal would scarcely have become less of a danger at the end of that time. No, the truth of the matter is that Mahler did not have the courage to say what he was really thinking but preferred to hide behind defensive, threadbare arguments. His letter, one has to conclude, was simply mendacious.

We do not know how Anna von Mildenburg reacted to the letter and how she dealt with the new situation. At all events, she did not take the veil but, if the reports may be trusted, began an affair with one of Mahler's friends in Hamburg, Hermann Behn, while in Vienna she allegedly enjoyed a fling with Siegfried Lipiner. We may assume that it was not easy for her to work in Vienna with her former lover, who both as director of the Court Opera and as a composer was given to increasingly bold experiments, but it says much for her artistic integrity that she played an active role in the operatic reforms undertaken by Mahler and Roller, triumphing as Isolde in their epoch-making production of *Tristan und Isolde* and also setting new standards as Beethoven's Leonore, Mozart's Donna Anna and Gluck's Aulidian Iphigenia. According to Alexander Witeschnik, she was 'a tragedienne of regal stature with her sorrowfully overcast, knowing Medusa's head and an elemental, fate-laden voice that resembled nothing so much as a force of nature, an illustrious artiste who was in every sense larger than life, the very embodiment of the Wagnerian music drama'.[44]

Mahler's later letters to Anna von Mildenburg reveal their once grand passion ending in sobriety and coolness. The following note was probably written in 1902: 'Without any sense of resentment and without wishing to hurt you, I am returning your letter unopened. – Believe me when I say that only the instinct for self-preservation can persuade me to do so, and I hope that in view of this you will get over the apparently wounding nature of such a reply.'[45] The last surviving note that passed between them strikes a tone of mild resignation that reflects Mahler's mood when he left Vienna for New York. On 7 December 1907 he drafted his famous letter bidding farewell to the members of the Court Opera. It must have occurred to him that there was one member of the ensemble whom he could not address in this impersonal way, and so he wrote separately to his former lover, a short note presumably penned the same day:

> My dear old friend! I have just written a letter bidding farewell to the 'honoured members' of the company. It will be pinned up on the notice board. But while I was writing it, it occurred to me that it does not include you and that in my eyes you stand *completely apart* from the others. I had also kept hoping to see you in person. But now you're in Semmering (which is, of course, more beautiful). And so I can only send you these few heartfelt words by way of farewell (from the theatre – not from Vienna, where I shall still be living) and clasp your hand in spirit. I shall always follow your career with all my old devotion and interest, and I hope that less turbulent times will one day bring us together again. At all events, you should know that even at a distance I shall remain your friend, a friend on whom you can count. I'm writing this amidst the most frightful upheaval. Fare well and keep going! Your old friend, Gustav Mahler.[46]

Anna Bahr-Mildenburg's reminiscences were published ten years after Mahler's death and, totally lacking in bitterness, are discreet to the point of self-denial. Those of his letters that she reproduces there understandably omit all mention of anything that would be unduly personal, but they none the less allow the reader to tell how close was the bond between composer and soprano. 'A common desire is bound to emerge, an encounter on the most basic spiritual level of a work must inevitably lead to a secret but altogether profound understanding that is uniquely capable of answering the creative artist's wishes' – with these words Anna von Mildenburg summed up three years of intense passion and twelve of artistic collaboration: she, too, saw her contribution as a 'sacred mission'.[47]

A Time of New Departures

In reflecting on Mahler's years in Hamburg, we have completely changed our perspective and methodology, abandoning our former chronological narrative and concentrating instead on a summary of the decisive changes of direction in his life. To return to our earlier narrative technique would simply lead to needless repetitions. What follows here is merely an attempt to provide a brief résumé of the outward changes in what was clearly a decisive period in Mahler's life.

Throughout his years as principal conductor of the Hamburg Opera, Mahler was tremendously busy, often to a point that seems altogether incredible. At no other period in his working life did he conduct so many performances. Between March 1891 and April 1897 he conducted a barely conceivable total of 715 performances. During the 1894/5 season, for example, he conducted 148 out of a total of 360, in other words, more than a third of the annual total. It is unlikely that a modern opera-house conductor would reach anywhere near this figure. In 2001/2, for instance, the general music director of the Bavarian State Opera conducted forty-six opera performances (and four concerts), a third of the number achieved by Mahler. (We shall say nothing of their respective fees.) The practical implications of this were spelt out in a letter that Mahler wrote to Ödön von Mihalovich in Budapest. His schedule between the middle and end of January 1893 was as follows: 16 January – the local première of Mascagni's L'amico Fritz; 17 January – Wagner's Siegfried; 18 January – L'amico Fritz; 20 January – Tristan und Isolde; 22 January – L'amico Fritz; 23 January – Fidelio; 24 January – Die Zauberflöte; 25 January – Lohengrin; 26 January – Tchaikovsky's Iolanta; 27 January – Die Walküre; 28 January – L'amico Fritz; 30 January – Hermann Goetz's Der Widerspenstigen Zähmung; and 31 January – L'amico Fritz.[48] It was no accident that, as we have noted, Mahler altered the way in which he spent his summer vacations in order to be able to devote his time to composition. In Hamburg, he continued to lead an unsettled existence, a point that emerges with some force from his constant changes of address: after initially taking rooms at the Hotel Royal on the Hohe Bleichen, he moved to rented accommodation in the Bundesstraße, then to the Fröbelstraße, the Parkallee and finally to the Bismarckstraße in the Hoheluft quarter of the city, where he lived with his two sisters and led a more or less settled existence.

Mahler's circle of friends in Hamburg was limited and yet his exchanges with them were intense – this, too, was a constant in his life. His closest contacts, both socially and professionally, were with Josef Bohuslav Foerster and also, of course, the young Bruno Walter, who arrived in the city in the autumn of 1894 to work as chorus master and conductor and with whom Mahler's relationship was like that of a father and son. For a time he was also close to Ferdinand Pfohl, although the two men were never close friends in the way that he was with Foerster and Walter. And yet it is striking that Mahler never used the familiar 'du' in his dealings with any of these men, this being a privilege accorded to only a handful of Mahler's older friends. With the exception of Anna von Mildenburg, he appears not to have sought any closer contact with anyone at the theatre – the sort of friendly dealings that he had with Wilhelm Hesch in Prague gave way increasingly to a sense of distance, something that he felt was necessary in order to maintain his own authority and avoid occluding the hierarchical relationship between the conductor and his singers. He also cultivated a number of contacts with members of Hamburg society. Among this group, pride of place goes to Hermann Behn, a patron of the arts with a profound love of music. Almost the same age as Mahler, he had studied law but because of his wealth never needed to practise his profession. Instead, he studied music for the love of it, studies that also took him to Anton Bruckner in Vienna and that enabled him to prepare a vocal score of Mahler's Second Symphony for piano duet. Together with the local businessman Wilhelm Berkhan, he helped to defray the expense of mounting the first performance of the Second Symphony in Berlin in December 1895. One of Behn's friends who subsequently became friendly with Mahler was Henriette Lazarus, a widow from Trieste, her salon on the Esplanade modelled on those of Henriette Hertz and Rahel Varnhagen that had flourished in Berlin in the heyday of German Romanticism. She was also an enthusiastic supporter of Bülow. Probably the closest friend of Mahler's sisters in Hamburg was Adele Marcus, a young widow with a small daughter. Six years older than Mahler, she had a room to let, and Mahler was one of the interested parties. Although he did not in fact take the room, he became friendly with her, a friendship cemented by their shared musical and literary interests. Rumours that they were lovers have no foundation in fact. Justine later went on holiday to Italy with Adele Marcus, while Mahler himself maintained a sporadic correspondence with her after he had left for Vienna.

Mahler's principal contacts outside Hamburg were initially those that he maintained with Vienna – there can be no doubt that long before he moved to Hamburg, he was already hoping that he would one day return to Vienna, even if we have no written evidence to support this claim. Vienna was the city of his dreams. The only surprise is that he achieved this goal as soon as he did. True, his contacts were few in number, nor was he in touch with any of the leading figures on the city's musical scene for he had left Vienna in 1880 as an unknown young musician. The only exceptions were Bruckner, whose Te Deum he performed in Hamburg in late March 1893, as he proudly informed the composer in a letter, and Brahms, whom he visited on several occasions in Bad Ischl while he was staying on the nearby Attersee. He was invariably much impressed by the surly and gruff old man, even though he must have known that Brahms had no idea what to make of his music. But even if Brahms was not an opera composer and had little to contribute to the debates about opera in Vienna, it was none the less clear to Mahler that he had tremendous authority and that he had scored a hit with him in December 1890, when he had

1 Mahler in the Dolomites (Fischleinboden, near Toblach) in 1909. All his life Mahler loved Alpine scenery where he could walk and swim.

2 Bernhard Mahler, Gustav's father whose 'choleric temperament repeatedly got him into trouble'.

3 Marie Mahler, Gustav's mother. 'Whenever his mother was ill in bed, as she often was with a migraine, [Gustav] would kneel behind her and pray intently, before asking her if she felt any better.'

4 A postcard showing the 'wretched little house' in Kalischt, Bohemia, where Mahler was born.

5 The earliest surviving photograph of Mahler, taken in 1865 or 1866. The downward-turning corners of his mouth dominated his features always, even when he smiled.

6 The Main Square in Iglau, Moravia where on special occasions a regimental band of soldiers would play, with trumpet, tuba and drums, delighting and mesmerizing the little boy Mahler.

7 Siegfried Lipiner who became Mahler's leading authority on all intellectual matters.

8 Mahler in 1881. At the age of twenty-one he had just completed his 'Opus 1', *Das klagende Lied*, and was miserably in love for the first time.

9 The 'Zum Höllengebirge' guest house at Steinbach on the Attersee, discovered by Mahler and his sisters in 1893. In 1894 Mahler built a little wooden 'composing hut' on the lake (*r., just behind the tree*) where he could work every morning in absolute seclusion.

10 Mahler and his sister Justine in 1899.

11 Anna von Mildenburg as Brünnhilde in Wagner's *Die Walküre*. At the time when Mahler was most in love with Anna he shared all his thoughts about his work and all his plans for the future with her.

12 The soprano Selma Kurz whose hallmark was her long, flawless trill. Mahler and she had an intense, though short-lived, love affair.

13 The house at Maiernigg on Wörthersee. After a morning's composing Mahler would return to the villa and swim from the jetty before lunch. His holiday routine was busy; he hated sitting around doing nothing.

14 Alma Schindler, *c.* 1898, the woman who would become Mahler's wife. She was an accomplished pianist and showed a certain talent for composing. Her beauty was matchless.

15 Mahler on his way to or from the opera house, Vienna, c. 1904.

Operndirigent Mahler.

16 Mahler triumphs over his predecessor Wilhelm Jahn: a 1897 cartoon by Theo Zasche.

17 The Vienna Court Opera House, c. 1900, then the most prestigious opera house in the world. Mahler held the post of director from 1897 until 1907.

conducted *Don Giovanni* in Budapest. Brahms died on 3 April 1897, the day before Mahler signed the preliminary contract for his Viennese engagement.

Far more remarkable than his dealings with these grand old men of the Viennese musical establishment was Mahler's relationship with Bayreuth and Cosima Wagner, a relationship that proved so useful to Anna von Mildenburg, though it could be argued that she would still have made her Bayreuth debut without Mahler's advocacy. Mahler had first attended the Bayreuth Festival in 1883, the year of Wagner's death, returning in 1889, 1891, 1894 and 1896. Cosima had first heard Mahler conducting one of her late husband's works – *Tannhäuser* – in Leipzig in November 1887, and from then on Bayreuth kept its eye on a conductor who was clearly extremely gifted but who, as Felix Mottl regretfully noted, was 'unfortunately a Jew'. And yet even in Bayreuth such a verdict can hardly have been completely annihilating. After all, it was enough that Jewish musicians revealed their Wagnerian credentials for Bayreuth to turn a blind eye to this failing. This was certainly the case with Carl Tausig and Josef Rubinstein and above all with Hermann Levi, who conducted the world première of *Parsifal* in 1882 and continued to be closely associated with Bayreuth until the end of his career, for all that he remains a classic example of the torments to which Jews were exposed in the Bayreuth of Wagner and his second wife. One wonders whether Mahler ever thought that he, too, would one day conduct in Bayreuth. Quite possibly he did, not least because Levi had shown him that even a Jew could do so and because there is little doubt that he was arguably the most fascinating Wagner conductor after Bülow. This certainly explains his attempts to build up a positive relationship with Cosima Wagner, although he also, of course, felt tremendous admiration for the composer's widow.

Mahler first came into close contact with her during the 1894 Festival. She knew perfectly well how much Wagner he had conducted in Hamburg for she took a strategic interest in such matters, not least because of the royalties. She had also asked him to coach the young Hamburg tenor Willi Birrenkoven for the part of Parsifal, a task that Mahler assumed with enthusiasm. His success, it may be observed in passing, was also noted by Strauss, who was on the music staff at the 1894 Festival, conducting all five performances of *Tannhäuser*. Cosima thanked Mahler by allowing him to visit Wahnfried between 28 July and 4 August and to attend performances of *Parsifal*, *Tannhäuser* and *Lohengrin*, which he watched from the family box. (*Parsifal* was conducted by Levi, *Lohengrin* by Mottl.) Mahler will no doubt have imagined standing on the podium in the 'mystic abyss', as Wagner himself had described the Bayreuth pit, but in the event it was not granted to him to do so. Writing to his sister Justine, who was currently staying at the family's summer refuge on the Attersee, he reported that he had been invited to Wahnfried almost every day and that his meetings with Cosima had always been cordial. He returned to Bayreuth in 1896 (there was no Festival in 1895) and attended performances of the *Ring*, five cycles of which were given under Richter, Mottl and Siegfried Wagner, whom Cosima was hoping to channel into a career in conducting. Strauss thought that Siegfried's conducting bordered on the catastrophic, but Mahler, who attended the cycle conducted by 'Fidi', as Siegfried was known within the family circle, adopted a much more diplomatic tone when he wrote to Cosima in the October of that year. To anyone reading between the lines it would be clear that he too was unhappy with Siegfried's conducting, but Cosima failed to spot the subtext and was delighted and grateful that a conductor as experienced in conducting her late husband's music dramas as Mahler had found her son so impressive, albeit with room for improvement.[49] At the same time – as we have already noted – Mahler was able to raise the subject of Anna von Mildenburg's engagement as Kundry in 1897, although his commitments in Vienna meant that he was unable to attend her Bayreuth debut.

Mahler had gained his post in Vienna not least as a result of the fact that in Hamburg he had belatedly converted to Catholicism. In the years around 1900 Cosima Wagner's position of power within the musical circles of her day extended far beyond the confines of Bayreuth, and it is known that she tried to prevent his appointment, even if we can only speculate on her reasons for doing so. One such reason may have been her abiding anti-Semitism, but it is more likely that she opposed his appointment because she wanted her favourite, Felix Mottl, to have the job. Mottl, she believed, would have ensured that Wagner's works dominated the repertory in Vienna to the exclusion of all else. Certainly there seems no reason to question the truth of a remark in a later letter to one of her female friends: 'I enjoy the best possible relations with Mahler and I am very happy to know that he is in Vienna. In almost every letter he assures me of his support for Bayreuth, something that he has often proved.'[50] Mahler had earlier demonstrated his support by conducting the Viennese première of Siegfried Wagner's *Der Bärenhäuter* in March 1899, by far the greatest success that Siegfried was ever to enjoy as an opera composer. Cosima again had cause to be grateful, but when a difference of opinion arose between Mahler and Siegfried, who conducted the last performance in the run, Cosima allowed all her old prejudices to boil to the surface in a typically Wagnerian manner: 'There was no dearth of semites either, and Mahler had in fact lured Siegfried into a kind of trap.'[51] In spite of this, dealings between Cosima and Mahler remained cordial, even if Cosima's side of the correspondence was marked by the occasional insincerity. Not until 1906, when illness obliged Cosima to withdraw from the running of the Bayreuth Festival, did their correspondence cease.

As for his own compositions, Mahler continued to be dogged by ill fortune. In Hamburg, his achievements as an opera conductor ensured that he was soon hailed as one of the leading figures on the German musical scene. Sooner or later, he was convinced, he would reach the very top of his career ladder. He was the principal conductor of one of the largest German opera houses, a house surpassed in importance only by Munich and Berlin. But as a composer he was still awaiting his breakthrough. The revised version of his First Symphony was not a success when it was performed in Hamburg on 27 September 1893 under his own direction. Even Ferdinand Pfohl, who as a critic was well disposed to him, regretted the absence of an overriding sense of structure. But the reactions were even more dismissive when Mahler conducted the work in Weimar on 3 June 1894. Much the same occurred on 4 March 1895, when he conducted the first three movements of his Second Symphony in Berlin within the context of a concert with the Berlin Philharmonic that was otherwise conducted by Strauss. Here, too, there was a failure on the part of audience and critics alike to understand the work. Among the audience was the composer Wilhelm Kienzl, who sat in one of the boxes alongside Strauss and Karl Muck and who recalled Strauss turning to him enthusiastically at a harmonically bold passage in the brass and saying: ' "Believe me, there are no limits to musical expression!" At the same time Muck, on my right, twisted his face into an unmistakable expression of horror, and the single word "Frightful!" escaped through his clenched teeth.'[52]

But the first performance of the complete Second Symphony, also in Berlin, on 13 December 1895 turned out to be a triumph. True, as we have noted, the audience was largely made up of musicians, including their dependants and students from the Conservatory, all of them drafted in to fill the hall when advance ticket sales had proved particularly poor. But the performance marked Mahler's first real success as a composer. Even he himself was overwhelmed to discover the effectiveness of the final movement, which he had not previously heard in performance. Although the result was exactly what he had imagined, he had never dared to believe that such an impact could be achieved. Even with his advancing fame as a composer, Mahler continued to be beset by such vicissitudes, and it was not until 12 September 1910, only a few months before his death, that the first performance of his Eighth Symphony in Munich finally brought with it the certainty that he and his music had found a place for themselves in the hearts of many listeners.

It remains to mention a further decisive change that took place in Mahler's life at this time, which led to the tactical masterstroke that he and his friends were able to undertake with an altogether unprecedented degree of virtuosity: his move to Vienna as conductor and, later, as director of the Vienna Court Opera. The event in question is closely bound up with that masterstroke in his career while also reflecting more deep-seated problems that affected not only Mahler's life in particular but the age in general. Of the various pieces of evidence that survive from this period, the most revealing is the letter that Mahler wrote to Ödön von Mihalovich in Budapest on 21 December 1896, which makes it clear that even before he arrived in Vienna he was already planning an assault on the directorship in addition to coveting the post of the Court Opera's principal conductor:

> This is to request you to do me a favour on which the whole pattern of my future life depends. The matter of the Conductor or Director post in Vienna is now acute. *My name* is among those receiving 'serious consideration'.
>
> Two circumstances are against me. First, I am told, is my 'craziness', which my enemies drag up over and over again whenever they see a chance of blocking my way. Second, the fact that I am Jewish by birth. As regards this latter point, I should not fail to inform you (in case you are not already aware of the fact) that I completed my conversion to the Catholic faith soon after my departure from Pest.[53]

On the central point, Mahler was undoubtedly right: his Jewishness was a serious, if not an insuperable, obstacle to his new appointment, Viennese anti-Semitism then being at its most virulent. But on the second point Mahler was lying, because at the time that he wrote this letter he had yet to convert to Catholicism. Not until two months later was he to take this step, a step documented by an entry in the baptismal register of the parish of St Ansgar in the Little St Michael's Church in Hamburg: on 23 February 1897 the then thirty-six-year-old Gustav Mahler from Kalischt in Bohemia was officially baptized by the local curate, a Herr Swider. The godfather was Theodor Meynberg. It is always embarrassing, not to say painful, to find a revered genius perpetrating an act of dishonesty like the present lie, but we have to ask what prompted Mahler to lie in the first place and whether we should not, rather, take issue with the circumstances that led a man of his probity to obfuscate a not unimportant step in his life. This raises the whole question of Mahler's relations with Judaism, a question that needs to be addressed before we can consider the call from the 'god of the southern climes' to this prodigal son in Hamburg.

Jewishness and Identity

Let me begin with a quotation:

> All [i.e. all Jewish composers] have assimilated the style that exists all
> around them, all have produced an oeuvre that is personal in style ...,
> and yet it cannot be said of any of them that they have changed the course of
> history or made a creative contribution in terms of *style* or *form*. . . . This
> transcendence of style, which is a transcendence of the second degree,
> seems to be beyond the scope of Jewish composers, because the Jew cannot
> break free from himself except in the abstract – and music is not an abstract.
> His soul is pegged to his body, for otherwise he would no longer be a Jew. . . .
> Mahler reveals himself in part through his recourse to popular melodies,
> to birdsong, fanfares and orchestral cataclysms – 'facts'! – and in part
> through the breadth of his symphonic forms; and it is because he does not in
> fact have a personal style but only a personal way of organizing a generally
> impersonal melodic dialectic (which is a personal way of *feeling*) that he
> reveals his personality through the breadth of his forms. In other words, he
> has recourse to *eloquence*. . . . This music is not Jewish music, it is the music
> of *Mahler*; but, using the language of us all, it signifies the modality of
> being Jewish.[1]

Surprisingly enough, this quotation is not taken from a text that was written
during the Third Reich or penned by a proto-Nazi author but is the work of an
internationally renowned conductor, Ernest Ansermet, whose performances of
the French repertory were held in high regard. His book *Les fondements de la
musique dans la conscience humaine* was first published in 1961 (a German
translation followed in 1985), but his ideas on Jewish composers failed to excite
any attention in their own day because his substantial tome has always been
regarded as unreadable by musicians and was largely ignored by musicologists.

Ansermet's curious comments need to be seen against the background of anti-Semitic trends in French musical life, which in turn were bound up, in part, with responses to Wagner's art and ideas in the final third of the nineteenth century, responses embodied in the work of that most influential composer and teacher Vincent d'Indy.

We may begin by asking whether Mahler was ever exposed to anti-Semitic resentment during his lifetime, and the answer is a resounding yes. The first campaign against him dates from 1885, when he was still only twenty-five and working as a conductor in Kassel. A newspaper article survives from this period, inveighing against Mahler as a Jew whom the local mayor had entrusted with the running of a major music festival at the expense of a German conductor above him in the theatrical hierarchy:

> In order that the whole world may see that in Kassel the Jew must play first fiddle on such occasions according to national liberal legal action, Mahler, a Jew who is currently assistant conductor at the Royal Court Theatre, has been named principal conductor.... This satisfied the different racial types, the Germans having all the work, while the Jew received all the credit. Oh, what fun it was to help turn a dear old Jew into a genius by writing and talking him up.[2]

This situation never changed but culminated in Vienna, a city described with some justification as a breeding ground for anti-Semitism in the German-speaking world in the years around 1900. By the end of 1896 Mahler had already begun to forge ties with Vienna and to prepare the ground for his appointment to the long-coveted position of principal conductor and, shortly afterwards, director of the Vienna Court Opera. By April 1897 the contract had been signed, Mahler having been baptized into the Catholic Church only two months earlier. But the days were long since over when conversion was enough to make a Gentile out of a Jew, and the Viennese press left Mahler in no doubt what he could expect from at least a section of its members.

On 14 April 1897, even before Mahler had conducted a note of music at the Court Opera, the *Reichspost* had informed its readers that:

> In our edition of 10 April we printed a note on the person of the newly appointed Opera Conductor, Mahler. At the time we already had an inkling of the origin of this celebrity and we therefore avoided publishing anything other than the bare facts about this unadulterated – Jew. . . . We shall refrain completely from any over-hasty judgement. The Jews' press will see whether the panegyrics with which they plaster their idol at present do not become washed away by the rain of reality as soon as Herr Mahler starts spouting his Yiddish interpretations [*mauscheln*] from the podium.[3]

The writer uses the word *mauscheln* to describe Mahler's platform manner, an old and ominous term of abuse directed at the German spoken by Jews. (Nowadays German linguisticians occasionally, if controversially, use the term 'West Yiddish' to distinguish this particular dialect from the true Yiddish dialect, 'East Yiddish'.) The word *mauscheln* – the language of Moses, or Moshe – was contentious even among Jews. In his famous German translation of the Pentateuch, the first edition of which was printed in Hebrew characters, Moses Mendelssohn sought to avoid all associations between *mauscheln* and a lack of education and a ghetto mentality. By the middle of the nineteenth century the great historian of Judaism, Heinrich Graetz, was already speaking of 'hideous *mauscheln*' and 'babbling gibberish'. It is no wonder, then, that anti-Semitically inclined non-Jews cultivated this negative stereotype in literature, onstage and in the form of caricatures and cartoons. From this point of view, *mauscheln* remained the decisive feature, allowing observers to identify even those Jews who had dispensed with the outward characteristics of Judaism in terms of their hairstyle and clothing. If the Viennese journalist applied the word *mauscheln* to Mahler's conducting in 1897, he was adroitly using a linguistic metaphor to imply the sort of physical characteristics that were traditionally ascribed to Jews, namely, violent movements of the extremities, a distinctive use of body language and swaying movements of the upper body – time and again writers and cartoonists pointed out that on the podium Mahler's movements were more fidgety than those of other conductors of the age, conductors whose style was much more understated. This point is brought out in a whole series of caricatures, although it is not always clear to what extent this emphasis is inspired by anti-Semitism. But in many cases, a comparison with older caricatures that are demonstrably part of the anti-Semitic tradition confirms beyond doubt that the intention is indeed anti-Semitic.

Although anti-Semitic attacks on Mahler came from only a certain section of the press, they remained a constant feature of his life from now on. Throughout his ten years as director of the Vienna Court Opera, everything that he did was more or less openly linked to the fact that he was Jewish. Particular indignation was caused by his retouchings to the instrumentation of the works that he conducted with the Vienna Philharmonic, notably the symphonies of Beethoven. On 4 December 1898, for example, the *Deutsche Zeitung* demanded that 'If Herr Mahler really wants to make corrections let him set about Mendelssohn or Rubinstein – that's something of course the Jews will never put up with – but let him just leave our Beethoven in peace.'[4] Such sentiments look forward to the infamous Protest of Richard Wagner's Own City of Music in April 1933 after Thomas Mann had delivered his lecture on the 'Sufferings and Greatness of Richard Wagner' in the Great Hall of Munich University and subsequently in other European cities. The musical scene in Munich was particularly short-sighted and reactionary at this time, embodied, as it was, in the figures of Hans Knappertsbusch, Hans Pfitzner and, unfortunately, Richard Strauss. The signatories refused to stand by and see Mann criticize 'German intellectual giants of enduring merit', to quote their inimitable phrase.[5] In 1897 the contributor to the *Deutsche Zeitung* had appealed to 'our Beethoven'. In 1933 no less illiberal voices spoke of 'our great German musical genius': others should evidently keep their distance, the 'others' including not only Jews like Mahler but also men of letters like Mann who, related by marriage to Jews, had been supportive of the Weimar Republic.

Anti-Semitic attacks on Mahler, whether overt or covert, were not limited to his activities as a conductor who re-instrumented the music of other composers, nor were they restricted to his work as the director of the Vienna Court Opera, whenever he dismissed popular singers. Above all, they were directed at his work as a composer. In general, the Viennese had not realized that in signing up their new director, they had got a composer as part of the bargain: by 1897, after all, Mahler was still largely unknown in this capacity. But his increasing fame went hand in hand with mounting controversy, forcing observers to confront the new situation. Nor were the anti-Semitic attacks on his work as a composer confined to Vienna but were found wherever his music was performed, especially when Mahler himself conducted, as he often did, so convinced was he that only in this way could he adequately introduce listeners to his unusual musical language.

In 1909 the respected critic and writer on music Rudolf Louis brought out a book under the title *Die deutsche Musik der Gegenwart* (German Music of the Present Day) that became an instant best-seller. The first book-length attempt to discuss German music in the wake of Wagner's death, it could not avoid mentioning Mahler, who was by then at the height of his controversial fame and who could rely on an army of supporters. Having assured his readers that he regarded anti-Semitic sentiments as foolish and crude, Louis then lobbed his grenade into the debate:

> What I find so hideously *repellent* about Mahler's music is its unequivocally *Jewish character*. . . . If Mahler's music were to *speak* Jewish, I might find it completely unintelligible. But I find it abhorrent because it *speaks with a Jewish accent*. In other words, it speaks musical German, but with the accent, the intonation and, above all, with the gestures of the eastern, all too eastern Jew. As a writer of symphonies, Mahler avails himself of the language of Beethoven and Bruckner, Berlioz and Wagner, Schubert and Viennese folk music – and one has to concede that he has acquired a tolerable grasp of the grammar and style of these languages. But with every sentence that he speaks he has the same effect on more sensitive listeners as the one that we would

5

55

feel if a comedian at the Budapest Orpheum [a cabaret in Vienna famous for its performances in a mixture of Yiddish and Viennese] were to declaim a poem by Schiller with no idea of how grotesque he appears in the mask of the German poet. The same inner contradiction invests Mahler's works with the same sense of embarrassing *inauthenticity*. Without noticing it himself – for I do not for a moment doubt in the subjective sincerity of Mahler's music – he plays a role that is, as it were, constitutionally impossible for him to carry off in any credible way.[6]

This was more dangerous and more pernicious than the attacks in newspapers notorious for their anti-Semitic opinions, for Louis was well respected in middle-class circles in the German-speaking world. Not only did he write for the *Münchner Neueste Nachrichten*, but with Ludwig Thuille he had also co-authored a standard work on harmony. He was certainly not known as an anti-Semite but was a widely read author whose books were to be found in the homes of all educated members of the middle class with an interest in music. But, like other writers, he accuses Mahler of musical *mauscheln*, adopting a line of argument all too familiar from the history of nineteenth-century anti-Semitism, when the increasingly successful emancipation of the Jews – their 'bourgeois amelioration', to quote the title of a well-known book from the end of the eighteenth century – was provoking more and more violent counter-reactions. The enemies of emancipation felt threatened by the acculturation of the German Jews and by their creative engagement with German culture. Such enemies now paid close heed to the gestures and language of the German Jews, and whenever they found examples of *mauscheln*, they were able to adopt a triumphalist tone and insist that the Jew would always remain a foreign element in the body politic. Much the same was true of Louis, who did not accuse Mahler of writing Jewish music, as he could easily have done, but complained, rather, that Mahler was trying to write German music, each note of which smacked of an ineradicable Jewishness. The old reproach that the Jews smelt differently – the 'foetor judaicus' was a commonplace among paranoid anti-Semites – was now applied to music: however virtuosic and brilliant the music of Jewish composers, it remained eclectic and mendacious as Jews were constitutionally incapable of being creative, and the worst part about it – or, rather, the best part about it, because it was this that made Jewish music so instantly identifiable – was that it spoke with a Jewish accent and had the speech patterns of the 'eternal Jew'. This, at least, was the common perception articulated by Louis and others.

These, then, were the principal charges that were laid at Mahler's door both during his lifetime and afterwards. The National Socialist press naturally clung to these stereotypes, even before 1933. In January 1929, for example, a reviewer in the *Völkischer Beobachter* wrote of a Munich performance of the *Lieder eines fahrenden Gesellen* that the work revealed 'the inner uncertainty and deracination of the superficially civilized western Jew in all his tragedy'. Mahler was

> false and insidious. The only characteristic that emerges with any authenticity is a hopeless melancholy, a denial of the world and a feeling of insecurity from which he extricates himself artificially by means of narcotic stimulants only to fall all the more deeply into a state of listlessness caused by his inferiority complex. It is a hopeless case.[7]

That such prejudices were still rife even after 1945 is clear from the passage in Ernest Ansermet's study cited above, a passage written around 1960. Many other examples of music reviews from the 1950s and 1960s – before the 'Mahler renaissance' got under way – could also be quoted in this context. It is depressing to discover the extent to which most of the critics of this period were convinced that none of the isolated performances of the composer's works would ever lead to a proper revival. In 1952, for example, a critic from Hanover thought nothing of lumping together Mahler and Heine by virtue of their 'association of naïveté and wit', except that Mahler apparently had 'none of Heine's western critical spirit': 'Mahler was a man of a more effeminate eastern type, but in a mysterious way both had succumbed to the magic of the German national character.'[8] Elsewhere we are told that Mahler

> lacked the uninhibitedness that helped Strauss, for example, to overcome many an obstacle, and yet he must have realized that his talents were limited. But he still set out with a superhuman will to transcend these limitations: with blood transfusions from folksong and art music he sought to increase his strength – and nothing is more disturbing than the profound resignation that is all that is left for the exhausted man to feel. . . . Sublimity clashes with the trivial, genuine emotion atrophies and becomes a studied construct, the composer's own ideas appear alongside others borrowed from elsewhere, and the disproportion between the actual content and the outer façade is impossible to overlook.[9]

These lines are not taken from the *Völkischer Beobachter* or *Der Angriff* but from one of the most popular concert guides of the 1950s and 1960s, Rudolf Bauer's *Das Konzert*, which first appeared in 1955, joining the best-seller list five years later when it was taken over by Germany's largest book club. It hardly needs to be said that the vast majority of the music critics and musicologists of this period – assuming they had not spent the war years in exile – had published assiduously during the Third Reich and now continued to write in much the same spirit as before, even if they eliminated the worst excesses of their National Socialist vocabulary. The anti-Semitic substance of critical responses to Mahler remained unchallenged, even if the word 'Jew' was never used, the Hanover critic's reference to the composer's 'more effeminate eastern type' being the exception that confirms the rule. The authors of such remarks could reckon on the fact that those of their readers who had read reviews and concert guides under the Third Reich knew what was meant by terms such as eclecticism and triviality, by the gap between intention and ability, by the hankering after empty effects, by the imitation of all forms and styles and by shallowness and saccharine sweetness. In Mahler's case these voices fell silent, at least in public, only when his international breakthrough had become unstoppable. In Germany, of course, anti-Semitic discourse was officially banned after 1945. But readers and listeners with sensitive hearing will have no difficulty in confirming that a residue of this type of argumentation can still be found today.

The time has come to address the question of the origins of these attitudes to Jewish composers and to ask whether Mahler was the first to suffer from such attacks. In fact their originator – the *diabolus in musica*, as it were – was none other than Richard Wagner. Writings on his anti-Semitism now fill entire book-cases. The correspondence cannot be regarded as closed. Far from it. As a result, the following account must be limited to a mere pointer to the source of all these attacks on Mahler and, by extension, on all other Jewish composers. The source is an article, 'Jews in Music', that Wagner published in two instal-ments in the *Neue Zeitschrift für Musik* in September 1850. The piece initially appeared under the pseudonym of 'K. Freigedank' ('Free Thought') but was reissued in booklet form in 1869, this time under Wagner's own name and with an introduction and a lengthy afterword.[10] Previous commentators have tended to claim that Wagner was the first writer to express his views on Jewish influ-ence on music and that he did so at a time when the modern concept of racial anti-Semitism did not yet exist – it is normally dated to the end of the 1870s, when the phrase 'anti-Semitism' was used for the first time. But writers on anti-Semitism have shown that even before this date there were already aggres-sive attempts to resist Jewish emancipation, attempts that found expression in a vast number of intemperate writings and pogrom-like measures in the years between 1810 and 1850. The world of music was initially only tangen-tially affected by these developments, although even before the appearance of Wagner's essay in 1850 there was already widespread resentment directed at Jews as performing artists and also as composers, Mendelssohn being the most prominent example. In Paris, too, there was already prejudice against Jewish composers such as Halévy and Meyerbeer during the 1830s and 1840s.

In short, Wagner was by no means the first in this field, not that this exonerates him, for he was the first to introduce any kind of system to the subject. By 1869, moreover, he was famous throughout Europe and able to add the weight of his name to the cause of anti-Semitism. This is not the place to trace the course of Wagnerian polemics, but it is striking that he was to prove the source of all the essential catchphrases that were to characterize anti-Semitic pamphleteering and that his influence went far beyond Mahler. Citing Mendelssohn and, above all, Meyerbeer, Wagner sought to show that Jewish musicians produced a confused contrafactum of the different forms and styles that had existed throughout history and that they attempted to make up for the absence of any real feeling by means of an assemblage of superficial effects. Jewish works of music were notable for a coldness and an indifference that bordered on the trivial and the absurd, the period during which music was dominated by Jews being characterized by its total lack of creativity. This was especially clear in the case of Meyerbeer. Although Meyerbeer is not mentioned by name in 'Jews in Music', contemporary readers would have had no difficulty identifying the anonymous butt of Wagner's barbs.

In his longer study, *Opera and Drama*, which he completed in January 1851, Wagner named names, dismissing Meyerbeer's music as a farrago of 'effects without causes', a phrase that quickly did the rounds. The republication of 'Jews in Music' in pamphlet form in 1869 revived the arguments and led to an embittered debate on the subject. The liberal writer Gustav Freytag, whose novel *Soll und Haben* features a number of shady Jewish characters, took issue with Wagner and listed the qualities that Wagner imputes to Jewish composers, finally asking his readers which composer best embodied these characteristics. Surely, he concluded, it was Wagner himself. This republication caused such a stir that from then on Wagner's arguments could no longer be ignored, allowing them to be reactivated by Mahler's critics in the years around the turn of the century. From here we can trace an unbroken line to the cultural politics of the Third Reich, which found in the writings of Wagner and the Bayreuth circle a welcome repository of clichés and catchphrases. Time and again anti-Semitic journalists appealed explicitly to Wagner, almost always referring in the process to his essay, 'Jews in Music'. Many writers have wondered why Wagner exerted such a powerful influence on contemporary Jews: Jewish musicians such as Carl Tausig, Josef Rubinstein and Hermann Levi flocked to Wagner's side, Jewish audiences attended performances of his works (only a small minority protested at his anti-Semitism), and not even Mahler could be swayed in his tremendous enthusiasm for Wagner. Although he must have been aware of Wagner's anti-Semitism, there is no evidence that he ever sought to distance himself from it.

What was Mahler's own attitude to his Jewish ancestry? It is a question that cannot be avoided, no matter how difficult it may be to answer. Unlike Wagner,

Mahler left no writings expressing his views on this or any other subject. Instead, we have to rely on his letters and on the reminiscences of his family and friends. He was born into a Jewish family in the south-eastern corner of Bohemia. In Iglau, the town to which the family moved soon after Mahler was born, there was initially no Jewish community with any proper organization to it, but when such an organization was finally established, it was Bernhard Mahler who sat on its committee. Very little Yiddish was spoken in this region, and so Mahler grew up speaking German. According to one of his earliest memories, he was still a small child when he protested at the singing in the local synagogue, suggesting that the family attended services there on a fairly regular basis. But we may also be right in assuming that while he was a student in Vienna, where he mixed with freethinkers and Nietzscheans such as Siegfried Lipiner and with men like Engelbert Pernerstorfer and Victor Adler, who went on to become prominent Socialists, he soon distanced himself from the faith of his forefathers, a faith that is unlikely to have been orthodox in character. Anti-Semitic attacks such as the one that he suffered in Kassel will have made it clear to him at an early date that his Jewish faith was an obstacle to his advancement – one thinks in this context of Heine's description of baptism as an 'entry ticket' to European civilization. By the winter of 1896/7, by which date Mahler was principal conductor in Hamburg and hoping to become conductor and director of the Vienna Court Opera, he still seemed surprised when writing to his friend Friedrich Löhr: 'The fact that I am Jewish prevents my getting taken on in any Court theatre. – Neither Vienna, nor Berlin, nor Dresden, nor Munich is open to me. The same wind is now blowing everywhere.'[11] Mahler's use of the word 'now' indicates that he had initially been unaware of this 'obstacle'. His childhood and adolescence will have been largely free from anti-Semitism. As we have already noted, it was not until the 1880s that a new and less tolerant regime began.

Having gradually moved away from orthodox Judaism, Mahler decided to convert to Christianity in 1897, in the middle of his negotiations with Vienna. 'Mahler is a Jew, I'll never get him through,' the administrative director of the Court Theatres, Eduard Wlassack, one of Mahler's patrons, is said to have exclaimed. But in a letter to Ödön von Mihalovich, Mahler himself reports a remark by the principal comptroller Prince Liechtenstein to the effect that 'things are not yet so bad in Austria that anti-Semitism can decide matters'.[12] Yet the obstacle still had to be removed. That Mahler waited until he was thirty-seven to remove it is an indication of the purely tactical nature of the step, a point reinforced by a letter to his young disciple Bruno Walter, who had asked him for his advice on the course that his life should take: 'But above all, you should convert and do your military service!'[13] Writing only weeks after his own conversion, Mahler was anxious that Walter should remove the two

most serious obstacles on the road to a career as a conductor. Shortly afterwards, he advised Walter to change his name and abandon the Jewish surname
Schlesinger in favour of the less stigmatizing Walter. That Mahler was not
entirely comfortable with his late conversion is clear from his repeated claim
that it had taken place earlier than was in fact the case. (We have already
quoted one particularly embarrassing example of this deceit.) Clearly he
preferred not to think that it was directly bound up with his Viennese appointment, although his anger may have been directed less at himself than at a
world which, pervaded by anti-Semitism, forced him to undertake such an act
of deception.

As for Mahler's beliefs, we can say only that their character is difficult to
define, a point to which we shall return in the wider context of his general
philosophical outlook. Alma, who – to put it mildly – was herself not free
from anti-Semitic sentiment, later insisted that her husband's conversion was
anything but opportunistic in character as he had always believed in Christ.
Indeed, she even uses the term 'Christian Jew', an expression commonly
applied to converts from Judaism whose Christianity was peculiarly fervent –
Mendelssohn was another such example. But Alma's assessment appears to
have been dictated by special interest. Mahler's private religion – if we may use
such an expression – was a highly individual mix of Goethean pantheism, a
belief in entelechy of a kind associated with both Goethe and Gustav Fechner,
namely, the notion of a creative destiny imposed on us by forces outside
ourselves, a religion of compassion in the spirit of Dostoevsky, a Nietzschean
independence and a profoundly felt natural religion. When Mahler used the
word 'God', he did not mean the Christian or the Jewish God but, as we shall
see in a later chapter, an amalgam of all this and much else besides.

There are plenty of examples of Jews such as the Marranos who were forcibly
converted but who retained their Jewish beliefs. But Mahler does not fall into
this category. Even as an adolescent he had clearly moved away from the faith
of his forefathers and, unlike Arnold Schoenberg in very different circumstances, he never returned to it. Mahler is sometimes cited as an example of the
problematical concept of 'Jewish self-hatred'. In particular, writers have drawn
attention to a letter that he addressed to his wife from Lemberg, where he was
giving two concerts on 2 and 4 April 1903: 'The most endearing part of it are
the Polish Jews that roam the streets here just like stray dogs in other places. –
It's highly amusing to observe them! My God, are these supposed to be my kith
and kin?! In the face of such evidence, all theories of racial origin appear more
ludicrous than I can tell you!'[14] Unsettling though such remarks may seem, we
must be wary of interpreting them as reliable evidence of the sort of Jewish self-
hatred that is discernible in the case of individuals such as Arthur Trebitsch and
Otto Weininger. Mahler was clearly prejudiced against Eastern European Jews,

but such prejudices were common and, indeed, normal among assimilated Western European Jews at this period. Very similar psychological mechanisms were later described by Jakob Wassermann, a non-convert who published an impressive set of memoirs under the title *Mein Weg als Deutscher und Jude* (an English translation appeared in 1933 as *My Life as German and Jew*).

There is no doubt that Mahler viewed his Jewish birth as a burden, and however much he may have protested at racial theories in his letter to his wife, he was no less able to escape from such ideas than any of his contemporaries. In a letter that he wrote in 1906 to the young Jewish conductor Oskar Fried, he spoke out quite openly on the subject: 'And don't forget that we can do nothing about our being Jewish, our chief mistake. We must merely try to moderate a little those superficial aspects of our nature which really *do* disturb, and to *give way as little as possible on important matters*.'[15] On another occasion he told Alfred Roller that he regarded his Jewish ancestry as a spur or incentive: 'If a person comes into the world with an arm that is too short, his other arm must learn to achieve even more and perhaps do things that two healthy arms could never have accomplished.'[16]

On the one hand, therefore, we find Mahler regarding his Jewish ancestry as a tormenting burden and sharing the prejudices of assimilated Western European Jews against those of their Eastern European counterparts who in the wake of Russian pogroms at the end of the nineteenth century fled to the West in increasing numbers. These refugees formed 'hordes of ambitious, trouser-selling youths from the inexhaustible Polish cradle', persuading the German nationalist historian Heinrich von Treitschke to coin the fatal phrase 'The Jews are our misfortune' in 1879. It was a phrase that the Nazi newspaper *Der Stürmer* was later to reprint on its title page every day. On the other hand, there is no evidence that – to use Anna Freud's expression – Mahler 'identified with the aggressor' in a way that is typical of Jewish self-hatred. Few men knew Mahler better than the artist and set designer Alfred Roller, who worked with him on his epoch-making productions at the Vienna Court Opera and who convincingly summed up the problem in the words: 'Mahler never hid his Jewish ancestry. But it gave him no pleasure.' Roller also reports the following remark: 'People should listen to my works and allow those works to affect them, either accepting them or rejecting them. But they should leave at home their positive or negative pre-judices against the work of the Jew. I demand this as my right.'[17] As we have seen, Mahler was denied this right. Even the anti-Semitic Alma admitted that he never denied his Jewish origins but tended, rather, to stress them, a point confirmed by Alphons Diepenbrock, one of Mahler's Dutch friends. But we need to remember that not to deny one's Jewish birth is one thing, whereas it is a completely different matter to see oneself as a Jew. Whenever Mahler felt rejected either as a human being or as a musician, he believed that it was as a Jew that he was being spurned. To that extent he undoubtedly regarded himself as a victim of the anti-Semitism of the age, even when that anti-Semitism may not have been present. There is also evidence, as previously noted, that he hated obvious displays of Jewishness, including Jewish jokes, no matter whether they were told by anti-Semites or Jews. He loved his wife's long flowing hair and when she pinned it up, he protested at her 'current Jewish look'.[18]

It is simply not possible to provide a definitive answer to the question of Mahler's relationship to Judaism and his own Jewish origins – no one who has taken any interest in what has been called the 'German-Jewish symbiosis' will be surprised at this inability to solve a problem that founders even on the definition of a Jew. The Halacha definition that is also applied in Israel, albeit controversially, argues that a Jew is someone with Jewish parents (in the case of a mixed marriage, the mother's Jewishness is paramount) or a convert to the religious precepts of Judaism. Set against this is the secular definition whereby those people are Jews who identify with the Jewish nation and its destiny. As we know, these differing definitions have led to test cases in Israel, and although judgements have been handed down from the highest secular and rabbinical courts in the land, the arguments have yet to be resolved. The Halacha also insists that baptized Jews remain Jews, being guilty only of infringing religious law. According to Halacha law, Mahler too must be regarded as a Jew. The problem with this definition emerges when we turn to the German-language *Jüdisches Lexikon* that was published in the 1920s: the author of the entry under 'Baptized Jews' can hardly contain his disgust at such people and even appends a list of baptized Jews intended to discourage others by naming and shaming their predecessors.

At the same time, however, the volume is evidently pleased to include an entry on Mahler in which the composer's baptism is mentioned, just as it is in the Mahler article in the *Encyclopedia Judaica*. (Conversely, the 1990 edition of the *Brockhaus-Enzyklopädie* makes no mention of Mahler's Jewish ancestry or of his baptism.) Once Mahler had abandoned his Jewish co-religionists, we can hardly regard him as a Jew any longer, at least to the extent that we are unwilling to follow Halacha law. In adopting this view of him we may be further encouraged by the fact that once he had outgrown his childhood he no longer observed any Jewish rituals. On the other hand, it is impossible to ignore Jean-Paul Sartre's famous definition of the Jew as someone who is regarded as such: in this sense, Mahler remained a Jew throughout his life. Perhaps we may combine both definitions and argue that a Jew is someone who regards himself as such and who identifies with Judaism or who is regarded by others as a Jew until such time as he himself comes to see himself as a Jew. (Here one thinks of the many Germans who said that it required Hitler to make them conscious of the fact that they were Jews.) This was certainly the line adopted by the a-religious, non-convert Sigmund Freud, when he explained in an interview in 1926: 'My language is German. My culture, my attainments, are German. I considered myself German intellectually, until I noticed the growth of anti-Semitic prejudice in Germany and German Austria. Since that time, I prefer to call myself a Jew'.[19]

A person who in this or a similar situation refuses to identify with Judaism, as Mahler refused to do, can hardly be described as a Jew. Here the individual's own definition of himself should be given greater weight than other people's definition of him. It is unsurprising that the undifferentiated use of the term 'Jew', especially when it is well-meaning, invariably leads to complications. Be that as it may, the various threads that bind a person to his Jewish ancestry need to be disentangled and examined one by one. Mahler did not regard himself as a Jew even though he was neither able nor willing to deny that he was born into a Jewish family. He felt remote from all aspects of Judaism, be they ritual, dress, hair or beard, and on occasion even spoke dismissively about them. Linguistically, too, he showed no trace of Western European Yiddish in the way he spoke. Towards the end of his life, an orchestral musician in New York addressed him as a German, prompting him to insist, rather, that he was from Bohemia. His famous remark that he was homeless three times over – as a Bohemian among Austrians, as an Austrian among Germans and as a Jew in the whole of the world, implying that he was forever an unwelcome intruder – is attested only by Alma and, like everything found only in her memoirs, it needs to be treated with caution. It may be the most famous sentence associated with Mahler, but doubts concerning its formulation are none the less in order.[20] But even if we take it literally, the phrase still does not allow us to conclude that Mahler defined himself as a Jew.

Alfred Roller believed that Mahler's attitude to Judaism was best characterized by the term 'compassion'. It was no doubt this compassion that prevented him from distancing himself more emphatically from his Jewish ancestry and from denying those origins altogether. At a time when a belief in race was still very deeply rooted, he was already prepared to cast doubt on racial theory. We shall perhaps come a little closer to this extraordinarily complex problem if we use the term that Arthur Schnitzler devised for his own attitude to Judaism: 'Gefühlsgemeinschaft', an 'emotional community' or commonality of feeling. Schnitzler was anything but a devout Jew but was a fully integrated agnostic whose command of the German language was second to none. In spite of this he did not abandon his Jewish religious community, even though he felt no real bond with it. Rather he felt close to other members of this community, which in his eyes replaced the increasingly obsolete concept of race. Freud said much the same:

I can say that I am as remote from the Jewish religion as from all others; that is to say, they are highly significant to me as a subject of scientific interest; emotionally I am not involved in them. On the other hand, I have always had a strong feeling of solidarity with my people and have also fostered it in my children. We have all remained in the Jewish confession.[21]

One senses something very similar in the case of Mahler, even if only in a much weaker form. It is an attitude documented by more than just his conversion. We may sum up the situation by suggesting that Mahler did not feel himself to be a Jew even if he sensed that there were links with his family's past. He hated negative Jewish qualities, at least as he understood them. He also hated anti-Semitism. If his conversion to Catholicism left him feeling uncomfortable, it was not because he had had to deny any articles of faith but because it had been a tactical manoeuvre. It will have been the admonishment of his superego, together with his compassion for those of his comrades who shared the same fate, that prevented him from distancing himself even more from his Jewish origins than he might perhaps have felt inclined to do. If we had to limit ourselves to a single definition, it might be that Mahler was not a Jew, but nor was he a Gentile. He came from a family that was still Jewish and that still played a part in the life of the local Jewish community but which in all likelihood could hardly be regarded as orthodox. His family had taken its first tentative steps on the road to assimilation, although a glance at Schnitzler's family shows just how much they still had to achieve in this regard. Mahler continued this journey with his typically intemperate determination and perseverance. In breaking free from the straitened circumstances of his family, which had taken generations to enter the ranks of the petty bourgeoisie, and in working his way up to one of the highest cultural positions in western Europe within a matter of barely twenty years, he left far behind him most of his forefathers' links with his Jewish faith. Nor should we forget that among his young friends both Lipiner and Löhr were baptized, as was his later brother-in-law, Arnold Rosé. But Mahler never forget where he came from. Nor did he seek to deny it. If his background became a burden to him, it was because the society in which he lived was impregnated with anti-Semitism to a degree altogether unknown to earlier generations.

We now have to ask whether Mahler wrote Jewish music. The question has to be put even if it has repeatedly been posed by anti-Semites. But it has also been asked by Mahler's supporters, even during his own lifetime. And it continues to be discussed to this day – much the same is true of Schoenberg, whose music was examined from this standpoint by the American musicologist Alexander L. Ringer in his 1990 book *Arnold Schoenberg: The Composer as Jew*. It will come as no surprise to discover that here, too, simple answers are ruled out, because any possible response is bound up with the answer to the question of what Jewish music is. There are two major encyclopaedias in the world that are dedicated to music, the English-language New Grove and the German *Die Musik in Geschichte und Gegenwart*. The latter has recently been completely revised, and the volume containing the article on 'Jewish Music' was published in 1996. The same difficulties arise over the definition of Jewish music as those that we encountered when discussing the Jewish identity. Indeed, it would be surprising if it were otherwise. The development of music is closely associated, of course, with the vicissitudinous fate of the Jews as a nation and as a religious community. During the diaspora local traditions played a considerable role, greater or lesser deviations from the liturgy depending on the extent to which the genres in question were already remote from the liturgy, having developed independently according to the Sephardi and Ashkenazi traditions. For a long time writers clung to the definition proposed by the musicologist Curt Sachs at the First International Congress on Jewish Music that took place in Paris in 1957: 'Jewish music is that music which is made by Jews, for Jews, as Jews.' This definition at least had the merit of memorability and is still occasionally found today. It is, as it were, the Halacha definition of Jewish music, the narrowness of which was quickly noted. A 'secular' rider was soon added, according to which all music with which Jews can identify should also be described as Jewish, although this inevitably raises the question of the role that Jews adopt when identifying with a particular type of music: religious Jews, cultural Jews or purely as music lovers. Take the example of Hermann Levi, the son of a rabbi from Gießen, who refused to convert to Christianity but conducted the first performances of *Parsifal* at the 1882 Bayreuth Festival, devoting himself with an abandonment bordering on self-sacrifice to music that could hardly be described as 'Jewish'.

In his 1992 book *Jewish Musical Traditions*, Amnon Shiloah emphasized the importance of intrinsic musical, geographical and historical aspects in any definition of Jewish music. Above all, however, he felt that the cultural context was important and rightly drew attention to the fact that performance practice is often decisive in defining the function of a particular Jewish musical identity. The author of the article on Jewish music in *Die Musik in Geschichte und Gegenwart* takes this definition as his starting point when arguing that Jewish music is music that combines formal, stylistic and semantic features of Jewish behaviour and culture. The whole of the substantial article adopts this same approach, tracing in minute detail the long history of the Jewish musical tradition. The entry ends with an account of the great cantors of the nineteenth century, including Salomon Sulzer in Vienna and Lazarus Lewandowski in Berlin. In the twentieth century, the writer draws attention to the importance of the national school of Jewish music in Russia between 1900 and 1930, a tradition that began life in

St Petersburg. Other twentieth-century composers who are mentioned here include Arnold Schoenberg, at least to the extent that he took an interest in Jewish themes, Leonard Bernstein and Dmitri Shostakovich, who, although not a Jew, used musical motifs from the Jewish tradition in works such as his Thirteenth Symphony and his song cycle *From Jewish Folk Poetry*. Other composers listed here are Ernest Bloch and Josef Tal, both of whom settled in Israel. But where are Meyerbeer, Mendelssohn and Mahler? They are not mentioned here, and rightly so, because, unless we are to take Wagner's anti-Semitic arguments seriously, none of them can be said to demonstrate any formal, stylistic or semantic signs of Jewish culture and Jewish behaviour.

At this point we could sit back and regard the argument as settled, were it not for the fact that Meyerbeer, Mendelssohn and Mahler – one lifelong Jew and two converts to Christianity, to stick to our existing terminology – are listed in all Jewish encyclopaedias as Jewish composers. Are these, then, examples of Jewish composers who wrote non-Jewish music? This is certainly the point of view adopted by the Jewish encyclopaedias in question and presumably also by non-Jewish encyclopaedias, even when they do not explicitly refer to Mahler's Jewishness. But the situation is not as simple as this, especially when we recall how even unbiased lovers of Mahler's music repeatedly claim that it sounds Jewish to them. Here we can at least appeal to Adorno, whose Mahler study of 1960 remains unsurpassed and who examined the Jewish element in Mahler's music, albeit only in passing: 'Possibly synagogal or secular Jewish melodies are rare; a passage in the Scherzo of the Fourth Symphony might most readily point in that direction.'[22] But the passage cited by Adorno is difficult to interpret in this way. Conversely, there are one or two other passages in which the listener may be able to sense the plaintive, jubilant tone of the clarinet as found in Eastern European klezmer music, but these passages are nowhere near enough to allow us to describe the whole of Mahler's output as 'Jewish'. He himself stressed on more than one occasion that as a small child in Iglau, on the border between Bohemia and Moravia, he listened with intense fascination to the local brass bands, running behind them and losing his way back home. He also listened to itinerant dance bands. These small groups of musicians also included Jewish players, of course, but the Hamburg musicologist Vladimir Karbusicky, himself a native of Bohemia, examined the musical impressions of Mahler's youth in a study that he published in 1978. While he was able to draw detailed attention to the influence of Bohemian and Moravian folk music, he has nothing to say on the subject of Jewish music.[23] Even if Jewish musicians were present in Iglau and its environs, they did not always play purely Jewish dance tunes and Jewish folk music but an indeterminable mixture of styles.

Mahler himself repeatedly emphasized the importance of the folk music from his region for his own early musical education. It was a point that he made at some length in an interview that he gave to a New York newspaper towards the end of his life.[24] But he insisted that what mattered was the way in which the material was reworked, not its origins. In the rare instances where Mahler alludes to this music or integrates it into his works, it is impossible to describe it as unequivocally Jewish, for it stems from the linguistic and cultural mix of Bohemian, Moravian, German and Jewish elements that was typical of the region where he grew up. Attempts by later writers to dissect these influences along coldly clinical lines are doomed to fail, and in the light of all that we know about Mahler's relations to Judaism, there can be no justification whatsoever for the claim that he consciously used and even parodied a particular Jewish musical element. It is unlikely that he would have quoted such material in an attempt either to assert his own identity as a Jew or, conversely, to imply a dismissive and malicious subtext. Rather, it is one of those many elements that Mahler amalgamated into his music, drawing no distinction between 'higher' and 'lower' forms but concerned only with its status within the symphonic context as a whole. To quote Adorno's inimitable description:

> The unrisen lower is stirred as yeast into high music. The rude vigour and immediacy of a musical entity that can neither be replaced nor forgotten: the power of naming is often better protected in kitsch and vulgar music than in a high music that even before the age of radical construction had sacrificed all that to the principle of stylization. This power is mobilized by Mahler. Free as only one can be who has not himself been entirely swallowed by culture, in his musical vagrancy he picks up the broken glass by the roadside and holds it up to the sun so that all the colors are refracted. . . . In the debased and vilified materials of music he scratches for illicit joys.[25]

To avoid all misunderstandings, I must stress that it is not my intention to remove every last trace of Jewishness from Mahler's music. Gershom Scholem was quite right to be exercised by the fact that well-meaning German writers of the post-war era have often shown a peculiar reluctance to use the word 'Jew' to describe Jews who do not necessarily insist on their Jewishness: 'After they were murdered as Jews, they are now glorified as Germans in a kind of posthumous triumph. To stress their Jewishness would be a concession to anti-Semitic theories. What a perversion!' In the same context, Scholem famously questions the 'myth of German-Jewish discourse', a form of discourse that he was able to regard only as the Jews' despairing cry echoing in the void:

> True, the total devotion to the German nation of so many people who describe themselves in their – numerous – autobiographies as being 'of Jewish extraction' because they otherwise had nothing in common with the

Jewish tradition, still less with the Jewish people, is one of the most moving and unsettling aspects of this process of alienation. The list of Jews who have been lost to the Germans is infinitely long, a catalogue of great and often astonishing gifts and achievements offered up to the Germans. . . . These people made a choice, and it is not our intention to contest the Germans' right to them. And yet it often leaves us feeling uncomfortable, for we sense the internal divisions in such lives. Even when they are conscious of being estranged from all that is 'Jewish', many of them reveal a quality that is felt by Jews and Germans alike – but not by the individuals concerned! – to be their Jewish substance. This is certainly true of such leading figures as Karl Marx and Ferdinand Lassalle and, closer to our own day, Karl Kraus, Gustav Mahler and Georg Simmel.[26]

At least to the extent that writers took heed of it at all, Scholem's radical refusal to pay lip service to the cosy debates about the 'German-Jewish symbiosis' brought a breath of fresh air to the difficult discussion over the relations between Germans and Jews, and yet there were times when Scholem tended to adopt an unduly Manichaean approach to the subject. Mahler, after all, is out of place in this list of names, each of which is *sui generis*: Kraus converted to Catholicism, only to abandon his newfound faith, while in the case of Simmel, it was the sociologist's father who had already converted to Christianity. As for Mahler, he did not 'offer himself up' to the Germans but refused to describe himself as a German. Nor did he distance himself from all things Jewish in the way that Kraus and Simmel did. We have already tried to approach this problem by suggesting that Mahler was not a Jew, but nor was he a Gentile. By not embracing the Germans and Austrians wholeheartedly, Mahler was spared the disappointment of rejection in its strictest form, but at the same time he exposed himself to a feeling of homelessness. He inhabited a world poised between past and future, a 'man of the air', to use a Jewish expression of the period: the roots that he put down were aerial roots. His manic restlessness, his sense of always being driven, his inability to relax, which made his wife ill, his tendency to bite his fingernails and even the nervous tic that made him stamp his foot and twitch his leg uncontrollably – in part, these are undoubtedly all examples of learned behaviour picked up while he was a child in a large family beset by health problems, but they may also be attributable to his sense of insecurity and to a feeling that he had no home to which he could return.

This is ultimately the only way to explain the letter that Mahler wrote to Bruno Walter in the summer of 1908 and that describes the events of the previous year, when his daughter Maria had died and his own heart disease was diagnosed. Here was a man at the height of his fame as a composer, a man who had already been acclaimed in New York as a world-famous conductor, a man who still had a wife and daughter – his marital crisis lay two years in the future – and who could feel proud of his own achievements as a composer, for he knew exactly who he was and what his music meant to him and others. And yet he was able to say of himself that he had suddenly lost all sense of clarity and reassurance and was standing 'vis-à-vis de rien' – he was facing the void.[27]

It remains to attempt at least a partial answer to the question how we might evaluate the Jewish element in Mahler's music if the criteria proposed by narrower definitions of the term are not applicable here. To answer this question we do not need to sink to the level of the unfazable anti-Semites. A glance at the debate that has taken place about Mahler during the last one hundred years allows us to distinguish three different groups. First, there are the anti-Semites who, as we have seen, insist that Mahler was Jewish. Then there is the Mahler faction that refuses absolutely to regard him as a Jewish composer. (Unsurprisingly, this group contains numerous assimilated Jews.) And finally there is the much smaller group that has attempted to think more seriously about the Jewish element in Mahler's music and to reclaim him for a new and more self-confident Jewishness. As early as the 1920s there was a debate in the columns of the journal *Der Jude* that involved writers of the standing of Arno Nadel, Paul Nettl, Heinrich Berl and Max Brod. Whereas Nadel argued for assimilation and claimed that Mahler wrote German music just as Meyerbeer wrote French music, Berl insisted that Mahler wrote Jewish music and, adopting a Zionist standpoint, demanded that all Jewish composers, including Schoenberg, should be mindful of their Jewish and Middle Eastern roots. He even went on to write a book on the subject, giving it the same title as Wagner's *Das Judentum in der Musik*.[28] For his own part, Max Brod voiced views that were only slightly less radical when he tried to bring Mahler and Judaism back into alignment. As late as 1961 he was still hailing Mahler as an example of a German-Jewish symbiosis – Scholem would have been delighted at this – but at the same time he insisted that with his predilection for marches Mahler had drawn his inspiration 'from the wellspring of Eastern European Jewish Hasidic folk music'. To assert that Mahler's music is characterized by march rhythms is, however, a bold claim to make. In attempting to explain away the fact that Mahler himself never referred to such traditions, Brod fell back on the simple expedient of declaring that these Jewish elements were all 'unconscious'.[29]

Even if Brod's attempt to demonstrate this point must ultimately be regarded as a failure, there remains much that is still worth considering. We have seen that the charge levelled by the anti-Semites that Mahler's music is trivial, eclectic, banal and derivative stems from Wagner's essay, but this in itself does not mean that it can be dismissed out of hand, for it has been raised even by critics who cannot be accused of anti-Semitism. And Mahler himself, after all, pre-empted all such reproaches by striking a note of irony. In 1896, while he was working on his Third Symphony, he wrote to Bruno Walter, 'Everyone knows by now that some triviality or other always has to occur in my work. But this time it goes beyond all bounds.'[30] Contemporaries noted from an early date that Mahler's symphonies contained elements that are not to be found in the works of his revered Brahms, for example, and even those of his champions who were receptive to his ideas had to struggle to make sense of this. When Mahler uses a posthorn or writes performance markings such as 'In a folk tone', 'Like the sound of distant bells' and 'Like the call of a bird', or when he writes for offstage orchestras, then even the most cloth-eared listeners must realize that he is striving to achieve effects different from those found in Brahms's Fourth Symphony or Bruckner's Eighth. For sceptical spirits, it was all too tempting to dismiss such elements as derivative and as substitutes for a lack of creativity. And this is certainly what happened, generally with an anti-Semitic intent.

Let us, however, also look at the way in which two adepts of the more recent period deal with this problem, neither of whom can be accused of anti-Semitism. Adorno refused to see any connection between Mahler's 'crudities' and his Jewish ancestry. Rather, he regarded both Mahler and his own teacher, Alban Berg, as advocates of the downtrodden masses, a point that emerges with peculiar force not just from his wonderful phrase about 'broken glass' but also from his earlier reference to the 'lower music' irrupting 'Jacobinically' into the 'higher'. Much later he addresses the Jewish question, but here he becomes oddly vague, insisting in the case of the Jewish element that

> One can no more put one's finger on this element than in any other work of art: it shrinks from identification yet to the whole remains indispensable. The attempt to deny it in order to reclaim Mahler for a conception of German music infected by National Socialism is as aberrant as his appropriation as a Jewish nationalist composer. . . . What is Jewish in Mahler does not participate directly in the folk element, but speaks through all its mediations as an intellectual voice, something non-sensuous yet perceptible in the totality.[31]

The reader would like Adorno to say more on this point, but he leaves us in the lurch and after alluding briefly and unsatisfactorily to 'the shrill, sometimes nasal, gesticulating aspect' of Mahler's late style, with its tendency to 'talk at cross purposes' – the anti-Semitic clichés are certainly a problem here – he turns abruptly and apparently with some embarrassment to another topic, leaving readers feeling that they are taking part in a conversation in which an unguarded remark has suddenly opened up a gaping abyss, which the speaker, after a brief moment of horror, then covers up by turning to far more innocuous matters.

Writing in the wake of Adorno, the German musicologist Hans Heinrich Eggebrecht has coined the phrase 'vocabular music' in an attempt to explain Mahler's ability to create a highly individual personal style out of 'high' and 'low' elements borrowed and picked up elsewhere. Time and again, eavesdroppers will hear concert-goers complaining that Mahler's music is 'second-hand'. And yet these same concert-goers insist that a single note of this music is enough to identify its composer. Second-hand and yet individual – even the most innocent listeners can grasp this apparent contradiction, leading them to seek to dismiss the problem in terms that are occasionally, but not always, anti-Semitic in character. Eggebrecht argues that Mahler used musical vocabularies from the tradition of both high art and popular culture, even famously drawing on the sounds of nature such as birdsong and cowbells, because he wanted to portray the world in its totality, depicting it in music that comes very close to language, hence the use of the term 'vocabularies'. Such music eschews the attempt to eradicate anything that might reveal the origins of individual elements – according to Mahler, in an interview that he gave in New York during the final years of his life, his own achievement as a composer was like that of a jeweller making an unpolished diamond sparkle. In Eggebrecht's view, this compositional method has something to do with the Jewish element in Mahler's music, and he draws a parallel between, on the one hand, the freedom of an approach that refuses to genuflect before the flotsam and jetsam of cultural possessions, still less to turn away from them in disgust, and, on the other, the homelessness of Mahler's Jewishness. In turn this existential restlessness is associated in Eggebrecht's view with the striking prevalence of marching, striding rhythms in Mahler's music.[32]

Whereas Adorno prefers a physiognomic argument (his monograph, after all, is subtitled 'A Musical Physiognomy'), Eggebrecht draws on comparisons of a linguistic nature. But both studies are conducted on the highest and most unambiguous level, and both ultimately suggest the impossibility of getting any closer to the Jewish element in Mahler's music in any rationally tangible way, whereas the attempt to monopolize Mahler for Zionist ends was always bound to fail. Within the context of any discussion about modernity and post-modernity it is perfectly possible to regard Mahler's 'polymaterial' procedure as a collage technique and as an example of plurality without trespassing on the quagmire of 'Jewishness in Music'. Perhaps the normally self-assured Adorno was right to express himself with unusual reticence when he wrote that the Jewish element 'shrinks from identification yet to the whole remains indispensable'.

Picking up Adorno's image, we might further analyse the light that falls through the broken glass of Mahler's relations to Judaism and break it down into other colours, and yet there still remains a residue that cannot be broken

down any further. Every writer who has examined the question of Mahler's
relations with Judaism must at some point confront a testimony known to a
broader readership since the mid-1980s or so, when a fuller – if by no means
complete – version of Natalie Bauer-Lechner's reminiscences was first made
available. An entry for 1901 reads:

> Mahler recalled a strange dream that he had had as a child – he must have
> been about eight at the time. It came to such vivid life before his mind's eye
> that he remained under its impression for a very long time and even today is
> unable to forget it. He told me: 'My mother, my brother Ernst and I were
> standing one evening at the window of our sitting room when my mother
> exclaimed: "God, what's happening!" The sky was filled with yellow mist; the
> stars were moving, following each other or devouring one another as if the
> world were ending. Suddenly I am outside in the marketplace. The fiery mists
> pursue me and when I look round, I can see in them an immense figure rising
> up, that of the Wandering Jew. His cloak, distended by the wind, towers over
> his shoulders like a vast hump; he is resting his right hand on a long staff
> surmounted by a gold cross. I find myself fleeing before him in frantic fear,
> but with a few steps he catches up with me and tries to force his staff on me
> (a symbol, as it were, of his eternally restless wanderings): at that point I wake
> up screaming with the most terrible fear.[33]

Re-imagined some thirty-five years after he had first dreamt it – assuming
that Mahler dreamt it at all in this form – this dream suggests that Ahasuerus
was a recurrent topos for him. But it would be wrong to reduce this topos to
the problems suffered by assimilated Jews in Central Europe in the years
around 1900. After all, Ahasuerus had in the course of the nineteenth century
become a literary figure extending far beyond the immediate Jewish context,
and not every restless composer, as Mahler undoubtedly was, could describe
himself as an Ahasuerus of the musical world. True, his Ninth Symphony
certainly does not end on a quietistic note, and the sketches for the Tenth
Symphony clearly reveal the signs of Mahler's deep-seated crisis. But nothing
suggests that the events surrounding the death of his daughter and the diagnosis of his heart disease in 1907 or Alma's affair with Walter Gropius in the
summer of 1910, which left him shaken to the very depths of his being and led
to his consultation with Sigmund Freud (and which affair, be it added, Alma
continued with Gropius without Mahler's knowledge), can in any way be
attributed to a tendency in the final years of his life to regard his Jewish origins
as profoundly problematic. Mahler's character remains ineluctably marked
by the infinitely complex life of an Austrian composer of Bohemian ancestry
who spoke German and who numbered Jews among his forebears, and to the

extent that the character and form of expression adopted by the artistic subject are indivisible, these attributes also characterized his work. All attempts to go beyond this observation and to seek concrete examples of Jewishness in his music must ultimately end in the mists and vapours of Mahler's childhood dream.

The Third Symphony

EVEN COMMITTED MAHLERIANS have always had difficulty with the Third Symphony, the opening movement of which seems immoderately distended – the slowest performance on record takes no fewer than thirty-seven minutes, more than the length of an entire symphony by Beethoven. And then there is the final movement, an affirmative-sounding Adagio lasting some twenty-five minutes, pursuing its leisurely course with its seemingly unshakeable belief in truth, beauty and goodness. Between these two extremes are four movements that could hardly be more heterogeneous. There are writers on Mahler who, for all their sympathetic response to the piece, regard it as a failure, arguing that elements that should have been welded together fall apart and that disparate ideas have been paratactically juxtaposed, to say nothing of the work's egregious gigantism. Others take a different view of the matter. Adorno, for example, conceded that objective difficulties might be suggested by the fact that the work is relatively rarely performed – certainly it receives fewer performances than the other three so-called 'Wunderhorn' symphonies – but he went on to attribute this circumstance to the fact that in the opening movement in particular Mahler ventured into territory that he was never again to explore: from this point of view, the Fourth Symphony undoubtedly gives the impression of a kind of neoclassical restraint after the excesses of the Third, which Mahler worked on in the main during his summer vacations in 1895 and 1896. The young Bruno Walter was present in Steinbach on the Attersee when Mahler played through the work on the piano during the summer of 1896 and was almost literally stunned by the power and novelty of the musical language within the work's symphonic world.[1] Walter uses the term 'primal sound', while Adorno describes its proportions as 'primeval'.

It is this work, above all, that commentators continue to associate with Mahler's idea of constructing an entire world, an ambition that undoubtedly culminates in the Third. It is worth quoting this famous sentence in context, a sentence that we must be grateful to Natalie Bauer-Lechner for noting down when she visited Mahler in Steinbach in the summer of 1895 and he told her 'jokingly' that he hoped he would finally 'earn applause and money' with a work that was 'pure humour and merriment, a great laugh at the whole world!' By the following day, however, he had become more serious and took back what he had said about the work's success, 'for people won't understand or appreciate its cheerfulness; it soars *above* that world of struggle and sorrow in the First and Second, and could have been produced only as a result of these'. And then comes the famous passage, this time with the important sentence in context:

> My calling it a symphony is really inaccurate, for it doesn't keep to the tradi-
> tional form in any way. But, to me 'symphony' means constructing a world
> with all the technical means at one's disposal. The eternally new and changing
> content determines its own form. In this sense, I must forever learn anew how
> to forge new means of expression for myself – however completely I may have
> mastered technical problems, as I think I may now claim to have done.[2]

Mahler's first two symphonies had been concerned with what we might call 'a hero's life', albeit not in the sense intended by Strauss in his symphonic poem of the same name, but here he aims for something even higher, because an 'Eroica' of the kind that he had achieved in his Second Symphony could not be surpassed by the same means and with the same musical language. He now set his sights much higher, even if they were aimed in a different direction, for what he now wanted to depict in his music was nothing less than the different stages in the development of animate nature. This quickly found expression in a conception that circulated among the composer's friends and supporters in a number of variants, all of them listing the titles of the individual movements. Significantly, Mahler then withdrew these movement headings and left no definitive version of them, even the most straightforward interpretation of which would require a discussion unto itself. Let us consider one of the later versions that comes from a letter that Mahler wrote to Max Marschalk in August 1896:

A Summer's Midday Dream
    Part One
    Introduction: Pan awakens.
    I. Summer marches in (Bacchic procession).
    Part Two
    II. What the flowers in the meadow tell me.
    III. What the animals in the forest tell me.

IV. What man tells me.

V. What the angels tell me.

VI. What love tells me.[3]

What we have here is clearly the ascent of all organic life to the very highest level, which is called not God but love, giving a cosmological dimension to the whole idea of constructing a world out of musical sounds. The roman numerals correspond to the symphony's individual movements. Mahler originally planned to add a seventh movement, 'Heavenly Life', but he then decided to reserve this for the finale of his Fourth Symphony. While working on the Third during the summer of 1896 he wrote to his lover Anna von Mildenburg: 'But just try to imagine such a major work, literally reflecting the whole world – one is oneself only, as it were, an instrument played by the whole universe.'[4] It is no accident that it is the Third Symphony above all that writers have used to illustrate their thesis that Mahler's symphonies can be compared to the great novels of the nineteenth century, as Adorno demonstrated with remarkable clarity, for the movement headings do indeed create the impression of chapter headings from a vast novel, even if that novel has no hero of the kind that may be imputed to the First and Second Symphonies.[5] The result is a poem about the whole world, a 'Commedia superhumana', to paraphrase the title that Mahler once gave to the last two movements of his First Symphony. His symphonies can certainly be viewed as symphonic siblings to the great realistic novels of the nineteenth century: the musical equivalents of a Balzac, Tolstoi, Keller or Dickens although closer to Mahler's heart, of course, were Cervantes, Sterne, Jean Paul and Dostoevsky, novelists who combined realism with fantasy and humour.

Particularly striking is Mahler's fondness for loquacious explanations of his Third Symphony, even if those explanations were not intended for wider consumption. No less striking is his comparison of himself to Zeus wrestling with Cronus or with Jacob wrestling with God (or, more accurately, the angel) or even with Christ on the Mount of Olives drinking to its bitter dregs the cup of cosmic suffering. Never again was Mahler to become involved in such rhetorical turmoil over a work. His explanations are full of contradictions, the subtle shades of meaning in the titles and their relative positions being far more random than one would imagine. Everything points to a feeling of uncertainty as to the meaning of a work which, lasting around one hundred minutes, overshadows everything that had gone before it. More than ever, Mahler evidently felt that the 'creator spiritus' was an unsettling, violent force that seized hold of the acolyte and left him deeply shaken, more a tsar than a father figure, to hark back to Adam Mickiewicz's expression. 'At such moments I am no longer my own master, but nor do I belong to you,' Mahler tried to reassure Anna von Mildenburg, explaining how he felt and why he needed a great deal of understanding from the people who loved him.[6] He granted Natalie Bauer-Lechner an even deeper insight into the workings of his heart, and since coquetry and self-regard were completely foreign to his nature, we may regard his remarks as utterly serious:

> It's frightening the way this movement seems to grow of its own accord more than anything else that I have done. The Second seems to me like a child in comparison. It is in every sense larger than life, and everything human shrinks into a pygmy world beside it. Real horror seizes me when I see where it is leading, the path the music must follow, and that it fell upon me to be the bearer of this gigantic work.[7]

It is above all the opening movement that makes the work as a whole seem so daring. That Mahler wrote it last of all seemed to him necessary, for otherwise he would not have had the courage to compose it. Before writing it, he had thought of giving it the heading 'Summer marches in', but by the time he had completed it, such innocuous jocularity no longer seemed appropriate, and it was now the idea of the great god Pan that he came to prefer: 'Pan awakens' he wrote at the head of the introduction. But even the image of a procession led by Bacchus or Dionysus no longer seemed suitable. In July 1896 he even thought of calling the work as a whole 'Pan: Symphonic Poems'.[8] The tenor of the piece is certainly one of terror-stricken panic, recalling Arnold Böcklin's *Pan Frightens a Shepherd*, a canvas that Mahler could well have known. The painting captures the heavy, brooding atmosphere of a hot summer's day, the sort of atmosphere that prompts Pan to inspire fear and terror in men and beasts, while shaking with laughter at his exploits. But Mahler said that the opening movement could also have been headed 'What the rocky mountains tell me', for life struggles to break free from immovable, inanimate matter, rising, growing and acquiring increasingly disparate forms until in the fifth movement it reaches the angels, who to words taken from one of the *Wunderhorn* poems sing their sweet-toned song. Finally, infinite love pours forth in the concluding Adagio. The Third and Ninth Symphonies both end, unconventionally, with an Adagio. Mahler himself claimed that he did not know the reason for this until he realized that only an Adagio could introduce the note of calm and immutability that he needed here.

The contrast between the first and second movements is even greater in the case of the Third Symphony than it was in the Second. How, after all, could a movement lasting a mere nine minutes assert itself in the face of one lasting more than thirty? The second movement is dancelike and retrospective in tone, making it difficult to justify the title 'What the flowers in the meadow tell me'. The overriding feeling is of a graceful exercise in style, a certain Biedermeier elegance that is already neo-Biedermeier and, as such, comparable to the neo-Rococo tone of the poems of Otto Julius Bierbaum, which Mahler did not, however, like. The middle section almost literally shimmers, suggesting the wind blowing over the grass. The third movement is headed 'What the animals in the forest tell me', although it was originally to be called 'What the cuckoo tells me', recalling the *Wunderhorn* song 'Ablösung'. Here the animals of the forest complain that a cuckoo that has been entertaining them has fallen to its death. They hope that it will be replaced by a nightingale. Mahler uses the song to propel the movement forward, its quaintly droll character representing a clear continuation of the 'Fish Sermon' in the Second Symphony. The posthorn episode that is central to this movement presumably has a literary basis to it, having been inspired by Nikolaus Lenau's poem 'The Postilion' ('Lieblich war die Maiennacht, Silberwölkchen flogen'), which tells of a postilion who stops at a graveyard in order to play the favourite song of a friend and colleague who is buried there. Ernst Decsey reports that he had written a review of the Third Symphony in which he mentions that while listening to the work, he had been reminded of Lenau's poem, whereupon Mahler had invited him to visit him and told him that he was right.[9] What Decsey could not have known is that in his fair copy of the full score Mahler had written 'The Postilion' over the posthorn's first entry.

The last three movements are in stark contrast to the first three – Mahler would not have been entirely wrong to see the break between the two parts after the third movement, rather than after the first. He realized that there was no 'normal' connection between the individual movements in the sense demanded by the symphonic tradition. In conversation with Natalie Bauer-Lechner, he admitted that he had originally intended such a connection, but in the end each movement had emerged as a self-contained and independent entity, something he was not disposed to regard as a failing.[10] None the less, the fourth, fifth and sixth movements form a more cohesive whole than the first three and create what Mathias Hansen has termed a 'large-scale movement', a point underscored by the fact that at the end of the fourth and fifth movements Mahler has added a note to the effect that there should be no break between the movements.

The fourth movement is a setting of the poem 'O Mensch! Gib acht!' from Nietzsche's *Also sprach Zarathustra*, sung here by a contralto soloist. The fact that Strauss's tone poem of the same name was first performed in the same year, 1896, as that in which Mahler completed work on his Third Symphony reflects the tremendous impact of Nietzsche's writings on freethinkers of this period, a group to which Strauss, throughout his entire life a free spirit and an agnostic, belongs more obviously than Mahler, who spent *his* life searching for God.[11] We have already seen that Mahler was bound to be drawn into Nietzsche's sway during his years of study in Vienna – no one who was friendly with Siegfried Lipiner could escape from that influence, and all who in the years around 1880 were young, progressive and anti-bourgeois were bound to become followers of Nietzsche. When judged by contemporary standards, Mahler's own enthusiasm for the philosopher is remarkably limited. According to Bruno Walter, Nietzsche's impact on Mahler was great but by no means lasting.[12] *Also sprach Zarathustra* impressed him with its linguistic brilliance, whereas its ideas tended, rather, to repel him. Above all, we need to remember that as a fanatical Wagnerian, Mahler could never follow Nietzsche down the road to apostasy and was indeed sharply critical of the philosopher for turning his back on Wagner. At the time that he was working on his Third Symphony, Mahler's enthusiasm for Nietzsche's skills as a writer were still so great that he was able to set one of his poems as its fourth movement. But within five years his attitude had changed considerably, and it annoyed him intensely when Alma suddenly revealed her half-digested thoughts on Nietzsche, whose 'utterly false and brazenly arrogant theories of masculine supremacy' he dismissed in a particularly venomous outburst even before they were married.[13] During the early days of their love he even demanded that Alma should burn an edition of Nietzsche's writings, a demand that she steadfastly and understandably refused to respect. Within a matter of only a few years, however, his attitude had become more tempered and he was again willing to concede that Nietzsche's language had a musical element to it, especially in *Also sprach Zarathustra*. He even acknowledged the philosopher's gifts as a composer.[14]

With its meditative character and its gently swaying carpet of sound, the fourth movement of the Third Symphony is permeated by the musical qualities of this intensely poetical language. The calming voice of the contralto soloist rises up from this carpet of sound and intones the words 'O Mensch!' (O man!) – if only all singers and conductors were to obey the performance marking here, 'With a mysterious expression – remaining quiet'. When at the end of the contralto's first verse the violins launch into a broad unison hymn which, as later writers have pointed out, is suspiciously similar to Sebastián de Iradier's immortal *La paloma*, the charge of triviality is not easy to refute. Mahler may have known this piece, although it seems unlikely that he consciously intended to quote it. In any case the rhythm of the original has been changed and the ending is different. But Mahler predicted this reproach too, and it did not trouble him. Banality could not be ignored by anyone wanting to construct a whole new world. High and low, sublime and trivial all find their place in Mahler's universe and are not excluded by any a priori decisions. This, too, was all part of the piece's polyphony. The concept of 'taste' and the lack of it was not in Mahler's vocabulary.

There is no finer illustration of Adorno's wonderful phrase – 'The unrisen lower is stirred as yeast into high music'[15] – than the Iradian raptness of this unison passage for the violins or the posthorn solo in which Mahler captures the artlessness and superficially banal rubato of a postilion who, with no artistic training, plays all the more fervently in consequence. The soloist is instructed to play this passage 'Freely, like the melody of a posthorn'. A precursor of the cornet, the posthorn is a difficult instrument to master – the philharmonic perfection that one finds today has something inappropriately sleek about it. In a letter he wrote to Bruno Walter in July 1896, Mahler parodied his critics:

> I am afraid the whole thing is again sicklied o'er with the notorious spirit of my humour, 'and there is frequent opportunity of pursuing my inclination to make a furious din'. Sometimes, too, the musicians play 'without taking the slightest account of one another, and here my savage and brutal nature reveals itself most starkly'. Everyone knows by now that some triviality always has to occur in my work. But this time it goes beyond all bounds. 'At times one cannot help believing one is in a low tavern or a stable.'[16]

The supposed naïveté of the fifth movement, with its sound of morning bells contrasting with the night-time sentiments of its Nietzschean predecessor, must be accepted as such by the listener, otherwise it risks recalling Nazarene art. The 'Beggars' Song of the Poor Children' from *Des Knaben Wunderhorn* is sung by a female choir accompanied by bells and by boys' voices doubling the bells and intoning the words 'Bimm Bamm' that Mahler added to the *Wunderhorn* poem. This, too, can work only if we are willing to forget its symphonic cynicism for four whole minutes. Mahler knew very well that this movement could not last a moment longer, otherwise he would have been accused of monumental kitsch, and yet his playful use of naïveté is inextricably linked to a subtle dramaturgical intent.

The final movement again offers Mahler's critics ample opportunity to take issue with his symphonic style, while its interpreters, too, are left feeling distinctly uncomfortable. Is the movement a monument to failure on the highest level? Or is it a record of arbitrariness and chance? Does it seem mechanistically grafted on to the rest of the work, which requires a positive climax here, inasmuch as it is all-embracing love that speaks? The link between the first and last movements that Mahler himself mentioned – the only one that he emphasized – is one between dull, petrified, inarticulate nature in the opening movement and the supreme articulation of the last, but it is not immediately apparent. After all, the unruly and eccentric colossus of the opening movement is difficult to reconcile with the sleekness and harmoniousness of the final one. No more is there a connection between the terrifyingly comic figure of the great god Pan and the marmoreal statue of the Greek Apollo that seems to stare at us here with hollow eye sockets. Were it not for the hierarchical structure built into the work, the listener might well take away the impression that it is not until thirteen years later, in the final Adagio of the Ninth Symphony, that we find the real answer to the question raised by the opening movement of the Third. Much about this last-named work remains a puzzle, and Mahlerians will find it hard to set aside their sense of uncertainty. And yet they may ultimately derive some consolation from Mathias Hansen's judgement of Solomon: 'This problem child runs the greatest risk of failing, and yet it also elicits the greatest attention and the most loving understanding.'[17]

The God of the Southern Climes: Vienna (1897–1901)

The Cabal

'Meanwhile I am telling the town a story of how to become president' – Ferdinand throws down this challenge to his father in Schiller's *Cabal and Love*. Our own challenge is to provide a dispassionate account of Mahler's rise to the position of opera director. It is worth examining the background to this episode in some detail as his rise to the head of what was then the most famous opera house in the world was a tactical masterstroke and a product of the workings of the most sophisticated cabal on the European arts scene at the end of the nineteenth century, the once nervous provincial conductor proving himself an undisputed master in this field.

Of course, he also had at his disposal a number of loyal and committed supporters headed by Natalie Bauer-Lechner, who was his closest confidante after his sister. She did much to promote Mahler's Vienna appointment, not least because she was able to reactivate her earlier contacts with Rosa Papier, an ex-singer who still had the best possible connections with the Vienna Court Opera, where she had enjoyed considerable personal success between 1881 and 1891 as the house's principal mezzo-soprano. Papier additionally had the ear and possibly also the heart of Privy Councillor Eduard Wlassack and, finally, she had taught Anna von Mildenburg. One of the increasing numbers of members of the middle class who rose to these elevated ranks in the country's administration, Wlassack was the administrative head of the offices overseeing all the court theatres in Vienna, a position he held from 1881 to 1893 and again from 1895 to 1903, with the result that he knew what went on in the theatre in a way that neither the intendant himself nor any other administrator could claim to do. The fact that Mahler had Rosa Papier on his side and, through her, Eduard Wlassack, was to prove his trump card, effectively assuring his position.

The head of all the court theatres at the decisive stage in the negotiations and, as such, Wlassack's superior, was Baron Josef von Bezecny, not to be confused with the Ferenc von Beniczky who had been responsible for Mahler's appointment in Budapest and who also helped Mahler in his present situation. Bezecny, whose name Mahler misspelled variously as Bezeczny, Besecny and even Besetzny – the latter possibly a pun on the verb *besetzen*, meaning 'to appoint' – had been Imperial and Royal Privy Councillor and section chief since 1885 and remained so until the start of 1898, long enough to take the decisive steps on Mahler's behalf. He was succeeded by Baron August Plappart von Leenheer, whose bureaucratic approach to his work was far less to Mahler's liking. Fortunately, the general administrator's superior, Prince Rudolf von und zu Liechtenstein, remained as well disposed to Mahler as Wlassack and Bezecny. He belonged to the family of Austrian aristocrats which, following the end of the monarchy, created the present-day state of Liechtenstein out of its estates in Vaduz. From 1896 to 1908 he was the chief comptroller to the emperor, entitling him to be addressed as 'Your Highness'. Still new to his job, he remained very much in the background, leaving his deputy, Prince Alfred Montenuovo, to take the decisions. Montenuovo, too, was well disposed to Mahler, withdrawing his support only towards the end of the Mahler era. When Liechtenstein died in 1908, Montenuovo became his successor. Among Mahler's closest associates at the court opera, two were particularly loyal, although neither was involved in Mahler's appointment: the company's artistic secretary Hubert Wondra, who, as living proof of Viennese nepotism, was a nephew of the director Wilhelm Jahn, and Mahler's own private secretary, Alois Przistaupinsky, whose name Mahler regularly shortened to 'Bschiss', an abbreviation both phonetically correct and affectionately meant.

In addition to these supporters at the heart of power, Mahler had other champions who were keen to see their old friend and acquaintance at the head of the Vienna Court Opera. Among them was Siegfried Lipiner, who, for all his low-profile involvement, was an intellectual éminence grise in the city. The composer Karl Goldmark had been a leading light in Vienna's musical life since the success of his opera *Die Königin von Saba* in 1875. He, too, had followed Mahler's career with a friendly eye and as a native Hungarian had taken a particularly close interest in his activities in Budapest, as he later did in Hamburg. The fact that Mahler signed his preliminary contract in Vienna on 4 April 1897, the day after Brahms's death, undoubtedly had a symbolic significance. Brahms had been ill for some time and had clearly not played an active role in Mahler's appointment in Vienna, and yet everyone in the city knew that ever since he had heard Mahler conduct *Don Giovanni* in Budapest, the revered composer had spoken of him in only the most generous terms, so that he must be regarded as at least a posthumous influence on Mahler's appointment. Among journalists, help was forthcoming from Ludwig Karpath, whom Mahler had met in Budapest and who had begun his career as a singer, in which capacity he had got to know Rosa Papier. But Karpath had then abandoned singing for journalism and had recently started to write for the *Neues Wiener Tagblatt*. His memoirs, *Begegnung mit dem Genius*, are an important source for our knowledge of the cabal surrounding Mahler's appointment as they contain a number of letters that are not to be found elsewhere. But Karpath's extreme vanity and his later falling-out with Mahler make him a not entirely reliable, if none the less important, contemporary witness.

Finally, we need to mention three of Mahler's friends from Budapest: Ödön von Mihalovich, Albert Apponyi and Ferenc von Beniczky, all of whom had remained convinced of Mahler's genius in spite of his inglorious departure from Budapest. They all used their contacts with Vienna – and they were all actively encouraged by Mahler to do so – in order to ensure that he achieved his goal. The evidence for the cabal is plentiful, allowing us to trace its course on an almost day-to-day basis, but, however fascinating the subject, we shall have to make do with merely a summary.

By the middle of 1896 at the latest, it is clear from Mahler's comments that he no longer felt happy in Hamburg. The initial impression is that he felt worn down by the treadmill of the theatre and could imagine bidding farewell to the opera by taking charge of a concert orchestra. In a letter to one of his friends in Budapest we even find him mentioning the idea of returning to Hungary, but this would have meant a return to the Royal Hungarian Opera. It is doubtful whether Mahler took this Hungarian option seriously, but it seems as if he was not over-fastidious on this point as long as he could get away from Hamburg. An offer from Budapest would at least have had tactical advantages. He had been in Hamburg for five years, longer than in any other theatre, and had exhausted the field of opportunities. By now he could work with the director, Bernhard Pollini, only by gritting his teeth and suppressing all negative feelings. His love for Anna von Mildenburg was also fading, and he additionally felt a sense of nostalgia, not for Iglau, which following his parents' death was now consigned to a phase in his past, but for Vienna, where he had spent the formative years of his life and where some of his oldest friends still lived. Above all, the Vienna Court Opera was the leading opera company in the world, and, if he was to pursue a career in opera, it was here that he would find the most brilliant position, a munificent salary and the finest singers and opera orchestra of the age. The brilliance of the position mattered less to him than the remuneration, which would help to alleviate his worries about providing for his brothers and sisters. Most important of all was the excellence of the performers. He knew that because of his various links with the city Vienna was the only place where he had a realistic chance of gaining such a position – neither Berlin nor Munich nor Paris nor New York offered such an opportunity, and even in London his connections were too tenuous to provide any hope of an appointment. In short, his Viennese ambitions were not entirely utopian.

Mahler's most candid insights into his emotional life at this time were vouchsafed in a letter to Friedrich Löhr, and there seems no reason to doubt in his sincerity when we find him writing to his friend, probably in the autumn of 1896:

> I am knocking about the world quite a lot now. I assure you it is a fight, a real one, in which one does not notice one is bleeding from a thousand wounds. In the lull one suddenly feels something moist, and only then realizes that one is bleeding. I find my 'successes' especially painful, for one is misunderstood before one has got out what one has to say. – I feel so homesick! Oh for a quiet corner at home! When shall I have earned that? I fear – only over yonder where all of us and all things shall be gathered together.[1]

Perhaps we should not take entirely seriously Mahler's claim to hanker after 'a quiet corner at home': such a desire to renounce the world would later become more pronounced, but in 1896 it was just a passing phase. He was still too motivated by burning ambition, still too convinced of all that he could achieve in the very highest position, for him to have been entirely serious. And if his homesickness was undoubtedly genuine, the 'quiet corner at home' was manifestly the director's office at the Vienna Court Opera. That the process had already been set in train by the autumn of 1896 is clear from a letter that Lipiner wrote on 21 November to the General Management of the Court Theatres – in other words, to Josef von Bezecny. Now preserved in the Vienna Municipal Archives, it relates to a meeting that had taken place between the two men, presumably a few days earlier, and is an attempt to counter rumours about Mahler's 'temperament' that were circulating in the city, rumours that threatened to make him seem unsuited to so diplomatically fraught a position. Mahler, Lipiner conceded, could sometimes be 'difficult', but it was always in pursuit of the highest goals. He could also demonstrate 'an often unbelievable patience'.[2]

Exactly four weeks later Mahler appealed directly to Bezecny. It is not entirely clear how we should interpret Mahler's remark that he had repeatedly been well received by his correspondent, as this implies a number of previous meetings about which we know nothing. But perhaps the two men had met while Mahler was working in Budapest. Alternatively, Mahler's brief visit to Vienna in June 1896 may have provided an opportunity for such an encounter. Whatever the answer, the two men evidently knew and respected each other. Above all, Bezecny respected Mahler. 'I hear from various sources', wrote Mahler, 'that the matter of the post of Conductor at the Vienna Court Opera will become urgent in the very near future.' There follow the usual remarks balancing modesty against self-esteem. But it is above all the end of the letter that speaks volumes for Mahler's subtle pride, for here he underlines the fact that if necessary he can extricate himself from his Hamburg contract at very short notice – he was to do so precisely three weeks later, by which date he was already confident of victory. At the same time he makes it clear that Bezecny should act quickly in order not to miss this unique, historic opportunity to appoint him: 'By a later date I may not be as free to take any decisions.'[3] This was a fraudulent claim. After all, Mahler had nothing in prospect apart from Vienna, but the threat was clearly effective, at least in the longer term. We shall shortly see why, in his letter to Bezecny, Mahler refers not to the post of director but to that of conductor. In order to ensure that his bridges were well and truly burnt, Mahler now adopted the high-risk strategy of exacerbating his simmering conflict with Pollini in Hamburg by openly declaring war on the company's senior stage manager, Franz Bittong, who years earlier had written a parody of *Die Meistersinger* that was intended as a satirical response to the reissue of Wagner's anti-Semitic essay, 'Jews in Music'.[4]

On the same day, 21 December, Mahler activated his links with Budapest, writing to Ödön von Mihalovich and indicating beyond doubt that his ambitions extended beyond the post of conductor to that of director. On the surface, his letter was concerned with Wilhelm Jahn, who had been director of the Court Opera since 1881 and one of its two principal conductors. The other was Hans Richter, whom we have already encountered on several occasions and who was also responsible for the Philharmonic concerts, leaving him less time for the opera. Jahn's regime in Vienna was not only the longest in the company's history, it was also extremely successful. He specialized in the Italian and French repertory (Massenet in particular was in his debt), while Richter took charge of the German repertory, including the works of Wagner, whose mature music dramas had been triumphantly staged in Vienna not least thanks to Richter. Richter, after all, had conducted the inaugural *Ring* in Bayreuth and thus acquired an aura of authority as a Wagnerian.

But it was now clear that Jahn's period in office was drawing to an end. He was old, ailing and tired, sixteen years of artistic and administrative responsibilities having taken their toll. It was no secret, therefore, that the general administrator's office needed to act. During the days and weeks leading up to Mahler's appointment, Jahn also had to contend with an eye operation – his eyesight had been failing for some time, with the result that not only had newer works to be played to him but he generally conducted from memory. It was no doubt this that persuaded Bezecny to dispense with Jahn's services: sixteen years was enough. In fact, Jahn saw this development as an attempt to lighten his burden both as a conductor and as the director of the Vienna Court

Opera. Clearly he had no intention of willingly giving up his two posts. True, he asked to resign in January 1897, but this was merely a tactical ploy. When Bezecny declined to accept his resignation, Jahn saw this as a vote of confidence. The prospective new conductor would help to lighten his burden of responsibility, something that was now desperately needed. Liechtenstein saw this as his chance to get rid of Jahn. But Bezecny was afraid of a scandal and wanted to avoid a confrontation, with the result that for the present he left Jahn in his post. (Coincidentally, this period also witnessed the end of another era, that of Max Burckhard, who had been running the Burgtheater since 1890 and who was a great admirer of the young Alma Schindler.) It was clear, however, to all concerned that the Vienna Court Opera was threatening to sink into tired routine and that however glorious its past may have been under Jahn, its future lay elsewhere. To that extent it seems apparent that if Mahler's name was considered, it was not only as conductor but also as director. No one seems to have thought of Richter, whose talents were evidently felt to be too one-sidedly Wagnerian and too limited to the concert hall. At fifty-three, moreover, he was considered old and too closely associated with Bayreuth to be able to do justice to the catholic operatic tastes of the Viennese.

The letter that Mahler wrote to Ödön von Mihalovich on 21 December 1896 – the same day as his letter to Bezecny – would seem to support the suggestion that the post of conductor was only intended as an interim step for both Mahler himself and for the Viennese court: 'This is to request you to do me a favour on which the whole pattern of my future life depends. In Vienna the matter of the conductor or, rather, of the director is now acute. *My name* is among those receiving "serious consideration". In other words, Mahler knew very well that the post of conductor was merely an interim step on the way to the directorship, something that he must have discussed with Bezecny or Wlassack or both. And yet even the term 'interim step' is not entirely correct, for Mahler remained the house's principal conductor even after he had become deputy director and then director: the post of director was therefore one that he held in addition to that of conductor. In his letter Mahler clear-sightedly points out that there were two factors that might still prove to be obstacles on the road to the director's office: his reputation as a difficult and even 'insane' person and his Jewish faith.[5] (We have already discussed his deception in claiming that he had converted to Christianity soon after leaving Budapest, whereas the actual date was five years later, February 1897.) If Lipiner assured Bezecny that Mahler could be 'difficult', but only in the service of his art, then it was presumably on Mahler's own instructions that he insisted on this point. Mahler also asked Mihalovich to call on the good services of Count Apponyi, while a second letter to Mihalovich, written the very next day, asks him to contact not only his former superior in Budapest, Ferenc von Beniczky, but also Counts Kinsky and Wilczek. 'Please, my dear friend, leave no stone unturned in this matter; only one more powerful thrust is needed in this affair to see me emerge victorious.'[6] Also of interest in this context is a letter that Mahler wrote to Mihalovich in the middle of January 1897, once again expressing his fears that his Jewish religion might yet thwart his designs on Vienna.[7] Above all, however, a powerful rival had suddenly appeared on the horizon in the person of Felix Mottl, leading Mahler to realize that he had been over-confident of victory.

Mottl was four years older than Mahler. He was born in Austria, closer to Vienna than Mahler, and had worked at the Vienna Court Opera as a répétiteur, a distinction not shared by Mahler. He had conducted in Bayreuth at every festival since 1886, representing the younger generation of conductors there. He had been court Kapellmeister in Karlsruhe since 1881 and, since 1893, the company's music director, revealing an unusual degree of loyalty to the house. He was a committed Wagnerian, but was also responsive to the music of other composers, notably Berlioz – he was the first conductor to mount a complete performance of the French composer's monumental two-part *Les Troyens*. And Mottl had another advantage over Mahler: he was not Jewish. He also had two eminent champions who weighed far more in the scales of public opinion than all of Mahler's foot soldiers. The first was Prince Metternich, the well-known scion of an illustrious Viennese family, while the other was Cosima Wagner, no less, who, in spite of her admiration for Mahler's work as a Wagner conductor who had earned Bayreuth's gratitude by coaching Anna von Mildenburg and Willi Birrenkoven, inevitably harboured serious doubts about the eligibility of a Jew. She placed the greatest hopes in Mottl, who, she believed, would guarantee that her late husband's works would find their fitting place in the Viennese repertory. No doubt she already knew that Mahler would perform at least as much Wagner as Mottl would have done, so that this consideration no doubt weighed less than Mahler's Jewish background. Cosima clearly used her connections with Vienna to champion Mottl's cause in the city, while also taking advantage of her respected position in the world of music and beyond as Wagner's widow and as the director of the only festival devoted to his unique genius. Whether she also used this position not just to support Mottl but also to belittle Mahler, we simply do not know.

As for Mahler's Jewish faith, we have already noted the evasive action that he took at the very last moment. Liechtenstein's comment that anti-Semitism was not the decisive factor in Austria gave him justifiable grounds for optimism. It was certainly a remarkable statement in a city which in the years around 1900 is generally believed to have been permeated with anti-Semitism. But Mahler's appointment proves that Liechtenstein was right. It is also worth recalling that the Kaiser had repeatedly refused to confirm Karl Lueger as the city's mayor largely because of the latter's blatant anti-Semitism. The synchronicity is striking: Mahler, a baptized Jew, signed his Viennese contract on 15 April 1897, and on the very next day the Kaiser confirmed Lueger in his post as mayor after he had already been elected to the post on no fewer than five occasions. The anti-Semitism that Mahler did indeed encounter is another matter or, rather, another side of the selfsame coin.

Mahler's appeals to his contacts in Budapest were not in vain, and in the course of January 1897 three letters fetched up on Bezecny's desk, Mihalovich, Apponyi and Beniczky all advocating Mahler's appointment with often identical phrases and emphasis, suggesting a concerted campaign. It is unclear what weight these letters carried, although they will not have been dismissed out of hand for all three writers could attest to Mahler's achievements as the director of a by no means insignificant opera company. By the beginning of February 1897 Mahler seems almost to have given up hope that his cabal would succeed, for a letter to Rosa Papier implies his belief that Mottl was marginally ahead in the race to the Vienna Court Opera. This will have rankled with Mahler, who needed assurance, not least because he had recently taken the risky step of resigning his post in Hamburg. In spite of this, his letters from this period reveal no signs of panic. Conversely, a premature rumour that Bezecny was about to step down left him profoundly agitated, prompting him to ask Rosa Papier to enquire of Eduard Wlassack how he should best proceed. In turn, dear old Karl Goldmark was asked to speak to Bezecny, although Karpath reports that Goldmark in fact did nothing. These events all took place in January 1897. By the end of February Mahler had converted to Christianity in Hamburg. And much of March was given over to an unusually lengthy concert tour, the first that Mahler had undertaken on such a scale. He travelled to Moscow, where he arrived on 12 March and three days later conducted works by Beethoven and Wagner. He then travelled to Munich via Berlin and conducted a concert of works by Wagner, Beethoven and Berlioz (two movements of the *Symphonie fantastique*!) with the Kaim Orchestra, the forerunner of the Munich Philharmonic. By 26 March he was in Vienna, where he spent little more than a day, but he will undoubtedly have used this time to continue his negotiations with Bezecny.

It is conceivable that a previously unpublished letter from Eduard Hanslick helped to seal the deal. Unfortunately, it is unclear to whom the letter was written, but since it has survived in the files of the general administrator's office, it seems likely that it was addressed to Bezecny. Alongside his idol Brahms, who died only a few days later, Hanslick was the most influential figure on Vienna's musical stage. He occupied a chair in aesthetics and the history of music at the University of Vienna and was also the city's leading music critic, contributing reviews to the *Neue Freie Presse*. Depending on one's point of view, he was famous or notorious as the head of the anti-Wagner faction, a point that also emerges from the present letter, dated 27 March 1897:

> Your Excellency,
>
> ... This is no private matter but one that concerns all opera lovers. I have just heard that Jahn's dismissal has been agreed – this is no great misfortune. The only two applicants worth considering are said to be MOTTL and MAHLER. But misfortune could be in store if – in my own humble opinion – Mottl were to become director. We know from his work in Karlsruhe that he loves and performs only Wagner, together with the whole of Wagner's evil imitators of German and French extraction. The fact that he also employs his wife[8] in leading roles and dignifies her with a standing that she does not deserve leads one to fear the worst. Conversely, it may be assumed on the strength of his achievements in Prague and Hamburg that Mahler will breathe new life into our opera without violating its classical traditions. Forgive me, Your Excellency, if on this occasion I ignore my own precept of never voting without first being asked to do so, but I wanted to get this off my chest. I can also assure you that I am speaking on behalf of the finest and most serious music lovers and connoisseurs. I am Your Excellency's most devoted servant, Dr Eduard Hanslick.[9]

We may assume that the die was cast during these final days of March 1897, because within days of his appearance in Budapest to conduct the second movement of his Third Symphony, Mahler was back in Vienna, where it was agreed that the details of his contract as Kapellmeister would be finalized on 3 April. Mahler seemed to be within reach of his goal, only for another anxious wait to wear down his already jangled nerves: he had misremembered the time of his meeting with the general administrator and arrived only after the latter had already left his office. Not until the next day did he finally sign the following document: 'I confirm that I am willing to accept an engagement as Conductor at the Vienna Court Opera Theatre for one year from 1 June at an annual salary of 5,000 (five thousand) florins, and that this declaration holds good until 15 April this year. Vienna, 4 April 1897.'[10] In short, this was a preliminary agreement or a declaration of intent, but for Mahler, at least, it was clear that this represented his breakthrough, which was confirmed on 15 April, when he signed his definitive contract, apparently deferring until 1 May the date on which he officially took up his new appointment.

By 8 April the *Wiener Abendpost* had already announced the name of the new Kapellmeister, an announcement followed up the next day by the *Neue Freie Presse*, the city's most important newspaper, which afforded proof of its reliability by renaming the conductor Heinrich Mahler and presciently asking what position he would hold in a house that already numbered Jahn, Richter, Johann Nepomuk Fuchs and Joseph ('Pepi') Hellmesberger among its roster of conductors. That same day, 9 April, Mahler also wrote to Eduard Wlassack, a letter that leaves us in no doubt that after the war of nerves and the success of his cabal, Mahler had no interest in adopting a triumphalist tone but was looking forward to the future with characteristic enthusiasm:

> It is now all-important for me to introduce myself artistically in Vienna as advantageously as possible; and to that end the period of Richter's absence seems to me the most propitious. I think the best would be a Wagner opera and *Fidelio*, which would represent both the main directions and should satisfy both the Wagnerians and the classicists. [It is no wonder that Mahler wanted to leap into the breach currently vacated by Richter, as these areas of the repertory were the very ones with which the latter was most closely associated.] The main thing after that would be to sketch out a plan of campaign for the next season and to prepare *new* productions and *new works* in such a manner that, with careful planning and full use of personnel and time, one new production and one new work could both be brought out together. This way we should already be able to make a start on widening this wretchedly restricted repertoire in the course of the coming season. And I know from experience that the public is very easy to win over as soon as it senses *things are looking up.*[11]

This was entirely typical of Mahler. He did not take a moment to allow his jangled nerves time to recover from the fray but lost no time in wrestling with the new problems that lay in his path: his battle cry was 'Attack!', an approach that had ensured success even in the face of Vienna's anti-Semitism, Bayreuth's opposition and powerful rivals. Of one thing he must have been certain: if he was unable to realize his plans to raise the local operatic industry to a new and artistically responsible level, then he would not be able to do so anywhere else in the world. And even if his later years in Vienna were overshadowed by the usual pattern of resigned acquiescence, it remains a fact that between 1903 and 1906 he and Alfred Roller were able to achieve almost everything that they set out to achieve, turning inside out the way in which opera was presented both here and elsewhere.

The Court Opera

The Vienna Opera can look back on a long and glorious, if occasionally vicissitudinous, history. It is easy to say that Mahler took over the leading operatic institution in the world – whatever Vienna's opera lovers may claim, it no longer enjoys this distinction – but there is no doubt that it deserved that accolade when he left it ten years later. Soon after the new medium of opera was invented in the early seventeenth century, the Emperor Ferdinand II did all in his power to ensure that operas, *intermedi, sacrae rappresentazioni* and whatever else these works may have been called were staged on special occasions, generally during the carnival season but also to celebrate birthdays and weddings. Among his successors, Leopold I continued this tradition, giving the first performance of Antonio Cesti's *Il pomo d'oro* in 1668, for example. But the audiences at these performances included only members of the court, together with diplomats and illustrious visitors. Opera abandoned the world of the court only when the Kärntnerthor-Theater was built in 1709 on the site of what is now the Hotel Sacher, directly behind today's State Opera on the Ringstraße. Court opera was performed in the Hoftheater am Michaelerplatz, a former ballroom refurbished as a theatre by Francesco Galli-Bibiena between 1698 and 1700 and used until 1744, when it was converted back into ballrooms. Gluck's first opera for Vienna, *Semiramide riconosciuta* (1748), was staged in the renovated Burgtheater, which remained in use until 1888, initially for operas, later predominantly for spoken drama. (The modern Burgtheater on the Ringstraße opened in the same year, 1888.) It was the Emperor Joseph II who rid the Burgtheater of Italian singers and replaced them with German plays and *singspiels*, while operas were staged at the Kärntnerthor-Theater, a division that survives to this day. Only when the actors were not performing was the Burgtheater available for operas. Mozart, for example, repeatedly – and, for the most part, successfully – attempted to have his operas performed here. Only *Die Zauberflöte* was staged at the Theater auf der Wieden, an opera with German words having no chance of being mounted at the Burgtheater.

The years between Mozart's death in 1791 and the July Revolution of 1830 were not the most golden in the history of Viennese opera. Apart from *Fidelio* at the Theater an der Wien, there were no new works worth mentioning. The Viennese theatre was dominated by Italian opera buffa. German *singspiels* by Süßmayr, Winter and Schenk gained an audience for themselves at the Imperial and Royal Court Opera Theatre at the Kärntnerthor, as it was called, followed, of course, by Rossini and the Italian bel canto operas of Bellini and Donizetti. Various impresarios, generally of Italian extraction, leased the house from the court and ran *stagione* seasons along more or less successful lines. But it was not until 1854 that the house acquired a certain degree of continuity when Karl Eckert became principal conductor and, in 1857, director, thereby establishing a local tradition whereby the principal conductor was also the general music director and general administrator all rolled into one. It was a tradition upheld by Wilhelm Jahn and Mahler and, later, by Felix von Weingartner, Franz

Schalk and Richard Strauss. As his name implies, Eckert was not Italian and so he hit on an idea that would probably never have occurred to his Italian predecessors and introduced the latest German operas to the house in the form of *Lohengrin* (1858) and *Tannhäuser* (1859).

Thus began the Vienna Opera's great Wagner tradition, a tradition that remained unimpaired by the fact that Wagner's own experiences in the city bordered on the traumatic. In the event, Eckert remained in the post for only three years and was followed by another Italian impresario, Matteo Salvi, who ran the company from 1861 to 1867, an interregnum not least because this was the decade when the magnificent new opera house was built on the Ringstraße, just across the road from the Kärntnerthor-Theater. Destroyed in the Second World War and rebuilt in 1955 in the form that is familiar today, the Imperial and Royal Court Opera Theatre in the New House opened on 25 May 1869 with a production of *Don Giovanni* under its new general administrator, Franz von Dingelstedt, a playwright by profession. He was followed by another conductor, Johann Herbeck, who was famous above all for his Wagner performances, although he was also a successful stage director, even if that post did not as yet exist as such. Herbeck was replaced in 1875 by Franz Jauner, a managing director with no experience of conducting and an example of the type of director familiar to Mahler from his dealings with Neumann, Staegemann and Pollini. Jauner immediately chalked up a success with Bizet's *Carmen*, which had opened to mixed reviews in Paris only a few months earlier. And he was also successful with Verdi, who conducted his Requiem and several performances of *Aida* at the Court Opera, ensuring that from now on the Italian composer was held in equally high esteem as Wagner among Vienna's opera enthusiasts. Only a few months later Wagner himself appeared in the city to conduct a benefit performance of *Lohengrin*, but although the performance was a success, Wagner never set foot in the city again. Hans Richter joined the company at more or less the same time as Jauner, his close association with Wagner implying the Master's imprimatur and guaranteeing idiomatic performances of his works.

Wilhelm Jahn was forty-five when he took up his appointment on 1 January 1881. He had been born in Moravia in 1835 and was therefore from a region not far from Mahler's own birthplace. His superior – and Bezecny's predecessor – was Baron Leopold von Hofmann. The years under Jauner and Jahn were a golden age for the Vienna Opera, a point that needs to be borne in mind when we assess Mahler's decade at the helm, a ten-year incumbency that came not at the end of a long period of dreary desolation and artistic insolvency but, rather, after a time of considerable success, even if some of the performances towards the end of this era fell short of the highest standards. And yet, even when we take this background into account, there is no denying the brilliance and

positively heroic rethinking of operatic life in Vienna, a rethinking that was
to affect the whole world of twentieth-century opera. The situation was helped
by the fact that Jahn and Richter worked well together, the former occupying
the twin posts of director and principal conductor, while the latter was effectively the deputy principal conductor. Interpretatively, however, they both
pursued very different careers, Jahn having a soft spot for the French and Italian
repertory, while Richter was firmly established as a Wagnerian. Jahn was fond
of Gounod, Bizet and Massenet as well as Verdi, and it is to his credit that he
introduced Massenet's *Manon* to Viennese audiences, scoring a tremendous
triumph in the process and following this up with the world première of
Werther in 1892. Jahn can also lay claim to the honour of ennobling Strauß's *Die
Fledermaus* by staging it at the Court Opera in 1894.

Any assessment of the revolutionary nature of Mahler's directorship also
needs to bear in mind that Jahn and Richter represented the older type of
German conductor: both were tall, powerfully built men with blond hair and
luxurious beards – anti-Semites would have described them as 'Aryan'. Richter
in particular bore a striking resemblance to the city's mayor, Karl Lueger. In
complete contrast was Mahler, small, thin, 'nervous', 'fidgety' and with a shock
of black hair. As such, he was the very embodiment of the stereotypical Jew –
a 'brimstone-back and blistered dwarf', to quote Wagner's description of his
Nibelung Alberich. For such a man to have seized control of the Vienna Opera
was hard to accept by all those whose thinking was coloured by German,
national and anti-Jewish, if not anti-Semitic, ideas. Two conductors could
not shoulder the burden of so large a house, and so Jahn and Richter were
assisted by three others, although none was particularly significant. Until 1884,
Wilhelm Gericke was responsible for the German repertory, a pallid figure
unable to inspire either the orchestra or the singers. Equally insignificant were
Johann Nepomuk Fuchs and Joseph ('Pepi') Hellmesberger, the latter the son
of a much more famous father: Joseph Hellmesberger Senior was the leader of
the Court Opera orchestra, the founder of a famous string quartet and director
of the Vienna Conservatory. Hellmesberger Junior's easy-going manner had
ensured that he was popular with the players, but otherwise he was held in low
esteem and was notoriously work-shy. Known above all as a wag, he succeeded
Mahler as the conductor of the Philharmonic concerts in 1901, an appointment that reflects badly on the orchestra's powers of judgement at this time,
even if it says much for their love of a quiet life.

The great strength of the Jahn era was its singers, for it was they who were
uppermost in the minds of contemporaries keen to hail the Vienna Court
Opera as the finest opera company in the world. Some of the great Wagnerian
singers of the Jauner era were still performing when Jahn took over in 1881,
including Amalie Materna, who had sung Brünnhilde in the inaugural

Bayreuth *Ring* in 1876; the heldentenor Hermann Winkelmann; the bass Emil
Scaria, who sang Gurnemanz in the world première of *Parsifal* in 1882 and
whose repertory included all of Wagner's bass and bass-baritone roles; and the
bel canto baritone Theodor Reichmann, a singer known for his nobility of
voice, even if his acting was less distinguished. In short, Jahn took over a
remarkable ensemble that he continued to develop, especially in the direction
of French and Italian opera. Josef Ritter from Salzburg was an acclaimed Don
Giovanni who could also sing Wagner's Alberich. And Jahn addditionally had
on his roster two singers ideally suited to Massenet and other composers
working in the same stylistic tradition: the soprano Marie Renard from Graz
(her real name was Pöltzl) and the Belgian tenor Ernest von Dyck, a round-
faced, somewhat portly former journalist, whose sense of style and mellifluous
tone made him an ideal exponent of the French repertory. His Des Grieux in
Manon was highly regarded by Massenet. He was also the first Werther. We
shall not be doing Mahler an injustice by claiming that his understanding of
vocal artistry was by no means the same as Jahn's. Like Wagner, he rated
dramatic expression more highly and regarded vocal refinement and beautiful
singing in the bel canto tradition as altogether secondary in importance.

On 16 May 1897 the morning edition of the *Breslauer Zeitung* published a
'Letter from Vienna' written by one of the paper's regular correspondents in
the Austro-Hungarian capital. Its author was the twenty-three-year-old Karl
Kraus, one of the most talented young journalists in a country with a long
tradition of such writing, the only difference being that Kraus was arguably
even more acerbic than his colleagues. In his article he offers an overview of
recent developments on Vienna's cultural scene, with particular emphasis on
the Court Opera:

> A new conductor has entered the Opera House recently with the panache of
> a Siegfried, and you can see in his eyes that he will soon have done with the
> bad old ways. Herr Mahler has conducted his first *Lohengrin* with a success
> which was unanimously acknowledged by the whole press. There is a rumour
> that he is soon to be made Director. Then, presumably, the repertoire of our
> Court Opera will no longer consist entirely of *Cavalleria rusticana*; native
> Austrian composers will no longer have their manuscripts returned to them
> unread (they will be returned read); and singers of merit will no longer be
> shown the door without reason. The new conductor is said to have given such
> effective proof of his energy that intrigues are afoot against him already.
> Mahler wrestling with insubordinate theatrical monsters [. . .].[12]

Two years later Kraus was to found his own newspaper, *Die Fackel*, and to
become the leading satirist in the German-speaking world. That he returned

to the subject of Mahler on many subsequent occasions is remarkable, given his almost complete lack of interest in music, the only exception being his fondness for French operettas. Written only days after Mahler's Court Opera debut, his present notice reveals a number of things. First, Mahler's future promotion to the post of director was an open secret – Kraus had no inside contacts at the Court Opera or with the general administrator's office but was merely repeating what was already common knowledge in the city. Second, the new conductor was exercising Viennese minds in a way normally reserved for the appointment of a new prime minister. (This, at least, is a tradition that Vienna has upheld to the present day.) Third, there were expectations that the repertory would change. (If Kraus specifically mentions *Cavalleria rusticana*, it is because its composer, Pietro Mascagni, had recently been acclaimed in Vienna when he had conducted performances of his runaway success, leading to a parody of the piece that was performed under the title *Krawalleria rusticana*, the German word *Krawall* meaning 'riot' or 'brawl'.) And, fourth, Mahler was already the object of powerful intrigue.

All four points were true. In the case of the last of them, we have already quoted the anti-Semitic piece that appeared in the *Reichspost* even before Mahler had conducted a note in the house: the Jewish press, it insisted, should take care that its panegyrics were not undermined once Herr Mahler had 'started his Jew-boy antics on the podium'. Nor was the *Reichspost* the only paper in Vienna to promote more or less anti-Semitic views. Throughout his life Mahler was careful not to engage openly with the anti-Semitism that was directed at him personally, still less to comment on the anti-Semitism that was almost universal at this time, but it is clear from a number of private remarks that he knew very well what was at stake here. Shortly after he had signed his preliminary contract, rumours again began to circulate about Bezecny's dismissal. On this occasion, they were not entirely groundless, because Bezecny did indeed lose his job in February 1898. On hearing of these rumours, Mahler was thrown into a state of extreme anxiety, prompting him to write to one of his journalistic allies in Vienna, Ludwig Karpath, and to ask whether the anti-Semitic newspapers would exploit the situation by claiming that Mahler's appointment had cost Bezecny his job. This was then followed by other rumours to the effect that a second conductor would be appointed alongside or even above Mahler. In short, he had every reason to be nervous. His preliminary contract was confirmed on 15 April, when he was still in Hamburg. A week later he conducted his final performance at the Hamburg Stadttheater. The evening began with Beethoven's 'Eroica' Symphony, followed by *Fidelio*, presumably with Anna von Mildenburg in the title role. The occasion was a triumph for Mahler. The stage groaned beneath the weight of all the flowers that he received, and the Hamburg correspondent of the *Neue Freie Presse* counted sixty curtain calls for the conductor – if true, it was a huge number. Mahler then travelled straight to Vienna, where he took rooms at the Hotel Bristol, while Justine remained behind in Hamburg to take care of the removal, which, as always, was relatively straightforward. Before the new season opened, brother and sister had found an apartment at 3 Bartensteingasse, a street running parallel to the Ringstraße and closer to the new Burgtheater than to the opera house, but still within reasonable distance.

The New Opera Director

Kraus was right when he observed that Mahler had taken up his new post with all the panache of a Siegfried. Once again – and, as it turned out, for the last time, for the situation in New York was to prove very different – he revealed all his old élan on assuming his new position, except that on this occasion he was resolved not to abandon the struggle as quickly as he had done in the past. And this time his resolve held firm. Indeed, it is significant that his appointments had been for progressively longer periods: in Bad Hall he had remained for only three months; in Laibach for seven; in Olmütz for a recidivist stint of only two months; in Kassel and Leipzig for two years each; in Budapest for two and a half years; in Hamburg for six years; and in Vienna for ten and a half years. One has the impression that on this occasion he drew on all his remaining reserves, both physical and mental, even if it meant driving to its limits a body which, lacking in strength, made up for that deficiency by sheer tenacity. Scarcely had he made his debut when he succumbed to a serious throat illness – presumably one of the attacks of purulent tonsillitis that were to plague him from now on – and was obliged to cancel all his remaining engagements during the last four weeks of the season, not resuming his duties until the beginning of August. In the light of all that we know about the history of Mahler's illnesses, this may be viewed from today's perspective as the writing on the wall. As we have seen from his letter to Wlassack, Mahler wanted to make his Viennese debut with a Wagner opera or *Fidelio*. At the end of April 1897 he met Jahn to discuss the matter, although Jahn seems not to have suspected that he was in the presence of his successor as the company's new director. Jahn generously offered him *Don Giovanni* – or *Don Juan*, to give it its German title – but, as he told Karpath, Mahler was unhappy with this choice, no doubt because he was fully aware of the horrendous difficulties of this work for singers, orchestral musicians and conductor, but he did not dare to decline the offer. But when Jahn decided to offer him *Lohengrin* instead, Mahler was overjoyed, knowing that he would create a far greater impression with it. Lengthy rehearsals were out of the question for a repertory piece of this nature, and it was only on the day of the performance, 11 May, that the new conductor was presented to the orchestra by Jahn – according to Karpath, no one in the entire theatre knew that this was the future director, but this seems unlikely, given the fact that rumours of Mahler's appointment were already circulating in the city. On this occasion Mahler at least had a chance to play through the prelude to Act One.

The evening's performance proved a triumphant success and he received a warm welcome, albeit on the part of the audience rather than the performers, whose initial response was one of uncertainty and reserve. But the reserve of the players, some of whom, of course, were petty-bourgeois anti-Semites hostile to the house's first Jewish conductor, grew less with each passing act, a development that can have had nothing to do with the conductor's conciliatory and winning personality but must have been based on his musical authority, which was in turn underpinned by his undoubted competence. Even the opening prelude was greeted by cheering, which increased as the evening progressed. Following the performance, an enthusiastic crowd gathered at the stage door, and the next day's reviews were correspondingly euphoric, at least if we exclude the anti-Semitic newspapers, whose critics refused to be talked round. Mahler was particularly pleased that it was above all young people and students at the Conservatory who waited for him and cheered him after the performance. As a young man, he had often suffered unspeakably when his ideas of what the music should sound like were inadequately realized. For the first time in his life he had now heard an outstanding orchestra and excellent singers coming close to that ideal, an ideal that he had carried in his head from Bad Hall to Hamburg and that had now become a reality.

In her memoirs, Natalie Bauer-Lechner reproduces a touching letter from an unnamed musician – presumably a member of the Court Opera orchestra – who wrote that not since Wagner's own performance of the work in 1876 had *Lohengrin* sounded as it did on this occasion: after Wagner and Bülow, Mahler was the greatest conductor he had known. Of course, Mahler had already had a chance to conduct an outstanding orchestra, but only in the concert hall, when he had, for example, rehearsed the second movement of his Third Symphony for Nikisch with the Berlin Philharmonic the previous November, but he had never had charge of such a body of players in the orchestra pit of an opera house. Whether or not the Vienna Court Opera was then the best opera company in the world is open to dispute, although there is much to be said in support of this claim, but what is beyond doubt is that the Court Opera orchestra was the finest opera orchestra in the world, a position that it retains even at a time when the house's standards in general have fallen. Mahler was swept along by the players' willingness to learn and by their ability to realize the conductor's intentions, whether or not they found the conductor himself sympathetic. After this inaugural *Lohengrin*, Mahler told Natalie that:

I got further with them in one rehearsal than after years with all the others. It's true that the acoustics of the Vienna Opera idealize the tone in a quite unbelievable way, whereas elsewhere bad acoustics make it coarser and more material. But the chief credit must go to Austrian musicianship: to the verve, the warmth and the great natural gifts that each player brings to his work.[13]

Mahler set about his new task with great enthusiasm, but it is remarkable that he initially made no attempt to revolutionize the stage, a development that had to wait until the beginning of 1903, when he staged *Tristan und Isolde* with Alfred Roller. Even so, we may be certain that he could already envisage a new way of presenting opera. After all, he had spent the last seventeen years working his way up from a tiny theatre producing operettas in the summer months to the Vienna Court Opera, allowing him to identify every last weakness of the current operatic scene, but he also knew that these weaknesses could not be overcome overnight. Happily, the orchestra was the least of his worries as it responded promptly to his new ideas. The singers, conversely, were more of a problem, not because they were bad – far from it – but because some were already too old to satisfy Mahler's demands, while others were unwilling or unable to accept a new performance style. In Hamburg, Anna von Mildenburg had shown him what an outstandingly talented singer could achieve – vocally, musically and dramatically – under his direction. He was determined to adopt a similar approach in Vienna, even if he needed to take his time. And yet there can be no doubt that he was resolved from the outset to bring about a new performance style onstage. That he tackled the problem in a level-headed way is an indication of his well-developed tactical intelligence. His most testing challenge was a complete reappraisal of production values. Viennese audiences were used to the fact that Jahn himself acted as stage director for important performances, ensuring that the singers were arranged in the most favourable positions amidst the most lavish scenery. Sometimes their positions may even have been meaningful and their movements credible. Until now, no one had demanded more of them. It had been sufficient for them to sing beautifully and for the orchestra to play as splendidly as they could. If Mahler had approached this problem with his usual dynamism, he would have encountered resistance on the part of the company and also on that of the audience. It says much for his great diplomatic astuteness that he waited almost six years before letting the cat out of the bag, an astuteness that is often overlooked. He also had to wait, of course, for a colleague like Alfred Roller to appear on the scene.

Mahler's contract as conductor was initially for one year, starting on 1 May 1897. Between then and his official debut on the 11th he had time to travel to Venice to see *La Bohème* – not Puccini's version, but the one by Leoncavallo, which at this period was still preferred to Puccini's, not least on account of the lasting success of *Pagliacci*. As chance would have it, however, Puccini's version was also being performed in another opera house in Venice – the decision by two Italian composers to set the same subject had caused considerable problems. Jahn had already reached an agreement with Leoncavallo to perform his version in Vienna, but when Mahler returned to the city, he told anyone willing to listen that Puccini's setting was infinitely preferable, a verdict confirmed by the history of opera, for all that history occasionally errs. After *Lohengrin*, Mahler went on to conduct *Der fliegende Holländer* and *Die Zauberflöte*. In the case of the latter, he was able to enlist the orchestra's sympathies by sending half of its members home or to the pub when he discovered to his dismay at the orchestral rehearsal that Mozart's *singspiel* was being performed with a huge Wagnerian orchestra. In his view this contradicted the whole spirit of the work.

The first new opera that Mahler added to the repertory was Smetana's *Dalibor*, which he conducted on 4 October 1897, in the process winning the public approval of the doyen of Vienna's music critics, Eduard Hanslick, whose behind-the-scenes advocacy of Mahler's appointment we have already mentioned. Hanslick was now seventy-two and, as such, the grand old man of Vienna's critics, but he was still tirelessly active. Readers familiar with him only as a critic of Wagner do not know him at all, for even today there is much that can still be learnt from his reviews, even from those critical of Wagner. He was also one of the wittiest and most pertinent critics of the second half of the nineteenth century. He concluded his review of *Dalibor* as follows:

> But it is the director, Herr Mahler, who has earned our special gratitude by performing *Dalibor*. He shares with Wilhelm Jahn the valuable ability to direct his attention not just to the score but also to the stage picture, in every case contributing sensitively to the work's dramatic and musical impact. Mahler has rehearsed *Dalibor* with keen understanding and meticulous care. No one familiar with the work will have failed to notice the way in which he brings out every subtlety of the score, while maintaining the harmonious unity of the whole and now and then enhancing its effectiveness by means of a modest cut or interpolation. Young, experienced and ambitious, he is, we hope, the man to breathe new life into our opera, which has recently grown weary and sleepy. The production of Smetana's *Dalibor* was without doubt a debt of honour that Austria's leading opera house needed to pay, both Hamburg and Munich long since having beaten us to the post. It will not be the last debt of honour that we shall have to thank Herr Mahler for paying off.[14]

This was Vienna's way of giving Mahler his letters patent. And even if Hanslick was later to be left utterly baffled by his first encounter with Mahler's own music, there is little doubt that he would have greeted Mahler's operatic reforms of the years after 1903 as enthusiastically as he greeted *Dalibor*, for it is clear that on the strength of his vast experience as a critic he sensed the new conductor's ability to revolutionize the stage.

In the middle of June 1897, four months before *Dalibor* opened, Mahler suffered from a sore throat. It was a bad omen. An abscess had to be removed, possibly from his tonsils, resulting in the first of many subsequent bouts of high fever and forcing Mahler to take to his bed for a few days, after which he joined Justine, Emma and Natalie in Kitzbühel, now that Steinbach on the Attersee was no longer a viable alternative. But Kitzbühel was suddenly struck by an outbreak of scarlet fever, and Mahler, anxious about the risk of infection, insisted that he and his party should leave, no doubt a wise decision in the light of his weakened condition. From Kitzbühel they travelled to Steinach on the Brenner and from there to Gries, Ridmanntal near Sterzing and finally Vahrn, also in South Tyrol, where they spent the rest of Mahler's sick leave. In the course of a brief excursion to the Pustertal they also visited Toblach, where Mahler was later to spend his final summer vacations in Europe.

In mid-July Mahler was obliged to interrupt his vacation in order to accept his appointment as the Vienna Opera's deputy director. By the end of July he was back in harness, his health restored. At that period the new season began in early August, which in view of Vienna's traditionally dusty summer heat can hardly have been an attractive proposition, but at this date this was of little concern to Mahler. In the course of the 1897–8 season he conducted 107 performances, not quite as many as he had done at the height of his stint of forced labour in Hamburg, but still a huge burden of responsibility when compared to the demands placed on today's conductors. At Liechtenstein's insistence, the outstanding business with Jahn was resolved when the latter was given a medal and urged to hand in his notice. Unlikely though it seems, Jahn is said to have been surprised by this turn of events, but he did as he was told, and on 8 October 1897 Mahler was appointed the house's artistic director with effect from 15 October. Never before had he signed such an advantageous contract, and nor would he do so again. As a civil-service appointment, it was for life and carried an annual salary of 12,000 florins, more than twice what he had received as the house's principal conductor. There was also a guaranteed pension of 3,000 florins, which he would receive no matter when he left the post. (Only a few years earlier, the Austro-Hungarian florin had been replaced by the crown, one florin being the equivalent of two crowns, but the florin was still retained for most calculations.) The pension was small in relation to Mahler's salary, but it was raised several times in the course of his appointment, so that by the time he left the company at the end of 1907 it was worth 7,000 florins. When taken with his sizeable income from America, it was

enough to keep him relatively affluent until the end of his life, a state of affairs
from which his wife and daughter were later to profit. As always, comparisons
with present-day prices are difficult to draw, all attempts at conversion
foundering on the differing purchasing power of the respective currencies.
Land prices and rents, for example, were considerably lower than today,
whereas clothing was markedly more expensive. It is no more than a vague
indication, therefore, to suggest that one crown was the equivalent of four
euros, giving an annual salary of between 90,000 and 100,000 euros. Nor
should we forget that the completely absurd fees commanded by leading
conductors today, some of whom receive ten times this amount, were not paid
in Mahler's day. For a court official, and especially for a musician, this was a
handsome sum, above all when we recall that, leaving aside the manner in
which they acquired their wealth, the only people who could really be
described as rich at this time were landowners, property owners and the
owners of large industrial concerns.

The hero of Carl Sternheim's play *Die Hose*, Theobald Maske, tells his wife in a
similar situation: 'I can now take responsibility for having a child with you.' Mahler
could have said the same. For the first time in his life, his family could feel financially secure and he could think of starting a family of his own – at thirty-seven
he was no longer young and by contemporary standards was already too old to
marry and have children. But even this prospect was not yet in sight. He was still
living with his two sisters in the Bartensteingasse. Emma did not move out until
the summer of 1898, when she married the cellist Eduard Rosé. Meanwhile, his
favourite sister Justine was seeing Eduard's brother, Arnold, the leader of the Rosé
Quartet, even if Mahler seems for a long time to have been oblivious to this fact.
Once Mahler had realized that he was unable to block Anna von Mildenburg's
Vienna appointment any longer, he had his hands full trying to channel what in
Hamburg had been a passionate affair into the calmer waters of collegial cooperation. There is no evidence of any other erotic entanglements on his part until
Selma Kurz joined the Vienna State Opera in the late summer of 1899. He was in
any case fully occupied conducting the aforementioned 107 performances during
his first season and, more generally, performing the duties of the house's artistic
director.

In reforming Vienna's opera industry, Mahler operated along rigorously
consistent lines, while adopting a diplomatic approach on all the decisive points.
Wherever he saw a real chance of success, he could be altogether uncompromising. But one has the impression that he reserved this attitude for minor skirmishes, while proving astonishingly flexible on more important matters. It may
appear inconsequential, for example, whether or not latecomers were admitted
during the performance. Today's standard reminder in programme booklets to
the effect that 'Latecomers cannot be admitted until a suitable break in the

performance' was a revolutionary innovation in Mahler's day. (The fact that complaisant ushers and pushy spectators continue to flout this rule is another matter.) Mahler introduced it initially for works that he himself deemed sacrosanct, namely, Wagner's music dramas, Mozart's *Don Giovanni* and Beethoven's *Fidelio*, and it is unclear whether it was then extended to the other works in the repertory. When Mahler told Wlassack what he was planning, the latter is said to have been appalled: 'That's not acceptable in Vienna.' But it was accepted, albeit with much head-shaking by many of the regulars. Even the emperor was apprised of the matter when an archduke objected to the withdrawal of his right to enter his box whenever he wanted. The emperor, too, responded by shaking his head: 'My God, the theatre is ultimately there for our own amusement, I don't understand this strictness, but the director's orders have to be obeyed.' As long as Liechtenstein was there to protect Mahler's back, then the latter could be reassured, knowing, as he did, that the emperor reacted angrily when members of his court tried to meddle in the running of the theatre and other institutions. It is reported that at one performance unrest broke out in the stalls when an usher admitted a latecomer. Mahler took note of the employee in question and afterwards read him the Riot Act. He dealt equally rigorously with the abuses of the claque, the group of professional clappers paid by individual singers to lead the applause for them. Mahler demanded that all his singers should sign a written undertaking not to maintain such groups of mercenary supporters. Although he apparently failed to eradicate the problem completely, the importance of the claque was nevertheless much diminished.

And there was another, far more important problem that Mahler tackled with no less rigour by restoring the cuts that were traditionally made in longer operas, especially Wagner's. We have already had occasion to mention Mahler's ruthlessness in cutting the whole of the fifth act of Meyerbeer's *Les Huguenots* for reasons that remain unclear. But he was ruthless only in the case of operas that he considered second-rate, as he unfortunately did with Meyerbeer's masterpiece. With Wagner's works, conversely, he adopted a different approach – one that, judged from today's perspective, is entirely understandable. The only cut in Wagner's works that continues to be sanctioned today is the famous one in the Love Duet in Act Two of *Tristan und Isolde*. All of his other works are now performed complete. But readers familiar with the historic recordings that were made at the Metropolitan Opera, for example, in the 1930s, 1940s, 1950s and in some cases even later will know that these performances involved massive cuts, resulting in drastically shorter performance timings, while also taking pressure off the singers. Such cuts were commonplace at the end of the nineteenth century. No one took exception to the fact that in every theatre apart from Bayreuth, David's account of the art of the Mastersingers was cut in Act One of *Die Meistersinger*, as was the scene between Sachs and Walther in Act Three;

or that Wotan's great monologue in Act Two of *Die Walküre* was reduced to a handful of phrases, that half of the scene between Wotan and Fricka was cut; and that in *Götterdämmerung* the scenes involving the Norns, Alberich and Waltraute were all removed in their entirety, resulting in the loss of some forty-five minutes of music.

Mahler refused to accept this – he respected Wagner's works too much to agree to such desecration, and so he insisted on performing them either uncut or virtually uncut, a point we now take for granted. He began with the *Ring*, which he gradually restored, performing it complete for the first time in Vienna in September 1898 in a new production on which he almost certainly worked very closely with the house's resident stage director, August Stoll. This was not yet the stage revolution that he was to undertake with Alfred Roller, and it is a matter for immense regret that what he achieved with *Tristan und Isolde* could not be extended to the *Ring*. His conducting of the cycle was almost universally acclaimed, but it will not have been clear to all his audience that he also directed the production as the name of the stage director was never included in programme booklets and playbills at this period. Mahler's success is all the more remarkable in that he was inevitably compared with Hans Richter, who had, as it were, been anointed by the Master himself and was regarded as Wagner's plenipotentiary on earth. At the same time, Mahler's interpretation must have struck even sympathetic Wagnerians as unusual. The review by the critic of the *Wiener Allgemeine Zeitung*, Gustav Schönaich, certainly gives pause for thought. Schönaich had heard Wagner himself conduct and had attended the inaugural *Ring* in Bayreuth but was relatively open-minded and certainly not disposed to prejudge the new conductor. His comments help to make clear what it was about Mahler's conducting that Wagnerians found so disconcerting:

> It is not a preference for slow or fast tempi, but rather his predilection for the effect of excessively dramatic contrasts which on occasion makes Mahler drag or hurry the tempo unduly. He often succeeds to a surprising degree in bringing out these contrasts – rarely, however, without in some way damaging the effect on the listener of what comes before and after. Allied to this is his close attention to detail and tendency to invest certain hidden features of the score with a significance that is perhaps not wholly their due. Not all themes are equally congenial to him. . . . The general trend of Mahler's tempi is certainly in the direction of hurry rather than slowness. . . . Though often splendid, spirited and well thought out, Mahler's conducting at times lacks the beautiful balance, and continuity of argument, and the majestic calm which is the strength of Richter's approach.[15]

Such an apparently impartial description deserves to be taken seriously. These are characteristics of Mahler at midpoint in his career, characteristics that time and again emerge from reviews of his conducting. The tendency to opt for extremes of tempo and to seek to capture and hold the listener's interest at the expense of balance and calm was a feature reminiscent of Kapellmeister Kreisler rather than more stolid practitioners of the art – and it is only natural that the essential characteristics of a conductor find expression in the way in which he conducts. Many of these qualities sound familiar. When we turn our attention to the great Wagner conductors of recent decades, it could be argued that the spirit of Hans Richter lived on in Hans Knappertsbusch, that of Mahler in Georg Solti or Leonard Bernstein – but this has nothing to do with their Jewishness or otherwise.

In order to perform Wagner's works uncut, outstanding singers are needed – this was as true in Mahler's day as it is now. The standard-bearers of the Jahn era were old and tired: Amalie Materna and Theodor Reichmann were no longer available or rapidly approaching retirement, and Emil Scaria was dead. Ernest van Dyck and Marie Renard, who had championed the French and Italian repertory under Jahn, were not to Mahler's liking: Van Dyck was fat and ungainly, and Renard relied on her pretty face and bell-like voice. Both were far removed from the spirit of the Wagnerian music drama in which the singing actor had an important part to play and which Mahler regarded as the model for all the works in the repertory. Intellectually, too, they were too limited to be capable of rethinking their approach to their profession. One by one, they left, as also did the American mezzo and, later, soprano Edyth Walker, who had arrived in Vienna two years before Mahler, proving indispensable as Fidès in Meyerbeer's *Le Prophète* and as Azucena in Verdi's *Il trovatore*. Singers like Van Dyck, Renard and Walker also had the disadvantage of performing a repertory that was of no real interest to Mahler. True, he conducted an unbelievably wide range of works during his early years in Vienna, but in his heart he hankered after the great dramatic operas of the past: Gluck, Mozart, Beethoven, Wagner and a handful of newer pieces. Of less interest to him were Rossini, Donizetti, Verdi, Meyerbeer, Gounod and Massenet. That he was guilty of seriously underrating some of these composers is, of course, another matter. As a result of this focus of interest, one of his principal tasks at the start of his appointment was to engage new singers.

The monumental figure of Anna von Mildenburg could be said to provide the yardstick by which Mahler's picture of the ideal singing actor could be measured. She set new standards not only as Brünnhilde, Isolde and Kundry but also as Ortrud, Donna Anna and Beethoven's Leonore. All other singers were inevitably judged by these standards, even if, as Mahler knew, they were unrealistically high. By the time that he left the company in 1907, Mildenburg's career was in decline, and although it is not true, as some writers have claimed, that she retired from the stage in 1909 (she appeared as Strauss's Klytämnestra as late as 1927), she pursued a freelance career once she had left the Vienna Court Opera. The daughter of an innkeeper from Weimar, Marie Gutheil-Schoder was intended to be Marie Renard's replacement, but she quickly outgrew her revered predecessor. Her voice was by no means as beguilingly beautiful as Renard's, so she initially encountered resistance on the part of Vienna's canary-fancying audiences, but she could lay claim to tremendous musicality, which Mahler particularly valued, and she eventually developed into an outstanding singing actress, taking her cue – by her own admission – from the leading actress of her age, Eleonora Duse. In particular, her Carmen succeeded in avoiding the old clichés of a hip-swinging, fiery-eyed beauty and created in its place a modern, fractured, nervous character. She moved to Vienna in 1900 and even sang Strauss's Elektra, while also championing the most modern composers, including Arnold Schoenberg.

In Mahler's eyes, Winkelmann's successor was the Danish tenor Erik Schmedes, who had been discovered by Pollini, arriving in Vienna from Dresden in 1898 and capturing the hearts of local audiences as the young Siegfried. He remained a member of the Vienna ensemble until he retired from the stage in 1924. Unlike Anna von Mildenburg, he lacked the ability to explore the depths of Wagner's tragic figures, but he could impress his audiences with his genuine humanity. With his sunny, cheerful disposition, this great bear of a man exerted an appeal that is best understood by readers familiar with Alma Mahler's early diaries. She flirted with him extensively, and after one performance of *Siegfried* noted that she would have been capable of anything if only he had been there and that he had made the blood run to her head.[16] What more can one say? It was no doubt this elemental impact that Mahler valued in the singer. Vocally, he will not have been satisfied with him, for Schmedes's surviving recordings reveal a powerful and even beautiful voice lacking the technical foundations necessary to achieve the sort of 'German bel canto' that Wagner wanted in his singers. Above all, his breathing technique was questionable.

A relative latecomer to Mahler's Vienna ensemble was the baritone Friedrich Weidemann, a native of Holstein, who joined the company in 1903, quickly becoming its leading Wagner baritone in roles such as Sachs and Wotan. Almost all of Mahler's singers left gramophone recordings, allowing us to recreate a composite picture of what they sounded like, and in Weidemann's case, too, it has to be said that his vocal technique lagged behind the sheer beauty of his voice and the inspiration of his expression. Mahler valued him particularly on account of his expressive singing, otherwise he would not have invited him to give the first performance of his *Kindertotenlieder* in 1905. As for bass singers, Vienna had not had an outstanding bass since Scaria's death in

1886, but in 1902 Mahler was lucky to be able to sign up Richard Mayr, the son of a Salzburg innkeeper. As everyone with an interest in the history of opera knows, Mayr was the leading interpreter of the role of Baron Ochs in Strauss's *Der Rosenkavalier*. Although he did not create the role in Dresden, he sang it at the first performance in Vienna in 1911, leaving his mark on the role and remaining its finest exponent even today, a position underscored not only by a gramophone recording but also by the many well-known photographs of him in the part. It is easy to forget that Mayr was not only a buffo bass. Immediately before joining the Vienna ensemble, he sang Hagen in Bayreuth and was later an ideal Marke and Gurnemanz. Mahler's old friend Wilhelm Hesch had come to Vienna shortly before he did, but health problems quickly led to the loss of his special qualities as a buffo bass.

Leo Slezak was a locksmith from Moravia who arrived in Vienna in 1901 and became the most radiant young heldentenor of his age. Here, too, a remarkable number of excellent recordings have survived and show how good he was. In this case, moreover, we shall have to acknowledge his outstanding technique and the brilliant top notes that allowed him to sing roles such as Arnold in Rossini's *Guillaume Tell*, Meyerbeer's tenor roles and, later, Verdi's Otello, as well as Lohengrin and Walther von Stolzing. With Schmedes in the heavier heldentenor roles and Slezak singing the lighter ones, Mahler had two performers who were the envy of practically every other opera house, the only possible exception being the Met in turn-of-the-century New York, where Jacques Urlus and Heinrich Knote were both appearing. In his hugely entertaining memoirs, Slezak wrote a touching tribute to his director in Vienna, highlighting his respect and unconditional willingness to do as he was told, even though it cannot always have been easy for the strict taskmaster and the practical joker to work together. No list of the singers who stood by Mahler through thick and thin would be complete without at least a brief mention of the baritone Leopold Demuth, famous in his day not only in Rossini's bel canto baritone roles but also as Wagner's Flying Dutchman; the *jugendlich-dramatisch* soprano Berta Foerster-Lauterer whom we have already met as the wife of one of Mahler's friends in Hamburg; the buffo tenor Hans Breuer, who was also an outstanding Mime; the character tenor Georg Maikl; and three sopranos, Bertha Kiurina, Lucie Weidt and Gertrude Förstel.

Not every singer could work with Mahler. Those who wanted only an easy life, happy to stick to the beaten path of well-tried routine and unwilling to be taken out of their comfort zone, were finished as far as Mahler was concerned, and for such singers he could really make life difficult: popular singers were dismissed, their dismissals turned against him by his enemies and used to hold him up to public ridicule in the form of cartoons and caricatures: 'Director Mahler driving away our favourites' was the caption to one such caricature.

Sometimes the anti-Semitic camarilla also seized on these facts to whip up resentment of the hated Jew at the head of the Vienna Court Opera. But there is no doubt that Mahler could not have carried out his reforms and achieved such impressive results if he had not had the support of a band of sworn allies drawn from the ranks of the company's leading singers, all of whom were prepared to submit to his dictatorial will and to place their own talents in the service of the cause that he represented. In her reminiscences, Marie Gutheil-Schoder recalled that:

> His great intelligence and philosophical approach to life and its manifestations left no room for the trivia of everyday existence. In his sympathies and antipathies he sometimes vacillated, it is true, but there was usually a reason why his feelings shifted. If he was disappointed in someone on whom he had lavished a great deal of time and attention, he would drop that person, just as he resented wasting his time and energy on inactivity. His irony was cutting and he was fond of venting it on those whom he found conceited, and he could be very angry if someone lacked the requisite seriousness during a performance! ... But to all who brought trust and loving understanding to Mahler's unique character and who responded to his genius and artistry with devotion and warmth, he opened up his heart, they gained the inestimable gift of his sympathy and interest and were even allowed the occasional glimpse into the very depths of his mind, depths that he anxiously hid from the world. He brought implacable rigour to the work that was essential to his creative urge. How often he would explain at the end of the first night of a new production: 'Well, I wish I could start the rehearsals all over again!' How serious he was in saying this is clear from the fact that in all the works he conducted and rehearsed new details would come to light in each and every performance, and musical climaxes were brought out which, unrehearsed, were the spontaneous expression of his powerful suggestive power, giving the performance the appearance of having been completely rethought.[17]

Selma Kurz

One of the singers who was a member of Mahler's Vienna ensemble has been deliberately ignored until now: Selma Kurz. But she can be ignored no longer, for she was without doubt the central love of Mahler's life between Anna von Mildenburg and Alma Schindler. It was a passion which, however brief, was none the less both violent and intense. For a long time the nature of their relationship was unclear, but the letters that Mahler wrote to the soprano and that were published in 1983 in the volume of reminiscences edited by the singer's daughter, Dési Halban, leave us in no doubt that the two of them had an affair.

Selma Kurz was born in Biala in Galicia in 1874. Like Mahler, she was Jewish and grew up in straitened circumstances. Her father was almost blind and earned a pittance repairing umbrellas. The cantor of the local synagogue needed soprano voices, male or female, and discovered the sixteen-year-old Selma Kurz, who was then sent to Vienna to study with Johannes Ress, having obtained financial support from one of the Esterházy princes. It has been claimed that she made her stage debut in Hamburg in 1895, in which case she would have met Mahler on this occasion. But although she signed a contract with Pollini, the appearance never took place, and it was not until 1899 that Kurz and Mahler met in Vienna. Her first engagement was in fact in Frankfurt in 1896, where, still only twenty-two, she sang roles such as Wagner's Elisabeth and Bizet's Carmen. Three years later she moved to Vienna. She auditioned for Mahler in the spring of 1898 as she no longer felt comfortable in Frankfurt, where she was being ogled by the local intendant. Mahler was enthusiastic about her singing and agreed to engage her on condition that she could extricate herself from her Frankfurt contract.

Selma Kurz made her dazzlingly successful Viennese debut as Mignon in early September 1899. Other major roles followed, initially in the *jugendlich-dramatisch* repertory, but later, and increasingly, in coloratura roles, after her phenomenal coloratura technique, including a flawless trill, was discovered more or less by chance. Her long trill quickly became her hallmark and can be heard on her many fine recordings, all of which attest to her uniqueness in this respect in the history of recorded sound. As with so many other high voices, anyone listening to these recordings today might wish for a little more emotion and expression, but this was the style at that time, a style common to all the virtuoso soprano roles in the French and Italian repertory. Inasmuch as Mahler was aware of certain weaknesses in this area, he was grateful for the fact that a singer of Selma Kurz's vocal stature almost literally fell into his lap.

His earliest notes and letters to her already reveal a particular affection. 'My dear little Kurz' is not the sort of salutation that he normally used for female singers. In the wake of his difficulties in dealing with the problem of Anna von Mildenburg, he had assured Rosa Papier and presumably himself as well that he would keep his distance from all the female members of his company, but in the case of Selma Kurz he quickly forgot his good intentions – what must Anna von Mildenburg have thought when she heard the rumours? After all, he had claimed that he would be driven from office if he continued his affair with her in Vienna.

Relations between Mahler and Selma Kurz became closer while they were rehearsing for the fifth Philharmonic concert in January 1900. Five of his own songs – two of the *Lieder eines fahrenden Gesellen* and three *Wunderhorn* settings – were sandwiched between works by Schumann and Berlioz. The local newspapers had already insinuated that Mademoiselle Kurz was Mahler's favourite singer, but even the elderly Eduard Hanslick was forced to concede that she had performed Mahler's 'extremely difficult' songs very well. Rumours were already rife even before the affair actually warranted such gossip. Anonymous letters circulated, even within the company, and since Mahler was never very circumspect in this regard, his more than artistic enthusiasm for the young soprano did not remain a secret for long. Events evidently took a decisive turn in Venice between 10 and 15 April 1900. Mahler left for Italy on 7 April, travelling via the Wörthersee and Abbazia in the company of Justine and Natalie. Purely by chance – or otherwise – Selma Kurz, too, happened to be in the city with an older female friend who acted as her chaperone, to use the somewhat malicious term of the time. Prior to the trip, Mahler had used the formal pronoun 'Sie' in his correspondence with the singer, but the very first note that he wrote on his return finds him adopting the intimate 'Du': 'My darling! I need to know how you are, whether the carriage was reserved, what your journey was like, how you slept and how you are. – I am still wearing everyone out and am most anxious to see you! Shall I see you for a moment this evening? Many *heart*felt greetings – your G.'[18]

The weeks that followed were extremely difficult for Kurz. Now twenty-five, she was, sexually speaking, almost certainly completely inexperienced but, as the director of the Vienna Court Opera repeatedly assured her, she had a great future ahead of her. She had been importuned by a director in the past, but now the situation was very different. Mahler was a different kind of person from Emil Claar in Frankfurt. Her elder by fifteen years, Mahler was a fascinating figure and his Jewishness was not a problem. But the fact that he was the director of the Vienna Court Opera weighed heavily on her mind. It is more than likely that in his impetuousness Mahler spoke of marriage, and yet this would have meant her giving up her career. We know from his relations with Anna von Mildenburg that Mahler thought no differently from most other men in his position. Whereas it may be possible today for the wife of a general administrator to be the company's prima donna, the practice is in dubious taste and was completely out of the question in Mahler's day. It was inconceivable that Mahler should resign and leave his wife to pursue her career, while it was equally out of the question that the soprano would move to Berlin or the Met, as this would have meant the couple's separation. And what about their children? It is all too easy to understand that Mahler should time and again have fallen for his female singers: their physical proximity in the rehearsal room and in the theatre, their shared love of opera, his gratitude for the singer's artistic, harmonious understanding and his monastic life outside his professional duties as a conductor – how else could he have found a wife, except perhaps among waitresses? And yet even on paper it is clear that

Mahler's notorious passion for his female singers was highly problematic, and it is no wonder that the woman whom he later married was not a performing artist but a young and inexperienced woman whose ambitions did not extend to opera, even if they included composition – and even this was ruled out by Mahler. All of these considerations must have flashed through Selma Kurz's mind. Although her letters to Mahler have not survived, there seems no reason to doubt that she was as passionate about him as he was about her, and yet she was still very young and insecure. Her advisers and maternal friends as well as her singing teacher would all have told her not to get involved or at least they would have counselled the most extreme caution. Much the same was true of Alma Schindler, but she, of course, chose to ignore all the nay-sayers.

Mahler's letters to his lover reflect his passion and nervous excitement and reveal how much he was taken aback by her fears and misgivings. The ability to empathize with others, especially with young women, was never one of his strong points. Thought processes and emotional worlds that were not his own were a closed book to him. At first he thought that the problems Selma Kurz was trying to deal with were the result of the ploys they were forced to adopt in public and of the need for secrecy whenever they met. His reaction to her evident complaints that he was too changeable was not very subtle but reveals the condescension of the older and wiser man that he also showed Alma Schindler: 'What you call my *moods* and what is grounded so deeply in my nature you do not yet understand because you are still too young to do so. That is why you often *mis*understand me. – But it doesn't mean that my love for you is wanting, still less that it is waning! Believe me – I was dumbstruck when I read this!'[19] Within days he seems to have sensed that he was losing Selma as she was not equal to the problems with which they were wrestling and that she thought he lacked the necessary certainty. The emphasis given to certain words in his letter to her is an indication of his strength of feeling and as such typical of a style that he always adopted whenever he was passionate about something:

> Selma, for God's sake, things simply *can't* go on like this! *Believe* me when I say that I love you and that my love is the *only* thing in my life and will always *remain* so! Just bear in mind that we are at the beginning of a long journey, a journey for which we need to be fresh, not *exhausted*. We must help each other. We are both affected by our *moods*, leading to the danger of constant *misunderstandings* even when we continue to assure each other that we *understand* one another! Let us continue to coexist, and let us *love* one another without worrying! [. . .] Yes, I am a complicated person – I'm often a mystery to myself – but this must be *one more reason* for you not to write me off as a subject of gossip and then to lower your *dear* little head just because

the cap happens to fit me on a purely superficial level. You should examine me yourself, my love – but don't *judge* me, just live and *love*! Only he who loves can see clearly![20]

Mahler was demanding too much. On the one hand, he was evidently not as devoted to the woman he loved as much as she might have expected (and here, too, we see behavioural patterns familiar from Mahler's later marriage), while on the other hand he showered her with his passion, presenting the young woman with insoluble problems for the future. How could a singer who had worked her way up from the poorest of backgrounds (a point that he should have understood very well) and who obviously had a major career ahead of her (this, too, should have been a familiar situation) guess that, far from 'judging' him, she should simply 'love' him? It is pointless to ask how he himself would have reacted if the roles had been reversed, for Mahler's thinking was no different from that of every other man at this period.

In the end the pressure proved too much for the singer, although it is not entirely clear why the relationship ended when it did. For Selma Kurz, the season in Vienna was over by the end of May and, physically and emotionally exhausted, she travelled to Marienbad to take the waters. Two weeks later Mahler set off for Paris to conduct three concerts with the Vienna Philharmonic at the Trocadéro and the Châtelet as part of the 1900 International Exhibition, where he also met Paul and Sophie Clemenceau, an acquaintanceship that was to prove very valuable. Mahler, too, was exhausted and unhappy with the way in which the concerts were promoted – it is said that they were announced as being 'Sous la direction de Monsieur Gustav MAHLHEUR'. Nor was he impressed by the acoustics of the Trocadéro. It is by no means unreasonable to assume that the severe migraine he suffered immediately before one of the concerts, forcing him to delay the start for half an hour while he lay, ashen-faced, in his dressing room, was bound up with the turbulent weeks that had just ended. By the time that he arrived at Maiernigg on the Wörthersee on 23 June – he had chosen the place the previous summer, although it was not until 1901 that his beautiful holiday home was to be built there – he could not go on. A letter that he wrote to Selma Kurz shortly after his arrival in Maiernigg shows that at least superficially he had recovered from the storms of the last few months. In it he strikes a note that is friendly but matter-of-fact and offers the soprano sound advice for looking after her voice and planning her future career. If we did not know the earlier letters, only the use of the familiar pronoun 'Du' would indicate what had taken place between the couple. The 'affair' lasted little more than six weeks, but it went deeper than is generally thought.

Selma Kurz was the last love of Mahler's life before Alma – with the exception of Alma, he was never again to be so infatuated with a woman. Perhaps the conclusion to be drawn from all this is that he would have done better to have married a singer and that for Mahler artistic accord was an essential ingredient of marriage, something he never achieved with Alma. Selma Kurz later married the distinguished Viennese surgeon Josef Halban, but it would appear from her daughter's volume of reminiscences that Mahler remained the great love of her life. Although her marriage was by no means unhappy, it burned only at a low heat, for she was incapable of recapturing the intensity of the weeks that she spent with Mahler. Her subsequent career was everything that she might have expected, and for decades she remained the darling of the Viennese, singing all over Europe and creating the role of Zerbinetta in the world première of the revised version of Strauss's *Ariadne auf Naxos* in 1916. She died in Vienna in 1933.

First Steps in the Direction of Reform

As we have already noted, Mahler's reform of Vienna's operatic scene pre-dates the production of *Tristan und Isolde* that opened in February 1903 but began on 11 May 1897 when he first raised his conductor's baton at the Vienna Court Opera. Some of his revolutionary measures have already been described: he banished the claque; he prevented latecomers from disturbing the performance; he lowered the house lights; both onstage and in the pit, he brought new and more rigorous standards to the works in the repertory; and he curtailed his singers' opportunities for extended leave of absence, when they could sign lucrative guest contracts with other houses. With his disciplinarian's gaze he would glower at latecomers as they tried to slip into the performance after the curtain had risen, and he would hiss at audiences that began to applaud during an important orchestral postlude or at the end of a scene. It is by no means far-fetched to claim that his behaviour acquired a certain attractiveness. Audiences wanted to be present when the new director was conducting and threw another of his famous tantrums. People everywhere spoke of his charisma with a mixture of admiration and awe. The name of the conductor was not mentioned on the daily playbills, and so most of the audience could not know who would be conducting the evening's performance until he appeared in the pit. It is said that a murmur would pass through the house whenever the small, pale man strode briskly towards the podium, his stormy features framed by a shock of black hair.

It was Mahler's first four years in Vienna that laid the foundations for the fascination and enthusiasm that he inspired in audiences and critics alike and that then allowed him to press ahead with even more far-reaching reforms. Such timing speaks volumes for the tactical skill of an artist said to be unworldly. His renewal of the repertory proceeded apace, but even antiquated productions that seemed to have reached the end of their days acquired a new lease of life when Mahler was conducting, and he proved a galvanizing influence after only a handful of rehearsals, in some cases re-studying the production. Curiously enough, his first entirely new production was Lortzing's *Zar und Zimmermann* – Mahler's attitude to German *Spieloper* was one of friendly respect, avoiding all sense of condescension. In turn this was followed by the local première of Smetana's *Dalibor*, a revival of *Die Zauberflöte*, the local première of *Eugene Onegin* and a new production of *Der fliegende Holländer*, all in the space of three months – no modern opera house would feel able to shoulder such a burden. That Mahler had no wish to be seen as a specialist in the German repertory is clear from his decision to mount performances of Bizet's *Djamileh*, Leoncavallo's *La Bohème*, a commitment that he took on complainingly but which he fulfilled to impressive effect, and Verdi's *Aida*. Verdi was far from being a favourite of his, and he would never have thought of equating Verdi and Wagner, yet he felt a certain respect for the Italian composer's later works. And, once he had assured himself that the musical apparatus was functioning effectively, he slowly began to take an interest in the staging of these works. Critical voices were first raised in October 1898, when he radically rethought the Wolf's Glen scene in a restudied production of *Der Freischütz*, replacing the usual ghost-train aesthetic by cloud projections on the backdrop and by the use of light and shade. But these changes were later silently reversed.

Shortly beforehand Mahler had conducted the first uncut performance of *Götterdämmerung* in the city, allowing the Norns to make their belated debut on the stage of the Vienna Court Opera and at the same time raising the question of how Wagner himself imagined them tossing the rope of destiny to one another. Mahler had enough experience of staging Wagner's works and of seeing them performed in Bayreuth to know that a literal presentation of this effect risked becoming involuntarily comic if the Norns failed to catch the rope. He instructed the singers to dispense with the rope completely and merely to mime the gestures. Fifty years later, Wieland Wagner could certainly have appealed to Mahler when staging this scene according to his New Bayreuth aesthetic.

Of course, Mahler was unable to conduct everything, and during his early years in Vienna he had to make do with Fuchs and Hellmesberger. Richter, too, was still on the music staff. It was an unsatisfactory situation, not least because Hellmesberger in particular was deeply rooted in mediocrity and made no secret of his hostility to Mahler. But an alternative conductor was soon found in Franz Schalk, whom Mahler knew and respected and who was brought to Vienna from Prague, becoming the house's principal conductor and from that point of view inheriting Richter's mantle. Richter was a far more distinguished conductor than

Jahn and had been the company's leading musical figure. Mahler knew his work from Bayreuth and respected him as a Wagner conductor, but he was undoubtedly right to think that for all his authority, Richter lacked even a vestige of genius: his performances may have been musically accurate, but for the most part they rarely came to life. None the less, Mahler showed him the respect that was his due and on taking up his new office wrote a scrupulously polite letter to which Richter replied with wounding coolness: once he had persuaded himself that Mahler's appointment would benefit the company, he would prove himself a good colleague.[21] Mahler never forgot this rebuff. Of course, Mahler's wish to shine as a Wagner conductor – and his brilliant debut in *Lohengrin* had proved that he could do so – was hardly calculated to make their long-term collaboration an attractive prospect. And with the exception of the anti-Semitic section of the press, Vienna's newspapers lavished such praise on Mahler's achievements that Richter felt that his own artistry had been impugned and began to think that all his good work for the company had suddenly been forgotten. It must remain an open question as to whether Richter, an old-guard Wagnerian and Bayreuthian, harboured anti-Semitic sentiments towards Mahler. Whatever the answer, he resigned in late February 1900 and withdrew to Manchester, where he was music director of the Hallé Orchestra. (One of his successors was John Barbirolli.) He also appeared frequently in London, where he had several useful contacts. He remained active as a conductor until 1911 – the year of Mahler's death – and then retired to Bayreuth. In consequence, it was Schalk who became Mahler's most important assistant. (Schalk became director of the Vienna State Opera after the First World War, for a time running the house in tandem with Strauss.)

But in 1901 Mahler also succeeded in luring Bruno Walter to Vienna. Walter was like a son to Mahler and remained loyal to him until his death, playing Kurwenal to Mahler's Tristan. In Vienna he was initially seen as a mere shadow of Mahler, not least on account of his youth, but he quickly developed a personality of his own. For a time they were joined by Ferdinand Löwe and, at the very end of Mahler's appointment in Vienna, by Alexander Zemlinsky, a former rival for the hand of Alma Schindler and now an outstanding opera conductor and a distinguished composer in his own right – Mahler conducted the first performance of his opera *Es war einmal*. But Zemlinsky was unable and, arguably, unwilling to remain in Vienna after Mahler left. Walter, conversely, remained until 1913, when he became general music director in Munich.

Richter's name is also associated with the musical directorship of the Vienna Philharmonic's concerts. Here, too, the changes that were necessary were very quickly implemented. The Vienna Philharmonic Orchestra had been founded by Otto Nicolai in 1842 from members of the Kärntnerthor-Theater orchestra, in other words, Court Opera musicians. By the time that Richter stepped down

as its principal conductor in September 1898 it could look back on a long
and glorious tradition. There had always been a close and, indeed, inevitable
link between the artistic directorship of the Philharmonic and the post of
conductor at the Court Opera. Richter had assumed this role on his arrival in
Vienna in 1875 and retained it until 1882, after which there was a twelve-
month interregnum, Richter's advocacy of Brahms – not yet the universally
admired composer that he was to become ten years later – gaining him a
number of enemies both inside the orchestra and within the wider public. For
a year, Jahn took over, but Richter then returned and held the post until 1898,
his twenty-two seasons in charge of the orchestra an impressive period in its
annals. It was only logical, of course, for Mahler to succeed him. If we ignore
the ineradicable anti-Semitism that accompanied Mahler wherever he
went, the initial relationship was entirely positive, not least because one of
Mahler's first acts on taking up his new post was to raise the salaries of the
orchestra's members. Such an action invariably improves relations, quite
apart from the fact that it was consistent with the social improvements that
Mahler had always championed for his musicians. Richter handed in his
notice, pleading health problems, not that these prevented him from fulfilling
his engagements in England. Mahler was elected the orchestra's new artistic
director on 24 September 1898. Richter had proposed him himself, his
alternative suggestion, Ferdinand Löwe, not being taken seriously. Mahler
immediately announced changes to the concert programmes, without,
however, going into detail. He had no interest in administration and rarely
attended the relevant meetings, an attitude immediately interpreted as
arrogance.

Mahler got off to a good start by programming the first complete performance of Bruckner's Sixth Symphony, but his decision to perform his own
Second Symphony on 9 April 1899 served merely to highlight the tensions
between at least a section of the orchestra and its new artistic director. It was
not that the performance was not a success. Indeed, the management of the
orchestra, whose members were court employees, specifically referred to the
success of the performance in its letter of thanks, but within the orchestra
there was a major coalition between its anti-Semitic members, the supporters
of Hans Richter who blamed Mahler for driving away their loyal vassal, and
those members who felt that music like Mahler's was unworthy of them. For a
long time the following season's concerts hung in the balance as a faction in the
orchestra tried to persuade Richter to return. Only when Richter declined and
Mahler, both scandalized and mortified, had kept the orchestra in suspense,
was a vote of confidence taken. Only then did Mahler agree to conduct the
next season's subscription concerts. The visit to the International Exhibition in
Paris in June 1900 – it was the orchestra's first foreign tour – proved sufficiently

successful to defuse the situation, although it had been preceded by a genuine scandal when Mahler had introduced a number of his own instrumental revisions to a performance of Beethoven's Ninth Symphony on 1 April. This is not the place to discuss the controversial question of Mahler's aim in undertaking changes both here and elsewhere, changes that often amounted to more than mere retouchings.

Mahler's working relationship with the Vienna Philharmonic continued to be fuelled by resentment and broke down completely in November 1900, when he conducted the local première of his First Symphony, the failure of which was almost complete. As we have noted, Hanslick held Mahler in high regard as the director of the Vienna Court Opera, but he concluded to his consternation that the new work belonged to a kind of music that to him was not music at all. (Even Mahler himself repeatedly conceded that his First Symphony was an extraordinarily difficult piece, more difficult, indeed, than its three successors.) Mahler could hardly be surprised that his audience, for the most part, refused to follow him. But he never forgave the orchestra for abandoning him on the platform, leaving him to face the booing alone, while the expression on their faces revealed their wish to distance themselves from the proceedings. From now on their relationship was irreparably soured, resulting in endless arguments whenever Mahler tried to curtail the players' activities away from the Court Opera and Philharmonic concerts or when he insisted that they should wear evening dress at opera performances – another of his reforms. He resigned as concert conductor in April 1901, explaining in his letter to the orchestra that his workload at the Opera and his health made it impossible for him to continue in the post. His reference to his health was not entirely far-fetched for only a short time earlier he had suffered from serious intestinal bleeding, a condition to which we shall shortly return. Even so, it remains a fact that at no point in his life had he worried about his own health when the task in hand was a matter close to his heart. The fact that his successor was none other than 'Pepi' Hellmesberger will have demonstrated to him that however wonderfully the orchestra may have played, it was not a sounding board for his own artistic goals in the concert hall – an orchestra capable of replacing him with Hellmesberger clearly had difficulty respecting his own high musical standards. It says much for the orchestra's professionalism that for the next six years their work with Mahler in the opera house was largely unproblematic and even committed. And we should also remember that Mahler's enemies were far from occupying every desk in the orchestra: Arnold Rosé, who was shortly to become his brother-in-law, was by no means alone in acknowledging Mahler's genius.

Never again did Mahler have to work as hard as he did during these early years in Vienna. His Herculean conducting achievement had to be combined with directorial responsibilities. This excessive workload led not only to an almost total suspension of his compositional plans, it also meant that his private life was practically non-existent – and even for an individual as ascetic as Mahler, this was an imposition. Everything he did was related to his work and his own creative endeavours. His extended vacations, with their physical exertions, were ultimately intended to toughen up his body, whose failings he recognized or suspected, and prepare himself for the tasks that lay ahead. Above all he needed to prepare for his work as a composer, which was for the most part restricted to the holidays, while the little free time that he had during the rest of the year, when he was busy conducting, had to be set aside for revising and elaborating his sketches and drafts.

The summer of 1897 had proved compositionally unproductive as a result of his frequent changes of address, while the following summer was spent recovering from another operation, during which he retired to the Villa Artmann at Vahrn in the South Tyrol, where he managed to complete only two *Wunderhorn* settings, 'Das Lied des Verfolgten im Turm' and 'Wo die schönen Trompeten blasen'. In 1899 Mahler and his entourage – now that Emma was married, it normally consisted only of Justine and Natalie – planned to spend the summer near Losenstein on the Enns but were unable to find suitable lodgings and so they moved on to Alt-Aussee, where they were visited by Siegfried Lipiner and, for a time, Arnold Rosé, whose presence seems not to have aroused Mahler's suspicions as far as Justine was concerned. Initially, it seemed as if the summer would pass by without any major compositional achievement, but then Mahler suddenly succeeded in drafting his Fourth Symphony in a single burst of creativity, allowing him to complete the work during the summer of 1900. Normal guest houses proved unsuited to such bursts of creativity, providing Mahler with a painful reminder of the long and unclouded idyll that he had enjoyed at Steinbach on the Attersee. Justine and Natalie decided to do what they could to help, and once Mahler had returned to Vienna, they set off in search of a permanent alternative. While visiting the Wörthersee, they bumped into Anna von Mildenburg, who contacted an amateur architect, Alfred Theuer, who himself owned a villa in Maiernigg. Theuer explained that it would ultimately be preferable for Mahler to build a holiday home of his own rather than renting a place and recommended a site that the owner was willing to sell on the shores of the lake near the village. There was also the possibility of leasing the land in the forest on the hillside above the house. Here a 'composing hut' could be built along the lines of the property at Steinbach, even if it would not command a view of the lake.

Mahler was summoned from Vienna and arrived in Maiernigg on 18 August 1899. He was satisfied with all the arrangements, and the purchase agreement was signed in September. Work on the building took longer than planned, with the result that in 1900 Mahler was unable to sleep in the new house and had to take rooms at the Villa Antonia. The 'composing hut', conversely, was already finished, so that for the first time since Steinbach he could work undisturbed from early morning to lunchtime. It was against this background that he was able to make rapid progress on his Fourth Symphony. By the following year the villa, too, was finished, and the summer months were almost uniquely productive from a compositional standpoint: Mahler completed the bulk of the *Kindertotenlieder* and made headway on his Fifth Symphony. Even today this setting impresses the visitor with its beauty, although the villa itself, now in private hands, is closed to the public. Mahler will not have imagined that he would ever have to abandon it. But in the summer of 1907 events took place that destroyed the idyll, and he never went back to the Wörthersee.

Let us return, however, to Mahler's serious illness in February 1901. On the 24th of the month he again had a busy schedule. During the day he conducted a lunchtime performance of Bruckner's Fifth Symphony, his final appearance with the Philharmonic – the psychological burden of his altercations with the orchestra will have left him emotionally drained. And in the evening he conducted *Die Zauberflöte* at the Court Opera. Later that night his health took a catastrophic turn for the worse. In a previously unpublished passage in her reminiscences, Natalie Bauer-Lechner reports that

> On Sunday night, to our extreme horror, Gustav suffered an intestinal haem-
> orrhage, and only the timely intervention of the doctor saved his life. The
> haemorrhage was so sudden and so violent that Gustav would have bled to
> death if he hadn't had a telephone, allowing Justi to summon Dr Singer, who,
> after various fruitless efforts of his own, was able to summon the surgeon
> Herr Hohenegg. ('An hour later and it would have been too late,' the latter
> said afterwards.) Gustav had already lost a lot of blood before he woke Justi,
> whom he had been reluctant to disturb. She found him in a pool of blood that
> Dr Singer was unable to staunch in spite of the iced water that he poured over
> him and bathed him in. Hohenegg finally stopped the flow of blood by vigor-
> ously tamponing the bleeding.

According to Natalie, Mahler later told her that 'As I stood on the threshold between life and death, I thought – as we are all bound to believe in such things – that it would almost have been better to have passed over straight-away! There seemed nothing terrible about quitting this life when one has put one's affairs in order. Indeed, I was almost repelled by the idea of returning to life.'[22] This dramatic account of the events on the night of the 24 February 1901 is unlikely to have been over-dramatized, although the world at large remained in the dark about the threat to Mahler's life. It provides us with a suitable opportunity to consider the history of Mahler's illnesses, an account that is bound to lead us to conclude that although he was a powerful swimmer and a tireless hiker who shouldered an unbelievable workload he, none the less, suffered from ill health throughout his adult life.

Mahler's Illnesses:
A Pathographical Sketch

'He was very often ill'
Anna Mahler on her father

'THIS IS HOW it is with typhus.' Thus begins the brief penultimate chapter of Thomas Mann's *Buddenbrooks*, after which the author describes in detail the aetiology of a typhoid sufferer, a description which, gleaned from scientific textbooks, was typical of Mann's whole methodology. By the end of the chapter, the reader knows that even though no patient is mentioned by name, it is young Hanno Buddenbrooks who is being described. At the end of the previous chapter we were told that while rhapsodizing so ecstatically at the piano, the boy was very pale and weak-kneed. It is Hanno whose death is laconically mourned in the final chapter, the musically highly gifted lad having succumbed to this hideous proletarian illness rather than to consumption, which in the nineteenth century was a sign of greater refinement. Mahler died from neither typhus nor tuberculosis nor even – and in spite of repeated claims to the contrary – from the egotistical brutality of his wife. (We shall consider Alma's contribution to her husband's final illness at a later point in our narrative.) He died from subacute bacterial endocarditis, or endocarditis lenta, an inflammation of the internal wall of the heart caused by a streptococcal infection. If the body was insufficiently strong to ward off the bacterial attack – and Mahler's previously weakened heart valves placed him in this category – then there was nothing that contemporary medicine could have done to help. There were no antibiotics to deal with such an illness, although even today endocarditis remains a serious and even a life-threatening condition.

The fifty-year-old Mahler was already relatively old, although his physical condition, albeit weakened by his diseased mitral valve, was otherwise sound. Indeed, he was in many respects astonishingly fit. He had been overworked throughout his whole life, and yet he had never collapsed beneath this burden.

Nor can it be said that he deliberately undermined his own health by overwork
or by alcohol or nicotine, both of which he enjoyed in moderation. But by the
autumn of 1910 he was beginning to suffer from a series of severe sore throats
which, more severe than any earlier symptoms in this regard, left him considerably weakened. It was not until 1928 that Alexander Fleming discovered
penicillin and, with it, the later use of antibiotics as a form of medical treatment, and a further twelve years were to pass before this treatment was put
into practice by Howard Florey and Ernst Chain. In short, it would have made
no difference if Mahler had contracted this illness ten years later. We shall later
have occasion to examine in greater detail this final illness, the onset of which
appears from all that we now know to date from the time of the rehearsals for
his Eighth Symphony in Munich in September 1910. Our present concern is to
see to what extent Mahler was a sick man all his life.

Even the briefest glance at Mahler's family history suggests that as far as
physical fitness goes, their genetic makeup was not of the best. Mahler's father
lived until he was sixty-two, his mother until she was fifty-two. From a
nineteenth-century perspective, this could be considered a good age. Indeed,
there is a certain irony to the fact that Marie Mahler was always seen as sickly,
the births of her fourteen children having left her physically worn out. And yet
in spite of this, she lived to be older than her son. It must give us pause for
thought that she is believed to have suffered not only from a bad hip or leg
but also from a weak heart, from which she presumably died – the surviving
sources make it impossible to be more precise. But it is striking that Mahler's
siblings died while they were still comparatively young, certainly far younger
than was normal in the second half of the nineteenth century. That only six out
of a total of fourteen children survived infancy is unusual in a family that
did not exactly live in the Iglau sewers. No documents have survived to indicate the cause of death of these infants, although it is striking that they were
all Mahler's brothers, whereas two of his sisters lived to be relatively old. The
third sister, Leopoldine, appears to have died of a brain tumour when she was
twenty-six. Justine lived to be seventy – she died in Vienna in August 1938 –
and Emma was fifty-eight when she died in Weimar in 1933. It is believed that
Ernst, whose death in 1875 at the age of only thirteen, left the young Mahler
deeply affected, succumbed to pericarditis, an inflammation of the membrane
enclosing the heart that at the time was generally ascribed to tuberculosis.
Alois, who has gone down in the family history as a wastrel who emigrated
to the United States, where he became a tolerably dependable if inconspicuous member of American society, evidently died of chronic myocarditis, an
inflammation of the muscular tissue of the heart often due to alcohol abuse. In
other words, two of Mahler's brothers, as well as his mother, died of heart
disease. In the case of neither Ernst nor Alois was there any question of a heart

attack but of ongoing conditions leading to irreparable damage to the heart. It is surely unusual to find so many coronary disorders within a single family and it suggests that there was a genetic predisposition within the Mahler family, even if such a diagnosis cannot be supported by any evidence.

In the case of Mahler, too, a heart condition was diagnosed four years before his final illness and independent of that illness. The episode in question took place in Maiernigg in July 1907. His daughter Maria died on the 12th and in the wake of her death Mahler's mother-in-law suffered a 'heart spasm' and Alma fainted. The local doctor, Carl Blumenthal, was summoned, and Mahler took the opportunity to ask him to examine his own heart, too. Regular health checks were totally alien to Mahler's whole nature and, indeed, unusual at this period. It seems likely that until then he had consulted doctors only when he was acutely ill. At all events, it is unlikely that he had ever had his heart examined: only auscultation was available at this time, electrocardiograms and X-ray examinations still lying far in the future. Blumenthal is said to have commented: 'Well, you've no cause to be proud of a heart like that.' Alma's comment, 'This verdict marked the beginning of the end for Mahler',[1] reflects her own medical ignorance and represents a completely unnecessary over-dramatization of the actual facts of the case. Understandably worried, Mahler immediately returned to Vienna and was re-examined by a heart specialist, Friedrich Kovacs, who, according to Alma's unsupported testimony, diagnosed a compensated congenital heart valve defect, a formulation which, medically speaking, is difficult to sustain. After all, no doctor at this period could ascertain whether a heart defect was congenital or acquired. If Mahler's defect had been congenital, then he is unlikely to have reached the age that he did. And if the valvular defect was compensated (and, as we have noted, Mahler had an extraordinary ability to push himself to the very limits of his physical endurance), then there could be no question of the beginning of the end, for Mahler had demonstrated with his physical and intellectual exertions that he was fitter than most people of his age – he was forty-seven when this diagnosis was made.

A second doctor in Vienna, Franz Hamperl, offered a less dramatic diagnosis in the form of a mild mitral stenosis. In other words, only one of the valves between the left vestibule and the left ventricle was slightly narrower than normal as a result of changes caused by inflammation, so that its function was somewhat impaired. Possibly it was a combined mitral vitium, meaning that the mitral valve did not close properly and tended to leak, while at the same time it did not open sufficiently. In turn this would lead to coronary insufficiency. But if, in the view of Mahler's doctors, his heart defect was 'compensated', then this would mean that the body had learnt to cope with a long-standing defect without showing any of the symptoms usually associated with such insufficiency, namely, shortage of breath and swollen legs, neither of which is attested in Mahler's case. Be that as it may, this diagnosis was far from being a death sentence for a man like Mahler who, by contemporary reckoning, had already completed three-quarters of his life expectancy without apparently suffering from any heart condition. Today the heart valve would probably be replaced, but such an operation was still a distant prospect in Mahler's day. Hamperl's diagnosis also had the advantage of ultimately allowing Mahler to ignore Kovacs's strict instructions to avoid all forms of strenuous exercise, which would have meant a complete change in Mahler's lifestyle.

Above all, the total avoidance of all physical activity beyond the occasional stroll – in other words, a ban on swimming and hiking – briefly turned Mahler into a hypochondriac who kept stopping to check his pulse. For a time he had followed Kovacs's orders, which admittedly reflected the current state of knowledge, but he soon noticed that his physical fitness was unimpaired and that it was now the lack of physical exercise that was making him ill. So he reverted to his former practices, albeit reducing them slightly, and was delighted to discover that they did him the world of good. On more than one occasion he reassured his friends that he felt as fit as he had done in the past. At least until the autumn of 1910 there can be no question of a serious deterioration in Mahler's health, as one would have expected with someone suffering from a weak heart. In short, Alma's claim that Blumenthal's diagnosis marked the beginning of the end for Mahler is no more than a widow over-dramatizing the situation.

Hamperl's diagnosis was to be confirmed by Mahler's final fatal illness. When Emanuel Libman of Mount Sinai Hospital in New York was asked for a second opinion by the Mahlers' regular doctor in the city, Joseph Fraenkel, he too found that in addition to endocarditis there was also an older, chronic mitral-valve defect with a presystolic-systolic heart murmur. But it must be stressed that this heart defect was not the cause of Mahler's death, even if it was a decisive factor in rendering his heart non-resistant to bacterial infection. We can no longer say whether a healthy heart would have succumbed to such a bacterial attack at a time when there was no known remedy, and yet it is correct to say that, medically speaking, such a valve defect is classified as a 'locus minoris resistentiae' – a point at which bacterial pathogenics such as the streptococcus that causes endocarditis can settle more readily than in healthy parts of the heart, not least because the inflammation leads to an enlargement of the surfaces that can serve as a colonization area.

In spite of all its imponderables, this diagnosis leads us, remarkably, to Mahler's twitching leg. When considering this characteristic, we already adduced the theory that this tic was a throwback to a childhood illness, chorea minor, more popularly known as St Vitus's Dance. If Mahler did indeed suffer from this illness as a child, then it is not unlikely that his mitral-valve defect remained as a consequence, albeit undetected, a diagnosis that has repeatedly been proposed by writers on the subject. The problem is that the evidence that Mahler suffered from this particular type of chorea is so slender that we simply cannot be certain: in short, the connection between his twitching leg and a childhood chorea is impossible to prove. In the case of a person as highly strung as Mahler, we may simply be looking at a nervous tic that he was not always able to control. In much the same way, it was only with difficulty that he was able to stop biting his fingernails at moments of nervous tension. This may or may not have been the case. Whatever the answer, it is likely that Mahler's mitral stenosis was the fatal consequence of a rheumatic illness or similar disease, and when we examine the frequency of Mahler's generally severe attacks of tonsillitis, then the link becomes more than likely: his striking susceptibility to this complex of symptoms may more plausibly be seen as the starting point for his final fatal illness than any congenitally weak heart.

One of our earliest indications of Mahler's extreme susceptibility to sore throats is a letter that he wrote to his friend Friedrich Löhr in the summer of 1885, when he was twenty-five. He was staying in Iglau and mentions that he has just recovered from a sore throat. It is never entirely clear what he understood by this term: was it a simple inflammation of the pharynx (pharyngitis), streptoc-cocal angina (an acute inflammation of the tonsils and pharynx) or a specific inflammation of the pharyngeal and/or palatine tonsils? Tonsillitis has long been treated by antibiotics and by a routine operation involving either a tonsillectomy (removal of the palatine tonsils) or an adenotomy (removal of the pharyngeal tonsils) as such illnesses often recur; and in the case of pathologically altered tonsils that frequently become infected, the pathogens may enter the blood-stream, causing other organs to become infected and leading to rheumatic disease, pyelitis and endocarditis. In some cases this may also mean the valvular heart defect from which Mahler suffered. It is more than likely that at some point in his life one of Mahler's illnesses pursued a course of this nature, and his biggest mistake, for which he himself must take full responsibility, is that he never underwent a tonsillectomy, which would have been entirely possible at this time, even if expensive and not without risk. A painful convalescence would also have been involved.

The point of no return clearly came in May–June 1897. Mahler had just taken up his new post as conductor at the Vienna Court Opera when a partic-ularly severe sore throat left him so weak that he was seriously ill for a month or more. This may have been the tonsillitis that led to his valvular heart defect. It started as a sore throat that he hoped to get over fairly quickly but which led to a relapse, forcing him to take to his bed again. As was often to be the case with such attacks, an abscess formed directly behind or next to his palatine

tonsils, a development that even today would be seen as a serious complication. In Mahler's day, too, it was customary to open the abscess surgically and
drain away the pus. But such an abscess can return, especially if the affected
tonsil or tonsils are not removed. A century ago it was unusual to combine
these two methods – lancing the abscess and, at the same time, removing the
palatine tonsils. Instead, doctors preferred to wait for the abscess to clear up
before considering whether to operate on the tonsils. A letter that Mahler
wrote to Anna von Mildenburg on 12 June 1897 indicates that his doctors
planned to perform this operation and that even at this date they assumed a
chronic condition: 'My throat is still in a dreadful state, and I fear I am going
to have to put up with one or two more abscesses. It appears, from what the
surgeon says, I have a neglected catarrh of the nose and throat and I have to
undergo daily treatment with silver nitrate. When I come back in August I
have to undergo another radical operation.'[2] At this point we could quote Alma
and argue that the beginning of Mahler's end dates from his decision, fourteen
years before his death, not to go ahead with this operation, which was presumably to remove his tonsils, a decision that stemmed from the fact that
outwardly, at least, he appeared to have made a full recovery and was afraid of
the painful recovery process that would follow an operation. No doubt he also
thought that he would have no time for what he regarded as a triviality. But in
this way he ensured that the focus of the disease, presumably already present
in his throat, was allowed to develop.

A further chance to intervene occurred at a later date, but by then it was almost
certainly too late. Following a severe sore throat during the rehearsals for the first
performance of his Eighth Symphony in Munich, Mahler consulted his doctor on
his return to Vienna in September 1910. The latter was no doubt in favour of a
tonsillectomy but according to Alma, he preferred not to operate because Mahler
was so sensitive to pain. Instead, he made do with cauterizing the affected area, as
he had done in 1909. During previous years he had suffered numerous severe
throat infections. In January 1901, for example, Natalie Bauer-Lechner reports
that Mahler rehearsed Beethoven's Ninth Symphony in a wretched, enfeebled
state that recurred in the middle of March 1902, when he conducted three
concerts in St Petersburg. We may assume that in his letters Mahler never
mentioned any minor attacks of this kind but only the more serious ones. Such
an attack came in September 1910, when he was rehearsing in Munich. His
temperature evidently continued to rise, as is typical of such illnesses. Afraid that
such a troublesome illness would render him unfit for work, Mahler immediately
had himself wrapped in hot packs, while the concert promoter, Emil Gutmann,
used hand towels to wipe away the floods of perspiration. Like many of
Mahler's other friends and admirers, Lilli Lehmann came to Munich for the
performance and was shocked to discover how sickly Mahler looked. Many other

observers commented on his appearance, too: he was as white as a sheet, his dark eyes burnt like coals in his ashen face, and it was only with the greatest effort that he was able to summon up his last remaining reserves of strength to conduct a performance that was to prove the greatest triumph of his career.

In retrospect Bruno Walter felt that Mahler was already marked out by death, an observation that is not entirely wide of the mark, for all that it is all too easy to see such links with hindsight. None the less, everything points to the fact that this severe sore throat, which he was unable to treat because of his concern for his symphony and which may in any case have been incurable, sowed the seeds of the illness that returned in New York in December 1910, leading to his final fatal illness two months later. It was a vicious circle to which Mahler ultimately succumbed, for it is highly likely that a severe sore throat – whether it was during his childhood or adolescence or not until 1897 is immaterial – led to the damage to his mitral valve. As a result of the accompanying bouts of fever, the increasingly severe sore throats and worsening attacks of tonsillitis that can no longer be distinguished from one another led to a further weakening of a body which even when it was healthy had been placed under severe strain by an altogether superhuman workload. By September 1910 Mahler's constitution was so weakened that it was unable to resist the new streptococcal attack that was concentrated on the already damaged heart and, more particularly, the heart's weakest point, the morbidly affected mitral valve. It was here that the infection settled and, finding a welcoming host, it spread to the rest of the body, finally leading to a breakdown of the body's entire defences.

It is unclear whether there were already signs of Mahler's heart defect before the latter was diagnosed in the summer of 1907. There are two independent accounts by reliable witnesses, Alfred Roller and Bruno Walter, who report that during rehearsals for a gala performance of *Lohengrin* in November 1905 Mahler kept rushing to and fro between stage and pit, moving the soloists and chorus members around the stage with a display of physical strength that onlookers found hard to credit, when Mahler suddenly stood still and clutched his heart. Both Roller and Walter were deeply shocked by such an unexpected move. But this cannot be regarded as the start of Mahler's fatal illness as it may simply have been an isolated instance of arrhythmia or nothing more serious than a stabbing pain in the chest. In itself the evidence is not compelling.

When compared to this causal link between Mahler's chronic bouts of tonsillitis and his final heart disease, all other ailments from which he suffered pale into insignificance. They none the less deserve to be mentioned as they complete our picture of Mahler's health, a picture that seems so depressing.

The second ailment from which Mahler suffered was haemorrhoids. Then as now this was an embarrassing complaint and to that extent it is less well documented, and yet there can be no doubt that in Mahler's case it was a serious, recurring ailment. We know practically nothing about Mahler's first recorded operation for haemorrhoids on 7 July 1889. He was then twenty-nine, unusually young for such an operation, for the swollen veins in the rectum and wall of the anus normally occur only in older people. None the less, this is an extraordinarily common complaint affecting some 80 per cent of the population at some point in their lives. Mahler suffered renewed internal bleeding in the autumn of 1893 and again in June 1895. On 3 September 1895 he wrote to Natalie Bauer-Lechner to tell her that the bleeding had started again and that he had no means of dealing with the problem – he had learnt by now to adopt a rather more candid approach to the subject and had no inhibitions about telling a female friend about his malaise.[3] On 24 February 1901, as we have already noted, he suffered the worst bleeding of his life. Although some sources claim that it took place during a performance of *Die Zauberflöte*, the severity of the haemorrhaging suggests that it began only afterwards. Whatever the truth of the matter, his doctors described it as life-threatening, tempting us to think that with Mahler everything was more dramatic than with other people, for haemorrhoidal bleeding is rarely life-threatening. In Mahler's case, however, it seems as if a serious vascular weakness had led to severe rectal diverticulation. The bleeding was finally staunched by tamponing the rectum, sitz baths and iced water having failed to help. Shortly afterwards Mahler underwent an operation, although its exact nature is unclear. Presumably it involved a total excision that dealt with the problem comprehensively as there are no further references to this particular ailment in Mahler's subsequent medical history. The only mystery remains an entry in Alma's diaries in January 1902 reporting 'an inflamed swelling' that was reduced by means of 'icebags, hot baths etc.'. Alma wondered whether it was 'because I resisted him so long', in other words, because she refused to have sexual intercourse with him. It remains unclear whether the swelling was in the region of the anus or if it affected the penis.[4]

A further tiresome chronic complaint that dogged Mahler throughout his life was his tendency to suffer from migraines. We have already mentioned the attack before his concert with the Vienna Philharmonic in Paris in June 1900, when he lay in his dressing room, as white as chalk, unable to move, with the result that the concert began half an hour late. (According to one source, the cause was annoyance at an anti-Semitic jibe from the orchestra.) Mahler suffered another severe migraine during his visit to St Petersburg in March 1902, which was also the newlyweds' honeymoon, allowing Alma to gain a clear idea of the health of a man who she had been warned was 'degenerate'. It is worth bearing in mind that at this time migraines were considered a woman's ailment. Statistically speaking, it is almost certainly the case that even today more women suffer from migraines than men. In Mahler's case this should not be taken to imply that he merely suffered from headaches of greater or lesser severity. Among his symptoms, rather, were extreme sensitivity to light and nausea, including vomiting, reducing him to a state of almost death-like paralysis. Mahler reacted with extreme sensitivity to all departures from his normal routine: if his hotel room or railway compartment was too warm (he preferred his bedroom to be cool or even cold) and if the meal at the inn disagreed with him, he would find himself suffering from a migraine. Aspirin and brisk walks were his way of dealing with less serious attacks, but they generally left him incapable of working, a condition that a high achiever like Mahler found hard to accept. Alma must have been reminded of a malicious remark by her friend Felix Muhr, who claimed that a doctor had told him that Mahler was incurably ill and growing perceptibly weaker, a remark made in December 1901, shortly before she and Mahler became engaged. Her reaction is significant, for she always believed that she was placing excessive demands on Mahler with a sexual appetite that she preferred to regard as a force of nature: 'Dear God, I shall nurse him like a child. I'll not be the cause of his downfall. I shall curb my longing & my passion – I want to make him better – restore him to health through my strength and youth, my beloved master.'[5] But when she thought that she had suffered enough privation and was squandering her strength and youth, she abandoned all pretence at self-sacrifice and lavished her unbridled passion and desire on Walter Gropius instead.

Mahler's problems were not restricted to his throat, anus and head but affected his entire gastro-intestinal tract. His life was marked by a whole series of contradictory diets, none of which he ever maintained for long, veering between a vegetarian regime and salted and smoked meat, and between whole-meal bread and pancakes with raisins, regardless of whether such experiments were good for him or not. On this point, too, he adopted his usual precept: however much the body might rebel, it still had to obey him. Mahler evidently had a particularly delicate digestive system. Indeed, it could be said that all his organs were more sensitive than those of ordinary mortals. As a result, his private remarks are full of references to his poor digestion, to air in his stomach, to stomach cramps and much else besides. Only towards the end of his life do things seem to have settled down.

If we add to this litany of complaints the recurrent mouth ulcers that can also lead to endocarditis, the occasional bout of lumbago and the spells of dizziness from which Mahler suffered at bedtime and which he finally reports having got rid of in the summer of 1905, we have a picture of dismaying clarity: throughout his life Mahler was seriously and chronically sick. At this point it would be possible, of course, to present the boldest conjectures on the link between genius and illness as proposed by Wilhelm Lange-Eichbaum, although there can be no question of any connection between genius and madness as propounded by Cesare Lombroso. One thinks of Franz Kafka and his lifelong obsession with his physical infirmities, including the years that he spent preoccupied with his pulmonary complaint, and its connection with his creative neurosis. It is tempting to presuppose such a link with Mahler, too, and, indeed, such a link has occasionally been advanced by writers on the subject,[6] but with unconvincing results. It is impossible to avoid the conclusion that although Mahler was chronically ill, he never felt that he was and never behaved as such. At least until the time of his final fatal illness, he clearly succeeded in regarding all physical disorders as disagreeable side effects of life, dealing with them without delay in order to be able to devote himself once again to his work. He is unlikely to have given any thought to the links between these recurrent problems, his medical knowledge being so limited that he did not regard a 'chronic sore throat' as a threat and never thought that such symptoms might have any more serious consequences. Only the diagnosis of his valvular heart defect threw him. But when far-reaching changes to his lifestyle turned out to be unnecessary he again felt subjectively well and, while he appears not to have forgotten the diagnosis entirely, he dealt with the information by repressing it.

Mahler's restless energy was no neurotic product of a permanent obsession with death, and the symptoms that we have described cannot be interpreted as evidence of a psychosomatic disorder, even if some of these symptoms invite psychosomatic explanations. Throughout his entire life he was manifestly preoccupied by the idea of death, but in a way that is true of all creative artists. His work proclaims this preoccupation, which varied only in its intensity over the course of his life. He would undoubtedly have subscribed to Thomas Mann's conviction in *The Magic Mountain* that we should prefer goodness and love and never allow death to dominate our thoughts. However remarkable it must seem, Mahler never regarded himself as someone who had been allotted just a short life. Only during his final illness would this thought have occurred to him, and even then there were moments when he was filled with hope and asked for medication to support his increasingly weakened heart.

On one point Alma was undoubtedly right, when she accused her husband of lacking the instinct for self-preservation.[7] He hated mollycoddling, not because he was obsessed with the notion of physical exercise but because he regarded it as a sin against the mind to allow the body to degenerate to the point when it could no longer meet the mind's demands. He once grew very agitated when his younger daughter Anna Justine – 'Gucki' – caught a chill. He was furious with her for having done so in spite of all attempts to toughen her up during their vacation in Toblach: 'We've made her go bare-legged, we've forbidden her warm clothing, and all that's come of it is – anaemia. Sad!'[8] For Mahler, illness and weakness were symptoms of an incorrect lifestyle, not the workings of fate to which we are haplessly exposed and which we need to counter by taking care of ourselves. As far as we know, Mahler consulted his doctor only when it was no longer possible to avoid doing so.

We may also observe this lack of any instinct for self-preservation whenever Mahler attempted to counter organic weaknesses by means of harsh measures, on which point, it is true, he was influenced by the beliefs of his own day. He tried various radical diets in an attempt to deal with his obviously weak stomach and intestines, not realizing that in the case of gastritis and other digestive disorders a combination of wholemeal bread and raw fruit and vegetables, however fashionable it may have been, was not necessarily the ideal solution. In spite of her inadequate medical knowledge, Alma was right when she told Mahler not to jump into the cold waters of the Wörthersee while his body was still hot from sunbathing, then to spend hours swimming in the lake before lying in the hot sun again, a routine he repeated several times a day. Unfortunately, her advice went unheeded. For a man who suffered from severe sore throats and tonsillitis, this was not an appropriate form of behaviour, but Mahler refused to see this and felt that he was right to try to toughen himself up in this way.

Karl Kraus spoke of Mahler taking up his new appointment in Vienna 'with the panache of a Siegfried', and it is indeed difficult not to be reminded here of Siegfried arriving at the Gibichung court in *Götterdämmerung*, when the hero introduces himself to the men who are to become his mortal enemies: 'I can offer you neither lands nor men, nor a father's house and court: I inherited only this body of mine; living, I waste it away.' Towards the end of his life, and under the influence of various philosophical writings to which we shall later return and which include the works of Gustav Theodor Fechner and Eduard von Hartmann, Mahler became ever more convinced that the body, with all its infirmities, was merely a mortal shell for the creative force that dwells within all creatures. Higher individuals, by which he understood creative men and women, had a kind of awareness of this creative energy working away within them, and they saw it as a challenge to rise to this task, hence the striving and permanent unrest, as Mahler called it, that constituted the artist's happiness and unhappiness – happiness in the few moments of perfection in a work, and unhappiness in the artist's constant struggle to deal with the adversities of life that stood in the way of his creativity. In an important letter that he wrote to Alma in the summer of 1909,[9] Mahler even went so far as to argue that works which are often described as immortal and that include *Die Meistersinger von Nürnberg*, Beethoven's Ninth Symphony, Goethe's *Faust* and, we may assume, his own symphonies, were mere husks, outer shells, like the bodies of the artists who created them. In spite of this, the products of this creative energy are necessary as manifestations that allow the individual to grow and that bring joy to the creator and to those who constitute the audience of these works. Like Fechner, Mahler regarded death as a transitional stage in our lives, just as the individual life was such a stage. In turn this explains why even during the serious crises of 1907 and 1910 Mahler neither longed for death nor feared it. And it also explains why he was unable to ascribe to the often serious symptoms of his manifold illnesses the importance that should ordinarily be ascribed to them.

The Fourth Symphony

W HEN THE DÜSSELDORF conductor Julius Buths informed Mahler of his decision to perform the composer's Fourth Symphony in the city in November 1903, Mahler wrote back to express his delight:

> So you mean to try to do the Fourth? This persecuted step-child that has so far known so little joy in the world. *I* am tremendously glad you like the work, and I can only hope that an audience educated by you will feel and understand as you do. My own experience in general has been that humour of this type (as distinct from wit or good humour) is frequently not recognized even by the best of audiences.[1]

When Mahler had conducted the first performance of his Fourth Symphony with the Kaim Orchestra in Munich in 1901, the work had found few friends. Prior to this performance, Mahler had run through the work with the Vienna Philharmonic, when the musicians had shown their old stubbornness with regard to his music, causing Mahler to complain with peculiar bitterness: 'And it is on this miserable rubbish-heap that I have to make a blossoming world arise!'[2] It had all sounded far too powerful, the finely spun threads of the work being covered by the broad brush strokes of the orchestra. For the present Mahler consoled himself with the thought that all the old animosities were to blame for this negative impression. The Munich orchestra was far better disposed towards him, even if it failed to reach the same high performance standards. Mahler took with him to Munich a young soprano from the Vienna Court Opera, Margarete Michalek, with whom his name has been amorously linked. He hoped that she would bring the requisite naïve immediacy and childlike spontaneity to the final movement, with its soprano solo, 'Wir genießen die himmlischen Freuden'.

In fact, the Munich première was far from being a resounding success. Local audiences still remembered the monumental Second Symphony, which had been performed in Munich the previous year. It, too, had proved unsuccessful, but audiences had assumed that Mahler would at least seek to match this gigantic work, if not to surpass it. Instead, they were taken aback by the neoclassical, seemingly domesticated Fourth, a work that was considerably shorter than the Second and scored for much smaller forces. Bemusement followed the opening movement, while the hissing after the second movement was louder than the applause. (In Mahler's day, hissing, not booing, was a sign of disapproval.) The Adagio inspired fewer signs of displeasure, and the final movement received the warmest applause of all, thanks, not least, to the soprano's contribution. Mahler saw himself confirmed in his suspicion that the good people of Munich would use the Second as a stick with which to beat the Fourth. Above all, he was angered by his colleagues who announced at the end of the final rehearsal that they would understand the piece only after the first performance, which they then proceeded to boycott. In Mahler's view, it was to Felix Weingartner's credit that he was the only prominent musician to attend the actual performance and to express his enthusiasm afterwards. Weingartner was to conduct the work several times in the course of the years that followed.

A few weeks later Mahler conducted the piece again, this time in Berlin, where the symphony was part of a programme otherwise conducted by Strauss. On this occasion the audience, at least, was more responsive, even if the critics were as hostile as they had been in Munich, where Theodor Kroyer had described the work as 'sickly, ill-tasting Supermusic', adding that 'the weeds that germinated in the Third Symphony, in which Mahler still manages to show himself from his better side, have burgeoned in this work into a thorny mass of noxious vegetation'.[3] In Berlin, Mahler at least had the satisfaction of hearing Strauss expressing what for him was real enthusiasm and even claiming that he himself could not have written anything like the Adagio.[4] Mahler had been proved right: audiences had problems with the strange humour of his Fourth Symphony, making the later and, indeed, the lasting popularity of the work seem positively disconcerting. After all, what are we to make of a 'symphonia humoristica' whose Scherzo, in second position, features the Grim Reaper playing a fiddle tuned a whole tone higher to ensure that it produces a particularly screeching, rough-sounding tone.[5]

Some three years had elapsed between the completion of the Third Symphony in 1896 and the start of work on the Fourth during the unsettled summer on the Aussee in 1899. It was the longest break from composition in the whole of Mahler's life. The main reason was, of course, his new post in Vienna, with its tremendous workload, not to mention his work with the Vienna Philharmonic, and perhaps also the mental exhaustion following his completion of the monumental Third Symphony and the question that he must have put to himself as to how he was to proceed. His refusal to be sidetracked from his creative work during the remaining years of his life seems also to have stemmed from his realization that he could not afford another such interruption. The Fourth's starkly contrasting resources, when compared to those of the Third, are one answer to the question of how best to proceed, and as such may be comparable to the answer proposed by Schoenberg in his opp. 6 and 8 Songs and First String Quartet after he had broken off work on his monumental *Gurre-Lieder* in 1903. And whereas the six movements of the Third Symphony are all so obviously disparate, the four movements of the Fourth are all thematically linked, culminating in the *Wunderhorn* song 'Das himmlische Leben', which was in fact originally intended for the Third Symphony. One of the last letters that Mahler wrote was to the Leipzig conductor and Mahlerian Georg Göhler in response to the latter's analysis of the Fourth. Mahler liked his analysis very much but missed any mention of the thematic links between the movements, links that were a matter of great importance to him.[6]

Mahler once told Natalie Bauer-Lechner that he really intended to write only a symphonic humoresque, but it had then turned into a normal-length symphony, whereas whenever he set out to write a normal symphony, it always ended up three times the length. It was probably Robert Schumann who introduced the term 'humoresque' to music when, appealing to Jean Paul, he gave the title to his op. 20 piano piece. For Schumann, who, among German composers, was the greatest admirer of Jean Paul's writings before Mahler, the term implied a felicitous combination of rapt infatuation and wit, but in the case of Mahler's Fourth Symphony there is a further deciding factor in the form of the eerily frightening element that was already prefigured in the Pan-like character of the introduction to the Third. Mahler explicitly reintroduces this element into the Fourth in ways that the naïve listener may neither suspect nor, indeed, hear. As he explained to Natalie Bauer-Lechner:

> What I had in mind here was extraordinarily difficult to bring off. Think of the undifferentiated blue of the sky, which is harder to capture than any changing and contrasting shades. This is the basic tone of the whole work. Only once does it become overcast and uncannily awesome – but it is not the sky itself which grows dark, for it shines eternally blue. It is only that it seems suddenly sinister to us – just as on the most beautiful day, in a forest flooded with sunshine, one is often overcome by a shudder of Panic dread. The Scherzo is so mystical, confused and uncanny that it will make your hair stand on end. But you'll soon see, in the following Adagio – where everything sorts itself out – that it wasn't meant so seriously after all.[7]

The very opening of the first movement presents its interpreters with a problem. The bells that are heard in the first three bars and that recur in several subsequent episodes initially remind the listener of the *Musical Sleigh Ride* attributed to Leopold Mozart and recall a spirit of childhood innocence, and most commentators accept this interpretation. But in doing so they overlook a passing remark that Mahler made to Natalie Bauer-Lechner in the context of the first performance in Munich: 'The first [movement] begins characteristically enough, with the bells of the Fool's Cap.'[8] In short, it was not the bells of a child's sleigh that Mahler had in mind here but a fool's cap fitted with bells, just as the mirror that Till Eulenspiegel holds up to his fellow human beings in Strauss's tone poem of 1895 – the work of Strauss's that Mahler conducted most often – is also set with bells. In this way Mahler establishes the semantic framework within which the piece as a whole is to be interpreted. This apparently seraphic symphony offers an alternative view of the world. As Adorno noted, nothing is as it appears on the surface. The result is a figurative work of irony that embraces anguish and terror as surely as it does the naïvely childlike. The Fourth Symphony dreams of a childhood for which we must grieve but which we can no longer trust. Mahler wanted the heavenly joys of the final movement, with its soprano solo, to be entrusted to a singer with a voice as youthful and childlike as possible. He certainly did not want a rich soprano voice. When Leonard Bernstein used a member of the Tölz Boys' Choir in his second complete recording of the symphony, he was not only praised for his decision, he was also completely right.

Mahler's humour in this 'humoresque' is clearly influenced by his reading of Jean Paul's 'Vorschule der Ästhetik', a text that we may assume he knew. In § 32 Jean Paul defines humour as 'the inverted sublime', destroying not the individual but the finite through its contrast with the idea.[9] According to Jean Paul, the humorist does not look down on earth from a higher world, thereby becoming conscious of its pettiness and vanity. Rather, he measures the world of infinity against the finite world and sees a connection between them, resulting in the laughter that contains within it both anguish and greatness. Just as there is a world humour, so there is a world irony that 'soars, singing and playing, not just above the errors of the world (just as the former does not merely soar above its follies) but also above all knowledge. Like a flame, it is free, consuming and delighting us, easily moved and yet rising only towards heaven'.[10] Irony professes to treat all that is absurd in the world and in human beings as if it were deadly serious. As such, it appears to depict everything objectively, praising it in its total irrationality and in that way deriving its effectiveness from the contrast between constant objectivization and the totality of the folly that is being criticized, and to that extent it is closely related to satire. In this sense Mahler's Fourth Symphony is a work of humour and irony – whether there is such a thing as humour and irony in music is an old argument rendered obsolete by the present piece. This is no doubt what Mahler meant when, speaking of irony and joviality in the same breath, he described the mood of the first three movements as follows: 'They breathe the joviality of a higher world, one unfamiliar to us, which has something awe-inspiring and frightening about it. In the last movement ("Das himmlische Leben") the child – who, though in a chrysalis-state, nevertheless already belongs to this higher world – explains what it all means.'[11] Humour and irony enter here, light-footed, which is yet another reason why Mahler reduces his forces in such a radical manner – how ironic that his malicious detractors so often accuse him of sounding over-blown. Mahler writes symphonic chamber music: 'There is no music on earth that can be compared with ours,' sings the soloist in the final movement. And the childlike, unsophisticated nature of the remark is under-scored by the singer's false emphasis on the first syllable of the word 'Musik'. Mahler was particularly proud of the work's subtle orchestration, a point that emerges with some force from his various attempts to compare the style of writing both in this movement and in the work as a whole with other images. On one occasion he spoke of a kaleidoscopic picture whose pieces were repeat-edly recombined and on another of the thousands of millions of droplets in a rainbow that seem to dissolve and yet which produce a brightly coloured picture. And on a third occasion he referred to the gossamer-like weave of a delicate shawl that could be folded as small as a nutshell but when unfolded would suddenly become unexpectedly large.

While working on the third movement, Mahler described it variously as an Adagio and an Andante, finally settling on the performance marking 'Ruhevoll' ('Calm'), its soaring stateliness suggesting a glimpse of the smile of Saint Ursula, who is mentioned in the fourth movement. Technically speaking, the third movement is a set of double variations, a technique favoured by Brahms but one which Mahler had hitherto eschewed. Here, too, Mahler provides his listeners with a puzzle, for the movement seems as if it is going to die away *pianissimo* on a wonderfully melancholic note. Shortly before the end we expect a coda to develop out of the *pianissimo* melody and fade away gently in a spirit of rapt transfiguration. But Mahler wants to provoke his listeners, and so he suddenly introduces a Luftpause, after which the coda begins with an Adornoesque 'breakthrough' as unexpected as it is inappropriate. With a *fortissimo* passage in all the brass and ascending and descending arpeggios and scales in the harp and strings, it could even be argued that Mahler places an ironic gloss on the cat-egory of the 'breakthrough': here it is, he seems to be saying, just when you least expect it, disturbing the slumber of the Adagio. But then it passes as quickly as it came, because instead of leading victoriously to the conclusion, the orchestral outburst ends abruptly, and the movement draws to its close, 'very tender and heartfelt' and 'dying away completely' in the flutes and high violins, just as it would have ended if its night-time rest had not been so rudely disturbed.

The performance marking at the start of the final movement is 'Sehr behaglich' (Molto comodo), while the singer is instructed to sing 'with an expression of childlike joviality, entirely without parody'. Mahler was evidently worried that listeners might somehow have noticed the inauthenticity of the first three movements and concluded, wrongly, that the final movement was meant to be a parody. In fact, the light that he sheds on the work at this point is refracted through several lenses. After all, the childlike soprano sings of heavenly joys but above all of murder and butchery, or, to be specific, the Massacre of the Innocents, albeit transferred to a heavenly context and to a different kind of victim. Those who are represented by the soprano lead an 'angelic existence', but these angels, for all their childlike innocence, are no different from earth's inhabitants. They, too, are guilty of killing in order to live. For them, too, there is the same guilty association between eating and being eaten. It is not ambrosia and nectar and manna that are the food of heaven but innocent animals: 'John lets the lamb go, and butcher Herod looks out for it! We lead a patient, blameless, patient, a dear little lamb to its death! St Luke slaughters the ox without a moment's thought or reflection.' This heaven is a slaughterhouse, and Herod, having butchered the children of Bethlehem, is rewarded by his being appointed a butcher here too, a task that he performs with ruthless concentration. Sts John and Luke do Herod's dirty work, while he watches over them. With all the brutal irony at his command, Mahler has given musical expression to the bad joke of the *Wunderhorn* song, 'Der Himmel hängt voll Geigen'.

The movement consists of four verses and a coda, the start of each new verse accompanied by shrill laughter by way of an ironic commentary. As Mahler noted, all four movements are closely connected, the bells of the opening movement returning here, but on this occasion they are combined with the shrill *fortissimo* of grinning piccolos and flutes, and with screeching clarinets that expose the apparent gentility of this congenial life in heaven for what it actually is, a travesty of life on earth. Mahler also set 'Das irdische Leben' – life on earth – with its embittered complaint of a starving child repeatedly consoled by its mother's promise of baked bread until it is too late. On earth children die of hunger, while in heaven the angels live it up, but at the expense of the innocent animals that are led to slaughter with childlike naïveté, so innocent, indeed, that they run towards their butchers' open knives: 'If you want deer or hare, they run towards you on the open road!' It is clear that this final movement cannot end on a note of warm-hearted sentimentality. There is no comforting conclusion, no sense of triumph, no wise smile. Instead, the movement dies away sombrely in the low notes of the harp and a final *morendo* on the double basses. The humoresque is stifled, choked by the course of the world. Here Mahler the ironist abandons the superior humour of Jean Paul's aesthetic outlook. The Adagio had tried to suggest that the Scherzo meant no ill, but the final movement undermines this brief assurance. Mahler might have said, Brechtian fashion, 'In me you have someone you cannot rely on.' Although programme notes may still mislead readers into thinking that the Fourth Symphony is imbued with the spirit of Mozart, the work turns out to be the most radical commentary on the course of the world that Mahler ever wrote.

Vienna in 1900: Alma as a Young Woman (1901–3)

Turn-of-the-Century Vienna

Mahler has far less in common with fin-de-siècle Vienna than is generally assumed to be the case, a remark that may surprise the reader, but one that is none the less prompted both by the need for accuracy and as a way of justifying the relative brevity of what follows. If the ensuing sketch turns out to be less detailed than expected, this is not so much because our picture of turn-of-the-century Vienna is now so clear and varied but because the list of famous names that is rattled off more or less automatically in this context – it includes such cultural giants as Gustav Klimt, Sigmund Freud, Karl Kraus, Adolf Loos, Theodor Herzl, Arthur Schnitzler, Hugo von Hofmannsthal, Joseph Maria Olbrich, Ernst Mach and Mahler himself, to name only the most important – gives a false impression in the specific case of Mahler. Although he contributed to the cultural life of the city between 1897 and 1907, his life was not shaped by turn-of-the-century Vienna. Rather, it was the Vienna of the years around 1875 that had left its mark on him, and that is an influence we have already examined elsewhere in all the requisite detail.

Mahler was not quite thirty-seven when he returned to Vienna in 1897. By now his thoughts and actions, his feelings and desires had all been clearly conditioned, leaving little to be added. Moreover, he continued to work tirelessly. He was now director of the Court Opera, with time to compose only during his summer vacations. He was also undertaking increasing numbers of guest engagements as a conductor, especially of his own works: who, after all, was better placed than Mahler himself – the greatest conductor of his age – to ensure that they received a fair hearing in the face of violent opposition from a hard core of recalcitrant listeners? Soon he was also to become the head of a family, at least to the extent that he had time for such a commitment. During his early years in Vienna he would often visit the city's cafés and even managed to get to the theatre – we know that he saw Molière's *Le Misanthrope* and Calderón's *El alcalde de Zalamea* at the Burgtheater. Only very rarely did he attend concerts, and even these visits were largely limited to his later years in Vienna, when works by protégés such as Schoenberg were being performed. On holiday, conversely, he often spent his free evenings attending operas and concerts in other towns and cities. The famous photographs that show him on his way to and from the Court Opera are typical: he trudges along, eyes unseeing, negligently dressed and apparently oblivious to passing trams and cars. The well-known oil painting by the caricaturist Theo Zasche, *The Ringstraße, Vienna* (1900), depicts a street filled with some of the city's most famous inhabitants, elbowing their way through the strolling crowd as if mere chance has brought them all here at the same time. Among them is Mahler. The image can hardly be described as realistic for Mahler is depicted sauntering along and carefully observing his surroundings, whereas exactly the opposite was the case. His appreciation of architecture and the visual arts was poorly developed, and from this point of view a city famed for its decorative arts could hardly engage his attention. That the Secession was the only Viennese art movement to inspire him to forge any closer contacts with the city was due entirely to Alma and her stepfather Carl Moll, who was a member of the group. Mahler also met Klimt – Alma's former idol – on the few occasions when he socialized with others.

In the spring of 1907, by which date Mahler was already planning to leave Vienna, Hermann Bahr published a book called simply *Vienna*. Although a native of Linz, Bahr was by then the city's most prolific critic and journalist – Karl Kraus continued to refer to him, ironically, as 'the gentleman from Linz'. The book was immediately impounded by the authorities in Vienna and for a time it was unobtainable. If it caused offence, this was not for moral or political reasons but because it was a venomous attack on the city written by one of its most perceptive critics:

> In the rest of Europe, Vienna is known for the fact that it is always Sunday there and that the spit is for ever turning on the hearth. It is also a Capua of the mind, where people live in a semi-poetic state that is dangerous to the whole. They also know the names of a number of waltzes by Lanner and Strauß: one of them is called 'Life Is a Dance', another one 'Glad To Be Alive', a third one 'Cheerful Even When Times Are Hard'. They also know a few choruses along the lines of 'The Viennese Never Go Under', 'Never Let the World See that You're Sad' and 'Always Be Merry', and also that it is the city of roast chickens, smart carriages and a world-famous sense of *Gemütlichkeit*. To the outside world it has retained this reputation as a city lulled by music and dancing, a city of harmless, slightly dissolute, rather inactive and incompetent

people who are none the less good and kind. But those who are fated to live here find this hard to believe. Rather, they are filled with anger.

And Bahr goes on to give vent to that anger, poking fun at the true Viennese who shower their city with scorn and contumely but who never think of leaving it. The true inhabitant of Vienna, Bahr concluded, hates his fellow citizens but cannot live without them. He despises himself but also finds himself a touching spectacle. He is permanently abusive towards others but demands that others praise him. He is always complaining and threatening but puts up with everything, except when people want to help him, and then he resists all proffered assistance. The Viennese are profoundly insecure. They never know how to react to others, how to judge them and how to behave. In order to find out what they should do, they ignore Goethe's advice which is that they should ask the opinion of beautiful women and rather turn to the Viennese institution that they idolize most of all: the theatre. For the true Viennese, the theatre does not imitate life, rather life imitates the theatre. Nowhere else are there so many talented people – people with a talent for politics and the arts. But this talent is left untapped and expresses nothing but itself. In short, it is hollow. However much talent there may be in the city, there is no one capable of embodying it.

And with this Bahr comes to the nub of his critique of Vienna, namely, a lack of real people in a city that is otherwise richly endowed. Here Bahr was clearly expressing his own personal disenchantment with a city that forced him to decamp to Salzburg with his wife, Anna von Mildenburg, whom he married in 1909, although, as Thomas Bernhard would have pointed out, it is questionable whether Salzburg was really preferable to Vienna:

Hence the horror that they feel when a real person appears in their midst. They are terrified. They want to creep away and hide. On the stage at least. For here they know that it will all be over in three hours. The Viennese can still bear reality in the form of pretence. And yet even here their admiration for Mitterwurzer, Kainz and Mildenburg still has more of the sense of a lascivious thrill to it, as though they are in the presence of a dangerous animal. And they are happy that these animals have been chained up by art. The Viennese have never tolerated a real person in their midst, not Beethoven, nor Schreyvogel, nor Hebbel, nor Kürnberger, nor Bruckner, nor Hugo Wolf, nor Waldmüller, nor Klimt, nor Burckhard, nor Mach, nor Mahler, no one. Real people are always kept in a cage of immense loneliness. The Viennese never let them enter their dear carefree easy lives.[1]

It is easy to see why the Viennese should have taken this amiss, and yet with his tremendous ability to sniff out trends and see which way the wind was blowing, Bahr struck a raw nerve: the Viennese – not just the anti-Semites among them – felt only malice towards Mahler. They were unable to abide the living presence of a genius going about his daily business. Mahler's disenchantment with the city, his ultimate resignation and the mendaciousness of the locals' grief when he returned to Vienna to die – all of this is explained by Bahr's clinical diagnosis.

In the twenty or so years during which Mahler had lived either in the Austrian provinces or Germany or in major cities such as Prague and Budapest, the dual monarchy had changed, and not to its own advantage. The fault lines were becoming increasingly visible and already allowing a glimpse of the catastrophe that was to be the First World War. A simple statistic may suffice here: between 1871 and 1917 Germany had five chancellors, whereas Hungary had seventeen prime ministers during the same period, Austria as many as twenty, a figure that points the way forward to the sort of conditions that obtained at the time of the Weimar Republic. Electoral reforms that were implemented in 1896 in response to mounting social pressure were only half-hearted at best, and it was not until 1907 that the decisive step was taken in this regard, by which date it was already too late. The planned reforms of a politician like Eduard Franz Joseph von Taaffe – the longest-serving prime minister in the dual monarchy at this period – were designed, by his own admission, to keep the two nations in a state of well-tempered dissatisfaction and in the longer term they were bound to fail. Nationalist aspirations in the multiracial state and the decline in political liberalism that was bound up with electoral reform had a disruptive and even a damaging effect. The suicide of Crown Prince Rudolf in Mayerling in 1889 was a severe blow not only for the emperor, whose wife, Elisabeth, was to be assassinated by an Italian anarchist nine years later, but also for the liberals who had placed their hopes in him – whether they were right to do so is another matter. In 1895 Count Badeni was appointed prime minister, and two years later he tried to solve the problem of the conflicting demands of the Czech and German languages in Bohemia and Moravia by giving them both equal status, only for the German-speaking population to react with undisguised fury, leading to a state of near civil war, the seismic repercussions of which were felt in Parliament itself, resulting in Badeni's downfall. Attempts on the part of his successors to turn back the clock in favour of the Germans, while making minor concessions to the Czechs, left both parties in the conflict dissatisfied and merely increased the tensions between them. Tensions also mounted between workers, members of the lower and upper middle classes, and between capital, industry and agriculture. It was entirely typical of the age that these mounting pressures led to an increasing radicalization of right- and left-wing politics.

From 1879 onwards, the German Liberal Party grew more and more unattractive and at the same time lost seats in Parliament. In 1891 a new party entered the lower house in the form of the Christian Socialists. Initially they had only four-teen representatives, but by 1911, the date of the last elections in pre-war Austria, there were seventy-six. Meanwhile, the Socialists made even greater gains, advancing from fifteen in 1897 – the first time they took part in an election – to eighty-seven in 1907. In 1911 that number then fell back slightly to eighty-two. Social democracy in Austria was largely the work of two of Mahler's old friends, Engelbert Pernerstorfer and Victor Adler. They had worked together on the German Liberals' programme in Linz in 1882, when they had been famous for their left-wing views. Another member of their group at that time was the radical nationalist member of Parliament, Georg von Schönerer, who was soon leading the Pan-German Party, with its explicitly nationalist and racist programme. Schönerer thus became the spokesman of an explosive mixture of anti-clericalism and anti-Semitism derived, not least, from the ideas of Wagner, to whom he was fond of appealing. The movement's watchword was 'Without Judea and Rome we shall build the German cathedral'. (Hitler paid tribute to Schönerer in *Mein Kampf*, while deploring his organizational and tactical errors.)

Thanks to his wild polemics and inflammatory politics, Schönerer soon found himself on the margins of the parliamentary system and had to make way for Karl Lueger, a far subtler tactician, who set himself up as the mouthpiece of the Christian Socialists in Vienna. With his 'cosier' variant of anti-Semitism ('I shall decide who is a Jew' was one of his more infamous remarks), he finally managed to become the mayor of Vienna in 1897 in the face of the emperor's opposition. Once again it is worth pointing out that this was the year in which Mahler returned to Vienna, where he found himself overwhelmed by a particularly viru-lent form of anti-Semitism that did not even spare the director of the Vienna Court Opera. Unlike Schönerer, Lueger was immensely popular in Vienna. 'Handsome Karl' cut an imposing figure with his Zeus-like features, his fine head of hair and a luxurious beard. He was also blessed with considerable gifts as an orator, a talent that he exploited to the full in appealing to the basest anti-Semitic and anti-modernist instincts, while politely distancing himself from the excesses bound up with such sentiments. He brought no new arguments to the debate but instead showed great skill in orchestrating the anti-Semitism that was already well established. That his efforts fell on fertile ground is clear from a widely publicized pamphlet, 'Our Father Lueger', which was circulated in the summer of 1896 in an attempt to shoot down resistance to a future Mayor Lueger:

> Our Father Lueger, who art in Vienna, hallowed be thy name, protect our Christian people, thy will be done to all Christian peoples on earth, give us no stock exchange but only Christian bread, forgive all debtors who have been betrayed by the hands of Jewish usurers as we forgive them that trespass against us, lead us not into temptation but deliver us from the Jewish evil. Amen.[2]

As in so many other respects, Vienna was to lead the way on the road to universal disaster, the city's anti-Semitism being fuelled and 'justified' by the arrival of Eastern European Jews. (Hitler's hatred of the Jews was another by-product of this development.) In 1880 there were 71,600 Jews in Vienna. Within a decade that number had risen to 118,500, and by 1900 it was 147,000. Like many assimilated Jews, Mahler, too, had difficulty with what Arnold Zweig called the 'Eastern European Jewish countenance'. But it made no difference to assimilated Jews or to former Jews like Mahler that they distanced themselves from their Eastern European brethren, for anti-Semites hated assimilated upper middle-class Jews from Vienna's exclusive residential areas at least as intensely as they hated the Jews from the ghettos of Poland and Galicia. Austrian Jews were invariably the losers in all these historical developments, and it made no difference how they defined themselves and how they behaved or whatever political positions they thought it appropriate to adopt. As so often, it was Arthur Schnitzler who found the pithiest phrases when in his novel *The Road to the Open* (1908) he devised the following dialogue between the cynical old Viennese Jew Salomon Ehrenberg and the Jewish Social Democrat Therese Golowski:

'I assure you, Therese, that you Jewish Social Democrats will suffer exactly the same fate as the Jewish Liberals and German Nationalists.'

'How's that?' Therese asked with her typical hauteur. 'In what way will we suffer exactly the same fate?'

'In what way? I'll tell you. Who created the liberal movement in Austria? The Jews! By whom were the Jews betrayed and abandoned? By the liberals! Who created the German Nationalist movement in Austria? The Jews. Who left the Jews in the lurch as if they were dogs? The Germans. Exactly the same will happen to you with Socialism and Communism. As soon as the soup has been served, you'll be driven from the table. It was always like that, and it will always remain so.'[3]

The journey from German Nationalism to Socialism that was undertaken by people like Adler, Pernerstorfer and Bahr himself was no less unusual than the one from German Nationalism to Pan-Germanism and anti-Semitism that was taken by Schönerer, for example. The breeding ground for many features of the sort of late Romantic Socialism that was widespread among intellectuals and artists at this time was a mixture of Marx, Nietzsche and Dostoevsky allied to a pre-Expressionist sentimentality based on the slogan that all men are brothers. All these features may be found in Mahler, too. Like Adler, he had not forgotten his humble background. Adler had worked as a doctor among the poor and knew from the sufferings of the inhabitants of Vienna's tenement buildings that the prosperity of the 1870s and later had a darker side to it. 'How can one be happy when a single creature still suffers on earth?' According to Alma, Mahler was fond of repeating this sentence of Dostoevsky's. She also adds that it was a favourite remark of other uninhibited egocentrics. According to Adler's widow, Mahler voted for the Socialist candidate in the 1901 elections, an act of astonishing boldness on the part of a director of the Court Opera. The name of the candidate was Victor Adler, but Mahler's decision to vote for him was almost certainly more than the result of their long-standing friendship.[4] Here, too, Mahler showed no trace of the attitude adopted by the writers of Young Vienna, a group of authors remote from politics and devoid of social concerns.

Nor did Mahler share the anxieties felt by the local bourgeoisie when the Socialists marched through Vienna for the first time on 1 May 1890, a march organized by Adler and, as such, felt to represent a different kind of threat from the one posed by Princess Metternich's Flower Festival that was held in the Prater each year. The sense of relief was tangible when the Viennese realized that the marching workers were well behaved and even picturesque, with none of the feared associations of a downtrodden proletariat ready to storm the bastions of social order. The sixteen-year-old Hugo von Hofmannsthal struck a precocious and blasé note: 'Vienna, 1 May 1890, Prater at 5 p.m. If the rabble rages in the streets, well then, my child, let them shout! For their loves and hates are vulgar! As long as they leave us time, let us devote ourselves to more beautiful things. Leave the rabble in the alleyways: empty phrases, hubbub, lies, pretence will fade away and vanish. The beautiful truth alone will survive.'[5] In the event, it was not the workers' movement that curtailed Young Vienna's aestheticist attempts to devote itself to beauty. Hofmannsthal's attitude cannot be entirely excused by reference to his tender years but was typical of the apolitical, otherworldly approach of his entire generation, an attitude that left even the resigned Naturalists and bohemian anarchists looking like militant activists. Hermann Broch criticized this attitude in his essay on Hofmannsthal, referring to the 'ethical indifference' that resulted when political thought atrophied and there was a concomitant increase in aesthetic thinking. In turn, he believed that this explained the decorative tendencies on the part of the overwhelming majority, who, creatively impotent, ended up worshipping at the shrine of naked hedonism.[6] A high achiever like Mahler was constitutionally incapable of such an outlook. According to Alma, he stumbled upon a May demonstration in 1905, when he was walking through the city. It was just as well behaved as it had been fifteen years earlier. For a time he joined the procession and returned home full of enthusiasm: these men, he said, were his brothers. They represented the future.[7]

In spite of all the country's inadequacies, it comes as no surprise to discover that it was in Vienna that Mahler was able to unlock his greatest potential in the opera house – he had already demonstrated that he could compose anywhere: all that he needed for that was mountains, green meadows and a lake, and these he could find all over Austria. Until shortly before the end of his tenure in Vienna, he was able to rely on the liberality of the court admin-istrators and on the tolerance of the emperor who, however vaguely, must have felt that his opera house was in the hands of a man of genius unlike any other in the history of an institution that had always been given preferential treat-ment. Such support undoubtedly had a productive and liberating effect on Mahler's work both as a conductor and as a reformer. From this point of view, it is even necessary to correct Robert Musil, who at the start of his novel *The Man Without Qualities* paints a picture of the legendary country of Kakania that claims that

> The country's administration was conducted in an enlightened, unobtrusive manner, with all the sharp edges cautiously smoothed over, by the best bureaucracy in Europe, which could be faulted only in that it regarded genius, and any brilliant individual initiative not backed by noble birth or official status, as insolent and presumptuous. But then, who welcomes inter-ference from unqualified outsiders? And in Kakania, at least, it would only happen that a genius would be regarded as a lout, but never was a mere lout taken – as happens elsewhere – for a genius.[8]

On this point Musil was wrong. Sigmund Freud and his vain attempts to obtain a chair at the University of Vienna no doubt confirmed him in his conviction, but it is one of the scarcely credible contradictions in the character of the city that although men of genius like Klimt and Mahler were hated and reviled, it was only in Vienna that they were able to work and that even if only for a limited period of time they received the money and organizational opportunities they needed to pursue their artistic goals unfettered by others. In the case of Mahler and his operatic reforms, there is no indication that the authorities ever tried to dictate his actions or influence his work. Only towards the end of his appointment did problems arise as a result of the sizeable box-office deficit and his increasingly lengthy periods of absence. We shall return to these problems in due course.

To the extent that Vienna and, more generally, Austria were willing to tolerate a genius at least for a time, especially when that genius added to the lustre of cultural institutions such as the Burgtheater and the Court Opera, then Bahr's scepticism was misplaced. Ultimately, however, he was to be proved right. He himself offers an explanation, however ambiguous, for Vienna's ability to tolerate Mahler as long as it did, at least as director of the Court Opera – the city's hostility to his music, conversely, continued to grow, starting with the

Vienna Philharmonic and eventually extending, with few exceptions, to the music-loving public as a whole. According to Musil, Kakania was

> just barely able to go along with itself. One enjoyed a negative freedom there, always with the sense of insufficient grounds for one's own existence, and lapped around by the great fantasy of all that had not happened or at least not yet happened irrevocably as by the breath of those oceans from which mankind had once emerged. Events that might be regarded as momentous elsewhere were here introduced with a casual '*Es ist passiert . . .*' – a peculiar form of 'it happened' unknown elsewhere in German or any other language, whose breath could transform facts and blows of fate into something as light as thistledown or thought. Perhaps, despite so much that can be said against it, Kakania was, after all, a country for geniuses; which is probably what brought it to its ruin.[9]

Broch offered a more accurate and pointed diagnosis than Musil when he spoke of a value vacuum in Austria at the end of the nineteenth century. Vienna, he went on, was the centre of that vacuum, joyously celebrating an apocalypse that affected the city's whole attitude to life and that was summed up in lines from *Die Fledermaus*, 'Glücklich ist, wer vergißt, was doch nicht zu ändern ist' ('Happy he who forgets what can't be changed'). Ever since Johann Strauß's operetta had received its first performance in Vienna in 1874, these lines had coloured all that the Viennese thought and felt. Those inhabitants whose interests were earthier parodied them as 'Glücklich ist, wer verfrißt, was nicht zu versaufen ist' ('Happy he who guzzles up all that can't be drunk'). They rejected Mahler's music because it showed them, trenchantly and even brutally, that although there was much that could not be changed, they should never forget what *could* be changed for the better. In the wistfulness of the transient it held out a promise of utopian happiness and described that happiness in music. But these same people then went on to acclaim Mahler when he presented them with the unvarnished truth of the great operas and music dramas in bold and rigorous performances that broke with all the comforting conventions of operatic routine. Vienna's art lovers were able to tolerate this because, as Bahr pointed out, it was all over in three or four hours at the most.

The feeling of superiority would have been intolerable if it had lasted any longer, for, however much they may have complained about the prevailing culture, few thought of abandoning it for good and of living in the rarefied heights to which Mahler himself aspired: the air was simply too thin, the earthy pleasures too few. The cultural historian Carl E. Schorske, to whom we owe a number of important studies of turn-of-the-century Vienna, has argued that by the middle of the nineteenth century two cultures coexisted in the city, representing two different sets of values: one was the rational culture of the law and the written word as embodied in the University and its brilliant traditions of philosophy, psychology, economics and jurisprudence, while the other was a culture of sensuality and charm manifest in the visual arts and the theatre. For the aristocracy and members of the middle class, this aesthetic culture was a symbol of social status and personal happiness, providing them with a feel-good factor found nowhere else in Europe. Once this aesthetic and emotional culture got out of hand and started to supplant a rational culture more closely linked to moral considerations, the result was a culture of self-indulgence that went hand in hand with moral indifference, as Karl Kraus was one of the first to point out. Feelings of decadence and pessimism had first made themselves felt in Europe at the start of the nineteenth century, most notably in France. In fin-de-siècle Vienna they produced the most exquisite frost patterns on windows looking out on grim reality – they are the same patterns as those seen by Schubert's wanderer in *Winterreise* – and the more luxuriant they became, the more opaque was the view of national tensions, economic crises and social ills. Behind these windows, however, there were plenty of opportunities for narcissism to thrive – the narcissism that fuelled turn-of-the-century art and helped that art to evolve in subtly differentiated ways. It is this atmosphere that is generally described as the fin de siècle.

The fin de siècle is best summed up as the feeling that contemporaries should avoid nationalist stereotyping, without drifting into the opposing Social Democrat camp. (As we have already noted, Mahler cannot be described as a fully paid-up member of this movement, but the mood still needs to be described in order to depict the context in which he operated.) It is the feeling of dissatisfaction towards state authority and imperialist expansionism, a feeling mitigated in the dual monarchy by a certain sentimental attachment to the old emperor – a final echo of this typically Austrian attitude may be found in Joseph Roth's novel *The Radetzky March*, with its desperate belief in monarchism. It is also the feeling of profound scepticism towards official religion. And it is the fascination with the fragmentation of the self that was diagnosed by empirio-criticism and that led to crises surrounding the identity of the self in the literature of Young Vienna. When Ernst Mach decreed that the self was irretrievably lost, contemporaries believed him, while attempting to counter his claim by means of yet greater refinement. Freud, it is true, sought to champion the threatened self at the expense of the id, but his theories found little favour, early psychoanalysis being regarded as a threat to bourgeois stability, exposing areas that risked undermining the double standards of the age. Mahler, of course, had no personal dealings with Freud until the two of them met for their famous walk in Leiden in 1910. There is no evidence that he knew more about Freud than any other educated person in Vienna during this period, although Klaus Pringsheim mentions a conversation with Mahler on the subject of the psychoanalyst. He then refers to Mahler in October 1910, after his meeting with Freud and shortly before his departure for his final visit to America. On another occasion Mahler's old friend Bertha Zuckerkandl asked him whether there was not a psychology of cities that could be applied to Vienna, for example, a city that produced men of genius, only to kill them off. 'Yes, you are right. Freud should add a psychology of cities to his list of publications. What terrible inner struggles there must have been during Vienna's formative years. Conflicting influences that give the character its duality. Unfortunately, you can't uncover the subconscious of a city.'[10]

We need to say more about the sense of fin de siècle as a characteristic feature of the age. Contemporaries felt that the legacy bequeathed by their fathers' generation, when rapid expansion had followed the founding of the Reich in 1871, often allowing art lovers to lead lives freed from the need to earn a living, was more of a burden than a blessing, and yet they lacked the strength to extricate themselves from the quagmire. At the same time, the obsessively detailed interest in the most minute workings of the psyche was seen to culminate in mysticism rather than self-knowledge. Allied to this was the fractured self-awareness of a generation of dilettantes who, looking down contemptuously on the philistines who went to the theatre to see operettas and unpretentious plays, may have acquired an exquisite taste for art but who themselves lacked the ability to create powerful masterpieces like those of Balzac, Tolstoy, Dostoevsky and Wagner, preferring to express themselves instead in the prose poem, the lyric drama and the Nietzschean review. Here, too, it is clear that Mahler's mighty symphonies belonged to a different generation with a different frame of mind – the artists of Young Vienna were all born between 1870 and 1880 and were thus ten or twenty years younger than Mahler. There was also a need to escape from the unnatural, mindless, barbaric present, a need that contemporaries met by seeking refuge in artificiality. None of the great fin-de-siècle writers, be they Huysmans or Maeterlinck, Schnitzler or Hofmannsthal, offers any true descriptions of nature, for which we have to turn, rather, to the symphonies of Mahler. Finally, there was an attempt at this time to place a positive gloss on the gloomy prospects held out by genetics and by current theories of degeneration. If contemporaries lacked the healthy young blood of an up-and-coming generation, they could at least sail down the river of European decadence, exposing their frayed nerve endings and perishing amid the convulsions of new sensations with all the dignity shown by the later Roman emperors while awaiting the barbarian hordes.

Perhaps the finest description of the spirit of the age is the one penned by the young Hugo von Hofmannsthal in his first essay on Italy's arch-decadent, Gabriele D'Annunzio:

We have nothing but a sentimental memory, a paralysed will and the uncanny gift for self-duplication. We watch our lives pass us by; we empty the cup betimes and yet remain perpetually thirsty . . .. We have, as it were, no roots in life and wander around among life's children like clairvoyant shades who are yet blind to the daylight. . . . People anatomize their own emotional lives or they dream. Reflection or fantasy, the image in a mirror or alternatively in a dream. Old furniture and new neuroses are modern. The psychological exercise of listening to grass grow is modern, as is splashing around in a purely imaginary world of wonders. Paul Bourget and the Buddha are modern, the dissection of atoms and playing ball with the universe; equally modern is the act of dissecting a whim, a sigh or a scruple; and modern, too, is the instinctual, almost somnambulistic abandonment to every manifestation of beauty, to a colour chord, a dazzling metaphor, a wonderful allegory.[11]

To sum up, this is not a diagnosis of Mahler's understanding of the age, for he held himself aloof from turn-of-the-century Vienna. But it *is* a diagnosis of the world inhabited by Alma Schindler, a world in which Mahler conducted and directed operas and composed. We must imagine that what found its way into his music and flowed out of it again, encountering bewilderment or enthusiasm, hatred or affection, was a process of osmosis. His music is not the immediate or unreflected expression of the fin de siècle but a part of the diagnosis of the age and a reflection on it.

The Secession

'To the age its art, to art its freedom'. These are the words emblazoned in letters of gold on the building housing the Vienna Secession, a structure designed by Joseph Maria Olbrich and erected in record time between April and November 1898 at the western end of the Karlsplatz, where it still stands. Even from a purely architectural standpoint, it was in marked contrast to the Artists' House next to the Musikverein on the other side of the square. It immediately came to symbolize the city with its floral dome, known to the locals as the 'golden cabbage'. Until now we have tended to stress the differences between turn-of-the-century Vienna and Mahler's musical imprint, but with regard to the Secession we need to adopt another point of view, a shift of perspective due to more than just Mahler's famous involvement in the exhibition of Max Klinger's Beethoven statue and the presentation of Gustav Klimt's Beethoven frieze and other works in the spring of 1902. As in other artistic centres across Europe, the years leading up to the turn of the century were marked by the emergence of a group of young painters and sculptors opposed to the dominance of traditional and academic views on art and eager to strike out on a path of their own.

In doing so, they seceded from the main body of artists and formed an association of their own, hence the term 'Secession'. First off the mark had been the
Munich Secession, whose artists had exhibited their work in Vienna in 1894,
encouraging their Viennese colleagues to follow suit. By 1897 – the year of
Mahler's appointment – they were able to announce their plans:

> A band of younger artists, inspired by their ideal and in spite of everything
> believing unshakeably in Vienna's artistic future, has now formed an
> Association of Visual Artists in Austria which, supported by a number of true
> and self-sacrificial art lovers, is called upon to work in a complementary, pure,
> ideal and artistic way without any cooperative or material considerations.

For today's readers, the names of those artists who from the outset formed
the core of the Secession represent all that was most significant about Viennese
art in the years around 1900: Gustav Klimt; Kolo Moser; Carl Moll, Alma
Schindler's stepfather; Alfred Roller, who was introduced to Mahler at the
Klinger exhibition and who soon became his most crucial associate in his
attempts to reform the operatic stage; Otto Wagner, who was the city's most
forward-looking architect before Adolf Loos; Joseph Maria Olbrich, who
designed the Secession's headquarters; and Josef Hoffmann. Only artists like
Oskar Kokoschka and Egon Schiele, born in 1886 and 1890 respectively, were
still too young to be members, although neither of them would have been the
artist he was without the Secession and the Wiener Werkstätte that was formed
shortly afterwards. The group was exceptionally disparate, its members having
little in common beyond their awareness that they formed the Viennese avant-
garde and that they wanted to bring local art closer to the world of art nouveau
or, as it was known in the German-speaking world, Jugendstil. A pronounced
interest in the arts and crafts movement set the Vienna Secession apart from
its slightly later counterpart in Berlin. From the outset there was a marked
tendency for the artists to fall into one of two different groups, those who were
interested in style and those whose thinking was coloured by Impressionist
ideas, leading ultimately to a further secession in 1905, when the artists associated with Klimt left the organization. In turn, a number of members of the
second group embraced an anti-urban, anti-cosmopolitan art.

The Secessionists' style was far from unified. Indeed, their only unifying
feature was their desire to organize exhibitions showcasing the whole range of
current trends in European art, which was then charting a wayward course on
the open sea between Impressionism, art nouveau, Expressionism and, vaguely
discernible on the horizon, abstract art. Also in evidence was a local variant of
the pluralism of the age that gave greater weight to the decorative element.
Particularly significant in this regard was Klimt's development from the

morbid Makart-influenced style of his early portraits to the shimmering pointillism of his landscapes and, finally, the Byzantine decorativeness of his maturity. Not until later were Kokoschka's radical Expressionism and Schiele's gaping sexual wounds to disturb their audiences and exercise the judiciary, while Klimt's no less lascivious drawings were for the most part kept from public view – not that this prevented him from becoming, quite rightly, the chief erotic artist of the Austrian avant-garde, suborning the senses of the young Alma Schindler, among others. Many of these artists were influenced by Wagner's idea of a synthesis of the arts and in some cases were also fired by pan-German political convictions. The movement's synthetic aspirations are well illustrated by the fact that 1902 was not only the year in which Klinger exhibited his Beethoven sculpture, it was also the year in which Isadora Duncan was allowed to perform her 'classical Greek' dances at the Secession. The same aspirations were also embodied in the organization's periodical, *Ver sacrum* (Sacred Spring). If the Secession's artists asserted their claims to freedom in their organization's motto, then this was in part a reflection of a serious disagreement that had arisen in 1900, when Klimt had been commissioned to create a new work for the Great Hall of the University, only for his painting *Philosophy* to encounter armed resistance. Similar protests were directed at his Beethoven frieze, a work that was Mahler's closest point of contact with the visual arts of his day and that was also the finest example of the Secession's aspirations to produce a total artwork in the spirit of Richard Wagner. What follows is a brief account of Mahler's contribution to this project, not a comprehensive assessment of Klimt's frieze, still less a disquisition of the exhibition as a whole.[12]

For the Secession's fourteenth exhibition, which was due to open in the middle of April 1902, the organizers planned something special – not just individual pieces were to be shown, but an entire room was to be the focus of a particular artwork and form a kind of temple. Its contents were designed to demonstrate what these young artists could create if they were commissioned to produce the kind of total artwork that they had not yet been officially invited to undertake. The inspiration was to be a work by an artist who, although only a corresponding member of the Secession, was acknowledged by old and young alike to be one of its leading figures: Max Klinger's monumental statue of Beethoven depicted a titanic, enthroned composer with an eagle at his feet. The starting point for Klinger's piece – now in the Gewandhaus in Leipzig – was the nineteenth century's cult of Beethoven, which he took to its furthest and ultimate lengths, combining, as he did, Wagner's image of Beethoven with Nietzsche's influential superman. Klimt was not the only artist who helped to design the room's interior, but his Beethoven frieze overshadowed all the other contributions to such an extent that they appeared to be secondary pieces. The overall conception was entrusted to Alfred Roller, although, according to Alma, it was not Roller but Carl Moll who had the idea of inviting Mahler to make a musical contribution to the opening ceremony.

In designing his Beethoven frieze, Klimt was concerned, above all, to depict the struggle between the lonely genius and the hostility and lack of understanding that characterize large sections of the world around him. The various panels reflect this interpretation, suggesting nothing so much as the stations of the Cross: they depict, in sequence, the longing for happiness; the sufferings of feeble humanity; the pleas addressed to a powerful individual – the artist – to fight the good fight on behalf of the weak; the hostile forces that are opposed to humanity and their champion and that are embodied in the terrifying figure of Typhon; illness, madness and death defeated by humanity's aspirations; the arts leading ultimately to a world of ideality; and, finally, a representation of Schiller's 'Ode to Joy' that had provided Beethoven with the words for his Choral Symphony: 'Joy, beautiful divine spark – this kiss to the whole world.' Klimt was inspired on every level by Klinger's view of Beethoven as an altogether titanic figure. But the artists of the Secession who paid this extraordinary tribute to Klinger and his work were clearly also thinking of the role of art and artists in the present day. This was a subject particularly close to Klimt's heart, for his paintings *Philosophy* and *Medicine*, which were intended for the Great Hall of the University, had provoked a veritable scandal when exhibited at the Secession in previous years. (His third commission, *Jurisprudence*, was not unveiled until 1903.) Most of the city's 'art lovers' and the majority of the teaching staff at the University dismissed his works as symbolically obtuse and in their depiction of nude bodies positively obscene. Klimt felt that he was battling with the Viennese over the place that was rightfully his in the city's artistic life, with the result that he saw himself as the knight in his Beethoven frieze. The claim that the knight resembles Mahler is difficult to sustain. True, Klimt may have thought of Mahler, who had fought and lost his battle with the Vienna Philharmonic only twelve months earlier. No less true is the fact that his position as a composer who championed the new and inaccessible was becoming increasingly precarious in Vienna. It is clear, moreover, from Karl Kraus's enthusiasm for 'Young Siegfried' at the Court Opera that the city's young and unruly artists and intellectuals saw Mahler as one of their own. But there is no question of any physical similarity between Mahler and the figure in the frieze. Indeed, Klimt himself would have regarded such a resemblance as trivializing in the extreme.

But Klimt's work is more than merely an expression of current disputes in the world of art. Far more important from Mahler's point of view was the artist's eclectic recourse to ideas associated with Wagner, whose essay on his own performance of Beethoven's Ninth Symphony in Dresden in 1846, for example, demonstrably left its mark on some of the details of Klimt's monumental frieze. Wagner, Klimt and Mahler all held the view that art alone was capable of leading disorientated humanity into a better world. 'Music is a sacred art,' sings the Composer in Hofmannsthal's libretto to Strauss's *Ariadne auf Naxos*. The artist is the high priest of this religious view of art. The tragedy and heroism of his own artistry that Klinger depicted in his statue of Beethoven were characteristics that Klimt and Mahler likewise divined in the composer. It made perfect sense that Beethoven and Wagner were Mahler's gods. And then there was Nietzsche, struggling with the philistines and idols of modernity – and even though Mahler was increasingly sceptical of Nietzsche from 1900 onwards, it was impossible for him to forget his old ties to the iconoclastic philosopher. Ideas about a comprehensive reform of culture designed to counter the debilitating interest in the whole problem of turn-of-the-century decadence were by no means unfamiliar to Mahler. The fact that he was best known and, indeed, notorious as a conductor of Beethoven and Wagner will also have played a part in the decision to invite him to participate in the venture – just over a year earlier his retouchings of the Ninth Symphony had given rise to arguments that the Viennese still remembered. (His legendary production of *Fidelio* at the Court Opera, conversely, did not take place until October 1904.)

It made sense, then, for the organizers to enlist Mahler's services if they wanted a musical element to their Secessionist artwork – and, given their claims to artistic universality, an opening ceremony without music would have been absurd, especially where Beethoven was the focus of interest. According to Alma, it was her stepfather, Carl Moll, who approached Mahler: the couple married in March 1902 and the exhibition opened on 15 April, not May, as claimed by Alma. We do not know when the earliest discussions between Mahler and the Secessionists took place, but he will have needed only a short time to prepare a suitable passage from the finale of the Ninth Symphony – the movement to which Klimt explicitly alludes – and to provide an arrangement of it. The original plan to perform the whole symphony with the Vienna Philharmonic, the Vienna Court Opera chorus and four vocal soloists foundered on reasons that are no longer clear – although it appears that the orchestra declared itself overworked and unable to appear, a reaction that is fully understandable in the light of the strained relations between the orchestra and its conductor, who could not compel his players to perform.[13] As a result, Mahler had to content himself with a wind-band arrangement of a passage from the final chorus performed by those members of the Court Opera orchestra who were willing to take part. Alma reports that the passage ran from 'Ihr stürzt nieder' to 'Überm Sternenzelt muß ein guter Vater wohnen', adding that when Klinger entered the hall to the strains of Beethoven's music, his eyes immediately filled with tears.[14]

At one of the preliminary rehearsals, probably on 12 April, the audience included Ludwig Hevesi, who loyally and enthusiastically observed the workings of the Secession: 'On the podium in the left-hand side aisle, Director Mahler was standing with his brass players and rehearsing a motif from the Ninth that he had arranged for trombones. In the evening, prior to the Klinger banquet at the Grand Hotel, an entirely private reception is planned at the Secession. Its members will welcome their beloved visitor and these strains of Beethoven's music will greet him as he enters.'[15] Mahler's involvement is not mentioned in the newspapers, leaving a number of questions open. Alma, for example, does not say exactly when Klinger was reduced to tears, but Hevesi leads us to assume that it was on the eve of the official opening that Mahler conducted this excerpt from Beethoven's symphony at the Secession, in other words, 14 April, and that it was not performed at the next day's official opening. But we cannot be certain. Even less clear is the excerpt that was performed. Hevesi speaks simply of a motif, whereas Alma refers to an entire passage from the final chorus. But a closer look at the score reveals that, no matter how it was arranged, this passage cannot have lasted more than a minute. Is it plausible that having abandoned their original plans for a complete performance of the symphony, the organizers, including Mahler, would have invested all this time and effort in an excerpt that can have been little more than a fanfare? Neither the score nor the parts that were used for this performance appear to have survived, but it is none the less tempting to think in terms of a longer excerpt rather than the same passage repeated several times. At least a few minutes would have been set aside for Beethoven's music.

Mahler will have felt at ease with the Secessionists, a feeling bolstered by his sense of solidarity with them, especially with Klimt, who in his own field had encountered exactly the same sort of resistance as Mahler had in his. All the members of the organization shared a common belief in the sacred mission of art and in the power of an art that embraced all the arts and all classes of society to change the world. The Secession was thus Mahler's closest point of contact with the artistic and intellectual aspirations of turn-of-the-century Vienna. None the less, it is worth remembering that until now Mahler had taken no obvious interest in the work of Klimt or Olbrich or Otto Wagner. Over and above any shared beliefs, it will have been Mahler's personal contacts with Moll and Klimt that inspired and encouraged him to lend his support to the venture. We do not know exactly when he met his future father-in-law, but it was presumably only after Alma had introduced him to the Moll household. It is unlikely that he got to know Klimt before early November 1901, when they were both invited to dine at the home of Emil and Bertha Zuckerkandl – this was also the evening when Mahler and Alma really got to know one another. It was presumably only during the preparations for the exhibition that Mahler was introduced to Alfred Roller, but the encounter soon led to closer contacts, including an invitation to supper at the newlyweds' home in May 1902, when another of the guests was Kolo Moser. The invitation also included the word 'Tristan' and thus looked forward to the epoch-making collaboration between Roller and Mahler whose first fruits were their new production of *Tristan und Isolde* in February 1903 – their plans must already have been discussed at the time of the Secession exhibition, for the initial set models were approved in June 1902.[16]

We do not know much more about contacts between Mahler and Klimt: although the two men remained in touch, Klimt appears to have visited the Mahlers only infrequently, but this was due in part, of course, to the fact that Alma had almost married him and, indeed, would have done so if cowardice had not prevented him. All three parties knew this, and it must have placed a certain strain on their relations. And yet the two men continued to respect each other and to take an interest in one another's work. In the context of a rather later episode in New York, Alma notes that her husband had developed a deeper interest in the visual arts: 'Mahler had no native feeling for painting; his mind was too much under the dominion of literature. Yet by degrees, through much looking and an exorbitant desire to know all that was to be known, he began to derive pleasure from pure painting and the ability to judge it. Moll, Klimt, Roller and Kolo Moser disputed the right to be his teacher.'[17] When Paul Stefan published his tribute to Mahler in 1910 to mark the composer's fiftieth birthday, Klimt – who was to survive Mahler by only seven years – contributed a textless reproduction of the knight from his Beethoven frieze.

A Salon Acquaintanceship

The name of Bertha Zuckerkandl takes us from the general to the particular: from our wider conspectus of turn-of-the-century Viennese culture to a narrower circle in the form of the most famous salon of the period, a place where many paths crossed. For Mahler, who had always maintained a respectful distance from the wider cultural context of which he was none the less a part, this was the path on which he met his future wife. As a literary and aesthetic phenomenon, the Viennese salon had flourished during the heyday of Romanticism and Biedermeier art in the first half of the nineteenth century, Fanny Arnstein's salon being the most important such meeting place at this time. By the end of the nineteenth century the tradition still existed, and observers could still catch an occasional glimpse of the older generation in the salons of Baron Todesco, the patron of the arts Nikolaus Dumba, the industrialist Ludwig Lobmeyr and the publisher Moritz von Gerold. The home of Josephine von Wertheimstein at Döbling was a place where representatives of

Old Europe – men like Ferdinand von Saar, Eduard Bauernfeld and Moritz von Schwind – could indulge their memories of an earlier age, the present generation having effectively forgotten their existence. The young Hugo von Hofmannsthal also had the honour of receiving an invitation, an honour he no doubt owed to his reputation as a precociously gifted poet whose earliest collection of verse was published under the pen name of Loris while he was still at school. When the 'old lady', as he called her, died in 1894, he wrote an eloquent obituary, his lifelong respect of the powerful ability of the precious and superannuated to exert a lasting sway drawing its strength from encounters such as this.

Bertha Zuckerkandl, by contrast, was a typical product of turn-of-the-century Vienna, her salon set apart from its predecessors not least by virtue of the fact that her principal means of communication was the still relatively recent invention of the telephone. She was four years younger than Mahler and the daughter of a successful journalist, Moritz Szeps, who had come to Vienna from Galicia and founded first the *Morgenpost*, then the *Neues Wiener Tagblatt*. As editor-in-chief of both, he was for half a century one of the most influential press barons in Vienna. Friendly with Crown Prince Rudolf, he advised the latter on political and personal matters. His daughter, too, had journalistic ambitions – an unusual career for a woman at this time. Her brother became editor-in-chief of the *Allgemeine Zeitung*, and for him she wrote articles and translated stage plays, mainly from the French. Her marriage to the eminent anatomist Emil Zuckerkandl in 1886 gave her a chance to lend the glamour of an upper-class salon to her far-flung attempts to infiltrate and consolidate the city's cultural scene. Her husband introduced her to his famous colleague Johann Schnitzler and the latter's son, Arthur. In turn, Schnitzler brought her into contact with Hugo von Hofmannsthal, through whom she met Richard Beer-Hofmann and Hermann Bahr. Bahr put her in touch with the writer Peter Altenberg, and so on.

Bertha's sister, Sophie, was married to Paul Clemenceau, a brother of Georges Clemenceau, who, after qualifying as a doctor, entered politics, championing Alfred Dreyfus and twice holding ministerial positions, initially as minister of the interior from 1906 to 1909 and then as prime minister from 1917 to 1920. In the latter capacity he was responsible for guiding France's fortunes during the final stages of the war and its aftermath. In Paris, Paul and Sophie Clemenceau formed the hard core of a group of enthusiastic Mahlerians that included another of Dreyfus's sympathizers, Georges Picquart, who was one of the first to become involved in the Dreyfus Affair when he exposed the tissue of lies surrounding the case. Another member of the group was Paul Painlevé, who likewise went on to become the country's prime minister. This band of loyal supporters followed Mahler whenever his concert tours brought him closer to Paris, and they also met him on their visits to Vienna.

Inasmuch as Bertha Zuckerkandl was an early champion of the Secession in turn-of-the-century Vienna, supporting the movement both through her journalism and through her salon, it was only a question of time before her address book included the name of Gustav Mahler, for all that the latter was notorious for his hatred of private gatherings, when he might find himself placed next to a guest with whom he had nothing to say.[18] The invitation duly arrived for 6 or 7 November 1901 – the sources differ, Bertha herself confusing the matter still further by giving 3 November 1900 as the date, although this is ruled out by other evidence. Alma's diaries suggest that it was 7 November 1901. According to Bertha's reminiscences, Mahler accepted the invitation in the course of a telephone call in which he passed on the good wishes of the Zuckerkandls' relatives in Paris, although this seems unlikely as Mahler had not been in Paris that year. Even so, Bertha's account of their telephone conversation is undeniably entertaining, Mahler insisting that he would not have to meet any of the other guests and that his diet consisted solely of wholemeal bread and apples grown in Meran in the Tyrol. At the same time, Alma's mother, Anna Moll, had apparently telephoned Emil Zuckerkandl to report that her daughter was spending all her time at the opera, returning home in tears and, pale and silent, rushing straight over to the piano. Knowing what was afoot, Zuckerkandl invited Alma to attend the same supper party as Mahler. However accurate the details of her account, Bertha's version of events is at least amusing and acutely perceptive: in order to provide Mahler with appropriate company, she also invited Hermann Bahr, Gustav Klimt and Max Burckhard, the former director of the Burgtheater, who had been more than just a fatherly friend to Alma. The guests launched into a discussion of the freedom of art in turn-of-the-century Vienna, each of the participants having a tale to tell about the erosions of that freedom and his manly attempts to resist it.

At the end of the meal the guests retired to the salon to relax, only for an argument to break out between Alma and the director of the Court Opera. She complained, somewhat presumptuously, that he had failed to give his response to a ballet submitted by Alexander Zemlinsky – her piano and composition teacher and also the man to whom she had been closer than to any other in her life so far. Such an extended silence, she went on, amounted to a snub. Her criticisms became increasingly strident, and Mahler's counterclaim that the piece was worthless did nothing to calm her. In the end he admitted defeat, promising to invite Zemlinsky to his office the very next day in order to discuss the matter. The ballet in question must have been *Der Triumph der Zeit* (*The Triumph of the Age*), a collaboration between Zemlinsky and Hofmannsthal, even if Alma erroneously calls it *Das goldene Herz* (*The Golden Heart*) – a further example of her unreliable memory. She does, however, state that it was a ballet by Hofmannsthal and that the composer worked on it during the first half of 1901 but never completed it. Conversely, it is strange that Mahler should have spoken so dismissively about Zemlinsky, whose opera *Es war einmal* he had introduced to the Court Opera repertory in 1900. Be that as it may, it seems entirely plausible that as he was leaving Mahler invited his hostess and Fräulein Schindler to the dress rehearsal of *Les Contes d'Hoffmann*, the first performance of a new production which Mahler conducted on 11 November 1901. Bertha Zuckerkandl takes up the story in a letter to her sister: 'Three weeks have gone by since then. Yesterday Alma and Mahler became engaged. Immediately after the evening with me he called on Alma's mother, Frau Moll, and was delighted by the atmosphere in their home – he thawed and forgot his ascetic view of the world, becoming young again and falling foolishly in love.'[19]

Alma recalled the fateful evening in her diary, and although her account differs on points of detail, it basically tallies with Bertha Zuckerkandl's. But with the publication of her diary, we also know that this legendary evening at the Zuckerkandls was not the first meeting between Mahler and Alma. They had first met more than two years earlier, when she had been on holiday with friends at Stambach near Goisern on Lake Hallstatt. She had been out cycling, a then fashionable sport that Mahler, too, enjoyed. On 11 July 1899, just outside Gosaumühle, Alma's group met Mahler's party, consisting of Mahler himself, his sister Justi, Arnold Rosé and an 'old woman', who may or may not have been Natalie Bauer-Lechner. Alma had repeatedly confided her infatuation with Mahler in her diary and shortly before their velocipedestrian encounter in the Salzkammergut she had written to ask him for his autograph. He had duly obliged, sending her a picture postcard of Aussee that was postmarked 5 July and adding the note: 'Sole authenticated and copyrighted signature: Gustav Mahler. Imitators are liable to prosecution.' But now she found it unsettling that he kept staring at her and that her beauty had clearly not left him unmoved. It is by no means implausible that he saw a connection between her and her request for his autograph:

Mahler is following us.

He soon overtook us, and we met some four or five times. Each time he struck up a conversation. Shortly before Hallstatt he dismounted. We were pushing our bikes, and he started up another conversation, staring hard at me. I jumped onto my bike and rode off into the distance. The Geiringers were angry: they'd wanted to introduce me, and he was expecting it too. Judging by the way he looked at me, he appears to have perceived the connection between myself and the postcard – which I found most embarrassing.

Anyway I feel absolutely no urge to meet him. I love and honour him as an artist, but as a man he doesn't interest me at all. I wouldn't want to lose my illusions either.[20]

This, then, was the first meeting between Mahler and Alma Schindler, not the evening at the Zuckerkandls almost two and a half years later, although it is this later encounter which, of the two, deserves to be described as 'fateful'.

Alma Schindler: A Portrait of a Very Young Woman

For her three female biographers Françoise Giroud, Susanne Keegan and Karen Monson, Alma Mahler-Gropius-Werfel née Schindler was a highly gifted artist, the victim of her own matchless beauty, and prevented from working as a composer in her own right by the domineeringly patriarchal Mahler, who tolerated no gods beside himself. Other observers – mostly men – see her differently. Strauss, for example, called her a 'dissolute woman', while Adorno is said to have described her in conversation as a 'monster'. The most ungallant description, however, is that of Elias Canetti in the third part of his autobiography, *The Play of the Eyes*. Canetti was friendly with the Mahlers' daughter, Anna, and in 1934 he was introduced to Alma: 'A large woman, over-flowing in all directions, with a sickly-sweet smile and bright, wide-open, glassy eyes.' This, then, was Canetti's first impression, the glassiness of Alma's stare the result of her intake of alcohol. She had gathered all her 'trophies' around her, namely, the score of Mahler's unfinished Tenth Symphony, with the composer's effusive marginalia referring to her, and the portrait that Kokoschka had painted of her as Lucrezia Borgia. Her sixteen-year-old daughter, Manon Gropius, then entered the room, leading Alma to wax lyrical about the 'Aryan' Gropius, the only man who was 'racially suited' to her. 'All the others who fell in love with me were little Jews. Like Mahler.'[21]

More recently, the German *littérateur* Hans Wollschläger has spoken of her 'complete inability to think a single coherent thought' and of her 'turgid gossip, hare-brained to the point of utter confusion' – Wollschläger was reviewing the first German edition of the complete correspondence between Alma and Mahler when it appeared in 1995.[22] Claire Goll painted an even more lurid portrait of Alma as Werfel's widow: 'In order to revitalize her fading charms, she wore gigantic hats with ostrich feathers, leaving us unsure whether she wanted to appear as a horse which, apparelled in black, traditionally precedes a funeral carriage or as a latter-day d'Artagnan. She was also powdered, rouged, perfumed and completely drunk. This bloated Valkyrie drank like a fish.'[23] Our picture of Alma Schindler has clearly changed over the years. Now, however, her recently published diaries for the years between 1898 and 1902, when she married Mahler, offer us a picture of fin-de-siècle Vienna seen from the standpoint of a young woman aged between nineteen and twenty-three. It is not the sort of picture that might be gleaned from Karl Kraus's *Die Fackel* or from Arthur Schnitzler's diary or from any of the reminiscences of other men and women of the period casting a nostalgic glance back over their lives. (It is worth mentioning in passing that Alma evidently read *Die Fackel* on a regular basis and even got to know its editor, even though there were never any close contacts between them.)

Alma was incapable of gazing down on a situation from Olympian heights but was torn to and fro by her feelings and moods and by her premature and immature assessments of people and events, a paper boat tossed about on the white crests of the waves of turn-of-the-century Vienna. Yet it is precisely this volatility that lends her jottings their immediacy. (It has to be noted, however, that towards the end of her life, Alma subjected their content to a censorious revisionary process. What was destroyed cannot be reconstructed, although passages that were merely blacked out have for the most part been deciphered.) The picture that emerges from these entries is bound to encourage us to qualify the negative views of Alma quoted a moment ago and help to explain much that would otherwise be hidden to anyone approaching the subject merely from Mahler's standpoint.

First and foremost, the diaries help to throw light on the problematical family structure. Alma's father, Emil Jakob Schindler, was a respected land-scape painter who died when she was only thirteen. Like Electra, she spent her whole life grieving for the loss of her father, and all her feelings of loneliness were bound up with the thought of Emil Schindler. Her mother very quickly married the artist Carl Moll, but Alma grew increasingly remote from her, especially after the birth of a stepsister. Although her stepfather was an avun-cular figure and by no means unsympathetic, there were repeated arguments with her mother. In the case of all her serious affairs before her marriage to Mahler – 'serious' in the fin-de-siècle sense of emotional involvement but physical abstinence – it is striking that she felt particularly attracted to much older men. Although earlier commentators had noted this fact, it was only with the publication of her diaries that it became clear to what an extent the loss of her father had played a decisive role in shaping her behavioural patterns. Gustav Klimt, the first great love of her life, was fifteen years older; Joseph Maria Olbrich was twelve years older; the heldentenor Erik Schmedes, whom she worshipped for his 'winning body' and bel canto approach to Wagner, was eleven years older; the Belgian Symbolist Fernand Khnopff was twenty-one years older; and Max Burckhard, the former director of the Burgtheater, was twenty-five years older. Alexander Zemlinsky, who was arguably the most important person in Alma's love life between Klimt and

Mahler, was only eight years older and, as such, the exception that confirms the rule. (Alma reproached him for not trusting himself enough with her.) Nineteen years her senior, Mahler redressed the balance.

Alma was a coquettish femme fatale who was still developing. She flirted unceasingly, the increasingly attractive centre of attention on the part of innumerable younger and older men. Her diaries make it clear that she was an erotic volcano, her sensuality almost untameable, a woman horribly drawn to the animalistic aspect of love. With a degree of detail that is bound to leave even the modern reader feeling slightly uncomfortable, she left little to the imagination when recording in her diary the expressions of her increasingly ungovernable sexuality. In her hands every Zola novel and Wagnerian vocal score became an erotic stimulus. It is significant that in the decisive weeks leading up to her engagement with Mahler her lack of sexual fulfilment had reached an unbearable level. The tender-hearted but all too bashful Zemlinsky was no more capable of quenching her raging thirst than she was herself. Fired by self-love, she was vain and flirtatious, delighting in all the compliments that she received wherever she went. But how could it be otherwise? After all, she was without doubt the most beautiful twenty-year-old in all the circles she frequented. Photographs from the period prove that the sweet little girls who filled the pages of the insatiable Schnitzler's catalogue of conquests could not hold a candle to her. The young Alma was tall, voluptuous and, in keeping with the ideal beauty of the age, a little Rubenesque. Even at this early date she had a tendency to look a little bloated, a tendency that became more pronounced with time. She had a magnificent head of hair and a round, soft-featured face of childlike beauty that was eye-catching even while she was still a young girl. She came from a well-respected family of artists, moving almost daily with perceptible assurance from the Secession and Musikverein to the Court Opera and Burgtheater, the object of male desire on the part of many of the leading representatives of all four of these institutions. She enjoyed sports and was an enthusiastic cyclist who was not afraid of falling off. Above all, she was gifted as an artist, although opinions of her abilities diverge. She was able to draw (a point well illustrated by her published diaries), she played the piano extremely well, and she wrote music.

Her piano playing served chiefly to allow her to revel in the works of her favourite composer, Wagner, and to give full rein to the feelings that she was unable to express in real life. Her cult of Wagner and his music was so all-encompassing that it has been difficult until now to gain an overview of it. In her eyes, he towered over Goethe and Arnold Böcklin, a saint whom she worshipped, like Ludwig II, to distraction. Her piano at home was a private altar at which she offered up sacrifices to Wagner. Good performances at the Court Opera induced in her a sense of ecstasy of positively orgasmic proportions. It was no accident that she was infatuated with the Wagnerian tenor Erik Schmedes, freely admitting that after a performance of *Siegfried* there was nothing she would not have done with him. Her Wagnerian fanaticism is undoubtedly connected to her anti-Semitism, an aspect of her character that has always occasioned surprise. With few exceptions, all Wagnerians at this time were almost by nature anti-Semites. 'No Jew can *ever* understand Wagner,' she noted in her diary after a performance of *Siegfried* in September 1899.[24] Her later dismissive references to Jews and all things Jewish are well documented, a point that Canetti was not slow to make. Her diaries, too, contain a whole catalogue of anti-Jewish remarks, although they cannot be said to amount to a coherent or consistent outlook. In July 1899 she called in at a local hostelry in Goisern and was disturbed by the endless jostling: 'A disgusting pack of Jews.'[25] There is absolutely no sense of self-irony when she describes herself elsewhere as a philo-Semite who stumbled at the occasional blow but who never lost her footing.[26] While lacking the systematic thinking that is part and parcel of anti-Semitism, Alma Schindler punctiliously mimicked the common prejudices of her age both in Vienna and elsewhere. In this she was confirmed by the anti-Semitism of her idol Wagner and by similar views within her own family, views that could not be shaken even by leading figures on the local cultural scene who, themselves Jewish, left a deep impression on her and included Zemlinsky and Mahler. But she was more selective when taking over the casual, everyday anti-Semitism that was to be found at every turn in fin-de-siècle Vienna and, indeed, elsewhere, the only exceptions being those towns and cities that did not have Jewish populations or where, even more rarely, Jews were positively welcomed.

In itself her decision to marry a Jew represents a significant rejection of the anti-Semitism of her age. (As we have already pointed out, the term 'Jew' is used here in the sense in which it was understood by Alma's contemporaries, Mahler's status in this regard being far from unequivocal.) She married Mahler in the face of opposition from her mother and stepfather, both of whom harboured anti-Jewish feelings – Carl Moll later joined the National Socialists, taking his own life in his mid-eighties in 1945. But it was impossible for her not to have been infected by the casual anti-Semitism of the age. She merely repeated such prejudices unthinkingly, while remaining ready to forget them as soon as she found a man attractive. Her parodies of Jewish characteristics made her the life and soul of all the parties she attended, but at the same time she felt sympathy for a friend who was the victim of an anti-Semitic hate campaign. As for Zemlinsky, her diaries contradict her later reminiscences and give the distinct impression that she would have married him if Mahler had not turned up at the very last moment. She was clearly deeply in love with Zemlinsky, and yet she baulked at the idea of marriage and of bringing 'little, degenerate Jew-kids' into the world, as she put it.[27] Even so, this thought did nothing to dampen her passion, and this consideration played no part in her decision to get to know Mahler, for all that she was advised not to marry a Jew – and this Jew in particular. Max Burckhard, Alma's fatherly friend who harboured more than fatherly feelings for her, summed up her contemporaries' response when her passion for Mahler became obvious: 'It would be a positive sin. A fine girl like you – and such a pedigree too. Don't spoil it all by marrying an elderly degenerate. Think of your children – it'd be a sin!'[28] Given Alma's youth, the age difference was certainly considerable when judged by the standards of the time and, with a pinch of salt, it would probably also be regarded as such today. But Burckhard's warning was also racially motivated – one is almost inevitably reminded of the term 'Rassenschande', which the National Socialists used for sexual relations with a non-Aryan. Certainly, it is clear from such a comment that ideas of a genetically sound Aryan race and a degenerate Jewish race were already percolating the thinking of even well-educated Germans – Burckhard was anything but an anti-Semitic backwoodsman. Indeed, Alma even thought of Burckhard as infected by Jewish ideas: 'I must admit, though, that the bad company he keeps is causing his pure, Aryan blood to semitify. He's even beginning to look Jewish.'[29]

Many writers have made fun of Alma's apparent tendency to collect men of genius as if they were butterflies. Indeed, she herself admitted that it was enough for a man of genius to look at her and she went weak at the knees. Her sensuality was easily roused, but pure manhood was not in itself sufficient to excite her. She also needed intellectual or artistic brilliance. In the case of Erik Schmedes, a strapping body and a beautiful voice were enough. Above all, he sang Wagner's heroic tenor roles. Before Zemlinsky arrived on the scene, it was Klimt who impressed her the most, and if he had not proved weak on one decisive point, then Alma would have gone down in history as Alma Klimt. But, instead, he came to an arrangement with Carl Moll and withdrew his candidacy following a visit to Italy when Alma almost became his lover. Klimt had the advantage of not being Jewish and of being considerably more attractive than Zemlinsky. If Klimt's reputation as a womanizer alarmed Alma, then it also made him more interesting in her eyes. A nightmare that she noted down in her diary and that might almost have come from a film by David Lynch reveals the extent of her feelings for Klimt:

I got undressed. – and suddenly I felt as if I were disgorging some slimy object. It hardened rapidly, only to melt again. I grasped it in my hands – it was nothing but a pair of blue eyes, blue eyes! I held the shadow in a stranglehold, thrust it from me. It cried out: I am your child – yours and Klimt's. More than once in your imagination you have conceived me – and now you deny my very existence.[30]

At the same time she ended her flirtation with Max Burckhard with the words: 'The minor excitement would not have harmed me. If only I knew whose turn it was now – it's terrible to be unoccupied.'[31] It was a sensation that Alma Schindler never had to endure for long. One wonders, however, whether her instinctual urges left her with any time to train as an artist.

This brings us to the question of Alma's compositional ambitions and Mahler's notorious insistence in his letter to her of 19 December 1901 that she must curb those ambitions if and when he married her. Although her surviving songs cannot be dated with any accuracy, they reveal an undoubted talent, but whether they demonstrate more than that remains questionable. Her composition lessons with the blind Bohemian pianist and organist Josef Labor were notable for his paternal forbearance. Her lessons with Zemlinsky, conversely, could have achieved something but in the end they remained too desultory. Antony Beaumont, the co-editor of Alma's diaries, argues on the basis of the music examples included in their pages that she lacked a musical ear and also a sound knowledge of theory and orchestration. As a result she never progressed beyond songs and short piano pieces. In a moment of anger Zemlinsky once dismissed her as 'only half a person', a woman who turned her hand to many things but never managed to complete anything.

It would be unfair to quote these opinions, were it not for the fact that Alma's diaries are full of self-criticisms on precisely this point. Even as a nineteen-year old, she was already striking a note of despair: 'In a word, I want to be a some-body. But it's impossible – & why? I don't lack talent, but my attitude is too friv-olous for my objectives, for artistic achievement.'[32] Towards the end of her diary, she even repeats Zemlinsky's dismissal of her abilities: 'I have this feeling that *nothing* really moves me. I am, truly, only half a person. I'm deeply saddened – no, I'm incapable of being *deeply* sad. Tepid – just tepid! I feel sorry for anyone who sincerely loves me. I'm disgusted at my behaviour.'[33] Alma's situation was hopeless, and the unspeakable loneliness and unhappiness to which she often refers are bound to leave the reader deeply affected. Even at the end of her life she still felt that she had not fully explored the whole range of her talents as a result of her inability to concentrate and her tendency to be all too easily distracted by her breathtaking beauty, so that she lacked the energy and industry to change a situation that she ascribed at times to her feminine existence and at others to individual failure. In the course of a discussion as to why women had achieved nothing notable in the field of music, she astonished her audience by arguing that women could achieve something as artists only as long as they merely copied from nature, hence their distinction as portraitists and landscape artists. But if the whole heart and mind were involved – and in the visual arts she named Böcklin as an example – then women must necessarily fail:

There is nothing like this with women, and there never will be because they have too little intellectual depth and philosophical training. They lack creative power. . . . And then there is music, of all the arts the one that is most difficult to understand and that is the most completely permeated by the mind – it comes entirely from the heart. Here there is no *copying* of nature – you wouldn't get beyond the sort of songs that imitate birdsong and millwheels. Here it is a question of reproducing a mood, and atmosphere is a momentary state involving the heart. And I – a young woman with such a small heart and an even smaller brain – I want to achieve something in this field? – Bah![34]

A woman who had learnt to think like this would be unable to develop much self-confidence as a composer. How could she remain steadfast when Mahler came along and asked her whether she could imagine herself working alongside him as his equal as a composer? Alma never broke free from these inhibitions.

She was undoubtedly considerably more gifted than the other daughters of upper middle-class parents in fin-de-siècle Vienna, and yet she was hardly another Fanny Mendelssohn. What puzzled her about Mahler from the outset was that he was so ruthless in pointing out her weaknesses – his ruthlessness may have been objectively justified but from a psychological and personal point of view it was little short of catastrophic. Undeterred by his great love for her, he even spelt out these weaknesses for her. Inwardly, she was forced to admit that he was right, but at the same time she inevitably felt humiliated whenever he tried to educate her, told her what she should be reading, shook his head at her half-baked philosophizing, chastised her for her superficiality and, in the ominous letter to which we have already referred, demanded that she should regard his own music as hers. In spite of claims to the contrary and notwithstanding Alma's own later attempts to rewrite history, this was not an outright ban on composition but merely reflected Mahler's all too sober observation that he could not envisage a marriage between two composers, hence his question – posed before it was too late – whether she saw things in the same light:

Let me speak in general terms. A husband and wife who are both composers: how do you envisage that? Such a strange relationship between rivals: do you have any idea how ridiculous it would appear, can you imagine the loss of self-respect it would later cause us both? . . . If you were to abandon *your* music in order to take possession of mine, and also to be mine: would this signify the end of life as you know it, and if you did so, would you feel you were renouncing a higher existence? Before we can think of forging a bond for life, we *must* agree on this question. What do you mean when you write:

'I haven't worked any more – since then!' 'Now I have to return to my work'
etc. etc.? What kind of work is this? Composition? Do you compose for your
own pleasure or for the benefit of mankind?[35]

We cannot call this a ban because by now Alma must have known what
she was letting herself in for. Nor was it a kind of blackmail but the spelling out
of a precondition for their planned marriage. It was a condition laid down
independently of the quality of her compositions which, as Mahler admitted
on more than one occasion, he simply did not know. One may dismiss this as
patriarchal or worse, but Mahler was not alone in holding this view – suffice it
to recall a letter that Freud wrote to his fiancée Martha Bernays in 1883
in which he expressed the very same convictions with regard to a woman's
role in life:

> It seems a completely unrealistic notion to send women into the struggle for
> existence in the same way as men. Am I to think of my delicate, sweet girl as
> a competitor? After all, the encounter could only end by my telling her, as I
> did seventeen months ago, that I love her, and that I will make every effort to
> get her out of the competitive role into the quiet, undisturbed activity of my
> home. . . .
>
> No, in this respect I adhere to the old ways, to my longing for my Martha
> as she is, and she herself will not want it different; legislation and custom have
> to grant to women many rights kept from them, but the position of woman
> cannot be other than what it is: to be an adored sweetheart in youth, and a
> beloved wife in maturity.
>
> There is so much more to be said on this subject, but I think we see eye to
> eye anyway.[36]

Martha Bernays had none of Alma Schindler's artistic ambitions, but she was
none the less a clever and self-possessed young woman not untouched by the
first stirrings of the movement for women's emancipation. Only four years
older than Mahler, Freud reacted with the same patriarchal condescension. No
matter how much he may have felt like any other young intellectual and
acknowledged that women were owed more rights, he could not conceive of a
woman as his rival or as a competitor.

On the other hand, it cannot be denied that Mahler was right – and no
amount of embittered feminist dogma will alter this fact. There is simply no
comparison between the short-breathed, atmospheric pointillism of Alma's
songs and the opening movements of the Fifth Symphony on which Mahler
was then working. It is doubtful whether Alma would ever have overcome the
opposition to female composers at this time and been taken seriously as a

composer, at least in the way that Mahler's contemporary, Ethel Smyth, was. But none of these considerations carries any weight when set aside Alma's reaction to Mahler's letter, a reaction confided in one of the final entries in her diary: 'It will leave an indelible scar. . . .'[37] And so it did, even if by the very next day Alma had voluntarily decided to abandon her own artistic ambitions out of her love of Mahler.

The young Alma Schindler's diaries cannot be called in evidence to support the spiteful comments that were quoted above. Rather, their author appears in the sort of gentle, transfigured light with which her father suffused his Austrian landscapes. True, she gives the impression of a coquette hopelessly in love with herself, unable to settle down but addicted to entertainment, while many of her opinions strike one as immature and supercilious. And yet the intensity with which she lived her life and her capacity for enthusiasm were unparalleled. What other man or woman of this period was prepared to live life so unsparingly? How much of the prudery of her age did she not have to overcome to keep such a matter-of-fact account of her irrepressible sexuality? How uninhibitedly she abandoned herself to the enjoyment of art, to which she responded with an unfailing depth of emotion! How drunkenly she imbibed the world of nature and how eloquently she described her experiences! There is humour to her descriptions of the way in which she soiled her clothing after drinking too much alcohol (her later alcoholism is mentioned here in astonishingly graphic terms) or how she had to run away down side streets, her garters torn to shreds, in order to escape from the attentions of importunate men. In the sexually charged atmosphere of turn-of-the-century Vienna such a sensual creature was bound to end up marrying prematurely or leading a life of libertinage, and of this she was incapable.

Alma Schindler was not the 'Bohemian Countess' Franziska zu Reventlow, but nor was she a suffragette. Rather, she was a versatile, highly talented, ravishingly beautiful woman who married too soon. The sexual and aesthetic experiences that the city had to offer her assailed her with such ferocity that any young woman was bound to bend like a reed in the wind. A woman who was successively and even simultaneously wooed by Gustav Klimt, Joseph Maria Olbrich, Kolo Moser, Max Burckhard, Alexander Zemlinsky and Gustav Mahler, and who ran from the opening of the Secession to a performance of *Die Walküre* at the Court Opera in order to revel in the sounds of Wagner's music, could scarcely evolve into an independent thinker. More than once her diaries describe her profound loneliness and thoughts of suicide, providing a background against which her unbridled love of life stands out with all the more shocking clarity. She simply had no time or opportunity to develop any strength of character of her own. Was Mahler the right man for her? It is doubtful, just as it is doubtful whether Alma was the right woman for Mahler. Her diaries provide the prehistory to this relationship, and at

least for the period that they cover, they help us to see her in a different light from
the one in which she has tended to appear until now.

Disorder and Early Sorrow: Preparations for a Wedding

The four months that passed between the fateful evening at the Zuckerkandls'
apartment on 7 November 1901 and the Mahlers' wedding in the Karlskirche on
9 March 1902 were a time of tension and turmoil for both Mahler and Alma. The
soirée at the Zuckerkandls certainly left Alma in a state of agitation: 'I must say,
I liked him *immensely* – although he's dreadfully restless. He stormed around the
room like a savage. The fellow is made *entirely* of oxygen. When you go near
him, you get burnt.'[38] It is a description that says much for the young woman's
powers of observation and art of characterization. Mahler left the party with
Max Burckhard, who lost no time in informing Alma that when he had told his
companion that she was a clever and interesting young woman, Mahler had
replied: 'I didn't care for her at first. I thought she was just a doll. But then I realized that she's also very perceptive. Maybe my first impression was because one
doesn't normally expect such a good-looking girl to take anything seriously.'[39] In
both Alma and Mahler a spark had been ignited. And the fire that had been lit
consumed them both with uncanny speed. Alma sensed that the incandescent
love that she had felt for Zemlinsky had suddenly cooled. She felt ashamed, was
overcome by self-doubt and wanted to destroy the 'poisonous weed' that was
growing inside her but was unable to resist its sway. Not everything about the
Court Opera director was to her liking. She did not care for his habit of singing
a particular phrase to make a musical point, nor did she like the way he articulated the letter 'r' – it is conceivable that he used a softer-sounding apical flap,
rather than the usual harder alveolar trill. Above all, she disapproved of the way
he smelled.[40] Alma had an acute sense of smell – time and again she had noted
in her diary that Zemlinsky smelled because he rarely washed, but to the extent
that Mahler's meticulous physical cleanliness was confirmed by other observers,
the same cannot have been true of him. Was it the clothing of the cigar smoker
whose smell she did not like? Or was it the infamous *foetor judaicus*, the
racially segregating smell of the Jew that many anti-Semites, including Arthur
Schopenhauer, believed that they could detect? We simply do not know. But it
remains a remarkable comment on the part of a woman who was distractedly in
love. At best, it is a symptom of her scruples and underlying lack of certainty.

Throughout the important first weeks and months of their courtship, both
parties felt profound uncertainty and ambivalence, and if these feelings were
more pronounced in the case of Alma, there is no doubt that Mahler too, albeit
for different reasons, was unable to commit himself unquestioningly to their
relationship. Far from exulting in a sense of effusive elation, they vacillated

between wild enthusiasm and the deepest of gnawing doubts. Already we may see here the seeds of the marriage's failure, a marriage to which Alma agreed only amidst extreme misgivings. These doubts never left her but were suppressed, only to resurface in moments of crisis, while constantly being fuelled and fomented by those members of her family and circle of friends who opposed her marriage to Mahler. She also had doubts about his music, music that caused her own to be suppressed. All these feelings find undisguised expression in one of the final entries in her diary prior to her wedding:

> If it ever comes to my marrying him, I must do everything *now* to stake *my* rightful claim . . . particularly in *artistic* questions. He thinks *nothing* of my art – and much of his own. And *I* think *nothing* of *his* art and much of my own. – That's how it is! Now he talks unceasingly of safeguarding *his* art. I *can't* do that. With Zemlinsky it would have been possible, because I have sympathy for his art – he's such a brilliant fellow. But Gustav is so poor – so *dreadfully* poor. If he knew *just* how poor he was – he would cover his face in shame. . . . And *I* am supposed to lie, lie for the rest of my life.[41]

And so she continued to vacillate. Did she love Mahler merely because he was the director of the Vienna Court Opera and a great conductor? Or was she attracted to his human qualities? Was he not too old, too ill and too degenerate, as a number of her friends insisted? Or was he a roué, as his future father-in-law furiously exclaimed when his wife went to see the director with their daughter? Many of these accusations were anti-Semitically charged, the Jews being the most degenerate of the degenerate in the eyes of many contemporaries. Even Alma herself saw the question of Mahler's Jewish ancestry as problematical, but as with Zemlinsky she was able to overlook it. She also found Mahler physically unattractive, neither as tall and imposing as the tenor Erik Schmedes nor as virile as Klimt. Although he had beautiful hands, he bit his nails, a habit that an aesthete like Alma found deeply offensive. Nor did burgeoning passion prevent her from ogling other men, and at a performance of *Die Meistersinger* on 12 December 1901, she began to flirt with a young doctor, Louis Adler, who was sitting in the same row. Deep and meaningful glances were exchanged, glances which, as she noted in her diary, bespoke unprecedented desire. Adler was also very attractive, with dark eyes: 'There's good stock for you. Mahler can't compete with that.'[42] To judge by his name, Adler was Jewish, and so Alma must have been using the word 'Rasse' not in a racial sense but as a synonym for 'Rassigkeit', hot-blooded sex appeal. Whatever the answer, it boded ill for the marriage of a passionate young woman boiling over with sensual desire. She also heard rumours of Mahler's affairs with Anna von Mildenburg, Selma Kurz and even Margarete Michalek, who had worked with Mahler on his Fourth Symphony. When she was reading through her diary at a later date, Alma added the words 'Later I discovered it was all lies!' In fact, it was Alma's note that was untrue, but it was all part of her lifelong ploy to portray Mahler as an ascetic right up to the time of his marriage, a man who feared women and who owed his discovery of a 'woman's delights and worth' – to quote Wagner's Loge – to Alma herself. As we know, the truth of the matter was rather different.[43]

Even so, we need to bear in mind that in contradistinction to Zemlinsky and, we may add, to Klimt, Alma always insisted that she harboured only 'the most sacred feelings' for Mahler, and the reason for these feelings emerges to shocking effect when she confides in her diary that her principal emotion was pity: 'He's sick, my poor dear, weighs under 10 stone – *far* too little. I shall care for him like a child. My love for him is infinitely touching.'[44] During his stroll with Mahler through the streets of Leiden in 1910, Freud was to speak of a Mary complex, but this Mary complex clearly had two sides to it: the large, voluptuous, 'Aryan' Alma saw herself as a mother imago holding the sickly little Jew in her lap in the manner of a Pietà, protecting and caring for him – hardly an encouraging portent for their future marriage. But nor should we forget that Alma's feelings for Zemlinsky, although very different, were not significantly affected by the fact that Zemlinsky was a Jew and, indeed, even smaller and more unattractive than Mahler – not that we would describe Mahler as unattractive. He also smelt even worse than Mahler.

And yet Alma's love continued to grow. Mahler even paraded the fact that he was much older than she was. And by means of the self-doubts that he passed on to her or that third parties dutifully retailed, he sought to silence his own doubts on the matter. In the course of the long walks that they took together, he explained to Alma that it was difficult to marry someone in a high but by no means secure position – in raising this objection, he clearly took it for granted that the two of them would marry. He also stressed his need for freedom and independence, while antagonizing her by trying to exert a schoolmasterly influence, notably when he advised her to burn her edition of Nietzsche's writings. He even compared their relationship to that between Sachs and Eva in *Die Meistersinger* – here, of course, he was on shaky ground, for Sachs renounces Eva in favour of the much younger and more presentable Walther von Stolzing. Alma was rightly annoyed at such a comparison, which she saw as a mere excuse. This critical phase in their relationship dates from early December 1901, predating by a few days Mahler's departure for Berlin, where he conducted his Fourth Symphony at a concert whose conducting duties he shared with Strauss. In fact, his tactics, however risky, seem to have been prompted by genuine doubts and misgivings. Shortly before he left for Berlin, he wrote a letter to Alma in which his profound love for her finds no less powerful expression than a patronizing didacticism that any young woman would surely have found intolerable:

> And sometimes I shall pause for thought with that 'distrustful' look on my face that so often surprises you. It isn't *mistrust* in the usual sense of the word, but *uncertainty* with regard to yourself and the future. My dearest, *learn to reply*! It's not at all easy, for one has to have weighed oneself in the balance, one has to know oneself. And *asking* is even harder. It can be learnt only in the light of a complete and intimate relationship with one's partner. My dearest dear, *learn to ask*!
>
> Yesterday you made a completely changed impression and appeared far more mature. I can sense that the past few days have opened you up, have revealed you. – And after my return, what then? – Then I shall ask: Do you *love* me? *More than yesterday*? Did you know me then, and do you recognize me now? And now, my love, my comrade, addio! Your Gustav.[45]

Throughout his absence in Berlin, Mahler continued to bombard Alma with long letters telling her to write more clearly ('Use bigger gaps between the characters') and speaking of his ambition to be understood and respected by his colleagues, a desire that had nothing to do with the ambition of the conductor and opera-house director: 'Please tell me if you understand what I mean and whether you can follow me. Alma! Could you stand by me and take all these burdens upon yourself – even to the point of humiliation – could you happily bear this cross with me?'[46] Is this the language with which one wins over a twenty-two-year-old woman? Marriage as a *via crucis* in the company of a vilified saviour of art? In her edition of her correspondence with Mahler, Alma changed 'can follow me' to 'want to follow me', a change that reflects the disquiet that Mahler's question caused in her.

Time and again Mahler condescended to Alma, adopting the position of the older, wiser and more educated man and telling her what she must do or give up or bear in mind, never for a moment thinking that he must adapt to her and take account of her own needs and limitations. His basic attitude was that she must raise herself to his level: 'On cloud-covered heights there dwell the gods,' the Wanderer proclaims in *Siegfried*, and it would be scant exaggeration to see the hand of the brilliant composer reaching down from these cloud-covered heights and grasping the hand of the young creature who, beautiful, naïve and untouched by the breath of the spirit and the highest art, is drawn aloft towards him. Mahler was at his most candid not in conversation with Alma but in a letter to his sister Justine. On 13 December 1901 – by which date Alma was already clear in her own mind about her future marriage – we find him writing to her: 'The dear girl herself is in quite a state, finding herself in a completely unfamiliar situation, to which I have to open both her eyes and my own. As I recently realized, she will have to mature considerably before I can consider taking such a momentous decision.'[47] Mahler's turn of phrase makes it sound ominously as if he were thinking of buying a piece of property rather than describing the love of his life. His tone of voice suggests a counterpart to Alma's attitude to him, an attitude in which a religious sense of pity was designed to place open ground between them. None of the famous marriages between artists that were entered into at this period began as inauspiciously as the one between Mahler and Alma.

And yet we should be wary of dismissing Mahler as no more than a cold-hearted schoolteacher who did not deserve his young bride. After all, his coolness was a cloak with which to shield the passion that took even him by surprise and which he, already a relatively old man, felt for this young woman. The many misgivings that beset him needed to be put into words. The more barriers that were placed in his way, the more he would be justified in feeling remorse: this was what she wanted – she had been duly warned. In another letter to his sister, he referred openly to the age gap between him and Alma and to the torment that it caused him: 'Only one thing still worries me: whether a person who is already growing old has the right to so much youthfulness and vigour, whether that person has the right to tether the spring to the autumn, to force his partner to forgo the summer. I know I have much to offer, but that is no fair exchange for the right to be young.'[48] There is no doubt that Mahler saw quite clearly what would be one of the problems that might – and indeed did – affect his marriage. Alma's affair with Walter Gropius is already prefigured in these words, and this includes more than just the cooling of the libido on the part of a much older man.

It is something of a miracle that in spite of the hail of warnings on the part of Alma's family and friends, and also in spite of her own profound doubts and misgivings and Mahler's avuncular but ultimately condescending attitude towards her, the real reasons for which were largely concealed from her, she remained steadfast. Anyone familiar with the true facts of the matter must regard her marriage as the most unlikely development of all. In normal circumstances, her relationship with Mahler would have remained a brief if impassioned liaison. It would presumably have been Mahler who took her virginity, but with that the affair would have been over. (It may none the less be recalled that Alma became pregnant even before she was married.) If we take a detailed look at the letters and diary entries from these decisive weeks, we shall see that it was ultimately Alma whose violent passion for Mahler helped her to overcome her misgivings. If she had hesitated even half as much as Mahler, failure would surely have followed. It was Alma's impetuous youth that overcame the ageing genius's emotional and moral scruples, although it remains open to question who was the ultimate victor here.

But there were still two further bridges to be crossed. One was a letter, the other a soirée at the home of Mahler and his sister. Initially, at least, Alma got on very well with Justine, even if in her later reminiscences she did not have a good word to say about her sister-in-law. In his letters to Justine, Mahler speaks of Alma's fondness for her. Only later are there any signs of a cooling off and talk of Justine's 'touchiness'.

Mahler's letter of 19 December 1901 is a remarkable document not only because it implicitly prevents Alma from composing any more music of her own, but also because, worryingly and even alarmingly, Mahler stakes every-thing on a single card, telling Alma any number of home truths and expressing himself so bluntly that the reader is left with the distinct impression that this was Alma's ordeal by fire and water. If she were able to withstand this scrutiny of her immaturity and lack of personal development, her relationship with Mahler could survive every other strain that might be placed upon it. But if it was unable to bear such an analysis, then it would be better if this passionate and troublesome affair ended without further ado. One thing is certain: Alma would never be able to claim that she had no idea of what lay in store. Mahler's 'ban' on her compositional activities is at the heart of this inordinately long letter, and it cannot be viewed in isolation for it is based on a view of Alma that amounts to nothing less than the belief that she was still immature as a person. It seems that the letter that prompted his reply had annoyed him for its super-ficiality. (Like all her letters to Mahler, it was destroyed by Alma herself.) Evidently she had mentioned a discussion with her former beau, Max Burckhard, that had revolved around her individuality. With the brutal honesty that he invariably evinced, especially when dealing with people who were important to him, Mahler simply denied that she had any individuality at all, at least in the higher sense:

Young, sympathetic and boundlessly delightful as you are, unsullied in body and soul, richly gifted, open-hearted and precociously self-assured, all this still makes no true individual of you. What you are for *me*, my Alma, what you could perhaps one day be for me – the highest and dearest part of my life, a faithful, valiant partner, who understands me and spurs me on to higher things, an unassailable fortress, who shields me from all my intrinsic and extrinsic enemies, a haven, a heaven, in which I can always submerge, retrieve and reconstitute myself – all this is so indescribably noble and beautiful – so much and so great – in a word: MY WIFE – but even this is still no individuality in the sense of those superior beings who determine the course of their own existence as well as that of mankind, and who alone bear that name.[49]

And Mahler then goes on to pick to pieces all of Alma's youthful enthusiasms and ideals, ideals buoyed up by the intellectual Zeitgeist and made up of a mixture of 'Schopenhauer's writings on womanhood, Nietzsche's utterly false and brazenly arrogant theories of masculine supremacy, the gut-rotting, murky fuddle of Maeterlinck and the public-house rhetoric of Bierbaum'. And he blames Alma's entourage – in particular Burckhard and Zemlinsky – for her subjective belief that she can maintain her own with the intellectual giants of the age. It is people like these who, inspired by her youthful beauty, have given her the deceptive feeling that she is intellectually and emotionally mature. (He could have said that they had given her this feeling in order to get her into bed with them, but he evidently preferred a more elegant turn of phrase here.)

Anyone who has read Alma's diaries in detail will be bound to agree with Mahler when, discussing the negative side of her personality, he goes on: 'My Alma, you have grown vain – . . . your vanity is a result of what these people think they see in you or would like to see in you. . . . With your charm, you serve such people as an uncommonly delightful, *agreeable* adversary, and one, moreover, who lacks the force of factual argument. Thus, in the belief that you are mutually benefiting mankind, you move together in ever-diminishing circles.' Unfortunately, Mahler went on, Alma was not entirely innocent of this immodesty on the part of people who regarded their own limited gossip as the centre of the universe. Mahler's diagnosis is hard to dispute, and he undoubtedly had a deeper and clearer view of the situation than the people in Alma's entourage, whose self-interest was all too apparent – only in the case of Zemlinsky was he manifestly unjust. And yet his assessment was both implacable and positively malicious. Above all, the candid expression of views that may have been modified in personal conversation and in that way acquired a more conciliatory tone reads like an official character reference when couched in the form of a letter – and such references are normally withheld from the candidate. Having dismissed this immature, albeit gifted, young woman as an inferior creature who might yet be capable of improvement – and it is clear that Mahler saw himself as an example of those 'higher existences' who can give artistic shape to other people's lives – Mahler presumes to inform her that she must give up composition if she is to marry him. He then broke off the letter in order to attend the final rehearsal of his Second Symphony. On resuming the letter, he insisted once again that his was the role of the composer and breadwinner, hers that of the loving companion and understanding comrade. 'Are you satisfied with that role? – I am asking *much* of you, *very much* – but I can and must do so, because I also know what I have to offer (and shall offer) in return.' It is striking that Mahler is so proud of what he can offer that he does not even think it necessary to go into detail and explain what it may involve. The final section of the letter strikes an even more sombre and forceful note, and at least from the standpoint of the modern reader becomes altogether insufferable:

Almschi, I beg you, read this letter carefully. Our relationship must not degenerate into a mere flirt. Before we speak again, we must have clarified everything, you must know what I demand and expect of you, and what I can give in return – *what you must* be for me. You must 'renounce' (your word) everything *superficial* and *conventional*, all vanity and outward show (concerning your individuality and your work) – you must surrender yourself to me *unconditionally*, make every detail of your future life completely dependent on my needs, in return you must wish for nothing except my *love!*

Mahler then demands that Alma reply by return of post.

This letter will come as a dreadful shock to you – I know it, Alma, and even if this is only cold comfort, you can well imagine that I am suffering just as much. I call to God, though aware that you have not yet made His acquaintance, to guide your hand, my love, in writing the truth and not letting yourself be led astray by ostentation. – For this is a moment of great importance, these are decisions that will weld two people together for eternity. I bless you, my dearest, no matter how you react. – I shall not write tomorrow, but wait instead for your letter on Saturday. A servant will be sent round and kept waiting in readiness. Many tender kisses, my Alma. And I beg you: be truthful! Your Gustav.

Mahler's letter has been quoted at length because it is arguably the most important one that he ever wrote to Alma. Its tone is ruthless, brutal, unadorned and honest and undoubtedly prompted by the profound need to get at the truth, and on a number of decisive points he had the truth on his side. But it is beyond question that no twenty-two-year-old woman could possibly know how to respond to such a letter. After all, he himself had observed her relative immaturity, and so it seems incredible that he should have regarded her reaction to his letter as an acid test that would allow him to tell whether two such different people could live their lives together. Her apparent ability to handle the shock caused by his letter and to pass the test that he had set her convinced him that she was mature enough to marry him, whereas it was in fact a further sign of her immaturity. All the problems and crises that later bedevilled their marriage were prefigured in this letter. We do not know whether Alma replied to it. All that we do know is her reaction to it, a reaction she confided in her diary when she found the letter waiting for her on her return home:

My heart missed a beat . . . give up my music – abandon what has until now been my life? My *first* reaction was – to pass him up. I had to weep – for then I understood that I loved him. Half-crazed with grief, I got into my finery and drove to 'Siegfried' in tears! . . . I feel as if a cold hand has torn the heart from my breast.

Mama & I talked it over until late at night. She had read the letter . . .! I was dumbfounded. I find his behaviour so ill-considered, so inept. It might have come all of its own . . . quite gently. . . . But like this it will leave an indelible scar . . .[50]

She took out the ominous letter again the next day:

I *forced* myself to sleep the night through. This morning I reread his letter – and suddenly I felt such warmth. What if I were to *renounce* [my music] *out of love* for him? Just forget all about it! I must admit that scarcely any music now interests me except his.

Yes – he's right. I must live *entirely* for him, to make him happy. And now I have a strange feeling that my love for him is deep & genuine. For how long? I don't know, but already *that* means much. I long for him *boundlessly*.[51]

If Mahler had been able to read Alma's diary, he would surely have felt confirmed in his view that she was immature and would have responded even more critically. His refusal to allow her to write music apparently caused her lifelong distress, but was it simply a tactical error? Would she have accepted his injunction if he had issued it at a later date and expressed it rather more circumspectly?

Another remarkable aspect of Alma's reaction is that it was confined to Mahler's ban on her activities as a composer, a ban that she accepted voluntarily and wholeheartedly. Conversely, she was not cut to the quick by Mahler's description of her as an immature woman who had not even completed the first step on the road to individuality and had no ideas of her own but merely parroted the inanities of the people around her, all of whom were as superficial as she was and who were repeating the fashionable remarks of others. None of this seems to have affected her. Rather, she was affected only by the single logical result of this criticism, namely, the insinuation that the music that she wrote was itself no more than a superficial mimicking of the music that was then in fashion, a reheating of a dish already served up by her teachers, Labor and Zemlinsky. Mahler's own conviction on this score was as implacable as it was logical: if only one of the partners in a marriage could work creatively as a composer, then it could only be Mahler himself, for he was a fully developed individual whose music improved and enriched humanity.

Alma was in no position to think through the implications of this attitude, and it did not occur to her that in the light of this letter marriage with a man like Mahler would not make her happy. Indeed, she did not even know how long this love, however deep and genuine, might last. Nor did she wonder what would happen if her love were to cool. Should her mother have done more to influence her here? Was Mahler, like the Burckhards and Zemlinskys of this world, not himself too dazzled by her beauty? Was he so convinced of his own Socratic abilities as to think that he could transform an immature future housewife and mother into a mature individual? It is impossible not to be reminded of a line in Wagner's *Lohengrin*: 'Thus misfortune enters this house.'

And then there was the evening when, to use Alma's expression, she was 'passed in review', an evening that she never forgot and that she described in detail in her reminiscences. It was the evening of 5 January 1902, when Mahler invited Alma and her parents, together with a few of his own closest friends from the 1870s, to his apartment in the Auenbruggergasse in order for the parties to get to know each other a little better, news of his engagement having appeared in all the local papers in the days just after Christmas. This had been a turbulent time for the couple. They had tried to make love on the afternoon of 1 January, but Mahler's erectile dysfunction had turned the occasion into a fiasco, reducing an already overwrought Alma to a state of near hysteria. Within two days, however, Mahler had made amends: 'Bliss and rapture,' Alma noted in her diary.[52] That the physical consummation of their love was followed so closely by the dispiriting evening at Mahler's apartment needs to be stressed. After she had desired it for so long, physical union with a man – and with this man in particular – seems to have swept aside all doubts and all the grounds for conflict that had still not been resolved, but within two days they had returned in the context of what had been planned as an innocent social get-together.

The guest list included not only Alma and her mother and stepfather but also the Lipiners, the Spieglers, Anna von Mildenburg, Kolo Moser and Justine Mahler and Arnold Rosé. Having failed to realize his early promise, Siegfried Lipiner, the Nietzschean Wagnerian and thaumaturge of 1870s Vienna, now led a reclusive life as librarian to the Imperial Senate. He had married his first wife, Anna née Hoffmann, in 1881 but they had been divorced since 1890. Anna, or 'Nina' as she preferred to be known, was a close friend of Mahler's and went on to become a mother figure to Bruno Walter, who felt that no one understood him as well as she did. On divorcing Lipiner, she had married Albert Spiegler in 1891. Trained as a doctor, Spiegler had sufficient independent means to work as a private tutor in the field of dietetics. He, too, had been a friend of Mahler's since the 1870s and was thus a guest on 5 January 1902. Lipiner's relations with his former wife appear to have been relatively harmonious, and in general he seems to have left a deep impression on all the women in his life, for they evidently tolerated his various escapades. At least this is the only possible explanation for the fact that the supper guests that evening in the Auenbruggergasse included not only Lipiner's ex-wife, but also his current spouse, Clementine, and his mistress, Anna von Mildenburg, who, unable to have Mahler, had sought consolation with his spiritual confidant. Also present was Arnold Rosé, the leader of the Court Opera orchestra. Mahler had finally discovered that his sister Justine, who was running his household in Vienna, had been secretly seeing Rosé, a discovery that apparently infuriated him – not least because he had failed to notice what was going on under his very nose. It was she who threw the party, an act of sisterly hospitality that was one of her last under Mahler's roof. The group was rounded off by the Secessionist artist Kolo Moser.

Such an illustrious and well-mixed group of interesting, clever and in part amiable individuals should have ensured that the evening passed off smoothly. But according to Alma, the supper party was a deliberate attempt to undermine her liaison with Mahler. It seems that there had already been contacts with Lipiner's group of friends, including a meeting at Mahler's apartment, where Alma met Lipiner for the first time. Among this group of Mahler's acquaintances ('His friends could not ever be friends of mine'[53]), Alma also numbered an 'old barrister, stupid and importunate', who was presumably Emil Freund, a friend of Mahler's from his grammar-school days in Iglau; and an old librarian, equally 'stupid and importunate', who must have been Friedrich Löhr. Turning to Lipiner, Alma quoted an apocryphal remark of Brahms: 'That lying hound of a Pole interests me.' The anti-Semitic undertone in this alleged put-down is unmistakable, for Lipiner hailed from Galicia, and at least the western half of Galicia was Polish. Anti-Semites regarded Polish and Russian Jews as the lowest of the low. But, unlike Brahms, Alma was not interested in Lipiner. If she described him as a 'lying hound of a Pole', it was to stress the anti-Semitic subtext of Brahms's ostensible slight, adding that he was 'an ill-natured, harsh-tempered brute – his eyes much too close together and surmounted by an enormous bald skull. He had a stammer; he was a bogus Goethe in his writing and a haggling Jew in his talk.'[54] Alma was evidently jealous of the fact that Mahler set such store by Lipiner and was envious of his education, in comparison to which her own seemed merely desultory and second-hand. In comparison to Mahler, too, this was an immense problem, prompting Alma to seek revenge by dismissing Lipiner's impressive erudition as altogether sterile.

Even on this first evening the atmosphere had been frosty. If Alma's account can be trusted, the other guests pried into her education, questioned her about Guido Reni, who meant nothing to her, and ridiculed her for reading Plato's

Symposium, a text that they claimed was far above her. Mahler could have seen this coming. Again and again the reader is struck by his lack of sympathetic understanding and unfamiliarity with the ways of the world. It would have been better if the 'full-dress review' had not taken place at all. Certainly, it was hardly necessary that it should do so. Writing with hindsight, Alma spoke of the 'grandiose and festive air which so completely belied the hollowness of that occasion'. In her diary she added an anti-Semitic dig to her sense of unease and rejection, claiming that all the other guests were 'conspicuously Jewish'. In general, it is noticeable that a person's Jewishness was overlooked only when he or she struck her as sympathetic, but if they were unsympathetic, then it suddenly became all-important. It was an attitude that she maintained all her life. For Lipiner and his circle, the situation was far from easy. Here, after all, was a young woman who, famous as a beauty throughout the city, was poised to take away their friend but who was incapable of competing with him or, indeed, with themselves on any artistic or intellectual level. They, too, were jealous and also, it seems, they lacked openness and tolerance. The atmosphere was poisonous. In her diary Alma admits that she wanted to shock the other guests with her unparalleled effrontery and when Anna von Mildenburg, fired by malice, asked her more successful rival for Mahler's favours, 'What is your opinion of Gustav's music?', she replied: 'I know very little of it, but what I do know I don't like.' This was simply untrue, for in a diary entry only shortly beforehand she had noted her increasing enthusiasm for it.[55] The temperature sank to below freezing point, but Mahler is said to have laughed and to have drawn Alma into an adjoining room.

Meanwhile, next door, her 'downfall' was being decreed. Alma's account makes it sound as if she was indulging her love of drama and trying to break down the bridges between her and Mahler's friends. In short, it is tempting to see it as yet another of her exaggerations. On this occasion, however, we may well be right to believe her, for a long letter has survived from Lipiner to Mahler that was written in the wake of this ominous evening in the Auenbruggergasse in reply to a letter from Mahler that has not survived. The letter seals the breach between Mahler and his old circle of friends and at the same time indicates that the supper party brought to the surface resentments which until then had simmered away unseen. Lipiner evidently felt that Mahler, at the pinnacle of his career and newly in love, no longer valued his old friends as much as he had done in the past and that he was now less willing to share his life with them. Lipiner sums up Mahler's attitude in the following sentence, which was presumably based on an actual remark of Mahler's: 'My dear Siegfried, you simply don't know how little I care about you all.'[56] When Lipiner goes on to complain about Mahler's habit of alienating even loyal friends and of dropping them only to pick them up again when it suited him, he is merely repeating a complaint repeatedly made by others: there was a high-handedness and a ruthlessness about the way in which he broke off relations with others and then renewed contact some time later. Lipiner reproaches Mahler for having spent the whole evening cosseting Alma even though he had spent most of the previous weeks with her, and for treating his old friends as mere extras in a scene designed to showcase the billing and cooing of the newly enamoured couple. Lipiner then turns his heavy guns on Alma. Did Mahler know what a risk he was running by marrying her? She had behaved in an unnatural, dishonest and foolish manner and was totally shameless. She had also been offensively disinterested in the other guests. 'I have always felt a chill in Alma's presence and the impression that she has left on me is not that of a woman who is at all bashful but one who is disagreeably disengaged, immodest and argumentative; I may say this precisely because I was not affected by it.' Her supercilious comments on Guido Reni and Plato merely served to demonstrate her 'lack of any natural feeling for all that is great and a want of respect and, indeed, a lack of all that is natural'. In short, Lipiner implied, how could such a woman understand what was great about Mahler's music? This letter seems to have precipitated the breach not only with Lipiner but also with all their other mutual friends.

Mahler's reaction has not survived, but we know that there was no further contact between the two erstwhile friends at least until such time as Bruno Walter attempted to bring them together again during one of the most turbulent periods in Mahler's life. As we have seen, the breach was caused by more than merely Alma's behaviour and Mahler's defence thereof. Mahler's relations with his old friends were no longer what they had been during the latter half of the 1870s. They had evidently imagined that the situation would be rather different when their student comrade returned to Vienna to run the musical life of the city. Moreover, Mahler and Lipiner had once argued violently over Wagner when Lipiner, referring to Wagner's relations with Liszt, had let slip a dismissive remark that Mahler took in bad part. Even so, one wonders why a ruined evening in Mahler's apartment should have had such repercussions. Mahler was bound to side with his fiancée when she found herself under attack from a band of conspirators who appeared to constitute a vipers' nest of petty jealousies and older rights, and who included one of Mahler's ex-mistresses. And yet a single conversation would have sufficed to resolve the situation and clear the air. There is only one psychologically convincing reason why Mahler suddenly abandoned an entire group of people who had been important to him for so long: it was painfully clear to him that his friends were right, even if the tone they adopted was wrong, but this was something that he was unable to admit to himself and others in the heady intoxication of his possession of the most beautiful woman in Vienna, a woman, moreover, who appeared to have survived every test. As the spokesman of the group, Lipiner merely said what Mahler himself knew, for all that his comments were undiplomatic and aggressively worded: neither as an artist nor as an intellectual nor yet as a mature woman was Alma Schindler a suitable wife for him. He forced himself to ignore these misgivings and at the same time to ignore the people from his past who shared these doubts and who, forgetting the sympathy and tolerance that they owed a woman like Alma, were all too quick to judge and summarily dismiss her.

There was a further victim who was left behind on the battlefield of this marriage: Natalie Bauer-Lechner. She deserves at least a brief excursus on her own significance and on that of her reminiscences. She was born in 1858, two years before Mahler, and began her career as a violinist, later switching to the viola. She was well known in her day as a member of the all-women Soldat-Roeger Quartet – a line-up as unusual in our own day as it was in hers. She first got to know Mahler in Budapest in the autumn of 1890, a meeting that marked the start of a twelve-year friendship. It would be no exaggeration to say that there were few other people who understood Mahler as well as she did. She was a fine musician and unusually clever, even if she had little experience of the world. She was also sensitive, and she loved and worshipped Mahler. Her reminiscences were first published in a much-abridged form in 1923 and in a fuller version in 1984. By general agreement they constitute the most valuable surviving record of Mahler's life apart from his own letters. As an impassioned pacifist she was imprisoned for one of her publications shortly before the end of the First World War. She died in 1921 at the age of sixty-three, two years before her reminiscences first appeared in print. She always said that Mahler and Lipiner were the two greatest men she had ever met – and there is no doubt that Mahler was the greater of the two. The sudden end of their friendship is shrouded in mystery, but there is no doubt that she was hopelessly in love with Mahler, who valued her highly for her utter devotion and understanding but who was not attracted to her physically: prematurely greying, she looked older than she was. Although more attractive than Anna von Mildenburg, she could not compare with the singer as an artist. Sometimes her doglike devotion grated on Mahler, but for many years she was effectively a part of the family and spent her summer holidays with them. Justine, too, liked her and valued her support in practical matters.

The breach came with Mahler's engagement to Alma Schindler at Christmas 1901. Until then, it is conceivable that Natalie harboured vague hopes that the apparently confirmed bachelor might still fall back on her, but now even this dim prospect faded from sight. Natalie attended the first Viennese performance of the Fourth Symphony on 12 January 1902 and left with Bruno Walter and his wife. The three of them discussed the work's hostile reception. But this is her last reference to Mahler in her reminiscences. In an unpublished passage in her own memoirs, Alma – constitutionally jealous and consumed by malevolence where other women were concerned – purports to recount the scene that led to the breach, claiming that Natalie had for a long time kept Mahler in the dark about the liaison between Justine and Arnold Rosé in order to 'blackmail' Justine – presumably in order to ensure that she remained close to Mahler. This is sheer malice on Alma's part, because Mahler opened himself up to Natalie in a way that he would never have done with an acquaintance who had been forced upon him. Alma then refers to the decisive conversation in the course of which Mahler accused Natalie of complicity with Justine, whereupon Natalie defended herself by declaring her love and attempting to embrace him. She is said to have begged Mahler to marry her, but he allegedly refused, claiming that he would love only a beautiful woman. In her desperation Natalie had insisted that she *was* beautiful, a point that Alma and Justine spitefully repeated whenever they could – one hopes that Mahler did not join in their malicious jibes. According to Alma, this was the last time that Mahler and Natalie spoke to each other. Her account raises more questions than it answers. But it is true that he detested scenes of this nature, and there is no doubt that something serious occurred.

Whatever the truth of the matter, Natalie's indispensable reminiscences end with the following sentences: 'Six weeks ago Mahler became engaged to Alma Schindler. If I wished to speak about this, I should find myself in the position of the physician who has to treat his nearest and dearest in a matter of life and death. In order, therefore, to bring this matter to an end, I place it in the hands of the supreme, eternal master!'[57] Unlike Lipiner, with whom he severed his links on account of Alma only to reforge them at a later date, Natalie disappeared without trace from Mahler's life, a disappearance difficult to understand when we read her reminiscences, which are characterized by their profound love and deep understanding. This is not to say that Mahler would have done better to marry Natalie, and yet there is not a single surviving line from Alma's pen that can compare to Natalie's in terms of its affection, loyalty and empathy.

Mahler and Alma were married in Vienna's St Charles's Church on 9 March 1902. It was a Catholic ceremony. The marriage register, which erroneously gives the date as 9 February, names two witnesses: Arnold Rosé, who was to marry Mahler's sister Justine the following day, and, on the bride's side, Alma's stepfather, Carl Moll.

The Fifth Symphony

WITH THE FIFTH Symphony we enter a new part of Mahler's symphonic world. He himself justified this statement by describing his first four symphonies as a tetralogy, and there is no doubt that they belong together, not least because of their links with various *Wunderhorn* poems. As a result they are often bracketed together as the *Wunderhorn* symphonies and as such distinguished from the instrumental symphonies of the middle period – the Fifth, Sixth and Seventh. The Eighth is in any case set apart from the others, while the Ninth and the unfinished Tenth are understandably classed as late works. One thing is certain: even in the case of the Fourth, Mahler had claimed that he was now in total control of his technical resources, and the Fifth finds him taking a further decisive step in this direction. Only in one respect did it turn out that he had not made as much progress as he had wanted, and that was in the field of instrumentation. Shortly before his death, he subjected the Fifth Symphony to a further fundamental overhaul in terms of its orchestration. In a letter to the conductor Georg Göhler, he admitted that even as a forty-year-old composer at the height of his powers, he could still commit the sort of mistakes that a novice might make: the experience acquired in his first four symphonies let him down – a new style needed a new technique. But while working on his Fifth Symphony he was not yet aware of this shortcoming.

During the summer of 1901, when he started work on the symphony, Mahler told Natalie Bauer-Lechner, in a relatively uncharacteristic expression of his own self-worth as a composer: 'It is the prime of a man's life; even if the inspiration does not reach the same high level as it once did, it is replaced by full strength and complete ability. I feel that I can achieve anything and that for a long time to come my resources will belong to me and obey me.'[1] The Fifth Symphony also represents a caesura inasmuch as Mahler stopped producing the lengthy programme notes that had characterized his earlier symphonies.

From now on, performers and commentators can no longer appeal to Mahler in the way that they had been able to do previously. However well-intentioned Mahler may have been in the past, he now realized that he was not doing himself or his works any favours by promulgating such programme notes and that any short-term advantages could in no way make up for the long-term damage that they caused. Nor should we forget that Mahler's association with Alma marked the end of his contacts with Natalie Bauer-Lechner. The Fifth Symphony was written in Maiernigg during the summers of 1901 and 1902. In February 1902, six weeks after he and Alma became engaged, Natalie stopped recording her conversations with Mahler, conversations that are of inestimable value for the light that they throw on his thoughts and feelings. It was, more-over, with particular care that Natalie had faithfully noted down his comments on his individual works. A conversation about the Fifth Symphony that took place during the summer of 1901 is the last of this kind to be recorded – Alma left only rudimentary jottings on Mahler's music, a state of affairs that stems from the fact that she unfortunately did not feel called upon to act as an Eckermann to her husband's Goethe.

Mahler's conversation with Natalie Bauer-Lechner is effectively limited to the symphony's third movement, its Scherzo, which was presumably the first of the five to be written and the first in which he experimented with his new musical style. The novelty about the Scherzo – and about the rest of the emerging score – is to be found in the unprecedented complexity of the writing. Drawing on one of his typical images, Mahler expressed this as follows: 'It is kneaded through and through till not a grain of the mixture remains unmixed and unchanged. Every note is charged with life, and the whole thing whirls round in a giddy dance.' And he went on to add an important pointer to his decision to abandon the world of the *Wunderhorn* songs and of the written or sung word in general: 'The human voice would be absolutely out of place here. There is no need for words, everything is purely musically expressed.'[2] Mahler was now certain, therefore, that everything he wanted to express could be expressed by purely musical means, something that had not been possible earlier. The orchestra was now able to absorb the written and sung word and render them dispensable. It alone now spoke more clearly than orchestra and singers, whether soloists or chorus, had previously been capable of doing. This was bound up, of course, with a reduction in the number of the work's poten-tial meanings or, rather, a reluctance to be precise as to what those meanings might be. The fewer the narrative structures that could be recounted by linguistic means, the less it was necessary to flag them up with linguistic images. Here we are once again reminded of Hans Heinrich Eggebrecht's term 'vocab-ular music' to describe Mahler's musical language, a term that Eggebrecht takes to mean structures within the music that hark back to material formed during the pre-compositional phase. These are musical phrases which, part of the common currency, can derive from all areas of music and which had previously never found their way into art music or, having once formed part of it, had sunk to the level of a commonplace. Here we may find an important key to understanding the notorious banalities and trivialities that are contained in Mahler's music but which are in fact elemental idioms. If listeners think that a particular passage sounds familiar, even if they cannot point to a concrete quotation, then this is an example of the sort of pre-existing material that Mahler needed and has nothing to do with eclecticism or paucity of invention. (It may be added in parentheses that with the single exception of his own songs and the *Bruder Martin* round in the First Symphony, Mahler never included direct quotations of other works in his music.)

Mahler created his symphonies out of this raw material that had left its mark on the world around him, from the singing of his childhood nanny to the strains of Bohemian musicians and the brass-band music played in garrison towns. He produced a new and infinitely varied idiom out of which he constructed the world of his symphonies, a world which, although artificial in the highest degree, is none the less linked to the real world through countless veins and arteries. The blood corpuscles that flow through these veins, turning the new body into a vital organism, are the elements that make up Mahler's vocabulary. These may consist of themes and motifs, but they may also express themselves harmonically as shifts from major to minor or as cadences. And they may also be conveyed in the choice of unusual instruments that found their way into Mahler's late Romantic symphony orchestra: cowbells, posthorn, guitar and mandolin are semantically charged signs that evoke certain extra-musical associations, recalling the last booming sound of the mountain slope before the hiker ascends to heights devoid of beasts and humans or suggesting the melancholy of a coach ride or a night-time serenade. The linguistic power of these scores extends even to their performance markings: 'In a folk tone', 'Like the song of a bird', 'Shyly' – these are all instructions that attest to this expressive quality. This same variety of expression is taken further than ever in the Fifth Symphony. Not even in the later works is it surpassed but merely more subtly differentiated.[3] Or we could put it another way: using a vocabulary that seems familiar and sometimes even intimately colloquial, Mahler expresses all that is unheard of and uncanny, all that is unsettling and upsetting. What was alien sounds familiar, and what is familiar now seems alien. Such an analysis may also be applied to Mahler himself, an individual who time and again seems to us to be so perplexing.

The very opening of the Fifth Symphony helps to explain what we mean by 'vocabular composition'. The first trumpet intones a fanfare alone before the full orchestra joins in, taking up the rhythm of the fanfare. For every musically educated listener, this rhythm recalls the opening of Beethoven's Fifth Symphony, where it is, however, differently instrumented. At the same time it is as banal as any trumpet fanfare – and Mahler was not thinking of a quotation or even an allusion here. But in the years around 1900 the musically uneducated Austrian listener might also be reminded of something altogether different, namely, the opening of the 'General marsch' associated with the Austro-Hungarian Army. The whole of the opening movement draws on the exceptional banality of this trumpet fanfare for its underlying gestures, the apparent triviality of the beginning generating a symphonic structure of extraordinary subtlety and complexity. The actual beginning of this 'Funeral March', as the opening movement is headed, is like a folksong that continues to evolve while alternating and combining with the highly rhythmical fanfare from the beginning, offering the world a funeral march of a kind never heard before. We may be tempted to imagine a scene in which the fanfare guides us to a field of battle, while the dirge takes us from the battlefield to a mass grave. In the first Trio section after figure 7, the movement strikes a note of positively cosmic terror, the performance marking 'Suddenly faster, impassioned, wild' ushering in a completely unexpected frenetic outburst that eventually relapses into the fanfare rhythm of the opening. Some commentators and performers see in this a gesture of hysterical screaming, an interpretation taken to its furthest extreme by Adorno, who writes that this music 'must have created an appalling impression at the time of its composition, retaining its power as a fearful dream of coming pogroms in which the piercing voice of the man ordering their murder combines with the screams of his victims. Passages such as these make it clear just how dangerous Mahler's music is in spite of its tonal resources: there is nothing pre-war about it.'[4] Rarely did Mahler write anything as daring as this. It was the starting point for Berg's Three Pieces op. 6 of 1914–15, especially the final piece, a march apparently written under the immediate impression of the assassination of Archduke Franz Ferdinand and his wife at Sarajevo in 1914 and also containing an echo of the final movement of the Sixth Symphony.

The second movement is no less complex than the first, not least because it uses material from the Trio section of the funeral march, but transforms the earlier terror into a melody that is unexpectedly tuneful. Here Mahler 'kneads' the material together in an altogether masterly manner that is impossible to overpraise: everything is interwoven, the most complex structures emerging from the most 'banal' beginnings, while radiant cantabile lines evolve out of themes that seem suited only to strident outbursts, only for them to be swallowed up or stifled as if their note of comfort had suddenly become untrustworthy. It is here, in bar 500, that we have an example of the familiar concept of a 'breakthrough'. There is something almost touching about the fact that

Mahler entered two arrows in the score at this point, an indication of his justified mistrust of performers whom he thought would fail to recognize it as a breakthrough. A chorale suddenly enters here in the most radiant of brass sonorities. The same chorale will later leave its mark on the end of the final movement. Here, however, it enters full-throatedly only to sink back again very quickly. In his own analysis of this passage, Mathias Hansen proposes the impressive image of an organ in full cry whose air supply is suddenly cut off, leading the sound to die away abruptly.[5]

The third movement is the Scherzo that Mahler mentioned in conversation with Natalie Bauer-Lechner. Its sheer length – almost twenty minutes in performance – means that it is no Scherzo in the traditional sense but a high point of Mahler's skill as a contrapuntalist. Using the basic pattern of a dance – principally waltz-like in character – he raises an edifice that almost defies the laws of architecture. He was fully aware of the difficulties of what he had designed, and while preparing for the first performance of the work with the Gürzenich Orchestra in Cologne in October 1904, he wrote to Alma:

That scherzo is an accursed movement! It will have a long tale of woe! For the next fifty years conductors will take it too fast and make nonsense of it. And audiences – heavens! – how should they react to this chaos, which is constantly giving birth to new worlds and promptly destroying them again? What should they make of these primeval noises, this rushing, roaring, raging sea, these dancing stars, these ebbing, shimmering, gleaming waves? What can a herd of sheep answer to an 'ancient lay 'mid brother-spheres', other than bleat?[6]

Mahler was to be proved right, and the Fifth Symphony continues to be one of his least popular works, a fate that it shares with the Sixth and Seventh, the two other instrumental symphonies from his middle period. But he was also right in his assessment of the way in which conductors would approach this movement: most take it too quickly and fail to observe the second half of the tempo marking 'Powerful, but not too fast'. The hectic quality of the movement as a whole should not be obtained by rushing it but should emerge of its own accord.

Whatever the standing of the work as a whole, it is the fourth movement – the Adagietto – that remains the single best-known movement in the whole of Mahler's output, a status that it owes to Luchino Visconti's film *Death in Venice*. The film did much to popularize Mahler's music and is by no means without merit. But the Adagietto is used throughout the film with the frequency of a leitmotif and, as such, is overexposed. (We shall have more to say on this point in our chapter on Mahler and posterity.) Even Mahler's own admirers have mixed feelings about this short movement, Mathias Hansen, for example, writing of its 'rutting sonorities'.[7] Here the crucial factor is again the way in which the movement is interpreted by the conductor and, above all, the latter's understanding of the tempo modifications. Briefly, the performer should not be tied down by the marking 'Sehr langsam' ('Very slow') that is found at the start of the movement but must also take account of later markings, including 'Do not drag', 'Pressing forward a little' and 'Flowing', which alternate with 'Slow' and 'Even slower' and, taken together, produce an organic whole. Among gramophone recordings, Bernard Haitink and the Berlin Philharmonic hold the record for the slowest performance of a movement that runs to only five pages in the printed score and for which they require a full fourteen minutes. One of Haitink's predecessors at the Concertgebouw, Willem Mengelberg, heard Mahler himself conduct the symphony in Amsterdam in March 1906 and although he recorded Mahler's timing for only this single movement, it was a little over seven minutes. Bruno Walter, too, was present at the first performance in Cologne in 1904 and he also adopts Mengelberg's tempo. Only in this way does the movement acquire the character of an intimate confession of love and lose its rutting fervour and sentimentality.

Mahler wrote the Adagietto during his first summer with Alma, and even commentators disinclined to adopt a straightforwardly biographical approach may abandon their reservations here: it is a musical declaration of love, a reading that Mahler and Alma confirmed when Mengelberg questioned him on the subject of the searingly expressive violin line that constitutes the movement's principal theme. He even added a kind of text to go with the violin theme: 'How I love you, / You my sun / I cannot tell you / with words / Only my longing / Can I pour out to you / And my love / My joy!'[8] Listeners tempted – perhaps a little indecorously – to sing these words to the violin line will find that they fit it. It is not clear, however, whether they were authorized by Mahler and Alma or whether it was Mengelberg himself who cobbled them together. But they are so similar in tone to the sort of poems that Mahler addressed to Alma that they may surely be regarded as authentic. It may be added that Strauss attended the final rehearsal of the work under Nikisch in Berlin in March 1905 and afterwards wrote very positively to Mahler on the subject, while criticizing the Adagietto and claiming that it served Mahler right that the audience had enjoyed this movement so much. As such, his letter serves merely to demonstrate the difficulty that people have when dealing with questions of 'taste'.[9]

The final movement is cast in the form of a rondo and causes Mahlerians even more problems than the Adagietto. Time and again critics have reproached Mahler for striking an unduly 'affirmative', dubiously positive note. It is a reproach that is directed above all at the final chorale, which now places the second-movement chorale under what might be termed the most impossible semantic pressure. There is no doubt that after the screams of the persecuted and tortured souls in the opening movement, this final apotheosis creates the effortful impression of a 'per ardua ad astra', and even Alma, not always sensitive to such niceties, was disturbed by the chorale, which she described as 'hymnal and boring', prompting Mahler to protest: 'Yes, but Bruckner –.' 'He, yes; but not you' was her instant rejoinder.[10] We are in a position similar to the one in which we found ourselves when discussing the final movement of the Third Symphony: is it figurative or literal? Commentators disposed to fall back on the notion of 'failure at the highest level' are guilty of presupposing that Mahler was trying to achieve something that he was unable adequately to express, hence the apparent superficiality of the ending. But it is clear that the chorale cannot be used in a straightforward way after it had been called into question in the second movement. The first three movements had already advanced so far into hostile, uncharted terrain that it must have seemed impossible to go beyond this and find a suitably climactic ending, so it is conceivable that Mahler opted for what Hansen has termed a 'compromise': the chorale and the wildly coruscating final stretta at the end of the symphony are used to give the impression that the astonishingly crass contradictions and inconsistencies that typify the first three movements above all can still be papered over with the tried and tested resources of the sort of apotheosis typical of symphonies from this and earlier periods.[11] It is worth bearing in mind that contemporary critics could make nothing of the first three movements, whereas they liked the Adagietto and praised the final movement as the high point of the piece. But the process of papering over the cracks is only partially successful, and the present apotheosis is no different from all the others like it in Mahler's output, conveying, as it does, an element that Adorno – writing in a different context – aptly summed up as that of 'extorted reconciliation'.

'Nothing is lost to you': Faith and Philosophy

FOR ALMA, IT was all very straightforward: 'He believed in Christ and had certainly not been baptised purely out of opportunism in order to get the job as director of the Vienna Court Opera.' As proof of Mahler's Christian faith, Alma cites a polemical remark of her own in which she had preferred Plato to Christ, prompting Mahler to write a letter in which he had vigorously opposed this view. He also, she went on, was deeply attracted to Catholic mysticism.[1] Although Alma herself had been brought up as a Catholic, her reading of Schopenhauer and Nietzsche meant that during the early weeks and months of their acquaintanceship, she had been something of a freethinker and, as a result, critical of religion, but Mahler had championed the teachings of Christ. As Alma later remarked, it was 'paradoxical that a Jew should hotly defend Christ against a Christian'.[2] It is worth recalling that Alma did not remain a freethinker and that in later life, when she wrote down her reminiscences and memoirs, she felt increasingly drawn to the Catholic Church, especially while she was still living in Austria and maintaining close contacts with some of its leading figures. She had a scandalous liaison with the Catholic cleric Johannes Hollnsteiner, for example, and the pseudo-Catholic *Song of Bernadette* by her third husband, Franz Werfel, will hardly have assumed its definitive form without her. Given her somewhat bigoted devotion to Catholicism towards the end of her life, her attempts to press Mahler into the service of the Catholic religion need to be treated with caution. In this context it is enough to cite the testimony of one of Mahler's closest confidants, Bruno Walter, to expose the problematical nature of Alma's claim. It was Walter, after all, who wrote that he 'could not call Mahler a believer'.[3] In spite of attempts by recent writers to turn Mahler into a Christian, doubts remain in order.

These doubts increase when we turn to the letter to which Alma was referring.[4] Here the reader will note with some surprise that Mahler was far from aligning himself with Christ or admitting to being a believer, as Alma sought to imply. Written in Munich in 1910, while Mahler was preparing for the world première of his Eighth Symphony, the letter was in fact intended to confirm a thesis that Alma had expressed in a letter which has not survived and that revolved around her comparison between Plato and Christ, a comparison that she herself claimed was not only self-evident but also entirely justified:

> All contrast is determined by milieu and Zeitgeist. On the one side, the radiance of culture in its highest form, with pupils and commentators of greatest intellectual brilliance; on the other, the darkness of a naive, infantile world, in which the child serves as a vessel for the marvels of worldly wisdom, an outcome of pure instinct, of a direct and intense way of looking at things and understanding them.[5]

For whatever reason, Alma falsified the meaning of this letter. Far from defending Christ against Plato, Mahler presents them both as equals and as two sides of the same coin, which is hardly the view of a Christian believer. Even more important is the opinion that he puts forward in a passage that precedes the one just quoted: the decisive element in Plato's thinking, he argues, was subsumed by Goethe's outlook on life, whereby all love is founded on procreation and creation, and procreation is an activity not only of the body but also of the soul. Nowhere was this better expressed than in the closing scene of *Faust*, Mahler's own musical setting of which he was currently rehearsing in Munich. In short, Goethe was the authority who assimilated the ideas of both Plato and Christ and fashioned them in a way that was compelling both philosophically and poetically. This certainly brings us much closer to Mahler's own faith.

Mahler was not a Christian in the sense of organized Christianity, which he had adopted for purely practical reasons and from which he maintained an inner distance, just as he remained aloof from the Jewish religion. But there is no doubt that he had a concept of God. Even so, it is difficult to say exactly what this concept was. His young follower, Oskar Fried, recalled that 'he was a God-seeker. With incredible fanaticism, with unparalleled dedication and with unshakeable love he pursued a constant search for the divine, both in the individual and in man as a whole. But he saw himself as divinely sent, a mission that suffused his entire being. His nature was religious through and through in a mystical, not a dogmatic, sense.' Fried's formulation is somewhat unfortunate, as Mahler certainly did not see himself as divinely sent. Rather, he thought of himself as the mouthpiece and vehicle of a divine mission. None the less, the gist of Fried's remark is worth taking seriously. Mahler's faith in his calling and his belief that he could fulfil his mission through his art was not unshakeable, and in moments of uncertainty he sought confirmation of his mission in his fellow humans, including the young people around him. 'And if he received no answer, no echo from my direction, if I was not immediately ready and willing to follow him wherever he desired to go, his face would become remarkably set and he would retreat into his impenetrable spiritual shell, a child enduring mortal disappointments and bewailing his divine origins.'[6] Fried's belief that Mahler was religious in a mystical but not a dogmatic sense is similar to Bruno Walter's and is confirmed by other observers. The God who is invoked in 'Urlicht', which Mahler set to music in the fourth movement of his Second Symphony, is not the God whose praise is extolled from church pulpits: 'I am from God and would go back to God!' insists the *Wunderhorn* poet. 'Dear God will give me a light, will light me to blissful everlasting life!'

Ernst Decsey reports a conversation with Mahler in the summer of 1909, when the composer had justified his faith in God by arguing that the materialism to which the nineteenth century had pinned its colours was incapable of satisfying him any longer. He recommended an essay by the Russian physicist Orest Danilovich Khvolson attacking the materialism championed by the popular and influential writings of Ernst Haeckel. 'When you see a complicated machine, a motor car,' Mahler told Decsey, 'you don't assume, do you, that there is no means of propulsion involved, because you can't see it? Well, don't you think there exists a concealed driving force within man?'[7] As we know, Mahler's bookshelves in Toblach included not only Khvolson's critique of materialism but also Alfred Brehm's multi-volume study of the life of animals, a choice of reading matter that says much about the composer's interest in all forms of life. Another book that formed part of his library and that he recommended to all his acquaintances was Friedrich August Lange's *History of Materialism*, which, first published in 1866, was no less successful than the writings of Ernst Haeckel that he criticized. A neo-Kantian, Lange attacked materialism for ignoring humanity's metaphysical needs.

Apart from Bruno Walter, Oskar Fried and a handful of other initiates, it was undoubtedly Alfred Roller who knew Mahler best of all, at least towards the end of his life. Roller, too, includes a number of important remarks about his friend and colleague's religious beliefs in the course of his characterization:

> He was deeply religious. His faith was that of a child. God is love and love is God. This idea came up a thousand times in his conversation. I once asked him why he did not write a Mass, and he seemed taken back. 'Do you think I could take that upon myself? Well, why not? But no, there's the Credo in it.' And he began to recite the Credo in Latin. 'No, I couldn't do it.'
>
> But after a rehearsal of the Eighth in Munich he called cheerfully across to me, referring to this conversation: 'There you are, that's my Mass.'

I never heard a word of blasphemy from him. But he needed no intermediary to God. He spoke with Him face to face. God lived easily within him. How else can one define the state of complete transcendency in which he wrote?[8]

This anecdote is quoted by many writers anxious to demonstrate that Mahler's thinking was grounded in Christianity.[9] But in order to sustain this interpretation, they are obliged to end the quotation with the words 'There you are, that's my Mass.' It is clear, however, from the passage that follows that Roller weakened the Christian connection by stating that Mahler needed no intermediary to God. Above all, the anecdote – and its authenticity is beyond doubt – proves the exact opposite of what many commentators have read into it. Mahler found it impossible to set the Nicene Creed that became the Credo of the Catholic Mass: 'I believe in one God, the Father almighty, Maker of heaven and earth and of all things visible and invisible. And in one Lord Jesus Christ. . . . And I believe in the Holy Ghost. . . . And I believe in one Catholic and Apostolic Church.' Mahler was unable to bring himself to set these lines. If he believed in an Almighty Father, it was in a wider sense than the one intended here. And if he had been honest with himself, this is where his setting of these lines would have had to end. If – 'cheerfully' and with a nod and a wink – he described his Eighth Symphony as his Mass, it was because it includes a setting of Hrabanus Maurus's Pentecostal hymn *Veni creator spiritus*. And in Mahler's eyes, the spirit of creation was not only the Holy Ghost but above all the *creator spiritus*. The second part of the work, conversely, is a setting of the final scene from *Faust II*, and there is no connection whatsoever between this scene and the Credo of the Catholic Church, unless it be the colourful resplendence of Catholic mysticism, a resplendence that fascinated Mahler as much as it did the elderly Goethe but which has nothing to do with Catholicism as such. In general, this final scene yields little to a Christian interpretation.

It is impossible to say for certain when Mahler was first introduced to the ideas of Gustav Theodor Fechner,[10] but it is more than likely that it was Lipiner who drew his attention to them for Lipiner had studied in Leipzig in 1876, when he had grown extraordinarily close to the much older man, who was at that time still teaching at the University. Fechner had developed a transcendental school of thought marked by the sort of natural philosophy that was typical of Romantic writers such as the German naturalist Lorenz Oken and which included all manner of mystical elements that many contemporaries regarded as wayward on account of Fechner's highly remarkable life and history of illness. His three-part investigation, *Zend-Avesta, or The Things of Heaven and the Beyond from the Standpoint of Natural Observation*, appeared in 1851 and rapidly achieved cult status among those readers who, unshackled by religious dogma, had no time for the crude materialism and empiricism of

the second half of the nineteenth century, with its growing reliance on technology. Even before this, Fechner had pseudonymously published a *Booklet on
Life after Death* that proved particularly popular in Austria. Of interest from a
Mahlerian perspective is Fechner's doctrine of the three stages of life: the
prenatal stage, life itself, and death. Every individual, Fechner argued, lived
three lives on earth. In his prenatal stage he lived alone in darkness, while the
second stage was spent sociably in the light. In the third stage his life became
interwoven with those of other spirits raised to a higher existence. Birth
marked the transition from the first to the second stage, while death was the
step from the second to the third stage. For Fechner, the earth was a more
animate being than man, while the earth and the other planets were in turn the
organs of a more animate world, just as men and women must be imagined as
the sense organs of the earth. This interpretation has repercussions for our
idea of death. If the individual who inhabits the animate earth serves as its eye,
for example, this eye closes only in order that it may enter a higher world, the
world of memory of the earth's soul:

> Just as the spirits of men and women are visions in a higher sense during
> their lives here on earth, so they are memories after their deaths. When a
> man briefly closes his eyes in life and his vision grows dim, then a memory
> awakens within him; and when man closes his eyes for ever in death and his
> intuitive existence grows dim, a life of memory awakens in a higher sense. . . .
> Now it is no longer individual visions that he experiences. Rather, his entire
> intuitive existence is raised up within him to a life of memory in a higher
> sense, a life which none the less still belongs to him as a person as much as
> the intuitive existence from which it derives.[11]

Because the metabolism is constantly changing, with the result that after a
while new matter sustains the same memories and the same consciousness,
Fechner concludes that in spite of physical change, there is psychic continuity.
In turn, it seemed to him possible that psychic reality might survive death.
During his life on earth, the active individual creates for himself something
that Fechner terms an 'active body' into which his soul passes when the body
dies. Our actions, whether visible or mental, continue to have an effect. The
survival of the individual after death is a survival of the soul with a new physical body. Just as we can recall earlier sense impressions without the corresponding stimulus, so our souls will continue to lead a life of memory even after our
bodies have decayed. In this new existence all the causal consequences of our
lives will become conscious to us. Until it finds a new body, this soul has no
sense organs and cannot, therefore, lead a life of visionary contemplation, but
it does have memories. In a new body, it can acquire new insights.

For a man like Mahler, who was looking for a meaning to life and death beyond the limitations of Judaism and Christianity, Fechner's world of ideas must have seemed like a revelation. Even as late as 1903, while fulfilling a concert engagement in Lemberg, he wrote to Alma: 'Between whiles I have avidly been reading *Zend-Avesta*, a book like an old, cherished friend, that brings one face to face with many things one has oneself seen and experienced.'[12] It was inevitable that the poetry of Friedrich Rückert should strike him as a faithful echo of Fechner's ideas. Rückert's lines in the *Kindertotenlieder*, 'What are only eyes to you in these days will be only stars to you in future nights', and his apostrophization of death as a 'journey to those heights', are entirely typical of Fechner, a point that occurred to Mahler at once, for in his letter to Alma of April 1903 he continues: 'Fechner's world is strangely like Rückert's; the two are closely related, and one side of me is deeply in accord with both of them. How few people know anything about *those* two! When you come to understand them, it will be a great step forward. Then you will be able to rid yourself of certain trivial ideas that are obscuring your vision and blinding you to reality.'[13]

Fechner's ideas, which Mahler had got to know as a young man (it is not clear whether he was reading Fechner's *Zend-Avesta* for the first time in 1903, although it seems more likely that he had read it before), were later combined with Goethe's even more crucial ideas on entelechy, a point that emerges with some force from an important letter that Mahler wrote to Alma in the summer of 1909, when he insisted that what matters is not man's works nor even the works of a man of genius but 'what a man creates of his own person, what his restless striving and vitality combine to *make* him'. It is this part of him that survives. What is decisive is not what he produces but his striving towards the light and towards the heights, in short, towards God: 'Draw increasingly on your inner strength (indeed you do!),' Mahler goes on; '*assimilate* as much of the world's beauty and power as you can (more than this one cannot do – and even then it is given only to the few). "Spread your wings," occupy your mind with all that is good and beautiful, never cease to grow (for that is true productivity).'[14] Mahler would certainly not have regarded Alma's attempts to turn him into a Catholic as the acts of an enlightened woman. Here, rather, we have the origins of his belief in immortality. In the Second Symphony this belief was still combined with the Christian doctrine of immortality, but, increasingly, it was to break free from it. The lines that Mahler added to Klopstock's hymn in the symphony's final movement include the following: 'O believe, my heart, O believe: nothing will be lost to you! What you longed for is yours, yes, yours! What you loved and strove for is yours!'

Fechner's writings were the crucial philosophical influence on Mahler during his youth, a point confirmed by many of the people who were close to him. Bruno Walter, for example, recalled that 'a lasting impression was made by Fechner's *Zend-Avesta*, and he delighted in *Nana, or the Spiritual Life of Plants* by the same author'.[15] In this last-named monograph, which dates from 1848, Fechner had extended the sphere of influence of the life of the spirit from humankind to animals and plants. It was only logical, therefore, that the belief in immortality should also apply to their spiritual lives as well. Alfred Roller records a moving example of Mahler's belief in the immortality of an insect's soul, and it is hard to resist its strange charm. Mahler was at home in Vienna with two visitors, one of whom was Roller. The conversation was interrupted by a troublesome fly, which Mahler tried to drive away by waving his hand at it. By chance he caught it such a blow that it fell to the floor, twitching and dying. In order to put it out of its misery, he raised his foot to squash it but for a long time held his leg in the air, clearly struggling with the decision: 'He gazed in distress at the crushed little corpse at his feet and with an agitated movement of the hand towards it, as if to calm and console it, he murmured: "There, there, don't fret: you too are immortal!" He turned away, wandered around the room, upset, and did not go on with what he had been saying'.[16] This is Mahler through and through: while sharing Fechner's belief that the whole of nature possessed an immortal soul, he would none the less grow uncertain, tormented, as he was, by the sufferings of the world, but imbued with a sense of profound respect in the face of life's mystery, a mystery which for him embraced both animals and plants. There is no doubt that he believed profoundly that the whole of nature was animated by God. If he can be said to have been a member of any religion, then it was a natural religion. Anna von Mildenburg, who was closer to him than anyone else at a decisive point in his life, recalled him suddenly stopping during a walk and listening to a bird or watching some other creature going about its business:

> This serenity always gave way to reflection and serious, pensive contempla-
> tion, an awareness of God's wisdom, will and influence. He always felt the
> miracle and the mystery, awestruck and with a touchingly childlike astonish-
> ment. He could not understand his fellow humans' indifference to these
> wondrous acts of nature.[17]

Whereas Fechner's importance for Mahler's world of ideas is well attested, the impact of a book by the German philosopher Hermann Lotze is rather more obscure. Of all Mahler's friends and acquaintances, only Bruno Walter refers to Lotze in a single sentence, but he insists that the writer's three-volume *Microcosm* (1856–64) was a key influence on Mahler and that it preoccupied his thoughts for some time. Lotze has gone down in the history of ideas as the founder of a system of teleological idealism that sought to demonstrate the validity of a causal mechanism for all that occurs in the outer and inner world. In this way he hoped to prove that this mechanism was understandable only as the expression of a morally purposeful world. This was an idea that Lotze elaborated above all in his *System of Philosophy* during the 1870s and 1880s. But Mahler will have been less interested in this aspect of his work than in his older study, whose subtitle, 'Attempt at an Anthropology', caught the interest of contemporaries inasmuch as Lotze's aim, especially in the second volume, was to write a history of the evolution of human culture at odds with the age's interest in natural science and in the way in which nature developed. In this sense, Lotze was the first systematic cultural anthropologist.[18] He rejected the idea that all living things develop according to an ascending scale from the lowest to the highest. In turn this hierarchy implied that all living things could be graded according to their value and significance, with man being placed above all other natural phenomena and regarded as an 'advance' on plants and animals. Within the context of the nineteenth century's belief in progress, this view also ascribed to humankind an absolute right to rule over lower forms on the evolutionary ladder.

Lotze's rejection of these prevailing ideas must have appealed to Mahler, who saw in nature a confirmation of the sheer fragility of the human race. Above all, it must have pleased him that Lotze stressed that the labours and efforts of bygone generations were not lost either to those who had undertaken them or to future generations. It was, Lotze believed, on this very misunderstanding that rationalistic historiography was based, with its assumption that the individual was willing to sacrifice his or her independent happiness to the continuing development of the whole. The problem could be resolved if one were to concede that loving commitment or self-sacrifice to the greater good were unthinkable unless the individual were himself to derive enjoyment from it. For Lotze, these finest aspects of human morality were additionally founded in the belief that individuals are preserved for ever: such individuals would be destroyed by all attempts at development if those attempts were themselves repeatedly destroyed. Lotze's belief in the eternal preservation of the individual clearly recalls Fechner's ideas, and it comes as no surprise to find that Lotze was a close friend and critical colleague of the older man:

> The presentiment that we are not lost to the future, that those who were here before us may have departed this earthly life but have not left all reality behind them and that, however mysterious the process may be, history progresses for them too: it is this belief that allows us to speak of a human race and of its history in the way that we do.[19]

This passage throws even clearer light on the lines that Mahler added to Klopstock's poem in his Second Symphony ('Nothing is lost to you') and on the

real reasons for his work ethic, including his fanatical desire to achieve: his
inspired gift for music had, he believed, been given to him to bring joy and
edification to himself and his closer contemporaries. And, irrespective of the
success or failure of his achievements, a distillation of that gift would be
preserved and would continue to leave its mark on future generations. The
sense of continuity, of rising to greater heights, was merely an expression of
what Mahler described as 'restless striving and vitality' in his letter to Alma,
qualities effectively given to all of us but felt to be an obligation only by higher
individuals, among whom Mahler numbered all great thinkers, scientists and
artists such as himself. It was an obligation which, as he himself admitted, was
unrelenting and often a source of pain and torment. A letter that Alban Berg
wrote to his later wife, Helene, in the summer of 1910 may serve to illustrate the
extent to which such ideas were rife among artists and intellectuals at this time.
Berg's premise was his inability to share his wife's tremendous love of animals:

> I find that on closer acquaintance animals (e.g. dogs) are also *human*, and for
> the present I've had my fill of them. After all, all that we ever strive to achieve
> is to pass from the mortal to the *divine*, and yet we know that it is nowadays
> no art to possess a soul because, as you rightly say, every dog has one. . . . It
> is no merit simply to possess a soul! *Unless a person uses it to achieve godlike
> goals*, then he is no different from the *dog* that has learnt to think and feel as
> a human being possessed of a soul.[20]

The letter that Mahler famously wrote to Alma in June 1909 draws above all on
the ideas of Fechner and Lotze in addition to those of Goethe. Here he expresses
his 'philosophy' at its most candid. Alma was currently staying at Levico in Italy,
where she had abandoned herself to a feeling of indolence, dissatisfaction and
sexual frustration. She evidently found Mahler's letters an effort to read and in her
replies appears to have struck a petulant, ill-humoured note. Mahler was clearly
reacting to such a letter in which Alma, as a frustrated composer and companion
to genius, had wondered whether life acquired its value and importance only
from creativity, a creativity which, as she understood it, she was prevented by her
husband from pursuing. Mahler's response was expressly intended to console her
and help her to understand herself better. As such, it is one of his most important
statements of intent and as a result deserves to be quoted at length. He begins by
considerably broadening his definition of creativity:

> Human beings – and probably all creatures on Earth – are incessantly
> productive.
>   At every level, this process is inseparable from the nature of life itself.
> When productive energy ceases to flow, its 'entelechy' dies with it, i.e. it needs

a new body to be reborn. On that level at which higher forms of humanity exist, the creative act (which comes to most people in the natural guise of procreation) is coupled with a gesture of self-awareness. On the one hand this enhances the process, on the other it makes *demands* on our moral judgement. And *this* is what causes creative people such *disquiet*. Apart from the few brief moments in the life of a genius when these conditions are met, it's the long intervening periods of infertility that test the awareness and provoke unrequitable longings. Indeed, the distinguishing feature of the chosen few is an unceasing and truly agonized sense of striving.

There follows the passage cited above, in which Mahler argues that what matters is not the works of these few people but what they become through restless striving and vitality. True creativity involves constant growth and the exercise of all that is beautiful and good. No doubt aware that Alma will have found it difficult to believe that in spite of his intense championship of the masterpieces of the past, he regarded these and his own works merely as by-products of a process of development leading to higher things, he then goes on to underline this point:

What we leave behind, no matter what it may be, is merely a husk, an outer shell. Die Meistersinger, the Choral Symphony, Faust – all these are nothing but discarded wrappings. In essence, our bodies are also no more than that! Now I am not saying that the act of creativity is pointless. Mankind needs it in order to grow, to *rejoice*, for that too is an expression of well-being and potency.[21]

For Mahler, the ideas of Fechner and Lotze guaranteed that his life as a creative artist was not in vain – 'O believe, you were not born in vain, you have not lived and suffered in vain' are among the lines that he added to Klopstock's poem in his Second Symphony. Even if his own works had a limited life – he once said that they would last around fifty years, after which they would give way to something different and new, for this was the way of the world – one crucial aspect of them could never be lost: the restless, incessant and painful struggle imposed on higher men and women. It was this that was truly immortal. And it was Fechner who insisted that souls did not 'merge' with one another in the afterlife. Rather, the soul's energy continued to live on after death in a personal, individual way even if the people who were still alive were unable to identify the previous soul's 'body'.

It is impossible not to be reminded here of Goethe's lines from *Faust II*, 'He who strives on and lives to strive / Can earn redemption still', lines that Mahler set to music in his own Eighth Symphony. And it is Goethe who inevitably comes to mind when we read the opening of Mahler's letter to Alma of June

1909, in which he uses the mysterious term 'entelechy', quoting it in inverted commas and claiming that it dies when productive energy ceases to flow and that it then needs a new body to be reborn. In our chapter on Mahler's reading matter, we already mentioned Goethe's towering importance for him. Like Jean Paul and Dostoevsky, Goethe held an unassailable position in his literary firmament, but, unlike them, he was also a thinker and a philosopher of the first order. And in the case of neither Goethe nor Mahler can their metaphysics be tied down to Christianity, for all that there are manifold links between them, links that are clearer in Goethe's case only because he was brought up in a culture that was more marked by Christianity.

Immediately before the lines quoted at the beginning of the last paragraph are two others, 'This noble spirit saved alive / Has foiled the Devil's will!', sung by Angels who, according to the accompanying stage direction, 'hover in the upper atmosphere, carrying FAUST's immortal part'. The 'Paralipomena' to *Faust II* includes an earlier version of this stage direction: 'Choir of Angels, carrying Faust's entelechy'. Derived from the Greek and meaning 'having a goal or perfection within itself', the term was coined by Aristotle to describe a formal principle necessary to guide a living organism along the path of self-development. According to Aristotle, all who are capable of achieving anything already contain within them the potential to do so. For Aristotle, entelechy was ultimately synonymous with energy and with both the movement towards perfection and the state of perfection itself. This idea was later taken up by Leibniz, who expanded the no less Greek concept of the monad (from *monas*, meaning 'unit') to that of entelechy. Initially it was the spiritual forces, or souls, that derived from the first monad, then incorporeal beings to which all phenomena can ultimately be traced back. Even as late as the nineteenth century, writers were still arguing that the representatives of monadism could be distinguished from the atomists by dint of the fact that monads were regarded as animate entities with spiritual properties, whereas atoms were inanimate. To put it at its simplest, the atomists were physicians, whereas the monadists were metaphysicians.

Goethe was familiar with the writings of both Aristotle and Leibniz and frequently used the term entelechy, often emphasizing it, especially in his conversations with Johann Peter Eckermann and in the stage direction cited above. But to the annoyance of his many commentators, his attempts to explain the term are frustratingly terse, a terseness all the more regrettable, given the weight and complexity of the idea in his writings. As a result, many of today's Goethe scholars are of the view that it was simply a synonym for 'soul'. After all, it matters little for the meaning of the end of the work whether it is Faust's entelechy, the part of him that is immortal, or his soul that the Angels carry off to Heaven. But Goethe also unthinkingly equated entelechy

and monad in a way that was particularly bold – whether this is epistemolog-
ically permissible is another question that need not detain us here. In one of
his conversations with Eckermann, he returned to the question of entelechy,
stating quite openly that 'Leibniz had similar thoughts about independent
beings, and indeed what we term an *entelecheia* he called a monad.'[22]

In other words, Goethe equated the terms entelechy and monad, which he
also regarded as synonymous with the soul that strives to bring to perfection
all that is enshrined within it. His concept of entelechy is also the basis of his
– and Mahler's – concept of immortality, his visionary belief that the soul lives
on and returns after death. Evidence of this comes from a letter that Goethe
wrote to his old friend, the composer Carl Friedrich Zelter, in the course of a
correspondence lasting thirty-three years. When Zelter suddenly lost his son
in March 1827, Goethe sent him his condolences in a brief but significant letter
that could have been written by Mahler himself:

> The circle of persons with whom I come most in contact seems to me like a
> roll of Sibylline leaves, which, being consumed by the flames of life, vanish,
> one after the other, into the air, thus making those that are left more precious,
> from moment to moment. Let us work, until we, in our turn, either before or
> after one another, are summoned by the Spirit of the Universe to return into
> ether. And may the Eternally-Living not deny us new activities, like those in
> which we have already been put to the test! Should He, father-like, add to
> these the remembrance and after-feeling of the rectitude and virtue we
> desired and achieved even in this world, we should assuredly but plunge all
> the more eagerly in amongst the wheels of this world's machinery.
>
> The Entelechean Monad must preserve itself only in restless activity; if it
> becomes its other nature, it can never, throughout Eternity, be in need of
> occupation.[23]

Here, too, we find the same ideas on entelechy and the 'restless striving and
vitality' that Mahler refers to in his letter to Alma, the similarities even
extending to verbal parallels. Mahler's thinking was clearly coloured by
Goethe's ideas. Indeed, the latter's conversations with Eckermann, which are
the source of much of what we know about his concept of entelechy, were
Mahler's *vade mecum*. A further passage in Eckermann attests to the distance
between Goethe's view of the subject and Christian teaching. Goethe was critical of the German writer on aesthetics, Karl Ernst Schubarth, for muddying
the waters of Christianity with philosophical concepts, arguing that the
Christian religion was a powerful entity in its own right and that it did not
need the support of philosophy. Nor did philosophy need religion to prove
doctrines such as that of immortality:

Man should believe in immortality; he has a right to this belief; it corre-
sponds with the wants of his nature, and he may believe in the promises of
religion. But if the philosopher tries to deduce the immortality of the soul
from a legend [i.e. from Christian religion], that is very weak and inefficient.
To me, the eternal existence of my soul is proved from my idea of activity; if
I work on incessantly till my death, nature is bound to give me another form
of existence when the present one can no longer sustain my spirit.[24]

Mahler says much the same in his letter to Alma: 'When productive energy
ceases to flow, its "entelechy" dies with it, i.e. it needs a new body to be reborn.'
Of course, Aristotle, Leibniz and Goethe would all have protested at Mahler's
phrase about the death of entelechy as this is precisely what it does not do. But
the concord between these various writers is otherwise complete, and there
seems little doubt that Mahler was in total agreement with Eckermann, who,
on noting down Goethe's thoughts, exclaimed enthusiastically: 'My heart, at
these words, beat with admiration and love. "Never," thought I, "was a doctrine
spoken more inciting to noble minds than this. For who will not work and act
indefatigably to the end of his days, when he finds therein the pledge of an
eternal life?' Ultimately, Goethe even argued for the ennoblement of 'higher'
individuals – the 'men of genius' referred to in Mahler's letter: 'I doubt not of
our immortality, for nature cannot dispense with the *entelecheia*. But we are
not all, in like manner, immortal; and he would manifest himself in future as
a great *entelecheia*, must be one now.'[25]

Readers who are inclined to dismiss these ideas of Goethe's as too periph-
eral to his thinking to be of any importance to Mahler's conceptual world may
care to consider a far more detailed text that has hitherto been largely ignored
by writers on Mahler because the composer himself does not refer to it. But it
is mentioned by Bruno Walter, who knew more about Mahler's conceptual
world than any other contemporary observer, including even Siegfried
Lipiner:

> The sun in the sky of his spiritual world was Goethe. He had a remarkable
> knowledge of his work, and, thanks to a unique memory, would quote
> endlessly from it. He was a constant reader of Goethe's conversations with
> Eckermann and others, and Goethe's discussion of immortality with Falk was
> one of the foundations of his intellectual life.[26]

In spite of the brevity of Walter's remark, the reference to Johann Daniel Falk
is worth looking at in greater detail. True, scholars have called into question
the authenticity of Goethe's conversations with Falk, a writer and social worker
who lived in Weimar and who is now best remembered as the author of the

German Christmas carol 'O du fröhliche, O du selige, gnadenbringende Weihnachtszeit'. But such doubts are irrelevant to Mahler, for he did not share them. The conversation that Goethe conducted with Falk on 25 January 1813 – the day on which Christoph Martin Wieland was buried in Weimar – constitutes his most detailed non-poetic statement on the subject of immortality, and even though he does not use the word 'entelechy', he expatiated on the ideas that he later expounded to Eckermann and Zelter. Wieland's death led Goethe to think that there could never be any question of the destruction of such lofty spiritual forces in nature, for nature never squandered its capital in that way. Appealing to Leibniz, he then expounded his belief that there exist in nature ultimate elements of all creatures, which he called souls or, rather, monads, just as he was to do later. But only important monads that were suited to more than an insignificant existence deserved to be called souls:

> The moment of death, which for that very reason can very well be called an act of dissolution, is the one at which the principal ruling monad releases all previous subordinates from their loyal service. . . . But all monads are by their very nature so imperishable that they cannot cease their activities at the moment of dissolution but continue to be active even at that moment. In this way they merely depart from their former relationship with the world in order to enter a new relationship without further ado. During this change, all depends on how powerful is the intention contained in this or that monad.

And, convinced that such a powerful intention was at work in both himself and in Wieland – and Mahler himself shared this belief – Goethe went on:

> As soon as we realize that this state of the world is eternal, then in much the same way we can accept that monads have no other aim than forever to share in the delights of the gods as forces that blissfully play their own part in creation. The evolving nature of Creation is entrusted to them. Whether they are invited to do so or not, they come of their own accord, passing along every road, descending from every mountain, arising from every sea and falling from every star. Who can stop them? I am certain that just as you see me here, so I have already been here a thousand times before and hope that I shall return here a thousand times in the future.[27]

This, then, was the one fixed point in Mahler's spiritual existence, a point that allows us to explain almost everything else in his life.

Writers on Goethe are now agreed that his oft-cited reference to redemption at the end of *Faust* has little to do with redemption in the Christian sense of the term. In his fair copy of the play, Goethe even put quotation marks round the lines 'He who strives on and lives to strive / Can earn redemption still.' According to Albrecht Schöne in his critical edition of *Faust*, 'it would be wrong to interpret these lines in the sense of a Christian doctrine of redemption. . . . The theology of the Cross did not find its way into the poem of *Faust*.'[28] Another recent writer, Jochen Schmidt, makes a similar point:

> Goethe helps himself to the Christian tradition with the same poetic freedom and with the same non-committal attitude to questions of philosophy as he does in the Classical Walpurgis Night, where he draws on the Greek tradition. In this last-named scene he stages Greek myth, while in the final scene it is Christian myth – and that is all. It is clear, not least from remarks by Goethe himself, that he adopted a mythological attitude to the Catholic veneration of the Virgin that is so important for the final section of *Faust* and that he did so in a non-polemical manner, distancing himself from the material in a way that is typical of the artist but not of the believer.[29]

In a second important letter to Alma from the summer of 1909, Mahler offers his own interpretation of the final scene of *Faust*. It is an altogether exceptional piece of exegesis, written without any knowledge of existing commentaries or secondary literature, by which he in any case set little store. And yet it hits the mark with its intuitive and remarkably sensitive understanding. Above all, Mahler recognizes very clearly that the central idea in this final scene is love: not Christian love, be it agape or caritas, but Eros – and not the earthly Eros of Mephistopheles but the 'eternal womanly', the Eros that guides us upwards by stages to ever greater perfection.[30] In his letter Mahler, using quotation marks, turns himself into Goethe's mouthpiece:

> '*Eternal Femininity* has *carried* us *forward*. We have arrived, we are at rest, we are in possession of that which on earth we could only desire or strive for. Christians speak of "eternal bliss", and for the sake of my allegory I have made use of this beautiful, sufficiently mythological concept – and the one most accessible to this era of world history.'[31]

In short, Mahler saw very clearly that this final scene in Goethe's vast drama was not grounded in the Christian religion. And if he set these lines to music in his Eighth Symphony, he did not do so in the spirit of Christianity. Mahler had come to Goethe through the natural philosophy of the Romantics and through his reading of Fechner and Lotze, and it was Goethe who had now shown him that it was possible to believe in the immortality of the soul and in redemption without being a Christian. The events that unfold in the final scene of *Faust*, which, set in a mountain ravine, describes the ascent of a soul that has been saved, rest on the idea of *apokatastasis panton*, an idea advanced by the third-century Christian theologian Origen and quickly rejected by Church orthodoxy. The concept is explained by Albrecht Schöne as a 'living, conciliatory return to God, embracing everything that once emanated from Him but which had grown estranged, losing its way and becoming lost, even the devils in hell'.[32] For a time Goethe thought of including Mephisto in the process of grace. It is a process that Mahler himself expressed in the fourth movement of his Second Symphony, with its setting of words from *Des Knaben Wunderhorn*: 'I am from God and would go back to God! / Dear God will give me a light, / Will light me to blissful everlasting life!'

There is no doubt that Mahler's beliefs were coloured by Christianity, just as he was initially touched as a child by the Jewish faith, but, his conversion notwithstanding, he moved away from both. He was no Ahasuerian Jew unable to escape from his faith, but nor was he a Christian or Catholic mystic, as Alma would have us believe. Like the later Goethe, he was inspired by Catholic mysticism, not as a believer but as an artist. Drawing on his reading of Fechner and Lotze and of Jean Paul and Dostoevsky, he had built up a belief in the immortality of the soul and in the importance of restless striving and creativity, a faith that then acquired an indestructible coherency through his acquaintance with Goethe's work. In this context it is impossible to overestimate the role played by Siegfried Lipiner, who was known as a Goethe expert in Vienna's intellectual circles and who in 1894 wrote his doctorate on 'Homunculus: A Study on *Faust* and Goethe's Philosophy'. Ultimately, too, the world of Friedrich Rückert's ideas acquired considerable importance. In one of the *Kindertotenlieder* that Mahler set, there are four lines that read: 'They have merely gone on ahead of us / And will not ask to come home again. / We shall overtake them on those hills / In the sunshine, the day is beautiful.'[33] Here we find a poetic echo of the congruence between Fechner and Rückert, two writers who knew one another, even if their contacts remained distant.

At the end of Mahler's life, a decisive role was played by Eduard von Hartmann's book *The Meaning of Life*, to which we shall return in the context of the composer's final weeks.

If Mahler used the word 'God', he did so very infrequently, and yet even on those occasions he meant something rather different from the Jewish or Christian God. What he meant was the supreme force and invisible creative power that he tried to explain to Ernst Decsey through his crude comparison with a motor car. It was this force that he found at a higher stage of reflection in the final scene of *Faust*, a scene from which 'God' is famously absent. In one of the earliest letters that Mahler wrote to Alma, even before they were married, it is clear that the word 'God' can be used for this force but that such a name is not necessary. It is also clear from the language he uses that faith is not bound to ecclesiastical doctrines:

> I believe you feel just as I do: we are fulfilled and united by a power that is beyond and above us. It will be our holy duty tacitly to respect that power. When at such a moment I speak the name of God out loud, the omnipotent sense of your love and of mine will make you realize that this is a power that prevails over both of us and hence holds us in its grasp *as one*.[34]

Today's Mahlerians have unfortunately largely lost sight of Richard Specht's splendid book on the composer, which was first published in 1913. It is devoted for the most part to an analysis of his works, and only forty or so pages are concerned with Mahler as a person. And yet these pages are among the finest characterizations of the composer and as such are worthy of taking their place alongside the reminiscences of Bruno Walter and Alfred Roller. Specht was not a close friend of Mahler but he had known him since 1895, when he was introduced to him in Hamburg. Specht includes a brief but impressive section on Mahler's view of the world consisting for the most part of his own *obiter dicta*. If Specht describes the composer as a 'pantheist', this term need not detain us here. Of greater importance in the present context is Specht's account of a lunch that he had with Mahler at his Hamburg apartment in 1895:

> I do not know how it happened or what event in the dim and distant future we were talking about, but I allowed myself to make some stupidly frivolous comment: 'That doesn't interest me,' I said; 'I'll be well gone by then; and even if I've come back, I shan't know anything about my former life.' A loud crash suddenly made us all start. Mahler had struck the table, causing the glasses to jump. 'How can someone like you say anything as thoughtless as that?' he screamed. 'We shall all return. The whole of existence has meaning only because of this certainty. It's a matter of complete indifference whether we recall an earlier stage of our existence at a later point of our return. What matters is not the individual and his memory and contentment but only the great movement towards perfection and the purification that increases with each incarnation. That is why I have to lead an ethical life in order to spare my ego, if it returns, a part of the journey and make its existence easier for it. That is my moral duty, regardless of whether my later self is aware of it or not and whether or not it will thank me for it.'[35]

The Sixth Symphony

M AHLER WAS DISTINCTLY uneasy as he set off for Essen on 20 May 1906 to prepare for the first performance of his Sixth Symphony. It was clear to him that the work once again placed extreme demands on its interpreters and listeners, even if those demands were different from those posed by its predecessor. From a purely superficial standpoint, the work is extraordinarily conventional: it has only four – classically ordered – movements, it has neither a chorus nor vocal soloists and, *horribile dictu*, it includes a repeat in its opening movement indicated at the end of its exposition (at figure 14) by a repeat sign. Mahler had only once before included such a repeat in a symphony. And yet the apparent conventionality is deceptive. He was also worried about the Essen Orchestra, for he knew that it was not as good as the Gürzenich Orchestra in nearby Cologne with which he had worked on his Fifth Symphony in October 1904. Begun during the summer of 1903 and completed in May 1905, the Sixth is scored for such vast resources that the Utrecht Orchestra had to be brought in to supplement the local forces. Mahler had earlier written to his friend Willem Mengelberg to ask whether the Utrecht players were competent, and Mengelberg had been able to reassure him. As a result the organizers were able to boast that the performance, which took place within the framework of the annual festival held by the Allgemeiner Deutscher Musikverein, would feature 110 orchestral players, a boast that dismayed Mahler by perpetuating the belief that he wrote only works of the most monstrous dimensions – the sobriquet of the 'Symphony of a Thousand' that was later pinned to the Eighth Symphony merely marked the low point of this development. But the initial rehearsals left him pleasantly surprised and encouraged him to describe the orchestra in a letter to Alma as 'splendid' – one of his favourite epithets.

Conversely, Mahler's comments on his new work are few and monosyllabic and effectively summed up in the word 'riddle'. In the autumn of 1904, for example, by which date the symphony was largely finished, he wrote to

Richard Specht: 'My Sixth will pose riddles that only a generation that has absorbed and digested my first five symphonies may hope to solve.'[1] As if to compensate, Alma evidently felt called upon to offer a biographical interpretation of the symphony, most successfully in the case of the opening movement's second subject, first heard at figure 8 (bars 77–9), after the implacably propulsive march rhythm of the earlier section has first died away. According to her reminiscences of her husband, Mahler came to her in Maiernigg in the summer of 1904 and claimed that he had captured her in this theme.[2] Even the most honourable writers have been convinced by this claim, with the result that the 'Alma theme' now haunts the corridors of Mahler scholarship. Only Adorno remained sceptical, finding in the theme an intentional triviality. Certainly, Alma would not have been proud of this portrait if she had listened to it closely, for the soaring line in the first violins strikes a somewhat ostentatious pose, confronting the listener and figuratively placing its hands on its hips in a gesture of smug complacency, suggesting a counterpart to the main theme of Strauss's *Don Juan*. Alma also claims that an arrhythmic passage in the third movement describes Mahler's little daughters tottering over the sand. Quite apart from the fact that Mahler's younger daughter was only a month old at this date and therefore incapable of walking at all, such an interpretation reduces the work to the level of a *Sinfonia domestica*. It is simply impossible to say any longer what may have been in Mahler's mind when he made these remarks, assuming that he made them at all.

More credible – not least because it is confirmed by another source – is the claim that Mahler seemed particularly upset by the rehearsals and performance of his Sixth Symphony. Following the final rehearsal in Essen, Alma and a number of Mahler's friends went to see him in his dressing room, where they found him pacing up and down, beside himself with grief, and sobbing and wringing his hands. Oskar Fried, Ossip Gabrilovich and the Düsseldorf conductor Julius Buths had no idea what to say. Then Strauss entered the room in high spirits, noticed nothing and left again in the same ebullient mood. Bruno Walter reports that Mahler was in fact depressed by the dismissive remark of a famous musician – although he does not name names, it is Strauss to whom he was referring and who, with his usual disarming honesty, had announced after the final rehearsal that the symphony as a whole and especially its final movement were over-instrumented. Klaus Pringsheim reports that Mahler subsequently fretted over the question why, after only a few rehearsals, Strauss was always able to make his works sound good, whereas he himself was invariably profoundly dissatisfied with whatever he had managed to achieve.[3]

There is a further aspect of the Sixth Symphony that is unusual: on no other occasion did Mahler reveal such uncertainty about the order of its movements.

Should the Scherzo be in second or third position and, as such, should it come before or after the Andante? Even in the autograph score, Mahler reversed the order of the movements and abandoned what is now their usual sequence of the Scherzo followed by the Andante, a sequence, be it added, that also makes much greater sense. It is believed that at both the first performance in Essen and the local première in Munich, the Andante was played in second position, although the programmes for the concert and the reports of the various critics do not always agree on this point.[4] The reason for Mahler's uncertainty is easy to see, for the propulsive rhythm of the beginning of the Scherzo is very similar to the opening of the first movement, and so Mahler was no doubt afraid that listeners would turn to each other and whisper: 'Look! He's repeating himself!' But all other arguments favoured the definitive order.

Mahler's sense of turmoil at the first performance of the work seems to have been unique, but it is bound up with the term 'Tragic' that was applied to the symphony when he conducted its first performance in Vienna in January 1907. It is a term that is still occasionally found even if it has never found general acceptance. It is also one which, as Bruno Walter confirms, Mahler himself used, although he must have known that even in his own day it had lost its sombre aura and that, much as today, it can be used for every routine idiocy. In 1886 the Wagnerian Felix Draeseke had called his Third Symphony his 'Tragica' and by his own admission had sought to give expression to Beethoven's tragic view of the world, a view that had found only inadequate expression in Beethoven's Third, Fifth and Ninth Symphonies. Reverting to purely instrumental forces, Draeseke had attempted to realize this aim using Wagner's extended orchestral language. That Mahler had no wish to write a 'Tragic Symphony' in the spirit of the age is already clear from the pomposity of the first movement's main theme. It is as if he were trying to say that if the official world of culture wanted a 'tragic' symphonic theme, then this would be it. A rhetorical, emotionally charged language is then employed to imply the entry of the hero or heroes of the Second and Third Symphonies into some hall of fame or other. In short, it is figurative music, implying an alternative 'what if?' of the kind that had long been Mahler's guiding principle. The final movement reveals that the nickname is not entirely unjustified, for otherwise Mahler would neither have used it himself nor sanctioned its usage. But first we need to cast a more detailed glance at the first three movements of the symphony.

That the entire work, with the exception of the intermezzo-like Andante, is based on a march rhythm that had been 'kneaded through and through' is clear from the interrelationship between the first and final movements: the first begins with this march, while the last one ends with the final twitchings of this rhythm in the timpani. But no one before Mahler would have dared to suggest that a march rhythm could also leave its mark on a Scherzo. The Sixth Symphony offers alarming proof that this is indeed possible. Mahler's marches are the best. His longest and most magnificent orchestral song is undoubtedly 'Revelge' of 1899, a song in which the implacable rhythm of the Sixth Symphony is already clearly prefigured. For the Andante, conversely, it is the fourth of the *Kindertotenlieder* that provided the model. Neither song is quoted directly, but in the case of the second of them, there is more than just an atmospheric echo. The link between the movements, which is considerably stronger than in the previous symphony, is created above all by the march-like character of 'Revelge' and, more specifically, by a formula that could hardly be conceived along simpler and at the same time more enigmatic lines. It is first found just before figure 7 in the opening movement and consists of a *fortissimo* major chord for three trumpets in F that fades away to a *pianissimo* minor chord in the same key to the accompaniment of the march rhythm in the timpani and a roll on the side drum. For all its primitive qualities, this shift from major to minor served Mahler in good stead and was used to work some of his greatest melodic miracles. But never did he use it as fruitfully as here. What can be achieved through two simple chords is altogether incredible, as Mahler the constructivist uses the simplest of materials to create towering edifices of sound, skyscrapers made, as it were, of mud bricks.

As we have already noted, the Scherzo achieves the rare feat of combining a traditional ländler with a march or, to put it another way, it allows a march to develop out of a ländler before the march is turned back into the ländler. We have previously observed Mahler's tendency to rob the Scherzo of its traditional stolidity and complacency and to turn it into something far more eerie and unsettling. And here he takes that process a stage further: suffice it to listen to the howling horns with their descending appoggiatura at figure 46 near the beginning of the movement – it sounds as if the players are being tortured. The shrieks of delight associated with the usual type of scherzo have been transformed into the sounds of physical anguish. The Andante stresses its intermezzo-like character to such an extent that it too begins to sound sinister. It is unrelated rhythmically and motivically to any of the previous or later movements but sings itself out, while having none of the intimacy of the Fifth Symphony's Adagietto. By evoking the atmosphere of the *Kindertotenlieder*, it comes close to what Adorno called the mystic cell of Mahler's symphonies inasmuch as the Fourth, Fifth, Eighth and Ninth Symphonies all contain clear allusions to these songs. This Andante cannot offer assurance, still less can it afford its listeners any comfort. Rather, the anguished outburst of the section starting at figure 100 – one of the greatest moments in the whole of Mahler's output – is an expression of unfathomable grief. The movement as a whole cannot staunch the emotions adumbrated in the first two movements and taken to their furthest extreme in the fourth and final movement but can merely offer its listeners a chance to catch their breath before that conclusion is reached.

The whole symphony, and especially its final movement, has something of a retraction about it, a retraction of all the 'positive' final movements before and since. Such a retraction is comparable to the one planned by Adrian Leverkühn in Thomas Mann's novel *Doktor Faustus* when his favourite nephew, Nepomuk Schneidewein, is snatched from him by the Devil. In turn, this would have been a retraction of Beethoven's Ninth Symphony and, more especially, its final movement, which famously embraces the whole of humanity. This fourth movement is one of the longest that Mahler ever wrote, a length that seems strangely at odds with the apparently classical formal balance of its three predecessors. It is also at odds with the 'positive' and 'affir-mative' endings found in practically all other symphonies. (As we have seen, these terms can be used only with quotation marks round them.) Mathias Hansen's formulation is undeniably apt: 'In the Sixth Symphony the joking stops, and it does so, moreover, with a decisiveness that may well go beyond all that can be depicted in art and even all that is capable of artistic expression.'[5] Here Mahler leaves behind him the world of 'as if'. This final movement threatens to annihilate all that has gone before it not only through its sheer length but also through the brutality of its sonorities. Even the cowbells, which in the opening movement still sounded like oases of peace in the midst of a confused world dominated by march rhythms, suggesting the final sounds of civilization that the hiker hears as he climbs higher up the mountain slope, now sound suddenly lost, like quotations from another, better world. And yet, as we have seen, Mahler succeeds, by dint of his supreme formal artistry, in forging a link between this final movement and the first two. The opening movement's march had suggested that things might take a turn for the worse, but nothing could have prepared us for just how bad things become. The final movement progresses towards its end, unstoppably, and the instrumentation on its own makes the point: never has a bass tuba sounded more primeval and aggressive than in the Sixth Symphony's final movement.

And then there are the hammer blows. It is believed that Mahler originally thought of having five such blows, but he then reduced this number to three, only for the third of them to be struck out. The question is whether we come any closer to Mahler's intentions by reinstating this blow in bar 783, shortly before the end of the work. (Among modern editors, Hans Ferdinand Redlich reintroduced it in his Eulenburg edition of the score.) Even in his own day, Mahler's use of a hammer in his orchestra encouraged stupid jokes and carica-tures, contemporaries evidently failing to understand that a composer could be so deadly serious. Mahler was keen for the instrument not to produce a metallic sound. Rather, it should resemble an axe striking at the very root of life itself. Alma was her usual unhelpful self when, adopting a biographical note, she related it all to her husband. According to her, Mahler claimed that the three hammer blows were the three blows of fate that strike the hero, the third of which fells him like a tree.[6] For Alma, this hero was, of course, Mahler himself. But doubts remain. Whereas the term 'hero' is unquestionably appropriate in the case of the Second and Third Symphonies, it misses the point of the Sixth. It is inconceivable that Mahler could ever have offered this as an interpretation of the work. At best, it would have been a prop for those listeners who were otherwise slow on the uptake.

It is clear beyond peradventure that the final movement of the Sixth deals with questions of finality, death and destruction and that it holds out no promise or prospect of any improvement, no sense of comfort or consolation. This being so, it is difficult to understand why Mahler described the third hammer blow as the decisive one, for in that case he would not have removed it. And when Alma then goes on to claim that these three blows befell Mahler himself, the third one of which struck him down, she can sustain this argument only by basing it on the theory that music can anticipate real life. If artists depict something terrible that affects them, then, according to Alma, they do so either after the event, as Rückert did when he wrote his *Kindertotenlieder* following the deaths of his own children, or because, as figures of genius, they possess a Cassandra-like gift to foresee the future. In other words, Mahler anticipated the death of his elder daughter in his *Kindertotenlieder*, while in his Sixth Symphony he foresaw the three blows of fate that Alma glossed as the death of his daughter, the diagnosis of his heart disease and her affair with Walter Gropius. But her theory demonstrates only that she had no real concept of the nature of artistic creativity. She could simply not conceive of the fact that her husband could write such a final movement at a time when he was at the height of his career as a conductor, administrator and opera reformer, and his music, although not universally admired, was finding a responsive audience and when, married to the most beautiful woman in Vienna, he had fathered two beautiful, healthy girls. So she interpreted his ability to compose such a supreme expression of negativity, at a time when everything about his outward life was supremely positive, as a sin that must inevitably be punished. And yet, even if we accept the inadequacy of Alma's approach, a number of aspects of the symphony remain puzzling. It ends with the minor-key element of the central major-minor formula played *fortissimo* by the winds towards the start of the symphony. This is then reduced to a pitiful *pianissimo* in the trumpets, followed by a final rebellious reassertion of the timpani repeating the march rhythm one last time and suggesting the convulsions of a body whose brain no longer gives out any signals. And with a final pizzicato in the strings, it is all over.

Discussing Adrian Leverkühn's own work of retraction, *The Lamentation of Doctor Faustus*, in Thomas Mann's novel *Doktor Faustus*, Serenus Zeitblom notes that:

> Here, toward the end, I find that the uttermost accents of sorrow are achieved, that final despair is given expression, and – but I shall not say it, for it would mean a violation of the work's refusal to make any concessions, of its pain, which is beyond all remedy, were one to say that, to its very last note, it offers any other sort of consolation than what lies in expression itself, in utterance – that is to say, in the fact that the creature has been given a voice for its pain. No, to the very end, this dark tone poem permits no consolation, reconciliation, transfiguration.[7]

As we know, Adorno helped Mann to write his novel, and although the recently published correspondence between the two men contains no proof that these passages in *Doktor Faustus* were inspired by Adorno's knowledge of Mahler's Sixth Symphony, a connection is none the less conceivable. Michael Gielen sees in the final movement the triumph of death as the logical culmination of the march rhythms that accompany the whole of the symphony.[8] Adorno's proposed reading of the end of the work comes in a radio lecture that deserves to be quoted here:

> In spite of the hammer blows, it would be futile to lie in wait in this final movement for the man who is said to be felled by fate. The music's commitment to unbridled emotion is its journey to death, undiminished revenge on Utopia exacted by the course of the world. Passages of open doubt retire behind others evocative of dull brooding and seething and of a roaring that draws ever closer. ... The catastrophes coincide with the climaxes. Sometimes it sounds as if in the moment of finite fire humanity might once again waken and the dead come to life again. Happiness flares up on the very brink of horror.[9]

Superficially, at least, the Sixth is no 'symphonia tragica', but, as Mahler rightly foresaw, it will no doubt always remains a 'symphonia enigmatica'.

Opera Reform – Early Years of Marriage – Mahler's Compositional Method (1903–5)

Opera Reform

Were it not for Alfred Roller, we would have no proof that Mahler never said 'Tradition is slovenliness', even though this phrase – or its German equivalent, 'Tradition ist Schlamperei' – is regularly cited in writings on the composer. The phrase must in any case seem strange coming from a composer as supportive of intellectual and artistic traditions as Mahler, a man who was a lynchpin in the development of music between two other composers no less aware than he was of the tradition within which they were operating: Brahms and Schoenberg. But Roller worked with Mahler on frequent occasions and insisted that what he actually said was 'What you theatre people call your tradition is mere convenience and slovenliness for you.'[1] This is rather different. Without Roller, moreover, the most fundamental shake-up of the operatic stage since the inception of the genre three centuries earlier would never have taken place, a revolution that involved the creation of the role of the opera director and of the modern stage in general. It is no accident that these reforms were carried out in parallel with similar developments in the spoken theatre, developments associated with the names of Otto Brahm and Max Reinhardt and bound up with turn-of-the-century ideas on theatrical reform, some of them positively utopian in character. Mahler and Roller were the first to seek to realize the theatrical visions of men like Adolphe Appia and Edward Gordon Craig, visions which in turn can be traced back to the idea of the total artwork formulated above all by Wagner in his writings in the middle of the nineteenth century. If Mahler and Roller were able to dispense this new wisdom in only what may be described as homoeopathic doses, then this was because no other approach was possible in a conservative court theatre at this period.

In two essays – *Art and Revolution* and *The Artwork of the Future* – that he wrote in the turbulent months between the Dresden Uprising of May 1849 and his flight to Zurich and decision to settle there later that year, Wagner demanded the reunification of the principal elements that made up the total artwork which he believed had flourished in classical Greece. Only when the egoisms of particular individuals had destroyed the community spirit of classical tragedy and the polity of ancient Athens was the great artwork of antique tragedy fragmented into its constituent parts. Rhetoric, sculpture, painting and music abandoned the round dance that they had once performed in amity, hence the development of opera, ballet and the spoken theatre as separate arts in bourgeois society. Wagner hoped that what he called the 'great revolution of humankind' would not only sweep away the social conditions that he abhorred but also bring about a rebirth of the total work of art. Just as humankind would one day be reunited in brotherly love, so the arts must necessarily be reunited as well. The great synthesis of the arts would embrace all the different genres and portray consummate human nature in all its immediacy. The dislocation of the arts that was typical of the modern period was a reflection of the particularism and egoism that characterized society. There had originally been three 'purely human' art forms, dance, music and poetry. Until now, they had never been united in opera but had simply coexisted under the aegis of a common 'treaty' (and we know from the *Ring* what Wagner thought about treaties). These three arts must now be joined by the three visual arts, architecture, sculpture and painting. For the 'artwork of the future', which was essentially drama and, more especially, music drama, this meant that architecture must provide the perfect theatre. The actor must now depict what sculpture and painting had hitherto achieved in their portrayal of humankind.

It was these six arts that had formed the total artwork during the heyday of ancient Greek art, but Wagner and his followers were not content with merely reviving Greek tragedy. In spite of its dreary isolation, music had none the less created the language of the orchestra, a magnificent new achievement embodied in its finest form, Wagner believed, in the symphonies of Beethoven. This achievement now had to be applied to the drama, which would lead to the emergence of the music drama and to its finest expression in the works of Wagner himself. To that extent these works could be described as 'the artwork of the future'. In short, the total artwork, or *Gesamtkunstwerk*, was not only what happened on the actual stage but also the whole of the building that was intended to recreate the sense of community between stage and audience, including a sense of community between the individual members of that audience. This also explains why the theatre that Wagner built in Bayreuth was amphitheatrical in design, with no side boxes or tiers from which the ruler's subjects could see far less than the prince himself in his centrally situated box. Another essential aspect of the total artwork was the involvement of the spectators, who would be absorbed by the events on the stage, a point on which

Wagner's idea remained very vague and one that he failed to realize even in Bayreuth.

The Swiss theorist and stage designer Adolphe Appia was the first man of the theatre to take up Wagner's ideas and raise them to a level which in theory at least went far beyond anything that Wagner had achieved at his first Bayreuth Festival in 1876. However visionary Wagner may have seemed in his earlier draft programmes, the realization of those visions fell far short of the ideal in the inaugural *Ring*. He was too corrupted by the bad taste of nineteenth-century scene painting to raise any objections to the set designs of Joseph Hoffmann or to their execution by Max and Gotthold Brückner, for all that the latter were among the most technically proficient scene painters of their age. Wagner himself was no doubt aware they were irredeemably old-fashioned and felt a general unease, prompting him to whisper to Malwida von Meysenbug, a mutual friend of his and Nietzsche's: 'Don't look too much! Just listen instead!' Such a comment hardly suggests the spirit of the total artwork. At least in his designs Appia achieved what Wagner had dreamt of.

But on one essential point he differed radically from Wagner: for Appia, it made no sense for the different branches of art to exist alongside one another as equals. Rather, there had to be a hierarchy among them, with acting as the most important, followed by the stage area, then light and, at the lower end of the scale, painting. Everything comes together in what Appia in a pioneering term described as the 'mise en scène'. The art of the 'mise en scène' – literally, the 'placing on stage' – was the art of developing in space what the dramatist had developed in time. In the 'word-tone-drama' – the neologism was Wagner's, and it was Wagner's works that Appia saw as the supreme expression of that concept – the music governs all the other elements, ordering them according to the demands of the action. It is the music that prescribes the performer's moves and in that way defines the stage area. This stage area should have nothing more to do with reality in the sense of the sort of crude naturalism propagated by the Meiningen school. Lighting and colour – essentially light on its own – should create a sense of space, which should take precedence over whatever actions were physically presented onstage. For Appia, light was in the same relationship to the performance as the music was to the score: it was the primary expressive element and as such was in stark contrast to the symbol, which provided a sense of orientation by means of mere allusion. Like music, light is able to express all that belongs to the inner-most essence of a phenomenon, a point that Appia stressed in his writings, which were published in the 1890s.

The second leading theatre reformer in turn-of-the-century Europe was Edward Gordon Craig. Unlike Appia, he had a chance to put his ideas into practice, even if only on a modest scale. It was effectively Craig who, with his greater sense of reality, invented the role of the director, arguing that the true task of the theatre was that of a stylized art form remote from any naturalism and that a demiurge was needed to control every aspect of the staging. If there were an artist who used actors, sets, costumes, lighting and movement in the right way and who became a master of movement, line, colour, rhythm and words, then the result would, he believed, be a new type of director who no longer had anything in common with the traditional stage manager, who merely indicated the actors' entrances and exits. In many ways Craig was even more radical than Appia for he finally found it disturbing to have a living human being onstage and developed the idea of the actor as an 'Über-Marionette' – the Nietzschean associations of the term were entirely typical of the age's enthusiasm for the champion of the *Übermensch*. Equally bold was Craig's concept of an adaptable stage area that could be rearranged for every performance, the only constant being the audience and the space in which it was accommodated. But the stage itself must be capable of permanent change, with the result that it should be as empty as possible. For both Appia and Craig, the art of the theatre was a creative art that existed independently of the art of the dramatist and musician. This re-evaluation of traditional priorities is no doubt one of the reasons why everyone involved in the theatre should find such theories so attractive.

Whereas Appia formulated his ideas in the years leading up to the turn of the century, Craig's writings on the theatre date in part from the following decade. In both cases, however, they were far ahead of their time and left few discernible traces on the theatre of their own day. Not until the 1920s were their ideas to find expression in the spoken theatre in the world of the German Expressionists, while it was only in the 1950s and 1960s that Bayreuth and music theatre in general finally took account of them. The only direct evidence of their influence in the years around the turn of the century may be found in the opera reforms of Mahler and Roller in Vienna. Roller had studied the available writings of both Appia and Craig, and although there is no actual proof of the fact, it is generally assumed that Mahler was at least familiar with the ideas of Appia. The work of both Appia and Craig was widely discussed in turn-of-the-century Vienna, and when Hermann Bahr noted in 1905 that he had detected Craig's influence in Roller's staging of *Don Giovanni*, then his observation was correct. When compared with the boldness of Appia's designs, Roller's work seems distinctly timid, and yet when we compare it with what was typical at this time not only in Bayreuth but during the whole of the nineteenth century, then Roller's designs could be said to have an explosive force mitigated only by the decorative style of the Vienna Secession. In this respect, Roller achieved on the stage of the Vienna Court Opera what Klimt had achieved in painting and Olbrich and Moser in the decorative arts. Roller was uniquely and astonishingly successful in giving Viennese audiences what they demanded in terms of their need for visual gratification, while subtly reducing the degree of naturalism in scene painting and allowing light, colour and air to create a hitherto unprecedented impact. That there were no real protests against his treatment of space and that he quickly came to be seen as the leading set designer of his age is an indication of his ability to get the prescription exactly right.

Only four years younger than Mahler, Roller was born in the Moravian city of Brno in 1864. His father was a painter and graphic artist and had written a successful textbook on the technique of etching. Roller moved to Vienna in 1884 to study law but soon switched to the visual arts and enrolled at the Academy of Fine Arts. He went on to co-found the Secession and came to the theatre through his encounter with Mahler. When Mahler left Vienna in 1907, Roller's interest in the Court Opera waned, and he ended his contract in 1909. While in New York, Mahler tried in vain to prepare the ground for Roller in the city, where he could have used his old comrade-in-arms. But Roller's impact on the history of the theatre was by no means over, for in 1911 he designed the sets and costumes for the Dresden première of Strauss's *Der Rosenkavalier*. For the next three-quarters of a century his designs were regarded as sacrosanct, leaving their mark on practically every other staging of the work throughout Europe and beyond. Only in the last twenty to thirty years have designers broken away from the weight of this tradition. Roller's work on *Der Rosenkavalier* brought him into contact with Hofmannsthal, Strauss and Max Reinhardt and led to further collaborations, including *Die Frau ohne Schatten* in Vienna in 1919 and the foundation of the Salzburg Festival in 1920. Roller designed the costumes for Hofmannsthal's *Jedermann* in the Festival's opening year and was also involved in the world première of Hofmannsthal's *Salzburger Großes Welttheater* two years later, as well as many of the Festival's productions of the operas of Mozart and Strauss that were central to the Salzburg repertory during the years that followed, many of them staged in collaboration with the director Lothar Wallerstein.

Perhaps the strangest commission that Roller received came in 1934, when he was almost seventy and was asked to design the sets and costumes for *Parsifal* at Bayreuth, an invitation ostensibly extended at the express request of Hitler. But the familiar anecdote that tells how the young art student found only one champion when he was turned down by the Vienna School of Arts and Crafts and that that champion was Alfred Roller belongs in the realm of myth. While we know that Hitler arrived in Vienna with a letter of recommendation to Roller that he had presumably obtained through private contacts, it seems that sheer timidity discouraged him from calling on the professor. But we also know that Hitler was so impressed by the stage productions of Mahler and Roller that even in later life he continued to express his admiration for Mahler and for the latter's understanding of Wagner. Although it was not until September 1907 that Hitler settled in Vienna, he had already spent a few weeks in the city in May 1906 and attended performances of Wagner's *Der fliegende Holländer* and, on the 8th of the month, *Tristan und Isolde*, a performance that we know from the Court Opera's records was conducted by Mahler.[2] It was no doubt these memories that prompted Hitler to extend the invitation to Roller in the 1930s. In his designs for Bayreuth, Roller fell back on tried and tested models, but, even so, these were more impressive than the nineteenth-century designs that still graced the stage of the fossilized Bayreuth Festival, where they inevitably encountered resistance. Roller died from tonsillar carcinoma in June 1935.

By the time that Mahler became director of the Vienna Court Opera, he had long since learnt from bitter experience that production values were nonexistent, whether at the smallest of provincial theatres or at the Hamburg Opera. With the help of all manner of assistants, he himself could see to the musical preparation of the various works in the repertory. But who could help him to sweep aside the fusty traditions of staging opera that had vexed him for decades? Alma hit the nail on the head when she claimed that, however varied her husband's interests, he lacked any real understanding of the visual arts, a lack that set him apart from most of the musicians of his age. This situation changed only when Alma introduced him to two of the artists of the Secession, Kolo Moser and Gustav Klimt, both of whom were keen to give him a helping hand. But Mahler's interest in the Wagnerian *Gesamtkunstwerk* had long made it clear to him that the success or failure of a production was determined not by individual parameters such as the singers or orchestra or the lovingly painted details of the stage sets but the overall impression, which meant that the staging as a whole must be accorded the same degree of importance as the other elements in the production. This emerges not least from the detailed memorandum that he addressed to the chief comptroller when complaining about the interference of the general administrator's office in his work. He also used the opportunity to spell out the rights and obligations of the director of the Court Opera, indicating that within two years of taking up office Mahler was already keen to assume overall responsibility and that he realized that all the elements in a performance were interrelated. It was also clear to him that the 'décor' needed to be improved:

In the theatre, unfortunately, purely musical successes are not successes *at all*. And if the attractiveness (or indeed the sheer *novelty*) of the stage setting – some detail that adds to the clarity, liveliness, harmoniousness of the décor or to that elusive correlation between stage and music – if its only consequence is that the performances are better attended, then the increased takings far outweigh the often quite insignificant cost of making the improvement. To block this expenditure may seem a small saving but in truth it often means a serious – but unfortunately not easily calculable – loss.[3]

And Mahler goes on to make an even more fundamental point:

> If one aspect of this performance is affected by another and often by something seemingly irrelevant, then this is merely a reflection of the complex and yet unified mechanism of the theatre and of the theatre administration, which is in fact an organism grounded in the interplay of its parts. This means that any interference in one of its parts affects all the others; that nothing is a matter of indifference here; and that the standards by which we can judge what is more or less important and more or less successful can be judged and maintained only within the field of operation itself, through the uninterrupted deployment of this machine.

Nowadays this must seem blindingly self-evident and common currency among all the members of a company, but in Mahler's day it was a completely new and revolutionary approach to the phenomenon of the theatre. The whole of the nineteenth century had demonstrated that parts of the whole could be stressed only at the expense of that whole, even though this misplaced emphasis did not preclude significant achievements on the part of singers or actors or musicians. But it was almost certainly Mahler who first expressed this standpoint in such emphatic terms.

Understandably Mahler sought a reliable and innovative colleague in the area with which he was least familiar. Initially it was the artist Heinrich Lefler whom he appointed head of scenic design. But Lefler did not meet all of Mahler's expectations, even if he represented an improvement on earlier standards, and so Mahler set about looking for a successor in the circles that he now frequented. He must have been impressed by Roller's designs for the Secession's headquarters in Vienna and especially by his fresco *Nightfall*, which Roller created around Max Klinger's vast sculpture in the Beethoven room. Until then, Roller had not worked in the theatre, unless he had helped the famous Viennese scene painters Carlo and Anton Brioschi, who worked chiefly for the Court Opera. It is conceivable that he assisted them during his youth in an attempt to earn some extra money, although there is no documentary evidence that he did so. Alma reports that at her husband's first meeting with Roller, the latter had deliberately provoked Mahler by claiming that he could bear to sit through a performance of *Tristan und Isolde* only by turning his back on the stage. Mahler had apparently then asked him to explain what the stage should look like if it was to warrant his attention. Roller had duly obliged, extemporizing an explanation, at the end of which Mahler had turned to Alma with the words: 'That's the man for me – I'll engage him!'[4]

Shortly afterwards – probably in May 1902 – Mahler invited Roller to have lunch with him, an occasion on which they were joined by Kolo Moser. The declared aim of the meeting was to discuss their planned collaboration on *Tristan und Isolde*. Mahler had already decided to invite Roller to design the sets, the Court Opera's resident designers, Lefler and Anton Brioschi, having been informed that their services would not be required. According to Mahler, they accepted this with a good grace, even though they did not know who was to replace them. Roller served his apprenticeship with Carl Maria von Weber's *Euryanthe*, which was staged in January 1903 under Mahler's direction. By 21 February 1903 their epoch-making production of *Tristan und Isolde* had been unveiled. Now not even the most critical observers had further reason to turn away from the stage and face the other way. Mahler was fortunate in terms of his cast: Anna von Mildenburg sang Isolde, while her Tristan was Alma's object of desire, the strapping Danish tenor Erik Schmedes. The affable basso profundo Richard Mayr sang Marke, and Brangäne was played by Hermine Kittel. In keeping with contemporary practice, neither Mahler nor Roller was named on the playbill, and yet it was as much to them, as to the singers, that the performance owed its success. Above all, it was they who ushered in a new era in staging opera, conscious, as they were, that so daring a work had never previously been fully explored on the stage. Of the singers, it seems likely that only Anna von Mildenburg's volcanic Isolde came up to Mahler's standards, and yet Alma reports that Mildenburg fought long and hard against the new sets, screaming that she would 'tear up the footlights' on the grounds that they were inartistic. But Alma's negative comments need to be treated with considerable scepticism, motivated, as they were, not only by the jealousy between two women but also by the feelings of jealousy of the art-loving amateur for the truly great singing actress.

As with *Der Rosenkavalier*, so with *Tristan und Isolde*, Roller's sets were to remain influential for decades. His sets for the opening act, for example, were on two levels, Isolde and Brangäne on floor level downstage, while Tristan and Kurwenal were positioned on a raised deck to the rear of the stage that was initially hidden from view by large red drapes. For the second act, Roller designed a castle garden at night, with stone benches and low walls, a clearly silhouetted black tree to the audience's right and a starry sky at the beginning turning to wan daylight at the end. In the third act the castle courtyard at Kareol was open to the sea but was pervaded by a sense of decay. At its centre was a vast white fortified tower that dominated the stage. Roller's designs for this and his later productions have for the most part survived and were the most decorative and colourful stage designs since those of Karl

Friedrich Schinkel, a feast for the eyes even when reproduced on the printed page.[5]

The reviews of the opening night give an idea of the overwhelming power of the performance. Max Graf, who later turned against Mahler, described the evening as a symphony in three movements. The opening act was red, the second one purple (Roller's designs are unclear on this point, though they inevitably represent only a single stage in the planning process, not the end result, which can be judged only in tandem with the lighting), and the third one grey. Over the performance as a whole wafted the flag of the Secession, while light and air made music alongside the Wagnerian orchestra, the basic chords of each act massing together in the form of its basic colour and basic light. What was so attractive about these designs, Graf continued, was their ability 'to vary the colour of a basic chord, spreading it out and changing it, bringing something of the subtle *Tristan* chromaticisms to the world of the decorative arts and creating musical impressions through the vibrations of air and colour. This is the first time that the modern Impressionist arts of painting have found their way on to the operatic stage.' Graf rightly relates this revolution to Wagner's ideas on the *Gesamtkunstwerk*, his only qualification being that Wagner might have been shocked by the designer's evident high-handedness.[6] Another prominent Viennese critic, Gustav Schönaich, was equally enthusiastic about the effects of light and colour but had reservations about the excessive darkness which meant that the lovers were barely visible in their second-act duet. It is clear from all the principal reviews that both on the present occasion and in the case of all their other collaborations over the space of a mere four years, Roller and Mahler succeeded in capturing the underlying mood of every situation and, indeed, of the work as a whole, and turning it into a symphony of colour, light and movement of unprecedented grandeur, the constituent parts so deftly interwoven as to create an indissoluble fabric of inextricable interrelationships.

The visual delights afforded by Roller's designs should not mislead us into thinking that the old-fashioned painted sets of Hoffmann, Brioschi and Lefler had simply been replaced by newer and more attractive Secessionist sets, as if Klimt had designed a frieze instead of Moritz von Schwind. Mahler and Roller wanted more than that. The spirit of the Secession was also the spirit of the *Gesamtkunstwerk*, a point clearly demonstrated by the very manner in which Klinger's Beethoven statue had been presented to the public. Nothing with any claims to be regarded as art could exist in isolation: what mattered was the way in which the arts harmonized with each other and belonged together. The critics in general lacked the ability to see what was so revolutionary about this process, Hermann Bahr alone demonstrating any real understanding in this regard:

Thus, what is called the atmosphere of a dramatic scene is the result of the scene; it does not exist until the scene creates it. And if, when the curtain rises, it is already evident in the setting before we have been prepared for it by the course of the drama, it cannot be effective. To begin with, Roller perhaps did not really grasp this, but he came to feel that the 'stylized' décor, the décor as an expression of an emotional atmosphere, must not appear until the feelings of the audience have been brought by the events on stage to the point where they actually demand to be reflected in the setting. This is the key to his designs, which fulfil a double function. At first they operate simply as a placard saying 'Imagine Tristan's ship, or Florestan's dungeon.' But then, when the stage atmosphere begins to affect the audience, when they lose their personal feelings and succumb to the dramatic transformation, they are no longer felt as just any old ship or any old prison but as an image of what has been heard: sounds become images.[7]

Bahr's description of an emotional mood becoming the mood of the staging captures the essential quality of Mahler's and Roller's reforms far more succinctly than all the wordy accounts of the critics. As a spokesman of the Young Vienna literary movement and its outright rejection of Naturalism, Bahr was well placed to understand the central concepts of the age: 'I – soul – nerves – mood.' Until then the young artists and intellectuals had taken little interest in the antiquated goings-on at the Opera, but now they suddenly saw a clear reflection of their own ideas and feelings on the stage of the venerable Vienna Court Opera. It was no wonder that they were enthusiastic about this development. The cult of Wagner that many of them had embraced had for the most part been centred on Wagner's music, music to whose overwhelming power it was possible to submit at the piano in arrangements for two or four hands – Arthur Schnitzler and Alma Schindler were two such adepts who wallowed in the Master's music in the privacy of their own music rooms. Until then – as Roller had noted – the joys of *Tristan und Isolde* were best experienced in the opera house with one's back to the stage. But such attitudes were no longer relevant. Even those listeners who laid claim to the most exquisite and most modern tastes in art – and they included the supporters of the Secession – could turn back to the stage with a sigh of relief and see there a reflection of their own choice tastes and sentiments. The power of Mahler's conducting and the vocal artistry of the leading Wagner singers of their day (in some respects Vienna's Wagnerian ensemble under Mahler was superior to its Bayreuth equivalent, even if there was a certain overlap) ensured that the baby was not thrown out with the bathwater: vocal standards remained high.

By the end of his work on *Tristan und Isolde*, Mahler knew that he had finally found the collaborator for whom he had been intuitively searching throughout the whole of his twenty galley years. It was not in his nature to waste words or to indulge in fulsome praise, but by Mahler's standards the letter that he wrote to Roller between the first and second nights of the new production is enthusiastic in the extreme:

My dear Herr Roller,

How you have put me to shame! For days I have been wondering how to thank you for all the great and wonderful things for which the Opera House and I owe you thanks. – And I have come to the conclusion that instead of trying to put anything into words, I should simply remain silent. – I know we are similar in one respect: in our completely unselfish devotion to art, even if we approach it by different roads. And I was also fully aware that you would not think me unappreciative or undiscerning if I did not try to put anything into words about what you have achieved and what you have come to mean to me.

And I should be very sad, as though it were some kind of farewell, over our saying such things to each other now, were I not joyfully certain that our collaboration hitherto is only a *beginning* and an indication of things to come.[8]

Mahler had changed the course of operatic direction. Heinrich Lefler was pensioned off to a post at the Vienna Academy of Art, and within three months of the first night of *Tristan und Isolde* Roller had been appointed head of the scenery workshop at the Vienna Court Opera with effect from 1 June 1903.

Mahler's success lent wings to his efforts. In Bayreuth in his youth he had experienced for himself the miracles of the invisible orchestra. He knew that he could not introduce this design to Vienna, where the breadth of the repertory would in any case have made it absurd. But he arranged for the pit to be lowered by 20 inches and at the same time to be extended to a total area of 635 square feet. (He had originally thought of lowering the pit by as much as five feet.) It had always disturbed him that the musicians could be seen by the audience, and in 1903 he was additionally troubled by the fact that the lights on the music stands detracted from the lighting effects that Roller was attempting to achieve on the stage. In an interview that he gave to the *Illustriertes Extrablatt* in September 1903, he stated that:

Putting the orchestra lower is important for a discreet orchestral sound and important for the purposes of discreet lighting. I purposefully avoid the words 'lighting effects'. We do not need crude effects, we want to make the *light* serve the theatre in *all* its grades, nuances and degrees of strength. To be always out for powerful effects is inartistic. But the matter does not end with the lighting; the whole of modern art has a part to play on the stage. Modern art, I say, not the Secession. What matters is the conjunction of all the arts.[9]

In other words, Mahler did not want to be pinned down to the Secession alone: the idea of the *Gesamtkunstwerk* manifestly lay behind all of his endeavours.

The next joint ventures between Roller and Mahler were initially eclipsed by their achievement over *Tristan und Isolde*. Their work on Hugo Wolf's *Der Corregidor* was overshadowed by the sad ending of the friendship between Mahler and Wolf, who died in an asylum in February 1903. Like Verdi's *Falstaff*, it turned out to be far less spectacular than their Wagnerian collaboration, and although Mahler himself conducted, we shall probably not go far wrong in assuming that neither work was as close to his heart as *Tristan und Isolde*. But this was certainly not the case with *Fidelio*, which opened on 7 October 1904. This was a work which Mahler rated as highly as Wagner's *opus metaphysicum*, the *Ring* and *Don Giovanni*, and had always been his *pièce de résistance*, the work that he programmed or at least requested for guest performances and for his debut appearances: it was a work with which he knew he could unleash the greatest impact. Here, then, was an opportunity to stage the piece under optimal conditions. And in this case he was able to play a more active role as a director than in the relatively static *Tristan und Isolde*. Not only does *Fidelio* contain a chorus, but he also had to work out credible moves with singers, some of whom were more willing than others. Time and time again he would jump up from the pit and climb up on to the stage, rushing to and fro, physically repositioning singers who were generally a foot taller and nearly five stone heavier, and demonstrating their relevant positions and moves in the way that Wagner had done at Bayreuth, but now as part of a completely different dimension within the overall action. We shall not go far wrong in regarding Mahler as the conductor and director whom Wagner spent his whole life hoping in vain to find as a collaborator.

In his set designs for *Fidelio*, Roller strove to achieve the greatest possible degree of simplification and at the same time monumentalization. The prison courtyard in Act One is one of his greatest designs.[10] The castle walls in the second and third acts of *Tristan und Isolde* likewise have a larger-than-life quality to them and are overpoweringly grey in colour. The gate through which the prisoners enter in *Fidelio* is part of a massive tower that seems to disappear upwards into the infinity of space. Only in the top left-hand corner of the stage, as seen from the audience's point of view, is there a scrap of blue sky that the prisoners can enjoy for the briefest of moments. It is clear from the way in which Roller has depicted Leonore – not as the sketch for a costume design but as a figure in a painting – that the moment presented here is the one at which the character, completely dwarfed by the vastness of the wall, rushes

into the courtyard with the words 'Abscheulicher! Wo eilst du hin!' The traditional solution to staging this opening act incorporated the exterior of Rocco's
house into the prison courtyard, thereby obviating the need for a scene change
and allowing the Biedermeier-like atmosphere of the opening numbers to
unfold beneath these walls, but this was a solution that Mahler and Roller
rejected as inimical to the mood of oppression and horror that pervades the
rest of the act. Instead, they created an interior set for Rocco's parlour, followed
by a change of scene to the prison courtyard. Mahler also cut Rocco's Gold
Aria, arguing that it held up and trivialized the action. However much he
may have respected the composers he loved, he was never squeamish about
making changes whenever he thought that retouchings or cuts could enhance
the effect that the composer in question was trying to achieve, an attitude
diametrically opposed to today's *werktreu* practices. Florestan's underground
dungeon had previously been represented by a spacious cellar, but Roller
reduced its commodious expanse to the dark and confining space so oppressively evoked in the orchestral introduction to this second act.

Equally unsatisfactory was the earlier attempt to bridge the gap between the
Dungeon Scene and the final scene outside the prison, where the light of
freedom contrasts with the blackness of the dungeon. In the past the change
was effected either by a lengthy scene change, during which the audience
remained seated in restless silence, or by a transformation as perfunctory as it
was awkward. In an older edition of the libretto, Roller discovered the stage
direction 'On the rampart' for this final scene and saw in it his opportunity to
bring out the contrast between extreme darkness on the one hand and extreme
brightness on the other. Although this required a break in the action while the
sets were noisily rebuilt, Mahler was unwilling to stand idly by in silence. Even
in Hamburg, he had had the revolutionary idea of performing the *Leonore*
Overture no. 3 at this point in the performance, an idea which is, however,
controversial as it clearly does not reflect Beethoven's own intentions. The
Prisoners' Chorus in the opening act likewise underwent a radical transformation. Today's opera-goer will be familiar with a whole series of ways of staging
this difficult scene, including even the non-appearance of the chorus, many
directors rejecting what they regard as the tired cliché of the prisoners stag-
gering in as a picture of wretchedness. Such an image was in fact invented by
Mahler and Roller: until then, the chorus had entered as quickly as possible,
grouped themselves picturesquely round the stage in positions that afforded a
clear view of the conductor and performed their party piece with all the enthusiasm of a glee club determined to demonstrate its power and tonal beauty.
Only in the wake of Roller and Mahler did it become customary to have these
victims of tyranny grope their way, one by one, out of their cells, emaciated,
half blinded by the light and scarcely able to walk or stand.

For all that it nowadays seems like a cliché, this was a revolutionary idea at the time. The critic of the city's leading liberal newspaper, the *Neue Freie Presse*, was Julius Korngold, the father of the child prodigy Erich Wolfgang. He was overwhelmed by this scene and rightly observed that Roller's sets were no longer an autonomous element in the theatrical experience but had entered into a symbolic relationship with the atmospheric elements of the action and the music. Korngold was concerned only that there may have been too much 'atmosphere' for an opera 'of the older kind'. Other newspapers, which had never made any secret of their chauvinist, German nationalist and anti-Semitic agenda, and who were against Mahler on principle and therefore also against Roller, took exception to the ingenious Spanish costumes that the masterly designer had created:

> Beethoven's music does not have a single glimmer of Spanish local colour. It is unadulteratedly German, without any foreign ingredient. The Spaniards strutting around on the stage really did not suit this German music but destroyed the mood from the very beginning. The fact that Director Mahler, in his ultranervous manner, believed it necessary to arrange Beethoven's music – which is not at all nervous but gloriously healthy – to suit his own personal taste by introducing all manner of novel nuances to the chosen tempo was of even less benefit to the overall impression.[11]

Not all of the new productions superintended by Mahler and Roller can be described here, but one further example, at least, deserves to be mentioned: their new production of *Don Giovanni*, which opened in December 1905, a month after their staging of *Così fan tutte* had launched a Mozart cycle that continued with *Die Entführung aus dem Serail*, *Le nozze di Figaro* and *Die Zauberflöte*, and that was mounted to commemorate the Mozart sesquicentenary in 1906. Roller's designs, notably for the Ball Scene at the end of the opening act, find him charting new territory in terms of stage machinery. Two or more towers delimited the stage area to the right and left, forming a kind of portal. These towers could be dressed and used in various ways but remained a constant presence, allowing for rapid scene changes, none of which lasted more than thirty seconds. They were also practicable, affording windows and balconies at various levels, depending on the requirements of the scene in question. They provided a continuum within which the scene could change, while restricting the vast width of the Court Opera stage, which, suited to French grand opera and the music dramas of Wagner, was less appropriate in the case of the more human dimensions of Mozart's operas. Roller alternated ingeniously between those scenes that took place downstage and others, such as the Ball Scene at the end of the opening act, in which the whole depth of the stage

was used, allowing the onstage bands to be positioned on a balcony at the very
back. And Roller's use of colour was even more intensely unbridled. The carpets
in Don Giovanni's banqueting hall were red, contrasting with the gold of the
tableware, while black cypresses framed the outdoor scenes at night. And a blue
sky gazed down impassively on the graveyard where Don Giovanni insults the
dead Commendatore. Once again the company's leading singers were pressed
into service: Friedrich Weidemann, a lyric baritone, was Don Giovanni; Donna
Anna was played by Anna von Mildenburg as a vengeful and unhinged fury;
and Marie Gutheil-Schoder, who had been a sensation as Carmen, provided a
more womanly, carefully crafted interpretation as Donna Elvira. And Mahler
himself conducted. Ludwig Hevesi, the leading authority on art in contemporary Vienna, grasped what was new and unprecedented about Roller's use of the
towers, which could be moved right downstage as far as the proscenium arch, a
solution that Mahler particularly liked because it meant that the audience could
be drawn further into the action, bringing the production closer to the basic
idea of a total work of art. According to Hevesi:

> For simple scenes, it is enough to have two pairs of towers to the left and
> right of the proscenium arch. For more complicated scenes more of them are
> used, where necessary. One such example is the Ball Scene, with its three
> orchestras and manifold entrances and exits. The towers are very simple,
> practicable structures with apertures at first-floor level that can serve as the
> windows of apartments and also as bays and balconies, sometimes decorated
> with rugs or, when they serve no purpose, covered with curtains. The result
> is an ideal structure, a kind of architectural passepartout creating an ideal
> space. This space is exactly as wide and as deep as the individual need
> requires it to be. In this way the stage cannot become a vast wasteland in
> which an individual character makes grotesquely exaggerated gestures in an
> instinctive desire to fill as much space as possible. As if as a by-product of this
> device, this caricature of operatic acting is dealt the coup de grâce.[12]

Hevesi clearly saw that with his work on *Don Giovanni* Roller had evolved
from being simply an inspired stage designer and become an inspired architect, a creator of space who positively demanded a new way of handling people
within that space, and this was what Mahler provided in his detailed work with
the singers, work that developed naturally out of Roller's designs.

Even if Roller's lack of diplomacy later caused Mahler certain difficulties,
the latter always knew that he would never find a better collaborator for his
vision of how he believed operas should be staged, a point well illustrated by
his attempts to lure Roller to the Met. They remained in contact until Mahler's
death. There is no surviving evidence that Mahler wrote to Roller at the end of

their work together, but no doubt it will have been enough for them to have spoken to one another. Nine years after Mahler's death, however, Roller summed up his own view of their collaboration in an article published in a special Mahler issue of the *Musikblätter des Anbruch*. Roller was a modest man, and so his reminiscences are concerned entirely with Mahler and not with his own role as a designer. Even so, he manages to distil the essence of their work together:

> He had the deepest contempt for all superficial ornamentation of the stage, for all that was purely decorative, for every ornamental detail that did not emerge with a sense of inner necessity from the overall conception of the production, no matter how splendid and beguiling that detail may have been. And it goes without saying that a man of his moral rectitude should indignantly reject all forms of kitsch. The vision of the sets had to spring entirely from the music, and it was by this that he judged their worth. If he was able to establish that worth, then he gladly submitted to every material demand. Once a scenic design was felt to be usable, he never hesitated to draw all the necessary consequences from it in terms of the acting and the way the moves were arranged. With his keen theatrical eye he was always able to identify in advance all the decisive points in the action and clearly foresee all the advantages and disadvantages that would follow if the concept were adopted. At the same time he himself was so brilliantly gifted as an actor that he had no difficulty in giving the singers the directions necessary for them to act out the scene in the appropriate way. Above all, however, he treated this aspect of his work on the production – the direction of the singers – in exactly the same way as all the others. In other words, he pointed out the goal, which in the case of the singers meant explaining in the individual rehearsals how the most perfect means of understanding was to be found in the music, after which they were given a free hand to create their roles on the stage on the strength of their own inner resources.[13]

Early Years of Marriage

At this point we need to turn back the clock to December 1901 and to the weeks leading up to Mahler's marriage to Alma. Above and beyond his ban on her activities as a composer, her diaries reveal how inwardly torn she was at this time. It is unnecessary to use the psychoanalyst's tools to read hidden meanings into her jottings and dreams, some of which she even took over into her memoirs, for those meanings are clear beyond peradventure. (Whereas her diary entries are generally authentic records of the actual moment, her memoirs and reminiscences of Mahler were written much later, albeit with the help of her diary. Mahler, of course, left no such intimate record of his activities.) Striking above all is the fact that Alma never for a moment succeeded in establishing a partnership between equals – but how could such a relationship have functioned, given the difference in their age and achievements? The insinuations of her friends and the scepticism of her parents left their mark on her. Was Mahler not too old for her? Too ill? Too Jewish? There is a distinct eagerness to the way in which she records a comment allegedly made by Mahler to his sister: 'Can autumn chain spring to its side?' Justine had evidently passed on this expression, which Mahler had used in a letter to her.[14]

Alma, unsurprisingly, had mixed feelings. On the one hand she was 'imbued with the holiest feelings' for Mahler,[15] looking up to him, feeling that he was her intellectual superior and sensing that he was right when he told her – in an entirely positive spirit – that they would go together like fire and water. But having to look up to him all the time was bound to lead in the longer term to a psychological crick in the neck. As a result, Alma attempted to convince herself that she should play the part of a mother caring for a poor and sickly child: 'I'm so afraid that his health will let him down – I can scarcely say. I can just see him lying in a pool of blood.'[16] Or was Alma trying to say that she *would like* to see her future husband lying in a pool of blood? But she felt that Mahler raised her aloft, whereas her dealings with the cynical Burckhard merely increased her sense of frivolity. She was embarrassed by her 'dirty jokes' whenever Mahler was around, for she admired his deadly seriousness, and yet she regarded him and his demands as highly restrictive: 'Are you happier when you live frivolously, unscrupulously, or when you acquire a beautiful, sublime outlook on life? . . . Freer in the former case, happier. [In the latter case] better – purer. Does that not hinder one's path to *freedom*?'[17] Self-reproaches alternate with outbursts of defiance. In the last of the diary's serial entries (a number of later ones were destroyed, leaving only a fragmentary record) Alma complains bitterly about the changed situation just seven weeks before her marriage:

> In the last few days everything has changed. He wants me different, completely different. And that's what I want as well. As long as I'm with him, I can manage – but when I'm on my own, my other, vain self rises to the surface and wants to be free. I let myself go. My eyes shine with frivolity – my mouth utters lies, streams of lies. And he senses it, knows it. Only now do I understand. I *must rise to meet him*. [For I live only in him.] . . . I must strive to become a real person, let everything *happen to me of its own accord*.[18]

With these words Alma's diary ends. But 'rising to meet' Mahler proved unduly effortful for a young woman who until then had known only acclaim, infatuation and enjoyment without needing to make any effort. She vacillated between recalcitrance and the realization that Mahler was right in principle when he encouraged her to abandon her frivolous ways – and by this he meant not erotic licentiousness but the overhasty, superficial way in which she judged art and her fellow humans, her grasshopper intellect and dilettantism, in short, all that Mahler hated the most. If he belittled her old friends such as Burckhard, Klimt and Zemlinsky, whom he came to value only at a later date, she no doubt felt that there was a grain of truth in what he said, but she also bridled at his criticisms because these people were important to her and she could see very well that he was exaggerating, clearly out of jealousy. And his own heroes – Lipiner and the latter's circle – did not strike her as in any way superior, only more Jewish, and that was something for which she did not particularly care.

Mahler was strict, too strict. Writing in her memoirs, Alma describes the sudden change that overcame him shortly before their marriage:

> He was full of suspicion and scented danger on every hand; and so a period of martyrdom set in for me. Everything in me which had so far charmed him became of a sudden suspect. My style of hairdressing, my clothes, my frank way of speaking, everything, in fact, was interpreted as being directed against him; I was altogether too worldly for him. Wrought upon by envious tongues and by his so-called friends, he lived a life of torment and inflicted torments a thousand times worse on me. Our lovely beginning had turned to gloom and misery.[19]

We may also recall that Alma had been an extremely rebellious adolescent who had behaved aggressively towards her stepfather and, precisely because her own father had been taken away from her at such an early date, had sought father figures in her life, including Burckhard, Klimt and Zemlinsky. Mahler was another father figure whose age and infirmities were such that Alma risked suffering another loss. Inner turmoil, infatuation and an overwrought sensuality were combined with the need to lean on an older man but also with the resolute desire not to let things get her down and with her insistence on remaining the most beautiful woman in Vienna. The result was a dangerous brew. As a result, Alma saw Mahler as a poor and sickly child whom she could cradle in her lap like a Pietà. There is no contradiction here. Rather, they are sides of one and the same coin. When she accuses him of jealousy, she admits with equal candour that she is envious of his composing. When he emerged from his composing hut in Maiernigg and, beaming with pleasure, told her about his work, she wept with sheer jealousy. And the fact that she admitted as much to him did not help the situation. In the autumn of 1902, she noted in her diary: 'I often feel as though my wings have been clipped. Gustav, why did you tie me to yourself – me, a soaring, glittering bird – when you'd be so much better off with a grey, lumbering one!'[20]

And then there are Alma's dreams. Their tone and bold imagery seem authentic, rather than a belated attempt to rewrite history when she set about editing her memoirs. Although she lived to be eighty-five, she was permanently sickly during her marriage with Mahler. And whereas he made every effort to suppress his major and minor ailments, she allowed herself the privilege and pleasure of letting the whole world know how much she was suffering. During one of her numerous periods of indisposition, she dreamt that Mahler was coming towards her at the end of a long suite of rooms, identifiable by his white face and black hair. This was in itself as terrifying as the appearance of Nosferatu in Murnau's film of the same name, but what made it even worse was that each time Mahler passed through one of the doors, a double of Mahler would step through the previous one. On another occasion Alma dreamt that she had received a pile of valuable drawings from which she was allowed to choose one. Mahler joined her and made holes in the drawings with the pen that he used when composing. He then drew both his legs up to his stomach and walked through the room like that. From every door miniature versions of Mahler emerged and strutted around the room in exactly the same fashion. Alma tried to take refuge in her own room, but these Mahlerian Rumpelstiltskins poured out of that one too.

Their first child, Maria Anna, later known as 'Putzi', was born on 3 November 1902. She was called 'Maria' after Mahler's mother, 'Anna' after Alma's. It was a breech delivery and correspondingly painful. Mahler had never been a father before and did not know how to handle these complications, and when they became critical, he started to pace the streets of the neighbourhood in a state of extreme agitation. When he heard about the breech delivery, he laughed out loud and exclaimed: 'That's my child. Showing the world straight off the part it deserves!'[21] Alma recovered only slowly from the birth, but there was another, more serious problem: 'I haven't the right love for my child yet.'[22] Her feelings stemmed not from the fact that the child was Mahler's and she had not yet sorted out her relationship with him, but because in spite of everything she loved him so much that there was no room for a child in their lives. Maria died in childhood. Their second daughter, Anna Justine ('Gucki'), suffered badly as a result of the difficulties that Alma had with her daughters by Mahler. Alma had more luck with Manon, her daughter by Walter Gropius, but she too was snatched away at an early age. Another dream is worth mentioning in the context of Alma's pregnancy-induced depression and needs no further commentary: 'A large green snake leaps up inside me, I tear at its tail – it won't come out – I ring for the servant – she pulls violently on it – suddenly she has the beast – it sinks down – in its mouth are all my internal organs – I am now hollow and empty like the wreck of a ship.'[23] We should probably not go far wrong in assuming that the marital problems Alma later tried to stigmatize as asceticism caused by Mahler's abstinence were in some way connected with her first pregnancy, after which she eviscerated herself and felt robbed of her sexual organs and at the same time of her sensuality.

There was also the complication caused by Anna von Mildenburg – and not only by her. Alma inevitably also heard the rumours about Mahler and Selma Kurz and the soprano Margarete Michalek. In the case of Anna von Mildenburg and Selma Kurz we are sufficiently well informed to be able to confirm their veracity, only in that of Margarete Michalek is their accuracy unclear. Even if Alma later consoled herself by claiming that they were no more than rumours and that Mahler had been a virgin when he married her, because he was afraid of women, she must have known better. Certainly, her diaries tell a different story. Selma Kurz disappeared from Mahler's life while continuing to be one of the leading lights of the Vienna Opera, but Anna von Mildenburg was temperamentally less inclined to step aside, and her brief fling with Siegfried Lipiner seems very much to have been a substitute for what she was prevented from having with Mahler: if Mahler himself was unavailable, then she would at least make do with a man of lesser genius from her lover's immediate circle. Alma evidently preferred not to know all the details of Mahler's relations with Anna von Mildenburg but told the outside world that Mahler had assured her that he had never been intimate with the soprano. Even so, the scenes that the singer made, her somewhat suspicious friendliness towards the young bride and her mortifying arrogance all left Alma feeling uncomfortable, and, amateur composer that she was, she was undoubtedly afraid that such a great artist represented a rival for Mahler's affections. In an attempt to placate Alma, Mahler seems to have made up all manner of tales, claiming, for instance, that in a vain attempt to rekindle their old passion, the singer had run around in the nude. Even after their marriage, the female singers at the Court Opera continued to be a thorn in Alma's flesh. She knew very well that Mahler was so addicted to his work that he had no time to get to know women outside the opera house, and it gave her pause for thought that all the affairs he was rumoured to have had were with singers working under him.

Even as late as January 1903 Alma was commenting on this situation in her diary, her embittered and agitated entry leaving us in no doubt about the inner turmoil that she was feeling:

Just returned from the Opera. Blocking rehearsal! Euryanthe! Nice rehearsal! Gustav let that WHORE drink from his glass! I stand SO in dread of her that I fear his coming home. When he is with Mildenburg or Weidt, his manner grows sweet and teasing, and he coos over them like a young love-bird – my God, may he NEVER come home! May I no longer have to live with him! I'm so upset, I can hardly write![24]

'Weidt' is the dramatic soprano Lucie Weidt. The 'whore' is presumably Anna von Mildenburg. If Alma was consumed by jealousy towards female singers, it was also because she blamed Mahler for the fact that she could no longer feel that she herself was an artist. 'Here I am no more than a housekeeper,' she complained from Maiernigg shortly after her wedding.[25] And she continued to be jealous of Anna von Mildenburg. The Mahlers' apartment in Vienna had to be redecorated each summer while the family was away on vacation. Mahler had to return earlier than the rest of the family and during this time had to make do with various temporary arrangements. In September 1903 Alma seems to have voiced her concerns, prompting Mahler to reply with unusual forcefulness: 'What gave you the idea that Mildenburg was staying with me at the Hietzinger Hof? Surely you know that she moved to Gumpendorfstrasse a year ago, over the road from the Lipiners? So there really was no need to make a fuss! Hell's bells [Himmelherrgottkreuztausenddonnerundhagelsappermentnocheinmal]!'[26]

Only weeks before her marriage, Alma confided in her diary that Mahler's position at the Opera was a powerful attraction and that she found it hard to distinguish between Mahler as a man and his influential post. But perhaps, she mused, Zemlinsky, too, would one day rise to an equally high position and that it might be more sensible to choose him instead:

> I don't know what to think, how to think – whether I love him or not – whether I love the director of the Opera, the wonderful conductor – or the man. . . . Whether, when I subtract the one, anything is left of the other. . . . What if Alex were to become famous? . . . One question *plagues* me: whether Mahler will inspire me to compose – whether he will support my artistic striving – whether he will love me like Alex. Because *he* loves me utterly.[27]

Alma was not being entirely honest here, for Zemlinsky – a man with a similar outlook to Mahler – had been critical of Alma's flightiness and of her superficiality and lack of concentration. What Zemlinsky undoubtedly lacked was Mahler's paternal authority. He was invariably willing to place his affection before criticism, whereas Mahler thought that he owed it to Alma to tell her the truth, for all that he loved her deeply.

If there was anything that poisoned Alma's relationship with Mahler more than his refusal to allow her to write music, it was her uncertainty and even hostility to his own compositions. It is clear from all that we have already noted that it was not the composer who overwhelmed her but the director of the Vienna Opera and the 'wonderful' conductor. The passage from which we have just quoted also includes the following remarks: 'And his art leaves me cold, so *dreadfully* cold. In plain words: I don't believe in him as a composer. And I'm expected to bind my life to this man.... I felt nearer to him from a distance than from near by.'[28] This entry is dated 3 December 1901, only three months before her marriage. In her reminiscences, too, Alma writes with disarming honesty about her feelings: 'I longed for music! Yes, for music ... that's strange. Our house was mostly quiet when Gustav Mahler returned home tired from the Opera. I longed for my own music because Gustav Mahler's music was initially alien to me and I drew close to it only through an extreme effort of will.'[29] In short, it was not emotion or love or enthusiasm that drew Alma to her husband's music but only an effort of will. Against such a background, expectations must have been low. True, there were moments when Alma felt or pretended to feel that she was moved by Mahler's music, and she may even have convinced herself that this was the case, notably in the summer of 1902 when he dedicated his Rückert setting, 'Liebst du um Schönheit', to her. And writing about the Eighth Symphony in her reminiscences, she noted that 'The floods of this great music and this man passed through my metaphysical body,'[30] adding that during the first performance in Munich she sat in her box almost swooning with excitement.

There is no reason to doubt that these remarks are not just as subjectively honest as those that attest to Alma's estrangement and frustration. Even as late as 1905 her feelings towards Mahler were as ambivalent as ever:

> But I can't give him all of my love. Why can't I? He was initially a stranger to me – and in many respects he still is. That is also one of the reasons why I cannot understand certain things about him – and when I can, that understanding drives me away from him. And yet there is so much here that is positive! I know that I genuinely love him and – now – that I simply couldn't live without him. He has taken so much from me that his presence is now my only support in life. I must now draw from the rest of my existence all that my brief life has to offer.[31]

There can be no doubt that after three years of marriage Mahler's libido was beginning to wane. A note in Alma's diary for the summer of 1905 refers explicitly to this problem:

> With Gustav I often don't know what to say. Before he even opens his mouth, I already know exactly what to expect. The past weeks have been tremendously hot, and I haven't felt like doing anything. Neither reading nor

working, nor anything else for that matter. I long for a husband – for I have
NONE. . . . But I feel too lethargic . . . even for that.[32]

Herein lies the seed of the catastrophic marital crisis that visited the couple in
the summer of 1910. Even before that Alma had flirted with attractive young
artists. After all, she did not need to get worked up about his fondness for
singers. Within her libidinous mindset only artists had a role to play: Klimt,
Zemlinsky and the strapping tenor Erik Schmedes. During her marriage it was
svelt musicians such as Ossip Gabrilovich who fired her passion without ever
tempting her to be unfaithful. Infidelity only became an issue with the architect Walter Gropius who, like Gabrilovich, was slimly built but who, unlike
him, was Aryan. There is an alarming report by one of Mahler's confidants, the
Swiss writer William Ritter, who attended the rehearsals for the Prague
première of the Seventh Symphony in 1908 and who reveals the yawning gulf
that existed between the couple at this time. Ritter is an incorruptible and
impartial witness who was deeply shaken by the eccentric attentiveness that
Mahler lavished on his wife at this time. During one of the final rehearsals he
sat her on her own at a table directly behind the conductor's podium. At the
end of the rehearsal, he stepped down from the podium and went over to his
wife like a sleepwalker with a harrowing expression of sadness and almost
despondency, sat down beside her and whispered something in her ear,
consuming her with his intensity. As for Alma:

> It was clear that she understood neither what was being said to her nor the
> music she had just heard, which she knew was written entirely out of rever-
> ence for her. . . . She forced a smile, . . . cast embarrassed looks to the left and
> the right. She was aware that we were all watching! And it made her so
> nervous, poor thing . . .! She felt not a jot of pity for the man of genius who,
> prostrated and entirely absorbed in his work, was virtually dying of love at
> her very feet.[33]

Their marriage got off to a very bad start, then, and even their honeymoon
failed to flatter Alma's jaded palate inasmuch as it took the form of a business
trip to St Petersburg, where Mahler conducted three concerts with the
Mariinsky Theatre orchestra. None of his own works featured on the
programmes, which for the most part included pieces by Mozart, Beethoven,
Wagner and Tchaikovsky. During the journey there, moreover, Mahler
suffered from a debilitating headache, an old complaint made worse on this
occasion by the overheated compartment. On his arrival in St Petersburg he
then caught a chill and it was only with difficulty that he was able to drag
himself to the concert hall. He stood on the podium, pale and emaciated, his

ashen face uplifted, his lips slightly parted. This, at least, is Alma's account. The letters that Mahler himself wrote to his sister from St Petersburg sound rather less dramatic, reporting, conversely, that it was Alma who was ill. This is one of the few occasions when we can compare Alma's detailed account with Mahler's own version of events, fuelling the suspicion that she was basically fond of exaggerating. Alma loved her husband most of all when he was ill, for then she could express without any inhibitions the overwhelming maternal love that she never felt for her children but only for the men in her life, especially when those men were small and ailing Jews like Mahler and Franz Werfel. Even though she herself never felt entirely well – for her, pregnancy was a physical torment from the outset – she was convinced that 'I knew once and for all that it was my mission in life to move every stone from his path and to live for him alone.'[34]

The couple's daily lives groaned beneath the burden of these manifold handicaps. Alma moved into Mahler's apartment. It was rented accommodation in a tenement block, but this was no ordinary tenement block. It had been built by Otto Wagner for his own needs and was a large structure of modestly modernist pretensions. Completed in 1891, it was situated in Vienna's third district at 5 Rennweg, only a few hundred yards from the Schwarzenbergplatz. The property is now 2 Auenbruggergasse, a tiny street running off the Rennweg towards the Strohgasse. Mahler lived on the fourth floor on the right-hand side of the building as seen from the Rennweg. He and his sisters had been living here since 19 February 1898. Emma married Eduard Rosé on 25 August 1898, and four years later Justine walked down the aisle with Eduard's brother Arnold. From then on the large and by no means unassuming apartment was occupied by Mahler and Alma, who remained there until 7 October 1909, although they spent the two years between 1907 and their definitive departure commuting between Vienna, New York and their summer home at Toblach. The apartment had a rectangular ground plan. We know from a sketch prepared by Alma that it was divided into a longer front part and a shorter rear section in the form of a letter J.[35] Five rooms overlooked the street: Mahler's bedroom and study, the dining room and shared living room and Alma's bedroom – from the outset, they slept in separate bedrooms. To the rear of the apartment lay the nursery, kitchen, a store and the bathroom. To the right of the main entrance was a maid's room. As a bachelor, Mahler had occupied the three large rooms overlooking the street and two of the smaller rooms. Prior to the birth of their daughter Maria, the couple rented two additional rooms that had previously been occupied by an army officer, who is said to have hated Mahler with such fury that he ordered his servant to turn up the gramophone to full volume whenever Mahler was trying to work. These new arrangements meant that the Mahlers now had three large rooms and two smaller ones, in addition to the bathroom, kitchen and servants' quarters. It was a spacious apartment believed to cover a surface area of 180 square metres (nearly 2,000 square feet) and as such was large enough for the Mahlers and their two children. Even Alma admitted to feeling comfortable there.

Finances and Everyday Life

If we may believe Alma, Mahler's finances were in a bad way when she married him in spite of the fact that he had been earning a respectable income for some time, beginning with the golden handshake that he had received when leaving Budapest. In Hamburg, his income had been that of a principal conductor. And in Vienna his salary was positively lavish by the standards of the time, not least when we consider that it included pension arrangements not only for Mahler himself as a civil servant for life but also for Alma in the event if his dying before her, an arrangement that was to stand Alma in particularly good stead. Specifically, Mahler's financial situation was as follows. (As always, comparisons with today's prices remain problematical.)

When he arrived in Vienna in 1897, Mahler's annual salary as a Kapellmeister was 5,000 florins, or approximately 40,000 euros. On 8 October 1897 he became director of the Vienna Court Opera on a basic salary of 6,000 florins supplemented by an extra 2,000 florins for his work as Kapellmeister and similar amounts that he received by way of a travel and housing allowance, making a total of 12,000 florins or 96,000 euros. It was agreed that he would receive a pension of 3,000 florins and that this would be raised to 4,000 after ten years – in the event, Mahler failed by just three days to remain in his post for ten years, but he was none the less awarded the increase. But that was not all. Mahler's basic salary was increased after a number of years to 7,000 florins, making an annual total of 13,000 florins, or 104,000 euros. Even by today's standards this is a respectable income, albeit considerably less than the sums that are nowadays commanded by general music directors and by the artistic directors of international orchestras, none of whom has to shoulder a workload comparable to Mahler's. The agreement terminating Mahler's contract that was drawn up by Prince Montenuovo and signed by Kaiser Franz Joseph was generous in the extreme: he received a one-off payment of 10,000 florins (80,000 euros) and an annual pension of 7,000 florins (56,000 euros). In the event of his death it was agreed that his widow would receive an annual pension of 1,000 florins (8,000 euros). Although this last-named sum may strike us as small, it was more generous than the average for the time. In general, then, Mahler was well paid, although this does nothing to alter the fact that for years he had amassed debts in caring for his whole family and that it was a long time before these could be paid off in full. Moreover, the house at Maiernigg was not cheap to build. These debts were certainly not due to the lavish lifestyle of an ascetic like Mahler but, as we know from his recurrent complaints, to the inability of all his brothers and sisters, including Justine, to manage their own finances. All of them lived beyond their means, convinced that their brother would help them out. We know from a postcard that Mahler sent to Alma in Maiernigg during the summer of 1905 that she received 500 florins a month for household expenses. By today's standards 4,000 euros sounds a lot of money, but we need to bear in mind that there were four mouths to feed as well as two servants on the family's payroll. None the less, these household expenses accounted for nearly half of Mahler's monthly income and presumably covered all the usual expenses, including clothing, shoes and food. The Mahlers also had to pay their own travelling expenses and a modest rent for their home in the Rennweg.

It was more than merely Alma's antipathy to Justine that led her to claim that the latter's profligacy had resulted in a mountain of debt that she estimated to be 50,000 gold crowns, a sum so high that Mahler had still not paid it off at the time of his wedding. Mahler's own letters to Justine, enjoining her to be less spendthrift, indicate that Alma was not wilfully slandering her sister-in-law, for all that she blamed Justine exclusively for the entire family's problems in this regard. It is unclear whether Justine was herself constitutionally extrava-gant or whether she simply found it easiest to give in to her siblings' escalating demands, but money was a constant theme throughout the years when Mahler was the family's only breadwinner. It would not be unduly cynical to say that the situation improved only when Leopoldine died in 1889, when Otto committed suicide in 1895 and when Emma and Justine married in 1898 and 1902 respectively. Only when Mahler himself married did he finally become free of the financial obligations to his family, but the mountain of debt that he had incurred continued to overshadow the early years of his marriage. According to Alma it took five years to pay off all these debts. When she confronted her sister-in-law, Justine is said to have remarked with a shrug of her shoulders: 'Well, if the worst had come to the worst, I would have gone begging with him from door to door.'[36]

Mahler's daily routine in Vienna followed the strictest of rituals. Unless he had conducting commitments that took him out of the country, the summer vacation might last from the middle of June to the end of August and was given over to composition and, in parallel with it, physical and mental recuperation. There was no time during the remaining months for creative work, for which Mahler required ever greater peace and quiet and could ill afford to be distracted by administrative chores or even by his work as a conductor and stage director. None the less, he was able to combine his daily workload in

Vienna with the task of elaborating the short score that he had produced during
the summer months. (We shall have more to say about Mahler's compositional
method in a later section of this chapter.) In 1902, for example, he returned
from his summer vacation in Maiernigg – his first with Alma – with the
completed Fifth Symphony. Even before his return to Vienna, he played it
through to Alma, the first time that he had done anything like this with her.
Back in Vienna, he devoted the winter months to the fair copy that could then
be submitted to the printer. Thanks to her above-average musical intelligence,
Alma was able to help in copying out and correcting the Fifth Symphony in
particular, and one has the feeling that she felt closest to Mahler in this
ancillary function.

For Mahler himself, extreme discipline was the order of the day. He would
get up at seven, have breakfast and then work at his desk on whichever
symphony was currently on the stocks. After barely ninety minutes, he would
leave for the Opera, where rehearsals, auditions and administrative chores
would occupy him all morning. Lunch had to be waiting for him when he
returned home at one. The journey on foot from the opera house to the
Rennweg took fifteen minutes. An attendant at the Opera would telephone his
apartment to announce that the director was on his way. Lunch was prepared,
and Mahler would ring when he arrived at the front door, so that the soup was
waiting for him on the table when he reached the fourth floor a few moments
later. Even the apartment door had to be open to save him from having to
fumble for his key. He would run through the apartment to the bathroom to
wash his hands before returning to the dining room. He would then have a
brief siesta for no more than half an hour. But soon even this short period of
rest was abandoned when Mahler began to feel that it was not conducive to a
healthy digestion. Instead he resorted to a brisk walk. During the summer
months this meant hiking through the mountains or along the shores of a lake,
but for the rest of the year he had to make do with walking four times round
the nearby Belvedere Gardens or, more prosaically, along the Ringstraße and
back. At five he would take high tea and at six would return to the opera house,
where performances generally began at seven, no difference being made
between a short work like *Fidelio* and a longer one such as *Tristan und
Isolde*. If Mahler was not conducting himself, he would watch part of the
performance or work in his office. Alma would collect him from the opera
house almost every day. If he was still working in his office, she would sit
in his box until he came to find her, and they would then go home together,
where a late and relatively frugal supper awaited them. As a result, Alma
never heard the end of several operas in the repertory. After supper, they
would sit for a while in their living room, talking, or Alma would read to her
husband.

Relations between Alma and Justine quickly cooled. They were simply too different in terms of their respective backgrounds. Alma was undoubtedly talented, a fêted beauty used to success, while Justine was an unattractive woman who for years had sacrificed her own life to that of her siblings, with no prospect of starting a family of her own. One has the feeling that Arnold Rosé was the first man in her life. By the time that they married, she was thirty, by contemporary standards an old maid with little chance of marrying. Her idolatrous love of her brother was a further seed of discord and the source of jealousy between the two women. The far more beautiful and lively Alma had taken away from her the only man who really mattered in her life, a man whom none could surpass. During his honeymoon trip to St Petersburg, Mahler wrote to tell her that 'I don't notice any difference at all between now and before! Isn't that remarkable? Hopefully, you feel this too.' Mahler meant no harm by this remark, but it was an insensitive thing to write, as was a later comment in another letter to Justine: 'My health is splendid – marriage seems to suit me very well.'[37] By now Justine's patience was at an end. Her own health was by no means 'splendid', and there was no comparison between a competent violinist like Arnold Rosé and her brother, a composer of genius. As we have seen, the relationship between brother and sister had never been incestuous but had become unhealthily interdependent following the loss of their parents and their shared concern for their siblings.

For all his love for his sister, Mahler must have heaved a sigh of relief when breaking free from Justine. But the same could not be said of her. Alma was a rival for Mahler's affections, the first to be taken seriously. Justine was deeply hurt by the fact that her brother did not miss their old companionship, and Alma no longer stood a chance. Whether or not it is true that Justine fainted at the stage door in Vienna when opening one of the letters from St Petersburg from which we have just quoted no longer matters. More revealing is the scene between Mahler and his sister that Alma reports with evident glee even though she did not witness it in person. Following a confrontation at the Court Opera, Justine is said to have wrung her hands and exclaimed: 'But, Gustav, after all, I am flesh of your flesh.' To which he replied: 'Dirt of your dirt, you mean.'[38]

One might have thought that the long summer holidays would have given the young couple an opportunity to enjoy each other's company, but Mahler's increasingly inflexible work routine made this impossible. Between 1902 – their first summer together as husband and wife – and the tragic events of 1907, when their daughter Maria died on 12 July, the couple spent their vacations at Maiernigg on the Wörthersee. Here Alma was soon obliged to adapt to Mahler's routine. Occasionally, tiresome news would arrive from the Court Opera in Vienna, but in general Mahler concentrated on his compositional work to such an extent that Alma saw little more of her husband than she did in Vienna.

During the summer of 1893 Mahler and his sisters had discovered Steinbach on the Attersee and by 1894 he had built a composing house here on the shore of the lake, absolute seclusion being a *sine qua non* for his mornings spent composing, for all that he otherwise valued convivial company. The Steinbach idyll, however, was not idyllic enough, for Mahler had to live in a guest house, and so it ended in the autumn of 1896. Although he was sorry to leave, the experience provided him with a model that he adopted from now until his death, separating the building in which he worked from the holiday home where he and his dependants lived. During the summer of 1897 Mahler had no holiday home at all, and it remained lodged in his memory as a uniquely grim experience, involving him, as it did, in an odyssey that took him from Kitzbühel to Vahrn, with a brief and prophetic visit to Toblach in the South Tyrol. Given his likely commitments at the Vienna Opera, it was clear that such a summer could not be repeated for, compositionally speaking, he produced almost nothing at all. The following summer, when the family returned to Vahrn, was not much better, nor was the summer of 1899, when they stayed at Alt-Aussee. With the exception of a number of *Wunderhorn* settings, Mahler produced nothing here either until the very end of his stay, when he was struck by his initial ideas for his Fourth Symphony. But lack of concentration prevented him from elaborating them. Where would he find a haven in which to develop his future plans?

Mahler had already returned to Vienna when Justine and Natalie Bauer-Lechner set off in search of a new property in early August 1899. Their quest took them to the Wörthersee, and here, as we have already had occasion to observe, they stumbled upon Anna von Mildenburg and were introduced to the architect Alfred Theuer, who quickly designed a comfortable but by no means ostentatious villa. Mahler returned to Maiernigg from Vienna in mid-August in order to inspect the place and see Theuer's plans, which filled him with enthusiasm. The next problem was to find a suitable plot of land. One measuring 3,000 square metres (nearly 11,000 square feet) was found right next to the lake beside the Villa Schwarzenfels, and Mahler proceeded to buy it for 4,000 florins. Given his annual salary of 12,000 florins, this was already a sizeable sum, and it did not include the cost of building a house on it. He borrowed the money from Justine, suggesting that even as director of the Vienna Court Opera he was not yet able to draw on unlimited resources. He had repaid the debt by the summer of 1905. In the woodland higher up the hillside was a further plot of land on which Mahler's 'study', as he called it, was to be built. It was surrounded by a fence in order to keep out visitors. (Impressively situated, the place is now a museum.) Work on both properties lasted a total of two years.

By the summer of 1900 the little house in the forest was finished, as always a simple structure comprising a single room. Justine described it in a letter to her sister Emma, who was by then living in Boston, where her husband had found work as a cellist: 'Gustav is in Paris, while I've been here in Maiernigg for five days now. I feel very much at my ease here, G.'s little house in the forest is like something out of a fairytale, as if it had been put there by magic, and the villa itself promises to be exceptionally beautiful.'[39] Even though the living quarters were not yet finished, Mahler was able to work again just as he had been used to in Steinbach, the first time for years that this had been possible. Able to complete his Fourth Symphony, he wrote to his friend Nina Spiegler:

> This summer, for me, has been so glorious that I feel myself really and truly braced for the coming winter.
> If I can keep this up in future – managing to get mental and physical repose in the summer – then I shall be able to lead a human sort of life even here in Vienna. . . .
> In this coming winter I shall myself make the fair copy of my work; and this will give me a foothold in all the stress of life, a foothold such as I have needed particularly in these recent years.
> One feels so utterly desolate when one has to survive without what is sacred to one.[40]

By the summer of 1901 the Mahlers' villa, too, was finished. A small and relatively narrow structure, it none the less offered all the amenities that Mahler needed and also had adequate space for his staff. Above all, he could be in his composing house within ten minutes. Alma did not particularly care for the villa. True, she liked the view, but the interior was furnished in a way she found too ornate, too typical of the late nineteenth century and, above all, too anti-Secessionist. Although she was able to remove some of its ornamental excesses, the basic fittings remained the same, and Mahler, less sensitive to such superficialities, was unable to invest any more money in the property. The house had two large verandas, one of them open, the other one closed. The open one went from the living room to Alma's bedroom, whereas the closed one led from the dining room to the guest room, which was very quickly converted into a nursery, a development welcomed by Mahler, who did not like overnight guests. On the first floor was Mahler's bedroom, the large balcony of which commanded the finest view of the lake. This room, with its large desk, also doubled as a study during the times when he was not working in his composing house. Adjoining it was a tiny closet with a washbasin. It was here that Mahler washed and dressed.

In Maiernigg, too, there was a meticulous regime. During the summer months Mahler got up between six and half past – earlier than he rose in winter. But he could go to bed earlier as he did not have to stay up for performances at the Court Opera and a late supper. As soon as he woke up, he told the cook to make him his breakfast, which she had to take to his composing house. She was instructed to return to the villa by a different route as Mahler did not want to see her on his way up the hill. By then he was generally so completely immersed in his music that he wanted at all costs to avoid a familiar face and obviate the need to react to it. Breakfast consisted of coffee with warm milk (the hut's only luxury was a spirit stove to warm the milk), wholemeal bread, butter and marmalade. By the time that Mahler arrived, the cook had already left, and he was able to warm the milk himself, frequently burning his fingers on the matches or the stove. Outside the house were a bench and a table where he took breakfast. The hut contained a grand piano, a bookshelf featuring mainly works by Goethe and Kant and a handful of scores, most of them by Bach. The hut had no basement and because of the surrounding trees was quite dark inside. Alma later thought that it was injurious to her husband's health as it tended to be damp and cold. Indeed, even Mahler himself is said to have admitted that the building ruined his health, for all that it was here that he wrote the principal works of his middle period, the happiest of the three periods, namely, his Fifth, Sixth, Seventh and Eighth Symphonies. His statement is undoubtedly an exaggeration, although it is equally clear that the hut's location exacerbated his tendency towards chronic angina.

He returned to the main building at midday and went to his room to change – he wore only his oldest clothes for work. He would then go down to the boathouse, where two small boats were kept. To the right and left of this boathouse were bathing cabins, each with its own little jetty stretching out over the lake. Experienced swimmer that he was, Mahler would dive into the water, swim far out into the lake, then whistle for Alma to come out of the house and wait for him by the bathing hut. He then swam back to the shore and lay in the sun for a while, before jumping back into the water and repeating this whole process until he felt ready for lunch. As before, the soup had to be waiting on the table – Mahler hated sitting around doing nothing. To an outsider this may have looked like a compulsive-neurotic disorder, but in fact it reflected Mahler's awareness of the constant need for meaningful activity.

The meal had to be frugal, non-fatty and unseasoned. Mahler spent much of his life experimenting with his diet, without, however, reaching a definitive solution. Max Burckhard was of the view that Mahler's diet would give anyone stomach trouble even if they had not previously been suffering from such a complaint. As we have already noted, Mahler suffered from digestive problems for most of his life, although they never amounted to anything particularly serious (except the haemorrhoidal bleeding in February 1901) and were certainly not the cause of his death. After the meal was over, Mahler would sit and talk for half an hour, after which came the obligatory walk, which in

Mahler's case was more of a run. Even with her earlier training as a cyclist, Alma had difficulty keeping up with him. At this period Mahler was still in excellent shape and would rush ahead, either leaving the villa directly or rowing across the lake to the opposite shore and beginning his walk there. Such walks could last three to four hours, and when Alma began to flag in the midday heat, Mahler would take her in his arms and say 'I love you', giving her renewed strength. He always carried around a notebook in order to keep a record of any musical ideas that struck him during this time. He would then step to one side of the path, leaving Alma to sit on the stump of a tree and recover her breath. Meanwhile, Mahler would beat time in the air and then continue to write in his notebook. On their return from their walk, Mahler would generally dive into the lake again and then, donning his working clothes, return to his composing house. He would finally come back down to the villa and after a relatively early supper he and Alma would spend the evening together, reading to one another or talking. The Mahlers were in bed by ten. Eight hours later a new day began. If Mahler had made more progress on his work than he had hoped for or if the daily routine had proved too tiring, he would occasionally go away for two or three days at a time as a kind of reward. Sometimes he set store by being on his own, but at other times he would take Alma with him. She enjoyed these excursions most of all because then she had her husband all to herself, undistracted by his work.

Mahler's Compositional Method

It was a complex and varied process that led from the first musical idea noted down during a walk to the printed score, and one, moreover, that often did not end even with the printed score, for Mahler tinkered obsessively, never satisfied with what he had achieved but repeatedly persuaded by the first performances of his works to undertake further improvements. A few examples may serve to illustrate this process.

Let us retrace our steps to the time of the Second Symphony.[41] While he was still working as a Kapellmeister in Leipzig, Mahler had decided that on completing his First Symphony in 1888 he would write an even bigger piece. The opening movement, to which he later gave the title 'Todtenfeier', was begun in Leipzig. He continued to work on it back at home in Iglau during the summer of 1888, completing the first draft on 8 August and the full score on 10 September. At the beginning of October he moved to Budapest as director of the Royal Hungarian Opera but was prevented from making any further progress on the symphony by his workload at the Opera, his worries about his family and the intrigues that were fomented against him. But the opening movement, itself unusually long, was finished, and in his despair at ever being able to complete the work, he decided for the time being to regard this opening movement as a finished piece. Giving it the title 'Todtenfeier', he turned it in this way into a kind of symphonic poem with programmatic aspirations. (He had already done the same with his First Symphony. Although a programme was not officially announced, it was initially trailed as a 'symphonic poem'.) In April 1891 Mahler became principal conductor of the Hamburg Opera, and it was now that he felt emboldened to return to composition. Initially, however, the summer months proved unproductive as a result of the upheaval of his move to the city and his frequent changes of address. Only when he discovered a refuge at Steinbach on the Attersee in the summer of 1893 did he find the necessary concentration to write the middle movements of the Second Symphony. The Scherzo is a fine example of Mahler's tendency to use his own existing songs as symphonic material, a feature that sets him apart from all the other great symphonists. The *Wunderhorn* song 'Des Antonius von Padua Fischpredigt' that forms the nucleus of the Scherzo was originally written for voice and piano before being orchestrated and then incorporated into the symphony. Mahler then set another *Wunderhorn* song, 'Urlicht', as the fourth movement of the symphony. Although little more than a brief transition, it none the less provides a necessary breathing space before the fifth and final movement.

In an important passage in her recollections of Mahler, Natalie Bauer-Lechner offers an insight into the process that led from song to symphonic movement. She had asked him how this initially unplanned expansion and transposition came about: 'It's a strange process! Without knowing at first where it's leading, you find yourself pushed further and further beyond the bounds of the original form, where potentialities lie hidden within it like the plant within the seed.'[42] And Mahler expressed similar sentiments about the second movement, the Andante moderato, the two main themes of which occur in a sketch dating back to his time in Leipzig. If he had kept them, it was no doubt in the belief that he would one day be able to make use of them:

'Here are two marvellous themes', said Mahler, 'that I picked up today from the sketch for the Andante of my Second Symphony. With God's help, I hope to finish both it and the Scherzo while I'm here.' When he has just been composing, he often seems, for a while, as if he were still in another world; and he confronts his own works as if they were completely foreign to him. 'I was always disturbed by those two little pieces of paper on which I had noted the themes – it was in Leipzig, when I conducted the *Pintos* there. I see now that they might well have bothered me. For the melody pours forth here in a full, broad stream; one idea is interwoven with the other, constantly branching out in an inexhaustible wealth of variations. And how choice and

delicate the end-product of this process of self-generation – if you could
follow its course right through, what a joy it would be to you!

'And that's the only way to create: in one grand sweep. It's no use playing
around with some poor little scrap of a theme, varying it and writing fugues
on it – anything to make it last out a movement! I can't stand the economical
way of going about things; everything must be overflowing, gushing forth
continually, if the work is to amount to anything.'[43]

It was very much during the late 1890s that Mahler's contacts with Natalie
Bauer-Lechner were at their closest and that she was able to record some of his
most powerful statements on his own creative process.

Fortunately, Natalie was inquisitive, and time and time again she would ask
what Mahler felt when he was composing or immediately before starting to do
so. As a violinist, she knew what music was, but she had no idea what composition meant. And Mahler expressed himself with total candour in a way that
was never to be the case at a later date, when he became more reserved and
mistrustful. He went on to refer to his first two symphonies as instances of the
link between life and art, a link that is so difficult for us to grasp:

> My two symphonies contain the inner aspect of my whole life; I have written
> into them everything that I have experienced and endured – Truth and
> Poetry in music. To understand these works properly would be to see my life
> transparently revealed in them. Creativity and experience are so intimately
> linked for me that, if my existence were simply to run on as peacefully as a
> meadow brook, I don't think that I would ever again be able to write anything
> worthwhile.[44]

As for the question of inspiration, Mahler had little more to say on the subject
than all the other creative artists of the time, arguing only that there was something mystical about it: the artist creates something as if prompted to do so by
an alien force, so that, unconscious of what he is doing, he is later incapable of
understanding how it came about. He felt that he was like a blind hen finding
a diamond. It was this process of inspiration that persuaded him of the existence of a higher being and also forced him to recognize the sanctity of the
creative process.

As an example of how this process works in practice, Mahler himself cited
the example of a passage in the fourth movement of his First Symphony, a
passage that – following Adorno – we may describe as the definitive 'breakthrough' in this work and that marks the transition from C major to the
symphony's home key of D major. Any other composer at this period would
have modulated from C major to C sharp major and thence to D major, but

Mahler wanted this D major to sound as if it had arrived completely out of the blue from another world. For a long time he resisted the idea of this freer and bolder modulation, finding it too daring and unconventional. Only with reluctance did he allow himself to be persuaded to adopt it, but when he did, he realized that it was the one truly great passage in the symphony. If the circumstances were favourable, Mahler explained, the inspirational and compositional process was unending, but it could also be a source of suffering for the composer, a point that he vividly illustrated by reference to an incident that occurred when he had wanted a certain movement to be in $4/4$ time only for him to be assailed by ideas in $3/4$ time. Natalie Bauer-Lechner asked him what he did with these uninvited guests. Mahler himself described them as 'unborn ideas' that arise when conditions are right and form a kind of primeval soup made up of ideas that cannot be used for the present. Far from being lost, they return at a later date – sometimes years later – just when they happen to be needed. This is what happened to him while he was working on 'Rheinlegendchen': an idea that had occurred to him three years earlier and that he had discarded at the time, evidently not even writing it down, suddenly came to mind again and proved wonderfully well suited to the new song.[45]

The task of giving written form to these ideas was a complicated process for Mahler, normally involving ten stages between the initial sketch and the printed score. As we have already seen, the initial idea would be jotted down during a walk and then transferred to music manuscript paper on Mahler's return home. On those rare occasions when no such paper was to hand, Mahler would draw the lines himself. The next stage was the sketch. Sketches may look very different, depending on the composer. Some composers produce their sketches on only a single stave, while others use several staves. Mahler generally used three, joined together with a brace.[46] This system allowed him, however cursorily, to indicate important thematic developments. One of the preliminary sketches for the opening movement of the Second Symphony, for example, already includes its main four-bar theme, noted down in total isolation before the start of the actual sketch and marked 'main theme'. This theme was clearly the starting point for Mahler's work on the movement. In the finished movement it appears only much later as the culmination of a lengthy and complex development. But it was present in Mahler's head from the very beginning.

The next, decisive stage with Mahler was the short score. At this point we need to recall that there have always been composers who have omitted all the earlier stages and launched straight into the full score. When working on Weber's *Die drei Pintos*, Mahler realized to his astonishment that Weber had proceeded in this way. Max Reger was to do so at a later date. With Mahler, the situation is far more complicated, for it encompasses every imaginable intermediary stage. The short score is a detailed draft on – normally – three to five staves arranged in the same order as the later full score. In other words, the high woodwind and brass are at the top, followed by the lower brass instruments, percussion and strings, with the violins above the violas, cellos and, finally, the double basses. Mahler's short scores were normally written on four staves, winds, strings and basses each having a different stave. An additional stave would be used in the case of a vocal line. In turn, the short score was the starting point for the full score in which the musical material was fully worked out for the first time. The next stage was the definitive autograph score that was intended to be used by the printer or engraver. It was this final process where Alma was able to help in the case of the Fifth Symphony. With Mahler, the term 'definitive' is perhaps ill-advised, for he continued to revise his scores even after their first performances. He would normally employ a professional copyist to prepare the printer's copy on the basis of his autograph – there were several excellent copyists in Vienna. Mahler would then correct and revise this printer's copy, and it was this *Stichvorlage* that was sent to the publisher or engraver. He would then receive back a set of proofs with which he was able to tinker to his heart's content. He often used these proofs when conducting the work's first performance as the full score had not always appeared in time. (The orchestral parts could be produced without the printer's copy of the full score.) The full score was then engraved on the basis of the corrected proofs, although for Mahler this was by no means the end of the matter, for the rehearsals and the first performance constituted the true baptism of fire for the new work. He conducted the first performances of all his first eight symphonies, the only exceptions being partial performances of individual movements, which he was willing to entrust to other conductors such as Felix Weingartner in the case of the Third Symphony. Only the Ninth Symphony and *Das Lied von der Erde* were posthumously premièred by Bruno Walter in Vienna and Munich respectively.

If Mahler was persuaded to alter a printed score, it was not because he was unsure about the work's formal design, the only exception to this general rule being the repeat sign that he added to the opening movement of the First Symphony. And he rarely altered the pitch of a note, for on matters such as this he never suffered any self-doubts. Conversely, he long remained uncertain about the instrumentation of his works, and it was this uncertainty that led to most of the often substantial changes that he undertook once he had heard the work in rehearsal and in performance. Using a razor blade he would scratch out individual notes and even whole lines, their replacements sometimes being entered on loose sheets of paper or indicated by means of corrections generally in blue crayon. At the time of the Second Symphony he was still a young and unknown composer with few chances of having his works performed, and at this stage in his career he suffered unspeakably for he evidently lacked the instrumentational imagination of other composers such as Richard Strauss. Once, when he was working on the Scherzo of his Second Symphony, he complained to Natalie Bauer-Lechner:

> If only I could hear it myself and finally take account of the rehearsal in order to see if I were barking up the wrong tree and whether something that strikes me as profound and significant were also profound and significant for others. Because if I cannot produce the same process in others – even if it is only in those few individuals on which any artist has to rely – and if I cannot summon up the same ideas as those that created my work inside me, I have created it in vain.
>
> How much I lose through not being able to try out my things in live performance! How much I could learn from that! It would be so important to me, as my way of treating the orchestra is particularly individual. For example, when scoring I perhaps over-emphasize certain things for fear that they might become lost, or sound too weak.[47]

It took a long time for Mahler to master this fear, which was responsible for his tendency to over-instrument certain passages in the works of his early and middle periods, although he would invariably revise these passages once he had heard them in performance. But the same fear also prompted the numerous performance markings that litter his scores, all of which have a single purpose: to ensure that the composer's wishes were clear even to the back desks of each section, so that nothing was lost and nothing came out wrongly. (Mahler knew orchestral players like the back of his hand.)

No other composer burdened his performers with so many instructions and requests. With today's top orchestras much of this advice is redundant, but during Mahler's own lifetime it was painfully necessary, so low were contemporary standards. 'Plaintive', 'singing', 'with a broad bowstroke', 'standing out', 'muted', 'change the bow frequently', 'keep the triplets flowing' and 'dying away' are all instructions to the players and conductor that go far beyond the traditional tempo and performance markings such as the addition or removal of mutes. Other instructions are purely technical: 'The cymbals should hang freely and be struck with sponge-headed drumsticks' is an instruction that was necessary because drumsticks normally had wooden heads at this time. In the case of the brass instruments, the most frequent instruction is 'bells raised', meaning that the sound should be directed upwards, rather than downwards or straight ahead, ensuring that the passages in question were not only appreciably louder but also much clearer. Nowadays few leading orchestras follow this instruction as the brass players are confident of achieving the impact intended by Mahler without the need for such additional effects. Nor was

Mahler at all squeamish when it came to advising his fellow conductors. At the start of the second movement of the Fifth Symphony, for example, we find the word 'ritenuto' over a single note – a dotted minim. In other words, the note must be held back. A similar marking occurs in the fourth bar of the same movement. Normally such markings apply to a passage that is at least a whole bar in length. To apply the marking to a single note – for the very next note is marked 'a tempo' – is odd, for no listener will be able to register it. And yet not even this was sufficient for Mahler, who added an asterisk over the notes in question and provided an explanation at the foot of the page: 'Note for the conductor. The sense of this *rit.* is, in both cases, a short pause, in order to drive toward the following chord with great force. *The figure itself* must be played in quick tempo.' In short, it is eminently possible to find in these works evidence to support the contemptuous term 'Kapellmeister music' that has often been applied to them: only a Kapellmeister could harbour such mistrust of his musicians and fellow conductors.

These markings were not the expression of a neurotic desire to control his performers or, if they were, then only in part. Mahler knew that the ultimate goal of any performance is clarity, and it was for the sake of this clarity that he sometimes over-instrumented his works, whether at the piano or at his desk. But he was no less willing to reduce the instrumentation if this served the same end. And he was proud that on this point he had no rivals:

> The area in which I believe I am ahead of the composers of the present and past when it comes to instrumentation is one that can be summed up in the word 'clarity'. I demand that everything should strike the ear just as it resounded in my own inner ear, and it is in order to meet this demand that I attempt to exploit all the resources at my disposal, right down to the very last of them. Each instrument should be used only at the right place in the score and only in the way that is most characteristic of it. Indeed, I even go so far as to insist that the violins perform cantabile passages and others requiring the greatest momentum on the E string, while the more sonorous notes and those associated with pain are played on the G string. [In general it was left to conductors and violinists to decide which strings to use.] I never use the middle strings to express passion as they do not sound right. These strings are far better suited to quiet passages that are veiled and mysterious. In such matters it is not a question of imagining some ideal that reality does not reflect.[48]

And Mahler went on to explain that all the laborious and detailed effort that this work cost him would be worth it if the outcome allowed the piece in question to withstand the ravages of time. In his earliest works, he concluded, he had had insufficient knowledge and skill and so he had needed to re-instrument them.

This explains why some of Mahler's symphonies were repeatedly reprinted. A closer look at the changes that the different versions contain reveals that their principal aim was a reduction in what might be termed the ambient noise.[49] By unleashing vast tonal resources, Mahler inevitably produced a level of sound that flew in the face of his ideal of clarity and that was in fact incompatible with it. Mahler spent his whole life struggling to achieve this balance, and the fact that in his Ninth Symphony, the Adagio from the Tenth and *Das Lied von der Erde* there is a definite tendency towards leaner textures suggests he had realized that the problem admitted of no solution. An example from the final movement of the Sixth Symphony may serve to illustrate this point, for the proofs contain one deletion after another. Sometimes it is the timpani and cymbals that are cut, on other occasions the triangle. Elsewhere the melodic line is no longer doubled by the trumpet, or else it is the side drum that is removed. Above all Mahler adopts a much more economical approach to the percussion and brass, the instruments that contribute the most to the sheer volume of the music. If new instruments are added, it is ones that produce far gentler sonorities such as the celesta and glockenspiel. Mahler clearly realized that it was possible to have too much of a good thing. The corresponding passages were not suddenly reduced from a thunderous roar to the gentlest of whispers, for they remain thunderbolts, but the effect now emerges more clearly and is not submerged in sheer noise. As Mahler observed, 'Composition demands the strictest self-criticism. The proportions, structure, climaxes and so on must not be sacrificed to some thing of beauty. Everything must be there in its rightful place, in an organic relationship with the whole and in a harmonious relationship to all its parts.'[50]

It remains to cast a brief glance at the publishing history of one of Mahler's major works: the Fifth Symphony may serve to illustrate the process in general.[51] In the whole history of music Mahler must surely be unique for the fact that the current critical edition of his works, which is being published under the aegis of the International Gustav Mahler Society of Vienna, is a collaborative venture on the part of no fewer than five different publishers, all of them eminent names in the world of music publishing: Bote & Bock, C. F. Peters, Schott, Universal Edition and Josef Weinberger. It is clear from this that Mahler's relations with his publishers were as complex and tempestuous as any love affair. His first four symphonies were published by two Viennese firms, Weinberger and Doblinger. The conductor Gustav Brecher, who was briefly employed at the Vienna Court Opera under Mahler before becoming principal conductor in Leipzig, was friendly with both Bruno Walter and Henri Hinrichsen, who was then running C. F. Peters in Leipzig, a considerably larger publisher than either Weinberger or Doblinger. Dissatisfied as always, Mahler parted company with Weinberger and was looking for a new home for his works. There is a certain lack of clarity concerning the contractual situation between Mahler on the one hand and, on the other, the publishing houses of Weinberger and Doblinger and the printing house of Eberle, which was run by Josef Stritzko. Eberle had engraved the First, Third and Fourth Symphonies as well as *Das klagende Lied*, and all had been distributed by Weinberger and Doblinger.

A surviving letter from Mahler to his legal adviser Emil Freund indicates that when he received an initial approach from Peters in July 1903 he felt obligated to Stritzko.[52] He asked Freund how he should respond to Peters's request to publish his Fifth Symphony. Should he ask Stritzko whether he was willing to pay as much as Peters? Legally speaking, Mahler was not tied to a particular publisher at this period and could pick and choose whom he wanted. He demanded 10,000 florins, a considerable sum of money when we recall that his annual salary as director of the Court Opera was 12,000 florins. But this sum also included all future royalties. It is impossible to say what these figures represent in today's terms, but it might suggest that an opera director who was also a composer and who was earning 100,000 euros a year would be able to sell his new symphony to a publisher for 80,000 euros. Hinrichsen was initially surprised at the size of Mahler's demand, and when the latter asked for 15,000 florins for his Sixth Symphony, the two men failed to agree and Mahler took his business to the firm of Christian Friedrich Kahnt. Had Mahler gone too far? Certainly not, for at more or less the same time Hinrichsen was prepared to pay Strauss 20,000 florins for his *Sinfonia domestica*. And yet not even this was enough for Strauss who, as the most astute of businessmen, demanded, and got, around 24,000 florins from Bote & Bock. And what possible comparison is there between a meretricious piece like the *Sinfonia domestica* and Mahler's Fifth? Yet it has to be admitted that at the time in question Strauss's work represented the better deal, achieving far more performances than Mahler's Fifth. Today the situation is reversed.

Be that as it may, Hinrichsen accepted Mahler's demands, however exorbitant he felt them to be, and in return acquired the rights to publish and distribute the Fifth Symphony, while Mahler retained the performing rights. The publisher's income was based chiefly on hire fees for the orchestral parts and the sale of conducting scores and, in the case of individuals wanting to study the work at home, piano reductions. (These were the days before symphonies started to appear on gramophone records.) The first performance of the Fifth Symphony under Mahler in Cologne on 18 October 1904 proved only a modest success, with the result that neither then nor later were the publisher's hopes fulfilled. (It was on the occasion of the Cologne première that

Hinrichsen first met his new composer.) It says much for the publisher that he was not deterred by this lack of success but expressed extreme interest in the Sixth Symphony, and it was only Mahler's own much-inflated demand that drove him away. Even as late as 1910 Hinrichsen reckoned that Mahler's Fifth Symphony had still not paid its way. During the six years since its first performance, it had been heard fewer than twenty times in all, in spite of which Hinrichsen was prepared – astonishingly – to consider a revised version of the score incorporating Mahler's many retouchings and to shoulder the burden of these costs. (Following Mahler's death, Hinrichsen remembered things differently and claimed that the composer had been willing to pay for the corrections himself.) In the run-up to the first performance, Mahler played through the symphony with his Viennese orchestra and even at this stage undertook several far-reaching changes. Others were made in the wake of the first performance. It needs to be remembered that the conducting score required 250 plates, the orchestral parts no fewer than 525 – and this for a symphony lasting barely seventy minutes. In short, considerable expense was involved. In the summer of 1910, moreover, Mahler declared that the old version of his Fifth Symphony should not be performed any longer as it was badly instrumented, and so he set about revising the score, a task that he completed early in 1911. But he died before the revised version could be published. The conductor Georg Göhler then set about attempting to produce such a version and received Mahler's own autograph copy from Alma, a copy that contained all the composer's changes. But for reasons of cost, Peters agreed to publish only the revised orchestral parts, leaving conductors to incorporate the necessary changes into the full score, which Peters even reprinted in the old edition. It was not until some years later that the conducting score and the miniature study score were aligned with the new parts.

The result of all these changes – and it is an accurate reflection of Mahler's working method – is that over the years the publishing house of Peters has brought out no fewer than seven versions of the Fifth Symphony: i) the study score that appeared in September 1904 and that may be regarded as the first version of the symphony; ii) the conducting score of November 1904 that contains numerous changes vis-à-vis its predecessor; iii) the conducting score that includes Mahler's changes of 1910–11 and that was published in November 1919 as a 'New Edition'; iv) the study score that appeared in April 1920 and that contains a further set of corrections, while also perpetuating errors that are the result of various misreadings; v) Erwin Ratz's critical edition of the first version of the score, which appeared in 1964 as part of the complete edition of Mahler's works and which has now been taken over by Peters's West German branch in Frankfurt am Main; vi) the corrected version of this edition that was superintended by Karl Heinz Füssl in 1989; and vii) Reinhold Kubik's new edition that was published as part of the complete critical edition in 2002. It is difficult to imagine a more complicated situation than this, and yet it merely reflects Mahler's attempts to achieve his ultimate goal of ever greater perfection.

The Seventh Symphony

I F IT HAD not been for its final movement, Mahler's Seventh Symphony might have been the firm favourite among audiences and performers of his music. He wrote it during two particularly happy summers in Maiernigg in 1904 and 1905, but by 1908 it had still not been performed, and so he turned to the impresario Emil Gutmann to ask whether the work could be given as part of a tour. Omitting to mention the cowbells and glockenspiel, he explained that it was scored for modest forces, the only unusual instruments being the guitar and mandolin in the fourth movement. 'It is my *best* work,' he concluded, 'and preponderantly cheerful in character.'[1] The idea of making the work the main draw on a tour came to nothing, and the symphony was finally premièred in Prague on 19 September 1908. Mahler's young supporters turned out in force and included Otto Klemperer, Bruno Walter and Artur Bodanzky, although, contrary to Alma's claim, Alban Berg was not among them. Mahler was in the best of spirits and continued to make corrections to the orchestral parts throughout the rehearsals. But the performance proved no more than a *succès d'estime*. Echoing his remarks to Emil Gutmann, Mahler wrote to Henri Hinrichsen, the head of Peters, to explain that 'the work is predominantly cheerful and humorous in character.'[2] But such a description is difficult to square with the heading of the symphony's second and fourth movements, 'Nachtmusik I' and 'Nachtmusik II'. Night is not traditionally a time of humour and cheerfulness, except possibly in the smoky atmosphere of a bar, and there is certainly no hint of such an atmosphere in the case of the present movements, both of which are nocturnes in the late eighteenth-century tradition. First found in the serenades of the period, such forms were then taken over into the piano pieces of composers like John Field and Frédéric Chopin, pieces sicklied over with the pale cast of melancholy. In using the term, Mahler will have thought of Mozart's *Eine kleine Nachtmusik* but also of Robert Schumann's four *Nachtstücke* op. 23. In turn, the expression will have been associated in the minds of both Schumann and Mahler with the *Nachtstücke* of E. T. A. Hoffmann. It is unclear whether Mahler was familiar at this date with Claude Debussy's *Nocturnes*, which he later conducted on two occasions, but they have little in common with his own 'Nachtmusiken'.

The second 'Nachtmusik' is serene in the spirit of a traditional serenade, although there is no denying that the two solo instruments, the guitar and mandolin, recall the popular Viennese idiom of *Schrammelmusik* and bring an element of inappropriate drollery to the movement as a whole, quite apart from the fact that the balance between these two plucked instruments and the rest of the orchestra is scarcely ever correct in the concert hall – perhaps only on a CD is it possible to hear the effect that Mahler intended. The first 'Nachtmusik' has something of a funeral march about it, and although Alma argued that when her husband wrote this movement, 'he was beset by Eichendorff-ish visions – murmuring springs and German romanticism',[3] we are reminded of an early *Wunderhorn* song like 'Der Schildwache Nachtlied' rather than of Joseph von Eichendorff. Moreover, if we accept Michael Gielen's idea that the Seventh Symphony was written from the inside outwards, it is the Scherzo which, framed by the two 'Nachtmusiken', is central to the work, whose outermost shell is provided by its opening movement and rondo finale.

We know that the two 'Nachtmusiken' were written in 1904 and that the two outer movements date from 1905. Unfortunately, we have no idea when the central Scherzo was composed. If it was the first of the five movements to be completed, Gielen's hypothesis would receive confirmation, and yet the hypothesis remains convincing whatever the true facts of the matter. A closer look at this central movement reveals nothing cheerful or humorous but only eeriness and ghostliness. The performance marking is 'Schattenhaft' ('Shadowy'), and ghostlike figures flit past like shadows in the muted or pizzicato strings over timpani and horns. Here Mahler recalls the third movement of his Second Symphony, and his explanation on that occasion could easily be adapted and applied to this later Scherzo: it is as if the listener has arrived outside a house in which a ball is taking place and can see the dancing couples through the window without being able to hear the music to which they are dancing. It is hard to think of Eichendorff's splashing fountains here, and even the two framing 'Nachtmusiken' are worlds removed from the mood of the poet's *Aus dem Leben eines Taugenichts*. Even so, the reference to Eichendorff is not entirely wide of the mark, whether it stems from Mahler himself or from his wife. It is not, however, *Aus dem Leben eines Taugenichts* or *Ahnung und Gegenwart* that spring to mind here but a poem such as 'Zwielicht' ('Twilight'):

> Dämmrung will die Flügel spreiten,
> Schaurig rühren sich die Bäume,

Wolken ziehn wie schwere Träume –
Was will dieses Graun bedeuten?
Hast ein Reh du lieb vor andern,
Laß es nicht alleine grasen,
Jäger ziehn im Wald und blasen,
Stimmen hin und wieder wandern.

[And twilight soon will spread its wings. The ghostly trees bestir themselves, and clouds drift past like heavy dreams – who'll rede the riddle of this dread? The deer you love above the rest should not be left to graze alone, for huntsmen's horns are all around, and voices wander to and fro.]

Schumann provided a wonderful setting of these lines, and Mahler was responding to them, too, in the Scherzo of his Seventh Symphony. And even if we may hear a serenade in the second 'Nachtmusik', it is no balmy summer night of the kind evoked by Carl Spitzweg: no strolling players have been invited by a young gentleman to perform at the foot of a lofty gable window. Rather, it is the sort of serenade that Eichendorff had in mind when he ended his poem 'Nachts' ('At Night') with the lines: 'Mein irres Singen hier / Ist wie ein Rufen nur aus Träumen' ('My wild-toned song is but a cry that comes from the world of dreams').

If we work our way outwards from the core of the symphony, then the humorous and cheerful aspects of the work grow remarkably diffuse, but we need to remind ourselves of Mahler's comment on the first three movements of his Fourth Symphony to the effect that we are dealing there with the cheerful serenity of a higher world, a serenity that for us has something eerie and frightening about it. These middle movements of the Seventh Symphony bring us back to Jean Paul's definition of humour. In other words, these ostensible nocturnal idylls are not played out in provincial towns of the Biedermeier era but are set in landscapes that remind us, rather, of Arnold Böcklin's more sombre paintings such as *The Ride of Death* and *Ruin by the Sea*, while the figures that flit past and peer out from behind the houses are those of James Ensor rather than Spitzweg. The alternative title of *Song of the Night* that has sometimes been adopted by concert promoters and record producers has not caught on and not brought the work the popularity that they and Mahler hoped for. Even today the Seventh Symphony remains Mahler's least popular symphony, a claim that would be confirmed by any performance statistics.

Even more puzzling than the middle movements are the outer movements. Marked 'Slow – Allegro', the first movement begins with what sounds suspiciously like a slow march played *pianissimo* by the full orchestra, from which a melody on the tenor horn breaks free, effortful and threatening, stretching itself until its very bones seem to crack. Various musical characters encroach on each other's territory, before becoming intertwined. Bright and darker colours alternate in a demonstration of the composer's supreme skill as an orchestrator, producing a chiaroscuro effect that is abruptly displaced by a furious, quicker march that develops a sense of tremendous forward momentum. The movement's manifold layers place extreme demands on orchestras and conductors alike, giving the impression that in terms of the multiple perspectives that it throws on our world of experience and emotion Mahler wanted to include everything that he normally distributes over an entire symphony. The movement culminates at bar 317 with a B major Adagio of overwhelming beauty that owes its effectiveness to swirling arpeggios in the harps and strings, suggesting the vision of a starry sky. We are no longer concerned with a hero's sufferings or happiness but with something higher and greater. Alma would have been better advised to describe this theme as the 'Alma theme', but few people would have believed her.

Mahlerians in general continue to have difficulty with the rondo-finale, and there are few movements in his output that have given rise to greater controversy. Indeed, the resultant debate, which can be only briefly examined here, has overshadowed the critical and practical reception of the piece in general. The movement begins and ends in C major. Although unusual in Mahler's output, this would not in itself be bad if the movement's overall character were not a kind of Über-major, expressing an excessive and explosive positivity in the form of a brilliant pyrotechnical display of all that is true and beautiful and good, accompanied by cymbals and bass drum as if the Janissaries' march from *Die Entführung aus dem Serail* had been instrumented by Strauss. The key of C major inevitably recalls Wagner's *Die Meistersinger von Nürnberg*, and there is indeed a hidden quotation from the opera. (Other commentators have even discovered a quotation from Franz Lehár's *The Merry Widow*.) There is a feeling here of strapping health and unbridled joviality that is hard to square with the mood of the final movement of the Sixth Symphony of only a short time earlier.

As an indication of the extreme range of interpretative possibilities, it is enough to cite only two. Writing in 1913, Richard Specht heard 'a cheerful and sunnily light-hearted joyousness in every note of this thunderous C major'.[4] This view was echoed by Paul Bekker, who belonged to the same generation as Specht and who, like him, took his hero at face value. His analysis of all of Mahler's symphonies was published in 1921 and remains a monumental example of a writer's ability to immerse himself wholly in a composer's works. He describes the final movement of the Seventh Symphony as a 'revelation of life transformed into music', while in the final moments, 'sun and earth, creator and creature, the divine and the earthly resound at one and the same time in a single great chord'.[5] A wholly different response is that of Adorno, a writer who can normally be relied on to strike a note of impassioned enthusiasm. Even as a young music critic in Frankfurt, he already had misgivings about this movement, and in his monograph on Mahler he offers a summation of those objections that is shocking in its negativity. Noting an egregious disproportion between the movement's resplendent form and its distinctly thin content, he bases his argument on the relentlessness of its diatonic harmonies, claiming that such sustained diatonicism inevitably results in a sense of monotony:

> Mahler was a poor yea-sayer. His voice cracks, like Nietzsche's, when he proclaims values, speaks from mere conviction, when he himself puts into practice the abhorrent notion of overcoming on which the thematic analyses capitalize, and makes music as if joy were already in the world. His vainly jubilant movements unmask jubilation, his subjective incapacity for the happy end denounces itself.[6]

Present-day interpretations of the Seventh Symphony are no longer satisfied with these two extreme positions and wonder whether a composer who had just completed the nihilistic finale of the Sixth Symphony could suddenly have written so stridently and tritely life-enhancing a work. If we accept this incongruity, we must conclude that the final movement of the Seventh Symphony cannot be taken seriously and that it is an 'ironic and in places even frivolous' movement, to quote Mathias Hansen.[7] Perhaps, then, the movement represents the recantation of a recantation. Or, alternatively, was Mahler trying to say that the final movement of his Sixth Symphony is one possible answer to life's questions and that the equivalent movement of the Seventh is another answer? If we add them together and divide them by two, is the result the sum total of our artistic responses to the ultimate problems of humanity? The question is unanswerable. At the start of the Seventh Symphony, the listener appears to set foot on firm ground, but this is undermined by the shadows of the night, and at the end, our night vision finely attuned, we are blinded by a dazzling sun and deafened by the battery of noise unleashed by the brass and percussion. Eichendorff's poem 'Twilight' ends with the words:

> Hast du einen Freund hienieden,
> Trau ihm nicht zu dieser Stunde,
> Freundlich wohl mit Aug und Munde,
> Sinnt er Krieg im tückschen Frieden.
> Was heut müde gehet unter,
> Hebt sich morgen neugeboren.

Manches bleibt in Nacht verloren –
Hüte dich, bleib wach und munter![8]

[If you have a friend on earth, do not trust him at this hour: words and glances feign his friendship. The peace is sham: he thinks of war. Whatever dies today, enfeebled, will rise newborn tomorrow. Much is lost at night – beware, be watchful and alert!]

The Administrator – Contemporaries – Signs of Crisis (1905–7)

The Administrator

If we wish to gain an overall view of Mahler's administrative responsibilities as director of the Vienna Court Opera, we need to take a step back before examining the final phase of his work for the company, a phase overshadowed by manifold problems.

Alma's claim that her husband had complete control over the Vienna Court Opera and was given a totally free hand by Kaiser Franz Joseph and his deputy comptroller, Prince Alfred Montenuovo, is difficult to sustain.[1] Above all, the impression that Mahler was allowed to do as he pleased by the general administrator of all the imperial and royal theatres is misleading. We may recall that at the time of Mahler's appointment the general administrator was Baron Josef von Bezecny, who was well disposed to the conductor, as also was Eduard Wlassack, the director of the chancellery and, as such, a far more important figure in terms of the day-to-day running of the theatre. Bezecny left office in February 1898 and was replaced by Baron August Plappart von Leenheer, who two years later was still being listed as interim director. With his appointment Mahler's situation changed, even if the change revealed itself only gradually. Wlassack, conversely, remained in office until May 1903. The post of general administrator was not a full-time appointment (Bezecny was also the director of a local bank) but an honorary position whose duties were largely performed by subordinate officials, and yet it was certainly enough to put a spanner in Mahler's works. The first confrontation between Plappart and his director concerned the latter's terms of service, including his rights and duties. Mahler had spent his galley years in various German opera houses and unlike Plappart he knew the depths to which such institutions could sink. As a result he was keen to maintain his right to decide on all important matters and not have to consult the general administrator's office on questions relating to the appointment and dismissal of singers and orchestral players. Under the terms of his service agreement, he was supposed to consult Plappart on all questions relating to leave of absence, including the periods when he himself was away on tour, in some cases conducting his own works – and it was this that proved particularly divisive and contentious.

An argument arose soon after Plappart's appointment that indicates the extent to which the balance of power was very different from the one described by Alma. At the end of 1898 Mahler tried to defend himself against a number of articles that had attacked him and his running of the opera house and that had appeared in various local papers whose anti-Semitism varied only in terms of its virulence. He was convinced that the attacks were due to indiscretions on the part of an individual member of the orchestra, most of whose players were hostile to him. He even thought that with the help of a graphologist he had managed to identify the culprit and wanted the general administrator's office to pay for the graphologist's report and institute proceedings against the person in question. Plappart sent Mahler packing and left him to pick up the bill.

Writers on Mahler have tended to describe Plappart as bureaucratic and narrow-minded, and there is no doubt that from the standpoint of Mahler and his friends this was true. But we do not know enough about him to say whether or not this assessment is fair. None the less, we may conclude that he had little interest in opera and was anxious only to ensure that a director who was regarded as stubborn was not given any unnecessary leeway and to avoid any form of conflict that might compromise his own position. Whether Plappart was anti-Semitic like many members of the Austrian aristocracy is uncertain, but it cannot be ruled out. The philo-Semites among the Austrian nobility must have been the exception. Fortunately, however, there was someone in this hierarchy who was well-disposed to Mahler and to whom he could – and did – turn in times of conflict, and that was Prince Montenuovo.

Montenuovo was second only to the senior comptroller, Prince Rudolf von und zu Liechtenstein, who remained in office from 1896 to 1908, in other words, for the whole of the period that Mahler held the post of director. And yet in spite of the fact that all the documents relating to Mahler bear Liechtenstein's signature, it seems to have been Montenuovo who was charged with the task of dealing with all matters appertaining to the opera. Bruno Walter recalled that Mahler's reports were submitted not to the general administrator's office in the Bräunerstraße, barely five minutes on foot from the Court Opera, but to Montenuovo in the Hofburg. Liechtenstein and Montenuovo were the general administrator's immediate superiors. It was to them that the director deferred. They were also the final court of appeal before the Kaiser, although the latter had no great interest in the opera, preferring the

Burgtheater and in particular its actresses, a point well illustrated by his long and touching and much-ridiculed liaison with the Burgtheater actress Katharina Schratt. And yet Franz Joseph may have sensed that Mahler was in a different league from the director of the Burgtheater at this period. Paul Schlenther had succeeded Alma's admirer, Max Burckhard, in 1898 and remained in office until 1910.

A number of anecdotes attest to the fact that Mahler resisted interference in his strict regime. On one occasion he is said to have been told to engage a particular soprano because she enjoyed the patronage of some aristocrat or other. Mahler duly auditioned the woman but refused to engage her because he did not think she was good enough. When it was borne in upon him that the Kaiser explicitly wanted this appointment, Mahler is said to have replied: 'All right, but I shall then add a note to the playbill, "Frau X, at the express desire of His Majesty the Kaiser". (According to a different version of the story, he is said to have retorted: 'I'm waiting for the Kaiser's orders to engage the lady.')

Mahler's strictness is attested above all by the instructions that latecomers should not be admitted once the performance had started, the only exceptions being the boxes and the areas set aside for standing room. In November 1897 the *Wiener Sonn- und Montagszeitung* published a satire under the heading of 'Regulations for Patrons of the Court Opera', according to which a cannon would be fired at the Arsenal at five o'clock in the afternoon, advising patrons that it was time to get ready for the opera. Moreover, on the day before the performance opera-goers had to inform their landlords of their intention of attending the opera, so that they could be urged to leave the building in good time. In order to avoid lengthy waits at the cloakrooms, all patrons would be issued with a standard opera cape at cost price. These capes could be removed with a single clasp and already bore the number of the cloakroom ticket emblazoned on their back.[2]

But let us return to Prince Montenuovo, of whom Bruno Walter provides a striking portrait in his autobiography:

Emperor Franz Joseph's Lord Steward, a grandson of the Austrian Princess Marie Louise whose second husband, after Napoleon, had been Baron Neipperg – Italianized into Montenuovo – was an elegant silver-haired man of medium height, his face adorned by a grey moustache and beard. He was cold and self-assured, rather dryly bureaucratic, but thoroughly reliable, and unshakable in his convictions. He deserved high praise for having resisted for ten years the intrigues and hostilities directed against Mahler. Men and women of high society, some of them even in the entourage of archdukes, were trying to gain his ear in their efforts to dethrone Mahler. And Mahler did not make things easy for Montenuovo either, though his heart was gladdened by the Prince's sincere esteem, by the sympathy under his dry manner.[3]

The rest of Mahler's administrative staff comprised his chancellery-appointed and devoted secretary Alois Przistaupinsky and the latter's assistants Ferdinand Graf, Carl Sageder, Alois Hartmann and Robert Kompass. To these names we may add those of the stage manager August Stoll and the chorus conductor Hubert Wondra, who also performed administrative tasks but on whom Mahler could not rely unconditionally, and the Court Opera's clerk, Carl Hasslinger, who dealt with minor day-to-day matters and who was a genuine jack of all trades for Mahler. (It was Hasslinger who would telephone to report that Mahler was on his way home for lunch.) This, then, was the motley crew who were brought into contact with Mahler by the latter's role as administrator: his personal factotum, his loyal secretary, his less than loyal chorus conductor, the bureaucratic and inartistic general administrator, the dry but supportive deputy comptroller and, at the very top, a relatively ignorant but tolerant Kaiser. Ranged against him was the press, which was largely hostile to him at the start of his appointment. Large sections were still hostile to him at the end.

Mahler initially made enemies by sweeping away ingrained operatic routine and inartistic bureaucratic practices and above all by his policy towards singers. (His arguments with the Vienna Philharmonic come under a separate heading.) An anti-Semitic caricature from a Viennese newspaper shows this very clearly.[4] In front of the Court Opera is a scarecrow with Mahler's badly drawn features, frightening away a flock of birds on whose backs it is possible to make out the names of prominent singers, including Reichmann, Naval, Renard and Forster, all of whom were allegedly driven away by Mahler. The caption beneath the caricature reads: 'Jew Mahler as a scarecrow driving away our finest singers!' And at the top is a second caption that reads: 'Reichmann too is going!' Theodor Reichmann was the famous baritone who had sung Amfortas in the first performances of *Parsifal* in Bayreuth in 1882. It is impossible to date the caricature, for according to the surviving records Reichmann remained a member of the Court Opera until his death in 1903. Perhaps it dates from a time when differences between the director and the baritone came to public attention. Reichmann was well known as a supreme exponent of bel canto – Bruno Walter, too, held him in high regard. By 1897, when Mahler joined the company, Reichmann was already past his best, but it was no doubt his lack of charisma onstage that Mahler found the most disappointing. Mahler was never squeamish about speaking his mind when he felt that a local favourite had passed his peak and that it was time for him to go. Moreover, not every type of voice was equally well represented when Mahler came to Vienna in 1897. A number of the names that appear in the caricature point to genuine conflicts, and the dismissal of these singers inevitably led a section of the press to attack Mahler, even though such dismissals might have been accepted as necessary or meaningful by any other director. And as the caricature indicates, Mahler's Jewishness was a further bone of contention. If he dismissed a non-Jewish singer, it was argued that Jewish hatred of non-Jews played a part in that decision. If he had signed up more Jewish singers, he would have been criticized for this, too, though in the event only Selma Kurz fell into this category.

Fortunately for Mahler, nearly all the singers he engaged proved a success, and it is clear that his enemies soon abandoned their attempts to attack his policy towards singers, for, however much local audiences may have missed the familiar faces, they were soon expressing their enthusiasm for their replacements. Mahler was not really an expert on voices but had an ear for vocal potential and an eye for dramatic talent. His problem was simply that his enthusiasms were frequently over-hasty and that on the strength of a single audition or guest appearance he would engage new singers who were unable in the longer term to meet the expectations that were placed in them. He was also volatile in his sympathies and antipathies, a shortcoming that was repeatedly held against him even by his friends and admirers. As such, it needs to be taken seriously. When Bruno Walter arrived in Vienna, he had to go off in search of singers in the provinces. He, too, admitted afterwards that a number of the decisions that Mahler took were misguided, but gradually an ensemble emerged that had no equal in Europe and that was particularly strong in the repertory that was closest to Mahler's own heart: Mozart, Beethoven and Wagner.

Contemporaries

'Mahler has often been reproached for performing very few new works,' wrote Paul Stefan in 1908. Stefan was an early Mahlerian, and his pamphlet, *Mahler's Legacy*, was in part a polemic against his idol's successor in Vienna, Felix von Weingartner.[5] The reproach, he went on, was misguided, because at the Vienna Court Opera nothing was as counterproductive as the failure of a new work. If several new works all proved a fiasco, then the director would have lost all credit in the eyes of his audiences and of the general administrator's office as well:

> Audiences at the Court Opera are conservative in terms of their social background and taste and shy away from anything that is unusual, preferring playfulness, memorable melodies and above all the most pointed dramatic impact. But what is acceptable to the average listener is unlikely to satisfy the most fastidious. The critics complain about the frivolousness of a new work and spoil audiences' enjoyment of it. No new work in recent years has appealed in its entirety to the Vienna Court Opera.

Stefan went on to draw attention to the fate of two operas in particular: Strauss's *Salome*, which in spite of Mahler's efforts was not staged at all, and Pfitzner's *Die Rose vom Liebesgarten*, which was mounted only with difficulty. In short, Stefan was right: there is no sign that under Mahler's stewardship there were any local or international premières that won a lasting place for themselves in the repertory. This, then, might be the only weak point in Mahler's administration. And yet it needs to be stressed that he did not take up his new post with the stated intention of turning the Court Opera into a centre of the avant-garde. Moreover, the years between 1897 and 1907 were oddly lacking in important new works, for all that the period between 1890 and 1920 were in general a time of plenty. Franz Willnauer has observed, quite rightly, that the true masterpieces of early twentieth-century opera – Strauss's *Elektra* and *Der Rosenkavalier*, Bartók's *Bluebeard's Castle*, Schreker's *Der ferne Klang*, Busoni's *Doktor Faust*, Pfitzner's *Palestrina* and Berg's *Wozzeck* – had not been written at the time that Mahler was director in Vienna.[6]

A glance at the performance statistics reveals a marked dearth of world premières and first performances. The first local première superintended by Mahler was Smetana's *Dalibor*, which entered the repertory in October 1897 alongside *The Bartered Bride*, a work that Jahn had introduced to Court Opera audiences the previous year. Mahler was always fond of Smetana's music, preferring it to that of Dvořák, whom he largely ignored as an opera composer, although *Rusalka* would surely have appealed to him. He had mixed feelings about late Verdi – the Italian composer was still alive when Mahler assumed office in 1897. If he ignored early and middle-period Verdi almost entirely, he was merely reflecting the German tradition in general. He once told Natalie Bauer-Lechner that Verdi had some wonderful ideas but that he tended to scatter them at random and string them together in no particular order. Only in his later works could he control his wealth of ideas and use them economically. In this regard Mahler had no hesitation in comparing Verdi with Albert Lortzing.[7]

Remarkably, however, Mahler failed to follow up this insight into the later Verdi by matching action to words. He twice conducted *Aida*, but there were no performances of *Don Carlo* or *Simon Boccanegra* in Vienna under his directorship. (It has to be admitted, however, that at this date neither work had been recognized as the masterpiece that it is.) And in 1907 Zemlinsky conducted *Otello*. Only in May 1904 did Mahler take any sustained interest in Verdi when he and Roller collaborated on *Falstaff*. Of the thirteen performances in this and the following two seasons, Mahler conducted only six, a clear sign that his heart was not in it – it is apparent from his possessiveness towards *Così fan tutte* that he did not willingly relinquish works to which he felt any attachment. His neglect of Verdi is perhaps his greatest sin of omission, and yet anyone

whose guiding stars were Gluck, Beethoven and Wagner and who shared
Wagner's contempt for 'foreign dross' could not be expected to place Verdi's
works on the same high level. But if Mahler maintained a kind of respectful
distance towards Verdi, he felt nothing but scorn for the *verismo* school and
for Puccini in particular. During his visit to Lemberg in early April 1903 he
took the opportunity to see *Tosca* at the local theatre and was impressed by the
standard of the performance as such:

> But the work itself! Act I: a Papal procession, accompanied by an inter-
> minable ding-dong of bells (which had to be specially imported from Italy).
> In Act 2 a *torture* scene with hideous screams, after which a man is stabbed
> to death with a sharp-pointed bread-knife. Act 3: panoramic view from a
> citadel over the city of Rome, to a gigantic bim-bam-bum with another bevy
> of bells – and an execution by firing squad. Before the shooting started, I got
> up and left. I need scarcely add that the score is a masterly sham; nowadays
> every shoemaker's apprentice is an orchestrator of genius.[8]

When *La Bohème* received its first performance at the Vienna Court Opera in
November 1903, Mahler unsurprisingly handed over the baton to Francesco
Spetrino, who was responsible for the company's Italian repertory. (Later it was
Bruno Walter whom Mahler invited to assume responsibilities of this nature.)
In her memoirs Alma recalls that Puccini attended the final rehearsals and that
he and Mahler 'had not a particle in common'. Mahler, moreover, could not
understand why his colleague ogled the royal box throughout the dress
rehearsal and demanded to be introduced to the archduchesses who were
sitting there.[9]

The real novelties were few and far between and nowadays create a
distinctly random impression: Siegfried Wagner's *Der Bärenhäuter*, which was
no doubt mounted as a favour to Cosima Wagner; Anton Rubinstein's *The
Demon*; Zemlinsky's *Es war einmal*; Richard Strauss's *Feuersnot*; Josef Forster's
Der dot mon (Forster was a representative of German *verismo* and unrelated to
Josef Bohuslav Foerster); Pfitzner's *Die Rose vom Liebesgarten*; and, the most
important new work of this period, Gustave Charpentier's *Louise*, which was
staged in March 1903. Of these, only the works by Zemlinsky and Forster were
world premières. *Louise* – an unusual example of French *verismo* crossed with
Impressionism – had received its first performance in Paris in February 1900.
Mahler was sent a copy of the vocal score and was initially put off by the background of a work that is set in the attics of contemporary Paris. No doubt he
was unpleasantly reminded of the bohemian subject matter already explored
by Puccini, but when he took a closer look at the score, he was much more
enthusiastic, telling Alma that the work was both brilliant and dramatic. He

accepted *Louise* without further ado, and the work was put into rehearsal. As was usually the case in Vienna at this time, it was double cast: the tenor lead of Julien was shared by Leo Slezak and Fritz Schrödter, while Louise was taken by Marie Gutheil-Schoder and Berta Foerster-Lauterer. Leopold Demuth played Louise's father in both casts.

Alma has left a lively account of the bohemian composer's arrival in Vienna to superintend the final rehearsals. According to her, Charpentier was unsophisticated but affable, spitting on the floor and biting his fingernails, something that she must have been used to from Mahler. He also flirted uninhibitedly with Alma, not that this prevented him from inviting a demimondaine to join him in Mahler's box. He immediately interfered in Mahler's production, having no time for the *verismo* staging that Mahler had in mind but seeking to replace it with something almost surreal. In the event, Mahler was so taken by Charpentier that he postponed the first night in order to allow the French composer to take control of the production. 'I was wrong,' he admitted. 'After all, the composer must know best.' Such an admission can by no means be taken for granted with a director and conductor of Mahler's exceptional standing. For all that the work remains on the fringes of the modern repertory, *Louise* was one of the few genuinely significant works that received their local première in Vienna during Mahler's decade of direction.

There were practically no real world premières during these years. A modest admirer of *Die Königin von Saba*, Mahler conducted the elderly Karl Goldmark's *Die Kriegsgefangene* in 1899. A two-act work, it did not fill an entire evening and had to be performed as part of a double bill with a ballet but disappeared from the repertory after only a few months. Zemlinsky's *Es war einmal* was the next world première in January 1900. It, too, proved short-lived and has only recently been rediscovered thanks to the medium of the gramophone. Josef Forster's *Der dot mon*, finally, was staged in February 1902. And that was it: three world premières in the space of ten years. All were conducted by Mahler himself, but none proved a lasting success. The end result was disappointing, and, as we have observed, the choice of new works limited.

Mahler enjoyed a close, if by no means unproblematic, relationship with two contemporary composers: Hans Pfitzner and Richard Strauss. Pfitzner is the Thersites of German musical history, although his political views tend rather to cast him in the role of a latterday Knight of the Doleful Countenance.[10] His polemics against Busoni, Bekker and all the other iconoclasts whom he accused of un-German activities were unfortunately seized on by the Nazis in support of their own nefarious cultural agenda. In his autobiography, which he wrote towards the end of his long life in the wake of the Second World War and which was posthumously published as *Impressions and Pictures from my Life*,

Pfitzner recalled that he had never shied away from crude anti-Semitic attacks whenever he sensed un-German thinking but that, adopting Karl Lueger's infamous motto, 'I shall decide who is a Jew', he was always ready to make exceptions if he encountered 'fundamentally German' Jews. His recollections of Mahler are marked by a mixture of gratitude and genuine emotion. A set of photographs has survived showing them both smoking cigars with Max Reinhardt in the garden of their host, Carl Moll. (These photographs were presumably taken at the time of the first performances of Pfitzner's *Die Rose vom Liebesgarten*.) Pfitzner never forgot his debt of gratitude to Mahler for staging his opera, and it is certainly striking that even at the time of the Third Reich he refrained from making any derogatory remarks about the outlawed Mahler, even though he could have scored highly with the authorities by doing so. Indeed, his whole attitude to Mahler was marked by a typical ambivalence.

Like his great mentor Wagner, Pfitzner was incapable of admitting that Jews might have any creative abilities of their own, and so he drew a careful distinction between Mahler the composer and Mahler the conductor with whom he was friendly. The composer, he wrote, had always been honest from a subjective point of view, pouring his heart's blood into his works. But, objectively speaking, Mahler had been dishonest, being incapable of rising above his Jewish nature. As a performer, conversely, he deserved the highest praise. Pfitzner recalled how he had arrived in Vienna feeling completely intimidated and put off by arrogant conductors who had hitherto treated him and his works with contempt, assuming they had not ignored him altogether. But Mahler, as famous as he was feared, had lavished the greatest care and attention on the music of a composer who, nine years his junior, was far from being established. He had also responded positively to all of Pfitzner's suggestions. As a result, the production of *Die Rose vom Liebesgarten* was an abiding light in its composer's life, and in recalling this experience, Pfitzner repeated a phrase that he had used on Mahler's death: 'In him there is love.'[11]

In fact, relations between Mahler and Pfitzner had started badly. *Die Rose vom Liebesgarten* had received its first performance in Elberfeld in 1901, after which Pfitzner had sent a copy of the score and libretto to Mahler but had met with little response. Mahler travelled to Krefeld in June 1902 to prepare for the first performance of his Third Symphony, and Pfitzner took the opportunity to call on the Mahlers at their hotel. Alma was always sympathetic towards Pfitzner, who, although not especially attractive to women, none the less had the occasional success and was currently trying to seduce Alma, or so she claims. In her memoirs she offers a highly dramatized account of Pfitzner's meeting with Mahler, on which she eavesdropped from an alcove in their hotel room. Speaking in a thin, high voice, Pfitzner poured out his unhappiness as a misunderstood artist who felt that a production of *Die Rose vom Liebesgarten* in Vienna was his last chance. Mahler, he insisted, was the only artist who could understand him. (Unfortunately we do not know what Pfitzner thought of Mahler's music at this period.) Mahler refused, coldly and tersely, arguing that the libretto was bad and the symbolism incomprehensible. Nor were there any singers in Vienna suitable for the main roles, an argument whose vacuity was spectacularly exposed when the performances finally went ahead. In his despair, Pfitzner slipped away towards the door, at which point Alma leapt out of her hiding place and squeezed his hand to show how deeply she sympa-thized with him – she had remembered Mahler's comments about his own beginnings as an unsuccessful composer. Perhaps the most remarkable aspect of all was that Mahler was not angry with Alma for her show of solidarity. For the present, however, the encounter produced no results. Then, in February 1904, Mahler was in Heidelberg for a performance of his Third Symphony and discovered that *Die Rose vom Liebesgarten* was being performed at the local theatre. Having made an effort to see the work onstage, he wrote to Alma to report on it:

> Yesterday I heard Die Rose vom Liebesgarten. The performance was very good, and fully confirmed my opinion of the work when I read the score. It brought me no new insights. My opinion of Pfitzner remains unchanged. A strong sense of atmosphere and very interesting range of orchestral colours. But too shapeless and vague. A perpetual jelly and primeval slime, constantly calling for life but unable to gestate. It evolves only as far as the invertebrates; vertebrates cannot follow. . . . The audience came with the best of intentions, but in such a stifling atmosphere of smog and mysticism, the interest waned.[12]

It remains open to question whether Mahler's initial impression, following his read-through of the score, or his later impression after he had seen the work onstage, was the right one. The present writer is not about to declare *Die Rose vom Liebesgarten* one of the most significant operas from the turn of the century. None the less, what we have here is a unique case of Mahler completely revising his judgement. Bruno Walter, too, recalled that Mahler had initially had a violent antipathy to the opera. Pfitzner no doubt thought that if Mahler changed his mind, it was above all because of Alma's enthusiasm and Walter's advocacy – Walter was one of the composer's earliest admirers and later gave the first performance of *Palestrina* in Munich. There are reasons for thinking that Mahler would have been as enthusiastic about this last-named work as Walter and the Mahlerian Thomas Mann. Alma and Walter refused to back down. Time and again Alma would leave a copy of the score of *Die Rose vom Liebesgarten* on Mahler's piano in the hope that he would look at it whenever he sat down at the instrument and played. Later, during the summer holidays, a copy of Pfitzner's First String Quartet arrived at Maiernigg, and after examining it at length, Mahler declared it a masterpiece. It remains unclear, however, why he was suddenly fascinated by the opera, but it is highly unlikely that he agreed to stage the work simply as a favour to Alma and Bruno Walter. We must assume, rather, that the positive aspects of the work, which emerge even from his negative-seeming letter to Alma, ultimately carried greater weight and overshadowed all other considerations.

Mahler's relations with Richard Strauss were both different and more complex and are the subject of a detailed study by Herta Blaukopf. At least as long as he was still writing symphonic poems, Strauss was the only composer whom Mahler could see as a serious rival but also as a comrade in arms.[13] It all began in October 1887 when Strauss, an assistant conductor at the Munich Opera, arrived in Leipzig to conduct his F minor Symphony. Mahler was deputy Kapellmeister there – only four years older than Strauss, he was already considerably higher up the career ladder than Strauss, who became director of the Vienna State Opera only long after Mahler's death. Conversely, Strauss enjoyed far greater public recognition as a composer. It seems to have been a mutual acquaintance, Max Steinitzer, who introduced these two aspiring composers and conductors. In a letter to Hans von Bülow, who was the mentor of and model for both men, Strauss spoke enthusiastically about Mahler, whom he described as a 'supremely intelligent musician and conductor', but he then committed the strategic error of commenting no less enthusiastically on Mahler's arrangement of Weber's *Die drei Pintos*, the first act of which Mahler had played to him on the piano. Bülow was sufficiently interested to obtain a copy of the score but was so appalled by what he discovered there that, adopting his typically caustic tone, he left Strauss in no doubt about his true feelings on the matter. Shocked in turn, Strauss obsequiously back-pedalled: the arrangement was indeed inept, a point he had unfortunately failed to note.

In spite of this there was frequent contact between Strauss and Mahler over the coming years, including a number of meetings, no doubt in Munich too. Their correspondence quickly assumed an increasingly intimate and friendly tone. At this stage in their respective careers, Mahler was successful as a conductor but felt misunderstood as a composer, whereas Strauss was moderately successful as a conductor, albeit still only an assistant conductor in Weimar at a time when Mahler was the principal conductor at the Hamburg Opera. As a composer, however, Strauss had firmly established himself as the head of a 'Young German' school thanks to works such as *Don Juan* and *Tod und Verklärung* (*Death and Transfiguration*). Mahler was sceptical about the symphonic poem as a genre and had little time for Franz Liszt, who had created this particular genre and whom he dismissed as the manufacturer of works both 'specious and meretricious'.

Relations between the two men remained cordial in spite of their rivalries, and Strauss even entered into negotiations with Pollini in Hamburg to take over Mahler's position as principal conductor, although in the event nothing came of the move. And yet Mahler, at least, quickly realized that he and Strauss were fundamentally different from one another, an insight that never left him. Particularly instructive from this point of view is a letter that Mahler wrote to Max Marschalk in December 1896. Marschalk had written an article on Mahler and had then sent a copy of it to him. Mahler did not acknowledge it, leading Marschalk to think that he had somehow upset the conductor. But Mahler was in fact very pleased with the piece. Above all, he explained, he was keen to stress the difference between himself and Strauss – and here we can sense not only the envy that he felt for his successful colleague but also his lack of willingness to conform to prevailing views about modern music: 'Permit me to differentiate myself throughout from Strauss – and to differentiate what you write about me from what the shallow Corybants say about that – forgive the harsh term – knight of industry! All the press's utterances about him reveal his knack of currying favour with his own kind.'[14]

Later in the same letter Mahler makes a number of derogatory remarks about *Also sprach Zarathustra*. The term 'knight of industry' inevitably recalls Adorno's polemical assault on Strauss in 1964: 'At a time when, musically too, the German middle classes were demonstrating features of a Freudian anal character, Strauss as a composer was revealing the gestures of an idealized major industrialist. He does not need to save: the resources are extremely lavish. He does not need to think of balancing the books but continues to produce unconcerned by such considerations.'[15] Even in his choice of words, Adorno took over the view of Strauss adopted by the Second Viennese School, specifically by his teacher Alban Berg, who had picked up these ideas from Mahler via Schoenberg. It was Mahler who once and for all defined the difference between himself and Strauss by reference to the concept of a knight of industry. But he was sufficiently objective to be able to acknowledge Strauss's abilities and above all to admit that Strauss was one of only a handful of contemporaries willing to champion his – Mahler's – own music. Josef Bohuslav Foerster reports that while he was still in Hamburg, Mahler obtained copies of every new work by Strauss, whom he regarded as his only real rival. Unfortunately there are few surviving records of Mahler's comments on his colleague's music. We know only that he regarded *Salome*, above all, as a masterpiece and did everything he could to mount a production of it at the Vienna Court Opera. He had got to know the work in May 1905 when Strauss played through parts of it to him on the piano at the Strasbourg Music Festival.

Mahler doubted whether a work as scandalous as *Salome* would ever find a place for itself in the repertory of Catholic countries, and yet he pursued the goal of mounting a production in Vienna with a resolve that shows he was not lying when he described the opera as Strauss's most important work.[16] Much of the correspondence between Mahler and Strauss is devoted to *Salome*. Mahler began by asking Strauss to send him the libretto in order for him to submit it to the censor's office. He already had a cast in mind, and it would in fact have been better than the one that had given the work's first performance in Dresden in December 1905. Strauss had agreed with Ernst von Schuch that Dresden would be given priority, but a second production in Vienna would clearly have helped to raise the work's public profile. Erik Schmedes would have sung Herod, Anna von Mildenburg Herodias and Friedrich Weidemann John the Baptist. Strauss wanted Selma Kurz to sing Salome, but Mahler pointed out that however vocally talented, she lacked the dramatic gifts for the role, and so he proposed Elsa Bland, a young dramatic soprano from Vienna, who did indeed go on to sing the part, but not under Mahler. In the event Mahler lost his battle with the censor, who argued that the presentation of such perverse sensuality was morally offensive. Mahler did everything in his power to reverse this decision. Strauss was understandably surprised by this turn of events, for in Dresden there had been no problems with the censor, which says much for the relative permissiveness of Kaiser Wilhelm's much-vilified Germany. By October 1905 it seemed as if the difficulties in Vienna had been overcome, encouraging Mahler to write to Strauss and, striking a triumphalist note, to explain that only a few minor changes would have to be made to the libretto. He proposed 'Bal Hanaan' as an alternative to Jochanaan, the censor having taken exception to this name.

But then, on 31 October, Mahler received a detailed report from the court censor, Emil Jettel von Ettenach, famously stating that 'the depiction of events that belong in the realm of sexual pathology' was unsuited to the stage of the Vienna Court Opera.[17] It is to Strauss's credit that he harboured no grudge against Mahler for this debacle, although the tremendous success of the Dresden première must have helped to cushion the blow. Moreover, he knew that Mahler had done all he could to bring about the performance: even Mahler's powers had their limitations. Vienna got to know *Salome* in the spring of 1907, when a visiting company from Breslau gave the local première. The first home-grown production took place at the Kaiser-Jubiläums-Theater in 1910, and the opera finally entered the Court Opera repertory in October 1918. Strauss wrote Mahler a letter of commiseration in March 1906: 'For heaven's sake do not let *Salome* give rise to a question of confidence. We need an artist of your determination, your genius and your outlook in such a position too badly for you to put anything at stake on *Salome*'s account. In the end we shall attain our ends without this!'[18]

The battle over *Salome* brought Mahler and Strauss closer together, and yet to Mahler it also demonstrated beyond all doubt that the two men were worlds apart as far as their aims and creative intentions were concerned. For Mahler this was a problem that he could resolve only with a certain degree of dishonesty, for the closer he drew to Strauss as man and artist, the more clearly his failings as a character became apparent, while at the same time he knew that of all the famous conductors of his day, none was doing more for him than Strauss. This is evident not from the correspondence that passed between the two colleagues, but from Mahler's letters to Alma. The differences between them were already apparent at the time of the Viennese performances of *Feuersnot* in late January 1902. This was the only Strauss opera that Mahler ever conducted. In her memoirs, Alma gives a lively account of the *Feuersnot* première, claiming that Strauss's wife, Pauline, spent the whole evening heaping abuse on her husband's 'shoddy work', while her husband talked only about money, calculating the royalties on his performances in Vienna and in general carrying on 'just like a commercial traveller': 'He had become an unashamed materialist, weighing his own advantage at every turn, a gambler on the stock exchange and an exploiter of the Opera. I saw Pfitzner and Schoenberg standing as stylites on either side of him and he as the worldling in between.'[19] Of course, all of Alma's accounts of Strauss and his wife are vitriolic in tone.

Strauss did himself no favours when, all unsuspecting, he started to read Alma's memoirs after the Second World War. His marginal jottings consist of a series of indignant exclamations, including 'Unbelievable' and 'All lies'. And he dismissed Alma with the words 'The inferiority complexes of a dissolute woman'. (The feeling was mutual.) But his anger was also directed posthumously at Mahler, whom he accused of ingratitude. After all, he had done a great deal to help his colleague, and although it was untrue to claim that he had conducted the world première of the First Symphony in Weimar in June 1894, he had certainly invited Mahler to conduct the first three movements of his Second Symphony in Berlin in 1895 at one of his own concerts and had given the Berlin première of the Fourth Symphony in 1901.

Nor did Strauss's advocacy end with Mahler's death. In August 1923, by which date Mahler's music had largely disappeared from concert programmes all over the world, he included the First Symphony in a concert that he gave with the Vienna Philharmonic at the Teatro Colón in Buenos Aires. One might think that Alma's animosity towards Strauss and his wife was a figment of a dissolute woman's imagination, but it was evidently shared by her husband. Following the opening night of *Feuersnot* in 1902, Mahler spent a few days in Semmering, recovering, and from there he wrote to Alma to describe the impression that Strauss had left on him during the performance itself and at the formal dinner afterwards. Picking up and confirming a dismissive comment of Alma's, he goes on:

Strauss has such a sobering influence; in his world one scarcely recognizes oneself. If those are the fruits that hang from the tree, how can one love such a tree? Your judgement hits the nail on the head. And I feel quite proud of you for spontaneously arriving at such an assessment. Rather live in poverty and walk the path of the enlightened than surrender oneself to Mammon, don't you agree? One day people will separate the wheat from the chaff – and when his day has passed, my time will come.[20]

One of Mahler's most famous remarks – 'My time will come' – is routinely quoted out of context, and yet it makes sense only against the background of his perception of himself as the polar opposite of Strauss. It does not need to be stressed that when taken with a pinch of salt and with the exception of two or three of Strauss's operas, Mahler's confidence has proved well founded. Their rivalry has survived their deaths, and it is difficult to find a music lover who holds both Mahler and Strauss in equal esteem. A choice has to be made between them. During their lifetime, they continued to grow apart, although only Mahler appears to have registered this fact. In early November 1905 we find him writing from Berlin: 'I had a very pleasant time with Strauss yesterday evening, but one cannot entirely disregard his offhanded, self-important attitude.'[21] And this growing sense of remoteness also coloured Mahler's otherwise high opinion of *Salome*. In May 1906, when Mahler was in Essen, preparing for the first performance of his Sixth Symphony, Alma wrote to him and let slip a dismissive comment of the work. Although Mahler defended the opera in his reply, there is no gainsaying the coolness of his response:

But now you *underestimate* the work, which really is a very significant one, though 'virtuosic' in the negative sense, as you rightly discerned. Wagner is something quite different. The further you develop in life, the more clearly you will sense the difference between those few great, *genuine* figures and the mere 'virtuosos'. I'm happy to see how *quickly* you're beginning to grasp such things. There's something *cold* about Strauss that has nothing to do with his talent but with his *character*. You can sense it, and it repels you.[22]

It will not have been easy for Mahler to hide these views from Strauss, whom he found not unsympathetic as a person, with the result that Strauss must have been appalled when forty years later he read these remarks of Mahler's, which Alma published in her memoirs, something she should most certainly have refrained from doing. The element of dishonesty that blighted his dealings with Strauss must have weighed heavily on Mahler, who was always sensitive on this point. Strauss, at all events, retained his sympathy for Mahler, and although it is difficult to describe their relationship as one of true friendship, there is no denying that he was genuinely shaken when he heard that Mahler had died.

Curiously enough, it was to Strauss that Arnold Schoenberg appealed when he wrote to the feared music critic of the *New York Times*, Olin Downes, in December 1948. Downes had reviewed a performance of Mahler's Seventh Symphony under Dimitri Mitropoulos and, referring to the piece, had ended his review with the words 'Chacun à son goût'. His attitude was not untypical of the arrogant condescension with which Mahler's music was viewed in the years after the Second World War, when it was by no means only former National Socialist writers who felt that Mahler's eclectic 'Kapellmeister music' was a passing phenomenon that had had its day. This was a view that was shared even by a doyen among critics such as Downes, who enjoyed a not inconsiderable reputation among many readers in the Anglo-American world. The elderly Schoenberg was furious with Downes for his sneering condescension and in this context cited Strauss, who, he claimed, had once expressed the greatest respect for Mahler's music. Schoenberg assumed that Downes had once written dismissively about Mahler and was now reluctant to change his mind. It is typical of Schoenberg's sense of justice that he also complains about a positive comment about his own music that Downes once made. Might not the readers of both reviews suspect that anyone who could write as unfoundedly about Mahler might be equally wrong about Schoenberg: 'If you would study the orchestral score you could not overlook the beauty of this writing. Such beauty is only given to men who deserve it because of all their other merits. You should not call me a mystic – though I am proud to be one – because this statement is based on experience.'[23]

Much to Schoenberg's surprise and annoyance, Downes published his letter in the *New York Times*, together with a rejoinder of his own, obliging the composer to react yet again. He was now furious at Downes for arguing that it was simply a matter of 'taste', for to Schoenberg's mind taste was by no means free from negative associations. But he admitted that the review had annoyed him not least because as a young man – between 1898 and 1908 – he had thought the same about Mahler as Downes did now. Only in the wake of a Pauline conversion had he become Mahler's most ardent champion. He also conceded that later, too, there had been a phase when he had been unwilling to study or listen to Mahler's music, so afraid was he that his old antipathy might return. But after settling in Los Angeles he had heard a moderately successful performance of the Second Symphony and had been both relieved and pleased to discover that Mahler's music had lost none of its power to convince him.[24] The only point worth mentioning here is his dating of the period when he disliked Mahler's music, for there is plenty of evidence that it did not last until 1908. True, Alma records Schoenberg's flippant answer to her question as to whether he was planning to attend the local première of Mahler's Fourth Symphony: 'How can Mahler do anything with the Fourth when he has already failed to do anything with the First?'[25] But this remark dates from 1902, and Schoenberg was notorious at this time for being an aggressive disputant with a fondness for aphorisms and paradoxes.

It is clear from a letter that Schoenberg wrote to Mahler in December 1904 that the former's conversion had already taken place by this time. His much later attempt to date this change of attitude to Mahler's departure for America makes little sense, for he had been one of the group of supporters who had said goodbye to their hero at the main station in Vienna. And his letter of 12 December 1904 was written under the immediate impact of the final rehearsal for the local première of the Third Symphony, which had taken place at noon that same day.[26] Like Saul on the road to Damascus, Schoenberg quite literally saw the light:

> In order to speak of the unheard-of impression which your symphony made on me, I cannot talk as one musician to another but I must speak as man to man. For: I have seen your soul naked, stark naked. It lay before me like a wild mysterious landscape with its horror-provoking shadows and ravines, and, next to these, joyful charming sunny meadows, idyllic resting places. I felt the symphony to be an experience of nature with its horror and evil and its transfiguring, tranquillizing rainbows. . . . I felt they were battles about illusions; I felt the grief of a disillusioned man, I saw good and evil forces struggling with each other, I saw a man in torturing agitation seeking for inner harmony; I could see it, a man, a drama, *truth*, most reckless truth. . . . I had to let off steam, please forgive me, I do not have medium feelings, it is either – or![27]

Mahler will have had difficulties with an effusive outburst like this, for such outpourings on the part of people he barely knew left him feeling uncomfortable. But from this time onwards Schoenberg and Zemlinsky were part of his inner circle. He called them Eisele and Beisele, alluding to their Jewish descent, although not in any malicious way. Alma, who was introduced to Schoenberg by Zemlinsky, has left a whimsical account of a frugal supper that the two men attended, an occasion when they went over to the piano to talk shop, egging each other on with doctrinaire and deliberately provocative remarks until both men left the flat, offended, swearing never to set foot in it again, while Mahler for his part vowed never to invite them back. But within a matter of weeks, Mahler, striking a note of disingenuousness, was asking: 'What's become of Eisele and Beisele?'[28]

From now on the 'Schoenberg circle', as it later came to be known, was a constant, close-knit group that was soon joined by Alban Berg, Anton Webern,

Egon Wellesz, Erwin Stein and Heinrich Jalowetz, all of whom had composition lessons with Schoenberg, in some cases at the recommendation of Mahler's boyhood friend, Guido Adler, who was now teaching musicology at the University of Vienna. Mahler watched these young people develop with a mixture of love and affection, and it is difficult to resist the impression that he regarded them as his adopted sons. Early in 1907 Mahler put himself in the firing line on their behalf on two separate occasions. On 8 February the Rosé Quartet and members of the wind section of the Vienna Philharmonic gave the first performance of Schoenberg's First Chamber Symphony op. 9 in the Musikvereinssaal. Alma reports that whole sections of the audience got up and noisily left the hall during the performance, prompting Mahler to rise to his feet and demand silence, a demand that was duly met. Schoenberg's First String Quartet op. 7 received its first performance three days before in the Bösendorfersaal, again with the Rosé Quartet. On this occasion, too, the performance threatened to descend to the level of a fiasco. One man stood up in front and hissed Schoenberg each time he came forward to take a bow. 'I must have a good look at this fellow who's hissing,' Mahler is said to have exclaimed as he confronted the man who was much larger than he was. The man raised his arm to strike Mahler, but Mahler's father-in-law, Carl Moll, tall and powerfully built, intervened and drove the belligerent booer from the hall. As he was leaving, the man cried out: 'Needn't get so excited – I hiss Mahler too!' There may be some truth in Alma's claim that following the performance of the Chamber Symphony, Mahler admitted to her: 'I don't understand his music, but he's young and perhaps he's right. I am old and I dare say my ear is not sensitive enough.'[29]

Many eyewitnesses, including Adorno, insist that of all Mahler's adepts, it was Anton Webern who was the most convincing interpreter of Mahler's music during the 1920s, although there is unfortunately no surviving evidence to support this assertion. And yet he too initially had problems with Mahler. Such problems are, of course, understandable when we recall that Webern's ideals were clarity, intelligibility and unambiguity, and that at the time when he began to take an enthusiastic interest in Mahler's music, Schoenberg's pre-atonal compositional ideal presupposed the greatest possible density of material from which a complex work had to develop organically. Everything to which the *jeunes fauves* of the Viennese musical scene aspired was at odds with the vast, universalist novels of which Mahler dreamt. At least after the *Gurre-Lieder*, Schoenberg was an aphorist when compared with the orotund rhetoric of Mahler, while Webern went even further in this direction with the extreme concision of his musical forms. Of all the members of this curious 'school', it was Berg who came closest to Mahler with his Orchestral Pieces op. 6, and yet even these three works last barely twenty minutes in all. To that extent,

Schoenberg was being entirely consistent when he was asked in an interview in 1909 who his mentors were and named Bach and Mozart, followed by Beethoven, Brahms and Wagner, rather than Mahler, whom he placed alongside Strauss and Reger as his least important influence. There is no contradiction here. Schoenberg loved Mahler as man and artist infinitely more than Strauss and Reger, but as a teacher and as a source of direct inspiration Mahler played only the most minor of roles. As Hanns Eisler put it in 1924, Schoenberg created new material in order to write music in the unified, self-contained tradition of the great classical composers. It was Schoenberg, Eisler concluded, who was the true conservative: he had even created a revolution in order to be reactionary.[30] Here Eisler identifies the difference between Schoenberg and Mahler, for Mahler created no new material but worked with existing resources, while breaking down the self-contained world of the classical composers and emancipating himself from them in order to describe the volcanic craters that were heaving and seething inside him. To that extent it is understandable that the younger generation of composers had reservations about Mahler and that they initially swore by Brahms, regarding the musical language of late Romanticism as something to be superseded. Against this background, Schoenberg's later praise of 'Brahms the progressive' was entirely logical, as was Zemlinsky's devotion to Brahms.

Much the same was true of Webern. In a diary entry of 1902 he noted that on working through Mahler's Second Symphony at the piano he had found much that struck him as studied and strange. In spite of this he regarded the reviews of the recent performance of the Fourth Symphony as spiteful and ridiculous, adding that Mahler was without doubt a brilliant conductor and a serious and profound composer.[31] In February 1905, some time after Schoenberg's Damascene conversion, Webern heard a repeat of Mahler's *Wunderhorn* and Rückert songs under the composer's own direction. He enjoyed the former but found the latter to be too sentimental – it is surprising to find the rigorously independent Webern repeating a common Mahlerian cliché. But the concert was notable above all for the fact that afterwards Webern had an opportunity to meet the composer in person, and from then on his enthusiasm for Mahler continued to grow.

Particularly relevant in this regard are the letters that Webern addressed to Alban Berg at the time of the posthumous first performance of *Das Lied von der Erde* in Munich on 20 November 1911 under the direction of Bruno Walter. Webern was in Berlin, Berg in Vienna, but neither of them could imagine missing the performance. 'Tell me,' Webern wrote to Berg, 'is it conceivable that we should not be there? For the first time since Mahler's death a new work by him! And we might be missing? Because of the eight-hour train journey? Financially speaking, it's possible, isn't it? I mean, it won't be easy, but it's possible. Presumably the same is true of you? We also have the time, I certainly do.' Webern read through the words of *Das Lied von der Erde* in a state of feverish excitement, scarcely able to wait for the date of the actual performance when he would be able to hear Mahler's music: 'For heaven's sake, what sort of music must it be?! I imagine I must be able to figure it out before I hear it. – Man, can you hold out till then? I can't!' Webern and Berg were both present when Mahler's unprecedentedly original music was heard for the first time, and even afterwards Webern found it difficult to calm down again:

As I've already told you, it's like the whole of life or, rather, the whole of experience passing by the soul of the dying man. The artwork makes things more dense; actuality evaporates and only the idea remains; that is what these songs are like. I could play this music for ever! Yes, now tell me, do you know what it is that creates this impression both here and in the utterances of other great people? Have you ever thought what happens when you hear this? What is this indefinable element? . . . I often think, yes, should one be allowed to hear this? Do we deserve to? But it is given to us to strive for ways of deserving it! Thrust your hand into your heart, tear out the filth, arise, 'Sursum corda' says the Christian religion. This is how Mahler lived, Schoenberg too. There is remorse, there is longing![32]

Berg never struck such an ecstatic note as this, but if we may trust the account of Adorno, who studied briefly with Berg, 'Berg's relationship to Mahler was enthusiastic and without reservation, above all with regard to the later works. We often played the four-hand arrangement of the second '*Nachtmusik*' from the Seventh, as well as much else by Mahler.'[33] There was always a portrait of Mahler in Berg's study. And Berg's enthusiasm for Mahler is no less clear from a letter that he wrote to his wife, Helene, in the autumn of 1912:

I've just played through Mahler's Ninth again. The first movement is the most glorious he ever wrote. It expresses an extraordinary love of this earth, the longing to live on it in peace, nature, to enjoy it completely, to the very depths of one's being, before death comes.

Berg then offers a brief analysis of this movement, an analysis which for all its brevity is the most moving ever penned. It ends with a two-bar quotation in which 'this heart, most glorious of human hearts that ever beat, may expand, ever wider, before it must stop beating for good.'[34] And when Webern conducted the Third Symphony in Vienna in May 1922, Berg was, of course, present. They may as well all give up, he wrote to Helene after one of the rehearsals: he could hardly bear to remain in the hall, so powerful was the music.[35] Mahler was infinitely comforted by the thought of being revered by this younger generation of composers who included among their number some of the finest musicians of turn-of-the-century Vienna, for it acted as an antidote to the dull aggression to which he was so often exposed by the performances of his works; and it seems likely that he would have been delighted by the way in which Berg's career developed, for the *Three Orchestral Pieces* and *Wozzeck* are both works in his own spirit. When Adorno first saw a copy of the score of the March from the *Three Orchestral Pieces*, he could not help exclaiming: 'That must sound like playing Schoenberg's Orchestral Pieces and Mahler's Ninth Symphony, all at the same time.' And Adorno also recalled Berg's reaction: 'I will never forget the look of pleasure this compliment – dubious for any other cultured ear – induced. With a ferocity burying all Johannine gentleness like an avalanche, he answered: "Right, then at last one could hear what an eight-note brass chord really sounds like." '[36]

There is no finer expression of the feelings of respect and reverence that these young musicians harboured for Mahler than the famous speech that Schoenberg delivered in Prague in March 1912 and that he repeated in Berlin and Vienna in the October and November of the same year. This speech is not only touching testimony to the admiration that they all felt for Mahler, it is also one of the most important texts on Mahler from the period before the First World War, an importance that it retains not only on account of its many detailed comments on Mahler's style of conducting and his instrumentation but also because it serves to refute the frequent charge of banality and senti-mentality. Above all, it is a hymn to genius in general and in particular expressed with all the passion that Schoenberg could muster at this period. When Schoenberg's *Theory of Harmony* appeared in the autumn of 1911, only a few months after Mahler's death, it bore a dedication to Mahler.[37] The first edition went on:

> The dedication was intended to give him some slight pleasure while he was alive. And it wished to express admiration of his works, his immortal compositions, and to testify that, while educated musicians pass them by with exaggerated shrugs of the shoulders, and even with contempt, these works are admired by somebody who also perhaps has some understanding. – Gustav Mahler had to do without greater pleasures than this dedication would have given him. This martyr, this saint had to leave us before he was able to do so much for his works that he was able to hand them happily over to his friends. – I would have been contented with giving him pleasure. But now that he is dead I would like my book to bring me some esteem, so that no-one can disregard me when I say: He was a truly great man.[38]

Schoenberg was present when Mahler was laid to rest, the musical reflex of his shock and dismay being the sixth of his op. 19 Piano Pieces, a work that dies away with the interval of a ninth in the bass beneath a sustained chord, without ever achieving proper closure.

Signs of Crisis

To the outside world it seemed as if Mahler's departure from the Vienna Court Opera at the end of 1907 had taken all the parties by surprise and that it was in the main a reaction to the increasingly virulent campaigns against him in a section of the local press, precipitating a sudden turn of events. But there is a simple and wholly plausible piece of evidence that refutes this theory. In 1906 – the actual details are unclear, but it may have been during a train journey to Essen at the end of May when Mahler conducted the first performance of his Sixth Symphony in the city – a music journalist by the name of Bernhard Scharlitt recorded a conversation with Mahler, the essential details of which he published a week after Mahler's death in the *Neue Freie Presse*. In the course of the conversation Mahler told Scharlitt that he would be leaving the Court Opera the following year – 1907 – because he had come to realize that the idea of a repertory opera company flew in the face of the demands that any modern director must make, demands before which even a genius like Wagner would have been bound to capitulate when confronted by the constraints of the industry. The principle of model performances that Mahler himself had upheld was for the most part no longer tenable, with the result that a few outstanding performances were undermined by others that fell far short of the ideal. Mahler went on to propose the idea of a second theatre in Vienna specifically for Mozart and Wagner that would operate during the summer months as a combination of a repertory opera company and a festival theatre, but such an idea, Mahler concluded, echoing Wagner's phrase about the 'music of the future', would not be realized for a long time to come. He knew that when he left Vienna in a year's time he would have exceeded his term. Even the greatest achievements were superseded. He wanted to leave at a time when the Viennese could still appreciate what he had done for them as the director of their Opera.[39]

There is no reason to doubt Scharlitt's account, for there is other evidence that points in the same direction and indicates that by May 1906 at the latest Mahler had already decided to resign from his post in Vienna. In short, his decision was not prompted by the crises and upheavals of the traumatic year of 1907. Mahler's reasons for ending such a glorious reign are many and various and can be understood only against the background of developments that were already taking place when his star still seemed to be shining at its brightest.

A brief glance at the performance statistics for this period reveals some remarkable findings. We may begin by recalling the astonishing number of 148 performances that Mahler conducted in Hamburg during the 1895–6 season: if we discount the theatre holidays, he was conducting an opera every other day. If he did not break this record in Vienna, it was because he now had other commitments as the director of the opera, quite apart from his increasing contribution to opera production. In spite of this he conducted 109 performances during his first full season in Vienna. We have already had occasion to point out that today's general music directors would conduct only about half this number and would have none of Mahler's other commitments. In no subsequent season did Mahler conduct as many performances.

In 1899–1900 the total was ninety-six, although this season also saw him conducting nine midday concerts with the Vienna Philharmonic, not including all the attendant rehearsals. By the following season he was conducting only fifty-five performances, and in 1901–2 the number was down to thirty-six, a reduction due not least to the arrival of Bruno Walter, whom Mahler felt that he could trust and who lightened the director's load both practically and psychologically. Moreover, Mahler's engagement and marriage also brought about changes to his private life. After that the figures pick up again, varying between thirty-seven and sixty during subsequent seasons. The final season ended prematurely with a performance of *Fidelio* on 15 October 1907, by which date Mahler had conducted only five performances.[40]

This reduction in the number of Mahler's engagements in Vienna can be explained by the increase in the number of performances of his own works that he conducted elsewhere, especially after the autumn of 1901. Indeed, this development would ultimately lead not only to one of the basic conflicts that prompted Mahler's resignation but also to many of the attacks that were launched against him by his enemies in the press. A few random dates and facts may help to illustrate this point.

Mahler conducted the first performance of his Fourth Symphony in Munich on 25 November 1901 and gave the Berlin première of the same work on 16 December 1901. On 9 June 1902 he superintended the first complete performance of his Third Symphony in Krefeld and on 23 January 1903 conducted a performance of his Fourth Symphony in Wiesbaden. In the course of the next twelve months he conducted his First Symphony in Lemberg on 2 April, his Second Symphony in Basel on 15 June and his Third Symphony in Frankfurt on 2 December. Between 22 and 25 October, moreover, he was in Amsterdam, conducting three concerts that included the local premières of his First and Third Symphonies. And not only were there the performances, there were also the journeys there and back, journeys that Mahler always made by train, generally at night in order to save time. He knew the railway timetable backwards and derived considerable pleasure from working out the best connections for Alma. By the years around 1900, trains in Central Europe had increased in speed, and yet this did little to reduce the time that Mahler spent away from Vienna. He would travel to the town or city where the concert was to be held three or four days in advance in order to be able to find adequate time for the rehearsals, something unavoidably necessary given the novelty of the works and the demands that they placed on local forces, even in the case of those as well disposed as the Concertgebouw in Amsterdam.

Mahler allowed himself little time to relax, and the physical effort should not be underestimated. He would often arrive back in Vienna in the early morning after a poor night's sleep on a hard bed in an overheated or freezing sleeper compartment, after which he would quickly change and have breakfast before rushing back to his office at the Court Opera. There were other occasions when he would board the night train immediately after a performance in Vienna. Even at this stage in his career, there were reports that he was wearing himself out prematurely, and in the light of his increasingly numerous tours and manifold other commitments, such reports cannot be dismissed out of hand: the hectic nature of these tours coupled with his own health problems must have contributed to his growing sense of exhaustion. Moreover, he often attended performances of his works under other conductors, helping with the preparations and fortunately encountering colleagues willing to heed his advice.

But it was in 1906 and 1907 that Mahler's foreign tours became most frequent and disruptive. He conducted his Fifth Symphony in Antwerp on 5 March 1906, repeating the same programme in Amsterdam on the 8th and remaining in the Dutch capital until the 10th for a performance of *Das klagende Lied*. And on 27 May he conducted the first performance of his Sixth Symphony in Essen. Normally his summer holidays were sacrosanct, but out of his love of Mozart and as a favour to the organizer, Lilli Lehmann, he conducted two performances of *Le nozze di Figaro* at the Salzburg Mozart Festival – a forerunner of the Salzburg Festival – on 18 and 20 August. On 8 November he conducted the local première of the Sixth Symphony in Munich and three days later was in Brno for his First. On 3 December he gave the Third Symphony in Graz, returning to the town on the 23rd for a repeat performance. The following year was no less busy. On 14 January he was in Berlin for a performance of his Third Symphony and from there he travelled to Frankfurt for a performance of the Fourth on the 18th. Two days later he conducted the First in Linz. Between 19 March and 16 April he was in Italy, an extended leave of absence that incurred the ire of Prince Montenuovo, more of which in a moment.

If Mahler subjected himself to the hectic pace and exhausting rigours of these foreign tours, it was not because of the relatively modest fees that they commanded. His financial situation had improved to such an extent that he no longer needed to worry about providing for his family, although he must also have been thinking about the time when he stepped down as director of the Opera and would be drawing only a pension. Moreover, Mahler hated travelling. So irritable was he that the slightest disturbances annoyed him: either the temperature was too hot or too cold, or he was distracted by the conversation of his fellow travellers in an adjoining compartment. The seats in the trains were badly sprung and he generally abhorred hotels, with the result that, surprisingly enough, he was always willing to stay with even vague acquaintances, preferring the concomitant lack of independence to the horrors of a hotel room. First and foremost, it was his concern about his compositions that drove him on.

Ida Dehmel, the wife of the poet Richard Dehmel whose poems were set by a number of Mahler's colleagues, including Strauss, Schoenberg and even Reger, has left a diary account of a conversation that she had with Mahler in mid-March 1905, when he was in Hamburg to conduct his Fifth Symphony, a performance that proved extraordinarily successful. He then travelled with her to Berlin and in the course of the journey told her how much he hated travel. In that case, she asked, why was he always travelling? Was it because of his children? She meant the children of his Muse, prompting Mahler to ask whether she meant these or his real-life children. The answer, he explained, was both: when he could no longer depend on his income as director of the Vienna Opera (and this remark confirms that even in 1905 he was already thinking of a time when he would no longer hold such a post), he would have to earn his living as a conductor. But the second reason revolved around his children in a figurative sense, a point well illustrated by his Fifth Symphony, which had recently been performed in Prague and Berlin and in both cases had proved a resounding failure. Mahler was referring to the performances under Leo Blech in Prague in February 1905 and in Berlin under Nikisch the following March, though he could also have mentioned the performance under Ernst von Schuch in Dresden the previous January. Only when he himself conducted the work, as he had done in Hamburg, was the outcome any different: 'We musicians are worse off than writers in that respect. Anyone can read a book, but a musical score is a book with seven seals. Even the conductors who can decipher it present it to the public soaked in their own interpretations. For that reason there must be a tradition, and no one can create it but I.'[41]

To this reason we may add another one: as we have already noted, Mahler needed to form an aural impression of the work that he had created at his desk. Manifestly he was not one of those composers whose inner ear can conjure up an exact idea of what the music will sound like in a performance, something that is hardly surprising when we recall the power and at the same time the subtlety of Mahler's music. As a young conductor, Klaus Pringsheim – the twin brother of Katia Mann – won for himself the right to be accepted into Mahler's inner circle. He was present, therefore, in Essen in May 1906 when the Sixth Symphony was being rehearsed, and he later recalled how Mahler, in sheer desperation, kept begging the trumpets to play louder, even though the result sounded like a hellish and incoherent din in the empty rehearsal room. Only when the players could blow no harder did the sound suddenly make musical sense, something that even the professionals sitting in the hall had not thought possible. Episodes such as these meant on the one hand that Mahler was forced to litter his scores with performance markings and instructions to the musicians and on the other that he had to discover through trial and error what the music would sound like, something he could do only through performances and more especially through rehearsals under his own direction. The passage under discussion may illustrate this point. The *fortissimo* marking for the trumpets would have suggested to any other conductor that he could be satisfied with a normal *fortissimo* at this point. But Mahler realized at the rehearsal in Essen that this normal *fortissimo* was not enough and so he asked the musicians to explore areas that at the time were evidently regarded by most listeners and even by musicians as non-musical noise, and yet it was only now that he achieved what he wanted. The passage in question was presumably at figure 158 in the final movement, where Mahler has added the note 'Bells raised!' to the *fortississimo* marking in order to increase the dynamics yet further.

When necessary, Mahler could be ruthless with his scores and in theory he granted this privilege to other conductors too. A significant example of this is attested by the composer and musicologist Egon Wellesz, who was present at the rehearsals for a performance of the Second Symphony in Vienna in 1907. This was Mahler's final concert in the city, not, as Wellesz claims, the last performance of one of his works during Mahler's own lifetime. At the words 'O Tod, du Allbezwinger' in the final movement, the soprano line is supposed to emerge radiantly from the orchestra, but although the soloist had a beautiful and expressive voice, it was not very large or penetrating. The trombones that accompany this passage are marked *pianissimo*, a marking as unusual as it is hard to achieve. In spite of repeated attempts to get the balance right, Mahler still felt that his intentions had not been realized. Finally he decided to strike out the trombones and, adopting a solemn tone, exclaimed: 'Hail to the conductor who in the future will change my scores according to the acoustics of the concert hall.'[42] And yet if a conductor were to obey this injunction today, he would be universally condemned. The anecdote is revealing, for it shows that Mahler's supreme demand for clarity did not shy away from even the most radical measures.

In short, there were very good reasons why Mahler took increasing pains over the performance of his own works. The tremendous intensity that he

initially brought to his job in Vienna and the enthusiasm and willpower that
he invested in his model productions should not blind us to the fact that his
own compositions were understandably more important to him than the most
successful performance of *Fidelio*. It is hard to avoid the impression that this
insight became increasingly clear to him as he grew older and he realized that
he had less and less time to complete the creative task that had been allotted to
him on earth, especially when he was increasingly distracted from that task by
the drudgery of his work at the Vienna Court Opera and by the parochial
intrigues that beset him. When he thought about the future of his works, feelings of euphoric certainty in the spirit of 'My time will come' alternated with
moments of resignation. During his final months in Vienna, his old friend
from Hamburg, Josef Bohuslav Foerster, renewed contact with him and
recalled his delight at the prospect of seeing more of his friends in Vienna – at
this stage Mahler envisaged spending the winter months in New York and the
summer in Vienna and Maiernigg. But he was also depressed by the frequent
attacks in the Viennese press and as a result resigned about the future of his
works:

> If I had no children, it would never occur to me to bother with publishing my
> compositions. How long does a work survive? Fifty years? Then along come
> other composers, another time, another taste, other works. What's the use of
> it? I need such vast resources, and who will take the trouble to rehearse my
> works properly? And even if someone invests the enthusiasm and the time,
> how can I be certain that he will understand my intentions? Better no
> performance at all than a bad one.[43]

How differently things turned out! For fifty years Mahler's works eked out a
pitiful existence on the fringes of the mainstream repertory until suddenly,
almost exactly fifty years after his death, they began to exercise an influence
which half a century later shows no signs of losing its impact.

If, in 1905, Mahler admitted to Ida Dehmel that he was neglecting his duties
as director of the Opera in order to devote himself to his own work as a
composer, then it is hard not to take seriously the criticisms of certain sections
of the Viennese public concerning his increasingly frequent absences from the
city. It was only Mahler's egocentricity that prevented him from feeling guilty
on this score. Moreover, he had never showed any staying power in matters
unrelated to his music, and it is all too typical of his career as a conductor and
an administrator that he began with tremendous aplomb but all too soon
threw in the towel. He was a sprinter, not a long-distance runner, or perhaps it
would be more accurate to describe him as a long-distance runner who started
the race too quickly and failed to maintain his initial pace. Fatally, too, he

undertook a superhuman workload during his early years in Vienna, setting standards that he was neither able nor ultimately willing to maintain and thereby committing a tactical error that led to justified criticism. That this criticism was cloaked in the mantle of anti-Semitism and pure Viennese destructiveness is another story.

Eloquent evidence of this criticism comes in the form of a caricature that appeared in *Die Zeit* on 20 January 1907 with the caption 'A month with the Director of the Vienna Court Opera'. The image is divided into four sections, each one of which gives a different reason for the director's absence: during the first week he was away rehearsing his latest symphony with the combined – and fictitious – orchestras of Kötzschenbroda, Langensalza and Apolda; during the second week he was hunting down a new instrument capable of producing hitherto untried sonorities; during the third week he was fully occupied reading the proofs of his recently completely Ninth Symphony; and he spent the fourth week in the administrative offices of the Court Opera, recovering from his earlier exertions.[44] Mahler knew very well that his increasingly frequent absences opened him up to criticism, but at some stage this became a matter of indifference to him, making it likely that his decision to leave his post was taken as early as 1905.

The Netherlands as an Oasis of Calm

Between 1903 and 1909 Mahler visited the Netherlands on four separate occasions, finding in its capital a haven of peace and in the circle of acquaintances around Willem Mengelberg and Alphons Diepenbrock a degree of friendship and love that he could not count on elsewhere. He had met Mengelberg at the first performance of his Third Symphony in Krefeld in June 1902, when the audience also included the two Dutch conductors Henri Viotta and Martin Heuckeroth, who were active in The Hague and Arnheim respectively. Diepenbrock was not present on this occasion but joined the group soon afterwards. It was presumably Mengelberg who invited Mahler to conduct his own works in the Netherlands.[45] He had been born in Utrecht in 1871, though his family came from the Rhineland. By 1895 he had succeeded Willem Kes as principal conductor of the recently founded Amsterdam Concertgebouw Orchestra, a post he retained until 1945, providing the orchestra with a rare sense of continuity and turning it into the internationally acclaimed body of players that it remains to this day.

Mengelberg was famous and, indeed, notorious for the meticulous preparation of his concert programmes, and there can be few other conductors whose scores are so peppered with entries relating to the tiniest details, turning them into multicoloured demonstrations of calligraphic mastery. On this point, too, he had much in common with Mahler, whose own scores were marked up in much the same way. There were times when Mengelberg would drive his musicians to distraction because he obliged them to spend up to half an hour tuning their instruments and talked incessantly during the rehearsals, so firmly convinced was he that all the important points could be communicated verbally. Together with Bruno Walter, he was the leading Mahler conductor of his generation, quite apart from which he also introduced Dutch audiences to the latest trends in symphonic music in the form of works by Debussy, Reger, Ravel, Stravinsky and Strauss. For a time he also conducted the Frankfurt Museum Orchestra and, in the 1920s, the New York Philharmonic, a commitment he apparently relinquished because of disagreements with Arturo Toscanini, who was the orchestra's other main conductor.

Mengelberg limited his activities to the concert hall and avoided the opera house altogether. Between the wars he was one of the most prominent of all European conductors, his emotional approach to the works that he conducted inviting comparisons with Wilhelm Furtwängler. Mengelberg's final years were overshadowed by controversy, for he maintained his links with German culture even after the Nazis had come to power and occupied the Netherlands. He even conducted in Nazi Germany. He was accused of being a collaborator and openly reviled by the many Dutch nationals who opposed the German occupation, with the result that a man who for fifty years had been the uncrowned king of his country's musical life was banned from making any further public appearances. He retired to Switzerland and died there, consumed by resentment, in 1951, almost exactly forty years after Mahler's own death. It remains unclear how he dealt with the fact that the works of a friend whom he had revered more than any other could not be performed in Germany, but there is a surviving recording that suggests that at least in the as yet independent Netherlands he retained his love of Mahler's music, for on 11 September 1939 – a few days after the outbreak of the war – he made the first complete recording of the Fourth Symphony, a release which in spite of its highly subjective and by modern standards far from faithful interpretation retains its special status among historic Mahler recordings: the fact that Mengelberg had heard Mahler himself conduct this work means that his recording undoubtedly contains much food for thought.

It was in Krefeld, therefore, in June 1902 that Mahler and his Dutch admirers first came into contact with each other. Mengelberg invited him to conduct two concerts with his Amsterdam orchestra in October 1903. The programmes would include the First and Third Symphonies. Unknown to Mahler, Martin Heuckeroth was currently planning to give the Dutch première of the Third Symphony in Arnheim a week earlier. It says much for the spirit of friendship that existed among these Dutch musicians that the rivalry caused no ill feeling, and it is said that when Mahler arrived in Amsterdam, he greeted Heuckeroth with the words: 'So you're Heuckeroth? I've heard it went very well. Where did you find the courage?'[46] Among the audience at the Amsterdam performance of the Third Symphony was Alphons Diepenbrock, who was to become the leading Mahlerian in the Netherlands after Mengelberg, albeit one whose views could also be coloured by criticism. Still largely unknown outside his native Holland, Diepenbrock was the first Dutch composer of international standing after centuries of obscurity. Two years younger than Mahler, he had a degree in classical languages and was qualified as a teacher. As a composer, he was largely self-taught, but on completing his first major work, a monumental Mass, in 1891, he devoted himself for the most part to composition, while giving private lessons in Latin and Greek in order to support his family. In his intellectual voraciousness, which found expression in many reviews and essays on questions of philosophy, history, literature and religion, he had much in common with Arrigo Boito, the late Verdi's highly gifted librettist and a distinguished composer in his own right. For the most part, Diepenbrock wrote vocal music for the concert hall, setting himself the highest standards with his choice of writers: Goethe, Hölderlin, Novalis and Nietzsche. His Novalis and Nietzsche settings, especially his cantata *Im großen Schweigen*, are all of the highest quality, their individual and instantly recognizable musical language springing from an amalgam of Wagner's orchestra and the influence of Strauss, Debussy and Mahler. Unfortunately gramophone recordings in recent years have failed to bring about a revival of Diepenbrock's fortunes.

Diepenbrock was fascinated by Mahler from the very outset. In a profoundly perceptive and keenly worded letter to one of his pupils he summed up his impressions of the Amsterdam performance of the Third Symphony in October 1903:

Last week I was introduced to Gustav Mahler. This man has left a deep impression on me. I heard his Third Symphony and admire it. The opening movement contains much that is ugly, but at a second and third hearing, when one knows what he is trying to say, it acquires a different aspect. Mahler is very simple and does not pretend to be a celebrity but acts his normal self. I have the greatest admiration for him. . . . Good-natured and naïve, sometimes even childlike, he looks out at the world with fairytale eyes from behind large crystal spectacles. He is modern in every respect. He *believes* in the future, which left me feeling that I am no more than a grieving 'Romantic'. I can tell you that his presence did me a world of good. I told him as much in a short and fairly emphatic letter, telling him that his music seems to possess the gift of 'transforming people' and of providing a sense of 'catharsis'. That is no small achievement.

Diepenbrock then added a few perceptive comments on the differences between Strauss and Mahler, arguing that the latter was almost entirely innocent of the 'neo-Prussian nickel-plating' that characterized Strauss's tone poems. Strauss had a telephone line to heaven that employed the usual urban networks, whereas Mahler's connection was much more direct.[47] By this date in his career, Mahler was far more wary of getting close to people than he had been in his youth, but he immediately felt a great fondness for both Diepenbrock and Mengelberg, while noting that in any exchange of ideas he could explore far greater depths with the former than with the more naïve Mengelberg, who was scarcely an intellectual at all. Whenever Mahler was in the Netherlands, he always ensured that Diepenbrock and his wife were invited to all the meals that he attended. It was only logical, therefore, that Diepenbrock should represent the Dutch Mahlerians at Mahler's burial service in Grinzing. But Mahler soon became friendly with Mengelberg too, and even during his first visit to Amsterdam he was invited to stay privately with the Mengelbergs. Such was his loathing of hotel accommodation that he invariably accepted these and similar invitations in spite of a number of unfortunate experiences in this regard. But with the Mengelbergs he was always happy: they lived only a few minutes away from the Concertgebouw, and their apartment was so large that Mahler's need for peace and quiet could be respected. On his final visit in October 1909, he wrote one of his whimsical entries in the Mengelbergs' guestbook: 'Ich lob' mir Hotel Mengelberg / das sicher ist der Engel Werk, / damit ein armer Musikant / findt manches mal der Heimat Land' ('I praise the Mengelberg Hotel that is undoubtedly the work of angels, so that a poor musician may find much to remind him of home there').

Mahler was first invited to Holland in the autumn of 1903 but was not entirely enthusiastic at the prospect. One of his favourite novels was *Max Havelaar* (1860), a work critical of Holland and her colonies, by Edward Douwes Dekker, who wrote under the name of Multatuli, which in Latin means 'I have borne much'. An important Dutch contribution to world literature, the novel revolves around its hero, Max Havelaar, and his foil, the narrow-minded Droogstoppel. Ever since Mahler and Alma had read the book, the name Droogstoppel had been synonymous in their minds with aggressively middle-class philistines in general. Mahler could not avoid detecting a certain prosperous narrow-mindedness in Amsterdam too and unchivalrously placed Mengelberg's wife among their number. But such was his initial enthusiasm for the country that he even considered settling in the Netherlands when he left Vienna, a plan which, not entirely serious, was soon abandoned. No doubt the Dutch countryside bordering on the North Sea failed to endear itself to a man who was fond of the Austrian mountains and lakes above all else. Even so, his visits to the museums of Amsterdam and his excursions to the North Sea, which are documented in photographs, gave him considerable pleasure, and he spoke enthusiastically of the wonderfully hazy light on the coast.

So successful were the performances of the First and Third Symphonies that Mahler was back in Amsterdam by October 1904. He was particularly pleased with the orchestra, whose Mahler tradition has been maintained to the present day by Bernard Haitink, Riccardo Chailly and Mariss Jansons. Dutch audiences, conversely, were less unanimous in their praise, a point made by Mengelberg himself, though Mahler's letters make no mention of this. Clearly it was enough for him to know that the orchestra was behind him, that an important conductor was championing his cause and that critics and a section of the public were willing to follow him – this meant infinitely more than he had ever encountered in Berlin or even Vienna. Moreover, Mengelberg may have been exaggerating in an attempt to highlight his own persistent efforts in support of Mahler's cause. In 1904 Mahler was able to combine his visit to the Netherlands with the first performance of his Fifth Symphony with the Gürzenich Orchestra in Cologne, whither he travelled on 12 October, only days after his epoch-making production of *Fidelio* in Vienna. Alma was prevented from accompanying him by one of her many illnesses. The Cologne performance took place on 18 October 1904, and the very next day Mahler continued his journey to Amsterdam, where he was warmly welcomed by his new friends. As before, he stayed with the Mengelbergs, and on this occasion he does not seem to have been unduly worried by Tilly Mengelberg's boorishness: 'Such kind, unpretentious people,' he described the couple in a note to Alma.[48]

Elisabeth Diepenbrock's diary entries for this period have survived and leave us in no doubt about the depth of her understanding for Mahler. Fons, as she called her husband, had an opportunity to play through his *Te Deum* to Mahler, who was sufficiently impressed to recommend the work to his colleague in Vienna, Franz Schalk, the conductor of the Gesellschaft der Musikfreunde's chorus. Mahler's enthusiasm was never based on tactical considerations or on the need to be polite, and so we may take his judgement seriously, not that it helped, for Schalk returned the score, refusing to conduct it but without giving any reason. As Mahler explained in a letter to his wife, the programme for the first Amsterdam concert on 23 October was nothing if not curious:

Just imagine, the programme for Sunday is as follows:
1. Symphony no. IV by G. Mahler
    Interval
2. Symphony no. IV by G. Mahler
   What do you think of that?

They're playing my work twice in a row – after the interval we start all over again. I'll be interested to see whether the audience will react more warmly the second time.[49]

Mahler was not mistaken in his optimistic assessment, for on the day after the concert we find him writing to Alma to report that the audience's reaction had been exactly as he had hoped. When compared with the 'imbecilic' audience in Cologne, which had responded with remarkable reserve to his Fifth Symphony, he felt that in spite of all its philistinism, his audience in Amsterdam could offer him something that he could not find even in Vienna. The audience's enthusiasm increased after the interval, and since he was pleased with the Dutch soloist, Alida Oldenboom-Lutkemann, a small and fat soprano with a voice of bell-like purity, the end of the work recalled a painting on a gold ground – exactly the sort of impression that he had envisaged. The performance was considerably more successful than that of the Third Symphony the previous year, when opinions had been divided. Two days later Mahler conducted his Second Symphony. This, too, was repeated, although not, of course, at the same concert but on the following evening. This represented a busy schedule, leaving Mahler with less time for socializing than in 1903. In spite of this he held a number of discussions with Diepenbrock that went deeper than those he was able to have with Mengelberg, whose taste in furnishings Mahler mocked. Mengelberg's father restored churches and had furnished his son's apartment in a neo-Gothic style, which for the Secessionist-minded Mahler, was exactly what Mengelberg deserved.

Mahler's next visit to the Netherlands took place eighteen months later, in March 1906, when he travelled directly from Vienna to Antwerp to conduct his Fifth Symphony, a work that the Berlin Philharmonic had performed in the town for spa guests in June 1905 under the now largely unknown conductor August Scharrer. From Antwerp, Mahler travelled to Amsterdam for performances of his Fifth Symphony, the *Kindertotenlieder* and two other songs. The soloist was the Dutch baritone Gerard Zalsman, who took over from the indisposed Friedrich Weidemann. As on his previous visits, Mahler was well satisfied with the performance and with the audience reaction. Two performances of Mahler's early cantata *Das klagende Lied* were planned for 10 and 11 March, but for reasons that remain unclear Mahler was summoned back to Vienna on ostensibly urgent business, leaving Mengelberg to take over the second performance. Mahler had, however, prepared the orchestra and chorus, and so the performance passed off without mishap. It is conceivable that he had to return to sort out problems in the run-up to a new production of *Le nozze di Figaro* and to resolve various disagreements that had arisen at the Court Opera, where the undiplomatic Roller had designed costumes for the planned

Lohengrin that were too expensive and too heavy for the singers to wear. He had also barred overweight chorus members from taking part in the performances. Mahler had to intervene. This was by no means the first time that Roller's brusqueness and arrogance had caused Mahler problems and got on his nerves. Elisabeth Diepenbrock reports that the *Kindertotenlieder* were not well received in Amsterdam and that after each song there was a rush for the exits. Diepenbrock allegedly told Mahler afterwards: 'I envy you your enemies.' But there is no mention of any of this in Mahler's own letters from this period. Even Diepenbrock initially had problems with the Fifth, although he later came round. It is interesting that alone among Mahler's contemporaries he recognized that the Adagietto was a love song.

The close and cordial relations between Mahler and the Netherlands now suffered their longest interruption, all plans for a return visit foundering on various obstacles, not least of which was Mahler's contract with New York, which kept him away from Europe for long periods, especially during the concert season. Not until October 1909 did Mahler and his Dutch friends meet again for the fourth and final time. His visit to see Sigmund Freud in Leiden in August 1910 took place amid great secrecy, and no one in Amsterdam knew about it. Strangely enough, there had in the meantime been something of a hiatus in Dutch interest in Mahler's music, the only recorded performance between January 1907 and October 1909 being the Fourth Symphony that the largely inexperienced Diepenbrock conducted on 26 March 1908. Mengelberg warned him not to undertake a piece that contains pitfalls for even experienced conductors, but his advice went unheeded. It was in this context that Mengelberg remarked that Amsterdam audiences were not unequivocal in their support of Mahler. This may also explain why Mengelberg did not wish to link his name and reputation to Mahler's music to the exclusion of all else and why he maintained a certain reserve during this period. Moreover, he took up a new post in January 1907, dividing his time between Amsterdam and Frankfurt, where he was principal guest conductor of the Museum Orchestra.

Mahler left Vienna for Amsterdam on 26 September 1909 and was met at the station by Mengelberg. As before, he stayed with the couple: 'The Mengelbergs are as warm-hearted and hospitable as ever, in a way that only the Dutch understand. Diepenbrock is a joy: profound and loyal.'[50] Mahler was also touched to discover that the orchestra had retained all its old loyalty. The players sent a deputation, asking him to conduct not only his Seventh Symphony, as planned, but also some other works by Beethoven and Wagner, so that they might have a chance to play this music under him. But the young Max Tak, who was then one of the orchestra's second violinists, reports that Mahler had lost none of his old tactlessness, and when he made fun of Mengelberg's habit of placing undue emphasis on metrical divisions in a score – and this while Mengelberg himself was in the hall – the orchestra took offence. One has the impression that as so often Mahler was simply oblivious to what he was doing, but the result was a degree of tension that was only resolved at the successful performances of the symphony, first in The Hague, and then in Amsterdam itself. Tak also reports that whereas Mahler's conducting style had formerly been restless and even fidgety, by 1909 he had discovered an almost eerie calm. During his first visit to the Netherlands, Mengelberg had asked him why he gripped his lapel with his free left hand, prompting Mahler to claim that this was a way of forcing himself to remain calm. By 1909 he was conducting almost entirely with his eyes and making only minimal use of the baton in his right hand. In this there is a striking parallel with Strauss, whose stoic deportment on the podium is attested by surviving film footage – what would we not give to have similar footage of Mahler? Even so, Tak went on, Mahler's beat was now stricter than it ever was with Toscanini, notorious though the latter was for his fanatical concern for precision.

One of Diepenbrock's pupils, Balthazar Verhagen, attended the performance in The Hague and, observing Mahler from close quarters, later recalled the tremendous impression left on him by his conducting. And he too attests that Mahler's style had changed a great deal, striking him as more relaxed than before. During a coach ride to Scheveningen, Mahler began to shiver and asked the driver to find a sunnier route. When Verhagen pointed out that the sun had already set, Mahler had smiled sadly and commented: 'Ah, no, people can't give us the sun.' Elisabeth Diepenbrock, too, reports that Mahler looked unwell and no longer trusted his own health, which is no wonder when we recall that since his last trip to the Netherlands he had been diagnosed as having a weak heart. While visiting another acquaintance, Mahler weighed himself, so we know that in 1909 he weighed sixty-one kilos (134 pounds, or nine and a half stone): given his height and slim build, this hardly suggests that he was seriously underweight. Indeed, Mahler himself is said to have expressed his satisfaction that he had not lost any weight. The carefree mood of earlier visits could not be recaptured. Mahler's walk in Scheveningen, with its overcast sky and shuttered hotels, depressed him. The North Sea in October can seem inconsolable to anyone fond of the green pastures and sun of the Alps in summer. 'I've no wish ever to return here,' Mahler, chilled to the marrow, is said to have exclaimed. His wish was to come true. It was left to Verhagen to sum up the mood of the Dutch Mahlerians: 'The restless wanderer fell like a meteor into our tranquil lives in The Hague. He hurled at our heads his mighty Seventh Symphony and silently departed – for ever.'[51] Having represented his fellow Dutch Mahlerians at Mahler's burial in Grinzing, Diepenbrock penned an obituary that expresses all the love and respect of the composer's friends in the Netherlands in language as simple as it is moving.[52]

The Finances of the Director of the Vienna Court Opera

At the end of May 1904, the general administrator of all the court theatres in Vienna, August Plappart, gave an interview to the *Neue Freie Presse* – the flagship of the liberal Viennese dailies – in which he expressed his satisfaction at the finances of his two biggest theatres, the Burgtheater and the Court Opera:

> We have every reason to be satisfied with the state of the Court Theatres. In both the Burg and the Opera the receipts have risen considerably, and in both theatres our expectations were exceeded. A few figures will illustrate this. In the Opera in the period from 1 January to 17 May, our takings amounted to 715,809 crowns. We had budgeted for receipts of 666,900 crowns in this period. So that in these four-and-a-half months the Opera showed a surplus of 48,909 crowns. In every single month the target was exceeded in both the Burg and the Opera. And the target for the coming year is always based on the receipts for the previous year. From 1 January 1903 to end of December the Opera's takings were 1,543,665 crowns. The target for this period was 1,485,900 crowns.[53]

Plappart then went on to draw attention to two facts that are as important today as they were a century ago: in spite of these healthy receipts, there could never be any question of a profit, because the opera house's budget amounted to 10,000 crowns a day. And, as the only fly in the ointment, new operas – unlike new plays – were never a box-office draw. With the exception of *Les Contes d'Hoffmann* – new to Vienna but not a new work – contemporary operas never caught on. Fortunately, audiences still flocked to the great repertory operas, a gratifying reflection of Mahler's successes with Mozart, Beethoven and Wagner.

In a word, the general administrator's office was more than happy with Mahler's directorship in 1903 and 1904, at least as far as the box office was concerned. The speed with which this situation could change has been meticulously documented by Franz Willnauer in his study of Mahler's years at the Court Opera.[54] The system that was used to calculate the company's future financial needs meant that then, as now, success was penalized. In budgetary terms, the Viennese Court Theatres operated according to the calendar year running from January to December rather than by season. If a year was particularly successful, the theatre was punished by having its projected income raised for the following year. This target would be reduced only if the theatre were less successful. Failures may have incurred censure but at least they lowered the bar when it came to planning for the future. Audits, conversely, were drawn up on the basis of the monthly box-office receipts and submitted in the middle of the year following the one to which the figures related. The projection fixed the level of the receipts that needed to be achieved, while at the same time restricting the house's outgoings in terms of staffing levels and other expenses. Mahler's successes meant that the projection was constantly being raised, but at the same time the company's outgoings had to remain unchanged: enhanced success was to be achieved with the same level of subsidy, the aim being to ensure that the grants awarded to all the court theatres to cover their inevitable deficits were kept as small as possible and even reduced in size.

A glance at the Court Opera's finances between 1903 and 1908 reveals that a deficit of 212,000 crowns was agreed for 1903. In the event, the shortfall turned out to be 264,000 crowns, requiring an extra subsidy of 52,000 crowns, an over-spend that seems to have been regarded as a venial sin. The following year, 1904, Mahler in fact achieved a feat beyond the capabilities of any present-day opera-house administrator: whereas the agreed deficit was 186,000 crowns, the actual shortfall turned out to be only 149,000 crowns: against all expectations, Mahler had helped the general administrator's office to save 37,000 crowns.

The rude awakening came in 1905. The projected deficit was again reduced, this time to 170,000 crowns, but on this occasion it was exceeded to the tune of 258,000 crowns, making a total shortfall of 428,000 crowns. Although Mahler made savings in 1906, he was unable to make up for the earlier mismanagement. Rumours about the director's failing fortunes attached themselves to these figures and soon reached the outside world, and there is no doubt that this, too, contributed to Mahler's increasing weariness with his position. It suddenly counted for nothing that he had spent the last eight years bringing in more money and running the company more efficiently. The poor figures for 1905 were repeated in 1907, by which date his heart was no longer in his job and he was absent for long periods. It is not entirely clear what went wrong in 1905, but three factors may perhaps explain the situation. First, Alfred Roller, who had helped to guarantee the company's artistic successes, was by no means unassuming in his demands. His surviving estimate for 1905 amounts to no less than 282,000 crowns. Second, the agreed deficit for 1905 was the punishment for a string of successes that meant that future estimates were increasingly curtailed. And, third, Mahler's long-term planning – it was he who initiated the modern practice of planning for more than a single season at a time – was artistically justified but financially imbalanced. Of the six new productions of 1905, four were the sort of new works that were feared by Plappart and his box-office managers, while only two were pillars of the repertory. True, Mahler had planned a major Mozart cycle for 1905 and 1906, promising (and delivering) full houses, but most of these productions were scheduled for 1906, hence the success of that year's season. In 1905, conversely, the company staged Pfitzner's *Die Rose vom Liebesgarten*, Ermanno Wolf-Ferrari's *Le donne curiose* (performed in German as *Die neugierigen Frauen*) and, in the form of a double bill, Leo Blech's *Das war ich* and Eugen d'Albert's *Die Abreise*. None of these proved a hit at the box office.

Ironically, then, it was Mahler's promotion of contemporary works that earned him his superiors' greatest censure, a situation made all the more ironical by the fact that with the exception of *Salome*, which he was prevented from staging, Mahler knew that none of these works was a masterpiece, hence his half-hearted efforts on their behalf. By law, the general administrator's office was required to communicate these findings to the comptroller's office, and it is to the credit of the latter that its records contain no criticism of Mahler, even though Plappart was no Mahlerian. Even so, the shortfall was so scandalous that Montenuovo and Mahler undoubtedly discussed the situation, although no record of their meeting survives. It is possible, however, that Montenuovo's blind faith in Mahler was suddenly called into question in the middle of 1906, when the figures for 1905 were submitted. However controversial, Mahler could easily be defended as long as he produced outstanding artistic and financial results, but a director hoppled by a financial deficit was altogether more vulnerable. There were two visible consequences of these problems: ticket prices were increased from the autumn of 1906, and the Court Opera's finances were subjected to closer scrutiny. Comparisons with the continuing success of the Burgtheater must have been difficult to stomach. We shall have no difficulty in imagining that Mahler's already waning interest in his post suffered a further setback at this juncture. If he had been honest with himself, he would have had to admit that the financial burden had arisen not least because he had unduly slackened the reins. In other words, the 1905 shortfall may well have been an additional factor in his decision to stand down in 1907.

Enemies and Friends

Mahler rarely made it easy for his friends to remain his friends, whereas he generally made it easy for his enemies to remain his enemies. Time and again he antagonized and frightened away even the most well-meaning contemporaries, for he had at least two qualities that impeded his dealings with others: he had much of the egocentricity of the genius, even if it fell short of the ruthless exploitation and Machiavellian manipulativeness of a man like Wagner, and he could not brook dishonesty, and so he set no store by sparing people's feelings when he thought that they deserved to be told the truth. As a young man Mahler was open and brutally honest, and he expected others to behave likewise. When he discovered that they rarely did, he became mistrustful and reserved, renewing contact with his student friends to the exclusion of all others, while never abandoning his own harshness of character or honesty of outlook. It is significant in this context that he made few new friends after he turned thirty. He was never polite for tactical reasons if he could not justify such an approach on practical or personal grounds. This did not preclude him from deploying his austere charms in seeking out fellow combatants and supporters. During his time in Vienna, for example, he courted a number of journalists, hoping to win them over to his cause, but quickly letting such people know that they were no longer welcome whenever the hopes that he had placed in them were disappointed, even when he knew that in dropping them, he may well have gained yet another influential enemy.

Mahler's famous fickleness was often due to this process of recognition, and yet there were other contacts that broke down for no apparent reason, so that even the people concerned were left at a loss. If he became annoyed with a person without the latter understanding why, then the breach was generally irreparable. In the case of the group of friends associated with Siegfried Lipiner, it was clear from an early stage that he was prepared to drop his closest and oldest acquaintances once he gained the impression – in this case it was the correct impression – that they had behaved badly towards his young wife. Mahler was incapable of talking such problems through. With Lipiner he was belatedly reconciled, but no such reconciliation took place with Natalie Bauer-Lechner.

Mahler was capable of the most raging fury – one is tempted to describe it as the rage of Achilles. Richard Specht, who knew him well and who wrote the first full-length study of Mahler, attributed both his infinite kindness and his insane rages to childlike aspects of his character, reminding us of Diepenbrock's reference to Mahler's 'good-natured' qualities and his 'fairytale eyes'. According to Specht, 'Just like a child, he would suddenly become trusting and then equally suddenly mistrustful. This mistrust could easily be stirred by an expression of casual malice or even an apparently involuntary smile or glance; and it could rarely be undone. Many were the sins that were committed against him and others as a result of this.'[55] Mahler's brusqueness and capriciousness were both childlike reactions to the world around him, making him easy to influence. He had the unfortunate tendency in everyday administrative matters to rely on incompetent advisers and assistants, which he did not only for the sake of his own convenience but also in order to avoid having to deal with the all-too-human aspects of life. He was remarkably short-sighted when it came to understanding human nature. He hated larger gatherings and regarded small talk as a criminal waste of time, so that if he had been sitting in a corner at a party and heard a remark that fired him with enthusiasm, he would leap to his feet and draw the person aside, forcing them

18 Mahler in Vienna, 1907, one of a famous series of shots of the composer in the rooms of the Court Opera.

19 Cartoon of Mahler from a Viennese newspaper. The caption reads 'Reichmann is going too!' and (*below*) 'The Jew Mahler as a scarecrow driving away our best singers'. Theodor Reichmann was a leading baritone at the Court Opera who had difficulties with Mahler.

20 Alfred Roller's design for the prison courtyard in Beethoven's *Fidelio*, mixed technique (1904).

21 The viola player, Natalie Bauer-Lechner, Mahler's closest confidante for many years. She was hopelessly in love with the composer.

22 'The Knight-in-armour, with Pity and Ambition', a detail of Gustav Klimt's monumental Beethoven frieze inside the Secession Building, Vienna. Klimt chose the knight figure as his contribution to a volume prepared for Mahler's fiftieth birthday (1910).

23 In the garden at Carl Moll's villa, with (*l. to r.*) Gustav Mahler, Max Reinhardt, Carl Moll and Hans Pfitzner.

24 Alma and her two daughters, Maria (*l.*) and Anna (*r.*), in 1906.

25 Mahler with his daughter Anna at Toblach in 1909.

26 Mahler, New York, 1909, principal conductor of the New York Philharmonic.

27 Cartoon from the time of the first performance of the Sixth Symphony in Vienna in January 1907. The caption reads: 'Oh my God, I have forgotten the motor horn! I can now write another symphony.'

28 Mahler conducting a rehearsal for his Eighth Symphony in the Munich Exhibition Hall, 1910.

29 One of the last photographs of Mahler, possibly taken in October 1910 on his final voyage from Europe to New York or on the return journey, April 1911. His face is already listless, his strength failing; he stands in his characteristic pose.

30 Auguste Rodin's bust of Mahler (1909).

31 Mahler's grave, Grinzing, Vienna. The stone was designed by Josef Hoffmann.

to divulge their opinions and showering them with his own. He was like a child assessing the usefulness of a new playmate. If at their next meeting he realized that he had encountered only a chance echo of his own ideas, he would drop the person in question and not bother with him again, once more incurring the charge of capriciousness that was repeatedly levelled at him. In Vienna it was rumoured that Mahler could be won over to a particular cause if the supplicant were to walk in front of him or behind him in the street or opera house and whistle a motif from one of his works. If he allowed himself to be taken in by such tricks, it was not out of superficial vanity but from child-like enthusiasm – only his most embittered enemies ever accused him of vanity. He was never able to distinguish properly between toadyism, fawning subservience and genuine affection.

When he realized too late that he had been deceived by other people, he would be incandescent with rage. Such rage was directed not only against the people who had failed to live up to his own high standards whereby all men were brothers, but also against himself for having allowed himself to be duped in the first place. At such times he could lose all sense of proportion and become unjust. Self-criticism and self-examination were alien to his nature. Richard Specht doubted whether Mahler ever really got to know other people. Alma's diaries are the clearest possible indication that she too had the feeling that her husband did not know her. If he valued another person and if that person let it be known that he was in difficulties, he could be inordinately helpful. The only entirely positive thing that the otherwise ambivalent members of the Court Opera orchestra and Vienna Philharmonic had to say about him was that no previous conductor had taken such an interest in their social situation and attempted to improve it, but they did not thank him for it. But if he helped someone who was not a member of his own circle of friends, he would do so in a more or less absent-minded way, implying that he was not to be troubled again. Specht is no doubt right to describe this attitude as the kindness of the egocentric unwilling to see the sufferings of others and at pains to put them from his mind. He was intolerant of other people's illnesses: 'Illness is a lack of talent,' he is reported to have said, presumably regarding such illnesses as a dereliction of duty. If a singer or an instrumentalist were to cancel, then that person was deemed to have sinned against the sacred task of serving art.

From that point of view it is entirely understandable that Mahler felt a hypochondriac's concern about the well-being of his own person. He knew how weak his own constitution was – if he struggled to overcome this weakness and punished his body mercilessly, it was because that body was not allowed to fail in its duty to serve the creative spirit. If he tried as far as possible to sweep aside all human limitations – and his work as director of the Vienna Court Opera brought him face to face with such limitations every working day – it was because they prevented him from carrying out his one true task in life. Specht reports that Mahler would adopt a utilitarian standpoint when assessing the people who were not members of his immediate circle of friends and judge them according to the ideas or information that they could offer him in return. Occasionally this system would break down, and he might find himself talking to someone about the state of music in Vienna only to find that the other person wanted to discuss natural philosophy, or someone whom he had planned to consult on a new diet suddenly turned out to be familiar with Mahler's music. He would then react with bewilderment and withdraw into his shell because his insistence on pigeonholing people had been called into question, requiring him to rethink his whole approach in ways that would cost him time and effort.

Mahler needlessly made enemies for himself even among those people who had not already shown him rejection and hatred. The composer Franz Schmidt apparently witnessed this for himself. Although his account is subjective and cannot be authenticated by other surviving sources, it none the less sounds plausible. Schmidt's fortunes have risen in recent years, and it is now generally felt that among Austrian composers of the turn of the century he ranks second only to Mahler. His great oratorio *Das Buch mit sieben Siegeln* has emerged from the shadows, and his Third and Fourth Symphonies are undoubtedly exceptional pieces. Thanks in part to Schmidt's own attempts at self-promotion, he was held up as Mahler's symphonic antithesis both during the latter's lifetime and more especially after his death, ultimately coming to be regarded as the guardian of the chauvinist Austrian legacy in contrast to that of the 'Jewish cosmopolitan' Mahler. When Schmidt's First Symphony won the Philharmonic Prize in 1900, this was seen in many quarters as a declaration of war on Mahler and his music. A sort of Austrian Pfitzner, Schmidt unfortunately fulfilled the hopes that were placed in him and in 1938 began to write a Hitlerian cantata, *Deutsche Auferstehung* (*German Resurrection*). An outstanding cellist in his youth, he joined the Vienna Court Opera orchestra in this capacity in 1896 and has left an embittered account of the difficulties caused him by the hostility of the orchestra's leader, Arnold Rosé. Schmidt wanted his de facto position as principal cellist to be formally recognized and, insisting on his rights, complained to Mahler, who hated such confrontations and left them to be dealt with by Rosé and the orchestra's board of directors. When Schmidt turned up in Mahler's office, the latter is said to have leapt to his feet and shouted at the cellist: 'What do you mean? Are you setting me conditions? Are you trying to play hard to get?' Schmidt's insistence infuriated Mahler yet further: 'You! You've exhausted my patience! Be careful! If you refuse to play for me or say one more word, you can consider yourself dismissed! I'm warning you!'[56]

This was presumably not an isolated case, and it certainly helps to explain why Mahler always had problems with collectives, especially in the form of orchestras and choruses. His conflicts with the Court Opera orchestra and the practically identical Philharmonic were the result of his inability to strike the right note with musicians who were musically and intellectually his inferiors – in this regard, Schmidt was probably the exception. When musicians realize that a conductor does not appreciate them, they can easily fall back on power games. Schmidt had made the mistake of thinking that he could influence Mahler by confronting him in person and that as the orchestra's best cellist he would get his way. But in this he misjudged Mahler, who was incapable of dealing with such situations. Like a terrier forced into a corner, he bared his teeth and went on the attack. Although he did not make good his threat of dismissing Schmidt, the cellist was now persona non grata. At the same time, Mahler had made an enemy of a man who was growing increasingly influential on the city's musical scene. He never forgave a person for driving him into a corner. Of course, he would have done better to find a new supporter, but in all decisive situations tactical considerations were always secondary.

But Mahler was also adept at intimidating former friends and supporters to such an extent that they abandoned him and even became his enemies. His dealings with the influential critic Ludwig Karpath represent a slightly less extreme form of this particular behavioural pattern. As we have seen, Karpath had been able to pull a few strings at the time of Mahler's appointment in Vienna. Mahler knew this and was correspondingly grateful, but an immoderate display of thanks would have contradicted his conviction that he owed that appointment not least to his own intrinsic merits. At this point Karpath committed a decisive error. At a party held shortly before the announcement of Mahler's engagement, Karpath boasted that it was to him that Mahler owed his appointment in Vienna. Alma, who was present on this occasion, passed this on to Mahler, who duly summoned Karpath to his offices. The result, according to Karpath's reminiscences, was a scene similar to the one that unfolded between Mahler and Schmidt. Having vented his fury, Mahler ended the encounter with a few words of reconciliation, but Karpath now felt offended that his role in Mahler's appointment had been belittled, and he was also angry with Alma for acting as a sneak. By his own account, he now avoided all further contact with Mahler, a point which, much to his credit, he later came to regret. Whatever the individual facts of the matter, Mahler could easily have picked up the threads of their former relations and renewed contact with a man who had once been one of his most impassioned supporters. But he did nothing at all. Karpath was not so dishonest as to align himself with Mahler's enemies, but his enthusiasm for his former hero cooled considerably in consequence of this episode.

As for Mahler's real enemies in Vienna, their number was legion. Their group psychopathology is worthy of a study of its own and would involve an examination of its motives and evasions, and of the hatred, betrayal and character assassination that were carried out in the name of journalism. Anti-Semitism was clearly a factor, albeit of varying intensity, but there were other reasons, too, for the hatred to which Mahler was exposed. Writing in January 1906, the ever perceptive Hermann Bahr observed that:

> Once again Mahler is being hounded, hounded, hounded! Why do they hate him so? Well, why do they hate Klimt so? They hate everyone who tries to be true to himself. That is what they cannot bear. 'Self-willed' and 'obstinate': the words themselves are a criticism. They cannot bear someone to have an opinion or a will of his own. They cannot bear the idea that someone should try to be free. And yet they wish they were free themselves. But do not dare. And are secretly ashamed that they are so cowardly. And avenge their bad conscience on the brave.[57]

Bahr was an astute psychologist and there is no doubt that he has struck a note of fundamental importance here. The hatred felt by people who were aware of their own inferiority towards a man as incommensurably great as Mahler has always been one of the most basic reasons for the hostility that he has incurred. And yet a closer examination of the subject reveals the need for a greater degree of differentiation. Karpath was not an isolated case but an instance, rather, of a phenomenon that could assume far more extreme forms. Mahler owed so much to people such as Karpath, but he showed himself to be ungrateful and did not make them his closest confidants and chief advisers not just behind the scenes in the Vienna Court Opera but in the musical life of the city as a whole. In the general administrator's office, too, there were people who were waiting for some token of Mahler's gratitude for having helped him to overcome all the anti-Jewish resistance in Vienna to the appointment of a former Jew as director of the Court Opera. And if he now failed to show the requisite gratitude, it was because ingratitude was a typically Jewish quality.

And then there was a whole series of famous singers in Vienna who had been local favourites until Mahler took up his appointment, even if their present achievements did not merit such adulation. They soon realized that the new director was deadly serious and not a man to be trifled with: so set in their old ways were they that they could not expect to retain their old positions. A few of them made an effort and showed renewed commitment, but others were too old or tired or cynical or lazy. They fell out of favour with the director, a point borne in on them by the tasks they were now expected to perform. Additionally deprived of the chance to avail themselves of the services of the claque, they were all too ready to supply the anti-Mahlerian press with titbits of gossip and scandal. Much the same was true of the orchestra. And a sizeable section of the audience was likewise alienated by Mahler's refusal to admit them after the start of the performance and by his insistence on darkening the auditorium even further, after the Bayreuth model, a development that not only prevented them from reading the word-books during the opera but also from consorting with other members of the audience. From the very outset there were intrigues and campaigns designed to make life impossible for the new director. Efforts were even made to expose him to erotic temptations in the hope that he would then be open to blackmail: not without good reason had Mahler been preceded to Vienna by the reputation of a man whose passions could easily be stirred by female singers – the case of Anna von Mildenburg was already well known, and his affair with Selma Kurz could not be kept quiet for long.

But there was also a section of the press that needed no excuse to attack Mahler. We have already quoted the *Reichspost* piece that appeared in April 1897 and that looked forward to the time when Mahler 'starts his Jew-boy antics at the podium'. The anti-Semitic press never wavered in its basic opposition to his appointment and remained unwilling to moderate its views. Other voices might become less strident or even fall silent, but only as long as Mahler was borne along on a wave of success. When his enthusiasm started to flag and his sensational productions with Roller began to seem run-of-the-mill and he preferred to conduct his own works out of town rather than appear in the pit of the Vienna Court Opera, the old voices of dissent were heard once again, rising to a new pitch of frenzy, especially from 1906. Prominent among these nay-sayers was Heinrich Reinhardt, a composer of operettas, including the successful *Das süße Mädel*, who was also, unfortunately, the music critic of the *Neues Wiener Journal*, a paper whose scattershot approach to Mahler criticism was nothing if not consistent. There were no depths to which Reinhardt was not prepared to stoop, however illogical he became in the process. For a long time he had complained about the absence of Gluck's operas from the repertory, but when *Iphigénie en Aulide* was finally staged, he dismissed the production as a completely pointless exhumation, no doubt relying on his readers' short memory. The anti-Mahler clique was centred upon a group of conspiratorial regulars at the Café Imperial. Richard Specht, to whom we owe a brilliant polemic directed at Mahler's enemies, characterized the group as follows:

Here was the epicentre of the hatred directed at Mahler. Here they discussed and gossiped and polemicized and played their parts as member of the critical general staff. Nor was it only music reviewers who contributed to the discussion: doctors, painters, librettists and those whom Mahler had failed to greet with a sufficient show of friendliness or whose invitations he had snubbed or whose lovers had had to leave the corps de ballet on account of their physical frailty or whose librettos had been rejected as unusable – all of them came together here to discuss whatever ways they could find to destroy Mahler.[58]

This war council was run by Robert Hirschfeld, a journalist who resented the fact that his undoubted talents found little scope for deployment in a second-rate rag, the *Wiener Abendpost*, with the result that he tried to reposition himself among the front rank of Viennese critics by dint of a particularly egregious aggressiveness. He had also prepared a performing edition of Mozart's *Zaide* for the Court Opera, an edition that he hoped would be an artistic and commercial success but which in the event disappeared from the repertory after only three performances, a state of affairs for which he inevitably blamed Mahler. Even more wounding to his personal vanity was Mahler's decision to ban him from his circle of friends following a brief initial interest. His need for attention having been brushed aside in this way, he became Mahler's most implacable enemy, and when the composer's Sixth Symphony received its first performance in Vienna on 4 January 1907, readers of the *Wiener Abendpost* were regaled by Hirschfeld's sneering sarcasm six days later:

If he [Mahler] were capable of expressing tragic feelings through the power of musical sound, he could readily dispense with the hammer and its fateful blows. But he lacks that inner, genuine creative strength. And so in his tragic symphony at the highest peak of excitement he reaches for the hammer. He cannot help it. Where music fails a blow falls. That is quite natural. Speakers whose words fail them at the decisive moment beat the table with their fists.[59]

After Hirschfeld, Mahler's most pugnacious opponents were Richard Wallaschek, who wrote for *Die Zeit*, Hans Liebstöckl and above all Paul Stauber, who was Hirschfeld's most obsequious vassal. Even Max Graf, who had initially proved supportive of Mahler, turned into a vehement critic. The court would never have forgiven Mahler for engaging in private feuds with individual journalists, and so he never reacted publicly to these attacks but repeatedly complained about them to his closest friends, revealing how deeply he was affected by them. In 1909 Stauber published a pamphlet under the title *Mahler's True Legacy* that was intended to counter the study by Paul Stefan in which Stefan had summed up Mahler's achievements at the Court Opera and attacked the director's successor, Felix von Weingartner. Stauber sought by every means in his power to ensure that the Mahler years appeared in the blackest possible light. Central to his pamphlet is an interminable list of singers who appeared under Mahler either on a trial basis or as guests and who were then not taken on permanently. Certainly there were a lot of these trial performances at this time, and there is no doubt that Mahler's uncertainty as a judge of voices played a role in this. But such a list cannot be paraded as a sign of wholesale failure. Stauber hypocritically praises Mahler's early years in Vienna but then in an attempt to topple the 'idol of the Mahler clique' feigns to detect a rapid decline in standards. In general Stauber paints an appallingly lurid picture of incompetence based on a handful of indisputably true facts and describes the second half of Mahler's decade in Vienna as follows:

> The opera house was bursting at the seams and threatening to fall apart, discipline was lax, the repertory in a worse shape than it had been under the blind and ailing Jahn. With only a handful of exceptions, of course, there was only one point on which the whole company – soloists, orchestra, chorus, ballet, administrative staff and stage crew – found themselves in agreement: their hatred of a director whose tyrannical whims unfortunately reached the level of rampant megalomania during his final period, making any further productive collaboration out of the question. His ruthlessness now knew no bounds.[60]

This was the language used to describe the director of the Vienna Court Opera. Such a tone would now be inconceivable except when it is felt that the rules of political correctness have been infringed. Only in Vienna are there still vestigial signs of this bellicosity in cultural matters, especially when an institution as sacrosanct as the State Opera is concerned. Everything that could be used to criticize Mahler was seized upon eagerly, generally against the background of anti-Semitism. A single example from Stauber's pamphlet will serve to illustrate this point. In its opening pages, Stauber refers to Paul Stefan as Mahler's advocate in absentia, describing him as 'Dr Paul Stefan *recte* Grünfeld', implying that Stefan has attempted to camouflage his Jewish origins behind an 'Aryan' name. A similar ploy was adopted when referring to Bruno Walter, whose real name was Bruno Schlesinger, the violin melody from the opening bars of the first melody of Mahler's Fourth Symphony being underlaid with the words 'Ich heiße Schlesinger, doch ich nenn mich Bruno Walter' ('My name is Schlesinger but I call myself Bruno Walter'). Nothing more needed to be said, for contemporaries knew what this meant: we shan't let the Jews get away with changing their names, we'll still catch them out.

The generally ill-received performances of Mahler's works in Vienna were particularly welcome fodder to these critics. That they were local premières rather than world premières speaks for itself. Mahler knew what to expect. The only one of his works to be premièred in Vienna was the revised version of *Das klagende Lied*. During his early years in the city only Reinhardt dared question the success of his work at the Opera. As we can see from Stauber, this early period was generally if hypocritically praised, but its duration became increasingly curtailed, while other targets were found, chief of which were Mahler's symphonies whenever they were performed in Vienna. But there was plenty of ammunition elsewhere: as we saw from the caricature reproduced above, there was criticism of Mahler for driving away the best singers, for insulting the orchestra, for dismissing members of the chorus and for failing to share his critics' view on visiting singers. And during the final years of his regime, Mahler opened himself up to criticism by neglecting his duties as director. On 3 April 1907, while he was visiting Italy on a particularly troublesome trip, the anti-Semitic and chauvinist *Deutsche Zeitung* plumbed new depths of malice:

> The last few days have once again provided striking illustration of the mismanagement from which the Vienna Court Opera is suffering at present. Director Mahler, having secured a huge income which can only be called exorbitant in view of his pernicious behaviour, is now away, 'travelling in symphonies' – peddling his own products – and in the meantime everything is going to wrack and ruin in the Court Opera. . . .
>
> Herr Mahler is doing a tour of Italy, gathering in laurels and even more money – we shall some time put together how many months' leave he has already extracted for his private affairs this year – and does not care in the least how his deputy in Vienna is coping with the Court Opera in the meantime.[61]

To the extent that contemporary discourse is no longer permeated by anti-Semitism, we need to stress the anti-Semitic subtext of this piece in the *Deutsche Zeitung*, the readership of which was well versed in spotting the relevant signs: for them, it was unnecessary to attack Mahler explicitly as a Jew. But the allusion was clear: the Court Opera's Jewish director was peddling his wares like some Jewish rag-and-bone man, even though he had extorted vast sums of money from the poor Kaiser and the imperial court, while offering them little in return.

But Mahler also had friends. Brusque, over-confident, standoffish and lost to the world both by choice and by circumstance, he was by no means adept at maintaining a circle of friends, and yet he retained the friendship of a sizeable group of people, most of whom he had got to know during the first thirty years of his life, although this is, of course, hardly exceptional in people's lives in general. As we have noted, he tended to ignore the pleasures and sufferings of others. The 'kindness of the egocentric' prevented him from forming

THE ADMINISTRATOR - CONTEMPORARIES - SIGNS OF CRISIS

friendships, and anyone who wanted to be his friend had to give up all hope of seeing his affection returned in full measure. Even Alma had cause to be dissatisfied on this score. That he none the less had a number of loyal friends says much for the charisma of genius in general.

In Vienna it was largely the group of friends around Siegfried Lipiner that remained Mahler's closest family, at least until the time of his marriage to Alma. A few more names may be added to this list. First and foremost there was Emil Freund, a childhood friend from Iglau who was a year older than Mahler and who had been practising law in Vienna since 1892. He was also Mahler's legal adviser, especially after 1897, when the latter returned to Vienna. Friedrich Löhr was likewise a year older than Mahler, who got to know him during his time at the University of Vienna. Löhr worked for a long time as a private tutor, but following the foundation of the University's Institute of Archaeology he obtained a permanent post there as secretary, functioning as a kind of non-professorial éminence grise. Löhr was the recipient of many of Mahler's most important early letters: in them the composer opened up his heart in a way that is the prerogative of youth. The brothers Heinrich and Rudolf Krzyzanowski were for a while Mahler's close companions, not only on their long walks together. Heinrich went on to become a Germanist, Rudolf a conductor like Mahler. Albert and Nanna (Nina) Spiegler were also close friends at least until the time of Mahler's marriage. He had been introduced to Albert Spiegler by Lipiner, who had been married to Nina. And then there was Guido Adler, another friend from Mahler's youth who remained unwavering in his support. Following his appointment to a chair in musicology at the University of Vienna, he taught many young musicians in the city, not least of whom was Webern.

With only a few of these friends – generally those from his youth – did Mahler use the familiar pronoun 'Du'. Lipiner was one of them, as, of course, were his brothers-in-law Arnold and Eduard Rosé, his in-laws Carl and Anna Moll (he was always far closer to Anna than to her husband) and, finally, Gerhart Hauptmann, whose fraternal feelings to his fellow men and women no doubt encouraged him to make the first move in the direction of greater intimacy. But Mahler could be just as cordial and friendly with people whom he did not address as 'Du'. He also stopped using the 'Du' form to former lovers once the affair was over: Anna von Mildenburg and Selma Kurz are the two most prominent examples of this punctiliousness on his part. Alfred Roller was a different matter. No one understood him better in his work as a director, and yet Mahler never progressed beyond a formal 'Dear Roller'. No doubt he was afraid that he might fall under an obligation and no longer be in control of his own decisions if he allowed himself to become too friendly. The companionship of the canteen was an abomination to him as was the fraternization of artists brought together by their work in the rehearsal room. As far as was possible, Mahler always kept his distance from such friendships, and although he tried to avoid seeming offensive and arrogant in this regard, he did not always achieve that aim.

He also avoided becoming too close to people who were not of his own generation. None of the young musicians in his entourage was as devoted to him as Bruno Walter, whom he treated as a kind of a son. And Walter was undoubtedly the most important conductor ever to come within his ambit of influence. But it would never have occurred to Mahler to use the 'Du' form to him. The same was true of Schoenberg, Berg and Webern. Mahler was even more circumspect in his dealings with critics. The elderly Eduard Hanslick lived long enough to take a benevolent interest in Mahler's early appearances in Vienna. Max Kalbeck, who was a friend and champion of Brahms, likewise belonged to the older generation of Viennese critics – he was ten years older than Mahler, to whom he was well disposed. Among the younger generation, it was Julius Korngold, Hanslick's successor on the *Neue Freie Presse*, who was most supportive of Mahler. Whether Korngold's support was tactically motivated because he hoped to enlist Mahler's services in promoting the career of his son, Erich Wolfgang Korngold, must remain an open question, though in June 1907 father and son were able to boast that Mahler had expressed his bemusement and enthusiasm when the ten-year-old Erich Wolfgang played him a cantata of his own composition. When asked how they might best encourage the boy's precocious talent, Mahler advised them to seek out Alexander Zemlinsky: 'He'll give him everything he needs.' When Zemlinsky was no longer teaching the young Korngold, he wrote to his former pupil: 'I hear you're now studying with X. Is he making any progress?' Two writers on music, Paul Stefan and Richard Specht, cannot be numbered among Mahler's closer circle of friends, and yet they remained his most loyal supporters long after he was dead. Specht published two monographs on Mahler in 1905 and 1913, laying down the guidelines for future studies, while Stefan edited the important collection of essays that was published in 1910 as a fiftieth-birthday tribute to Mahler, the most important journalistic honour that he received. Stefan was always proud to report that when Mahler heard about the volume, he apparently expressed his shock: 'You are, after all, my friend. You'll ensure that it does me no harm.' Away from Vienna, there were three writers in particular who believed in Mahler's genius and published various writings on the subject: Ernst Nodnagel, Ludwig Schiedermair and Max Marschalk, who wrote for the *Vossische Zeitung* and who was Gerhart Hauptmann's brother-in-law.

Hauptmann was one of Mahler's greatest admirers, an admiration no doubt communicated to him by his brother-in-law, for Hauptmann himself had only a limited understanding of music. He and Mahler appear to have met at a dinner party at the home of Max Burckhard in Vienna, when the other guests included Hauptmann's second wife, Margarete Marschalk, whom he was to marry in 1904, and Josef Kainz, the greatest actor of his age. From then on, the Mahlers and Hauptmanns met almost every time that the latter were in Vienna. Alma was given the task of keeping an eye on Margarete, who had the habit of spending vast sums of money whenever she went shopping in Vienna. Alma claims that Hauptmann felt great tenderness for Mahler, a feeling that the latter did not fully reciprocate. Hauptmann told her that Mahler expressed in clear terms what he himself felt only chaotically. He – Hauptmann – had received more from Mahler than from any other person. But, according to Alma, Hauptmann's slowness of mind and convoluted way of speaking, which Thomas Mann caricatures in the figure of Peeperkorn in *The Magic Mountain*, annoyed the volatile and punctilious Mahler. Hauptmann was then working on *Emanuel Quint*, and so the two men discussed the figure of Christ. A previously unpublished letter that Mahler wrote to Hauptmann on 7 March 1904, no doubt shortly after their first encounter, is couched in such unusually cordial terms as to make Alma's claims barely tenable. The letter also attests to the charm that Mahler could exert if his correspondent seemed to be worth the effort:

Let's say what's on our minds so that nothing is lost in the course of careers that will unfortunately keep us apart for far too long: that we belong together and that the bond that has been forged so quickly without our intending it shall continue to exist with our conscious knowledge and intent. You need only to know that my life here is lonely and silent to judge how much it has become a welcome habit in recent days to meet you and to talk and think about everything that has been building up in me over the course of the years. And this was only the beginning – only an initial attempt to reach an agreement on what we feel and our way of expressing ourselves, just as two people do who meet on the shore after a long sea journey and discover to their inexpressible delight that they are from the same country. Every afternoon in recent days I have felt that I had to collect you from the Hotel Sacher for a stroll, so that we might walk through the streets and squares together and enjoy the hour and not think of the ones that were to follow.[62]

Among the writers in Vienna who repeatedly championed Mahler's cause, pride of place goes to Hermann Bahr. The two men never became friends, in spite of Bahr's concerted attempts at a closer relationship, but Bahr got his own back by marrying Mahler's cast-off lover, Anna von Mildenburg. Another writer who repeatedly spoke out in defence of Mahler was Felix Salten, the

influential cultural critic who was the author of both *Bambi* and, in all likelihood, the pornographic classic *Josefine Mutzenbacher*. Only with the publication of Arthur Schnitzler's complete diaries has it become possible to judge
Mahler's importance for Schnitzler. It was known that Paul Stefan had invited
Schnitzler to contribute to his 1910 tribute, but otherwise Schnitzler made no
public statements on the composer, and even in his letters Mahler plays only a
marginal role. But a glance at Schnitzler's diaries reveals the remarkable fact
that he attended almost all of Mahler's concerts in Vienna and many of
Mahler's opera performances, all of them faithfully recorded in his diary, albeit
without any more detailed information. One is tempted to speak of Schnitzler's
idolization of Mahler. It helped, of course, that of all the writers associated with
Young Vienna, it was Schnitzler who had the closest links with music, even if
those links are rarely reflected in his writings. He played the piano to a high
standard, often performing duets with his mother. Together they worked
through the recently published piano-duet versions of Mahler's symphonies,
which in the years before the rise of the gramophone were the only way of
getting to know such music within the privacy of one's own home. Richard
Specht recalls that following the publication of his Sixth Symphony, Mahler
discovered that Schnitzler – an author he knew only in passing for he rarely
read contemporary literature – had been deeply moved by the sombre vision
of the symphony's final movement. Mahler was galvanized: 'This Schnitzler
must be a wonderful fellow!' And he expressed the wish to meet the writer as
soon as possible, complaining that in Vienna people took far too little interest
in important contemporaries, a reluctance inspired either by fear of the
unknown, by the wish not to appear importunate or by the desire not to be
reckoned a member of a clique. In a letter that he wrote after Mahler's death,
Schnitzler admits that he met the composer only once at the Rosés in October
1905 – perhaps this was the meeting that was arranged after Mahler had
expressed the wish to get to know him. To the extent that Schnitzler was
extremely reserved when it came to meeting people outside his own very
narrow circle of friends, who included Hofmannsthal, Beer-Hofmann and
Salten, closer contact was out of the question. Mahler, too, never frequented
the city's literary circles, quite apart from the fact that he was too bound up in
his work at the Opera and too cut off from the rest of the world during the
summer months to be able to look much further than his own immediate
circle of acquaintances.

But Schnitzler's contribution to the 1910 volume is clear evidence of the
veneration that he felt for Mahler. He initially intended it as a message
addressed to Mahler directly, but Stefan asked him to change the wording on
the grounds that even three years after he had stepped down from his post at
the Court Opera, Mahler's standing in the city remained precarious, making

any association of personal good wishes with a public show of support problematical in the extreme. In his reply to Stefan, Schnitzler acknowledged the validity of the editor's argument, while also confessing his inability to find the right words to pay tribute to a figure as exceptional as Mahler precisely because he was so devoted to his art, but for Mahler's sake he would try to find the right turn of phrase. The final version may be cited as an example of the profound effect that Mahler had on Schnitzler:

> Of all the composers who are writing music today – and many of them are genuinely dear to me – none has given me more than Gustav Mahler, for he has given me joy and emotion of a kind that I owe to only the greatest of men. I have scarcely ever felt the urge to offer an aesthetic or critical explanation of the ultimate reasons for our most powerful artistic experiences; and it seems to me that such an attempt is even more hopeless when applied to music whose primeval laws are based on the rigid roots of mathematical formulas and whose ultimate effects are decided within the most remote and metaphysically vague limitations. All that is left to me, therefore, just as it is often left as a final refuge for more pedantic music lovers, is to trust my own innate feelings and to voice my gratitude for what I have received. It is a wonderful feeling to be allowed to express such thanks on a day which, perhaps filled with more hope than it is with fulfilment, signifies the high point of a gifted artist's life.[63]

In spite of its formulaic language, the present statement and, more especially, Schnitzler's far less formal diary entries leave us in no doubt about their author's capacity for being moved by Mahler's music, making it all the more regrettable that the two men never became friends: Mahler was of a literary bent and particularly receptive to great literature and yet he never forged any closer links with any of Vienna's leading writers. He could hardly have found a truer friend and a more kindred spirit than he would have done with Schnitzler.

In the case of Karl Kraus there is not even any evidence of a personal meeting with Mahler, an omission possibly due to the fact that Alma may have got to know Kraus in her youth but failed to take away any very positive impressions of him. Moreover, Kraus had even less understanding of music than Schnitzler. True, he was certainly not unmusical, as is clear from surviving recordings in which his declamation of couplets and scenes from Offenbach's operettas reveals a tremendous musicality even though he never learnt to read music. But this seems to have been the full extent of his knowledge of music, and there is no evidence that he ever attended any concerts. And his monastic lifestyle and preference for working at night left him just as isolated as Mahler. Here, too, we have good reason to regret that the two men never got to know each other because – as Mahler said of himself and Strauss – they were like two miners digging the same seam from opposite sides. Each strove in his own way to combat slovenliness (in Kraus's case it was linguistic slovenliness) and to wage war on ignorance and indolence, corruption and nepotism, Vienna's false *Gemütlichkeit* and the debasement of great art to the point where it was used to decorate the homes of middle-class philistines. As a result, they often found that they shared the same enemies in the Viennese press. Above all, Kraus sensed that there was a fundamental anti-Semitism to almost all the attacks on Mahler, attacks that he pilloried in turn. Mahler never expressed his views on Kraus, whereas there is some evidence that Kraus recognized Mahler's significance. On several occasions he defended Mahler, the Viennese press being in his eyes the cause and embodiment of practically every ill.

Schoenberg admired Kraus almost as much as Mahler, and in May 1906 he wrote to Kraus as the most implacable critic of the local press, attempting to interest him in seeing Mahler as the victim of that press. Schoenberg offered to call on Kraus with Zemlinsky and tell him about the background to the various campaigns against Mahler. We do not know whether this meeting ever took place. But Schoenberg appears to have approached Kraus again in May 1907, when the attacks on Mahler reached their high point. Kraus replied to the effect that at that particular juncture he was unable to take a stand on Mahler's behalf but would be happy to offer Schoenberg space in the pages of *Die Fackel* to come to Mahler's defence. Unfortunately Schoenberg did not take Kraus up on his offer. Instead, Kraus contributed a handful of remarks on the situation.[64] But Kraus was on hand when Mahler lost the musical directorship of the Vienna Philharmonic's concerts and when the local newspapers – especially the ones that had spearheaded the campaign against him – shed crocodile tears on the composer's death. After all, he knew how much mediocrities and the depraved hate all that is exceptional.

It seems that on one occasion Kraus did go to the opera in order to hear Mahler conduct a work by his favourite composer, Offenbach, whose *Les Contes d'Hoffmann* Mahler staged in November 1901. Thirty years later Kraus still remembered this performance when he saw Max Reinhardt's production in Berlin, the director's last major undertaking in the city before he left the country for a life of exile. Kraus had no time for Reinhardt and had invariably been critical of his work. He was appalled by the 1931 production: 'Quite apart from the repeated mistreatment of the music, the total inadequacy of the production was clear not least from the relatively unmutilated Antonia act which even for those who do not retain a memory of Gustav Mahler's magnificent production demonstrates a poverty of invention that would put any average municipal opera house to shame.'[65] For thirty years, then, Kraus had retained a memory of Mahler's magnificent production.

In Paris, too, Mahler had an eminent and devoted circle of friends to which we have already referred. It was Bertha Zuckerkandl who introduced Mahler to her sister Sophie and her brother-in-law Paul Clemenceau. Through them he got to know Paul's brother, Georges. After studying medicine, Georges had embraced a career in politics and in the wake of the Franco-Prussian War of 1870–1 joined the far left. He was entirely on the side of the Dreyfusards during the Dreyfus Affair of the mid-1890s and published Zola's famous article, 'J'accuse', in his newspaper, *L'Aurore*. The other hero of the Dreyfus Affair was Colonel Georges Picquart, a figure perhaps even more impressive than Zola in that he was not a member of the left wing and needed to overcome a soldier's ingrained prejudices against the left and, more especially, against a 'Jewish traitor' like Dreyfus. Following Dreyfus's conviction, Picquart was appointed chief of the army's intelligence section, in which capacity it became painfully clear to him that the real traitor was Major Ferdinand Walsin-Esterhazy and that it was his own colleague Major Hubert-Joseph Henry who was responsible for the campaign of vilification directed at Dreyfus. For defending Dreyfus, Picquart was demoted and transferred overseas and it was only slowly that he was rehabilitated. He and Dreyfus were finally pardoned in 1906, when Picquart was promoted to the rank of brigadier-general. Georges Clemenceau was the French prime minister from 1906 to 1909 and again from 1917 to 1920. His brother and comrade-in-arms, the latter's wife Sophie and Georges Picquart formed the nucleus of Mahler's fan club in Paris. To their names must be added those of the mathematician and politician Paul Painlevé, who himself later served as the prime minister of the French Republic in two separate terms, and Baron Guillaume de Lallemand.

This illustrious group of supporters was unwilling to be outdone in its enthusiasm for Mahler. Picquart spoke fluent German and was highly cultured. He and Lallemand played Mahler's symphonies in the same arrangements for piano duet as those used by Arthur Schnitzler and his mother. Mahler had followed the Dreyfus Affair with a mixture of close interest and indignation, his sensitivity to anti-Semitism leaving him in no doubt as to the origins of the affair, and so he was delighted to meet the leading Dreyfusards and especially the chief protagonist in the affair, who was still not fully rehabilitated at the time of their first encounter. Like many others, the anti-Jewish Alma had been angered by the pro-Dreyfus campaign in Vienna's liberal press and, like Karl Kraus, she was intuitively hostile to Dreyfus. If she changed her allegiance, it was almost certainly because of her friendship with Bertha Zuckerkandl and Sophie Clemenceau rather than any real enthusiasm for Dreyfus. Of all these French Mahlerians, it was Picquart whom Mahler liked most of all, and whenever they came to Vienna he would arrange for a kind of Dreyfus festival to be mounted at the Court Opera with particularly distinguished casts. These Parisian Mahlerians were, so to speak, the political pendant to the purely musical faction in Amsterdam.

This list of Mahler's friends would not be complete without a mention of a handful of individuals headed by Arnold Berliner. A physicist by training, Berliner had been director of AEG before turning increasingly to writing textbooks and editing scholarly journals, foremost of which was *Die Naturwissenschaften* (*Natural Sciences*). Mahler, who owned a copy of his basic handbook on physics, had been introduced to Berliner in Hamburg, where the latter was working for AEG, and had taken English lessons with him. He later moved to Berlin. Mahler invariably consulted him on questions relating to modern science. They remained in contact until Mahler's death. Berliner took his own life in 1942, when he was due to be deported from his flat in the capital. A manuscript containing his reminiscences of Mahler is no longer extant. Mahler's other friends in Hamburg included the musician Hermann Behn, who is remembered for preparing piano arrangements of the symphonic repertory, including Mahler's own music. The composer Josef Bohuslav Foerster and his wife, the soprano Berta Foerster-Lauterer, were also friendly with Mahler both in Hamburg and later in Vienna, where Berta was engaged at the Opera. A number of other figures accompanied Mahler only briefly on his journey through life. In Leipzig they included the musician and journalist Max Steinitzer. As we have observed, Mahler was by no means adept at forming friendships, making the foregoing phalanx of friends all the more impressive.

The Eighth Symphony

M AHLER HAD A very clear idea of the quality of his music, and at no point in his life was he assailed by self-doubts on that score. And yet he was never tempted to insist on his own importance in a spirit of self-celebration. All the more remarkable is it, therefore, that in the case of his Eighth Symphony he abandoned his usual reserve. In mid-August 1906, for example, he wrote to Willem Mengelberg, a letter that also helps us to identify the work's *terminus ad quem*:

> I have just finished my Eighth – it is the grandest thing I have done yet – and so peculiar in content and form that it is really impossible to write anything about it. Try to imagine the whole universe beginning to ring and resound. These are no longer human voices, but planets and suns revolving. – More when I see you.[1]

In spite of this, it is worth recalling that there are Mahlerians who, while acknowledging that Mahler's symphonies continued to improve in quality, exclude the Eighth from this development, seeing it as unique and significant, yet held back by regressive tendencies. Quite apart from its eruptive genesis, Mahler had the impression that in many respects the Eighth was different from all his previous symphonies. Four years were to pass between the completion of the work and its first performance in Munich on 12 September 1910, an occasion to which we shall return in due course. But it is striking that throughout this period Mahler made little attempt to have the work performed. One wonders whether deep-seated doubts had belatedly started to assail him about the work's relevance, a suggestion that has sometimes been made in the past. But he was at least able to see how enthusiastic his supporters were whenever he showed them the score. In late September 1909 he played excerpts from it to Mengelberg and Diepenbrock and afterwards wrote to

Alma 'It's funny: the work always makes the same, typically powerful impression. It would be absurd if my most important work happened to be the easiest to understand.'[2] It needs to be stressed that Mahler was still describing his Eighth Symphony as his most important work a year after he had completed *Das Lied von der Erde* and shortly after he had put the finishing touches to the Ninth. After all, there is no doubt that if Mahlerians all over the world were asked to name the composer's most important works, it would be *Das Lied von der Erde* and the Ninth Symphony that came out at the top of the list.

Mahler saw things differently. By late June 1910, by which date he was in Munich, working on the preliminary round of rehearsals for the first performance of the Eighth, his enthusiasm had reached new heights and he struck a note that would be unbearably smug in the case of any other composer but which is moving in Mahler's case precisely because it is so unusual: 'I've already heard every passage in detail at least once, and "do believe he's a genius!" So far the world has experienced nothing of the kind, and billions of years ago those primeval cells were pretty well organized, if one considers that even then they contained the seed of future works such as this.'[3] 'I do believe he's a genius' are words attributed to the leader of the St Petersburg orchestra following a performance of Mahler's Fifth Symphony under the composer's direction in 1902. Since then Mahler and Alma often quoted the phrase to each other, half in jest. But there is no sense of jesting in what follows, for all its relaxed tone. Particularly striking is Mahler's reference to the growth of monads, or entelechy, that had long been associated in his mind with the whole project that was his Eighth Symphony.

For Mahler, the special status of the Eighth stemmed not only from its unusual form as a symphonic cantata, but also, we may assume, from its exceptional genesis. Ever since he had developed his technique of composing only during his summer vacation, he had never managed to complete a whole symphony in the course of a single summer. In terms of the psychology of the creative artist, it seems very much to have been the pressure to use the summer months for this purpose that led to a creative block at the start of each vacation. This might explain Alma's claim that during the first two weeks of his summer holidays in Maiernigg in 1906 – the last summer that was completely carefree for Mahler – her husband produced nothing at all. But in a later letter to Alma, Mahler remembered things differently:

> In art, as in life, I rely entirely on spontaneity. If I were *obliged* or *compelled* to compose, I know for sure that I couldn't put a single note to paper. Four years ago, on the first morning of our summer in Maiernigg, I went up to my shack, resolved to take it easy (for I was in dire need of rest at the time) and to gather new strength. – As I entered that all-too-familiar room, the creator

spiritus took possession of me, held me in its clutches and chastised me for eight weeks, until the work was all but finished.[4]

It was the 'creator spiritus' that is invoked in the opening bars of the symphony and that raged for up to eight weeks between mid-June and mid-August 1906, undoubtedly a record for such a large-scale work lasting some eighty minutes in performance. Indeed, there are even some accounts that suggest the creative burst lasted only six weeks in all.

The words that Mahler set are taken from two different sources, the Pentecostal hymn attributed to Hrabanus Maurus (c. 780–856), who was Abbot of Fulda from 822 to 842 and Archbishop of Mainz from 847, and the final scene from Part Two of Goethe's *Faust*, 'Mountain Gorges, Forest, Cliff, Wilderness', also known as the 'Anchorites' Scene', anchorites being the devout hermits who live in caves in the mountains and provide the staffage for this scene. The harnessing together of these two texts has given rise to countless misunderstandings and even bewilderment for there seems to be no connection between the ninth-century father of the Church and the nineteenth-century prince of poets. The most famous expression of this attitude was voiced by Hans Mayer, whose training was literary rather than musical and who asked, rhetorically: 'Should we also mention the theologically and poetically absurd idea of trying to force together the hymn, "Veni creator spiritus", and the Chorus Mysticus from Part Two of *Faust* in an attempt to forge a musical and spiritual entity?' There was, Mayer argued, a 'monstrous discrepancy' between the two texts.[5] Dieter Borchmeyer, on the other hand, has pointed out that the discrepancy is not in fact as great as it appears and that Goethe not only knew and valued the 'Veni creator spiritus' (a point that Mahler cannot have known) but even prepared a German translation and asked his friend Carl Friedrich Zelter to set it to music.[6] Zelter evidently made several attempts to do so but in spite of frequent reminders from Goethe he failed to complete the setting. Particularly interesting is Goethe's interpretation of this Pentecostal hymn as an appeal to genius and, as such, a work likely to speak to all strong and intelligent people.[7] It was this that attracted Mahler to the hymn, for it reflects his faith in the power of creativity. In short, this setting is Goethean rather than Catholic in spirit.

That the work's perspective is counter-chronological, with *Faust* adumbrating the Pentecostal hymn, rather than the other way round, is clear from the symphony's genesis. While conducting two performances of *Le nozze di Figaro* in Salzburg in August 1906, Mahler spoke at length with Richard Specht, who made a note of their conversation after the composer's death. Mahler had explained that it had long been his intention to set the final scene from *Faust*, including the words of the Mater Gloriosa. All earlier attempts to set these words, he claimed, had been too saccharine or weak. He was undoubtedly thinking of Liszt's *Faust* Symphony, which ends with a setting of the Chorus Mysticus. In the case of Schumann's version, he was perhaps a little unjust. But the idea was evidently a long-standing one, albeit a little vague. At that point Mahler had stumbled upon a copy of a book containing Hrabanus Maurus's hymn and in a flash had seen before his mind's eye the whole of the symphony's opening section, to which the final scene from *Faust* had struck him as the 'answer'.[8] Mahler also had a very specific passage in mind, allowing him to forge a link between two texts that seem to inhabit completely different worlds and ages. This is the plea for light to fire our senses in the middle of Hrabanus Maurus's hymn: 'Accende lumen sensibus, / Infunde amorem cordibus' – 'May light fire our senses, pour love into our hearts.' (Goethe's translation of these lines is both freer and bolder: 'Ignite lights in our senses, joyful courage in our hearts.') At the final rehearsal in Munich, Mahler drew Webern's attention to this passage: 'The passage *accende lumen sensibus* forms the bridge to the concluding section of *Faust*. This spot is the cardinal point of the entire work.'[9] Of course, Mahler knew Goethe far better than the world of medieval Catholicism, and so he must have been particularly touched to discover that the Pentecostal hymn anticipates Goethe's quasi-religious approach to light: 'Light and spirit, the former ruling in the physical world, the latter in the moral world, are the highest conceivable indivisible energies,' we read in one of Goethe's *Maxims and Reflections*.[10]

Mahler was of course aware that formally speaking he was striking out in an entirely new direction with this work, and on this point too he said as much to Richard Specht. It surprised him that there had been no previous symphony that involved singing from start to finish. In his Second, Third and Fourth Symphonies he himself had used the human voice to summarize ideas which, as he put it, could be expressed only at extreme length in a purely symphonic form. But now he was using the human voice as a musical instrument – the opening movement, Mahler explained, was entirely symphonic in form and yet sung from beginning to end. He could have added that the second movement does at least have a lengthy, purely instrumental introduction.

The opening movement is the more conventional of the two, a conventionality positively demanded by the woodcut-like nature of the text as compared to the elderly Goethe's sublime way with words. When set beside the polyphonic miracles of the Fifth, Sixth and Seventh Symphonies, there is no getting round the fact that the Eighth reveals a reduction in the work's compositional complexity to the point where the textures are predominantly homophonic. Of course, Mahler did not suddenly lose his skills as a composer. Rather, he was concerned to provide an archaic, hymn-like guise for an archaic, hymnic text, and to that extent his recourse to the oratorio tradition in his choral writing is a reflection of his need to put across his message as clearly as possible. From that point of view he would certainly not have agreed with those commentators who regard this as a stepping back or even as a regressive move. If we accept this, there remain enough details which, each wondrous in its own way, contribute to the overall impact of the work. The simple expedient of repeating the thunderous cry of 'Veni', a repeat not anticipated by the poet, and of adding the trumpets and trombones to underscore this fanfare-like appeal, is enormously effective. The descending fourth of the first 'Veni' provides a germ cell for the whole of the opening part, and yet it also leaves its mark on the second part of the symphony, too, as does the call of 'Accende', which acquires its incandescent quality from the fact that – nonsensically from a linguistic point of view – there is a decisive pause between the first and second syllables, a pause that some conductors take as a licence to disrupt the flow of the music completely: a few milliseconds on the part of a sensitive conductor will make all the difference here.

Once one has heard this moment in a good performance, the power of the uplift is unforgettable, and even the elderly Adorno could still write enthusiastically about it in a performance of the work under Webern in Vienna. Together with the leaping intervals at 'Infirma nostri corporis', the uplift and the downward plunge of the 'Veni creator spiritus' and the 'Accende lumen sensibus' form the basic musical material of the work as a whole. The greater density of the second part does not make it easy for the listener to recognize the extent to which the motivic material of the first part has left its mark on the second movement, a circumstance that already invalidates the reproach that concert reviewers continue to level at the work even today, namely, that the two halves do not hang together. The texts may date from periods that are a thousand years apart, but, musically speaking, the two parts may be described as twins which, although they may not initially look alike, share the same genetic material.

The second part begins in E flat minor, a reaction against the E flat major of the end of the first part. The introduction is arguably the most magnificent section of the entire work. After the wildly jubilant note of the 'Gloria' that ends the first part of the symphony and that includes the full organ, the listener is left dazzled. Mahler does not say how long the break should last, but the beginning of the second part leaves itself and the listener time to recover. We are reminded of a man who, blinded by the snow, gradually regains his sight and realizes just how high his route has brought him. The outlines become clearer and a vast space opens up inhabited by an unprecedented wealth of detail. Over the gently drifting sounds of the muted first violins, the vista slowly opens up, and we can see both downwards, where the pizzicato cellos and double basses pick out our laborious ascent, and upwards, where flute and clarinet make it plain that the highest point has not yet been reached. A vast gulf opens up between the highest and lowest instruments, suggesting an infinite expanse, and only gradually does the middle register fill with the entry of additional winds. No less magnificent is the first choral entry, 'Waldung, sie schwankt heran', the words disjointedly stammered by the chorus as it brings life to this primeval and supernatural world, following Goethe's instructions as if they were stage directions for a *Symphonie dramatique* – Berlioz's *Symphonie fantastique* and *La Damnation de Faust* were evidently two of the models for this scene. These strange and sporadic syllabic sounds reveal a compositional boldness that looks forward to word settings of a much later period.

Only when the Pater Ecstaticus enters with his 'Ewiger Wonnebrand', to be followed by a regular line-up of soloists, does it become impossible to avoid associations of a string of arias sung by members of a glee club taking their turns on the podium. If Goethe's scene seems barely stageable, Mahler's setting resembles nothing so much as a concert performance of an opera. Many writers have pointed out that the ending of Goethe's play defies a theatrical presentation, Albrecht Schöne, for example, asking whether only film could do justice to it. This non-performable aspect of the work becomes a problem for Mahler only because, swayed by his feelings of respect for the original, his setting of the words gives musical prominence to one mythically mystical figure after another, each of whom is accompanied by puzzling descriptions and who sings words that are uniquely difficult to understand. It is not until its final section that the work once again breathes air from other planets. Indeed, there is an almost perceptible jolt when the Chorus mysticus enters with the words 'Alles Vergängliche' and draws us back to the peak of Mahler's inventive powers. It is no accident that in terms of its musical language and atmosphere this chorus recalls the final section of the Second Symphony, bringing the work to an end with a similarly powerful climax.

The Eighth Symphony continues to divide opinion. It is often performed on festive occasions and to that extent may be compared to Wagner's *Die Meistersinger von Nürnberg* and Beethoven's Ninth. At the same time, however, Adorno raised such serious objections to it in his influential book on Mahler that one rubs one's eyes in amazement at finding a Mahlerian of his eminence venting his spleen on the work in this way. Dismissing it as a 'giant symbolic shell', Adorno argued that the work's authority derived from the dogmatic and canonical gesture of its words. It was a representation of the collective spirit, anticipating an age of collectivism that Mahler sensed but which he would have done better to have resisted, instead of joining in. Here Adorno even uses the term 'offence' to sum up his attitude to Mahler's inability to resist this temptation, an extreme expression of stigmatizing opprobrium that reflects the disappointment of the lover at an error on the part of the object of his desire.[11] But the Eighth Symphony has also been accused of selling out to the desire on the part of Wilhelmine Germany to create a total work of art that would establish and celebrate values in an age devoid of values.

Essentially, this is the same discussion as the one we had over the final movement of the Seventh Symphony when compared to that of the Sixth, except that no one has yet dared to interpret the Eighth as a work of inauthenticity, a work of 'what if?', with its own inbuilt critique. But by this date in his career Mahler was conceptually and musically too bound up with the logical consequence of his increasingly radical style for such a reproach to appear at all convincing. Why should he have attempted to create a gigantic work of total art in 1906, at a time when such a work was largely discredited? Composing music to accompany the unveiling of Klinger's titanic monument to Beethoven is not the same as composing music in the spirit of that monument. True, the Second Symphony contains hints of that approach, and yet even there they are already nipped in the bud. There is no reason why a concept that Mahler was unable to realize in 1890 should suddenly have been resurrected in 1906 after the radically progressive instrumental symphonies of the composer's middle period. But nor is it possible to interpret the two parts of this dramatic symphonic cantata as an undercover critique of the Holy Ghost or of the belief in a Creator or of the idea of erotic love hymned at the end of *Faust*. Mahler's exegetes are faced with the problem that whereas the note of affirmation struck by the previous symphonies may be read as a negation in disguise, this is emphatically not true of the Eighth. And whereas Adorno and many like him may be able to get away with the notion of 'brokenness' as a central element in Mahler's style, this does not help us in the case of the Eighth. Attempts to look back to the earlier works raise more questions than they answer. The Eighth stands on its own, casting no backward glances, an assertion with which Mahler, too, would no doubt have agreed. We may suppose that in his Pentecostal creative frenzy Mahler did not fully notice how he had abandoned the most advanced bridgeheads of his compositional style when setting two texts that were particularly close to his heart: the hymn to the spirit of creativity and the hymn to all-embracing erotic love, as Mahler explained in an important letter to Alma dated June 1909.[12] In short, Mahler was unaware that he was in part reverting to a kind of conservatism that he had left behind him with his First Symphony. Adorno's critique is by no means far-fetched, even if we may reject its angry tone.

Recent writers have tended to defend the work at all costs and treated it as the monumental piece that Mahler never intended it to be, and yet in advancing this view, they have very real difficulty ignoring the more problematical aspects of the piece.[13] If Mahler noticed too late that he had allowed the creator spiritus to blind him to weaknesses in the work – they are weaknesses only when judged by his own high standards – then he buried this understanding deep in his heart, for at no point did he voice any doubts or reservations. It seems reasonable to assume that inasmuch as he viewed the creative process as something sacrosanct, he felt that it was no longer permissible to rework or improve the result of this *furor*. Its sanctity stemmed not from the fact that he prided himself on being a Sturm und Drang genius before whose abilities he prostrated himself in awestruck obeisance but because – especially in the case of his Eighth Symphony – he saw himself as the mouthpiece of a higher principle: entelechy had chosen him, and the spiritus creator had whipped him into submission over an eight-week period until he produced the piece.

In the letter that he wrote to Alma on 8 June 1910, Mahler struck out a sentence: 'If something is expected of me, I never shirk it.'[14] The Eighth Symphony, with its two texts combined in this particular way, demanded to be composed; entelechy had forced this task upon him as a result of his old love of the end of Goethe's drama and a chance encounter with an old book on moral edification. It was not up to him to question the validity of this Pentecostal experience. And when the work's first performance four years later brought him the supreme rewards of such enthusiastic devotion on the part of so many people, it was understandably difficult for him to weigh up the respective merits of the undeniably weaker passages in the score and the equally undeniable power of those passages that continue to leave their mark on listeners today. To quote the closing lines of *Faust*, even earth's insufficiency here finds fulfilment.

Annus Terribilis
(1907)

If we view the operations of one of the leading musico-dramatic institutions in Germany – the Imperial and Royal Court Theatre – from the outside, we shall find ourselves faced by a motley assortment of performances of the most varied kind and the most contradictory styles. The only thing that emerges with any clarity from all this is that none of these performances bears the stamp of correctness and that if it takes place at all, it is not from inner necessity but because of some dire outward circumstance. It is impossible to point to a single performance in which the end and the means are in total accord. In every case, lack of talent, the faulty training or inappropriate use of certain singers and the inadequate preparation and resultant insecurity of others, to say nothing of the rough and listless delivery of the chorus, gross blunders in the production, the almost complete inability to arrange the onstage action, the crude and senseless acting of some members of the cast and, finally, the grave errors and negligence in the interpretation and performance of the music, with its neglect of nuance and lack of coordination between orchestra and singers, make themselves felt somewhere or other in a more or less disturbing and even offensive manner. Most of these performances bear all the hallmarks of a heedless devil-may-care attitude against which the efforts of individual singers to step outside the artistic framework by seeking applause for their particular achievements appear all the more repellent and make the performance as a whole seem altogether absurd.[1]

IN SPITE OF appearances, the foregoing is not a philippic directed at Mahler by critics such as Reinhardt, Hirschfeld and Liebstöckl but is taken from a memorandum that Wagner published in the Viennese *Botschafter* in 1863, his aim being to nudge the Court Opera closer to the goal of 'ennobling the nation's morals and taste', a goal already pursued by the Emperor Joseph II. Like Mahler, Wagner had learnt all about the opera industry from the inside, working his way up through the ranks and, on the basis of experiences not dissimilar to Mahler's, proposing concrete suggestions for improving the situation: the number of performances, he argued, should be cut by half, French and Italian operas should be performed by non-subsidized commercial companies, and the running of the opera company should be divided up among three directors with individual responsibilities for voice, orchestra and staging. (Forty years before Mahler, Wagner was already advocating the creation of a director's post with greater powers than was usual at this period.) Ultimately Wagner was moving in the direction of a festival-type administration similar to the one that he later implemented in Bayreuth, his emphasis on the German repertory necessarily leading to the exclusive promotion of his own particular works.

We have already had occasion to quote Mahler's resigned remark from 1906, when he noted the impossibility of raising an opera company that operated almost every day to the level that he had in mind. It was a logical consequence of Wagner's admonitions of 1863. Shortly before he stepped down from his post, Mahler gave a long interview to his old shield-bearer Ludwig Karpath in the course of which he observed that:

> No theatre in the world can be maintained at such a pitch that each performance is like the next. And it is this that repels me about the theatre, for of course I should like all performances to be on the same high level and to achieve an ideal that it is simply not possible to attain. No one was able to achieve this before me, and no one will do so after me. And since I have come to this conclusion after ten years in the post, I am leaving a post that was at my disposal right up to the time that I took my definitive decision, a point that I can you assure you is true.[2]

Clearly Mahler was no longer thinking of the idea, expressed in conversation with Bernhard Scharlitt a year earlier, of a summer festival of works by Mozart and Wagner in a theatre on the Kahlenberg, for example – the sort of festival that was to be established fifteen years later in Salzburg. After all, he himself had described it as a pipe dream and evidently did not see himself as being in any position to pursue such a project, especially in Vienna, where he would have had to face a strong headwind. We can only speculate on his attitude to the Salzburg Festival, but from everything we know, it seems that he would have been enthusiastic about it. In his model productions with Roller, he had always succeeded in achieving the standards that he (and Wagner) had had in mind, but those achievements were limited to these performances, and only when he taxed his resources to their limits. Mahler's work with Roller led to a veritable revolution in the theatre but it necessarily meant a reduction in the number of performances that Mahler conducted. To that extent Mahler was following Wagner's advice, but it applied only to the performances that he himself conducted, not to those delegated to other conductors. Nor was there any point in arguing in favour of a reduction in the number of performances – if he had suggested halving their number, as Wagner had proposed, his superiors would simply have doubted his sanity. Let us not forget that before Mahler arrived in the city, no one in charge of the Vienna Court Opera had demanded improved production values and higher dramaturgical standards. As long as the orchestra and singers were up to the mark, then everyone was happy. What Mahler and Roller did, they achieved on their own initiative. Recent decades had seen an increase in the number of performances, an increase shared by every court theatre of the period, for this was the only way in which income could be increased – ticket prices were already too high for them to be raised any further. To do so was not a viable alternative.

It was a source of considerable despair for Mahler that although he gradually managed to raise the standard of the performances of works by Gluck, Mozart, Beethoven and Wagner that he himself directed and conducted, bringing them up to the sort of level that Wagner had had in mind and that was the starting point for Mahler's own theatrical vision, the other works in the repertory – French operas from Meyerbeer to Massenet and Italian operas from Rossini to *verismo* – remained on the same low level that Wagner had rightly pilloried forty years earlier. (It may be added in passing that in the case of the French and Italian repertory, Mahler demonstrated the sort of Austro-German arrogance that was typical of his age and that can be traced back to Wagner's own views on the subject.) Musical standards were raised only when Mahler succeeded in signing up a whole series of new conductors willing to invest more time in this area of the repertory: Franz Schalk from 1900, Bruno Walter from 1901, Francesco Spetrino from 1903 and Alexander Zemlinsky from 1907. All were conductors of an eminence previously unknown at the Court Opera. In this regard, Mahler was completely lacking in vanity and set no store by wanting his star to shine more brightly in the company of lesser lights. But after a number of years of self-sacrificial work in harness to Vienna's opera industry, it had become clear to him that his own work as a composer was more and more important to him and that he needed to champion his music himself. Titurel's admonition in Wagner's *Parsifal*, 'My son Amfortas, are you officiating?', had long kept him in his post, serving the great masterpieces of music, but Titurel's voice was growing weaker, and Mahler's duties were starting to tire him.

But there were two things above all that increased this sense of weariness. First, there was Mahler's failed attempt to get Strauss's *Salome* staged at the

Court Opera, a failure that affected him deeply and left him feeling not only embittered but also embarrassed vis-à-vis Strauss: regarded by many outsiders as the plenipotentiary of the musical life of Vienna, he had been unable to persuade his own company to stage the one modern work that he held in the highest regard and that was being staged by other Court Theatres in Germany and elsewhere. The *Salome* affair was not the main reason for his resignation, but it was an important stage in that process. Richard Specht was exaggerating when he claimed that 'it was clear to him that he would go from the moment that he failed to defeat sanctimonious servility and in the face of the court theatre's censorship to force through a performance of the most brilliant music drama of the turn of the century',[3] but there is none the less a grain of truth to his statement. The second hard fact was the horrendous deficit of 1905 and the concomitant feeling that although his superiors had reacted with surprising restraint, Mahler had lost some of the support that he had enjoyed until then. Even so, we must be wary of assuming that this decision was a fait accompli, as Specht and many of Mahler's friends later claimed, for the evidence is far from unequivocal.

There are signs, easy to overlook but none the less significant, that Mahler's actions were by no means single-minded and his decision far from final, for in the middle of April 1907, shortly after his return from Italy, we find him writing to Julius von Weis-Osborn in Graz and expressing the hope that he will see his correspondent again soon, perhaps in the company of the latter's friend, Ernst Decsey, at a performance of Gluck's *Iphigénie en Aulide*. The production had opened on 18 March and was the last time that Mahler and Roller worked together. But there is nothing in Mahler's letter to indicate that he regarded this as their final collaboration, for he writes that 'I think it is the best thing Roller and I have achieved so far. Anyway we have advanced a fair distance along our road'.[4] This hardly sounds as if Mahler had been carrying around with him his letter of resignation in his back pocket. Rather, one has the impression that he had every intention of continuing his work with Roller and advancing further down the road that they had chosen for themselves.

Even so, the year 1907 started badly and continued in the same vein. With hindsight, Mahler's decision to resign looks like the logical consequence of these events, but was in fact the result of complex developments that might have ended differently if Mahler's mood had not been so black and if sections of the local press had not surpassed themselves in terms of their hate campaign against him. As we have seen, Mahler had made up his mind in principle to leave his post in Vienna, and yet the situation could have turned out differently if circumstances had been more favourable. It may be added in passing that neither of the terms 'dismissal' or 'discharge' is the right one here. Mahler's appointment was for life, so that he could not simply announce his resignation.

And if he had decided to throw in the towel, he would have forfeited all his rights, especially his own pension and Alma's widow's pension. Mahler was always worried about his financial situation, and so resignation was never an issue. As a result, his only option was to ask the emperor to 'relieve' him of his post, to quote the official terminology. In short, he had to be allowed to retire and in that way to draw his pension. Once he was in receipt of this pension, he could no longer work in Vienna either as a conductor or a theatre administrator, a point codified in the decree that the emperor later signed. But there was nothing to prevent Mahler from assuming a similar position elsewhere.

There is a certain symbolic rightness to the fact that the press campaign against Mahler began on 1 January 1907 and continued virtually unabated until the day of his resignation. The witch-hunt was launched by a certain Hans Puchstein in the *Deutsches Volksblatt*. It needs to be remembered that in a city with as many newspapers as Vienna it was not one or two that were against Mahler but practically all of them, even if the few that spoke out in his defence were among the most influential and liberal. The fact that the left-of-centre *Neue Freie Presse* was on the whole pro-Mahler may give the impression that the composer had important friends in the city, but the paper's readership represented only a small part of Vienna's population. All who subscribed to Pan-German ideals and held conservative views and whose opposition to the Jews ranged from covert prejudice to open anti-Semitism supported Georg von Schönerer or Karl Lueger and read the *Wiener Mittagszeitung*, the *Reichspost*, the *Wiener Sonn- und Montagszeitung*, the *Ostdeutsche Rundschau*, the *Deutsche Zeitung*, the *Deutsches Volksblatt*, the *Österreichische Volkszeitung* or the *Montags-Revue*. (In several cases, the paper's Pan-German agenda was manifest from its title, while Karl Kraus renamed the *Deutsches Volksblatt* 'our Christian Taagblaatt' in deference to its sheep-like readership.) All of them capitalized on the witch-hunt against Mahler, and although their attacks amounted to small-arms fire when set beside the big guns of the *Neue Freie Presse*, the combined effect was substantial. And so Puchstein opened the proceedings in the *Deutsches Volksblatt*, regretting the gaps in the Court Opera repertory (and in doing so identifying an undeniable weak point in Mahler's direction, for the house's repertory was distinctly one-sided) and criticizing the director's choice of singers, a criticism always likely to go down well in a city obsessed with voices. In particular Puchstein attacked two of the singers whom Mahler held in especially high regard, Selma Kurz and Marie Gutheil-Schoder. The former was said to be a dispassionate singing machine, the latter technically wayward. In both cases, there was a certain truth to Puchstein's comments, but in privileging these negative aspects to the exclusion of all others, he failed to take account of Kurz's vocal artistry and Gutheil-Schoder's outstanding gifts as a singing actress.

On 4 January 1907 Mahler introduced his Sixth Symphony to Viennese audiences at the city's Musikverein. Significantly, the orchestra that he used was neither the Philharmonic nor the Court Opera orchestra but that of the Konzertverein, which had invited him to conduct one of its concerts devoted to new works. By local standards, the performance was remarkably successful both with the general public and with the orchestra. But there was a hard core of Mahler's opponents, whose protest took the form of children's trumpets blown from the balcony. Yet this was as nothing when compared with the reviews, the majority of which were negative in tone. But even Mahler's old supporters had difficulty with a work that is undoubtedly hard to digest. After all, the composer himself had said that it posed riddles that could be solved only by listeners familiar with its five predecessors. He may also have committed the error of subtitling the piece in the programme his 'Tragic' symphony, a description seen by many critics as challenging Beethoven. Even Max Kalbeck, Brahms's friend and biographer and essentially well disposed to Mahler, barely knew where to begin with the work. Mahler had been profligate with his instrumental resources, Kalbeck wrote, and was wrong to use 'the primitive tools of barbaric natural music and folk music', by which he meant the cowbells, switch and, of course, the infamous hammer blows that caused a considerable stir. (In a further revision, Mahler had eliminated the third of these blows. The question of whether or not it should be reinstated continues to divide opinion.)

Writing in the *Neue Freie Presse*, Julius Korngold remained the most sympathetic of Mahler's critics, and yet even he had problems with the piece. Alluding to Haydn's 'Surprise Symphony' (known in German as the 'Symphonie mit dem Paukenschlag'), he expressed particular reservations about the work's final movement, asking whether it was in fact possible 'for the ear to accommodate the extreme polyphony that is inflicted on the listener in the tangle of voices of modern scores'. Turning to the instrumentation, he missed the smooth blending together of the different elements, hearing instead a realistic juxtaposition of them and even instrumental dissonances. He concluded that although the Sixth Symphony represented an advance on Mahler's earlier works in terms of its unified symphonic structure, its realistic effects would tax any listener's nerves and ultimately become intolerable. Not for the first time and certainly not for the last, other critics objected that the outward resources lavished on the work merely sought to paper over its inner hollowness. As Max Vancsa wrote in *Die Wage*, 'If you take away the vast forces for which it is scored, no sense of tragic emotion remains, and only a minimum of emotion in general.'[5]

The leaders of the anti-Mahler faction naturally gave their all. We have already quoted from Robert Hirschfeld's review in the *Wiener Abendpost*, comparing the hammer blows with an orator thumping his fist on a desk because he has run out of ideas. Writing in the *Neues Wiener Journal*, Heinrich Reinhardt went even further: 'Brass! Plenty of brass! An unprecedented amount of brass! Even more brass! Nothing but brass! And that was just the opening movement. The second movement is the third because the third one is the second. The contrapuntal and thematic writing is nil.' And Reinhardt went on to infer the current state of the Court Opera from the musical qualities of the symphony: 'The Vienna Court Opera has sunk to a new low that few people would have thought possible.' Nor was this his final insult, for he proceeded to claim that it was with 'rabbit-like fecundity' that Mahler produced a new, larger-than-life work each year, the latest specimen revealing the most 'hopeless lack of ideas'. In the *Illustriertes Wiener Extrablatt*, Hans Liebstöckl likewise spoke of a 'shameful impoverishment of invention' and 'impotence of inspiration'. Mahler was 'on a permanent pilgrimage', atoning for works that were an expression of 'original sin'. 'He is still writing in exactly the same way that he did at the beginning. The only thing new is the celesta and the cowbells in the orchestra.' If these passages have been quoted, it is not because they differ substantially from earlier reviews of Mahler's music but because they indicate the tone that was struck at the start of 1907, a tone which, in contrast to earlier campaigns, continued to resonate until the writers had achieved their declared aim of destroying the hated director and wounding him where he was most vulnerable: his own compositions, the singers whom he engaged, his work at the Court Opera (although it was only with difficulty that his enemies were able to criticize his own productions) and his increasing absences from Vienna.

Mahler had only a few days in which to regain his breath before Richard Wallaschek, writing in *Die Zeit* on 12 January, heaped more coals on the fire. Wallaschek had the temerity to rubbish the recent productions of Mahler and Roller, to complain about the state of the repertory and to report that the singers at the Court Opera were increasingly unhappy about the fact that while Mahler was pleased to grant himself frequent leaves of absence, he almost never allowed his singers to sign lucrative deals out of town – a complaint which, although true, was out of date. Mahler had realized that he could no longer refuse to grant such permission to his singers, with the result that he had for some time adopted a more liberal approach to such requests. Until now he had abided by his maxim of not reacting to such reproaches in the press, but a change was in the offing. In the course of a conversation with Montenuovo he asked his superior whether it was time to take an official stance on such attacks. It is unclear if Montenuovo had already lost confidence in Mahler or whether he was merely opposed to such a stance in this one particular case, but, whatever the answer, he let it be known that he considered such a show of support to be inopportune. Mahler should respond by showing his critics what he was capable of as an artist – Montenuovo was thinking specifically of the first night of *Die Walküre*, which was due to take place on 4 February. Produced at a particularly critical time, this staging found appreciably more detractors than the earlier achievements of the tried and tested team of Mahler and Roller. Many of the reviewers found the stage too dark and the costumes too modern, while the fact that Siegmund wore a brown wig rather than the usual blond one kept the columnists exercised for a period of several days. Mahler's position was now so precarious that even critics who had previously lacked the confidence of their convictions, suddenly found that the conductor's tempos were far too idiosyncratic.

The month of February also marked the first signs of trouble within the company itself. The first night of a new production of Auber's *La Muette de Portici* was planned for the end of the month. An important and, indeed, remarkable example of French grand opera, the work centres on the silent role of Fenella, normally taken by a trained dancer. The Court Opera wanted to break with this tradition and to cast Marie Gutheil-Schoder in the part, an exceptionally talented singing actress who was, however, afraid that people would say that she had finally lost her voice. The house accordingly reverted to the idea of a dancer but one of exceptional merit. Party to this decision were Bruno Walter, who was to conduct the first night, the company's stage manager, August Stoll, and Roller, who had developed an interest in the ballet – in this he differed from Mahler, who remained relatively indifferent to this particular art form. Roller even thought of choreographing a ballet himself and calling it *Rübezahl*, the same title as Mahler's unfinished opera. (Alma's account of this episode is typically confusing.) Roller suggested casting the young dancer Grete Wiesenthal as Fenella. She had already made a name for herself with her novel style of dancing, and the literary figures of New Vienna – especially Hugo von Hofmannsthal – lay at her feet. Roller and Walter ensured that they had Mahler's support and were confident that the young dancer would be a sensation. Unfortunately, the ballet master, Josef Hassreiter, felt, not unreasonably, that he had been passed over and created a scandal by offering to resign. Mahler supported his friend and colleague, though he must have known that Roller had been wrong to go over the ballet master's head. Indeed, Roller's high-handed, non-conciliatory manner had made more enemies than friends in Vienna and made Mahler's position more difficult.

Although a compromise was found, allowing Wiesenthal to alternate with another dancer, the scandal was soon being reported in the press, culminating in a further meeting between Mahler and Montenuovo, to whom Hassreiter had gone running. 'This is the first time you have condoned an irregularity since you have directed the Opera,' Montenuovo is said to have rebuked

Mahler. 'My sense of duty will not allow me to overlook it.'[6] It is no longer possible to say whether Alma was right when she writes that from this moment onwards Montenuovo, unable to get over his annoyance, had looked for an opportunity to get rid of Mahler, but if her account of the meeting is correct, then it is clear that Montenuovo was beginning to withdraw his support: the press campaigns against the director, the increasingly sour atmosphere within the house and Mahler's own behaviour were not without their consequences.

The next incident was waiting just around the corner. In the wake of the new production of Gluck's *Iphigénie en Aulide* that had opened on 18 March and that was more favourably received by the critics than *Die Walküre* had been, Mahler and Alma set off for Italy, a tour which, planned some time earlier, involved two concerts in Rome and one in Trieste. In Rome Mahler conducted the Accademia di Santa Cecilia in two mixed programmes that included only one of his own compositions: the Adagietto from his Fifth Symphony. In Trieste he introduced his First Symphony to Italian audiences. The photographs that were taken in the course of this tour show a relaxed Mahler behaving for all the world like a tourist rather than a hounded conductor. He was in fact away for almost four weeks, during which time he conducted only three concerts, an undertaking which by his own standards must have seemed more like a holiday. Such a break could hardly be begrudged him, and yet it is questionable whether such a lengthy absence was wise when the situation in Vienna was so tense. Unsurprisingly, it was seen as an affront. But if Mahler was already resolved to give up his post at the end of the year, the way in which his visit to Italy was viewed in Vienna may well have been a matter of some indifference to him. A letter that Roller wrote to his wife at the end of April suggests that Mahler was inwardly resolved on such a step. As such, it is at odds with the letter to Julius von Weis-Osborn quoted earlier: 'The Opera is really in a mess as a result of Viennese roguery. I admire Mahler for maintaining his equanimity and for taking things step by step like the knight in [Ludwig Uhland's ballad] "Schwäbische Kunde". It seems that now – on 1 May it will be ten years since he was appointed director – all available forces are coming together to bring about his downfall. If only people knew how much he'd like to go!'[7]

Mahler's relaxed expression in the photographs taken in Rome does not in fact reflect the tense situation in Vienna, for another problem was already preying on his mind. The tenor Fritz Schrödter had served the house well in the past and even taken part in performances of Mahler's music, but he was one of those singers whose powers were noticeably waning and who tried to compensate by means of a display of truculence. Mahler would have liked to have got rid of him but realized that this would cause the usual commotion, reviving the old accusation of 'Mahler the Jew driving away the best singers'. As a result he had suggested extending Schrödter's contract but on a reduced salary. Schrödter was furious and brooded on reprisals, for which Mahler's extended absence offered ample opportunity. Within days of his return to Vienna, Mahler could read in the local papers that Schrödter had flatly turned down the director's offer of a new contract and that he had used his influence with court officials to ensure that he was re-employed under the old conditions. Such a blatant affront to the director's authority made an already difficult situation infinitely worse.

On 21 April, at the height of the Schrödter affair, Mahler suffered a further humiliation that affected him all the more deeply for being so unexpected. Until now, it had never occurred to anyone to boo a performance under Mahler's direction, but this is precisely what happened during the performance of *Tristan und Isolde* on 21 April. It is not entirely clear from surviving accounts when the booing broke out, although it seems as if it was directed in the main at the visiting bass Felix von Kraus, who was singing King Marke. But any boos for a singer engaged by Mahler were effectively aimed at Mahler too, and he certainly got the message. Although his friends tried to assure him that it was merely a childish prank on the part of a handful of goaded opera-goers, he himself is said to have remarked that if his audience had abandoned him, then it was time for him to go. His resistance was beginning to fail him, and his plans to find an alternative to running the intractable Court Opera were taking on clearer form, while his disgust at the press campaigns against him continued to grow. There are no surviving letters in which he vents his feelings at these developments – this will have been reserved for private conversations with his friends and with his wife. But a single sentence shows how much he was wounded by all this. In June, his old friend Arnold Berliner wrote to ask him whether the rumours about his resignation were true: 'It is all quite true. I am going because I can no longer endure the rabble.'[8] Mahler's turmoil and agitation are clear not least from the fact that instead of signing this brief note with his own name, he initially signed himself 'Berliner'.

Meanwhile, the Mahlers' extended visit to Italy had had a sequel that appears to have been the final straw for Montenuovo. Here, too, we have only Alma's testimony when she claims that Mahler had intended to play a trick on the Court Opera in order to extend his leave of absence. Prior to his departure he had announced that he would be away until only just after Easter but planned to submit a request from Italy, asking to be allowed to remain in the country in order to conduct the third concert in Trieste, thereby presenting the company with a fait accompli. But he appears to have given away his hand by noting down the dates of his entire month-long absence in the main ledger. One of Mahler's increasingly numerous enemies in the company took this ledger to the general administrator's office, leading to another meeting with Montenuovo, presumably before Mahler left for Rome. It seems as if he had repeatedly threatened to step down from his post, a threat that worked only as long as he could rely on Montenuovo's support. But the situation had changed, and Mahler was apparently shocked and surprised when, far from protesting, Montenuovo took up the idea and suggested that both parties should seriously consider the matter. Mahler had crossed the Rubicon, and even if he now regretted his offer, he could no longer back down without losing face. It looks as if both men were later taken aback at the repercussions of their conversation, and it is believed that Montenuovo made one final attempt to persuade Mahler to remain, but as the result of an incautious remark to a journalist Mahler had now made it impossible for him to remain in his post without a serious loss of face.

Mahler's Resignation

Events followed hard on each other's heels during the month of May. Although it remains a matter for speculation, it is conceivable that two illnesses in Mahler's family tipped the scales. Alma was ill when she returned from Italy. True, she had often been ill in recent years, but on this occasion she needed an operation, details of which are unknown. And then, in early May, Anna succumbed to scarlet fever. During the first five months of this *annus terribilis* Mahler was frantically busy. He had been worn down by the attacks launched against him by the press and could no longer count on the loyalty of his superiors, a loyalty that he himself had tested to the limits. He could no longer remain in a house where his work was more and more of a torment. He needed to be set free by a final liberating blow. It will have been in early May that Mahler took his definitive decision to resign. Already the rumours in the city were rampant. Writing retrospectively, Paul Stefan observed that:

> Mahler's fate was sealed with ultimately breakneck speed. *Die Walküre* was perhaps the most perfect production in this theatre in living memory, a performance such as people dream about. Storms of applause thundered around Mahler's head before the second act – he never accepted an audience's thanks and avoided any greeting. A weary man thanked them. And indignation after indignation, affairs, sensations, announcements. Time and again it was rumoured that he was definitely leaving, hoping for liberation and freedom from the tyranny of art. *Iphigenia in Aulis*, wonderful acting before an empty house, and a work for listeners other than those who were there as subscribers. *Othello*. Disquiet, announcements, announcements. An address signed by

the best names in Vienna begged Mahler to remain. He left, finally, in June, he really left.[9]

Dated 11 May, the document to which Stefan refers here is undoubtedly impressive, containing, as it does, not just the best, but the very best, names in Vienna and reflecting the enormous impact that Mahler's activities had had on the intellectual and artistic elite of the city. Written after all the decisions had been taken, it begins by summing up Mahler's ten-year directorship, which was said to have enriched the city

> by your ability to recreate favourite works in an entirely novel and impressive way and lay bare their essence and lend them musical expression, and by a magnificent series of artistic feats whose achieved aim was the implementa-tion of a new style of performance, but above all – and perhaps even more than through any individual achievements – by your great example of meeting the implacable demands of a rigorous cultivation of art, which you did by sweeping away thoughtless prejudices in a manner free from any cult of personality.

The writers went on to condemn the press campaign against Mahler, before concluding by expressing

> the thanks of a number of people who owe you a very great deal, people in whom these works, in the form that you have given to them through your magnificent interpretations, have remained indelibly alive and who were privileged to receive decisive and lasting impressions as a permanent gift and who know, finally, what you mean to us and what you will always mean to us.[10]

This document is in fact curiously ambiguous in character, for at no point is Mahler invited to remain – presumably the signatories knew that it was too late for such a request, only the final phrase holding out the promise of a change of heart. Even so, the list of sixty-nine signatories is exceedingly impressive, the only notable absentee being Specht, who no doubt initiated the move and who may well have declined to sign it because he had already been denounced as one of Mahler's closest supporters. The following roll call, which features only those names that are still familiar to us today, is a wistful reminder of the enviable state of Vienna's cultural scene in 1907: there were the writers Peter Altenberg, Hermann Bahr, Richard Beer-Hofmann, Hugo von Hofmannsthal, Alfred Polgar, Felix Salten, Arthur Schnitzler, Jakob Wassermann and Stefan Zweig; the architects and artists Josef Hoffmann,

Gustav Klimt and Kolo Moser; the actors and theatre managers Max Burckhard, Josef Kainz, Adolf von Sonnenthal and Hugo Thimig; the physician Josef Breuer; the distinguished anatomist Emil Zuckerkandl and his wife, Bertha; and, finally, the composer Arnold Schoenberg. At the beginning of June, Sigmund Freud, Ernst Mach and Lilli Lehmann were among many other personalities to add their names to this tribute. We do not know how Mahler reacted to this appeal, but we may assume that he was moved and touched by it. It is by no means certain that he knew how much he was admired and even worshipped by Vienna's elite, for he cannot have been personally acquainted with many of the signatories.

By the second half of May the speculation reached fever pitch. On 17 May, the *Illustriertes Wiener Extrablatt* announced that 'Director Mahler has indicated to a prominent personality his intention of leaving his position at the Court Opera next autumn'. Five days later the pro-Mahler *Neue Freie Presse* reported that 'In artistic circles rumours have been circulating for some time that Director Mahler is planning to leave his position. Several discussions between the Second Chief Comptroller Prince Montenuovo and Director Mahler have given these rumours added stimulus'. And by 23 May the anti-Mahlerian *Neues Wiener Journal* was no longer in any doubt on the matter: 'The resignation of Gustav Mahler, on which we carried a report a few days ago, can already be treated as definite. The reasons which have caused the Director of the Court Opera to take this decision are obvious. The conditions at the theatre have made an artistic crisis inevitable, which Herr Mahler no longer feels capable of overcoming.'[11] The *Neues Wiener Journal* was well informed, and four days later Mahler asked to be relieved of his post.

In order to counter the rumours, Mahler asked to see his old comrade-in-arms Ludwig Karpath and granted him a lengthy interview that took place during a walk along the Ringstraße on 4 June and that appeared in edited form in the *Neues Wiener Tagblatt* on the 5th. (A fuller version was published in Karpath's reminiscences in 1934.) Mahler used this platform to deny in the strongest possible terms all the reports that were circulating about him. It was being claimed, for example, that he had clashed with Schrödter, who had demanded Mahler's dismissal by the Kaiser. Mahler stressed that he was leaving of his own volition as he wanted to be completely independent. Above all, he had realized that, the opera industry being what it was, it was impossible to ensure that every performance was of the same high standard. The 1905 deficit had been repaid, and the house would be ending the present financial year with a healthy surplus. Money was not an issue as he was planning to leave his post before an intended increase in his pension. (In the event, this increase was granted to him.) But recent weeks had been very hard for him, precipitating his decision to leave. To prevent any demonstrations for or against his directorship, he would not be conducting any further performances between now and the expiry of his contract. (Mahler was unable to hold to this resolve.) And he would not be accepting any other appointments. He would have to remain in his post only until such time as a successor was found.[12]

Mahler mentioned the name of Felix Mottl – it was an open secret that the general music director of the Munich Opera was the preferred candidate in influential circles. Mottl's greatest champion was Princess Pauline Metternich, the granddaughter of the great Austrian statesman, who had married her uncle Richard Metternich, Austria's ambassador in Paris from 1859 to 1870, when the couple had returned to Vienna. Culturally speaking, Pauline Metternich was the éminence grise of the Viennese court, organizing parades, celebrations and exhibitions. She had never liked Mahler and for a long time had championed Mottl, prompting Karl Kraus to suspect that Mahler had stumbled over the princess's train. We shall later examine the question why it was not Mottl who succeeded Mahler but Felix von Weingartner. In the event Mottl died only weeks after Mahler, collapsing while conducting a performance of *Tristan und Isolde* in Munich and dying a few days later.

Writing in the *Neue Freie Presse* on 4 June, Julius Korngold still found it difficult to believe the rumours: 'Is it true that we are losing Mahler?' He recounted the events of the last few weeks, carefully weighing them up and showing great understanding for Mahler. He alone dared to take Mahler's character as the starting point of his disquisition:

> Like all men of genius, Mahler is essentially naïve by nature, and as in his symphonies, so in his character, there is a remarkable element of naïveté mixed in with keen rationality. This explains all his infringements of the most trivial rules of caution and wisdom in life, and there are many people in his immediate circle who have not hesitated to take advantage of this. It would have been easy for Mahler to win over people outside his workplace, people who would have included the mightiest in the land. After all, they were looking everywhere for this intelligent and fascinating man. He refused to be found – by anybody. He was always consumed by his own ideas, assailed by an incessant flood of artistic inspiration. A great loner in a position held by someone traditionally beset on all sides; simple, lacking in all sense of need, a man innocent of all posturing, a child in the circle of his own kind.

And Korngold ended by striking a prophetic note: 'The day will come when the importance of the "Mahler era" will be clearly felt and will seem like some wondrous legend of a brilliant time at the Court Opera.'[13]

None of the surviving documents allows us to say exactly how Mahler's retirement was seen from the immediate perspective of Montenuovo and, ultimately, the Kaiser, although a paper headed the 'Most Humble Submission by the Most Loyally Obedient Second Chief Comptroller Prince Alfred Montenuovo Relating to Changes in the Running of the Court Opera' and submitted on 2 October 1907 offers a retrospective assessment of the situation. It had taken until then to sort out all the uncertainty about Mahler's successor. Felix von Weingartner had been born in Zara (now Zadar) in Dalmatia on 2 June 1863 and, like Mahler and Mottl, was Austrian. And, as Montenuovo rightly noted, he was one of the finest contemporary conductors, worthy of being ranked alongside Mahler, Schuch, Mottl, Nikisch and Muck. During the 1890s he had been a conductor at the Berlin Court Opera and also directed the Hofkapelle's symphony concerts. Although he stepped down from his post at the Opera, he continued to conduct the symphony concerts, having signed a contract that would have kept him in Berlin until 1921. (By this date the orchestra had in fact long since ceased to exist.) The Viennese court used all its diplomatic skills to free him from the fetters of his Prussian contract, allowing Montenuovo to present to the Kaiser a successor to Mahler who enjoyed the highest reputation and who owed nothing to Viennese intrigue. That his period in office was relatively brief and by no means as glorious as might have been expected was due to many reasons that we shall examine in due course. Above all, however, he underestimated the one point that Korngold had rightly anticipated: although Mahler may have been hated as long as he ran the company, this period was soon transfigured in people's memories, and as a director and as a conductor Weingartner was judged by Mahler's standards and found wanting.

Before Montenuovo could introduce Weingartner to the Kaiser, he first had to list the reasons for Mahler's departure, and in the elegant chancellery language that considered all press campaigns and petty arguments beneath its dignity, he attributed that departure to Mahler's increased activities away from the Court Opera and to his ever more frequent absences:

On the occasion of a discussion that I held with him last April on conditions in the Court Opera and the disadvantages bound up with such absences, he declared that he now saw his true task in life in the world of artistic activity that he was then pursuing and that he could not forgo increasingly frequent and lengthy leaves of absence, not least because in his view the institution did not suffer in consequence. On the strength of my own experience I was unable to share this view, and so Mahler felt persuaded to express his inclination to resign from running the Court Opera.[14]

There is no doubt that in his arid bureaucratic language Montenuovo had identified the root cause of the problem, while high-mindedly passing over all the secondary reasons, which evidently did not belong in such an official document as this.

This is not the first time we have had occasion to observe how anxious and at the same time how astute Mahler could be when dealing with matters of finance. A letter that he wrote to Montenuovo almost certainly at the height of the crisis in the middle of May shows how tenaciously and successfully he fought to maintain his financial position after he stepped down as director – the modest circumstances of his early youth and the years when he was responsible for the welfare of his brothers and sisters had left a lasting mark on him.[15] It was entirely legitimate for him, therefore, to think of his family's provision. (It will be remembered that his heart disease had not yet been diagnosed.) According to the terms of his contract, he was entitled to a pension of 11,000 crowns after ten years, but that period was not yet up. He argued in his letter that he had geared his entire lifestyle to the pension that he would have received after thirteen years in harness: 14,000 crowns. He asked to be granted that sum. Of particular interest is his justification for this demand: he had stepped down, he explained, 'through no fault of my own' but as the result of 'an unforeseen chain of events', an explanation that sits ill with the true facts of the matter. He also demanded a one-off payment of 20,000 crowns and an assurance that his wife and children would continue to be entitled to a widow's pension. Montenuovo took his time before replying, a delay due not least to the arguments over Mottl and Weingartner.

It seems likely that Montenuovo spoke to the Kaiser in May or June in order to discuss Mahler's settlement, but it was not until 10 August that he wrote to Mahler from his summer vacation in Semmering to inform him that the Weingartner case had been resolved and that the Kaiser had agreed to all of Mahler's financial requests and demands. Whether or not the court was aware of what it had lost in Mahler, its generosity is clear from the icing on Montenuovo's cake: although Mahler's rank in the civil list was only that of a senior civil servant, he was awarded a widow's pension equivalent to that of a privy councillor.[16] Another two months were to pass before Montenuovo could summarize all these points in his submission to the Kaiser. Of some interest in this context is the clause in the decree relieving Mahler of his post and stating that Mahler could not work as an administrator or even as a conductor in any of Vienna's theatres, otherwise he would lose his pension. On 5 October, three days after Montenuovo's submission, the Kaiser's decree had been signed, summarizing his subordinate's report and naming Weingartner as Mahler's successor. As Weingartner was not available until 1 January 1908, Mahler was asked to stay on until the end of the year. With a positively Prussian sense of duty he not only agreed to this request but helped to prepare the forthcoming season, which he did with an apparent sense of liberation now that the decision had finally been taken.

New Perspectives

An undated letter to the Berlin impresario Norbert Salter, probably written in May, reveals that Mahler lost no time in casting around for alternative employment. It must have been clear to him that he and his family could live only relatively modestly on the pension that he had been accorded. Even though this pension was lavish by any standards, it was still less than half the 36,000 crowns that he had received while in office. It had taken him a long time to pay off the debts that the rest of his family had amassed, with the result that he and Alma had had little time to enjoy the benefits of his well-paid post. The house in Maiernigg was necessary for the Mahlers' summer vacations but it had to be staffed and maintained, while Mahler's concert tours brought him little extra income – a reasonable way of topping up his salary as director of the Vienna Court Opera, but inadequate if his only additional income was his pension. And so we find Mahler writing to Salter: 'I am at present so overwhelmed with projects and offers that – especially as no successor to me has yet been found – I cannot yet reply to any of them. Naturally I must first take a long look at things. The best will be for you to collect everything you receive connected with me, and we shall discuss the matter when I come to Berlin in the *very near* future. I dare say America will be inevitable for me.'[17]

We may well be right in assuming that the number of projects and offers to which Mahler refers was substantially smaller than he claims it to have been. At all events, he was not open to offers from every quarter, as he wanted his correspondent to believe. Vienna would, of course, have been the most practical solution, but this was ruled out by the provisions of his pension settlement. Nor could there be any question of his taking over the running of another opera house – he had no wish to repeat the experiences of the past. And, in any case, which opera house could it have been after he had already run the world's leading company? Anything else would have felt like a relegation. Nor could Mahler consider the post of principal conductor at a court opera house, for where was the director whom Mahler would allow to boss him around, quite apart from the fact that the salary attached to such a position fell far short of his expectations. The only possibility in this regard would have been the musical directorship of the Bayreuth Festival (one wonders how the Festival would have turned out), but Mahler was of course clear in his own mind that Wagner would have turned in his grave at the thought of a 'former Jew' running his Festival. And Cosima would have killed herself first.

All that remained in Germany and Austria was the possibility of taking over a leading orchestra, but here, too, there were only two orchestras worth considering: the Vienna and the Berlin Philharmonics. The former was ruled out by the bitter experiences that Mahler had had with this orchestra in the past, while the Berlin Philharmonic was in the best possible hands with Arthur Nikisch, a magus of the podium who was to retain control of both the Berlin orchestra and the Leipzig Gewandhaus Orchestra until his death in 1922. It would never have occurred to the Berliners to swap the world-famous maestro for a conductor like Mahler, who had the reputation not only for being difficult but for preferring composition to conducting. The Berlin Philharmonic was emphatically not one of the offers with which Mahler had been 'overwhelmed'. In the light of all this, it makes sense that he ended his letter to Salter by noting that America was 'inevitable' if he wanted to achieve anything. He had never been to the country, and his knowledge of English was no better than it had been when he visited London in 1892, but he knew very well that he could earn a small fortune in a country whose cultural life was in the ascendant, and he also knew that the German repertory was being rebuilt at the Metropolitan Opera after the death of Anton Seidl, who had already done much in this regard. Finally, he knew that the Met's director, Heinrich Conried, was really called Heinrich Cohn. A native of Bielitz in Silesia, he had begun his career as an actor in the Austrian provinces and is even said to have appeared briefly on the boards of the Vienna Burgtheater, only for his diminutive stature to impede his career on the stage. He had succeeded Maurice Grau as the lessee of the Metropolitan Opera in February 1903, Grau's successes in this regard having turned the post into a highly lucrative one. The house was owned by the Metropolitan Opera and Real Estate Company, and so the lessee was not a court appointee as Mahler had been in Vienna. If the company was properly run, the lessee could earn considerable amounts of money. Mahler and Conried made contact astonishingly quickly – we do not know when this was or who instituted the contact, but presumably it was Salter. By 4 June Mahler was on the night train to Berlin to enter into negotiations with Conried, who was currently staying in the Prussian capital.

Conried had inherited a company that was in the pink of financial health. The Met had moved into its new premises in 1883, an outwardly unprepossessing building known to the locals as a yellow-brick brewery and situated on Broadway between Thirty-Ninth and Fortieth Streets. Its auditorium, conversely, was a magnificent temple to the arts affectionately known as the 'Golden Horseshoe' and seating some 3,000 patrons. As such, it was larger than most European houses. Before 1883 and for a short time afterwards there was a rival company in the Academy of Music on Fourteenth Street. Since 1966 the Met has been housed in the Lincoln Center in an even larger building inimical to intimate effects. One of the oldest of American opera houses, it soon acquired a reputation as a Mecca for the world's great singers. During the 1880s, moreover, the German conductor Leopold Damrosch was instrumental in establishing German opera at the Metropolitan Opera. Following his premature death in 1885, he was succeeded by Anton Seidl, who introduced the majority of Wagner's mature music dramas to astonished New York audiences, turning Wagner's works into one of the cornerstones of the repertory and importing eminent singers from Germany and Austria, including Amalie Materna, Bayreuth's first Brünnhilde. By the 1890s German opera from Beethoven to Wagner had come to dominate the Metropolitan repertory, a dominance that played no small part in Mahler's decision to accept a position with the company. His old friend Lilli Lehmann appeared here in all her leading roles, especially Isolde. Max Alvary, with whom Mahler had worked in London in 1892, sang his first Wagner roles in New York. And Albert Niemann, the first Bayreuth Siegmund and Wagner's Paris Tannhäuser, was also a Metropolitan Opera regular. By the date of Seidl's early death in 1898, the German repertory and Wagner in particular were firmly established at the Met. Maurice Grau, who ran the company from 1891 until his retirement in 1903, was fortunate in being able to engage singers of the calibre of Édouard and Jean de Reszke. Jean was regarded as the leading dramatic tenor of his day, at home in both Wagner and the Italian and French repertory. In the autumn of 1903, Grau also signed up a young tenor from Naples, an engagement that was to prove momentous, for Enrico Caruso was to become the most successful singer of the early twentieth century and one of the principal attractions of the Met, where he sang an unhealthily large number of performances. Although Caruso and Mahler never worked together, they were none the less in close contact with one another, as is clear from the caricatures of the composer produced by the tenor, who was also an excellent draughtsman.

Conried was initially able to reap the rewards of his predecessors' hard work, but in 1906 – and herein lies an important precondition of Mahler's engagement – he found himself having to face a serious challenge in the new Manhattan Opera House that was being run by Oscar Hammerstein. Hammerstein, too, was a German Jew. The son of a building contractor from Stettin, he moved to America at an early age and after working for a time in a cigarette factory eventually became one of his new country's most successful theatre producers. Over the years he is said to have built no fewer than thirteen theatres, a number of which he also ran. (His grandson, Oscar Hammerstein II, was the librettist of some of the most successful American musicals, including *Show Boat and Oklahoma!*) Hammerstein set about challenging the hegemony of Conried and the Met. It had been clear from the rivalry between the old Academy of Music and the Met that New York did not need two large opera houses, and so Conried found himself fighting a battle for his company's very existence, but fortune was on his side. Although Hammerstein was able to engage Alessandro Bonci as his leading tenor, Conried had Caruso, who was already on his way to becoming an international star. The ailing Conried retired in 1908, before the rivalry between the two houses had been settled, and it was not until Hammerstein, financially crippled by a further operatic enterprise in Philadelphia, retired in 1910 that the Met, under its new director Otto Kahn, was finally able to claim victory.

Back in 1907, Conried was understandably anxious to increase the Met's drawing power, and to this end he introduced three measures in particular. Hammerstein having made a name for himself with his brilliant successes in the French repertory, Conried decided against entering into direct rivalry in this area but built up the Italian repertory instead, rightly believing that in Caruso he held the strongest hand. Secondly, he signed up the Russian bass Fyodor Chaliapin, who had already proved a sensation in western Europe, although in the event his larger-than-life, hyper-realistic acting style found fewer supporters among New York's opera lovers than it had done elsewhere, while American audiences, used to the polished and stylish singing of a bygone era, responded less warmly to the bass's indifference to the bel canto tradition. Conried's third ploy – and it is the one that brings us back to Mahler – was to consolidate the German repertory by bringing in new singers such as Berta Morena and, later, Leo Slezak and new conductors. It was not unknown in New York that the most electrifying Wagner performances in Europe were those that had been conducted by Mahler in Vienna. A successor to Seidl still had to be found, and when Conried, who regularly visited Europe in his search for new and talented artists, heard that Mahler was about to step down from his post in Vienna, his excitement is not hard to imagine.

Conried's was not the first offer that Mahler received from New York. As early as February 1887, while he was still a minor conductor in Leipzig, he had written to Friedrich Löhr to announce that 'At the same time I have received an offer from New York, an invitation to replace Anton Seidl – perhaps I shall end up by accepting it!'[18] There is also a surviving letter to Lilli Lehmann that Mahler wrote in late April or early May 1898 and in which he reports that he has received a request from New York to conduct fifty concerts a season and become director of the National Conservatory of Music.[19] Neither plan came to anything. Concrete negotiations with Conried seem to have started in May 1907. (As so often, Mahler's unfortunate tendency not to date his letters proves a nightmare for his biographer.) The go-between was Norbert Salter, while

Mahler's negotiating team in Vienna appears to have been Roller and Rudolf Winternitz, who ran a fashion house in Vienna that worked closely with the Court Opera's costume department. The negotiations opened with a series of skirmishes, prompting Mahler to ask Salter if, in the event of his failing to come to an arrangement with Conried, Hammerstein might be interested in him. His letter even suggests that Hammerstein had already signalled his interest. Conried wanted to sign Mahler up for six months and also offered to arrange a number of concerts for him. Mahler replied to the effect that if nothing came of his 'dismissal' by the Kaiser, he could make himself available for a period of only eight weeks. But if his resignation was accepted, then he could come for six months. At the end of May Mahler telegraphed to Conried to announce that everything was fine and that he would be travelling to Berlin in early June to 'draw up our battle-plan'.[20]

Mahler took the night train to Berlin on 4 June and put up at the Hotel Kaiserhof, where Conried, too, was staying. Having changed and breakfasted, he went to see Conried, apparently in the company of Winternitz. They continued to discuss the details of the contract, suggesting that everything was not yet 'fine', the principal sticking point being the length of time that Mahler would be present in New York. Here there was a yawning gulf between the parties' goals, Conried wanting to keep Mahler in New York as long as he could, while Mahler was keen to earn as much money as he could in the shortest possible time, the strangeness of the New World filling him with feelings of apprehension, quite apart from the fact that he knew he would never find time to compose in New York. He was determined not to take on any new commitments that were as onerous and as time-consuming as those in Vienna. But he reached a provisional agreement with Conried in Berlin on 5 June and in a letter that was repeatedly interrupted by various distractions he communicated its contents to Alma. For six months' work in New York he would receive 125,000 crowns, a breathtaking increase on the 36,000 crowns that he had been receiving for ten months' work in Vienna. He agreed to work at the Met for four years, during which time he reckoned on being able to earn half a million crowns. As an alternative plan, which was evidently drawn up in case he was unable to free himself from his contract in Vienna, he would visit New York each year for between six and eight weeks, for which he would be paid 50,000 crowns a year, making a total of 200,000 crowns over a four-year period.

The situation in Vienna was now made more complicated by the fact that Mottl was unable to break his contract with Munich. The prince regent Luitpold was not willing to lose this pillar of the city's musical life, leaving Montenuovo feeling duped, for he had in principle accepted Mahler's request to be relieved of his post but could not let him go without at the same time being able to put forward the name of a successor. It looks as if Montenuovo, overcome by remorse, now tried to discourage Mahler from leaving, even though both men had already agreed on his departure. But Mahler, armed with his still secret contract with Conried and its altogether fabulous conditions, was in an exceptionally strong position and so he rejected Montenuovo's overtures. For several weeks Montenuovo could come up with no successor, but at least Mahler's assurance that he would remain until the end of the year gave him some breathing space. If necessary he could even have forced Mahler to stay longer by refusing to let him go. Negotiations with Weingartner soon got under way, although even as late as early August it looked as if Weingartner would be obliged to remain in Berlin. By 9 August, however, everything had been sorted out. These developments also help to explain why Franz Joseph was able to sign Mahler's dismissal papers at the same time as Weingartner's provisional appointment on 5 October. Mahler was home and dry, because even in the unlikely event of his having to remain in his post, he could still carry out his American tours. For the present, Montenuovo, who knew of the negotiations going on behind his back, insisted that Conried should make no public announcement until his dealings with Weingartner had been brought to a satisfactory conclusion. Although Montenuovo's plans may for a time have been thrown into confusion, by August everything had fallen into place.

Conried and Mahler met again in Vienna on 21 June, and on this occasion both men brought their seconds with them, Ernest Görlitz and I. C. Coppicus in the case of Conried, Roller and Winternitz in that of Mahler. (Quite why Winternitz should have played such an important role in these negotiations remains unclear.) The definitive contract between Mahler and Conried was signed in Vienna on 21 June, the wily Conried describing himself as 'President of the Conried Metropolitan Opera Co.'[21] This definitive contract looked rather different from the one that Mahler and Conried had provisionally agreed upon in Berlin, a fact that earlier writers on Mahler have tended to ignore. It reduced Mahler's visits to New York to the basic minimum that he himself had initially proposed, namely, three months at the height of the winter season. Specifically, Mahler agreed to arrive in the city between 20 and 25 January each year and to make himself available within two days of his arrival. Particularly interesting is the final clause of all: Mahler would not be obligated to conduct *Parsifal*. The origins of this clause can be traced back to a letter that Wagner wrote to King Ludwig II of Bavaria, insisting that the work should remain the preserve of Bayreuth. Attempts were soon being made to overturn this ban, but Mahler would never have acted in the face of his idol's wishes. In fact, Conried had already mounted a production of *Parsifal* at the Met in December 1903, a production that was regarded by many Wagnerians, and especially by Bayreuth, as an act of sacrilege and decried as a 'rape of the Grail'. The fact that Conried was Jewish made it easy for Bayreuth's anti-Semites to compare his crime to Alberich's rape of the Rhinegold and to invest the Met's director with the features of a rapacious Jew in a caricature of the period. In an addendum to the contract, which was not signed until September, it was agreed that Mahler would take up his duties four weeks earlier than originally specified and that he would receive an extra 25,000 crowns in consequence. Otherwise Mahler's season would last from the end of January to the end of April every year from 1908 to 1911. During this four-year period Mahler received 300,000 crowns: in other words, his fee was more than twice what he received in Vienna, even though he was doing only a third of the work. Conried also paid his travel expenses between Europe and America and first-class hotel accommodation and board. For the first year at least, Alma, too, would be paid for in terms of travel and accommodation. Under the terms of his contract, Mahler could accept no other work in America but was free to undertake engagements elsewhere. If he were to fall ill, he would receive no fee – in the event, Mahler was no longer bound by the terms of Conried's contract when he finally succumbed to his last fatal illness. Not even the most experienced professional businessman well versed in contract law could have negotiated his contract as tenaciously and as success-fully as this allegedly otherworldly artist.

Mahler's prospects for the next four years now seemed rosier than he could possibly have imagined only a short time previously. None the less, he bridled at the forced labour of his work at the Met with reluctant and arrogant singers, an orchestra whose members could not hold a candle to their counterparts in Vienna, an ignorant public, a foreign language, life in vast, dark hotel complexes in Manhattan, and long sea crossings between the two continents – in short, nothing to rouse his enthusiasm. Quite the opposite, in fact. But the chance to earn so much money in a concentrated three-month period and to spend the rest of the year composing and promoting his own music, without being interrupted each autumn with the start of the new opera season, fired his imagination. After a terrible period of uncertainty and of the most unwelcome haste to which he was ever subjected, he had finally succeeded in breaking free. The future lay at his feet. He felt in the best of health. He had survived all the burdens that had been placed upon him, and only his old attacks of migraine had returned with redoubled force, he told Alma in a letter that he wrote to her from the Hochschneeberg, whither he had retired on his own on 23 June, the day after the Vienna opera season finished. He then returned to the capital for a day, before heading back to the mountains. Then, on 30 June, he caught the train to the Wörthersee, where he was joined by Alma and the couple's two daughters. By the evening of the 30th the family was together again, and their best holiday for years could begin.

The Onset of Horror

A laconic letter to Arnold Berliner of 4 July hints at the coming horror without as yet revealing its full import: 'We have had frightful bad luck! I shall tell you when we next meet. Now my elder daughter has scarlet fever – diphtheria!'[22] His younger daughter, Anna, had already caught scarlet fever at the beginning of May, after previously having suffered a scalded hand as the result of an accident on the part of her English nanny, Maud Turner. Her recovery had been slow. Because of the danger of infection, Anna had gone to stay with her grandparents, while Mahler himself had taken rooms in a hotel. According to Anna's later reminiscences, her father blamed her grandparents for returning her to the family hearth too soon, with the result that Maria became infected. It may be added here that the diagnosis of scarlet fever *and* diphtheria is scientifically unsustainable. Whereas the symptoms may initially be the same, there is no doubt that Maria was suffering from diphtheria and that scarlet fever would not have killed her. Diphtheria bacteria and scarlet fever streptococci are two different pathogens, so that anyone suffering from scarlet fever cannot infect another person with diphtheria. To that extent, Anna's grandparents may be absolved of any blame. Anna seemed to have recovered when her elder sister, in actual fact the healthier of the two, succumbed to what appeared to be the same illness.

A century ago scarlet fever was one of the commonest of all childhood diseases. As with Mahler's own fatal illness, the discovery of antibiotics has largely put an end to the horrors of scarlet fever. The accompanying skin rash was painful and unpleasant but not life-threatening, the only risk arising from the high temperature that sometimes affected the patient but which could be combated with quinine, bed rest and cold compresses. Even a century ago healthy children normally recovered from scarlet fever, as was the case with Anna Mahler, but inflammation of the mucous membrane caused by scarlet fever might cause complications, leading contemporary medicine to conclude that the fever had developed into diphtheria. Thus we find Brockhaus's encyclopaedia claiming in 1894 that 'inflammation of the mucous membrane may assume varying degrees of seriousness and even take on the character of diphtheria'. Vaccination has led to the virtual elimination of diphtheria in the modern world but even now it remains substantially more dangerous than scarlet fever. In Mahler's day there was no antidote to either. Diphtheria was dangerous because inflammation of the pharyngeal cavity and larynx might lead to asphyxiation, not just as a result of the inflammation itself but through neuroparalysis, which might paralyse the muscles of the larynx, to say nothing of the delayed effects of damage to the cardiac muscle. Even today, therefore, it is by no means exceptional for doctors to perform a tracheotomy in order to improve the patient's breathing. But neither vaccination nor antibiotics were available for Maria Mahler. Brockhaus gives an idea of what she and her parents had to endure in consequence:

> As for the course that diphtheria takes, the illness generally begins suddenly with a high temperature, shivering and tiredness, difficulty in swallowing, a swelling of the lymph glands in the jaw and a whitish deposit on the mucous membrane of the tonsils and pharynx, a coating that spreads fairly quickly to other areas. These white areas cannot be wiped clean, and if an attempt is made to remove them by force, the area will be left raw and bloody. Left to themselves, they break off and leave discoloured, putrid ulcers that cause an extremely foul smell in the mouth. If the inflammation and the formation of these deposits spreads to the pharynx, the patient quickly grows hoarse, followed by complete voicelessness, coughing, wheezing and in the case of small children asphyxiation. Diphtheria of the nasal cavity can be recognized by nosebleeds and a malodorous suppurating discharge from the nostrils.

This is what happened to Maria Mahler, the couple's elder daughter, who in photographs always looked healthier and more ebullient than her sister, Maria being a strikingly beautiful, gifted child who, as Bruno Walter wrote after her death, seemed to exude more than average energy and vitality. Within three days of the Mahlers' arrival in Maiernigg, the first symptoms had started to appear. It is unlikely that the child could have been saved even if the family had been in Vienna. Given the diagnosis, her chances of surviving were poor. Her final illness lasted not two weeks, as Alma later recalled, but only ten days. Mahler withdrew to his room, while a storm raged outside, and a red sky provided a backdrop to these implacable events. 'In this weather, in this raging storm, I'd never have sent the children outside' – Alma's forebodings when Mahler wrote his *Kindertotenlieder* seemed to have been confirmed in the most terrible way imaginable. The doctor treating the child, Carl Victor Blumenthal, attempted a tracheotomy during the night of 10/11 July. Alma recalls running along the shore of the lake, screaming, until the child's English nanny found her and announced that it was all over, meaning, in fact, that the operation was over. But it made no difference. Throughout the rest of the night and the whole of the following day the child lay in Alma's bed, eyes wide open, gasping for breath, while Mahler – according to Alma – fled the house, unable to bear the sight and sound of his dying daughter. She finally passed away early on the morning of the 12th.

Alma's mother had arrived from Vienna, but it was all too much for her, too, and during a walk by the lake, she suffered a heart spasm, apparently at the very moment that the tiny coffin was being lifted into a cart and taken away to

Klagenfurt. Mahler came down to the lakeside, his face distorted with grief, while Alma recalled retrospectively that it was 'almost a joy' for her to fall into a deep faint. Mahler, Alma and Anna Moll retired indoors like frightened birds, feeling that if they were to emerge from their room, they might never come back. Blumenthal now had to minister to the needs of both women, prompting Mahler to suggest, by way of a distraction, that the doctor should examine his own heart, too, as his wife was always expressing her concern on that score. Blumenthal did as he was asked and afterwards famously remarked 'Well, you've no cause to be proud of a heart like that.' The sounds that he heard indicated a heart-valve defect, a diagnosis that we examined in detail in an earlier chapter. For Mahler and his wife, life in their beautiful house in Maiernigg and work in the composing house in the forest behind it now became impossible. Precipitately they packed their belongings and fled from the Wörthersee. Alma spent the rest of the summer at Schluderbach in the Tyrol, a village to the south of Toblach at the intersection of the roads to Cortina and Misurina in an area familiar to Mahler from his earlier visits to the Dolomites. He himself travelled to Vienna for a few days in order to prepare for his final season and to consult a heart specialist, Friedrich Kovacs. He left Maiernigg on 17 July in the company of Richard Nepallek, a Viennese neurologist whom Alma knew and who had come to Maiernigg to offer the couple his support and deal with all the formalities following Maria's death, Mahler and Alma themselves being incapable of carrying out these tasks.

In the course of the train journey back to Vienna, Mahler wrote to Alma, arguably one of the strangest letters that he ever penned. It begins: 'Dearest, we're sitting here in the dining car, and our eyes are in our stomachs (what a shame neither of you is here, you'd revel in it). I beg you, now your two guardians have left, don't *overdo* things and keep a hold on everything.' A day later he wrote again, this time reporting that he had put up at the Hotel Imperial, had a bath, eaten some ham, heard the first garbled reports on his resignation and slept extremely well, so that he was now feeling fine.[23] These are entirely normal letters, except that they are not normal in the context of the catastrophe that had struck only a few days earlier. Did Mahler really not have anything better to do a week after the terrible death of his elder daughter than to report that he had slept well and enjoyed a slice of ham? These letters are puzzling in the extreme. Such total disregard for all that had happened and the cheerful tone that he adopts here – was it all just an attempt to protect himself from the tragedy? A tragically ironic stance? Not one of the letters that he wrote during these weeks and months refers to what had taken place. There is not even the merest hint. That they do not reflect the real Mahler is clear from a letter that Bruno Walter wrote to his parents in the middle of September: 'He has been completely broken by it; outwardly one sees nothing, but anyone who knows him knows that inwardly he is completely washed up. She seems to bear it more easily, with tears and philosophizing. I really don't know how anyone can bear anything like this.'[24] Alma later wrote that the death of their daughter drove a wedge between the couple, claiming that Mahler unconsciously blamed her for the child's death. After a few days in Vienna, during which time he received Kovacs's partial confirmation of Blumenthal's diagnosis, Mahler joined Alma in Schluderbach, and in the middle of August the couple returned to Maiernigg. In the face of all the claims that they left Maiernigg following their daughter's death and never returned, it is worth noting that according to Alma they did not feel as uncomfortable as they had thought they would. But in spite of this, they did not return there the following year.

We can only speculate on Mahler's reaction. A year later, however, he wrote an important letter to Bruno Walter that allows us a far deeper insight into his inner workings than he normally granted others. Indeed, it is perhaps the most disturbing letter that he ever wrote, for it describes his attempts to deal with the tragedy. In a note to the published edition, Walter himself adds 'I suppose I had suggested that Mahler should read Feuchtersleben's *Diatetics of the Soul*.' One of Walter's favourite titles, Ernst von Feuchtersleben's study had first appeared in 1838 and been reprinted forty-five times by 1883. (An English translation was published in 1852.) It was one of the most successful best-sellers of the age, highly regarded by Grillparzer and others, and a forerunner of all those self-help manuals that nowadays seek to guide a disorientated society. Just as a correct diet should help to redress the body's imbalance, so the soul needed the right sustenance, for outer balance must be matched by inner balance. For a perennial optimist like Walter, this may well have been the right reading matter, but for the emotionally fragile Mahler it was bound to seem an ineffectual product of the bourgeois Biedermeier age, the equivalent of an attempt to cure pneumonia with lime-blossom tea. His reply to Walter's letter, which is no longer extant, was correspondingly prickly:

What is all this about the soul? And its sickness? And where should I find a remedy? On a visit to Scandinavia? That would have been no more than a distraction. It was only here, in solitude, that I could come to my senses and regain a sense of awareness. – Ever since I was overcome by panic and terror, as I was at that time, I have tried only to avert my eyes and stop listening. – If I'm to find the way back to myself, I must surrender to the horrors of loneliness. But basically I am speaking only in riddles, because you do not know what went on inside me and what is still going on inside me; but it is certainly not a hypochondriac's fear of death, as you suppose. That I must die was something I already knew. – But without trying to explain or describe something for which there are perhaps no words at all, I shall say only that at a single blow I have lost all the clarity and calm that I had ever struggled to achieve; and that I stood vis-à-vis de rien and that at the end of my life I am like a beginner who has to learn how to walk and stand. – Is this a mental outlook that must be fought with a psychiatrist's weapons, as you imply? And as for my 'work', there is something distinctly depressing about having to learn everything over again. I cannot work at my desk. Inner activity must be accompanied by outer activity.

Mahler then reports on his racing pulse and the fear that he feels at even a modest increase in physical activity, especially since such violent physical activity had always been the motivating force behind his creative work:

Imagine Beethoven having both his legs amputated as the result of an accident. If you know how he lived his life – do you think that after this he could have drafted even a single movement of a quartet? And this can hardly be compared with my own situation. I admit that, superficial though it may seem, this is the greatest calamity that has ever befallen me. I have to start a new life – and here too I am a complete beginner.[25]

Here, too, there is no mention of his daughter's death but only of his heart diagnosis, with its serious consequences in terms of severely reducing his physical movements and of the need to keep checking his pulse, which for Mahler was a positively unhealthy thing to do. With hindsight we may well be inclined to think that averting his eyes and no longer listening was his way of attempting to mitigate the horror of the situation. Like the letter as a whole, it suggests that a massive shift had taken place in Mahler's psychological makeup. He simply could not handle his doctor's diagnosis concerning his heart disease – a diagnosis initially more serious than it actually was – coming so soon after the death of his daughter. The phrase 'at a single blow' implies that he had to link the two hammer blows in an attempt to come to terms with them. The loss of his daughter was something with which he could not cope – certainly not through his forced jollity immediately after the catastrophe – and so he attempted to hide it away inside a lesser problem in the hope that it would become more bearable. If Mahler was still claiming that his life had fallen apart a whole year after the catastrophe and in doing so apparently referring to his doctor's diagnosis about his own state of health, then he did so not from heartlessness but in an attempt not to overtax his ability to come to terms with the situation and to allow his psyche time to deal with what was manageable.

It was not Ernst von Feuchtersleben who could help Mahler in the summer of 1907 but only another, more powerful source of consolation: 'Ja, gib mir Ruh, ich hab Erquickung not' ('Yes, give me peace, I need refreshment'). According to Alma, it was during this period that Mahler sought comfort in

Hans Bethge's *Die chinesische Flöte*, a collection of free adaptations of Chinese poetry. Alma claims that a friend of her father, Theobald Pollak, had given a copy of this slender volume to Mahler several years earlier, but this is impossible as the book was not published until the autumn of 1907. It seems that Alma is mixing up the Bethge edition with an older book of poems by Li-Tai-Po. She also claims that her husband singled out a number of the poems which he intended to set to music at a later date and that he took out the volume again under the weight of the blows of fate that rained down on him in the summer of 1907. The poems, she writes, are immeasurably sad, which is not in fact true, as Bethge's selection – like Mahler's own – includes poems that are light-hearted and cheerful alternating with others that strike a more tragic tone. There is no doubt that Mahler was motivated by feelings similar to those expressed by Bethge himself in his introduction to the collection:

> The very first time that I came across poems from the Chinese, I was altogether enchanted. What a lovely lyric art I found here! I felt a timidly diaphanous delicacy of lyric sounds, I gazed into an art of words that is entirely filled with imagery and that sheds light on a world of wistful nostalgia and the mysteries of existence, I felt a slight lyric trembling, an outpouring of symbolism, something tender and airy like moonlight, and an emotional gracefulness that reminded me of a flower.[26]

It is impossible to say for certain whether Mahler got to know Bethge's volume in 1907 or not until 1908.[27] Alma was fond of rewriting history, adapting events to suit her own perception of them, highlighting some events and combining others whenever it helped to heighten the drama of the situation. If she is right when she asserts that Mahler began work on the initial sketches for *Das Lied von der Erde* in Schluderbach in the summer of 1907, it can have been no more than the first tentative steps of the kind that Mahler would record in his sketchbooks during his walks. Most of the work on the score was undertaken during the summer of 1908. Be that as it may, the qualities that drew Mahler to these poems are as clear from the ones that he did not set as from those that he did. Among the former group is the following, a sad little poem by an unknown poet:

> Der Herbstwind reißt die Blätter von den Bäumen,
> Sie wirbeln durch die kalte Luft zur Erde;
> Ich sehe ihnen ohne Mitleid zu
> Mit starren Augen.
>
> Mein Herz war einsam, da sie kamen. Einsam
> Seh ich sie wandern. Trauer füllt mein Herz,

So wie die Täler sich mit Schatten füllen
Beim Nahn des Abends.

Die winterlichen Stürme werden bald
Das Wasser wandeln zu Kristall. Jedoch
Sobald der Lenz kommt, springen alle Bäche
In neuer Wonne!

Sobald der Lenz kommt, will ich auf die Gipfel
Der Berge steigen! Sonne, liebe Sonne,
Erbarme dich, laß meines Herzens Trauer
Dann endlich schmelzen.

[The autumn wind tears the leaves from the trees, they whirl to the ground through the cold air, I watch them, pitiless, with staring eyes. My heart grew lonely when they came. Lonely I see them drift. Sadness fills my heart just as they fill the valleys with shadows as evening approaches. The winter storms will shortly turn the water to crystal. But when spring comes, all the brooks will leap with joy again! As soon as spring comes I'll climb up to the summits of the mountains! Sun, dear sun, take pity on me and let my heart's sadness melt at last.]

These lines make it clear why Mahler did not return to Rückert and his *Kindertotenlieder*, which had once captured his imagination. Rückert had wallowed in his pain too pitilessly and too monomaniacally, and Mahler had followed him without restraint, retracing his lines with garish colours. Now screams of protest and outrage had to be replaced by delicacy, sadness and a slight sense of trembling in order to give expression to all that he had suffered, and for this Bethge's reworked poems were ideal. Just as, in the poem that we have just quoted, grief finally melts away beneath the sun of life, so in the final movement of *Das Lied von der Erde*, the quietistic tone that is struck by Wang-Wei's poem is further intensified by Mahler's additional lines. Whereas Bethge's version ends with the words 'Die Erde ist die gleiche überall, / Und ewig, ewig sind die weißen Wolken' ('The earth is everywhere the same, and forever, forever are the white clouds'), Mahler expands this passage and adds greater weight to its underlying sentiments: 'Die liebe Erde allüberall blüht auf im Lenz / und grünt aufs neu! / Allüberall und ewig blauen licht die Fernen! / Ewig, ewig!' ('Everywhere the dear earth blossoms in spring and grows green again! Everywhere and forever the distance shines bright and blue! Forever . . . forever!'). *Das Lied von der Erde* is one of the vessels into which Mahler poured his attempt to achieve clarity and calm by wresting them back again.

As far as Mahler's work commitments were concerned, the rest of the year ran smoothly after Montenuovo's brief attempt to rescind his resignation had been nipped in the bud. The reader may be inclined to ask why the general administrator, August Plappart von Leenheer, played no part in these developments, but the answer is simple: Plappart had left his post on 30 June 1906, and the post remained unfilled. Mahler had charge of no more new productions, his last collaboration with Roller having been Gluck's *Iphigénie en Aulide* back in March, a production that had played to half-empty houses. In the event, Mahler's resolve not to appear on the podium at the Court Opera could not be maintained as there were a number of performances that still needed to be conducted, at least until such time as the official decree, with all its financial provisions, had been duly ratified by the Kaiser. In such matters, Mahler was punctilious, not wanting to be accused of insubordination until his pension had been properly sorted out. He used his prerogative as director to arrange the performances in such a way that in September and October the house seemed to be mounting a kind of secret Mahler Festival. Once again he revisited the greatest successes of his ten-year tenure in Vienna: *Don Giovanni, Le nozze di Figaro, Die Zauberflöte, Die Walküre, Iphigénie en Aulide* and *Fidelio* – only *Tristan und Isolde* was missing. In keeping with the standard practice of the period, the audience did not know who was conducting until the door to the pit opened, and Mahler or some other conductor emerged. But everyone was aware that sooner or later he would conduct his very last performance in Vienna. In early October he travelled to Frankfurt and Wiesbaden – it was the last time he applied for, and was granted, leave of absence – in order to conduct works by Beethoven and Wagner at a concert in Wiesbaden on the 9th with the Kaim Orchestra from Munich. The age of orchestral tours had already begun.

No one could have known at the time that a repertory performance of *Fidelio* on 15 October would be the last time that Mahler conducted at the Court Opera. We do not know whether Mahler himself was aware of the significance of the occasion. Ludwig Karpath even gives the impression that he was standing in for another conductor. Be that as it may, the audience accorded him an ovation. Alma, still weakened by the summer's events, then went to take the waters at Semmering, and on the 19th Mahler left for three concerts in St Petersburg and Helsinki, or Helsingfors as it was then known. (Finland was under Russian control, although from 1905 it had enjoyed a certain autonomy.) His concerts in St Petersburg took place on 26 October and 9 November and included works by Beethoven, Berlioz and Wagner, whereas the concert in Finland on 1 November featured his own Fifth Symphony, which he conducted for the final time. His long letters to Alma are full of melancholy reminiscences of their honeymoon trip to St Petersburg in 1902. They are also filled with his sad and persistent reminders to write to him more often and with expressions of his own disquiet about her health – Alma, too, was thought to have a bad heart. Throughout it all, it is impossible to avoid the feeling that he was afraid of losing her too. On his first evening in Helsingfors, where he arrived after an eight-hour train journey from St Petersburg, Mahler attended a concert conducted by Robert Kajanus, one of the leading figures in the musical life of his country. Among the works performed were two by Jean Sibelius, his op. 16 *Spring Song* and the *Valse triste* op. 44. Mahler was deeply disappointed: 'The first composition was a standard piece of kitsch spiced with a national sauce prepared from the "Nordic" harmonies we know only too well. Yuck.'[28] But when he met Sibelius, he was forced to admit that he was extremely sympathetic as a person. Sibelius was naturally interested in what Mahler could do for him in New York, a hope that in the event remained unfulfilled. Mahler also got to know the most famous Finnish painter of the period, Akseli Gallen-Kallela, and went sailing with him through the Finnish skerries. They stopped off at the home of the architect Eliel Saarinen to warm up, and while they were there, Gallen unpacked his easel and started to paint Mahler's portrait. It was by now dark and massive logs were hissing and crackling in the hearth as if in a smithy. Gallen's portrait shows Mahler face-on, his head resting in his right hand, the glow of the fire reflected in his face and in the lenses of his glasses. It is the most impressive likeness of him after Rodin's.

In St Petersburg, Mahler's performance of his Fifth Symphony caused mainly bewilderment. The audience included representatives of two very different generations of Russian musicians: Nikolay Rimsky-Korsakov and Igor Stravinsky. Rimsky-Korsakov found the instrumentation 'coarse and clumsy' and dismissed the work as a whole as an 'arrogant improvisation' by a composer 'who never knows what will happen in the next bar'. Stravinsky, who for a time studied privately with Rimsky, was only twenty-five years old at this time and later recalled Mahler's striking appearance on the podium rather than the work, which evidently left very little of an impression on him.

By 12 November Mahler was back in Vienna, where he conducted a performance of his Second Symphony on the 24th, his final appearance in the city as a conductor. Reactions to the piece were no different from those that he had endured during the previous ten years. To put it mildly, they were mixed. Of course, the reviewers were also tempted to use the occasion to combine a critique of the concert with a more general survey of Mahler's years in the city. It is unnecessary to quote from any of them as the picture had not changed. Events now moved quickly. In the rider to his agreement with Conried, Mahler had promised to sail from Cherbourg on 12 December. Now only three weeks remained to prepare for the trip and take his leave of Vienna, a leave-taking that assumed various ceremonial forms. Using highly official language he bade farewell to the members of the Court Opera in a printed letter in which, with typically unwavering honesty, he did nothing to hide the problems that the two parties had had to face. He struck the right tone from the outset: 'Instead of the whole, the complete creation, that I had dreamt of, I leave behind something piecemeal and imperfect – as man is fated to do.' And he went on: 'In the throes of the battle, in the heat of the moment, neither you nor I have been spared wounds, or errors. But when a work has been successfully performed, a task accomplished, we have forgotten all the difficulties and exertions; we have felt richly rewarded even in the absence of the outward signs of success. We have all made progress, and so has the Institution for which we have worked.' He ended with a barbed remark, specifically excluding from his message of gratitude all those who had obstructed his work in the course of the last ten years: 'Please accept my hearty thanks, you who have helped forward my difficult and often thankless task, who have supported me and have fought at my side.'[29]

The extent to which Mahler's relations with the company and with his superiors had broken down is abundantly clear from the fact that no one felt it necessary to arrange an official farewell for the departing director who had turned the Vienna Opera into the leading and most progressive opera house in the world. The relief at finally getting rid of the difficult genius far outweighed any sadness at his departure, to say nothing of the people who had spent the last ten years intriguing against him and who now looked forward to a time when they could drink to Weingartner's health and to an easier life without Mahler. But Weingartner had barely arrived in Vienna as the great white hope for the future when he discovered what loyalty meant to the locals. In his reminiscences he had no hesitation in stressing that Mahler's great legacy consisted in little more than a clapped-out ensemble and dubious production values. Nor was he squeamish about the means that he used in getting his way, reintroducing the old cuts in *Die Walküre* and ruining the legendary *Fidelio* by cutting the *Leonore* Overture no. 3 between the last two scenes of the opera and instead playing the *Leonore* Overture no. 2 at the start of the performance. It was with this restudied *Fidelio* that Weingartner introduced himself to Viennese audiences on 23 January 1908. But without the *Leonore* Overture, there was no time for the scene change required by Roller's sets, preventing the final scene from creating so brilliant an effect. At this point Weingartner reverted to the old prison courtyard from Act One, thereby losing one of the great coups of the Roller–Mahler production. By the same token, the chorus at the end of the opening act was allowed to stand downstage as a group and trumpet its wretchedness to the audience.

It now turned out that Mahler had more supporters than he had thought, for a section of the audience, including people who did not necessarily lament the director's departure, had in the meantime grown to like the Mahler–Roller *Fidelio* and voiced their protests at Weingartner's interference with it, protests that Weingartner believed could only be the work of a pro-Mahler political clique. But perhaps it included people who had always protested because it was in their nature to do so. Mahlerians such as Paul Stefan trembled with rage and disgust at Weingartner's violation of the work, and writers on Mahler have followed his lead. It is interesting, however, to note that Alfred Roller found the changes neither particularly bad nor particularly good. In a long letter that he wrote to Mahler in New York on the eve of the 1908 restudied revival, Roller describes what their joint achievement looked like in his successor's hands. If Mahler had been hoping for a picture of a natural disaster – he was always keen to hear negative comments about Weingartner – then he will have been disappointed, for Roller offers a surprisingly neutral account of the proceedings, before concluding: 'On the whole, a quite businesslike and, as it strikes me, a rather philistine production without any particular inspiration or go; it does not exactly ruin the opera but neither does it do anything to reveal its depths. Weingartner seems to have the orchestra well in hand. His conducting, certainly, seems to me rather pedestrian. I have no sense of an overarching structure.'[30] Weingartner would not be deflected from his course, so firmly convinced was he that everything that was anti-Mahler would go down well in Vienna. But local perceptions of Mahler among at least a section of the press and public had been transformed, and to the extent that Weingartner, for all that he was a fine conductor, was judged by his predecessor's standards and found wanting, he was left with little choice but to sever his connections with Vienna in 1911.

In a handful of brief private letters Mahler took his leave of a number of individuals, including Anna von Mildenburg. It is hard to avoid the impression that he had a bad conscience that because of their former relationship his dealings with her in Vienna had been so formal and distant. Zemlinsky and Schoenberg were invited to afternoon coffee, while Bruno Walter received a letter assuring him that their bond required no words to underline it. But Mahler's admirers were not content to leave it at that. Presumably at the instigation of the loyal and assiduous Paul Stefan, it was decided that Mahler should be given a proper send-off at the station. The printed invitation was signed by Webern and Stefan as well as two pupils of Zemlinsky and Schoenberg, Karl Horwitz and Heinrich Jalowetz, and asked the composer's admirers to present themselves at the Westbahnhof at 8.30 on Monday 9 December. 'Since the aim is to surprise Mahler with this demonstration, it seems imperative not to confide in persons close to the press.'[31] Some two hundred people responded to the invitation, including, of course, Berg and Schoenberg, Roller and Klimt. Alma does not say whether Mahler was genuinely surprised but described the send-off as follows:

> They were all drawn up when we arrived, flowers in their hands and tears in their eyes, ready to board the train and deck out our compartment with

flowers from roof to floor. When we drew slowly out it was without regret or backward glances. We had been too hard hit. All we wanted was to get away, the farther the better. We even felt happy as Vienna was left behind. We did not miss our child, who had been left with my mother. We knew now that anxious love was of no avail against catastrophe, and that no spot on earth gives immunity. We had been through the fire. So we thought. But, in spite of all, one thing had us both in its grip – the future.[32]

According to Alma, Mahler insisted during the journey that he was taking his leave of repertory opera but expressed his happiness that he had contrived to hide from the public the fact that he was making bricks without straw. According to another account, Klimt is said to have commented only 'It's over' on the forecourt at the Westbahnhof. In Paris the Mahlers put up at the Hotel Bellevue and in the evening attended a performance of *Tristan und Isolde* at the Palais Garnier. The Tristan was Ernest van Dyck, who had appeared to great acclaim in Vienna, but the Mahlers left before the end. On 12 December, in keeping with the terms of Mahler's contract, they set sail from Cherbourg aboard the *Kaiserin Auguste Viktoria*. Mahler was seasick. They arrived in New York on 20 December. A new era was beginning, although it was to be very much shorter than planned.

31

Das Lied von der Erde

I N EARLY SEPTEMBER 1908 Bruno Walter received a letter from Toblach inviting him to meet Mahler for lunch in Vienna on the 5th: 'I have been hard at work (from which you can tell that I am more or less "acclimatized"). I myself do not know what the whole thing could be called. I have been granted a time that was good, and I think it is the most personal thing I have done so far. Perhaps more about that when I see you.'[1] The work to which Mahler was referring here was *Das Lied von der Erde*.

The first edition of Hans Bethge's *Die chinesische Flöte* was published by Insel-Verlag of Leipzig in 1907. Hans Bethge (1876–1946) was a writer with a doctorate in Romance literature. A native of Dessau, he later moved to Berlin.[2] *Die chinesische Flöte* contains adaptations of eighth-century Chinese poems based on German, French and English translations, Bethge himself not being conversant with Chinese. The volume was remarkably successful, no doubt because it tapped into a vein of japonaiserie already mined by Jugendstil artists. Bethge built on the success of the collection and published adaptations of Indian, Japanese and Persian poetry. It is worth mentioning here that one of Sou-Chong's most famous arias in Franz Lehár's *The Land of Smiles* and a favourite of the tenor Richard Tauber derives from Ma-Huang-Tschung's 'The Spurned Lover' in Bethge's anthology. Lehár's version reads: 'Von Apfelblüten einen Kranz / Legt ich der Lieblichsten vors Fenster / In einer Mondnacht im April' ('I laid a garland of apple blossoms before my sweetheart's window one moonlit night in April'), whereas Bethge's version is: 'Von Birnbaumblüten einen Kranz / Legt ich der Herrlichsten vors Fenster / In einer Mondnacht im April' ('I laid a garland of pear-tree blossoms before the most glorious woman's window one moonlit night in April'). This is not the place to discuss the poetic or philological merits of Bethge's adaptations. What matters is that they cast a spell on Mahler, who until then had taken very little interest in Chinese or oriental literature, unless we count individual poems by the Orientalist

Friedrich Rückert. Most of Mahler's work on *Das Lied von der Erde* can be dated to the summer of 1908. Alma's claim that the earliest sketches date from 1907 is almost certainly ruled out by the fact that the anthology was probably not published until the autumn of that year. Mahler may also have revised the score in 1909, but in general he began work on it in July 1908 and had completed it by September.[3] The first performance was conducted by Bruno Walter on 20 November 1911 six months after Mahler's death. It took place in the Munich Tonhalle. The orchestra was that of the local Konzertverein, and the soloists were both American, Sarah Jane Cahier ('Mrs Charles Cahier') and William Miller. After the interval Walter conducted the Second Symphony as part of a memorial concert organized by the loyal Emil Gutmann.

Das Lied von der Erde is a puzzling work for Mahler's admirers and also for scholars. That we are dealing here with one of his most important works was clear from a very early date, but exactly what sort of a work is it in terms of musical history? Is it a cycle of orchestral songs, as its main heading claims, or is it, rather, a 'symphony for tenor and contralto (or baritone) voice and orchestra', as its subheading states? Mahler seems initially to have envisaged the former alternative and planned to write a piece modelled on Berlioz's *Les Nuits d'été*, for example, but in the course of his work he appears to have given increasing prominence to the goal of overcoming the hitherto strict division between symphony and song. The result is what Hermann Danuser has described as 'one of the most radical dovetailings of existing genres in the whole history of music until then'.[4] The three middle movements, 'Von der Jugend', 'Von der Schönheit' and 'Der Trunkene im Frühling', most clearly resemble lieder in terms of their character and length, whereas the introductory and dramatically assured 'Das Trinklied vom Jammer der Erde', which lasts a full eight minutes, and, above all, the final movement, 'Der Abschied', which, at almost thirty minutes, lasts nearly as long as the previous five movements together, both go far beyond anything that we might define as a song. 'Der Abschied' in particular constitutes a final symphonic Adagio similar to those that end the Third and Ninth Symphonies. Indeed, it is this final movement that most encourages us to define the work as a symphony, even though the concept of a song cannot be abandoned altogether. The secret of the work's unusual impact lies in the sense of a *coincidentia oppositorum*, a union of opposites, song and symphony no longer being forced beneath the same yoke, as is otherwise the case with Mahler, but allowed to flow freely into one another as if at the end of a lengthy tradition. The boldness of the concept is subsumed by the purity of its realization. Nor is the fact that the work has six movements particularly exceptional: so, too, has the Third Symphony.

The existential scope of the work is already clear from its opening movement. The refrain, 'Dunkel ist das Leben, ist der Tod' ('Life is dark, and so is death'), is taken over from Bethge's adaptation of the original poem by Li-Tai-Po and marks out the extremes between which the song-symphony operates, for these lines are not those of a lament but of an ecstatically ebullient drinking song. The strident, gleaming tone of the opening, which places inordinate demands on the tenor's power and penetration, is achieved by means of the tension inherent in the interval of a second, while the vaguely exotic character of the work as a whole stems from the use of pentatonic elements that had not previously been a part of Mahler's musical language. Instead of being built around the usual major and minor modes, the work is based on a five-note scale associated with central and eastern Asia. Other examples of pentatonicism that may be familiar to the reader are Puccini's *Turandot* and Lehár's aforementioned *Land of Smiles*, in particular the song 'Von Apfelblüten einen Kranz', in which pentatonicism is used insistently to suggest a particular exoticism. The other distinguishing feature of the musical language of *Das Lied von der Erde* is its prevailing diatonicism. In this case, however, the pentatonic colouring rescues it from the charge levelled against the unadulterated diatonicism of the final movement of the Seventh Symphony.

The second song, 'Der Einsame im Herbst', bears the performance marking 'Etwas schleppend. Ermüdet' ('Somewhat dragging. Weary'). 'Weary' is not so much a tempo marking as an instruction to the performer on how to interpret the piece. The muted first violins move sinuously and yet lethargically in hexachords, and the lake above which the autumn mists float appears to be ruffled. The first oboe adds its plaintive strains. This could almost be a quotation from the start of the scene between Pimen and Grigory in Mussorgsky's *Boris Godunov*. Even the situation is similar: Pimen is writing his chronicle by the light of an oil lamp, while the words that Mahler has set here include the phrase 'My little lamp guttered with a hiss'. Autumn and weariness settle like mildew on the lonely Chinese poet, who lives in a little hut on the shores of a lake. The sense of uplift at the words 'Sonne der Liebe, willst du nie mehr scheinen' ('Sun of love, will you never shine again?') is as vain as it is brief, and the end of the question, 'Um meine bittern Tränen mild aufzutrocknen' ('And dry up tenderly my bitter tears'), sinks back into the lethargy of the opening in which nature and the soul are attuned with one another. The world of nature is apportioned to the supporting violins, the sighs of the soul to the plaintive woodwind. The fact that the soul can find no secure basis for certainty or trust is reflected in the almost complete absence of a bass register and the spare textures of the instrumentation, which is chamber-like in its diaphanous lightness.

Mahler never came closer to Impressionism in music than in the third movement, 'Von der Jugend', plein-air painting of the most gossamery kind. There could hardly be a starker contrast than with 'Der Einsame im Herbst'. In the earlier song we encountered a man utterly alone and able to contemplate only death as a form of release, whereas here we have a friend among friends, with-drawing momentarily from the pavilion in the centre of a small lake, and with a sense of pleasure and inner calm watching and listening to his friends as they drink and talk and write poetry. Mahler links the two songs together by appearing to repeat the basic figure from 'Der Einsame im Herbst' at the start of 'Von der Jugend'. This time, however, it is entrusted not to the *strascinando* violins but to the flute and oboe, which leap along in typically cheeky fashion – the notes on the printed page reveal the inner relationship more clearly than their aural impression. The strings are marked '*saltando*' ('leaping'), and the tenor voice, too, leaps like a ball on a fountain, almost chuckling, filled with a very real zest for life and intense vitality. There is something particularly ingeni-ous about Mahler's treatment of the text, with its reference to a mirror image: 'Auf des kleinen, kleinen Teiches stiller, stiller Wasserfläche zeigt sich alles wunderlich im Spiegelbilde.' ('On the little pool's still surface everything is strangely mirrored.') Twelve-note technique would, of course, have provided a simple solution to this problem in the form of retrograde, inversion and retro-grade-inversion. But this was not an option available to Mahler, and so he used individual notes and even entire sections that appear to mirror each other.

The fourth song, 'Von der Schönheit', likewise uses mirror effects. Here the poet describes young women on the riverbank, their delicate outlines reflected in the water. Whereas the earlier song had described an all-male society, here we have its counterpart in the form of a group of young women, albeit one startled by a party of wild-eyed men on horseback. This gives Mahler a chance to interpolate what is almost certainly the briefest quick march in his output, an agitated wild hunt that bursts into the *comodo dolcissimo* idyll with unex-pected and alarming brutality and is by no means as harmless as the text would have us believe. The male principle drives away all porcelain-like delicacy and subtlety, even if it passes across the stage with lightning speed. The narrator grows breathless and proves incapable of providing a precise account of events in so low a register – the passage is barely singable, a feature due not to the inability of the singer or to Mahler's incompetence but to the situation, which takes the narrator's breath away. The most beautiful of the women casts agitated, languorous glances in the direction of the wildest of the young men, but as the violas die away the sense of bewilderment remains long after the song has ended: the virginal idyll has been destroyed for good.

In the fifth song, 'Der Trunkene im Frühling', the singer who had launched the cycle with the opening drinking song seems to have woken up from one of his many drunken stupors. But perhaps this song is sung by the 'lonely man in autumn', who had sought refuge from his loneliness in drink. The fact that 'Der Einsame im Herbst' is sung by the alto and not by the tenor, who sings the two drinking songs, should not carry undue weight, not only because the alto can be replaced by a baritone but also because these are not songs associated with specific roles: it is the alto who embodies the lonely *man*. Mahler paints an inimitable portrait of a drinker (the poem's original title) but also of a 'drunken man' – including the Nietzschean connotations of that term that are also found in Alfred Mombert's anthology of poems, *Der himmlische Zecher* (The Celestial Toper) that appeared in 1909. For this toper, real life and the world of dreams merge as one, and he is incapable of distinguishing any longer between daytime, dreams and drinking. The reeling motion of the song and its rapid shifts reflect the drunkard's vacillating frame of mind, but beneath the satirical surface there is something self-destructive, and we shall probably not go far wrong in seeing behind this apparently happy drunkard the figure of Wagner's ailing Tristan reeling across the stage: 'Verfluchter Tag mit deinem Schein! Wachst du ewig meiner Pein?' ('Accursed day with your bright light! Do you watch forever over my torment?')

But it is the final song, 'Der Abschied', that ultimately confirms our definition of the work as a symphony. On hearing the first five songs, a keeper of the seal of the great musico-aesthetic tradition might argue that for all the sophistication and delights of the work, they do not justify its subtitle as a 'symphony', but the final movement suddenly raises the whole work to the level of the great symphonic tradition and retrospectively exudes an authority that lifts the miniatures and snapshots of the previous movements to expressive heights unparalleled in Mahler's output. This final movement – the word 'song', which had earlier been appropriate, no longer does it justice – is worthy of taking its place alongside the greatest of Mahler's Adagios, while surpassing them in terms of its ability to achieve the same effect with far more economical means. Never has the unfathomable loneliness of the human soul been laid so bare and seemed as vulnerable as it does here. This is also the only time that Mahler has combined two separate poems, Mong-Kao-Jen's 'In Erwartung des Freundes' and Wang-Wei's 'Der Abschied des Freundes', linking together the two phases of expectation and valediction in a single movement, albeit with a number of changes to both texts. Expectation and valediction now appear as the two sides of the same coin, and this coin is loneliness and death. (It may be added in passing that if the mezzo-soprano or baritone soloist sits down during the long orchestral interlude, then they have the most disruptive effect imaginable on the flow and cohesion of this movement.)

Until now, even in 'Der Einsame im Herbst', sadness had seemed relatively light-footed, with violin figurations and plaintive solo woodwind. But the final movement begins with the performance marking 'Schwer' ('Heavy'). By retaining his extremely translucent, chamber-like instrumentation, Mahler ensures that this heaviness is achieved not through massive orchestral effects but simply through a low pizzicato in the double basses and cellos, semibreves in the harps, a tam-tam struck *pianissimo*, two horns also marked *pianissimo* and the contrabassoon in its lowest register. This is repeated twice before the first oboe enters with a characteristic turn that will later leave its mark on the final movement of the Ninth. The use of extreme contrast that had characterized the earlier movements is now replaced by a uniform mood of bleakness culminating in the extraordinarily spare textures of the middle section at 'Es wehet kühl im Schatten meiner Fichten', where the solo voice is accompanied only by a pedal point in the double basses and the turn in the upper register of the flute, the melancholic fluttering of the bird of death seeming to derive from the end of the Second Symphony. At the phrase 'O Schönheit!', there is a sense of optimism and uplift, only for a veiled funeral march to usher in the orchestral interlude that leads to the second, concluding poem by Wang-Wei, starting with the words 'Ich stieg vom Pferd'. Mahler found this subjective perspective too direct and so he objectified the farewell by simply changing the personal pronoun from 'I' ('Ich') to 'he' ('Er') and instructing the singer to interpret these lines 'in a narrative tone, without expression'. The range is very narrow, making it difficult to distinguish between narrative economy or neutrality and total weariness.

The work ends with a sevenfold repeat of the word 'Ewig' ('forever'/'eternal'). Mahler found a bold solution to the problem of how to end a symphony that somehow has to reach a conclusion while at the same time implying the infinity and open-endedness of human hopes and longings and sufferings: the ideas of closure and open-endedness are intertwined like death and life. To that extent the work could also be called 'The Song of Life and Death'. Over a basic C major tonality the voice moves seven times from E to D, remaining on the second degree of the scale with a hovering persistence instead of completing the obvious final step to C. The final chord is a triad with added sixth (C–E–G–A), the note A producing a dissonance that avoids the shrillness of the famous nine-note chord in the fragmentary Tenth Symphony but which, combined with the vocal line of the soloist, none the less invests this ending with a sense of delicate suspension. On the one hand, then, Mahler avoids closure, while on the other hand providing the work with a conclusion that represents an expanded form of the *Grundgestalt* of A–G–E that shapes the work as a whole.[5] *Das Lied von der Erde* does not end and yet it ends, prolonging life and death in the evolutionary scale and cycle of nature – earth – and extending them into eternity.

Starting Afresh: New York
(1908–11)

A New City – a New Opera House

In Mahler's day the crossing from Cherbourg to New York lasted a whole week. The couple put up at the Hotel Majestic, a huge conglomeration of six tower blocks arranged in parallel in two groups of three, overlooking Central Park West on the corner of Seventy-Second Street. A postcard to Mahler's mother-in-law indicates that they were staying on the eleventh floor. The hotel seems not to have been entirely to the Mahlers' liking, for on their next visit they stayed at the Savoy on Fifth Avenue at the corner of Fifty-Ninth Street and the south-eastern corner of Central Park, where Central Park South and Fifth Avenue intersect. It was also substantially closer to the Met, which lay between Thirty-Ninth and Fortieth Street on the one hand and between Seventh Avenue and Broadway on the other. Moreover, the Savoy was popular with singers like Caruso, who stayed there whenever they were appearing at the Met.

Neither Mahler nor Alma knew New York when they arrived on 20 December 1907. It had changed enormously during the period since 1880, when electric lighting was installed on Broadway, ushering in the city's transformation into an international capital. Two years later the first electric power station began operating. The Gilded Age was a time of economic prosperity that was gradually established in the wake of the Civil War and that developed with increasing speed. The leading New York families were said to consist of the four hundred men and women who every January were invited by Caroline Astor to a vast ball at her home. Their fortunes had been made earlier in the century, but the Gilded Age finally gave them an opportunity to spend them ostentatiously. In addition to foundations and hospitals, a new and attractive institution like the Metropolitan Opera, where they owned boxes, naturally came within their purview. The Astors, for example, had made millions trading in furs and real estate back at the beginning of the century and had continued to add to their wealth in the course of the years that followed – in the end it was said that they owned half of Manhattan. The Vanderbilts owed their fortune to property and stock-market speculations, while the Rockefellers, who had moved to New York from Cleveland, owed theirs to oil. Their fairytale wealth helped to support the Met and, by extension, funded the lavish terms of Mahler's contract. The 1880s were a golden age in New York's cultural history, enjoying a boom from which the city continues to benefit even today: in 1880 the Metropolitan Museum of Art was opened, the Met in 1883, Carnegie Hall, where Mahler was to conduct the New York Philharmonic, followed in 1891, the city's neoclassical Public Library in 1902. Meanwhile, the year 1895 had seen the inception of a particular type of unscrupulous journalism, when William Randolph Hearst bought the *Morning Journal* and sought to defeat his rival Joseph Pulitzer by any means available. The story of this struggle is enshrined in Orson Welles's film classic *Citizen Kane*, Hearst being the model for Charles Foster Kane.

Brooklyn Bridge was opened to traffic in 1883, and within five years New York, Brooklyn, Queens and Staten Island could unite to form America's largest city. With a population of three and a half million, it was exceeded only by London and Paris. So attractive was New York that it proved a magnet for immigrants from Europe. Traditionally, they came from Ireland, Germany, Scandinavia and Italy, but by the end of the century the largest influx was of Russian Jews who, fleeing from the increasing number of pogroms at home, sought refuge not only in western Europe but also in America and especially in New York. Mahler did not like these immigrants, above all the ones who had got on in the New World and who were currently working at the Met – he regarded them as the main reason for the house's desperate artistic plight, although he would presumably have had no answer to the question as to how an American opera house could function at the end of the nineteenth century with only American artists in a land with no operatic tradition to look back on.

Having barely set foot in the city, Mahler rushed off to the Met to see the house for himself. Everything there was new to him. According to Alma, it was only now that he discovered that he would be making his debut with *Tristan und Isolde*. And yet even if this was news to him, it will have been an agreeable surprise, for he knew that *Tristan und Isolde* and *Fidelio* were the two pieces with which he could win over an audience in a twinkling, always assuming that the cast was right. He held his first orchestral rehearsal on 23 December and at once gave notice of his rigorous approach, breaking off within minutes and insisting that all other rehearsals in the house be discontinued as he claimed not to be able to hear his own players. The chorus was currently rehearsing in the foyer, as was its wont. Until then no other conductor had been able to do anything about this unfortunate situation, even though it was impossible to close the doors to the auditorium sufficiently tightly to keep out extraneous noises. But Mahler got his way. For the opening night on the first day of the new year, his cast was all that he could have dreamt of: his Isolde was the Swedish-American soprano Olive Fremstad, arguably less convincing as an actress than Anna von Mildenburg, but blessed with a fuller and more radiant voice, as her few surviving recordings make clear. Mahler had not previously worked with the Munich heldentenor Heinrich Knote, but he seems to have been enthusiastic about him. Knote's recordings are all excellent and show that of all the great Wagner tenors of his time he was arguably the most modern and closest to today's ideal. The only comparable singer in Mahler's day was Leo Slezak in Vienna, but he did not sing heavy roles like Tristan and Siegfried. When compared with Erik Schmedes in Vienna and Carl Burrian at the Met, both of whom produced a thick and viscous tone, Knote was slimmer, more youthful and also more expressive, his outstanding technique fully equal to all the demands of a part like Tristan, which is notorious for ruining voices. In the second act in particular, few Wagner tenors are able to stay in tune in the *piano* passages of the Love Duet, but Knote proved that it is possible to sing even these difficult sections of the score with perfect intonation and tonal beauty. Mahler was beside himself with pleasure and showered Knote with compliments. In terms of their vocal beauty and purity of intonation, Fremstad and Knote were evidently preferable to Mildenburg and Schmedes, just as the Met's famous ensemble in general was superior to its no less famous counterpart in Vienna.

The reviews of the first night were ecstatic. Fremstad was making her role debut as Isolde and was exceptionally well received, but it was Mahler – introduced to local audiences as the 'eminent conductor from Vienna', his activities as a composer largely overlooked – who was undoubtedly the star of the evening. W. J. Henderson, the much-feared critic of the *New York Sun*, observed that Mahler's guiding hand was discernible in every detail. And although Mahler's tempos had occasionally departed from those that were familiar from New York's Wagner tradition, the 'eloquent variety of Wagner's instrumentation was displayed by the simple process of bringing out clearly every solo phrase, while the harmonic and contrapuntal background was never slighted'. Other writers stressed the lucidity and powerful rhythmic quality of Mahler's conducting and his ability to create tremendous climaxes. It is clear from these reviews that neither the audience nor the local critics had heard Wagner's music conducted like this before.

There is an interesting account of the fascination exerted by Mahler's conducting debut at the Met, interesting not least for the comparison that it draws with Alfred Hertz, the company's principal conductor, who was mainly responsible for the German repertory. The account is that of a Russian-born pianist and critic who later persuaded Toscanini to conduct the NBC

Symphony Orchestra and later still became the network's director of music. In 1908 Samuel Chotzinoff was still a young music lover lucky enough to be present when Mahler made his Met debut:

> Mahler came out hurriedly and climbed swiftly into the conductor's chair. His profile was sharp and arresting. He looked and behaved quite unlike Hertz. His gestures were economical and precise. The prelude sounded different. It was not as lush as with Hertz. There were fewer retards and accelerations. There was a severity about this interpretation that, strangely enough, heightened both its sensuousness and its suspense. The curtain went up, the invisible sailor sang his precarious measures, and suddenly the orchestra and Isolde plunged me into waves of strong, beautiful, rugged sound. For the first time I could remember, I heard distinctly the words Isolde was singing. My eyes turned to Mahler to find a reason. He was 'riding' the orchestra with the calculated sureness of a master trainer, at one moment curbing it to a crafty balance between it and the voice on the stage, at another giving it its head as it raced alone. Perhaps at certain climaxes he was too solicitous for the voice. Though I heard the words and the voice, I was sensible of the reins on the orchestra, and I did not feel the thrill and elation of a great fusion of both, which I had expected. Nevertheless, it was an entirely new *Tristan* for me. Now at last I knew how Wagner should sound. Hertz had misled us. Wagner could be as clear, as understandable, as lucid as *Aïda*.[1]

Chotzinoff's testimony is informative not least because, although writing retrospectively, he avoids the clichés and sweeping generalizations of New York's resident critics and provides us with one of the most precise analyses and succinct characterizations of Mahler's conducting that have come down to us. As many observers confirmed, Mahler had abandoned the eccentric gestures of his youth and adopted a stricter and more economical style of conducting. Moreover, he preferred a Wagnerian sound that was lean-textured and yet muscular, embodying the phenotype closest to his own physical appearance – such links do indeed exist and are by no means far-fetched. He eschewed an excessive use of rubato. And, above all, he favoured the voice over the orchestra. Presumably Chotzinoff was unaware that in striving for clarity, Mahler was in fact aspiring to Wagner's own ideal attitude to the relationship between words and music. Like most Wagner conductors then as now, Hertz was unable to resist the temptation to give the orchestra its head and drown even singers like Fremstad and Knote. In contrast, Mahler's rigour and austerity were clearly felt to be unusual and yet uncommonly fascinating.

All surviving accounts of Mahler's conducting indicate that towards the end of his life he created an impression similar to the one made by his New York

rival, Arturo Toscanini, at the end of *his* career. The young theatre director
Peter Brook heard the elderly Toscanini at one of his final concerts in London.
He was expecting a 'spectacular whirlwind of passionate gesticulation and
demonic movement', but instead he found himself watching a frail figure

> beating time with tiny, almost imperceptible movements of one hand. And he
> listened. . . . The almost motionless old man was all attention, and such was
> the clarity of his mind, such was the intensity of his feeling, that there was
> nothing further he had to do. He needed only to listen, to let the music take
> shape for his inner ear, and the outer sound called towards him by his
> listening matched what he needed to hear.[2]

New York's second most important critic after Henderson was Henry E.
Krehbiel, who wrote for the *New York Tribune*. He had heard of Mahler's
exploits in Vienna and expected that the conductor would sweep away the
cobwebs from the Met's musty stage with no less revolutionary ardour, but in
this he was being unrealistic, for how could Mahler have achieved such a feat
in only a week? From the outset Krehbiel was carping in his criticisms of
Mahler, and when disagreements later arose over Krehbiel's contribution to the
programme notes of one of Mahler's concerts, he became the conductor's most
outspoken critic. Henderson, too, later backed away from his initial enthusiasm, not least because he did not know what to make of Mahler's music on
the rare occasions when it was performed by the New York Philharmonic, with
the result that Mahler forfeited the support of the city's two most important
critics. True, there was never the same vicious campaign against him as there
had been in Vienna and certainly none of the anti-Semitic undertones and
overtones of that campaign, but the result was a perceptible cooling in Mahler's
initial enthusiasm for the musical life of New York. With few exceptions, he
never had any luck with his 'superiors'. Krehbiel's obituary of Mahler was a
truly infamous piece of writing, far worse than any of his reviews and, as such,
a classic example of a posthumous character assassination. In spite of all this,
the audience at the performance on 1 January 1908 was captivated and
rewarded Mahler with a standing ovation. Even Mahler himself was surprised
at the scope of his success.

Although the singers left little to be desired, the same could not be said of
the orchestra or of the house's production values, at least when compared to
those in Vienna, a point that Mahler noted at once – one wonders whether he
had harboured any illusions in this regard. A glance at the names of the singers
with whom he worked at the Met will confirm that he will have had no
complaints – and almost all of them left gramophone recordings, allowing us
to build up a mental picture of the sound of the Met's ensemble. They included

not only Caruso (with whom he never worked) as *primus inter pares* but also the American contralto Louise Homer; the Italian character baritone Antonio Scotti, who was the finest Scarpia of his age and Mahler's Don Giovanni; the tenor Alessandro Bonci, a *lirico spinto* who had abandoned Hammerstein for Conried; Johanna Gadski, who sang both Donna Elvira and Brünnhilde and who was second only to Olive Fremstad as a *hochdramatisch* soprano; and Berta Morena, who came to New York at Mahler's suggestion and sang Leonore in his *Fidelio*. For Wagner's tenor roles, Mahler had at his disposal not only Knote but also Carl Burrian and, for two seasons, Erik Schmedes. They were the three leading heldentenors in the world. For roles such as Zerlina in *Don Giovanni*, Mahler could choose between Marcella Sembrich and Geraldine Farrar, the former drawing to the end of an illustrious career, the latter still at the start of hers. Emmy Destinn, the finest *jugendlich-dramatisch* soprano of the age, was his Mařenka in *The Bartered Bride* and Lisa in his final series of performances of *The Queen of Spades* in March 1910, a production in which his old comrade-in-arms from Vienna, Leo Slezak, took the part of Hermann. Slezak appeared in only four seasons at the Met: in spite of his successes as Verdi's Otello and Wagner's tenor heroes, he felt ill at ease in the New World and soon returned to Vienna and the Tegernsee. We do not know whether Mahler liked Fyodor Chaliapin, who sang Leporello in *Don Giovanni*, but it is unlikely that the musical liberties that the Russian bass took will have been to Mahler's taste. On the other hand, the singer reports in his memoirs that at the first rehearsal for *Don Giovanni*, Mahler complained that none of the singers showed the commitment that he was used to. New York's audiences – the Vanderbilts, the Morgans, the Astors and the Rockefellers, who had financed the building of the new house, making land available and continuing to make donations in order to keep the company afloat (the theatre was literally built around the boxes that they owned), together with all the older moneyed families and many of the nouveaux riches – valued the opera for reasons other than those for which Mahler revered this art form. Then as now the Met's philosophy was centred on its singers' performances and its magnificent interior.

Of the company's conductors, the valiant Anton Seidl had been by far the most significant to date, so that it is all the more to Conried's credit that he hit on the idea of appointing Mahler, a decision that then encouraged Otto Kahn to sign up Toscanini. According to Alma, Conried had ultimate authority over the productions, and there is no doubt that in this regard there could be no talk at the Met of opera productions that could be compared to those achieved in Vienna by Mahler and Roller. All the productions that were taken over or restudied by Mahler – the last-named group includes *Fidelio, Le nozze di Figaro, The Bartered Bride* and *The Queen of Spades* – were officially placed in the hands of the house producer, Anton Schertel, but we may be certain that, starting with his revival of *Fidelio*, Mahler took a personal interest in what happened on the stage, albeit not to the extent that he had done in Vienna. Previous writers on Mahler have sometimes given the impression that at the Met he was too tired to care about anything any longer but that he simply carried out his conducting duties and ignored all other aspects of the performance. Alma claims that Mahler 'did not care' about the staging,[3] and although this may have been true of the first run of performances of *Tristan und Isolde*, it could certainly not be said of what followed. For *Don Giovanni* on 23 January 1908 Mahler is said to have demanded fifteen rehearsals with orchestra and soloists, which was undoubtedly far more than was usual at the Met. And for *Fidelio*, his first genuinely new production on 20 March 1908, he will at least have attempted to transfer his old working methods to the new house, and not merely by reproducing Roller's sets. Indeed, in one of his letters, he states explicitly that his aim was to conduct *and* to direct. Even if he had come to New York with the firm intention of not allowing himself to be worn down by the opera industry as much as he had been in Vienna, he was bound to attempt to sweep away the wretched conditions that he found there. If he had stayed any longer in New York, he might even have agreed to succeed Conried, and we should now be speaking of a Mahler era at the Met as well as in Vienna.

With the exception of the singers, Mahler took only a few days to realize that conditions at the Met were in urgent need of improvement. But it was also clear to him that he could not achieve this alone and that the only person who could help him was Roller. In an uncharacteristically detailed letter that he wrote four weeks after his arrival in New York, he invited Roller to join him in America, beginning with a uniquely intemperate diagnosis: 'As a result of the *absolute* incompetence and fraudulent activities of those who have for years had control over the stage in matters of business and art (managers, producers, stage managers, etc.), almost all of whom are immigrants, the situation at the Opera is bleak.'[4] The locals, he went on, were better qualified, for although the tastes of the audiences and of the multimillionaires who held the reins of power were corrupt, at least they were not as blasé as their counterparts in Vienna but were hungry for the new and extremely eager to learn. No doubt to Roller's complete bewilderment, Mahler went on to spell out what was happening behind the scenes at the Met: he had barely arrived in New York before he had been offered Conried's post. There is no doubt that Conried was seriously ill – Alma diagnosed his illness as tabes, a wasting disease that marked one of the final stages of syphilis. Mahler does not mention this, but merely states that Conried was completely discredited, mainly as a result of unfairness and tactlessness. It looks as if New York's operatic millionaires had

had their eye on Mahler for some time and that the enormous success of his *Tristan und Isolde* reinforced the desirability of his appointment. Mahler lost no time in turning down the offer, which apparently came as a surprise to him. He had not shaken off the burden of his Vienna appointment to take on a similar workload in New York. Above all, the directorship would have required him to spend nine months of every year in America, putting an end to the freedoms that he had only recently acquired. He goes on in his letter to Roller: 'As you have guessed, I quite decisively refused. But I expressed my willingness to continue assisting the management, in some capacity, in artistic matters, and in any case to continue conducting and producing.'

Having failed to enlist Mahler's services, the authorities cast around for an alternative and approached Giulio Gatti-Casazza, who was currently running La Scala in Milan, with Toscanini as his music director. According to Mahler, the plan was to appoint Gatti-Casazza as Conried's successor, entrust the Italian repertory to Toscanini and leave the German repertory with Mahler himself – as always, it was Italian and German operas that formed the twin pillars of the Metropolitan repertory. Mahler seems not to have suspected that this decision would spark one of the decisive conflicts that would make it impossible for him to remain at the Met. After all, he should have known that Toscanini was making a name for himself with his spectacular Wagner performances at La Scala. Was it likely that a man as ambitious as Toscanini would allow himself to be reduced to conducting no more than Puccini and Verdi in New York? But this conflict still lay in the future.

For the present Mahler was keen for Roller to come to New York and assume responsibility for the sets and costumes at the Met, for in Mahler's view these were in urgent need of an overhaul. Roller's responsibilities, Mahler went on, would allow him excellent prospects without any of the administrative chores with which he had had to contend in Vienna. And he would have ample funds at his disposal, although he would have to negotiate the terms himself and secure complete freedom of action and authority over everything concerning the stage. Roller could arrange things in such a way that he would need to spend only five months a year in New York and in return should demand a salary of fifteen thousand dollars. Roller's reply has not survived. Letters between New York and Vienna took almost two weeks to arrive, and Mahler had written twice more before he received Roller's first surviving answer. In the first of these letters he was still hopeful that Roller might be appointed head of productions. By now, however, Conried's successor had been announced as Giulio Gatti-Casazza in tandem with Andreas Dippel, a former tenor with whom Mahler had worked in Vienna. But Mahler still regarded himself as 'hovering as a kind of spirit over the waters', as he put it in his letter of 15 February 1908. During the intervening weeks, moreover, Roller had received a visit from Rawlins Cottenet, a member of the Metropolitan Board who had come to conduct negotiations with him in Vienna. In this context, it is worth noting that in his first letter to Roller, Mahler had mentioned that at the Met Roller had a reputation for 'squandering millions', a reputation that Roller must now be at pains to repudiate. But between 15 and 27 February – the dates of Mahler's second and third letters to Roller – events had taken an unfortunate turn. Roller's reputation seems not to have improved, and Cottenet evidently had nothing positive to report on his meeting with Vienna's self-assured designer, while Gatti-Casazza and perhaps also Dippel saw no reason to spend yet more money on a post whose raison d'être was unclear and to lumber themselves with a designer generally regarded as difficult, especially since the task of stage manager was currently in the conscientious and trouble-free hands of Anton Schertel.

Mahler's third letter attests to his annoyance and helplessness: 'Things have taken a turn that I cannot yet entirely assess. This much seems clear to me: that someone has put a spoke in my wheel.' And Mahler concludes on a note of disillusionment: 'I no longer believe an offer will be made to you.'[5] Roller's reply to this letter reflects his own disappointment, for he clearly felt that his days at the Vienna Court Opera were numbered – his permanent appointment did indeed end in 1909. Roller, too, was unsure why nothing had come of the matter: perhaps his faulty English was to blame or – and he considered this the most likely explanation – Gatti-Casazza was responsible. The reasons can no longer be disentangled, although it looks as if all the foregoing factors played a part. Gatti-Casazza was undoubtedly afraid of Mahler's power, especially as a 'spirit hovering over the waters' aided and abetted by the loyal Roller. The episode has been recounted at length since it seems likely that it had the same effect on Mahler as the *Salome* debacle in Vienna. It was the first intrigue that affected him in a city that he had thought immune to intrigue, and it also represented a bitter defeat less than two months after his triumphant *Tristan und Isolde*. One could say that from now on his days at the Met were numbered. Even when he was still confident that Roller would be appointed, he had told the latter that he did not intend to remain at the Met for more than two seasons. When it became clear that Roller would not be appointed, he told Mengelberg in no uncertain terms: 'I am quite entranced with this country, even though the artistic satisfaction to be got out of the Metropolitan is very far from what it might be. But now I must finally do something for my family.'[6]

The optimism of the first few days proved as fleeting as a spring shower. In his letters Mahler repeatedly praised native American culture and contrasted it with that of the 'loathsome Germans' who blamed American conditions for their failure to make any impression in the New World and who spoke ill of America when they returned to Europe. (There is some truth to the suggestion that resentment against the German Jews in New York also played a part in this negative assessment.) During the early part of February, when Mahler thought that something might come of Roller's appointment in New York, he wrote a long letter to his father-in-law, Carl Moll: 'If I were still theatre-oriented, I would have found here, as never before, the arena for my restless energies. Now I must be satisfied, however, with "stocking the larder" for Almschi and Gucki as well as I can.'[7] Once again Mahler stresses that his only concern is to provide for his family, the unspoken implication being that a time would come when he could no longer do so. Everything he did was done on the basis of 'If I remain healthy' – the phrase recurs with striking frequency in his letters of this period. The events of the previous summer had left him profoundly shocked, although there were still the occasional flashes of his old wit and good humour. He explained his daily routine to his father-in-law:

I am constantly loafing. – That is work one never sees the end of. My working schedule is of uncommon simplicity. When I arise, I have breakfast. Hereafter my conscience assaults me for a time (always depending on the weather). Afterwards I idle away my chores. Then comes lunch. Thereupon I must rest for a few hours on doctor's orders. When I get up, it is snack time. From then until dinner I would have some time. But those wretched habits are so diffi-cult to conquer. Right – now and then I also conduct and hold rehearsals.[8]

It is not clear where Mahler picked up his ideas about American innocence and good humour, although one suspects that he was responding like any modern visitor to America, whose initial impression is invariably that the Americans are incredibly friendly and uncomplicated. The picture that we are able to form of Mahler's contacts outside the Met suggests that those contacts were limited in the extreme. Alma reports that during these initial weeks and months in New York, Mahler often spent half the day in bed at the Majestic, sleeping, reading and even taking his meals there in order to spare his heart for the rehearsals and performances, as his doctor had insisted. Only after the 1908/9 season did he start to regain confidence in his physical abilities: the tremendous workload that he shouldered as conductor of the New York Philharmonic is one that he could not have taken on if he were still following doctor's orders. Having decided to ignore a holiday that meant nothing to him now that he had lost his elder daughter and left his younger one in Europe, he found his first Christmas in America a particularly dispiriting experience. Alma felt abandoned and homesick, leading to the realization that a deep gulf divided her from her husband. The German impresario Maurice Baumfeld rescued the couple from their brooding introspection and invited them to spend Christmas with him. Only when a group of actors joined them did the

Mahlers flee: they cared little for the company and the most dissolute among them was called 'Putzi', the term of affection that they had used for Maria, their late daughter. But where would the Mahlers have found convivial entertainment? Most of the ex-Germans who were working at the Met and, more generally, on the cultural scene in New York were not to the Mahlers' liking. Conried, who was in any case tarred by the same brush, was ill, and neither Mahler nor his wife spoke adequate English. Even during his years in Vienna he had felt little inclination to mix with singers, whom he found uneducated and uncultured – not all of them were of Lilli Lehmann's intellectual calibre – and he was in any case anxious to maintain his distance.

Only slowly did Mahler forge any closer contacts. There was Caruso, the outstanding singer and brilliant caricaturist, who entertained and sometimes annoyed his colleagues with his practical jokes. And then there were some of the other singers from Europe whom Mahler learnt to tolerate and whose number included Heinrich Knote. Knote had an American brother-in-law, the famous physician Leon Corning, described by Alma as a Hoffmannesque figure, morbidly avaricious and the inhabitant of a haunted house that the Mahlers were invited to visit. Towards the end of Mahler's first season in New York – he left on 23 April after only four months in the city – the couple got to know another important person, Joseph Fraenkel, whom both Mahler and Alma found sympathetic, witty, spontaneous and even a little splenetic, but always original. He had moved to New York from Vienna ten years earlier and had made a name for himself as a neurologist and psychiatrist. Mahler was particularly taken by his theory on ears, according to which we can control all our other organs with the single exception of the ears, which alone reveal the naked truth about a person. The Mahlers duly made a party game of judging new acquaintances by their ears. Fraenkel said of himself that he divided people into those with whom he lived and those on whom he lived. Of all the people whom Mahler met in New York, Fraenkel seems to have been the one who inspired him the most: it was the last great friendship of his life. Fraenkel inevitably became the Mahlers' personal physician in New York and initially had to deal with Alma rather than her husband: typically she reacted to the new and difficult situation by showing symptoms of a weak heart and a nervous breakdown. Mahler, who was in fact more at risk than his wife, largely forgot his own illnesses and fretted over Alma. Fraenkel had also made a point of getting to know New York and loved the city's artistic treasures, proving an excellent guide. What Alma does not reveal in her published reminiscences is that Fraenkel fell hopelessly in love with her, although it is unclear to what extent he let her know his feelings. All that we know for certain is that after Mahler's death he invited Alma to marry him, an invitation that she turned down. Shortly afterwards the confirmed bachelor married one of Alma's friends.

Events continued to run their course at the Met throughout the months of February and March 1908. Once Conried had left, Mahler was free to choose whether to stay or leave, for his contract had been with Conried or, rather, with the company to whom the Met was leased. He had no hesitation in publicly announcing that with Conried's departure his own contract was no longer valid but declared his willingness to make himself available as a conductor at least for the coming season. In the middle of March he signed a new contract, this time with the most powerful man at the Met, Otto H. Kahn. Kahn hailed from Mannheim but now worked for the banking firm of Kuhn, Loeb and Co. in New York. A board of management without a representative from the world of banking was as inconceivable then as it is now, and so Kahn was a member of the board of the Metropolitan Opera and Real Estate Company, which looked after the interests of the leading families who financed the Met. As such, he was responsible for finding a successor to Conried. While he was in Milan, negotiating with Gatti-Casazza (he would rather have had Toscanini as his director, but the latter turned him down), Andreas Dippel was appointed manager in New York. For two years the two directors functioned as a team, but Gatti-Casazza then assumed overall control, a position he maintained until 1935 – these were the Met's golden years.

Under the terms of his new contract with Kahn, Mahler would continue to spend three months in New York and also had a chance to conduct concerts not only for the company itself but also independently, allowing him to increase his income and present himself to local audiences as a concert conductor. Kahn assured Mahler that the 'two Italian gentlemen' – Gatti-Casazza and Toscanini – valued their colleague's artistry, while Mahler for his part had apparently expressed his diplomatic belief that he could 'look forward to developments under the new regime with confidence'.[9] The truth of the matter is that Mahler's doubts about his future at the Met had in the meantime grown considerably. Whatever Conried's failings, he had at least spoken the same language in every sense of the term, whereas the same could not be said of Gatti-Casazza. Quite apart from the fact that he had never had a high opinion of Italian impresarios, Mahler knew that Gatti-Casazza was too committed to a repertory that he had always held in low regard and was unlikely to sympathize with his ambitions for the German repertory.

The performances that Mahler had conducted at the Met left him feeling dissatisfied. Even his first new production in the United States, *Fidelio* on 20 March, had failed in this respect, for although he had tried to bring the stage to life, Mahler was bound to realize that he no longer had the strength and inclination to invest as much energy in the proceedings as he had done in Vienna. The reviews were again very good and in some cases even ecstatic. Although there were no complaints on this occasion about the absence of any revolution in the staging of the work, in spite of excellent performances from Berta Morena and Carl Burrian in the main roles, Mahler was forced to admit that even though this may have been the best *Fidelio* ever seen in New York, it still fell some way short of his achievements in Vienna.

It was not only these experiences and the vague prospect of having to work with the 'Italian gentlemen' but also, and above all, the failure of his attempts to bring Roller to New York that persuaded Mahler to look for fresh woods and pastures new. And these pastures contained not an opera house but a concert hall.

Within weeks of his arrival in America, Mahler had received an approach from the Boston Symphony Orchestra. Karl Muck had conducted part of the orchestra's season, and now a successor was needed. Mahler turned down the invitation and instead recommended his colleague from Amsterdam, Willem Mengelberg, describing the orchestra in a letter to Mengelberg as the best in America and worthy of being placed alongside the Vienna Philharmonic. But nothing came of all this. Meanwhile Mahler had already received an invitation from Walter Damrosch to conduct three concerts with his New York Symphony Society in the spring of 1908. Damrosch was the son of the Met pioneer Leopold Damrosch, who had come to America from Breslau and run the Met briefly before dying in harness in 1885. Mahler's contract with Conried had explicitly precluded such activities, and so these concerts had to be postponed until the winter of 1908/9, finally taking place between late November and the middle of December. Three concerts were given, the second of which included the local première of Mahler's Second Symphony. Mahler's new contract with Kahn left him with a freer hand than previously and allowed him to lend an ear to what can only be termed a bold plan, to which he gave ebullient expression in a letter that he wrote to his mother-in-law, Anna Moll, in late March.

These new contacts had been forged in the immediate aftermath of his successful performances of *Fidelio* and came from a Ladies' Committee made up of several New York socialites eager to immortalize themselves in the city's cultural life and with spare capital at their disposal – money earned by their husbands. As the talk of the town, Mahler seemed to them to be the ideal figure to lead such an enterprise. At the Met it was the older money that set the tone and there was little scope for these *nouvelles riches* at the opera, whereas the city's up-and-coming orchestral scene could certainly benefit from a makeover. By local standards, the New York Symphony Orchestra under Damrosch was a worthy institution, even if Mahler thought less highly of it than others did, but the city's second orchestra, the New York Philharmonic Society, was in a poor way, and it was this that the Ladies' Committee under Mrs George R. Sheldon decided needed its help. According to Mahler:

I am moving, or rather 'things' are moving, towards the formation of a Mahler Orchestra entirely at my disposal, which would not only earn me a good deal of money, but also give me some satisfaction. Everything now depends on the New Yorkers' attitude to my work. – Since they are completely unprejudiced I hope I shall here find fertile ground for my works and thus a spiritual home, something that, for all the sensationalism, I could not achieve in Europe. A tree needs such ground if it is not to die.[10]

At the end of April the committee's plans were made public and involved a series of gala concerts under Mahler at Carnegie Hall during the coming season – Carnegie Hall was to be the scene of all his concerts in New York. Mahler was to be given the chance to form a new orchestra made up of the finest musicians of New York and Brooklyn and promoted under the not espe-cially attractive working title of the Greater New York Orchestra. This festival orchestra would then form the nucleus of a permanent ensemble that would be conducted by other conductors. For the present, however, Mahler was its sole music director. In the event this plan came to nothing for reasons that need not concern us here. Instead the committee contented itself with revitalizing the New York Philharmonic under Mahler. His contract as principal conductor was announced in February 1909, and his first two concerts duly took place in late March and early April. His first concert in his new function was held in Carnegie Hall on 4 November 1909. During the two seasons remaining to him in New York, Mahler conducted the almost incredible total of ninety-five concerts with the New York Philharmonic, a total all the more remarkable for taking place within such a limited timeframe.

Between 1 January and mid-April 1908 Mahler conducted twenty-seven performances at the Met, a by no means negligible number. The critics regarded *Don Giovanni* and *Fidelio* as his finest achievements, although he himself no doubt derived the greatest satisfaction from his very first appear-ance in the Met pit conducting *Tristan und Isolde*. Despite his best efforts, neither *Die Walküre* nor *Siegfried* came up to his expectations. His four months in New York were ultimately a time of disappointment, the impres-sions that he took away with him dispiriting rather than inspiring, and yet the Mahlers' mood by the date of their departure for Europe was better than it had been when they set off. Their memories of the previous summer and of their first Christmas without Putzi were slowly starting to fade. The unique prospect of conducting his own orchestra was an exciting one and would make up for all the annoyance that Mahler had had with the Vienna Philharmonic and all the insults that he had suffered. The engagement even offered him a chance to introduce his own music to America. Clearly Mahler was deluding himself on this point, and disillusionment was not long in coming, although his reputation was now sufficient for him to be able to avoid the aggressive responses that his music had encountered in Vienna.

The First Summer in Toblach

Mahler and Alma arrived in Cuxhaven, Germany, on 2 May 1908. Her suspicion that she had bound her fate to that of an old man was confirmed when she disembarked and a porter, offering to help her with her luggage, remarked: 'Your father need not bother.' From there they travelled to Hamburg and then to Wiesbaden, where Mahler had to conduct a performance of his First Symphony. After ten days in Vienna he then took the train to Prague, where a concert on 23 May provided him with an opportunity to spend time with two young admirers, Otto Klemperer and Artur Bodanzky. Bodanzky was later to work at the Met. Not until the middle of June could Mahler embark on his summer holiday.

On fleeing from Maiernigg the previous summer, Mahler and Alma had spent some time at Schluderbach, eight miles south of Toblach, which is the highest point in the Val Pusteria and at the same time the watershed between the Black Sea and the Adriatic. On this occasion they took rooms at the Trenkerhof in Alt-Schluderbach, high on the mountainside between Toblach and Schluderbach, a spacious and well-kept farm with a first floor that could be rented in its entirety. The 1900 edition of Bruckmann's illustrated travel guide for Toblach and the Ampezzo Valley describes the ascent from the Val Pusteria to an area popular with visitors and does so in glowing colours:

> Since the opening of the railway in 1871, tourism has enjoyed an unsuspected upturn throughout the whole of the Val Pusteria. Not only have tourists and day-trippers discovered the natural beauty of the various valleys, descriptions of which have drawn new armies of admirers every year, but visitors have found in the Val Pusteria some wonderful locations for longer summer holidays, places between two thousand and six thousand feet above sea level that have invited them to linger from spring to late autumn and that soon came to enjoy a reputation as places to spend the summer inasmuch as the local population has demonstrated a very real understanding in dealing with the demands of foreign tourists.[11]

In 1887 Crown Prince Friedrich Wilhelm spent three weeks in Toblach, contributing to the popularity of the place and, indeed, to that of the region as a whole. But Bruckmann's description also makes it clear why Mahler, in search of peace and quiet, did not look for accommodation in Toblach itself but away from the village, where the quiet Trenkerhof commanded a wonderful view of the valley. A small composing house was also run up very quickly, closer to the main building than any of Mahler's previous huts. The Trenker family, which still owns the property, was amazed at the size of Mahler's entourage. In the 1930s the landlord's stepdaughter could still recall the arrival of no fewer than three pianos, one of which was placed in the hut, while the others were accommodated in the main building. Director Mahler, as he was still known, rose at six each morning and set off for his hut, which he additionally surrounded by a fence, a structure further raised in height when a number of apprentices climbed over it. On earlier visits to the region, including one in June 1906, Mahler had fallen in love with the countryside around Toblach. According to Bruckmann's travel guide, 'fertile fields, green meadows, light-barked larch forests alternating with darker spruce forests and neat little farmhouses between them create a picture of loveliness.' It was this that Mahler liked. There was only one serious difference from the places where he had spent all his previous summers: there was no real lake in which he could bathe. In the light of his recent diagnosis, Mahler presumably no longer wanted to risk placing undue stress on his heart by swimming, an activity that had once been so important to him.

In general the summer of 1908 was overshadowed by the events of twelve months earlier. Difficult though it may be for us to accept this today, Mahler had been deeply unsettled by the diagnosis of a 'compensated heart-valve defect'. Several factors must be borne in mind here. Today such a diagnosis would hardly occasion such a reaction, for an operation would replace the damaged valve, and only the need to take blood-thinning agents would remind the patient that they had undergone such an operation at all. But in Mahler's day this diagnosis was final: nothing could be done to repair the damaged valve. He knew that heart disease was endemic in his family and will have remembered that his mother was dead by the time she was fifty-two. He had received his own diagnosis at the age of forty-seven and must have wondered how much time he himself had left. He had always ignored his illnesses and worked hard to toughen up a body not naturally capable of phys-ical endurance, taking it beyond its natural limitations and forcing it into submission. He now over-reacted to the diagnosis of 1907. Had he been sensible, he would have told himself that up to the time of the diagnosis he had not been substantially inhibited in what he could achieve, even if by the stan-dards of the time he was already quite an old man. Like a child obliged to watch something terrifying after successfully closing its eyes to the horror, he reacted with a panic attack and a sensitivity to illness out of all proportion to the facts. Not until 1910 did he regain his trust in his body, a long process that began, hesitatingly, in the summer of 1908 and that would no doubt have continued if it had not been interrupted by the profound shock of his discovery of Alma's affair with Walter Gropius and the severe angina brought on by the first performance of his Eighth Symphony in Munich.

Two letters that Mahler wrote to Bruno Walter during the summer of 1908 are an indication of his inner turmoil and sense of disorientation at this time. We have already quoted from the earlier of the two, with its reference to Mahler's finding himself staring into the void. The second – it was probably written slightly earlier – is less overtly dramatic in tone but certainly no less moving. Mahler notes that he has not only found somewhere else to spend the summer but that he has had to change his whole way of life, a way of life hitherto bound up with his working method. He now realized more clearly than ever that the long walks, the mountaineering and the long periods spent swimming were not just intended to toughen up his body or to relax but were the conditions that he needed to work, conditions that had all the attributes of an obsessional neurosis. Just as one artist might need the smell of rotting apples, another a bottle of Rotspon and a third a neat row of twenty well-sharpened pencils and file-card boxes, so Mahler needed an ambulant alternative:

> For many years I have been used to constant and vigorous exercise – roaming about in the mountains and woods, and then, like a kind of jaunty bandit, bearing home my drafts. I used to go to my desk as a peasant goes into his barn, to work up my sketches. Even spiritual indisposition used to disappear after a good trudge (mostly uphill).

And the same was true of physical indisposition: how often was Mahler not able to master his migraines by means of a brisk walk! But this was now over. Mahler admits that his hypochondria, previously kept under control, had now been allowed free rein. He felt worse than in winter as the loneliness of his Toblach refuge tempted him into auscultating his inner life – feeling his heart and taking his pulse merely made him feel worse than he was, a point that should have given pause for thought to the doctors who were treating him: 'Since I have been in the country I have been feeling worse than I did in town.' For the first time in his life, he went on, he wished that the holidays were over – this was the worst thing that a man like Mahler could have said about this summer. Even worse was the realization that there was nothing he could do except work. The restrictions placed on him restricted his productivity, which in turn had the effect of a drug withdrawal. The glorious scenery was ruined for him now that it had become clear that until now he had been able to enjoy it only when he knew that his work on a new piece had advanced to the point where it could be worked over during the winter. He was now painfully aware that his capacity for enjoyment was severely limited:

It is wonderful here. If only I could have enjoyed something like this once in my life after completing a work! – For that, as you know for yourself, is the only moment when one is really capable of enjoying things. At the same time I am noticing a strange thing. I can do nothing but work. Over the years I have forgotten how to do anything else. I am like a morphia-addict, or an alcoholic, who is suddenly deprived of his drug. – I am now exerting the sole remaining virtue I have: patience![12]

If the context were not so depressing, we should be forced to smile at the thought of Mahler praising patience as a virtue.

The terrible sense of bewilderment and disorientation did not last. The holidays began with visits from various Viennese friends who, after the Mahlers' lengthy absence in America, were naturally keen to see them again. Although such visits were by no means unusual, Mahler found them on this occasion extremely tiresome. But finally he found inspiration and made substantial progress on *Das Lied von der Erde*. The sketches for the third movement are dated 1 August, those for the first 14 August, for the fourth 21 August and for the sixth 1 September. A letter to Carl Moll indicates that he had more or less regained his balance and that he was even looking forward to a visit from his in-laws. Even here, of course, self-interest played a role for he could now feel less guilty at neglecting Alma. In a letter to his old friend from Hamburg, Adele Marcus, he notes that he is feeling calmer and refers to a passage from Goethe's conversations with Eckermann to which we shall return in a moment.

To the extent that Mahler had no intention of returning to America before the middle of November and because on this occasion he had no season to prepare in Vienna, he could have extended his stay at Toblach. But the Toblach idyll ended in early September because he needed to travel to Prague for the first performance of his Seventh Symphony with the Czech Philharmonic, followed five weeks later by the Munich première of the same work with the local Tonkünstler Orchestra. Mahler left Toblach by the night train on 5 September and breakfasted at the Café Schwarzenberg, opposite the Café Imperial, where he met Roller. He had lunch with Carl Moll and Bruno Walter at Meißl und Schadn and left that same afternoon for Prague. The run-up to the performance was an exceptionally happy time for Mahler. The orchestra was generally well disposed to him, although their close links with Vienna meant that some of their members had been adversely influenced by colleagues in the Court Opera orchestra. As always, Mahler was at his most relaxed when surrounded by his younger admirers, who on this occasion included Walter, Bodanzky and Klemperer. Klemperer, who was then a conductor at Prague's German Opera, later recalled that Mahler had twenty-four rehearsals, though this number is probably an exaggeration. He was amazed at Mahler's way of working: after each rehearsal with the orchestra, Mahler would take the parts back to his hotel room and make improvements. His young admirers offered to help, but he preferred to do it all himself. They often spent the evenings at Mahler's hotel, and Klemperer recalled that, no doubt as a result of the good progress that Mahler had made on *Das Lied von der Erde* that summer, he was particularly relaxed and repeatedly made dismissive jokes about his successor in Vienna, Felix von Weingartner, heedless of who might be listening. Alma remembered things differently, and Mahler emerges from her memoirs as highly strung and harassed, not least as a result of his doubts about the instrumentation of his latest symphony – it should not be forgotten that three years had elapsed since he had completed work on the score: he must have wondered whether the symphony would still sound as he had imagined it and if every detail in the score would stand up to his present scrutiny. Klemperer also recalled Mahler speaking dismissively of Hugo Wolf: he had dared to describe Wolf's song 'Gebet' ('Herr, schicke, was du willst') as a success, prompting a black look from Mahler.

The most detailed account of the two weeks that Mahler spent in Prague is the one left by William Ritter, a Swiss writer whose reminiscences, unlike his articles and comments on Mahler's works, are of considerable interest. Ritter was seven years younger than Mahler, an arts journalist who wrote for French and Swiss newspapers and who had been living in Munich since 1901. He had attended the first performance of the Fourth Symphony in November 1901 and immediately fell under Mahler's spell, following his career at first hand, writing about him and eventually being accepted into the composer's inner circle. He reports on the chaotic rehearsals in Prague's Exhibition Centre, which doubled as a banqueting hall. Mahler seems to have borne all this with an unusual degree of composure. The final rehearsal was attended by some of the leading figures in Czech musical life, including Vítězslav Novák, Josef Suk and Otakar Ostrčil. The actual performance was relatively successful, the two 'Nachtmusiken' and the Scherzo being applauded. Indeed, the applause after the second 'Nachtmusik' was such that in keeping with contemporary practice any other conductor would have had to repeat it. The noisy finale was presumably taken at face value and acclaimed, only the opening movement occasioning some bewilderment. When Schoenberg heard Ferdinand Löwe conduct the same work in Vienna over a year later, he wrote to Mahler, who was by then in New York:

> I had the impression of perfect repose based on artistic harmony; of something that set me in motion without simply upsetting my centre of gravity and leaving me to my fate; that drew me calmly and pleasingly into its orbit – as though by that force of attraction which guides the planets in their

courses, which leaves them to go their own way, influencing them, certainly, but in a manner so measured and preordained that there are never any sudden jolts.

This may sound a little bombastic perhaps. Nevertheless, it seems to me to express one thing which I supremely felt: I have put you with the classical composers. But as one who to me is still a *pioneer*.[13]

For Mahler, one of the less agreeable aspects of the summer of 1908 was the need to prepare for the forthcoming season at the Met. Above all, he was discouraged by the prospect of having to work with the two 'Italian gentlemen'. A letter from the Met's co-director, Andreas Dippel, reached Mahler in Toblach in the middle of July. Dippel was himself in Europe and had met Gatti-Casazza in Vienna. He had even hoped to travel on to Toblach to see Mahler, but had to postpone the visit, which seems in the end not to have taken place. In a long letter he informed Mahler about his meeting with Gatti-Casazza, a letter that already anticipates some of the problems that lay ahead. It seems that Mahler had previously made two demands that Dippel addressed in his letter. The first concerned the appointment of the Italian conductor Francesco Spetrino, whom we have already encountered at the Vienna Court Opera, where he was responsible for works in the Italian repertory that Mahler himself was not prepared to conduct and that Bruno Walter could not shoulder on his own. Mahler was evidently so pleased with Spetrino's work in Vienna that he wanted him to join him at the Met. Dippel agreed, and Spetrino was duly signed up from the start of the 1908/9 season. But it is clear from the company's annals that he left the Met at the end of the season, when Mahler's influence was starting to wane. It is easy to imagine that Gatti-Casazza and Toscanini had no wish to see their bailiwick at the Met invaded by a conductor favoured by Mahler. Mahler's second demand was that *Tristan und Isolde* should be newly staged in Roller's Viennese sets and according to the concept that he had evolved with his designer. It says much for his ambitions at the Met that he was so disenchanted by what had been billed as a new production that he suggested remedial action of a particularly intransigent kind. With this, Mahler's darkest forebodings were confirmed. He should have known that Gatti-Casazza and, above all, Toscanini had harboured Wagnerian ambitions of their own in Milan.

In 1895, even before taking up his post at La Scala, Toscanini had conducted a performance of *Götterdämmerung* in Turin that was the first to use Italian forces and had gone on to conduct *Tristan und Isolde* in Turin. He seemed determined to dazzle Italian audiences with his Wagnerian credentials: his first new production at La Scala was *Die Meistersinger von Nürnberg* in December 1898, followed a year later by *Siegfried* and in December 1900 by *Tristan und Isolde*.

Toscanini could even be described as the prime mover in introducing Italian
audiences to the works of a composer previously known only for *Lohengrin*. In
short, Toscanini wanted to be more than just the greatest Verdi and Puccini
conductor of his day, an accolade that was already his: he also wanted to challenge all his rivals as a Wagnerian, a challenge that culminated in Bayreuth in
1930 and 1931, when at Siegfried Wagner's invitation he conducted performances of *Tannhäuser, Tristan* and *Parsifal*. If Toscanini did not outclass the great
German conductors of the time, he was none the less a serious Wagnerian alternative to a conductor like Wilhelm Furtwängler. Mahler was unwilling and
unable to compete in the Italian repertory but now he saw himself faced with the
keenest of rivals in the field in which he felt himself most at home.

This, then, was the first of Mahler's problems, a sheepish Dippel having been
forced to concede that nothing could come of a new *Tristan* under Mahler's
direction and using Roller's sets, for his co-director had already informed him
that he had bought the 1900 Milan sets and would be using them in New York.
Dippel claimed that there was nothing he could do in the face of a fait
accompli. Moreover, Roller had blotted his copybook by making what Dippel
regarded as exorbitant demands for the sets for a new production of *Le nozze
di Figaro* that Mahler was planning to stage at the Met in January 1909. But the
real sticking point came at the end of Dippel's letter to Mahler. He reminded
his correspondent that he had agreed to share Wagner's operas with Hertz and
Toscanini:

> I think that you will not make it into a federal question if Toscanini conducts
> a few Tristan performances before your arrival, in the Milanese *mise-en-scène*
> familiar to him. It is generally known that for a foreigner, who wishes to show
> that he can also conduct Wagner in addition to the Italian repertoire, it is
> easier to make his debut with Tristan than with another opera, and that espe-
> cially because of the soloists, with whom it is relatively simpler to come to an
> understanding in such a work.[14]

This was a gauntlet thrown down to Mahler. It was true, of course, that he
could not take charge of the entire Wagnerian repertory at the Met and could
certainly not expect the company to schedule its Wagner performances to
coincide with his own brief sojourns in the city. During the previous season,
for example, Hertz had conducted performances of *Die Walküre, Siegfried* and
even of *Tristan und Isolde*, but it was a completely different matter if Toscanini
were to sink his claws into *Tristan und Isolde*, the very work with which Mahler
himself had made his debut, and if he were to do so, moreover, in new sets:
it would be like a visiting card from a new principal conductor, while
Mahler's own performances the previous season would be made to look like

the swansong of a bygone age, especially since he had been refused a new production of the work. Quite apart from any personal vanities and sensitivities, Mahler could not tolerate such a slight, which was only made worse when Dippel offered him *L'elisir d'amore* and *Don Pasquale* by way of compensation. If not downright brazen, such an offer was at least stupid and lacking in tact. Was Mahler supposed to conduct Donizetti, while Toscanini was introduced as Wagner's new plenipotentiary? Even the more concrete plans for productions of *The Bartered Bride* and *The Queen of Spades* were hardly calculated to make up for Toscanini's Alberich-like theft of Wagner's gold. In the same letter Dippel also made it unmistakably plain that 'a division of the German opera from the Italian, that we had both expected, will not take place under the regime that has been created', leaving Mahler in no doubt that his days at the Met were numbered. 'One thing alone do I want, the end', he could echo Wotan's outburst: 'And Alberich will see to that end!' The prospect of his own orchestra will have helped to sugar the pill.

But Mahler decided to show his teeth and demonstrate his old fighting spirit. He refused to tolerate the affront that the foolish Dippel had inflicted at Gatti-Casazza's instigation, and in his reply he concentrated almost exclusively on the *Tristan* affair:

> It is inconceivable to me that a new production of *Tristan* should be put on without my being consulted in any way, and I cannot give my consent. Further, I expressly stated when the contract was being discussed, *as you yourself can witness*, that I wished to keep in my hands for the ensuing season those works which I had already rehearsed and conducted in New York. I was given every assurance that this would be so, and it was only at your request and desire that I abstained from having it put in writing in the contract. If recently – out of consideration for the wishes of my colleague – I gave a free hand to the new Director, it was with the express exception of *Tristan*. – I took very special pains with *Tristan* last season and can well maintain that the form in which this work now appears in New York is my intellectual property. If Toscanini, for whom, though unknown to me, I have the greatest respect, and whom I consider it an honour to be able to salute as a colleague, were now to take over *Tristan* before my arrival, the work would obviously be given an entirely new character, and it would be quite out of the question for me to resume my performances in the course of the season. I must therefore urgently request that it shall be reserved for me to conduct and not put in the repertory until after 17th December.[15]

Mahler's decisive intervention proved effective, and although Toscanini made his North American and Met debut on 16 November, before Mahler returned to New York, it was in *Aida*, with an all-star cast that included Emmy Destinn, Louise Homer, Enrico Caruso and Antonio Scotti. But Toscanini's decision to slip in a performance of *Götterdämmerung* on 10 December with two of Mahler's *Tristan* singers, Erik Schmedes and Olive Fremstad, looks like an act of blatant provocation, even though Mahler had not yet conducted this work at the Met. But at least it was not *Tristan und Isolde*. On this point Mahler got his way, and it was not until a year later that Toscanini was able to conduct this last-named work, by which time Mahler had already left the Met, returning only for *The Queen of Spades*. Alma's claim that Toscanini did indeed make his New York debut conducting *Tristan und Isolde*, and that he spent the rehearsal period making malicious remarks about Mahler, is untrue. She also claims that she and her husband attended a performance of *Tristan und Isolde* under Toscanini and found it full of 'distressing' nuances. Conceivably she was referring to Toscanini's *Götterdämmerung* in December 1908, although there is no other evidence to support this claim. Conversely, we have Bruno Walter's testimony that after hearing Toscanini conduct *Tristan und Isolde* in November 1909, Mahler exclaimed that 'He conducts it in a manner entirely different from ours, but his way is magnificent.'[16] Toscanini, conversely, was not so magnanimous. As an old man, he told an acquaintance that Mahler's *Tristan und Isolde* had had no passion, but he was tired and ill at the time. Even more dismissive was another remark: Mahler was simply 'crazy'.[17] Mahler may have reported a victory in this final skirmish of his career, but the war had been won by the Italians. Toscanini remained at the Met until the summer of 1915, and it was only the events in wartime Europe and his affair with Geraldine Farrar, who tried to force him to leave his wife and children, that ended his reign at the Met. No other great conductor has shaped the artistic fate of the company since the days of Mahler and Toscanini.

Mahler's Second Season

Mahler and Alma arrived back in New York for his second season on 21 November 1908. Although the general public may not have known it, all the signs indicated that he would not be remaining at the Met for long. True, he had announced at an early date that he would not be staying for ever at the Met, but not even he could have imagined that he would be there for such a short space of time. But there is no indication that the situation was a source of any sadness. Ultimately the conditions at the Met had left him deeply disillusioned, and his initial enthusiasm and belief that local taste was uncorrupted and that audiences were ready to listen to new and unfamiliar works had quickly evaporated. The singers, admittedly, were outstanding, but the orchestra could not compare with its counterpart in Vienna, and the production values were below even those that Mahler found waiting for him in Vienna in 1897. His attempts to remedy the situation had proved a failure, and even in his own particular field – the Wagner repertory – he now found himself facing a serious rival. To the extent that this rival was an ally of the new director, Mahler no longer had a future at the Met. In the circumstances, his musical commitment is remarkable. He conducted the revival of *Tristan und Isolde* and three further performances; he also conducted *Fidelio*; and there were two new productions: *Le nozze di Figaro* on 13 January 1909 and *The Bartered Bride* on 19 February, the latter the first time that the work had been heard in New York. (Chicago had staged the opera in Czech in 1893, but Mahler opted for Max Kalbeck's German version.) The cast of *Le nozze di Figaro* included Marcella Sembrich as Susanna, who was shortly to bid farewell to the company with a final gala performance, Emma Eames as the Countess, Geraldine Farrar as Cherubino, Adamo Didur as Figaro and Antonio Scotti as the Count. Musically speaking, it came up to the highest standards and was well received by critics and audiences alike. And the same was true of *The Bartered Bride*, which, given audiences' unfamiliarity with the work, could not have been expected. The cast included the matchless pairing of the Czech soprano Emmy Destinn as Mařenka and the Berlin tenor Karl Jörn as Jeník, though it is less clear how the Italian bass Adamo Didur coped with the German dialogue as Kecal. Mahler, however, must have been delighted to demonstrate his old love of Smetana's music.

After only twelve weeks his second season at the Met ended on 26 March 1909 with a performance of *Le nozze di Figaro*. Meanwhile, his three concerts with Damrosch's New York Symphony Orchestra had taken place between 29 November and 13 December 1908. Here Mahler must have realized that his victories in the pit of the Metropolitan Opera, however hard-won, could not necessarily be repeated in the concert hall. Krehbiel smugly opined that the third concert, comprising works by Beethoven, Wagner and Weber, was 'more inciting and exciting than satisfying'. The second of the concerts provided Mahler with a chance to introduce his Second Symphony to American audiences. Presumably he chose the Second in the knowledge that it was the most popular and effective of his symphonies. And yet the performance fell short of the high expectations that he had placed in the piece. Clearly it would be difficult to find the 'fertile soil' and 'spiritual home' for his works that he had envisaged only recently: the ground was stonier and the home less hospitable than he had imagined. Although he did not know the New York Symphony Orchestra, it enjoyed a decent reputation, making his disappointment all the greater. As he wrote to his Swiss supporter, William Ritter, 'I am at present busy rehearsing my 2nd, unfortunately with utterly inadequate forces. America for the moment has no idea what to make of me; (in my opinion she has no idea of what to make of any art, and that has perhaps been ordained in the cosmic plan).'[18]

Mahler's comments are as acerbic as they are unequivocal: his disappointment at his experience at the Met can be heard resonating in these lines, while his hopes of finding an orchestral alternative seemed destined to fail as well. Nor can he have been under any illusions about the reception accorded to his Second Symphony: at best his achievements at the Met inspired respect and even civility, but many listeners were probably not even aware that he was also a composer. And every conductor who wrote music at that time – and the same is basically still true today – had to endure the reproach that he wrote only Kapellmeister music. If W. J. Henderson, writing in the *New York Sun*, was entirely positive in his assessment, albeit a little too anxious to please, Lawrence Gilman in *Harper's Weekly* trotted out all the old arguments: Mahler's music was not original; it lacked individuality and imagination; and it lacked 'that which no purpose can assure and no determination compel: the wind of inspiration'.[19] Mahler knew what was going on. He had already heard such comments, whether spoken or unspoken. Even his own efforts, on which he had mostly been able to rely in the past, had been insufficient to inspire a wave of enthusiasm in the hearts of his listeners. But at least he could still place his hopes in a better orchestra, the Mahler Orchestra, even though he must have known that this would not change the situation in any substantial way. By now he will have been thoroughly discouraged and realized the impossibility of finding a spiritual home in America. The fact that he conducted only his First and Fourth Symphonies, together with the *Kindertotenlieder* and his arrangement of two of Bach's suites, with the New York Philharmonic says much for his profound sense of resignation. His inner departure from New York began on 8 December 1908 with the American première of his Second Symphony.

But Mahler still had his final hand to play. The plan to form an orchestra of his own foundered on insuperable logistical and financial difficulties, and it is an irony of musical history that it should be Toscanini for whom NBC created a new orchestra in 1937, allowing him to make his legendary recordings of operas and concerts. Between 1928 and 1936 Toscanini was also music director of the New York Philharmonic: here, too, the Italian's superior constitution triumphed for he lived to be almost twice as old as Mahler. Back in 1908, the New York Philharmonic Society had fallen on hard times, and so the Ladies' Committee and a number of influential figures in the city's musical life decided to reorganize it and bring in new blood. Mahler's association with the orchestra was announced in mid-February 1909, his contract probably signed at the end of March. He quickly joined in the search for new musicians and even made enquiries of Bruno Walter in Vienna, asking him whether this or that player from the Vienna Philharmonic or Konzertverein might be interested in travelling to New York – anxious to avoid ill feelings, he insisted that the enquiry was strictly confidential. He conducted his first concert with the old New York Philharmonic on 31 March and his second on 6 April. The programme on these occasions comprised works by Schumann, Beethoven and Wagner, and the reviews were very good and even euphoric. Here, at least, there were grounds for a glimmer of hope. Although rumours were circulating that Mahler would be conducting as many performances at the Met in 1909/10 as he had done the previous season, he had long since made up his mind to decline any such invitation. But he was keen not to cause an open breach with the company, and so he agreed to conduct Tchaikovsky's *The Queen of Spades*, a work that had been close to his heart since his acquaintance with the composer in Hamburg in 1892/3. Indeed, the plan had already been adumbrated in Dippel's letter of July 1908. Staged in March 1910, it was the only new production that Mahler agreed to conduct that season.

By early June he was back in Vienna, where he received a remarkable letter from Engelbert Humperdinck containing an equally remarkable offer: Mahler was to become the general administrator of a new Wagner Theatre in Berlin, which was to be built in the Friedrichstraße along the lines of the Bayreuth Festspielhaus. Humperdinck had been appointed president of the Great Berlin Opera Society only a few weeks earlier, a society intended to provide an alternative to the old opera house on Unter den Linden, which was completely over-subscribed and geared to the needs of the court. Mahler's answer has not survived, but it seems unlikely that he would have lent his support to a venture intended to rival Bayreuth. Although his loyalty to Cosima Wagner was by no means unconditional, there was no doubt of his devotion to Wagner and to his life's work. In the event, plans for a Wagner Theatre in the Friedrichstraße came to nothing, and all that remained of the project was the later Deutsches Opernhaus in the new Bismarckstraße in the western half of the city, the forerunner of the present Deutsche Oper.

In all the turmoil surrounding him, Mahler was tossed to and fro between hope and despair, and his feeling of being chained to the Met, where he sometimes conducted every two or three days, left him complaining that he was in the eye of the storm. In another key letter to Bruno Walter, who was his closest confidant during these months and evidently the beneficiary of confidences more intimate than those he entrusted to his wife, Mahler reported that he still felt himself to be the victim of a profound crisis whose roots lay eighteen months in the past, even if its character had now changed. He now saw everything in a new light, felt himself to be in a state of flux and would not be surprised if he suddenly found himself in a new body, like Faust in the final scene of Goethe's drama, when the angels wrest Faust's immortal soul from the clutches of Mephistopheles. Mahler seems to have felt like Faust shortly before he is blinded: 'My way has been to scour the whole world through. / Where was delight, I seized it by the hair; / If it fell short, I simply left it there, / If it escaped me, I just let it go. / I stormed through life, through joys in endless train, / Desire, fulfilment, then desire again; / Lordly at first I fared, in power and speed, / But now I walk with wisdom's deeper heed.' Of course, Mahler had not seized every passing delight, and he was currently not walking with wisdom's deeper heed, but he had certainly stormed through life, composing and conducting. He grants Walter an even deeper glimpse into his tormented soul:

> How absurd it is to let oneself be submerged in the brutal whirlpool of life! To be untrue to oneself and to those higher things above oneself for even a single hour! But writing that down like this is one thing – on the next occasion, for instance, if I now leave this room of mine, I shall certainly again be as absurd as everyone else. *What* is it then that *thinks* in us? And what acts in us?
>
> Strange! When I hear music – even while I am conducting – I hear quite specific answers to all my questions – and am completely clear and certain. Or rather, I feel quite distinctly that they are not questions at all.[20]

Ever since his youth Mahler had thought about the meaning of life. Fechner's ideas, which had been exercising him at this time, no longer seemed to be sufficient. He had always rejected materialism as conceived by Ernst Haeckel, and, as we have already noted, books such as Hermann Lotze's *Mikrokosmos* were now more important to him. It is surely significant that it was at about this time that he learnt to observe himself and to regard his soul as the equal of his body – he had developed a particular interest in this Faustian element in the summer of 1906, while he was working on his Eighth Symphony, but many of his friends confirm that *Faust* was part of his permanent reading and that he could quote whole sections from the play. Nor is it mere chance that he now renewed contact with Siegfried Lipiner, whom he had abandoned so abruptly in 1902. And so we find him writing to Bruno Walter: 'I can't help thinking very often of Lipiner. Why don't you ever write anything about him? I should like to know whether he still thinks the same way about death as he did eight years ago, when he told me about his very peculiar views (at my somewhat importunate request – I was just convalescent after my haemorrhage).' And he ends the letter by asking Walter to give Lipiner and Nanna Spiegler his warmest wishes. One thing above all is striking about this letter of January 1909: by writing of a 'tremendous crisis', Mahler is thinking along lines very different from those of six months earlier, when his letter to Walter was marked by confusion and despair. On this occasion,

Mahler's awareness of the crisis is associated – much to his own surprise – with a cheerful serenity. It is not quietism, for it is only when he is listening to or performing music that his questions are answered or no longer seem so important. When he starts to brood on them, conversely, he continues to drift along, clutching at every passing straw. But nor is it a longing for death, for he stresses that he is more than ever in love with life and with the 'sweet habits of existence'. At the same time he appears to observe the world's hurly-burly with a gentle smile and a shake of the head. His fifty years of storming through life elicit a similar reaction. No doubt he was conscious of the fact that his commitments in America were still far from over, but he had already started to move on, a move that meant his mind was also turning to thoughts of death. This was not new, of course – the previous year he had told Bruno Walter that he had always known he must die – but he now seems to have been drawing closer to a more self-evident and relaxed attitude to death, which had been preoccupying his thoughts since the summer of 1907.

Between 19 and 30 April 1909 the Mahlers were in Paris, where preparations were already under way for a performance of the Second Symphony planned for April 1910. Once again Mahler looked up his old friends, Sophie and Paul Clemenceau, Georges Picquart, who in a total reversal of his fortunes was now his country's minister of war, Paul Painlevé and Guillaume de Lallemand. Also, Carl Moll had had an inspired idea: both in honour of Mahler's work in Vienna and in anticipation of his fiftieth birthday, he had proposed commissioning a bust of Mahler from Auguste Rodin, the most famous sculptor of his age. A portrait bust, generally made of bronze, cost forty thousand francs. Although a man of means, Moll could not afford such a fee, but Clemenceau managed to persuade Rodin of Mahler's importance. Rodin had little interest in music and although he had exhibited on several occasions at the Vienna Secession, he apparently had only a vague idea who Mahler was. For Clemenceau's sake he agreed to reduce his fee to twelve thousand francs for a bronze bust and five copies. In the event Rodin prepared several more for his own use, which explains why copies of his highly expressive piece can be seen all over the world (Ill. 30). Moreover, there are two slightly different originals, together with a marble bust of a wholly different character, the sitter's features hewn from the marble block with a visionary intention that has nothing to do with the likeness of a portrait, allowing Rodin to exhibit the piece as a figure from the eighteenth century and even give it the title 'Mozart', a title by which it is still known today. This is not as absurd as it may sound, for Rodin had told Mahler's companions that the latter's head was a mixture of Benjamin Franklin, Frederick the Great and Mozart.

Mahler had not previously sat for a painter or sculptor (Gallen-Kallela's sketch of 1907 does not count) and initially turned down the request but later allowed himself to be talked round by the claim that Rodin had been so inspired by his features that he absolutely had to make a bust of him. (Mahler apparently did not know that good money changed hands.) Mahler was sceptical when he arrived for his first sitting but soon became interested in Rodin and his working method, which, according to Alma, consisted not in hollowing out a lump of clay but in applying layer upon layer of clay to a small wooden base and then shaping it with his bare hands. Mahler spoke very little French, whereas Rodin spoke no language apart from French, but the two men soon seem to have reached an understanding, and when Mahler returned to Paris the following April, he was keen that Rodin should attend his concert and hear his Second Symphony, which the sculptor appears to have done.

A Reconciliation

By 1 May 1909 the family was back in Vienna – on this occasion Anna Moll had returned with them from New York. They spent a number of extremely enjoyable weeks in the city, during which time Alma noted that Mahler was more relaxed and looked younger than he had done for a long time. And for the first time since 1907 he was susceptible to life's more innocent pleasures. He also busied himself with his plans for the New York Philharmonic and ensured that the American violinist Theodore Spiering, who was currently working in Berlin, was appointed its leader. In a fit of his old perfectionism he even addressed the problem of the orchestra's timpani. Above all, however, these weeks in May saw a reconciliation between Mahler and Siegfried Lipiner and with the latter's circle, a reconciliation that was brought about by Bruno Walter. Evidence for this comes from a letter that Mahler wrote to Alma from Toblach on 13 June: 'I'm enclosing the letter from Fritz [Löhr] to show you why I'm making my peace with my old friends and acquaintances. Be so kind as to support me in this. Let's hope that all the joy and happiness it causes will reflect on us – I know it will. For me it's a great consolation to have straightened everything out with Lipiner – and "to love as long as love can last"'.[21] These lines reveal an extraordinary lack of understanding of his wife and of human nature in general, for Mahler must have realized that for Alma the severance of his ties with Lipiner and the latter's camarilla, as she saw it, was the great triumph of the early days of her marriage. She loathed Lipiner – even in old age this hatred was unabated. And now she was expected to help her husband mend this particular fence? How well did Mahler really know his wife?

We do not know any further details about his reconciliation with Lipiner but only that Walter, acting as a go-between, took Mahler to see Lipiner at the Imperial Council Library where the latter was earning his living, practically forgotten by the wider intellectual public. Mahler will not have found this an easy step to take, for he always had difficulty admitting to his mistakes. But it was presumably he who took the first step or at least persuaded Bruno Walter to do so. It says much for his changed attitude to the world that he was willing to pick up where he had left off more than seven years earlier. The break was by no means one-sided, for Lipiner, too, was arrogant and overbearing, but, unlike Mahler, he was additionally sensitive and vulnerable as a result of the fact that after such a promising start his literary and philosophical gifts had dried up and he was now completely ignored by the outside world. People who failed to share his own delusions of grandeur had no chance of getting through to him. Even at a much earlier date he and Mahler had argued over Wagner so intransigently that for a whole year they had refused to speak to each other. It makes sense, therefore, that it was Mahler who, from his position of superiority, made the first move towards reconciliation. The relief that he clearly felt is evidence of the fact that he had never really come to terms with the break. It is evident that if he was driven back to Lipiner, it was because of his profound insecurity and his inability to answer questions about the meaning of life and death by means of music, including even his own music. It matters little that Lipiner's surviving writings do not really provide answers to these questions, for what is important is that Mahler himself believed that they might. After all, Lipiner was the only real philosopher among his closer circle of friends. And, according to Bruno Walter, Lipiner fulfilled the expectations placed in him. 'Trivial causes had separated the friends for years,' he begins his explanation, somewhat trivializing the true facts of the matter:

> he now forcefully sought him out and demanded that this clear and lofty spirit should share with him the certainty of the view of the world in which he found peace. The joy with which Mahler spoke to me of those conversations will always be to me a happy and touching memory. Lipiner put the essence of these talks into a poem entitled 'Der Musiker spricht', and presented it to Mahler on his fiftieth birthday. But even this source could not finally slake his thirst. 'What Lipiner says about it is wonderfully deep and true,' he said to me, 'but you have to be Lipiner to find certainty and peace in it.'[22]

Mahler received this poem the following summer and found it inspirational, telling Walter that it was the finest poem ever written and henceforth carrying it around in his wallet. It was Lipiner's Nietzschean belief in the permanence of our essential humanity even after death that was crucial to Mahler at this stage in his life, when it was reinforced by insights gleaned from Goethe and Fechner. The poem acquires additional significance from the fact that Mahler received it only days before the worst crisis of his life, which was triggered by Alma's affair with Gropius: and yet even these lines were incapable of consoling him.

This is not the place to discuss whether this poem is as magnificent as Mahler thought. What caught his attention was undoubtedly the skilful and, indeed, virtuosic mimicry of the language of Part Two of *Faust* on the one hand and of Nietzsche on the other. But the poem's underlying ideas must also have appealed to Mahler, quite apart from the fact that he was flattered to think that as a musician he had inspired a poem of this kind. Lipiner's concern was the power of the spirit of creativity that Mahler had recently invoked in the first part of his Eighth Symphony, with its setting of Hrabanus Maurus's Pentecostal hymn. Lipiner's counterpart to Hrabanus Maurus's 'creator spiritus' is the 'creative spirit' which, powerful and violent, 'glows' in countless spirits, a creative force that is also a ruling spirit and which even God Himself worships because the human spirit, embodied here in the musician's melody, is man's only way of approaching the deity. On this highest stage of human consciousness, a kind of *catena aurea* is produced, a great round dance of the spirit and, indeed, of spirits in general, stretching out into infinity – the same round dance as that performed by the Chorus of Blessed Boys in the final scene of *Faust*, where they are ushered in by Pater Seraphicus: 'Rise then higher: as you rise, shall / Growth unnoticed bless your throng. / As in pure eternal wise shall / God's own presence make you strong. / Thus sustained in spheres supernal, / Spirits find their heavenly food: / Love revealed, the love eternal, / Flowering in beatitude.' Of course, Mahler did not receive Lipiner's poem until the summer of 1910, but, as Walter points out, there is no doubt that it sums up the essence of the conversations that he had with Lipiner in Vienna in May 1909. It comes as no surprise, therefore, to find that the entire nucleus of this world of ideas can be discerned in the letters that Mahler wrote to Alma in the summer of 1909.

On 9 June, Mahler took his wife and daughter and the latter's governess to the health resort of Levico near Trent, where Alma hoped to recover her health, which continued to be a cause for concern. This was by no means the first such visit to a spa, and her frequent periods of indisposition during her marriage to Mahler are bound to give pause for thought. Since she lived to be eighty-five, we must inevitably ask ourselves whether it was only organic reasons that laid her up, often for weeks at a time, or whether it was the unsatisfying nature of her marriage that affected her in psychosomatic ways. There are also repeated references to alcohol abuse, a problem that beset her throughout her entire life. We do not know how the ascetic Mahler reacted to this – there are only infrequent hints that he even noticed the problem at all. This, at least, is the only possible interpretation of a line in a letter to his mother-in-law expressive of his relief: 'This time I can give you the best of news about Almscherl. She is really blossoming – is keeping to a splendid diet, and has *entirely* given up alcohol, looking younger every day.'[23] There were good reasons for the Levico cure: in March, Mahler had written to his father-in-law from New York and ended his letter with the remarkable sentence, 'Alma is very well. About her present state she has doubtless written to you herself. She has been relieved of her burden. But this time she actually regrets it.'[24] In the absence of an alternative explanation, we must assume that Alma had had a miscarriage or an abortion, which Mahler refers to with an extraordinarily business-like coldness: in the light of the loss of their elder daughter, a third child would surely have meant a lot to the couple. Whatever the answer, it is clear from the phrase 'this time' that this was not the first such occurrence. Alma spent four weeks in Levico. After leaving her there, Mahler travelled straight to Toblach, and throughout the following weeks, letters were the chief means of communication between them. As a result, this health cure produced some of the most important and substantial letters that Mahler ever wrote to Alma. Two in particular stand out, one containing his interpretation of the final scene of Part Two of *Faust*, the other offering a detailed description of his whole outlook on life. We have quoted from both of them elsewhere in this volume.

But Alma had other concerns and other worries that could hardly be alleviated by references to entelechy and the artist's incessant productivity. At no point in her life had she felt as lonely and isolated as she did during these months. She, too, was still affected by the events of 1907 but in a different way from Mahler. While he was wrestling with thoughts of death and the afterlife and on the importance of his work as a composer, Alma, as so often, was more down to earth. She turned thirty in 1909 and by the standards of the day was no longer young. But nor was she old enough to give thought to her own impending death. In spite of her various illnesses, she did not feel as if she were about to die. While Mahler brooded on death, she thought about her failed marriage, her lack of sexual fulfilment and her thwarted ambitions as a composer. Following the death of his daughter and the diagnosis of his heart disease, Mahler grew even more withdrawn than before. Alma, too, had needed time to process all this, but she was basically healthier by nature and nor was she distracted by hectic conducting duties or the isolation of the composer. It seems that feelings of rejection returned in the summer of 1909 that were every bit as violent as those that had assailed her in the early weeks of her marriage. Following the birth of her daughter Maria, she had felt that the child did not need her and that she herself did not love the child in the right way – today we would describe this as post-natal depression. But now she had the same feelings with regard to her younger daughter, Anna: this was the date at which mother and daughter first became estranged, a sense of alienation from which Anna was to suffer all her life. Much later Alma was sufficiently honest with herself to make the following entry in her diary:

Gustav gave her a loving wave. Was that it? I don't know – but suddenly I
knew: this child must go . . . *and at once. In God's name.* . . . Away with the
thought! Away with the accursed thought. But the child was dead a few
months later. Freud explains these desires as perverted fear . . . Gustav's death
too – I wanted that. I once loved another and he was the wall over which I
could not climb.[25]

This is unequivocal. And it was around these thoughts that Alma's mind grav-
itated during the four weeks that she spent in Levico, a period that undoubtedly sowed the seeds for the upheavals of the summer of 1910.

In her reminiscences Alma leaves us in no doubt about her mental state in
Levico:

I was in a state of profound melancholy. I sat night after night on my balcony,
weeping and looking out at the crowd of gay and happy people, whose laughter
grated on my ears. I longed to plunge myself into love or life or anything that
could release me from my icy constraint. We exchanged letters daily on abstract
topics. He got anxious about me and at last he came to see me.[26]

And yet even this brief visit began on a discordant note:

When he got out of the train I failed to recognize him. Wishing to look his
best he had gone to the barber at Toblach before he left, and he had been
given a close crop while he read the newspaper without giving a thought to
what was going on. The sides of his head were shorn as close as a convict's
and his excessively long, thin face, deprived now of all relief, was unrecogniz-
ably ugly. I could not get used to the transformation and after two days he
sadly departed again.[27]

If Mahler was unsettled by this dispiriting visit, he succeeded in concealing it, for
none of his comments during these weeks gives anything away. As usual, he will
not have taken his wife's 'whims' very seriously. He wrote to his mother-in-law:
'Almschi has been sending me thoroughgoing letters of lamentation, from which
I deduce that she is finding the cure very strenuous.'[28] He had learnt nothing, and
the situation was to deteriorate far more before his eyes were opened. All his
other letters paint a picture of him as completely relaxed and cheerful. He asked
his mother-in-law to send him some honey, some ink for a fountain pen and a
key ring. With the help of his lawyer Emil Freund he negotiated a contract with
Emil Hertzka, the head of Universal-Edition, for his Eighth Symphony. And he
continued to make plans for his forthcoming season in New York. Among his
surviving letters is a cry for help addressed to Bruno Walter, whom he needed to

assist him in drafting a programme of twenty-four concerts with the New York Philharmonic. Above all, however, he had completed *Das Lied von der Erde* and made good enough progress on his Ninth Symphony.

Mahler's joviality was neither forced nor superficial but was the result of a mixture of profound seriousness and a newfound inner equilibrium, a state that was to last exactly a year. The finest portrait of Mahler during this summer of 1909 is the one painted by the music critic Ernst Decsey and published within weeks of the composer's death in 1911. Decsey was invited to visit Mahler at Toblach:

> '*Vita fugax*' [This fleeting life] ... I can still hear the deep, metallic voice pronouncing these words as the sun went down over the snow-fields of Toblach, casting them in its reddish glow. It was one of his favourite sayings and will remain in my memory for ever, for when he uttered it ... *vita fugax* ... there was a hint of his desperation at not being able to check the headlong rush of this fleeting life, at not being able to fill every hour of his existence with the riches of his imperial mind, at not being able to turn every moment into one of action. He was a man who was consumed by himself. A fire glowed constantly within him; one never spent an hour with Gustav Mahler in which it did not burst forth, in which one did not gain something from him. This way he had of throwing himself into things, which gave his life fulfilment even if his work remained unfinished, was not a passing mood, it was his fundamental nature.

Decsey then goes on to report how, returning from a long walk, Mahler exclaimed: 'I get such pleasure from the world! How beautiful the world is! How can any fool say: I am indifferent to it all. Anyone who says that is a clod. Man is a marvellous machine, of course, but anyone who says that is a pile of shit.' 'To be happy is a gift,' Mahler said on another occasion. A path through a field bathed in the evening light prompted the remark 'What a story that path has to tell!' And finally he compared a motor car with a human being in justi-fying his belief in a God of Creation.[29] Mahler spent this summer drawing breath: he felt a greater sense of mental balance, and his body, too, was working better than it had been, now that he no longer paid so much heed to his doctor's orders. Decsey reports that the two of them took long walks together. He seemed to have regained his strength.

In early October the Mahlers gave up their flat in the Auenbruggergasse. Now that he had to spend longer periods in New York as a result of his new contract with the New York Philharmonic and the summer months would henceforth be spent in Toblach, there seemed no point in paying for accommodation in Vienna. For shorter periods they could stay with the

Molls, but they also toyed with the idea of having a house specially built for them either in Vienna itself or nearby. Alma, who was considerably more practical than her husband in such matters, packed up all their possessions and placed them in storage. Mahler had mixed feelings about leaving the flat in which he had spent such a key period in his life – he had moved into it with Justine in February 1898. He then spent a few days with the Redlich family at Göding in Moravia, where he put the finishing touches to *Das Lied von der Erde*. During this time Alma and Anna both had their tonsils removed (if only Mahler had had the same operation!). And at the end of September he travelled to Amsterdam for the final time to conduct his Seventh Symphony. He then went straight to Paris, where on 8 October he joined up with Alma and Anna and had a number of additional sittings with Rodin. The Mahlers left Cherbourg on 13 October for the third of their four visits to America.

The New York Philharmonic

The third season that Mahler spent in New York was the first one wholly devoted to the newly reconstituted New York Philharmonic, the only exception being his final project at the Met, a new production of Tchaikovsky's *The Queen of Spades*, of which he conducted only four performances. This was the first time since he had ceased to run the Vienna Opera that he was a principal conductor with wide-ranging responsibilities. When he had left Vienna, he had not anticipated this, but the situation was now different. The Met had proved a bitter disappointment, and the New York Philharmonic was his only clear alternative as a source of serious money. The orchestra had undergone far-reaching changes. Of the 102 musicians who had made up its numbers in the spring of 1909, only fifty-six were still the same ones at the time of Mahler's first concert in the November of that year. Only two of the old woodwind players remained. The new leader, Theodore Spiering, who was Mahler's personal choice, guaranteed the new spirit of the orchestra. There was, however, a significant change from Mahler's working practices at the Met, for he now shouldered a far greater burden than he had done at the opera, where he had conducted twenty-seven performances during his first season and twenty-three during his second. Even when we take account of the short time that he was in New York and throw in the necessary rehearsals, we are still left with the impression that his commitments during this period were as nothing when compared to those that he took upon himself during his early years in Vienna, when he had the additional burden of his administrative duties. But Mahler can hardly have planned for what he had to take on in his third season in New York, and yet it was clear to him that running an orchestra single-handedly was very different from working on the conducting staff in an opera house.

Above all, the season was now substantially longer. During Mahler's second season at the Met, his first performance had been on 23 December, his last on 26 March – a total commitment of three months in total. But now his season lasted from 4 November to 2 April, two months longer, and was originally planned to comprise forty-three concerts, a number which in the event was increased to forty-seven. During his second season, 1910/11, no fewer than sixty-five concerts were planned, and of these he completed forty-nine between early November 1910 and 21 February 1911, when his final fatal illness took its toll. All in all, this was a workload reminiscent of his worst excesses of over-exertion. A glance at his diary for January 1910 may give some idea of this burden. The final concert of 1909 took place on New Year's Eve, after which Mahler had a few days' rest before three more concerts on 6, 7 and 8 January. There were further concerts on 14, 16 and 17 January, the last of these in Philadelphia. A new programme on the 20th was repeated on the 21st, and yet another new programme on the 26th was repeated in Brooklyn two days later. The month ended with a special concert on the 30th, giving a total for the month of eleven concerts. While some of the programmes were the same, there were also numerous rehearsals to conduct. There could be no question of Mahler taking things easy. And yet, incomprehensibly, Alma gives the impression in her reminiscences that it was all plain-sailing. Mahler occasionally admitted that it was a strenuous schedule but repeatedly stressed that he was up to it. And whereas in Vienna he had also had to shoulder a heavy burden of administrative responsibility, he was able to concentrate in New York on choosing the programmes and conducting the concerts. A man with a seriously weak heart could not have handled this schedule, and the impression occasionally given by writers that Mahler was already dying by the end of 1909 is misleading if not downright false.

With Bruno Walter's help, Mahler had ensured that the concerts were extremely varied. Indeed, it soon turned out that they were too highly spiced for conservative American tastes. They were divided into four different series: eight normal subscription concerts that were repeated on the afternoon of the next day; a cycle of six Beethoven concerts; a further series described, somewhat curiously, as 'historical concerts'; and a series of five popular concerts held on Sunday afternoons. A handful of these concerts were repeated, in some cases outside New York. If we ignore the two concerts that Mahler conducted with the 'old' Philharmonic Society in March and April 1909, the concert with which he launched his incumbency on 4 November 1909 inevitably seems strange by today's standards. Indeed, all the concert programmes at the end of the nineteenth century and beginning of the twentieth century seem strange in our eyes, although it is conceivable that in fifty years from now, they will no longer look so odd. Central to the programme on

4 November was Beethoven's 'Eroica' Symphony, preceded by the same composer's overture *Die Weihe des Hauses* and followed by Liszt's *Mazeppa* and Strauss's *Till Eulenspiegel*. As such, it was typical of all Mahler's New York programmes, for Beethoven was his favourite 'classical' composer and *Till Eulenspiegel* was his party piece in the modern repertory. Equally inconceivable to modern tastes is the concert at which Mahler conducted all four of the overtures for *Leonore/Fidelio*. The reviews were polite, noting that orchestral standards had risen, even if they still fell short of the ideal. Only Mahler's critical nemesis, Henry Krehbiel, still found much to say: the conductor's approach to Beethoven was too fussily detailed for his liking, too concerned with colour and bombast and too little interested in nobility and dignity. This was the tone that Krehbiel was to adopt from now on.

At Mahler's first 'historical' concert, the programme proved too much for New Yorkers' palate, even if their bewilderment was shown only in expressions of polite reserve. It consisted of his controversial arrangement of Bach, a Handel aria, Bach's Violin Concerto in E major, excerpts from operas by Rameau and Grétry and Haydn's Symphony no. 104. Since eighteenth-century music was almost never performed in the concert hall at this time in America, the term 'historical' concert is understandable. Mahler's Bach Suite was a world première. When it appeared in print, it did so under the (German) title 'J. S. Bach: Suite from his Orchestral Works with Written-Out Continuo Arranged for Concert Performance by Gustav Mahler'. Mahler had arranged movements from the second and third of the four Orchestral Suites, allotting the continuo part to an organ and prevailing on Steinway & Sons to modify one of their pianos so that it sounded like a harpsichord. According to the printed programme, 'Mr. Mahler will play the Bach Klavier in the compositions of Bach and Handel'. This 'Bach Klavier' was an unusual instrument as far as the music lovers of the time were concerned, for in Mozart's operas, for example, the recitatives were accompanied on a modern piano. The critics were baffled by the unusual programme, and there seems little doubt that their reaction will have been shared by the audience, whose tastes were limited to the period between Beethoven and Tchaikovsky. To have the conductor conduct from the keyboard was also a novel experience, allowing Krehbiel to claim that there was a lack of precision in the performance.

It would be wrong to suggest that Mahler's first season as principal conductor of the New York Philharmonic was a failure, for it was a major event in the city's musical life. Mahler was the most famous conductor in Europe (Toscanini was still far from achieving this status), he had been a sensation at the Met, however briefly, and he was now in the process of ushering in a glorious future for an orchestra whose fortunes he had revived. This, at least, is how his audiences viewed the situation, and so, too, did most of the critics.

And yet there were reservations that were to increase with the passage of time. Neither the orchestra nor the audience, which was attuned to superficial spectacle and glamour, could really warm to this austere Savonarola of music, which is how many of them regarded Mahler. It is clear from radio interviews given by members of the orchestra during the 1960s that almost all of them were afraid of Mahler. The thin little man radiated a tremendous authority and knew how to exert it whenever he was cross or annoyed. Latecomers were an abomination to him, and he refused to put up with fidgeting or gossip during his rehearsals. Even fifty years later one member of the orchestra could still recall Mahler asking one of the double basses to play a particular passage on his own since he suspected him of poor intonation. The man declared that he was too nervous to do so. Mahler went on rehearsing. Half an hour later he broke off again: 'Are you still nervous?' 'Yes.' The same conversation was repeated thirty minutes later, at which point Mahler finally called it a day. At the start of the next day's rehearsal, Mahler asked the player again. By this point he was a bundle of nerves. 'I didn't sleep all night and I'm still very nervous.' 'You know, you have no business to play in a symphony orchestra,' retorted Mahler. 'You should be playing in the back room of a saloon.'[30] If eyewitnesses are right when they claim that Mahler was far more mild-mannered in New York than he had been in Vienna, it is easy to understand the sort of reign of terror which, from an orchestral player's perspective, he must have exerted in Vienna.

But how did Mahler himself view his new place of work and his musicians? We may recall how dismissive he was of the New York Symphony Orchestra. He should now have been more satisfied, but he was not. He wrote to Bruno Walter in the middle of December, after his first series of concerts: 'My orchestra here is the true American orchestra. Untalented and phlegmatic. One fights a losing battle. I find it very dispiriting to have to start all over again as a conductor. The only pleasure I get from it all is rehearsing a work I haven't done before. Simply making music is still tremendous fun for me. If only my musicians were a bit better!'[31] It was a sobering assessment after so many hopes on all sides – this, then, was the Mahler Orchestra, assembled at his own suggestion and tailored to his own needs. In fact the depressed tone of Mahler's letter to Walter may be explained in part by the fact that it was written in the wake of the first American performance of his First Symphony at the third subscription concert on 16 December 1909. It will be recalled that he had conducted his Second Symphony in the city a year earlier, while Walter Damrosch had already given the American première of the Fourth in November 1904, and the Fifth had been heard in Boston in February 1906, when the piece was performed no fewer than four times. In short, the First, Fourth and Fifth Symphonies were familiar to audiences and critics, even if only from hearsay. The First was compared to the other two and found wanting. All the critics, even the most well-meaning, revealed a fundamental misunderstanding of Mahler's music, complaining about its instrumentation, its musical commonplaces and its lack of both beauty and expressive power – all the old clichés. By now Mahler must have realized that he would never find his artistic home in New York. All his dreams had been blighted by a premature frost, a depressing discovery that he none the less bore with remarkable equanimity thanks to his newfound composure. 'The day before yesterday I did my First here! Apparently without getting much reaction' – and that is all that he had to tell Walter. Far more important for him was to revisit a work from his past, and, eager to confess his feelings, he revealed his response to Walter with rare immediacy:

All of these works give me a peculiar sensation when I conduct them. A burning pain crystallizes: what a world this is that rejects such sounds and patterns as something antagonistic! Something like the funeral march and the storm that then breaks out seem to me like a burning denunciation of the Creator. And in each new *work* of mine (at least up to a certain period) this cry again and again goes up: 'Not their father art thou, but their tsar!' [This favourite phrase of Mahler's comes from Lipiner's translation of Mickiewicz's 'Todenfeier'.] That is – what it is like *while I am conducting*! Afterwards it is all instantly blotted out. (Otherwise one just could not go on living.) This strange reality of visions, which instantly dissolve into mist like the things that happen in dreams, is the deepest cause of the life of conflict an artist leads. He is condemned to lead a double life, and woe betide him if it happens that life and dream flow into one – so that he has appallingly to suffer in the one world for the laws of the other.[32]

On one point at least Mahler was more satisfied than he ever had been in Vienna: 'The audiences here are very lovable and relatively better mannered than in Vienna. They listen attentively and sympathetically.' But Mahler's prevailing mood was a mixture of estrangement and mounting homesickness. He ends his letter by asking Walter to pass on his good wishes to all his friends, foremost among whom he names Lipiner: 'I am immensely looking forward to the time when I can be together with everyone again! Oh that I may be granted that for a span of time!'[33] By this he meant a time 'after America', when he would have earned enough money to spend the whole year in Vienna or its environs and would be in regular contact with his younger and older friends, including Lipiner and Friedrich Löhr, Albert and Nanna Spiegler, Bruno Walter and Roller, Schoenberg, Zemlinsky and Berg, Carl and Anna Moll, Foerster, Adler and the few critics who he felt understood him, namely, Richard Specht, Paul

Stefan and Julius Korngold. The fact that the idea of bringing his American activities to an end sooner rather than later was no passing whim is clear from a letter to Roller from early January 1910. Here he states specifically that if the pressures on him continue as before he will remain in America no more than a year and then return to Europe for good. For a time he toyed with the idea of settling in the Netherlands, and it was not entirely in jest that he mentioned that he and Alma had found a new game in choosing a place to live: Paris, Florence, Capri, Switzerland and the Black Forest were all mooted. Shortly before his death he did indeed begin to make plans for a property near Vienna, 'where the sun shines and beautiful grapes grow', as he explained to Roller.[34]

Also at the start of 1910 Mahler suddenly found himself in the disagreeable position of having to defend himself and Alma from his circle of friends in Vienna, a situation that recalled the turbulent days of their engagement. He had evidently written a letter to Guido Adler that is no longer extant but which Adler interpreted to mean that Mahler's life in New York was a picture of unadulterated horror. Mahler clearly got wind of this. The picture peddled by Adler to his Viennese friends is one of a conductor working harder than he had ever done in Vienna, under conditions unworthy of him, and egged on by Alma, who was allegedly interested only in leading an extravagant lifestyle and flattering her social ambitions and egomania. Mahler used the relative peace and quiet of New Year's Day to defend himself against these charges. Nor did he mince his words but began by defending his American engagement with the argument that he needed conducting as a counterbalance to composition and that the directorship of a concert orchestra was proving invaluable for instrumenting his own works, an experience denied him in the opera house. There is, however, something a little imbalanced about his rhetorical question 'Can I help it if Vienna chucked me out?' Is this really how he now saw his departure from the city? Nor, he went on, would his Viennese pension guarantee the degree of comfort that he felt was his entitlement after nearly thirty years of hard labour. 'So I welcomed the chance of the American offer, which provided me not only with an occupation suited to my tastes and abilities, but also with a good salary that will soon enable me to spend what years remain to me in a manner befitting one's human dignity.' He does not mention the various sources of annoyance in New York: his dissatisfaction with the orchestra and the lack of enthusiasm for his own works. What he does say, however, is that Alma has been grievously wronged by all this gossip, for she was a loyal companion who shared all his intellectual interests and a sensible, level-headed housekeeper to whom he owed all the affluence and order in his private life. Such language sounds as if it has been lifted straight out of a character reference. In the event, Adler appears not to have received this letter, for Alma found the original among her husband's papers after his death.[35]

Settling In

If Alma's account can be trusted, then the Mahlers led more active social lives during their third winter in New York than they had done on their previous visits, Mahler himself apparently deriving a remarkable degree of pleasure from the numerous dinner invitations that he received from the city's leading families. On one occasion they even spent an evening at the home of President Theodore Roosevelt's sister-in-law at Sagamore Hill, Oyster Bay. She showed them round the President's house, Roosevelt currently being away in Africa, pursuing his favourite sport of big-game hunting. They also consulted a drunken medium, Eusapia Palladino, who wore a peasant's shawl round her head and made dark prophecies about Mahler, claiming that he was in danger. Although they did not know what to make of all this, the séance certainly gave them pause for thought. At one point a mandolin flew through the air and slightly injured Mahler. This was a period when theosophy and spiritualism were all the rage – at more or less the same time Baron Schrenck-Notzing was making a similar impression on Thomas Mann in Munich. At the home of Louisine Havemeyer the Mahlers saw some of the art treasures that wealthy Americans were then able to acquire. The anthropophobic eccentric Louis Tiffany asked Mahler whether he could observe some of his orchestral rehearsals unobserved. By way of thanks he invited the Mahlers to visit him at his home, a sign of special favour. His palatial residence contained lighting effects of every kind. The *Parsifal* prelude was being played on an organ – this was one work by Wagner that Mahler had never conducted. Tiffany himself hovered in the background, surrounded by a pall of smoke from the hashish to which he was addicted.

With a vague shudder of apprehension the Mahlers also had themselves taken to Chinatown and an opium den. This sort of visit was fashionable at this period as a kind of after-dinner entertainment, the detective who accompanied the party with a loaded revolver merely adding to the sense of titillation. The Chinese addicts could be seen on bunks and stretchers, sleeping off the effects of their intoxication and reminding Alma of a baker's shop with human loaves. They also visited a Salvation Army hostel, where they heard a wheezing harmonium and the eerie singing of men and women prepared to play the part of repentant sinners in return for a cup of coffee and a roll. But it was the Jewish quarter that repelled them the most. 'Are *these* our brothers?' Alma asked Mahler. According to her reminiscences, he shook his head in despair, a plausible reaction in the light of his earlier comments about the Jews he had seen in Lemberg. There were also social and official engagements that generally went no further than a formal dinner, which had the advantage of ending early, allowing the Mahlers to be home at a reasonable hour, while for the other guests the night was still young.

But these months also saw the emergence of closer links with a circle of friends and acquaintances who included Joseph Fraenkel, the violinist Franz Kneisel, a Viennese painter called Carl Hassmann, Ernest Schelling and his wife, and Prince Paul Troubetzkoy, the brother of the famous sculptor Wladimir Troubetzkoy and, according to Alma, a 'wild, handsome Russian' – at this period she was becoming increasingly attracted to wild and handsome men, especially if they were young. Other people with whom the Mahlers became acquainted during these months were the journalist Carlo di Fornaro, who had made a name for himself exposing abuses in the American penal system; the English writer Poultney Bigelow, who had been friendly with Wilhelm II before he became Kaiser, later forfeiting the latter's sympathies by writing a book that was critical of his former friend; and the American graphic artist, Charles Dana Gibson, whose empty-headed socialite wife asked Alma how such a beautiful woman could ever have brought herself to marry such a hideous, old and altogether impossible man like Mahler. Alma does not seem to have been particularly surprised that the woman's response to all her counter-arguments was a 'contemptuous smile'. Whether Mahler really found all this as insanely interesting as Alma claims must remain an open question, but Mahler no doubt made an effort to put on a brave face as he knew that this was one of the ways of ensuring that his young and voracious wife could bear to remain in a world in which she was always going to feel a stranger. From this point of view, Guido Adler was not entirely wrong.

There is no need to describe in greater detail the events of the rest of the season. As we have already noted, Mahler's programmes were exceptionally varied, especially at the popular Sunday concerts, where a Bizet aria might rub shoulders with the 'Eroica', Handel's Largo with the Funeral March from *Götterdämmerung*, with a Massenet aria and the *Meistersinger* Overture thrown in for good measure. The other programmes were dominated by Beethoven – a source of common ground for Mahler and his American audiences. For him, Tchaikovsky's symphonies were not on the same high level. Still less was Rachmaninov's Third Piano Concerto in which the composer himself played the solo part. But Mahler must have been delighted to have Ferruccio Busoni as the soloist in Beethoven's Fifth Piano Concerto. Busoni was the only virtuoso of this time who was Mahler's intellectual equal, and a genuine bond of friendship sprang up between the two men. They had in fact known each other for years, Busoni having performed under Mahler in Vienna in 1899. In March 1910 Mahler conducted Busoni's *Turandot* Suite in New York, prompting the composer to write to his wife: 'With what love and unerring instinct this man rehearsed! Artistically, and humanly, it was both gratifying and warming.'[36] It was a touching coincidence that Busoni's *Berceuse élégiaque* was on the programme of the final concert that Mahler ever conducted. His delight in performing his own works was by now much diminished. But at the end of January he presented his *Kindertotenlieder* with Ludwig Wüllner as the soloist. The reactions in the press ranged from respect to open bewilderment. This time it was Henderson who was the most critical: 'Mr. Mahler feels but he does not create.'[37] Mahler's final production at the Met, Tchaikovsky's *The Queen of Spades*, opened in early March, with Emmy Destinn as Lisa and Leo Slezak as Hermann. This was the first time since Vienna that he had worked with the waggish heldentenor. Never previously staged in America, the work was politely received, but audiences failed to warm to it, and after four performances it disappeared from the repertory until 1965. Mahler seems to have been in a sombre mood at the rehearsals and was unusually stern with the singers and musicians. Although internationally acclaimed, Emmy Destinn was so terrified of the conductor that she had to flee from one of the rehearsals. Mahler conducted his fourth and final performance of the work on 21 March. It was the last opera he ever conducted. The family boarded the *Kaiser Wilhelm* on 5 April and set sail for Cherbourg, a crossing that marked the end of Mahler's penultimate season in New York.

33

The Ninth Symphony

M AHLER'S NINTH SYMPHONY is shrouded in the myth of the late work – in this case the last work that the composer completed. By the time that Bruno Walter and the Vienna Philharmonic gave its first performance in Vienna on 26 June 1912, Mahler had been dead for over a year, although respect for the dead certainly did not prevent some of the critics in the audience from dismissing the piece as inferior to the Eighth and complaining that it was shallow and threadbare. In the case of the Eighth, Mahler had been surprisingly forthcoming, making his silence in the case of the Ninth all the more striking. His only comment on it – and it is remarkable for its neutral, non-committal tone – comes in a letter that he wrote to Bruno Walter from Toblach in August 1909, while he was busy working on the score. This was the only time after the Eighth that Mahler completed an entire symphony of comparable length in the space of a single summer:

> I have been working very hard and am just putting the finishing touches to a new symphony. Unfortunately my vacation is also nearly finished – and as always I am in the tiresome position of having to rush back to town still quite breathless from composing, and to start work again. Well, that just seems to be my lot. The work itself (insofar as I know it, for I have been writing away at it blindly, and how that I have begun to orchestrate the last movement I have forgotten the first) is a very satisfactory addition to my little family. In it something is said that I have had on the tip of my tongue for some time – perhaps (as a whole) to be ranked beside the Fourth, if anything. (But quite different.)[1]

When set alongside Mahler's enthusiastic comments on his Eighth Symphony, this sounds almost as if he were referring to an inferior piece, rather like a father failing to find the necessary degree of enthusiasm for yet another addition to his family. None of Mahler's own remarks would support the view that in the eyes of many of his admirers, it is his Ninth, rather than his Eighth, that is his finest achievement. Alma claims that he used the word 'symphony' to describe *Das Lied von der Erde* only as part of the work's subheading and that he refused to number it, so superstitious was he. Only on completing his Ninth Symphony did he heave a sigh of relief. Inasmuch as Bruno Walter makes a similar claim, we may well be inclined to believe Alma on this occasion, although doubts about this version of events remain in order, or at least about the extent to which Mahler intended his comments to be taken seriously.

The myth of the late work – and it is sufficient to recall Beethoven's late quartets and Bruckner's Eighth and unfinished Ninth – also affects our perception and interpretation of the symphony. Or take a different example, Brahms's *Four Serious Songs*, which was the composer's penultimate work. When he sets the words from Ecclesiasticus, 'O death, how bitter is the remembrance of thee to a man that liveth in his possessions, unto the man that hath nothing to vex him', it is impossible not to think of the composer's own death only a few months later. Much the same has happened in the case of Mahler's Ninth Symphony, Paul Bekker setting the lofty tone in 1921: 'An attritional song, not really created for the ears of this world, it tells of the afterlife. Mahler himself died because of it. His instinctive urge for the truth had been met. He had seen God in that final revelation that it is given to us to encompass with our eyes here on earth: God as death. The unwritten subheading of the Ninth Symphony is "What death tells me".[2] Bruno Walter supports Bekker when he writes about the link between the final section of *Das Lied von der Erde* – which Mahler had returned to and revised after completing his Ninth Symphony – and the Ninth, which he demanded should be called 'The Farewell', identifying the feeling of departure as the music's motivating force. The greatest temptation for any biographer or commentator on an artist's work is to invoke an intimate link between his life and works, and in the case of a composer such a temptation is almost impossible to resist, especially when we recall that both Walter and Bekker were authorities on the subject. If, on the basis of the Ninth Symphony, we infer the sort of man that Mahler must have been in the summer of 1909, then we are left with the picture of someone who had already started to distance himself from the world as a result of the deeply unsettling experiences of the summer of 1907 – and who was now a different person, seemingly dematerialized, concerned only with thoughts of the afterlife and, in the face of his imminent death, taking his leave of all that he loved in the world. Of course, the music of the Ninth Symphony and especially its final movement can easily contribute to such an impression, especially because there is no denying that as a result of the crisis of 1907, Mahler's outlook on the world had changed in far-reaching ways. And yet we need to mistrust such short-sighted conclusions, for the reality of the situation was very different.

The impression given by Mahler during these summer months in Toblach in 1909 cannot be squared with the cliché-ridden picture of him that is suggested by some writers. At the end of June we find him writing to his old friend Arnold Berliner. At this date he was still on his own, as Alma was taking the waters at Levico, and so he invited Berliner to visit him, offering him a good bed, lots of books to read and plenty of free time. Although Mahler would of course be busy composing during the morning, they could talk, eat and walk during the after-noons and evenings: 'It is marvellous here and is certain to restore you in body and soul. I guarantee you bread and butter and sound boots for the entire rest of your life. I shan't even begrudge you ham!'[3] During the day Mahler enjoyed being on his own, but in the evening he missed his wife and daughter and was annoyed by the noisy inhabitants of the Trenkerhof. Visitors were coming and going all the time and included Oskar Fried, Gustav Brecher and Emil Freund, with whom Mahler practised what for him was the fascinating technique of deep breathing. Previously he used to complain about hordes of unannounced visitors, but now he seemed genuinely pleased to see them. He wrote to his mother-in-law and asked her to send him some ink for his fountain pen, some peppermint oil and a jar of real honey – 'not that disgusting liquorice syrup' served up by his housemaid. In a long letter to Alma he talks exclusively about problems with the servants following the departure of Kathi, the parlourmaid, who had never been able to get on with Mahler. Alma tended to side with her servants in order to make common cause with them in her disagreements with her husband, and she did so with Kathi, too, making Mahler so cross that he wrote angrily to Alma to complain that she had served the Trenkerhof's own butter rather than the better-quality Niederdorf variety. The Trenkers' butter, he complained, stank like liquid manure.[4] In the light of all these details we are bound to ask ourselves whether these are the letters of a composer who is no longer of this world. If the music of the Ninth Symphony seems impossible to square with this man, then this is because the links between life and art are more complex than any dreamt up by conventional wisdom.

When judged by the 'excesses' of the earlier symphonies, the Ninth is a work of classical restraint. It avoids extremes, reverts to four-movement form and uses no voices or cowbells or hammer or immoderately large orchestra. Even in terms of its length, it is by no means excessive by Mahler's standards. But within this classical restraint, which also finds expression in the work's basic-ally lyrical character and its interweaving of song and symphony, we find a newly intensified expressivity, an expressivity within what is generally a low dynamic range that emerges in the opening movement from the inarticulate and the unutterable and which in the final movement slips back into the unut-terable as it dies away. The very beginning of the opening Andante comodo is unheard of in the most literal sense of that term. The cellos and two horns seem to enter from another world, hesitantly, gropingly and murmuringly, in a rhythm that has been described by Michael Gielen as the 'rhythm of death' and that certainly suggests extrasystolic arrhythmia. Never before had Mahler used such short musical ideas over such long periods, some of them little more than a bar in length. The listener is reminded of someone waking up from a troubled dream and muttering to himself, trying to articulate what he has experienced before sinking back into silence and sleep. What Mahler depicts here with unique immediacy is a crisis of music's ability to speak. The new music of the Second Viennese School is adumbrated here not only in the actual articulation but also in the abandonment of classical forms such as first-movement sonata form and variation technique which, however much he may have tested them to their limits, Mahler had continued until now to regard as binding. Further evidence of this development may be found in the weakening grip of traditional tonality, notably in the third movement. But this is not the place to discuss the much-debated question as to whether the Ninth is the last work of the older type of music or the first work of the newer type.

The Ninth Symphony is more or less coeval with a famous text that is an example of literary modernism and that suggests a certain shared experience. Hugo von Hofmannsthal's 'Chandos Letter' dates from 1902. In it a fictitious Lord Chandos in Elizabethan England writes to his friend Francis Bacon and describes his experience of losing the ability to string together coherent thoughts and phrases. The abstract words that are needed to articulate opinions decay in his mouth – he says – like putrid mushrooms. Everything disintegrates, breaking down into ever smaller parts and refusing to be harnessed together in a single concept.[5] The term 'crisis of language' has frequently been applied to this text but scarcely begins to do it justice. No doubt Hofmannsthal was familiar with the debates about the crisis in language that were fashionable at this period and that were prefigured by Nietzsche, playing a part in Viennese empirio-criticism and finding particularly striking expression in Fritz Mauthner's *Contributions to a Critique of Language* in 1901/2. To this Hofmannsthal adds a profound sense of crisis affecting not only our consciousness but also our very existence, a crisis triggered in his own case by the loss of the poet's youthful ability to write verse with apparently instinctive ease. Of course, there is a fundamental difference between Hofmannsthal's situation and that of the much older Mahler in terms of their physical and mental lives, but each of them was responsive to the signs of a crisis that affected not only their age in general but their individual lives in particular.

That Mahler's own crisis had left him shaken to the very roots of his being is clear from his letter to Bruno Walter in which he speaks of staring into the abyss. That crisis continued to resonate in him, and the opening movement of the Ninth Symphony is in part an attempt to give musical expression to these experiences. Mahler also felt, no doubt, that the materials that he had hitherto used to construct his worlds of sound were no longer sufficient to articulate the experiences of the last two years. The opening movement is an expression of this experience and poses a question that the final movement then attempts to answer. It is not surprising that at the end of his letter to Lord Chandos, Hofmannsthal suggests that his crisis may be surmounted by non-linguistic means: 'And the whole thing is a kind of feverish thinking, but thinking using material that is more immediate, more fluent, more white-hot than words. It is a kind of eddy – not the sort that seems to lead directly into the abyss in the eddies of language but one that somehow takes me into myself and into the deepest womb of peace.'[6] As Elektra says, just before she collapses in the triumph of death: 'He who is as happy as we are should do but one thing: say nothing and dance!' Hofmannsthal was profoundly convinced that dance, mime and music must come to the assistance of language and that they may even replace it in order to end its crisis. From now on his own works were to be influenced by this feeling. Unlike the Eighth Symphony and *Das Lied von der Erde*, both of which are permeated by the spoken word, the 'speechless' Ninth Symphony is the answer to Lord Chandos's questions, and it provides this answer in a more immediate, more fluent and white-hot way than language itself could ever do.

Two themes soon break free in the opening movement, the first a lyrical theme in the major, the second, closely related to it but more dramatic, in the minor. But the dynamic level remains largely unchanged. No overarching structures emerge, for the musical argument continues to be made up of very small particles, albeit varied with extreme artistry but not in the sense of classical variation technique. Writers fail to agree on whether it is still possible to identify the old elements of a sonata movement – exposition, development section, recapitulation and coda – in this curious movement. Should the utterly unique episode from bar 376 onwards be described as the end of the recapitulation or as a trio? The impression that it creates is confusing and, puzzlingly, that of a sinfonia concertante that is not of this world: flutes and piccolo in their highest register and horns, trumpets and low strings perform a shadow play that seems to be part of a surrealist's dream. Neither the dreamer nor the person to whom it is recounted seems able to understand it, for it fails to produce a consistent meaning. Supported by only a handful of woodwinds, the flute leads us upwards to dizzying heights, at which point the sound turns yellow, thinning out to harmonics in the harp, strings and piccolo, no longer a sound but merely the noise of scraping. This opening movement has something of a negative manifesto about it and seems to want to demonstrate that traditional means can no longer be used for a symphonic argument. Each time that the movement no longer knows how to go on, it attempts to fall back on

material from which it believes it was developed, but like a falling moun-
taineer, it reaches out and grasps only the air, for the material from the beginning of the movement is in itself already fragmented and no longer capable of
building up and supporting the musical argument.[7]

The second movement is ländler-like in character and from that point of
view appears familiar enough, but on this occasion the mood acquires an
implacable and brutal aspect, a mood intensified by the use of cinematic
straight cuts in which different dance modes and tempos are abruptly juxtaposed by means of double bar-lines and changes in the tempo markings.
Striking a note of self-irony, Mahler himself once noted that his music needed
to embrace the trivial, but here the principle is relentlessly taken to its furthest
extreme, especially in the second waltz.

The third movement is a Rondo-Burlesque, and on this occasion it is the
burlesque element that is taken to its furthest extreme. The final fugue in
Verdi's *Falstaff* begins with the words 'Tutto nel mondo è burla' ('Everything in
the world is a joke'). This was a work that Mahler himself conducted, and even
though he had previously held Verdi's operas in low regard, he admitted that
he had learnt much from the older Verdi's art of knowing what to leave out.
The term 'burlesque' derives from Italian *burla*. (As a young man Mahler's
friend and rival Richard Strauss had written a *Burleske* for piano and
orchestra.) It implies a musical joke, but in the Ninth Symphony the joke is
violent and malicious. Far too often Mahler's music has been over-interpreted
and described as 'music written on the eve of the First World War' or even as
'music that anticipates genocide'. In much the same way numerous works of
literature have been said to look forward to catastrophes and disasters with
more prescience than politicians and cultural commentators. The biographer
admits to being sceptical about such 'presentiments'. True, Mahler's sympathy
with the downtrodden and humiliated is evident in his music, and he was infinitely more sensitive to stupidity and brutality, aggression and vulgarity than the
average person who embodies these qualities, but he did not anticipate the
First World War, and his deserters, marches and funeral processions do not
move ineluctably towards the firebreak of this conflict in particular but only of
war in general. Listeners who hear persecution and pogroms in Mahler's
music are right to do so, but like all great music, it depicts the universal rather
than the historically specific. And yet the third movement of the Ninth has a
quality that seems to represent the exception that confirms the foregoing rule.
The auto-aggression of this raging whirlwind takes the mild irony of the
'Fischpredigt' Scherzo from the Second Symphony and raises it to a level that
is barely tolerable.

Six months before his death Franz Schubert wrote an Allegro in A minor for
piano duet. In spite of its brevity (although it may have been intended as the

first movement of an unfinished sonata), it is one of the most disturbing works from this period in his life. He or his publisher called it *Lebensstürme* (*Life's Storms*). In comparison, the third movement of Mahler's Ninth Symphony is like one of life's tornados, depicting the course of the world, in all its empty bustle, with an acuity found in no other movement that he wrote. It is hard not to be reminded here of the long letter that Mahler wrote to Bruno Walter in January 1909, reporting on the consequences of the great crisis of 1907 and his resultant thirst for life but also his thoughts on death, thoughts he wanted to discuss with Siegfried Lipiner:

> How absurd it is to let oneself be submerged in the brutal whirlpool of life! To be untrue to oneself and to those higher things above oneself for even a single hour! But writing that down like this is one thing – on the next occasion, for instance, if I now leave this room of mine, I shall certainly again be as absurd as anyone else. *What* is it then that *thinks* in us? And what acts in us?[8]

This 'whirlpool of life' is at the heart of the third movement, but whereas the letter describes it from the outside and adopts a sceptical and ironic tone, the music captures our attempts to break free from it. Clearly Mahler had in mind here a society moving increasingly rapidly and ever more blindly towards the abyss – the movement, after all, is a harried march. Mahler could certainly have been reminded of Loge's words at the end of *Das Rheingold*: 'Ihrem Ende eilen sie zu, die so stark im Bestehen sich wähnen' ('They're hurrying on towards their end, though they think they will last for ever').

The fourth and final movement is an Adagio that quickly assumed the character of a testamentary disposition – assuming that we do not reserve that privilege for the opening Andante-Adagio of the unfinished Tenth Symphony. This fourth movement is the quintessential Mahlerian Adagio. At the risk of sounding crass, one could say that the listener who hears this Adagio and is not moved on the very deepest level should abandon all further attempts to come to terms with Mahler. He is lost to Mahler, just as Mahler is lost to him. The basic building block of this movement is a very simple figure, a turn, a type of ornament in which the main note alternates with its two auxiliaries a step above and below. As such, this figure consists of no more than four notes, the second and fourth of which are repeated. It was originally performed very quickly, but in the hands of Bruckner and Wagner, for example, it became both slower and more emphatic, expressive of the deepest emotion. The turn had already provided the underlying character of 'Der Abschied' in *Das Lied von der Erde*, at the beginning of which it is heard five times in succession on the oboe, unforgettably memorable and incisive, first on C, then on D and then on F, conjuring up the boundless loneliness of this valedictory moment. In the

Adagio of the Ninth, the turn occurs with even greater frequency and becomes even more expressive, having already been heard in the first movement and at the end of the third, where it constitutes one of those Mahlerian islands of bliss in the midst of life's whirlpool, while failing to achieve the status of a final destination. Only in the final movement does this turn achieve this aim, but at a price. Here Mahler harks back not only to *Das Lied von der Erde* but also to the fourth of the *Kindertotenlieder* ('Oft denk ich, sie sind nur ausgegangen'), from which he reworks two decisive passages. The turn-based theme builds to a *fortissimo* climax in the strings, after which the movement's second subject enters, ghost-like, in the highest register of the first violins. The contrabassoon, cellos and double basses then add their voices in their lowest register. Here a soul spreads wide its wings in order to span the void that has opened up and that otherwise would be unbearable. The music then reverts to its opening character, leading to a sense of uplift and a climax in bar 118, the sheer weight of which could not have been foreseen. The turn motif returns in the *fortissimo* trombones, which invest it with a power that is hard to credit, while the violins insist on a high E flat in bar 168 that could – and should – provide the starting point for a development in any direction apart from the one that actually follows, namely, the complete extinction of the music over the space of the last twenty-six bars.

Starting with the Adagissimo – in itself an extremely unusual tempo marking – Mahler deploys what Hans Heinrich Eggebrecht, in his analysis of this final movement, calls 'his whole arsenal of vocables expressive of grief':[9] the chromatic three-note descent, the whole-tone step downwards, the semitone step up and down and the turn. Following this expression of grief, there is, however, no gesture of consolation, still less of affirmation. Following a direct quotation from the fourth of the *Kindertotenlieder* ('im Sonnenschein! Der Tag ist schön auf jenen Höhn') played by the first violins with 'heartfelt emotion', the music trickles away to a *pianissisimo*, before dying away completely in the second violins, violas and cellos. As listeners we long for this movement to end as soon as possible, but Mahler extends our agony, drawing out the music to literally intolerable lengths – there are performances in which the resistance of many listeners to the unbearable nature of this ending finds expression in increasing restlessness. Normally the word 'blood-curdling' is used only in the context of screams, but one is tempted to speak of a blood-curdling dying away in the case of the present movement. Hans Heinrich Eggebrecht has described this passage as follows:

> In terms of its musical shape and message, the epilogue to the Ninth Symphony is written into the Adagio and, indeed, into the symphony as a whole from the very beginning: it is not the world that breaks in from outside

at the end but the 'other world' that is brought about and achieved by the composition as the actual subject, a state of attainment identical with the dissolution into silence and the 'dying away' of the subject.[10]

In his book *Real Presences*, George Steiner has ascribed to poetry, art and music the ability to bring us into the most direct contact with things that do not belong to us. It is the aim and privilege of the aesthetic experience to create a continuum between temporality and eternity, between matter and spirit and between the individual and the 'other', turning them into an enlightened presence. On one point Steiner even places music on a higher plane than poetry and the visual arts. There is music, he writes, 'which conveys both the grave constancy, the finality of death and a certain refusal of that very finality'.[11] As an example of this transcendent power of music, Steiner cites the slow movement of Schubert's String Quintet – and who would contradict him? But those listeners who also find this power in Mahler's music, most notably in the final movement of the Ninth Symphony, may feel that – in the words of the last of the *Kindertotenlieder* – they are 'in their mother's house'.

Crisis and Culmination
(1910)

Between Tobelbad and Toblach

Mahler's final summer began in the best of all possible moods, at least as far as he himself was concerned. He seems to have been oblivious to the fact that Alma was dissatisfied with her life as a wife and mother, although his eyes were about to be brutally opened. The couple arrived back in Europe on 11 April, looking forward to a week in Paris that would see a performance of the Second Symphony at the Châtelet with the Orchestre des Concerts Colonne. They were particularly keen to see their old friends and forge closer links with Mahler's French colleagues, but their plans began to unravel almost straightaway. One of their first engagements was a formal dinner given by Gabriel Pierné, who had just taken over the Colonne Orchestra from its founder, Édouard Colonne. A native of Metz, Pierné had studied under Massenet and César Franck and made a name for himself as an organist. Although it has now been forgotten, his oratorio *La Croisade des enfants* enjoyed considerable success in the first decade of the twentieth century. The other guests at the dinner included Debussy, Dukas, Fauré and Alfred Bruneau, who was famous as a representative of naturalism in music and for his settings of Zola. In short, they were the crème de la crème of French music of the period. Also in attendance were Paul and Sophie Clemenceau. According to Alma, Mahler felt uncomfortable in this company. Although he had conducted some of Debussy's orchestral works and Dukas's *The Sorcerer's Apprentice*, he was never able to summon up much enthusiasm for French Impressionism in music. By the same token, some of the younger musicians in Paris felt a decided antipathy to German music. Their older colleagues had grown up as the Wagnerian faithful, but the younger generation bridled against the all-powerful influence of the Germans, and Wagner himself had forfeited French sympathies with his egregiously anti-French outlook during the Franco-Prussian War of 1870–1.

The chauvinistic attitudes that coloured French musical politics in the wake of France's defeat continued to simmer until boiling over in 1914, spectacularly so in the case of Debussy. We know from Debussy's reviews that he never missed an opportunity to defend French music in the face of its Teutonic counterpart. All of this helps to explain the great interest that has been taken in Alma's account of the performance of Mahler's Second Symphony that he conducted on 17 April: in her reminiscences she claims that much to Mahler's annoyance Debussy, Dukas and Pierné ostentatiously left the hall during the second movement and that they complained afterwards that the music was too Schubertian for their taste, and even Schubert, they went on, was too Viennese and Slav for them. What is particularly remarkable about all this is that their scandalous discourtesy is not mentioned in any other source. True, a lone voice is said to have cried out 'Down with German music', but such a sensational demonstration of dissent would surely have remained lodged in the memory of other members of the audience. Moreover, we know that Dukas was a paragon of courtesy and refinement. The previous evening Mahler had done him the honour of attending a performance of his only opera, *Ariane et Barbe-Bleu*, at the Opéra-Comique and made a point of congratulating him at the end of the opening act. Here, too, Alma is clearly fantasizing when she claims that by the end Mahler had been very bored, for it is unlikely that a listener who had warmed to the opening act of this masterpiece would not have been even more impressed by the second and third acts. It seems unlikely, then, that the sophisticated Dukas, whom Mahler had treated so courteously and respectfully on the 16th, should have behaved so boorishly on the 17th. That Pierné was among the boors is even more unlikely, for not only had he hosted the dinner in Mahler's honour, he was also the music director of the orchestra that had extended the invitation to Mahler. He also conducted the first half of the evening's programme. A conductor who entrusts the baton of his own orchestra to a colleague does not walk out on the following performance.

The only member of this group who could conceivably have committed such an act of discourtesy was Debussy, a composer notorious for his abruptness and asperity. Following the concert he is said to have commented to the Comtesse Greffulhe, a famous Parisian beauty, 'There you have your Mahler', deliberately mispronouncing the composer's name as 'Malheur'. He was undoubtedly one of the most violently anti-Teutonic French musicians of the age. A friend recalled that in August 1914, shortly after the outbreak of the First World War, he vented his spleen on Germany and German music:

'Ouf', he said with disgust, 'those people drink whether they are thirsty or not! Everything with them is '*en gros*'. A theme must be long, regardless of its contents or value; the longer the better. Then another interminable episode and then another endless theme. Then, after sixteen quarts of beer, they begin a development so long, so long, that there is scarcely room in this house to hold it. Take, for instance, the symphonies of Mahler (which he, of course, pronounced Mal-air), with its thousand voices and whips, submarines and whatnot ... Or Monsieur Strauss, who is clever in that he knows how to write nothingness itself ... Well, my friend, with it all, their noise does not sound any louder than the finale to Beethoven's Fifth, produced by a small orchestra with only the addition of a contrafagott!'[1]

In short, Debussy is the only member of the group whom we could imagine being capable of such a demonstration, and yet even in his case the few surviving scraps of evidence point in contradictory directions, making it difficult to know whether the incident took place at all, at least in the way described by Alma. None the less, the anecdote has proved tenacious. Suffice it to have drawn attention to this clash between German and French music. Apart from this alleged scene, the concert was a success, even if – as in New York – respect prevailed over enthusiasm.

From Paris the Mahlers travelled to Rome, briefly breaking their journey in Vienna. Mahler had already visited Italy for a series of concerts in the spring of 1907, a tour that had caused him annoyance with the authorities in Vienna. In Rome he was due to conduct three concerts with the same orchestra as before, the Accademia di Santa Cecilia, although in the event only two took place. Mengelberg had just conducted a number of other concerts with the orchestra and had remained behind in the city in order to see Mahler. He had been very dissatisfied with the standard of playing and advised Mahler to be stern with them. Mahler did not need telling twice, and his rudeness towards the players led to serious difficulties. Their numbers were depleted, several of their colleagues having already left for a lucrative tour of Latin America, and the demanding programme – Wagner, Strauss, Tchaikovsky and Mahler's own Bach Suite – suffered accordingly. According to Alma, Mahler laid into the players, armed only with a dictionary, his Italian being to all intents and purposes limited to 'stupidità' and 'indolenza'. As a result, he found it necessary to cancel the third concert, something he had never done before. Alma seems to have tried to persuade him to abide by the terms of his contract, a stance which, to judge by a surviving passage in their correspondence, led to an argument between them.

By 3 May the couple were back in Vienna, where Mahler was able to rest for a few days. Otherwise his time was taken up preparing for the first performance of his Eighth Symphony in September. He had completed the work in the summer of 1906 but thanks to the difficulties of performing such a monumental piece, to say nothing of his commitments in New York, he was seriously behindhand with plans for its publication and performance. The vocal score was not published until the end of April 1910, the full score not until late January 1911, by which date the first performance had already taken place. Emil Hertzka of Universal-Edition had assured Mahler that vocal scores for the soloists and choral parts would be ready by the beginning of 1910. Mahler's first concrete mention of a performance comes in a letter he wrote to Emil Gutmann from New York in the autumn of 1909. It was to be another year before the performance finally took place, but the demands were immense from both a musical and a logistical point of view. Not only was this the first time that Mahler had written anything on this scale but the choir and soloists, too, were faced with unusual demands, although the challenges faced by the orchestra were not substantially greater than those posed by the earlier symphonies. That the performance went ahead in the face of Mahler's misgivings and prevarications is due to the Munich impresario Emil Gutmann. Readers may be surprised to discover that Mahler was initially opposed to the performance. But his experiences in the past had led him to think that it was better to forgo a performance than to have to make do with one that was bad or merely mediocre. And if Gutmann had not been able to overcome all of Mahler's objections with his unflagging enthusiasm, then the latter would have been denied the greatest triumph of his life and would not have heard the work at all.

Gutmann was born in Vienna but from 1906 ran a concert agency from the Theatinerstraße in Munich. He had promoted the first performance of the Seventh Symphony in the city in October 1908, a performance that Mahler had given in the Odeon-Saal with the Kaim Orchestra, which was named after its founder, Franz Kaim, but which was disbanded in 1908, only to be reconstituted almost immediately as the Munich Tonkünstler Orchestra. By the date of the first performance of the Eighth Symphony it had been renamed yet again as the Konzertverein Orchestra. It is now known as the Munich Philharmonic. Gutmann, who was last heard of in an asylum in the 1920s, was therefore running an enterprise that was still very recent and in which contacts and connections were no less important than they are today, but he was soon successful, otherwise he would not have been asked to organize a festival of music that lasted for half the year and that was held in conjunction with the 1910 Munich Exhibition. The extensive complex of exhibition halls on the Theresienhöhe had been built in 1907 and even included a small theatre, the Munich Artists' Theatre. In 1908 there had been a gala concert under Mottl in the Odeon and the traditional Mozart and Wagner festivals in the Residenztheater and the Prinzregententheater. The plans for 1910 were even more ambitious, not least because the events now coincided with the ten-year cycle of the Oberammergau Passion Play – it was hoped to attract pilgrims from Oberammergau to Munich, although in this the organizers were disappointed. The October Festival was also celebrating its centenary. The largest of

GUSTAV MAHLER

the exhibition halls was turned into a concert hall (it still exists) and was intended to facilitate the performance of monumental works like Mahler's Eighth Symphony, which was rumoured to suffer from gigantomania. There were also art exhibitions and a visit from Max Reinhardt's German Theatre from Berlin. The musical events began with a commemoration of the centenary of Schumann's birth and continued with a series of concerts featuring the symphonies of Beethoven, Brahms and Bruckner with the Konzertverein Orchestra under its principal conductor Ferdinand Löwe – Löwe was a Mahlerian, although Mahler held him in low regard as a conductor. A number of choral concerts were followed at the end of June by a week-long Strauss Festival, with gala performances in the Prinzregententheater and concerts with the Vienna Philharmonic. The festival was to culminate with the world première of Mahler's Eighth Symphony on 12 September, with a repeat performance the following day.

Mahler's letters to Gutmann, together with a sketch that Gutmann wrote, admiring Mahler's organizational skills, reveal the extent not only of the composer's involvement in the preparations but also the impresario's commitment to the realization of this exceptional project. In fact their relationship was initially soured by Gutmann's insistence on promoting the piece as the 'Symphony of a Thousand', a marketing ploy designed to drum up interest in the work. It is a title that has stuck. Mahler defended himself vigorously against such a stratagem, repeatedly complaining in his letters about a Barnum & Bailey mentality – a reference to the largest American circus of the time. Gutmann duly dropped the name, a decision made all the easier by the fact that it had already served its purpose. In planning the rehearsals, he met all of Mahler's demands, and one is bound to admire the obstinacy and even the implacability with which the composer insisted on these requirements, for it was, of course, in Gutmann's interests to keep the number of the rehearsals to a minimum in order to save costs. Time and again in his letters Mahler threatened to abandon the whole affair – and he would never have allowed a performance to go ahead with another conductor after he himself had introduced all his previous works to the world. And in the unlikely event of Mahler permitting another conductor to take over, Gutmann would undoubtedly have felt that without the legendary conductor from Vienna, who now had a second home in New York, the whole affair would have been somehow incomplete.

Mahler's main concern was that the choirs would not be ready in time, for ordinary choirs and ordinary chorus rehearsals were inadequate for what he had in mind. Moreover, the exceptional size of the exhibition hall required exceptional forces, making Gutmann's nickname of the 'Symphony of a Thousand' an accurate reflection of the number of performers needed, especially the choirs, which totalled 850 singers in all. Add the number of orchestral players and the soloists, and the total was not far short of a thousand. The Riedel-Verein of Leipzig and the Singverein of the Gesellschaft der Musikfreunde in Vienna both provided 250 singers, while the children's chorus was made up of 350 children from the Central Singing School in Munich. (Nowadays there are rarely more than fifty or sixty children involved in performances of the Eighth.) Mahler fussed and fretted over all this with tireless attention to detail. But he was also concerned to engage the right soloists, for he was well aware of the demands that he was placing upon them, especially the tenor, whom he originally envisaged as a Wagnerian heldentenor with the necessary power and penetration. There were times when he considered using two tenors, one for each half. Although he had admired Heinrich Knote in New York, he was not convinced that Knote was up to the musical demands of the first half. He wrote off Leo Slezak without further ado, knowing that Slezak would have neither the time nor the inclination for such an assignment. In the end Mahler's choice fell on Felix Senius from Berlin, a singer whose appearances were limited to the concert hall but with whom Mahler seems ultimately to have been satisfied. Histories of the Munich Philharmonic proudly refer to this performance as the most important ever given by the orchestra, but its chroniclers invariably omit a remark that Mahler made in January 1911, when he told Gutmann that 'the Munich orchestra has treated me in most unfriendly fashion'.[2]

But Mahler still had to get through a summer that was to shake him to the very foundations of his being. The present writer admits with some hesitation to having difficulties with the events of these months, not so much because the surviving evidence is poor or because what happened is beyond the scope of human experience and understanding. Rather, these events depict our 'hero' in such a desperate and hopeless situation, a character who, for all his contradictions, was none the less a great man but who seems simply to fall apart. If it were not for the unfinished Tenth Symphony, which reveals Mahler at the very peak of his abilities and powers of concentration, for all that this summer's events left their mark on almost every page of the score, one might be tempted to assume that it was a breakdown that also affected his powers of creativity. That this was not the case provides us with at least a modicum of reassurance in a tangled skein of events that shows a man completely derailed after having apparently only recently come to terms with the shock of 1907. After the death of his daughter and the diagnosis of his heart valve defect, this was the third of the hammer blows from the Sixth Symphony. And even if as a composer he had removed that blow, as a man he could no longer avoid it.

We have already examined the problematical nature of the Mahlers' marriage. Although Alma's account of this summer of 1910 conceals more than it reveals, other sources leave us in no doubt about what actually happened. Her reminiscences of Mahler and her volume of memoirs were both written on the basis of her diaries and letters and present a prettified picture of reality, but those passages that escaped her censorship are already sufficiently revealing. Two remarks in particular allow us to suspect what was going on beneath the surface. In her autobiography, she writes that 'this strange marriage with Gustav Mahler – this abstraction – had left me inwardly a virgin for the first ten years of my conscious life. I loved Mahler's mind, but his body was vague to me'. And in her reminiscences of Mahler she writes about the height of the crisis in 1910: 'I knew that my marriage was no marriage and that my own life was utterly unfulfilled.'[3] The young Alma was a highly sensual creature but sexually inexperienced, and her first physical contact with her future husband was a fiasco. If this initial fiasco was followed by 'joy upon joy', this phase was to give way in turn to an insidious attenuation of the so-called pleasures of marriage. It is one of the principal delights of the age in which we live to take a prurient interest in the sex lives of the famous, but the present writer is interested in this aspect of the Mahlers' marriage only to the extent that it can throw light on decisive phases and events in Mahler's life. All the signs point to the fact that Mahler lost interest in his wife and that his libido was directed instead towards his career as a conductor and his work as a composer. Freud later confirmed this, but he could do so only because Mahler, who was normally puritanically taciturn in such matters, told him so. This basic tendency on Mahler's part to abstain from sexual relations with his wife must have been considerably increased after the disastrous summer of 1907, when the death of his daughter, the diagnosis of his heart valve defect, which made his latent hypochondria immeasurably worse, the concern to compose even more quickly in the face of his uncertain life expectancy and his nervousness about the unpredictable burden of work awaiting him in New York, will all have contributed to a further loss of libido, thereby reinforcing a pre-existing tendency.

We have already quoted passages describing Alma's horror of her husband and her infinite sense of distance from him. Indeed, she even confirms this in her memoirs. At the same time, however, she repeatedly stressed her love for Mahler, suggesting a permanent state of simultaneous attraction and repulsion. That she never really loved or understood Mahler's music was something that she herself admitted on more than one occasion, even if she then repeatedly denied it as if shocked by her own admission. She was deeply hurt by the fact that in adopting the role of her mentor he dismissed the very thing that she herself held dearest in her life, namely, her ambitions as an artist and more especially as a composer. She could not tell that the exaggerated praise heaped on her gifts by men such as Max Burckhard and Gustav Klimt was designed to obtain her favours but took everything at face value. Even the insanely infatuated Alexander Zemlinsky, who was far more honest in his criticisms, had discovered how sensitive she could be. It was this unhappy combination of several factors that made her marriage such a disaster: her long-standing scepticism towards a man whom she regarded as old and not especially attractive and who, as her friends had predicted, had proved sickly and whom she always regarded as a Jew (her anti-Semitism never entirely deserted her, for all that it was repeatedly suppressed), together with Mahler's superior attitude, which, although unintended, merely added psychologically to the age difference between them; the channelling of his energies into his work; and, finally, his partial, if never total, lack of sexual interest in his wife. When Alma refers to her husband's conversation with Freud, she mentions not only Mahler's fixation on his 'stricken' mother and his wish to rediscover her imago in his wife but also a fixation of her own: 'I too always looked for a small, slight man, who had wisdom and spiritual superiority, since this was what I had known and loved in my father.'[4] This is a convincing self-diagnosis when we recall Mahler and Franz Werfel but far less so when we include Gropius and Kokoschka. But it is doubtful whether Alma had already gained this insight by the summer of 1910.

Alma's diaries, whether from the time of her marriage or later, tell a rather different story. Here we read of an ugly scene, only the first half of which found its way into her memoirs, the remainder having been censored. We have already mentioned how she had to stand by and watch two female singers at the opera billing and cooing with Mahler, whereas as soon as he returned home, he was the detached and weary husband who demanded to be looked after. According to her diary, Mahler tried to fondle her when he returned home, but she thrust him away, telling him that he disgusted her. 'The next day we had it out in the Stadtpark. He said he felt clearly that I did not love him. He was right. After what happened, everything in me was cold.'[5] Shortly afterwards she felt that she did indeed love him, but outbursts such as this were far from passing storms. We can well imagine the doubts that assailed Mahler – almost certainly from the very outset: after all, we recall his sombre reflections on whether autumn should chain itself to spring. The sheer force of his breakdown when he discovered his wife's affair with Gropius was due in part to the fact that it merely confirmed long-standing fears that he had never been able to resolve. In 1905 there was another scene in which Alma freely admitted that she had always found Mahler's smell 'unsympathetic', to which he replied:

'That is the key to a lot – you have acted against your nature.' How right he is, I alone know. He was a stranger to me – in many ways he remains a stranger to me and, I believe, will always do so. And I have already suffered so much because of this. And that is why there is so much that I cannot understand – or sometimes, if I could, it drives me away from him. That,

knowing this, we can continue to live together?! Duty? Children? Habit? No
– I know that I really love him and that at present I couldn't live without him.[6]

Alma was nothing if not honest, an honesty that she forfeited only in the case
of her affair with Walter Gropius, which she hid from the world until Mahler
was dead. Her comments here are revealing. But what are we to make of her
reference to Mahler's 'unsympathetic' smell, which she claims played a role
only during her engagement and the early part of her marriage? How is this
related to the 'disgust' that she felt after the birth of their first daughter? We can
only speculate on whether the *foetor judaicus* was subliminally involved here,
the claim that the Jews smelt different being one of the bases of anti-Semitism.
And what about the sentence that ends this revealing entry: 'He's taken so
much from me that his presence is now my only support.' To be dependent on
someone who had allegedly taken everything from her must have struck her
as deeply traumatizing. It is entirely logical, therefore, that we find the first
signs of yearning during this summer of 1905. These months in Maiernigg
were hot, and Alma had nothing to do but copy out Mahler's music. Otherwise
she felt listless, driven only by sensuality. She could yearn only for a man, she
commented at the time, but she did not have one.

Even more eloquent are some of the diary entries made long after Mahler's
death. An oppressive dream that Alma had at the height of her affair with
Oskar Kokoschka could hardly be more revealing – or macabre. It is a scene
that could come straight out of Ken Russell's film about Mahler, although it
apparently escaped his notice. Alma and Kokoschka are in bed in a ship's
cabin, with the dying Mahler beneath them. The ship's doctor advises them to
find another cabin as the body will soon start to smell. They leave the cabin in
search of an alternative but after wandering around for some time they find
themselves back at their starting point. By now, however, the dead Mahler has
disappeared. The physical loathing of Mahler and the smell of his body has
here become the worrying smell of his corpse, and the sexual embrace with the
lover who was able to meet Alma's needs after Gropius assumes the form of a
gesture of contempt for the dying Mahler but at the same time is prevented
from taking place until the corpse has disappeared. The situation could hardly
be clearer. Time and again Mahler plays an important role in Alma's diaries,
the frequency of his appearances in no way reduced by the passage of time.
Again and again she asks her old question of fate: was she right to marry a Jew?
Readers who may be surprised that in spite of – or because of – her marriage
to Franz Werfel, Alma continued to be exercised by anti-Jewish feelings will
find from her diaries that she never gave up her prejudices in this regard, even
though she may largely have airbrushed them out of her published texts. On
one occasion she notes that the Jews had brought the Aryans the spirit but in

return devoured their hearts, on another that it was possible to have relationships with Jews but that one should never marry them. Following her experiences with Gropius, Kokoschka and Werfel and her discovery that Kokoschka's and Werfel's sexual predilections bordered on the perverse, she realized that there was a connection between a man's importance and his morbid sexuality. Although her comments on Mahler may be less extreme than her remarks on the other men in her life, it is significant that she describes him as psychologically impotent. He had been able to possess her only when he caught her unawares during the night. From the outset they had had separate bedrooms, so that during the final years of their marriage she had simply locked her bedroom door, a decision he evidently accepted without demur.

The locked bedroom door is the key to a disastrous marriage. Alma clearly never asked herself whether it is possible to describe someone as psychologically impotent who is none the less capable of consummating a marriage and whether a locked bedroom door is not likely to make the problem worse. In the summer of 1910 a young, Aryan, gifted and good-looking architect by the name of Walter Gropius beat at this locked door. He was by no means the first young man who restored Alma's faith in her physical attractiveness. Pfitzner, too, had worshipped her, but although she had held him in high regard as a creative artist, he was not the man to awaken her slumbering sexuality in spite of the fact that, as Zemlinsky had shown, not all such men needed to be heroes. Although the pianist and conductor Ossip Gabrilovich was Jewish, he was good-looking in his way, a wild young Russian who had studied the piano with Anton Rubinstein and who was a year older than Alma. He also worshipped Mahler. During the summer or winter of 1907 the couple drew closer together, a point that Alma stresses in her diaries, where she notes the link with her daughter's death and the way in which she felt broken, sick, ugly and old in consequence. Gabrilovich was the first man in a long time to tell her that he loved her. In her memoirs Alma admits that she became emotionally involved with him. While Mahler was working, the couple gazed out of the window at a moonlit meadow and exchanged a kiss – according to Alma, it was no more than this. Each time they saw each other, their feelings were rekindled. Much later in New York, Gabrilovich is said to have taken his leave of Alma by playing a Brahms Intermezzo. Mahler, who had already retired for the night, had apparently been suspicious and eavesdropped on their conversation, afterwards asking Alma to explain herself. She claims that she had a clear conscience and was able to defend her actions, even though, as she admits in her memoirs, she was close to suicide. On that occasion she was able to suppress her urges and desires, but Gropius changed all that.

It needs to be said at the outset that Alma's account of the events that took place in Tobelbad and Toblach is designed to mislead the reader. At no point does she admit that she slept with Gropius or that their relationship continued until Mahler's death and that it was later resumed. As a result, her reminiscences are of only limited use here, while her memoirs dismiss this episode even more cursorily. (The German editor, Willy Haas, excised it completely, whereas the American edition at least retains a reference to it.) At the time that he met Alma, Gropius was far from being the famous architect that he was later to become. Still only twenty-seven, he was four years younger than Alma, an age difference that must have flattered her. He had studied architecture in Munich and his native Berlin and spent some time working for the great Jugendstil artist and theatre reformer Peter Behrens. Gropius had just set up his own business in Neu-Babelsberg.[7] By the spring of 1910 he was exhausted from running that business and also suffering from the effects of a persistent chill. His doctor advised him to take the waters at Tobelbad. Writers have repeatedly confused Tobelbad with Toblach. Tobelbad is in fact near Graz, and it was to Tobelbad that Mahler took his ailing wife on 1 June 1910, together with their daughter Anna and the latter's English nanny. The following day he returned to Vienna in order to organize the preliminary rehearsals for his Eighth Symphony. Alma had scarcely unpacked her suitcase when she met Gropius for the first time on 4 June. She would soon be thirty-one and was no longer the most beautiful young woman in Vienna, but she was still attractive, now somewhat fuller of figure, a buxom beauty, voluptuous and imposing, a schoolboy's dream in frills and furbelows. Not until she turned forty did she start to look her age and her face and figure turned pudgy, a process evident from photographs of the period. In 1910 she had largely reduced her alcohol intake, which had threatened to rise to dangerously high levels, and this will have added to her attractiveness. It is clear from photographs that the twenty-seven-year-old Gropius was slim and relatively tall, with intensely piercing eyes and a moustache that made the age difference less apparent. He had already had the occasional affair, but Alma was undoubtedly the first genuinely impressive woman in his life, a thoroughbred of a woman. Gropius's biographer, Reginald Isaacs, notes that his subject invariably became involved with women who were either married or in some way unavailable, which he attributes to an over-developed mother fixation. It is a diagnosis amply confirmed by the immoderately intimate letters that Gropius wrote to his mother. She too was a powerful woman – Isaacs thinks it significant that her son was drawn to other emotionally strong women.[8]

The doctor who was treating Alma and presumably Gropius, too, introduced the pair to each other. Alma gives the impression that Gropius was a young madcap who, much to her surprise, fell in love with her, but the truth of the matter is that for both parties it was a *coup de foudre* of a kind that Alma had not known since her adolescence, certainly not with her husband. On the day of their first meeting, they had supper together, then went for a walk, before sitting by a stream and talking well into the night. In the course of the next few days, nature took its course, as writers of the turn of the century might have put it. Alma and Gropius had time to allow their affair to develop, for it was not until 30 June that Mahler returned: the lovers had three and a half weeks together, although the affair cannot have been easy to hide in a tiny resort, where Alma was still the wife of the director of the Vienna Court Opera and where they were under the constant scrutiny of Anna, the child's nanny and the prying eyes of the spa doctors and various other visitors.

As always, Mahler was completely self-absorbed, although not so much that he was not unsettled by Alma's increasingly infrequent news. She had never been a great correspondent, and Mahler had often had occasion to complain about her laziness. When she did write, her large and unwieldy handwriting filled the pages so quickly that the content of her letters was in no way reflected in their length. Whether or not it was an unfortunate coincidence, it is striking that shortly after leaving Alma, Mahler wrote to say how much he would enjoy spending some time in an out-of-the-way place like Tobelbad, calm and free from care and relieved of the need to work. 'That's something we've never done together!' he truthfully noted.[9] But, as always, such ideas quickly faded. Mahler could not seriously imagine a life in which he could idle away his time. On his way back from Tobelbad, he visited a monastery, perhaps one of the places he had in mind as a retirement home before the couple finally bought a plot of land at Semmering. In a further letter he attempted to put Alma's mind at rest. She had evidently asked him whether he still found her attractive. At remarkable length he sought to reassure her that he had just found her particularly youthful-looking, a claim that rather contradicts the whole point of her visit to Tobelbad. Back in Vienna for rehearsals with the chorus of the Musikverein, he took time off to visit a little castle at Pöchlarn, a trip on which he was accompanied by Carl Moll, the surgeon Josef von Winter and the latter's wife, Josefine. Josefine kept a note of the outing and records that Mahler was in the best of moods, enjoying a meal of ham and eggs followed by apples and nuts. He then travelled to Leipzig to work on his Eighth Symphony with the chorus of the Riedel-Verein. There is something distinctly unsettling about the way in which Mahler kept writing to Alma during this period, expressing his love with peculiar forcefulness. He knew nothing, of course, about Gropius, but he must have sensed that his love for his wife and, more especially, her love for him needed rekindling as a matter of some urgency. As a result his letters reveal a wholly unprecedented enthusiasm in the way in which he looks forward to a life of comfort with Alma and to seeking out an idyllic country house for when they return to Europe for good. He must have felt that in their eight years of marriage the needs of his much younger wife had been neglected. But he certainly did not suspect that it was already too late. He even did something that Alma insisted he had never brought himself to do: he asked his father-in-law to obtain a tiara for Alma, which she received on her next birthday – the fact that Mahler mistook the date may or may not be significant.

Around 20 June, while he was rehearsing in Munich, Mahler became uneasy. Alma's letters were becoming increasingly monosyllabic and sibylline. 'After yesterday's sad letter,' he began on 21 June, 'I'm worried not to have heard from you at all today. Are you concealing something from me? I keep sensing something between the lines.'[10] She was indeed hiding something from him, and Mahler, his reputation as an insensitive egomaniac notwithstanding, noticed this very clearly. At the same time he wrote to his mother-in-law, 'I am so perturbed by Almschi's letters, which have such a peculiar tone. What on earth is going on?' He asked her if he should travel to Tobelbad rather than Toblach, as planned.[11] By 25 June, however, he could bear it no more and telegraphed Alma to announce that he would be coming to Tobelbad to see her. But, mindful of the shock he had given her in Levico, he promised not to visit the barber's first. He told her how much he was looking forward to seeing her, that he was exhausted and that he had strained a muscle in his upper arm, something he had never previously done, although such problems are not uncommon with conductors. His heart, however, was fine. He left for Styria on the 30th. How Alma received him we do not know. Nor do we know how Mahler reacted to the atmosphere between them. But it looks as if he left again two days later, suspecting nothing and travelling directly to Toblach, where he was wanting to make a start on his Tenth Symphony. Although it may seem odd that he spent his fiftieth birthday alone in Toblach, this is not a reflection of his isolation but was his express desire. He never marked his own birthdays, which he regarded as a waste of time and energy. He had also asked people not to send him cards or presents, although letters and telegrams arrived by the score. He seems not to have been angered by this.

We do not know when he received his finest birthday tribute, the festschrift that was soon to become his epitaph and which he nowhere mentions in writing. When Paul Stefan had first raised the idea with him, he had expressed his concern that it might do him more harm than good. It was not one of those collections of articles traditionally given to academics to mark their birthday or retirement. Rather, Stefan had had the idea of producing a portrait of Mahler by means of a series of dedicatory essays. (We have already referred to Schnitzler's contribution.) The frontispiece was a photograph of Rodin's marble bust of Mahler, while the final image was the Knight from Klimt's Beethoven frieze, a portrait based on Mahler, albeit not in a literal sense. A series of more general pieces opened the volume and were written by Guido Adler, Gerhart Hauptmann and the pianist and composer Conrad Ansorge.

Angelo Neumann and Max Steinitzer provided portraits of Mahler as a young theatre conductor. But the bulk of the volume was devoted to Mahler's years in Vienna and the list of contributors reads like a veritable who's who of prominent figures in the city's cultural life. Surprisingly, perhaps, the most authoritative contribution is the one by Hugo von Hofmannsthal, who was far from being a member of Mahler's circle of friends or a part of the city's musical life, and who never made any other public statements on the subject. None the less, a previously unpublished letter from Mahler to Hofmannsthal, probably written at the time of his departure from the Court Opera, indicates that Hofmannsthal had joined in the general manifestations of friendship and admiration by giving him a present, presumably one of his own books. But Mahler's letter appears to have led to no further dealings between the two men:

My dear Herr von Hofmannsthal! I should like to have shaken your hand in person, which is why I have kept delaying my thanks for your kind gift from one day to the next. But now – as generally happens, everything that one should and would like to do finally builds up – I can thank you only by letter, but I should like to express the hope that we may often meet in future. Two such fellows should really not keep walking past each other. And so I hope to see you after the holidays – at your own place or at mine! Your most devoted servant, Gustav Mahler.[12]

Hofmannsthal's contribution to Stefan's volume makes one regret all the more that the two men had no further contact:

Where there is a mind, there is an effect. Wherever it is activated, it comes into conflict with matter; it is opposed by inertia, inadequate understanding and sheer misunderstanding, but it overcomes them, and it is the atmosphere surrounding this struggle that is interesting: such interest does not need to be added here. A chaotic, truly heterogeneous entity assumes a rhythmic form, sometimes even involving convulsions; the hostile and dull elements come together in a particular relationship, reacting to each other in ways that could hardly have been predicted, and the art lover will note with delight, the philistine with astonished reluctance that a living whole can develop from many dead elements but only, of course, through the miracle of a creative mind. Such a drama was Gustav Mahler's directorship of the Vienna Opera.[13]

The final section of the volume was devoted to fellow composers. While Richard Strauss and Max von Schillings offered platitudes rather than detailed assessments, and Max Reger contributed a page of music (a contribution all the more remarkable in that there is no evidence of any closer contact between the two men), the pieces by Bruno Walter and the critic Georg Göhler are notable for their profound and affectionate understanding. In short, a finer tribute has never been offered to a composer. This volume and the first performance of the Eighth Symphony are eloquent testimony to the fact that after twenty-five years of struggling with a hostile world Mahler had entered the memory and awareness of his age in ways that would never be forgotten.

Confusion

It is not entirely clear when Alma left Tobelbad for Toblach, but it must have been around 15 July. She had had several more weeks in which to enjoy the state of euphoria occasioned by her love of Gropius, for he too had remained in Tobelbad, the spa treatment for twenty-seven-year-olds lasting a remarkable length of time at this date. The disaster was triggered by the impassioned letter to Alma that he addressed to 'Herr Director Mahler' or 'Herr Gustav Mahler' and that arrived on 29 July. Writers continue to puzzle over whether Gropius 'made a mistake in the stress of emotion', as Alma puts it with disdainful reserve, or whether he intended the letter for Mahler. In his biography of Gropius, Reginald Isaacs offers an important clue when he notes that Gropius not only took up with married or attached women but always felt an urge to make contact with their husbands. Alma and Gropius had agreed that he would send his letters to Toblach poste restante and address them, fairly transparently, 'A. M. 40'. In old age, Gropius assured Mahler's biographer Henry-Louis de La Grange that it was all a mistake on his part.[14] But one aspect of this whole disastrous affair remains puzzling. Mahler was generally not at home when the postman arrived, and so Alma would place his letters on the piano in the Trenkerhof, so that he would see them as soon as he came in, hence her description of him sitting down at the piano on opening the letter and asking 'What is this?' with a voice choked by emotion. Alma must surely have recognized Gropius's handwriting as this can hardly have been the first letter that he wrote to her in the two weeks since they had been together in Tobelbad. At the very least the postmark 'Tobelbad' could have told her who the letter was from. She was bound to assume the worst if her young lover was writing to her unsuspecting husband. She could at least have opened the letter and on discovering its contents have spirited it away. That it was not a confession intended for Mahler is clear from Alma's reaction to Gropius, but it is equally clear that Mahler cannot have read the letter from beginning to end. It evidently contained references to the sex that the lovers had had together. After collecting two later letters from Gropius from the post office, she wrote to him on 31 July:

I fetched two letters from you yesterday. A. M. 40 – everything in order. Now I understand what happened the day before yesterday *less and less*. The only thing that makes me believe that you deliberately addressed your letter to Herr G. Mahler is the passage in today's letter: 'Did your husband not notice anything? Tell me everything, I shall always understand you correctly!!' Otherwise I should have to assume that you were confused, which is what I'd rather do . . . – Since it has come out more or less by accident & not as the result of some open admission on my part, he's lost *all* trust, *all* faith in me! *Just think* – the letter in which you wrote *openly* about all the secrets of our nights of love was addressed to: Herr Gustav Mahler – Toblach – Tyrol. Is that what you *really intended*? And he *almost* read it. With febrile yearning I await your letter, in which you must clear all this up. I *hope* that you can say *something* to save yourself & me.[15]

Mahler had evidently not read the whole of Gropius's letter and had failed to reach the passage in which he had referred explicitly to the sexual pleasures that he had enjoyed with Alma – presumably Alma tore the letter from his hands or he refused to read any further. Although the letter has not survived, we can imagine that it would have begun with an expression of endearment. Be that as it may, it is conceivable not only that Gropius deliberately addressed the letter to Mahler but also that Alma deliberately placed it on the piano in the hope of resolving the issue. But she cannot have known what would happen next. And she evidently hoped to avoid any further confrontation by asking Gropius not to come to Toblach, albeit in vain. He wrote. 'Your letter makes me horribly anxious for you both. No tragedy! I'll go out of my mind if you don't call me to come over. I want to justify myself before you both and to clear up the mystery!'[16]

Alma was inwardly torn and confused. The wild despair with which Mahler now assailed her with tokens of his love and with his profound dismay seems to have caught her off-guard. If she had been hoping to provoke a response with her affair, she had succeeded beyond all measure. This at least would explain her mounting uncertainty: 'For my part I am now experiencing something that I had not thought possible. Namely, that Gustav's love is so boundless – that my remaining with him – in spite of all that has happened – means life to him – and my leaving – will be his death. . . . Gustav is like a sick, magnificent child.' It is more than likely that in writing this, she was repeating Mahler's own words. She then asked Gropius how he imagined what might happen next: 'What would happen if I . . . decided on a life of love with you. Oh – when I think about it, my Walter, that I should be without your love for my whole life. Help me – I don't know what to do – what I have the right to.'[17] In spite of the fact that Alma begged Gropius not to travel to Toblach, there was no stopping him. He told her that he wanted to comfort her and to be comforted in turn. It is strange to think of the young adulterer wanting to offer comfort. To Alma? To Mahler? Although no longer a child, he seems to have reacted to this difficult situation in a not entirely mature way.

Gropius arrived in Toblach some time around 5 August. Alma claims to have seen him standing beneath a bridge and to have told Mahler, who responded by saying 'I'll go and bring him along myself.' Mahler apparently went down to the bridge and found Gropius, although it is unclear how he recognized him. He brought him back to the farm, leading the way with a lantern, and then left the couple alone together. In the American edition of her memoirs, Alma writes that Gropius had already asked Mahler to give up his wife. During their discussion, Mahler paced up and down in his room, where two candles had been lit and a Bible lay open on the table. 'Whatever you do will be right,' he said. 'Make your decision!' But, as Alma adds, 'I had no choice'. Clearly she felt that there was an element of emotional blackmail in Mahler's comment and that his very life hung on her decision.[18] The next morning she took Gropius to the station and remained with Mahler. The draft of a letter from Gropius to Mahler has survived. Whether or not Mahler received it is unclear. 'Unfortunately we had very little to say to each other – it pains me that I can only hurt you. At least let me thank you for the generosity with which you met me and allow me to take your hand one last time.'[19]

But how did Mahler himself react to these events, which robbed him of his clarity of vision and peace of mind at least as much as the events of 1907, when, to quote his own expression in his letter to Bruno Walter, he had been left staring into the abyss? No letter has survived similar to the one that he wrote to Walter. He was always reserved by nature and reluctant to allow others to share in his sufferings and pleasures. Even as a young man he had few people to whom he would open up, Friedrich Löhr being the only significant example at this time. Later Siegfried Lipiner and Bruno Walter seem to have fulfilled a similar function, whereas Natalie Bauer-Lechner was his confidante only in matters relating to music. But it is one thing to speak of the death of a daughter and a diseased heart, another to admit that one's wife has been unfaithful and one's marriage is a failure. Certainly he could never have confided in friends like Lipiner, who would have seen in his admission a validation of their basic mistrust of Alma. And Bruno Walter was too much of a substitute son and a young supporter to be drawn into such a confession. Such crises are not discussed with much younger people, however intimate they may otherwise be. Perhaps it would have been possible for Mahler to talk about what had happened after one or two years, but such a luxury was not to be granted him. It seems, then, as if he spoke to no one about what had taken place. Above all, it looks as if Mahler may have discussed his marital problems with Freud and even have touched on their sexual component, but that he never said anything to Freud about Alma's affair with Gropius. Anna Moll also knew about the affair and thus became an accomplice. And it seems likely that Carl Moll was aware of what was going on. Conversely, we do not know whom Gropius told about his affair. It is distressing to see how completely isolated Mahler was in the greatest crisis of his life. Our only information about his reaction to it is to be found in part in Alma's reminiscences, which as always remain unreliable and on this occasion cannot even be corrected by reference to other surviving sources, and in part in Alma's letters to Gropius and the brief notes and poems that Mahler placed on his wife's dressing table or pillow during this period in August 1910.

Alma used the new situation to settle old scores. Everything that had been building up in her over the years now poured out in long walks with Mahler, triumphantly aware, as she now was, that she finally had his attention. According to her later reminiscences they would walk along beside each other, weeping aloud for days at a time. They then summoned Anna Moll, who enjoyed the trust of both of them. In her memoirs Alma writes that she now realized that she could never leave Mahler and told him so, a confidence that left him overjoyed. Always jealous, he had none the less not reckoned on the fact that Alma's flirtatious nature could ever produce such results. All his former misgivings now struck him as justified and all too true. Like Othello, he could have told himself that he had 'not those soft parts of conversation / That chamberers have; or for I am declined / Into the vale of years – yet that's not much – / She's gone. I am abused, and my relief / Must be to loathe her. O curse of marriage, / That we can call these delicate creatures ours / And not their appetites!' At the same time – as she admitted in her memoirs – Alma kept from Mahler the fact that her love for him had cooled. What kept her with him, she explained, was her sense of responsibility and the fear that he would not survive her loss. What she did not say was that she can have had only a vague idea of what life would be like with Gropius, who was a complete non-entity when compared with Mahler. It seems unlikely that they discussed the problems with their sex life – for a puritan like Mahler, this was never a subject that he could mention, and presumably he hoped that it was not an issue for Alma – and we must never lose sight of the fact that men born in the nineteenth century commonly held the view that a woman had few sexual impulses of her own beyond motherhood and obedience to her husband. It is unclear whether Mahler ever knew that Gropius had given Alma the sort of sexual pleasure that Mahler himself had never been able to do. It is not even clear whether Mahler realized that his wife had had sex with Gropius, but he must at least have suspected as much. On Alma's side there was no doubt about the importance of finding sexual gratification with Gropius. The lack of inhibition that we encountered in her adolescent diaries will also have overwhelmed Gropius and left him reeling. Alma was largely innocent of the prudishness of the upper middle-class women of her day – one wonders whether Gropius was aware in advance of the primal force of her femininity. She wrote to him at the end of August, blaming her husband for all her ailments, including her problems with her heart and gall bladder:

> I feel that for my heart and all my other organs nothing is worse than enforced asceticism. I mean not only sensual desire, the lack of which has turned me prematurely into a detached, resigned old woman, but also the continuous rest for my body ... Now I am in bed ... I am with you so intensely that you must feel me.[20]

It is unlikely that any of this came out in the long conversations that took place between Alma and Mahler. She was prevaricating, as is understandable. Certainly, she was by no means certain at this time that she would remain with Mahler. Her letters to Gropius speak of a life spent together in sexual fulfilment: 'When will the time come when you lie naked next to me at night, when nothing can separate us any more except sleep? ... I know that I only live for the time when I am wholly yours.' Dated early September, this letter was signed 'Dein Weib' – 'your wife'. For Alma, sex and motherhood were inseparable, on which point she was still a child of her time: 'My Walter, I want your child – and I'll cherish it and care for it until the day when, without regret but secure and calm, we can sink into each other's arms, smiling and for ever. Write to me, Walter, whether you still feel this as strongly today as you did a month ago.'[21] Mahler and his fate play no part in this picture of intoxicated happiness and vision of the future. When Alma refers to a time in which she could exist for Gropius alone and cherish his child until she and her lover were united, she was clearly looking forward to a time when her old and ailing husband was no longer alive. A divorce was never an option for Alma.

In his own way, Mahler wrestled with the angel, reacting as a child might have done. Normally his eyes remained dry, but now he could not stop crying. The doors between their separate bedrooms were now left open so that he could hear the sound of his wife's breathing. Or he would appear like a ghost at her bedside, causing her to start up in alarm. More than once he lay on the floor of his composing hut, crying – this was how Alma found him when she went to fetch him for lunch. On one occasion he fainted. Alma's account of this incident dates from the end of August, not from the height of the crisis. Like the rest of the family, he had caught a sore throat from the child's nanny – a harbinger of the serious attack of angina that affected him in Munich. Alma found him lying on the ground outside his bedroom, a lit candle beside him.

He recovered only slowly from this attack, but three days later he left for Leiden for his meeting with Freud.

Mahler's notes and poems for Alma are our most accurate reflection of the events of this period. The picture that we can see in this mirror comes perilously close to a case of personality dissociation. Space does not permit a detailed account of these documents, which are in any case undated, making it impossible to be sure of their chronology. They include lines such as the following, committed to paper in a state of some agitation:

My darling, my lyre,
   I am possessed by dark spirits; they have cast me to the ground. Come and dispel them. Abide by me, my rod and staff. Come soon today, that I may rise up. Here I lie prostrate and await you; and silently I ask whether I may still hope for salvation, or whether I am to be damned.[22]

Another note seems to have been written by way of a reaction to Alma's assurance that she would not leave him. Although her claim that she still loved him seems implausible, he was clearly sufficiently desperate to accept it at face value: 'Beloved! I slept wonderfully, but not for a moment did my senses slumber. Never again shall I lack that blissful certainty: *she loves me*! These words are my life's essence. If I may no longer speak them, I am dead.' Although Mahler himself presumably never intended it, comments like these placed his wife under the most enormous pressure. The tension that he felt at this time even finds expression in verse:

   Holdeste! Liebste!
   Mein Saitenspiel!
   Und mein Sturmlied!
   Du Herrliche! O könnt ich Töne finden –
   mein stammelnd Seufzen Dir in Worten künden!
   Mein Athem ist – mein Wesen nicht mehr meins!
   Nicht ich mehr – ich bin von mir selbst geschieden
   – nicht eher kann mich Himmelsruh befrieden
   als bis ich trunken deines süssen Weins!

   Der Lenz hat mich und dich zu sich bezwungen.
   Ich gab mich gleich, nicht hab ich erst gerungen
   Ich starb – wie gern – und süss küsst er mich wach!
   Die Töne brausen – wüthen mir im Herzen
   die heissen Worte flammen – Hochzeitskerzen –
   Es strömt mein Wesen dir in's Brautgemach!

[Fairest, dearest one, / My lyre, / My storm-song, / You wondrous being! What music could I write / Whose words conveyed to you my mortal plight? / My breath, my very being is not mine! / No longer one, my self and I are driven forth – / And find no rest in heaven nor on earth, / Until they've slaked their thirst with your sweet wine. / The springtime forced itself on our alliance, / I yielded instantly, without defiance. / I died – how gladly – and its kiss restored my life. / The notes fly high, my heart beats quicker – / The words, like wedding candles, burn and flicker – / My very being flows to you, my wife.]

On one occasion Mahler kissed his wife's 'little slippers' a thousand times. Elsewhere he coins increasingly outrageous variants on Alma's pet names, finally producing such Dadaist forms as 'Almschilitzili' and 'Almschilitzilitzilitzi', which he then proceeds to use on frequent occasions. Matter-of-fact contemporaries will say that Mahler was merely making a fool of himself, but his biographer is bound to see in all this a case of ego regression tending towards infantilism, for this is exactly how children express themselves, crying uncontrollably, throwing themselves on the ground, kissing slippers and using diminutive forms of words such as 'Almschilitzilitzilitzi', together with all the other childish stammerings: one reads this with a mixture of dismay, emotion and pity. This is how children react when the object of their love threatens to withdraw, but adults, too, can react in this way when they lose control of the ego and the fear of loss and loneliness risks gaining the upper hand. The text of Mahler's note referring to the slippers would seem to suggest that Alma shared his bed in order to calm him down: 'You took mercy on me.'

The reference to ego regression is not intended to sound dismissive, and such a process never arrives out of the blue. The more perceptive of Mahler's friends and acquaintances repeatedly drew attention to the fact that this austere genius also had a pronounced element of childishness about him that they noted with astonishment and bewilderment precisely because it was so difficult to square with the public image of the imperious dictator and implacable prophet of art. The conductor Oskar Fried observed that 'he would retreat into his impenetrable spiritual shell, a child enduring mortal disappointments and bewailing his divine origins'.[23] For his part, Richard Specht commented that 'He was really a great child. ... He was spontaneously trusting or suspicious, like a child. ... Most of all, he craved love as a child does. He needed love, understanding, tenderness as few others do.'[24] We must remember that psychoanalysts working in the field of artistic creativity have long believed that this creativity is inconceivable without a certain amount of ego regression. The ego regresses to a more primitive stage such as sleep, imagination, intoxication and psychoses in which it is weakened, but it can also be observed in the case of various kinds of creative activity. In his pioneering work on illusion and dreams in Wilhelm Jensen's *Gradiva*, for example, Freud showed that the daydream, with its great feats of imagination, has clear analogies with artistic creativity in general. In the daydream the ego regresses to a more primitive state of imagined wish fulfilment and gives other forces a freer rein than is permitted by the waking state, with its censorship controls. Mahler's behaviour during the greatest crisis of his life strikes us as both strange and at the same time all too familiar.

Ernst Kris built on Freud's ideas and used them as the starting point for a psychoanalytical theory of artistic creativity. In Kris's view, the ego – and without a powerful ego, artistic achievement is inconceivable – manipulates the phenomenon of regression in the sense that it adapts it to its own ends, facilitating the controlled regression that triggers creative forces and ideas before regaining the upper hand in the actual creative process. In this way Kris distinguishes between the inspirational phase in which controlled regression is permitted and the working-out phase, when the ego has to regain control.[25] Mahler's behaviour during a crisis that was all the more dangerous in that the crisis of three years earlier had yet to be properly processed should not be taken to mean that a seriously narcissistic individual simply carried on like a child. Rather, a genius whose psychological make-up involved a certain degree of ego regression and whose childish characteristics had been noted long before this crisis and accepted as part of his personality, merely behaved in a way that conflicted with the demands of the social mores of his age.

And there is something else that needs to be mentioned to complete our picture of the events that unfolded at the Trenkerhof in Alt-Schluderbach in July and August 1910: Mahler's rediscovery of his wife's songs. In her reminiscences, she gives the impression that she went for a walk with Anna and on her return heard her songs, long locked away, being played on the piano. Mahler had apparently then come out to greet her with the words: 'What have I done? These songs are good – they're excellent. I insist on your working on them and we'll have them published. I shall never be happy until you start composing again. God, how blind and selfish I was in those days!'[26] Alma dates this incident to the time after Mahler's return from Leiden, but it is clear from her letters to Gropius that it in fact took place on 9 August. This is not the place to discuss the artistic merits of Alma's songs, not least because there are other, albeit contradictory, studies available. Susanne Rode-Breymann has summarized all the arguments in favour of a positive assessment and made a compelling case for them, while Jörg Rothkamm has tried to show that Alma did not revise them on her own but received substantial help from Mahler, who gave these fourteen surviving songs the form in which they have come down to us. He warns against overestimating Alma's abilities and tends to see Mahler himself as their co-composer.[27] In advancing this view, Rothkamm draws on the unpublished correspondence between Alma and Gropius – a thousand or so letters have survived, and some of the important ones have been cited in the foregoing pages. It seems that Alma was by no means exaggerating when she wrote retrospectively about Mahler's enthusiasm. In fact, she seems, rather, to have downplayed his response. And so we find her telling Gropius on 14 August 1910: 'Only now shall I really have something from G. – he wants to read difficult works with me – he's already playing music.' A day later we read: 'The most *ardent* desire of my life has again become clear to me. G. wants to spend his life encouraging me in my work.' And even more astonishingly:

> My joy is now the love and *admiration* that G. is devoting to *my* music. He plans to devote his future life to *this* alone, and I, who had already doubted in such happiness, can scarcely believe it. He plays nothing else all day long and says they are simply *inspired*. – Well, to be *honest*, I knew that my things are 'good' – and if I have dragged my children around with me *in secret* for the last eight years – I still *knew* that they were a success – and simply believed it was a woman's lot to have to renounce all *this* happiness when I got married.

And that was not all:

> For me, it is a bridge back to life. Suddenly I'm in love with the world once again. . . . Gustav lives for these songs – his own works are 'a matter of indifference' to him – he plays them to himself as soon as I am out of the room and finds in them a clearer expression of my whole being than when he talks to me in person.

Alma implies that it was Mahler himself who said that his previous nine symphonies and the tenth, on which he was then working, were a matter of indifference to him, and we can well believe her when she writes that this is what he said. Most astonishingly of all, she herself seems to have taken these remarks seriously. Anyone who were to claim today that Mahler's nine symphonies are a matter of indifference next to Alma's fourteen songs would merely make himself look foolish. A shooting star cannot be compared with a planet. In her reminiscences, Alma, too, refers to this overestimation of her talents. This does not mean that her songs are worthless. They deserve to be performed, for they reveal an astonishing sense of atmospheric values, of the subtleties of their word-setting and even melodic inventiveness. In short, they are the work of a talented composer, not the sort of genius revealed in a single one of the *Lieder eines fahrenden Gesellen*. Anyone who claims that Alma could have enjoyed a great career as a composer but was brutally prevented from doing so by her husband is on very shaky ground.

There is no denying that Mahler's response to his wife's talent was not only very foolish, it was also wrong. As Jörg Rothkamm has written:

> We must be careful not to transfer to Alma herself the undeniably impressive artistic potential of the people who gravitated towards her in the course of her life. Of course she was inspired by them, albeit not to the extent that she herself inspired and supported other artists. For a life as a composer she lacked mainly the intransigent will and compulsion to write music and the tenacity to complete a large-scale work.[28]

Alma knew exactly what set her apart from Mahler, and in a letter that she wrote to Gropius from New York in November 1910 she admitted that 'Everything he does, he does so *completely* – so *comprehensively* – you can really learn from *this* how one should live.'[29] Did Mahler himself really believe that all his own works were worthless next to his wife's songs? Clearly he wanted *her* to believe it. They were sacrifices offered up to Aphrodite, and they certainly had an effect. His self-abasement contributed to the fact that she at least found it easier to live with him and was able to continue with her marriage, albeit with the constant prospect of one day being able to live with Gropius, either after divorcing her husband or after his death. But it also has to be said that Alma found Gropius too immature as a person and too undistinguished as an architect to be able to provide her with the lifestyle to which she was accustomed. This is clear from a further letter that she wrote to him from Toblach in August 1910: 'I must now see if I can put up with this life at least until I can call you or, rather, until you call me. Until you are ready and can stand on your own two feet in the world, so that I can follow you with every happiness and you do not need to be afraid to take me home.'[30] The picture that Alma subsequently painted of a painfully rebuilt marriage is false, for she merely put off the prospect of a life with Gropius, treating the present situation with dilatory indifference and delaying a final decision. Fortunately Mahler interpreted the situation differently, at least for the present, and it must have seemed as if his sacrifices had paid off.

It is impossible to offer a final verdict on the whole terrible confusion of these weeks in Tobelbach and Toblach, which left all three participants profoundly shaken, Mahler most of all. It is no secret that Alma has always been criticized by Mahler's supporters, starting with Lipiner and continuing down to the present time. We have already had occasion to quote from the malicious accounts of Canetti and Adorno, a malice offset by the affection that Adorno's teacher, Alban Berg, felt for Alma. We have also quoted from the review of the German edition of the correspondence between Mahler and Alma by the German writer Hans Wollschläger, who did not have a single good word to say about Alma and who referred to her pompous and hare-brained conversations, the queasy dilettantism of her compositions and her lazy vacillation between submission and domination – this is strong stuff.[31] Nor does he sidestep the difficult question about Alma's complicity in Mahler's death: both Canetti and Adorno believed that she had murdered her husband, although neither was fully familiar with the facts of the Gropius affair. Wollschläger went even further: 'Mahler's death agony began not in 1907 with the diagnosis of his bad heart, which Alma, fully aware of what she was doing, did everything in her power to exaggerate, but in August 1910, with the letter which Gropius even in old age claimed he had wrongly addressed "by mistake"'.

Wollschläger was right to assert that Mahler's death can be traced back to August 1910, but it began with the throat infection that he caught from Anna's nanny. This time it was not one of his usual sore throats but a serious illness, that was not recognized as such, leading to a collapse that he effortfully overcame in order to make the journey to Leiden. It then returned with unprecedented force in early September, obliging him to take to his bed before he could find the strength to resume rehearsals of his Eighth Symphony. We have already discussed the medical connection in our chapter on Mahler's various illnesses: his basic condition was such that it was only a question of time before one of his numerous infections affected his already damaged heart. This could have happened at any time. In the event, it was the two bouts of infection in August and September 1910 that prepared the ground for the streptococcal attack to which he ultimately succumbed. To what extent this powerful psychological shock undermined his physical health is unclear. It is a question that raises the issue of psychosomatic links that cannot be established more than a century after the event and of which the actors themselves were only dimly aware. There is some truth to the serious reproach levelled at Alma by Wollschläger and others like him, but it is difficult to know how to evaluate it in relation to Mahler's physical condition. Nor is it possible to identify any specific moral guilt on Alma's part. Should she have spared him all this? She knew, of course, that he was not well but she could not know how precarious his health in fact was.

Throughout the spring and early summer of 1910 Mahler was busier and at the same time more relaxed than he had been since 1907. He had survived the heart diagnosis of three years earlier and showed every sign of improving. As his recent season in New York had demonstrated, his capacity for work was almost completely restored – certainly he himself saw things in this light. Alma cannot have had the impression that in embarking on her affair with Gropius she was delivering the fatal blow to a man who was already dying. If she felt that Mahler would not survive their separation, this did not mean that he would die if she left him and that she herself would be to blame for his death, but simply that he could not envisage life without her. There is not a scrap of evidence to suggest that even Mahler himself felt that he was dying during the summer of 1910. Alma does not deserve the moral opprobrium of posterity for embarking on an affair with Gropius. After eight years of a frustrating marriage she believed that she deserved it. The foundations of that marriage had been shaky from the outset, and for that she cannot be held entirely responsible. Autumn had chained itself to spring, the over-ripe to the immature. No blessing could accrue to such a match. Mahler ignored Hans Sachs's maxim in *Die Meistersinger von Nurnberg*, justifying his renunciation of the younger Eva: 'My child, I know a sad tale about Tristan and Isolde: Hans Sachs was wise and wanted none of King Marke's happiness.' One does not have to worship Alma blindly to realize that she did not murder her husband. A quite different question is the matter of her continuing affair with Gropius and the lies that this entailed – but by then Mahler was already dying. Emotionally speaking, he never really recovered. Alma spent the rest of her life feeling guilty, and she paid for her passion not least by the fact that her marriage to Gropius was a fiasco. This also explains the macabre cult of the dead Mahler that characterized her life – Canetti saw only the most negative aspect of this. In February 1919 her son Martin, who was born while she was still married to Gropius but whose father may in fact have been Werfel, fell critically ill – he died soon afterwards. In her diary an agitated Alma noted that although Kokoschka and Werfel were gifted men, they were no more than 'microbes' beside Mahler: 'I suddenly know with terrible clarity that I love Gustav and only Gustav, and that since his death I have always been seeking and have never found – and never will.'[32]

It is a mark of genius that even in extreme situations the person in question is still able to work, as Mahler did while organizing the first performance of his Eighth Symphony with iron resolve and even starting work on his Tenth. Gropius had been gone for only a few days when Mahler returned to his composing hut, Alma's reassurance that she would remain at his side apparently restoring his creative powers. Even so, he was shaken to his very foundations. The fragility of his mental state is clear from lines that he wrote for Alma on the music manuscript paper intended for his Tenth Symphony: 'For my dearest one, / My absent, omnipresent friend: / The time has come, the quill is in my hand – / Yet the idea continually eludes me. / To me the staves are like some desert land, / Their five straight lines a mirage that deludes me. / For still I am as dazzled by that light / Which shone on me at Aphrodite's sight.' The Anacreontic garb in which these lines are dressed finds altogether more disturbing expression in the famous scribblings in the short score of the Tenth Symphony. 'Tod! Verk! Erbarmen!! O Gott! O Gott! Warum hast Du mich verlassen? Dein Wille geschehe!', we read in the short score of the third movement. The word 'Verk' has caused a certain amount of mystery, but it appears from a sketch now in the Bavarian State Library that it is an abbreviation of 'Verkündigen' and refers to the *Todesverkündigung*, or Annunciation of Death, in Act Two of *Die Walküre*, Mahler evidently drawing an analogy between the encounter of Brünnhilde and Siegmund and his own situation.[33] The lines may therefore be translated: 'Death! Annunciation! Have mercy! My God, my God, why hast thou forsaken me? Thy will be done!' On the title page of the second Scherzo we read 'The Devil dances it with me! Madness, seize me, accursed that I am! Destroy me, that I may forget I exist, that I may cease to be, that I . . .'. At this point the line breaks off, although we may imagine it continuing with words such as 'ever existed' or 'may perish'. At the end of this same movement Mahler has written: 'You alone know what it means. Ah! Ah! Ah! Farewell my lyre! Farewell / farewell / farewell / farewell / ah! ah!' And at the end of the final movement, Mahler has added the words: 'To live for you! To die for you! Almschi!'

In a series of conversations about Mahler's symphonies that he held with the critic Paul Fiebig, the conductor Michael Gielen expressed a widespread unease at these effusive comments, which he said made him feel uncomfortable. 'If he had added anything like this at the time of the First Symphony, I would have accepted it, but here it amounts to a kind of exhibitionism that I find simply embarrassing.'[34] But exhibitionism is a wilful externalization of something that would have been better kept hidden. Mahler was no exhibitionist, but we ourselves have become voyeurs who have to deal with the fact that these self-revelations have been put into circulation. These 'springtime cries of a servant from the depths', to quote from a poem by Brentano, were not intended for public scrutiny, not even for Alma. Conversely, the surprising dedication of the Eighth Symphony was intended to be seen by Alma: 'To my dear wife Alma Maria', a dedication added at the very last minute to the vocal score of the work. Mahler had never planned this. Rather, it was a spontaneous expression of the panic that had seized him. Here, too, he was trying to placate a capricious goddess – Mahler called her Aphrodite – with sacrificial gifts. It is not exhibitionism when a tormented soul commits its distress to paper. Readers seeking an example of exhibitionism may care to consider the young Elias Canetti's account of a visit that he paid to Alma in the early 1930s:

> Less than six feet from her stood the vitrine in which the score of Mahler's unfinished tenth symphony lay open. My attention was called to it, I stood up, went over and read the dying man's cries of distress – it was his last work – to his wife, his 'Almshi [*sic*], beloved Almshi', and more such intimate, desperate cries; it was to these most intimate pages that the score had been opened. This was no doubt a standard means of impressing visitors. I read these words in the handwriting of a dying man and looked at the woman to

whom they had been addressed. Twenty-three years later, she took them as if they were meant for her now. From all who looked at this showpiece she expected the look of admiration due to her for this dying man's homage, and she was so sure of the effect of his writing in the score that the vapid smile on her face expanded into a grin. She had no suspicion of the horror and disgust I felt. I did not smile, but she misinterpreted my gravity as the piety due to a dying genius, and since all this was happening in the memorial chapel she had erected to her happiness, she took my piety as one more homage to herself.[35]

On 25 August, Mahler, by now more or less over his angina but still emotionally fragile, set off for Leiden for his repeatedly postponed consultation with Sigmund Freud. To quote Brentano:

> Weh der Raum wird immer enger,
> Wilder, wüster stets die Wogen,
> Herr, o Herr! ich treib's nicht länger,
> Schlage deinen Regenbogen.

[Woe, the space is getting smaller, wilder and more desolate the waves. Lord, O Lord! No longer can I bear it. Span the heavens with your rainbow.]

Freud and Mahler's Sufferings – A Stroll through Leiden

Even before Alma had arrived in Toblach from Tobelbad, Mahler had suffered an upsetting experience in his composing hut, as he later told Bruno Walter. Startled by a vague noise, he had looked up from his desk and seen something 'frightfully dark' burst through the window. He had jumped up, appalled, and found himself facing an eagle that seemed to fill the whole room. (In another version it is a smaller bird of prey.) The bird quickly vanished, but Mahler had scarcely recovered from his initial shock when a crow that had been pursued by the eagle flew out from under the sofa and made good its escape, also through the window. Mahler had always been horrified at these manifestations of nature red in tooth and claw, and now such a demonstration intruded upon his compositional work, and the incident left an indefinable impression on him.[36] During the spring of that same year Freud had developed an interest in another bird of prey, a vulture, which he believed had visited the infant Leonardo da Vinci as he lay in his cot. In fact the artist remembered the bird as a kite, but Freud mistakenly translated Leonardo's *nibio* as a vulture. The vision served as the starting point for a far-reaching investigation into the artist's latent homosexuality and intellectual curiosity and, more generally, the suppression of our physical urges, sublimation and questions of neurosis and artistry. As such, the essay is arguably Freud's most important contribution to the psychoanalysis of the creative artist in general.[37] We do not know whether Mahler told Freud about his own experience with an eagle when he met him for a consultation in Leiden at the end of August 1910.

The first six months of 1910 had been a particularly trying time for Freud. At the end of March the Second International Psycho-Analytical Congress had taken place in Nuremberg, when simmering conflicts had broken out in unexpected ways. Sándor Ferenczi had tried to weaken the influence of the Viennese contingent by proposing Zurich as the group's future centre and Carl Gustav Jung as its president. The Viennese members, led by Alfred Adler and Wilhelm Stekel, had opposed a move manifestly designed to limit the perceived preponderance of Jews in the movement, but they were unable to prevent Jung from being elected the association's president, something that Freud expressly supported. As we know, this presidency was short-lived, but Freud could not have known this at the time. A visit to southern Italy was planned as a diversion, and Freud chose Ferenczi as his travelling companion, for he preferred to undertake these journeys without his family in tow. But before the two men left Paris on 1 September, Freud could look forward to a pleasant few weeks relaxing in the Netherlands. The North Sea was chosen as the rest of the family was only a day's journey away in Hamburg, where Freud's mother-in-law, Emmeline Bernays, was seriously ill. She died at the end of October.

Freud left Vienna for the Netherlands in the middle of July, initially visiting The Hague, then moving on to Noordwijk, where he stayed at the Noordzee Guest House. It was presumably here that he received Mahler's first telegram, asking for a consultation. The date of this initial approach cannot be established with any certainty, but it is unlikely to have been before Mahler found out about his wife's affair: it was this that triggered a move that cannot have been easy for Mahler to make. This does not mean that Mahler – an earlier remark expressing his scepticism about psychoanalysis notwithstanding – may not already have thought of consulting Freud in the belief that the latter could help him to come to terms with the events of 1907. Freud normally had no time for such enquiries while he was on vacation, but in Mahler's case there were several reasons to be less squeamish: both men were from Jewish families from the same part of the Austro-Hungarian Empire, Freud from Moravia, Mahler from the border between Bohemia and Moravia; both had a love-hate relationship with Vienna, where they had both encountered resistance aplenty and suffered many a personal attack; both had achieved a good deal in the face of opposition, Mahler more than Freud, who was never actually offered a professorial chair; and both were now nationally, even internationally, acclaimed. Although Freud felt little interest in music as opposed to literature, the visual arts and archaeology, he was none the less sympathetic to Mahler's work in Vienna. There is no evidence that they had met previously, and although the tight-knit nature of Vienna's cultural world might tempt one to question this claim, the very different circumstances of their lives make it at least plausible. Both men hated the local cultural scene, with its coffee shops, invitations and balls, and both were completely absorbed in their work. Freud never attended the opera or concerts, and Mahler did not frequent the company of psychoanalysts. Even such kindred spirits as Freud and Arthur Schnitzler had taken years to forge any contacts, Freud avoiding any meeting out of what he called 'fear of meeting his double'.

It is unclear who advised Mahler to seek out Freud. The latter's biographer, Ernest Jones, thought that it was the Viennese psychoanalyst Richard Nepallek, who was close to the Molls and who had helped the Mahlers at the time of their crisis in 1907. But it seems more likely that the idea came from Bruno Walter, who had undergone treatment a few years earlier, at a time when Freud was by no means the first port of call for artists and intellectuals. He has left an amusing account of his experience in his memoirs. Neuralgic-rheumatic pain in his right arm having reached the point where it called his whole professional career into question and all traditional treatments having proved ineffectual, Walter consulted Freud, expecting to be questioned about sexual aberrations in infancy, but instead he was asked whether he knew Sicily. On answering 'no', Walter was told to take the night train to Italy and forget about his arm and his work. Walter did as he was told, and although the journey was not in itself enough to cure him completely, he managed to get rid of the symptoms after a period of only a few months.[38]

Freud responded to Mahler's telegram by proposing a date, which Mahler turned down by return of post. The whole performance was repeated three times, Freud no doubt seeing in it an example of some obsessional neurosis. He then announced that he had to return to Paris at the end of August, thereby placing Mahler under greater pressure to reach a decision. Mahler himself had to be in Munich in early September to prepare for the performances of his Eighth Symphony, and in October he was returning to New York to fulfil his commitments as music director of the Philharmonic Society. As a result, the only small window of opportunity was the final week of August, when Freud would be in Leiden, staying with his colleague Jan Rudolf de Bruine-Groeneveldt, which is why he suggested Leiden as a place to meet. Mahler's links with the Concertgebouw and with colleagues such as Diepenbrock and Mengelberg meant that for him the Netherlands was a less exotic travel destination than it was for Freud. The result was a meeting which by any standards was exceptional, initially at the hotel where Freud was staying and then in the course of a walk through the streets of the town, a stroll lasting several hours. Thanks to the letters and telegrams that Mahler, in a state of some agitation, sent to his wife during this period, we can date these events with some accuracy: he left Innsbruck on 25 August, arriving in Cologne the next day and returning to Austria on the 27th. In other words, his consultation with Freud can only have taken place on the afternoon of the 26th or the morning of the 27th – as we shall see in a moment, Freud recalled that it was during the afternoon that he met Mahler.

If Mahler consulted Freud, it was not because of a bad arm. Not all writers who have described this meeting as significant or meaningful have been aware of just how momentous and memorable it was. Imagine, instead, a meeting between Freud and Karl Kraus. Although Kraus was regarded as an interesting case in Freud's circle, a single remark from Kraus along the lines of his famous dictum that 'psychoanalysis is the disease whose cure it purports to be' would have been enough to put an end to the thought of any further consultation. Or what about Freud and Klimt, Schiele or Kokoschka? No such encounter took place. Or Freud and Hofmannsthal? In spite of the psychopathological background of *Elektra*, the two men were never in contact, and even as late as 1908 Hofmannsthal was still describing Freud as a vain and narrow-minded mediocrity. In the case of Schnitzler, his contacts with Freud remained friendly but distant. Mahler was the only eminent figure from legendary turn-of-the-century Vienna to have any close contact with Freud, even if that contact lasted less than a day. Nor is it really possible to speak of Mahler as a patient, even though Freud himself used the term 'analysis' when referring to their meeting. In short, it was an extraordinary encounter between the Napoleon of the musical scene of Vienna and New York and the Goethe of psychoanalysis. One might expect that such a momentous meeting would have left a mass of source material, but there are in fact only a few brief accounts of it, all of them vitiated by having been written long after the event.

Nearly a quarter of a century later, one of Freud's pupils, Theodor Reik, asked his mentor about the encounter, prompting Freud to reply on 4 January 1935: 'I analyzed Mahler in Leyden for a whole afternoon in the year 1912 (or 1913?)' – Freud was clearly wrong on this point, and evidently he no longer recalled the year of Mahler's death:

> If I may believe reports, I achieved much with him in that time. He felt he needed to see me because his wife was at that time rebelling against the withdrawal of his libido. In highly interesting probings through his life we laid bare his love conditions, in particular his Holy Mary complex (Mother fixation). I had plenty of opportunity to admire this man of genius's capacity for psychological understanding. No shaft of light was thrown at the time on the symptomatic façade of his compulsive neurosis. It was as if one was digging a single deep tunnel through a puzzling building complex.[39]

The second account is taken from Ernest Jones's biography of Freud. He too picked up the idea of a 'Mary complex', claiming that Freud went on to say to Mahler:

'I take it your mother was called Marie. I should surmise it from various hints in your conversation. How comes it that you married someone with another name, Alma, since your mother evidently played a dominating part in your life?' Mahler then told him that his wife's name was Alma Maria, but that he called her Marie!

There follows the famous and oft-quoted remark of Mahler's that is said to offer an explanation for the juxtaposition of emotional depth and vulgarity in his compositions, a juxtaposition that he said ruined everything. (It may be questioned in parentheses whether Mahler really expressed himself in this way.) As a child, he explained, he had witnessed a painful scene between his brutal father and his mother. In his despair he ran outside, where the song 'Ach, du lieber Augustin' was being played on a barrel organ.[40] Jones's whole account needs to be treated with more circumspection than has been the case until now, for it rests on a comment that Freud made in person to Marie Bonaparte in 1925, thirty years before Jones set down his recollections of it in print. A single error is enough to raise doubts about its reliability. While it is true that Mahler initially wanted to call his fiancée Marie, in the end he stuck to Alma and its numerous derivatives. Essentially, however, this version tallies with Freud's much more authentic account in his letter to Theodor Reik.

The third account is that of Alma in her reminiscences, where she adds a further detail in the form of a remark that she reproduces as direct speech. Freud had allegedly reproached Mahler: 'How dared a man in your state ask a young woman to be tied to him?' And Freud is said to have gone on:

'I know your wife. She loved her father and she can only choose and love a man of his sort. Your age, of which you are so much afraid, is precisely what attracts her. You need not be anxious. You loved your mother, and you look for her in every woman. She was careworn and ailing, and unconsciously you wish your wife to be the same.'[41]

Alma can only agree with Freud, which in itself raises a question over the accuracy of her quotation, adding that Mahler was reassured by these explanations but refused to accept Freud's conclusion that he was suffering from a mother fixation. This contradicts the accounts of both Freud himself and Ernest Jones, for it is impossible to identify a mother fixation if the person undergoing analysis is not prepared to acknowledge it himself. Freud, however, specifically claimed that 'We laid bare his Mother fixation' – and he is unlikely to have been using the royal 'we' here.

In his writings Freud often referred to his patients in coded form, and it seems strange that he would not also have mentioned Mahler, who was by far the most famous object of his analysis. Curiously enough, no previous writer has thought of looking for traces of Mahler in Freud's published writings, and yet such a search proves unexpectedly fruitful. In 1918 Freud published a series of three essays on the psychology of love that had initially appeared separately. The first was published in 1910 under the title 'A Special Type of Choice of Object Made by Men', the second in 1912 as 'On the Universal Tendency to Debasement in the Sphere of Love'.[42] Both essays contain analogies with the case of Mahler. In the first, these parallels are undoubtedly weaker and must in any case rest on coincidence as the piece was evidently written before Freud left for his summer vacation in 1910, but in the second they are far more striking. Both essays deal with the issue that was at the very heart of Mahler's own problems, namely, an immoderate mother fixation and the transfer of the image of the careworn, ailing mother to the wife.

But the parallels go even further. In his study of the choice of object made by men, Freud includes among the 'necessary conditions for loving' that of the 'injured third party': in other words, the man in question chooses as the object of his love not a woman who is free but one on whom another man can 'claim right of possession'. From this point of view, Walter Gropius would have been an ideal case for study. But Mahler represents a less intense form of this condition, for he had told Alma before they became engaged: 'If only you had had a love affair or were a widow, it would be all right.'[43] Symptomatic of the second precondition is its close connection with jealousy, for only then does the man's passion reach its full height and the woman acquires her 'full value': Mahler's reaction to Alma's affair with Gropius is a good example of this type of symptom. Freud traces all these different types of behaviour back to a single source:

> The object-choice which is so strangely conditioned, and this very singular way of behaving in love, have the same psychical origin as we find in the loves of normal people. They are derived from the infantile fixation of tender feelings on the mother, and represent one of the consequences of that fixation. ... In our type, on the other hand, the libido has remained attached to the mother for so long, even after the onset of puberty, that the maternal characteristics remain stamped on the love-objects that are chosen later, and all these turn into easily recognizable mother-surrogates.[44]

It is sufficient at this point to draw attention to the fact that when Mahler first got to know Alma, not only did he want to call her Marie after his mother, but he was also disappointed that she did not look to have suffered very much. He complained about this to his mother-in-law, prompting the worldly-wise and at the same time prophetic reply: 'Don't worry – that will come.'[45]

Until such time as any evidence emerges to show that Freud reworked the manuscript of this essay before it appeared in print in the autumn of 1910, we must accept the foregoing parallels as no more than remarkable coincidences. But this is no longer possible or necessary in the case of the second essay, 'On the Universal Tendency to Debasement in the Sphere of Love', which first appeared in 1912 and which deals with 'psychical impotence' – the very same diagnosis as the one proposed by Alma in the unpublished passage from her diary that we quoted a moment ago. Freud, of course, had expressed himself in more general terms in his letter to Reik and had spoken of a 'withdrawal' of Mahler's 'libido'. Jones expresses this same idea more directly when he claims that following his conversation with Freud, Mahler regained his sex drive. As the most general pathogenic reason for 'psychical impotence', Freud singles out an 'incestuous fixation on mother or sister, which has never been surmounted'. In this context it will be recalled that from the early 1890s to the time of his marriage in 1902, Mahler shared his apartment and invariably went on holiday with his sister, Justine, who was eight years younger and who self-sacrificingly ran his household and forwent any family life of her own. She was apparently incapable of marrying until her brother had begun his affair with Alma Schindler – the fact that she got married on the very next day is significant. There is absolutely no reason to think that there was an incestuous relationship between Mahler and his sister, but an element of unconscious fixation may none the less have played a role here.

For Freud, the love lives of such people remained divided, a division that finds expression in art in the dichotomy of sacred and profane love:

Where they love they do not desire and where they desire they cannot love. They seek objects which they do not need to love, in order to keep their sensuality away from the objects they love; and, in accordance with the laws of 'complexive sensitiveness' and of the return of the repressed, the strange failure shown in psychical impotence makes its appearance whenever an object which has been chosen with the aim of avoiding incest recalls the prohibited object through some feature, often an inconspicuous one.[46]

Following the emotional upheavals of 1907 Mahler had devoted all his energies to his work as a composer – after all, it was not a case of writer's block that he wanted to discuss with Freud. His desire embraced the depths of animate nature, thoughts of death and immortality as mediated by his reading of Goethe and Fechner and his conversations with Lipiner. It was certainly not directed at his wife, for all that he continued to love her. But, following the hammer blows of the past three years, she now bore the marks of careworn suffering that Mahler had missed for so long. Now, however, this feature reminded him all too palpably of his mother.

It seems clear Freud was later given information that persuaded him that his conversation with Mahler had helped his patient. At all events, Mahler was spared any further buffetings during the months that remained to him, even if only because he never discovered that Alma was secretly continuing her affair with Gropius. During his train journey back to Austria, he wrote her a poem whose literary merits need not detain us but which deserves to be quoted here for what it tells us about the most brilliant person whom Freud ever analysed in person. Not only is it an unusual and spontaneous reaction to a psychoan-alytical conversation with the father of psychoanalysis, it also attests to Mahler's subjective belief that after only a single afternoon this remarkable encounter between the two men had produced a positive result – whether this is in fact possible is contested more vigorously than ever by the opponents of psychoanalysis:

> Nachtschatten sind verweht an einem mächt'gen Wort,
> Verstummt der Qualen nie ermattend Wühlen.
> Zusammen floss zu einem einzigen Akkord
> Mein zagend Denken und mein brausend Fühlen.

> *Ich liebe Dich!* – ist meine Stärke, die ich preis
> die Lebensmelodie, die ich im Schmerz errungen,
> *O liebe mich!* – ist meine Weisheit, die ich weiss,
> der Grundton, auf dem jene mir erklungen.

> *Ich liebe Dich!* – ward meines Lebens Sinn
> Wie selig will ich Welt und Traum verschlafen,
> *O liebe mich!* – Du meines Sturms Gewinn!
> Heil mir – ich starb der Welt – ich bin im Hafen![47]

[The nightmare's dispelled by force of persuasion, / Dispersed are the torments of self-contemplation, / In one single chord my hesitant notions / Converge with the power of searing emotions. / '*I love you!*': three words that support and maintain me, / Life's melody rising from sorrow and pain. / *O love me!* – three words that I know, that sustain me, / The bass-note to each and to every refrain. / '*I love you!*': three words that remain what I live for. / With joy will I forfeit the world all around. / *O love me!* – you that tempests blew ashore! / Bless me – dead to the world – my haven found.]

By way of a postlude, it is worth adding that at an auction held by Sotheby's of London in May 1985, two of the objects on offer were letters from Freud. The first was dated 23 May 1911 and was written within days of Mahler's death. It was addressed to Mahler's lawyer, Emil Freund, and reads:

> Dear Dr Freund,
>
> Since I have discovered from the newspapers that you are dealing with the estate of Director Mahler, I take the liberty of rendering my statement of account with the deceased, which amounts to 300 crowns. This is based on a consultation with him that lasted several hours and took place in Leiden (the Netherlands) in August 1910, to where I travelled from Noordwijk a. Z. in response to his urgent summons. Your most devoted servant, Prof. Dr Freud.

Sotheby's estimate for this invoice was £3,000–5,000. The second letter was a typewritten note, signed by Freud and acknowledging receipt of the three hundred crowns from Emil Freund 'for medical services rendered'.[48]

Munich and the First Performance of the Eighth Symphony

Mahler travelled to Munich on 3 September for the final rehearsals for the first performance of his Eighth Symphony. Physically he had still not fully recovered from the throat problems that had plagued him all summer, and psychologically, too, he was still somewhat frail, in spite of Alma's assurances and Freud's diagnosis and advice. Alma followed her husband to Munich a few days later, a delay that he filled by writing her three long letters that demonstrate the tremendous energy he was still capable of generating. Several times he refers to himself as a 'schoolboy' awaiting his 'Saviour':

> Freud is quite right: this utter dependence on you has always been latent in me, you have always been my light and the centre of my universe. Admittedly, the inner light that shines over us all, and the consciousness of sanctity – no longer diminished by inhibitions – heightens these sensations infinitely. What torment, what pain that you can no longer reciprocate them. But just as love always engenders love, fidelity always wins through to fidelity, and as long as Eros remains the master of men and gods, I too shall succeed in winning back what was once mine, in regaining the heart that once beat for me and can indeed be united only with mine on its journey towards God and serenity.[49]

The editors of these letters are right to speak of Mahler's total submission. At this point Mahler suffered a further bout of throat infections and this time he took to his bed at the Hotel Continental, no longer dismissing the illness with the ease with which he had done in the past but summoning a doctor as he needed to be fully recovered by the time that the rehearsals resumed. The doctor decided against swabbing his throat but prescribed a new type of medicine designed to reduce the inflammation. For his part, Mahler wrapped himself in blankets collected from the rest of the hotel, hoping to sweat out the infection, a treatment that had helped him in the past. For three hours he lay prone, sweating profusely. Emil Gutmann called to visit him and turned white as a sheet, fearing that the two concerts would be jeopardized. He helped by wiping Mahler's face with a towel. On 4 September Mahler was still seriously ill in bed, and the first rehearsal was scheduled for the morning of the 5th. What he went through, physically and mentally, is hard to describe. His final letter to Alma before she left for Munich finds him vacillating between euphoria and animal fear as to whether she really loved him. Time and again he had to hear her assurances, which provided him with what he called 'joy without rest', a phrase taken from Goethe's poem 'Rastlose Liebe' ('Restless Love'). Since Alma was lying, she will have offered this assurance only reluctantly.

Between 5 September and the final rehearsal on the 11th Mahler more or less pulled himself together, although there are many eyewitness accounts from friends who came to Munich for the performances and who, not having seen him for a year or more, were shocked at his appearance: he looked drawn, there were signs of the *facies hippocratica*, his erect bearing was no longer in evidence, his face was as white as a sheet, his eyes were unnaturally bright, and he had lost the little extra weight that he had put on in America, leaving him looking emaciated, a picture of wretchedness. Lilli Lehmann was aghast at what she saw and could barely sit through the second half of the performance, so upsetting did she find the whole experience. Gutmann wrote of his admiration for the magnificent way in which Mahler, in spite of everything, remained in command of the massed forces on the platform and kept firm control of the logistics of the undertaking as a whole. In the course of the preliminary rehearsals in Vienna, Leipzig and Munich he had welded the choruses together to form a homogeneous whole and initiated the soloists into the unusual challenges of their parts. Now they had to be combined with the orchestra. Mahler's technique consisted in giving each group the feeling that it was on its own contribution that the success or failure of the whole exercise depended and that it therefore had to concentrate on its own particular task. The individual groups were to leave it to him to bring them together as a single entity. When a trumpeter had great difficulty with an exposed top C, Mahler explained that this was no ordinary top C but a cry, a vital function of music that finds expression in this trumpet, and with that the problem was solved. Mahler enjoyed a particularly close working relationship with the 350 children in the chorus. As his daughter Anna later recalled, he took them seriously, while evincing an attitude towards them that was loving, involved and yet humorous. A Viennese journalist reports that at one of the final rehearsals Mahler sat down on his conductor's chair, cupped his hands together and called a cheerful 'Good Morning' to the children, which they echoed equally cheerfully.

Together with five other halls, the vast space had been built in 1907 for the 1908 Munich Exhibition. It was a structure of iron, reinforced concrete and glass, and the hall was filled with light during daytime hours. The podium, which may be seen in photographs of Mahler rehearsing the symphony, was necessarily huge. Not even today's large concert platforms can accommodate more than five hundred performers, whereas here space had to be found for twice that number. Roller drew up a series of designs showing how the platform should be divided into sections with rostra and steps in order to avoid having the performers all on the same level, an arrangement impossible for acoustical reasons and also because of the sightlines. Mahler not only refused to have the work promoted as his 'Symphony of a Thousand', he also declined to sanction the publication of an explanatory introduction, and so it was not until the following year, when Mengelberg conducted the work in Berlin, that Richard Specht was invited by Universal-Edition to write such a guide.

While Mahler was working like a madman, Alma invited Gropius to Munich – and here the moral imperative starts to take effect. She met him by the back door of the Hotel Regina, where he was staying, and probably also in the hotel itself. Mahler began rehearsals on Monday 5 September and with two exceptions held two rehearsals a day, partly in the main exhibition hall and partly in the Tonhalle in the Türkenstraße. The final public rehearsal took place on the morning and afternoon of Sunday 11 September, with the first performance on the Monday evening and a repeat performance on the Tuesday. Otto Klemperer attended the rehearsals and helped Mahler in various ways, at least to the extent that the latter was prepared to accept assistance. But Klemperer had to leave before the actual performance in order to conduct *Lohengrin* in Hamburg. He later recalled how accommodating Mahler had been in dealing with his own work:

The soloists and the orchestra were there, but not the choir. Even so, it was wonderful. I must say that for the first time I felt that I was in the presence of a great composer. But he was still not satisfied with the scoring. During rehearsals he kept making small changes. He would say, 'No, take this for two clarinets, or this alone, or this louder or softer.' Some years before he died, he said, 'The trouble is I cannot orchestrate.' He was never satisfied. He always wanted more clarity, more sound, more dynamic contrast. At one point during the rehearsals for the Eighth Symphony he turned to some of us in the auditorium and said, 'If, after my death, something doesn't sound right, then change it. You have not only the right but the duty to do so.'[50]

It was almost alarming to see all the prominent figures who, genuine or soi-disant, streamed into the Munich Exhibition Hall on that Monday evening in September 1910. In addition to various members of the house of Wittelsbach, Paul Clemenceau and his wife had come from Paris, together with Auguste Rodin and the composers Camille Saint-Saëns and Paul Dukas. Strauss was there, of course. (A selection from his works had been one of the earlier high-points of the festival). Other composer-colleagues were Alphons Diepenbrock, Max von Schillings and Max Reger, also, strangely enough, Nietzsche's friend the composer Heinrich Köselitz ('Peter Gast'). And so, too, were Lilli Lehmann, Siegfried Wagner from Bayreuth, Max Reinhardt, Arnold Berliner and the critic Oskar Bie from Berlin, and the conductors Willem Mengelberg and Leopold Stokowski. Pfitzner seems to have been prevented from attending by his new position in Strasbourg. But it was Vienna that fielded the largest delegation: Anna von Mildenburg and her husband Hermann Bahr and Anton Webern, the tenor Erik Schmedes, Kolo Moser, Carl Moll, Alfred Roller and Bruno Walter. Zemlinsky had attended some rehearsals, and possibly the first performance. Franz Schalk was present, having conducted some of the rehearsals in Vienna, albeit not to Mahler's satisfaction as he had meddled with some of his tempos. Schalk sought repeatedly to champion Mahler's cause, both during the composer's lifetime and after his death. Other members of the audience included Thomas Mann, who did not have far to come, although it seems that one of Mahler's closest friends, the writer Gerhart Hauptmann, did not attend. Arthur Schnitzler, Hugo von Hofmannsthal and Stefan Zweig, often mentioned as being present, were definitely not in Munich. Last, but not least, Walter Gropius was in the audience.

Bruno Walter recalled the rehearsals and the performance:

Those were great days for us who shared in the rehearsals of the Eighth. The hand of the master controlled the vast array without apparent effort. All concerned, including the children, who adored him at once, were filled with a solemn elevation of mood. What a moment it was, when at the zenith of his career, and, little as we knew it, soon to be called from us by the hand of fate, he took his place amid the applause of the thousands filling the vast auditor-ium, in front of the one thousand performers – above all at the point where the *Creator spiritus*, whose fire inspired him, is called on and a thousand voices utter the cry expressing his whole life's longing – *Accende lumen sensibus, infunde amorem cordibus!* As the last note died away and a storm of applause surged towards him, Mahler stepped up to where, at the top of the platform, the chorus of children stood. He went along the line shaking their outstretched hands as they cheered him. This tribute of love from the young filled him with hope for the future of his work and gave him deep joy.

During rehearsals his friends had anxiously noted many signs of physical weakness. But at the performance he seemed at the height of his powers. The lift of his spirit gave his tired heart its old vigour. This was, however, the last time he conducted a composition of his own; he never heard his last two works.[51]

Mahler had never known such an enthusiastic response from an audience or from his fellow performers. As he himself will have realized, an essential part in his own reaction must have been played by his ability to control the sheer mass of sound and the vast resources for which the work is scored – that element of the piece which Adorno, hesitating between scepticism and admiration, termed a 'giant symbolic shell'. Conversely, Mahler was probably unaware of the unedifying discussion that arose in the newspapers of the time, wondering whether such a hypertrophic work was not in fact typical of 'Jewishness in music' – the sort of 'effects without causes' that Wagner had complained about in Meyerbeer. But even if he had been aware of it, Mahler would hardly have allowed himself to become worked up by these comments by his 'superiors'.

Far more important to Mahler was undoubtedly the token of gratitude that he received from Thomas Mann, who was able to meet the composer in person for the first time after the concert. A few days later he wrote to Mahler:

My dear Sir,

I was incapable of saying, that evening in the hotel, how deeply indebted to you I was for the impressions of 12th September. It is an imperative necessity to make at least some small acknowledgement, and so I beg your acceptance of the book – my latest – which I send you herewith.

It is certainly a very poor return for what I received – a mere feather's weight in the hand of the man who, as I believe, expresses the art of our time in its profoundest and most sacred form.

It is but a trifle.

Perhaps it may afford you tolerable entertainment for an idle hour or two.

Yours sincerely,
Thomas Mann[52]

The book was *Royal Highness*. It is unlikely that Mahler read it as he had little time for contemporary literature. Moreover, Mann's suggestion that it might entertain Mahler 'for an idle hour or two' will hardly have whetted his curiosity for the whole concept of 'an idle hour' was alien to him, and he had never felt the need for 'entertainment'.

The Mahlers returned to Vienna on 14 September 1910 and stayed with the Molls. They were due to return to New York in the middle of October. Meanwhile, rumours had begun to circulate in Vienna that Mahler would be returning to the Court Opera. Weingartner's days there were numbered – he left in February 1911. If a revival of Cornelius's *Der Barbier von Bagdad* is regarded by historians as the most important event that took place during the whole of Weingartner's regime, then – regardless of one's respect for this undervalued work – we can hardly be under any illusion about the standing of this period in the Court Opera's history. According to newspaper reports of the time, there was even a discussion between Montenuovo and Mahler, but there is no evidence that such a meeting took place, and Mahler himself always dismissed the report as a canard. He had no wish to return to the post of director, although it is conceivable that he would have considered a position as a guest conductor when he returned from New York and that such a position would not have been without its attractions if he had chosen to live in Vienna or its immediate surroundings. But when it became clear that the next director would be Hans Gregor, who took up his post on 1 March 1911, the matter resolved itself, for Mahler had heard only the most unfavourable reports about the director designate. Instead he turned his attentions to buying a house near Vienna as a kind of retirement home, a plan that he had been entertaining for some time. The contract was signed by Emil Freund on 3 November, by which date the Mahlers were already back in New York. Under its terms Mahler paid forty thousand crowns for Farm no. 17 at Breitenstein on the Semmering. The sellers were Josef Hartberger Junior and Maria Hartberger.

During all this upheaval, Mahler also took steps to ensure the livelihood of Arnold Schoenberg: in August he sent him eight hundred crowns, in early October he bought three of his paintings, an anonymous acquisition that Schoenberg found out about from Webern only after Mahler's death, and Mahler attended the final rehearsal for a performance of Schoenberg's String Quartets opp. 7 and 10, which the Rosé Quartet performed to mark the opening of an exhibition of Schoenberg's paintings. Both Schoenberg and Zemlinsky were once again invited to supper with the Mahlers. According to Alma, it was on this occasion that Schoenberg said to her: 'I promise you never to argue with Mahler again. From today on he can shout at me as hard as he likes. I shall never take offence. My mind is made up. And it is because I love him.'[53] Mahler spent part of this period revising his Fourth Symphony and correcting the proofs of the Eighth. The couple then left Vienna separately, planning to meet up again on board the *Kaiser Wilhelm II*. Mahler travelled to Berlin, where he saw a number of his friends, including Oskar Fried, before boarding the ship in Bremen. Alma left two days earlier, presumably with the excuse of calling on the couple's friends in Paris, but in reality for very different reasons. This was her last opportunity to see Gropius before she returned to America, and she planned the meeting with great precision and sophistication:

> Rendez-vous would be Munich.
>
> I'll be leaving on Friday 14 October at 11.55 on the Orient Express from Vienna. My bed is no. 13 in the second sleeping car. I've not yet been into town and so I don't know your answer. I'm writing on the off-chance. I'd advise you (if you're coming) to book your sleeping-car ticket in the name of Walter Grote from Berlin – G[ustav] is leaving two days later and may ask to see the list. Please answer as soon as possible. A. M. 50.[54]

Gropius boarded the train in Munich – it was the last time that he saw Alma before Mahler's death.

The Fragmentary Tenth Symphony

W ITH THE RELEASE in 2000 of a recording of Mahler's Tenth Symphony by the Berlin Philharmonic under Sir Simon Rattle in what the packaging described as 'a performing version of Mahler's draft, prepared by Deryck Cooke, in collaboration with Berthold Goldschmidt, Colin Matthews and David Matthews', a debate that had been going on for eighty years appeared to have been settled: Mahler's Tenth Symphony had finally come of age. And now that a leading Mahlerian such as Michael Gielen has overcome his initial scepticism and taken this version into his repertory, its widespread acceptance is assured, ensuring its victory over other performing versions. The protracted history of this fragment and attempts to complete it is too complex to be examined in detail here,[1] but what is important is that not even the opening movement has come down to us in the sort of condition in which Mahler performed his other symphonies, nor even in the state in which he left the Ninth Symphony and *Das Lied von der Erde*, neither of which he lived to perform. Not even the publication in 2003 of the sketches that now form part of the Moldenhauer Archives in the Bavarian State Library alters this fact. To date there have been at least six attempts to produce a performing version on the basis of this heterogeneous material. During her lifetime Alma Mahler approached both Schoenberg and Shostakovich, asking whether they would be willing to undertake such a challenge. As early as 1924, Ernst Krenek, who was for a time her son-in-law, had collaborated with Franz Schalk and Alexander Zemlinsky on a performing version of the first and third movements that Schalk conducted in Vienna in the October of that year. By the 1950s there was something of a race to complete these disparate drafts, a race ultimately won by the English musicologist Deryck Cooke. In his foreword to the published edition, Cooke refuses to describe his version as a reconstruction or a completion but as a glimpse into Mahler's workshop, and yet the wider public has come to regard this version as Mahler's Tenth – after all, who reads the small print in a score or a programme booklet? But listeners who now have a chance to hear the third movement, with its portentous title of 'Purgatorio', certainly have food for thought even if they are not familiar with the complex genesis of this version. That it lasts less than four minutes is an indication of the fact that Mahler's purgatories could be short and painless. And yet the impression given by publishing houses, record companies and performers that something authentic and finished is being presented is more than problematical.

Mahler began work on his sketches for his Tenth Symphony in Toblach between 6 and 17 July 1910, in other words, between his fiftieth birthday and Alma's arrival from Tobelbad. And he put them to one side on 3 September, without ever returning to them. Instead, his time was taken up with the exhausting preparations for the first performance of his Eighth Symphony and planning his season of concerts in New York, his journey to America and the frantic activity bound up with this season, which was brought to a premature end by the onset of his final fatal illness. Clearly he had no opportunity – or he did not look for an opportunity – to take out his sketches again after 3 September.[2] The catastrophic events of the summer of 1910 left clear traces on them. But in order to avoid any misunderstandings, it needs to be stressed that neither the conception of the symphony nor the resultant sketches are a 'response' to the events that overwhelmed Mahler in July and August 1910. Rather, they predate those events. Even so, these events are reflected in the sketches and caused Mahler to break off work on the score, and may even have discouraged him from elaborating them in the course of his final winter. It is unnecessary to repeat the heart-breaking comments that Mahler added to the sketches – even quoting them once is arguably once too often. But they suggest that during the final months of his life he lacked the emotional strength to take out these sketches again. This was a task that was to be left to a later age.

There will perhaps continue to be conductors who are content to perform only the opening Adagio, just as there are conductors who still perform Berg's *Lulu* in its two-act version, rather than in the three-act version completed by Friedrich Cerha. (In every other way, the two cases are barely comparable.)

This opening movement is by far the most fully worked out part of the score, especially in terms of its instrumentation. It is an uncommonly impressive Adagio, but one that reveals more 'moderate' features when compared with the Adagio of the Ninth Symphony and, as such, is more firmly embedded in the great tradition of the symphonic Adagio, notably the Adagios of Bruckner – not only his incomplete Ninth Symphony but also the opening movement of his Third. Melancholy and meditative in character, the first subject-group is vaguely reminiscent of the opening of Act Three of *Tristan und Isolde*, but we do not know whether Mahler intended this as a homage to one of the gods of his youth and whether he might have toned it down in the final version of the piece, but there is no doubt that the spare textures of the sketches would have been more densely harmonized: at one point in the sketches for this movement he writes the word 'polyphonic'. But however impressive this movement may be from a melodic and atmospheric point of view, it would not have remained as it is in the sketches – this *arte povera* was not Mahler's last word on the subject. If there is a reason for performing this movement, it is to acquaint ourselves with one of the most disturbing of Mahler's creations, disturbing precisely because of the stark contrast that exists between its innovative language and its initially retrospective character.

I am thinking in particular of the famous nine-note chord that buries its way into our consciousness in bar 206 and again in bar 208: to paraphrase Mahler, the world had heard nothing like it, at least the world in which his harmonic language had operated until then. Seeming to come from another world, a powerful tutti chord in A flat minor erupts into an adagio passage that restores the mood of the beginning. From this chord there develops a wind chorale that draws attention to itself by dint of its unusual dissonances – it sounds like a Bruckner chorale groping its way towards atonality. Starting in bar 203 from a sustained A in the violins, a new chord is built up in four steps, culminating in the nine-note chord in bars 206 and 208, a chord that has nothing to do with the functional harmony that Mahler had embraced hitherto and that cannot be explained by that traditional harmonic language. Initially we hear only the a'' in the first violins, then the five-note chord G sharp-B-D-F-A, before the C sharp is added in the bass and C-E flat-G above it. At no previous point in Mahler's output had it been possible to predict this emancipation of the dissonance.

The consequences of this nine-note chord for his subsequent output must remain the object of speculation. While it would be wrong to abandon our former scepticism concerning any alleged link between Mahler's life and music, there does seem to be a legitimate explanation for this unprecedentedly bold harmony in that it may well be inspired by the catastrophic events that unfolded in Toblach during the summer of 1910. The chord was evidently added to the first movement only when Mahler was already working on the sketches to the final movement, for it is only here that the whole passage appears in its initial form. Mahler evidently wanted to use so powerful a passage in the opening movement, too, and to create an overarching structure, hence his decision to add it to the earlier movement as well. The connection between Alma's infidelity and this terrible dissonance – terrible for listeners in 1912, whereas from today's perspective it is terrible for reasons other than purely musical ones – is irrefutable, for the sustained a'' of the first violins, like the a' in the third trumpet in bars 206 and 208, surely refers to her. Less convincing, by contrast, is the recently revived hypothesis that Mahler is referring to this chord in the poem that he wrote to Alma immediately after his encounter with Freud, the first verse of which ends with the lines 'Zusammen floss zu einem einzigen Akkord / Mein zagend Denken und mein brausend Fühlen' (literally, 'My hesitant thinking and raging feelings flowed together in a single chord'). It matters little whether Mahler sketched out this chord before he travelled to Leiden or only after his return. What matters is that if Mahler had been thinking of the chord in his poem, it could only have been as an expression of otherworldly consonance, for the chord in the poem refers to the love between the couple, a love that Mahler urgently invokes and that he hopes to win back. For a nine-note dissonance to express the longed-for restitution of marital harmony would have come suspiciously close to a Freudian slip or an example of self-mortifying irony.[3]

However inadequate these comments, they may none the less suffice. The harrowing circumstances in which these sketches were produced, their puzzling character, the aura of the late work whose incompleteness cannot, however, be blamed on the composer's final fatal illness – all of this places the fragmentary Tenth Symphony in the realm of speculation. It is by no means illegitimate or symptomatic of a lack of piety to want to listen to Deryck Cooke's 'performing version', but the listener is simply deluding himself if he thinks that what he can hear is Mahler's Tenth Symphony. The work is not by Mahler, and if it has found a place for itself in the concert hall, then scepticism is in order. The objections of various Mahler experts are far from being invalidated by the increasing refinements to Cooke's performing version or by the alternative versions proposed by others. Although Cooke's version seems to have gained an unstoppable momentum, it is still worth reminding ourselves of Adorno's warning, which has lost none of its pertinence:

The draft has by no means been developed to the point where we can guess where it was heading. Its own laws remained shrouded in darkness. With an epico-musical composer like Mahler what is significant is the apparently insignificant and the detail which, incessantly newly produced, is always changing. And for that the fragment offers insufficient purchase. One does not need to fall victim to puritanical zeal or to fetishize the genius when one mistrusts attempts that cannot achieve their intended aim and that merely cause confusion. . . . Even the opening movement would be better honoured by our reading it in silence, rather than by being exposed to performances in which the unrealized becomes the imperfect.[4]

'My heart is weary' – The Farewell

How Men of Genius Die

'How gentle and calm as the sea were your life and death, Wutz, you contented little schoolmaster!' one of Mahler's favourite authors, Jean Paul, writes at the start of the 'kind of idyll' that constitutes his life of Maria Wutz of Auenthal. 'The calm and mild sky of a late summer surrounded your life not with clouds but with fragrance: the stages of your life were the fluctuations and your death was the plucking of a lily whose leaves flutter on standing flowers – even outside the grave you slept gently!'[1] Mahler's life and death were anything but gentle and as calm as the sea. He was no contented musician, and it would never occur to anyone remotely familiar with his life to describe it as a kind of idyll. Mahler had nothing in common with Maria Wutz. The death of great men is generally seen as very different from that of provincial schoolmasters. Take the following example:

He lay in the final agony, unconscious and with the death-rattle in his throat, from 3 o'clock, when I arrived, until after 5 o'clock; then there was suddenly a loud clap of thunder accompanied by a lot of lightning which illuminated the death-chamber with a harsh light (there was snow in front of the house). After this unexpected natural phenomenon, which had shaken me greatly, he opened his eyes, raised his right hand and, his fist clenched, looked upwards for several seconds with a very grave, threatening countenance, as though to say, 'I defy you, powers of evil! Away! God is with me.' It also seemed as though he were calling like a valiant commander to his faint-hearted troops: 'Courage, men! Forward! Trust in me! The victory is ours!'

As he let his hand sink down onto the bed again, his eyes half closed. My right hand lay under his head, my left hand rested on his breast. There was no more breathing, no more heartbeat! The great composer's spirit fled from this world of deception into the kingdom of truth.[2]

Anselm Hüttenbrenner's account of Beethoven's death suggests that this is how a Titan dies, nature providing elemental funeral music in the form of thunder and lightning and driving snow. Another observer of the same event, Andreas Johann Wawruch, the composer's principal physician at the time of his death, reports on a similar natural spectacle, adding the rhetorical question: 'What would a Roman augur have concluded about his apotheosis from the fortuitous unrest of the elements?'[3] According to an ineradicable legend, Mozart's burial was accompanied by rain, snow and hail – it is possible that these conditions preceded the interment but that the weather quickly improved. A similar spirit permeates accounts of the last words or gestures of great men and women. In the case of Mozart, he is said to have puffed up his cheeks to imitate the timpani in his Requiem – a work likewise shrouded in mystery. As Wolfgang Hildesheimer remarks in his biography of Mozart, 'The last hours and the death of a genius are also subject to aesthetic censure: they must provide some undisputed beauty for reverent generations to come; they must also have the stuff of tradition, "last words", last gestures.'[4] No 'last words' of Mozart have come down to us, whereas according to Alma, Mahler repeatedly spoke the name 'Mozartl' – an Austrian diminutive of the composer's name – while dying.

It is now generally accepted that Goethe did not say 'More light' on his deathbed. According to another version, he spoke of the approach of spring, when there was a greater chance of recovery. The truth of the matter is that the cause of death – almost certainly a heart attack brought on by his bronchitis – left him with little time to utter any dying words. In Goethe's case we have the highly realistic account of his final moments by his personal physician, Carl Vogel, who reports on his contorted features, sunken eyes, ashen face and chattering teeth, an account undoubtedly closer to the truth but hardly Titanic in spirit. When great men die, the elements are thrown into disarray: according to the French Classicists, they die 'un beau trépas'. Goethe is one of the few to be spared such concomitant phenomena, whereas in the case of Napoleon – if we may believe his biographers – the whole of nature was in turmoil. The sober historian Adolphe Thiers was unable to persuade his readers to accept his own version of events, whereby the weather on the day the deposed emperor died was calm and sunny. Chateaubriand talks of rain and storms, Emil Ludwig of a storm that uprooted two trees outside Napoleon's house. De Bradi describes an uncanny calm abruptly broken by a violent tempest like a powerful cannonade, while others claim that a thunderclap was heard in distant Flanders at the moment that Napoleon died. Yet others insist that they saw a comet. Of course, there is a venerable precedent to all of these reports: 'And, behold, the veil of the temple was rent in twain from the top to the bottom, and the earth did quake, and the rocks rent; and the graves were opened.'

And what about Mahler? Alma describes his death-rattle lasting several hours. 'That ghastly sound ceased suddenly at midnight on 18th May during a tremendous thunderstorm. With that last breath his beloved and beautiful soul had fled.'[5] It has to be added at this point that she was not in fact present in the room when Mahler died. According to Bruno Walter, when the coffin was taken from the clinic to the cemetery chapel, 'a storm broke and such torrents of rain fell that it was almost impossible to proceed'.[6] Paul Stefan describes the moment at which the coffin was lowered into the ground: 'The rain had ceased, a wonderful rainbow became visible, and a nightingale's voice was heard through the silence. Then fell the last clods, and all was over.'[7] Alma had no hesitation in investing Mahler's death with the features of Christ's Passion: 'On the evening after, he was washed and his bed made. Two attendants lifted his naked emaciated body. It was a taking down from the cross.'[8] Last words also include last signs and portents in the form of signals from another world, a world that no longer makes sense to those who are shameless enough to survive the great man's death. Goethe, for example, is said to have drawn symbols in the air with his forefinger and then, when he no longer had the strength to raise his arm, on the blanket of his bed. Alma, too, claims to have seen Mahler conducting with one of his fingers on the quilt.

Faced with the death of any great figure whom we admire unreservedly, we inevitably ask ourselves questions as to whether their deaths were not premature or senseless and whether they might have gone on to create yet greater masterpieces. Given the greatness of the Ninth Symphony and of the unfinished Tenth, no one will claim that Mahler had passed the peak of his powers and was merely repeating himself. Quite the opposite, a constant development is discernible, and there is widespread agreement that these two works, together with *Das Lied von der Erde*, represent the pinnacle of his achievement. And even if we find it hard to imagine any further increase in his powers, there is no reason to suppose that the Tenth would have been followed by a period of creative stagnation or even decline. It is quite different when an artist appears to have reached the end of his career and put his house in order and his will to live is broken or at least so impaired that death seems a welcome comforter, even if the artist himself is ultimately reluctant to accept this. The elderly Goethe is a case in point. He had not reached the stage of desiring death, but he was conscious of the fact that the harvest had been gathered in. This was emphatically not true of Mahler.

It is also generally believed that the death of great men, like any powerful event, is heralded by portents, including comets and other celestial phenomena. But in spite of all the crises and catastrophes and threats to his health, Mahler did not see his death coming and certainly did not long for it. There are a number of chiefly American studies of a psychoanalytical bent that speak of a deep-rooted death wish on Mahler's part. Such writers claim that he was obsessed by the death of so many of his brothers in their infancy and early youth and above all by that of his favourite brother, Ernst, and that this obsession found expression in the fratricide in *Das klagende Lied* and that it went on to dominate his entire life as a covert driving force. Such claims can be dismissed out of hand. Mahler never stopped thinking about death, but there is no evidence that he had a relaxed approach to his own mortality. In principle he shared Thomas Mann's view in *The Magic Mountain* that 'for the sake of goodness and love, man shall let death have no sovereignty over his thoughts'. His discussions with Lipiner and his belief in entelechy were ultimately an attempt to come to terms with death. The only candid remark of his to have come down to us is the one that we have already quoted from his letter to Bruno Walter: he had always known that he must die. And when, in the very next breath Mahler denies having a hypochondriac's fear of death, we know that we can believe him.[9] And yet the crisis of 1907 had shaken the very foundations of his own private view of the world, and it needed considerable effort on his part, lasting several years, to pull himself together again. An element of effusiveness remains, and there seems little doubt that Mahler would not have subscribed to the tone of Mozart's famous remark in a letter to his father:

> When looked at closely, death is the true goal of our lives, and for a number of years I've familiarized myself with this true friend of man to such an extent that his image is no longer a source of terror to me but is comforting and consoling! And I give thanks to my God that He has given me the good fortune of finding an opportunity – you understand what I mean – of realizing that death is the *key* to our true happiness. – I never go to bed without thinking that – young as I am – I may no longer be alive the next morning – and yet no one who knows me can say that I'm sullen or sad in my dealings with them – and for this blessing I give daily thanks to my creator and with all my heart wish that all my fellow creatures may feel the same.[10]

This is not the place to discuss the extent to which Mozart may have been echoing intellectual and literary models of his age or, conversely, expressing his very own profound convictions. Suffice it to say that Mahler did not share this quietistic calm: his sense of inner equilibrium was fragile and effortfully achieved, so that it could all too easily be shaken by any passing crisis.

The Last Season in New York

We cannot be sure about Mahler's basic mood during the final months of his life and whether he had learnt to cope with the events of the summer of 1910, but the surviving sources seem to indicate that, astonishingly, he survived the third hammer blow more resiliently than the previous two. On the other hand, a man like Mahler was never able to cope with events of this nature. And yet it seems that he believed Alma and that he had survived the Gropius affair or, rather, he interpreted her assurances in such a way that he was able to believe that he had survived it. He remained unaware of the fact that she was continuing her passionate affair behind his back, not only in Munich, where his attention was taken up with rehearsals for his Eighth Symphony, but also in the sleeping carriage from Munich to Paris and probably also in Paris, too. Nor did he know that letters continued to pass to and fro between New York and Berlin. Ever since he had suffered a severe attack of streptoccocal angina in Munich in September 1910, he was marked out by death, a colourful metaphor that in the present case has medical support. Yet he was by no means sick at heart. As we have noted, many of his friends were struck by his wretched appearance at the rehearsals and performances in Munich. And yet the snap-shot photographs that were taken in Munich's Hofgarten at this time do not show a dying man, and the same is true of the pictures taken of him in New York that winter.[11] It will be recalled that the Viennese impresario Maurice Baumfeld invited the Mahlers to spend Christmas with him and his family in his New York apartment in 1907. In his reminiscences of the composer, which were published soon after the latter's death, he discusses the winter of 1910/11 in terms that could hardly be more unequivocal:

> In the first half of the final winter he had been in a particularly happy frame of mind. Full of the most grandiose plans which, contrary to his usual custom, he actually confided in others. He was filled with the serene joy of life that is typical of advancing age. Since he knew that he and his family were financially secure for the rest of his life, he wanted to spend a few years – 'anyway it won't be all that long' – enjoying the unfettered existence of an independent artist. Living only for his compositions, for which he expected full recognition only from a later age, and looking forward to a time of cheerful contemplation within the circle of those friends with whom he was glad to spend hour upon hour.[12]

It is unclear how we should interpret the phrase 'anyway it won't be all that long'. Does it mean that he would not be able to hold out for long without conducting? Rather, it suggests that he had a limited life expectancy, but even then it does not imply a presentiment of death or a longing for death, but merely the sober realization that his health was seriously impaired and that his family did not expect him to live for long. But why should he not live to be more than sixty, like his father? Whatever the answer, nothing suggests that he expected to be dead within a matter of months. Even what appears to be his last surviving letter – it was written to Emil Hertzka of Universal-Edition and arrived in Vienna on 21 February, the day of Mahler's last concert, so it will have been posted around the 13th, exactly a week before the onset of his final illness – contradicts this claim, for Mahler says quite clearly that he plans to return to New York for the following season. His family knew that he had a weak heart, but such was his tremendous energy that he had recovered from every exertion and achieved incredible feats of endurance. The present situation seemed no different. To all intents and purposes he looked to be fully recovered. During the crossing to America, he was in the best of moods and even took part in an onboard concert, accompanying the famous Irish tenor John McCormack.

The couple arrived in New York on 25 October. At the end of November he wrote to Emil Freund in Vienna: 'I am pretty well at the moment, with a frantic amount of work, which I am coping with very well. Alma and Gucki are, I'm afraid, not in the best of health.'[13] And to his Munich impresario, Emil Gutmann, who had performed miracles in organizing the performances of the Eighth Symphony in September, he wrote, probably in December: 'It is as good as certain that I shall return next season.'[14] This is not the tone adopted by someone paralysed by a presentiment of death. Mahler's resolve was unbroken, and he certainly needed his strength, for his commitments had increased, the Philharmonic Society wanting him to conduct even more concerts than in previous seasons. At the same time, however, his difficulties with some of the Society's organizers took a turn for the worse. Within days of his arrival in New York he gave one of his rare interviews to *The Etude*. In the course of it, he was particularly voluble, expatiating on the influence of the folksong on national styles, on the importance of good music during a child's formative years and the inclusion of folk elements, real or apparent, in symphonic music, an aspect of his own music that has often been criticized. Conversely, his comments on the capabilities and potential of black Americans would now be dismissed as an egregious example of political incorrectness. Music such as ragtime, he insisted, was simply substandard and attempts to incorporate it into American art music should be avoided at all costs. Neither Scott Joplin nor George Gershwin could have appealed to Mahler in their defence. People were not all the same, Mahler concluded, and 'red-skinned aborigines' needed centuries to evolve to an advanced ethnological level.[15]

Mahler's fortunes as conductor and music director of the New York Philharmonic were by no means as brilliant during his final season in the city as they had been previously. If we are to judge him by his own high standards, we shall be forced to conclude that, his initial triumphs at the Met and Carnegie Hall notwithstanding, his American years were not a success. Not even his experience and authority were enough to restore the Met to an even keel, nor was he able to find a new artistic home in America for his own music, while his tremendous commitment to the New York Philharmonic failed to achieve the desired results.[16] Mahler did not die at the peak of his personal happiness and artistic triumphs – the first performances of the Eighth Symphony had taken place a full eight months earlier, a date that had also marked the low point in his marriage. After three years in New York, the Viennese maestro's novelty had worn off. The number of subscribers to his concerts fell slightly but perceptibly. The critics no longer reviewed each Mahler concert as if it were a sensation. Instead, it was Toscanini who was now the talk of the town. At the very moment that Mahler was writing to Gutmann to say that he was planning at least one more season in New York, the organizers of the Philharmonic concerts seem to have started to discuss the question of his successor. In this he himself was partly to blame, for, as with the Met, he had hesitated to sign a long-term contract but had committed himself only to one season at a time – and even this commitment had been made with some reluctance. Understandably, orchestras and their boards of management, to say nothing of their shareholders, are never keen on such ad hoc arrangements.

Mahler conducted his Fourth Symphony on 17 and 20 January 1911 in the version that he had spent the previous summer meticulously revising. Although he was very pleased with the way the work now sounded, a number of critics again complained about music that struck them as so unusual. Mahler's programmes contained fewer novelties than before, but instead there were more repeats, a change intended to make his work easier but which in fact meant that the concerts received less attention, with the result that the Guarantors' Committee insulted Mahler by setting up a programme committee designed to assist him in planning his concerts. This was an act of brazen effrontery, and Mahler interpreted it as such.

Strong-headed and undiplomatic as ever, Mahler also made mistakes when dealing with the orchestra. Even before this, he had developed the habit of seeking out a confidant in every orchestra with which he worked closely and using that person in furthering his own ends. Collectives tended to make him anxious, which he tried to overcome by high-handedness and a show of force. All the more important, then, were the individuals on whom he believed he could rely and who would report on the mood within the orchestra but whom their orchestral colleagues regarded, rather, as spies and collaborators. His brother-in-law Arnold Rosé had been one such figure in the Court Opera orchestra in Vienna. It was a situation that led to animosities, for all that Rosé's outstanding musicality lent him a certain authority. In the case of the New York Philharmonic, Mahler singled out a second violinist by the name of Theodor Johner, but Johner had less natural authority than Rosé. The orchestra mutinied against him and by extension against Mahler, insisting on the spy's dismissal. As always, Mahler dug his heels in and, insisting on retaining Johner's services, turned the whole wretched affair into a battle of wills. But whereas in Vienna he had been the all-powerful director of the Opera, in New York he was no more than the de facto principal conductor: the real power lay in the hands of the committee that ran the orchestra. The players went running to the committee, and Mahler lost the battle.

In the middle of February he was summoned to the home of Mary Sheldon, whose unequivocal support he no longer enjoyed. The only member of the committee to have retained her unquestioning loyalty was Minnie Untermeyer, but on her own there was little that she could do. The immensely wealthy Mary Sheldon evidently gave Mahler to understand that even great artists have to serve the needs of the society that finances them. Mahler had to climb down and accept Johner's dismissal. According to Alma he returned from this meeting incandescent with anger and shaking with fury. His shivering may also have been a harbinger of his final fatal illness, although it could have been brought on by the agitation that he was feeling. These events took place only a few days before the onset of his final illness and undoubtedly hastened it. His final concerts following this confrontation were overshadowed by his deep-seated anger towards the orchestra and its committee and by an equally deep-seated antipathy towards him on the part of large sections of the orchestra and its committee. It was on this low point that their association ended, for all that it had begun so gloriously. It is unlikely that in the wake of these events Mahler thought seriously about returning to New York for a further season.

He conducted his very last concert at Carnegie Hall on 21 February. It was an Italian-themed programme, with works by three contemporary Italian composers, Leone Sinigaglia, Giuseppe Martucci and Marco Enrico Bossi, Mendelssohn's 'Italian' Symphony and Busoni's *Berceuse élégiaque*, which Busoni, who was present at the performance, had written on the death of his mother and which, he told his wife, Mahler did not conduct quite as well as his *Turandot* Suite. None the less, the success of the performance was such that the mutual regard in which the two composers held each other and which dated back to their first meeting in Vienna in 1899 will undoubtedly have increased. Mahler was unable to conduct the repeat of the concert three days later, when the orchestra's leader, Theodore Spiering, whom Mahler had himself engaged, took over all the works in the programme with the exception of Busoni's *Berceuse élégiaque*, which Busoni himself conducted. Spiering conducted the remainder of the concerts that season: it seems to have become clear very soon that Mahler would be unable to do so, even though the rest of the world continued to be assured that he would be returning to the podium very quickly.

The harmonious relationship between husband and wife that Alma describes in her reminiscences of these final months in America rests on a deception. By 8 November, Mahler had completed his first three concerts of the season and, as seems to be confirmed by an unclear photograph, he went for a walk in Central Park with his daughter. Alma used his absence to write to Gropius from her desk in the Savoy Hotel:

> You float before me like a figure of light – a most beautiful youth – and you determine my actions. When shall I see you in person? When? Shall I see you again just like a god created you – for only a god can achieve anything of this kind? I want to absorb all your beauty. The perfection of us both must surely produce a demigod.[17]

Alma's mother had long known about the affair and with a sound mother's instinct clearly sided with the stronger – and younger – couple. One has the feeling that she had already written off Mahler, who for his part called her 'Mummy' and clearly regarded her as a substitute for his own mother, who had died twenty-two years earlier. Let us hope that he suspected nothing. In a letter that she wrote to Gropius from Vienna on 13 November 1910 Anna Moll noted that

> the sad thing is that one cannot do anything at present – one has to leave it all to time, but I firmly believe that for both of you your love will survive all this. I have such boundless trust in you and am convinced that you love my child so much that you will do nothing to make her even more unhappy.[18]

It must remain Alma's secret how she managed to deal with Mahler's childlike high spirits as he kissed lips that had just sealed a letter to Gropius. The whole of her cult of her dead husband, as described by Canetti, and her insistence on carrying on like Mary Magdalene throughout Mahler's final illness were clearly the expression of a guilty conscience. She can scarcely have seen herself as innocent of her husband's death.

Mahler fell over himself in his attempts to show Alma his affection. He invited her to Niagara Falls and in general was more charming and attentive than he had ever been before. Initially, at least, these final months were not overshadowed, except by problems with the orchestra. The couple began to take an interest in theosophy and the occult and studied books by C. W. Leadbeater and Annie Besant, the latter a former associate of Helena Blavatsky, that were *le dernier cri* in Europe and America. The Mahlers tried closing their eyes to see what colours they could see. 'We were very near together in those days.' For Christmas 1910 Mahler gave his wife vouchers to spend on 'a fine spree along Fifth Avenue'. Some days earlier he had gone out 'with a very solemn air', taking his chequebook with him, something he otherwise never did, so great was his fear of losing it. He laid out her presents on a table, but there was something about the situation that Alma claimed to have found distinctly unsettling:

> A pang of icy dread gripped me, when I saw, on a table all for me, that long mound of presents covered with a white cloth and smothered in roses. I snatched off the covering. Mahler stood idly by. But his sadness soon vanished and my dread premonition also, for I was touched to the heart by all the lovely things he had thought of without any regard for his own likes and dislikes.[19]

Mahler also took a greater interest in his daughter Anna than he had ever done before. She was then six, an age at which Mahler, who was unable to relate to infants, could begin to treat her as a person. As an old woman, Anna gave several interviews in which she spoke about her father and her mother. (With Alma she always had what, to put it mildly, was a problematical relationship.) She had the piercing eyes and profile of her father. When she was young, it was her mother's gentler features that predominated, but in old age she came to look just like her father. People who knew Anna, including her lovers, claimed that she was more attractive than her mother, inevitably triggering feelings of jealousy in the latter. In adulthood she made no secret of the fact that as a small child there was something terrible about the atmosphere at home, where her father was always revising his scores and needed peace and quiet for his work, but whenever he spent time with her, he was loving and understanding. She sometimes went roller-skating in Central Park but kept falling over. Each time her father patiently set her on her feet again. Even as an old woman, there was one detail Anna remembered very clearly: her father used to eat meat that was badly overcooked. As she realized very clearly, he really did not want to eat meat at all, as he had never entirely abandoned the vegetarian ideas of his youth but believed that he needed meat as a source of strength. But it could not look or taste like meat. It had to be dried out and shrivelled up – if it tasted terrible, it could not be a sin against the spirit. Anna also remembered watching him scratching out notes in a manuscript and exclaiming 'Papi, I wouldn't like to be a note.' 'Why not?' he asked. 'Because then you might scratch me out and blow me away.'[20] Mahler was delighted by her answer. The scratched-out notes were an integral part of his Ninth Symphony, which he continued to work on as long as he could. Evidently he did not return to his Tenth Symphony during his final winter.

After another tiring series of concerts, Mahler again fell ill on 20 February. It seemed to be the usual sore throat. Joseph Fraenkel examined him and suggested that he should pull out of the concert the following evening. Mahler pointed out with some justification that this would not be the first time he had conducted a concert with a high temperature. Frozen to the marrow, he made his way to Carnegie Hall wrapped in blankets. During the interval he felt even worse but continued with the concert. On returning to his hotel, he was given an aspirin and put to bed. By the next morning he seemed to be much better, the fever had gone and, with it, the infection. Mahler's good spirits returned. The attack appeared to have followed its usual course, just as it had done for years, so that there seemed little reason to be anxious. But suddenly the whole situation changed. The fever returned, initially in a mild form, then stronger, only for it to recede, before returning again with yet greater virulence. This was unusual, and it was also unsettling for Mahler, who knew his own body and his reactions very well. For her part, Alma seems not to have been unduly unsettled as yet. Initially they thought it was influenza. But when Mahler collapsed again, just as he had done in Toblach the previous summer, Fraenkel grew concerned, and on this occasion Mahler seems to have sensed that the situation was serious, although he could still call on his humour to help him. 'You will be in great demand when I am gone,' he told Alma, 'with your youth and looks. Now who shall it be?'[21] And he drew up a list from which Gropius's name was conspicuous by its absence. Alma was forced to laugh, even though she, too, was now conscious of the gravity of the situation. On another occasion he told her to look after his retouched scores of the symphonies of Beethoven and Schumann, claiming – mistakenly – that they were valuable. He was still able to attend a rehearsal for one of his concerts on 3 March, when Frances Alda, the famous New Zealand soprano who was married to the Met's director, Giulio Gatti-Casazza, sang one of Alma's songs, 'Laue Sommernacht'. Alma attended the actual concert and was able to report that the song had been well received, which pleased Mahler.

From now on Mahler's health got worse by the day. It probably did not take Fraenkel long to suspect a case of endocarditis, for he knew that his friend and patient had a heart valve defect and that he had suffered from recurrent bouts of throat infection. But he had no means of verifying this diagnosis, and so he turned to Emanuel Libman, who had studied with the world's leading authority on such matters, William Osler. Libman worked at the Mount Sinai Hospital, where he specialized in inflammatory heart diseases. Much later he developed an interest in a nonbacterial form of endocarditis now known as Libman endocarditis. Libman visited Mahler at his hotel and began by confirming not only Fraenkel's diagnosis of a heart valve defect but also his suspicion that Mahler was suffering from a subacute endocarditis. The symptoms were clear. The spleen was enlarged, petechiae – small lesions – were visible on the conjunctivae and skin, and, most worryingly, there was a slight clubbing of the fingers, a condition found when the heart is no longer able to supply the blood with sufficient oxygen. Inasmuch as the fingertips and toes are the parts of the body that are furthest from the heart, this under-provision of oxygen is most clearly apparent here. The fingertips swell and become rounded. If the fingers are particularly narrow, as they were with Mahler, then the clubbing is especially noticeable, encouraging the comparison with a drumstick. This suspicion still needed to be confirmed by a blood culture. This was a relatively new method of diagnosis and it was expensive. Nowadays we have laboratories in which thousands of diagnoses can be made every day on the basis of small quantities of a patient's blood, using expensive equipment, so that it is hard for us to imagine how difficult this procedure was in Mahler's day. Considerable quantities of blood had to be drawn using thick cannulae. Libman asked his young assistant, George Baehr, to take the samples and prepare the cultures. Baehr later recorded his impressions:

> On arrival I withdrew 20 ml. of blood from an arm vein with syringe and needle, squirted part of it into several bouillon flasks and mixed the remainder with melted agar media which I then poured into sterile Petri dishes. After 4 or 5 days of incubation in the hospital laboratory, the Petri plates revealed numerous bacterial colonies and all the bouillon flasks were found to show a pure culture of the same organism which was subsequently identified as *streptococcus viridans*.[22]

The bacterium is described as 'viridans' because it looks green under a microscope. When Mahler was examined shortly afterwards by André Chantemesse in Paris, the famous bacteriologist was delighted by the 'marvellous state of development' in Mahler's streptococci. 'Just look at these threads – it's like seaweed.'[23] It is hard not to be reminded of the Doctor in Berg's *Wozzeck*. This diagnosis confirmed Fraenkel's worst fears – Alma claims that his hair turned white overnight – and effectively sounded Mahler's death knell. It was still possible to support the circulation and give Mahler a blood transfusion, although this was not in fact attempted because of the patient's impaired state of health and the risks bound up with such a course of treatment. He was given anti-streptococci vaccinations, but these produced no significant results. Before the discovery of penicillin, none of this would have been of any medical use. The streptococci had settled on the damaged parts of the heart. They could also, of course, have infected a healthy heart, but in a damaged heart they had a far better chance of developing. In such cases the heart valves increasingly fail, the lungs can become congested, causing Mahler to have choking fits. And embolisms can occur in other organs if parts of the bacterial colony are carried in the bloodstream. The kidneys can fail and be the immediate cause of death, as was evidently the case with Mahler. And there can also be multiple organ failure. Mahler's final illness lasted three months. It was not a merciful death.

Mahler's fever dropped when the blood samples were taken, leading Alma – foolishly and senselessly, but forgivably – to feel a renewed sense of hope. Revealing her medical ignorance, she writes in her memoirs that 'Probably it would have been a good thing if he had been bled'.[24] Baehr reports that Mahler insisted on knowing the truth. No doubt he was not told the whole truth, but only that his illness was life-threatening. Since Mahler had no medical under-standing, it was easy to conceal things from him, and so he was given the impression that it was still possible to alleviate his condition. Collargol injec-tions were tried, which were as effective as incense cones during an outbreak of cholera. Fraenkel was all in favour of consulting a bacteriologist in Europe. This, too, was a cosmetic solution, since neither he nor Libman had any hope for their patient's recovery, and they duly prepared Alma to expect the worst. Chantemesse was one of the most eminent bacteriologists in Europe, and Paris had the additional advantage that it was home to many of the Mahlers' friends. And so it was decided to take the patient back to Europe as long as he was still capable of travelling.

Alma's mother – the procuress and confidante – was given one final chance to help her son-in-law. She came to New York as quickly as she could, and her resolve and energy proved useful, for Alma had relapsed into one of her frequent bouts of weak-willed inactivity. Although Anna Moll almost set the whole apartment alight with a spirit stove, she was otherwise a great help. Maurice Baumfeld visited Mahler on the day before his departure and found him lying on a couch by the open window, covered in blankets, tired and emaciated, his face ravaged by his illness. Little Anna was playing in the room. Mahler was still lucid and asked about the latest gossip in the musical life of New York but showed little reaction when he was told. Baumfeld had the distinct feeling that Mahler was 'receding further into the distance with every passing hour'.[25] On the day of the departure – 8 April – Mahler refused the stretcher that was offered him. Leaning on Fraenkel for support, he dragged himself to the hotel lift. The lobby had been cleared by the hotel's solicitous staff in order to spare him the stares of inquisitive strangers. At the side entrance he was collected by the waiting car of Minnie Untermeyer, the last of the Philharmonic Society's board members to remain loyal to him.

Once onboard, Mahler was taken straight to his cabin. Fraenkel gave Alma all the necessary instructions, warning her not to call in the ship's doctor and then saying goodbye to Alma and Mahler, whom he knew he would never see again. Mahler still felt sufficiently strong to get up nearly every day and take the air in a secluded part of the deck. It was on one such occasion that the last two photographs of him were taken. On one of them he is seen sitting on a crate-like structure on the upper deck next to Alma, who is turned towards him. His right leg is raised and rests on the railing. There is nothing to indicate that he is a dying man, but he is too far from the camera for us to be able to make out his face. Indeed, there is some suggestion that this photograph may date from his previous crossing. The second picture is more powerfully expressive. Here he is seen leaning against the railings in a position entirely typical of him, his left leg bent around his right leg, his left arm resting elegantly on the railing and a walking stick in his right hand, the stick apparently wedged between the planks. He is wearing the same suit as the one seen in photographs taken during his voyage to America only a few months earlier, a sturdy, tweed-like travelling suit, while his hat is familiar from the Munich snapshots from the previous September. Some writers have sought to date this photograph to October 1910, and certainly it seems surprising that Mahler still had the strength to stand, fully dressed, on deck, suggesting that the photograph may not have been taken in April 1911. On the other hand, there is no denying that his features reveal a dramatic decline in his health when compared with images from the previous autumn and winter. The negligent stance is deceptive, and the observer will find it hard to avoid the feeling that the stick is the only support for the composer's infirm body. It is, however, his face that reveals the true facts of the matter. The tremendous energy that we can see in his eyes and mouth in all his other photographs has been replaced by a despondent and enfeebled emptiness. His lips had always been thin, but his once expressive mouth is now so contracted as to express only bitterness, the corners turned down to such an extent that they seem to pass into the chin, while the deep furrows running from the nose to the cheekbones bulge visibly. The eyes are lifeless, like candles that have been snuffed out. It is the last photograph ever taken of Mahler. It is impossible to look at it for long.

Return

Other passengers on board the ship included Ferruccio Busoni and a 'young Austrian' who annoyed Alma by his attentions. Later, on the train from Cherbourg to Paris, he also got on Mahler's nerves by telling his daughter unsettling stories. It was the young Stefan Zweig.[26] Mahler refused to see anyone, and Alma admitted no one to his presence, so that Busoni was able to keep his colleague's spirits up only by writing down 'crazy specimens of counterpoint' and having them delivered to the Mahlers' cabin. Busoni never forgot this crossing with Mahler and only a few days after his death he wrote to a fellow pianist, Egon Petri, to say that he was 'completely devastated' by what had happened: 'I had just gained a friend in him; it strikes me as completely implacable.'[27] Zweig watched events unfold on the quay at Cherbourg with an importunate curiosity that finds expression in a particularly precious piece of prose:

> He lay there, deathly pale, motionless, his eyelids shut. The wind had blown his greying hair to one side, his rounded brow stood out clear and bold and beneath it the hard chin that was the seat of his thrusting will. His emaciated hands lay folded wearily on the blanket. For the first time I saw him weak, this man who had once been consumed by fire.
>
> This silhouette – unforgettable, unforgettable! – was set against the grey infinity of sky and sea. There was boundless sorrow in this sight, but also something transfigured by greatness, something that died away on a note of sublimity, like music.[28]

In her reminiscences, Alma claims, rather more prosaically, that Zweig had offered to help with the Mahlers' luggage but that he vanished at the critical moment.

The Mahlers put up at the Hôtel Élysée on 16 April, where they were joined by Carl Moll. The next day there was a flicker of ghost-like hope, for when Alma got up, she discovered Mahler sitting on the balcony, fully dressed, and demanding breakfast. He even began to plan for the future. Something should be done about Peter Cornelius's opera *Der Barbier von Bagdad*, he insisted. It was, he said, a wonderful piece. He then ordered an 'electric automobile' in order to visit the Bois de Boulogne, for it was a beautiful day. The beauty of the city and of the weather briefly revived him, but the effort proved too much, and by the end he was at death's door, his head resting in his mother-in-law's lap. Now he, too, lost all hope. Until now there had been no talk of a desire or readiness to die. Of course, his feelings had vacillated between euphoria and despair and sometimes a mixture of the two, but now his strength began to fail him. He had always exuded life and driven his feeble body beyond its natural limits, and it was this vital spark that kept him going for a full three months. But by 18 April Mahler had abandoned all hope for his future recovery, and even then it took another month before his life was finally snuffed out. During this period he spoke a lot with Anna Moll in order to spare his wife. He told her that he wanted to be buried at Grinzing next to his daughter and that there was to be no music and no speeches at his funeral. And only the word 'Mahler' was to be placed on his tombstone: 'Any who come to look for me will know who I am, and the rest do not need to know.'[29] In the event, the Secessionist artist Josef Hoffmann who designed the timeless tombstone added only the word 'Gustav'.

Alma adds another detail that should be noted, albeit with reservations. According to her reminiscences Mahler spoke at length about the companions of his youth, by which he meant Lipiner and his circle: 'They spun webs around me like spiders. They stole my life away. They kept me apart, from jealousy and envy. But I am to blame too. Why did I let it happen? My life has all been paper!'[30] And he apparently kept repeating this final sentence. One is tempted to think that Alma was giving free rein to the ineradicable hatred that she felt for Lipiner and for all who had influenced her husband before she met him, including his sister Justine. It is altogether implausible that Mahler would have expressed himself in such negative terms, especially after his rapprochement with Lipiner, something he had welcomed so sincerely and which there is no reason to think had turned sour. Bruno Walter, who brought the old friends together again, would surely have noticed if there had been a renewed cooling off, but he says absolutely nothing. The final sentence, 'My life has all been paper', may, however be different, as it has an authentic Mahlerian ring to it, for all that it is disconcertingly unexpected.

Is it conceivable that all nine completed symphonies were just 'paper' and that Mahler regretted having written them? For more than a century these works have fired the imagination of several generations of music lovers, moving them and inspiring them. Such an expression flies in the face of Mahler's lifelong approach to the creative process, although it is certainly possible that his profound despair in the face of death provoked such depressing thoughts. Although it must sound slightly fatuous to say so, death came at a particularly unfortunate time for Mahler: whatever he may have tried to tell himself, he had dealt with his marital crisis on only the most superficial level; his activities in New York had taken a distinctly unfavourable turn; his wonderful vision of life with family and friends in Semmering, where he could devote himself to composition, was still far from being realized; and he had only just made a start on his Tenth Symphony. Ultimately, however, one remains incredulous precisely because from Alma's perspective a sentence such as 'My life has all been paper' confirms her permanent struggle for affection and at the same time reinforces her own belief that she was right to turn her back on music that she had never been able or willing to embrace in all its significance and that had never justified such extreme commitment. A far more credible picture is drawn by Bruno Walter, who hurried to Paris to be with his dying mentor. And yet he too reports on a negative attitude towards Mahler's own works, confirming Alma's account, albeit in less dramatic terms:

There he lay, the tormented victim of an insidious illness that now affected his spirit as well as his body. His mood was sombre and dismissive. When, in an effort to turn his mind to more cheerful matters, I cautiously raised the subject of his own works, his remarks were, for the first time, wholly pessimistic.

Sometimes a spark of his old humour was rekindled, but generally Walter felt only a kind of disinterestedness far removed from the man he knew and loved, but it was all that he needed to make clear to him the hopelessness of Mahler's situation. Walter made one last attempt to cheer him up by reminding him of the house that he was planning at Semmering, prompting Mahler to reply sadly: 'That would be nice, but my only desire now is to be allowed enough digitalis to keep my heart going.'[31] Walter had to return to Vienna, and when he next saw Mahler in the clinic in the city, the latter was already in a coma.

The reason why the Mahlers had travelled to Paris was André Chantemesse, an eminent bacteriologist at the Pasteur Institute, but he could do no more than confirm Libman's diagnosis and express his delight at the cultures beneath his microscope. Mahler's condition continued to deteriorate and in her helplessness Alma summoned Franz Chvostek from Vienna, who was really a specialist in diseases of the thyroid gland and liver but who enjoyed a legendary reputation in Vienna as a diagnostician. He was on holiday in Trieste when the summons reached him, but he came at once to Paris. Of course, not even he could help, but Mahler knew him, and since Chvostek knew how to deal with such patients, he sought to cheer him up by joking that Mahler would soon recover: 'Now then, Mahler, what's all this about? Working too hard, that's what it is. You'll have to knock off for six months or a year. You've brought it on yourself – you can't treat your nerves that way, you know.'[32] Mahler was delighted by Chvostek's jocular tone and could not wait to return to Vienna with him, as Chvostek suggested. He wanted to live or die in Vienna, not Paris. On 21 April Mahler was transferred to Dr Defaux's clinic at Neuilly, where he received the serum therapy prescribed by Chantemesse. But it produced no results. Mahler started to suffer from choking fits, with additional symptoms of angina pectoris, and after three weeks at the clinic, Mahler could take no more. The medical opportunities in Paris seemed to be exhausted, which is hardly surprising, since they had been non-existent in the first place. On the night of 11/12 May 1911 Mahler and his party boarded the train to Vienna.

In Vienna a competition was in progress to decide who could shed the biggest crocodile tears. On 28 April the *Illustriertes Wiener Extrablatt* had published a collage of two photographs and a drawing on its title page. One of the photographs showed Defaux's clinic at Neuilly, the other the doctor himself, while the drawing depicted Mahler, fully dressed and lying on a couch, with Defaux next to him in conversation with his patient. Viennese patriotism felt violated. For all that he had been persecuted and vilified by the majority of the local papers, this great man, not to say this genius, was 'one of us'. So why was he being treated in Paris? Until only recently, the *Neues Wiener Journal* had led the field in attacking Mahler, but now it rejoiced when the terminally ill composer finally arrived back in Vienna on 12 May:

Mahler is an example of the way in which so much strength is dissipated when torn from its native soil and natural habitat. . . . He has been obliged to submit to *foreign methods of treatment* at the hands of doctors who struck him as strangers, until the sudden decisiveness of those around him set him free. . . . A genius from a caring state is not exposed in this way to life's superficial vicissitudes. Such a genius has a home in which to move freely and work creatively.

And the writer went on to inveigh against Mahler's enemies of old: 'Austria now has the honour of being the country to which Mahler longed to return: it was his last request to return to a country where, as he himself emphasized, he belongs. But, in truth, it has not done all that it could have done to deserve this honour.' Karl Kraus reproduced these passages in *Die Fackel*, adding only a single sentence: 'Thus spake the *Neues Wiener Journal*, after organizing the Mahler witch-hunt.'[33] As he lay dying, Mahler generated more interest than he had ever done as the Court Opera's controversial director. His final days became the subject of sensational speculations. Bertha Zuckerkandl wrote to her sister Sophie Clemenceau in Paris, where it seems that Mahler's French friends had not been allowed to visit him:

The moment the press announced that Mahler was seriously ill and on his way home, the city was seized by a show of demonstrative grief – the same people who, when he was healthy and active, had driven away the very man who had sacrificed himself for their sake.

Under sensational headlines the press issued daily bulletins from his bedside. Sentimental anecdotes were peddled by people who affected to be touched by them. In the salons and coffee houses there was a veritable fire-work display of memories of the glorious age of opera under Mahler. His brilliant *Don Giovanni* . . . His magnificent *Fidelio* . . . His ebullient *Figaro*! . . . Never again will people see anything like it! . . . The same sneering gentlemen who had spat on every Mahler performance now wanted to belong to the inti-mate circle of Mahlerians.

And the Loew Sanatorium, where the dying man lay, protected by Alma, was surrounded each day by hundreds of people.[34]

The journey from Paris to Vienna had itself been a media event, although it bore no resemblance to the scene in Ken Russell's Mahler film in which the ailing composer is shown pale and coughing but cheerful and sitting upright in his train carriage. The truth of the matter is that Mahler spent the whole journey lying in his sleeping compartment, incapable of standing up. At each of the larger stations journalists came onboard, hoping to hear news of his condition. Mahler was told about them and apparently did not find their interest excessive. The Loew Sanatorium was located in the Mariannengasse in Vienna's ninth district, between the Alserstraße and the Lazarettgasse. For Mahler, it was no more than a place to die. In the train, Chvostek had warned Alma that even if Mahler recovered, he would spend the rest of his life in a wheelchair with his mind impaired. A demented Mahler in a wheelchair was neither conceivable nor desirable. The steps that the doctors took in the Loew Sanatorium were gestures of helplessness, nothing more. Swellings appeared on the patient's legs, and radium was applied. He was still sufficiently lucid to notice the countless baskets of flowers that arrived for him, including one from the Vienna Philharmonic that apparently gave him particular pleasure. Arnold Berliner came from Berlin and was one of the last people whom he saw. Mahler grasped his hand and said 'My dear friend', then turned his face to the wall. His daughter was brought to see him and he is said to have told her to 'be a good girl'.[35] In old age, Anna Mahler was no longer able to remember this, her ability to deal with unpleasant experiences being sufficiently well developed to suppress details of this kind. She remembered only that when her mother came to tell her that her father was dead, she replied: 'Don't. I know'.[36]

The final stage in Mahler's death throes began with the onset of pneumonia on 14 May. On the 17th he fell into a coma, although his fingers continued to tremble on the blanket, which Alma interpreted as conducting. Chvostek increased the dose of morphine, and shortly after eleven o'clock on the evening of the 18th it was all over. Apart from the medical staff, Carl Moll was the only member of the family to be with Mahler at the end. But it was the sculptor Anton Sandig, rather than Moll, who took the death mask. Alfred Roller and other close friends took their leave of Mahler in his hospital room. Roller reports that by the time he came to see Mahler, the signs of Mahler's weeks of wrestling with death had already etched themselves into his face, whereas Klimt, who came later, noted a change to something more solemn and calm, a kind of sublime beauty, which, he claimed, is how the death mask depicts Mahler. On this point the biographer scarcely has the authority to contradict those who saw Mahler on his deathbed, but anyone seeing the death mask – at the 2010 Viennese Mahler exhibition, for example – will gain a feeling less of sublimity than of the final struggle for life, a life to which the dying man clung with every fibre of his being. The *facies hippocratica* overshadows all attempts to heroicize and aestheticize death. In his will he had left instructions that his heart should be pierced with a sharp instrument, a practice still common at this time to ensure that death had indeed occurred.

Mahler was not unprepared to meet death. As we have seen, the thought of it had haunted him since the summer of 1907, without, however, exerting a hypochondriac's hold on him. Of course, he had always been impressed by the

thoughts on life and death of his old philosophical mentor Gustav Theodor
Fechner:

> We must never believe that death will spirit us away to a completely different
> world. Even after death we shall continue to inhabit the same earthly world
> as the one in which we now live; only we shall comprehend this world by
> other means and pass through it with greater freedom. In the world through
> which we now effortfully trudge, we shall one day float effortlessly. Why plant
> a new garden when flowers bloom in the old garden, flowers to which our
> new lives will open our eyes and provide us with new senses with which to
> enjoy them? The same earthly plants serve the caterpillars and butterflies, but
> they must strike them both in different ways. And whereas the caterpillar
> clings to a single plant, the butterfly flies freely over the whole of the garden.
> On earth we can see nothing of the people who preceded us into the afterlife.
> But what can the caterpillar see that tells it of the life of the butterfly? What
> does the chicken in the egg know about the life of the bird? ... It is only
> because we have earthly eyes that we cannot see those souls who have already
> been born into a new life, even though these people are among us and around
> us and live and work within us.[37]

We could express this a little differently using the lines of Friedrich Rückert
that Mahler set in slightly altered form in the fourth of his *Kindertotenlieder*:

> Oft denk' ich, sie sind nur ausgegangen!
> Bald werden sie wieder nach Hause gelangen!
> Der Tag ist schön! O, sei nicht bang!
> Sie machen nur einen weiten Gang!
>
> Jawohl, sie sind nur ausgegangen
> Und werden jetzt nach Hause gelangen!
> O, sei nicht bang, der Tag ist schön!
> Sie machen nur den Gang zu jenen Höhn!
>
> Sie sind uns nur vorausgegangen
> Und werden nicht wieder nach Haus verlangen!
> Wir holen sie ein auf jenen Höhn
> Im Sonnenschein! Der Tag ist schön auf jenen Höhn!

[I often think they have just gone out. They'll soon be coming home again.
It's a beautiful day. No, do not be afraid. They have only gone for a long walk.
Yes, they have just gone out and will now be returning home. Don't be afraid,

it's a beautiful day, they are only walking to those heights. They've just gone
on ahead of us and won't want to return home. We shall overtake them on
those heights in the sunshine. It's a beautiful day on those heights.]

If his despair during the final stage of his life was not too demoralizing, Mahler
will have drawn strength from these ideas and additionally recalled Lipiner's
thoughts on death, allowing him to regard the via dolorosa of his final months
as painful pebbles beneath his feet on his way to Rückert's heights.

The last book that Mahler read was Eduard von Hartmann's *The Problem
of Life*. Alma has left a vivid account of the way in which Mahler tore the
pages from this 440-page book because he no longer had the strength to hold
it in its bound form. Hartmann had been an engineer and an army officer
before turning to philosophy, in which he was essentially self-taught. His first
published work, *Philosophy of the Unconscious*, appeared in 1869 and was a
tremendous popular success. Hartmann set out to combine Schopenhauer's
doctrine of the will with the late Schelling's metaphysics and Hegel's thoughts
on the world-historical process. Thanks to his use of the term 'unconscious'
thirty years before Freud, Hartmann continues to interest writers even today,
although he cannot be regarded as a precursor of psychoanalysis. In both of
the aforementioned works he seeks to explain the dialectic between will and
representation as attributes of an unconscious substance that is said to
underpin all our lives and actions. He later questioned some of the issues that
were then exercising modern physics and sought to resist the inexorable
advance of Darwinism, proving a powerful critic of a mechanistic view of the
world and a leading proponent of vitalism. In *The Problem of Life*, which
appeared in 1906, Hartmann sums up these views, while dealing at length with
his opponents and with more recent writings on the subject. The first part of
the book is historical and traces the theory of evolution in the wake of Darwin,
discussing the pros and cons of mechanism and vitalism in modern biology,
while making clear the author's own support of vitalism and pointing out that
the physical and chemical laws that had filled the century of progress with such
enthusiasm were not enough to produce the forms of life as we know them.
Hartmann's aim was to re-establish a peaceful coexistence between natural
science and natural philosophy, and on this point he was bound to excite
Mahler's interest, since the latter's curiosity about the latest findings in physics,
as communicated to him chiefly by Arnold Berliner, was not that of a man who
believed implicitly in progress but of someone whose views were also coloured
by the natural philosophy of Goethe and the Romantics.

In the second, and final, part of his book, Hartmann considers death, and it
will have been this section that interested Mahler the most. The author opens
his chapter with the following consideration: 'Behind all life, death lurks like a

spectre. Why? Why must all that is born die, since life itself does not die but continues in new generations?'[38] And at the end of this chapter Hartmann comes close to answering the question that exercised the dying Mahler. Hartmann observes that the change from one generation to the next and the replacement of the old by the new is indispensable if life is to evolve at all. Even the most brilliant mind must at some point fall short of the demands of the age in terms of its ability to adapt. 'The world always needs new generations that can adapt to the new conditions with a fresh and impartial consciousness in order to raise evolution to a higher stage. Death in old age can therefore be justified from a teleological point of view, even if it cannot be justified in terms of life's outward aims.'[39] In reading these lines, Mahler may well have thought of Arnold Schoenberg, whom he sought to help during his final illness. Hartmann felt that it was better for the individual consciousness to step aside when that person had completed his role in life and better if the prejudiced individual were replaced by his unprejudiced counterpart, as he puts it. 'At the same time, however, the fact that people die when they are old reminds us of our other insight, namely, that no individual creature exists for its own sake but only to sacrifice itself on the altar of nature as a whole, nature whose meaning lies in the spiritual life of the whole.'[40]

If Mahler was reading Hartmann's book for the first time in 1911, this passage will have reminded him of his own convictions about entelechy as set forth in his letter to Alma of June 1909.[41] We may recall that it had long been his belief that entelechy, which expresses itself in creativity, is not bound to a single body. Rather, it migrates to another body when that other body dies. The works that the genius produces are mortal and fleeting, a skin or husk, and this is true, Mahler believed, of even great works, including his own. The only thing that lasts is what man makes of himself and what he becomes by dint of restless striving. All of this chimed in a quite remarkable way with Hartmann's thoughts on the continuation of life and the meaning of death. And this brings us back to the summer of 1909, when, driven on by his thoughts about death, Mahler had renewed contact with Lipiner. These thoughts had preoccupied him since the summer of 1907 and represented a position very different from the one he had previously held. In early May 1908 he held a lengthy discussion with Adele Marcus in Hamburg, in the course of which they touched on the afterlife. Back in Toblach, Mahler sent her a copy of Goethe's conversations with Eckermann, a book that he always carried round with him. And he drew her attention to particular passages which, he said, might provide her with more information about the mystery that they had discussed.

In particular, Mahler directed her to the conversation between Goethe and Eckermann on 10 January 1830, when Goethe read aloud the scene from *Faust* in which his hero travels to 'the mothers'. Eckermann himself then developed a theory about the significance of these 'mothers', a theory that Mahler took to be Goethe's. The interior of the earth is imagined here as a vast empty space with no corporeality, and it is here that the 'mothers' live outside space and time. They are the creative, preservative principle that is the starting point for all existence:

> Whatever ceases to breathe returns to them as a spiritual nature, and they preserve it until a fit occasion arises to come into existence anew. All souls and forms of what has been, or will be, hover about like clouds in the vast space of their abode. . . . All this is, indeed, no more than a poetic creation; but the limited human mind cannot penetrate much further, and is contented to find something on which it can repose. Upon earth we see phenomena, and feel effects, of which we do not know whence they come and whither they go. We infer a spiritual origin – something divine, of which we have no notion, and for which we have no expression, and which we must draw down to ourselves and *anthropomorphize*, that we may in some degree embody and make comprehensible our dark forebodings.[42]

It seems as if Mahler was helped through his final weeks by a combination of Goethe's concept of the 'mothers', Hartmann's ideas on growth, dissolution and renewal, and Mahler's own belief in entelechy. But there can be no question of a return to Christian or Jewish or other religious convictions such as we often find at the end of people's lives. All in all, one has the impression that when he died, Mahler was not at peace with himself or with the wider questions of life and death.

'And later that same day the world was respectfully shocked to receive the news of his death.' It is impossible not to quote the final sentence of Thomas Mann's novella, *Death in Venice*, not least because the outward appearance of his writer, Gustav von Aschenbach, is modelled, in part, on Mahler, who had left such a profound impression on Mann at the time of the first performance of his Eighth Symphony in Munich. Barely twenty-four hours after his death, Mahler's coffin was taken to the cemetery chapel at Grinzing, a transfer attended by Bruno Walter, who reports on the storm and heavy rain. There the coffin lay until midday of 22 May. Alma had announced her husband's death in the Viennese press:

> In her own name and in that of her daughter Anne [*sic*] Maria and all her relatives, Alma Maria Mahler announces the death of her dearly beloved husband, father etc. Gustav Mahler, who was released from his long and serious suffering on Thursday 18 May, before midnight, in his fifty-first year. The mortal remains of the dearly departed will be blessed in the parish church at Grinzing at 3 o'clock on Monday, the twenty-second of this month, and laid to eternal rest in the local cemetery.[43]

Mahler had already written his will in April 1904. In the briefest possible terms, Alma is appointed his sole heir and his descendants limited to the statutory portion of his estate. Carl Moll is appointed their guardian, Emil Freund as Mahler's executor.[44] Alma attended neither her husband's death nor his burial. She had contracted a serious case of pneumonia, and Chvostek had ordered her to remain in bed. Moll and Arnold Rosé made the necessary arrangements. A large group of mourners numbering around five hundred followed the coffin from the church to the grave. The church was not the tiny cemetery chapel, where the coffin had been laid out, but the parish church in Grinzing. The cemetery lies on a hill just before the centre of the village, on the left-hand side of the road when approaching from Vienna.

There is a surviving photograph of the burial, showing Mahler's coffin on a horse-drawn carriage and accompanied by uniformed attendants, while another photograph depicts part of the funeral procession, which included many friends, both close and not so close. Guido Adler and Fritz Löhr were there, as were Bruno Walter, Alfred Roller, Arnold Schoenberg and presumably also Alban Berg, Paul Stefan, Richard Specht and, from the Netherlands, Alphons Diepenbrock – Mengelberg seems to have been prevented from attending. The Court Opera was well represented, foremost among the mourners being its new director, Hans Gregor, whom Mahler held in such low regard. Anna Bahr-Mildenburg was there, of course, as were Leo Slezak and Erik Schmedes. Julius Epstein, Mahler's old piano teacher, came to pay his respects to his much younger pupil. Other mourners included Gustav Klimt, Emil Hertzka from Universal-Edition, Hermann Bahr and Hugo von Hofmannsthal. The family was represented by Justine and Arnold Rosé. We do not know whether Emma was there. Josef Bohuslav Foerster attended the ceremony with his wife Berta and later recalled how small the coffin seemed, almost like a child's. Silence reigned:

> It was at this moment – not a word was spoken through it all – that the world seemed to stand still for an instant, and a great sigh was uttered by all who were present. Then, as before, there followed a silence as sublime as it was hallowed.[45]

Foerster was not given to embroidering his narrative, and so we may well believe him when he writes that somewhere in the vicinity a bird sang a disjointed springtime melody, irresistibly reminding him and no doubt the others of the final movement of the Second Symphony:

> There, above a world shaken to its very foundations by the horrors of the Last Judgement, a solitary bird soars aloft, as high as the clouds themselves, the

last living creature, and its song, free of all terror and free of all sadness, fades away, quietly, ever so quietly, as, sobbing convulsively, its final note coincides with the entry of the trumpets that call both the quick and the dead to the judgement seat.[46]

Moll and Rosé threw the first clods of earth on the coffin. A few days later Hofmannsthal wrote to a friend, the Countess Ottonie von Degenfeld:

> Mahler was buried the other day. I stood by the open grave among a jostling crowd of people and threw earth into it, and I felt the most unfathomable sadness for Mahler, felt the whole bitter weight of a loss that nothing would ever make good. Then, as I was leaving, I suddenly understood that men will similarly lose something when I myself die and that one day someone may be sad at heart in consequence, just as I am now sad because of Mahler, to whom I spoke only once in my life. At that moment, the unfathomable nature of an existence like mine no longer seemed oppressive.[47]

Arnold Schoenberg left a disconcerting painting of this scene, the open grave like a gaping wound in a mound inflamed by yellows and greens and reds.

We began this chapter with Jean Paul, and we shall end it with Jean Paul. In his novel *Titan* the quirkily humorous librarian Schoppe, who has taught the hero Albano all he knows, dies after being placed in an asylum, where he does indeed go mad when confronted by his alter ego Siebenkäs, the hero of an earlier novel by the same author. The narrator writes his Requiem:

> You have nothing more to do here on earth, you firm and rigorous spirit, and a gentle, playful sun poured its rays into the final evening storm in your breast, filling it with roses and gold. The earth and all things earthly from which the fleeting worlds are formed was far too small and light for you. For behind life you sought something higher than life, not your self, no mortal, no immortal, but the eternal, all-first God. – *Appearances* here on earth – evil as well as good – were a matter of indifference to you. You now rest in real *being*, death has swept away the whole sultry cloud of life from your dark heart, and the eternal light is revealed, a light that you sought for so long; and you, its beam, live again in the fire.[48]

Mahler and Posterity

'DO YOU HAVE to be there in person when you become immortal?' This was Mahler's answer when he was asked by a friend why he did not do more to ensure that his works were performed and better known: 'Sooner or later, they themselves will do whatever is necessary.'[1] Rather more famous are two other remarks by Mahler: first (and it is doubtful that this originated from Mahler himself), that he was homeless three times over and, second, 'My time will come.' But, as so often, we need to take a closer look at the context from which this sentence comes, for although the basic interpretation remains the same, it acquires a more nuanced aspect. When Mahler wrote it, he was attempting to distance himself from Richard Strauss and referring specifically to Strauss's attitude following the first performance in Vienna of his opera *Feuersnot*, when the composer turned out to be obsessed with success and with the royalties that would accrue to him as a result. Mahler was clearly disenchanted by the whole aura surrounding Strauss:

> Rather live in poverty and walk the path of the enlightened than surrender oneself to Mammon, don't you agree? One day people will separate the wheat from the chaff – and when his day has passed, then my time will come. Would that I could live to see it at your side! But you, my Lux, will certainly live to see it, I hope, and you will remember the time when you had not yet learnt to distinguish the sun through the mist. Do you remember, in the Stadtpark, when everyone saw the sun as a hideous red stain?[2]

In short, Mahler was seeking to distance himself from Strauss and to see an inverse relationship between his own fate and that of a colleague and rival whom he respected but did not love.

Mahler's hope that he would live long enough to see his time come turned out to be deceptive, but from every other point of view he was proved right.

Strauss's reputation has sunk since the interwar period and is now limited to the indestructible popularity of a handful of operas. His other stage works have more or less disappeared from the repertory, and his tone poems play only a marginal role in the concert hall and, interestingly enough, are conducted chiefly by those conductors who have little time for Mahler. Moreover, Alma died in 1964 and was able to witness the beginning of the international wave of enthusiasm for Mahler's works that began around 1960 and to divert part of the resultant lustre to her own person. Mahler himself seems not to have doubted that his time would come, only about the date when this process would begin. And so we find him writing to a French journalist in 1906 when the latter offered to promote his works in Paris: 'I sometimes feel I shall not live to see "my time"; and then an echo from an unknown world comes just at the right moment.'[3] A third remark, again taken from a letter to Alma, is strangely moving and prophetic. Mahler was preparing for the first performance of his Fifth Symphony in Cologne in October 1904. However valiant, the Gürzenich Orchestra inevitably had problems with the Scherzo, prompting Mahler to comment: 'Would that I could perform my symphonies for the first time fifty years after my death!'[4] And it was indeed about fifty years after his death that his works finally entered the repertory.

Writers now refer so routinely to a 'Mahler renaissance' that it is impossible to avoid this term, however unsatisfactory it may be. Strictly speaking, a renaissance can be enjoyed only by something that already existed in a thoroughly stable form and that needed only to be reborn to achieve its former greatness. But there can be no question of this in Mahler's case, for it was not until 1960 that Mahler was first acknowledged as a composer of international importance and his works first entered the repertory. Throughout the period from 1911 to 1960 he was a controversial figure, his works attacked and despised well before they were officially banned in those countries in which the racial doctrines of the National Socialists robbed all Jewish composers of the air that they needed to breathe and, where possible, deprived them of their lives. But nor would it be true to claim that Mahler's works disappeared without trace between 1911 and 1960 and that only then were they exhumed. Even during this period his music was passionately championed by enthusiasts in the concert hall and among audiences and loved by a minority, while being denigrated and reviled by the majority. As we have already indicated, a by no means unimportant role in this state of affairs was played by anti-Semitism. Within days of Mahler's death the *Alldeutsches Tagblatt* made it clear to its Viennese readers that the object of its hatred had certainly not disappeared with his passing:

He was buried in Grinzing on Monday 22 May, the former director of the Court Opera and conductor of the Philharmonic. He was undoubtedly a

Jewish patriot and lived entirely for Judah. The reports about him were, of course, written by people like him and were so inordinately effusive as to be worth handing down to posterity as cultural curiosities. There were vast numbers of wreaths whose ribbons were covered with dedications to the Nibelung dwarf who came to power from the darkness of the pariahs, and there was once again a fine opportunity for people to kowtow to the Jews like the good citizens that they are.[5]

This was not an isolated instance of anti-Semitism. Rather, it set the tone that was to remain typical of responses to Mahler's works, even if it was not always expressed in such virulent terms but more or less skilfully concealed behind specious arguments.

A second example must suffice. On 26 June 1912 Bruno Walter conducted the world première of Mahler's Ninth Symphony with the Vienna Philharmonic in the city's Musikvereinssaal. On 20 November 1911, moreover, he had given the first performance of *Das Lied von der Erde* in Munich. Together, these performances represented a pioneering feat which, if the First World War had not intervened, would perhaps have laid the foundations for a continuous tradition of performing Mahler's works. Walter's actions were hailed by Mahlerians as an act of ordination but provoked rather different reactions in other quarters. Writing about the Ninth Symphony in the *Ostdeutsche Rundschau* a certain Heinrich Damisch complained that

The whole thing is one gigantic weed in the symphonic garden, a weed from which a new cross-beam for the temple of disgusting indecency may be carved. It is with increasing brazenness that criminals and psychopaths are violating music, that unique gift from heaven that the gods still allow us in an age of the most sobering reality. And, seated in boxes and galleries, the mob howls its approval for this music, which it welcomes either out of snobbism or from self-conceit. Perhaps we may yet be saved from all this impropriety by the sense of aesthetic shame on the part of those noble-minded women whose sensitivities lie close to eternal nature: perhaps they will rescue us from such art and from this culture from the Orient, for it is from here that those people have come who busy themselves debasing what is good, raising aloft what is evil, reviling the dead and deceiving the living.[6]

Although Damisch avoids the word 'Jew', the anti-Semitic thrust of his attack was clear to every reader. During the years that followed, Damisch developed the views expressed here. It is worth adding that he played a significant part in the establishment of the Salzburg Festival and although he had to moderate his ideas in the wake of the Second World War, he still held an influential position in the International Mozarteum Foundation in Salzburg and received one of Austria's highest awards for services to his country.

The First World War shook the cultural life of Europe to its very core, and yet this seemed as if it might be Mahler's chance of a breakthrough, for many commentators have heard in his marches a prefigurement of war. During the winter of 1918/19 there was a small-scale Mahler cycle in Vienna under the direction of Bruno Walter, who was by now general music director in Munich and whose love of Mahler remained constant, for all that he rarely conducted the middle symphonies. Ernst Bloch referred specifically to Mahler, while exaggerating his importance as a 'Jewish prophet'.[7] The organizational and artistic high point of the first great Mahler wave after 1918 was undoubtedly the Mahler Festival that was mounted in Amsterdam in 1920. This was the first time that Mahler's works had been presented in their entirety, accompanied by a series of lectures. The guiding hand was that of Willem Mengelberg, together with his nephew Rudolf, who was a writer on music. One of the lectures was given by the Italian composer Alfredo Casella, a rare example of a Mahlerite in his native country. Other lecturers were Guido Adler, Felix Salten, Richard Specht and Paul Stefan, whose Mahlerian enthusiasms had failed to find a fertile soil in Vienna – Herta Blaukopf was the first writer to recognize the true significance of this Mahler Festival in Amsterdam.[8] Universal-Edition published a booklet to mark this exceptional occasion. Mahler's works were performed on alternate days between 6 and 21 May, all of them with the Concertgebouw Orchestra under Mengelberg in a unique act of love and devotion. The festival organizers also honoured Mahler's spirit by including a series of chamber recitals featuring works by Max Reger, Alphons Diepenbrock, Alfredo Casella, Claude Debussy, Maurice Ravel, Alexander Scriabin, Carl Nielsen, Josef Suk, Igor Stravinsky and Arnold Schoenberg.

The publication that commemorated these events also included press reviews and indicates that the festival was enthusiastically reviewed as far apart as London and New York. And it ends with a list of foreign visitors demonstrating the power of Mahler's music to bring nations together, especially nations divided until recently by war. In turn this led to the suggestion that another, even larger festival should be organized at which former enemies should present their latest and most important contributions to the field of music, creating a forum for the artistic and academic exchange of new ideas. A committee was set up to pursue this plan, and Willem Mengelberg was proposed as its honorary president. Among the manifesto's signatories were Casella, Schoenberg and Nielsen and the Berlin critic Oscar Bie. The significance of this suggestion can perhaps be judged from a comparison between this slender publication of 1920 and the monumental volume published seventy-five years later to mark the 1995 Amsterdam Mahler Festival.[9]

The Amsterdam Festival raised the question of whether Mahler's time had finally come. Nine years after his death, his breakthrough seemed inevitable, especially when one reads the lively debates about his music in reviews and publications of the period. In the autumn of 1920 Mahler's young disciple Oskar Fried was able to mount a Mahler cycle in Vienna, although it is significant that he used not the Philharmonic but the Vienna Symphony Orchestra and that there were no accompanying lectures or discussions. None the less, Mahler's works were all performed with the exception of the Eighth Symphony. In the reviews the old animosities alternated with a new enthusiasm, and it seemed that not even in Vienna were people left cold by Mahler any longer. In 1923/4 Thomas Mann's brother-in-law Klaus Pringsheim organized a relatively major Mahler cycle in Berlin, Hermann Scherchen began to explore Mahler's works in Leipzig, and in Wiesbaden, where Mahler had conducted on more than one occasion, there was a small Mahler festival. The first half of the 1920s confirmed Mahlerians in their view that their hero's time had come, an impression underscored by the dates of the most important books on Mahler that were published at this time. As early as 1918 the leading critic Paul Bekker had brought out a slender volume, *The Symphony from Beethoven to Mahler*, the very title of which scandalized many contemporaries. His major study, *Gustav Mahler's Symphonies*, appeared three years later and continues to be an important introduction to the composer's music. It also had a decisive and generally underrated influence on Adorno's picture of Mahler. The final page includes a brief but impressive bibliography, beginning, chronologically, with Ludwig Schiedermair's 1901 study of Mahler and also listing works by Paul Stefan, Richard Specht, Guido Adler and Artur Neißer.

Alfred Roller's iconography, with its unparalleled physical description of the composer, appeared in 1922; Natalie Bauer-Lechner's reminiscences in 1923, albeit in a heavily abridged edition; and Alma's first edition of Mahler's correspondence in 1924, an affectionately designed tribute, with photographs and a facsimile of one of Mahler's letters. Vienna's leading avant-garde music journal, the *Musikblätter des Anbruch*, had devoted a whole issue to Mahler as early as 1920. Also in Vienna, Webern conducted a performance of the Third Symphony in 1922 at one of the Workers' Symphony Concerts organized by the city's active Social Democrats under David Josef Bach. From then on Webern was regarded as one of the finest Mahler conductors of his age, although his reputation barely extended beyond the confines of Vienna. Zemlinsky, too, championed Mahler's works in both Vienna and Prague. When Franz Schalk conducted the fragmentary Tenth Symphony at the Vienna State Opera in a performing edition by Ernst Krenek, Mahler's ship of state seemed finally to be home and dry. But appearances proved to be deceptive.

In 1922 the leading Berlin critic Adolf Weißmann, who had already made a
name for himself with level-headed books on prima donnas and virtuosos,
published a study under the title of *Music in Crisis*, which sought to relate developments in music since the turn of the century to the upheaval of the First
World War and the overthrow of middle-class values. One chapter is devoted to
Mahler and begins with the laconic statement: 'There is a Mahler problem.'[10]
Although Weißmann was himself Jewish – or perhaps precisely because of that
fact – he was obsessed with Mahler's Jewishness. While chastising those writers
who regarded the 'problem of race', as it was called at this time, as central to
their critique of Mahler, he insisted that Mahler's own Jewishness could not be
gainsaid and that it found expression in features such as his internationalism
and universal aspirations. And he then went on to list the clichés that we know
only too well from our chapter on Mahler and Jewishness and which continue,
even today, to bedevil debates on the composer:

> He wants to sing songs that are autochthonous and Austrian, but he is
> haunted, tormented and burdened in a hundred different ways: as a man of
> the modern age, as a fervent epigone, and as a Jew. All of this affects his
> music, which is driven by a demon. Hence the countless contradictions in his
> works. Hence a certain profound shallowness, a half-creative irony that seeks
> to turn base metal into gold. Hence, too, his inspired sonorities that counter-
> feit the idea of woods and meadows. And overriding everything, as a
> hallmark of his race, there is something Christ-like, something that strives for
> sanctity.[11]

Weißmann ends his chapter on Mahler with words that betray his whole
uncertainty and that are typical of interwar critics and music lovers who, while
not actually hating Mahler, were somehow puzzled and exercised by music
that they did not want to let into their lives: 'His life is more valuable than his
music, which is largely rooted in his all-compelling ability to recreate the
works of others. As a result he remains a passing phenomenon, with no sense
of fulfilment to him. And yet it is impossible to think of him without profound
emotion.'[12]

This, then, was the position regarding Mahler after 1918: while revered by an
increasingly large group of Mahlerians and raised to the status of a modern classical composer at the Mahler Festival in Amsterdam in 1920, he was at the same
time hated or at least mistrusted by a far greater number of music lovers and
experts, whether real or self-appointed. In the first Austrian Republic, Mahler's
standing remained precarious, and attempts to erect a monument to him, which
originated in part with Alma, failed to make much progress – in a city in which
one of the main streets was named after its anti-Semitic mayor, Karl Lueger, it was

not so easy to establish a memorial to Mahler. And Mahler's name was inevitably added to the Index of the new Third Reich. There is abundant evidence of this. Suffice it to mention Theodor Fritsch's *Handbook on the Jewish Question* and the notorious *Lexicon of Jews in Music* by Theo Stengel and Herbert Gerigk. Less well known is the *Musical ABC of Jews* that appeared in Munich in 1935. The entry on Mahler begins with a clear allusion to Wagner's polemics of the 1850s:

> He is generally regarded as the typical representative of the noisy hooligans; he wrote monstrous works for the concert hall such as the 'Symphony of a Thousand' whose mass of instruments serves only to cover up its pitiful lack of melodies and desolation. By always hankering after empty effects, his works are as quintessentially Jewish as his ancestry. He came from a Jewish brandy bar and had himself baptised only later in Vienna.[13]

At least until the Third Reich's annexation of Austria in 1938, the situation in Vienna was very different. Under its federal chancellor Engelbert Dollfuß and, following his assassination, Kurt von Schuschnigg, the authoritarian *Ständestaat* that was established under the constitution of 1 May 1934 sought to make Mahler the quintessential Austrian composer of the recent past. Presumably the chances that three living composers, Franz Schmidt, Joseph Marx and Julius Bittner, would enjoy this privilege were regarded as extremely slim. But in promoting a Jewish composer like Mahler, a regime whose authoritarianism was plain for all to see could at least score points for tolerance when compared with the hated National Socialist government in neighbouring Germany. Although Austria could look back on a long tradition of anti-Semitism, this was not one of the *Ständestaat*'s defining ideologies, as it was in the case of Germany. Moreover, Alma Mahler entertained close links with a number of Austrian leaders as well as with prominent Austrian Catholics influential in the running of the country. Among her admirers were Kurt von Schuschnigg, Hans Pernter, who was in charge of the arts section at the Ministry of Education, and Ernst Rüdiger von Starhemberg, who had once marched alongside Hitler at the Feldherrnhalle in Munich and who was now the leader of the Austrian Patriotic Front.

In post-war Austria, Mahler's finest hour came in May 1936, when Bruno Walter conducted performances of the three works that were best suited to prestigious performances, namely, the Second and Eighth Symphonies and *Das Lied von der Erde*. Driven from Germany, Walter had evinced a pronounced sympathy for the 'New Austria', a point that he shared with Ernst Krenek, who was briefly married to Mahler's daughter. At the same time, Walter delivered a lecture that helped to underline his position as Mahler's heir and prophet and guaranteed that the picture of Mahler became more soft-edged and less angular – this is a mere statement of fact and is not intended to belittle Walter's achievements or his

profound love of Mahler's music. Walter's love of harmony, which also encouraged a Christian interpretation of the Second and Eighth Symphonies, was
well suited to the country's basically Catholic ideology. Krenek sounded a similar
note. In an essay that he wrote in 1941 for the American edition of his book on
Mahler, Walter praised Mahler's works as sprung from the spirit of Christian
eschatology.[14]

But the situation soon changed. It is interesting to observe the way in which
conductors who continued to conduct Mahler's works while Austria was still
independent suddenly stopped doing so without a word of complaint. Leopold
Reichwein was one such conductor. So, too, was Clemens Krauss, an eminently
gifted Austrian who was the friend and librettist of Strauss. Few people know
that until 1938 Krauss was a committed Mahlerian but ignored his works
thereafter. Equally interesting is the case of Wilhelm Furtwängler. In the
minds of many observers even today, he could have been the greatest Mahler
conductor of his age if he had wanted to be. After 1945 he conducted only the
Kindertotenlieder and the *Lieder eines fahrenden Gesellen*, including a famous
recording with Dietrich Fischer-Dieskau. Until 1933 Furtwängler's repertory
included the First, Second, Third and Fourth Symphonies. But his notebooks
reveal that under the Third Reich he sought increasingly to distance himself
not only from Mahler's works, which were in any case banned, but also
from those of Richard Strauss. Furtwängler's greater interest in Beethoven,
Bruckner, Brahms and Wagner encouraged him to speak with mounting
scepticism of Mahler, Reger and Strauss, three turn-of-the-century composers
whom he invariably bundled together and whom he now regarded as symptomatic of a development in the direction of gigantomania. Such artists were
'able to bring "skill" so much to the fore because the lack of dominant spiritual
strength is so marked in them. In Mahler, Reger, Strauss and Debussy, technique begins to distance itself from experience, to become high-handed. The
disappearance of substance, an aesthetic formed by the age and also the form
of the audience, is characteristic.'[15] Furtwängler was no anti-Semite and was
not playing the anti-Jewish card here, but he none the less comes close to
repeating Wagner's jibe about 'effects without causes', technique remote from
experience amounting to more or less the same thing in his estimation. It is
hardly surprising that, given his views on the subject, Furtwängler felt no great
desire to conduct Mahler's works again after 1945.

Much the same is true of Karl Böhm, a conductor far more willing to
compromise than Furtwängler. Böhm had conducted the occasional performance of a Mahler symphony before 1938 since it was opportune to do so. But
he had no difficulty in forgoing Mahler in Nazi Germany, where he pursued
his wartime career, and even when the war was over, his passion for Mahler
was not rekindled. Herbert von Karajan was a more complicated case, just as

his attitude to National Socialism was more ambivalent than that of either Furtwängler or Böhm. Like Furtwängler, Karajan had concentrated on the three Bs, Beethoven, Bruckner and Brahms, and also conducted a good deal of Wagner, but, unlike Furtwängler, he had no problems with either Verdi or Richard Strauss. Indeed, some of his greatest successes had been in Strauss's operas and symphonic poems. He had already turned sixty when he decided in 1970 that there was now room in his life for Mahler. During the 1960s both Leonard Bernstein and Georg Solti – two conductors whom the pathologically ambitious Karajan regarded as his keenest rivals – had proved surprisingly successful in conducting Mahler's works, and so Karajan decided to bite the bullet, scoring such a success with *Das Lied von der Erde* that he was tempted to explore other works by a composer to whom he had previously not felt attracted. But Mahler invariably takes his revenge on bandwagon-hoppers. Even with the Berlin Philharmonic, Karajan was never able to establish himself as a leading Mahler conductor. His interpretations were always controversial, and his recordings remain so, except for a thrilling live performance of the Ninth Symphony. None the less – and whatever his reasons – he deserves some credit for initially tackling two of the less frequently performed symphonies, the Fifth and the Sixth. In the case of the Sixth, Wolfgang Stresemann, who was the orchestra's general administrator at this period, recalls that there was no overlooking Karajan's uncertainty with regard to Mahler, whose music he dismissed as 'Kapellmeister music'. He had also wanted to make a major cut in the symphony's final movement and had been discouraged only by Stresemann's admonitions.[16]

But we are starting to get ahead of ourselves and need to return to the immediate post-war period. There seemed little place for Mahler in a continent that had been left ravaged by war and little chance for the sort of upturn in his fortunes that had occurred after 1918. Indeed, there were many critical voices only too happy to express the view that Mahler's time was now over. Many of these agenda-setters had actively supported the National Socialists in both Austria and Germany, and after a brief pause to rethink their position had once again set to work. As we have already had occasion to note, they had no difficulty in regaling their readers with their old anti-Semitic prejudices, while merely removing the most offensive expressions. But even outside this circle, there was the widespread belief that it was no longer necessary to take any more interest in Mahler. Stravinsky was the man of the moment, and attempts by Adorno to hold up the Second Viennese School as a counterweight remained limited in what they achieved. In Adorno's *The Philosophy of New Music* of 1949, Mahler's name is occasionally mentioned as an undisputed authority, chiefly in the context of Alban Berg, but he could hardly be pressed into service as a radical forebear of new music. Above all, Adorno's writings had for the present little impact on the concert-going public or on musical journalism.

Two random examples of typical attitudes to Mahler during this post-war period may be cited here. When Bruno Walter conducted Schubert's 'Unfinished' and Mahler's First Symphony in Munich in early October 1950, one of the press seats was occupied by Karl Heinz Ruppel, who was to go on to become one of the Federal Republic's most prominent music and theatre critics. Writing in the *Süddeutsche Zeitung*, he noted that

> The main work on the evening's programme was Gustav Mahler's D major Symphony, the first of nine, and it was not without a sense of shock that one encountered it. For here one is confronted by a genuine tragedy – the tragedy of a spiritual individual who in the second half of the nineteenth century strove to escape from the complexities and problems of a highly civilized existence. This is not a question of the natural creativity of a composer who, as a genius of the ethos of the artist and as an intellectually supremely well-organized child of a late-flowering age, was a universal rather than an original phenomenon. No, what one finds so disturbing on renewed acquaintance with his First Symphony is a tragic error: Mahler thought that it was still possible in the years around 1890 to write a pastoral symphony.

And Ruppel describes the third movement as 'an example of genuine inspiration in which the tragic flaw in Mahler's nature – the very thing that everywhere else prevented him from achieving creative perfection – itself becomes creative and finds magnificently moving expression'.[17] We do not need to plumb the depths of Rudolf Bauer's concert guide – quoted in our chapter on Mahler and Jewishness – to rediscover all the old formulas which, even when clothed in faint praise, retain their dismissive character: Mahler lacked originality, he was a tragic figure and was prevented from achieving perfection as a creative artist. If this was the opinion of one of the most prominent critics of the period, what could one expect from his less eminent colleagues?

One final example may serve to illustrate the levels to which provincial critics could sink. In May 1951 the First Symphony finally received its first performance in Hanover. The town's leading critic began his review:

> After a long time music lovers can finally make up their own minds about a composer who was as widely admired at the turn of the century as he has been vilified since then. There is no doubt that most of today's listeners have moved away from most of his symphonies, which, far from being timeless, were closely bound up with their age. Even so, it is worth our while to listen to his First Symphony, which is crammed full of inspired details, even if its

Wunderhorn ideas and its orchestration, which is sometimes downright theatrical in its hankering after effects, have lost their appeal for us today.[18]

These two specimens of German music journalism are entirely typical of the situation in the 1950s, making the sudden change in Mahler's fortunes after 1960 all the more remarkable.

Various suggestions and suppositions have been advanced to explain this sudden shift, and there seems little doubt that a number of factors came together at this time. The centenary of the composer's birth was a reason to hold major Mahler festivals. The two most important ones took place in New York and Vienna. Leonard Bernstein's cycle with the New York Philharmonic began to appear that same year on LP. The Berlin publishing house of Bote & Bock brought out Erwin Ratz's new edition of the Seventh Symphony, the first volume in a planned critical edition that was a collaborative effort between the International Gustav Mahler Society in Vienna and the five different publishers who owned the rights to Mahler's works. Ratz had been editor-in-chief since 1955. The edition remains incomplete, although only a handful of minor works still have to be included. Even so, it has repeatedly become clear that the older volumes need revising as new sources have come to light. Another impetus came from the record industry. Even during the era of 78 rpm records, there had been recordings of complete symphonies, but it required the introduction of 33 rpm records in 1948 to make a complete cycle a viable option. The early Mahler cycles under Bernstein, Haitink and Solti were conceivable only in the age of the long-playing record.

Related to this was the introduction of stereophonic sound in 1958. By the Mahler centenary of 1960 this development was well into its stride. The leading Mahler biographer of this period, Kurt Blaukopf, was particularly interested in the sociology of music and repeatedly stressed the significance of stereophonic sound to the Mahler boom. After all, Mahler's scores contain so many instructions to the performers that are akin to stage directions affecting the dramaturgical use of sonority, including the use of offstage bands and distant cowbells, that monophonic recordings of his music, lacking the spatial-ization of the sound that became possible with stereo, were bound to remain rudimentary. On this point, Blaukopf even believed that stereo recordings were preferable to performances in the concert hall, where they had to contend with the pitfalls of problematical acoustics:

> The best studio recordings of recent times can at last give us a sound image closer to Mahler's intentions than almost any concert performance. .... Thanks to the techniques of electro-acoustic recording and reproduction, textual purity can be preserved and Mahler's original intention, as manifested

in his notation, fulfilled. The stereo record has been the salvation of these works.[19]

Adorno's slender but immensely important monograph on Mahler appeared in 1960. Its significance was quickly appreciated, even though its conceptual and stylistic demands mean that it was never destined to achieve a widespread impact. Other writers who began to publish on Mahler at around this time include Donald Mitchell, whose four-volume disquisition on Mahler's works began in 1958 and ended in 2007 with a collection of essays covering a whole half-century. The first volume of Henry-Louis de La Grange's monumental and exhaustive study appeared in English in 1973, before being continued in French between 1979 and 1984. A new English edition, begun in 1995, will run to four volumes. Kurt Blaukopf's tremendously influential account of Mahler's life and works appeared in 1969 and was followed in 1976 by a magnificent documentary study produced in collaboration with his wife, Herta, and translated that same year into English. A revised edition of the German version was published in 1993. Mahler's letters had first appeared in print in 1924 in an edition superintended by Alma. A much enlarged edition by Herta Blaukopf appeared in 1982, a revised edition in 1996. Herta Blaukopf was also responsible for editions of Mahler's correspondence with Strauss and a number of other contemporaries, while numerous other articles added considerably to our knowledge of the composer. The study of Mahler's music published in 1982 by the German musicologist Hans Heinrich Eggebrecht ranks alongside Adorno's monograph as one of the most important German-language publications in this regard. The profound three-volume study by the Hamburg musicologist Constantin Floros appeared between 1977 and 1985. The third of these volumes, devoted to the symphonies, was published in an American translation in 1993. Floros's Berlin colleague Hermann Danuser published a volume of essays on Mahler in 1991 and the following year edited an anthology of articles by other writers spanning several generations. These are only the most important stages on the road of Mahler scholarship.

For all its derogatory associations, the term 'Mahler boom' is by no means unjustified. If the 1960s witnessed his breakthrough as a composer, the 1970s brought a degree of popularization which, as so often, was not without a certain trivialization. In this context it is impossible to avoid mentioning Luchino Visconti's film *Death in Venice*, which ensured that the Adagietto from the Fifth Symphony came to be regarded as an example of sentimentalized kitsch. Unfortunately, the use of this music in the film has come to be equated with the film itself, with the result that *Death in Venice* is now routinely dismissed as little more than a tear-jerker. Such a dismissal is unfair, for it is in fact a quite remarkable film, stylistically assured, very well acted and of great aesthetic appeal. And the link between Mahler and the main character in Thomas Mann's short story was already suggested by Mann himself, at least on a physical level, so that it was by no means unreasonable of Visconti to re-locate the poet Gustav von Aschenbach and place him in a musical landscape. But the interpretation of the Adagietto that Visconti used is almost unbearable. Presumably for legal and financial reasons he avoided any of the famous recordings and recorded a new version of questionable aesthetic merit that is notable above all for its element of kitsch. There seems little doubt that it was with *Death in Venice* that Mahler came to be seen as a composer who is easy on the ear. Even nowadays there are few television films on the subject of Vienna around 1900 and on decadence and fin-de-siècle culture in general that do not use Mahler as background music. And the same is true of cinema films with any artistic pretensions. But we do not need to worry unduly about this. Mahler's music can bear it, and if a handful of listeners develop an interest in this background music, then this trivialization may be said to have a positive side to it.

Fifty years ago it would have been hard to find a composer who claimed Mahler as his model – in Germany only Karl Amadeus Hartmann comes to mind. Today the situation is different, although it seems that the trend may now be in decline. Stravinsky was a notorious Mahlerian nay-sayer, but once that influence had faded, there were increasing numbers of composers willing to admit to their debt to Mahler, the most famous undoubtedly being Shostakovich, whose fortunes in the West were long overshadowed by the perception of him as a product of Stalinist policies in music. Now he has taken his rightful place on the international stage, and the traces of Mahler's influ-ence on his music are palpable. His official pronouncements on Mahler amounted to little more than clichés, but in private he admitted to an intense love of Mahler. Time and again he acknowledged that *Das Lied von der Erde*, and especially the final movement, invariably moved him to tears. Many composers of the older generation have proclaimed their allegiance to Mahler. Pierre Boulez as a conductor has championed him. Luciano Berio used the Scherzo from Mahler's Second Symphony as the template for the third move-ment of his five-movement *Sinfonia* of 1968/9, producing a collage-like work that at the time created quite a stir and even today remains highly effective. In 1988/9 Alfred Schnittke wrote a quartet movement in A minor as a second movement for Mahler's fragmentary piano quartet. And Wolfgang Rihm admitted in a conversation some years ago that after his early infatuation with Mahler's music, he moved away from it, only to return to it with renewed affec-tion. Rihm credits Mahler's influence in the early 1970s with warning avant-garde composers of the dangers of adopting the sort of over-academic musical language that they had promoted since the time of the Darmstadt Summer

Schools. Instead, Mahler's music was able to offer the dramaturgy of the great novel, epic grandeur and exuberance, for which the composer needed no superficial tricks of an illustrative or literary kind. It was, Rihm concluded, Mahler's intellectual and spiritual insistence on the here and now that made him a contemporary of the future, to quote the subtitle of Kurt Blaukopf's 1969 study.[20] Peter Ruzicka has expressed himself in not dissimilar terms. In the mid-1990s the New York jazz musician Uri Caine approached Mahler's music using a collage-like method of adaptation designed to make the music sound unfamiliar, the success of which owed something to his problematical insistence on the Jewish element in this music. Unless appearances are deceptive, then Mahler's influence on the latest generation of European composers is no longer as great as it was on those who are now fifty and older. But this may be a false impression and unreliable as the basis of a prognosis.

Mahler is here to stay. He has asserted himself and achieved an international popularity that fills concert halls and sells CDs. For a composer who was so controversial during his lifetime and afterwards, this is exceptional. Mahler festivals such as those held in Amsterdam in 1995 and the Mahler cycle that was given in Munich in 2002 now play to sold-out houses. When Sir Simon Rattle took over as principal conductor of the Berlin Philharmonic in that year, he sought to impose his own personal stamp on the orchestra in part through Mahler's Fifth Symphony, which he conducted at the first concert he gave in the wake of his appointment. Performed under the full glare of the world's media spotlight, the concert was immediately released on CD.

No one should think that the old antipathies to Mahler, still occasionally coloured by anti-Semitic prejudices, have been erased by the composer's newfound popularity. Such undertones are still discernible, even if they are no longer expressed with quite the same virulence as before – for that we have to thank the fact that Mahler is now a mainstream composer and that anti-Semitism remains unacceptable, even if that taboo is no longer as powerful as it once was. The continuing existence of reservations about Mahler is clear from even the most cursory glance at those conductors who champion Mahler's works and those who do not. The former category includes Claudio Abbado, Maurice Abravanel, John Barbirolli, Rudolf Barshai, Leonard Bernstein, Gary Bertini, Pierre Boulez, Riccardo Chailly, Gustavo Dudamel, Ivan Fischer, Valery Gergiev, Michael Gielen, Carlo Maria Giulini, Bernard Haitink, Daniel Harding, Jascha Horenstein, Eliahu Inbal, Mariss Jansons, Otto Klemperer, Paul Kletzki, Kirill Kondrashin, Rafael Kubelík, James Levine, Lorin Maazel, Zubin Mehta, Dimitri Mitropoulos, Kent Nagano, Vaclav Neumann, Roger Norrington, Jonathan Nott, Seiji Ozawa, Simon Rattle, Fritz Reiner, Hermann Scherchen, Carl Schuricht, Giuseppe Sinopoli, Georg Solti, Leopold Stokowski, George Szell, Klaus Tennstedt, Michael Tilson Thomas and Bruno Walter – an incomplete but sufficiently impressive list. But at least as interesting is the list of those conductors who have given Mahler a wide berth. Of the older generation, suffice it to name Ernest Ansermet, Karl Böhm, Sergiu Celibidache, Ferenc Fricsay, Wilhelm Furtwängler (after 1933), Eugen Jochum, Herbert von Karajan (until the 1970s), Erich Kleiber, Hans Knappertsbusch, Pierre Monteux, Charles Munch, Wolfgang Sawallisch, Arturo Toscanini and Günter Wand. More recently, Carlos Kleiber, Riccardo Muti and Christian Thielemann have likewise avoided Mahler – Thielemann conducted the Eighth Symphony in Munich in 2010.

It is striking that among the conductors who are contemptuous of Mahler, there are many who have established themselves as Brucknerians of the first order. The evident incompatibility between Bruckner and Mahler from an interpretative point of view is a remarkable phenomenon. (There are, of course, exceptions, but these merely confirm the rule.) Celibidache and Wand are the best-known examples of this. Wand once noted that in Bruckner's music there are no musical statements of a 'private' nature, only impersonal and supra-personal ones. The conclusion would seem to be that Mahler's music is far too 'private' for a conductor like Wand, too personal, too exhibitionist and too soul-baring. Or is it because Bruckner's music is emphatically Christian in character? At all events, we need to be wary of claiming that Mahler conductors must necessarily be Jewish, for there is at least one significant counter-example: Daniel Barenboim may have worked tirelessly to introduce Wagner's music to Israel in spite of the nominal boycott that still exists there, but for a long time he fought shy of Mahler. In 2007, however, he conducted the First, Fifth, Seventh and Ninth Symphonies in Berlin, together with *Das Lied von der Erde*. For a conductor to wait until he is over sixty to demonstrate such a commit-ment to Mahler is surely unique in the history of music.

Mahler today and tomorrow: it is difficult to imagine Mahler becoming any more popular than he is now. Rather we may anticipate a decline in that popu-larity when the last vestiges of any sort of cultural education disappear for good, for Mahler's music needs not only technical reproduction but also a constant revitalization through the experience of live performances; and to the extent that his works are expensive to perform, they are a costly pleasure that society must be willing to afford. His music and his person are so weighed down with clichés that even the most incompetent review of a concert or a recording parrots the same old phrases about a homeless Jew, inwardly torn apart, a prophet both strict and zealous, a man lost to the world, sometimes also the first terrible husband of the famous Alma Mahler-Werfel – the music itself tends sometimes to disappear behind this wall of clichés. Above all, a knowledge and understanding of his music runs the risk of vanishing with the disappearance of middle-class musical culture and its technologies and techniques, including the ability to read music. This is not to belittle the purely emotional experience of Mahler, which is clearly still an international phenomenon. Listeners who are moved by Mahler's music will initially, at least, be won over by it. This is already a lot, but it is not enough. Listeners who merely allow themselves to be overwhelmed by the intoxication of this music will simply remain in thrall to it and never achieve a state of impassioned understanding.

Mahler remains a problematical phenomenon. Adorno once wrote a short essay to which he gave the title 'Die Wunde Heine' ('The Heine Wound'). He was referring to the inability of German readers, long before National Socialism, to come to terms with Heinrich Heine's virtuosity and with the natural fluency of his poetic and linguistic expression, which was the opposite of autochthonous homeliness and hence hinted at the failure of Jewish emancipation. As we have already had occasion to note, this could scarcely be said to apply in every detail to Mahler, who was some sixty years younger than Heine. But in reactions to Mahler, the same wound continues to fester and bleed. It is no wonder that, as Adorno observed, Heine's true nature was revealed not in the songs of those composers such as Schubert and Schumann who set his poems to music but in the composer who did not set them, Mahler. For it is in Mahler's songs about army deserters and in his funeral marches such as that of the Fifth Symphony and, finally, in the strident shifts between major and minor tonalities of the *Wunderhorn* songs, that the music of Heine's poetry ultimately comes to vibrant life. There is also a Mahler wound, which will not close as long as human society lacks the desire for reconciliation. His music speaks of this lack with a clarity that is found in the works of few other composers.

Abbreviations

AME   Alma Mahler-Werfel, *Erinnerungen an Gustav Mahler* (Zurich am Main and Berlin 1971); trans. Basil Creighton as *Gustav Mahler: Memories and Letters*, ed. Donald Mitchell and Knud Martner, 4th edn (London 1990)

AME   (1949) Alma Mahler, *Gustav Mahler: Erinnerungen und Briefe*, 2nd edn (Amsterdam 1949)

AMML   Alma Mahler-Werfel, *Mein Leben* (Frankfurt am Main 1960); Engl. trans. *And the Bridge is Love: Memories of a Lifetime* (London 1958)

AMTB   Alma Mahler-Werfel, *Tagebuch-Suiten 1898–1902*, ed. Antony Beaumont and Susanne Rode-Breymann (Frankfurt am Main 1997); trans. Antony Beaumont as *Diaries 1898–1902* (London 1998)

BWGM   Bruno Walter, *Gustav Mahler: Ein Porträt* (Wilhelmshaven 1981); trans. Lotte Walter Lindt (London 1990)

BWTV   Bruno Walter, *Thema und Variationen: Erinnerungen und Gedanken* (Frankfurt am Main 1947); trans. James Galston as *Theme and Variations: An Autobiography* (New York 1946)

DLG I   Henry-Louis de La Grange, *Gustav Mahler: Chronique d'une vie*, 3 vols (Paris 1979–84)

DLG II   Henry-Louis de La Grange, *Gustav Mahler*, 4 vols (Oxford 1995–; vols 2–4 published so far)

GMB   Herta Blaukopf (ed.), *Gustav Mahler: Briefe* (Vienna 1996); partial Engl. trans. by Eithne Wilkins, Ernst Kaiser and Bill Hopkins as *Selected Letters of Gustav Mahler*, ed. Kurt Martner (London 1979)

GMBA   Henry-Louis de La Grange and Günther Weiß (eds), *Ein Glück ohne Ruh': Die Briefe Gustav Mahlers an Alma* (Berlin 1995); trans. Antony Beaumont as *Gustav Mahler: Letters to his Wife* (London 2004)

GMFB   Stephen McClatchie (ed.), *Gustav Mahler: 'Liebste Justi!' Briefe an die Familie* (Bonn 2006); originally published in English as *The Mahler Family Letters* (Oxford 2006)

GMMB   Franz Willnauer (ed.), *Gustav Mahler: 'Mein lieber Trotzkopf, meine süße Mohnblume'. Briefe an Anna von Mildenburg* (Vienna 2006)

GMRSB   Herta Blaukopf (ed.), *Gustav Mahler – Richard Strauss: Briefwechsel 1888–1911* (Munich 1988); trans. Edmund Jephcott as *Gustav Mahler – Richard Strauss: Correspondence 1888–1911* (London 1984)

GMUB   Herta Blaukopf (ed.), *Gustav Mahler: Unbekannte Briefe* (Vienna and Hamburg 1983); trans. Richard Stokes as *Mahler's Unknown Letters* (London 1986)

HDMZ   Hermann Danuser, *Gustav Mahler und seine Zeit* (Laaber 1991)

HEMM   Hans Heinrich Eggebrecht, *Die Musik Gustav Mahlers*, 2nd edn (Munich 1986)

HKBGM   Herta and Kurt Blaukopf (eds), *Gustav Mahler: Leben und Werk in Zeugnissen der Zeit* (Stuttgart 1994)

IGMG   Internationale Gustav Mahler Gesellschaft

KBMD   Kurt Blaukopf (ed.), *Mahler: Sein Leben, sein Werk und seine Welt in zeitgenössischen Bildern und Texten* (Vienna 1976); trans. Paul Baker and others as *Mahler: A Documentary Study* (New York and Toronto 1976)

MHGM   Mathias Hansen, *Gustav Mahler* (Stuttgart 1996)

NBL   Herbert Killian (ed.), *Gustav Mahler in den Erinnerungen von Natalie Bauer-Lechner* (Hamburg 1984); partial trans. by Dika Newlin as *Recollections of Gustav Mahler by Natalie Bauer-Lechner*, ed. Peter Franklin (London 1980)

NLM   Norman Lebrecht, *Gustav Mahler im Spiegel seiner Zeit* (Zurich and Sankt Gallen 1990); originally published in London in 1987

NMF   Nachrichten zur Mahler-Forschung

RMA   Zoltan Roman, *Gustav Mahler's American Years (1907–1911): A Documentary History* (Stuyvesant, NY, 1989)

RMU   Zoltan Roman, *Gustav Mahler and Hungary* (Budapest 1991)

TWAM   Theodor W. Adorno, *Mahler: Eine musikalische Physiognomik* (Frankfurt am Main 1960); trans. Edmund Jephcott as *Mahler: A Musical Physiognomy* (Chicago 1992)

WMWO   Franz Willnauer, *Gustav Mahler und die Wiener Oper* (Vienna 1993)

Notes

Chapter 1. What Did Mahler Look Like? An Attempt at a Description

1. AMML 29. Throughout the main text, *Mein Leben* and its English-language equivalent, *And the Bridge is Love*, are referred to as Alma's 'memoirs'. (For full bibliographical details, see the list of abbreviations on p. 707.) Conversely, the term 'reminiscences' is reserved for Donald Mitchell's edition of her *Erinnerungen an Gustav Mahler*, available in English as *Gustav Mahler: Memories and Letters* (AME). In general, references to the German edition are to the one published in Frankfurt am Main in 1971, although occasionally the second edition, published in Amsterdam in 1949, is preferred as this contains documents not taken over into the 1971 edition. For these and other abbreviations used in the notes, the reader is referred to the list of abbreviations on pp. 707–8.
2. BWGM 17; Engl. trans. 17–18.
3. Ferdinand Pfohl, *Gustav Mahler: Eindrücke und Erinnerungen aus den Hamburger Jahren*, ed. Knud Martner (Hamburg 1973), 16.
4. BWGM 19; Engl. trans. 20.
5. NBL and Alfred Roller, *Die Bildnisse von Gustav Mahler* (Leipzig and Vienna 1922), 9–28. Roller's description of Mahler is included in Norman Lebrecht's *Mahler Remembered* (London 1987), 149–65, and taken over from there by Gilbert Kaplan in *The Mahler Album* (New York and London 1995), 15–28. A revised edition of Kaplan's *Mahler Album* was published in 2011.
6. Kaplan, *The Mahler Album* (note 5).
7. AME 42.
8. Roller, *Die Bildnisse* (note 5), 15.
9. Roller, *Die Bildnisse* (note 5), 15.
10. NBL 82; Engl. trans. 84.
11. Pfohl, *Gustav Mahler* (note 3), 17.
12. Pfohl, *Gustav Mahler* (note 3), 17.

Chapter 2. Small Steps: Kalischt and Iglau (1860–75)

1. NBL 62; Engl. trans. 69.
2. KBMD, fig. 4, 6.
3. See Wilma Iggers (ed.), *Die Juden in Böhmen und Mähren: Ein historisches Lesebuch* (Munich 1986), 15–17, and Natalia Berger (ed.), *Wo sich Kulturen begegnen: Die Geschichte der tschechoslowakischen Juden* (Prague 1992).
4. GMB 318; for the letter heading, see GMB 25; not in the Engl. trans.
5. This incident is known from the unpublished section of NBL, cited here from NLM 33; Engl. trans. 12.
6. AME 30–1.

7. See Susan M. Filler, 'The Missing Mahler: Alois (Hans) in Chicago', *Neue Mahleriana*, ed. Günther Weiß (Berne, and New York 1997), 39–45.
8. Alma Rosé is the subject of a study by Richard Newman and Karen Kirtley, *Alma Rosé: Vienna to Auschwitz* (Portland, OR 2000).
9. NLM 28–30.
10. NBL 69.
11. Theodor Fischer, 'Aus Gustav Mahlers Jugendzeit', *Deutsche Heimat: Sudetendeutsche Monatsschrift für Kunst, Literatur, Heimat und Volkskunde*, vii (1931), 264–8.
12. NBL, typescript in the archives of the IGMG, 12.
13. On klezmer music, see Rita Ottens and Joel Rubin, *Klezmer-Musik* (Munich and Kassel 1999); on the early influences on Mahler's musical development, see Vladimir Karbusicky, *Gustav Mahler und seine Umwelt* (Darmstadt 1978).
14. Fischer, 'Aus Gustav Mahlers Jugendzeit', cited in NLM 20; Engl. trans. 20 (emended).
15. NBL, typescript in the archives of the IGMG, 11–12.
16. Ibid.
17. *Počátek cesty: Gustav Mahler a Jihlava v archivních pramenech*, ed. Jihlava Municipal Archives (Jihlava 2000). Although this volume is advertised as bilingual, the English translations by Nora Martišková are so woefully unidiomatic as to render the publication unusable by English-speaking readers.
18. Quoted from the facsimile in *Počátek cesty* (note 17), 90.
19. GMB 31; Engl. trans. 55.
20. GMB 25; not in the Engl. trans.

Chapter 3. Studies in Vienna (1875–80)

1. Hermann Broch, 'Hofmannsthal und seine Zeit', *Schriften zur Literatur*, i: *Kritik* (Frankfurt am Main 1975), 111–284.
2. Robert A. Kann, *Geschichte des Habsburgerreiches 1562 bis 1918*, 3rd edn (Vienna, Cologne and Weimar 1993), 331.
3. On the Ringstraße, see the comprehensive documentary study by Renate Wagner-Rieger (ed.), *Die Wiener Ringstraße: Bild einer Epoche*, 11 vols (Vienna 1969–79); see also Carl E. Schorske, 'Die Ringstraße, ihre Kritiker und die Idee der modernen Stadt', *Wien: Geist und Gesellschaft im Fin de siècle* (Munich 1994), 23–109.
4. Broch, 'Hofmannsthal und seine Zeit' (note 1), 175.
5. NBL 157–8; Engl. trans. 146.
6. On Hans Rott, see Heinz-Klaus Metzger and Rainer Riehn (eds), *Hans Rott: Der Begründer der neuen Symphonie* (Munich 1999) (= Musik-Konzepte 103/4); see also the important documentation in Uwe Harten (ed.), *Hans Rott (1858–1884)* (Vienna 2000).
7. For quotations from Krzyzanowski's jottings, see Thomas Leibnitz, ' "Ja, er ist meinem Eigensten so verwandt . . .": Hans Rott und Gustav Mahler. Notizen zu einer tragischen Beziehung', *Gustav Mahler: Werk und Wirken*, ed. Erich Wolfgang Partsch (Vienna 1996), 73–5. The complete text has been published by Uwe Harten (note 6).
8. NBL 70–1; not in the Engl. trans.
9. Dietrich Fischer-Dieskau, *Hugo Wolf: Leben und Werk* (Berlin 2003), 372–4.
10. HKBGM 26; Engl. trans. 154 (emended).
11. HKBGM 27; Engl. trans. 154 (emended).
12. Arnold Schoenberg, 'Brahms, der Fortschrittliche', *Stil und Gedanke: Aufsätze zur Musik* (Frankfurt am Main 1976), 35–71; trans. Leo Black as 'Brahms the Progressive', *Style and Idea*, ed. Leonard Stein (London 1975), 398–441, esp. 401.
13. HKBGM 28–9; Engl. trans. 156.
14. NBL, typescript in the archives of the IGMG, fol. 26/27 III.
15. GMBA 286; Engl. trans. 239.
16. NBL, unpag. typescript in the archives of the IGMG.
17. NBL 32; Engl. trans. 37.

18. See the excellent account by Herta Blaukopf, 'Mahler an der Universität: Versuch, eine biographische Lücke zu schließen', *Neue Mahleriana*, ed. Günther Weiß (Berne and New York 1997), 1–16.

19. Theodor Fischer, 'Aus Gustav Mahlers Jugendzeit', *Deutsche Heimat: Sudentendeutsche Monatsschrift für Kunst, Literatur, Heimat- und Volkskunde*, vii (1931), 264–8, esp. 267.

20. The standard study on the Pernerstorfer circle remains William J. McGrath, *Dionysian Art and Populist Politics in Austria* (New Haven 1974); see also William J. McGrath, 'Mahler und der Wiener "Nietzsche-Verein"', *Nietzsche und die jüdische Kultur*, ed. Jacob Golomb (Vienna 1998), 210–24.

21. Friedrich Nietzsche, *Sämtliche Briefe*, 8 vols, ed. Giorgio Colli and Mazzino Montinari (Munich and Berlin 1986), v.346–7.

22. See the brief but accurate account in Peter Sprengel, *Geschichte der deutschsprachigen Literatur 1870–1900* (Munich 1998), 224–5, where Sprengel draws attention to the affinities between Lipiner's *Prometheus* and Carl Spitteler's mythopoeic rhapsody, *Prometheus und Epimetheus*, of 1880.

23. BWTV 190; Engl. trans. 159–60.

24. Richard Kralik, *Tage und Werke: Lebenserinnerungen* (Vienna 1922), 59.

25. Friedrich Eckstein, '*Alte unnennbare Tage!*' (Vienna 1936), 112–13.

26. BSB, Ana 600, B, I, 2 b/Poisl, quoted in Sigrid von Moisy, 'Gustav Mahlers Briefe', *Gustav Mahler: Briefe und Musikautographen aus den Moldenhauer-Archiven in der Bayerischen Staatsbibliothek* (Munich 2003), 53–4.

27. GMB 30–3; Engl. trans. 54–7.

28. HKBGM 31–2; Engl. trans. 158.

29. Mahler's letter of 14 March 1880 to Anton Krisper in Hans Holländer, 'Unbekannte Jugendbriefe Gustav Mahlers', *Die Musik*, xx (1928), 807–13, esp. 811; see also Engl. trans. of GMB, 62.

30. GMB 37; Engl. trans. 387 (emended).

Chapter 4. The Summer Conductor: Bad Hall (1880)

1. Hans Holländer, 'Unbekannte Jugendbriefe Gustav Mahlers', *Die Musik*, xx (1928), 807–13, esp. 809; see also Engl. trans. of GMB, 60 (emended) (letter to Anton Krisper, 18 Feb. 1880).

2. GMB 32–3; Engl. trans. 56–7 (letter to Josef Steiner, 19 June 1879).

3. GMB 30; Engl. trans. 54 (letter to Josef Steiner, 17–19 June 1879).

4. GMB 33; Engl. trans. 57 (emended) (letter to Emil Freund, June 1879).

5. GMB 34; Engl. trans. 58 (emended) (letter to Anton Krisper, postmarked 22 Sept. 1879).

6. GMB 35; Engl. trans. 59 (emended) (undated letter to Anton Krisper, [between late Nov. and 14 Dec. 1879]).

7. Johann Wolfgang von Goethe, *The Collected Works*, xi: 'The Sorrows of Young Werther', trans. Victor Lange (Princeton, NJ 1995), 20 and 36.

8. GMB 37; Engl. trans. 62 (letter to Anton Krisper, postmarked 3 March 1880).

9. GMB 205; Engl. trans. 200 (undated letter to Max Marschalk, [4 Dec. 1896]).

10. Jacob and Wilhelm Grimm, *Kinder- und Hausmärchen*, ed. Heinz Rölleke, 3 vols (Stuttgart 1980), i.166.

11. On this point and on *Das klagende Lied* in general, see Janina Klassen, 'Märchenerzählung: Anmerkungen zum "Klagenden Lied"', *Gustav Mahler durchgesetzt?*, ed. Heinz–Klaus Metzger and Rainer Riehn (Munich 1999), 8–32 (= Musik-Konzepte 106).

Chapter 5. Emotional Ups and Downs in Laibach (1881–2)

1. GMB 39–40; Engl. trans. 64–5 (emended) (letter to Emil Freund, 1 Nov. 1880).

2. Stefan Zweig, *Die Welt von Gestern* (Frankfurt 1953), 89–90; trans. as *The World of Yesterday* (New York 1943), 88–9.

3. See Jens Malte Fischer, *Richard Wagners 'Das Judentum in der Musik': Eine kritische Dokumentation als Beitrag zur Geschichte des Antisemitismus* (Frankfurt 2000).

4. GMFB 350; Engl. trans. 251 (letter to Justine Mahler, 17 Dec. 1893).

5. NBL 124; Engl. trans. 118.
6. KBMD 229; Engl. trans. 226.
7. Indeed, it was not until the mid-1930s that the existence of a three-movement version came to light, and not until 1969 was it properly rediscovered both in the concert hall and on record, albeit in a hybrid version that combined the first version of the opening movement with the revised versions of the other two sections. The first version of Mahler's bold 'op. 1' was finally revealed to the world only in 1997, when Kent Nagano performed the piece to compelling effect in Manchester, a performance also released on compact disc. Since then there are only two versions in which *Das klagende Lied* should be performed: either the two-movement revised version or, preferably, the original version in three movements. Hybrid versions are not acceptable.

Chapter 6. For the Last Time in the Provinces: Olmütz (1882–3)

1. GMFB 49; Engl. trans. 20–1 (letter from Marie Mahler to Gustav Mahler, 15 Dec. 1882).
2. HKBGM 47–8; Engl. trans. from Kurt Blaukopf (ed.), *Mahler: A Documentary Study*, trans. Paul Baker and others (New York and Toronto 1976), 166.
3. GMB 43–4; Engl. trans. 17 (letter to Friedrich Löhr, 12 Feb. 1883).
4. HKBGM 45; Engl. trans. 168 (emended).
5. GMB 47; Engl. trans. 73 (emended) (letter to Friedrich Löhr, July 1883).

Chapter 7. Presentiment and a New Departure: Kassel (1883–5)

1. The present chapter is based on the detailed researches of the Kassel dramaturge Hans Joachim Schaefer in *Gustav Mahler: Jahre der Entscheidung in Kassel 1883–1885* (Kassel 1990).
2. GMB 48; Engl. trans. 74 (letter to Friedrich Löhr, 19 Sept. 1883).
3. GMB 50; trans. from Kurt Blaukopf (ed.), *Mahler: A Documentary Study* (New York and Toronto 1976), 170 (undated letter to Gustav Lewy, [late Oct. 1883]).
4. GMB 51; trans. from *Mahler: A Documentary Study* (note 3), 170 (emended) (undated letter to Hans von Bülow, [25 or 26 Jan. 1884]).
5. Quoted from Schaefer, *Gustav Mahler* (note 1), 45.
6. GMB 52; Engl. trans. 76 (emended) (undated letter to Friedrich Löhr, [April 1884]).
7. GMB 56; Engl. trans. 80 (emended) (undated letter to Friedrich Löhr, [late Aug. 1884]).
8. GMB 57; Engl. trans. 81 (emended) (letter to Friedrich Löhr, 1 Jan. 1885; Löhr argues that Mahler was alluding to Jean Paul here.)
9. See Schaefer, *Gustav Mahler* (note 1), 79.
10. Schaefer, *Gustav Mahler* (note 1), 82.
11. GMB 66; Engl. trans. 89 (letter to Friedrich Löhr, 5 July 1885).

Chapter 8. The Avid Reader: Mahler and Literature

1. GMB 141–2; Engl. trans. 153 (undated letter to Friedrich Löhr, [late 1894 or Jan. 1895]).
2. On Mahler's song texts, see the present writer's detailed examination in 'Das klagende Lied von der Erde: Zu Gustav Mahlers Liedern und ihren Texten', *Jahrhundertdämmerung: Ansichten eines anderen Fin de siècle* (Vienna 2000), 90–110, esp. 90–4.
3. Achim von Arnim and Clemens Brentano, *Des Knaben Wunderhorn: Alte deutsche Lieder*, ed. Heinz Rölleke, 3 vols (Stuttgart 1987), iii.119–20.
4. NBL 165; Engl. trans. 155–6.
5. TWAM 57; Engl. trans. 38.
6. Hans Moldenhauer, *Anton von Webern: A Chronicle of his Life and Work* (London 1978), 75–6.
7. Karl Kraus, 'Bekenntnis', *Gedichte*, ed. Christian Wagenknecht (Frankfurt 1989), 93.
8. Rudolf Borchardt, *Prosa III* (Stuttgart 1960), 340.
9. Hans Wollschläger, ' "Der Gang zu jenen Höhn" ', *Friedrich Rückert: Kindertotenlieder* (Frankfurt and Leipzig 1993), 38–9.

10. Herta Blaukopf, ' "Bücher fresse ich immer mehr und mehr": Gustav Mahler als Leser', *Mahler-Gespräche*, ed. Friedbert Aspetsberger and Erich Wolfgang Partsch (Innsbruck 2002), 96–8.
11. GMBA 307; Engl. trans. 257 (letter to Alma Mahler, 12 Jan. 1907).
12. GMBA 282; Engl. trans. 236 (letter to Alma Mahler, 16 Aug. 1906).
13. GMBA 206; Engl. trans. 168 (letter to Alma Mahler, 28 June 1904).
14. NLM 238; Engl. trans. 255.
15. GMBA 180; Engl. trans. 144 (letter to Alma Mahler, 29 Jan. 1904).
16. GMBA 249; Engl. trans. 207 (letter to Alma Mahler, 6 June 1905).
17. NLM 236; Engl. trans. 253.
18. NLM 241; Engl. trans. 260–1 (revised).
19. NBL 198; Engl. trans. 178.
20. Richard Specht, *Gustav Mahler* (Berlin 1913), 35; a different version of this anecdote may be found in AME 155; Engl. trans. 126.
21. Specht, *Gustav Mahler* (note 20), 35.
22. Fyodor Dostoevsky, *The Brothers Karamazov*, trans. David McDuff (London 2003), 308.
23. Jean Paul, *Ideen-Gewimmel* (Munich 2000), 53.

Chapter 9. Becoming Mahler: Prague (1885–6)

1. GMB 67; Engl. trans. 90 (letter to Friedrich Löhr, 10 [July] 1885).
2. Heinrich Grünfeld, *In Dur und Moll: Begegnungen und Erlebnisse aus fünfzig Jahren* (Leipzig and Zurich 1923), 19.
3. GMB 68; Engl. trans. 94 (letter to Friedrich Löhr, 28 Nov.–28 Dec. 1885).
4. Jitka Ludvová has documented every surviving trace of Betty Frank in 'Betty Frank, Gustav Mahlers Prager Freundin', *Gustav Mahler und Prag* (Prague 1996), 23–56.
5. KBMD 173; Engl. trans. 174.
6. HKBGM 64–5; Engl. trans. 175 (emended).
7. HKBGM 65; Engl. trans. 176.

Chapter 10. The First Symphony

1. GMB 92; Engl. trans. 111–12 (undated letter to Friedrich Löhr, [March 1888]).
2. NBL 173; Engl. trans. 157.
3. GMB 169–70 and 171–2; Engl. trans. 177–8 and 178–81 (letters to Max Marschalk, 20 and 26 March 1896).
4. Bruno Walter, *Briefe 1894–1962*, ed. Lotte Walter Lindt (Frankfurt 1969), 48–52 (letter to Ludwig Schiedermair, 6 Dec. 1901).
5. GMB 277; Engl. trans. 262 (undated letter to Max Kalbeck, [20 Nov. 1900?]).
6. NBL 138; Engl. trans. 131.
7. These and later comments on individual works are based in part on the writings of Theodor W. Adorno, Paul Bekker, Hermann Danuser, Hans Heinrich Eggebrecht, Constantin Floros, Mathias Hansen and Donald Mitchell.
8. NBL 173; Engl. trans. 157.
9. TWAM 61; Engl. trans. 41.
10. MHGM 55.
11. Mahler's own detailed comments on his First Symphony may be found in NBL 172–6; the Engl. trans. (157–61) is incomplete.
12. Eduard Hanslick's review originally appeared in the *Neue Freie Presse* on 20 Nov. 1900 and is quoted here from Renate Ulm (ed.), *Gustav Mahlers Symphonien: Entstehung – Deutung – Wirkung* (Munich and Kassel 2001), 70.
13. Ferdinand Pfohl, *Gustav Mahler: Eindrücke und Erinnerungen aus den Hamburger Jahren*, ed. Knud Martner (Hamburg 1973), 64–7.
14. RMA 313–14.
15. GMB 396; Engl. trans. 346 (undated letter to Bruno Walter, [18 or 19 Dec. 1909]).

Chapter 11. Life's Vicissitudes: Leipzig (1886–8)

1. GMB 68; Engl. trans. 94 (letter to Friedrich Löhr, 28 Nov.–28 Dec. 1885).
2. GMB 78; Engl. trans. 101 (corrected) (undated letter to Friedrich Löhr, [Oct.? 1886]).
3. GMB 79; Engl. trans. 102 (letter to Max Staegemann, 6 Nov. 1886).
4. HKBGM 68; Engl. trans. 177.
5. HKBGM 68; Engl. trans. 177.
6. GMB 87; Engl. trans. 109 (undated letter to Friedrich Löhr, [early May 1887]).
7. Ethel Smyth, *Impressions that Remained*, 2 vols (London 1923), ii.174–5.
8. GMB 88–9; Engl. trans. 109 (undated letter to Friedrich Löhr, [4 Jan. 1888]).
9. Cosima Wagner, *Das zweite Leben: Briefe und Aufzeichnungen 1883–1930*, ed. Dietrich Mack (Munich 1980), 191 (letter from Cosima Wagner to Hermann Levi, 19 June 1889).
10. NBL 175; Engl. trans. 159.
11. GMB 92; Engl. trans. 112 (undated letter to Friedrich Löhr, [March 1888]).
12. GMB 93–4; Engl. trans. 113 (letter to Max Staegemann, 16 May 1888).

Chapter 12. Notes on Mahler's Songs

1. Readers who wish to pursue their understandable interest in Mahler's songs are referred, once again, to Mathias Hansen's brief but lucid account in MHGM and to Peter Revers, *Mahlers Lieder: Ein musikalischer Werkführer* (Munich 2000).
2. GMB 57; Engl. trans. 81 (emended) (letter to Friedrich Löhr, 1 Jan. 1885).
3. Rudolf Baumbach, *Lieder eines fahrenden Gesellen*, 4th edn (Leipzig 1882), 1.
4. GMB 322; Engl. trans. 282 (letter to Ludwig Karpath, 2 March 1905).
5. NBL 193; Engl. trans. 173.
6. Johann Wolfgang von Goethe, 'Rezension von Des Knaben Wunderhorn', *Sämtliche Werke nach Epochen seines Schaffens* (Munich 1988), vi/2.602–16.
7. Jean Paul, 'Speech of the Dead Christ from the Universe that There Is No God' from 'Siebenkäs', *Sämtliche Werke*, ed. Norbert Miller (Munich and Vienna 1987), i/2.270–5.
8. NBL 135; this passage is not in the Engl. trans.
9. NBL 194; Engl. trans. 174.
10. AMML 32; Engl. trans. 60.
11. MHGM 248.

Chapter 13. Lowland Dreams: Budapest (1888–91)

1. The fullest account of Mahler's time in Budapest is Zoltan Roman's documentary study, *Gustav Mahler and Hungary* (Budapest 1991) (= RMU).
2. GMB 95; this letter is not included in the 1979 Engl. trans. (undated letter to Max Steinitzer, [early summer 1888]).
3. On Mihalovich and his later letters to Mathilde Wesendonck, in which Mahler plays an important role, see Inge Birkin-Feichtinger's article, 'Ödön von Mihalovich's Mahler-Bild aus der Sicht von Briefen an Mathilde Wesendonck aus den Jahren 1889–97', *Studia Musicologica Academiae Scientiarum Hungaricae*, xliii (2002), 41–51.
4. Ludwig Karpath, *Begegnung mit dem Genius* (Vienna 1934), 11–12; Engl. trans. from Kurt Blaukopf (ed.), *Mahler: A Documentary Study*, trans. Paul Baker and others (New York and Toronto 1976), 182.
5. HKBGM 77; Engl. trans. 183.
6. GMB 97; Engl. trans. 117 (undated letter to members of the Budapest Opera, [before 10 Oct. 1888]).
7. GMB 98; Engl. trans. 118 (letter to Max Staegemann, 20 Dec. 1888).
8. HKBGM 78; Engl. trans. 184.
9. HKBGM 79; Engl. trans. 184.
10. RMU 200.

11. RMU 59.
12. Lilli Lehmann, *Mein Weg*, 2nd edn (Leipzig 1920), 367; trans. Alice Benedict Seligman as *My Path Through Life* (London 1914), 388.
13. HKBGM 88; Engl. trans. 190 (emended).

Chapter 14. The Conductor

1. Franz Werfel, *Gedichte* (Berlin, Vienna and Leipzig 1927), 321.
2. Elias Canetti, *Masse und Macht* (Hamburg 1960), 455–6; trans. Carol Stewart as *Crowds and Power* (London 1962), 396.
3. Mary Lawton, *Schumann-Heink: The Last of the Titans* (New York 1929), 360.
4. NBL 31; Engl. trans. 35.
5. H. C. Robbins Landon, *Beethoven: His Life, Work and World* (London 1992), 174–5.
6. Schließmann's caricature is reproduced in Kurt Blaukopf (ed.), *Mahler: A Documentary Study*, trans. Paul Baker and others (New York and Toronto 1976), pl. 194.
7. Gilbert Kaplan, *The Mahler Album* (New York and London 1995), pl. 194.
8. This caricature is reproduced on p. 274 of K. M. Knittel's excellent article, ' "Ein hypermoderner Dirigent": Mahler and Anti-Semitism in *Fin-de-siècle* Vienna', *19th Century Music*, xviii (1995), 257–76.
9. NBL 56; Engl. trans. 58.
10. NLM 246; Engl. trans. 267–8.
11. BWGM 71; Engl. trans. 81.
12. Josef Bohuslav Foerster, *Der Pilger: Erinnerungen eines Musikers* (Prague 1955), 386.
13. BWGM 71; Engl. trans. 81–2.

Chapter 15. The Second Symphony

1. GMB 172–3; Engl. trans. 180 (letter to Max Marschalk, 26 March 1896).
2. See GMBA 87–9; Engl. trans. 64–5; GMB 172–3; Engl. trans. 180 (letter to Max Marschalk, 26 March 1896); and NBL 40; Engl. trans. 43–4.
3. Georg Christoph Lichtenberg, *Schriften und Briefe*, 6 vols (Munich 1967–92), i.223–4.
4. GMB 302; Engl. trans. 269 (letter to Julius Buths, 25 March 1903).
5. Rudolf Stephan, *Gustav Mahler: II. Symphonie c-Moll* (Munich 1979), 74–5.
6. TWAM 179; Engl. trans. 136.
7. Alban Berg, *Briefe an seine Frau* (Munich and Vienna 1965), 21; trans. Bernard Grun as *Alban Berg: Letters to His Wife* (New York 1971), 32 (emended).

Chapter 16. Self-Realization: Hamburg (1891–7)

1. Josef Bohuslav Foerster, *Der Pilger: Erinnerungen eines Musikers* (Prague 1955), 352–3; the Titian canvas is reproduced in Kurt Blaukopf (ed.), *Mahler: A Documentary Study*, trans. Paul Baker and others (New York and Toronto 1976), pl. 100.
2. BWGM 20; Engl. trans. 20–21.
3. HKBGM 91; Engl. trans. 192.
4. Modeste Tchaikovsky, *The Life & Letters of Peter Ilich Tchaikovsky*, ed. Rosa Newmarch (New York 1973), 675.
5. Foerster, *Der Pilger* (note 1), 92–3; Engl. trans. from Blaukopf, *Mahler: A Documentary Study* (note 1), 193.
6. Marie von Bülow, *Hans von Bülows Leben dargestellt aus seinen Briefen* (Leipzig 1921), 510.
7. GMB 118; Engl. trans. 139 (undated letter to Friedrich Löhr, [28 Nov. 1891]).
8. GMB 117; Engl. trans. 138 (undated letter to Friedrich Löhr, [28 Nov. 1891]).
9. GMB 117; Engl. trans. 138 (undated letter to Friedrich Löhr, [28 Nov. 1891]).
10. GMB 141; Engl. trans. 152 (undated letter to Friedrich Löhr, [late 1894 or Jan. 1895]).
11. GMB 119; Engl. trans. 140 (undated letter to Emil Freund, [late autumn of 1891 or winter of 1891/2]).

12. HKBGM 96; Engl. trans. 195.
13. GMB 121-2; Engl. trans. 141-2 (undated letter to Arnold Berliner, [9 June 1892]).
14. Hermann [Herman] Klein, *Thirty Years of Musical Life in London 1870-1900* (London 1903), 365-6.
15. GMB 123; Engl. trans. 142-3 (undated letters to Arnold Berliner, [29 June and 14 July 1892]).
16. Dan H. Laurence (ed.), *Shaw's Music*, 3 vols (London 1989), ii.650 ('Siegfried at Covent Garden', originally published in *The World* on 15 June 1892).
17. Herman Klein, *The Golden Age of Opera* (London 1933), 163-4.
18. Ferdinand Pfohl, *Gustav Mahler: Eindrücke und Erinnerungen aus den Hamburger Jahren*, ed. Knud Martner (Hamburg 1973), 11.
19. Pfohl, *Gustav Mahler* (note 18), 26-8.
20. BWGM 24; Engl. trans. 26.
21. Anna Bahr-Mildenburg, *Erinnerungen* (Vienna and Berlin 1921), 14; Engl. trans. from Blaukopf, *Mahler: A Documentary Study* (note 1), 202-3.
22. BWGM 23; Engl. trans. 25.
23. Jean Paul, 'Vorschule der Ästhetik', *Sämtliche Werke*, ed. Norbert Miller and others (Munich and Vienna 1987), i/5.125; see also Julian Johnson, *Mahler's Voices: Expression and Irony in the Songs and Symphonies* (Oxford 2009), 127-32.
24. Anna von Mildenburg, 'Aus Briefen Mahlers', *Moderne Welt*, iii/7 (1921), 13; quoted from NLM 101-2; Engl. trans. 90-1. Mildenburg is more forthcoming here than in her *Erinnerungen* of the same year.
25. GMUB 246-7; Engl. trans. 232 (undated letter to Wilhelm Zinne, [30 May 1895]). Mahler writes 'Geheimrad', a pun compounding 'Geheimrat' (privy councillor) and 'Rad' (bicycle).
26. GMBA 297-8; Engl. trans. 248 (telegram to Alma Mahler, 6 Nov. 1906). The whole telegram is written in doggerel rhyme.
27. NBL, typescript in the archives of the IGMG, 3.
28. AME 81; Engl. trans. 55.
29. On Mahler's visits to Steinbach, see Herta Blaukopf, 'Das Häuschen am Attersee', *Gustav Mahler in Steinbach am Attersee*, ed. IGMG (Vienna n.d.), 3-5. See also the account by Mahler's nephew, Alfred Rosé, who travelled to Steinbach with his mother in 1928 and received a first-hand report from her: Alfred Rosé, 'From Gustav Mahler's Storm and Stress Period', *Canadian Music Journal*, i (1957), 21-4, reproduced in the Engl. edition of NLM 67-71.
30. BWGM 30; Engl. trans. 33.
31. GMUB 234; Engl. trans. 220 (undated letter to Cosima Wagner, [late Oct. 1896]).
32. GMB 156; Engl. trans. 169-70 (undated letter to Anna von Mildenburg, [21 Nov. 1895]).
33. GMMB 40-41 (letter to Anna von Mildenburg, 29 Nov. 1895).
34. NBL 180-1; Engl. trans. 163-4.
35. Anna Bahr-Mildenburg, *Darstellung der Werke Richard Wagners aus dem Geiste der Dichtung und Musik: Tristan und Isolde. Vollständige Regiebearbeitung sämtlicher Partien mit Notenbeispielen* (Leipzig and Vienna 1936).
36. GMMB 54 (letter to Anna von Mildenburg, 10 Dec. 1895).
37. AME 70; Engl. trans. 44.
38. GMMB 77-8 (letter to Anna von Mildenburg, 7 Feb. 1896).
39. GMMB 95-6 (letter to Anna von Mildenburg, 19 May 1896).
40. GMMB 149 (letter to Anna von Mildenburg, 21 July 1896).
41. GMMB 219 (letter to Anna von Mildenburg, 14 May 1897).
42. HKBGM 124-5; Engl. trans. 212.
43. GMMB 244-5 (undated letter to Anna von Mildenburg, [?24 July 1897]).
44. Emil Pirchan, Alexander Witeschnik and Otto Fritz, *300 Jahre Wiener Operntheater* (Vienna 1953), 190-1.
45. GMMB 316 (undated letter to Anna von Mildenburg, [March 1902]).
46. GMMB 225 (letter to Anna von Mildenburg, 7 Dec. 1907).
47. Bahr-Mildenburg, *Erinnerungen* (note 21), 32.
48. HKBGM 97; Engl. trans. 195.

49. GMUB 234–5; Engl. trans. 219–21 (undated letter to Cosima Wagner, [late Oct. 1896]).
50. GMUB 218; Engl. trans. 205 (emended) (letter from Cosima Wagner to Marie von Wolkenstein, 2 July 1899).
51. GMUB 221; Engl. trans. 207 (undated letter from Cosima Wagner to Marie von Wolkenstein, [after 11 Dec. 1899]).
52. Wilhelm Kienzl, *Meine Lebenswanderung* (Stuttgart 1926), 143; Engl. trans. from Blaukopf, *Mahler: A Documentary Study* (note 1), 201.
53. HKBGM 118; Engl. trans. 207–8.

Chapter 17. Jewishness and Identity

1. Ernest Ansermet, *Les fondements de la musique dans la conscience humaine et autres écrits*, ed. Jean-Jacques Rapin (Paris 2000), 670–2.
2. Hans Joachim Schaefer and others, *Gustav Mahler: Jahre der Entscheidung in Kassel 1883–1885* (Kassel 1990), 62.
3. HKBGM 122; Engl. trans. 210 (*Die Reichspost*, 14 April 1897).
4. HKBGM 132; Engl. trans. 218 (*Deutsche Zeitung*, 4 Nov. 1898).
5. See Hans Rudolf Vaget, *Im Schatten Wagners: Thomas Mann über Richard Wagner* (Frankfurt 1999), 232–3.
6. Rudolf Louis, *Die deutsche Musik der Gegenwart* (Munich and Leipzig 1909), 182.
7. Dr B., *Völkischer Beobachter* (Munich edn) (26 Jan. 1929).
8. Wolfgang Schlüter, *Niedersächsische Zeitung* (19 Nov. 1952).
9. Rudolf Bauer, *Das Konzert*, rev. edn (Berlin 1961), 403.
10. See Jens Malte Fischer, *Richard Wagners 'Das Judentum in der Musik': Eine kritische Dokumentation als Beitrag zur Geschichte des Antisemitismus* (Frankfurt 2000). The introduction to this documentary volume deals with the present problem in some detail.
11. GMB 140; Engl. trans. 152 (undated letter to Friedrich Löhr, [late 1894 or Jan. 1895]).
12. HKBGM 119 (undated letter to Ödön von Mihalovich); Engl. trans. 208 (dated 25 Jan. 1897).
13. GMB 246; Engl. trans. 231 (a sentence has been inadvertently omitted from the English translation) (undated letter to Bruno Walter [late May or early June 1897]).
14. GMBA 144; Engl. trans. 114 (letter to Alma Mahler, 31 March 1903).
15. GMUB 55; Engl. trans. 55 (undated letter to Oskar Fried, [Aug. 1906]).
16. Alfred Roller, *Die Bildnisse von Gustav Mahler* (Leipzig and Vienna 1922), 25.
17. Roller, *Die Bildnisse von Gustav Mahler* (note 16), 25.
18. GMBA 304; Engl. trans. 255 (letter to Alma Mahler, 10 Jan. 1907).
19. Freud in an interview conducted in English in 1926, cited by Peter Gay, *A Godless Jew: Freud, Atheism, and the Making of Psychoanalysis* (New Haven 1987), 139.
20. AME 137; Engl. trans. 109.
21. Gay, *A Godless Jew* (note 19), 122 (letter from Sigmund Freud to an unnamed correspondent, 27 Jan. 1925).
22. TWAM 192; Engl. trans. 149.
23. See Vladimir Karbusicky, *Gustav Mahler und seine Umwelt* (Darmstadt 1978).
24. RMA 442–5.
25. TWAM 54; Engl. trans. 36.
26. Gershom Scholem, 'Juden und Deutsche', *Judaica II* (Frankfurt 1970), 33.
27. GMB 367–8; Engl. trans. 324 (letter to Bruno Walter, 18 July [1908]).
28. Heinrich Berl, *Das Judentum in der Musik* (Berlin and Leipzig 1926).
29. Max Brod, *Gustav Mahler: Beispiel einer deutsch-jüdischen Symbiose* (Frankfurt 1961), 20 and 19.
30. GMB 191; Engl. trans. 189 (letter to Bruno Walter, 2 July 1896).
31. TWAM 192; Engl. trans. 149.
32. HEMM 287–9.
33. NBL 185; not in Engl. trans.

Chapter 18. The Third Symphony

1. BWGM 32–3; Engl. trans. 3.
2. NBL 35; Engl. trans. 40.
3. GMB 196; the Engl. trans. (192–3) reproduces only the German without a translation (letter to Max Marschalk, 6 Aug. 1896).
4. GMB 187; the Engl. trans. (190) is abridged and misdated (undated letter to Anna von Mildenburg, [28? June 1896]).
5. HDMZ 152–4.
6. GMB 187; Engl. trans. (190) incomplete (undated letter to Anna von Mildenburg, [28? June 1896]).
7. NBL 59; Engl. trans. 61.
8. NBL 60; Engl. trans. 63.
9. NLM 239; Engl. trans. 257.
10. NBL 56; Engl. trans. 59.
11. See Anette Unger, *Welt, Leben und Kunst als Themen der 'Zarathustra-Kompositionen' von Richard Strauss und Gustav Mahler* (Frankfurt 1992).
12. BWGM 102; Engl. trans. 118.
13. GMBA 107 and 62; Engl. trans. 81 and 19 (letter to Alma Mahler, 19 Dec. 1901).
14. NLM 201; Engl. trans. 210.
15. TWAM 53–4; Engl. trans. 36.
16. GMB 190–1; Engl. trans. 189 (letter to Bruno Walter, 2 July 1896).
17. MHGM 95.

Chapter 19. The God of the Southern Climes: Vienna (1897–1901)

1. GMB 199; Engl. trans. 193 (undated letter to Friedrich Löhr, [autumn 1896]).
2. HKBGM 117; Engl. trans. 207.
3. GMB 211–12; not in Engl. trans. (letter to Josef von Bezecny, 21 Dec. 1896).
4. Franz Bittong, *Die Meistersinger, oder: Das Judenthum in der Musik. Parodistischer Scherz in 1 Akt* (Berlin [1871]), reproduced by Jens Malte Fischer, *Richard Wagners 'Das Judentum in der Musik': Eine kritische Dokumentation als Beitrag zur Geschichte des Antisemitismus* (Frankfurt 2000), 329–52.
5. RMU 166 (letter to Ödön von Mihalovich, 21 Dec. 1896).
6. RMU 167 (letter to Ödön von Mihalovich, 22 Dec. 1896).
7. RMU 168–9 (undated letter to Ödön von Mihalovich, [mid-Jan. 1897]).
8. This was the soprano Henriette Standthartner, Mottl's first wife (1866–1933), whom he married in 1893. They later separated, but she refused to divorce him, and it was only on his deathbed that he was able to marry his second wife, the soprano Zdenka Fassbender (1879–1954). (Mahler was not the only conductor to promote the stage careers of the women in his life.)
9. HHStA Wien, Gen. Intendanz, 897, K 165 (no. 491) (letter from Eduard Hanslick, 27 March 1897).
10. HKBGM 121; Engl. trans. 210.
11. HKBGM 122; Engl. trans. 210.
12. HKBGM 123; Engl. trans. 211 ('Wiener Brief', *Breslauer Zeitung*, 16 May 1897).
13. NBL 87; Engl. trans. 89 (emended).
14. Eduard Hanslick, 'Dalibor', *Am Ende des Jahrhunderts: Musikalische Kritiken und Schilderungen* (Berlin 1899), 65–6.
15. KBMD 157; Engl. trans. 147–8.
16. AMTB 481; Engl. trans. 269 (entry of 24 March 1900).
17. Marie Gutheil-Schoder, *Erlebtes und Erstrebtes: Rolle und Gestaltung* (Vienna and Leipzig 1937), 19–20.
18. Dési Halban (ed.), *Selma Kurz: Die Sängerin und ihre Zeit* (Stuttgart and Zurich 1983), 88.
19. Halban, *Selma Kurz* (note 18), 89.
20. Halban, *Selma Kurz* (note 18), 89.
21. Ludwig Karpath, *Begegnung mit dem Genius* (Vienna and Leipzig 1934), 66–7.
22. NBL, typescript in the archives of the IGMG.

Chapter 20. Mahler's Illnesses: A Pathographical Sketch

1. AME 151; Engl. trans. 122.
2. GMB 247; Engl. trans. 227 (letter to Anna von Mildenburg, 12 June 1897).
3. NBL 38; not in Engl. trans.
4. AMTB 752; Engl. trans. 468 (entry of 6 Jan. 1902).
5. AMTB 738; Engl. trans. 456 (emended) (entry of 9 Dec. 1901).
6. See, for example, Peter Ostwald, 'Gustav Mahler: Health and Creative Energy', *A 'Mass' for the Masses: Proceedings of the Mahler VIII Symposium, Amsterdam 1988*, ed. Eveline Nikkels and Robert Becqué (Rijswijk 1992), 100–2.
7. AME 96; Engl. trans. 69.
8. GMBA 393; Engl. trans. 331 (letter to Alma Mahler, 25 June 1909).
9. GMBA 385–6; Engl. trans. 324 (letter to Alma Mahler, 20? June 1909).

Chapter 21. The Fourth Symphony

1. GMB 305; Engl. trans. 272 (letter to Julius Buths, 12 Sept. 1903).
2. NBL 198; Engl. trans. 177–8.
3. HKBGM 153–4; Engl. trans. 230 (review by Theodor Kroyer first published in *Die Musik*, i [1901/2], 548–9).
4. NBL 203; Engl. trans. 184.
5. NBL 179; Engl. trans. 162.
6. GMB 428; Engl. trans. 372 (letter to Georg Göhler, 8 Feb. 1911).
7. NBL 162; Engl. trans. 151–2.
8. NBL 202; Engl. trans. 182.
9. Jean Paul, 'Vorschule der Ästhetik', *Sämtliche Werke*, ed. Norbert Miller (Munich and Vienna 1987), i/5.124–6.
10. Jean Paul, 'Vorschule der Ästhetik' (note 9), i/5.156.
11. NBL 198; Engl. trans. 178. (It is a foolhardy translator who disagrees with Dika Newlin, but it seems to the present translator that the standard translation of 'Heiterkeit' as 'serenity' is wide of the mark and that a meaning closer to the joviality of comic opera – in German, 'heitere Oper' – is more appropriate here.)

Chapter 22. Vienna in 1900: Alma as a Young Woman (1901–3)

1. Hermann Bahr, 'Wien', *Sinn hinter der Komödie* (Graz and Vienna 1965), 71–3.
2. Leaflet from 1896 quoted in *Arthur Schnitzler: Materialien zur Ausstellung der Wiener Festwochen 1981* (Vienna 1981), 66.
3. Arthur Schnitzler, 'Der Weg ins Freie', *Gesammelte Werke*, 6 vols (Frankfurt 1961–7), i.696–7.
4. KBMD 228; Engl. trans. 225.
5. Quoted in Ludwig Greve and others (eds), *Jugend in Wien: Literatur um 1900* (Munich 1974), 87.
6. Hermann Broch, 'Hofmannsthal und seine Zeit', *Kommentierte Werkausgabe*, ed. Paul Michael Lützeler, 13 vols (Frankfurt 1974–81), i.170.
7. AME 110; Engl. trans. 82.
8. Robert Musil, *Der Mann ohne Eigenschaften* (Hamburg 1952), 33; trans. Sophie Wilkins and Burton Pike as *The Man Without Qualities* (London 1997), 29.
9. Musil, *Der Mann ohne Eigenschaften* (note 8), 35; Engl. trans. 31.
10. NLM 264; Engl. trans. 288.
11. Hugo von Hofmannsthal, 'Gabriele D'Annunzio', *Gesammelte Werke, Reden und Aufsätze*, ed. Bernd Schoeller and Rudolf Hirsch, 10 vols (Frankfurt 1979), i.174–6.
12. See, above all, Marian Bisanz-Prakken, *Gustav Klimt: Der Beethovenfries. Geschichte, Funktion und Bedeutung* (Salzburg 1977).
13. See DLG II, ii.512–13.
14. AME 62–3; Engl. trans. 37.
15. Ludwig Hevesi, *Acht Jahre Secession* (Vienna 1906), 383.
16. GMB 293; Engl. trans. 262 (undated letter to Alfred Roller, [May 1902]).

17. AME 189; Engl. trans. 160.
18. Bertha Zuckerkandl, *Österreich intim: Erinnerungen 1892–1942* (Frankfurt 1970), 38–43.
19. Zuckerkandl, *Österreich intim*, 43 (Bertha Zuckerkandl's letter to Sophie Clemenceau, 30 Nov. [1901]).
20. AMTB 318; Engl. trans. 163 (entry of 11 July 1899).
21. Elias Canetti, *Das Augenspiel: Lebensgeschichte 1931–1937* (Munich and Vienna 1985), 59–61; trans. Ralph Manheim as *The Play of the Eyes* (London 1990), 51–3.
22. *Frankfurter Allgemeine Zeitung* (5 Dec. 1995), L 9.
23. Claire Goll, *Ich verzeihe keinem* (Munich and Zurich 1980), 174.
24. AMTB 371; Engl. trans. 195 (entry of 22 Sept. 1899).
25. AMTB 316; not in Engl. trans. (entry of 9 July 1899).
26. AMTB 180; Engl. trans. 89 (entry of 29 Jan. 1899).
27. AMTB 694; Engl. trans. 421 (entry of 28 July 1901).
28. AME 42; Engl. trans. 18.
29. AMTB 586; Engl. trans. 345 (entry of 18 Oct. 1900).
30. AMTB 422; Engl. trans. 225 (entry of 13 Jan. 1900).
31. AMTB 612; not in Engl. trans. (entry of 1 Jan. 1901).
32. AMTB 11; Engl. trans. 5 (entry of 9 Feb. 1898).
33. AMTB 662; Engl. trans. 400 (entry of 22 April 1901).
34. AMTB 165–6; not in Engl. trans. (entry of 21 Dec. 1898).
35. GMBA 108; Engl. trans. 82 (letter from Mahler to Alma Schindler, 19 Dec. 1901).
36. Sigmund Freud, *Briefe 1873–1939* (Frankfurt 1968), 82–3; trans. Tania and James Stern as *Letters of Sigmund Freud* (New York 1992), 76 (letter from Sigmund Freud to Martha Bernays, 15 Nov. 1883).
37. AMTB 745; Engl. trans. 462 (entry of 20 Dec. 1901).
38. AMTB 724; Engl. trans. 443 (entry of 7 Nov. 1901).
39. AMTB 725; Engl. trans. 444 (entry of 8 Nov. 1901).
40. AMTB 731; Engl. trans. 449 (entry of 3 Dec. 1901).
41. AMTB 744–5; Engl. trans. 461 (entry of 19 Dec. 1901).
42. AMTB 740; Engl. trans. 457 (entry of 12 Dec. 1901).
43. AMTB 741; Engl. trans. 458 (entry of 13 Dec. 1901).
44. AMTB 746; Engl. trans. 463 (entry of 22 Dec. 1901).
45. GMBA 75; Engl. trans. 52 (undated letter to Alma Schindler, [8 Dec. 1901]).
46. GMBA 84; Engl. trans. 61 (undated letter to Alma Schindler, [12 Dec. 1901]).
47. GMBA 85; Engl. trans. 61 (undated letter to Justine Mahler, [13 Dec. 1901]).
48. GMBA 97; Engl. trans. (emended) 72 (undated letter to Justine Mahler, [15 Dec. 1901]).
49. GMBA 105; Engl. trans. 79 (undated letter to Alma Schindler, [19 Dec. 1901]).
50. AMTB 745; Engl. trans. 462 (entry of 20 Dec. 1901).
51. AMTB 745; Engl. trans. 462 (entry of 21 Dec. 1901).
52. AMTB 751; Engl. trans. 467 (entry of 5 Jan. 1902). For reasons that are unclear, the German edition of GMBA mistakenly dates this entry 3 Jan., but the error has been corrected in the Engl. trans. (cf. GMBA 124; Engl. trans. 96).
53. AME 50; Engl. trans. 25.
54. AME 51; Engl. trans. 26.
55. AMTB 745; Engl. trans. 462 (entry of 21 Dec. 1901).
56. Lipiner's letter was first published in its entirety by Eveline Nikkels, *'O Mensch! gib acht!': Friedrich Nietzsches Bedeutung für Gustav Mahler* (Amsterdam 1989), 108–12.
57. NBL 204; not in Engl. trans.

Chapter 23. The Fifth Symphony

1. NBL 192; not in Engl. trans.
2. NBL 193; Engl. trans. 173.
3. HEMM 67–9.
4. Theodor W. Adorno, 'Zweiter Mahler-Vortrag', *Gesammelte Schriften*, 20 vols (Frankfurt 1997), xviii.596.
5. MHGM 117.

6. GMBA 220–1; Engl. trans. 179 (letter from Gustav Mahler to Alma Mahler, 14 Oct. 1904). (The quotation comes from the Prologue in Heaven in Goethe's *Faust*, ll. 243–4.)

7. MHGM 112.

8. Quoted in Truus de Leur, 'Gustav Mahler in the Netherlands', *Gustav Mahler: The World Listens*, ed. Donald Mitchell (Amsterdam 1995), i.15–40, esp. 37.

9. GMRSB 90; Engl. trans. 75 (letter from Richard Strauss to Gustav Mahler, 5 March 1905).

10. AME 74; Engl. trans. 47.

11. MHGM 122.

Chapter 24. 'Nothing is lost to you': Faith and Philosophy

1. AMML 28; cf. Engl. trans. 27–8.

2. AME 45; Engl. trans. 20.

3. BWGM 99; Engl. trans. 115.

4. GMBA 430–1; Engl. trans. 361–3 (letter from Gustav Mahler to Alma Mahler, 18 June 1910).

5. GMBA 431; Engl. trans. 363 (letter from Gustav Mahler to Alma Mahler, 18 June 1910).

6. NLM 172; Engl. trans. 174–5 (emended).

7. NLM 235–6; Engl. trans. 252 (emended).

8. Alfred Roller, *Die Bildnisse von Gustav Mahler* (Leipzig and Vienna 1922), 26.

9. See Constantin Floros, *Die geistige Welt Gustav Mahlers in systematischer Darstellung* (Wiesbaden 1977), 123–4.

10. On Fechner and his world of ideas, see Michael Heidelberger, *Die innere Seite der Natur: Gustav Theodor Fechners wissenschaftlich-philosophische Weltauffassung* (Frankfurt 1993).

11. Gustav Theodor Fechner, *Zend-Avesta*, ed. Friedrich Panzer (Wiesbaden n.d.), 180–1.

12. GMBA 148; Engl. trans. 117–18 (letter from Gustav Mahler to Alma Mahler, 2 April 1903).

13. GMBA 148; Engl. trans. 118 (letter from Gustav Mahler to Alma Mahler, 2 April 1903).

14. GMBA 386; Engl. trans. 324 (undated letter from Gustav Mahler to Alma Mahler, [20] June 1909).

15. BWGM 101; Engl. trans. 117.

16. Roller, *Die Bildnisse von Gustav Mahler* (note 8), 24.

17. NLM 103; Engl. trans. 91 (emended).

18. It is not possible to discuss Lotze's philosophy and cultural anthropology in adequate detail here. For the most recent and fullest account of his ideas, see Reinhardt Pester, *Hermann Lotze: Wege seines Denkens und Forschens. Ein Kapitel deutscher Philosophie und Wissenschaftsgeschichte im 19. Jahrhundert* (Würzburg 1997). On *Mikrokosmos*, see especially pp. 255–7.

19. Hermann Lotze, *Mikrokosmos* (Leipzig 1909), iii.51. See also Pester, *Hermann Lotze* (note 18), 269–71. Lotze's approach here is far more muted than that adopted by Fechner, whose divagations on the subject are markedly more discursive and mystical.

20. Alban Berg, *Briefe an seine Frau* (Munich and Vienna 1965), 175 (letter from Alban Berg to Helene Berg, 4 Aug. 1910). (This passage is not included in Bernard Grun's 1971 Engl. trans.)

21. GMBA 385–6; Engl. trans. 324 (undated letter from Gustav Mahler to Alma Mahler, [20] June 1909).

22. Johann Peter Eckermann, *Gespräche mit Goethe in den letzten Jahren seines Lebens* (Berlin and Weimar 1982), 345; trans. John Oxenford as *Conversations of Goethe with Eckermann and Soret* (London 1913), 443 (entry of 3 March 1830).

23. Hans Günter Ottenberg and Edith Zehm (eds), *Briefwechsel zwischen Goethe und Zelter in den Jahren 1799 bis 1832* (Munich 1991), i.981–2; trans. Arthur D. Coleridge as *Goethe's Letters to Zelter* (London 1892), 281–2 (letter from Goethe to Zelter, 19 March 1827).

24. Eckermann, *Gespräche mit Goethe* (note 22), 265; Engl. trans. 360 (entry of 4 Feb. 1829).

25. Eckermann, *Gespräche mit Goethe* (note 22), 412 (entry of 1 Sept. 1829).

26. BWGM 102; Engl. trans. 118–19.

27. Flodoard von Biedermann (ed.), *Goethes Ausgewählte Gespräche* (Leipzig 1912), 203–5 (entry of 25 Jan. 1813).
28. Johann Wolfgang von Goethe, *Faust*, ed. Albrecht Schöne (Frankfurt 1999), 784.
29. Jochen Schmidt, *Goethes Faust: Erster und zweiter Teil. Grundlagen – Werk – Wirkung* (Munich 1999), 288.
30. Schmidt, *Goethes Faust* (note 29), 289.
31. GMBA 389; Engl. trans. 327 (undated letter from Gustav Mahler to Alma Mahler, [22] June 1909).
32. Goethe, *Faust* (note 28), 788.
33. Friedrich Rückert, *Kindertodtenlieder*, ed. Hans Wollschläger (Frankfurt 1993), 303.
34. GMBA 91; Engl. trans. 67 (letter from Gustav Mahler to Alma Schindler, 14 Dec. 1901).
35. Richard Specht, *Gustav Mahler* (Berlin 1913), 52.

Chapter 25. The Sixth Symphony

1. GMB 318; Engl. trans. 277 (undated letter from Gustav Mahler to Richard Specht, [autumn 1904]).
2. AME 97; Engl. trans. 70.
3. NLM 187; Engl. trans. 193.
4. See Karl Heinz Füssl, NMF, xxvii (1992), 3–5 and Gastón Fournier-Facio, 'The "Correct" Order of the Middle Movements in Mahler's Sixth Symphony', *Discovering Mahler: Writings on Mahler, 1955–2005*, by Donald Mitchell (Woodbridge 2007), 633–47.
5. MHGM 135.
6. AME 97; Engl. trans. 70.
7. Thomas Mann, *Doktor Faustus* (Berlin and Frankfurt 1949), 775–6; trans. John E. Woods as *Doctor Faustus* (New York 1999), 515.
8. Michael Gielen and Paul Fiebig, *Mahler im Gespräch: Die zehn Sinfonien* (Stuttgart and Weimar 2002), 127.
9. Theodor W. Adorno, 'Dritter Mahler-Vortrag', *Gesammelte Schriften*, 20 vols (Frankfurt 1997), xviii.621–2.

Chapter 26. Opera Reform – Early Years of Marriage – Mahler's Compositional Method (1903–5)

1. Alfred Roller, 'Mahler und die Inszenierung', *Musikblätter des Anbruch*, ii (1920), 273.
2. See Brigitte Hamann, *Hitlers Wien* (Munich and Zurich 1996), 42–6; trans. Thomas Thornton as *Hitler's Vienna: A Dictator's Apprenticeship* (New York and Oxford 1999), 26–7. A complete chronicle of Vienna Court Opera performances during Mahler's years in the city is held by the IGMG and confirms all of Hamann's suppositions on this point.
3. HKBGM 135; Engl. trans. 219. The second part of this quotation is taken from the same document in Manfred Wagner, *Alfred Roller in seiner Zeit* (Salzburg and Vienna 1996), 71.
4. AME 80; Engl. trans. 54.
5. Roller's designs are reproduced in Wagner, *Alfred Roller in seiner Zeit* (note 3). The *Tristan* designs appear on p. 132.
6. Max Graf, *Die Wiener Oper* (Vienna and Frankfurt 1955), 163–5.
7. Hermann Bahr, *Tagebuch* (Berlin 1909), 38; Engl. trans. from HKBGM 238.
8. GMB 301; Engl. trans. 267–8 (undated letter from Gustav Mahler to Alfred Roller, [between 22 Feb. and 3 March 1904]).
9. HKBGM 171; Engl. trans. 235 (*Illustriertes Extrablatt*, Vienna, 9 Sept. 1903).
10. See the designs reproduced in Wagner, *Alfred Roller in seiner Zeit* (note 3), 134.
11. *Deutsches Volksblatt* (8 Oct. 1904), quoted by Wagner, *Alfred Roller in seiner Zeit* (note 3), 83.
12. Ludwig Hevesi quoted by Wagner, *Alfred Roller in seiner Zeit* (note 3), 90.
13. Roller, 'Mahler und die Inszenierung' (note 1), 274.
14. AME 47; Engl. trans. 22; see also GMBA 97; Engl. trans. 72 (undated letter from Gustav Mahler to Justine Mahler, [15 Dec. 1901]).

15. AMTB 747; Engl. trans. 464 (entry of 23 Dec. 1901).
16. AMTB 747; Engl. trans. 463 (entry of 22 Dec. 1901).
17. AMTB 747; Engl. trans. 463 (entry of 22 Dec. 1901).
18. AMTB 752; Engl. trans. 468 (entry of 16 Jan. 1902).
19. AME 49; Engl. trans. 25.
20. AMML 33; Engl. trans. 33.
21. AME 75; Engl. trans. 49.
22. AMML 33; Engl. trans. 33.
23. These dreams are described in AMML 35–6; not in the Engl. trans.
24. GMBA 138; Engl. trans. 109 (diary entry of 8 Jan. 1903).
25. GMBA 135; Engl. trans. 106 (diary entry of 10 July 1902).
26. GMBA 166; Engl. trans. 132 (undated letter from Gustav Mahler to Alma Mahler, [4 Sept. 1903]).
27. AMTB 731–2; Engl. trans. 449 (entry of 3 Dec. 1901).
28. AMTB 731; Engl. trans. 449 (entry of 3 Dec. 1901).
29. AMML 40; not in the Engl. trans.
30. AMML 48; not in the Engl. trans.
31. AMML 37–8; partially available in the Engl. trans. 34.
32. GMBA 254; Engl. trans. 212 (diary entry of 6 July 1905).
33. William Ritter quoted in GMBA 366–7; Engl. trans. 308.
34. AME 59; Engl. trans. 34.
35. NMF, vii (1980), 14.
36. AME 62; Engl. trans. 36.
37. GMFB 503–4; Engl. trans. 369–70 (undated letter from Gustav Mahler to Justine Mahler, [17 March 1902]).
38. AME 82; Engl. trans. 55–6.
39. GMFB 459–60; Engl. trans. 337 (undated letter from Justine Mahler to Emma Mahler, [third week of June 1900]); see also Herta Blaukopf, 'Villa Mahler am Wörthersee', *Gustav Mahler am Wörthersee* (Klagenfurt n.d.), 7. The present information on the villa at Maiernigg is based on Herta Blaukopf's account.
40. GMB 270; Engl. trans. 242 (letter from Gustav Mahler to Nina Spiegler, 18 Aug. 1900).
41. See Rudolf Stephan, *Gustav Mahler: II. Symphonie c-Moll* (Munich 1979).
42. NBL 27; Engl. trans. 32.
43. NBL 25; Engl. trans. 29.
44. NBL 26; Engl. trans. 30.
45. NBL 28; not in the Engl. trans.
46. This point is well illustrated by the list assembled by Rudolf Stephan (ed.) in *Gustav Mahler: Werk und Interpretation* (Cologne 1979).
47. NBL 29–30; partial trans. in Engl. trans. 34.
48. NBL 62; not in the Engl. trans.
49. This is the expression used by Stephan, *Gustav Mahler* (note 46), 63.
50. NBL 64; not in the Engl. trans.
51. This development is well documented by Eberhardt Klemm, 'Zur Geschichte der Fünften Sinfonie von Gustav Mahler', *Jahrbuch Peters 1979* (Leipzig 1980), 9–116.
52. GMB 304; Engl. trans. 270 (undated letter from Gustav Mahler to Emil Freund, [24–8 July 1903]).

Chapter 27. The Seventh Symphony

1. GMB 360; Engl. trans. 312 (undated letter from Gustav Mahler to Emil Gutmann, [early 1908]).
2. See Eberhardt Klemm, 'Zur Geschichte der Fünften Sinfonie von Gustav Mahler', *Jahrbuch Peters 1979* (Leipzig 1980), 51 (undated letter from Gustav Mahler to Peters, [5 Dec. 1907]).
3. AME 117; Engl. trans. 89.
4. Richard Specht, *Gustav Mahler* (Berlin 1913), 251.
5. Paul Bekker, *Gustav Mahlers Sinfonien* (Berlin 1921), 265.

6. TWAM 180–1; Engl. trans. 137.
7. MHGM 151.
8. Joseph von Eichendorff, *Werke in einem Band*, ed. Wolfdietrich Rasch (Munich 1955), 11–12.

Chapter 28. The Administrator – Contemporaries – Signs of Crisis (1905–7)

1. The most detailed account of Mahler's activities as director of the Vienna Court Opera is WMWO, esp. 149–56.
2. This satire was rediscovered by Willi Reich and published under the title 'Ein heiteres Dokument aus der Mahler-Zeit', *Österreichische Musikzeitschrift*, xix (1964), 26–8.
3. BWTV 183; Engl. trans. 152–3.
4. The caricature is reproduced by Gilbert Kaplan, *The Mahler Album* (New York and London 1995), no. 293, unfortunately without a source reference.
5. Paul Stefan, *Gustav Mahlers Erbe* (Munich 1908), 9.
6. WMWO 75–90, esp. 79.
7. NBL 146; Engl. trans. 138.
8. GMBA 146–7; Engl. trans. 116 (undated letter from Gustav Mahler to Alma Mahler, [1 April 1903]).
9. AME 63; Engl. trans. 37.
10. See Jens Malte Fischer, 'Hans Pfitzner: The Very German Fate of a Composer', *Music and Nazism*, ed. Michael H. Kater and Albrecht Riethmüller (Laaber 2003), 75–98; see also the comprehensive study by Sabine Busch, *Hans Pfitzner und der Nationalsozialismus* (Stuttgart 2001).
11. Hans Pfitzner, 'Eindrücke und Bilder meines Lebens', *Sämtliche Schriften*, ed. Bernhard Adamy (Tutzing 1987), 556–692, esp. 690–2.
12. GMBA 182–3; Engl. trans. 146 (undated letter from Gustav Mahler to Alma Mahler, [1 Feb. 1904]).
13. The relationship between Mahler and Strauss is documented by Herta Blaukopf's edition of their correspondence, GMRSB, which also includes a lengthy afterword.
14. GMB 205; Engl. trans. 200 (undated letter from Gustav Mahler to Max Marschalk, [4 Dec. 1896]).
15. Theodor W. Adorno, 'Richard Strauss', *Gesammelte Schriften*, 20 vols (Frankfurt 1997), xvi.565–6.
16. GMB 328; Engl. trans. 298 (undated letter from Gustav Mahler to Albert Neisser, [mid-Dec. 1905?]).
17. The court censor's decision is reproduced in WMWO 200–1; see WMWO 189–209 for the events surrounding plans to stage *Salome* in Vienna; and see GMRSB for the correspondence between Mahler and Strauss.
18. GMRSB 118; Engl. trans. 93 (letter from Richard Strauss to Gustav Mahler, 15 March 1906).
19. AME 53; Engl. trans. 28.
20. GMBA 129; Engl. trans. 100 (letter from Gustav Mahler to Alma Schindler, 31 Jan. 1902).
21. GMBA 266–7; Engl. trans. 222 (letter from Gustav Mahler to Alma Mahler, 8 Nov. 1905).
22. GMBA 279; Engl. trans. 233 (undated letter from Gustav Mahler to Alma Mahler, [22 May 1906]).
23. Arnold Schoenberg, *Letters*, ed. Erwin Stein (London 1974), 261 (undated letter from Arnold Schoenberg to Olin Downes, [mid-Dec. 1948]). (Schoenberg wrote in English.)
24. Schoenberg, *Letters* (note 23), 263–5 (undated letter from Arnold Schoenberg to Olin Downes, [Dec. 1948]).
25. AME 105; Engl. trans. 78.
26. This letter cannot have been written after the official concert on 14 Dec. 1904, as claimed by Hans Heinz Stuckenschmidt in his biography of Schoenberg (Zurich 1974), 95. The date was corrected in Humphrey Searle's Engl. trans. (London 1977), 103.
27. Stuckenschmidt, *Schönberg* (note 26), 95–6; Engl. trans. 103 (letter from Arnold Schoenberg to Gustav Mahler, 12 Dec. 1904).
28. AME 105; Engl. trans. 78.

29. AME 140; Engl. trans. 112.
30. Hanns Eisler, *Musik und Politik* (Leipzig 1973), 15.
31. Webern's views on Mahler may be found in Anton Webern, *Weg und Gestalt* (Zurich 1961), 15–17.
32. Webern, *Weg und Gestalt* (note 31), 19–21.
33. Theodor W. Adorno, 'Berg: Der Meister des kleinsten Übergangs', *Gesammelte Schriften* (note 15), xiii.359; trans. Juliane Brand and Christopher Hailey as *Alban Berg: Master of the Smallest Link* (Cambridge 1997), 28.
34. Alban Berg, *Briefe an seine Frau* (Munich and Vienna 1965), 238–9; trans. Bernard Grun as *Alban Berg: Letters to His Wife* (London 1971), 147–8 (emended) (undated letter from Alban Berg to Helene Berg, [autumn 1912?]).
35. Berg, *Briefe an seine Frau* (note 34), 483; Engl. trans. 298 (letter from Alban Berg to Helene Berg, 24 May 1922).
36. Adorno, 'Berg' (note 33), 352; Engl. trans. 22.
37. Schoenberg's Prague speech on Mahler is reproduced in Arnold Schönberg, *Stil und Gedanke: Aufsätze zur Musik* (Frankfurt 1976), 7–24. The English version that appears in *Style and Idea: Selected Writings of Arnold Schoenberg* (Berkeley 1984), 449–72, is the 1948 revision partially translated by Schoenberg himself and edited by Dika Newlin.
38. The complete version of the dedication is reproduced in Stuckenschmidt, *Schönberg* (note 26), 127–8; Engl. trans. 137–8.
39. NLM 200–1; Engl. trans. 208–10. The text of Bernhard Scharlitt's interview with Mahler was first published in the *Neue Freie Presse* on 25 May 1911 and reprinted in *Musikblätter des Anbruch*, ii (1920), 309–10.
40. This includes all of Mahler's conducting commitments in Vienna and is based on the statistics held by the IGMG that are also available online.
41. NLM 173–4; Engl. trans. 177.
42. NLM 214; Engl. trans. 225. Wellesz's 'Reminiscences of Mahler' first appeared in *The Score* on 28 Jan. 1961, 54–6.
43. Josef Bohuslav Foerster, *Der Pilger* (Prague 1955), 703; Engl. trans. from NLM 216–17 (emended).
44. GMBA 314; Engl. trans. 263.
45. The principal facts and documents relating to Mahler and the Netherlands have been collected by Eduard Reeser (ed.) in *Gustav Mahler und Holland: Briefe* (Vienna 1980).
46. Reeser, *Mahler und Holland* (note 45), 8.
47. Reeser, *Mahler und Holland* (note 45), 10.
48. GMBA 225; Engl. trans. 183 (undated letter from Gustav Mahler to Alma Mahler, [20 Oct. 1904]).
49. GMBA 225; Engl. trans. 184 (undated letter from Gustav Mahler to Alma Mahler, [21 Oct. 1904]).
50. GMBA 412; Engl. trans. 347 (undated letter from Gustav Mahler to Alma Mahler, [1 Oct. 1909]).
51. Reeser, *Mahler und Holland* (note 45), 29.
52. Reeser, *Mahler und Holland* (note 45), 108–10.
53. See HKBGM 173–4; Engl. trans. 236.
54. WMWO 172–88.
55. Richard Specht, *Gustav Mahler* (Berlin 1913), 24–5.
56. NLM 118–19; Engl. trans. 110–11 (emended).
57. HKBGM 184; Engl. trans. 243.
58. Richard Specht, 'Mahlers Feinde', *Musikblätter des Anbruch*, ii (1920), 278–87.
59. HKBGM 190; Engl. trans. 246.
60. Paul Stauber, *Vom Kriegsschauplatz der Wiener Hofoper: Das wahre Erbe Mahlers* (Vienna 1909), 46–7.
61. HKBGM 192; Engl. trans. 248.
62. IGMG Hauptmann 1/985 (copy of letter from Gustav Mahler to Gerhart Hauptmann, 7 March 1904).
63. Arthur Schnitzler's contribution to Paul Stefan (ed.), *Gustav Mahler: Ein Bild seiner Persönlichkeit in Widmungen* (Munich 1910), 67. The first version of this tribute and

Schnitzler's letter to Stefan are reproduced in Arthur Schnitzler, *Briefe 1875–1912* (Frankfurt 1981), 625–7 and 955–6.

64. See Friedrich Pfäfflin, 'Karl Kraus und Arnold Schönberg: Fragmente einer Beziehung', *Karl Kraus* (Munich 1975), 127–9.

65. Karl Kraus, *Die Fackel*, xxxiii (March 1932), 8.

Chapter 29. The Eighth Symphony

1. GMB 335; Engl. trans. 294 (undated letter from Gustav Mahler to Willem Mengelberg, [18? Aug. 1906]).

2. GMBA 413; Engl. trans. 348 (undated letter from Gustav Mahler to Alma Mahler, [1 Oct. 1909]).

3. GMBA 431–2; Engl. trans. 363 (undated letter from Gustav Mahler to Alma Mahler, [20 June 1910]).

4. GMBA 424; Engl. trans. 356–7 (undated letter from Gustav Mahler to Alma Mahler, [8 June 1910]).

5. Hans Mayer, 'Musik und Literatur', *Gustav Mahler*, ed. Rainer Wunderlich Verlag (Tübingen 1966), 142–56, esp. 145–51.

6. Dieter Borchmeyer, 'Gustav Mahlers Goethe und Goethes Heiliger Geist: Marginalie zur *Achten Symphonie* aus aktuellem Anlaß', NMF, xxxii (1994), 18–20.

7. Johann Wolfgang von Goethe, *Sämtliche Werke nach Epochen seines Schaffens*, ed. Karl Richter and others, 33 vols (Munich 1985–98), xvii.749 ('Maximen und Reflexionen', no. 762).

8. Richard Specht (1913), quoted in: *Gustav Mahler, VIII. Symphony. Critical edition* (Universal Edition, Vienna 1977), Preface by Karl Heinz Füssl (unpaginated).

9. Hans and Rosaleen Moldenhauer, *Anton von Webern* (London 1978), 135.

10. Goethe, *Sämtliche Werke* (note 7), xvii.749 ('Maximen und Reflexionen', no. 1202).

11. TWAM 182–3; Engl. trans. 138–9.

12. GMBA 388–90; Engl. trans. 326–8 (letter from Gustav Mahler to Alma Mahler, 22(?) June 1909).

13. Christian Wildhagen's otherwise impressive analysis, *Die 'Achte Symphonie' von Gustav Mahler: Konzeption einer universalen Symphonik* (Frankfurt 2000), tends in the same direction.

14. GMBA 424; Engl. trans. 356 (undated letter from Gustav Mahler to Alma Mahler, [8 June 1910]).

Chapter 30. *Annus Terribilis* (1907)

1. Richard Wagner, 'Das Wiener Hof-Operntheater', *Gesammelte Schriften und Dichtungen*, 10 vols (Leipzig 4/1907), vii.272–95, esp. 275; trans. William Ashton Ellis as *Richard Wagner's Prose Works*, 8 vols (London 1892–9, R1993–5), iii.361–86, esp. 366.

2. Ludwig Karpath, *Begegnung mit dem Genius* (Vienna and Leipzig 1934), 184–5.

3. Richard Specht, 'Mahlers Feinde', *Musikblätter des Anbruch*, ii/7–8 (1920), 285.

4. GMB 343; Engl. trans. 300 (undated letter from Gustav Mahler to Julius von Weis-Osborn, [April 1907]).

5. See Juliane Wandel, *Die Rezeption der Symphonien Gustav Mahlers zu Lebzeiten des Komponisten* (Frankfurt 1999), 120–2. The following quotations are all taken from this study.

6. AME 145; Engl. trans. 117.

7. Manfred Wagner, *Alfred Roller in seiner Zeit* (Salzburg and Vienna 1996), 105 (letter from Alfred Roller to his wife, 29 April 1907).

8. GMB 343; Engl. trans. 301 (undated letter from Gustav Mahler to Arnold Berliner, [17 June 1907]).

9. Paul Stefan, *Das Grab in Wien: Eine Chronik 1903–1911* (Berlin 1913), 79–80.

10. Quoted in WMWO 260–1.

11. See HKBGM 193–4; Engl. trans. 248.

12. Karpath, *Begegnung mit dem Genius* (note 2), 183–5.

13. Julius Korngold in the *Neue Freie Presse* of 4 June 1907, quoted in WMWO 262–7.
14. WMWO 272–5.
15. AME (1949) 405–7; Engl. trans. 300–1 (undated letter from Gustav Mahler to Alfred Montenuovo, [early summer 1907]).
16. AME (1949), 407–8; Engl. trans. 301–2 (letter from Alfred Montenuovo to Gustav Mahler, 10 Aug. 1907).
17. HKBGM 195; Engl. trans. 249.
18. GMB 85; Engl. trans. 107 (undated letter from Gustav Mahler to Friedrich Löhr, [18 Feb. 1887]).
19. GMUB 105–6; Engl. trans. 96–7 (undated letter from Gustav Mahler to Lilli Lehmann, [late April/early May 1898]). (The discovery of a copy of a letter among Alma Mahler's papers at the University of Pennsylvania provides a more accurate date than was available to Herta Blaukopf at the time when the German edition of this volume was published in 1983.)
20. RMA 22.
21. RMA 30–3.
22. GMB 344; Engl. trans. 301 (letter from Gustav Mahler to Arnold Berliner, 4 July 1907).
23. GMBA 324–5; Engl. trans. 272–3 (undated letter from Gustav Mahler to Alma Mahler, [18 July 1907]).
24. Bruno Walter, *Briefe 1894–1962* (Frankfurt 1969), 95.
25. GMB 367–8; Engl. trans. 324 (emended) (letter from Gustav Mahler to Bruno Walter, 18 July 1908).
26. Hans Bethge, *Die Chinesische Flöte* (Leipzig 1907), 103.
27. See GMBA 360; not in the Engl. trans.
28. GMBA 344; Engl. trans. 290 (undated letter from Gustav Mahler to Alma Mahler, [30 Oct. 1907]). According to Alma, the phrase 'Pui Kaiki' ('Yuck') was Gucki's attempt at the expression of disgust, 'Pfui Teufel').
29. WMWO 213; Engl. trans. from Kurt Blaukopf (ed.), *Mahler: A Documentary Study*, trans. Paul Baker and others (New York and Toronto 1976), 250–1 (emended).
30. AME (1949), 421–6; Engl. trans. 310–13, esp. 311 (letter from Alfred Roller to Gustav Mahler, 22 Jan. 1908).
31. A facsimile of this document appears in GMBA 351; not in the Engl. trans.
32. AME 155–6; Engl. trans. 126.

Chapter 31. *Das Lied von der Erde*

1. GMB 371; Engl. trans. 326 (undated letter from Gustav Mahler to Bruno Walter, [early Sept. 1908]).
2. See Eberhard Bethge, 'Hans Bethge und das *Lied von der Erde*', NMF xxxv (1996), 18–20.
3. The two most comprehensive accounts of the work are Hermann Danuser's outstanding study (Munich 1986) and Stephen E. Hefling's Cambridge Music Handbook (Cambridge 2000). See also HDMZ 204–43.
4. HDMZ 204.
5. See the excellent analysis in HDMZ 212–43.

Chapter 32. Starting Afresh: New York (1908–11)

1. NLM 220; Engl. original 232.
2. Peter Brook, *Threads of Time: A Memoir* (London 1998), 84–5.
3. AME 157; Engl. trans. 129.
4. GMB 348; Engl. trans. 309 (letter from Gustav Mahler to Alfred Roller, 20 Jan. 1908).
5. GMB 356; Engl. trans. 317 (letter from Gustav Mahler to Alfred Roller, 27 Feb. 1908).
6. GMB 355–6; Engl. trans. 314 (undated letter from Gustav Mahler to Willem Mengelberg, [24 Feb. 1908]). The final sentence is missing from the Engl. trans.
7. RMA 82 (letter from Gustav Mahler to Carl Moll, 16 Feb. 1908).
8. RMA 82 (letter from Gustav Mahler to Carl Moll, 16 Feb. 1908).

9. RMA 102 (letter from Kuhn, Loeb & Co. to Gustav Mahler, 18 March 1908).
10. GMB 361; Engl. trans. 319 (emended) (undated letter from Gustav Mahler to Anna Moll, [March 1908]).
11. *Bruckmanns Illustrierte Reiseführer: Toblach und das Ampezzo-Thal* (Munich n.d.), 6.
12. GMB 365; Engl. trans. 322 (undated letter from Gustav Mahler to Bruno Walter, [summer 1908]).
13. AME (1949) 446–8; Engl. trans. 325–6 (letter from Arnold Schoenberg to Gustav Mahler, 29 Dec. 1909).
14. RMA 151 (letter from Andreas Dippel to Gustav Mahler, 9 July 1908).
15. AME (1949) 431; Engl. trans. 316–17 (undated letter from Gustav Mahler to Andreas Dippel, [July(?) 1908]).
16. BWTV 361; Engl. trans. 306.
17. Harvey Sachs, *Toscanini* (London 1978), 105.
18. GMUB 150–1; Engl. trans. 146 (undated letter from Gustav Mahler to William Ritter, [postmarked New York 8 Dec. 1908]).
19. The principal reviews are reproduced in RMA 181–3.
20. GMB 374–5; Engl. trans. 329–30 (undated letter from Gustav Mahler to Bruno Walter, early 1909]).
21. GMBA 379; Engl. trans. 318 (letter from Gustav Mahler to Alma Mahler, 13 June 1909). The 'joy and happiness' mentioned by Mahler refer to Löhr's announcement of the birth of a son; the quotation is adapted from Ferdinand Freiligrath's poem 'Der Liebe Dauer'.
22. HKBGM 216; Engl. trans. 259.
23. GMB 426; Engl. trans. 371 (undated letter from Gustav Mahler to Anna Moll, Jan./Feb. 1911]).
24. GMB 381; Engl. trans. 333 (undated letter from Gustav Mahler to Carl Moll, [10 March 1909]).
25. Alma's previously unpublished diary entry quoted by Jonathan Carr, *The Real Mahler* (London 1997), 154.
26. AME 181; Engl. trans. 151.
27. AME 181; Engl. trans. 151.
28. GMB 386; Engl. trans. 339 (undated letter from Gustav Mahler to Anna Moll, [summer 1909]).
29. NLM 235–6; Engl. trans. (emended) 251–2.
30. Excerpts from William Malloch's 'Mahlerthon' currently available from Sony Classical on *Bernstein/Mahler: The Complete Symphonies* (88697-45369-2).
31. GMB 396; Engl. trans. 346 (undated letter from Gustav Mahler to Bruno Walter, [18 or 19 Dec. 1909]).
32. GMB 396; Engl. trans. 346 (undated letter from Gustav Mahler to Bruno Walter, [18 or 19 Dec. 1909]).
33. GMB 397; Engl. trans. 347 (undated letter from Gustav Mahler to Bruno Walter, [18 or 19 Dec. 1909]).
34. GMB 401; Engl. trans. 350 (letter from Gustav Mahler to Alfred Roller, 6 Jan. 1910).
35. GMB 398–400; Engl. trans. 348–9 (letter from Gustav Mahler to Guido Adler, 1 Jan. 1910).
36. Ferruccio Busoni, *Briefe an seine Frau*, ed. Friedrich Schnapp (Erlenbach-Zurich and Leipzig 1935); trans. Rosamond Ley as *Ferruccio Busoni: Letters to his Wife* (London 1938), 161 (letter from Ferruccio Busoni to his wife, 12 March 1910).
37. RMA 333 (Henderson's review in the *New York Sun*, 27 Jan. 1910).

Chapter 33. The Ninth Symphony

1. GMB 392; Engl. trans. 341 (undated letter from Gustav Mahler to Bruno Walter, [Aug. 1909]).
2. Paul Bekker, *Gustav Mahlers Sinfonien* (Berlin 1921), 340.
3. GMB 385; Engl. trans. 337 (undated letter from Gustav Mahler to Arnold Berliner, [20 June 1909]).
4. GMBA 402–3; Engl. trans. 388–9 (undated letter from Gustav Mahler to Alma Mahler, [8 July 1909]).

5. Hugo von Hofmannsthal, 'Ein Brief', *Gesammelte Werke in zehn Einzelbänden*, ed. Bernd Schoeller (Frankfurt 1979–80), vii.461–71.
6. Hofmannsthal, 'Ein Brief' (note 5), vii.471.
7. This is the line of argument adopted by Friedhelm Krummacher in his outstanding analysis of this oft-examined movement, 'Struktur und Auflösung: Über den Kopfsatz aus Mahlers IX. Symphonie', *Gustav Mahler*, ed. Hermann Danuser (Darmstadt 1992), 300–23.
8. GMB 375; Engl. trans. 329 (undated letter from Gustav Mahler to Bruno Walter, [early 1909]).
9. HEMM 251–3.
10. HEMM 253.
11. George Steiner, *Real Presences* (London 1989), 226.

Chapter 34. Crisis and Culmination (1910)

1. Roger Nichols, *Debussy Remembered* (London 1992), 210.
2. GMUB 85; Engl. trans. 84 (letter from Gustav Mahler to Emil Gutmann, 31 Jan. 1911).
3. AMML 44; this passage is not included in the Engl. trans.; and AME 201; Engl. trans. 173.
4. AME 203; Engl. trans. 175.
5. Jonathan Carr, *The Real Mahler* (London 1997), 143.
6. Carr, *The Real Mahler* (note 5), 200.
7. The standard biography of Gropius is Reginald Isaacs's two-volume *Walter Gropius: Der Mensch und sein Werk* (Berlin 1983–4). Unfortunately, the posthumously published American edition, which appeared in Boston in 1991 under the title *Gropius: An Illustrated Biography of the Creator of the Bauhaus*, is compromised by three shortcomings. First, the text was cut by around a third; second, the translations from the German originals are often alarmingly inaccurate; and, third, a number of the documents relating to the affair between Gropius and Alma are wrongly dated, a failing that also affects the German edition. For the correct dates, see Jörg Rothkamm, 'Wann entstand Mahlers Zehnte Symphonie? Ein Beitrag zur Biographie und Werkdeutung', *Gustav Mahler durchgesetzt?*, ed. Heinz-Klaus Metzger and Rainer Riehn (Munich 1999), 100–22 (= Musik-Konzepte 106). Writings on Gropius and Alma that predate Isaacs's study are compromised by their failure to take account of these decisive documents. This is a failure that also affects Karen Monson's biography of Alma.
8. Isaacs, *Walter Gropius* (note 7), i.447 n.118; not in the Engl. trans.
9. GMBA 423; Engl. trans. 355 (undated letter from Gustav Mahler to Alma Mahler, [6 June 1910]).
10. GMBA 432; Engl. trans. 364 (undated letter from Gustav Mahler to Alma Mahler, [21 June 1910]).
11. GMB 410; Engl. trans. 359 (undated letter from Gustav Mahler to Anna Moll, [c. 20 June 1910]).
12. Copy of undated letter from Gustav Mahler to Hugo von Hofmannsthal in the Egon Wellesz Collection, Lincoln College, Oxford, F 13 Wellesz 1397 (c. 1907).
13. Paul Stefan (ed.), *Gustav Mahler: Ein Bild seiner Persönlichkeit in Widmungen* (Munich 1910), 16.
14. GMBA 442–3; this editorial passage was not included in the Engl. trans., but see DLG II iv.843.
15. See Isaacs, *Walter Gropius* (note 7), i.99; Engl. trans. 33–4 (emended); for the correct date see Rothkamm, 'Wann entstand?' (note 7), 108 (undated letter from Alma Mahler to Walter Gropius, [31 July 1910]).
16. Isaacs, *Walter Gropius* (note 7), i.99; Engl. trans. 34 (emended) (undated letter from Alma Mahler to Walter Gropius, [summer 1910]).
17. Isaacs, *Walter Gropius* (note 7), i.100; Engl. trans. 34 (emended) (undated letter from Alma Mahler to Walter Gropius, [summer 1910]).
18. AME 202; Engl. trans. 174.
19. Rothkamm, 'Wann entstand?' (note 7), 109 (undated draft of a letter from Walter Gropius to Gustav Mahler, [5 or 6 Aug. 1910]).

20. Isaacs, *Walter Gropius* (note 7), i.102; Engl. trans. 35 (emended) (letter from Alma Mahler to Walter Gropius, 27 Aug. 1910).
21. Isaacs, *Walter Gropius* (note 7), i.103; Engl. trans. 35 (emended) (letter from Alma Mahler to Walter Gropius, 27 Sept. 1910).
22. See GMBA 446–54; Engl. trans. 375–83. It is with some reluctance that the present translator questions a colleague as distinguished as Antony Beaumont, but the word 'Saitenspiel' that Mahler uses here and later surely means the instrument, not the act of playing on it. Many writers of the Romantic period, from Chamisso and Eichendorff to Grillparzer and Geibel, used 'Saitenspiel' in the sense of 'lyre'.
23. NLM 172; Engl. trans. 175.
24. NLM 181; Engl. trans. 182–4.
25. Ernst Kris, *Psychoanalytic Explorations in Art* (New York 1952); and *Selected Papers of Ernst Kris* (New Haven 1975), 263–71.
26. AME 204; Engl. trans. 176.
27. See Susanne Rode-Breymann, *Die Komponistin Alma Mahler-Werfel* (Hanover 1999) and Jörg Rothkamm, 'Wer komponierte die unter Alma Mahlers Namen veröffentlichten Lieder? Unbekannte Briefe der Komponistin zur Revision ihrer Werke im Jahre 1910', *Die Musikforschung*, liii (2000), 432–45.
28. Rothkamm, 'Wer komponierte?' (note 27), 445.
29. Rothkamm, 'Wer komponierte?' (note 27), 445 (letter from Alma Mahler to Walter Gropius, 16 Nov. 1910).
30. Rothkamm, 'Wer komponierte?' (note 27), 435 n.28 (letter from Alma Mahler to Walter Gropius, 10 Aug. 1910).
31. Hans Wollschläger, 'Scharf angeschlossener Kettenschmerz', *Frankfurter Allgemeine Zeitung* (5 Dec. 1995), L 9.
32. Carr, *The Real Mahler* (note 5), 219.
33. Hartmut Schaefer, 'Die Musikautographen von Gustav Mahler', *Gustav Mahler: Briefe und Musikautographen aus den Moldenhauer-Archiven in der Bayerischen Staatsbibliothek* (Munich 2003), 216.
34. Michael Gielen and Paul Fiebig, *Mahler im Gespräch: Die zehn Sinfonien* (Stuttgart and Weimar 2002), 212.
35. Elias Canetti, *The Play of the Eyes*, trans. Ralph Manheim (London 1990), 51–2.
36. BWGM 53–4; Engl. trans. 61–2.
37. Sigmund Freud, 'Leonardo da Vinci and a Memory of his Childhood', *The Standard Edition of the Complete Psychological Works of Sigmund Freud*, ed. James Strachey, 24 vols (London 2001), xi.57–137.
38. BWTV 213; Engl. trans. 181.
39. Theodor Reik, *The Haunting Melody* (New York 1953), 342–3 (letter from Sigmund Freud to Theodor Reik, 4 Jan. 1935).
40. Ernest Jones, *Sigmund Freud: Life and Work*, 2nd edn, 3 vols (London 1956–8), ii.89.
41. AME 203–4; Engl. trans. 175.
42. Sigmund Freud, 'A Special Type of Choice of Object Made by Men' and 'On the Universal Tendency to Debasement in the Sphere of Love', *The Penguin Freud Library*, ed. James Strachey, 15 vols (Harmondsworth 1991), vii.227–42 and 243–60.
43. AME 54; Engl. trans. 29.
44. Freud, 'A Special Type of Choice' (note 42), vii.235.
45. AME 203; Engl. trans. 175.
46. Freud, 'On the Universal Tendency' (note 42), vii.251.
47. GMBA 452; Engl. trans. 381 (undated poem from Gustav Mahler to Alma Mahler, [27 Aug. 1910]).
48. *Music, Continental Manuscripts and Printed Books* (London 1985) (Sotheby's catalogue for auction on 9–10 May 1985), Lots 142 and 143. Freud's invoice of 23 May 1911 was auctioned again in New York on 17 June 1992, when the reserve was $12,000–18,000; see *Fine Books and Manuscripts* (17 and 18 June 1992), Lot 29. The receipt is dated 24 Oct. 1911.
49. GMBA 457–8; Engl. trans. 387 (undated letter from Gustav Mahler to Alma Mahler, [5 Sept. 1910]).

50. Peter Heyworth, *Conversations with Klemperer* (London 1973), 34.
51. BWGM 51–2; Engl. trans. 58–9. The two works referred to here are *Das Lied von der Erde* and the Ninth Symphony, which Walter introduced to audiences in Munich and Vienna in 1911 and 1912 respectively.
52. Thomas Mann, *Briefe 1889–1936* (Frankfurt 1979), 88; Engl. trans. from AME 342 (undated letter from Thomas Mann to Gustav Mahler, [Sept. 1910]).
53. AME 210; Engl. trans. 182.
54. Isaacs, *Walter Gropius* (note 7), i.104; Engl. trans. 35 (emended) (letter from Alma Mahler to Walter Gropius, 12 Oct. 1910).

Chapter 35. The Fragmentary Tenth Symphony

1. For an analysis of the whole work see Jörg Rothkamm, *Gustav Mahlers Zehnte Symphonie: Entstehung, Analyse, Rezeption* (Frankfurt am Main and New York 2003).
2. See the detailed account by Jörg Rothkamm, 'Wann entstand Mahlers Zehnte Symphonie? Ein Beitrag zur Biographie und Werkdeutung', *Gustav Mahler durchgesetzt?*, ed. Heinz-Klaus Metzger and Rainer Riehn (Munich 1999), 100–22 (= Musik-Konzepte 106). Rothkamm has also examined the performing edition of Deryck Cooke and Berthold Goldschmidt, *Berthold Goldschmidt and Gustav Mahler: Zur Entstehung von Deryck Cookes Konzertfassung der X. Symphonie* (Hamburg 2000).
3. This thesis is also advanced by Jörg Rothkamm in his otherwise convincing account of the work in *Gustav Mahlers Zehnte Symphonie* (note 1). See also his analysis of the symphony in Renate Ulm (ed.), *Gustav Mahlers Symphonien: Entstehung – Deutung – Wirkung* (Munich and Kassel 2001), 302–11. For an examination of the latest state of research on the sketches of the Tenth Symphony, see Hartmut Schaefer, *Gustav Mahler: Briefe und Musikautographen aus den Moldenhauer-Archiven in der Bayerischen Staatsbibliothek* (Munich 2003), 190–225.
4. Theodor W. Adorno, 'Fragment als Graphik: Zur Neuausgabe von Mahlers Zehnter Symphonie', *Gesammelte Schriften*, 20 vols (Frankfurt 1997), xviii.253.

Chapter 36. 'My heart is weary' – The Farewell

1. Jean Paul, 'Die unsichtbare Loge', Jean Paul, *Sämtliche Werke*, ed. Norbert Miller (Munich and Vienna 1987), i/3422.
2. H. C. Robbins Landon, *Beethoven: Sein Leben und seine Welt in zeitgenössischen Bildern und Texten* (Zurich 1970), 391; Engl. trans. (London 1992), 233. (Hüttenbrenner's report first appeared in the Graz *Tagespost* on 23 Oct. 1868.)
3. Robbins Landon, *Beethoven* (note 2), 390; Engl. trans. 232. (Wawruch's account first appeared in the *Neue Zeitschrift für Musik* on 12 June 1843.)
4. Wolfgang Hildesheimer, *Mozart* (Frankfurt 1980), 370; trans. Marion Faber as *Mozart* (New York 1982), 359.
5. AME 230; Engl. trans. 201.
6. BWGM 57; Engl. trans. 63.
7. NLM 284; Engl. trans. 313–14.
8. AME 230; Engl. trans. 201.
9. GMB 367; Engl. trans. 375 (letter from Gustav Mahler to Bruno Walter, 18 July 1908).
10. Cliff Eisen (ed.), *Wolfgang Amadeus Mozart: A Life in Letters*, trans. Stewart Spencer (London 2006), 527 (letter from Wolfgang Amadeus Mozart to Leopold Mozart, 4 April 1787).
11. Gilbert Kaplan (ed.), *The Mahler Album* (New York and London 1995), plates 126–9 and 137–40. It may be added in passing that the figure identified by Thomas Mann's brother-in-law, Klaus Pringsheim, as his brother-in-law is more likely to be William Ritter.
12. NLM 275; Engl. trans. 301–2 (emended).
13. GMB 423; Engl. trans. 369 (undated letter from Gustav Mahler to Emil Freund, [21 Nov. 1910]).
14. GMB 425; Engl. trans. 370 (undated letter from Gustav Mahler to Emil Gutmann, [Dec. 1910–Jan. 1911]).

15. NLM 265–8; Engl. original 288–93.
16. See the detailed summary of Mahler's last season in RMA 373–7.
17. Reginald Isaacs, *Walter Gropius: Der Mensch und sein Werk*, 2 vols (Berlin 1983–4), i.105; not in the Engl. trans. (letter from Alma Mahler to Walter Gropius, 8 Nov. 1910).
18. Isaacs, *Walter Gropius* (note 17), i.105; Engl. trans. (Boston 1991), 36 (emended) (letter from Anna Moll to Walter Gropius, 13 Nov. 1910).
19. AME 214; Engl. trans. 186.
20. NLM 250–5; Engl. trans. 274–8.
21. AME 219; Engl. trans. 190.
22. DLG II iv.1230.
23. AME 227–8; Engl. trans. 198.
24. AME 221; Engl. trans. 192.
25. NLM 274; Engl. trans. 301.
26. AME 225; Engl. trans. 195–6. Here he is described only as a 'young Austrian', who remained unidentified under the partial publication of the uncensored version of Alma's reminiscences in DLG II.
27. Ferruccio Busoni, *Briefe an Henri, Katharina und Egon Petri* (Wilhelmshaven 1999), 146.
28. NLM 278; Engl. trans. 306.
29. AME 226; Engl. trans. 197.
30. AME 226; Engl. trans. 197.
31. BWGM 55; Engl. trans. 62–3.
32. AME 228; Engl. trans. 198.
33. Karl Kraus, 'Der Ankläger', *Die Fackel* (May 1911), 7.
34. NLM 283; Engl. trans. 312 (emended).
35. AME 230; Engl. trans. 200.
36. NLM 255; Engl. trans. 278.
37. Gustav Theodor Fechner, *Zend-Avesta: Gedanken über die Dinge des Himmels und des Jenseits vom Standpunkte der Naturbetrachtung*, ed. Max Fischer (Leipzig 1922), 242–3. Fechner's book first appeared in 1851.
38. Eduard von Hartmann, *Das Problem des Lebens* (Bad Sachsa im Harz 1906), 289.
39. Hartmann, *Das Problem des Lebens* (note 38), 309.
40. Hartmann, *Das Problem des Lebens* (note 38), 309.
41. GMBA 385–6; Engl. trans. 324 (undated letter from Gustav Mahler to Alma Mahler, [?20 June 1909]).
42. Johann Peter Eckermann, *Gespräche mit Goethe in den letzten Jahren seines Lebens* (Berlin and Weimar 1982), 331–3; trans. John Oxenford as *Conversations of Goethe with Eckermann and Soret* (London 1913), 423–4 (entry of 10 Jan. 1830).
43. *Neues Wiener Tagblatt* (20 May 1911), reproduced in GMBA 468; Engl. trans. 392.
44. GMBA 486; not in the Engl. trans. (Mahler's last will and testament of 27 April 1904).
45. Josef Bohuslav Foerster, *Der Pilger* (Prague 1955), 706.
46. Foerster, *Der Pilger* (note 45), 706.
47. Hugo von Hofmannsthal/Ottonie Gräfin Degenfeld, *Briefwechsel*, ed. Marie Therese Miller-Degenfeld (Frankfurt 1974), 142–4, esp. 144 (letter from Hugo von Hofmannsthal to Ottonie Degenfeld, 26 May 1911).
48. Jean Paul, *Sämtliche Werke*, (note 1), i/3.800–1. Bruno Walter was the first to quote this passage in the context of Mahler's death. There is no more appropriate epitaph than this; see BWTV 241; Engl. trans. 207.

Chapter 37. Mahler and Posterity

1. NBL 186; Engl. trans. 166. (The 'friend' is not identified and appears not to be Natalie Bauer-Lechner herself.)
2. GMBA 129; Engl. trans. 100 (emended) (undated letter from Gustav Mahler to Alma Mahler, [31 Jan. 1902]).
3. GMB 331; Engl. trans. 290–1 (undated letter from Gustav Mahler to Josef Reitler, [June 1906]).

4. GMBA 220–1; Engl. trans. 179 (undated letter from Gustav Mahler to Alma Mahler, [14 Oct. 1904]).

5. *Alldeutsches Tagblatt* (31 May 1911), quoted in Juliane Wandel, *Die Rezeption der Symphonien Gustav Mahlers zu Lebzeiten des Komponisten* (Frankfurt 1999), 233. This study is admirably well documented and allows a deep insight into the battles surrounding Mahler, a subject treated only cursorily in the present biography.

6. Gerhard Scheit and Wilhelm Svoboda, *Feindbild Gustav Mahler: Zur antisemitischen Abwehr der Moderne in Österreich* (Vienna 2002), 77–8.

7. Ernst Bloch, *Geist der Utopie* (first published 1918) (Frankfurt 1973), 89–90.

8. Herta Blaukopf, 'Amsterdam 1920: Sechs Zeitzeugen feiern Mahler', *Muziek & Wetenschap*, v (1995), 347–9.

9. C. Rudolf Mengelberg (ed.), *Das Mahler-Fest Amsterdam Mai 1920* (Vienna and Leipzig 1920); and Donald Mitchell (ed.), *Gustav Mahler: The World Listens* (Haarlem 1995).

10. Adolf Weißmann, *Die Musik in der Weltkrise* (Stuttgart and Berlin 1922), 104.

11. Weißmann, *Die Musik* (note 10), 106.

12. Weißmann, *Die Musik* (note 10), 117.

13. Christa Maria Rock and Hans Brückner (eds), *Das musikalische Juden-ABC* (Munich 1935), 56.

14. See Scheit and Svoboda, *Feindbild Gustav Mahler* (note 6), 92–4.

15. Wilhelm Furtwängler, *Aufzeichnungen 1924–1954* (Wiesbaden 1980), 186; trans. Shaun Whiteside as *Notebooks 1924–54* (London 1995), 114.

16. Wolfgang Stresemann, '*Ein seltsamer Mann . . .*' *Erinnerungen an Herbert von Karajan* (Frankfurt and Berlin 1990), 234–6.

17. Karl Heinz Ruppel, concert review in the *Süddeutsche Zeitung* (4 Oct. 1950), 3.

18. Erich Limmert, concert review in the *Hannoversche Allgemeine Zeitung* (8 May 1951).

19. Kurt Blaukopf, *Gustav Mahler oder der Zeitgenosse der Zukunft* (Munich 1980), 273–4; trans. Inge Goodwin as *Gustav Mahler* (London 1973), 253. (The Engl. trans. is based on the first German-language edition of 1969.)

20. Wolfgang Rihm, *Ausgesprochen: Schriften und Gespräche*, 2 vols (Winterthur 1997), i.237–9.

Select Bibliography

The literature on Mahler has grown to the point where it is no longer possible to retain an accurate overview of it, although Simon Namenwirth attempted to do so in 1987 (see Bibliography). More recent writings are covered by the *Nachrichten zur Mahler-Forschung* (see Journals), which at least for German speakers remains the most useful pointer to new publications, in many cases also including a review. What follows is by necessity a mere fraction of what is available.

Works

Gustav Mahler: Sämtliche Werke. Kritische Gesamtausgabe, published by the Internationale Gustav Mahler Gesellschaft of Vienna in association with Bote & Bock, C. F. Peters, Schott Musik International, Universal Edition and Josef Weinberger. (For a full list of contents, see www.gustav-mahler.org)

Bibliography

Filler, Susan M. *Gustav and Alma Mahler: A Research and Information Guide*, 2nd edn (New York and London 2008)
Namenwirth, Simon Michael. *Gustav Mahler: A Critical Bibliography*, 3 vols (Wiesbaden 1987)

Journals

Nachrichten zur Mahler-Forschung, ed. Internationale Gustav Mahler Gesellschaft of Vienna (published approximately twice a year since 1976; unfortunately the British Union Catalogue of Music Periodicals lists no complete sets in Great Britain)

Iconographical Studies

Kaplan, Gilbert (ed.). *The Mahler Album* (New York and London 1995; rev. edn New York and London 2011)
Roller, Alfred. *Die Bildnisse von Gustav Mahler* (Leipzig and Vienna 1922)

Discographies

Fülöp, Peter (ed.). *Mahler Discography* (New York 1995; rev. edn Toronto 2010)
Smoley, Lewis. *The Symphonies of Gustav Mahler: A Critical Discography* (Westport 1986)
——. *Gustav Mahler's Symphonies. Critical Commentary on Recordings since 1986* (Westport 2000)

Handbooks

Barham, Jeremy (ed.). *The Cambridge Companion to Mahler* (Cambridge 2007)
Mitchell, Donald and Andrew Nicholson (eds). *The Mahler Companion*, 2nd edn (Oxford 2002)
Sponheuer, Bernd and Wolfram Steinbeck (eds). *Mahler Handbuch* (Stuttgart 2010)

Documentation

Blaukopf, Herta and Kurt (eds). *Gustav Mahler: Leben und Werk in Zeugnissen der Zeit* (Stuttgart 1994) (this is a revised edition of the following entry, but with the plates removed)
Blaukopf, Kurt (ed.). *Mahler: Sein Leben, sein Werk und seine Welt in zeitgenössischen Bildern und Texten* (Vienna 1976); trans. Paul Baker and others as *Mahler: A Documentary Study* (New York and Toronto 1976)
Brenner, Helmut and Reinhold Kubik. *Mahlers Welt: Die Orte seines Lebens* (Salzburg and Vienna 2011)
Dvořák, Petr (ed.). *Počátek cesty: Gustav Mahler a Jihlava v archivních pramenech/Journey's Beginning: Gustav Mahler and Jihlava in Written Sources* (Jihlava 2000) (this invaluable collection of documents is unfortunately rendered unusable by the poor Engl. trans.)
Karbusicky, Vladimir. *Mahler in Hamburg: Chronik einer Freundschaft* (Hamburg 1996)
Klemm, Eberhardt. 'Zur Geschichte der Fünften Sinfonie von Gustav Mahler', *Jahrbuch Peters 1979* (Leipzig 1980), 9–116
Klukanová, Ludmila. *Jihlava Gustavu Mahlerovi* (Jihlava 2000)
Kuna, Milan (ed.). *Gustav Mahler a Praha/Gustav Mahler und Prag: Zur 110. Wiederkehr seines Wirkens in Prag 1885/1886* (Prague 1996) (contains two articles in Czech, with German translations, by Erich Steinhard and Jitka Ludvová)
Lebrecht, Norman. *Mahler Remembered* (London 1987); trans. into German as *Gustav Mahler im Spiegel seiner Zeit* (Zurich and Sankt Gallen 1990)
Martner, Kurt. *Mahler's Concerts* (London 2010)
Meylan, Claude (ed.). *William Ritter: Chevalier de Gustav Mahler. Écrits, correspondance, documents* (Berne 2000)
Reeser, Eduard (ed.). *Gustav Mahler und Holland: Briefe* (Vienna 1980)
Reilly, Edward R. (ed.). *Gustav Mahler and Guido Adler: Records of a Friendship* (Cambridge 1982); trans. into German as *Gustav Mahler und Guido Adler: Zur Geschichte einer Freundschaft* (Vienna 1978)
Roman, Zoltan. *Gustav Mahler's American Years (1907–1911): A Documentary History* (Stuyvesant, NY, 1989)
——. *Gustav Mahler and Hungary* (Budapest 1991)
Schaefer, Hans Joachim and others. *Gustav Mahler: Jahre der Entscheidung in Kassel 1883–1885* (Kassel 1990)
Vondenhoff, Bruno and Eleonore (eds). *Gustav Mahler Dokumentation: Sammlung Eleonore Vondenhoff. Materialien zu Leben und Werk*, 3 vols (Tutzing 1978–97)

Catalogues

Kubik, Reinhold and Thomas Trabitsch (eds). *Gustav Mahler und Wien* (Vienna 2010)
Kühn, Hellmut and Georg Quander (eds). *Gustav Mahler: Ein Lesebuch mit Bildern* (Zurich 1982)
La Grange, Henry-Louis de (ed.). *Gustav Mahler: Un homme, une œuvre, une époque* (Paris 1985)
Mengelberg, Rudolf (ed.). *Das Mahler-Fest Amsterdam Mai 1920: Vorträge und Berichte* (Vienna and Leipzig 1920)
Mitchell, Donald (ed.). *Gustav Mahler: The World Listens* (Haarlem 1995)
Moisy, Sigrid von and Ulrich Montag (eds). *Gustav Mahler: Briefe und Musikautographen aus den Moldenhauer-Archiven in der Bayerischen Staatsbibliothek* (Munich 2003)

Stephan, Rudolf (ed.). *Gustav Mahler: Werk und Interpretation. Autographe, Partituren, Dokumente* (Cologne 1979)
Wiener Festwochen (ed.). *Gustav Mahler und seine Zeit* (Vienna 1960)

Letters

Blaukopf, Herta (ed.). *Gustav Mahler: Unbekannte Briefe* (Vienna and Hamburg 1983); trans. Richard Stokes as *Mahler's Unknown Letters* (London 1986)
—— (ed.). *Gustav Mahler – Richard Strauss: Briefwechsel 1888–1911* (Munich 1988); trans. Edmund Jephcott as *Gustav Mahler – Richard Strauss: Correspondence 1888–1911* (London 1984)
——. *Gustav Mahler: Briefe*, rev. edn. (Vienna 1996); partial Engl. trans. by Eithne Wilkins, Ernst Kaiser and Bill Hopkins as *Selected Letters of Gustav Mahler*, ed. Kurt Martner (London 1979)
Halban, Dési (ed.). *Selma Kurz: Die Sängerin und ihre Zeit* (Stuttgart and Zurich 1983)
Hansen, Mathias (ed.). *Gustav Mahler: Briefe* (Leipzig 1981)
Isaacs, Reginald. *Walter Gropius: Der Mensch und sein Werk*, 2 vols (Berlin 1983–4); partial Engl. trans. as *Gropius: An Illustrated History of the Creator of the Bauhaus* (Boston 1991)
La Grange, Henry-Louis de and Günther Weiβ (eds). *Ein Glück ohne Ruh': Die Briefe Gustav Mahlers an Alma* (Berlin 1995), in collaboration with Knud Martner; trans. Antony Beaumont as *Gustav Mahler: Letters to his Wife* (London 2004)
McClatchie, Stephen (ed.). *Gustav Mahler: 'Liebste Justi!' Briefe an die Familie* (Bonn 2006); trans. as *The Mahler Family Letters* (Oxford 2006)
Mahler, Alma Maria (ed.). *Gustav Mahler: Briefe 1879–1911* (Berlin 1924)
——. *Gustav Mahler: Erinnerungen und Briefe* (Amsterdam 1940, rev. 1949); trans. Basil Creighton as *Gustav Mahler: Memories and Letters*, ed. Donald Mitchell and Knud Martner, 4th edn (London 1990)
Willnauer, Franz (ed.). *Gustav Mahler: 'Mein lieber Trotzkopf, meine süße Mohnblume': Briefe an Anna von Mildenburg* (Vienna 2006)
—— (ed.). *Gustav Mahler: Verehrter Herr College! Briefe an Komponisten, Dirigenten, Intendanten* (Vienna 2010)

Contemporary Accounts and Memoirs

Bahr-Mildenburg, Anna. *Erinnerungen* (Vienna and Berlin 1921)
Eckstein, Friedrich. *'Alte unnennbare Tage!' Erinnerungen aus siebzig Lehr- und Wanderjahren* (Vienna 1936)
Foerster, Josef Bohuslav. *Der Pilger: Erinnerungen eines Musikers* (Prague 1955)
Gutheil-Schoder, Marie. *Erlebtes und Erstrebtes: Rolle und Gestaltung* (Vienna and Leipzig 1937)
Karpath, Ludwig. *Begegnung mit dem Genius* (Vienna and Leipzig 1934)
Kienzl, Wilhelm. *Meine Lebenswanderung* (Stuttgart 1926)
Killian, Herbert (ed.). *Gustav Mahler in den Erinnerungen von Natalie Bauer-Lechner* (Hamburg 1984); trans. Dika Newlin as *Recollections of Gustav Mahler by Natalie Bauer-Lechner*, ed. Peter Franklin (London 1980)
Klemperer, Otto. *Meine Erinnerungen an Gustav Mahler und andere autobiographische Skizzen* (Zurich 1960); trans. J. Maxwell Brownjohn as *Minor Recollections* (London 1964)
Mahler-Werfel, Alma. *Mein Leben*, ed. Willy Haas (Frankfurt 1960) (the Engl. original was written in collaboration with E. B. Ashton and published in 1958 under the title *And the Bridge is Love: Memories of a Lifetime*; there are substantial differences between the two publications)
——. *Erinnerungen an Gustav Mahler*, ed. Donald Mitchell (Zurich 1971); for an Engl. trans., see Letters
——. *Tagebuch-Suiten 1898–1902*, ed. Antony Beaumont and Susanne Rode-Breymann (Frankfurt 1997); trans. Antony Beaumont as *Diaries 1898–1902* (London 1998)
Pfohl, Ferdinand. *Gustav Mahler: Eindrücke und Erinnerungen aus den Hamburger Jahren*, ed. Knud Martner (Hamburg 1973)

Stefan, Paul. *Gustav Mahlers Erbe* (Munich 1908)
—— (ed.). *Gustav Mahler: Ein Bild seiner Persönlichkeit in Widmungen* (Munich 1910)
——. *Das Grab in Wien: Eine Chronik 1903–1911* (Berlin 1913)
Walter, Bruno. *Thema und Variationen: Erinnerungen und Gedanken* (Frankfurt am Main 1947); trans. James A. Galston as *Theme and Variations* (New York 1946)
——. *Gustav Mahler: Ein Porträt* (Wilhelmshaven 1981); trans. Lotte Walter Lindt as *Gustav Mahler* (London 1990)
Zuckerkandl, Bertha. *Österreich intim: Erinnerungen 1892–1942*, ed. Reinhard Federmann (Frankfurt 1970)

Biographies and General Studies on Life and Works

Adler, Guido. *Gustav Mahler* (Vienna 1916)
Blaukopf, Kurt. *Gustav Mahler oder der Zeitgenosse der Zukunft* (Vienna 1969, repr. 2011); trans. Inge Goodwin as *Gustav Mahler* (London 1973)
Carr, Jonathan. *The Real Mahler* (London 1997); trans. into German as *Gustav Mahler: Biographie* (Düsseldorf and Munich 1997)
Feder, Stuart. *Gustav Mahler: A Life in Crisis* (New Haven 2004)
Floros, Constantin. *Gustav Mahler*, 3 vols (Wiesbaden 1977–85); the third volume was translated into English by Vernon and Jutta Wicker as *Gustav Mahler: The Symphonies* (Portland, Oregon 1993)
——. *Gustav Mahler: Visionär und Despot* (Zurich and Hamburg 1998)
Franklin, Peter. *The Life of Mahler* (Cambridge 1997)
Hilmes, Oliver. *Witwe im Wahn: Das Leben der Alma Mahler-Werfel* (Munich 2004)
Karbusicky, Vladimir. *Gustav Mahler und seine Umwelt* (Darmstadt 1978)
Keegan, Susanne. *The Bride of the Wind: The Life and Times of Alma Mahler* (London 1991)
Kennedy, Michael. *Mahler*, 2nd edn (Oxford 2000)
La Grange, Henry-Louis de. *Mahler: A Biography* (London 1974)
——. *Gustav Mahler: Chronique d'une vie*, 3 vols (Paris 1979–84)
——. *Gustav Mahler. Vienna: The Years of Challenge (1897–1904)* (Oxford and New York 1995)
——. *Gustav Mahler. Vienna: Triumph and Disillusion (1904–1907)* (Oxford and New York 1999)
——. *Gustav Mahler: A New Life Cut Short (1907–1911)* (Oxford and New York 2008)
Lebrecht, Norman. *Why Mahler? How One Man and Ten Symphonies Changed Our World* (London 2010)
Mitchell, Donald. *Gustav Mahler: The Early Years*, ed. Paul Banks and David Matthews (Woodbridge 2003)
——. *Gustav Mahler: The Wunderhorn Years: Chronicles and Commentaries* (Woodbridge 2005)
——. *Gustav Mahler: Songs and Symphonies of Life and Death: Interpretations and Annotations* (Woodbridge 2002)
——. *Discovering Mahler: Writings on Mahler 1955–2005*, ed. Gastón Fournier-Facio (Woodbridge 2007)
Monson, Karen. *Alma Mahler: Muse to Genius. From Fin-de-Siècle Vienna to Hollywood's Heyday* (Boston 1983) (a German trans. was published in Munich in 1985)
Müller, Karl-Josef. *Mahler: Leben – Werke – Dokumente* (Mainz 1988)
Niekerk, Carl. *Reading Mahler: German Culture und Jewish Identity in fin-de-siècle Vienna* (Rochester, NY 2010)
Principe, Quirino. *Mahler* (Milan 1983)
Schiedermair, Ludwig. *Gustav Mahler: Eine biographisch-kritische Würdigung* (Leipzig 1901)
Schreiber, Wolfgang. *Gustav Mahler in Selbstzeugnissen und Bilddokumenten* (Reinbek 1971)
Seele, Astrid. *Alma Mahler-Werfel* (Reinbek 2001)
Specht, Richard. *Gustav Mahler* (Berlin 1905)
——. *Gustav Mahler* (Berlin 1913) (not identical to the foregoing title)
Stefan, Paul. *Gustav Mahler: Eine Studie über Persönlichkeit und Werk* (Munich 1910, R1981)
Wagner, Manfred. *Alfred Roller in seiner Zeit* (Salzburg and Vienna 1996)

Wagner, Mary H. *Gustav Mahler and the New York Philharmonic Orchestra Tour America* (Lanham 2006)

Willnauer, Franz. *Gustav Mahler und die Wiener Oper* (Vienna 1993)

Musical Style, Works

Adorno, Theodor W. *Mahler: Eine musikalische Physiognomik* (Frankfurt 1960); trans. Edmund Jephcott as *Mahler: A Musical Physiognomy* (Chicago 1992)

Andraschke, Peter. *Gustav Mahlers IX. Symphonie: Kompositionsprozeß und Analyse* (Wiesbaden 1976)

Barham, Jeremy. *Perspectives on Gustav Mahler* (Aldershot, Hants 2005)

Bekker, Paul. *Gustav Mahlers Sinfonien* (Berlin 1921)

Cardus, Neville. *Gustav Mahler: His Mind and his Music* (London 1965)

Cooke, Deryck. *Gustav Mahler: An Introduction to his Music* (London 1980)

Danuser, Hermann. *Gustav Mahler: Das Lied von der Erde* (Munich 1985)

——. *Gustav Mahler und seine Zeit* (Laaber 1991)

—— (ed.). *Gustav Mahler* (Darmstadt 1992)

Del Mar, Norman. *Mahler's Sixth Symphony* (London 1980)

Duse, Ugo. *Gustav Mahler* (Turin 1973)

Eggebrecht, Hans Heinrich. *Die Musik Gustav Mahlers*, 2nd edn (Munich 1986)

Franklin, Peter. *Mahler: Symphony No. 3* (Cambridge 1991)

Geck, Martin. *Von Beethoven bis Mahler: Die Musik des deutschen Idealismus* (Stuttgart and Weimar 1993)

Gielen, Michael and Paul Fiebig. *Mahler im Gespräch: Die zehn Sinfonien* (Stuttgart and Weimar 2002)

Greene, David B. *Mahler: Consciousness and Temporality* (New York 1984)

Hansen, Mathias. *Gustav Mahler* (Stuttgart 1996)

Harten, Uwe (ed.). *Hans Rott (1858–1884)* (Vienna 2000)

Hefling, Stephen E. *Mahler Studies* (Cambridge 1997)

——. *Mahler: Das Lied von der Erde (The Song of the Earth)* (Cambridge 2000)

Hilmar-Voit, Renate. *Im Wunderhorn-Ton: Gustav Mahlers sprachliches Kompositionsmaterial bis 1900* (Tutzing 1988)

Hilmes, Oliver. *Im Fadenkreuz: Politische Gustav-Mahler-Rezeption 1919–1945* (Frankfurt 2003)

Indorf, Gerd. *Mahlers Sinfonien* (Freiburg im Breisgau, Berlin and Vienna 2010)

Johnson, Julian. *Mahler's Voices: Expression and Irony in the Songs and Symphonies* (Oxford 2009)

Kolleritsch, Otto (ed.). *Gustav Mahler: Sinfonie und Wirklichkeit* (Graz 1977)

Krummacher, Friedhelm. *Gustav Mahlers III. Symphonie: Welt im Widerbild* (Kassel 1991)

Matter, Jean. *Connaissance de Mahler: Documents, analyses et synthèses* (Lausanne 1974)

Metzger, Christoph. *Mahler-Rezeption: Perspektiven der Rezeption Gustav Mahlers* (Wilhelmshaven 2000)

Metzger, Heinz-Klaus and Rainer Riehn (eds). *Gustav Mahler* (Munich 1989) (= Musik-Konzepte Sonderband)

—— (eds). *Gustav Mahler: Der unbekannte Bekannte* (Munich 1996) (= Musik-Konzepte 91)

—— (eds). *Gustav Mahler durchgesetzt?* (Munich 1999) (= Musik-Konzepte 106)

Nikkels, Eveline and Robert Becqué (eds). *A 'Mass' for the Masses: Proceedings of the Mahler VIII Symposium Amsterdam 1988* (Rijswijk 1992)

Odefey, Alexander. *Gustav Mahlers 'Kindertotenlieder': Eine semantische Analyse* (Frankfurt 1999)

Op de Coul, Paul (ed.). *Fragment or Completion? Proceedings of the Mahler X Symposium Utrecht 1986* (The Hague 1991)

Painter, Karen (ed.). *Mahler and His World* (Princeton and Oxford 2002)

Partsch, Erich Wolfgang (ed.). *Gustav Mahler: Werk und Wirken* (Vienna 1996)

Reed, Philip (ed.). *On Mahler and Britten: Essays in Honour of Donald Mitchell on his Seventieth Birthday* (Woodbridge 1995)

Reik, Theodor. *The Haunting Melody: Psychoanalytic Experiences in Life and Music* (New York 1953, R1983)

Revers, Peter. *Gustav Mahler: Untersuchungen zu den späten Sinfonien* (Hamburg 1985)

——. *Mahlers Lieder: Ein musikalischer Werkführer* (Munich 2000)

Revers, Peter and Oliver Korte (eds). *Gustav Mahler: Interpretationen seiner Werke*, 2 vols (Laaber; announced for 2010)

Rothkamm, Jörg. *Gustav Mahlers Zehnte Symphonie: Entstehung, Analyse, Rezeption* (Frankfurt am Main 2003)

Ruzicka, Peter (ed.). *Mahler – eine Herausforderung* (Wiesbaden 1977)

Samuels, Robert. *Mahler's Sixth Symphony: A Study in Musical Semiotics* (Cambridge 1995)

Schadendorf, Miriam. *Humor als Formkonzept in der Musik Gustav Mahlers* (Stuttgart and Weimar 1995)

Schäfer, Thomas. *Modellfall Mahler: Kompositorische Rezeption in zeitgenössischer Musik* (Munich 1999)

Scheit, Gerhard and Wilhelm Svoboda. *Feindbild Gustav Mahler: Zur antisemitischen Abwehr der Moderne in Österreich* (Vienna 2002)

Schoenberg, Arnold and others. *Gustav Mahler* (Tübingen 1966)

Sponheuer, Bernd. *Logik des Zerfalls: Untersuchungen zum Finalproblem in den Symphonien Gustav Mahlers* (Tutzing 1978)

Sponheuer, Bernd and Wolfram Steinbeck (eds). *Gustav Mahler und die Symphonik des 19. Jahrhunderts* (Frankfurt 2000)

Stephan, Rudolf. *Gustav Mahler: IV. Symphonie G-Dur* (Munich 1966)

——. *Gustav Mahler: II. Symphonie c-Moll* (Munich 1979)

——. *Mahler-Interpretation: Aspekte zum Werk und Wirken von Gustav Mahler* (Mainz 1985)

Stuppner, Hubert (ed.). *Mahler a Dobbiaco/Mahler in Toblach* (Milan 1989)

Tadday, Ulrich (ed.). *Gustav Mahlers Lieder* (Munich 2007)

Ulm, Renate (ed.). *Gustav Mahlers Symphonien: Entstehung – Deutung – Wirkung* (Munich and Kassel 2001)

Unger, Anette. *Welt, Leben und Kunst als Themen der 'Zarathustra-Kompositionen' von Richard Strauss und Gustav Mahler* (Frankfurt 1992)

Vogt, Matthias Theodor (ed.). *Das Gustav-Mahler-Fest Hamburg 1989: Bericht über den Internationalen Gustav-Mahler-Kongreβ* (Kassel 1991)

Wandel, Juliane. *Die Rezeption der Symphonien Gustav Mahlers zu Lebzeiten des Komponisten* (Frankfurt 1999)

Weiβ, Günther (ed.). *Neue Mahleriana: Essays in Honour of Henry-Louis de La Grange on His Seventieth Birthday* (Berne and New York 1997)

Wildhagen, Christian. *Die 'Achte Symphonie' von Gustav Mahler: Konzeption einer universalen Symphonik* (Frankfurt 2000)

Wilkens, Sander. *Gustav Mahlers Fünfte Symphonie: Quellen und Instrumentationsprozeβ* (Frankfurt 1989)

Wollschläger, Hans. *Der Andere Stoff: Fragmente zu Gustav Mahler* (Göttingen 2010)

Zychowicz, James L. (ed.). *The Seventh Symphony of Gustav Mahler: A Symposium* (Cincinnati 1990)

——. *Mahler's Fourth Symphony* (Oxford 2000)

Index

NOTE: GM = Gustav Mahler; Alma refers to his wife, Alma Mahler. In the subheadings Mahler's symphonies are ordered numerically.

Abbado, Claudio 704
Abravanel, Maurice 704
Accademia di Santa Cecilia, Rome 622
Adler, Alfred 648
Adler, Guido 31, 481, 632, 689
  and band music in Iglau 30
  and Budapest appointment 181–2
  and letter on GM's hardships in America
    607, 609
  and Mahler Festival in Amsterdam 694
  musicology chair at Vienna 74, 182, 511
  and Viennese Academic Wagner
    Society 63
Adler, Louis 371
Adler, Salomon 76
Adler, Victor 76, 77, 84, 230, 259, 344, 345–6
Adorno, Theodor W. 129, 391, 449, 695
  on Second Symphony 207
  on Third Symphony 274, 276, 279
  on Fourth Symphony 336
  on Fifth Symphony 388
  and Sixth Symphony 410, 415
  on Seventh Symphony 461–2
  on Eighth Symphony 523, 524–5, 659
  on Tenth Symphony fragment 665
  and Alma Mahler 361, 410, 643, 644
  on Berg and GM 483, 485
  'The Heine Wound' 706
  on Jewish element in GM's work 266,
    267, 270, 271
  and Mann's Doktor Faustus 415
  monograph on GM 702
  and Second Viennese School 699–700
  on Strauss 475
  on Webern 481

Ahasuerus figure 272
Albani, Emma 591
Albert, Eugen d' 172, 501
Allmers, Hermann 168
Altenberg, Peter 358
Alvary, Max 218–19, 545
Amsterdam
  Concertgebouw Orchestra 491, 495,
    497–8, 694
  Mahler Festival 694–5, 696
Ansermet, Ernest 251–2, 256, 705
Ansorge, Conrad 632
anthropology, Lotze's evolutionary ideas
  398–400
anti-Semitism
  Alma Mahler 261, 361, 364–5, 371, 380,
    381, 517–18, 627, 628–9
  and anti-modernity 198
  in Austro-Hungarian Dual Monarchy 15,
    344–5
  in Budapest 180, 183, 186
  and critical responses to GM 82–3, 124,
    145, 198, 252–7, 298, 429, 467, 507, 510
  and economic uncertainty 51, 52
  emergence after Austro-German dual
    alliance 46
  fate of Jewish composers under Third
    Reich 692
  foetor judaicus 370, 628
  and gesticulation of Jews and conductors
    198, 253
  GM as target 248, 252–7, 261–2, 294,
    296, 316, 465, 467–8, 507, 510
  GM as target after death 692–3, 693–4,
    696–7

GM's indifference to in those he
  admired 60, 104, 132, 247, 258
historical roots and emancipation of
  Jews 255, 257, 706
and Jewish lack of creative energy 82–3,
  251, 255, 258
and linguistic stereotyping 253, 254–5
and Pan-German nationalism in Austria
  46, 63–4, 344, 345
rise of Third Reich and GM's reputation
  696–7
in Vienna 47, 49, 51, 250, 252–3, 254,
  259, 288–9, 296, 344–5, 465, 692–3
and Vienna Philharmonic post 316
Wagner and circle 60, 63, 80, 83, 104,
  141, 157, 247, 248, 257–8
see also Jews
Appia, Adolphe 416, 418, 419
Apponyi, Albert 284, 287, 289
Aristotle 402
Arnim, Achim von 126–7, 129, 170,
  172, 174
Arnoldson, Sigrid 144
art in Vienna of 1870s 42–54
see also Secessionist art and artists
Astor family 568–9
Attersee, Austria 228, 230–2, 236–7, 301, 443
Austria
  Mahlerian conductors and shifts in
    allegiance 698–9
  resistance to memorial to GM 696–7
  Ständestaat and GM's reputation 697–8
  see also Austro-Hungarian Dual
    Monarchy
Austro-German dual alliance (1879) 46
Austro-Hungarian Dual Monarchy
  Ausgleich (1867) 12–13, 46–7
  Jews in 13–15, 19, 31
  political uncertainty at fin de siècle 343–6
  rivalry between Vienna and Budapest
    179–80
  tensions and Vienna of 1870s 46–52
  see also Budapest and GM's Royal Opera
    post; Franz Joseph; nationalist
    movements and dual monarchy;
    Prague; Vienna

Bach, David Josef 695
Bach, Johann Sebastian 157
Bad Hall and GM's summer post 90–8, 105
Badeni, Kasimir Felix von 343
Baehr, George 677
Bahr, Hermann 132, 210, 237, 358, 359,
  658, 689
  and anti-Semitism in Vienna 345, 506
  defends GM 506, 513, 538
  on Roller's designs 419, 424–5

Vienna and attitudes towards GM
  341–3, 347–8
Bahr-Mildenburg, Anna see Mildenburg
Balzac, Honoré de 276, 350
band music 25–6, 30–1, 266
Barbirolli, Sir John 315, 704
Barenboim, Daniel 705
Barshai, Rudolf 704
Bartók, Béla 186
Baudelaire, Charles 130
Bauer, Rudolf 256–7, 700
Bauer-Lechner, Natalie 2, 5, 695, Ill 21
  breach with GM on marriage to Alma
    236, 383–4, 386, 502
  and GM's First Symphony 148, 150, 151
  and GM's Second Symphony 204–5,
    448–9
  and GM's Third Symphony 275, 277, 278
  and GM's Fourth Symphony 335, 336
  and GM's Fifth Symphony 385, 386
  and Die drei Pintos 164
  and GM's affair with Marion von
    Weber 166
  on GM's appearance and characteristics
    5, 7
  on GM's childhood 13, 25, 32
  and GM's childhood compositions 27–8
  on GM's collaboration with Wolf 64–5
  on GM's compositional method 153–4,
    173, 448–50, 452
  on GM's health 319–20, 326, 328
  and GM's life-threatening haemorrhage
    319–20
  on GM's musical sensibilities as child 20
  on GM's praise for Vienna Opera
    performers 298–9
  on GM's views on Bruckner's limitations
    72–3
  on GM's views on Rott's talent 57
  on GM's views on Verdi 469
  on GM's Wandering Jew 272
  holidays with Mahlers 230, 232,
    318–19, 444
  on Justine's family burden 228–9
  on Anna von Mildenburg's move to
    Vienna 241–2
  as musician 383
  on polyphony at fair 128–92
  reminiscences and insight into GM's
    work 386
  reminiscences and reliability of 20,
    383, 384
  on Rückert Lieder and GM's emotions 175
  unrequited love for GM 165, 236,
    242, 383–4
  and Vienna Opera appointment 282
Bauernfeld, Edward von 103, 358

Baumbach, Rudolf 170–1, 172
Baumfeld, Maurice 577–8, 670, 678
Baumgarten, Moritz 86, 93, 99, 108
Bayreuth Festival 57, 142–3
    GM recommends Anna von Mildenburg
        233, 247, 248
    GM visits 113, 134, 230, 247–8
    and Neumann's touring company 141
    Parsifal as preserve of 548–9
    Roller's designs 420–1
    and Wagner's total artwork ideas
        417–18, 419
Beaumont, Antony 366
Bechstein, Ludwig 97
Beer-Hofmann, Richard 358, 538
Beethoven, Ludwig van 25, 115
    account of death 666–7
    conducting style 195–6
    GM and Roller's *Fidelio* staging
        427–9, Ill. 20
    and Secession art 351, 353–5, 424, Ill. 22
    veneration and anti-Semitism 253, 254
Behn, Hermann 243, 246, 518
Bekker, Paul 461, 612, 695
Bellini, Vincenzo 30, 37, 292
Benedix, Roderich 52
Beniczky, Ferenc von
    and GM in Budapest 180, 181, 184,
        185, 189
    and Vienna appointment 284, 287–8, 289
Benjamin, Walter 136
Berg, Alban 475, 480–1, 560, 658, 689
    and Adorno 270, 483, 699
    and Alma Mahler 643
    and GM's work 207, 388, 482–4
    Lulu 131, 663
    on soul of man and animals 400
    Wozzeck 129
Berg, Helene (*née* Nahowski) 207, 400
Berio, Luciano 703
Berkhan, Wilhelm 246
Berl, Heinrich 269
Berlin, Wagner Theatre plan 593
Berlin Philharmonic Orchestra 203, 204,
        249, 390, 704
Berliner, Arnold 536, 550, 613, 658
    GM's letter from London 219–20
    as source of scientific information
        126, 518
    visits dying GM 684
Berlioz, Hector 61, 62, 125, 195
Bernays, Martha 368
Bernstein, Leonard 195, 199, 266, 336,
        699, 701, 704
Bertini, Gary 704
Besant, Annie 674
Bethge, Hans 554–6, 562–3, 564

Bezecny, Baron Josef von 283, 285–7, 289,
        296, 464
Bianchi, Bianca 189
Bie, Oskar 658, 694
Bierbaum, Otto Julius 168, 278
Bigelow, Poultney 609
Birrenkoven, Willi 247, 288
Bittong, Franz 286
Bizet, Georges 184, 293, 294, 309, 314, 609
Bland, Elsa 476
Blaukopf, Herta 131, 133, 474, 694, 702
Blaukopf, Kurt 701–2
Blavatsky, Helena 674
Blech, Leo 488
Bloch, Ernst 694
Blumenthal, Carl Victor 323, 551, 552, 553
Böcklin, Arnold, *Pan Frightens a
        Shepherd* 277
Bodanzky, Artur 458, 582, 585
Bohemia 12–13
    Jews in 14, 15, 19, 31
    linguistic divisions 141–2, 343
    musical influences on GM 266–7
    nationalist movements 46, 343
Böhler, Otto 197
Böhm, Karl 698, 705
Boito, Arrigo 493
Bonci, Alessandro 573
Bondy, Abraham 16
Borchardt, Rudolf 130–1
Borchmeyer, Dieter 521
Börne, Ludwig 134
Bossi, Marco Enrico 673
Boston Symphony Orchestra 580
Bote & Bock (music publishers) 454,
        455, 701
Boulez, Pierre 703, 704
Brahm, Otto 416
Brahms, Johannes 337, 380
    as Beethoven Prize judge 58, 105
    and Bruckner 72, 73–4
    as child prodigy 25
    friendship with GM 73–4, 246–7
    GM's respect for work 73–4
    impressed with GM in Budapest 187, 283
    and Leipzig Gewandhaus 157
    and New German School 61, 62,
        71–2, 182
    and 'New Symphony' 57
    and rebuttal of Rott 58
    and 'Schoenberg circle' 482
    songs and choice of poets 168
    status in Vienna 61
    on symphony problem 149–50
    Wagner rivalry 61, 62, 63, 71–2
Brecher, Gustav 613
Brehm, Alfred Edmund 126, 133, 394

Brentano, Clemens 126–7, 129, 138, 170, 172–3, 174
Brentano, Franz 74
Breuer, Hans 307
Brioschi, Anton 422, 423
Brioschi, Carlo 422
Broch, Hermann 346, 348
  on Vienna 42–3, 53–4
Brod, Max 269
Brook, Peter 572
Broz, Jan (Johannes Brosch) 26, 29
Bruckner, Anton 154, 246, 705
  and Brahms 72, 73–4
  as Conservatory teacher 55, 59
  GM's ambivalent view of 72–3, 73–4
  and New German School 62, 72
  support for Rott and 'New Symphony' 57–8
Brückner, Gotthold 113, 143, 418
Bruneau, Alfred 620
Büchner, Georg 95, 129, 173, 174
Budapest and GM's Royal Opera post 167, 178–90, 222–3
  Hungarian nationalism 179–80, 183, 189–90
  linguistic problems 179, 180, 183, 184, 185–6
  press responses to appointment and work 183, 184, 185, 189, 190
  secret negotiations to leave for Hamburg 187–8, 190, 211
Bülow, Cosima von see Wagner, Cosima
Bülow, Hans von 67, 125, 145, 196, 213–15
  admiration for GM's conducting 209, 213–14, 215
  antipathy to GM's work 164–5, 214–15, 217, 474
  death and memorial service 205, 215
  rebuffs GM's youthful effusion 118–20
Burckhard, Max 370, 376, 539
  advises Alma against GM 365
  Alma's liaison with 359, 362, 366, 375, 432, 433
  and Burgtheater 287, 466
  on GM's diet 446
Burrian, Carl 570, 573, 580
Busoni, Ferruccio 1–2, 125, 138, 609–10, 673
  and GM's final voyage 679–80
Busse, Carl 170
Buths, Julius 206, 333, 410

Cahier, Sarah Jane 563
Caine, Uri 704
Calderón de la Barca, Pedro 205, 341
Callot, Jacques 151
Canetti, Elias

  on Alma Mahler 361, 364, 643, 644, 645, 646–7, 674
  on conductors 192–3
Carltheater, Vienna 12
Caruso, Enrico 6, 545, 546, 573, 578
Casella, Alfredo 694
Celibidache, Sergiu 705
Celtic culture and Telyn Society 76–7
Cervantes, Miguel de 126, 138, 276
Chailly, Riccardo 495, 704
Chaliapin, Fyodor 546, 573
Chantemesse, André 677, 678, 682
Charpentier, Gustave 470–1
Chinese poetry 554–6, 562–4, 566, 567
Chopin, Frédéric 69, 458
Chotzinoff, Samuel 571
Christian Socialists in Vienna 344
Chvostek, Franz 682, 684
Claar, Emil 310
claque and GM's reforms 303, 313, 506–7
Clemenceau, Georges 358, 517
Clemenceau, Paul 312, 358, 517, 595, 620, 658
Clemenceau, Sophie 312, 358, 517, 595, 620, 658, 683
Colonne, Édouard 620
Colonne Orchestra, GM conducts 620, 621
Concertgebouw Orchestra in Amsterdam 491, 495, 497–8, 694
Conried, Heinrich 544–9, 573, 574–5, 578, 579, 580
Conservatory see Vienna Conservatory and GM as student
Cooke, Deryck 662–3, 665
Corning, Leon 578
Cottenet, Rawlins 576
Craig, Edward Gordon 416, 418–19
Czech nationalism 141
  and anti-Semitism 15
  and linguistic divisions 141–2
  tension in dual monarchy 46–7, 343–4
Czech Philharmonic Orchestra, GM conducts 585–6

Damisch, Heinrich 693–4
Damrosch, Leopold 545, 580
Damrosch, Walter 580, 591
Danuser, Hermann 563, 702
Death in Venice (film) 389, 702–3
Debussy, Claude 620, 621–2, 698
Decsey, Ernst
  on Third Symphony 278
  on GM in Toblach 133, 601
  on GM's conducting style 198–9
  on GM's faith 394, 407
  on GM's feelings towards Wolf 66
  on GM's literary tastes 132, 133, 134

Defaux, Clément 682
Dehmel, Ida 488
Dehmel, Richard 168, 488
d'Elvert, Christian 22
Delius, Frederick 158
Demuth, Leopold 307, 471
Destinn, Emmy 573, 610
Dickens, Charles 126, 138, 276
Didur, Adamo 591
Diepenbrock, Alphons 261, 491, 658, 689
    friendship with GM 493–4, 496, 497,
        498, 519–20
Diepenbrock, Elisabeth 495, 497, 498
diphtheria 550–1
Dippel, Andreas 575, 576, 579, 587, 588,
    589, 593
Doblinger (music publishers) 454–5
Doepler, Carl Emil 143
Donizetti, Gaetano 104, 117, 184, 292,
    305, 589
Dostoevsky, Fyodor 77, 129, 133, 136–8,
    260, 346
Downes, Olin 479
Draeseke, Felix 411
Dreyfus, Alfred 358, 517–18
Dual Monarchy see Austro-Hungarian
    Dual Monarchy
Dudamel, Gustavo 704
Dukas, Paul 219, 620, 621, 658
Duncan, Isadora 353
Duse, Eleonora 236, 306
Dvořák, Antonín 469, 646
Dyck, Ernest van 295, 305, 561

Eames, Emma 591
Eberle (printing house) 455
Eckermann, Johann Peter 402, 403, 404
    'mothers' theory 687–8
Eckert, Karl 292–3
Eckstein, Friedrich 84
Eggebrecht, Hans Heinrich 271, 386–7,
    618–19, 702
Ehrlich, Josef 78
Eichendorff, Joseph von 459–60, 462
Eisler, Hanns 482
Elgar, Edward 176
Elizza, Elise 107
Elmblad, Johannes 143
entelechy 137, 260, 397, 400–8, 520, 526,
    687–8
Epstein, Julius 40–1, 54, 55, 67,
    70, 689
Erkel, Ferenc 180, 186
Erkel, Sándor 180–1, 182, 186, 190
Essen Orchestra, GM conducts 409, 410,
    411, 489
evolutionary ideas 398–400, 686

Falk, Johann Daniel 134, 404–5
Farrar, Geraldine 573, 590
Fauré, Gabriel 620
Fechner, Gustav Theodor 78, 331, 332, 399,
    400, 401, 594
    on death 685
    GM's belief in entelechy 260, 397, 407
    Zend-Avesta and GM's interest in 395–8
Ferenczi, Sándor 648
Feuchtersleben, Ernst von 553
Fibich, Zdenek 142
Fiebig, Paul 646
Fischer, Franz 113
Fischer, Heinrich A. 29
Fischer, Ivan 704
Fischer, Theodor
    on character of GM 32, 39
    childhood memories 23, 29, 30–1,
        39, 96, 97
    Literary Club member 75
    on Mahlers' home in Iglau 22–3
    on student days 68
Fischer-Dieskau, Dietrich 65, 698
Floros, Constantin 702
Foerster, Josef Bohuslav 205, 475,
    490, 518
    friendship with GM in Hamburg
        208–10, 211, 214, 215, 245
    on funeral of GM 689–90
    on GM's conducting skills 200–1
Foerster-Lauterer, Berta 208, 307, 471,
    518, 689
Fornaro, Carlo di 609
Förstel, Gertrude 307
Forster, Josef 470, 471
Fraenkel, Joseph 324, 578, 609, 675–6,
    677, 678
Frank, Adolf 114
Frank, Betty 143–4, 147
Frank, Gustav (cousin) 75, 91, 99
Franz Joseph, emperor of Austria and
    king of Hungary 12, 13, 45–6, 50,
    288–9, 343
    and Vienna Opera 303, 464, 465–6, 541,
        542
Fremstad, Olive 570
Freud, Anna 261
Freud, Sigmund 34, 272, 347, 349–50,
    539, 641
    GM's consultation 372, 497, 626, 627,
        636–7, 647–55
    and Jewish identity 263–4
    on woman's role 368
Freund, Emil 94, 108, 613, 660
    and disturbed state of GM 100, 101
    as friend and correspondent 99, 100,
        101, 380, 511, 671

as GM's legal adviser and executor 455,
511, 600, 655, 689
GM's letters to 101, 217–18, 455, 671
Literary Club member 75
Freytag, Gustav 258
Fricsay, Ferenc 705
Fried, Oskar 261, 393–4, 410, 613, 640, 695
Friedjung, Heinrich 48–9, 76
Fritsch, Theodor 697
Fuchs, Johann Nepomuk 291, 294, 314
Fuchs, Robert 54, 55, 59, 67, 105
Furtwängler, Wilhelm 698, 699, 705
Füssl, Karl Heinz 457

Gabrilovich, Ossip 410, 438, 629
Gade, Niels Wilhelm 158
Gadski, Johanna 573
Gallen-Kallela, Akseli, portrait of GM 558
Galli-Bibiena, Francesco 292
Gareis, Fritz 198
Gast, Peter (Heinrich Köselitz) 658
Gatti-Casazza, Giulio 575, 576, 579, 587,
589, 676
Genée, Richard 52
Gergiev, Valery 704
Gericke, Wilhelm 294
Gerigk, Herbert 697
German nationalism
and Telyn Society 76–7
and tension in Dual Monarchy 343–4
German Reich
anti-Semitism 253–4
Austro-German dual alliance (1879) 46
economic depression 51–2
German Romanticism 98, 172–3
'German-Jewish symbiosis' 267–8
Gernsheim, Friedrich 59
Gesamtkunstwerk (total artwork) 353,
416–18, 421, 424, 427
Gesellschaft der Musikfreunde 54
Gibson, Charles Dana 609
Gielen, Michael 415, 459, 614, 646, 662, 704
Gilman, Lawrence 592
Gilsa, Baron Adolph von und zu 112, 115,
118, 120, 123, 124
Giorgione, The Concerto 209–10
Giroud, Françoise 361
Giulini, Carlo Maria 704
Gluck, Christoph Willibald 116, 142, 147,
243, 292, 305, 470, 507, 529, 530, 535,
557
Goethe, Johann Wolfgang von
accounts of death 667, 668
on Des Knaben Wunderhorn poems 173–4
and entelechy 401–7, 687–8
Faust 401–3, 405–7, 521–4, 525, 526,
593–4, 598

Faust and Eckermann's 'mothers'
theory 687–8
GM's admiration and interest in 133–4,
137, 260, 393, 397, 400, 401–7
GM's setting of 'Anchorites' Scene'
521–4, 525, 526, 598
GM's youthful identification with
Werther 94–5
Göhler, Georg 335, 385, 456, 634
Goldberg, Albert 166–7
Goldmark, Karl 80, 105, 222, 283, 289
Goldschmidt, Berthold 662
Goll, Claire 361
Gounod, Charles 104, 146, 294, 305
Graetz, Heinrich 253
Graf, Ferdinand 467
Graf, Max 424, 508
Grau, Maurice 544, 545
Great Berlin Opera Society offer 593
Greater New York Orchestra 581
Gregor, Hans 660, 689
Greif, Martin 97–8
Grengg, Karl 219
Grieg, Edvard 158
Grimm, Jacob 96–7, 114–15
Grimm, Wilhelm 96–7, 114–15
Gropius, Manon (Alma's daughter) 361, 434
Gropius, Martin (Alma's son) 645
Gropius, Walter
affair with Alma 272, 329, 361, 374,
438, 628
meets Alma in Tobelbad 629–31
mistaken letter to GM and fallout 627,
634–45, 663, 664–5
mother fixation and unattainable women
630, 652
in Munich for Eighth Symphony 657, 658
ongoing affair after revelation 654, 657,
660–1, 670, 674
unpublished correspondence with
Alma 641–2, 643
Gruber, Max von 76
Grünfeld, Alfred 140
Grünfeld, Heinrich 140
Grünfeld, Moritz and family 34
Gutheil-Schoder, Marie 199, 306, 308, 430,
471, 531, 534
Gutmann, Emil 326, 458, 563, 656, 671
and Eighth Symphony Munich première
623, 624, 625

Haas, Willy 630
Habsburg Empire and role of Vienna 45–6
Haeckel, Ernst 394, 594
Haffner, Karl 52
Haitink, Bernard 390, 495, 701, 704
Halban, Dési 308, 313

Halban, Josef 313
Halévy, Ludovic 52, 257
Hamburg
  First Symphony performed in 149, 150–1
  friends in 245–6
  GM's post at Stadttheater 208–50
  GM's success in post 218, 225–6,
    248–9, 296–7
  history of opera house 211
  repertory and work load 245
  secret negotiations to leave Budapest
    187–8, 190, 211
  Vienna appointment and departure for
    240–4, 284–5, 286, 296–7
Hammerstein, Oscar 545–6, 547
Hamperl, Franz 323–4
Handel, George Frideric 211, 604, 609
Hansen, Mathias 154, 173, 176, 278, 281,
    413, 462
  and Fifth Symphony 389–90, 391
Hansen, Theophil von 54
Hanslick, Eduard 310, 512
  admiring review of Vienna Opera
    Dalibor 300–1
  as 'Brahmin' 62, 71
  on Bruckner's Third Symphony 72
  GM's appraisal of 221
  negative review of First Symphony
    156, 317
  university teaching 74
  and Vienna appointment 156, 289–90
  and Wagner 60, 71, 290
Harding, Daniel 704
Harris, Sir Augustus 219
Hartmann, Alois 467
Hartmann, Eduard von 331, 407, 686–7,
    688
Hartmann, Karl Amadeus 703
Hasslinger, Carl 467
Hassmann, Carl 609
Hassreiter, Josef 534
Hauptmann, Gerhart 126, 131, 511,
    512–13, 632, 658
Havemeyer, Louisine 608
Haydn, Joseph 72, 215, 532, 604
Hearst, William Randolph 569
Hebbel, Friedrich 47
Heine, Heinrich 19, 256, 259, 706
Heinzel, Richard 56, 74
Hellmesberger, Joseph ('Pepi'), Junior
    291, 294, 314, 317
Hellmesberger, Joseph, Senior 54,
    68–9, 294
Helsinki, GM conducts in 557, 558
Henderson, W. J. 570, 592, 610
Herbeck, Johann 72, 293
Hermann, Abraham (grandfather) 16–17

Hermann, Marie see Mahler, Marie (mother)
Hermann, Theresia (grandmother) 17
Hertz, Alfred 570, 571, 588
Hertzka, Emil 600, 623, 671, 689
Herzl, Theodor 340
Hesch, Wilhelm 246, 307
Heuckeroth, Martin 491, 492–3
Hevesi, Ludwig 44, 356, 430
Heyworth, Peter 67
Hildesheimer, Wolfgang 667
Hilgermann, Laura 143
Hiller, Ferdinand 157
Hinrichsen, Henri 454–6, 458
Hirschfeld, Robert 508, 532
Hitler, Adolf 344, 345, 420–1
Hoffmann, Anna (Nina), see Spiegler, Nanna
Hoffmann, E. T. A. 1, 138, 151
Hoffmann, Josef 223, 352, 538, 680
Hoffmann, Joseph 143, 418
Hoffmann-Matscheko, Nina 136
Hofmann, Leopold von 293
Hofmannsthal, Hugo von 358, 658
  ballet 359–60
  and burial of GM 689, 690
  'Chandos Letter' 614, 615
  on decadence of fin-de-siècle era 350–1
  Elektra and Anna von Mildenburg 233–4
  festschrift contribution 633
  GM's attitude to work of 131–2
  Roller's designs 420
  and Young Vienna movement 346
Hölderlin, Johann Christian Friedrich 138
Holländer, Hans 98
Hollnsteiner, Johannes 392
Homer, Louise 573
Horenstein, Jascha 704
Horwitz, Karl 560
Hrabanus Maurus 521, 522–3, 598
Hülsen, Botho von 112, 115, 118
Humperdinck, Engelbert 593
Hungarian nationalism 179–80, 183, 189–90
Hüttenbrenner, Anselm 666–7
Huysmans, Joris-Karl 350

Ibsen, Henrik 133, 136
Iglau (Jihlava) 12, 13–14, 17–19, Ill. 6
  cultural life 30
  GM conducts in 108
  GM performs in 69, 113
  GM's childhood 22–41
  GM's visits home as young man 99–100,
    108, 113, 124, 147, 166, 230
  Jewish community 259
  Mahler family homes 21–3, 165
  Municipal Archives and GM's
    schooling 33–6
  music of 266–7

Inbal, Eliahu 704
Indy, Vincent d' 252
International Exhibition, Paris (1900)
312, 316
International Gustav Mahler Society 454, 701
Iradier, Sebastián de 279
Isaacs, Reginald 630, 634
Italy, GM visits 299–300, 535–6, 536–7, 622

Jahn, Wilhelm 61, 195, 234, 283, 291,
299, 316
and GM's succession 286–7, 297–8,
301, 305
and Vienna Opera golden age 293–5
Jalowetz, Heinrich 481, 560
Jansons, Mariss 495, 704
Jauner, Franz 60–1, 293
Jean Paul (*pseud. of* Johann Paul Friedrich
Richter) 133, 134–6, 137, 175, 226,
666, 690
on friendship of books 138–9
GM visits birthplace 113, 134
'humouresque' and Fourth Symphony
335, 336, 338–9
and titles in GM's First Symphony
135, 150
Jews
attraction of Wagner 83, 258
conditions in pre-war Austria-Hungary
13–15, 19, 259, 345
end of liberalism after 1879 German
alliance 46, 259
fate of composers under Third Reich 692
Jewish music question 264–73, 697
klezmer music 31, 266
legal definition and identification
as 262–3
respect for education in pre-war
Europe 19
see also anti-Semitism
Joachim, Joseph 61, 73, 157
Jochum, Eugen 705
Johner, Theodor 672–3
Jones, Ernest 649, 651, 653
Jörn, Karl 591
Joseph II, Kaiser 15, 16, 292, 527
Joukowsky, Paul von 113
Jude, Der (journal) 269
Jugendstil 43, 352
Jung, Carl Gustav 648

Kafka, Franz 329–30
Kahn, Otto H. 546, 573, 579
Kahnt, Christian Friedrich 455
Kaim Orchestra in Munich 289, 333,
557, 623
Kainz, Josef 539

Kaiser, Emil 109
Kajanus, Robert 558
Kalbeck, Max 107, 153, 512, 532
Kalischt (Kaliště), Bohemia 12, 13, 14, 17, 99
Kann, Robert A. 46, 47
Kant, Immanuel 126, 446
Kaplan, Gilbert 3
Karajan, Herbert von 698–9, 705
Karbusicky, Vladimir 266
Karpath, Ludwig 109, 296, 297–8, 557
GM on *Wunderhorn* poems 172
on GM's arrival at Budapest Opera 182–3
and GM's churlishness 505, 506
interview with GM on leaving
Vienna 528, 539–40
and Vienna appointment 283–4, 289,
505, 506
Kassel theatre and GM's post 68, 112,
113, 114–24
anti-Semitic newspaper article 252
strict working and moral ethic 115–16
wide-ranging repertory and work load
116–17
Keegan, Susan 361
Keglevic, Count István 180
Kes, Willem 491
Khnopff, Fernand 362
Khvolson, Orest Danilovich 394
Kienzl, Wilhelm 186, 249
Kittel, Hermine 423
Kitzbühel as holiday destination 301
Kiurina, Bertha 307
Kleiber, Carlos 705
Kleiber, Erich 158–9, 705
Klein, Herman 220
Kleist, Heinrich von 116, 136
Klemperer, Otto 67, 212, 458, 582
conducting style 195
and GM in Prague 585–6
on GM's striving for perfection 657–8
Kletzki, Paul 704
klezmer music 31, 266
Klimt, Gustav 341, 347, 359, 421, 539
and Alma Schindler 353, 357, 362,
365, 433
attends GM's send-off from Vienna
560, 561
and GM's death 684, 689
knight image and GM 354, 357, 632
Secession and Beethoven frieze 351,
352–5, 356, Ill. 22
Klinger, Max 351, 353–4, 355, 356, 424
Klopstock, Friedrich Gottlieb 128, 205, 215
Knappertsbusch, Hans 254, 705
Kneisel, Franz 609
Knote, Heinrich 307, 570, 573, 578, 625
Knüpfer, Paul 161

Kokoschka, Oskar 352, 353, 361, 628, 629, 645
Komlóssy, Ferenc 186
Kompass, Robert 467
Kondrashin, Kirill 704
Konzertverein Orchestra in Munich 623, 624
Korngold, Erich Wolfgang 176, 429, 512
Korngold, Julius 429, 512, 532, 540
Kovacs, Friedrich 323, 324, 552, 553
Kralik, Heinrich 83
Kralik, Richard 82–3
Kraus, Felix von 536
Kraus, Karl 131, 268, 341, 349, 531, 540
  admiration for GM's *Contes d'Hoffmann* 516–17
  defence of GM 515–16, 683
  Die Fackel 295, 362, 516, 683
  poetry and spiritual message 130
  positive review of Vienna appointment 295–6
Krauss, Clemens 698
Krehbiel, Henry E. 572, 591, 604
Krenek, Ernst 662, 695, 697, 698
Krenn, Franz 54–5, 67
Kris, Ernst 641
Krisper, Anton
  as friend in Vienna 55, 56, 64, 86
  GM lodges with parents in Laibach 103
  GM's letters 56, 86, 93, 94–5, 98, 101
  venereal disease and insanity 56, 100, 101, 102
Kroyer, Theodor 334
Krzyzanowski, Heinrich 510
  as friend in Vienna 55, 56, 59
  walking tours 95, 113, 164, 166
Krzyzanowski, Rudolf 69, 72, 510
  conducting career 56
  as friend in Vienna 55, 56, 62, 64
  walking tours 95, 164
Kubelík, Rafael 704
Kubik, Reinhold 457
Kurz, Selma (*later* Halban) 199, 302, 308–13, 371–2, 435, 468, 531, Ill. 12

La Grange, Henry-Louis de 634, 702
Labor, Josef 366
Lachner, Vincenz 162
Ladies' Committee of New York Philharmonic Society 580–1, 592–3, 605, 673
Laibach (Ljubljana) and GM's position 102–5, 108
Lallemand, Baron Guillaume de 517, 595
Lange, Friedrich August 126, 394
Lange-Eichbaum, Wilhelm 329
Langhans, Carl Ferdinand 158

latecomers and GM's reforms 225, 302–3, 313, 466, 507
Lauterer, Berta *see* Foerster-Lauterer, Berta
Lazarus, Henriette 246
Leadbeater, Charles 674
Lefler, Heinrich 422–4, 426
Lehár, Franz, 461, 562, 563
Lehmann, Lilli 186–7, 326–7, 487, 539, 545, 546, 656, 658
Leibniz, Gottfried Wilhelm 402, 403, 405
Leiden
  GM conducts in 644
  GM consults Freud in 647–55
Leipzig
  Conservatory 157–8
  Gewandhaus Orchestra 157, 158, 161
  GM's position at Stadttheater 123, 146–7, 157–67
  Neumann as opera promoter 141, 158
  performance of *Die drei Pintos* 164
  performance of *Don Giovanni* 165
Lemcke, Karl 168
Lenau, Nikolaus 278
Lenbach, Franz von 44
Leonardo da Vinci 126, 647, 730
Leoncavallo, Ruggero 299, 300, 314
Leschetitzky, Theodor 54
Lessing, Gotthold Ephraim 27–8
Levi, Hermann 113, 165, 167, 247, 265
Levine, James 704
Lewy, Gustav 92, 100, 102, 109, 112
liberalism in Austria
  crisis and 1879 defeat 46, 49–50, 343–4
  GM and student critiques 83–4
  Ringstraße as expression of 48–9, 50
Libman, Emanuel 324, 676–7
Lichtenberg, Georg Christoph 205
Liebstöckl, Hans 508, 533
Liechtenstein, Prince Rudolf von und zu 259, 283, 287, 288, 301, 303, 465–6
Liliencron, Detlev von 168
Lipiner, Clementine 380
Lipiner, Nanna *see* Spiegler, Nanna
Lipiner, Siegfried 100, 126, 243, 259, 264, 318, Ill. 7
  Alma on GM's regret at friendship 680–1
  Alma's introduction and GM's break with 379–80, 381–3, 502
  and Anna von Mildenburg 436
  anti-Semitic responses to work 79, 80, 82–3
  circle in Vienna 55, 63–4, 75–84, 278–9, 381–3, 502, 511, 681
  failure to achieve potential 80–1, 597
  influence on GM's ideas and beliefs 395, 407

Nietzsche and *Prometheus Unbound* 78,
79, 81, 82
reconciliation with GM and poem 80,
594, 596–8, 606, 681, 687
Renatus poem 79, 81–2
as translator 203
and Vienna appointment 283, 285
views on death and GM 594, 597, 617,
669, 686, 687
Wagner and visit to Wahnfried 79–80
Liszt, Franz 149, 186, 474
and New German School 61–2, 106, 182
Literary Club in Vienna 75
Loew Sanatorium, Vienna 683, 684
Löhr, Friedrich 123, 164, 264, 380, 689
on affair with Marion von Weber 163
as family friend 188, 216, 217, 230,
510, 511
GM on Bülow 215
GM on *Lieder eines fahrenden
Gesellen* 170
on GM's conducting 146
GM's letters to 109, 111, 113, 117–18,
121, 124, 125, 140, 143, 148, 259,
285, 325, 511
visits GM in Prague 144, 146
Löhr family 188, 189
Löhr, Uda 188, 216, 230
Lombroso, Cesare 329
London, GM conducts in 219–20
Loos, Adolf 43–4, 48, 352
Lortzing, Albert 157, 469
Lösch, Josef 231
Lotze, Hermann 398–400, 407, 594
Louis, Rudolf 254–5
Löwe, Ferdinand 315, 316, 586, 624
Lueger, Karl 49, 288–9, 294, 344, 531
Ludwig II, King of Bavaria 363, 548

Maazel, Lorin 704
McCormack, John 671
Mach, Ernst 349 539
Mackay, John Henry 168
Maeterlinck, Maurice 132, 350, 376
Magyar nationalism in Budapest 179–80,
183, 189–90
Mahler, Abraham (great-great-grandfather)
16
Mahler, Alma (wife, *née* Schindler, *later*
Gropius *then* Werfel) Ills 14 & 24
advice against marrying GM 328, 329,
371, 374
'Alma's theme' in Sixth Symphony 410
ambivalent feelings towards GM and
crisis in marriage 626–9, 636–7
anti-Semitism 261, 361, 364–5, 371, 380,
381, 517–18, 627, 628–9

appearance and beauty 240, 361, 363
appraisal of GM's work 371, 381, 391,
436–7, 626, 681
artistic talent 363
birth of children 434–5
on breach with Natalie Bauer-Lechner 384
Catholicism 392
on Charpentier 471
on Chinese poetry and grieving GM 554–5
on Christianity of GM 260, 392–3
and clothes for GM 8
and completion of Tenth Symphony
fragment 662
as composer and GM's demand for
renunciation 363, 366–9, 371, 375–9,
433–4, 626–7
as composer and GM's rediscovery of
her songs 641–3, 676
copies music for GM 442
courtship period 370–84, 431–4
cult of Mahler after his death 645,
646–7, 668, 674, 696, 705
and death of daughter Maria 550–3
dedication of Eighth Symphony to 646
descriptions of 361–2
as distant mother 434, 599–600
dreams 434–5, 628
and Dreyfus Affair 517–18
drinking and alcoholism 361, 369,
598, 630
father figure attraction 627, 651
on female lack in creative arts 366–7
and final illness and death of GM 667,
668, 674, 676, 677, 678–9, 680–1, 684,
688, 689
first meeting(s) with GM 359–61, 370
and Fraenkel in New York 578
as freethinker 392
on French rudeness during GM's Second
Symphony in Paris 621
and Freud's analysis of GM 627, 651–2
frivolous nature and effort of 'rising to
meet' GM 432–4, 437
generation gap with husband 75, 374,
432, 582, 627, 645, 651
GM defends against Adler's gossip 607
GM's poems to 639–40, 654, 664–5
on GM's view of Toscanini 590
Gropius affair *see* Gropius, Walter
on harsh childhood of GM 24, 34
and Hauptmanns 513
health during marriage 434, 439, 537,
557–8, 578, 598–9, 630, 638
and health of GM 323, 324, 326, 328,
329, 331, 432, 439
honeymoon in St Petersburg 438–9
humour lost on 227–8

Mahler, Alma (*cont.*)
  as influence on GM's work 390, 410
  and interpretation of GM's work 410, 414
  jealousy and denial of GM's previous
    relationships 210–11, 235, 372, 384,
    435–6
  on Jewish identity of GM 261
  and Justine 229, 375, 379, 384, 441,
    443, 681
  lack of commentary on GM's
    work 386
  lack of descriptive powers 1
  and *Das Lied von der Erde* 563, 612
  life as young woman 361–70, 431–4
  and Lipiner friendship and
    reconciliation 596, 680–1
  love affairs and flirtations 85–9, 306,
    362–3, 364, 365–6, 369, 392, 438,
    609, 629
  and Maiernigg holiday home 443, 445,
    446, 447, 552, 553
  and markings on Tenth Symphony
    manuscript 645–7
  marriage to GM: early years 431–47;
    feelings of isolation and crisis of
    1910 438, 599, 600, 625–32, 634–56
  and Anna von Mildenburg 210–11, 234,
    235, 238, 371–2, 423, 435–6
  on Montenuovo and GM's departure
    from Vienna 535
  in New York 577–8, 608–9
  Nietzsche reading and GM's disapproval
    279, 372, 392
  on parents-in-law 20
  'passed in review' evening 379–83
  and Pfitzner 472–4
  as pianist 363–4
  publication of GM's letters 234, 361,
    644–5, 695, 702
  publication of memoirs 477, 478, 626,
    629–30, 636, 674
  published diaries 359–61, 361–2, 366,
    369, 371, 432, 433–4
  on Puccini 470
  repulsion at GM's physical presence 600,
    626, 627–8
  and Roller's meeting with GM 422–3
  and Rome cancellation 622
  and Rückert Lieder 176
  on Secessionist exhibition 355
  on send-off from Vienna 560–1
  sexual nature 363–4, 369, 371, 626,
    628, 637–8
  sexual relations with GM 328, 329,
    374, 435, 437–8, 626, 627, 629, 637,
    638, 650
  and Strauss 361, 477–8

  on student life at Conservatory 62
  and Toblach and GM's domestic
    difficulties 613
  tonsillectomy 602
  as unreliable witness 20, 24, 263, 439,
    555, 629–30, 674
  and 'unsympathetic smell' of GM
    627, 628
  Wagner worship 363–4
  and Werfel 192
  on Wolf's breakdown 65
Mahler, Alois (brother) 21, 23, 188, 216,
    229, 322–3
Mahler, Anna Justine (daughter) 138, 330,
    434, 598, 697, Ills 24 & 25
  and Canetti 192
  distant relations with mother 561,
    599–600
  and father's death 684
  memories and memoirs of father 11,
    226–7, 656–7, 675
  scarlet fever 537, 550
  in Tobelbad 630, 631
  tonsillectomy 602
Mahler, Bernard (great-grandfather) 16
Mahler, Bernhard (father) Ill. 2
  background and family 13–19
  birth of GM 13, 14, 17
  as book-lover 19, 22, 133
  as distiller 14–15, 17–18
  enterprising nature 18
  illness and death 100, 110, 113, 188,
    228–9, 322
  Jewishness 14–15, 19–20, 22, 259
  marriage 16–17, 20
  photograph of 23
  and son's distractedness 32
  and son's musical talent 27, 29, 39–40,
    41, 68
  as strict disciplinarian 20, 33
Mahler, Emma Marie Eleonor (sister, *later*
    Rosé) 21, 188, 216, 229, 439, 441
  death 322
  and Dostoevsky test 137
  family holidays at Attersee 230
  marriage to Eduard Rosé 228,
    302, 445
Mahler, Ernst (brother) 21, 22–3, 37–8,
    216, 322–3, 669
Mahler, Gustav
  admiration of 'Schoenberg circle' 479–85
  appearance and characteristics 1–11, 59,
    109, 133, 140; Alma's shock on
    convict's haircut 600; bad habits 6,
    7–8, 268, 371; beard and incarnations
    8, 84, 91–2, 144–5, 196; and clothing
    8–9; and *The Concerto* painting

209–10; as conductor 196–7, 198–9,
493; 'demonic' impressions 2, 198–9;
in final days 679; height and stature 3;
laughter 5, 9–10; as non-Aryan
conductor 294; physical activity and
fitness 3–5, 9, 95, 110–11, 230, 318,
323, 442, 446–7, 583, 584; seriousness
and melancholic aspect 10–11, 24;
shape of skull 6–7; short-sightedness
8, 31–2, 91; tone of voice and accent
10, 84; 'twitching foot' and gait 2, 5–7,
84, 324–5; *see also* portraits and
likenesses *below*
books and reading 32–3, 75, 77–9, 82–3,
125–39, 394; *see also* literary
influences *below*
character 187, 220–32; ambitious streak
118, 160–1, 226, 243–4, 250, 287–8;
anger 10, 224–5, 308, 502, 503, 504–5;
anxiety over work and money 167,
181, 215–16, 217, 284; as child 32,
36–7; childlike ego regression during
marital crisis 640–1; childlike
egocentrism 502–3, 640, 641; childlike
naïveté in Vienna post 540; danger of
drawing parallels with music and state
of mind 612–14; day-dreaming and
distractedness 32, 221, 222, 600;
defeatism and self-doubt 217, 249,
410, 452; 'difficult' reputation 285,
287, 313; discipline of daily routine
441–2, 445–7; disconcerted by
prostitute 221–2; disconcerting
directness with friends 501–3;
dismissal of birthdays 632; energy and
impatience in career 178–9, 222, 446;
expediency and economy with truth
70–1, 112, 243, 250; Freud's analysis
and 'Mary complex'/mother fixation
650–4; high standards cause
misjudgement as tyrant 187, 194, 224;
high-handedness with friends 381–2;
insecurity and Jewish background
268; intensity and constant striving
601; introspective nature 32, 93, 636;
lack of vanity 8, 9, 110, 503; loneliness
in Hamburg 217–18; loneliness in
New York 577–8; love of animals and
nature 221, 226, 398, 601; love and
extremes of emotion 86–9, 121–2,
238–40; melancholy and despair
100–2, 181, 218–19, 268–9; mood
swings and volatility 86–9, 93–5,
99–102, 217–18, 222, 223–4, 468;
moral standards 132, 226; patronizing
approach to young women in life
237–8, 240, 310–12, 366, 367–8, 371,

373–4, 375–9, 627; sense of humour
and irony 162, 220, 226–8, 275, 280,
333, 334, 336–7, 338–9; sociability on
holiday 230, 613; social skills and
tactlessness 161–2, 222, 227, 240,
497–8, 502–3; unsympathetic
impression 221
childhood and early youth 12–41;
accordion playing and love of band
music 25–6, 30–1, 266; Ahasuerus
dream 272; background as German-
speaking Jew 13–15, 259, 263, 267;
birth 13, 14, 17; early childhood in
Iglau 23–41; education in Judaism 19,
20; estrangement from Judaism 20, 88;
family history 16–18, 264; first
compositions 27–8, 69, 84–5;
imaginative feats 36–7; music lessons
26–7, 29; musical sensibilities and
skills 20, 24–9, 33–4, 36–7, 103–4;
piano recitals 26, 33–4, 37, 39; school
days 33–6, 67, 140; Schwarz's
petitioning of parents 39–41;
simultaneous studies in Iglau and
Vienna 34–5, 67, 69–70; as Vienna
Conservatory student 28, 34–5, 37,
39–41, 54–89
compositional practice and process
447–57; Natalie Bauer-Lechner's
accounts of 153–4, 173, 448–50, 452;
'composing houses' and holiday
arrangements 173, 228, 230, 231, 236–7,
245, 318–19, 441, 443–7, 520–1,
582–90; eagle in composing hut 647–8;
fear of misinterpretation of work 452–3,
488–91; instrumentation problem
451–2, 453–4, 488–9, 657–8; and living
quarters in Hamburg 209–10; need for
silence 62, 231; and opera house
schedules 111–12, 178, 189, 231, 318,
441–2; plans to devote more time to
670, 681; publication of work 454–7,
622–3, 701; revisions 451–2, 454, 456,
489, 532; stages in writing score 450–1;
use of sketchbook/notebook 173, 447,
448, 555
as conductor 191–201; acquisition of skills
67–8; Bad Hall as first appointment
90–8, 105; Budapest Opera post 167,
178–90, 222–3; calmer style in later
career 200, 224, 498; concert tour
before Vienna post 289; conducting
style 109–10, 145, 146, 195, 196–201,
253, 498; critical responses *see* critical
and public reception of work *below*;
dedication and empathy with
performers 198, 199, 211–12, 213, 308,

Mahler, Gustav: as conductor (*cont.*)
571; disappointment at New York
musicians 572, 590, 605; distant
relations with colleagues 245–6, 578; on
emotions on conducting own work
606; energetic working method 110–11,
146, 195, 196, 197–9, 200, 224–5, 253;
exacting standards and demands on
performers 103–4, 111, 117–18, 145,
160–1, 187, 193–4, 198, 208, 223–6,
307–8, 528–9, 605, 622; foreign concert
tours and performances 299–300,
535–6, 536–7, 557, 620, 621, 622;
foreign tour absences compromise
Vienna post 486–91, 510, 533, 541–2;
guest conducting concerts in America
580–1, 602–6; Hamburg Opera
position 187–8, 190, 208–50; heavy
work load 116–17, 245, 317–18, 321–2,
486–8, 490–1, 528–9; Kassel position
68, 112, 113, 114–24, 252; lack of
leadership skills 194–5; Laibach season
as principal conductor 102–5, 108;
Leipzig Opera position 123, 146–7,
157–67; London season 219–20;
'magnetism' and charisma 220, 225–6,
313, 511; nervous agitation 187, 193,
198, 253; New York *see* New York
Metropolitan Opera post *and see* New
York Philharmonic Orchestra; Olmütz
position 104, 105, 108–12; opera likes
and dislikes 104–5; of own work
199–200, 203, 254, 309–10, 316–17,
390, 451, 486–91, 510, 606, 610, 622–5,
655–9; and pay and conditions for
musicians 224, 503; performance from
memory in Prague 146; in Prague
140–7, 167; return to Prague 585–6;
and Secessionist exhibition (1902) 354,
355–7; in Vienna *see* Vienna Court
Opera appointment and tenure *and see*
Vienna Philharmonic Orchestra; and
Wagner repertory 142–3, 159–60,
184–6, 212–13, 218–20, 297–8, 303–5,
569–70, 571; Wagner repertory and
reinstatement of cuts 303–4, 559;
Wagner repertory and restaging in
Vienna 314, 423–6; Wagner repertory
and Toscanini in New York 575,
587–90, 591
critical and public reception of work:
First Symphony 155, 156, 249, 317,
700–1; Second Symphony 203, 249,
316, 333–4, 591–2, 621; Fourth
Symphony 333–4, 482, 672; Fifth
Symphony 558; Sixth Symphony
532–3; anti-Semitic responses 82–3,

124, 145, 198, 252–7, 296, 298, 429,
467–8, 507, 510; Bülow's negative
responses 164–5, 214–15, 217; as
conductor in Budapest 185, 189, 190;
as conductor in Hamburg 212–13,
296–7; as conductor in Kassel 117,
252; as conductor in London 219, 220;
as conductor in New York 570–1,
579–80, 592, 604–5, 610; as conductor
in Prague 145–6; as conductor in
Vienna 295–6, 298, 300–1, 304–5,
532–3, 557; *Das klagende Lied* 107;
posthumous evaluations 696–7;
Vienna Opera staging reforms 424–5,
429, 430, 533, 534, 559–60; *see also*
performance of work *below*
and death of daughter Maria 550–4
and death of Wagner 110
early compositions 27–9, 69, 84–5, 95
English language skills 219–20, 518, 578
as father 9–10, 675
festschrift for 50th birthday 357, 512,
514–15, 632–4
final illness and death 6, 321, 324, 327,
666–90; attention to Alma and Anna
674–5; fatal illness 675–8, 682, 684;
Grinzing burial 680, 688, 689–90; and
presentiment of death 668–9, 670–1,
680–1; professional commitments in
New York 671–3, 675–6; regrets 680–1;
voyage home 6, 678–90; will 689
financial circumstances: anxiety over
work and money 181, 215–16, 217,
284, 531, 542; Budapest salary and
pay-off 183, 190, 216; as Conservatory
student 68; early conducting positions
105, 108, 112; Hamburg salary 216,
224; and New York contracts 547, 549,
577, 579, 580; publication fees and
royalties 455; and success of *Die drei
Pintos* 166; Vienna Opera contract
and benefits 301–2, 440–1, 540, 542,
543; Vienna Opera years 440–7, 543
friends 501–18; Alma's account of GM's
regret 680–1; Conservatory circle
55–66; direct honesty and
egocentrism 501–4; enemies in
Vienna 504–10; familiarity and use of
'Du' 511–12; isolation during Gropius
affair 636–7; Lipiner/Pernerstorfer
circle 55, 63–4, 75–84, 278–9, 381–3,
502, 511, 681; reconciliation with
Lipiner 596–8, 681, 687; and social life
in New York 577–8, 608–9
health and lifestyle 321–32, 498;
abscesses and operation to remove
241, 301, 325–7; cycling skills 227;

delicate digestive system 329, 331, 446; eating and drinking habits 222–3, 322, 329, 331, 359, 442, 446, 613, 675; endocarditis as fatal illness 676–8, 682; family history 322–3, 583; final illness and contributing factors 188, 321, 322, 324, 325–7, 644, 673, 675–8, 682, 684; genius and ailments 329–30; haemorrhoids and internal bleeding 188, 222, 317, 319–20, 327–8; heart problems 5, 21, 223, 321, 322–7, 552, 644, 676–7; hypochondria after diagnosis of heart condition 553–4, 583–4; life-threatening haemorrhage 319–20, 328; loss of libido and marital crisis 626, 627, 629, 637, 638, 650, 653; and Maiernigg composing hut 446; migraines 8, 222, 312, 3 28–9, 438–9, 549; New York and routine in 577; physical activity and fitness 3–5, 9, 95, 110–11, 230, 318, 321, 323, 442, 446–7, 583, 584, 601; possible causes of 'twitching leg' 5–6, 324–5; and professional work load 317, 321–2, 326–7, 487; robust attitude to illness 330–1, 503; smoking 223, 322; throat illnesses and tonsillitis 241, 297, 301, 322, 325–7, 638–9, 655–6, 670, 675–6, 682; vegetarianism 64, 83, 101, 110, 222, 675

holidays 123, 167; composing arrangements in Steinbach 228, 230–2, 236–7, 245, 301, 443; daily routine 443, 445–7; isolation in Scandinavia 218, 230; Maiernigg and 'composing hut' 173, 318–19, 441, 443–7, 520–1, 543, 551, 552, 553; preference for mountains and lakes 100, 230; Toblach and 'composing hut' 301, 582–5, 600–1, 611, 613, 632, 647; walking and physical activity 4, 9, 95, 113, 164, 230, 318, 442, 446–7, 583, 584, 601

ideas and beliefs 260, 392–408; attitude to Christianity and God 260, 392–5, 397, 406–8; childhood prayers 24, 27; compassion as religion 77, 129, 137–8, 226, 260, 263, 398; conversion and Catholicism 228, 248, 250, 252, 259–60, 289, 394–5; and creative works 331–2, 400–8; on death and immortality 331, 332, 396–8, 403–8, 595, 612, 617, 668–9, 684–8; entelechy and striving for perfection 137, 397, 400–8, 520, 526, 687–8; and existential crisis in New York 593–5,

614–15, 617; Fechner 260, 395–8, 400, 401; German nationalist sympathies 64, 76–7; Goethe 133–4, 260, 393, 397, 401–7, 593–4, 598, 687–8; Lotze 398–400; Nietzsche 77–9, 83–4, 279, 355; pantheistic view of nature 87, 93–4, 232, 260, 398; socialist sympathies 345–6; views on racial difference in America 576–7, 671; work and divine purpose 393–4, 399–408; see also Jewishness below

intellectual energy 74–84, 222

Jewishness 14, 31, 226, 251–73; Ahasuerus figure 272; ambivalent attitude towards 259–60, 261–2, 263, 264, 272–3; anti-Semitic attitudes towards 248, 252–7, 261–2, 296, 371, 465, 467–8, 507, 510, 692–3, 696; appearance and comments on 2, 198, 294; and Budapest position 180, 183, 186; conversion to Catholicism 228, 248, 250, 252, 259–60, 289; critics and anti-Semitism 82–3, 124, 145, 198, 252–7, 296, 298, 429, 466, 507, 510; family background 259, 263, 264; impact in childhood 19, 20; indifference to anti-Semitism in those admired 60, 104, 132, 247, 258; Jewish music question 264–73, 697; and 'Jewish self-hatred' 260–1; prejudice towards German Jews in America 576–7; as threat to Vienna appointment 287, 288–9

literary influences 27–8, 38, 88, 125–39, 202–3; Chinese poetry 554–6, 562–4; Eichendorff 459–60, 462; Hofmannsthal's 'Chandos Letter' 614, 615; and *Das klagende Lied* 96–9; *Des Knaben Wunderhorn* 126–9, 170–1, 172–3, 232, 277, 280, 335; Jean Paul 134–6; and redefinition of symphony 135–6; titles of Third Symphony 276; and youthful angst 94–5; *see also* Goethe; *see also* Rückert; *and see* books and reading *above*

love affairs and relationships: early tragedy of unrequited lover 100; first loves 85–9, 94–5, 99, 100–1; Betty Frank in Prague 143–4; Selma Kurz 308–13; Anna von Mildenburg in Hamburg 210–11, 223–4, 228, 234–44; Johanna Richter in Kassel 114, 118, 120–3, 170; Marion von Weber as first great love 148–9, 162–4, 166; youth and sexual reticence 102

marriage to Alma: composing skills and letter demanding renunciation 366,

Mahler, Gustav: marriage to Alma (*cont.*)
367–8, 371, 375–9, 433–4; concern
over age gap 374, 432, 627, 645, 651;
courtship and preparation for
wedding 370–84, 431–4; crisis of
1910 438, 599, 600, 625–32, 634–56,
663; daily routine 441–2, 445–7; early
years 431–40; family and friends
introduced to 379–83; first meeting(s)
Alma Schindler 359–61; honeymoon
in St Petersburg 438–9, 443; ignorance
of Gropius affair and visit to Tobelbad
631–2; last months and attempts to
please 645–6, 674–5; mistaken letter
and fallout from Gropius affair 627,
634–45, 663, 664–5; renewed interest
in Alma's compositions 641–3, 676;
see also Mahler, Alma
   musical influences: band music 25–6,
30–1, 266; Chinese poems 555, 556,
562–4, 566, 567; deserter imagery 129,
173, 616; early loves 85–9, 94–5,
148–9; fairy stories as source 96–8;
folk element in music 266–7, 270, 671;
grand passion for Marion von Weber
163, 166; historical turbulence 52;
Jewish music 31; literary influences
126–31, 135–6, 170–1, 202–3; love for
Alma 390; love of nature 93–4, 172–3,
231–2; marital crisis and Tenth
Symphony 663, 664–5; Rott's
contemporary work 57, 59; Wagnerian
passion as young man 62–3, 113, 258
   operatic works: *Argonauts* overture 84,
95; *Die drei Pintos* ('out of Weber')
162, 164–6, 167, 474; *Herzog Ernst von
Schwaben* (unknown fragment) 28–9,
38, 85; *Rübezahl* 64–5, 84–5, 95, 108
   performance of work: First Symphony
156, 249, 317, 605–6, 700–1; Second
Symphony 203–4, 246, 249, 316,
333–4, 489, 591–2, 620, 621, 697;
Fourth Symphony 333, 495–6, 605–6,
672; Fifth Symphony 389, 456, 488,
495, 496, 558, 605–6; Sixth Symphony
409, 410, 411, 489, 532–3; Seventh
Symphony in Prague 585–6; Eighth
Symphony 622–3, 624–5, 655–9, 697;
Ninth Symphony 693–4; *Das klagende
Lied* 106–7; foreign tours and absences
compromise Vienna post 486–91, 510,
533, 541–2; *Kindertotenlieder* 496, 497,
610; *Das Lied von der Erde* 693–4, 697;
in Netherlands 491–8; in New York
591–2, 605–6, 610; posthumous
performances and interpretations
662–3, 665, 698–9, 701–2, 703; and

revisions 451–2, 456, 458, 532; songs
in Vienna repertoire 309–10; *see also*
critical and public reception of work
above
   as pianist 26–7, 33–4, 37, 39, 67, 68, 69,
104, 108, 113
   as piano teacher and accompanist 26–7,
68, 86, 108
   poems 88–9, 122–3, 239–40, 639–40,
654, 664–5
   portraits and likenesses 3; caricatures
and Jewishness 253; Caruso sketch 7;
as conductor 197, 198; death mask 7,
684; Gallen-Kallela portrait 558;
Klimt's knight 354, 632; photographs
6–7, 7–8, 9, 10–11, 223, 228, 535, 670;
photographs in childhood and youth
24, 31–2, 91; photographs in Vienna
Opera years 341; photographs on
voyage home 678–9; Rodin's bust 6,
595–6, 602, 632
   posterity and reputation 572, 691–706;
festivals and celebrations 694–5, 696,
701, 704; as influence on other
composers 703–4; and 'My time will
come' statement 691–2; popularity of
Death in Venice 702–3; postwar lack
of enthusiasm for 699–701; present-
day conductors' attitudes to 704–5;
publications and scholarship 702;
resistance to memorial in Austria
696–7; revival of interest in late
twentieth century 490, 692, 701–6;
stereo recordings of work 701–2, 704;
Third Reich and 'problem of race'
696–7; twentieth-century conductors
and interpretations 662–3, 665, 698–9,
701–2, 703
   pride in Eighth Symphony 519–20
   prizes and competitions 58, 67, 69, 84, 105
   programme music and symphonic work
135–6, 149–50, 151–3, 156, 202–3,
203–6, 448
   religion *see* Jewishness *and see* ideas and
beliefs *above*
   responsibility for brothers and sisters
100, 167, 188, 216–17, 441, 543, 577
   songs 126–31, 168–77, 188; conservative
choice of material 168–9; *Des Knaben
Wunderhorn* songs 126–9, 169, 170,
171–5, 204, 206, 231, 309–10, 335, 394,
448; interrelation with symphonies
169, 173, 175, 204, 206, 335, 412, 448,
563, 618; *Kindertotenlieder* 129–30,
131, 169, 170, 176–7, 319, 412, 496,
497, 610, 618, 685–6; *Das klagende
Lied* cantata 29, 85, 93, 95–8, 105–7,

150; *Lieder eines fahrenden Gesellen* 88, 114, 122, 124, 126–8, 147, 148, 153, 155, 169–72, 256, 309–10; *Lieder und Gesänge* 170, 172; 'Revelge' 173–5, 412; Rückert Lieder 129–31, 168, 170, 175–7, 556
symphonies: First Symphony 135, 136, 148–56, 165, 167, 188, 202, 249, 317, 449–50, 700–1; Second Symphony 166, 188, 202–7, 215, 231, 246, 249, 316, 333–4, 394, 397, 399–400, 447–9, 482, 489, 591–2, 620, 621, 697; Third Symphony 173, 231–2, 236–7, 270, 274–81, 480, 492, 493; Fourth Symphony 266, 274, 318, 319, 333–9, 482, 495–6, 672; Fifth Symphony 135, 319, 385–91, 442, 454, 455–7, 488, 495, 496, 558, 702–3; Sixth Symphony 409–415, 454, 462, 489, 532–3; Seventh Symphony 458–63, 479, 497–8, 585–7; Eighth Symphony 135, 249, 394, 409, 437, 519–26, 598, 622–3, 624–5, 646, 655–9, 697; Ninth Symphony 135, 169, 280–1, 483, 520, 611–19, 693; Tenth Symphony fragment 625, 645–6, 662–5; *Das Lied von der Erde* (song-symphony) 169, 482–3, 520, 555, 556, 562–7, 585, 612, 617–18, 693, 697; 'Todtenfeier' movement 166, 447–8
on tradition and slovenliness 145, 416
'vocabular music' 271, 386–8
Mahler, Isidor (brother) 21
Mahler, Justine Ernestine (sister, *later* Rosé) 23, 216, 246, 373–4, 689, Ill. 10
and Alma 229, 375, 379, 380, 384, 441, 443, 681
appearance 228
and Natalie Bauer-Lechner 384
death 21, 322
and family holidays 230, 318–19, 444–5
financial management and GM's debts 441
Freudian relationship with GM 443, 653
illness after nursing parents 4, 188, 228–9
marriage to Arnold Rosé 21, 228, 302, 439, 443
on response to Second Symphony 203
shares house with GM 21, 188, 228, 238, 297, 302, 380, 439, 441
Mahler, Leopoldine (sister, *later* Quittner) 21, 22–3, 441
death 188, 216, 322
Mahler, Maria Anna (daughter) 10–11, 268, 434, Ill. 24
illness and death 323, 414, 550–4
Mahler, Marie (Maria, grandmother, *née* Bondy) 16, 17

Mahler, Marie (mother, *née* Hermann)13, 19, Ill. 3
close relationship with son 20–1, 23, 24
health 20–1, 38, 322, 583
illness and death 100, 113, 188, 228–9, 322
marriage 16–17, 20
photograph of 23
and son's musical abilities 27
Mahler, Otto (brother) 217, 229, 230, 441
Brahms and Bruckner debate 73–4
inconsistent character 216
musical talent 21, 29, 188, 216
suicide 21
Mahler, Simon (grandfather) 14–15, 16, 17
Mahler (film) 20, 683
Mahler Festival in Amsterdam 694–5, 696
Mahler Orchestra plan in New York 580–1, 592–3, 605, 673
Maiernigg on Wörthersee 173, 312, 318–19, 441, 443–7, 520–1, 543, 551, 552, 553, Ill. 13
Maikl, Georg 307
Makart, Hans 44–5
Malloch, William 728
Manhattan Opera House, New York 545–6, 547
Manheit, Jacques (Jakob) 109–11
Mann, Thomas 321, 330, 513, 669
Aschenbach and GM's similarities 688, 703
bitterness of schooldays 36
Buddenbrooks 321
Doktor Faustus and GM's Sixth 413, 415
and first performance of the Eighth Symphony 658, 659
reaction to Wagner lecture 253–4
Visconti's *Death in Venice* 389, 702–3
Wolf and art from life 66
Marcus, Adele 246, 585, 687–8
Marie Louise, Archduchess of Austria 466
Marschalk, Margarete 513
Marschalk, Max 95, 96, 148–9, 151–2, 202, 204, 275, 475, 512
Marschner, Heinrich 116, 144
Martucci, Giuseppe 673
Marx, Karl 268, 345
Mascagni, Pietro 296
Massenet, Jules 286, 294, 295, 305, 529, 609, 620
Materna, Amalie 294–5, 305, 545
Matthews, Colin and David 662
mauscheln as derogatory term 253, 255
Mayer, Hans 521
Mayr, Richard 307, 423
Mehta, Zubin 705
Méhul, Étienne-Nicolas 110, 112
Meilhac, Henri 52

Mendelssohn, Felix 157, 257, 258, 260, 266
Mendelssohn, Moses 253
Mendelssohn, Fanny 367
Mengelberg, Tilly 494, 495
Mengelberg, Willem 409, 657, 658, 689
  conducting career 491–2, 497, 580,
    622, 694
  friendship with GM 491, 495, 496,
    497–8, 519–20
  and Mahler Festival in Amsterdam 694
  and tempo for Fifth Symphony 390
Merezhkovsky, Dimitri 126
Metropolitan Opera *see* New York
  Metropolitan Opera post
Metternich, Pauline 540
Meyerbeer, Giacomo 104, 162, 257, 258, 266
Meysenbug, Malwida von 79, 81–2, 418
Michalek, Margarete 333, 371–2, 435
Mickiewicz, Adam 80, 202–3, 276
Mihalovich, Ödön von 245, 259
  and Budapest appointment 182, 184
  and Vienna appointment 250, 284, 286,
    287–8, 289
Mildenburg, Anna von (*later* Bahr-
  Mildenburg) 55, 120, 186–7, 658, 689,
  Ill. 11
  achievement and talent as singer 232–4,
    243, 299, 305–6
  affair with GM in Hamburg 210–11,
    223–4, 228, 234–44
  and Alma's 'passed in review' evening
    379, 380, 381
  Alma's view of 210–11, 234, 235, 238,
    371–2, 423, 435–6
  appearance 235–6
  discreet memoirs 244
  fading of affair and move to Vienna 235,
    240–4, 284, 302, 309
  first impression of GM 223–4, 234
  GM recommends for Bayreuth 233,
    247, 248
  and GM's dedication in work 198, 199
  on GM's delight in nature 398
  on GM's sense of humour 227
  letters from GM 210–11, 234–5, 236–7,
    238–9, 242–3, 244, 276–7, 326, 560
  and Maiernigg holiday home 318
  marriage to Bahr 342
  and Pollini's exploitation of performers
    211–12, 233
  and power as attraction 436
  and Vienna Court Opera 241–3, 423, 430
Miller, William 563
Mitchell, Donald 702
Mitropoulos, Dimitri 479, 705
Moll, Anna (Alma's mother, *formerly*
  Schindler) 362, 364, 379, 511, 561, 613

  and courtship of Alma and GM 359,
    360, 378, 653
  and death of granddaughter 323, 550,
    551–2
  and Gropius affair 637, 674
  help in GM's final illness 678, 680
  shared appreciation of Rosegger with
    GM 132
Moll, Carl (Alma's stepfather) 223, 362,
  365, 379, 384, 472, 481, 511, 585, 631,
  658, 680, Ill. 23
  and death of GM 684, 689, 690
  and death of granddaughter 550
  GM's letter on life in New York 577
  and Gropius affair 637
  and National Socialists 364
  and Rodin bust of GM 595, Ill. 30
  and Secession 341, 352, 354, 355, 356
monadism and entelechy 402–3, 405, 520
Mondheim-Schreiner, Alexander 103
Monson, Karen 361
Montenuovo, Prince Alfred 283, 464,
  465–6, 487, 501
  and GM's departure from Vienna Opera
    535, 536–7, 541–3, 547–8, 557
  and press attacks on GM 533–4
Monteux, Pierre 705
Moravia 12–13
  Jews in 14, 15, 19, 31
  musical influences on GM 266–7
  nationalist movements 46, 343
Morena, Berta 546, 573, 580
Mörike, Eduard 97, 168
Moscheles, Ignaz 158
Moser, Kolo 352, 357, 379, 380, 421, 423,
  539, 658
Mottl, Felix 247, 539
  as applicant for Vienna post 248, 288,
    289, 290
  as candidate to succeed GM in Vienna
    540, 547–8
  refuses Budapest position 181, 182
  Viennese Academic Wagner Society 63
Mozart, Leopold 336, 731
Mozart, Wolfgang Amadeus 24–5, 29, 292
  death and burial 667, 669
  GM conducts 104–5
  Don Giovanni: restaging of in Vienna
    429–30; performance of in Leipzig 165
  and Rodin bust 595
Muck, Karl 142–3, 249, 580
Muhr, Felix 329
Müller, Wilhelm 88, 122, 171
Multatuli (i.e. Edward Douwes Dekker)
  126, 494
Munch, Charles 705
Münden Grand Music Festival 123–4

Munich
  Exhibition (1910) and Eighth Symphony
    623–4, 657–9, Ill. 28
  GM's work in 289, 333–4, 585, 623–5,
    655–9
  reactionary music scene 253–4
  see also Kaim Orchestra in Munich
Munich Philharmonic Orchestra 623, 625
music publishers 454–7
Musical ABC of Jews 697
Musil, Robert 347, 348
Muti, Riccardo 705

Nadel, Arno 269
Nagano, Kent 705
Nahowski, Helene see Berg, Helene
Napoleon, accounts of death 667
National Socialism 255–7, 261, 365
  and GM's posthumous reputation 692,
    697, 698–9
nationalist movements and Dual Monarchy
    46–7, 343–4
  and anti-Semitism in Austria–Hungary
    15, 63–4, 344
  German nationalism and Telyn Society
    76–7
  Hungarian nationalism 179–80, 183,
    189–90
  linguistic divisions in Budapest 179, 183,
    184, 185–6
  linguistic divisions in Prague 141–2
Naumann-Gungl, Virginia 120
Nepallek, Richard 552, 649
Nestroy, Johann Nepomuk 91
Netherlands
  GM meets Freud 647–55
  GM visits 491–8
Nettl, Paul 269
Neuilly clinic 682
Neumann, Angelo 219
  festschrift contribution 633
  in Leipzig 141, 158
  in Prague 123, 141, 142–3, 144, 145, 146,
    160, 167
  as Wagner promoter 141
Neumann, Vaclav 705
New German School 61–2, 71–2, 106, 182
'New Symphony' 56–8, 150
New York Metropolitan Opera post 497,
    602, 608–10
  dissatisfaction with achievements at 572,
    576–7, 579–80, 590–2, 671–2
  first season 568–82
  guest conducting opportunities 580–1,
    591–2
  hopes for collaboration with Roller in
    574, 575–7, 580, 588

preliminaries to 544–9
refusal of director's post 574–5
second season and impending departure
    590–6
singers and GM's conducting 570, 571,
    572–3
third and last season in New York 673
Tristan und Isolde as opening
    performance and signature 569–71,
    588–90
Wagner repertory and conflict with
    Toscanini 575, 587–90, 591
wealthy sponsors 568–9, 573, 574–5, 580
work load 602, 603, 607
New York Philharmonic Orchestra
  GM conducts 580–1, 592, 602–6,
    609–10, 671–3, 675–6
  relations end on low point 672–3
New York Philharmonic Society 671
  Ladies Committee and Mahler
    Orchestra plan 580–1, 592–3,
    605, 673
New York Symphony Orchestra, GM
    conducts 580, 591–2, 605
Nicolai, Otto 116, 315
Nielsen, Carl August 694
Niemann, Albert 545
Nietzsche, Friedrich Wilhelm 27, 214, 260,
    355, 372
  Brahms faux pas 63
  condemnation of Jean Paul 134
  GM and Reading Society 77–9, 83–4
  GM's Third Symphony and Zarathustra
    278–9
  Lipiner and Prometheus Unbound 78, 79,
    81, 82
  'Nietzsche societies' 78, 83
  and Wagner 77–8, 83, 279
Nikisch, Arthur 67, 145, 166, 212, 390, 544
  conducting style 158–9, 196
  conducts GM's work 488
  rivalry with GM in Leipzig 146–7, 158–61
Nodnagel, Ernst 512
Norrington, Sir Roger 705
Nott, Jonathan 705
Novalis 493

Offenbach, Jacques 52, 91, 515, 516
Olbrich, Joseph Maria 351, 352, 356, 362
Oldenboom-Lutkemann, Alida 493
Olmütz and GM's position 104, 105, 108–12
Osler, William 676
operettas 91, 104
orchestral musicians, working conditions
    224, 503
ornament in Vienna 43–5, 48, 346
Ozawa, Seiji 705

Painlevé, Paul 358, 517, 595
Palladino, Eusapia 608
Panizza, Oskar 168
Pan-German sentiment in Austria 46,
    63–4, 76–7, 344, 345, 353
    and press campaign against GM 531–4
Paoli, Betty 82
Papier, Rosa 55, 124, 234, 241–2, 282,
    289, 309
Paris 561
    French antipathy towards German music
        620–2
    GM conducts Second Symphony in
        620, 621
    GM's final visit for treatment 680,
        682, 683
    GM's supporters in 358–9, 517–18,
        595, 683
    International Exhibition (1900) 312, 316
    visits for Rodin bust 595–6, 602, Ill. 30
Pauline (first love) 85, 88
Paumgartner, Bernhard 55
Paumgartner, Hans 55
Pernerstorfer, Engelbert 230
    circle in Vienna 55, 75, 83–4
    political leanings 63, 76, 77, 259, 344, 345
    and Telyn Society 76, 77
Perron, Karl 161
Peters, C. F. (music publishers) 454–5,
    456–7, 458
Pfitzner, Hans 168, 223, 254, 629, 658, Ill. 23
    GM and production of Die Rose vom
        Liebesgarten 469, 471–4
Pfohl, Ferdinand
    on appearance of GM 2, 4, 5, 6
    on character of GM 221, 222–3
    and First Symphony 156, 249
    friendship with GM 209, 221–3, 224,
        243, 245
    on voice and laugh of GM 9–10
Picquart, Georges 358, 517–18, 595
Pierné, Gabriel 620, 621
Piloty, Karl von 44
Plappart von Leenheer, Baron August 283,
    464–5, 499, 500, 501, 557
Poisl, Josephine 85, 86, 94, 95, 99, 100–1
Pollak, Theobald 555
Pollini, Bernhard (Baruch Pohl) 219, 241,
    286, 309, 475
    exploitation of performers 211–12, 233
    GM's difficult relationship with 211–12,
        240, 284, 286
    secret negotiations with GM 187–8, 211
polyphony 128–9, 279
Popper, David 182
Prague
    GM boards as schoolboy in 34, 140

GM as conductor at Landestheater
    140–7, 167
GM returns to conduct own work 585–6
    linguistic divisions and cultural life 141–2
Pressburg, Wenzel 29
Pringsheim, Klaus 349–50, 410, 489, 695
Proksch, Anna 18
Przistaupinsky, Alois 283, 467
psychoanalysis
    death wish attributed to GM 668–9
    and ego regression 640–1
    Kris and theory of creativity 641
    see also Freud, Sigmund
Puccini, Giacomo 470
Puchstein, Hans 531

Quittner, Ludwig 188

Rachmaninov, Sergei 753
Rameau, Jean-Philippe 604
Raimund, Ferdinand 53
Rattle, Sir Simon 705
Ratz, Erwin 456, 701
Raul, Emanuel 109
Ravel, Maurice 492, 694
'Reading Society of Viennese German
    Students' 77–9, 82, 83
Redlich, Hans Ferdinand 413
Reger, Max 633–4, 658, 698
Reichmann, Theodor 295, 305, 467
Reichwein, Leopold 698
Reik, Theodor 650, 651, 653
Reinecke, Carl 157
Reiner, Fritz 705
Reinhardt, Heinrich 507, 510, 533
Reinhardt, Max 223, 416, 420, 472, 516,
    658, Ill. 23
Renard, Marie 295, 305, 306
Reni, Guido 380, 382
Reszke, Édouard de 545
Reszke, Jean de 545
Richter, Hans 61, 67, 105, 220, 248, 304
    and Budapest Opera 180, 181
    conducting style 195, 198
    and Vienna Opera 286, 287, 291, 293,
        294, 314–15
    and Vienna Philharmonic 315–16
Richter, Johanna 114, 118, 120–3, 170
Rihm, Wolfgang 703–4
Rimsky-Korsakov, Nikolay 558
Ringer, Alexander L. 264
Ritter, William 438, 586, 591–2
Rode-Breymann, Susanne 641
Rodin, Auguste 658
    bust of GM 6, 595–6, 602, 632, Ill. 30
Rohde, Erwin 78
Roller, Alfred 223, 327, 585, 658, 689, Ill. 20

and appearance of GM 2–4, 5, 8
and ballet productions 534
Bayreuth Festival designs 420–1
costs of designs 500
and dying GM 684
on GM and immortality of fly 398
GM's appreciative letter 426
on GM's desire to leave Vienna Opera 535
GM's formal relations with 511
GM's hopes of collaboration in
    New York 574, 575–7, 580, 588
on GM's Jewishness 261, 263
GM's New York appointment and role in
    420, 547, 548, 574–6
on GM's religious beliefs 394–5
iconographic study of GM 2, 695
lack of diplomacy 496–7, 534
Munich Exhibition designs 657
New York post 588
Salzburg Festival designs 420
and Secession 352, 354, 356–7, 419–20,
    422, 424
and 'tradition is slovenliness'
    statement 416
tribute to GM's artistic integrity and
    collaboration 431
Vienna Opera collaboration and reform
    291, 416, 419–21, 422–31, 496–7, 500,
    528–9, 530, 533, 534, 557, 559–60
on Weingartner's productions 560
Rome, GM visits and conducts in
    535–6, 622
Roosevelt, Theodore 608
Rosé, Alma (niece) 21
Rosé, Arnold 264, 317, 318, 379, 380, 511
dispute with Franz Schmidt 504
and GM's burial 689, 690
as GM's orchestra confidant 672
marriage to Justine 21, 228, 302, 439, 443
Rosé, Eduard 302, 445, 511
Rosé, Emma see Mahler, Emma Marie
    Eleonor
Rosé, Justine see Mahler, Justine Ernestine
Rosé Quartet 21
Rosegger, Peter 132
Rossini, Gioachino 104
Roth, Joseph 349
Rothkamm, Jörg 641–2, 643
Rott, Hans 150
as friend in Vienna 55, 56–9, 64
mental instability 58, 100, 101, 102
possible influence on GM's work 57, 59
responses to work 56–8
Rubinstein, Anton 65, 470, 629
Rubinstein, Josef 247, 253, 258
Rückert, Friedrich 32, 126, 414, 562–3
and Fechner's ideas 397, 407

GM's song settings 129–31, 168, 175–7,
    556, 685–6
Ruppel, Karl Heinz 700
Russell, Ken, Mahler 20, 683
Ruzicka, Peter 704

Sachs, Curt 265
Sageder, Carl 467
St Petersburg
    concerts before New York 557–8
    honeymoon and concerts in 438–9, 443
Saint-Saëns, Camille 658
Salten, Felix 513–14, 538, 694
Salter, Norbert 543, 544, 546–7
Salvi, Matteo 293
Salzburg Festival 420, 487, 528, 693–4
Samaroff, Olga 137
Sandig, Anton 684
Sartre, Jean-Paul 262
Sawallisch, Wolfgang 705
Scandinavian holiday 218, 230
Scaria, Emil 113, 295, 305, 306–7
scarlet fever 550
Schalk, Franz 314, 315, 495–6, 529, 658
    and Tenth Symphony fragment 662, 695
Scharlitt, Bernhard 485, 528
Scheffel, Joseph Victor von 116
Schelling, Ernest 609
Scherchen, Hermann 192, 695, 705
Schertel, Anton 574, 576
Schiedermair, Ludwig 152–3, 512
Schiele, Egon 352, 353
Schiller, Friedrich 19, 116, 255, 282, 354
Schillings, Max von 633, 658
Schindler, Alma see Mahler, Alma
Schindler, Emil Jakob (Alma's father) 362
Schinkel, Karl Friedrich 211, 424
Schlenther, Paul 466
Schließmann, Hans 197
Schmedes, Erik 307, 423, 570, 658, 689
    Alma's flirtation with 306, 362,
        364, 365
    in New York 573
Schmidt, Franz 504–5
Schmidt, Jochen 406
Schnittke, Alfred 703
Schnitzler, Arthur 4, 358, 658
    diaries and depth of feeling for GM
        514, 515
    festschrift contribution 514–15
    GM's attitude to work of 131–2
    GM's belated friendship with 649
    Jewishness and sense of community
        263, 264
    on plight of Jews 345
    and sexual 'problem' of times 102
Schnitzler, Johann 358

Schopenhauer, Arthur 77, 79, 80, 370, 376, 392, 686
Schoenberg, Arnold 260, 335, 479–85, 658
  on Brahms and Wagner 71–2, 73, 482
  and burial of GM 689, 690
  circle of friends and admiration for GM 480–5
  as defender of GM 479–81, 484, 516, 539
  friendship with GM 480–1, 484–5, 560, 660
  GM's Dostoevsky challenge 136
  and GM's music 479–80, 481–2, 586–7
  GM's practical support for 481, 660, 687
  and Jewish music question 264, 266, 269
  and Mahler Festival in Amsterdam 694
  and Tenth Symphony fragment 662
Scholem, Gershom 267–8
Schönaich, Gustav 304, 424
Schöne, Albrecht 406, 407, 524
Schönerer, Georg von 63–4, 344, 345, 531
Schorske, Carl E. 348–9
Schott (music publishers) 454
Schratt, Katharina 243, 466
Schreker, Franz 54, 469
Schrödter, Fritz 471, 535–6, 539
Schubarth, Karl Ernst 403
Schuber, Hermann 90
Schubert, Franz 171–2, 177, 616–17
Schuch, Ernst von 123, 204, 476, 488
Schuler, Alfred 81
Schumann, Robert 98, 125, 157, 335
Schumann-Heink, Ernestine 193–4
Schuricht, Carl 705
Schütz, Heinrich 115
Schwarz, Gustav 39–40, 41
Schwarzenberg, Prince Friedrich 47
Schwind, Moritz von 151, 358, 424
Scott, Sir Walter 96
Scotti, Antonio 573
Secessionist art and artists 341, 351–7, 359, 419–20, 424, 427
  reaction against ornament 43–4, 48
Seelau 99
Seidl, Anton 145, 158, 160, 219
  creates opening for GM in Prague 142–3
  and New York Met 544, 545, 573
Sembrich, Marcella 573
Semper, Gottfried 45, 48
Senius, Felix 625
sex and threat of venereal disease 101–2
Shakespeare, William 133
Shaw, George Bernard 67, 220
Sheldon, Mary (Mrs George R.) 580–1, 673
Shiloah, Amnon 265
Shostakovich, Dmitri 266, 662, 703
Sibelius, Jean 558

Simmel, Georg 268
Sinigaglia, Leone 673
Sinopoli, Giuseppe 705
Sittard, Josef 212–13
Sladky, Jakob 29
Slezak, Leo 199, 307, 471, 570, 625, 689
  in New York 546, 573, 610
Slovenia and nationalism 103
Smetana, Bedřich 142, 469
Smyth, Ethel 163, 369
social democracy in Austria 76, 77, 83, 344, 345
Solti, Sir Georg 699, 701, 705
Specht, Richard 18, 409–10, 512, 514, 689
  on Dostoevsky and GM 136
  on enemies of GM 507–8
  and GM on intention in Eighth Symphony 521–2
  on GM's beliefs in immortality 408
  on GM's childlike egocentrism 502, 503, 640
  and GM's resignation from Vienna Opera 530, 538
  guide to GM's work 657
  and Mahler Festival in Amsterdam 694
  on Seventh Symphony 461
Speidel, Ludwig 62
Spetrino, Francesco 470, 529, 587
Spiegler, Albert 88, 379, 511
Spiegler, Nina ('Nanna')(née Hoffmann, formerly Lipiner) 379–80, 445, 511, 594
Spiering, Theodore 596, 602, 673
Spitzweg, Carl 460
Spohr, Louis 115, 195, 196
Staegemann, Max 147, 159, 160–1, 162, 164, 184
  and Goldberg affair 166–7
Stauber, Paul 508–9, 510
Stefan, Paul
  and burial of GM 668, 689
  on GM's weariness and resignation in Vienna 537–8
  and Mahler Festival in Amsterdam 694
  Mahler's Legacy and defence of GM 468–9, 508, 509
  organizes festschrift 357, 512, 514–15, 632–4
  organizes send-off from Vienna 560–1
Stein, Erwin 481
Stein, Lorenz von 77
Steinbach, Austria 228, 230–2, 236–7, 301, 443, Ill. 9
Steiner, George 619
Steiner, Josef 39, 99
  Herzog Ernst von Schwaben story 28, 38
  letters from GM 86–8, 93–4
Steinitzer, Max 164, 181, 474, 518, 633

Stekel, Wilhelm 648
Stengel, Theo 697
Stephan, Rudolf 207
Sterne, Laurence 126, 276
Stokowski, Leopold 137, 658, 705
Stoll, August 304, 467, 534
Strauß, Johann, conducts Wagner in
    Vienna 60
    Die Fledermaus 45, 52–3, 294
Strauss, Pauline 477
Strauss, Richard 215, 470, 616, 633, 658
    and Alma Mahler 361, 477–8
    Also sprach Zarathustra 278, 475
    anti-Semitism 254
    as conductor 67, 196, 203, 247, 474, 498
    Diepenbrock on 494
    Don Juan as symphonic poem 149, 150
    Elektra and Anna von Mildenburg 233–4
    first meeting with GM in Leipzig 164
    GM's relations with man and work 64,
        132, 167, 471, 474–9, 530, 691–2
    GM's view of difference to self 475,
        477, 691
    and GM's work 164–5, 167, 214, 249,
        390, 410, 474
    materialistic outlook 475, 477, 478, 691
    and modern conductors 698, 699
    and music publishers 455
    posterity and reputation 691–2, 698
    published correspondence with GM 702
    and Roller 420
    Salome and Vienna Opera 469,
        475–6, 529–30
    songs and choice of poets 168, 172
    Third Reich and view of 698
    Till Eulenspiegel 336
    and Wagner family 247, 248
Stravinsky, Igor 558, 699, 703
Streicher, Theodor 172
Stresemann, Wolfgang 699
Strindberg, August 136
Stritzko, Josef 455
Sturm, Franz 26, 29
Sucher, Rosa 219
Suk, Josef 208, 586, 694
Sullivan, Sir Arthur 158
summer theatres in resorts 90–1
Suppé, Franz von 91, 104
Svoboda, Wilhelm, 733, 739
symphonic music and 'New Symphony'
    57, 150
syphilis 102
Szilágyi, Arabella 185
Szell, George 705

Taaffe, Eduard Franz Joseph von 343
Tak, Max 497–8

Tauber, Richard 562
Tausenau, Richard 102
Tausig, Carl 247, 258
Tchaikovsky, Piotr Ilyich 166, 213, 165, 593
Telyn Society 75–7, 83
Tennstedt, Klaus 705
Thalberg, Sigismond 37
theatre reforms 416–20
Theuer, Alfred 318, 444
Thielemann, Christian 705
Third Reich and GM's work 697, 698–9
Thomas, Michael Tilson 705
Thuille, Ludwig 255
Tiffany, Louis 608
Titian 209–10, 715
    The Concerto 209–10
Toblach holiday home 301, 582–5, 600–1,
    611, 613, 632, 647
    Gropius affair and confrontation 635–6
Tolstoy, Leo 350
tone poems 150
Toscanini, Arturo 498, 572, 573, 579, 592,
    672, 705
    conflict with GM in New York 575,
        587–90, 591
total artwork (Gesamtkunstwerk) 353,
    416–18, 421, 424, 427
train travel and foreign tours 486–7, 488
Treiber, Wilhelm 115, 116, 119
    feud with GM in Kassel 117–18, 120,
        123, 124
Treitschke, Heinrich von 261
Trenker family 583
Troubetzkoy, Prince Paul 609
Turner, Maud 550

Überhorst, Karl 112
Ujházy, Ede 184
Unger, Rabbi 33, 35
Universal-Edition (music publishers) 454,
    600, 623, 657, 671, 694
University of Vienna 74–5, 354
Untermeyer, Minnie 673, 678
Urlus, Jacques 307
Utrecht Orchestra 409

Vancsa, Max 532
Vanderbilt family 569, 573
Varnhagen, Rahel 246
vegetarianism and Wagnerism 64, 83, 101,
    110, 222
venereal disease and effects 56, 58, 100,
    101–2
Venice, GM visits 299–300
Verdi, Giuseppe, GM's neglect 104, 469,
    469–70
Verhagen, Balthazar 498

Victorin, Franz 29
Vienna 42–54
    anti-Semitism in 47, 49, 51, 250, 252–3,
        254, 259, 288–9, 296, 344–5, 465, 692–3
    architecture 42, 48–9
    art and Secession 351–7, 359, 419–20,
        424, 427
    Bahr's critique 341–3
    cholera epidemic (1873) 51
    fin-de-siècle era 340–57
    genius and city's tolerance of 347–8
    GM as student in see Vienna
        Conservatory and GM as student
    GM's changes of address as young man
        92–3, 108
    GM's homesickness for 284–5, 606–7
    GM's marital home 439–40, 601–2
    GM's plans to return after America
        606–7, 660
    GM's return for death 682–90
    Grinzing grave 680, 688, 689, Ill. 31
    opera see Vienna Court Opera
    ornament and reaction against 43–5,
        48, 346
    political role and building of Ringstraße
        47–9, 50
    political uncertainty 343–6
    press and anti-Semitism on death of GM
        692–3
    press campaign against GM 507–10, 516,
        531–4, 536, 539, 558, 683
    press and return of dying GM 682–3
    salons 357–8
    stock market collapse (1873) 50–2
    'value vacuum' in fin-de-siècle era
        348–51
    and Wagner cult 59–64, 83
    World Fair (1873) 50, 51
Vienna Conservatory and GM as student
        28, 34–5, 37, 54–89
    absence of conducting classes 67
    circle of friends 55–66
    compositions and state of mind 69,
        84–9
    course change from piano to
        composition 67
    and musical backdrop in Vienna 71–4
    nature of studies and achievements
        66–71, 74–5
    petitioning of parents and entrance to
        39–41
    prizes 67, 69, 84
Vienna Court Opera Ill. 17
    dual posts of conductor and director
        286–7, 292–3, 301–2, 316
    finances and deficit 499–501, 529, 530,
        539–40

GM at see Vienna Court Opera
        appointment and tenure
    historical background 291–5
    presence at GM's funeral 689
    repertory and conservatism 468–70, 499,
        500–1
    rumours of GM's return 660
    strength of singers 294–5
    Wagner tradition 60–1, 293, 314
    Wagner's critique 527–8, 529
    and Wolf's Der Corregidor 65–6, 427
Vienna Court Opera appointment and
        tenure 240, 248, 249–50, 259,
        282–320, 419–31, 464–518
    anti-Semitic attacks on GM 252–3, 254,
        296, 465, 466–7, 507–10, 516
    campaign behind appointment
        282–91, 505
    campaign to remove 490–1, 506–10,
        531–4, 535–7, 539, 558, 683
    compromising absences to conduct own
        work 486–91, 510, 533, 541–2
    conducting roster 294, 314–15,
        529–30
    delight with responsiveness of musicians
        298–9
    as director and finances of opera house
        499–501, 530, 539–40
    directorial authority and administrative
        duties 464–8, 499–501, 534–5, 536
    and dual post as director 301–2, 316,
        464–8, 499–501
    festschrift as tribute to 633
    final performance and farewell 244, 557,
        558–61
    friends and enemies 501–18
    GM's 'difficult' reputation 285, 287,
        313, 465
    opening performance 297–8
    plans for opera reform 299, 302–8,
        313–20, 466
    reforms in staging and productions 314,
        347, 416–31, 528–9, 533, 534,
        559–60
    repertory and contemporary composers
        468–85, 499, 501, 530
    resignation and interim period before
        New York 543–9
    resignation and prelude to 485–91,
        527–43
    resignation and supporters' tributes
        538–9, 540–1
    reviews of GM 295–6, 298, 300–1,
        304–5, 532–3
    singers and GM's administration
        305–8, 466, 467–8, 506–7, 509,
        531–2, 533, 535–6

Vienna Philharmonic duties 316–17, 319, 486, 504–5
  work load 317–18, 486, 490–1, 528–9
Vienna Philharmonic Orchestra 161, 315–17, 486, 684
  anti-Semitism and GM's productions 253
  reluctance to perform Bruckner 72–3, 74
  resignation on health grounds 317
  trials of GM's relations with 224, 316–17, 319, 333, 355, 465, 504–5
  Walter's posthumous performances of GM's work 693
Vienna University, GM studies at 74–5
Vienna Werkstätte 43, 352
Viennese Academic Wagner Society 63, 64
Viotta, Henri 491
Visconti, Luchino, *Death in Venice* 389, 702–3
'vocabular music' 271, 386–8
Vogel, Carl 667
Volkelt, Johannes 81

Wagner, Cosima (*formerly* Bülow) 113, 119, 185, 233
  anti-Semitism 248, 288
  GM visits Wahnfried 247–8
  on hearing Mahler's *Tannhäuser* in Leipzig 165, 247
  and Vienna appointment 248, 288
Wagner, Otto 49, 352, 356, 439
Wagner, Richard 125, 162
  admiration felt by GM and circle 57, 59–60, 62–3, 83, 161
  anti-Semitism 60, 63, 80, 83, 104, 141, 157, 257–8
  Brahms rivalry 61, 62, 63, 71–2
  and Bülow 119
  conducting style 196
  effect of death on GM 110
  French antipathy towards 620
  influence on Secession art 353, 354–5, 424
  'Jews in Music' article 104, 157, 257–8
  as late starter 25
  on Leipzig and 'Jewish music' 157
  Lipiner at Wahnfried 79–80
  Makart visit 45
  Mann's lecture on 253–4
  Neumann's promotion of work 141
  and New German School 61–2, 71, 72
  in New York Met repertoire 545
  Nibelungenlied 76
  and Nietzsche 77–8, 83, 279
  Opera and Drama 258
  and opera reform 303–5, 416–18, 527–8
  Parsifal and Bayreuth 113, 548–9
  performance cuts and GM's reinstatement 303–4, 559

reception in Vienna 60–4, 83
  total artwork concept (*Gesamtkunstwerk*) 353, 416–18, 421
  vegetarianism 64, 83, 101, 222
  and Vienna Opera 293, 527–8, 529
  see also Mahler, Gustav: as conductor, and Wagner repertoire
Wagner, Wieland 314
Wagner, Siegfried 248, 470, 658
Walker, Edyth 305
Wallaschek, Richard 508, 533
Wallerstein, Lothar 420
Walter, Bruno (*formerly* Schlesinger)
  and Third Symphony 231–2, 269–70, 274, 280
  and Seventh Symphony 458
  and Ninth Symphony 611, 612, 693
  age gap and GM's formal relations 512
  on Alma's beauty 240
  and anti-Semitism 509
  and appearance of GM 2, 5, 210
  and burial of GM 668, 688, 689
  on concentration of GM 222
  conducting studies 67
  on conducting style of GM 199, 200, 201
  as conductor 192, 390
  as conductor at Vienna Opera and Philharmonic 315, 470, 486, 529, 534, 693
  conducts GM's work after death 451, 563, 611, 693, 694, 697–8, 705
  on critical remarks and GM's despair 410
  on demands of GM on performers 225–6
  on dying GM's pessimism 681–2
  festschrift contribution 634
  first impression of GM 1
  and Freud consultation 649
  friendship with GM 245, 560, 585
  on GM's choice of singers in Vienna 468
  on GM's view of Toscanini 590
  on Goethe and GM 134, 404
  on health of GM 327
  ignorance of Dostoevsky 137
  Jewishness and GM's advice on 259–60
  letters from GM 156, 268–9, 280, 562, 584–5, 593–4, 600–1, 611, 614, 617
  and *Das Lied von der Erde* 482, 562, 563, 612, 693, 697
  on Lipiner 82
  on Lotze's influence on GM 398
  on Maria's death and effect on GM 551, 552–4
  on Montenuovo 466
  and Munich Exhibition performance 658–9

Walter, Bruno (cont.)
New York letters from GM 592–3, 593–5
and New York Philharmonic concert
programme 603
and Pfitzner's work 473–4
and players for New York Philharmonic
592–3
and posthumous reputation of GM 697–8
on programme music and GM's
views 152–3
and reconciliation with Lipiner 596–7,
681
and religious belief of GM 392
and Nanna Spiegler 379
Steinbach visit 231–2
and Werfel poem 192
Wand, Günter 705
Wandering Jew figure 272
Wassermann, Jakob 261, 538
Wawruch, Andreas Johann 667
Weber, Captain Carl von 162, 163–4
Weber, Carl Maria von 104–5, 114, 115
Die drei Pintos and completion by GM
162, 164–6
Weber, Caroline von 162
Weber, Marion von 148–9, 162–4, 165
Weber, Max Maria von 162
Webern, Anton 130, 480–83, 522, 560,
658, 660
and GM's work 481, 482–3, 523, 695
Wedekind, Frank 126, 131
Weidemann, Friedrich 306, 430
Weidt, Lucie 307, 435–6
Weinberger, Josef (music publishers) 454–5
Weingartner, Felix von 334, 451
as GM's successor in Vienna 540, 541,
543, 548, 559–60, 586, 660
and Stefan's defence of GM 468–9, 508
Weininger, Otto 64, 260
Weis-Osborn, Julius 530, 535, 726
Weißmann, Adolf 696
Wellesz, Egon 481, 489
Werfel, Franz 192, 392, 628, 629, 645
Wieland, Christoph Martin 134, 314, 405
Wiener Werkstätte 43, 352
Wiesenthal, Grete 534–5
Wieland, Christoph Martin 134,
314, 405
Wild, Dortchen 96
Wilde, Oscar 132
Wilhelm I, Kaiser 165
Wilhelm II, Kaiser, 609
Willnauer, Franz 210, 469, 499
Winkelmann, Hermann 66, 295
Winter, Josef and Josefine
von 631
Winternitz, Rudolf 547, 548

Witeschnik, Alexander 243
Wlassack, Eduard 259, 282, 289, 291,
303, 464
Wolf, Hugo 92, 111
anti-Semitism 60, 63, 64
choice of poets for songs 168
and collaboration on Rübezahl 64–5, 84
Der Corregidor 64, 65, 427
enforced departure from Conservatory
68–9
as fervent Wagnerian 59–60, 62, 63
as friend of GM in Vienna 55,
59–61, 62
friendship breaks down 64–6, 68–9,
427, 586
nervous breakdown and insanity 65–6,
101, 102, 427
Wolff, Hermann 214
Wolf-Ferrari, Ermanno 501
Wollschläger, Hans 131, 361, 643–4
Wondra, Hubert 283, 467
World Fair in Vienna (1873) 50, 51
Wörthersee see Maiernigg on
Wörthersee
Wüllner, Ludwig 610

Yiddish and mauscheln 253, 255
Young Vienna movement 346, 349, 350,
425, 514

Zasche, Theo 341
Zelter, Carl Friedrich 521
Zemlinsky, Alexander 54, 136, 658
and Alma Schindler 359, 362–3, 364–5,
370, 372, 376, 433, 627, 629
Alma's hesitation before marriage
to GM 436
on Alma's musical talent 366
Alma's unflattering description 1
ballet composition 359–60
and Brahms 482
conducts at Vienna Opera 315, 529
friendship with GM 480, 512, 560, 660
and GM's legacy 695
and performing version of Tenth
Symphony 662
works performed at Vienna Opera
470, 471
Zichy, Count Géza 189–90
Zinne, Wilhelm, 227, 716
Zola, Emile 363, 517, 620
Zuckerkandl, Bertha 350, 356, 357, 358–61,
517, 539, 683
Zuckerkandl, Emil 356, 358, 359, 539
Zweig, Arnold 345
Zweig, Stefan 101, 102, 192, 538, 658
and GM's final voyage 679, 680

Acknowledgements

POETS RARELY NEED advisers or colleagues willing to cast a careful and critical eye over their manuscripts, whereas the writers of biographies can generally not get by without them. The author feels obliged to list a whole series of individuals and institutions.

My first debt of gratitude is to Herta Blaukopf, the doyenne of international Mahler scholarship (now no longer alive), whose unparalleled knowledge of every aspect of Mahler's life and works proved invaluable. Together we were also able to share memories of her late husband, Kurt Blaukopf, whose biography of 1969 was the first to open many readers' eyes to the composer's personality. It continues to occupy a crucial place in the history of responses to Mahler. Tobias Heyl was more than merely a professional and outstanding editor: his own enthusiasm for this music and for its composer was both inspiring and immensely helpful.

It is more than fifty years since Arnfried Edler introduced me to the name of a composer that at the time meant as little to me as it did to many others. To Bruno Maderna and Michael Gielen I owe my first life-affirming encounters with Mahler's symphonies – and I am tremendously grateful for the fact that today I am able to speak to Michael Gielen about the composer. I am no less grateful to Dietrich Fischer-Dieskau, who in the 1960s was responsible for my earliest impressions of Mahler's songs and with whom I have more recently held many an amiable discussion. Today no one sings Mahler's songs better than Thomas Hampson – it is not least because of this that the present study is dedicated to him. It was Michael Krüger who on the Orient Express between Salzburg and Munich gave this book its first important impetus and who has kept it on track since then. In Berlin, Efim Etkind lent me a helping hand at the start of what was to prove a very long journey, and I am only sorry that he did not live to witness its completion. Yosef and Ophra Yerushalmi likewise offered me their encouragement. Wolfgang Rihm gave me one particularly important piece of advice – his music has repeatedly cast its spell on me whenever Mahler has not been playing next to my desk. Peter Roth advised me on medical questions, which unfortunately play such a major part in this book. Many years ago I asked Hermann Danuser whether he thought that a longer study of Mahler made any sense, and he answered with an emphatic 'yes'. Mahler's English biographer, Jonathan Carr (who died in 2008), lent me his support as a colleague. At the Bavarian State Library, Sigrid von Moisy and Hartmut Schaefer generously allowed me to examine the material that they were preparing for an exhibition of the library's Mahlerian holdings. The priceless documents that are now available in Munich, especially those from the collection of Hans Moldenhauer, have turned the city into one of the principal centres of international Mahler scholarship – a development that came just in time to benefit the present study. The late Günther Weiß generously allowed me to see his catalogue essay before it went to press. The eminent Mahler scholar Knud Martner made a number of helpful corrections and comments.

Many institutions have supplied me with material and factual information. The Internationale Gustav Mahler Gesellschaft in Vienna granted me access to its important holdings and provided me with a complete list of all Mahler's appearances as a conductor at the Vienna Court Opera. (I am especially grateful to Frank Fanning in this respect.) Other institutions to which I am indebted are the Bavarian State Library, Munich; the University of Western Ontario, which currently houses the Mahler–Rosé Collection; the Bibliothèque Musicale Gustav Mahler in Paris; the Austrian Theatre Museum in the person of Frau Weißenböck for the then unpublished papers of Anna Bahr-Mildenburg; the Austrian National Library; the Municipal and Regional Library of Vienna; the Van Pelt Library at the University of Pennsylvania, Philadelphia, for the Mahler-Werfel Collection; the Pierpont Morgan Library, New York; the Metropolitan Opera Archives and the New York Public Library for the Bruno Walter Collection.

I am especially grateful to the Institute for Advanced Study in Berlin, where I was able to give the present study its initial shape while working on other projects. I am also deeply grateful to the Hampsong Foundation for funding the English translation.

I do not need to explain what this book owes to my wife – to quote from Mahler's 'Blicke mir nicht in die Lieder', 'Bees, when they build their cells, let no one watch them either'.

This book is no more than the fulfilment of a promise that I once made to a large grey stone in Vienna.